SECOND
EDITION

ABNORMAL PSYCHOLOGY

Robin S. Rosenberg
University of California at San Francisco

Stephen M. Kosslyn
Minerva Schools at the Keck Graduate Institute

WORTH PUBLISHERS
A Macmillan Higher Education Company

Senior Vice President, Editorial and Production: Catherine Woods
Publisher: Kevin Feyen
Associate Publisher: Jessica Bayne
Executive Marketing Manager: Katherine Nurre
Developmental Editor: Thomas Finn
Director of Print and Digital Development: Tracey Kuehn
Associate Managing Editor: Lisa Kinne
Media Editor: Anthony Casciano
Editorial Assistant: Catherine Michaelsen
Photo Editor: Robin Fadool
Photo Researchers: Roman Barnes and Donna Ranieri
Project Editor: Christine Cervoni, TSI Graphics, Inc.
Art Director: Barbara Reingold
Cover Designers: Barbara Reingold and Lyndall Culbertson
Interior Designers: Charles Yuen and Lyndall Culbertson
Production Manager: Barbara Anne Seixas
Composition and Line Art: TSI Graphics, Inc.
Anatomical and Studio Art: Matthew Holt, Keith Kasnot, and Chris Notarile
Printing and Binding: RR Donnelley
Cover Art: coloroftime/E+/Getty Images

Library of Congress Control Number: 2013955446

ISBN-13: 978-1-4292-4216-5
ISBN-10: 1-4292-4216-7

Printed in China

Third printing
Worth Publishers
41 Madison Avenue
New York, NY 10010
www.worthpublishers.com

To our families

Robin S. Rosenberg is a clinical psychologist in private practice in both Menlo Park and San Francisco, California. She is board certified in clinical psychology by the American Board of Professional Psychology, and has been certified in clinical hypnosis.

Courtesy of Robin Apple

Dr. Rosenberg is a fellow of the American Academy of Clinical Psychology, member of the Academy for Eating Disorders, President of the Santa Clara County Psychological Association, member of the California Psychological Association Ethics Committee, and assistant clinical professor at the University of California at San Francisco. She has taught psychology classes at Lesley University and Harvard University.

Dr. Rosenberg received her B.A. in psychology from New York University, and her M.A. and Ph.D. in clinical psychology from the University of Maryland, College Park. She completed her clinical internship at Massachusetts Mental Health Center, had a postdoctoral fellowship at Harvard Community Health Plan, and was a staff member at Newton-Wellesley Hospital's Outpatient Services. Dr. Rosenberg specializes in treating people with anxiety disorders, eating disorders, depression, and sexual dysfunctions.

In addition, Dr. Rosenberg writes about fictional popular culture figures and the psychological phenomena their stories reveal. She is author of *Superhero Origins: What Makes Superheroes Tick and Why We Care* and *What's the Matter with Batman? An Unauthorized Clinical Look Under the Mask of the Caped Crusader*, as well as college-level psychology textbooks. She is the editor of *The Psychology of the Girl With the Dragon Tattoo; The Psychology of Superheroes; Our Superheroes, Ourselves;* and *What Is a Superhero?* Dr. Rosenberg is also a blogger at *Psychology Today* and the *Huffington Post*.

Stephen M. Kosslyn is the Founding Dean of the Minerva Schools at KGI (Keck Graduate Institute). Previously, he served as Director of the Center for Advanced Study in the Behavioral Sciences and as Professor of Psychology at Stanford University.

Courtesy of Mark Estes

Kosslyn also is the former chair of the Department of Psychology, Dean of Social Science, and John Lindsley Professor of Psychology at Harvard University. He received a B.A. from UCLA and a Ph.D. from Stanford University, both in psychology.

Kosslyn's research has focused primarily on the nature of visual cognition, visual communication, and individual differences; he has authored or coauthored 14 books and over 300 papers on these topics. Kosslyn has received the following accolades: the American Psychological Association's Boyd R. McCandless Young Scientist Award, the National Academy of Sciences Initiatives in Research Award, the Cattell Award, a Guggenheim Fellowship, and the J-L. Signoret Prize (France). He has honorary Doctorates from the University of Caen, the University of Paris Descartes, and University of Bern. Kosslyn has been elected to Academia Rodinensis pro Remediatione (Switzerland), the Society of Experimental Psychologists, and the American Academy of Arts and Sciences.

◻ LIST OF CHAPTERS

CONTENTS

CHAPTER 10

Eating Disorders................................297

CHAPTER 11

Gender and Sexual Disorders.......................327

☐ CHAPTER 16
Ethical and Legal Issues 503

□ PREFACE

his is an exciting time to study psychopathology. Research on the entire range of psychological disorders has blossomed during the last several decades, producing dramatic new insights about psychological disorders and their treatments. However, the research results are outpacing the popular media's ability to explain them. We've noticed that when study results are explained in a news report or an online magazine article, "causes" of mental illness are often reduced to a single factor, such as genes, brain chemistry, irrational thoughts, or social rejection. But that is not an accurate picture. Research increasingly reveals that psychopathology arises from a confluence of three types of factors: neurological (brain and body, including genes), psychological (thoughts, feelings, and behaviors), and social (relationships, communities, and culture). Moreover, these three sorts of factors do not exist in isolation, but rather mutually influence each other. It's often tempting to seek a single cause of psychopathology, but this effort is fundamentally misguided.

We are a clinical psychologist (Rosenberg) and a cognitive neuroscientist (Kosslyn) who have been writing collaboratively for many years. Our observations about the state of the field of psychopathology—and the problems with how it is sometimes portrayed—led us to envision an abnormal psychology textbook that is guided by a central idea, which we call the *neuropsychosocial approach*. This approach allows us to conceptualize the ways in which neurological, psychological, and social factors interact to give rise to mental disorders. These interactions take the form of feedback loops in which each type of factor affects every other type. Take depression, for instance, which we discuss in Chapter 5: Someone who attributes the cause of a negative event to his or her own personal characteristics or behavior (such attributions are a psychological factor) is more likely to become depressed. But this tendency to attribute the cause of negative events to oneself is influenced by social experiences, such as being criticized or abused. In turn, such social factors can alter brain functioning (particularly if one has certain genes), and abnormalities in brain functioning affect one's thoughts and social interactions, and so on—round and round.

The neuropsychosocial approach grew out of the venerable biopsychosocial approach—but instead of focusing broadly on biology, we take advantage of the bountiful harvest of findings about the brain that have filled the scientific journals over the past two decades. Specifically, the name change signals a focus on the brain itself; we derive much insight from the findings of neuroimaging studies, which reveal how brain systems function normally and how they have gone awry with mental disorders, and we also learn an enormous amount from findings regarding neurotransmitters and genetics.

Although mental disorders cannot be fully understood without reference to the brain, neurological factors alone cannot explain these disorders; rather, mental disorders develop through the complex interaction of neurological factors with psychological and social factors. Without question, psychopathology cannot be reduced to "brain disease," akin to a problem someone might have with his or her liver or lungs. Instead, we show that the effects of neurological factors can only be understood in the context of the other two types of factors addressed within the neuropsychosocial approach. (In fact, an understanding of a psychological disorder cannot be reduced to any single type of factor, whether genetics, irrational thoughts, or family interaction patterns.) Thus, we present cutting-edge neuroscience research results and put them in context, explaining how they illuminate issues in psychopathology.

Our emphasis on feedback loops among neurological, psychological, and social factors led us to reconceptualize and incorporate the classic diathesis-stress model (which posits a precondition that makes a person vulnerable and an environmental trigger—the diathesis and stress, respectively). In the classic view, the diathesis was almost always treated as a biological state, and the stress was viewed as a result of environmental events. In contrast, after describing the conventional diathesis-stress model in Chapter 1, we explain how the neuropsychosocial approach provides a new way to think about the relationship between diathesis and stress. Specifically, we show how one can view *any* of the three sorts of factors as a potential source of either a diathesis or a stressor. For example, living in a dangerous neighborhood, which is a social factor, creates a diathesis for which psychological events can serve as the stressor, triggering an episode of depression. Alternatively, being born with a very sensitive amygdala (a brain structure involved in fear and other strong emotions) may act as a diathesis for which social events—such as observing someone else being mugged—can serve as a stressor that triggers an anxiety disorder.

Thus, the neuropsychosocial approach is not simply a change in terminology ("bio" to "neuro"), but rather a change in basic orientation: We do not view any one sort of factor as "privileged" over the others, but regard the interactions among the factors—the feedback loops—as paramount. In our view, this approach incorporates what was best about the biopsychosocial approach and the diathesis-stress model.

Our new approach should lead students who use this textbook to think critically about theories and research on etiology, diagnosis and treatment of mental disorders. We want students to come away from the course with the knowledge and skills to understand why no single type of findings alone can explain psychopathology, and to have compassion for people suffering from psychological disorders. One of our goals is to put a "human face" on mental illness, which we do by using case studies to illustrate and make concrete each disorder. These goals are especially important because this course will be the last psychology course many students take—and this might be the last book about psychology they read.

The new approach we have adopted led naturally to a set of unique features, as we outline next.

Unique Coverage

By integrating cutting-edge neuroscience research and more traditional psychosocial research on psychopathology and its treatment, this textbook provides students with a sense of the field as a coherent whole, in which different research methods illuminate different aspects of abnormal psychology. Our integrated neuropsychosocial approach allows students to learn not only how neurological factors affect mental processes (such as executive functions) and mental contents (such as distorted beliefs), but also how neurological factors affect emotions, behavior, social interactions, and responses to environmental events—and vice versa.

The 16 chapters included in this book span the traditional topics covered in an abnormal psychology course. The neuropsychosocial theme is reflected in both the overall organization of the text and the organization of its individual chapters. We present the material in a decidedly contemporary context that infuses both the foundational chapters (Chapters 1–4) as well as the chapters that address specific disorders (Chapters 5–15).

In Chapter 2, we provide an overview of explanations of abnormality and discuss neurological, psychological, and social factors. Our coverage is not limited merely to categorizing causes as examples of a given type of factor; rather, we explain how a given type of factor influences and creates feedback loops with other factors. Consider depression again: The loss of a relationship (social factor) can affect thoughts and feelings (psychological factors), which—given a certain genetic predisposition (neurological factor)—can trigger depression. Using the neuropsychosocial approach, we show how disparate fields of psychology and psychiatry (such as neuroscience and clinical practice) are providing a unified and overarching understanding of abnormal psychology.

Our chapter on diagnosis and assessment (Chapter 3) uses the neuropsychosocial framework to organize methods of assessing abnormality. We discuss how abnormality may be assessed through measures that address the different types of factors: neurological (e.g., neuroimaging data or certain types of blood tests), psychological (e.g., clinical interviews or questionnaires), and social (e.g., family interviews or a history of legal problems).

The research methods chapter (Chapter 4) also provides unique coverage. We explain the general scientific method, but we do so within the neuropsychosocial framework. Specifically, we consider methods used to study neurological factors (e.g., neuroimaging), psychological factors (e.g., self-reports of thoughts and moods), and social factors (e.g., observational studies of dyads or groups or of cultural values and expectations). We show how the various measures themselves reflect the interactions among the different types of factors. For instance, when researchers ask participants to report family dynamics, they are relying on psychological factors—participants' memories and impressions—to provide measures of social factors. Similarly, when researchers use the number of items checked on a stressful-life events scale to infer the actual stress experienced by a person, social factors provide a proxy measure of the psychological and neurological consequences of stress. We also discuss research on treatment from the neuropsychosocial framework.

During times of political unrest, violence, or terrorism, rates of trauma-related disorders are likely to increase.

The clinical chapters (Chapters 5–15), which address specific disorders, also rely on the neuropsychosocial approach to organize the discussions of both etiology and treatment of the disorders. Moreover, when we discuss a particular disorder, we address the three basic questions of psychopathology: What exactly constitutes this psychological disorder? What neuropsychosocial factors are associated with it? How is it treated?

Pedagogy

All abnormal psychology textbooks cover a lot of ground: Students must learn many novel concepts, facts, and theories. We want to make that task easier, to help students come to a deeper understanding of what they learn and to consolidate that material effectively. The textbook uses a number of pedagogical tools to achieve this goal.

Feedback Loops Within the Neuropsychosocial Approach

This textbook highlights and reinforces the theme of feedback loops among neurological, psychological, and social factors in several ways:

- In each clinical chapter, we include a section on "Feedback Loops in Understanding," which specifically explores how disorders result from interactions among the neuropsychosocial factors. We also include a section on "Feedback Loops in Treating," which specifically explores how successful treatment results from interactions among the neuropsychosocial factors.

- We include neuropsychosocial "Feedback Loop" diagrams as part of these sections. For example, in Chapter 7 we provide a Feedback Loop diagram for understanding posttraumatic stress disorder and another for treating posttraumatic stress disorder.

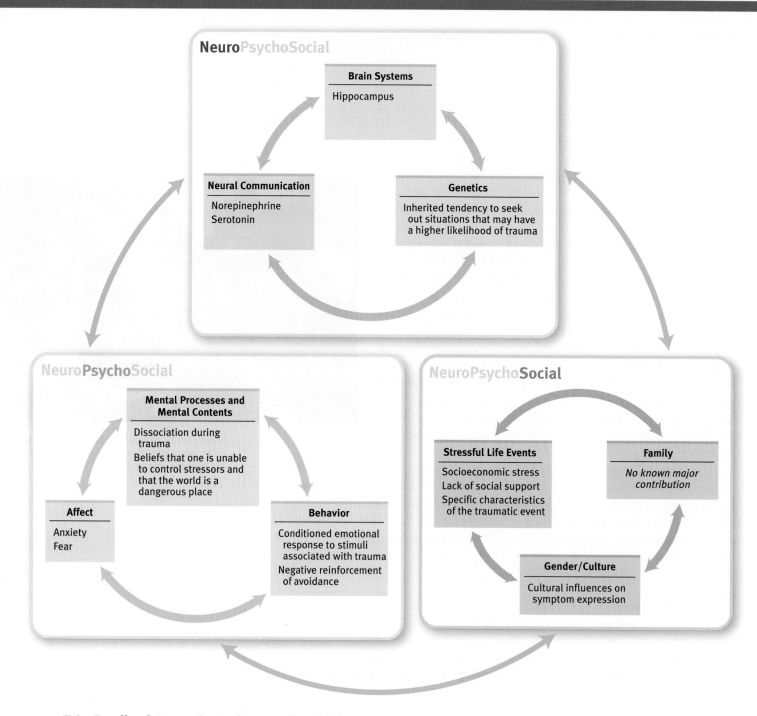

FIGURE **7.2 • Feedback Loops in Understanding PTSD**

These diagrams illustrate the feedback loops among the neurological, psychological, and social factors. Additional feedback loop diagrams can be found on the book's website at: www.worthpublishers.com/launchpad/rkabpsych2e.

- The Feedback Loops in Understanding diagrams serve several purposes: (1) they provide a visual summary of the most important neuropsychosocial factors that contribute to various disorders; (2) they illustrate the interactive nature of the factors; (3) because their overall structure is the same for each disorder, students can compare and contrast the specifics of the feedback loops across disorders.

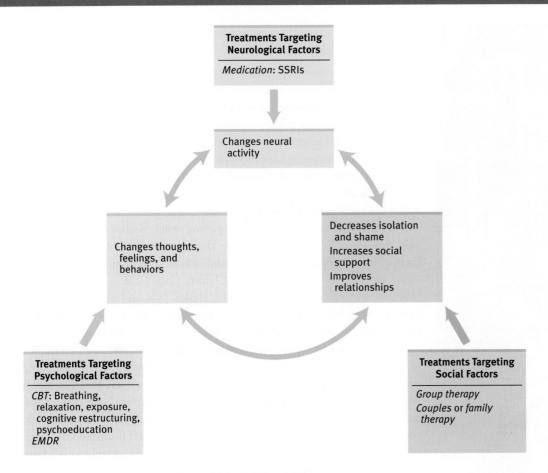

FIGURE **7.3 • Feedback Loops in Treating PTSD**

- Like the Feedback Loops in Understanding diagrams, the Feedback Loops in Treating diagrams serve several purposes: (1) they provide a visual summary of the treatments for various disorders; (2) they illustrate the interactive nature of successful treatment (the fact that a treatment may directly target one type of factor, but changes in that factor in turn affect other factors); (3) because their overall structure is the same for each disorder, students can compare and contrast the specifics of the feedback loops across disorders.

Clinical Material

Abnormal psychology is a fascinating topic, but we want students to go beyond fascination; we want them to understand the human toll of psychological disorders—what it's like to suffer from and cope with such disorders. To do this, we've incorporated several pedagogical elements. The textbook includes three types of clinical material: *chapter stories*—each chapter has a story woven through, traditional third-person cases (*From the Outside*), and first-person accounts (*From the Inside*).

Chapter Stories: Illustration and Integration

Each chapter opens with a story about a person (or, in some cases, several people) who has symptoms of psychological distress or dysfunction. Observations about the person or people are then woven throughout the chapter. These chapter stories illustrate the common threads that run throughout the chapter (and thereby integrate the material), serve as retrieval cues for later recall of the material, and show students how the theories and research presented in each chapter apply to real people in the real world; the stories

Tom Wargacki/WireImage/Getty Images

Using this book's definition of a psychological disorder, did either of the Beales have a disorder? Big Edie exhibited distress that was inappropriate to her situation; both women appeared to have an impaired ability to function. The risk of harm to the women, however, is less clear-cut.

humanize the clinical descriptions and discussions of research presented in the chapters.

The chapter stories present people as clinicians and researchers often find them—with sets of symptoms in context. It is up to the clinician or researcher to make sense of the symptoms, determining which of them may meet the criteria for a particular disorder, which may indicate an atypical presentation, and which may arise from a comorbid disorder. Thus, we ask the student to see situations from the point of view of clinicians and researchers, who must sift through the available information to develop hypotheses about possible diagnoses and then obtain more information to confirm or disconfirm these hypotheses.

In the first two chapters, the opening story is about a mother and daughter—Big Edie and Little Edie Beale—who were the subject of a famous documentary in the 1970s and whose lives have been portrayed more recently in the play and HBO film *Grey Gardens*. In these initial chapters, we offer a description of the Beales' lives and examples of their very eccentric behavior to address two questions central to psychopathology: How is abnormality defined? Why do psychological disorders arise?

The stories in subsequent chapters focus on different examples of symptoms of psychological disorders, drawn from the lives of other people. For example, in Chapter 6 we discuss football star Earl Campbell (who suffered from symptoms of anxiety); in Chapter 7 we discuss the reclusive billionaire Howard Hughes (who suffered from symptoms of obsessive-compulsive disorder and who experienced multiple traumatic events); and in Chapter 12 we discuss the Genain quadruplets—all four of whom were diagnosed with schizophrenia.

We return often to these stories throughout each chapter in an effort to illustrate the complexity of mental disorders and to show the human side of mental illness, how it can affect people throughout a lifetime, rather than merely a moment in time.

From the Outside

The feature called *From the Outside* provides third-person accounts (typically case presentations by mental health clinicians) of disorders or particular symptoms of disorders. These accounts provide an additional opportunity for memory consolidation of the material (because they mention symptoms the person experienced), an additional set of retrieval cues, and a further sense of how symptoms and disorders affect real people; these cases also serve to expose students to professional case material. The *From the Outside* feature covers an array of disorders, such as cyclothymic disorder, panic disorder, transvestic disorder, and separation anxiety disorder. Often several *From the Outside* cases are included in a chapter.

From the Inside

In every chapter in which we address a disorder in depth, we present at least one first-person account of what it is like to live with that disorder or particular symptoms of it. In addition to providing high-interest personal narratives, these *From the Inside* cases help students to consolidate memory of the material, provide additional retrieval cues, and are another way to link the descriptions of disorders and research findings to real people's experiences. The *From the Inside* cases illuminate what it is like to live with disorders such as agoraphobia, obsessive-compulsive disorder, illness anxiety disorder, alcohol use disorder, gender dysphoria, and schizophrenia, among others.

Learning About Disorders: Consolidated Tables to Consolidate Learning

In the clinical chapters, we provide two types of tables to help students organize and consolidate information related to diagnosis: DSM-5 diagnostic criteria tables, and Facts at a Glance tables.

DSM-5 Diagnostic Criteria Tables

The American Psychiatric Association's manual of psychiatric disorders—the Diagnostic and Statistical Manual of Mental Disorders, 5th edition (DSM-5)—provides tables of the diagnostic criteria for each of the listed disorders. For each disorder that we discuss at length, we present the DSM-5 diagnostic criteria table; we also explain and discuss the criteria—and criticisms of them—in the body of the chapters themselves.

Facts at a Glance Tables for Disorders

Another important innovation is our summary tables for each disorder, which provide key facts about prevalence, comorbidity, onset, course, and gender and cultural factors. These tables are clearly titled with the name of the disorder, which is followed by the term "Facts at a Glance" (for instance, *Obsessive-Compulsive Disorder Facts at a Glance*). These tables give students the opportunity to access this relevant information in one place and to compare and contrast the facts for different disorders.

New Features

This edition has two new features: *Current Controversy* boxes and *Getting the Picture* critical thinking photo sets.

Current Controversies

New to this edition, each clinical chapter includes a brief discussion about a current controversy related to a disorder—its diagnosis or its treatment. Examples include whether the new diagnoses in DSM-5 of mild and major neurocognitive disorders are net positive or negative changes from DSM-IV, and whether eye movement desensitization and reprocessing (EMDR) provides additional benefit beyond that of other treatments for posttraumatic stress disorder. These discussions help students understand the iterative and sometimes controversial nature of classifying "problems" and symptoms as disorders, and whether and when treatments might be appropriate. Many of these discussions were contributed by instructors who teach Abnormal Psychology—including: Ken Abrams, Carleton College; Randy Arnau, University of Southern Mississippi; Glenn Callaghan, San Jose State University; Richard Conti, Kean University; Patrice Dow-Nelson, New Jersey City University; James Foley, College of Wooster; Rick Fry, Youngstown State University; Farrah Hughes, Francis Marion University; Meghana Karnik-Henry, Green Mountain College; Kevin Meehan, Long Island University; Jan Mendoza, Golden West College; Meera Rastogi, University of Cincinnati, Clermont College; Harold Rosenberg, Bowling Green State University; Anthony Smith, Baybath College; and Janet Todaro, Salem State University.

Getting the Picture

Also new to this edition are brief visual features that help to consolidate learning, which we call *Getting the Picture*: We offer two photos and ask students to decide which one

📷 **GETTING THE PICTURE**

Imagine that you know that both of these women are afraid of getting fat and believe themselves to be overweight. If you had to guess based on their appearance, which of these models would you think didn't meet all the criteria for anorexia nervosa and instead had a partial case? The woman on the right is more likely to have a partial case because, based on these photos, she does not appear to be significantly underweight.

best illustrates a clinical phenomenon described in the chapter. Each chapter contains several of these features.

Summarizing and Consolidating

We include two more key features to help students learn the material: end-of-section application exercises and end-of-chapter summaries (called *Summing Up*).

Thinking Like a Clinician: End-of-Section Application Exercises

At the end of each major section in the clinical chapters, we provide *Thinking Like a Clinician* questions. These questions ask students to apply what they have learned to other people and situations. These questions allow students to test their knowledge of the chapter's material; they may be assigned as homework or used to foster small-group or class discussion.

End-of-Chapter Review: *Summing Up*

The end-of-chapter review is designed to help students further consolidate the material in memory:

- Section Summaries: These summaries allow students to review what they have learned in the broader context of the entire chapter's material.

- Key Terms: At the end of each chapter we list the key terms used in that chapter—the terms that are presented in boldface in the text and are defined in the marginal glossaries—with the pages where the definitions can be found.

- At the very end of *Summing Up*, students are directed to the online study aids and resources pertinent to the chapter.

Integrated Gender and Cultural Coverage

We have included extensive culture and gender coverage, and integrated it throughout the entire textbook. You'll find a complete list of this coverage on the book's catalog page. Some of our coverage of culture and gender include:

- *Facts at a Glance* tables provide relevant cultural and gender data for each specific disorder
- Cultural differences in evaluating symptoms of disorders in psychological research, 63, 66
- Cultural differences in assessing social factors in psychological assessment, 75, 103–104
- Gender and cultural consideration in depressive disorders, 127
- Suicide—cultural factors, 150
- Cultural influence of substance abuse, 263
- Alcoholism rate variations by gender and culture, 271–273, 411
- Gender and culture differences in schizophrenia, 377
- Oppositional defiant disorder—cultural considerations for diagnosis, 468
- Gender differences in different types of dementia (Table 15.9), 501

Media and Supplements

The second edition of our book features a wide array of multimedia tools designed to meet the needs of both students and teachers. For more information about any of the items below, visit Worth Publishers' online catalog at www.worthpublishers.com.

LAUNCHPAD WITH LEARNINGCURVE QUIZZING A comprehensive Web resource for teaching and learning psychology, LaunchPad combines rich media resources and an easy-to-use platform. For students, it is the ultimate online study guide with videos, e-Book, and the LearningCurve adaptive quizzing system. For instructors, LaunchPad is a full course space where class documents can be posted, quizzes are easily assigned and graded, and students' progress can be assessed and recorded. The LaunchPad for our second edition can be previewed at: www.worthpublishers.com/launchpad/rkabpsych2e. You'll find the following in our LaunchPad:

The **LearningCurve** quizzing system was designed based on the latest findings from learning and memory research. It combines adaptive question selection, immediate and valuable feedback, and a game-like interface to engage students in a learning experience that is unique to them. Each LearningCurve quiz is fully integrated with other resources in LaunchPad through the Personalized Study Plan, so students will be able to review with Worth's extensive library of videos and activities. State-of-the-art question analysis reports allow instructors to track the progress of individual students as well as the class as a whole. The many questions in LearningCurve have been prepared by a talented team of instructors including Kanoa Meriwether from the University of Hawaii, West Oahu, Danielle Gunraj from the State University of New York at Binghamton, and Anna Aulette Root from the University of Capetown.

- **Diagnostic Quizzing** developed by Diana Joy of Denver Community College and Judith Levine from Farmingdale State College includes more than 400 questions for every chapter that help students identify their areas of strength and weakness.

- An **interactive e-Book** allows students to highlight, bookmark, and make their own notes, just as they would with a printed textbook. Digital enhancements include full-text search and in-text glossary definitions.

- **Student Video Activities** include more than 60 engaging and gradeable video activities, including archival footage, explorations of current research, case studies, and documentaries.

- **The *Scientific American* Newsfeed** delivers weekly articles, podcasts, and news briefs on the very latest developments in psychology from the first name in popular science journalism.

COURSESMART E-BOOK The CourseSmart e-Book offers the complete text in an easy-to-use, flexible format. Students can choose to view the CourseSmart e-Book online or download it to a personal computer or a portable media player, such as a smart phone or iPad. The CourseSmart e-Book for *Abnormal Psychology*, Second Edition, can be previewed and purchased at www.coursesmart.com.

Also Available for Instructors

The *Abnormal Psychology* video collection on Flash Drive and DVD. This comprehensive collection of more than 130 videos includes a balanced set of cases, experiments, and current research clips. Instructors can play clips to introduce key topics, to illustrate and reinforce specific core concepts, or to stimulate small-group or full-classroom discussions. Clips may also be used to challenge students' critical thinking skills—either in class or via independent, out-of-class assignments.

INSTRUCTOR'S RESOURCE MANUAL, by Kanoa Meriwether, University of Hawaii, West Oahu and Meera Rastogi, University of Cincinnati: The manual offers chapter-by-chapter support for instructors using the text, as well as tips for explaining to students the neuropsychosocial approach to abnormal psychology. For each chapter, the manual offers a brief outline of learning objectives and a list of key terms. In addition, it includes a chapter guide, including an extended chapter outline, point-of-use references to art in the text, and listings of class discussions/activities, assignments, and extra-credit projects for each section.

TEST BANK, by James Rodgers from Hawkeye Community College, Joy Crawford, University of Washington, and Judith Levine, Farmingdale State College: The test bank offers over 1700 questions, including multiple-choice, true/false, fill-in, and essay questions. The Diploma-based CD version makes it easy for instructors to add, edit, and change the order of questions.

PRESENTATION SLIDES are available in three formats that can be used as they are or can be customized. One set includes all the textbook's illustrations and tables. The second set consists of lecture slides that focus on key themes and terms in the book and include text illustrations and tables. A third set of PowerPoint slides provides an easy way to integrate the supplementary video clips into classroom lectures. In addition, we have lecture outline slides correlated to each chapter of the book created by Pauline Davey Zeece from University of Nebraska-Lincoln.

Acknowledgments

We want to thank the following people, who generously gave of their time to review one or more—in some cases all—of the chapters in this book. Their feedback has helped make this a better book.

REVIEWERS OF THE FIRST EDITION

Eileen Achorn, University of Texas at San Antonio

Tsippa Ackerman, Queens College

Paula Alderette, University of Hartford

Richard Alexander, Muskegon Community College

Leatrice Allen, Prairie State College

Liana Apostolova, University of California, Los Angeles

Hal Arkowitz, University of Arizona

Randolph Arnau, University of Southern Mississippi

Tim Atchison, West Texas A&M University

Linda Bacheller, Barry University

Yvonne Barry, John Tyler Community College

David J. Baxter, University of Ottawa

Bethann Bierer, Metropolitan State College of Denver

Dawn Bishop Mclin, Jackson State University

Nancy Blum, California State University, Northridge

Robert Boland, Brown University

Kathryn Bottonari, University at Buffalo/SUNY

Joan Brandt Jensen, Central Piedmont Community College

Franklin Brown, Eastern Connecticut State University

Eric Bruns, Campbellsville University

Gregory Buchanan, Beloit College

Jeffrey Buchanan, Minnesota State University–Mankato

NiCole Buchanan, Michigan State University

Danielle Burchett, Kent State University

Glenn M. Callaghan, San Jose State University

Christine Calmes, University at Buffalo/SUNY

Rebecca Cameron, California State University, Sacramento

Alastair Cardno, University of Leeds

Kan Chandras, Fort Valley State University

Jennifer Cina, University of St. Thomas

Carolyn Cohen, Northern Essex Community College

Sharon Cool, University of Sioux Falls

Craig Cowden, Northern Virginia Community College

Judy Cusumano, Jefferson College of Health Sciences

Daneen Deptula, Fitchburg State College

Dallas Dolan, The Community College of Baltimore County

Mitchell Earleywine, University at Albany/SUNY

Christopher I. Eckhardt, Purdue University

Diane Edmond, Harrisburg Area Community College

James Eisenberg, Lake Erie College

Frederick Ernst, University of Texas–Pan American

John P. Garofalo, Washington State University–Vancouver

Franklin Foote, University of Miami

Sandra Jean Foster, Clark Atlantic University

Richard Fry, Youngstown State

Murray Fullman, Nassau Community College

Irit Gat, Antelope Valley College

Marjorie Getz, Bradley University

Andrea Goldstein, South University

Steven Gomez, Harper College

Carol Globiana, Fitchburg State University

Cathy Hall, East Carolina University

Debbie Hanke, Roanoke Chowan Community College

Sheryl Hartman, Miami Dade College

Wanda Haynie, Greenville Technical College

Brian Higley, University of North Florida

Debra Hollister, Valencia Community College

Kris Homan, Grove City College

Farrah Hughes, Francis Marion University

Kristin M. Jacquin, Mississippi State University

Annette Jankiewicz, Iowa Western Community College

Paul Jenkins, National University

Cynthia Kalodner, Towson University

Richard Kandus, Mt. San Jacinto College

Jason Kaufman, Inver Hills Community College

Jonathan Keigher, Brooklyn College

Mark Kirschner, Quinnipiac University

Cynthia Kreutzer, Georgia Perimeter College, Clarkston

Thomas Kwapil, University of North Carolina at Greensboro

Kristin Larson, Monmouth College

Dean Lauterbach, Eastern Michigan University

Robert Lichtman, John Jay College of Criminal Justice

Michael Loftin, Belmont University

Jacquelyn Loupis, Rowan-Cabarrus Community College

Donald Lucas, Northwest Vista College

Mikhail Lyubansky, University of Illinois, Urbana-Champaign

Eric J. Mash, University of Calgary

Janet Matthews, Loyola University

Dena Matzenbacher, McNeese State University

Timothy May, Eastern Kentucky University

Paul Mazeroff, McDaniel University

Dorothy Mercer, Eastern Kentucky University

Paulina Multhaupt, Macomb Community College

Mark Nafziger, Utah State University

Craig Neumann, University of North Texas

Christina Newhill, University of Pittsburgh

Bonnie Nichols, Arkansas NorthEastern College

Rani Nijjar, Chabot College

Janine Ogden, Marist College

Randall Osborne, Texas State University–San Marcos

Patricia Owen, St. Mary's University

Crystal Park, University of Connecticut

Karen Pfost, Illinois State University

Daniel Philip, University of North Florida

Skip Pollack, Mesa Community College

William Price, North Country Community College

Linda Raasch, Normandale Community College

Christopher Ralston, Grinnell College

Lillian Range, Our Lady of Holy Cross College

Judith Rauenzahn, Kutztown University

Jacqueline Reihman, State University of New York at Oswego

Sean Reilley, Morehead State University

David Richard, Rollins College

Harvey Richman, Columbus State University

J.D. Rodgers, Hawkeye Community College

David Romano, Barry University

Sandra Rouce, Texas Southern University

David Rowland, Valparaiso University

Lawrence Rubin, St. Thomas University

Stephen Rudin, Nova Southeastern University

Michael Rutter, Canisius College

Thomas Schoeneman, Lewis and Clark College

Stefan E. Schulenberg, University of Mississippi

Christopher Scribner, Lindenwood University

Russell Searight, Lake Superior State University

Daniel Segal, University of Colorado at Colorado Springs

Frances Sessa, Pennsylvania State University, Abington

Fredric Shaffer, Truman State University

Eric Shiraev, George Mason University

Susan J. Simonian, College of Charleston

Melissa Snarski, University of Alabama

Jason Spiegelman, Community College of Beaver County

Michael Spiegler, Providence College

Barry Stennett, Gainesville State College

Carla Strassle, York College of Pennsylvania

Nicole Taylor, Drake University

Paige Telan, Florida International University

Carolyn Turner, Texas Lutheran University

MaryEllen Vandenberg, Potomac State College of West Virginia

Elaine Walker, Emory University

David Watson, MacEwan University

Karen Wolford, State University of New York at Oswego

Shirley Yen, Brown University

Valerie Zurawski, St. John's University

Barry Zwibelman, University of Miami

REVIEWERS OF THE SECOND EDITION

Mildred Cordero, Texas State University

Brenda East, Durham Technical Community College

Jared F. Edwards, Southwestern Oklahoma State University

Rick Fry, Youngstown State University

Kelly Hagan, Bluegrass Community & Technical College

Jay Kosegarten, Southern New Hampshire University

Katherine Lau, University of New Orleans

Linda Lelii, St. Josephs University

Tammy L. Mahan, College of the Canyons

David McAllister, Salem State University

Kanoa Meriwether, University of Hawaii, West Oahu

Bryan Neighbors, Southwestern University

Katherine Noll, University of Illinois-Chicago

G. Michael Poteat, East Carolina University

Kimberly Renk, University of Central Florida

JD Rodgers, Hawkeye Community College

Eric Rogers, College of Lake County

Ty S. Schepis, Southwest Texas State University

Gwendolyn Scott-Jones, Delaware State University

Jason Shankle, Community College of Denver

Jeff Sinkele, Anderson University

Marc Wolpoff, Riverside Community College

Many thanks also go to our Advisory Board for the helpful insights and suggestions:

Randy Arnau, University of Southern Mississippi

Carolyn Cohen, Northern Essex Community College

Christopher Dyszelski, Madison Area Technical College

Brenda East, Durham Technical Community College

Rick Fry, Youngstown State University

Jeff Henriques, University of Wisconsin

Katherine Noll, University of Illinois at Chicago

Marilee Ogren, Boston College

Linda Raasch, Normandale Community College

Judith Rauenzahn, Kutztown University

Susan Simonian, College of Charleston

For double checking our DSM-5 information, we want to give a loud shout out of thanks to:

Rosemary McCullough, New England Counseling Associates

Jim Foley, College of Wooster

Although our names are on the title page, this book has been a group effort. Special thanks to a handful of people who did armfuls of work in the early stages of bringing the book to life in the first edition: Nancy Snidman, Children's Hospital Boston, for help with the chapter on developmental disorders; Shelley Greenfield, McLean Hospital, for advice about the etiology and treatment of substance abuse; Adam Kissel, for help in preparing the first draft of some of the manuscript; Lisa McLellan, senior development editor, for conceiving the idea of "Facts at a Glance" tables; Susan Clancy for help in gathering relevant literature; and Lori Gara-Matthews and Anne Perry for sharing a typical workday of a pediatrician and a school psychologist, respectively.

To the people at Worth Publishers who have helped us bring this book from conception through gestation and birth, many thanks for your wise counsel, creativity, and patience. Specifically, for the second edition, thanks to: Jessica Bayne, our acquisitions editor and rock; Thomas Finn, our development editor who went over and over and over each chapter with good humor, patience, and a needed "outside" eye; Jim Strandberg, our pre-development editor, whose advice, support, and amazing attention to detail were sorely appreciated; Christine Cervoni and her crew at TSI Graphics for getting the manuscript ready to become a book; Babs Reingold (again), art director, for her out-of-the-box visual thinking. We'd also like to thank Roman Barnes and Robin Fadool for their help with photo research; Eileen Lang and Catherine Michaelsen for helping prepare the manuscript for turnover; Anthony Casciano for helping to wrangle our supplements and media packages; and Kate Nurre for marketing our book. And a special note of thanks to Carlise Stembridge for organizing and helping us with our advisory board.

On the personal side, we'd like to thank our children—Neil, David, and Justin—for their unflagging love and support during this project and for their patience with our foibles and passions. We also want to thank: our mothers—Bunny and Rhoda—for allowing us to know what it means to grow up with supportive and loving parents; Steven Rosenberg, for numerous chapter story suggestions; Merrill Mead-Fox, Melissa Robbins, Jeanne Serafin, Amy Mayer, Kim Rawlins, and Susan Pollak, for sharing their clinical and personal wisdom over the last three decades; Michael Friedman and Steven Hyman, for answering our esoteric pharmacology questions; and Jennifer Shephard and Bill Thompson, who helped track down facts and findings related to the neurological side of the project.

Robin S. Rosenberg

Stephen M. Kosslyn

ABNORMAL PSYCHOLOGY

CHAPTER **1**

The History of Abnormal Psychology

"Big Edie" (Edith Bouvier Beale, 1894–1977) and her daughter, "Little Edie" (Edith Beale, 1917–2002), lived together as adults for 29 years. Their home was a 28-room mansion, called Grey Gardens, in the chic town of East Hampton, New York. But the Beales were not rich society women, entertaining in grand style. They had few visitors, other than people who delivered food to them daily, and they lived in impoverished circumstances. For the most part, they inhabited only two of the second-floor rooms and an upstairs porch of a house that was falling apart. These intelligent women were not simply poor recluses, though. They were unconventional, eccentric women who flaunted the rules of their time and social class.

Let's consider Big Edie first. In her later years, Big Edie had difficulty walking, and her bedroom was the hub of the Beale women's lives and full of squalor. It contained a small refrigerator, a hot plate on which food was heated or cooked, and up to 52 cats. The room had two twin beds, one for Little Edie, the other for Big Edie. Big Edie made her bed into an unusual nest of blankets (no sheets). Cats constantly walked across the bed or rested on it; because the women didn't provide the cats with a litter box, the bed was one of the spots the cats left their droppings. Big Edie's mattress was so soiled that the grime and the cat droppings were indistinguishable.

Big Edie hadn't left the house in decades (except for one occasion; Sheehy, 1972) and would let Little Edie out of her sight for only a few minutes before yelling for her to return to the bedroom. When Big Edie fell off a chair and broke her leg at the age of 80, she refused to leave the house to see a doctor, and refused to allow a doctor to come to the house to examine her leg. As a result, she developed bedsores that became infected and she died at Grey Gardens 7 months later (Wright, 2007).

Abnormal psychology
The subfield of psychology that addresses the causes and progression of psychological disorders; also referred to as *psychopathology*.

Psychological disorder
A pattern of thoughts, feelings, or behaviors that causes significant personal *distress*, significant *impairment* in daily life, and/or significant *risk of harm*, any of which is unusual for the context and culture in which it arises.

Little Edie was also unusual, most obviously in her style of dress. Little Edie always covered her head, usually with a sweater that she kept in place with a piece of jewelry. She professed not to like women in skirts, but invariably wore skirts herself, typically wearing them upside down so that the waistband was around her knees or calves and the skirt hem bunched around her waist. She advocated wearing stockings *over* pants, and she suggested that women "take off the skirt, and use it as a cape" (Maysles & Maysles, 1976).

ALTHOUGH BOTH OF THESE WOMEN WERE ODD, could their behavior be chalked up to eccentricity or did one or both of them have a psychological disorder? It depends on how *psychological disorder* is defined.

The sort of psychologist who would evaluate Big Edie and Little Edie would specialize in **abnormal psychology** (or *psychopathology*), the subfield of psychology that addresses the causes and progression of psychological disorders (also referred to as *psychiatric disorders*, *mental disorders*, or *mental illness*). How would a mental health clinician—a mental health professional who evaluates or treats people with psychological disorders—determine whether Big Edie or Little Edie (or both of them) had a psychological disorder? The clinician would need to evaluate whether the women's behavior and experience met three general criteria for psychological disorders.

The Three Criteria for Determining Psychological Disorders

Big Edie and Little Edie came to public attention in 1971, when their unusual living situation was described in the national press. Health Department inspectors had raided their house and found the structure to be in violation of virtually every regulation. "In the dining room, they found a 5-foot mountain of empty cans; in the upstairs bedrooms, they saw human waste. The story became a national scandal. Health Department officials said they would evict the women unless the house was cleaned" (Martin, 2002). The Beales were able to remain in their house after Big Edie's niece (Jacqueline Kennedy Onassis, the former first lady) paid to have the dwelling brought up to the Health Department's standards.

To determine whether Big Edie or Little Edie had a psychological disorder, we must first define **psychological disorder**: a pattern of thoughts, feelings, or behaviors that causes significant personal *distress*, significant *impairment* in daily life, and/or significant *risk of harm*, any of which is unusual for the context and culture in which it arises (American Psychiatric Association, 2013). Notice the word *significant* in the definition, which indicates that the diagnosis of psychological disorder is applied only when the symptoms have a substantial effect on a person's life. As we shall see shortly, all three elements (distress, impairment, and risk of harm) do not need to be present; if two (or even one) of the elements are present to a severe enough degree, then the person's condition may merit the diagnosis of a psychological disorder (see Figure 1.1). Let's consider these three elements in more detail.

FIGURE 1.1 • Determining a Psychological Disorder: Three Criteria The severity of a person's distress, impairment in daily life, and/or risk of harm determine whether he or she is said to have a psychological disorder. All three elements don't need to be present at a significant level: When one or two elements are present to a significant degree, this may indicate a psychological disorder, provided that the person's behavior and experience are not normal for the context and culture in which they arise.

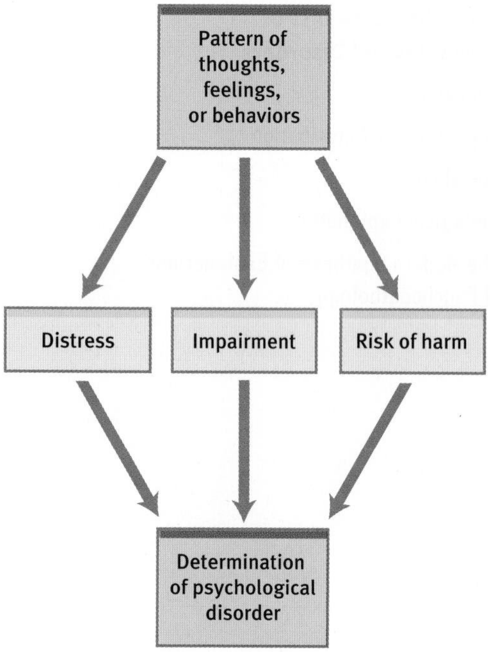

Distress

Distress can be defined as anguish or suffering, and all of us experience distress at different times in our lives. However, when a person with a psychological disorder experiences distress, it is often *out of proportion* to a situation. The state of being

distressed, in and of itself, does not indicate a psychological disorder—it is the degree of distress or the circumstances in which the distress arises that mark abnormality. Some people with psychological disorders exhibit their distress: They may cry in front of others, share their anxieties, or vent their anger on those around them. But other people with psychological disorders contain their distress, leaving family and friends unaware of their emotional suffering. For example, a person may worry excessively but not talk about the worries, or a depressed person may cry only when alone, putting on a mask to convince others that everything is all right.

Severe distress, by itself, doesn't necessarily indicate a psychological disorder. The opposite is also true: The absence of distress doesn't necessarily indicate the absence of a psychological disorder. A person can have a psychological disorder without experiencing distress, although it is uncommon. For instance, someone who chronically abuses stimulant medication, such as amphetamines, may not feel distress about misusing the drug, but that person nonetheless has a psychological disorder (specifically, a type of *substance use disorder*).

Big Edie and Little Edie Beale were clearly unconventional and eccentric. But did either of them have a psychological disorder? Psychological disorders involve significant distress, impairment in daily life, and/or risk of harm.

Did either Big Edie or Little Edie exhibit distress? People who knew them describe the Beale women as free spirits, making the best of life. Like many other people, they were distressed about their financial circumstances; but they in fact had real financial difficulties, so these worries were not unfounded. Little Edie did show significant distress in other ways, though. She was angry and resentful about having to be a full-time caretaker for her mother, and the documentary film *Grey Gardens* (as well as the HBO film and Broadway play of the same name) clearly portrays this: When Big Edie yells for Little Edie to return to her side, Little Edie says in front of the camera, "I've been a subterranean prisoner here for 20 years" (Maysles & Maysles, 1976).

Although Little Edie appears to have been significantly distressed, her distress was reasonable *given the situation*. Being the full-time caretaker to an eccentric and demanding mother for decades would undoubtedly distress most people. Because her distress made sense in its context, it is not an element of a psychological disorder. Big Edie, in contrast, appears to have become significantly distressed when she was alone for more than a few minutes, and this response is unusual for the context. We can consider Big Edie's distress as meeting this criterion for a psychological disorder.

Impairment in Daily Life

Impairment is a significant reduction of a person's ability to function in some important area of life. A person with a psychological disorder may be impaired in functioning at school, at work, in taking adequate care of himself or herself, or in relationships. For example, a woman's drinking problem may interfere with her ability to do her job or to attend to her bills; a middle-aged, married man's continually worrying about his increasing baldness—spending hours and hours each day "fixing" his hair—might impair his ability to get to work on time.

Where do mental health clinicians draw the line between normal functioning and impaired functioning? It is the *degree* of impairment that indicates a psychological disorder. When feeling "down" or nervous, we are all likely to function less well—for example, we may feel irritable or have difficulty concentrating. With a psychological disorder, though, the degree of impairment is atypical for the context—the person is impaired to a greater degree than most people in a similar situation. For instance, after a relationship breakup, most people go through a difficult week or two, but they still go to school or to work. They may not accomplish much, but they soon

We don't know why this woman is so upset, but being persistently upset at work might qualify as an impairment—a significant reduction in a person's ability to function in some important area of life, such as work. Researchers have attempted to measure the effects of impairment associated with psychological disorders on the ability to function at work: For every 100 workers, an average of 37 work days per month are lost because of reduced productivity or absences due to psychological disorders (Kessler & Frank, 1997).

Psychosis
An impaired ability to perceive reality to the extent that normal functioning is difficult or not possible. The two types of psychotic symptoms are hallucinations and delusions.

Hallucinations
Sensations that are so vivid that the perceived objects or events seem real, although they are not. Hallucinations can occur in any of the five senses.

Delusions
Persistent false beliefs that are held despite evidence that the beliefs are incorrect or exaggerate reality.

begin to bounce back. Some people, however, are more impaired after a breakup—they may not make it out of the house or even out of bed; they may not bounce back after a few weeks. These people are significantly impaired.

One type of impairment directly reflects a particular pattern of mental events: A **psychosis** is an impaired ability to perceive reality to the extent that normal functioning is difficult or not possible. The two forms of psychotic symptoms are hallucinations and delusions. **Hallucinations** are sensations that are so vivid that the perceived objects or events seem real, although they are not. Hallucinations can occur in any of the five senses, but the most common type is auditory hallucinations, in particular, hearing voices. However, a hallucination—in and of itself—does not indicate psychosis or a psychological disorder. Rather, this form of psychotic symptom must arise in a context that renders it unusual and impairs functioning.

The other psychotic symptom is **delusions**—persistent false beliefs that are held despite evidence that the beliefs are incorrect or exaggerate reality. The content of delusions can vary across psychological disorders. Common themes include a person's belief that:

- other people or organizations—the FBI, aliens, the neighbor across the street—are after the person (*paranoid* or *persecutory delusions*);
- his or her intimate partner is dating or interested in another person (*delusional jealousy*);
- he or she is more powerful, knowledgeable, or influential than is true in reality and/or that he or she is a different person, such as the president or Jesus (*grandiose delusions*);
- his or her body—or a part of it—is defective or functioning abnormally (*somatic delusion*).

Were the Beale women impaired? The fact that they lived in such squalor implies an inability to function normally in daily life. They knew about hygienic standards but didn't live up to them. Whether the Beales were impaired is complicated by the fact that they viewed themselves as bohemians, set their own standards, and did not want to conform to mainstream values (Sheehy, personal communication, December 29, 2006). However, their withdrawal from the world can be seen as clear evidence that they were impaired. Perhaps they couldn't function in the world and so retreated to Grey Gardens.

The women also appear to have been somewhat paranoid: In the heat of summer, they left the windows nailed shut (even on the second floor) for fear of possible intruders. The women's social functioning was impaired to the extent that their paranoid beliefs led to strange behaviors that isolated them. In addition, their beliefs led them to behave in ways that made the house so uncomfortable—extreme temperatures and fleas—that relatives wouldn't visit. And Big Edie's distress at being alone for even a few minutes indicates that her ability to function independently was impaired. It seems, then, that a case could be made that both of them—Big Edie more so than Little Edie—were impaired and not functioning normally.

Risk of Harm

Some people take more risks than others. They may drive too fast or drink too much. They may diet too strenuously, exercise to an extreme, gamble away too much money, or have unprotected sex with multiple partners. For such behavior to indicate a psychological disorder, it must be outside the normal range. The criterion of danger, then, refers to symptoms of a psychological disorder that lead to life or property being put at risk, either accidentally or intentionally. For example, a person with a psychological disorder may be in danger when:

- depression and hopelessness lead him or her to attempt suicide;
- hallucinations interfere with normal safety precautions, such as checking for cars before crossing the street;

- a distorted body image and other psychological disturbances lead the person to refuse to eat enough food to maintain a healthy weight, which in turn leads to malnutrition and medical problems.

Psychological disorders can also lead people to put other people's lives at risk. Examples of this type of danger include:

- auditory hallucinations that command the person to harm another person;
- suicide attempts that put the lives of other people at risk, such as driving a car into oncoming traffic;
- paranoia so extreme that a parent kills his or her children in order to "save" them from a greater evil.

The house in which Little Edie and Big Edie lived had clearly become dangerous. Wild animals—raccoons and rats—roamed the house, and the ceiling was falling down. But having too little money to make home repairs doesn't mean that someone has a psychological disorder. Some might argue that perhaps the Beale women simply weren't aware of the danger. The women were, however, aware of *some* dangers: When their heat stopped working, they called a heating company to repair it, and ditto for the electricity. They had a handyman come in regularly to repair fallen ceilings and walls, and to fill holes that rats might use to enter (Wright, 2007). It's hard to say, however, whether they realized the extent to which their house itself had become dangerous.

On at least one occasion in her early 30s, Little Edie appears to have been a danger to herself. Her cousin John told someone about "a summer afternoon when he watched Little Edie climb a catalpa tree outside Grey Gardens. She took out a lighter. He begged her not to do it. She set her hair ablaze" (Sheehy, 2006). From then on, her head was at least partially bald, explaining her ever-present head covering.

Aside from Little Edie's single episode with the lighter, it's not clear how much the Beale women's behavior led to a significant risk of harm. Big Edie recognized most imminent dangers and took steps to ensure her and her daughter's safety. The women were not overtly suicidal nor did they harm others. The only aspect of their lives that suggests a significant risk of harm was the poor hygienic standards they maintained.

Context and Culture

As we noted earlier, what counts as a significant level of distress, impairment, or risk of harm depends on the context in which it arises. That human waste was found in an empty room at Grey Gardens might indicate abnormal behavior, but the fact that the plumbing was out of order for a period of time might provide a reasonable explanation. Of course, knowing that the human waste was allowed to remain in place after the plumbing was fixed would probably decide the question of whether the behavior was abnormal.

In addition, the Beales appeared to have delusions—that people wanted to break into the house or kidnap them, and that then-President Nixon might have been responsible for the 1971 "raid" on their house by the town health inspectors (Wright, 2007). But these delusions aren't necessarily as farfetched as they might

Tom Wargacki/WireImage/Getty Images

Using this book's definition of a psychological disorder, did either of the Beales have a disorder? Big Edie exhibited distress that was inappropriate to her situation; both women appeared to have an impaired ability to function. The risk of harm to the women, however, is less clear-cut.

TABLE 1.1 • Psychological Disorders: Facts at a Glance

- Psychological disorders are a leading cause of disability and death, ranked second after heart disease (Murray & Lopez, 1996).

- About half of all Americans will likely develop at least one of 30 common psychological disorders, such as those related to depression, anxiety, or substance abuse, over the course of their lives; in half of the cases, symptoms will begin by age 14 (Kessler, Berglund, et al., 2005).

- Those born more recently have a higher likelihood of developing a psychological disorder than those born earlier (Kessler, Berglund, et al., 2005).

- Within a given year, about 25% of Americans experience a diagnosable or diagnosed mental disorder; of these cases, almost one quarter are severe (Kessler, Chiu, et al., 2005).

- Disadvantaged ethnic groups—Hispanics and Blacks—do not have a higher risk than others for psychological disorders overall (Breslau et al., 2005).

How do we define "risk" or "danger" in different cultural environments? How does culture impact our understanding of abnormal behavior?

Culture
The shared norms and values of a society that are explicitly and implicitly conveyed to its members by example and through the use of reward and punishment.

sound. Their house *was* broken into in 1968, and, as relatives of Jackie Kennedy, they had cars with Secret Service agents posted outside their house while John F. Kennedy was president.

Behavior that seems inappropriate in one context may make sense in another. Having a psychological disorder isn't merely being different—we wouldn't say that someone was abnormal simply because he or she was avant-garde or eccentric or acted on unusual social, sexual, political, religious, or other beliefs (American Psychiatric Association, 2013). And as we've seen with the Beales, the effects of context can blur the line between being different and having a disorder. Table 1.1 provides additional information about psychological disorders.

Culture, too, can play a crucial role in how mental illness is diagnosed. To psychologists, **culture** is the shared norms and values of a society; these norms and values are explicitly and implicitly conveyed to members of the society by example and through the use of reward and punishment. Different societies and countries have their own cultures, each with its own view of what constitutes mental health and mental illness—even what constitutes distress and how to communicate that distress. For example, in some cultures, distress may be conveyed by complaints of fatigue or tiredness rather than by sadness or depressed mood. Some sets of symptoms that are recognized as disorders in other parts of the world are not familiar to most Westerners. One example, described in Case 1.1, is *koro*, a disorder that arises in some people from countries in Southeast Asia. Someone with *koro* rapidly develops an intense fear that his penis—or her nipples and vulva—will retract into the body and possibly cause death (American Psychiatric Association, 2013). This disorder may break out in clusters of people, like an epidemic (Bartholomew, 1998; Sachdev, 1985). Similar genital-shrinking fears have been reported in India and in West African countries (Dzokoto & Adams, 2005; Mather, 2005).

CASE 1.1 • FROM THE OUTSIDE: Cultural Influence on Symptoms

Although most cases of *koro* appear to resolve quickly, in a minority of cases, symptoms may persist.

A 41-year-old unmarried, unemployed male from a business family, presented with the complaints of gradual retraction of penis and scrotum into the abdomen. He had frequent panic attacks, feeling that the end had come. The symptoms had persisted more than 15 years with a waxing and waning course. During exacerbations he spent most of his time measuring the penis by a scale and pulling it in order to bring it out of [his] abdomen. He tied a string around it and attached it to a hook above to prevent its shrinkage during [the] night. . . . He did not have regular work and was mostly dependent on the family.
(Kar, 2005, p. 34)

In addition, cultural norms about psychopathology are not set in stone but can shift. Consider that, in 1851, Dr. Samuel Cartwright of Louisiana wrote an essay in which he declared that slaves' running away was evidence of a serious mental disorder that he called "drapetomania" (Eakin, 2000). More recently, homosexuality was officially considered a psychological disorder in the United States until 1973, when it was removed from the *Diagnostic and Statistical Manual of Mental Disorders (DSM)*, the manual used by mental health clinicians to classify psychological disorders.

Let's examine the behavior of the Beales within their context and culture. Big Edie's father claimed that his ancestors were prominent French Catholics; she and her siblings grew up financially well off. Big Edie was a singer and a performer, but, as a product of her time, she was expected to marry well (McKenna, 2004). Her father arranged for her to wed New York lawyer Phelan Beale, from a socially prominent Southern family (Rakoff, 2002). Little Edie was born about a year later, followed by two brothers. Big Edie was very close to her daughter, even keeping her out of school when Little Edie was

📷 GETTING THE PICTURE

Which photo shows a person more likely to have a psychological disorder based on the voluntary changes made to his/her skin? Answer: It depends on the cultural context. The scarring of the man in the left is intentional and common in his West African tribe, and hence would not be considered a sign of abnormality—but such scarring might be a sign of something abnormal in some Western cultures. However, cultures shift over time, and what is abnormal in one time and place may not be in another. For example, ear gauging (shown on the right) used to be found in African tribes but not in the West, but recently some young people in Western culture have adopted this practice.

11 and 12, ostensibly for "health reasons." However, Little Edie was well enough to go to the movies with her mother every day and on a shopping trip to Paris (Sheehy, 2006).

After she was married, Big Edie continued to sing, to write songs with her accompanist, and even to record some of those songs. At that time, however, cultural conventions required a woman of Big Edie's social standing to stop performing after marrying, even if such performances generally were limited to social functions. Big Edie's need to perform was almost a compulsion, though, and she would head straight to the piano at family gatherings.

In 1934, when Little Edie was 16, Big Edie and her husband divorced; divorce back then was much less common and much less socially acceptable than it is today. This event marked the start of Big Edie's life as a recluse (Davis, 1969). By 1936, the house and grounds began to suffer from neglect (Davis, 1996). In 1942, Big Edie's husband stopped supporting her financially after she showed up late for their son's wedding, dressed inappropriately—another time when Big Edie's behavior was unusual for the context and culture. Big Edie's father set up a trust fund for her, which provided a small monthly allowance, barely enough to pay for food and other necessities.

Like her mother, Little Edie was artistically inclined. She aspired to be an actress, dancer, and poet. In 1946, she left home to live in New York City and work as a model, but her father disapproved of this, as he had disapproved of his wife's musical performances (Sheehy, 2006).

In 1952, after 6 years of being separated from her daughter, Big Edie became seriously depressed (Sheehy, 2006), although there is no information about her specific symptoms. She spent 3 months calling Little Edie daily, begging her to return to Grey Gardens. Eventually, Little Edie moved back to take care of Big Edie. When she did, her artistic aspirations became only dreams and fantasies. *Grey Gardens* vividly captures Little Edie's disappointment at the path her life took—becoming a round-the-clock caretaker to her mother, a disappointed woman herself.

So far, we've seen that psychological disorders lead to significant distress, impairment in daily life, and/or risk of harm. We've also seen that the determination of a disorder depends on the culture and context in which these elements occur. A case could be made that the Beale women did have psychological disorders; let's consider each woman in turn. Big Edie exhibited significant distress when alone for more than a few minutes; her reclusiveness and general lifestyle suggest an impaired ability to function independently in the world—perhaps to the point where there might have been a risk of harm to herself or her daughter. Her behavior and experience appear to satisfy the first two criteria, which is enough to indicate that she had a psychological disorder. Moreover, Big Edie suffered from depression at some point after Little Edie moved to New York, and she experienced enough distress that she begged her daughter to return to Grey Gardens.

As for Little Edie, her distress was appropriate for the context and thus would not meet the first criterion. Her ability to function independently, though, appears to have been significantly impaired, which also increased the risk of harm to herself and her mother. It appears that she, too, suffered from a psychological disorder. However, these conclusions must be tentative—they are based solely on films of the women and other people's descriptions and memories of them.

Now that we know what is required to determine whether someone has a psychological disorder, we'll spend the rest of this chapter looking at how psychopathology has been explained through the ages, up to the present.

Thinking Like A Clinician

Suppose Pietro was hearing the voice of a deceased relative, and he was from a culture where such experiences were considered normal—or at least not abnormal. But he was distressed about hearing the voice, to the point where he was having a hard time doing his job. Should Pietro be considered to have a psychological disorder? If so, why? If not, why not? What additional information would you want to help you decide, if you weren't sure?

Views of Psychological Disorders Before Science

Psychological disorders have probably been around as long as there have been humans. In every age, people have tried to answer the fundamental questions of why mental illness occurs and how to treat it. In this section, we begin at the beginning, by considering the earliest known explanations of psychological disorders.

Ancient Views of Psychopathology

Throughout history, humans have tried to understand the causes of mental illness in an effort to counter its detrimental effects. The earliest accounts of abnormal thoughts, feelings, and behaviors focused on two possible causes: (1) supernatural forces and (2) an imbalance of substances within the body.

Supernatural Forces

Societies dating as far back as the Stone Age appear to have explained psychological disorders in terms of supernatural forces—magical or spiritual in nature (Porter, 2002). Both healers and common folk believed that the mentally ill were possessed by spirits or demons, and possession was often seen as punishment for some religious, moral, or other transgression.

In the ancient societies that understood psychological disorders in this way, treatment often consisted of *exorcism*—a ritual or ceremony intended to force the demons to leave the person's body and restore the person to a normal state. The healer led the exorcism, which in some cultures consisted of reciting incantations, speaking with the spirit, and inflicting physical pain to induce the spirit to leave the person's body (Goodwin et al., 1990). This belief in supernatural forces was common in ancient Egypt and Mesopotamia and, as we shall see shortly, arose again in the Middle Ages in Europe and persists today in some cultures. Although it is tempting to regard such a view of psychopathology and its treatment as barbaric or uncivilized, the healers were simply doing the best they could in trying to understand and treat devastating impairments.

Archaeologists have found evidence of *trephination*, the boring of a hole in the skull, dating as far back as 7,000 years ago. In some ancient cultures, insanity was thought to arise from supernatural forces; one explanation for trephination is that the hole allowed these supernatural forces to escape. Treatment for mental illness is usually related to the prevailing explanation of the cause of the mental illness.

Carlos Munoz-Yague/Science Source

Imbalance of Substances Within the Body

Throughout history, some societies have understood psychological disorders as arising from imbalances of one or more bodily substances.

Chinese Qi

Healers in China beginning in the 7th century B.C.E. viewed psychological disorders as a form of physical illness, reflecting imbalances in the body and spirit. This view rests on the belief that all living things have a life force, called *qi* (pronounced "chee," as in *cheetah*), which flows through the body along 12 channels to the organs. Illness results when *qi* is blocked or seriously imbalanced; to this day, this view underpins aspects of Chinese medicine. Even today, Chinese treatment for various problems, including some psychological disorders, aims to restore the proper balance of *qi*. Practitioners use a number of techniques, including acupuncture and herbal medicine.

Ancient Greeks and Romans

Like the ancient Chinese, the ancient Greeks viewed mental illness as a form of bodily illness arising from imbalances (U.S. National Library of Medicine, 2005). Specifically, mental illness arose through an imbalance of four *humors* (that is, bodily fluids): black bile, blood, yellow bile, and phlegm. Each humor corresponded to one of four basic elements: earth, air, fire, and water. The ancient Greeks believed that differences in character reflected the relative balance of these humors, and an extreme imbalance of the humors resulted in illness—including mental illness. Most prominent among the resulting mental disorders were *mania* (marked by excess uncontrollability, arising from too much of the humors blood and yellow bile) and *melancholy* (marked by anguish and dejection, and perhaps hallucinations, arising from too much black bile). The goal of treatment was to restore the balance of humors through diet, medicine, or surgery (such as bleeding—letting some blood drain out of the body—if the person were diagnosed as having too much of the humor blood).

Beginning with the physician Hippocrates (460–377 B.C.E.), the ancient Greeks emphasized reasoning and rationality in their explanations of natural phenomena, rejecting supernatural explanations. Hippocrates suggested that the brain—rather than any other bodily organ—is responsible for mental activity, and that mental illness arises from abnormalities in the brain (Shaffer & Lazarus, 1952). Today, the term *medical model* is used to refer to Hippocrates' view that all illness, including mental illness, has its basis in biological disturbance. Galen (131–201 C.E.), a Roman doctor, extended the ideas of the Greeks. Galen proposed that imbalances in humors produced emotional imbalances—and such emotional problems in turn could lead to psychological disorders.

Forces of Evil in the Middle Ages and the Renaissance

The almost naked man is being beaten by priests in order to drive out the devil (the devil is kneeling in front of another priest). Such punishments or torture were attempts to "cure" mental illness, which was believed to arise from the devil.

With the rise of Christianity in Europe, psychopathology came to be attributed to forces of evil. During the Middle Ages (approximately 500–1400 C.E.), the Greek emphasis on reason and science lost influence, and madness was once again thought to result from supernatural forces. However, at this time mental illness was conceived as a consequence of a battle between good and evil for the possession of a person's soul. Prophets and visionaries were believed to be possessed or inspired by the will of God. For example, French heroine Joan of Arc reported that she heard the voice of God command her to lead a French army to drive the British out of France. The French hailed her as a visionary. In contrast, other men and women who reported such experiences usually were believed to be possessed by the devil or were viewed as being punished for their sins. Treatment consisted of attempts to end the possession: exorcism, torture (with the idea that physical pain would drive out the evil forces), starvation, and other forms of punishment to the body. Such inhumane treatment was not undertaken everywhere, though. As early as the 10th century, Islamic institutions were caring humanely for those with mental illness (Sarró, 1956).

During the Renaissance (approximately the 1400s through the 1600s), mental illness continued to be viewed as a result of demonic possession, and witches were held responsible for a wide variety of ills. Indeed, witches were blamed for other people's physical problems and even for societal and environmental problems, such as droughts or crop failures. As before, treatment was primarily focused on ridding the person of demonic forces, in one way or another.

During this period, people believed that witches put the whole community in jeopardy through their evil acts and through their association with the devil (White, 1948). The era is notable for its witch hunts, which were organized efforts to track down people who were believed to be in league with the devil and to have inflicted possession on other people (Kemp, 2000). Once found, these "witches" were often burned alive. The practice of witch burning spread throughout Europe and the American colonies:

> Judges were called upon to pass sentence on witches in great numbers. A French judge boasted that he had burned 800 women in 16 years on the bench; 600 were burned during the administration of a bishop in Bamberg. The Inquisition, originally started by the Church of Rome, was carried along by Protestant Churches in Great Britain and Germany. In Protestant Geneva 500 persons were burned in the year 1515. Other countries, where there were Catholic jurists, boasted of as many burnings. In Treves, 7,000 were reported burned during a period of several years.
> (Bromberg, 1937, p. 61, quoted in White, 1948, p. 8)

Rationality and Reason in the 18th and 19th Centuries

At the end of the Renaissance, rational thought and reason gained acceptance again. French philosopher René Descartes proposed that mind and body are distinct and that bodily illness arises from abnormalities in the body, whereas mental illness arises from abnormalities in the mind. Similarly, according to the 17th-century British philosopher John Locke, insanity is caused by irrational thinking, and so could be treated by helping people regain their rational, logical thought process.

However, the theory that deficits in rationality and reason caused mental illness did not lead to consistent approaches to treatment. In the Western world, the mentally ill were treated differently from country to country and decade to decade. As we see in the following sections, various approaches were tried in an effort to cope with the mentally ill and with mental illness itself.

Asylums

The Renaissance was a time of widespread innovation and enlightened thinking. For some people, this enlightenment extended to their view of how to treat those with mental illness—humanely. Some groups founded **asylums**, institutions to house and care for people who were afflicted with mental illness. In general, asylums were founded by religious orders; the first of this type was opened in Valencia, Spain, in 1409 (Sarró, 1956). In subsequent decades, asylums for the mentally ill were built throughout Europe.

Before long, though, criminals and others who weren't necessarily mentally ill were sent to asylums, and the facilities became overcrowded. Their residents were then more like inmates than patients. At least in some cases, people were sent to asylums simply to keep them off the street, without any effort to treat them.

Perhaps the most famous asylum from this era was the Hospital of St. Mary of Bethlehem in London (commonly referred to as "Bedlam," which became a word meaning "confusion and uproar"). In 1547, that institution shifted from being a general hospital to an asylum used to incarcerate the mad, particularly those who were poor. Residents were chained to the walls or floor or put in cages and displayed to a paying public, much like animals in a zoo (Sarró, 1956). Officials believed that such exhibitions would deter people from indulging in behaviors believed to lead to mental illness.

Asylums were initially meant to be humane settings for those with mental illness. A victim of their success, asylums became overcrowded as a result of an influx of criminals and people with medical illnesses. With overcrowding, the primary purpose of asylums became incarceration rather than treatment, as was true of the Hospital of St. Mary of Bethlehem ("Bedlam") in the early 18th century, illustrated here.

Pinel and Mental Treatment

The humane treatment of people with psychological disorders found a great supporter in French physician Phillipe Pinel (1745–1826). He and others transformed the lives of asylum patients at the Salpêtrière and Bicêtre Hospitals (for women and men, respectively) in Paris: In 1793, Pinel removed their chains and stopped "treatments" that involved bleeding, starvation, and physical punishment (Porter, 2002). Pinel and his colleagues believed that "madness" is a disease; they carefully observed patients and distinguished between different types of "madness." Pinel also identified *partial insanity*, where the person was irrational with regard to one topic but was otherwise rational. He believed that such a person could be treated through psychological means, such as reasoning with him or her, which was one of the first mental treatments for mental disorders.

Moral Treatment

In the 1790s, a group of Quakers in England developed a treatment for mental illness that was based on their personal and religious belief systems. Mental illness was seen as a temporary state during which the person was deprived of his or her reason. **Moral treatment** consisted of providing an environment in which people with

Asylums
Institutions to house and care for people who are afflicted with mental illness.

Moral treatment
Treatment of the mentally ill that involved providing an environment in which people with mental illness were treated with kindness and respect and functioned as part of a community.

©Burstein Collection/Corbis

Humanitarian Dorothea Dix worked tirelessly for humane treatment of the mentally ill in the United States (Viney, 2000).

mental illness were treated with kindness and respect. The "mad" residents lived out in the country, worked, prayed, rested, and functioned as a community. Over 90% of the residents treated this way for a year recovered (Whitaker, 2002), at least temporarily.

Moral treatment also began to be used in the United States. Around the time that Pinel was unchaining the mentally ill in France, Doctor Benjamin Rush (1745–1813), a physician at the Pennsylvania Hospital in Philadelphia, moved the mentally ill from filthy basement cells to rooms above ground level, provided them with mattresses and meals, and treated them with respect.

In the 1840s Dorothea Dix (1802–1887), a schoolteacher who had witnessed the terrible conditions in the asylums of New England, also began to support moral treatment. She engaged in lifelong humanitarian efforts to ensure that the mentally ill were housed separately from criminals and treated humanely, in both public and private asylums (Viney, 2000). Dix also helped to raise millions of dollars for building new mental health facilities throughout the United States. Her work is all the more remarkable because she undertook it at a time when women did not typically participate in such social projects.

Moral treatment proved popular, and its success had an unintended consequence: Unlike private asylums, public asylums couldn't turn away patients, and thus their population increased tenfold, as the mentally ill were joined by people with epilepsy and others with neurological disorders, as well as many who might otherwise have gone to jail. As a result, public institutions housing the mentally ill again became overcrowded and underfunded, and moral treatment—or treatments of any kind—were no longer provided (Porter, 2002). Sedation and management became the new goals.

Thinking Like A Clinician

Why might explanations of mental illness as arising from supernatural forces have been popular for so long? How does a given treatment follow from beliefs about the cause of mental illness? Can you think of at least two specific examples where beliefs about the cause of mental illness have shaped treatments in different ways?

The Transition to Scientific Accounts of Psychological Disorders

Each of the prescientific explanations of psychological disorders proved inadequate. There is, however, one positive legacy from the prescientific era: The mentally ill came to be regarded as ill, and so were treated humanely, at least in some places and some eras. If the Beales had lived in the 18th century or earlier, they might have ended up in Bedlam on display. If the Beales were diagnosed today, they would almost certainly receive treatments that would enable them to function more effectively in the world. Let's now consider the crucial transition from prescientific times to today.

Freud and the Importance of Unconscious Forces

Sigmund Freud (1856–1939), a Viennese neurologist, played a major role in making the study of psychological disorders a science. He not only developed new methods for both diagnosis and treatment (many of which are still in use today) but also proposed a rich and intricate theory, which continues to have massive influence on many clinicians.

Initially Freud, influenced by the French neurologist Jean-Martin Charcot, used hypnosis with his patients in Vienna. Although he had some success, he found that not everyone was equally hypnotizable and that patients' symptoms often returned. This led Freud to develop another method to help patients with hysteria: *free association*, a technique in which patients are encouraged to say whatever thoughts occur to them. Free association was part of Freud's treatment that involved talking—often referred to as the "talking cure"—which rested on his idea that mental disorders in general arise in part because of unconscious conflicts. His idea was that talking freely would help a person to reduce his or her unconscious conflicts and so provide some relief from the psychological disorder.

Psychoanalytic Theory

Freud developed a far-reaching theory of the origins, nature, and treatment of psychopathology based on both his work with patients (who were mostly middle-class and upper-middle-class women) and his observations about himself. His **psychoanalytic theory** (the Greek word *psyche* means "mind") proposes that thoughts, feelings, and behaviors are a result of conscious and unconscious forces continually interacting in the mind. Psychoanalytic theory also suggests that the mind is organized to function across three levels of consciousness:

- The *conscious* consists of thoughts and feelings that are in awareness; this is normal awareness.

- The *preconscious* consists of thoughts and feelings that a person does not perceive, but that can be brought voluntarily into conscious awareness in the future.

- The *unconscious* includes thoughts and feelings that cannot be perceived or called into awareness on command, but which have power to influence a person.

According to Freud, people have sexual and aggressive urges from birth onward. Freud argued that when we find such urges unacceptable, they are banished to our unconscious, where they inevitably gain strength and eventually demand release. Unconscious urges can be released as conscious feelings or thoughts, or as behaviors. Freud believed that abnormal experiences and behaviors arise from this process. For example, according to psychoanalytic theory, one woman's extreme fear of eating dust arose from unconscious sexual impulses related to "taking in" semen (the dust symbolically represented semen; Frink, 1921).

Freud (1923/1961) also distinguished three psychological structures of the mind—the id, the ego, and the superego:

- The **id** is the seat of sexual and aggressive drives, as well as of the desire for immediate gratification of physical and psychological needs. These physical needs (such as for food and water) and psychological drives (sexual and aggressive) constantly require satisfaction. The id is governed by the *pleasure principle*, seeking gratification of needs without regard for the consequences.

- The **superego**, the seat of a person's conscience, works to impose morality. According to Freud, the superego is responsible for feelings of guilt, which motivate the person to constrain his or her sexual and aggressive urges that demand immediate gratification. People with an inflexible morality—an overly rigid sense of right and wrong—are thought to have too strong a superego.

©Bettmann/Corbis

In Freud's view, mental illness is caused by unconscious conflicts that express themselves as psychological symptoms. He revolutionized treatment of psychological disorders by listening to what patients had to say.

• Meanwhile, the **ego** tries to mediate the id's demands for immediate gratification and the superego's high standards of morality, as well as the constraints of external reality. Normally, the ego handles the competing demands well. However, when the ego is relatively weak, it is less able to manage the conflicts among the id, superego, and reality, which then cause anxiety and other symptoms.

Figure 1.2 shows how the three mental structures are related to the three levels of consciousness.

One of Freud's lasting contributions to the field of psychopathology—and all of psychology, in fact—is his notion of the unconscious, the thoughts and feelings that cannot be perceived or called into awareness on command, but which have power to influence a person.

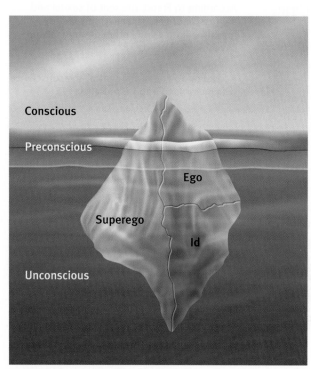

FIGURE 1.2 • Freud's Iceberg Metaphor of the Organization of the Mind Freud proposed that the mind is made up of three structures: id, ego, and superego. Each person is aware (conscious) of some of what is in his or her ego and superego; some of the preconscious contents of the ego and the superego can be brought into awareness, and some of those contents—along with all of the id—remain unconscious.

Ego
According to Freud, the psychic structure that is charged with mediating between the id's demands for immediate gratification and the superego's high standards of morality, as well as the constraints of external reality.

Psychosexual stages
According to Freud, the sequence of five distinct stages of development (oral, anal, phallic, latency, and genital) through which children proceed from infancy to adulthood; each stage has a key task that must be completed successfully for healthy psychological development.

Neurosis
According to psychoanalytic theory, a pattern of thoughts, feelings, or behaviors that expresses an unresolved conflict between the ego and the id or between the ego and the superego.

Psychosexual Stages

Freud also identified five distinct stages of development (the oral, anal, phallic, latency, and genital stages) through which children proceed from infancy into adulthood. Four of these stages involve particular *erogenous zones*, which are areas of the body (the mouth, genitals, and anus) that can satisfy the id's urges and drives. Freud called these five stages **psychosexual stages** because he believed that each erogenous zone demands some form of gratification and that each stage requires that a person successfully complete a key task for healthy psychological development. All of these stages arise during infancy or childhood, although they may not be resolved until adulthood, if ever. An unresolved conflict or issue from an earlier stage, which leaves the person focused on issues related to that stage, is referred to as a *fixation*. For example, according to Freud (1905/1955), people with a fixation at the oral stage use food or alcohol to alleviate anxiety.

Mental Illness, According to Freud

Freud proposed two general categories of mental illness: neuroses and psychoses. A **neurosis** is a pattern of thoughts, feelings, or behaviors that expresses an unresolved conflict between the ego and the id or between the ego and the superego.

Freud (1938) defined *psychosis* as a break from reality characterized by conflict between the ego's view of reality and reality itself. (Note that this is *not* the current conventional definition of psychosis—an impaired ability to perceive reality, such as arises with hallucinations—used by most mental health clinicians and researchers, and which we use in the rest of this textbook.) According to the psychoanalytic view, then, schizophrenia involves a psychosis because it is an escape from reality into one's own internal world (Dorcus & Shaffer, 1945).

Freud was also revolutionary in proposing that parents' interactions with their child are central in the formation of personality. For instance, parents who are too strict about toilet training their toddler may inadvertently cause their child to tend to become fixated at the anal stage.

Defense Mechanisms

In addition to proposing an explanation for how internal psychological conflict arises, Freud, along with his daughter, the noted psychoanalyst Anna Freud (1895–1982), suggested how such conflicts are resolved: The ego frequently employs unconscious

TABLE 1.2 • Common Defense Mechanisms

Defense Mechanism	How the Defense Mechanism Transforms the Conflict	Example
Repression (considered to be the most important defense mechanism)	Unintentionally keeping conflict-inducing thoughts or feelings out of conscious awareness	You "forget" about the time you saw someone getting mugged across the street.
Denial	Not acknowledging the conflict-inducing thoughts or feelings to oneself (and others)	You are addicted to painkillers but won't admit it, even though the addiction has caused you to miss work.
Rationalization	Justifying the conflict-inducing thoughts, feelings, or behaviors with explanations	After a father hits his daughter, he justifies his behavior to himself by saying it will build her character.
Projection	Ascribing (projecting) the conflict-inducing thoughts or feelings onto others	Instead of admitting that you don't like a classmate, you say the person doesn't like you.
Reaction formation	Transforming the conflict-inducing thoughts or feelings into their opposite	Your feelings of attraction to your colleague at work are transformed into distaste and disgust, and you begin to feel repulsed by the colleague.
Sublimation	Channeling the conflict-inducing thoughts or feelings into less-threatening behaviors	When a father's frustration and anger at his teenage daughter mount, he channels his feelings by going for a 20-minute run.

defense mechanisms, which work to transform the conflicts in a way that prevents unacceptable thoughts and feelings from reaching consciousness. If successful, defense mechanisms can decrease anxiety (see Table 1.2).

Psychoanalytic Theory Beyond Freud

Psychoanalytic theory has been modified by Freud's followers; these variations fall under the term *psychodynamic theory* and have attracted many adherents. Psychodynamic theorists have focused on areas that Freud did not develop fully:

• normal versus abnormal development of the self (Kohut, 1971);

• the contribution of additional sources of motivation, such as feelings of inferiority (Ansbacher & Ansbacher, 1956);

• the development and work of the ego (Hartmann, 1939);

• the possibility that our species has certain inborn and unconscious archetypes (an *archetype* is an abstract, ideal characterization of a person, object, or concept) that underlie some aspects of motivation (Jung, 1983).

   In addition, Karen Horney (1885–1952) and other psychologists conducted research on the ways that moment-to-moment interactions between child and parent can contribute to psychological disorders (Horney, 1937; Kernberg, 1986; Sullivan, 1953). This emphasis on the contribution that an infant's social world can make to psychopathology is one of the lasting contributions of psychodynamic theory. Treatment based on psychodynamic theory is generally referred to as *psychodynamic therapy*. Various modifications of psychodynamic therapy have been developed based on specific alterations of Freud's theory.

Evaluating the Contributions of Freud and His Followers

One challenge to psychodynamic theory is that its guiding principles, and those of its corresponding treatments, rest primarily on subjective interpretations of what patients say and do. Another challenge is that the theory is not generally testable using

Defense mechanisms
Unconscious processes that work to transform psychological conflict in order to prevent unacceptable thoughts and feelings from reaching consciousness.

Mental processes
The internal operations that underlie cognitive and emotional functions (such as perception, memory, and guilt feelings) and most human behavior.

Mental contents
The specific material that is stored in the mind and operated on by mental processes.

scientific methodologies. For instance, according to psychodynamic theory, a fear of eating dust could be due to a sublimation of sexual impulses or a reaction formation to an unconscious desire to play with fecal matter (see Table 1.2). The problem is not that there can be more than one hypothesis based on psychodynamic theory, but rather that there is no evidence and no clear means for obtaining evidence that either hypothesis (or both) is correct.

Nevertheless, psychodynamic theory rested on a fundamental insight that was crucial for the development of later theories and treatments: **Mental processes** are the internal operations that underlie cognitive and emotional functions (such as perception, memory, and guilt feelings) and most human behavior. In addition, psychodynamic theory's focus on **mental contents**—the specific memories, knowledge, goals, and other material that are stored and processed in the mind—has led to much fruitful research. Furthermore, the notion that some mental processes and mental contents are hidden away from consciousness has proven invaluable to understanding psychopathology.

The Humanist Response

Some psychologists, such as Abraham Maslow (1908–1970), reacted adversely to Freud's ideas, especially two notions: (1) that mental processes are mechanistic (with the same sort of cause-and-effect relations that govern all machines), driven by sexual and aggressive impulses, and (2) that humans don't really have free will because our behavior is in response to unconscious processes. These psychologists proposed a different view of human nature and mental illness that came to be called *humanistic psychology*, which focuses on free will, innate goodness, creativity, and the self (Maslow, 1968).

Carl Rogers (1902–1987) proposed that symptoms of distress and mental illness arise when a potential route to personal growth is blocked, as can occur when a person lacks a coherent and unified sense of self or when there is a mismatch—an *incongruence*—between the ideal self (the qualities a person wants to have) and the real self (the qualities the person actually has) (Rogers, 1942). For example, suppose a woman believes she should *always* be energetic (ideal self), but her real self is someone who is often energetic, but not always. The incongruence between the two selves can lead her to feel bad about herself, which in turn creates feelings of apathy and guilt.

Rogers developed *client-centered therapy* to help people reduce such incongruence and to help them create solutions to their problems by releasing their "real selves." In accordance with this approach of self-empowerment, Rogers (1942) stressed that his *clients* were not *patients* who are seen to be "sick" and lacking in power. Referring to people as "clients" indicated that they had control over their own lives and were interested in self-improvement through engagement with mental health services (Kahn, 1998).

Although the emphasis on self-empowerment has proven useful, the humanist approach, like all approaches, falls short on its own as a general method for conceptualizing and treating mental illness. As we shall see, other factors (e.g., biological and social) must be considered.

Thinking Like A Clinician

Based on what you have read, why do you think Freud's theory has less influence today than it once had? Why might certain aspects of psychodynamic theory continue to influence modern perspectives?

Scientific Accounts of Psychological Disorders

In the early 20th century, advances in science led to an interest in theories of psychological disorders that could be tested rigorously, generating hypotheses that could be proven or disproven. Several different scientific approaches (and accompanying theories) that emerged at that time are still with us today; they focus on different aspects of psychopathology, including behavior, cognition, social interactions, and biology. These scientific accounts and theories have thrived because studies have shown that they explain some aspects of mental illness. Let's examine these modern approaches to psychopathology and how they could explain Big Edie and Little Edie's thoughts, feelings, and behavior.

Behaviorism

All of the views discussed so far focus on forces that affect mental processes and mental contents. However, some psychologists in the early 20th century took a radically different perspective and focused only on directly observable behaviors. Spearheaded by American psychologists Edward Lee Thorndike (1874–1949), John B. Watson (1878–1958), and Clark L. Hull (1884–1952), and, most famously, B. F. Skinner (1904–1990), **behaviorism** focuses on understanding directly observable behaviors rather than unobservable mental processes and mental contents (Watson, 1931). The behaviorists' major contribution to understanding psychopathology was to propose scientifically testable mechanisms that may explain how maladaptive behavior arises (Skinner, 1986, 1987). These psychologists focused their research on the association between factors that trigger a behavior and on a behavior and its consequences; the consequences influence whether a behavior is likely to recur. For instance, to the extent that using a drug has pleasurable consequences, a person is more likely to use the drug again.

The pleasurable feelings that can be induced by consuming alcohol often serve as reinforcers, prompting people to engage in the behavior again (and again, and again).

At about the same time in Russia, Nobel Prize–winning physiologist Ivan Pavlov (1849–1936) accidentally discovered an association between a reflexive behavior and the conditions that occur immediately prior to it (that is, its antecedents), an association created by a process sometimes referred to as *Pavlovian conditioning* (Pavlov, 1936). He studied salivation in dogs, and he noticed that dogs increased their salivation both while they were eating (which he predicted—the increased salivation when eating is a reflexive behavior) and *right before* they were fed (which he did not predict). He soon determined that the dogs began salivating when they heard the approaching footsteps of the person feeding them. The feeder's footsteps (a neutral stimulus) became associated with the stimulus of food in the mouth, thus leading the dogs to salivate when hearing the sound of footsteps; the dogs' past association between the feeder's footsteps and subsequent food led to a behavior change.

Pavlov investigated the reflexive behavior of salivation, and other researchers have found that reflexive fear-related behaviors (such as a startle response) can be conditioned in the same fashion. These findings contributed to the understanding of how the severe fears and anxieties that are part of many psychological disorders can arise—how neutral stimuli that have in the past been paired with fear-inducing

Behaviorism
An approach to psychology that focuses on understanding directly observable behaviors in order to understand mental illness and other psychological phenomena.

objects or events can, by themselves, come to induce fear or anxiety. We will consider such conditioning in more detail in Chapter 2.

Among the most important insights of behaviorism, then, is that a person's behavior, including maladaptive behavior, can result from *learning*—from a previous association with an object, situation, or event. Big Edie appears to have developed maladaptive behaviors related to a fear of being alone. This may have been a result of past negative experiences with (and the resulting associations to) being alone, perhaps by neighborhood boys playing tricks on her when they knew she was home alone.

Behaviorism ushered in new explanations of—and treatments for—some psychological disorders. The behaviorists' emphasis on controlled, objective observation and on the importance of the situation had a deep and lasting impact on the field of psychopathology. However, researchers also learned that not all psychological problems could readily be explained as a result of maladaptive learning. Rather, mental processes and mental contents are clearly involved in the development and maintenance of many psychological disorders. This opened the door for cognitive psychology.

The Cognitive Contribution

Psychodynamic and behaviorist explanations of psychological disorders seemed incompatible. Psychodynamic theory emphasized private mental processes and mental contents; behaviorist theories emphasized directly observable behavior. Then, the late 1950s and early 1960s saw the rise of *cognitive psychology*, the area of psychology that studies mental processes and contents starting from the analogy of information processing by a computer. Researchers developed new, behaviorally based methods to track the course of hidden mental processes and characterize the nature of mental contents, which began to be demystified. If a mental process operates on mental contents like a computer program operates on stored data, direct connections can be made between observable behavior, as well as personal experiences, and mental events.

Cognitive psychology has contributed to the understanding of psychological disorders by focusing on specific changes in mental processes and mental contents. For instance, people with *anxiety disorders*—a category of disorders that involves extreme fear, panic, and/or avoidance of a feared stimulus—tend to focus their attention in particular ways, creating a bias in what they expect and remember. In turn, these biased memories appear to support the "truth" of their inaccurate view about the danger of the stimulus that elicits their fear. For instance, a man who is very anxious in social situations may pay excessive attention to whether other people seem to be looking at him; when people glance in his general direction, he will then notice the direction of their gaze and infer that they are looking at him. Later, he will remember that "everyone" was watching him.

Other cognitive explanations of psychological disorders focused on distortions in the content of people's thoughts. Psychiatrist Aaron Beck (b. 1921) and psychologist Albert Ellis (1913–2007) each focused on how people's irrational and inaccurate thoughts about themselves and the world can contribute to psychological disorders (Beck, 1967; Ellis & MacLaren, 1998). For example, people who are depressed often think very negatively and inaccurately about themselves, the future, and the world. They often believe that no one will care about them; or, if someone does care, this person will leave as soon as he or she sees how really inept, ugly, or unlovable the depressed person is. Such thoughts could make anyone depressed! For cognitive therapists, treatment involves shifting, or *restructuring*, people's faulty beliefs and irrational thoughts that led to psychological disorders.

Cognitive therapy might have been appropriate for the Beale women, who had unusual beliefs. Consider the fact that Little Edie worried about leaving her mother alone in her room for more than a few minutes because she might come back and find her mother dead (Graham, 1976). Big Edie also had unusual beliefs. One time, a big kite was hovering over Grey Gardens and she called the police, concerned that the kite was a listening device or a bomb (Wright, 2007).

The focus on particular mental processes and mental contents illuminates some aspects of psychological disorders. But just as behaviorist theories do not fully address why people develop the *particular* beliefs and attitudes they have, cognitive theories do not fully explain why a person's mental processes and contents are biased in a *particular* way. Knowledge about social and neurological factors (i.e., factors that affect the brain and its functioning) helps to complete the picture.

Social Forces

We can view behavioral and cognitive explanations as psychological: Both refer to thoughts, feelings, or behaviors of individual people. In addition to these sorts of factors, we must also consider social factors, which involve more than a single person. There is no unified social explanation for psychological disorders, but various researchers and theorists in the last half of the 20th century recognized that social forces affect the emergence and maintenance of mental illness. Many of these social forces, such as the loss of a relationship, abuse, trauma, neglect, poverty, and discrimination, produce high levels of stress.

One of the social factors that occurs earliest in life is *attachment style*, which characterizes the particular way a person relates to intimate others, and it begins in infancy. Researchers have delineated four types of attachment styles in children:

📷 **GETTING THE PICTURE**

The type of attachment an infant forms with her parent can have profound implications later in life. Which photo might illustrate a secure attachment? Although we can't tell for sure from one snapshot, children like the one on the right, who are not upset when their mother is going to leave the room, often show signs of a secure attachment.

1. *Secure attachment.* Those who become upset when their mother leaves but quickly calm down upon her return (Ainsworth & Bell, 1970).

2. *Resistant/anxious attachment.* Those who become angry when their mother leaves and remain angry upon her return, sometimes even hitting her (Ainsworth & Bell, 1970).

3. *Avoidant attachment.* Those who had no change in their emotions based on mother's presence or absence (Ainsworth & Bell, 1970).

4. *Disorganized attachment.* Those who exhibit a combination of resistant and avoidant styles and also appear confused or fearful with their mother (Main & Solomon, 1986).

Among American children, those with an insecure attachment style (the last three styles listed above) are more likely to develop symptoms of psychological disorders (Main & Solomon, 1986; Minde, 2003).

Research on social factors also points to the ways that relationships—and the social support they provide—can buffer the effects of negative life events (Hyman et al., 2003; Swift & Wright, 2000). For example, researchers have found that healthy relationships can mitigate the effects of a variety of negative events, such as abuse (during childhood or adulthood), trauma, discrimination, and financial hardship. The opposite is also true: The absence of protective relationships increases a person's risk for developing a psychological disorder in the face of a significant stressor (Dikel et al., 2005). (Note that *stressor* is the technical term used to refer to any stimulus that induces stress.)

The Beale women experienced many stressors: financial problems, the dissolution of Big Edie's marriage, and, in later years, social isolation. Their extended family and their community ostracized them, at least in part because they were independent-minded and artistic women. In addition, Little Edie endured her own unique social stresses: Both her parents were excessively controlling. Her father restricted her artistic pursuits, and Little Edie could scarcely leave her mother's room before her mother was calling urgently for her to return; this intense attachment and close physical proximity echo their relationship when Little Edie was a child.

Like the other factors, social factors do not fully account for how and why psychological disorders arise. For instance, social explanations cannot tell us why, of people who experience the same circumstances, some will go on to develop a psychological disorder and others won't.

Biological Explanations

In 1913 it was discovered that one type of mental illness—which was then called *general paresis*, or *paralytic dementia*—was caused by a sexually transmitted disease, syphilis. The final stage of this disease damages the brain and leads to abrupt changes in mental processes, including psychotic symptoms (Hayden, 2003). The discovery of a causal link between syphilis and general paresis heralded a resurgence of the medical model, the view that psychological disorders have underlying biological causes. According to the medical model, once the biological causes are identified, appropriate medical treatments can be developed, such as medications. In fact, antibiotics that treat syphilis also prevent the related mental illness, which was dramatic support for applying the medical model to at least some psychological disorders.

Since that discovery, scientists have examined genes, neurotransmitters (chemicals that allow brain cells to communicate with each other), and abnormalities in brain structure and function associated with mental illness.

What biological factors might have contributed to the Beales' unusual lifestyle and beliefs? Unfortunately, the documentaries and biographies about the two women have not addressed this issue, so there is no way to know. All we know is that one of Big Edie's brothers was a serious gambler, another died as a result of a drinking problem, and one of her nieces also battled problems with alcohol; taken together, these observations might suggest a family history of impulse control problems. We might be tempted to infer that such tendencies in this family reflect an underlying genetic predisposition, but we must be careful: Families share more than their genes, and common components of the environment can also contribute to psychological disorders.

In fact, this is where the medical model reveals its limitations. Explaining psychological disorders simply on the basis of biological factors ultimately strips mental disorders of the broader context in which they occur—in thinking people who live in families and societies—and provides a false impression that mental disorders arise from biological factors alone (Angell, 2011). As we shall see throughout this book, multiple factors usually contribute to a psychological disorder, and treatments targeting only biological factors usually are not the most effective. In the next section we discuss in greater detail this multiple-perspective approach and the model we will use throughout this text.

The bacterium *Treponema pallidum* is responsible for the sexually transmitted disease syphilis. Left untreated, syphilis eventually causes severe brain damage that in turn gives rise to abrupt changes in mental processes, including psychotic symptoms.

Alfred Pasieka/Science Source

The Modern Synthesis of Explanations of Psychopathology

In the past several decades, researchers and clinicians have increasingly recognized that psychological disorders cannot be fully explained by any single type of factor or theory. Two approaches to psychopathology integrate multiple factors: the *diathesis–stress model* and the *biopsychosocial approach*.

The Diathesis–Stress Model

The diathesis–stress model is one way to bring together the various explanations of how psychological disorders arise. The **diathesis–stress model** rests on the claim that a psychological disorder is triggered when a person with a predisposition—a *diathesis*—for the particular disorder experiences an environmental event that causes significant stress (Meehl, 1962; Monroe & Simons, 1991; Rende & Plomin, 1992). Essentially, the idea is that if a person has a predisposition to a psychological disorder, a particular type of stress may trigger its occurrence. But the same stress would not have that effect for a person who did not have the predisposition; also, a person who did have a diathesis for a psychological disorder would be fine if he or she could avoid those types of high-stress events. Both factors are required.

For example, the diathesis–stress model explains why, if one identical twin develops depression, the co-twin (the other twin of the pair) also develops depression in less than one quarter of the cases (Lyons et al., 1998). Because identical twins share virtually 100% of their genes, a co-twin should be guaranteed to develop the disorder if genes alone cause it. But even identical twins experience different types and levels of stress. Their genes may be virtually identical, but their environments are not; thus, both twins do not necessarily develop the psychological disorder over time. The diathesis–stress model is illustrated in Figure 1.3.

A diathesis may be a biological factor, such as a genetic vulnerability to a disorder, or it may be a psychological factor, such as a cognitive vulnerability to a disorder, as can occur when irrational or inaccurate negative thoughts about oneself contribute to depression. The *stress* is often a social factor, which can be acute, such as being the victim of a crime, or less intense but chronic, such as recurring spousal abuse, poverty, or overwork. It is important to note that not everybody experiences the same social factor in the same way. And what's important is not simply the objective circumstance—it's how a person *perceives* it. For example, think about roller coasters: For one person, they are great fun; for another, they are terrifying. Similarly, Big Edie and Little Edie didn't appear to mind their isolation and strange lifestyle and may even have enjoyed it; other people, however, might find living in such circumstances extremely stressful and depressing. Whether because of learning, biology, or an interaction between them, some people are more likely to perceive particular events and stimuli as stressors (and therefore to experience more stress) than others. The diathesis–stress model was the first approach that integrated existing, but separate, explanations for psychological disorders.

The Biopsychosocial and Neuropsychosocial Approaches

To understand the bases of both diatheses and stress, we need to look more carefully at the factors that underlie psychological disorders.

Three Types of Factors

Historically, researchers and clinicians grouped the factors that give rise to psychological disorders into three general types: *biological* (including genetics, the

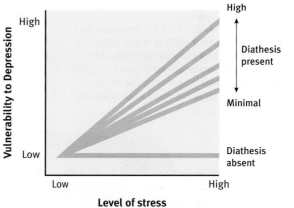

FIGURE 1.3 • The Diathesis–Stress Model According to the diathesis–stress model of depression, people who are more vulnerable to depression (high diathesis) will become depressed after experiencing less stress than people who are less vulnerable to depression (low or absent diathesis). Put another way, given the same level of stress, those who are more vulnerable to depression will develop more symptoms of depression than those who are less vulnerable.

Diathesis–stress model
A model that rests on the idea that a psychological disorder is triggered when a person with a predisposition—a diathesis—for the particular disorder experiences an environmental event that causes significant stress.

Biopsychosocial approach
The view that a psychological disorder arises from the combined influences of three types of factors—biological, psychological, and social.

structure and function of the brain, and the function of other bodily systems); *psychological* (thoughts, feelings, and behaviors); and, *social* (social interactions and the environment in which they occur). The **biopsychosocial approach** to understanding psychological disorders rests on identifying these three types of factors and documenting the ways in which each of them contributes to a disorder.

The biopsychosocial approach leads researchers and clinicians to look for ways in which the three types of factors contribute to both the diathesis (the predisposition) and the stress. For instance, having certain genes (a biological factor), having biases to perceive certain situations as stressful (a psychological factor), and living in poverty (a social factor) all can contribute to a diathesis; similarly, chronic lack of sleep (a biological factor), feeling that one's job is overwhelming (a psychological factor), or having a spouse who is abusive (a social factor) can contribute to stress.

However, two problems with the traditional biopsychosocial approach have become clear. First, the approach does not specifically focus on the organ that is responsible for cognition and emotion, that allows us to learn, that guides behavior, and that underlies all conscious experience—namely, the brain. The brain not only gives rise to thoughts, feelings, and behaviors, but also mediates all other biological factors; it both registers events in the body and affects bodily events.

Second, in the biopsychosocial approach, the factors were often considered in isolation, as if they were items on a list. Considering the factors in isolation is reminiscent of the classic South Asian tale about a group of blind men feeling different parts of an elephant, each trying to determine what object the animal is. One person feels the trunk, another the legs, another the tusks, and so on, and each reaches a different conclusion. Even if you combined all the people's separate reports, you might miss the big picture of what an elephant is: That is, an elephant is more than a sum of its body parts; the parts come together to make a dynamic and wondrous creature.

Researchers are beginning to understand how the three types of factors combine and affect each other. That is, factors that researchers previously considered to be independent are now known to influence each other. For example, the way that parents treat their infant was historically considered to be exclusively a social factor—the infant was a receptacle for the caregiver's style of parenting. However, more recent research has revealed that parenting style is in fact a complex set of interactions between caregiver and infant. Consider that if the infant frequently fusses, this will elicit a different pattern of responses from the caregiver than if the infant frequently smiles; if the infant is fussy and "difficult," the caregiver might handle him or her with less patience and warmth than if the infant seems happy and easygoing. And the way the caregiver handles the infant in turn affects how the infant responds to the caregiver. These early interactions between child and caregiver (a social factor) then contribute to a particular attachment style, which is associated with particular biases in paying attention to and

The whole elephant cannot be described by a group of blind men if each of them is feeling only a small part of the animal's body. In the same way, past explanations of psychological disorders that focused on only one or two factors created an incomplete understanding of such disorders.

perceiving emotional expressions in faces (psychological factors; Fraley & Shaver, 1997; Maier et al., 2005).

In fact, some researchers who championed the biopsychosocial approach acknowledged that explanations of psychological disorders depend on the interactions of biological, psychological, and social factors (Engel, 1977, 1980). But these researchers did not have the benefit of the recent advances in understanding the brain, and hence were not able to specify the nature of such interactions in much detail.

These problems led to a revision of the traditional biopsychosocial approach, to align it better with recent discoveries about the brain and how psychological and social factors affect brain function. We call this updated version of the classic approach the *neuropsychosocial approach*, which is explained in the following section.

The Neuropsychosocial Approach: Refining the Biopsychosocial Approach

The neuropsychosocial approach has two defining features: the way it characterizes the factors and the way it characterizes their interactions. As we discuss below, this approach emphasizes the brain rather than the body (hence the *neuro-* in its name) and maintains that no factor can be considered in isolation.

Emphasis on the Brain Rather Than the Body in General As psychologists and other scientists have learned more about the biological factors that contribute to psychological disorders, the primacy of the role of the brain—and even particular brain structures and functions—in contributing to psychological disorders has become evident. Ultimately, even such disparate biological factors as genes and bodily responses (e.g., the increased heart rate associated with anxiety) are best understood in terms of their relationship with the brain. Because of the importance of the brain's influence on all biological functioning involved in psychological disorders, this book generally uses the term *neurological* rather than *biological* and the term *neuropsychosocial* rather than *biopsychosocial* to refer to the three types of factors that contribute to psychological disorders.

Emphasis on Feedback Loops Neurological, psychological, and social factors are usually involved simultaneously and are constantly interacting (see Figure 1.4). These interactions occur through feedback loops: Each factor is affected by the others and *also* feeds back to affect the other factors. Hence, no one factor can be understood in isolation, without considering the other factors. For example, problems in relationships (social factor) can lead people to experience stress (psychological factor); in turn, when people feel stressed, their brains cause their bodies to respond with a cascade of events. As you will see throughout this book, interactions among neurological, psychological, and social factors are common.

In short, the **neuropsychosocial approach** can allow us to understand how neurological, psychological, and social factors—which affect and are affected by one another through feedback loops—underlie psychological disorders (Kendler, 2008).

In the next chapter, we will discuss the neuropsychosocial approach to psychological disorders in more detail, examining neurological, psychological, and social factors as well as the feedback loops among them. In that chapter, we will also continue our evaluation of the Beales and the specific factors that might contribute to their unusual behavior. In subsequent chapters, we will consider the stories of various other people.

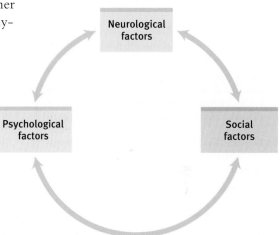

FIGURE **1.4 • The Neuropsychosocial Approach** According to the neuropsychosocial approach, neurological, psychological, and social factors interact with one another via feedback loops to contribute to the development of psychopathology.

Neuropsychosocial approach
The view that a psychological disorder arises from the combined influences of neurological, psychological, and social factors—which affect and are affected by one another through feedback loops.

Thinking Like A Clinician

Imagine that you are a clinician, and Natasha comes to see you about her depression. She tells you that she had a "chemical imbalance" a few years ago, which led her to be depressed then. Based on what you have read, which of the various modern perspectives was she adopting? What other types of causes could she have used to explain her depression? How would the two integrationist approaches (diathesis–stress and neuropsychosocial) explain Natasha's depression? (*Hint:* Use Figures 1.3 and 1.4 to guide your answers.) What do the two approaches have in common, and in what ways do they differ from each other?

☐ SUMMING UP

The Three Criteria for Determining Psychological Disorders

- A psychological disorder is a pattern of thoughts, feelings, or behaviors that causes significant distress, impaired functioning in daily life, and/or risk of harm.

- The distress involved in a psychological disorder is usually out of proportion to the situation.

- Impairment in daily life may affect functioning at school, at work, at home, or in relationships. Moreover, people with a disorder are impaired to a greater degree than most people in a similar situation. A psychosis is a relatively identifiable type of impairment that includes hallucinations or delusions.

- A psychological disorder may lead to behaviors that create a significant risk of harm to the person or to others.

- Mental health clinicians and researchers recognize that context and culture in part determine whether a person's state involves significant distress, impairment, or risk of harm.

Views of Psychological Disorders Before Science

- The oldest-known view of psychopathology is that it arose from supernatural forces, either magical or spiritual. Ancient and modern Chinese views of psychopathology consider its cause to be blocked or significantly imbalanced *qi*. The ancient Greeks attributed mental illness to an imbalance of bodily humors. The term *medical model* refers to Hippocrates' view that illness (including psychological disorders) results from a biological disturbance.

- The Middle Ages saw a resurgence of the view that supernatural forces cause psychopathology: Mental illness was viewed as the result of demonic possession; witch hunts were frequent. By the end of the Renaissance, however, the mentally ill began to be treated more humanely.

- In the years immediately following the Renaissance, mental illnesses were thought to arise from irrational thinking, but this approach did not lead to consistent treatment.

- In the 1790s, Pinel championed humane treatment for those in asylums in France. In other European settings, patients were given moral treatment.

- In the United States, Benjamin Rush initiated the effort to treat the mentally ill more humanely; similarly, Dorothea Dix strove to ensure that the mentally ill were housed separately from criminals and treated humanely.

The Transition to Scientific Accounts of Psychological Disorders

- Freud played a major role in making the study of psychological disorders a science, largely by developing new methods for diagnosis and treatment; he also proposed an extensive theory of psychopathology. Freud's methods included hypnosis and free association.

- According to Freud's psychoanalytic theory, thoughts, feelings, and behaviors result from conscious and unconscious forces—such as sexual and aggressive urges. Moreover, he proposed that the mind is structured to function across three levels of consciousness: the conscious, the preconscious, and the unconscious.

- Freud proposed three psychic structures in the mind—id, ego, and superego—which are continually interacting and negotiating.

- According to Freud, each person passes through five psychosexual stages from infancy to adulthood, of which four involve particular erogenous zones. For healthy psychological development, each stage requires the successful completion of a key task.

- Various forms of psychodynamic therapy have been proposed, each drawing primarily on a different aspect of psychodynamic theory. A drawback of psychodynamic theory is that it has proven difficult to test scientifically.

- Humanistic psychologists such as Carl Rogers viewed psychodynamic theory as too mechanistic and opposed to free will. Rogers proposed that symptoms of distress and mental illness arise when a potential route to personal growth is blocked, as can occur when there is incongruence between the ideal and real selves. Rogers developed client-centered therapy to decrease incongruence in clients.

Scientific Accounts of Psychological Disorders

- Psychologists Edward Thorndike, John Watson, Clark Hull, and B. F. Skinner spearheaded behaviorism, focusing on directly observable behaviors rather than unobservable mental processes and mental contents. They investigated the association between a behavior and its consequence, and proposed scientifically testable mechanisms to explain how maladaptive behavior arises. Behaviorism helps explain how maladaptive behavior can arise from previous associations with an object, a situation, or an event.

- Pavlov discovered and investigated what is sometimes referred to as Pavlovian conditioning—the process whereby a reflexive behavior comes to be associated with a stimulus that precedes it. Pavlovian conditioning helps explain the severe fears and anxieties that are part of some psychological disorders.

- Cognitive psychology has led to the scientific investigation of mental processes and mental contents that affect how people pay attention to stimuli and develop biases in what they expect and remember. Such biases in turn can confirm the inaccurate views that perpetuate a psychological disorder. Aaron Beck and Albert Ellis each focused on how people's irrational and inaccurate thoughts about themselves and the world can contribute to psychological disorders, and each developed a type of treatment to address the irrational and inaccurate thoughts.

- Social forces that help explain psychological disorders include difficulties with attachment and the role of relationships in buffering negative life events.

- Psychological disorders cannot be fully explained by any single type of factor or theory. One approach to integrating different factors is the diathesis–stress model, which proposes that if a person has a predisposition to a psychological disorder, stressors may trigger its occurrence.

- The biopsychosocial approach rests on the idea that both diathesis and stress can be grouped into three types of factors: biological, psychological, and social. Recent research allows investigators to begin to understand the role of the brain in psychological disorders and the feedback loops among the three types of factors. For these reasons, this book uses the term *neuropsychosocial* rather than *biopsychosocial*.

Key Terms

Abnormal psychology (p. 4)

Psychological disorder (p. 4)

Psychosis (p. 6)

Hallucinations (p. 6)

Delusions (p. 6)

Culture (p. 8)

Asylums (p. 13)

Moral treatment (p. 13)

Psychoanalytic theory (p. 15)

Id (p. 15)

Superego (p. 15)

Ego (p. 16)

Psychosexual stages (p. 16)

Neurosis (p. 16)

Defense mechanisms (p. 17)

Mental processes (p. 18)

Mental contents (p. 18)

Behaviorism (p. 19)

Diathesis–stress model (p. 23)

Biopsychosocial approach (p. 24)

Neuropsychosocial approach (p. 25)

More Study Aids

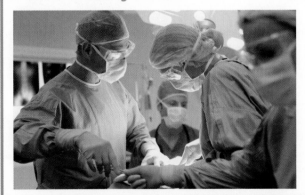

For additional study aids related to this chapter, including quizzes to make sure you've retained everything you've learned and a Student Video Activity exploring early hospital treatments for severe mental disorders, go to: www.worthpublishers.com/launchpad/rkabpsych2e.

Chris Ryan/OJO Images Ltd./Alamy

CHAPTER **2**

Understanding Psychological Disorders: The Neuropsychosocial Approach

As we saw in Chapter 1, clearly the Beale women had odd thoughts and feelings and engaged in unusual behaviors. As we asked in Chapter 1, were they merely eccentric? Did Big Edie or Little Edie (or both of them) have a psychological disorder? Could either of them have had more than one psychological disorder? If one or both had a disorder, how could we understand why? The neuropsychosocial approach allows us to consider the factors that lead someone to develop a psychological disorder, which is known as its **etiology**.

Let's consider the Beale women in terms of the neuropsychosocial approach. First, we can ask about *neurological* factors: Was something abnormal about their genes or brains? Perhaps their neurons or neurotransmitters functioned abnormally, and that led to their odd behavior. Second, we can ask about *psychological* factors: How might their thoughts and feelings have motivated them, and what role might their mental processes have played? And third, we can ask about *social* factors, such as their financial circumstances, their family relationships, the straitlaced society they were members of, and other cultural forces affecting them.

AT ANY MOMENT IN A DAY OF THE BEALES' LIVES (or anyone's life, for that matter), all three types of factors are operating: neurological, psychological, and social. Depending on the state of a person's brain (which is affected, for example, by various chemicals produced by the body), social factors (such as an angry friend or a stressful job interview) have a greater or lesser impact. This impact in turn affects psychological factors (the person's thoughts, feelings, and behaviors) in different ways. And then the psychological factors can affect both neurological factors and social factors, continuing the interaction among these different influences. Thus, considering only

Etiology
The factors that lead a person to develop a psychological disorder.

29

one type of factor would lead to an incomplete understanding of psychological disorders. That is why we consider each type of factor—neurological, psychological, and social—in detail (see Figure 1.4 in Chapter 1). It is important to note, however, that the neuropsychosocial approach does not focus on each type of factor individually; rather, we must always consider how the three factors interact and affect one another via feedback loops.

⬚ Neurological Factors in Psychological Disorders

Big Edie had always been unconventional. She didn't seem to care what other people thought of her behavior. And although she loved performing—seemingly to the point of compulsion—she was a recluse for most of her adult life, seeing almost no one but her children. How did such a lifestyle arise? And what about Little Edie's paranoid beliefs? Could neurological factors account for the odd beliefs and behaviors of this mother and daughter? In fact, accumulating research indicates that genes can contribute to the development of disorders by affecting both the structure and function of the brain (Gottesman, 1991; Greenwood & Kelsoe, 2003; Hasler et al., 2004).

Neurological factors that contribute to psychological disorders include abnormalities in the structure of the brain, in the operations of specific chemicals, and in specific genes. Researchers and clinicians sometimes focus on neurological factors when they explain psychopathology—noting, for example, that depression is correlated with abnormal levels of a particular chemical (serotonin) in the brain or that an irrational fear of spiders develops partly from an overly reactive brain structure involved in fear (the amygdala; Larson et al., 2006). However, as you know, the neuropsychosocial approach maintains that explanations based on neurological factors alone rarely provide the whole story. Each thought, feeling, and behavior, as well as each social experience and the environment in which we live and work, affects our neurological functioning. In other words, as noted above, the three types of factors typically interact with one another through *feedback loops*. Neurological factors contribute to psychopathology, but they must be considered in the context of the other factors.

To understand the role of neurological factors in explanations of psychopathology, we next consider brain structure and function, neurons and neurotransmitters, and genetics and the ways that genes interact with the environment.

Brain Structure and Brain Function

The brain is the organ of thinking, feeling, and behavior, and thus it must play a key role in psychopathology. In the following sections, we start our discussion with the big picture by considering the overall structure of the brain and its organization into large systems. Then we turn to increasingly more detailed components, considering how individual brain cells interact within these systems.

A Quick Tour of the Nervous System

Psychopathology involves deficits in how a person thinks, feels, and behaves. The brain, of course, is ultimately responsible for all of these functions. Let's briefly consider how different parts of the brain contribute to cognitive and emotional capacities when the brain is structured and functions normally. In later chapters, when we need to know more to understand a specific psychological disorder, we'll look more closely at specific parts of the brain and how they can malfunction.

The Central Nervous System and the Peripheral Nervous System

The central nervous system (CNS) has two parts: the brain and the spinal cord. The CNS is the seat of memory and consciousness, as well as perception and voluntary action (Smith & Kosslyn, 2006). However, the CNS is not the only neurological foundation of our internal lives. The peripheral nervous system (PNS) also plays an important role and is of particular interest in the study of psychopathology.

The Peripheral Nervous System

Like the CNS, the PNS is divided into two parts, in this case the sensory-somatic nervous system and the autonomic nervous system (see Figure 2.1). The *sensory-somatic nervous system* is involved in connecting the brain to the world, via both the senses (inputs) and the muscles (outputs). The *autonomic nervous system (ANS)* is probably of greater relevance to psychopathology, in part because it plays a key role in how we respond to stress. The ANS controls many involuntary functions, such as those of the heart, digestive tract, and blood vessels (Goldstein, 2000; Hugdahl, 2001).

The ANS itself has two major components: the sympathetic nervous system and the parasympathetic nervous system. The *sympathetic nervous system* revs you up so that you can respond to an emergency: It speeds up the heart (providing more blood and oxygen to the limbs) and dilates the pupils of the eyes (making you more sensitive to light). The sympathetic system also slows down functions that are not essential in an emergency, such as those involved in digestion. The result of the sympathetic nervous system's being activated is called the *fight-or-flight response* (or the *stress response*, because it occurs when people experience stress).

The other part of the ANS is the *parasympathetic nervous system*, which settles you down after a crisis is over: The parasympathetic nervous system slows the heart, contracts the pupils, and increases the activity of the digestive tract. The parasympathetic system typically counteracts the effects of the sympathetic nervous system, and psychopathology may arise if it fails to do so effectively. In fact, dysfunctional activity in the parasympathetic nervous system has been associated with various psychological problems, such as anxiety disorders, disruptive behavior, and hostility (Pine et al., 1998).

The Four Brain Lobes

Let's now focus on one part of the CNS, the brain. As shown in Figure 2.2, the brain has four major lobes, back to front: occipital lobe, parietal lobe, temporal lobe, and frontal lobe. The brain is divided into two hemispheres (or half-spheres), left and right, and each hemisphere has all four lobes. We start with the back of the brain.

When the eyes are stimulated by light, they send neural impulses into the brain; the first area to process this information in detail is the *occipital lobe*, which is at the very back of the brain. This lobe is entirely dedicated to the function of vision.

Two major neural pathways lead forward from the occipital lobes. One extends up into the *parietal lobe*, at the top, back of the brain. This lobe processes spatial information, such as the relative location of objects. The parietal lobe also has other functions, including a role in self-awareness. The second neural pathway from the occipital lobe leads down to the *temporal lobe* (so named because it lies under the temple),

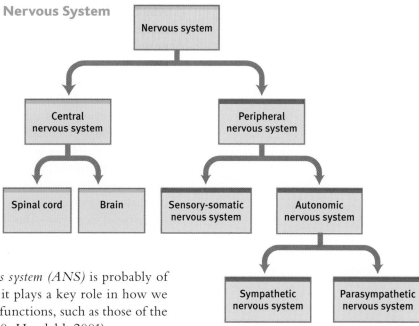

FIGURE 2.1 • The Nervous System
The autonomic nervous system (ANS) is part of the peripheral nervous system (PNS), and malfunctioning of the ANS can produce abnormal responses to stress.

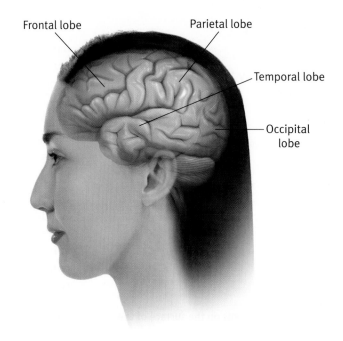

FIGURE 2.2 • The Lobes of the Brain

which stores visual memories, processes auditory information, and decodes the meaning of speech; the temporal lobe also contributes to conscious experience. Abnormal functioning in the temporal lobe can produce intense emotions, such as elation when a person is manic (Gyulai et al., 1997).

Both the parietal lobe and the temporal lobe send information to the *frontal lobe*, which is located right behind the forehead. The frontal lobe plays crucial roles in feeling emotions and using emotional responses in decision making, as well as in thinking and problem solving more generally; it is also involved in programming actions and controlling body movements. Because these functions are so important to the vital activities of planning and reasoning, the frontal lobe is sometimes referred to as the seat of *executive functioning*; its role is much like that of the head of a successful company—an executive—who plans the company's future and formulates responses to obstacles that arise. Abnormalities in the frontal lobe, and in executive functioning, are associated with a variety of disorders, including *schizophrenia*, a psychological disorder characterized by profoundly unusual and impaired behavior, expression of emotion, and mental processing (Bellgrove et al., 2006; Morey, Inan, et al., 2005).

The Cortex and Beneath the Cortex

The **cerebral cortex** is the outer layer of cells on the surface of the brain that overlays all four of the lobes. Contained in the cerebral cortex is the majority of the brain's **neurons**, the cells that process information related to our physical, mental, and emotional functioning. Most of the brain functions just described are carried out primarily in the cortex of the corresponding lobes. But many important brain functions are carried out in *subcortical areas*, beneath the cortex, as shown in Figure 2.3.

The *limbic system* (key parts of which are shown in the left half of Figure 2.3) plays a key role in emotions; among its most important components are the hypothalamus, the hippocampus, and the amygdala:

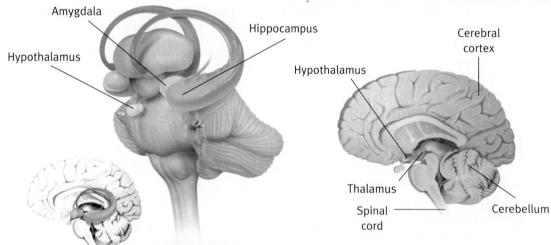

FIGURE 2.3 • Key Subcortical Brain Areas

- The *hypothalamus* governs bodily functions associated with eating, drinking, and controlling temperature, and it plays a key role in many aspects of our emotions and in our experience of pleasure (Swaab, 2003).

- The *amygdala* is central to producing and perceiving strong emotions, especially fear (LeDoux, 2000).

- The *hippocampus* works to store new information in memory of the sort that later can be voluntarily recalled (Squire, 2004).

In addition to components of the limbic system, other important subcortical structures include the thalamus, the basal ganglia, and the cerebellum. Both physical abnormalities and abnormal levels of activity in these subcortical brain areas can contribute to psychological disorders, as we will discuss in later chapters when relevant.

Neurons

Now that you know essential functions that different parts of the brain perform, it's time to discuss *how* these functions occur. All brain activity depends on neurons, and malfunctions of neurons often contribute to psychological disorders (Lambert &

Cerebral cortex
The outer layer of cells on the surface of the brain.

Neurons
Brain cells that process information related to physical, mental, and emotional functioning.

Kinsley, 2005). The brain contains numerous types of neurons, which have different functions, shapes, and sizes. Most neurons interact with other neurons. In some cases, neurons *activate*, or act to "turn on," other neurons; in other cases, neurons *inhibit*, or act to "turn off," other neurons. We can classify neurons into three main types:

- *Sensory neurons* receive input from the sense organs (eyes, ears, and so on).
- *Motor neurons* carry output that stimulates muscles and glands.
- *Interneurons* lie between other neurons—sensory neurons, motor neurons, and/or other interneurons—and make up most of the neurons in the brain.

Sets of connected neurons that work together to accomplish a basic process, such as making you recoil when you touch a hot stove, are called **brain circuits**; sets of brain circuits are organized into **brain systems**, which often can involve most of an entire lobe—or even large portions of several lobes. Many forms of psychopathology arise because specific brain circuits are not working properly, either alone or as part of a larger brain system.

To understand brain circuits, consider an analogy to a row of dominoes: When one domino falls, it causes the next in line to fall, and so on, down the line. Similarly, when a neuron within a brain circuit is activated, it in turn activates sequences of other neurons. However, unlike a domino in a row, the average neuron is connected to about 10,000 other neurons—and thus a complex pattern of spreading activity occurs when a brain circuit is activated, which usually ends up involving a large brain system. For each input, a brain system produces a specific output—for instance, an interpretation of the input, an association to it, or a response based on it. Ultimately, it is the pattern of activated neurons that is triggered—by a sight, smell, thought, memory, or other event—that gives rise to our cognitive and emotional lives. A pattern of neurons firing makes us desire that third piece of chocolate cake or causes us to recoil when a spider saunters out from behind it. Brain systems allow us to think, feel, and behave.

Psychopathology can arise when neurons fail to communicate appropriately, leading brain systems to produce incorrect outputs. For example, people with schizophrenia appear to have abnormal circuitry in key parts of their frontal lobes (Pantelis et al., 2003; Vidal et al., 2006). To understand such problems—and possible treatments for them—you need to know something about the structure and function of the neuron and its methods of communication.

The Cell Body

To see how neurons can fail to communicate appropriately, we must take a closer look at them. Figure 2.4 shows that a neuron has three parts: a receiving end, a sending end, and a middle part, called the *cell body*. When a neuron has been sufficiently stimulated (typically by signals from other neurons), very small holes in the cell's outer covering (its "skin") open, and the neuron's internal balance of chemicals changes to the point where the neuron "fires." It is this firing that sends information to other neurons (Lambert & Kinsley, 2005).

Each neuron registers the sum to- tal of inputs, both those that try to stimulate it to fire and those that try to inhibit it from firing. The neuron, then, balances the two sorts of inputs against each other and only fires if the stimulating influences substantially outweigh the inhibiting ones (Kandel et al., 2007). To understand how firing occurs, we need to look at two other major parts of the neuron: the axon and the dendrites.

Brain circuits
Sets of connected neurons that work together to accomplish a basic process.

Brain systems
Sets of brain circuits that work together to accomplish a complex function.

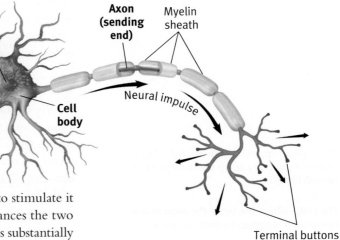

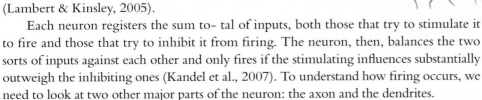

FIGURE 2.4 • The Neuron

The Axon, Dendrites, and Glial Cells

The *axon* is the part of the neuron that sends signals to other neurons. The axon is a long, threadlike structure, some of which is covered by a layer of fatty material, known as the myelin sheath, that insulates it electrically; the axon includes the terminal buttons. Although each neuron has only a single axon, it often branches extensively, allowing signals to be sent simultaneously to many other neurons (Shepherd, 1999).

When a neuron has been stimulated to the point that it fires, a wave of chemical activity moves from the cell body down the axon very quickly. This wave is called an **action potential**. When the action potential reaches the end of the axon, it typically causes chemicals to be released. These chemicals are stored in structures called *terminal buttons*, and these chemicals affect other neurons, muscles, or glands. If stimulation does not cause a neuron to fire when it is supposed to, the circuit of which the neuron is a part will not function correctly—and psychopathology may result. Let's consider why a neuron might not fire when stimulated appropriately.

We've seen that neurons fire after they are stimulated, but how are they stimulated? Two ways: First, they are stimulated at their *dendrites*, which receive signals from other neurons. Dendrites, like axons, are highly branched, so a single neuron can receive many different signals at the same time. Received signals move along the dendrites to the cell body (Kandel et al., 2007). Second, in some cases, neurons receive inputs directly on their cell bodies. Such inputs are produced not only by other neurons but also by *glial cells*. Glial cells are involved in the "care and feeding" of neurons, and act as a kind of support system (in fact, *glial* means "glue" in Greek; Lambert & Kinsley, 2005). The brain has about 10 times as many glial cells as neurons. Researchers have learned that glial cells do much more than provide support services; they can directly stimulate neurons, and they play a role in modulating input from other neurons (Parpura & Haydon, 2000).

Given the roles of neurons and glial cells in brain function, it is not surprising that researchers have found that at least some patients with psychological disorders (specifically, the sorts of mood disorders we consider in Chapter 5) have abnormally low numbers of both types of cells. One possible reason for such deficits may be that stress early in childhood (and even to the mother, prior to a child's birth) can disrupt the development of both neurons and glial cells (Zorumski, 2005).

Chemical Signals

The way neurons communicate is crucial for understanding psychopathology. In many cases, psychological disorders involve faulty signaling among neurons, and effective medications operate by altering the ways in which signals are produced or processed (Kelsey et al., 2006). Subsequent chapters of this book will describe how particular signaling problems contribute to some psychological disorders and how certain medications compensate for such problems. To understand these problems with chemical signaling, we now need to consider what happens at the synapse, what neurotransmitters do, the nature of receptors, and what can go wrong with chemical communication among neurons.

The Synapse

When a neuron fires, chemicals are released at the terminal button. Those chemicals usually contact another neuron at a **synapse**, which is the place where the tip of the axon of one neuron nestles against another neuron (usually at a dendrite) and sends signals to it. Most of the time, the sending neuron is not physically connected to the receiving neuron, though. Instead, the chemicals carry the signal across a gap, called the *synaptic cleft*, shown in Figure 2.5. Events at the synapses can go awry, which can underlie a variety of types of psychopathology.

Neurotransmitters

The chemicals that are released by the terminal buttons are called **neurotransmitters**. It is worth looking briefly at the major neurotransmitters that play roles in psychological disorders. However, keep in mind that no neurotransmitter works in

Action potential
The wave of chemical activity that moves from the cell body down the axon when a neuron fires.

Synapse
The place where the tip of the axon of one neuron sends signals to another neuron.

Neurotransmitters
Chemicals that are released by the terminal buttons and cross the synaptic cleft.

isolation and that no psychological disorder can be traced solely to the function of a single neurotransmitter. Nevertheless, as shown in Table 2.1, imbalances in some of these substances have been linked, to some extent, with certain psychological disorders.

You may have noticed in Table 2.1 that the descriptions of what the neurotransmitters do are fairly general. There's a reason for this: The effects of neurotransmitters depend in part on the nature of the receiving neurons. Thus, we must next look more closely at what's on the receiving end of these chemical substances. The information in the following section is also crucial if we are to understand how various drugs work to treat psychopathology.

Chemical Receptors

A neuron receives chemical signals at its **receptors**, specialized sites that respond only to specific molecules (see Figure 2.5). Located on the dendrites or on the cell body, receptors work like locks into which only certain kinds of keys will fit (Kelsey et al., 2006; Lambert & Kinsley, 2005). However, instead of literally locking or unlocking the corresponding receptors, the neurotransmitter molecules *bind* to the receptors and affect them either by exciting them (making the receiving neuron more likely to fire) or by inhibiting them (making the receiving neuron less likely to fire). We noted earlier that a sending neuron can make a receiving neuron more or less likely to fire, and now we see how these effects occur: The sending neuron releases specific neurotransmitters.

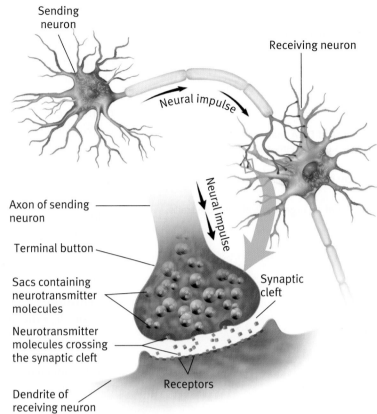

FIGURE 2.5 • The Synapse

Receptors
Specialized sites on dendrites and cell bodies that respond only to specific molecules.

TABLE 2.1 • Major Neurotransmitters, Their Major Functions, and Commonly Associated Disorders

Neurotransmitter	Major functions	Associated disorders or problems
Dopamine	Reward, motivation, executive function (in frontal lobes), control of movements	*Too little:* attention-deficit/hyperactivity disorder *Too much:* inappropriate aggression, schizophrenia
Serotonin	Mood, sleep, motivation	*Too little:* depression and obsessive-compulsive disorder *Too much:* lack of motivation
Acetylcholine	Storing new information in memory, fight-or-flight response	*Too little:* delusions *Too much:* spasms, tremors, convulsions
Adrenaline (also called epinephrine)	Attention, fight-or-flight response	*Too little:* depression *Too much:* over-arousal, feelings of dread or apprehension
Noradrenaline (also called norepinephrine)	Attention, fight-or-flight response	*Too little:* distractibility, fatigue, depression *Too much:* anxiety disorders, schizophrenia
Glutamate	Registering pain, storing new information in memory	*Too little:* schizophrenia *Too much:* substance abuse
Gamma-amino butyric acid (GABA)	Inhibits brain activity in specific areas	*Too little:* anxiety, panic disorder (possibly) *Too much:* lack of motivation
Endogenous cannabinoids	Emotion, attention, memory, appetite, control of movements	*Too little:* chronic pain *Too much:* eating disorders, memory impairment, attention difficulties, schizophrenia (possibly)

Sources: Based on Bressan & Crippa, 2005; Buchsbaum et al., 2006; Eger et al., 2002; Giuffrida et al., 2004; Goddard et al., 2001; Kalivas & Volkow, 2005;Meana et al., 1992; Muller & Schwarz, 2006; Mundo, Richter, et al., 2000; Nemeroff, 1998; Nutt & Lawson, 1992; Rao & Lyketsos, 1998; Wilson & Nicoll, 2001.

Reuptake
The process of moving leftover neurotransmitter molecules in the synapse back into the sending neuron.

Hormones
Chemicals that are released directly into the bloodstream that activate or alter the activity of neurons.

Genes
Segments of DNA that control the production of particular proteins and other substances.

Genotype
The sum of an organism's genes.

Phenotype
The sum of an organism's observable traits.

Abnormal Communications Among Neurons

How can communications among neurons at the synaptic cleft go awry, and thereby lead to psychological disorders? Scientists point to at least three ways in which such communications can be disrupted.

First, neurons might have too many or too few dendrites or receptors, making the neurons more or less sensitive, respectively, to even normal amounts of neurotransmitters in the synaptic cleft (Meana et al., 1992). Second, the sending neurons might produce too much or too little of a neurotransmitter. Third, the events after a neuron fires may go awry (Kelsey et al., 2006). In particular, when a neuron fires and sends neurotransmitter chemicals to another neuron, not all of these molecules bind to receptors. Rather, some of the molecules linger in the synaptic cleft and need to be removed. Special chemical processes operate to **reuptake** these leftover neurotransmitters, moving them back into the sending neuron. Sometimes reuptake does not operate correctly, which may contribute to a psychological disorder.

Hormones and the Endocrine System

Hormones are chemicals that are released directly into the bloodstream that activate or alter the activity of neurons. For example, some hormones play a key role in helping animals respond to stressful situations by altering the functioning of the ANS (Kandel et al., 2007). However, traumatic events can disrupt this often-helpful mechanism and contribute to psychological disorders such as depression (Claes, 2004).

Hormones are produced by glands in the *endocrine system*, which secretes substances into the bloodstream. Hormones affect various organs throughout the body. *Cortisol* is a particularly important hormone, which helps the body to cope with challenges by making more resources available; cortisol is produced by the adrenal glands (which are located right above the kidneys) and abnormal amounts of cortisol have been linked to anxiety and depression.

The Genetics of Psychopathology

Researchers knew about the inheritance of traits long before the discovery of DNA (deoxyribonucleic acid, the long molecule that contains many thousands of genes). Everyone knows that people "take after" their parents in some ways that have nothing to do with learning, and genes are responsible for this resemblance. Genes affect not only physical traits but also the brain and, through the brain, thinking, feeling, and behavior; moreover, genes can affect how vulnerable people are to particular psychological disorders (Plomin et al., 1997, 2003).

In the middle of the 20th century, James Watson and Francis Crick identified **genes**, which correspond to segments of DNA that control the production of particular proteins and other substances (see Figure 2.6). Genes are *expressed* when the information in them is used to produce proteins and other substances, which both produce biological structures (including the parts of the neurons) and affect biological processes (such as reuptake). For many traits, gene variants—referred to as *alleles*—determine how the trait is manifested. The sum of an organism's genes is called its **genotype**. In contrast, the sum of its observable traits is called its **phenotype**, which results from how the genotype is expressed in a particular environment.

FIGURE 2.6 • DNA

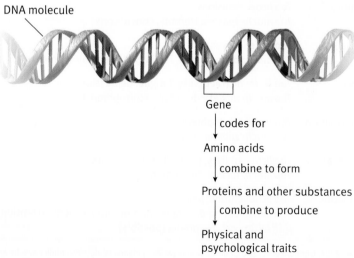

DNA molecule

Gene
↓ codes for
Amino acids
↓ combine to form
Proteins and other substances
↓ combine to produce
Physical and psychological traits

For most traits, many genes work together to cause particular effects. Sets of genes give rise to traits, such as height, that are expressed along a continuum, and the joint actions of these genes produce **complex inheritance** (Plomin et al., 1997). Traits that arise from complex inheritance cannot be linked to a few distinct genes, but rather emerge from the interactions among the effects of numerous genes. Almost all psychological disorders that have a genetic component, such as schizophrenia and depression, arise in part through complex inheritance (Faraone et al., 2001; Plomin et al., 2003).

Behavioral Genetics

Studies that investigate the contributions of genes to mental illness rely on the methods of **behavioral genetics**, which is the field that investigates the degree to which the variability of characteristics in a population arises from genetic versus environmental factors (Plomin et al., 2003). With regard to psychopathology, behavioral geneticists consider these questions: What is the role of genetics in causing a particular mental disorder? What is the role of the environment? And what is the role of interactions between genes and the environment?

Throughout this book, we discuss the relative contributions of genes and the environment to the development of specific mental disorders. We must always keep in mind, however, that any conclusions about the relative contributions of the two influences are always tied to the specific environment in which the contributions are measured. To see why, consider the following example (based on Lewontin, 1976). Imagine three situations in which we plant two apple trees of the same variety, one of which has genes for large apples and one of which has genes for small apples.

In the first case, we keep the environment the same for the two trees. Unfortunately for them, however, it is not a very friendly environment: The soil is bad, the trees are in the shade, and there isn't much water. Both trees produce small apples. In this case, the environment overshadows the genetic influence for large apples.

In the second case, the trees are luckier. For both trees, the soil is rich, the trees are in the sun, and they receive plenty of water. What happens? The tree with genes for large apples produces larger apples than the tree with genes for small apples.

In the third case, the tree with genes for large apples is planted in the impoverished environment, and the tree with genes for small apples is planted in the favorable environment. Now, the tree that has genes for small apples might produce bigger apples than the tree with genes for large apples because the environmental conditions have favored the former and acted against the latter.

As this example makes clear, for trees and other organisms—including humans—the influence of genes must be described in relation to the environment in which they function. In other words, genes and environment interact through *feedback loops*—and in fact, that's why the phenotype depends on how genes function in a specific environment. The same genes can have different effects in different environments. A research finding of a certain degree of genetic influence on a disorder in one environment does not necessarily have any relationship to the degree of genetic influence on the disorder in other environments. For example, the fact that genes can predispose an individual to alcoholism has different effects in the alcohol-embracing culture of France and the alcohol-shunning culture of Pakistan.

Heritability

Behavioral genetics characterizes the relative influence of genetic factors in terms of the heritability of a characteristic. **Heritability** is an estimate of how much of the variation in that characteristic within a population (in a specific environment)

Complex inheritance
The transmission of traits that are expressed along a continuum by the interaction of sets of genes.

Behavioral genetics
The field that investigates the degree to which the variability of characteristics in a population arises from genetic versus environmental factors.

Heritability
An estimate of how much of the variation in a characteristic within a population (in a specific environment) can be attributed to genetics.

Monozygotic twins
Twins who have basically the same genetic makeup because they began life as a single fertilized egg (zygote), which then divided into two embryos; also referred to as *identical twins*.

Dizygotic twins
Twins who developed from two fertilized eggs and so have the same overlap in genes (50%) as do siblings not conceived at the same time; also referred to as *fraternal twins*.

It is not easy to sort out the effects of genetics from those of the environment by studying identical twins. Each twin has unique experiences even before he or she is born: One twin may get fewer nutrients or be exposed to more toxins while in the mother's womb; that is, there can be different environments for the twins even before birth. Such differences can result in differences in behavior.

can be attributed to genetics. For example, the heritability of *generalized anxiety disorder* (which is characterized by worry that is not associated with a particular situation or object, as we will discuss in detail in Chapter 6) is about .32 in citizens of Western countries (Hettema, Neale, & Kendler, 2001). This means that about one third of the variation in generalized anxiety disorder in this population is genetically determined.

There is no sure-fire research method for assessing heritability. Many variables can affect the results. For example, if researchers find a similar prevalence of a mental disorder in children and their parents, can they assume genetic inheritance? Not necessarily; they would have to rule out any effects of the environment that might be operating. It is difficult to assess "the environment" for a given person. The environment must be understood not in objective terms but rather in terms of how situations and events are perceived and understood. For instance, for siblings in a given family, does having divorced parents constitute the same environment? Not exactly: A child's age at the time of parents' divorce can influence how the child experiences the divorce. A preschooler might believe he or she somehow caused the divorce, whereas an older child—who is more mature cognitively, emotionally, and socially—is less likely to make that inference (Allison & Furstenberg, 1989; Hoffman, 1991). Researchers can entirely avoid such age effects between siblings by studying twins.

Twin and Adoption Studies

Twin studies compare some characteristic, or set of characteristics, in two groups of twins, identical and fraternal. Identical twins have basically the same genetic makeup, because they began life as a single fertilized egg (or *zygote*) that then divided to become two embryos. Such twins are **monozygotic** (*mono-* means "one"). Fraternal twins begin life as different fertilized eggs, and so are **dizygotic** (*di-* means "two"). Fraternal twins are like any other nonidentical siblings in terms of their genetic similarity: They have about 50% overlap in the genes that vary among humans. When researchers compare the characteristics of monozygotic twins and dizygotic twins, controlling as much as possible for the environment, they can attempt to draw conclusions about the relative contribution of genes to those characteristics in that environment. For instance, such studies have suggested that schizophrenia is about 50% heritable (Gottesman, 1991). However, we must be cautious about such estimates: Not only can identical twins have slightly different genetic makeups but they also begin to have different experiences before birth—in fact, one twin is usually heavier and larger at birth because of differences in the amounts of nutrients the two fetuses receive in the womb (Cheung et al., 1995; Hollier et al., 1999).

Sometimes researchers try to discover the roles of genes and the environment in mental disorders by conducting *adoption studies*: They study twins who were separated at birth and raised in different homes, then compare them to twins who were raised in the same home. In addition, researchers also study biologically unrelated children who were adopted and raised together, then compare them to unrelated children who were reared in different homes. But even in adoption studies, it's not easy to disentangle the effects of genes and the environment. The reason is that genetic differences influence the environment—a relationship that is characterized by the *reciprocal gene–environment model*. For instance, suppose that a pair of twins has genes that lead them to be high-strung and very active. Even if these twins are raised apart in different environments, their parents may react similarly to them—trying to keep them calm and out of trouble, which might mean that they wouldn't be taken on family outings as often as children who are less of a handful. The point is that even in different adopted households, genes can influence how twins are treated and what they experience. Thus, although twin and adoption studies can be fascinating, their findings must be interpreted cautiously.

The problems with twin and adoption studies have led many researchers to take advantage of recent technological advances in genetics: It is now possible to assess, inexpensively and quickly (for many genes), whether a particular person has a specific allele of a gene (Schena et al., 1995). Researchers have used such techniques to attempt to find associations between the presence or absence of specific alleles and psychological disorders. For example, Rasmussen and colleagues (2006) found that people who develop schizophrenia relatively late in life tend to have one particular allele of a certain gene.

Feedback Loops in Understanding Genes and the Environment

We've seen how genes can affect the environment, but—to the surprise of many—the genes themselves are also affected by the environment, including psychological and social factors (Slavich & Cole, 2013). We consider the feedback loops between the environment and the genes in the following two sections.

The Environment Affects the Genes

Many people seem to think of genes as instructions for building the brain and the body, guiding the construction process and then ceasing to function. For many genes, this is not so. Even in adulthood, a person's genes are regulated by the environment (Hyman & Nestler, 1993). Consider a simple example: Did you ever try to learn to play piano? If you did, your fingers were probably sore after even a half-hour of practice. But if you stuck with it, you could play for longer and longer periods with no discomfort. What happened? Your muscles got stronger. But how? When you first began, the stress of using your fingers in new ways actually damaged the muscles (which is why they felt sore). Then, a series of chemical events inside the muscle cells of your fingers *turned on* genes in the nuclei of these cells. These genes directed the cells to produce more proteins, to build up the muscles, which made them stronger. If you stopped playing for a period of time, those genes would turn off, and the muscles would become weaker. This is why your fingers might be sore when you first resumed playing after having taken a long break.

The point is that some genes are activated, or turned on, as a result of experience, of interacting with the world (Kandel et al., 2007; South & Krueger, 2011). This is true of genes in the brain that produce neurotransmitters and that cause new synapses to form. In fact, when you learn something, genes in your brain are turned on, which causes new connections among neurons to be formed. This is true even when you learn maladaptive behaviors, which can produce, among other problems, a *phobia*—an intense, irrational fear of an object or situation. Moreover, genetic factors can contribute to a neurological vulnerability for a psychological disorder. For example, genetic factors can lead a person to be prone to learning maladaptive behaviors. However, researchers have found that the same genes are associated with a number of different mental disorders. This probably occurs because these genes affect shared neural functions that have been disrupted (Cross-Disorder Group of the Psychiatric Genomics Consortium, 2013). It seems likely that if a person inherits genes that can underlie such fundamental dysfunctions, different environmental stressors can trigger the dysfunction in different contexts, leading to different disorders.

However, genes are not destiny. More often than not, having specific genes does not determine behavior but rather predisposes a person to be affected by the environment in certain ways. That is, genes can predispose a person for a specific disorder, but those genes may have that effect only when triggered by psychological or social factors.

The Genes Affect the Environment

We've just seen that the environment affects the genes, and we've already noted that the reverse also occurs. Let's now look in more detail at ways in which the genes affect the environment. Many researchers (e.g., Plomin et al., 1997; Scarr & McCartney, 1983) distinguish three ways in which genes affect the environment—passive interaction, evocative interaction, and active interaction:

1. *Passive interaction*. The parents' genes affect the child's environment—and the child passively receives these influences. For instance, some parents avoid social groups because they are shy, which is in part a result of their genes; this means that their child has relatively few social experiences. The child may not have inherited the parents' shy temperament, but the parents' genes nonetheless act through the environment to affect the child.

2. *Evocative interaction* (also called *reactive interaction*). A person's inherited traits encourage other people to behave in particular ways, and hence the person's social environment will be affected by his or her genes. For example, if you are very tall and heavy-set, others may respond to you somewhat cautiously—in a way they would not if you were short and frail. Similarly, others may approach or avoid you (fairly or not!) in response to your temperament (e.g., shy, calm, high-strung); any specific temperament will appeal to some and not to others. Thus, even your circle of friends will be somewhat determined by your genes, and those friends will then affect you in certain ways, depending on their own characteristics.

3. *Active interaction*. Each of us actively seeks out some environments and avoids others, and our genes influence which environments feel most comfortable to us. For example, a person who is sensitive to environmental stimulation might prefer spending a quiet evening at home curled up with a good book instead of going to a loud, crowded party at a friend's house.

The interactions between genes and the environment involve all the factors considered by the neuropsychosocial approach and hence create complex feedback loops. Once the environment (including social factors, such as one's choice of friends) has been influenced by genes, the environment in turn affects the genes (as well as one's knowledge, beliefs, attitudes, and so on).

Again, the import of these observations for psychological disorders is clear. Genes can put a person at risk for a particular psychological disorder, but other factors—psychological and social—can influence the expression of the genes. And the specific psychological and social factors that affect a person arise, in part, from that person's genes (which affect, for example, aspects of his or her appearance). Thus, even though genes may make some people vulnerable to specific kinds of mental illness, the path from genes to illness is neither straight nor inevitable.

Thinking Like A Clinician

Dominic is adopted, and his biological father was an alcoholic; alcoholism has a genetic component. Dominic's adoptive parents are very religious and don't drink alcohol. Suppose scientists determine that, among alcoholics, a particular brain area has an abnormally high level of activity of the neurotransmitter dopamine. Further suppose that Dominic has too much activation of dopamine neurons in this area. Does this mean that his brain is wired like that of an alcoholic, and he should just resign himself to eventually becoming an alcoholic? How might psychological and social factors affect dopamine levels?

Psychological Factors in Psychological Disorders

Both of the Beale women had idiosyncratic ideas and inclinations. For instance, Little Edie, in talking about World War II, expressed an unusual view about who should be soldiers and sent off to fight a war—people who are not physically healthy and hardy. With such people as soldiers, she claimed, the war would be over sooner (Maysles, 2006). In addition, Big Edie was known to command Little Edie to change her attire, repeatedly, up to 10 times each day (Maysles, 2006). Psychological factors, such as learning, can help to account for people's beliefs and behavior. Could aspects of Big Edie's and Little Edie's views and lifestyle have been learned? And how might their emotions—such as Big Edie's fear of being alone or Little Edie's resentment of her mother's control—influence their thoughts and behavior? Let's examine the role that previous learning, mental processes and contents, and emotions can play in psychological disorders.

Behavior and Learning

As we saw in Chapter 1, psychological disorders involve distress, impaired functioning, and/or risk of harm. These three elements can be expressed in behaviors, such as occurs when people disrupt their daily lives in order to avoid feared stimuli or when they drink too much alcohol to cope with life's ups and downs. Many behaviors related to psychological disorders can be learned. As we shall see, some psychological disorders can be explained, at least partly, as a consequence of one of three types of learning: classical conditioning, operant conditioning, and observational learning.

Classical Conditioning

In a landmark study of an 11-month-old infant, known as "Little Albert," John B. Watson and Rosalie Rayner (1920) demonstrated how to produce a phobia. The researchers conditioned Little Albert to be afraid of white rats, using the basic procedure that Pavlov used when he conditioned his dogs (see Chapter 1), except in this case the reflexive behavior was related to fear rather than salivation. To do this, they made a very loud sound immediately after a white rat (which was used as the neutral stimulus) moved into the child's view; they repeated this procedure several times. Whenever Little Albert subsequently saw a white rat, he would cry or exhibit other signs of fear. The process that generated Little Albert's fear of white rats is called **classical conditioning**—a type of learning that occurs when two stimuli are paired so that a neutral stimulus becomes associated with another stimulus that elicits a reflexive behavior; classical conditioning is also referred to (less commonly) as Pavlovian conditioning. By experiencing pairings of the two stimuli (the white rat and the loud noise in the case of Little Albert), the person comes to respond to the neutral stimulus alone (the white rat) in the same way that he or she had responded to the stimulus that elicited the reflexive behavior (the loud noise).

How, specifically, does classical conditioning occur? Using the lingo of psychologists, the stimulus that reflexively elicits a behavior is called the **unconditioned stimulus (UCS)**, because it elicits the behavior without prior conditioning. In the case of Little Albert, the loud noise was the UCS, and the behavior it reflexively elicited was a startle response associated with fear. Such a reflexive behavior is called an **unconditioned response (UCR)**. The neutral stimulus that, when paired with the UCS, comes to elicit the reflexive behavior is called the **conditioned stimulus (CS)**.

Classical conditioning
A type of learning that occurs when two stimuli are paired so that a neutral stimulus becomes associated with another stimulus that elicits a reflexive behavior; also referred to as *Pavlovian conditioning.*

Unconditioned stimulus (UCS)
A stimulus that reflexively elicits a behavior.

Unconditioned response (UCR)
A behavior that is reflexively elicited by a stimulus.

Conditioned stimulus (CS)
A neutral stimulus that, when paired with an unconditioned stimulus, comes to elicit the reflexive behavior.

Before Classical Conditioning

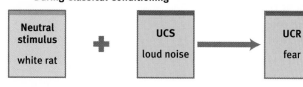

During Classical Conditioning

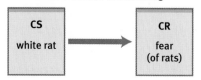

After Classical Conditioning

FIGURE **2.7 • Classical Conditioning of a Fear: Little Albert**

Conditioned response (CR)
A response that comes to be elicited by the previously neutral stimulus that has become a conditioned stimulus.

Conditioned emotional responses
Emotions and emotion-related behaviors that are classically conditioned.

Stimulus generalization
The process whereby responses come to be elicited by stimuli that are similar to the conditioned stimulus.

Operant conditioning
A type of learning in which the likelihood that a behavior will be repeated depends on the consequences associated with the behavior.

Reinforcement
The process by which the consequence of a behavior *increases* the likelihood of the behavior's recurrence.

It is called the conditioned stimulus because its ability to elicit the response is *conditional* on its being paired with a UCS. In Little Albert's case, the CS was the white rat. The **conditioned response (CR)** is the response that comes to be elicited by the previously neutral stimulus (the CR is basically the same behavior as the UCR, but the behavior is elicited by the CS). In Little Albert's case, the CR was the startle response to the rat alone (and ensuing fear-related behaviors, such as crying and trying to avoid the rat). The process of classical conditioning is illustrated in Figure 2.7.

Although various reflexive behaviors, such as salivation, can be classically conditioned (Pavlov, 1927), the ones most important for understanding psychopathology are those related to emotional responses such as fear and arousal (Davey, 1987; Schafe & LeDoux, 2004). When emotions and emotion-related behaviors are classically conditioned, they are referred to as **conditioned emotional responses**. People who have the personality characteristic of being generally emotionally reactive—referred to as being high in *neuroticism*—are more likely to develop conditioned emotional responses than are people who do not have this personality characteristic (Bienvenu et al., 2001).

Conditioned responses can also *generalize*, so that they are elicited by stimuli that are similar to the conditioned stimulus, a process called **stimulus generalization**. For instance, Little Albert became afraid not only of white rats but also of other white furry things. He even became afraid of a piece of white cotton! His fear of rats had generalized to similar stimuli.

As we shall see in detail in later chapters, classical conditioning is of interest to those studying psychological disorders because it helps to explain various types of anxiety disorders (particularly phobias, such as Little Albert's phobia), substance abuse and dependence (Hyman, 2005), and the development of specific types of sexual disorders (Domjan et al., 2004).

Operant Conditioning

Operant conditioning is a type of learning in which the likelihood that a behavior will be repeated depends on the consequences associated with the behavior. Operant conditioning usually involves voluntary behaviors, whereas classical conditioning usually involves reflexive behaviors. With operant conditioning, when a behavior is followed by a positive consequence, the behavior is more likely to be repeated. Consider Big Edie's behavior of crying out for Little Edie to come back into the room. Little Edie then returns to the room (a positive consequence), making it more likely that Big Edie will cry out for Little Edie to return in the future. When a behavior is followed by a negative consequence, it is less likely to be repeated. For instance, the last time Big Edie left Grey Gardens was in 1968, when she and her daughter went to a party at a friend's house; upon returning home, the Beale women discovered that thieves had taken $15,000 worth of heirlooms. It seemed to Big Edie that her behavior (leaving the house) was followed by a negative consequence (the theft), and so she never left again.

Psychologist B. F. Skinner showed that operant conditioning can explain a great deal of behavior, including abnormal behavior, and operant conditioning can be used to treat abnormal behaviors (Skinner, 1965). As we shall see throughout this book, operant conditioning contributes to various psychological disorders, such as depression, anxiety disorders, substance abuse disorder, eating disorders, and problems with self-regulation in general. Operant conditioning relies on two types of consequences: reinforcement and punishment; each can be either positive or negative.

Reinforcement

A key element in operant conditioning is **reinforcement**, the process by which the consequence of a behavior *increases* the likelihood of the behavior's recurrence. The consequence—an object or event—that makes a behavior more likely in the future is called a *reinforcer*. In the case of Big Edie's fear of being alone, the behavior was Big Edie's calling out to her daughter to return to her room, and it was followed by a reinforcer: Little Edie's return to her mother's side.

We need to consider two types of reinforcement: positive reinforcement and negative reinforcement. **Positive reinforcement** occurs when a desired reinforcer is *received* after the behavior, which makes the behavior more likely to occur again in the future. For instance, when someone takes a drug, the chemical properties of the drug may lead the person to experience a temporarily pleasant state (the reinforcer), which he or she may want to experience again, thus making the person more likely to take the drug again.

In contrast, **negative reinforcement** occurs when an aversive or uncomfortable stimulus is *removed* after a behavior, which makes that behavior more likely to be repeated in the future; note that negative, in this instance, does not necessarily mean "bad." For example, suppose that a man has a strong fear—a phobia—of dirt. If his hands get even slightly dirty, he will have the urge to wash them and will be uncomfortable until he does so. The act of washing his hands is negatively reinforced by the consequence of removing his discomfort about the dirt, which makes him more likely to wash his hands again the next time they get a bit dirty. Negative reinforcement is often confused with punishment; as we see next, however, the two are very different.

Punishment

Positive reinforcement and negative reinforcement both *increase* the probability of a behavior's recurring. In contrast, **punishment** is a process by which an event or object that is the consequence of a behavior *decreases* the likelihood that the behavior will occur again. Just as there are two types of reinforcement, there are two types of punishment: positive punishment and negative punishment. **Positive punishment** takes place when a behavior is followed by an undesirable consequence, which makes the behavior less likely to recur. In other words, an undesired stimulus is added in response to a behavior. For example, imagine that every time a young boy sings along with a song playing on the radio, his older sister makes fun of him (an undesirable consequence): In the future, he won't sing as often when she's around. That boy has experienced positive punishment.

Negative punishment occurs when a behavior is followed by the *removal* of a pleasant or desired event or circumstance, which decreases the probability of that

Positive reinforcement
The type of reinforcement that occurs when a desired reinforcer is *received* after a behavior, which makes the behavior more likely to occur again in the future.

Negative reinforcement
The type of reinforcement that occurs when an aversive or uncomfortable stimulus is *removed* after a behavior, which makes that behavior more likely to be produced again in the future.

Punishment
The process by which an event or object that is the consequence of a behavior *decreases* the likelihood that the behavior will occur again.

Positive punishment
The type of punishment that takes place when a behavior is followed by an undesirable consequence, which makes the behavior less likely to recur.

Negative punishment
The type of punishment that takes place when a behavior is followed by the *removal* of a pleasant or desired event or circumstance, which decreases the probability of that behavior's recurrence.

📷 GETTING THE PICTURE

In which photo are the students, at least in theory, receiving positive punishment? Answer: The students in the left photo. School detention is an attempt at positive punishment: Imposing the consequence of detention on students who exhibit troublesome behaviors should decrease the likelihood of those behaviors' occurring in the future.

TABLE 2.2 • Four Types of Operant Conditioning

Type of conditioning	How it occurs	Result	Example
Positive reinforcement	Desired consequence is produced by behavior.	Increased likelihood of the behavior	A pleasant effect from drug use makes drug use *more likely* to recur.
Negative reinforcement	Undesired event or circumstance is removed after behavior.	Increased likelihood of the behavior	The uncomfortable feeling of having dirty hands is relieved by washing them (which makes such washing *more likely* to recur).
Positive punishment	Undesired consequence is produced by behavior.	Decreased likelihood of the behavior	A sister's humiliating comment about her brother's singing along with the radio makes future singing in her presence *less likely* to recur.
Negative punishment	Pleasant event or circumstance is removed after behavior.	Decreased likelihood of the behavior	Removing a television from a teenager's room after he stays out too late makes staying out too late *less likely* to recur.

behavior's recurrence. Negative punishment occurs, for example, when a teenager stays out too late with friends and then her parents take away for a week her access to television (or cell phone, e-mail, use of the car, or something else she likes). Big Edie's father tried to use negative punishment to modify her behavior: He decreased her monthly allowance, repeatedly reduced her inheritance, and even told her that he was doing this because of her eccentric behavior. His attempts at negative punishment did not work, however, which indicates that the consequence he picked—taking away some money—was not meaningful enough to Big Edie. The four types of operant conditioning are compared in Table 2.2.

Receiving frequent punishments or negative criticisms is associated with depression in some people: Over time, some individuals who experience such aversive events eventually give up trying to avoid or escape them and become depressed. Martin Seligman and his colleagues suggested that this giving up is learned through operant conditioning (Miller & Seligman, 1973, 1975). The process appears analogous to what happens to animals in similar circumstances. Consider a classic study by Overmier and Seligman (1967): When caged dogs were electrically shocked, at first they would respond to the shocks, trying to escape from them by moving to a different part of the cage. But when they could not escape the continued shocks, they eventually stopped responding and simply endured, huddling on the floor. Even after they were put in a new cage in which they could easily avoid the shocks by moving, they remained on the floor. This phenomenon, whether in animals or humans, is called **learned helplessness**: In an aversive situation where it seems that no action can be effective, the animal or person stops trying to escape (Mikulincer, 1994). Learned helplessness is considered to underlie certain types of depression. For example, sometimes people are emotionally abused—continually criticized, humiliated, and belittled—and no matter how hard they try to be "better" (and so prevent the abuse), the emotional abuse continues. When people in such a situation give up trying, they may become depressed and become vulnerable to a variety of stress-related problems.

Feedback Loops in Understanding Classical Conditioning and Operant Conditioning

Let's suppose that a student gave a presentation that didn't go well, and some classmates snickered during one part (social factor). Let's also suppose that this student had an inherited vulnerability (a neurological factor; Stein & Gelernter, 2010) that increased his or her risk of developing a conditioned emotional response—in this case, to making presentations (Mineka & Zinbarg, 1995). And let's further suppose that the student developed negative, irrational thoughts about public speaking (psychological factor; Abbott & Rapee, 2004; Antony & Barlow, 2002). The three sorts of factors, fueling each other, can increase the likelihood that the student will develop a *social phobia*—an intense fear of public humiliation or embarrassment, accompanied by an avoidance of social situations likely to elicit this fear.

Learned helplessness
The state of "giving up" that arises when an animal or person is in an aversive situation where it seems that no action can be effective.

Observational Learning

Not all learning involves directly experiencing the associations that underlie classical and operant conditioning. **Observational learning** (also referred to as *modeling*) results from watching what happens to others (social factor; Bandura et al., 1961); from our observations, we learn ways to behave as well as develop expectations about what is likely to occur when we behave the same way (psychological factor). Observational learning is primarily a *psychological* factor: The key is mental processes (who and what behaviors are paid attention to, how the information is perceived and interpreted, how motivated the individual is to imitate the behavior). However, social factors are also involved, which include who the model is, his or her status, and his or her relationship to the observer. For instance, people who have high status or are attractive are more likely to hold our attention—so we are more likely to model their behavior (Brewer & Wann, 1998).

People who are uncomfortable in particular social situations may leave such situations as early as possible; this early departure is negatively reinforced because, once they leave, they no longer feel uncomfortable. Such negative reinforcement of social anxiety can contribute to a psychological disorder called social phobia—unreasonable anxiety or fear in social situations.

Through observational learning, children can figure out what types of behavior are acceptable in their family (Thorn & Gilbert, 1998), even if the observed behaviors are maladaptive. For example, when children observe parents managing conflict through violence or by drinking alcohol, they may learn to use such coping strategies themselves. From a young age, Little Edie spent much of her time with her mother, and during the 2 years she was kept out of school, she was with her mother practically day and night. Thus, in her formative years, Little Edie had ample opportunity to watch her mother's eccentric behavior and may have modeled her own eccentric behavior on that of her mother. Further, observational learning and operant conditioning can work together: When Little Edie modeled her behavior after her mother's, she was no doubt reinforced by her mother.

Mental Processes and Mental Contents

As noted in Chapter 1, both mental processes and mental contents play important roles in the etiology of psychological disorders. Let's take a closer look at these two types of contributing factors.

Mental Processes

We all have biases in our mental processes; hearing the same conversation, we can differ in what we pay attention to, how we interpret what we hear, and what we remember. With some psychological disorders, mental processes involved in attention, perception, and memory may be biased in particular ways:

- *Attention* results in selecting certain stimuli, including those that may be related to a disorder (van den Heuvel et al., 2005). Women with an eating disorder, for instance, are more likely than women without such a disorder to focus their attention on the parts of their bodies they consider "ugly" (Jansen et al., 2005) or on words related to food (Brooks et al., 2011).

- *Perception* results in registering and identifying specific stimuli, such as spiders or particular facial expressions of emotion (Buhlmann et al., 2006). As one example of bias in perception, depressed people are less likely than nondepressed people to rate neutral or mildly happy faces as "happy" (Surguladze et al., 2004).

- *Memory* involves storing, retaining, and accessing stored information, including that which is emotionally relevant to a particular disorder (Foa et al., 2000).

Observational learning
The process of learning through watching what happens to others; also referred to as *modeling*.

Cognitive distortions
Dysfunctional, maladaptive thoughts that are not accurate reflections of reality and contribute to psychological disorders.

Consider the disorder *illness anxiety disorder*, which is marked by a preoccupation with bodily sensations, combined with a belief of having a serious illness despite a lack of medical evidence. People suffering from illness anxiety disorder have a memory bias: They are better able to remember health-related words than non–health-related words (Brown, Kosslyn, et al., 1999), which is not surprising considering that the disorder involves a preoccupation with illness.

Thus, various mental processes can contribute to psychopathology by influencing what people pay attention to, how they perceive various stimuli, and what they remember. In turn, these alterations in mental processes influence the content of people's thoughts by shifting their awareness of various situations, objects, and stimuli.

Mental Contents

The contents of people's thoughts can play a role in whether someone develops a psychological disorder. Psychiatrist Aaron Beck (1967) proposed that dysfunctional, maladaptive thoughts are the root cause of psychological problems. These dysfunctional thoughts are **cognitive distortions** of reality. An example of a dysfunctional belief is a woman's conviction that she is unlovable—that if her boyfriend *really* knew her, he couldn't love her. Cognitive distortions can make a person vulnerable to psychological disorders and are sometimes referred to as *cognitive vulnerabilities* (Riskind & Alloy, 2006). Beck (1967) also argued that recognizing these false and dysfunctional thoughts and adopting realistic and adaptive thoughts can reduce psychological problems. Cognitive distortions can be a result of maladaptive learning from previous experiences. A man with a classically conditioned fear of rodents, for instance, may come to believe that rodents are *dangerous* because of the fear and anxiety he experiences when he's with them. Operant conditioning can also give rise to cognitive distortions. For instance, a child who is repeatedly rejected by her father can grow up to believe that nobody could love her. In this case, the conditioning could have occurred when, every time she tried to hug her father, he turned away. Cognitive distortions and biased mental processes affect each other. Several common cognitive distortions are presented in Table 2.3.

People who get anxious about public speaking often have the dysfunctional belief that audience members will laugh and jeer; this belief is a cognitive distortion. This woman is enjoying herself at a soccer game but laughter like this is what many people are afraid of when they think about speaking in public.

TABLE 2.3 • Cognitive Distortions

Cognitive distortion	Definition	Example
All-or-nothing thinking	Seeing things in black and white	You think that if you are not perfect, you are a failure.
Overgeneralization	Seeing a single negative event as part of a never-ending pattern of such events	While having a bad day, you predict that subsequent days will also be bad.
Mental filter	Focusing too strongly on negative qualities or events, to the exclusion of the other qualities or events	Although your overall appearance is fine, you focus persistently on the bad haircut you recently had.
Disqualifying the positive	Not recognizing or accepting positive experiences or events, thus emphasizing the negative	After giving a good presentation, you discount the positive feedback you received and focus only on what you didn't like about your performance.
Jumping to conclusions	Making an unsubstantiated negative interpretation of events	Although there is no evidence for your inference, you assume that your boss didn't like your presentation.
Personalization	Seeing yourself as the cause of a negative event when in fact you were not actually responsible	When your parents fight about finances, you think their problems are somehow your fault, despite the fact that their financial troubles weren't caused by you.

Source: Copyright © 1980 by David D. Burns, M.D. Reprinted by permission of HarperCollins Publishers, William Morrow. For more information see the Permissions section.

Mental health professionals need to keep in mind, however, cultural factors that may contribute to what appear to be maladaptive cognitive distortions but in fact reflect appropriate social behavior in a patient's culture. For instance, some cultures, such as that of Japan, have a social norm of responding to a compliment with a self-deprecating statement. It is only through careful evaluation that a clinician can discern whether such self-deprecating behavior reflects a patient's attempt to show good manners or his or her core maladaptive dysfunctional beliefs about self.

Emotion

Many psychological disorders include problems that involve emotions: not feeling or expressing enough emotions (such as showing no response to a situation where others would be joyous or sad), having emotions that are inappropriate or inappropriately excessive for the situation (such as feeling sad to the point of crying for no apparent reason), or having emotions that are difficult to regulate (such as overwhelming panic) (Aldao & Nolen-Hoeksema, 2010; American Psychiatric Association, 2013).

But what, specifically, are emotions? To psychologists, an **emotion** is a short-lived experience evoked by a stimulus that produces a mental response, a typical behavior, and a positive or negative subjective feeling. The stimulus that initiates an emotion could be physical: It can be a kiss, the positive comments on an essay you get back from a professor, or the sounds of a tune you listen to on your computer. Alternatively, the stimulus can occur only in the mind, such as *remembering* a sad occasion or tune or *imagining* your perfect mate.

Mental health clinicians and researchers sometimes use the word **affect** to refer to an emotion that is associated with a particular idea or behavior, similar to an *attitude*. *Affect* is also used to describe how emotion is expressed, as when noting that a patient has **inappropriate affect**—the patient's expression of emotion is not appropriate to what he or she is saying or to the situation. An example is a person laughing at a funeral or talking about a happy event while looking sad or angry. **Flat affect** is a lack of, or considerably diminished, emotional expression, such as occurs when someone speaks robotically and shows little facial expression. People with some psychological disorders, such as schizophrenia, frequently display inappropriate or flat affect. Other people may exhibit **labile affect**, a pattern in which affect changes very rapidly—too rapidly. Labile affect may indicate a psychological disorder; for instance, some people with depression may quickly shift emotions from sad to angry or irritable.

In the film *Grey Gardens*, Little Edie and her mother often displayed inappropriate affect, and Little Edie's emotions were sometimes labile, rapidly changing from anger to happy excitement to relative calm. For instance, at one point, Big Edie recounts that when Little Edie had moved to New York City, Big Edie wanted Mr. Beale to return to Grey Gardens. Little Edie immediately started yelling, "You're making me very angry!" (Maysles & Maysles, 1976), even though one moment before she had been relatively calm, and they were talking about events that had transpired over 20 years earlier.

A **mood** is a persistent emotion that is not attached to a stimulus. A mood lurks in the background and influences mental processes, mental contents, and behavior. For example, when you wake up "on the wrong side of the bed" for no apparent reason and feel grumpy all day, you are experiencing a type of bad mood. Some psychological disorders, such as depression, involve disturbances in mood.

Emotions and Behavior

Emotions and behavior dynamically interact. On the one hand, emotion can change behavior. People are more likely to participate in activities and behave in ways that are consistent with their emotions (Bower & Forgas, 2000). For instance, when people

Girl Ray/Getty Images

Some disorders are characterized by inappropriate affect—expressions of emotion that are inappropriate to the situation. We can imagine a situation where this young man's laughter—which may be just a reaction to a funny joke—might be a sign of inappropriate affect if he had just heard bad news.

Emotion
A short-lived experience evoked by a stimulus that produces a mental response, a typical behavior, and a positive or negative subjective feeling.

Affect
An emotion that is associated with a particular idea or behavior, similar to an attitude.

Inappropriate affect
An expression of emotion that is not appropriate to what a person is saying or to the situation.

Flat affect
A lack of, or considerably diminished, emotional expression, such as occurs when someone speaks robotically and shows little facial expression.

Labile affect
Affect that changes inappropriately rapidly.

Mood
A persistent emotion that is not attached to a stimulus; it exists in the background and influences mental processes, mental contents, and behavior.

Emotions and behavior have a reciprocal relationship: Changing behavior can change emotion, which this depressed person is trying to do by exercising.

Mental processes can affect emotions, such as occurs when a person attributes a bad grade to negative qualities about himself or herself, which in turn leads to poor mood.

are sad, they tend to hunch their shoulders and listen to slow music rather than upbeat music; when people are afraid, they tend to freeze, like a deer caught in the headlights; and when people are depressed, they often don't have the inclination or energy to see friends, which can lead to social isolation. On the other hand, a change in behavior can lead to a change in emotion. When people who are depressed make an effort to see friends or engage in other activities that they used to enjoy, they often become less depressed (Jacobson et al., 2001).

Emotions, Mental Processes, and Mental Contents

Emotions affect behavior as well as mental processes and mental contents. In fact, emotions and moods contribute to biases in attention, perception, and memory (Demenescu et al., 2010; MacKay & Ahmetzanov, 2005; Mogg & Bradley, 2005; Yovel & Mineka, 2005). For example, when feeling down, people are more likely to see the world through "depressed" lenses, to have a negative or pessimistic slant in general; not only will they find it easier to remember past periods of sadness, but they will also tend to view the future as hopeless; they will see more reasons to be sad than will people who aren't down (Lewis & Critchley, 2003).

The causality also works in the other direction: Mental processes can affect emotions. For example, emotions are affected by attributions. That is, we all regularly try to understand why events in our lives occur, and thus make *attributions*, assigning causes for particular occurrences. A person's mood can be affected by the attributions he or she makes. For instance, college students who tend to attribute negative events to general, enduring negative qualities about themselves ("I am stupid") are more likely to become depressed after a negative event (such as getting a bad grade) (Metalsky et al., 1993).

Emotional Regulation and Psychological Disorders

Difficulty in regulating emotions and related thoughts and behaviors can lead to three types of problems (Cicchetti & Toth, 1991; Weisz et al., 1997):

1. *Externalizing problems* are characterized by too little control of emotion and related behaviors, such as aggression, and by disruptive behavior. They are called externalizing problems because their primary effects are on others and/or their environment; these problems are usually observable to others.

2. *Internalizing problems* are characterized by negative internal experiences, such as anxiety, social withdrawal, and depression. Internalizing problems are so named because their primary effect is on the troubled individual rather than on others; such problems are generally less observable to others.

3. *Other problems* include emotional or behavioral problems that do not fit into these categories. This "other" category includes eating disorders and learning disorders (Achenbach et al., 1987; Kazdin & Weisz, 1998).

Significant difficulty in regulating emotions can begin in childhood and last through adulthood, forming the basis for some disorders.

Neurological Bases of Emotion

Emotion is a psychological response, but it is also a neurological response. We can learn much about the psychological aspects of emotion by considering how it arises from brain function. For example, research by Richard Davidson and colleagues, conducted largely by measuring the brain's electrical activity, have demonstrated that there are two general types of human emotions, approach emotions and withdrawal emotions, each relying on its own system in the brain. *Approach emotions* are positive emotions, such as love and happiness, and tend to activate the left frontal lobe more than the right. *Withdrawal emotions* are negative emotions, such as fear and sadness, and tend to activate the right frontal lobe more than the left (Davidson, 1992a, 1992b, 1993, 1998, 2002; Davidson et al., 2000; Lang, 1995). Researchers have also found that people who generally have more activation in the left frontal lobe tend to be more optimistic than people who generally have more activation in the right. This is important because depression has been associated with relatively less activity in the left frontal lobe (Davidson, 1993, 1994, 1998; Davidson et al., 1999). As a result of genetics, learning, or (most likely) some combination of the two, some people are temperamentally more likely to experience positive (approach) emotions, whereas others are more likely to experience negative (withdrawal) emotions (Fox et al., 2005; Rettew & McKee, 2005).

Temperament

Temperament is closely related to emotion: **Temperament** refers to the aspects of personality that reflect a person's typical emotional state and emotional reactivity (including the speed and strength of reactions to stimuli). Temperament is in large part innate, and it influences behavior in early childhood and even in infancy. Temperament is of interest in the study of psychological disorders for two reasons (Nigg, 2006a): First, specific types of temperament may make a person especially vulnerable to certain psychological disorders, even at an early age. For instance, people who are temperamentally more emotionally reactive are more likely to develop psychological disorders related to high levels of anxiety. Second, it is possible that in some cases a psychological disorder is simply an extreme form of a normal variation in temperament. For instance, some researchers argue that social phobia is on a continuum with shyness but is an extreme form of it; shyness involves withdrawal emotions and lack of sociability, and is viewed as a temperament (Schneider et al., 2002).

The Beale women had unusually reactive temperaments—they reacted strongly to stimuli. One or the other of them would respond to a neutral or offhand remark with emotion that was out of proportion: hot anger, bubbling joy, or snapping irritability. It's not a coincidence that mother and daughter seemed similar in this respect. Much evidence indicates that genes contribute strongly to temperament (Gillespie et al., 2003); in fact, some researchers report that genes account for about half of the variability in temperament (Oniszcenko et al., 2003). Researchers have associated some aspects of temperament to specific genes, such as genes that affect receptors for the neurotransmitter dopamine and a gene involved in serotonin production, and have shown that these genes can influence depression and problems controlling impulses (Nomura et al., 2006; Propper & Moore, 2006). Genes that affect dopamine receptors have also been shown to influence emotional reactivity (Oniszcenko & Dragan, 2005). However, these genes have stronger effects on children raised in harsh family environments; as we stressed earlier, the effects of genes need to be considered within the context of specific environments (Roisman & Fraley, 2006; Saudino, 2005).

C. Robert Cloninger and his colleagues have proposed one particularly influential theory of temperament, which describes temperament in terms of four dimensions—novelty seeking, harm avoidance, reward dependence, and persistence—each of which is associated with a brain system that relies predominantly on a particular neurotransmitter, as shown in Table 2.4 (Cloninger, 1987b; Cloninger et al., 1993).

In fact, researchers have found associations between genes and these dimensions of temperament (Gillespie et al., 2003; Keltikangas-Järvinen et al., 2006; Rybakowski et al., 2006). The specific results suggest that temperament arises from the joint activity of many different genes.

Fear involves a reflexive activation of the amygdala, not necessarily accompanied by any cognitive interpretation of the stimulus. Other emotions, such as guilt, depend on such interpretation. The ease of treating an emotional problem may be related to the nature of the underlying mechanism that gives rise to the experience of that emotion.

Temperament
The aspects of personality that reflect a person's typical emotional state and emotional reactivity (including the speed and strength of reactions to stimuli).

TABLE 2.4 • Cloninger's Four Temperaments

Temperament	Description	Hypothesized related neurotransmitter	Associated disorder(s)
Novelty seeking	Searching out novel stimuli and reacting positively to them; high levels can lead to being impulsive, avoiding frustration, and easily getting angry	Dopamine	With a high level, disorders that involve impulsive or aggressive behaviors
Harm avoidance	Reacting very negatively to harm and avoiding it whenever possible	Serotonin	With a high level, anxiety disorders
Reward dependence	Degree to which past behaviors that have led to desired outcomes in the past are repeated	Norepinephrine	With a low level (in combination with high impulsivity), substance use disorders
Persistence	Making continued efforts in the face of frustration when attempting to accomplish something.	Possibly dopamine	With a low level, attention-deficit/hyperactivity disorder

Thinking Like A Clinician

Maya is depressed; she's often tearful and feels hopeless about the future and helpless to change the negative things in her life. Give specific examples of the ways that types of learning might have influenced her negative expectations of life and led to her current depression. (It's okay to speculate here, but be specific.) Based on what you have read, how can Maya's thought patterns and emotions lead to her feeling depressed (or make the depression worse)?

☐ Social Factors in Psychological Disorders

We exist in a world filled with social forces: our relationships with family, friends, colleagues, and neighbors; the messages we receive through the media; the norms of our culture. These social forces help to shape who we become. They can help to protect us from developing psychological disorders, or they can make us more vulnerable to or exacerbate psychological disorders. Social forces begin to exert their influence before adulthood, and they can affect each generation differently, as a culture changes over time. For instance, the more recently an American is born, the more likely he or she is to develop a psychological disorder (Kessler, Bergland, et al., 2005), perhaps because of social trends such as the increased divorce rate, an increased sense of danger, and a diminished sense of local community (Twenge, 2000).

Consider Big Edie and Little Edie. The social factors that influenced them include their relationships with other members of their family, their financial circumstances, the prevailing community and cultural standards of appropriate behavior for women—and the discrimination they encountered. Let's examine in more detail each type of social factor—family, community, and culture—as well as the stress they can create.

Family Matters

Certain aspects of family life form the basis for the type of attachment a child has to the primary caregiver, which influences how a child comes to view himself or herself and learns what to expect from other people. Other family-related social factors include the style of interaction among family members, child maltreatment, and parental psychological disorders. All of these factors can contribute to the emergence or persistence of psychological disorders.

Family Interaction Style and Relapse

If family members exhibit hostility, voice unnecessary criticism, or are emotionally overinvolved, then the family environment is characterized by **high expressed emotion**. Based on what we know of the Beale women, their family environment would likely be classified as high expressed emotion. Consider these typical comments by Big Edie to her daughter: "Well, you made a rotten breakfast," followed moments later by, "Everything is perfectly disgusting on account of you" (Maysles & Maysles, 1976). Big Edie and Little Edie were also clearly overinvolved with each other: They spent virtually all their waking hours together, participated in all aspects of each other's lives, and responded to each other in exaggerated ways.

British researchers found that among people with schizophrenia, those whose families showed high expressed emotion were more likely to have the disorder recur; the same association between high expressed emotion and relapse has been found in other studies in the United States and China (Butzlaff & Hooley, 1998; Yang et al., 2004). This may be because high expressed emotion is associated with family members' belief that the patient has the ability to control his or her symptomatic behaviors, which sometimes leads the family members to push the patient to change (Miura et al., 2004). Unfortunately, these exhortations may well backfire: Instead of encouraging the patient to change, they may produce the sort of stress that makes the disorder worse! When family members are educated about the patient's disorder and taught more productive ways of communicating with the patient, relapse rates generally decline (Miklowitz, 2004).

High expressed emotion is not associated with relapse in all cultural or ethnic groups; members of different groups interpret such emotional expression differently. Among Mexican American families, for instance, the family member with schizophrenia is more likely to have a recurrence if the family style is the less common one of being distant and aloof; high expressed emotion is not related to recurrence (Lopez et al., 1998). And among African American families, high expressed emotion is actually associated with a better outcome (Rosenfarb et al., 2006). One possible explanation is that in African American families, confrontations are interpreted as signs of honesty (Rogan & Hammer, 1998) and may signal love and caring.

High expressed emotion
A family interaction style characterized by hostility, unnecessary criticism, or emotional overinvolvement.

Loungepark/Getty Images

Although high expressed emotion is associated with relapse in a European American family member with schizophrenia, this is not true among Mexican Americans; the likelihood of relapse of a patient with schizophrenia in a Mexican American family is higher when family members are emotionally distant. The family shown here does not appear to be emotionally distant.

Child Maltreatment

Child maltreatment comes in various forms—neglect, verbal abuse, physical abuse, and sexual abuse—and is associated with a higher risk for a variety of psychological disorders (Cicchetti & Toth, 2005; Green et al., 2010; Naughton et al., in press), including personality disorders (Battle et al., 2004; Bierer et al., 2003). Child maltreatment exerts its influence indirectly, through the following:

• *An altered bodily and neurological response to stress.* For instance, children who have been maltreated have higher baseline levels of cortisol than do children who have not been maltreated. Such alteration of the stress response in those who have been maltreated continues into adulthood (Tarullo & Gunnar, 2006; Watts-English et al., 2006).

• *Behaviors that are learned as a consequence of the maltreatment.* Maltreatment may result in a type of learned helplessness, so the children are more likely to be victimized as adults (Renner & Slack, 2006).

• *Biases in discriminating and responding to facial expressions.* For instance, children who have been physically abused are more likely to perceive photographs of faces as conveying anger than are children who have not been physically abused (Pollak et al., 2000).

Social support
The comfort and assistance that an individual receives through interactions with others.

- *Difficulties in attachment.* Children who have been maltreated are less likely to develop a secure type of attachment than are children who have not been maltreated (Baer & Martinez, 2006).
- *Increased social isolation.* Children who have been physically abused report feeling more socially isolated than children who have not been physically abused (Elliott et al., 2005).

However, not everyone who experienced maltreatment as a child develops a psychological disorder (Haskett et al., 2006; Katerndahl et al., 2005).

Parental Psychological Disorders

Another family-related factor that may contribute to psychological disorders is the presence of a psychological disorder in one or both parents (Pilowsky et al., 2006). It is difficult to pinpoint the specific mechanism responsible for this association, however, because it could be due to any number—or combination—of factors. For instance, a parent may transmit a genetic vulnerability for a psychological disorder to a child. Alternatively, the specific patterns of interaction between an affected parent and a child may lead to particular vulnerabilities in learning, mental processes, cognitive distortions, emotional regulation, or social interactions—any or all of which can increase the risk of a psychological disorder as the child grows older (Finzi-Dottan & Karu, 2006).

What is clear is that the association between a parent's having a psychological disorder and the increased risk of the child's later developing a psychological disorder isn't solely a result of genetic vulnerability. For instance, when depressed mothers received treatment, their symptoms improved, and so did their children's symptoms of anxiety, depression, and disruptive behaviors. The more positively a mother responded to her treatment, the less likely her children were to continue to have symptoms (Weissman, Pilowsky, et al., 2006; Wickramaratne et al., 2011). And consider children of women who had depressive symptoms: When such children went to preschool, they had fewer emotional and behavioral problems than did the children who spent their preschool years at home with their mothers full time (Herba et al., in press.)

Community Support

Social support—the comfort and assistance that an individual receives through interactions with others—can buffer the stressful events that occur throughout life (Silver & Teasdale, 2005). Conversely, a lack of social support can make people more vulnerable to various psychological disorders (Scarpa et al., 2006). College students who experience high levels of stress, for instance, are less likely to be depressed if they have relatively high levels of social support (Pengilly & Dowd, 2000).

The Beale women did not have much social support in their extended family or community, but they had each other, which clearly played a role in limiting whatever distress they may have felt about their lifestyle and circumstances. Little Edie noted, "My mother really was the most extraordinary member of the family. She was always singing. . . . I was happy to be alone with mother because we created the sort of life we liked, and it was very private and beautiful" (Wright, 2007, p. 17). Had the Beale women not supported each other and shared good times, the symptoms of psychological disorders that they displayed might have been worse.

Social Stressors

Living in poverty is associated with a higher rate of psychological disorders. Another social factor associated with psychological disorders is discrimination. Let's examine these two factors—socioeconomic status and discrimination—in more detail.

Mike Theiler/Getty Images

Social support can lessen the detrimental aftereffects of a stressful event such as an untimely death. People who do not have such support have a higher risk of developing a psychological disorder.

Socioeconomic Status

Socioeconomic groups are defined in terms of education, income, and occupational level; these indicators are sometimes referred to collectively as *socioeconomic status (SES)*. People from low SES backgrounds have a higher rate of psychological disorders than people from higher SES backgrounds (Costello et al., 1996, Mittendorfer-Rutz et al., 2004; Ramanathan et al., 2013). Socioeconomic factors may contribute to the development of psychological disorders in several ways. One theorized mechanism is through **social causation**: socioeconomic disadvantages and stress *cause* psychological disorders (Freeman, 1994). Specifically, the daily stressors of urban life, especially as experienced by people in a lower socioeconomic level, trigger mental illness in those who are vulnerable. For instance, living with inadequate housing, very limited financial means, and few job opportunities corresponds to the stress component of the diathesis–stress model discussed in Chapter 1 (Costello, Compton, et al., 2003). Case 2.1 describes Anna, whose depression was precipitated by financial stressors.

CASE 2.1 • FROM THE OUTSIDE: Depression and Social Selection

Anna was a single mother in her 30s when she sought treatment for her depression. At the time, she was having difficulty getting out of bed and was struggling to maintain order and basic routines at home for herself and her children. She had separated from her husband and lost her job 5 years prior to her first visit to the clinic. Since that time she had been struggling financially. She had a number of part-time jobs to try to make enough money to keep her family fed and clothed. However, she was often short of funds and felt very worried and stressed by their straitened [sic] financial situation. She noted she often felt worse after the summer as she became overwhelmed by the demands of a new school year and the thought of Christmas. As a result of encountering difficulty finding a permanent full-time position, her confidence waned, and she feared that she had lost her job skills. She had recently returned to school to take some business courses to update and extend her qualifications. . . .

Anna expressed regrets about her divorce. She had not realized at the time what a massive and difficult journey it would prove to be. She regretted uprooting her children and found her worries about money very stressful and disconcerting because she had never had to worry about finances before. Anna was a committed and dedicated mother who, even as she struggled to feed her children, put on a happy face to hide her stress because she did not want to worry them.

(Watson et al., 2007, pp. 83–84)

Another mechanism that may be responsible for the connection between psychological disorders and low SES is **social selection**, the hypothesis that those who are mentally ill "drift" to a lower socioeconomic level because of their impairments (Mulvany et al., 2001; Wender et al., 1973). Social selection is sometimes referred to as *social drift*. Research suggests that the relationship between psychological disorders and SES cuts both ways: Low SES both contributes to disorders and is a consequence of having a disorder (Conger & Donnellan, 2007; Fan & Eaton, 2001; Johnson et al., 1999).

A study by Jane Costello and colleagues (Costello, Compton, et al., 2003) tested the influence of social selection and social causation on psychopathology in children. These researchers tracked more than 300 Native American children between the ages of 9 and 13 for 8 years; the children were seen annually. At the start of the study, over half of the children were living in poverty. Halfway through the study, a casino opened on the reservation, raising the income of all the Native American families and pulling one quarter of them above the poverty line. Before the casino opened, children whose families were below the poverty line had more psychiatric symptoms than children whose families were above it. After the casino opened, the number of

Social causation hypothesis
The hypothesis that the daily stressors of urban life, especially as experienced by people in a lower socioeconomic class, trigger mental illness in those who are vulnerable.

Social selection hypothesis
The hypothesis that people who are mentally ill "drift" to a lower socioeconomic level because of their impairments; also referred to as *social drift*.

psychiatric symptoms among children who were no longer living in poverty was the same as among those who had never lived in poverty. Once the socioeconomic disadvantages and accompanying family stress were removed, children functioned better, and their symptoms improved—an outcome that supports the role of social causation in this setting (Rutter, 2003).

Discrimination, Bullying, and War

Being the object of discrimination is associated with an increased risk of distress and psychological disorders (Bhui et al., 2005; Chakraborty & McKenzie, 2002; Mays & Cochran, 2001; Simons et al., 2002). Women, for example, may experience sexual harassment and assault, limitations on their freedom (such as a prohibition against working outside the home), or glass ceilings (unstated limits on social or occupational possibilities). Such experiences may lead to increased stress and vulnerability to psychological disorders. Consider that sexual harassment of women in the workplace is associated with subsequent increased alcohol use by those women (Freels et al., 2005; Rospenda, 2002). Similarly, members of ethnic, racial, or sexual minority groups may experience harassment at—or discrimination in—school, housing, or jobs, which can create a sense of powerlessness and lead to chronically higher levels of stress (Bhugra & Ayonrinde, 2001; Mills et al., 2004; Williams & Williams-Morris, 2000), which in turn increases the risk for developing psychological disorders.

The stigma and discrimination encountered by some gays and lesbians can make them—and others experiencing discrimination—more vulnerable to psychological disorders (Herek & Garnets, 2007; Mays & Cochran, 2001).

In addition, whereas discrimination involves negative behavior toward someone because of his or her status as a member of a particular group (based on ethnicity, race, religion, sexual orientation, or another characteristic), *bullying* involves negative behavior that may be unrelated to the victim's membership in an ethnic, racial, or other group. Research indicates that being a victim of childhood bullying can contribute to psychological problems in childhood and adulthood (Arseneault et al., 2008; Copeland et al., 2013; Sourander et al., 2009), and it is particularly likely to lead to internalizing problems.

Finally, war often inflicts extreme and prolonged stress on soldiers and civilian victims. How an individual responds to the effects of war is determined by a variety of factors (discussed at length in Chapter 7), such as proximity to the fighting and the duration of combat. After mandated extended tours of duty for American soldiers in Iraq and Afghanistan, at least 20% of returning troops had symptoms of posttraumatic stress disorder or depression (Tanielian & Jaycox, 2008).

Culture

Every culture promotes an ideal of healthy functioning—of a "normal" personality—and a notion of unhealthy functioning. These ideals differ somewhat from culture to culture and can shift over time (Doerfel-Baasen & Rauh, 2001). Some cultures, such as those of many Asian, Latin American, and Middle Eastern countries, are *collectivist*, placing a high value on getting along with others; in such cultures, the goals of the group (family or community) traditionally take precedence over those of the individual. In contrast, other cultures, such as those of Australia, Canada, the

GETTING THE PICTURE

Which family immigrating to the United States is more likely to experience stressful acculturation? Answer: The family on the left will probably have a more stressful acculturation; they come from a collectivist culture, with different values. The family on the right comes from an individualist culture (the Netherlands) that has values more similar to those of the United States.

United Kingdom, and the United States, are *individualist*, valuing independence and autonomy; the goals of the individual take precedence over the goals of the group (Hui & Triandis, 1986). In either case, if an individual has personality traits that are different from those valued by the culture, other people's responses to the person may lead him or her to feel humiliated and to develop poor self-esteem, which increases the risk of developing psychological disorders.

In addition, moving from one culture to another often leads people to adopt the values and behaviors of the new culture, a process that is termed *acculturation*. This can be very stressful and can create tension between parents—who moved to the new culture as adults—and their children, whose formative years were spent in the new culture. As these children grow up, they may be forced to choose between the values and views of their parents' culture and those of the new culture, which can be stressful and can make them more likely to develop psychological disorders (Escobar et al., 2000). However, the degree to which acculturation is stressful and increases the risk for psychological disorders depends on other factors, such as the degree of difference in values between the native and new cultures, the reasons for leaving the native country (for example, traumatic causes for leaving, such as war and famine, can have strong effects), the change in SES status that results from immigration, and the degree of discrimination encountered in the new culture. In the absence of these other factors, moving to a new culture is not necessarily associated with later psychological disorders (Kohn, 2002).

Thinking Like A Clinician

Gonsalvo and Bill, roommates, are both first-year college students. Gonsalvo has left his family and country and moved to another continent to study in the United States; Bill's family lives a few hours' drive away. What social factors may influence whether either young man develops a psychological disorder during their time at college? Be specific about possible factors that might lead *each man* to be vulnerable. What social factors may protect them from developing a disorder? What additional information would you want to help you answer these questions, and how might such information affect your predictions?

A Neuropsychosocial Last Word on the Beales

We conclude this chapter by briefly examining how neurological, psychological, and social factors might have affected each other via feedback loops in the case of Big Edie and Little Edie. Both women were artistic, unconventional, and independent (psychological factor), but their social class and the time in which they lived made their behavior "inappropriate," leading them to be discriminated against within their extended family and community (social factor). In turn, the social constraints of their day prevented them from having jobs or careers, and so they were unable to support themselves; they were financially dependent on others (social), which created its own stress (neurological and psychological). These external realities, in turn, may have heightened their feeling that people were out to get them (psychological factor). Moreover, it is possible that they had neurological characteristics—such as emotional reactivity—that predisposed them to behave in certain ways, which in turn evoked certain responses from others.

We will draw on the neuropsychosocial approach—considering all three types of factors *and their feedback loops*—to understand the various psychological disorders discussed in this book. Neurological factors (genetics, brain structure and function, and bodily responses), psychological factors (learning and behavior, mental processes and mental contents, and emotions), social factors (social stressors, relationships, family, culture, and socioeconomic status), and the interactions among these factors all play a role in explaining psychological disorders.

SUMMING UP

Neurological Factors in Psychological Disorders

- The nervous system has two major parts: the central nervous system (CNS), which is composed of the brain and spinal cord, and the peripheral nervous system (PNS), which is composed of the sensory-somatic nervous system and the autonomic nervous system (ANS).

- The ANS controls many involuntary functions, such as those of the heart, blood vessels, and digestive tract. The ANS has two major components: the sympathetic nervous system and the parasympathetic nervous system.

- The brain is divided into two hemispheres, left and right; each has four lobes: occipital lobe (involved in vision), parietal lobe (e.g., involved in processing spatial information and self-awareness), temporal lobe (e.g., involved in processing auditory information, including speech, and memory), and frontal lobe (e.g., site of executive functioning).

- Subcortical (beneath the cortex) areas of importance include the limbic system, which plays a key role in emotions, key parts of which are the hypothalamus, the amygdala, and the hippocampus.

- There are three types of neurons: sensory neurons, motor neurons, and interneurons. Neurons communicate with each other to create patterns of activation in brain circuits, which in turn are organized into large brain systems; these systems may be disrupted in cases of psychopathology.

- There are many types of neurotransmitters, which play different roles in the brain; imbalances of neurotransmitters can contribute to psychological disorders.

- Hormones, chemicals produced by glands in the endocrine system, can affect the functioning of neurons.

- Genes can influence the development of psychopathology. Heritability is an estimate of how much of the variation of a characteristic across a population, *in a specific environment*, is determined by genes.

- Behavioral geneticists may use twin and adoption studies to determine the relative influences of genes and environment.

Psychological Factors in Psychological Disorders

- Three types of learning can contribute to psychological disorders: classical conditioning of emotional responses such as fear and anxiety; operant conditioning of voluntary behaviors through positive and negative reinforcement and punishment; and observational learning, which can guide the observer's behaviors and expectations.

- Mental processes and mental contents play important roles in the etiology and maintenance of psychological disorders.

- Emotional disturbances contribute to some psychological disorders. Such disturbances include not feeling or expressing emotions to a normal degree and having difficulty regulating emotions.

- Emotions, behaviors, mental contents, and mental processes are often intertwined, and so disturbances in one will affect the others. Moreover, a person's attributions and mood can affect each other.

- Emotions involve both a psychological and a neurological response to a stimulus.

- Having a particular temperament may make a person especially vulnerable to certain psychological disorders, even at an early age. Evidence indicates that genes contribute strongly to temperament; however, the effects of genes need to be considered within the context of specific environments.

- Temperament is conceived of as having four dimensions: novelty seeking, harm avoidance, reward dependence, and persistence. Cloninger proposed that each of these dimensions is associated with the action of a particular neurotransmitter.

Social Factors in Psychological Disorders

- Social factors can help protect us from developing psychological disorders, or they can make us more vulnerable to or exacerbate psychological disorders. Such factors begin to exert their influence before adulthood.

- A family's style of interacting that involves high expressed emotion can contribute to relapse in patients with schizophrenia from particular ethnic or cultural groups.

- Being maltreated as a child indirectly contributes to the development of psychological disorders by increasing stress, teaching maladaptive behaviors, promoting biases in discriminating among and responding to facial expressions, creating difficulties in attachment, and increasing social isolation.

- Psychological disorders in parents can contribute to psychological disorders in their children, although it is difficult to pinpoint the specific mechanism through which this influence occurs.

- Social support can buffer against stress, and a lack of social support can make people more vulnerable to psychological disorders.

- Low SES is associated with a higher rate of psychological disorders; both social causation and social selection contribute to this relationship.

- Being the object of discrimination is associated with an increased risk of distress and psychological disorders.

- Different personality traits and behaviors are valued in different cultures; thus, acculturation can lead to conflict among family members, creating stress and a risk of psychological disorders.

Key Terms

Etiology (p. 29)
Cerebral cortex (p. 32)
Neurons (p. 32)
Brain circuits (p. 33)
Brain systems (p. 33)
Action potential (p. 34)
Synapse (p. 34)
Neurotransmitters (p. 34)
Receptors (p. 35)
Reuptake (p. 36)
Hormones (p. 36)
Genes (p. 36)
Genotype (p. 36)
Phenotype (p. 36)
Complex inheritance (p. 37)
Behavioral genetics (p. 37)

Heritability (p. 37)
Monozygotic twins (p. 38)
Dizygotic twins (p. 38)
Classical conditioning (p. 41)
Unconditioned stimulus (UCS) (p. 41)
Unconditioned response (UCR) (p. 41)
Conditioned stimulus (CS) (p. 41)
Conditioned response (CR) (p. 42)
Conditioned emotional responses (p. 42)
Stimulus generalization p. 42)
Operant conditioning (p. 42)
Reinforcement (p. 42)
Positive reinforcement (p. 43)
Negative reinforcement (p. 43)
Punishment (p. 43)
Positive punishment (p. 43)

Negative punishment (p. 43)
Learned helplessness (p. 44)
Observational learning (p. 45)
Cognitive distortions (p. 46)
Emotion (p. 47)
Affect (p. 47)
Inappropriate affect (p. 47)
Flat affect (p. 47)
Labile affect (p. 47)
Mood (p. 47)
Temperament (p. 49)
High expressed emotion (p. 51)
Social support (p. 52)
Social causation hypothesis (p. 53)
Social selection hypothesis (p. 53)

More Study Aids

For additional study aids related to this chapter, including quizzes to make sure you've retained everything you've learned and a Student Video Activity exploring the power a community can have in treating individuals suffering from mental illness, go to: www.worthpublishers.com/launchpad/rkabpsych2e.

Photodisc

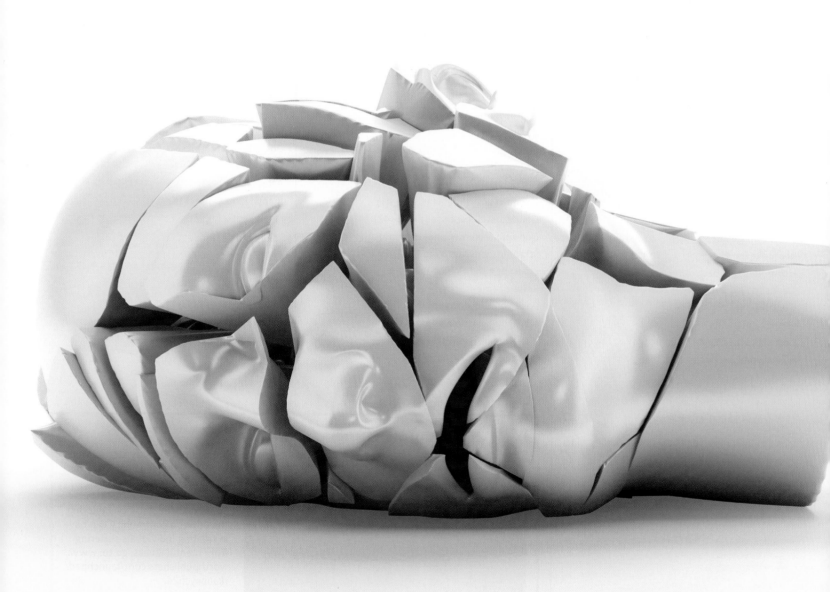

CHAPTER **3**

Clinical Diagnosis and Assessment

Jeannette Walls had an unusual childhood. She and her three siblings—Lori, Brian, and Maureen—had smart, engaging parents who taught them each to read by the time they were 3, explained and demonstrated scientific principles to them, instilled a love of reading and appreciation for the arts, and made their children each feel that they were special. As Jeannette Walls recounts in her memoir, *The Glass Castle* (2005), her father, Rex, was an intelligent man who was a skilled electrical engineer. Her mother, Rose Mary, was an artist and had trained to be a teacher. Yet Rex had difficulty holding onto jobs, and most of the time Rose Mary didn't have a paying job. Both parents gave their children enormous freedom to explore and experiment; they also often left the children to fend for themselves.

Rex and Rose Mary would uproot and move the family in the middle of the night, sometimes giving the kids 15 minutes to pack their things and pile into the car. They'd leave town in order to avoid bill collectors or child welfare officials, moving to whatever small town caught Rose Mary's and Rex's fancy. Neither parent spent much time fulfilling the many daily responsibilities of parenting, such as preparing meals. For instance, even at the age of 3, if Jeannette was hungry, she knew not to ask her parents for something to eat but to make it herself. She figured out how to make hot dogs: put water in a pot and boil the dogs, standing on a chair by the gas stove in order to do it. During one stint of hot dog making when she was 3, her dress caught on fire. She was so severely burned that she was hospitalized for 6 weeks and had skin grafts. Her hospital stay ended when her father had a fight with her doctor about whether her bandages should remain on; her father carried Jeannette from her hospital room in the middle of the night and out to the car, where her family was waiting for her. They headed out of town to wherever the road took them; Jeannette's scars never properly healed.

Jeannette Walls

THE FAMILY REFERRED TO THIS AND OTHER LATE NIGHT MOVES from one dusty town to another as doing "the skedaddle." A few months after taking Jeannette out of the hospital, the family did the skedaddle again. During Jeannette's early childhood, Rex would get a job as an electrician or an engineer (often making up stories about previous jobs he'd had or degrees he'd earned). When they left a town, Rex would explain to the family that they were running from federal investigators who were chasing him for some unnamed episode in the past; Rose Mary admitted to the children that frequently they were running from bill collectors. Sometimes they moved simply because Rex was bored.

Rex and Rose Mary tried to make their tumbleweed life into an adventure for their children, and they succeeded to some extent when the children were young. However, the parents' own problems got in the way of their responsibilities. During most of Jeannette's school years, her family was so poor that the children ended up eating only one meal a day—the lunch leftovers at school that they were able to scavenge from the trash. When Rex would lose his job, sometimes he'd stay home. He drew up blueprints for a solar-powered "glass castle" or worked on his design for a tool that would find gold in rocks. And increasingly during Jeannette's childhood, he'd gamble and drink. In what Jeannette describes as his "beer phase," Rex would drive fast and sing loudly. When he began to drink the "hard stuff," Rose Mary would get frantic because Rex would become angry: He'd beat his wife, throw furniture around, and yell. Then he'd collapse.

Rose Mary, under duress from her children and the threat of visits from child welfare officials, tried two different stints of working as a teacher, but she hated it so much that she had a hard time getting out of bed to get ready for work, and she had difficulty doing the paperwork required by the job. After a year, Rose Mary refused to work anymore; she claimed that she needed to put herself first—to paint, sculpt, and write novels and short stories—even though Rex still was not working and there was no other regular income.

Did Rex and Rose Mary have psychological disorders? To answer that question, we must return to the criteria for a psychological disorder that we discussed in Chapter 1: a pattern of thoughts, feelings, or behavior that lead to distress, impairment in daily life, and risk of harm, within the context of the culture. Did Rose Mary or Rex experience significant distress? Remarkably, Jeannette's account of her family conveys little sense that her parents were distressed by their situation. What about impaired functioning? The fact that neither parent was able to hold a job consistently certainly indicates impairment in daily life.

With regard to risk of harm, Rose Mary and Rex put themselves and their children at risk countless times in various ways: They—and their children—regularly went without food (and neither parent was sufficiently motivated to earn money in order to buy food). Rex repeatedly drove while intoxicated, sometimes at 90 miles an hour or more. The family members' physical safety was put at risk in other ways. One night when Jeannette was 10 years old, she woke up to find a vagrant sexually groping her. When the children asked their parents to close the front and back doors at night, their parents refused: "They wouldn't consider it. We needed the fresh air, they said, and it was essential that we refuse to surrender to fear" (Walls, 2005, p. 103). The parents put themselves at risk of harm in other ways, including intense fighting. For example, during one fight, Rex and Rose Mary went at each other with knives—and then their fighting suddenly switched off, and the couple ended up laughing and hugging. Rose Mary admitted to her children that she was an "excitement addict," and her quest for excitement and Rex's drinking and related behavior often led the family into dangerous situations.

According to Jeannette's descriptions, then, both Rex and Rose Mary Walls would seem to have had some type of psychopathology. On what basis should you evaluate and classify their behavior? How would a mental health professional go about identifying their specific psychological problems? How should you go about determining whether a specific diagnosis is warranted? For mental health professionals, a **diagnosis** is the identification of the nature of a disorder (American Psychiatric Association, 2013). A diagnosis is made by assigning a patient's symptoms to a specific classification. Classifying a set of symptoms as a disorder allows you to know more than was initially apparent. Depending on how much is known about a given disorder, a diagnosis may suggest the disorder's possible causes, its course over time, and its possible treatments. In Rex's case, for example, a diagnosis for his pattern of drinking and related behavior would be what mental health clinicians call *alcohol use disorder* (which we discuss in more detail in Chapter 9). Having a diagnosis might allow one to infer why he—and other people with the same set of symptoms—may have developed the disorder and whether the symptoms would be likely to shift in frequency or intensity over time. Moreover, the diagnosis might indicate that certain types of treatment, such as those based on behavioral principles (see Chapter 2), might be more effective than other types of treatment.

A diagnosis is based on information about the patient obtained through interviews, observations, and tests. Such information is part of a **clinical assessment**—the process of obtaining relevant information and making a judgment about mental illness based on the information. Clinical assessments often go further than providing information needed to make a diagnosis. They also can provide information about the specific ways in which and the degree to which an individual is impaired, as well as about areas of functioning that are not impaired. When we discuss the mental health—or mental illness—of Rex and Rose Mary Walls, we are trying to approximate a clinical assessment based on the words—and judgments—of their daughter, Jeannette—someone who knew them intimately. Rex died at the age of 59. Were he alive today and it were possible to make a clinical assessment of him and Rose Mary, we would be in a position to determine with greater confidence whether either of them could be diagnosed with a psychological disorder.

Diagnosing Psychological Disorders

Rose Mary and Rex Walls created an endurance contest for their growing children. A typical example was when Lori was diagnosed by the school nurse as severely nearsighted and in need of glasses. Rose Mary didn't approve of eyeglasses, commenting, "If you had weak eyes . . . they needed exercise to get strong" (Walls, 2005, p. 96). Rose Mary thought that glasses were like crutches.

Rex had unusual beliefs as well. He told his family that he couldn't find a job in a coal mining town because the mines were controlled by the unions, which were controlled by the mob. He said he was nationally blackballed by the electricians' union in Arizona (where he had previously worked), and in order to get a job in the mines, he must help reform the United Mine Workers of America. He claimed that he spent his days investigating that union.

Unusual beliefs may not have been the only factor that motivated Rose Mary and Rex's behavior; they also seemed to have a kind of "tunnel vision" that led them to pay attention to their own needs and desires while being indifferent to those of their children. When Jeannette was 5 and the family was again moving, her parents rented a U-Haul truck and placed all four children (including the

Diagnosis
The identification of the nature of a disorder.

Clinical assessment
The process of obtaining relevant information and making a judgment about mental illness based on the information.

youngest, Maureen, who was then an infant) and some of the family's furniture in the dark, airless, windowless back of the truck for the 14 hours it would take to get to their next "home." Rex and Rose Mary instructed the children to remain quiet in this crypt—which was also without food, water, or toilet facilities—for the entire journey. The parents also expected the children to keep baby Maureen silent so that police wouldn't discover the children in the back: It was illegal to transport people in the trailer. What explanation did the parents give their children for locking them up this way? They said that only two people could fit in the front of the truck.

In order to determine whether Rex and Rose Mary Walls had psychological disorders, we would have to compare their behavior and psychological functioning to some standard of normalcy. A diagnostic *classification system* provides a means of making such comparisons. Let's first examine general issues about classification systems and diagnosis and then consider the system that is now most commonly used—the system described in the most recent edition of the *Diagnostic and Statistical Manual of Mental Disorders.*

Why Diagnose?

You may have heard that categorizing people is bad: It pigeonholes them and strips them of their individuality—right? Not necessarily. By categorizing psychological disorders, clinicians and researchers can know more about a patient's symptoms and about how to treat the patient. To be specific, classification systems of mental disorders provide the following benefits:

- They provide a type of shorthand, which enables clinicians and researchers to use a small number of words instead of lengthy descriptions.

- They allow clinicians and researchers to group certain abnormal thoughts, feelings, and behaviors into unique constellations.

Without a classification system for psychological disorders, the problems that Pete Wentz, Jessica Alba, and Keith Urban appear to have suffered from—bipolar disorder, obsessive-compulsive disorder, and substance abuse, respectively—would be nameless. Among other purposes, a classification system allows clinicians to diagnose and treat symptoms more effectively, allows patients to know that they are not alone in their experiences, and helps researchers to investigate the factors that contribute to psychological disorders and to evaluate treatments.

- A particular diagnosis may convey information—useful for both clinicians and researchers—about the etiology of the disorder, its course, and indications for its treatment.

- A diagnosis can indicate that an individual is in need of attention (including treatment), support, or benefits.

- Some people find great relief in learning that they are not alone in having particular problems (see Case 3.1).

CASE 3.1 • FROM THE OUTSIDE: On Being Diagnosed with a Disorder

Sally, an articulate and dynamic 46-year-old woman, came to share her experiences with our psychiatry class. For much of her adult life, she had suffered from insomnia, panic attacks, and intense fear. Then, six years ago, a nightmare triggered memories of childhood sexual abuse and she was finally diagnosed with posttraumatic stress disorder.

Being diagnosed, she told us, was an intense relief.

"All those years, I thought I was just crazy," she said. "My whole family used to call me the crazy one. Once, my brother called my mom and asked, 'So, how's my crazy sister?' But all of a sudden I wasn't crazy any more. It had a name. It had a real reason. I could finally understand why I felt the way I did,' she said."

(Rothman, 1995)

A Cautionary Note About Diagnosis

Having a classification system for mental illness has many advantages, but assigning the appropriate diagnosis can be challenging. For example, clinicians may be biased to make—or not make—particular diagnoses for certain groups of people. Patients, once diagnosed with a disorder, may be stigmatized because of it (Ben-Zeev et al., 2010). In what follows, we examine the possibilities of bias and stigma in more detail.

A **diagnostic bias** is a systematic error in diagnosis (Meehl, 1960). Such a bias can cause groups of people to receive a particular diagnosis disproportionately, on the basis of an unrelated factor such as sex, race, or age (Kunen et al., 2005). Studies of diagnostic bias show, for example, that in the United States, Black patients are more likely than White patients to be diagnosed with schizophrenia instead of a mood disorder (Gara et al., 2012; Trierweiler et al., 2005). Black patients are also prescribed higher doses of medication than are White patients (Strakowski et al., 1993).

When a mental health clinician is not familiar with the social norms of the patient's cultural background, the clinician may misinterpret certain behaviors as pathological and thus be more likely to diagnose a psychological disorder. So, for instance, the clinician might view a Caribbean immigrant family's closeness as "overinvolvment" rather than as normal for that culture.

Other groups, such as low-income Mexican Americans, may have their mental illnesses underdiagnosed (Schmaling & Hernandez, 2005). Part of the explanation for the underdiagnosis may be that the constellation of symptoms experienced by some Mexican Americans does not fit within the classification system currently used in North America; another part of the explanation may be language differences between patient and clinician that make accurate assessment difficult (Kaplan, 2007b; Villaseñor & Waitzkin, 1999).

Bias is particularly important because when someone is said to have a psychological disorder, the diagnosis may be seen as a stigmatizing label that influences how other people—including the mental health clinician—view and treat the person. It may even change how a diagnosed person behaves and feels about himself or herself (Ben-Zeev et al., 2010; Eriksen & Kress, 2005). Such labels can lead some

Diagnostic bias
A systematic error in diagnosis.

people with a psychological disorder to blame themselves and try to hide their problems (Corrigan & Watson, 2001; Reinberg, 2011). Feelings of shame may even lead them to refrain from obtaining treatment (U.S. Department of Health and Human Services, 1999). Great strides have been made toward destigmatizing mental illness, although there is still a way to go. One organization devoted to confronting the stigma of mental illness is the National Alliance for the Mentally Ill (nami.org), which has a network of advocates—called StigmaBusters—who combat incorrect and insensitive portrayals of mental illness in the media.

Reliability and Validity in Classification Systems

Classification systems are most useful when they are reliable and valid. If a classification system yields consistent results over time, it is **reliable**. To understand what constitutes a reliable classification system, imagine the following scenario about Rose Mary Walls: Suppose she decided to see a mental health clinician because she was sleeping a lot, crying every day, and had no appetite. Further, she consented to have her interview with the clinician filmed for other clinicians to watch. Would every clinician who watched the video clip hear Rose Mary's words and classify her behavior in the same way? Would every clinician diagnose her as having the same disorder? If so, then the classification system they used would be deemed reliable. But suppose that various clinicians came up with different diagnoses or were divided about whether Rose Mary even had a disorder. They might make different judgments about how her behaviors or symptoms fit into the classification system. If there were significant differences of opinion about her diagnosis among the clinicians, the classification system they used probably is not reliable.

Problems concerning reliability in diagnosis can occur when:

- *the criteria for disorders are unclear* and thus require the clinician to use considerable judgment about whether symptoms meet the criteria; or
- *there is significant overlap among disorders*, which can then make it difficult to distinguish among them.

However, just because clinicians agree on a diagnosis doesn't mean that the diagnosis is correct! For example, in the past, there was considerable agreement about the role of the devil in producing mental disorders, but we now know that this isn't a correct explanation (Wakefield, 2010). Science is not a popularity contest; what the majority of observers believe at any particular point in time is not necessarily correct. Thus, another requirement for any classification system is that it needs to be **valid**. The categories must characterize what they are supposed to be classifying. Each disorder should have a unique set of criteria that correctly characterize the disorder.

The reliability and validity of classification systems are important in part because such systems are often used to study the etiology of a psychological disorder, its **prognosis** (the likely course and outcome of the disorder), and whether particular treatments will be effective. In order to use a classification system in this way, however, the **prevalence** of each disorder—the number of people who have the disorder in a given period of time—must be large enough that researchers are likely to encounter people with the disorder. (A related term is *incidence*, which refers to the total number of new cases of a disorder that are identified in a given time period.)

In sum, a classification system should be reliable and valid in order to be as useful as possible for patients, clinicians, and researchers. Next, we'll examine a commonly used classification system for psychological disorders—the system in the *Diagnostic and Statistical Manual of Mental Disorders (DSM)*.

Reliable
A property of classification systems (or measures) that consistently produce the same results.

Valid
A property of classification systems (or measures) that actually characterize what they are supposed to characterize.

Prognosis
The likely course and outcome of a disorder.

Prevalence
The number of people who have a disorder in a given period of time.

The Diagnostic and Statistical Manual of Mental Disorders

Suppose that child welfare officials had spoken with Rex and Rose Mary Walls and required that the parents be evaluated by mental health professionals. How would a mental health clinician go about determining whether or not either of them had a disorder? What classification system would the clinician probably use? The classification system that most clinicians use in the United States is found in the *Diagnostic and Statistical Manual of Mental Disorders*, which is currently in its fifth edition. This guide, published by the American Psychiatric Association (2013), describes the characteristics of many psychological disorders and identifies *criteria*—the kinds, number, and duration of relevant symptoms—for diagnosing each disorder. This classification system is generally *categorical*, which means that someone either has a disorder or does not.

A different classification system, used in some parts of the world, is described in the *International Classification of Diseases* (ICD). The World Health Organization (WHO) develops the ICD, with its 11th edition released in 2017. The primary purpose of the ICD is to provide a framework for collecting health statistics worldwide. Unlike the DSM, however, the ICD includes many diseases and disorders, not just psychological disorders. In fact, until the sixth edition, the ICD only classified causes of death. With the sixth edition, the editors added diseases and mental disorders. Current versions of the mental disorders sections of the ICD and the DSM have been revised to overlap substantially. Research on prevalence that uses one classification system is now generally applicable to the other system.

The Evolution of DSM

When the original version of the DSM was published in 1952, it was the first manual to address the needs of clinicians rather than researchers (Beutler & Malik, 2002). At that time, Freud-inspired, psychodynamic theory was popular, and the DSM strongly favored the psychodynamic approach in its classifications. For example, it organized mental illness according to different types of conflicts among the id, ego, superego, and reality, as well as different patterns of defense mechanisms employed (American Psychiatric Association, 1952). The second edition of the DSM, published in 1968, had only minor modifications. The first two editions were criticized for problems with reliability and validity, which arose in part because their classifications relied on psychodynamic theory. Clinicians had to draw many inferences about the specific nature of patients' problems, including the specific unconscious conflicts that motivated patients' behavior.

The authors of the third edition (DSM-III), published in 1980, set out to create a classification system that had better reliability and validity. Unlike the previous editions, DSM-III:

- did not rest on the psychodynamic theory of psychopathology (or on any other theory);

- focused more on what can be observed than on what can be inferred;

- listed explicit criteria for each disorder and began to use available research results to develop those criteria; and

- included a system for clinicians and researchers to record diagnoses as well as additional information—such as related medical history—that may affect diagnosis, prognosis, and treatment.

Ferris Jabr

The Diagnostic and Statistical Manual (DSM) evolves over time as research and changing social views lead to changes in the disorders listed and the criteria for those disorders. DSM is currently in its fifth edition.

TABLE 3.1 • The 22 Categories of Mental Disorders in DSM-5

Neurodevelopmental Disorders
Schizophrenia Spectrum and Other Psychotic Disorders
Bipolar and Related Disorders
Depressive Disorders
Anxiety Disorders
Obsessive-Compulsive and Related Disorders
Trauma- and Stressor-Related Disorders
Dissociative Disorders
Somatic Symptom and Related Disorders
Feeding and Eating Disorders
Elimination Disorders
Sleep–Wake Disorders
Sexual Dysfunctions
Gender Dysphoria
Disruptive, Impulse Control, and Conduct Disorders
Substance-Related and Addictive Disorders
Neurocognitive Disorders
Personality Disordersw
Paraphilic Disorders
Other Mental Disorders
Medication-Induced Movement Disorders and Other Adverse Effects of Medication
Other Conditions That May Be a Focus of Clinical Attention

Source: Diagnostic and Statistical Manual of Mental Disorders, Fifth Edition, American Psychiatric Publishing, 2013.

Comorbidity
The presence of more than one disorder at the same time in a given patient.

TABLE 3.2 • Summary of DSM-5 Diagnostic Criteria for Schizophrenia

- At least two or more *positive symptoms* (termed positive because they indicate the presence of an—extreme or distorted version of—typical behavior), each present for at least 1 month.

  - Delusions: Unusual, persistent and entrenched beliefs.

  - Hallucinations: Sensations so vivid they seem real, although they are not.

  - Scrambled speech: Thoughts appear disconnected, sentences are incoherent and words can be jumbled.

  - Significantly disorganized or catatonic behavior: Difficulty with daily tasks such as planning a meal or daily hygiene and physical immobility.

- Some *negative symptoms* (termed negative because they indicate the *absence* of typical behavior), such as a failure to express or respond to emotion; slow, empty replies to questions; or an inability to initiate goal-directed behavior.

- Social and/or work-related dysfunction since the onset of symptoms. The functioning level since the onset of the symptoms is significantly below the prior level.

Source: Diagnostic and Statistical Manual of Mental Disorders, Fifth Edition, American Psychiatric Publishing, 2013.

The weaknesses of DSM-III led to DSM-IV, published in 1994, which specified new disorders and revised the criteria for some of the disorders included in the previous edition. In 2000, the American Psychiatric Association published an expanded version of DSM-IV that included more current information about each disorder, such as new information about prevalence, course, issues related to gender and cultural factors, and **comorbidity**—the presence of more than one disorder at the same time in a given patient. This revised edition is called DSM-IV-TR, where *TR* stands for "Text Revision." The list of disorders and almost all of the criteria in DSM-IV-TR were not changed, but the text discussion of the disorders was revised. DSM-IV and DSM-IV-TR defined 17 major categories of psychological problems, and nearly 300 specific mental disorders.

In 2013, the American Psychiatric Association published the fifth edition, DSM-5, which includes over 300 disorders (depending on how you count) across 22 categories, as shown in Table 3.1 (American Psychiatric Association, 2013). The new edition was intended to address criticisms of DSM-IV and to incorporate more recent research findings about disorders that relate to the diagnostic criteria, and into what category they best fall. However, many have criticized DSM-5 as not addressing the flaws in DSM-IV and being *less* based on research than the previous edition (Frances, 2013; Greenberg, 2013). In fact, the National Institute of Mental Health, which funded research that used DSM-IV diagnoses to categorize patient's symptoms, will not fund research using DSM-5 diagnoses (Insel, 2013).

The edition number went from Roman numbers (IV) to Arabic numbers (5) because the mental health professionals in charge of creating DSM-5 envisioned the fifth edition as "a living document," with "Web-based releases" of refinements to the manual over time (5.1, 5.2, and so on; Kupfer, 2012). However, the idea of a living document with frequent updates has been criticized as creating confusion for clinicians and problems for researchers who need to compare results from studies across the updates (Rosenberg, 2013a).

The Evolution of DSM-5

The jury is still out on whether DSM-5 is an improvement over the previous edition, DSM-IV-TR. To understand some of the factors that led to the creation of DSM-5, we will use the example of the diagnosis of schizophrenia (see Table 3.2); this disorder is discussed in more detail in Chapter 12. The issues raised in the discussion that follows apply to most DSM-5 disorders.

Subjectivity in Determining Clinical Significance

Various editions of DSM have been criticized because their criteria require mental health professionals to draw subjective opinions. Consider the symptoms of schizophrenia in Table 3.2. DSM-5 instructs the clinician to determine whether, because of these symptoms, the individual's functioning is "markedly below the level achieved prior to the onset." (American Psychiatric Association, 2013, p. 99) Part of the problem is that this decision, to a certain extent, is subjective. DSM-5 does not specify what, exactly, *markedly* means. Not all professionals would consider the same patient's dysfunction marked *enough* to qualify. These problems are complicated further if the clinician relies on the patient's description of his or her previous level of functioning; the patient's view of the past may be clouded by the present symptoms.

In a similar vein, consider the disorders known as *adjustment disorders*, which are characterized by a response, such as distress, that is "out of proportion to the severity or intensity of the stressor" (American Psychiatric Association, 2013, p. 286). The clinician must determine whether an individual's response is proportional. However, different people have different coping styles, and what seems to one clinician like an excessive response may be deemed normal by another clinician (Narrow & Kuhl, 2011).

Disorders as Categories, Not Continuous Dimensions

The criteria for disorders in DSM-5 are structured so that someone either has or does not have a given disorder. It's analogous to the old adage about pregnancy: A woman can't be a little bit pregnant—she either is or isn't pregnant. But critics argue that many disorders may exist along continua (continuous gradations), meaning that patients can have different degrees of a disorder (Kendell & Jablensky, 2003).

Consider, for example, two young men who have had the diagnosis of schizophrenia for 5 years. Aaron has been living with roommates and attending college part time; Max is living at home, continues to hallucinate and have delusions, and cannot hold down a volunteer job. (*Hallucinations* are sensations that are so vivid that the perceived objects or events seem real, although they are not, and *delusions* are persistent false beliefs that are held despite evidence that the beliefs are incorrect or exaggerate reality.) Over the holidays, both men's symptoms got worse, and both were hospitalized briefly. Since being discharged from the hospital, Aaron has had only mild symptoms, but Max still can't function independently, even though he no longer needs to be in the hospital. The categorical diagnosis of schizophrenia lumps both of these patients together, but the intensity of their symptoms suggests that clinicians should have different expectations, goals, treatments, and prognoses for them. As shown in Figure 3.1, on a dimensional scale, one of them is likely to be diagnosed with mild schizophrenia, whereas the other is likely to be diagnosed with severe schizophrenia.

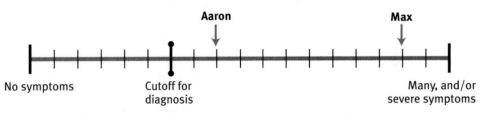

To address this general criticism, DSM-5 includes optional dimensional scales for some disorders; clinicians can rate the severity of symptoms (from mild to severe). For instance, DSM-5 includes a set of scales to rate each of eight symptoms related to schizophrenia. However, such ratings are optional and the decision to diagnose a patient is still categorical (McHugh & Slavney, 2012).

FIGURE 3.1 • A Disorder as on a Continuum If a disorder such as schizophrenia is best characterized along a continuum, then two people, Aaron and Max, diagnosed with schizophrenia but with different severity or numbers of symptoms, would fall at different points on the continuum. Aaron has fewer symptoms and is able to function better than Max. According to DSM-5, they both have the same disorder. However, their illnesses have different courses and prognoses and will likely require different types of treatment. None of this information is captured by the categorical diagnostic system of DSM-5.

People with Different Symptoms Can Be Diagnosed With the Same Disorder

For many DSM-5 disorders, including schizophrenia, a person needs to have only some of the symptoms in order to be diagnosed with the disorder. For example, in Table 3.2, a person needs to have only two out of the five symptoms. Consider three people who have been diagnosed with schizophrenia: One has delusions and hallucinations. Another has disorganized speech and disorganized behavior but *no* delusions or hallucinations. And a third person classified as having schizophrenia has negative symptoms and delusions, but not disorganized behavior or hallucinations. Taken together, these three people with schizophrenia display *heterogeneous* symptoms: The sets of symptoms are different from each other. Nevertheless, the three people are classified with the same disorder according to DSM-5. People with different combinations of symptoms may have developed the disorder in different ways, and different treatments might be effective. Thus, the DSM-5 diagnostic system may obscure important differences among types of a given mental disorder (Malik & Beutler, 2002).

Duration Criteria Are Arbitrary

Each set of criteria for a disorder specifies a minimum amount of time that symptoms must be present for a patient to qualify for that diagnosis (see the last bullet point in Table 3.2). However, the particular duration, such as that noted for bipolar disorder (which requires that the symptoms be present for at least 1 week), is often arbitrary and not supported by research (Brauser, 2012; Greenberg, 2013).

Some Sets of Criteria Are too Restrictive

Some categories of disorders in DSM-5 include two types of diagnoses that can be used when a person's symptoms do not meet the necessary minimum criteria for the disorder that is the best fit, but the person is nonetheless significantly distressed or impaired. At least for some categories of disorders in DSM-IV, this type of diagnosis (called *not otherwise specified* in DSM-IV) was the most frequent diagnosis in the category (Keel et al., 2011). The two types in DSM-5 are *Other Specified* _____ (fill in the blank with the category of disorder) and *Unspecified* _____. With the former, the clinician notes why—in what ways—the criteria are not met (e.g., the symptoms have not yet been present long enough); with the latter, the clinician chooses not to specify why the criteria are not met. Thus, people might be diagnosed with either of these "other" type disorders because their symptoms do not meet the minimum duration necessary for a diagnosis of a specific disorder; alternatively, they might be diagnosed with one of these "other" disorders because they don't have enough symptoms to meet the criteria for that specific disorder.

Psychological Disorders Are Created to Ensure Payment

With each edition of DSM, the number of disorders increased, reaching over 300 with DSM-5. Does this mean that more types of mental disorders have been discovered and classified? Not necessarily. This increase may, in part, reflect economic pressures in the mental health care industry (Eriksen & Kress, 2005). Today, in order for a mental health facility or provider to be paid or a patient to be reimbursed by health insurance companies, the patient must have symptoms that meet a DSM-5 diagnosis. The more disorders that are included in a new edition of DSM, then, the more likely it is that a patient's treatment will be paid for or reimbursed by health insurance companies. But this does not imply that all of the disorders are valid from a scientific perspective.

To address the criticism about the growing number of disorders, the authors of DSM-5 set out to maintain or reduce the total number of disorders. To achieve this goal, and still add new disorders, in some cases disorders have been consolidated: for instance, what was a disorder in DSM-IV may now be a subtype of another disorder in DSM-5. Using such "accounting" methods, the authors of DSM-5 claim to have achieved their goal while at the same time potentially increased the types of symptoms for which health insurance payment may be possible.

Social Factors Are Deemphasized

Perhaps because DSM-5 does not generally address etiological factors (the causes of a disorder), it does not explicitly recognize social factors that *contribute* to disorders. DSM-5 states that its diagnoses are not supposed to apply to conflicts that are mainly between an individual and society but rather to conflicts within an individual (American Psychiatric Association, 2013). However, this distinction is often difficult to make (Caplan, 1995). For instance, people can become depressed in response to a variety of social stressors: after losing their jobs, after they are exposed to systematic discrimination, after emigrating from their native country, or after experiencing other social and societal conflicts.

Social factors are further deemphasized in DSM-5 with the presumption of neurobiological causes of mental illness, at least with some categories of disorders, such as neurodevelopmental disorders and neurocognitive disorders.

Comorbidity Is Common

About half of the people who have been diagnosed with a DSM-IV disorder have at least one additional disorder; that is, they exhibit comorbidity (Kessler et al., 2005). This will probably be true with DSM-5 because the criteria for many disorders have not become more stringent (which would reduce the number of people diagnosed with the disorders); in fact, in some cases, the criteria in DSM-5 have actually become *less* stringent, so that they apply to more people. This high comorbidity raises the question of whether some disorders in DSM-5 are actually distinct. For instance, half of the people who meet the criteria for *major depressive disorder* also have an anxiety disorder (Kessler et al., 2003). Such a high rate of comorbidity suggests that these two types of DSM-5 disorders often represent different facets of the same underlying problem (Hyman, 2011; Kendler et al., 2011). This possibility raises questions about validity and makes DSM-5 diagnoses less useful to clinicians and researchers.

DSM-5 Is Unscientific and Lacks Rigor

The process leading up to the publication of DSM-5 has been criticized on a number of grounds, some of which stem from a rush to meet a publication deadline that some argued was set arbitrarily. Criticisms include (Strakowski & Frances, 2012):

- Proposed diagnoses and criteria were not adequately *field-tested*: Mental health professionals in various types of settings (e.g., hospitals, clinics) tried using the new manual to diagnose patients. Unfortunately, these field tests showed disappointingly low reliability for some disorders (Ghaemi, 2012; Greenberg, 2013). That is, using the new criteria, mental health clinicians didn't agree on what diagnosis was most appropriate for a given patient. After field testing, some of the criteria were revised, in the hope of increasing reliability, and these new criteria (and wording) were supposed to have another round of field testing.

- However, the planned final stage of research on the new criteria was cancelled because of pressure to meet the planned publication deadline. One consequence is that the wording of the criteria that were tested in earlier phases isn't the wording in the final version of DSM-5; problems with reliability and validity of the diagnoses are thus more likely (Greenberg, 2013).

- Many disorders were proposed as additions to DSM-5, some of which were very controversial, and others were placed in a section of the manual (equivalent to an appendix) for disorders that need further study before being accepted into the regular part of the manual. An example is *attenuated psychosis syndrome*, which was originally named *psychosis risk syndrome* because the diagnosis is for people thought to be *at risk* to develop a psychotic disorder. Given the controversial nature of such disorders, some researchers argued that they should not have been included even in an appendix because the implications of adding the new disorder, and of deciding its criteria for further study, were not thought through well enough (Cornblatt & Correll, 2010).

As Allen Frances, organizer of and contributor to several previous DSM editions (DSM-III, DSM-IV, DSM-IV-TR) noted about DSM-5:

Each change in a DSM is an opportunity for clinical and forensic misuse, with unpredictable and harmful unintended consequences. Changes are also costly to psychiatric research in direct ways, such as the cost of changing instruments midstream, and even more importantly in indirect ways, such as the [difficulty comparing research results

One criticism of DSM-5 is that social factors that contribute to psychological disorders—such as being laid off from work, which apparently was the case for this man—are not incorporated into the diagnosis (Greenberg, 2013). This doesn't mean to imply that this man, who was looking for help in Los Angeles, has a disorder.

for a given disorder using diagnostic criteria that differ across editions]. . . It might be worth the risks and costs of DSM-5 changes if there were compelling science supporting them, but there isn't.

(Strakowski & Frances, 2012).

Although the criticisms of DSM-5 must be taken seriously, the clinical chapters of this book (Chapters 5–15) are generally organized according to DSM-5 categories and criteria. The DSM has been, to date, by far the most widely used classification system for diagnosing psychological disorders.

The People Who Diagnose Psychological Disorders

Who, exactly, are the mental health professionals who might diagnose Rex or Rose Mary Walls, or anyone else who might be suffering from a psychological disorder? As you will see, there are different types of mental health professionals, each with a different type of training. The type of training can influence the kinds of information that clinicians pay particular attention to, what they perceive, and how they interpret the information. However, regardless of the type of training they receive, all mental health professionals must be licensed in the state in which they practice (or board certified, in the case of psychiatrists); licensure indicates that they have been appropriately trained to diagnose and treat mental disorders.

Clinical Psychologists and Counseling Psychologists

A **clinical psychologist** generally has a doctoral degree, either a Ph.D. (doctor of philosophy) or a Psy.D. (doctor of psychology), that is awarded only after several years of coursework and several years of treating patients while receiving supervision from experienced clinicians. People training to be clinical psychologists also take other courses that may include neuropsychology and psychopharmacology. In addition, clinical psychologists with a Ph.D. will have completed a *dissertation*—a major, independent research project. Programs that award a Psy.D. in clinical psychology place less emphasis on research.

Clinical neuropsychologists are a particular type of clinical psychologist. Clinical neuropsychologists concentrate on characterizing the effects of brain damage and neurological diseases (such as Alzheimer's disease) on thoughts (that is, mental processes and mental contents), feelings (affect), and behavior. Sometimes, they help design and conduct rehabilitation programs for patients with brain damage or neurological disease.

A **counseling psychologist** might have a Ph.D. from a psychology program that focuses on counseling or might have an Ed.D. (doctor of education) degree from a school of education. Training for counseling psychologists is similar to that of clinical psychologists except that counseling psychologists tend to have more training in vocational testing, career guidance, and multicultural issues, and they generally don't receive training in neuropsychology. Counseling psychologists also tend to work with healthier people, whereas clinical psychologists tend to have more training in psychopathology and often work with people who have more severe problems (Cobb et al., 2004; Norcross et al., 1998). The distinction between the two types of psychologists, however, is less clear-cut than in the past, and both types may perform similar work in similar settings.

Clinical psychologists and counseling psychologists are trained to perform research on the nature, diagnosis, and treatment of mental illness. They also both provide *psychotherapy*, which involves helping patients better cope with difficult experiences, thoughts, feelings, and behavior. Both types of psychologists also learn how to administer and interpret psychological tests in order to diagnose and treat psychological problems and disorders more effectively.

Clinical psychologist
A mental health professional who has a doctoral degree that requires several years of related coursework and several years of treating patients while receiving supervision from experienced clinicians.

Counseling psychologist
A mental health professional who has either a Ph.D. degree from a psychology program that focuses on counseling or an Ed.D. degree from a school of education.

Psychiatrists, Psychiatric Nurses, and General Practitioners

Someone with an M.D. (doctor of medicine) degree can choose to receive further training in a residency that focuses on mental disorders, becoming a **psychiatrist**. A psychiatrist is qualified to prescribe medications; psychologists in the United States, except for appropriately trained psychologists in New Mexico and Louisiana, currently may not prescribe medications. (Other states are considering allowing appropriately trained psychologists to prescribe.) But psychiatrists usually have not been taught how to interpret and understand psychological tests and have not been required to acquire detailed knowledge of research methods used in the field of psychopathology.

A **psychiatric nurse** has an M.S.N. (master of science in nursing) degree, plus a C.S. (clinical specialization) certificate in psychiatric nursing; a psychiatric nurse may also be certified as a psychiatric nurse practitioner (N.P.). Psychiatric nurses normally work in a hospital or clinic to provide psychotherapy; in these settings, they work closely with physicians to administer and monitor patient medications. Psychiatric nurses are also qualified to provide psychotherapy in private practice and are permitted in some states to monitor and prescribe medications independently (Haber et al., 2003).

Although not considered a mental health professional, a *general practitioner* (GP), or family doctor (the doctor you may see once a year for a checkup), may inquire about psychological symptoms, may diagnose a psychological disorder, and may recommend to patients that they see a mental health professional. Responding to pressure to reduce insurance companies' medical costs, general practitioners frequently prescribe medication for some psychological disorders. However, studies have found that treatment with medication is less effective when prescribed by a family doctor than when prescribed by psychiatrists, who are specialists in mental disorders and more familiar with the nuances of such treatment (Lin et al., 2000; Wang et al., 2005; Wilson et al., 2003).

Mental Health Professionals with Master's Degrees

In addition to psychiatric nurses, some other mental health professionals have master's degrees. Most **social workers** have an M.S.W. (master of social work) degree and may have had training to provide psychotherapy to help individuals and families. Social workers also teach clients how to find and benefit from the appropriate social services offered in their community. For example, they may help clients to apply for Medicare or may facilitate home visits from health care professionals. Most states also license *marriage and family therapists* (M.F.T.s), who have at least a master's degree and are trained to provide psychotherapy to couples and families. Other therapists may have a master's degree (M.A.) in some area of counseling or clinical psychology, which indicates that their training consisted of fewer courses and research experience, and less supervised clinical training than that of their doctoral-level counterparts. Some counselors may have had particular training in *pastoral counseling*, which provides counseling from a spiritual or faith-based perspective.

Table 3.3 reviews the different types of mental health clinicians.

Psychiatrist
A mental health professional who has an M.D. degree and has completed a residency that focuses on mental disorders.

Psychiatric nurse
A mental health professional who has an M.S.N. degree, plus a C.S. certificate in psychiatric nursing.

Social worker
A mental health professional who has an M.S.W. degree and may have had training to provide psychotherapy to help individuals and families.

TABLE 3.3 • Clinicians Who Diagnose Mental Disorders

Type of clinician	Specific title and credentials
Doctoral-level psychologists	Clinical psychologists (including clinical neuropsychologists) and counseling psychologists have a Ph.D., Psy.D., or Ed.D. degree and have advanced training in the treatment of mental illness.
Medical personnel	Psychiatrists and general practitioners have a M.D. degree; psychiatrists have had advanced training in the treatment of mental illness. Psychiatric nurses have a M.S.N. degree and have advanced training in the treatment of mental illness.
Master's-level mental health professionals	Social workers with a master's degree (M.S.W.), marriage and family therapists (M.F.T.), and master's level counselors (M.A.) are mental health clinicians who have received specific training in helping people with problems in daily living or with mental illness. Psychiatric nurses have master's level training.

Assessing Psychological Disorders

People came to know about Rose Mary and Rex Walls through the eyes of their daughter, Jeannette. In her memoir, Jeannette reports incidents that seem to be clear cases of neglect and irresponsible behavior. How might a mental health clinician or researcher have gone about assessing Rose Mary's or Rex's mental health? Although mental health clinicians might read Jeannette Walls's memoir, hear her speak about her parents, or even see brief video clips of Rose Mary Walls, the information conveyed by those accounts isn't adequate to make a clinical assessment: Jeannette's memoir—and Rose Mary's brief statements on videotape—portray what Jeannette and the video directors chose to include; we don't know about events that were not discussed or portrayed, and we don't know how accurate Jeannette's childhood memories are. Other people's accounts of an individual's mental health generally provide only narrow slices of information—brief glimpses *as seen from their own points of view*, none of which is that of a mental health clinician in this case. Without use of the formal tools and techniques of clinical assessment, any conclusions are likely to be speculative.

Were it possible to obtain information about Rose Mary and Rex Walls directly, what specific information would a clinician want to know in order to make a diagnosis and recommendations for treatment? More generally, what types of information are included in a clinical assessment?

A complete clinical assessment can include various types of information regarding the three main categories that underlie the neuropsychosocial model:

- *neurological and other biological factors* (i.e., the structure and functioning of brain and body),
- *psychological factors* (i.e., behavior, emotion and mood, mental processes and contents, past and current ability to function), and
- *social factors* (i.e., the social context of the patient's problems, the living environment and community, family history and family functioning, history of the person's relationships, and level of financial resources and social support available).

Most types of assessment focus primarily on one type of factor. We'll consider assessments of each of these main types of factors in the following sections.

Assessing Neurological and Other Biological Factors

In some cases, clinicians assess neurological (and other biological) functioning in order to determine whether abnormal mental processes and mental contents, affect, or behaviors arise from a medical problem, such as a brain tumor or abnormal hormone levels. In other cases, researchers seek to understand neurological and other biological factors that may be related to a particular disorder because this information might provide clues for possible treatments. Although neurological and other biological factors are not generally part of the DSM criteria for diagnosing mental disorders, the search for neurological and other biological markers or indicators of various psychological disorders has proceeded at a rapid pace over the past decade. It is clearly only a matter of time before these sorts of factors will be part of the standard diagnostic criteria for many psychological disorders (Lieberman, 2011).

Assessing Abnormal Brain Structures with X-Rays, CT Scans, and MRIs

Some psychological disorders, such as schizophrenia, appear to involve abnormalities of the *structure* of the brain. This is why clinical assessments sometimes make use of scans of a patient's brain. *Neuroimaging techniques* provide images of the brain. The oldest neuroimaging technique involves taking pictures of a person's brain using *X-rays*. A computer can then analyze these X-ray images and reconstruct a three-dimensional image of the brain. **Computerized axial tomography (CT)** (*tomography* is from a Greek word for "section") builds an image of a person's brain, slice by slice, creating a CT scan (sometimes called a CAT scan).

A more recent technology, **magnetic resonance imaging (MRI)**, makes especially sharp images of the brain, which allows more precise diagnoses when brain abnormalities are subtle. MRI makes use of the magnetic properties of different atoms. By detecting different atoms and combining the signals into images, MRI can indicate the location of damaged tissue and can reveal particular parts of the brain that are larger or smaller than normal. For instance, an MRI can reveal the shrinkage of brain tissue that typically arises with chronic alcoholism (Rosenbloom et al., 2003); had Rex Walls had an MRI, it might well have shown that his brain had such shrinkage.

CT scans and MRIs can provide amazing images of the structure of the living brain, which may provide information that can help to diagnose psychological conditions. For example, some people with schizophrenia have larger ventricles (interior, fluid-filled spaces in the brain) than do people who do not have the disorder (Schneider-Axmann et al., 2006). These larger ventricles may occur, at least in part, because some of the surrounding brain tissue is smaller than normal (Gaser et al., 2004).

Assessing Brain Function with PET Scans and fMRI

Some mental disorders are associated not with abnormal brain structures (physical makeup) but rather with abnormal brain *functioning* (how the brain operates). The brain can also produce abnormal thoughts, feelings, and behaviors because it functions inappropriately. Researchers use different types of brain scans to assess brain functioning.

We've just talked about how certain neuroimaging techniques can reveal brain structure, but how can researchers observe brain functioning? A key fact is that when a part of the brain is active, more blood (which transports oxygen and nutrients) flows to it, a little like the way that more electricity flows into a house when more appliances are turned on.

The neurons draw more blood while they are sending and receiving signals than they do when they are not activated, because the activity increases their need for oxygen and nutrients. Because neurons in the same area of the brain tend to work together, specific areas of the brain will have greater blood flow while a person performs particular tasks.

In the field of psychopathology, researchers use functional neuroimaging to identify brain areas related to specific aspects of a disorder. For example, in one study, researchers asked participants with social phobia, who were afraid of speaking in public, to speak to a group and also to speak in private while their brains were scanned.

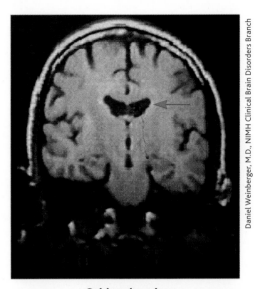

Schizophrenia

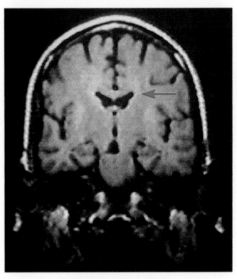

No schizophrenia

People with schizophrenia tend to have abnormally large ventricles (fluid-filled spaces in the brain). Compare the two MRI images above: The ventricles are indicated by the red arrows.

Computerized axial tomography (CT)
A neuroimaging technique that uses X-rays to build a three-dimensional image (CT or CAT scan) of the brain.

Magnetic resonance imaging (MRI)
A neuroimaging technique that creates especially sharp images of the brain by measuring the magnetic properties of atoms in the brain.

Positron emission tomography (PET)
A neuroimaging technique that measures blood flow (or energy consumption) in the brain and requires introducing a very small amount of a radioactive substance into the bloodstream.

Functional magnetic resonance imaging (fMRI)
A neuroimaging technique that uses MRI to obtain images of brain functioning, which reveal the extent to which different brain areas are activated during particular tasks.

Neuropsychological testing
The employment of assessment techniques that use behavioral responses to test items in order to draw inferences about brain functioning.

Speaking in public activated key parts of the limbic system, particularly the amygdala, more than did speaking in private (Tillfors et al., 2001). As noted in Chapter 2, the amygdala is involved in strong emotion, particularly fear. This part of the brain was not activated when people without a social phobia were tested. Other researchers have reported similar results for other sorts of phobias (Pissiota et al., 2003).

The functional neuroimaging technique used in the study of social phobia just described was **positron emission tomography (PET)**, one of the most important methods for measuring blood flow (or energy consumption) in the brain. PET requires introducing a very small amount of a radioactive substance into the bloodstream. While a person performs a task, as active regions of the brain take up more blood they take up more of the radioactive substance than do less active regions. The relative amounts of radiation from different areas of the brain are measured and sent to a computer, which constructs a three-dimensional image of the brain that shows the levels of activity in the different areas. In PET images, higher radiation (greater activity) typically is illustrated with brighter colors.

Functional magnetic resonance imaging (fMRI) is currently the most widely used method for measuring human brain function. When a region of the brain is activated, it draws blood more quickly than the oxygen carried by the hemoglobin in the blood can be used. This means that red blood cells with oxygenated hemoglobin accumulate in the activated region—and this increase is what is measured in an fMRI scan. Brain regions that are not activated (or are activated less strongly) when a person is performing a particular task (such as speaking in public or looking at pictures) draw less blood, and the oxygen carried by the blood gets used up. The difference in oxygen levels due to brain activity is reflected in the fMRI images.

The advantages of fMRI over PET include the absence of radiation and the ability to construct brain images showing activation that occurs in just a few seconds. Disadvantages include the requirement that a participant must lie very still in the narrow tube of a noisy machine (which some people find uncomfortable).

Neuropsychological Assessment

An assessment of neurological factors may include **neuropsychological testing**, which uses behavioral responses to test items in order to draw inferences about brain functioning. Assessing neuropsychological functioning allows clinicians and researchers to distinguish the effects of brain damage from the effects of psychological problems (for example, disrupted speech can be caused by either of these). Neuropsychological assessment is also used to determine whether brain damage is contributing to psychological problems (for example, frontal lobe damage can disrupt the ability to inhibit aggressive behavior).

Neuropsychological tests range from those that assess complex abilities (such as judgment or planning) to those that assess a relatively specific ability (such as the ability to recognize faces). Other neuropsychological tests, such as the Bender Visual-Motor Gestalt Test-II (2nd edition) (Bender, 1963; Brannigan & Decker, 2003), assess more complex functions. Patients are shown a series of drawings that range from simple to complex and are asked to reproduce them. This test assesses the integration of visual and motor functioning, which involves many distinct parts of the brain. The test may be used to help diagnose various problems, including learning disorders and memory problems (Brannigan & Decker, 2006).

Robin Nelson/PhotoEdit

The Rey Osterrieth Test requires the test-taker to copy a complex figure, and then draw it from memory; the test assesses visual perception, organizational ability, and memory.

Assessing Psychological Factors

During an assessment, clinicians and researchers often seek to identify the ways in which psychological functioning is disordered and the ways in which it is not. For instance, a clinical assessment would shed light on the extent to which Rex Walls's problems were primarily a result of his drinking or arose from underlying distress or impairments that may have been masked by his pronounced drinking.

Certain areas of psychological functioning—mental processes and mental contents, affect, and behavior—are often directly related to DSM-5 criteria for specific disorders. Further, these areas are frequently the most relevant for determining a person's current and future ability to function in daily activities.

Mental health researchers and clinicians employ a variety of assessment techniques and tools to evaluate psychological functioning, including interviews and tests of cognitive and personality functioning. Which tools and techniques are used depends on the purpose of the assessment.

Clinical Interview

An important tool used to assess psychological functioning is the **clinical interview**, a meeting between clinician and patient during which the clinician asks questions related to the patient's symptoms and functioning. A clinical interview provides two types of information: the content of the answers to the interview questions, and the manner in which the person answered them (Westen & Weinberger, 2004). Questions may focus on symptoms, general functioning, degree and type of impairment, and the patient's relevant history. Clinicians generally use three types of interviews: unstructured, structured, or semistructured.

In an *unstructured interview*, the clinician asks whatever questions he or she deems appropriate, depending on the patient's responses. The advantage of an unstructured interview is that it allows the clinician to pursue topics and issues specific to the patient. However, different clinicians who use this approach to interview the same patient may arrive at different diagnoses, because each clinician's interview may cover different topics and therefore gather different information. Another problem with unstructured interviews is that the interviewer may neglect to gather important information about the context of the problem and the individual's cultural background.

In a *structured interview*, conversely, the clinician uses a fixed set of questions to guide the interview. A structured interview is likely to yield a more reliable diagnosis because each clinician asks the same set of questions. However, such a diagnosis may be less valid, because the questions asked may not be relevant to the patient's particular symptoms, issues, or concerns (Meyer, 2002b). That is, different clinicians using a structured interview may agree on the diagnosis, but all of them may be missing the boat about the nature of the problem and may diagnose the wrong disorder.

A *semistructured interview*, discussed in more detail later, combines elements of both of the other types: Specific questions guide the interview, but the clinician also has the freedom to pose additional questions that may be relevant, depending on the patient's answers to the standard questions.

Observation

All types of interviews provide an opportunity for the clinician or researcher to observe and make inferences about different aspects of a patient:

- *Appearance.* In addition to obvious aspects of appearance (whether the person has bathed recently and is dressed appropriately), signs of disorders can sometimes be noted by carefully observing subtle aspects of a person's appearance. For example, patients with the eating disorder bulimia nervosa (to be discussed in Chapter 10) may regularly induce vomiting; as a result of repeated vomiting, their parotid glands, located in the cheeks, may swell and create a somewhat puffy look to the cheeks (similar to a chipmunk's cheeks).

Clinical interview
A meeting between clinician and patient during which the clinician asks questions related to the patient's symptoms and functioning.

- *Behavior.* The patient's body language, facial expression, movements, and speech can provide insights into different aspects of psychological functioning:

  ◦ *Emotions.* What emotions does the patient convey? The clinician can observe the patient's expression of distress (or lack thereof) and emotional state (upbeat, "low," intense, uncontrollable, inappropriate to the situation, or at odds with the content of what the patient says).

  ◦ *Movement.* The patient's general level of movement—physical restlessness or a complete lack of movement—may indicate abnormal functioning.

  ◦ *Speech.* Clinicians observe the rate and contents of the patient's speech: Speaking very quickly may suggest anxiety, mania, or certain kinds of substance abuse; speaking very slowly may suggest depression or other kinds of substance abuse.

  ◦ *Mental processes.* Some behaviors reveal characteristics of mental processes. Do the patient's mental processes appear to be unusual or abnormal? Does the patient appear to be talking to someone who is not in the room, which would suggest that he or she is having hallucinations? Can the patient remember what the clinician just asked? Does the patient flit from topic to topic, unable to stay focused on answering a single question?

Behaviors observed during a clinical interview can, in some cases, provide more information than the patient's report about the nature of the problem. In other cases, such observations round out an assessment; it is the patient's own report of the problem—its history and related matters—that provides the foundation of the interview. In any case, the clinician must keep in mind that "unusual" behavior should perhaps be interpreted differently for patients from different cultural backgrounds.

Patient's Self-Report

Some symptoms cannot be observed directly, such as the hallucinations that characterize schizophrenia, or the worries and fears that characterize some anxiety disorders. Thus, the patient's own report of his or her experiences is a crucial part of the clinical assessment.

At some point in the interview process, the clinician will ask about the patient's history—past factors or events that may illuminate the current difficulties—and the patient will report such information about himself or herself. For example, the

🖸 GETTING THE PICTURE

Does how someone look play a role in assessment? If these models were actually clients you saw in an emergency room, the appearance of which model would likely provide a clinician with important information to follow up on during an assessment? Answer: Both. The model on the left appears disheveled, suggesting the possibility of depression or psychosis, whereas the animation of the person on the right might indicate mania or substance use.

clinician will ask about current and past psychological or medical problems and about how the patient understands these problems and possible solutions to them. The clinician will inquire about substance use, sexual or physical abuse or other traumatic experiences, economic hardships, relationships with family members and others, and thoughts about suicide. The patient's answers help the clinician put the patient's current difficulties in context and determine whether his or her psychological functioning is maladaptive or adaptive, given the environmental circumstances (Kirk & Hsieh, 2004).

Some patients, however, intentionally report having symptoms that they don't actually have or exaggerate symptoms that they do have, either for material gain or to avoid unwanted events (such as criminal prosecution); such behavior is the hallmark of **malingering**. For instance, a malingering soldier may exaggerate his or her anxiety symptoms and claim to have posttraumatic stress disorder in order to avoid further combat. Malingering contrasts with **factitious disorder**, which occurs when someone intentionally falsely reports or induces medical or psychological symptoms in order to receive attention. Whereas both malingering and factitious disorder involve deception—inventing or exaggerating symptoms—the motivations are different. Unlike those with malingering, people with factitious disorder do not deceive others about the symptoms for material gain or to avoid negative events.

Most patients intend to report their current problems and history as accurately as possible. Nevertheless, even honest self-reports are subject to various biases. Most fundamentally, patients may accurately report what they remember, but their memory of the frequency, intensity, or duration of their symptoms may not be entirely accurate. As we noted in Chapter 2, emotion can bias what we notice, perceive, and remember.

Another bias that can affect what patients say about their symptoms is *reporting bias*—inaccuracies or distortions in a patient's report because of a desire to appear in a particular way (Meyer, 2002b). In some cases, patients may not really know the answer to a question asked in a clinical interview. For instance, when asked, "Why did you do that?" they may not have thought about their motivation before and may not *really* be aware of what it was but instead create an answer on the spot (Westen & Weinberger, 2004). In other cases, people's psychological functioning is sufficiently impaired that they confuse their internal world—their memories, fears, beliefs, fantasies, or dreams—with reality, which leads to inaccuracies in self-reports.

Thus, although a patient's self-report is important, it has limitations. Similarly, when interviewing children, the clinician must be sensitive to the fact that they may lack adequate insight and/or the verbal ability to reliably report their mental health status.

Semistructured Interviews

Because clinicians sometimes want to be sure to cover specific ground with their questions, they may use a semistructured interview format, asking a list of standard questions but formulating their own follow-up questions. The follow-up questions are based on patients' responses to the standard questions. One set of questions that assesses a patient's mental state at the time of the interview is the *mental status exam*. In a mental status exam, the clinician asks the patient to describe the problem, its history, and the patient's functioning in different areas of life. Other standard questions in the mental status exam probe the patient's ability to reason, to perform simple mathematical computations, and to assess possible problems in memory and judgment. The clinician uses the patient's answers to the standard questions to develop hypotheses about possible diagnoses and difficulties with functioning, and then asks other questions to obtain additional information. For instance, as part of the mental status exam, patients

GSO Images/Getty Images

Some problematic behaviors may be obvious to a mental health professional while interacting with a patient. Other behaviors, which occur infrequently or only in specific types of environments, such as avoiding stepping on cracks (which some people with obsessive-compulsive disorder do) are less likely to be observed. If the patient doesn't view these behaviors as a problem, he or she may not report them.

Malingering
Intentional false reporting of symptoms or exaggeration of existing symptoms, either for material gain or to avoid unwanted events.

Factitious disorder
A psychological disorder marked by the false reporting or inducing of medical or psychological symptoms in order to receive attention.

As part of the mental status exam, patients are asked whether they know their own name, the date and year, and who is currently president. Patients who do not know these facts may have some type of memory impairment. Further tests will be done to determine the specific memory problems, their cause, and possible treatments.

are routinely asked whether they remember their own name, the date and year, and who is president. If the patient doesn't remember correctly who the current president is, the clinician might ask other, more detailed questions involving different aspects of memory—such as memories of other languages spoken, of more distant events or important personal events in the recent past—which may reflect an underlying neurological problem. People from other cultures may answer some of the questions in a mental status exam in unconventional ways, and clinicians must take care not to infer that "different" is "abnormal."

A mental status exam assesses cognitive, emotional, and behavioral functioning broadly, and the standard questions are not designed to obtain specific information that corresponds to the categories in DSM-5. The interviewer can arrive at a diagnosis based on answers to both standard and follow-up questions, but the goal of the mental status exam is more than diagnosis: It creates a portrait of the individual's general psychological functioning. The mental status exam contrasts with another semistructured interview format, the *Structured Clinical Interview* for DSM (SCID; First et al., 1997, 2002). The SCID is generally used when the interview is part of a research project and is designed to assist the researcher in diagnosing patients according to DSM criteria.

Clinical interviews provide a wealth of information about the patient's symptoms and general functioning, as well as about the context in which the symptoms arose and continue. However, a thorough clinical interview can be time-consuming and may not be as reliable and valid as assessment techniques that utilize tests.

Tests of Psychological Functioning

Many different tests are available to assess various areas of psychological functioning. Some tests assess a relatively wide range of abilities and areas of functioning (such as intelligence or general personality characteristics). Other tests assess a narrow range of abilities, particular areas of functioning, or specific symptoms (such as the ability to remember new information or the tendency to avoid social gatherings).

Cognitive Assessment

One tool to assess cognitive functioning is an intelligence test. Clinicians typically use the *Wechsler Adult Intelligence Scale*, 4th edition (WAIS-IV, revised in 2008), or the *Wechsler Intelligence Scale for Children*, 4th edition (WISC-IV, revised in 2003), depending on the age of the patient. Numerical results of these tests yield an *intelligence quotient* (IQ); the average intelligence in a population is set at a score of 100, with normal intelligence ranging from 85 to 115. IQ scores of 70 to 85 are considered to be in the *borderline* range, and scores of 70 and below signify mental impairment. However, the single intelligence score is not the only important information that the WAIS-IV and WISC-IV provide. Both of these tests include subtests that assess four types of abilities:

- *verbal comprehension* (i.e., the ability to understand verbal information);

- *perceptual reasoning* (i.e., the ability to reason with nonverbal information);

- *working memory* (i.e., the ability to maintain awareness and mentally manipulate new information); and

- *processing speed* (i.e., the ability to focus attention and quickly utilize information).

In addition, the WAIS-IV and WISC-IV are devised so that the examiner can compare an individual's responses on each of the subtests to the responses of other people of the same age and sex. Information about specific subtests helps the examiner determine the individual's pattern of relative strengths and weaknesses in intellectual functioning.

Current versions of intelligence tests have been designed to minimize the influence of cultural factors, in part by excluding test items that might require cultural knowledge that is unique to one group (and would thus put members of other groups at a disadvantage) (Kaufman et al., 1995; Poortinga, 1995).

Personality Assessment

Various psychological tests assess different aspects of personality functioning.

Inventories In order to assess general personality functioning, a clinician may use an *inventory*—a questionnaire with items pertaining to many different problems and aspects of personality. An inventory can indicate to a clinician what problems and disorders might be most likely for a given person. Inventories usually contain test questions that are sorted into different *scales*, with each scale assessing a different facet of personality. The most commonly used inventory is the *Minnesota Multiphasic Personality Inventory*, 2nd edition (MMPI-2; Butcher et al., 1989); see Table 3.4 for

TABLE 3.4 • A Sample of MMPI®-2 Scales

Scale	Sample Item	What Is Assessed
? (Cannot Say)	The score is the number of items that were unanswered or answered as both true and false.	An inability or unwillingness to complete the test appropriately, which could indicate the presence of symptoms that interfere with concentration.
L (Lie)	Sometimes want to swear (F)	Attempts to present himself or herself in a positive way, not admitting even minor shortcomings.
F (Infrequency)	Something wrong with mind (T)	Low scores suggest attempts to try to fake appearing to have "good" mental health or psychopathology; high scores suggest some type of psychopathology.
K (Correction)	Often feel useless (F)	More subtle attempts to exaggerate "good" mental health or psychopathology. This scale is also associated with education level—more educated people score higher than those with less education.
1. Hs (Hypochondriasis)	Body tingles (F)	An abnormal concern over bodily functioning and imagined illness.
2. D (Depression)	Usually happy (F)	Symptoms of sadness, poor morale, and hopelessness.
3. Hy (Hysteria)	Often feel very weak (T)	A propensity to develop physical symptoms under stress, along with a lack of awareness and insight about one's behavior.
4. Pd (Psychopathic Deviate)	Am misunderstood (T)	General social maladjustment, irresponsibility, or lack of conscience.
5. Mf (Masculinity–Femininity)	Like mechanics magazines (T for women)	The extent to which the individual has interests, preferences, and personal sensitivities more similar to those of the opposite sex.
6. Pa (Paranoia)	No enemies who wish me harm (F)	Sensitivity to others, suspiciousness, jealousy, and moral self-righteousness.
7. Pt (Psychasthenia)	Almost always anxious (T)	Obsessive and compulsive symptoms, poor concentration, and self-criticism.
8. Sc (Schizophrenia)	Hear strange things when alone (T)	Delusions, hallucinations, bizarre sensory experiences, and poor social relationships.
9. Ma (Hypomania)	When bored, stir things up (T)	Symptoms of hypomania—elated or irritable mood, "fast" thoughts, impulsiveness, and physical restlessness.
10. Si (Social Introversion)	Try to avoid crowds (T)	Discomfort in social situations and preference for being alone.

Note: (T) indicates that when the item is marked as true, it contributes to a high score on the scale; (F) indicates that when the item is marked as false, it contributes to a high score on the scale. The dark green rows above refer to the *validity scales*, and the light green rows refer to the *clinical scales*.

FIGURE 3.2 • An MMPI-2 Profile This is the MMPI-2 profile of a depressed 47-year-old man. His highest clinical scores are on the D and Pt scales, followed by Pd and Si. People with this profile typically are significantly depressed, agitated, and anxious. They may brood about their own deficiencies and have concentration problems (Greene, 2000).

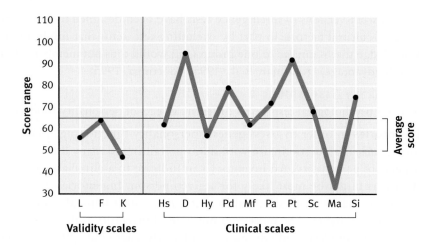

the scales, and Figure 3.2 for the sample profile. Originally developed in the 1930s to identify people with mental illness, it was revised in 1989 to include norms of people from a wider range of racial, ethnic, and other groups and to update specific items; the scores were recalibrated in 2003, in a form referred to as the MMPI-2-RF, where the new suffix stands for "Restructured Form." The MMPI-2 consists of 567 questions about the respondent's behavior, emotions, mental processes, mental contents, and other characteristics. The respondent rates each question as being true or false about himself or herself. Test-takers generally require about 60 to 90 minutes to complete the inventory. (There is also a short form, with 370 items.) The MMPI-2 has been translated into many languages and is used in many different countries.

Projective Tests Psychologists may also wish to assess facets of patients' personalities that are less likely to emerge in a self-report, such as systematic biases in mental processes. In a **projective test**, the patient is presented with an ambiguous stimulus (such as an inkblot or a group of stick figures) and is asked to make sense of and explain the stimulus. For example, what does the inkblot look like, or what are the stick figures doing? The idea behind such a test is that the particular structure a patient imposes on the ambiguous stimulus reveals something about the patient's mental processes or mental contents. This is the theory behind the well-known *Rorschach test*, which was developed by Herman Rorschach (1884–1922). This test includes 10 inkblots, one on each of 10 cards. The ambiguity of the shapes permits a patient to imagine what the shapes resemble. Although the Rorschach test may provide information about some aspects of a patient's personality and mental functioning, it does not accurately assess most aspects of psychological disorders (Lilienfeld et al., 2000; Wood et al., 2001).

The Rorschach test is a projective test that consists of inkblots. Patients are asked what each inkblot—like the one here—looks like. The Rorschach test is based on the idea that the test-taker imposes a structure onto the ambiguous inkblot; the patient's responses are thought to reveal something about himself or herself.

Another projective test, the *Thematic Apperception Test (TAT)*, uses detailed black-and-white drawings that often include people. The TAT was developed by Christiana Morgan and Henry Murray (1935) and is used to discern motivations, thoughts, and feelings without having to ask a person directly. The patient is asked to explain the drawings in various ways: The clinician may ask the patient what is happening in the picture, what has just happened, what will happen next, or what the people in the picture might be thinking and feeling. Like the Rorschach test, the TAT elicits responses that presumably reflect unconscious beliefs, desires, fears, or issues (Murray, 1943). Responses on the TAT may be interpreted freely by the clinician or scored according to a scoring system. However, only 3% of clinicians who use the TAT rely on a scoring system (Pinkerman et al., 1993).

Projective test
A tool for personality assessment in which the patient is presented with ambiguous stimuli (such as inkblots or stick figures) and is asked to make sense of and explain them.

As part of the Thematic Apperception Test, patients are asked to describe the motivations, thoughts, and feelings of people portrayed in various drawings. Some clinicians consider a patient's answers to reflect unconscious beliefs, feelings, and desires.

Assessing Social Factors

Symptoms arise in a context, and part of a thorough clinical assessment is collecting information about social factors. To some extent, the context helps the clinician or researcher understand the problems that initiated the assessment: How does the patient function in his or her home environment? Are there family factors or community factors that might influence treatment decisions? Is the patient from another culture, and if so, how might that affect the presentation of his or her symptoms or influence how the clinician should interpret other information obtained as part of the assessment?

The importance of social and environmental factors in making an assessment is illustrated by Arthur Kleinman (1988) in examples such as this: If a man has lost energy because he has contracted malaria, has a poor appetite as a result of anemia (due to a hookworm infestation), has insomnia as a result of chronic diarrhea, and he feels hopeless because of his poverty and powerlessness, does the person have depression? His symptoms meet the criteria for depression (as we shall see in Chapter 5), but isn't his distress a result of his health problems and social circumstances and their consequences? Summing up his experiences as depression might limit our understanding of his situation and the best course of treatment.

Family Functioning

As noted in Chapter 2, various aspects of family functioning can affect a person's mental health. This was certainly true of the Walls family, where Rex's drinking and irresponsibility led Rose Mary to become overwhelmed and to "shut down"—staying in bed for days and crying. Similarly, their marriage appeared to have a role in Rex's drinking problem (Walls, 2005).

In order to assess family functioning, clinicians may interview all or some family members or ask patients about how the family functions. Some clinicians and researchers try to assess family functioning more systematically than through interviews or observations. For example, the *Family Environment Scale* (Moos & Moos, 1986) requires family members to answer a set of questions. Their answers are integrated to create a profile of the family environment—how the family is organized, different types of control and conflict, family values, and emotional expressiveness. Such information helps the clinician or researcher to understand the patient within the context of his or her family and identifies possible areas of family functioning that could be improved (Ross & Hill, 2004).

The subtle dynamics that develop in a family, such as one sibling's feeling that the other is favored, can have far-reaching implications.

Clinicians should inquire about the problems and strengths of a patient's community, such as the presence of violence and the sources for support. Such information helps us understand the wider context of the patient's symptoms, as well as interventions that might be helpful.

Community

When making a clinical assessment, a clinician should try to learn about the patient's community in order to understand what normal functioning is in that environment. As we saw in Chapter 2, people who have low socioeconomic status (SES) are more likely to have psychological disorders. These people live in poorer communities, which tend to have relatively high crime rates—and so they are more likely to witness a crime, be a victim of crime, or to live in fear. What, then, is "normal" functioning in this context?

In an effort to understand a patient within his or her social environment, "community" may be defined loosely; it can refer not only to where the patient lives but also to where he or she spends a lot of time, such as school or the workplace. Some jobs and work settings can be particularly stressful or challenging, and a comprehensive assessment should take such information about a patient into account. Consider that some work settings place very high demands on employees—high enough that some may become "burned out" (Aziz, 2004; Lindblom et al., 2006). Symptoms of burnout (a psychological condition, though not a psychological disorder in DSM-5) include feeling chronically mentally and physically tired, dissatisfied, and performing inefficiently—which resemble symptoms of depression (Maslach, 2003; Mausner-Dorsch & Eaton, 2000).

The clinician should also assess the patient's capacity to manage daily life in his or her community, considering factors such as whether the patient's psychological problems interfere with the sources for social support and ability to communicate his or her needs and interact with others in a relatively normal way. Similarly, the clinician may be asked to determine whether the patient would benefit from training to enhance his or her social skills (Combs et al., 2008).

Culture

To assess someone's reports of distress or impairment, a clinician must understand the person's culture. Different cultures have different views about complaining and how to describe different types of distress or other symptoms, which influence the amount and type of symptoms people will report to a mental health clinician—which, in turn, can affect the diagnosis a clinician makes. For instance, White British teenagers with anorexia nervosa say they are afraid of becoming fat and report being preoccupied with their weight (both symptoms are part of the criteria set for anorexia); in contrast, British teenagers of South Asian background do not report these symptoms but are more likely to report a loss of appetite (which is not part of the criteria set; Tareen et al., 2005). Thus, the reported symptoms of the British teenagers of South Asian background may not meet enough of the criteria for a diagnosis of anorexia—although they may still have significant distress, impairment, or risk of harm.

Such cultural differences may underlie, at least in part, the dramatic differences in the apparent rates of serious mental illness across countries, shown in Figure 3.3 (WHO World Mental Health Survey Consortium, 2004). (A mental illness was considered *serious* if the individual was unable to carry out his or her normal activities for at least 30 days in the past year.) These rates were based on data gathered in face-to-face interviews. Notice how much higher the rates are in the United States than in other developed and developing countries. One explanation for this discrepancy is that Americans are less inhibited about telling strangers about their psychological problems. People in other countries might have minimized the frequency or severity of their symptoms.

To help clinicians assess cultural factors, DSM-5 includes a 16-question *Cultural Formulation Interview.* Specifically, responses to this set of questions help clinicians to

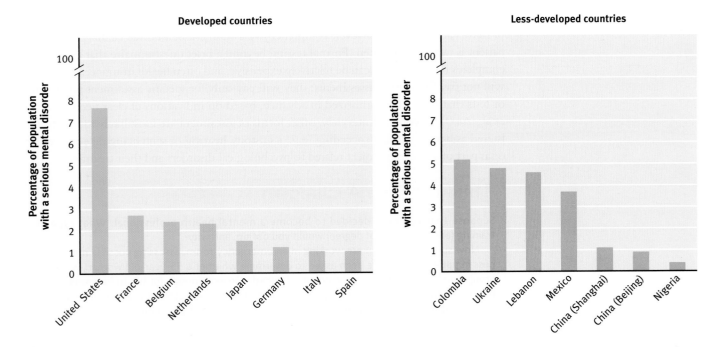

FIGURE **3.3 • Rates of Serious Mental Illness Across Countries** From 2001 to 2003, the World Health Organization conducted surveys to measure the prevalence of serious mental disorders in the populations of various countries. The results revealed significant differences among countries (WHO World Mental Health Survey Consortium, 2004).

Source: Copyright 2004 by the American Medical Association. For more information, see the Permissions section.

understand how culture and cultural identity might influence the ways that patients explain and understand their problems. These factors, in turn, may influence diagnosis and treatment (American Psychiatric Association, 2013).

Assessment as an Interactive Process

Mental health researchers and clinicians learn about patients from assessing psychological and social factors and, to a lesser extent, neurological and other biological factors. Information about each type of factor should not be considered in isolation but rather should influence how the clinician understands the other types of information.

Knowledge of psychological factors must be developed in the context of the patient's culture. Psychiatrist Paul Linde (2002) recounts his experiences working in a psychiatric unit in Zimbabwe: The residents of that country generally understand that bacteria can cause an illness such as pneumonia, but they nonetheless wonder why the bacteria struck a particular individual at a specific point in time (a question that contemporary science is just beginning to try to answer). They look to ancestral spirits for an answer to such a question, even when a particular person is beset with mental rather than physical symptoms. In Zimbabwe, the first experience of hallucinations and delusions is viewed as a sign that the individual is being called to become a healer, a *n'anga*, and not as an indicator of mental illness.

Thus, knowledge of the patient's culture influences how an outside researcher such as Linde understands the symptoms. When a patient in Zimbabwe claims to be hearing voices of dead ancestors, Linde undoubtedly interprets this symptom somewhat differently than he would if a White, American-born patient made the same claim. At the same time, knowledge of a patient's family history of chronic schizophrenia (which may indicate a neurological factor—genetic, in this case) will also influence the interpretation of the patient's symptoms.

Clearly, the way that each type of factor is assessed can influence how the other types of factors are assessed. However, comprehensive assessment of all three factors in the same patient is rarely undertaken. Formal testing beyond a brief questionnaire that the patient completes independently can be relatively expensive, and often health insurance companies will not pay for routine assessments; they will pay only for specific assessment procedures or tests that they have authorized in advance, based on indications of clear need (Eisman et al., 2000). Beyond an interview, other forms of assessment are most likely to be administered as part of a legal proceeding (e.g., a custody hearing or sentencing determination) or as part of a research project related to psychological disorders and their treatment.

Thinking Like A Clinician

Suppose that you have decided to become a mental health professional. What type of training (and what type of degree) would you obtain, and why?

Now suppose that you are working in an emergency room, assessing possible mental illness in patients. You have been asked to determine whether a 55-year-old woman, who was brought in by her son, has a psychological disorder severe enough for her to be hospitalized. Based on what you have read, if you could use only one assessment method of each type (neurological, psychological, and social), what methods would you choose, and why?

Diagnosing and Assessing Rose Mary and Rex Walls?

Now that you know something about diagnosis and assessment, let's review what we know—and what we don't know—about Rose Mary and Rex Walls, starting with Rex, using the neuropsychosocial approach.

We know that he drank alcohol—regularly and to excess. In fact, he drank so much and so chronically that when he stopped drinking, he developed *delirium tremens* (also known as the DTs)—withdrawal symptoms marked by hallucinations and shaking. He clearly would have been diagnosed as having *alcohol use disorder*. (Disorders related to misuse of alcohol and other substances are discussed in Chapter 9.)

We don't know whether the tall tales he told about himself were delusions or merely attempts to make himself look good in his own eyes and those of other people. Based on Jeannette's descriptions of her father, it appears that Rex also strove to be the center of attention. This pattern of self-centered behavior suggests that he may have had a personality disorder (specifically, what is known as *narcissistic personality disorder*, and possibly other personality disorders, discussed in Chapter 14).

What about Rose Mary? Based on Jeannette's descriptions of her mother's difficulties. Rose Mary may have suffered from depression. It is possible, though, that certain behaviors instead may have been expressions of anger and resentment about feeling forced to work when her husband was so irresponsible. She was bitter that she hadn't become a famous artist and blamed her lack of success on her children. In addition, given her own preoccupations with her worth as an artist, even as her children were starving, she may well have had *narcissistic personality disorder*.

However, again we need to be cautious: No mental health clinician can know with certainty what, if any, specific disorder Rose Mary or Rex Walls may have had. We cannot make a direct clinical assessment of neurological, psychological, or social factors; we can only infer such factors from their daughter's account, which does not provide the kind of information needed to make an accurate clinical assessment.

Finally, clinicians and researchers diagnosing and assessing patients must keep in mind the possibility that symptoms of a psychological disorder can arise from medical problems. Only after ruling out medical illnesses can a mental health clinician or researcher have confidence in a diagnosis of a psychological disorder.

☐ SUMMING UP

Diagnosing Psychological Disorders

- Among other purposes, classification systems for diagnosis allow (1) patients to be able to put a name to their experiences and to learn that they are not alone; (2) clinicians to distinguish "normal" from "abnormal" psychological functioning and to group together similar types of problems; and (3) researchers to discover the etiology, course, and effectiveness of treatments for abnormal psychological functioning.

- Classification systems have drawbacks: (1) They can be subject to diagnostic bias—perhaps on the basis of the patient's sex, race, or ethnicity; and (2) for some people, being diagnosed with a psychological disorder is experienced as stigmatizing, which changes how the person feels about himself or herself or is seen by others.

- Classification systems should be both reliable and valid.

- The most commonly used classification system in the United States is the *Diagnostic and Statistical Manual of Mental Disorders*, presently in its fifth edition (DSM-5). The DSM-5 generally does not focus on etiology but instead focuses on what can be observed rather than inferred and lists explicit criteria for each disorder.

- DSM-5 has been criticized on numerous grounds, including:

  ○ What constitutes clinically significant distress or impaired functioning is subjective and can vary widely from one clinician to another.

  ○ Most disorders are classified as categorical rather than as on continua.

  ○ The way the criteria are structured leads heterogeneous groups to be diagnosed with the same disorder.

  ○ The duration criteria can be arbitrary and not necessarily supported by research.

  ○ Many diagnoses have been created in order to ensure payment from health insurance providers. Moreover, diagnoses have been added for disorders that clearly are medical problems.

  ○ Social factors that lead or contribute to psychological disorders are deemphasized.

  ○ There is a high comorbidity rate: Half the people diagnosed with one disorder have at least one other disorder.

- Psychological disorders are generally diagnosed by clinical and counseling psychologists, psychiatrists, psychiatric nurses, and social workers. Other clinicians in a position to diagnose psychological disorders include general practitioners, pastoral counselors, and marriage and family therapists.

Assessing Psychological Disorders

- Neurological and other biological factors may be assessed using various methods. Neuroimaging techniques can assess brain structure (X-rays, computerized axial tomography, and magnetic resonance imaging) and brain function (positron emission tomography and functional magnetic resonance imaging). Neuropsychological testing can assess brain functioning.

- Various methods are used to assess psychological factors. These include the clinical interview, observing the patient, patient self-report, and reports of others involved in the patient's life. Specific aspects of psychological functioning can be assessed through tests of cognitive abilities, and personality functioning can be assessed with inventories, questionnaires, and projective tests.

- Some techniques used to assess psychological factors also can be used to assess social factors—such as family functioning—as well as to provide a more detailed portrait of the patient's community and culture. These social factors affect and are affected by neurological and psychological factors.

Key Terms

Diagnosis (p. 61)
Clinical assessment (p. 61)
Diagnostic bias (p. 63)
Reliable (p. 64)
Valid (p. 64)
Prognosis (p. 64)
Prevalence (p. 64)
Comorbidity (p. 66)
Clinical psychologist (p. 70)
Counseling psychologist (p. 70)
Psychiatrist (p. 71)
Psychiatric nurse (p. 71)
Social worker (p. 71)

Computerized axial tomography (CT) (p. 73)
Magnetic resonance imaging (MRI) (p. 73)
Positron emission tomography (PET) (p. 74)
Functional magnetic resonance imaging (fMRI) (p. 74)

Neuropsychological testing (p. 74)
Clinical interview (p. 75)
Malingering (p. 77)
Factitious disorder (p. 77)
Projective test (p. 80)

More Study Aids

For additional study aids related to this chapter, including quizzes to make sure you've retained everything you've learned and a Student Video Activity exploring how to assess antisocial behavioral patterns, go to: www.worthpublishers.com/launchpad/rkabpsych2e.

Form Advertising/Alamy

CHAPTER **4**

Research Methods

Suppose you are a psychologist at a college counseling center. A student, Carlos, comes to the center because he's been depressed since his girlfriend, Liana, broke up with him 5 weeks ago. Liana's rejection came out of nowhere, as far as Carlos is concerned. He feels abandoned and alone. He has been spiraling downward since the breakup, feeling irritable and sad, sleeping a lot, and without appetite. He was just fired from his on-campus job because of his poor attitude. He doesn't care much about his classes or schoolwork. During your sessions with Carlos, he seems preoccupied with his relationship with Liana and worries that no other woman will ever love him.

Carlos is not the only student on campus to have this type of problem. You've noticed that a surprising number of students seeking help at the counseling center are depressed and have recently broken up with a boyfriend or a girlfriend. Like Carlos, these students frequently report feeling hurt, rejected, and unlovable. Some even think about suicide.

You wonder, though, whether the depression that many of these students are experiencing is a result specifically of their breakups. Perhaps they were depressed before the breakup—and that contributed to the failure of the relationship. In Carlos's case, perhaps his depression started earlier (although he hadn't realized it), and Liana got sick of his being down in the dumps. On the other hand, maybe a lot of the students would not have become depressed if their relationships had not ended.

HOW CAN YOU DETERMINE WHETHER THE STUDENTS ARE DEPRESSED because their relationships ended, or whether their relationships ended because they were depressed? In this chapter, we explore specific methods that psychologists use to study psychopathology and its treatment, the challenges associated with the use of the different research methods, and the ways in which researchers address those challenges.

Scientists often collect quantitative data (numerical measurements, such as how many symptoms someone has, the number of weeks symptoms have been present, or how many people in the family have similar symptoms).

Using the Scientific Method to Understand Abnormality

Perhaps your observations about depression and relationship breakups are based simply on a coincidence: People—particularly young people—are frequently beginning and ending relationships, and depression and breakups occur completely independently of each other. Many of the depressed students coming to the counseling center have had prior bouts of depression. In such cases, a breakup would not necessarily be the culprit, because those people might have had another bout of depression regardless. Alternatively, there may be a causal connection between breaking up and depression—but it could go either way, with either one leading to the other.

To determine whether the breaking up of a relationship can in fact lead to depression, you would use the **scientific method**, which is the process of gathering and interpreting facts that generally consists of the following steps:

1. Collect initial observations
2. Identify a question
3. Develop a hypothesis that might answer the question
4. Collect relevant data to test the hypothesis
5. Develop a theory
6. Test the theory

The Scientific Method

How can the scientific method help researchers learn more about the association between breakups in relationships and depression or, more generally, about how a psychological disorder such as depression arises?

Collect Initial Observations

The first step in the scientific method is to collect initial observations. Sometimes the initial observations lead immediately to the next steps, but other times they lead the researcher to describe the phenomenon more carefully and systematically by collecting data. **Data** are methodical observations, which often include numerical measurements of phenomena. Scientific facts are based on such data. Data about depression and breakups, for instance, might include responses to a questionnaire on which people who have recently gone through a breakup rate their moods and functioning.

Properly collected data can be **replicated** under identical or nearly identical conditions: Any other researcher, using the same collection method, should obtain a second set of data with the same characteristics as the first. For example, if a researcher at another college's counseling center gave the same questionnaire about mood and functioning to a different group of students who'd recently suffered a breakup, that researcher would be trying to replicate the data.

Identify a Question

The process of explaining a set of observations begins by asking a specific question. Let's say that your observations have led you to ask this question: "Why do some people get depressed after a relationship ends rather than bounce back?" The question identifies an area where properly conducted research can point toward an answer.

Scientific method
The process of gathering and interpreting facts that generally consists of collecting initial observations, identifying a question, developing a hypothesis that might answer the question, collecting relevant data, developing a theory, and testing the theory.

Data
Methodical observations, which include numerical measurements of phenomena.

Replication
The process of repeating a study using the same data collection methods under identical or nearly identical conditions to obtain data that should have the same characteristics as those from the original study.

Develop and Test a Hypothesis

After identifying a question, a researcher forms a *hypothesis*. A **hypothesis** is a preliminary idea that is proposed to answer the question about a set of observations. Hypotheses are important in part because they direct the researcher to make specific additional observations (which may include making precise measurements). The most common kinds of hypotheses propose a way to understand differences in measurements of a variable in different circumstances (such as differences in rates of depression when no breakup has occurred versus soon after a breakup) or to establish a relationship between different variables. *Variables* are measurable characteristics of the object or event of interest; for example, mood (rated on a scale ranging from very positive to very negative) is a variable. For instance, a hypothesis might address *which people* are likely to get depressed or *why* some people are likely to get depressed. Let's say you develop this hypothesis: People who suffered a major loss during childhood (such as the death of a parent) are more likely to get depressed after a relationship ends during adulthood. Your hypothesis involves two variables: (the presence or absence of) childhood loss and depression.

After the researcher has a hypothesis, he or she must test it by collecting new data. If the resulting data are as expected, the hypothesis is supported. But if the data are inconsistent with the hypothesis, the researcher must think again—and try to develop a new hypothesis and then test it. And even when the data generally are consistent with the hypothesis, often some aspect of the data were unexpected, which leads to new hypotheses to be tested.

The scientific method is used to determine whether a hypothesis—such as the idea that a relationship's breaking up can lead to depression—is correct. The process of research on psychopathology often begins with observations that lead to a hypothesis about either the factors that may contribute to psychological disorders or the aspects of treatment that may be particularly helpful.

Develop a Theory

After enough data are collected and hypotheses are confirmed or disconfirmed, the researcher proposes a **theory**, which is a principle or set of principles that explains a set of data. A theory provides an answer to the question identified by the researcher. For example, you might theorize that depression is particularly likely to arise in adults after a relationship ends if they, as children, suffered a loss and there was nothing they could do to control or manage the situation. That is, according to this theory, the child forms an enduring association between loss and a sense of helplessness, and it is the feelings of helplessness that produce depression. According to this theory, when later in life the adult experiences a loss, this triggers the associations to helplessness, which in turn leads the adult to become depressed.

Test the Theory

The next step of the scientific method is to test the theory by collecting and examining additional data. The theory leads to **predictions**, hypotheses that should be confirmed if a theory is correct. So, for instance, your theory focuses on people who not only had a significant loss during childhood but also felt that they could not control or manage the situation. The theory predicts that children who felt particularly helpless after a loss would be more likely as adults to become depressed after a relationship breaks up. Data can then be collected to address this specific prediction: In addition to questionnaires about early loss and mood and functioning, an additional questionnaire might ask about memories of feeling helpless. You could then test people who did or did not have an uncontrollable loss during childhood by giving them increasingly difficult puzzles; as a measure of current feelings of helplessness, you would assess how easily participants give up trying to solve the puzzles. You would predict that people who experienced a loss as a child would be more likely to feel—and behave as if they were—helpless currently, *and* that these people would become depressed after a relationship breaks up. Many methods can be used to test the predictions made by a theory, and we'll see what these are in the following section.

Figure 4.1 provides a summary of the steps of the scientific method.

Hypothesis
A preliminary idea that is proposed to answer a question about a set of observations.
Theory
A principle or set of principles that explains a set of data.
Predictions
Hypotheses that should be confirmed if a theory is correct.

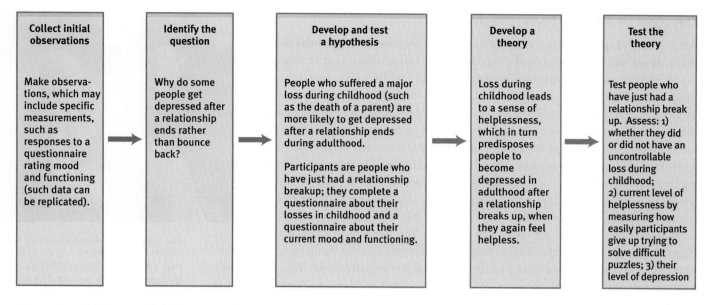

Collect initial observations	Identify the question	Develop and test a hypothesis	Develop a theory	Test the theory
Make observations, which may include specific measurements, such as responses to a questionnaire rating mood and functioning (such data can be replicated).	Why do some people get depressed after a relationship ends rather than bounce back?	People who suffered a major loss during childhood (such as the death of a parent) are more likely to get depressed after a relationship ends during adulthood. Participants are people who have just had a relationship breakup; they complete a questionnaire about their losses in childhood and a questionnaire about their current mood and functioning.	Loss during childhood leads to a sense of helplessness, which in turn predisposes people to become depressed in adulthood after a relationship breaks up, when they again feel helpless.	Test people who have just had a relationship break up. Assess: 1) whether they did or did not have an uncontrollable loss during childhood; 2) current level of helplessness by measuring how easily participants give up trying to solve difficult puzzles; 3) their level of depression

FIGURE **4.1 • Steps of the Scientific Method**

Types of Scientific Research

Any individual researcher does not need to go through the entire sequence of steps in the scientific method to be doing science. Moreover, psychologists may employ different research methods when they work on different phases of the sequence and when they attempt to answer different questions; such methods include experiments, quasi-experiments, correlational research, case studies, and meta-analysis. As we review the various research methods, we will point out both their major strengths and their weaknesses.

Conducting Research with Experiments

Ideally, researchers prefer to employ **experiments**, which are research studies in which investigators intentionally manipulate one variable at a time and measure the consequences of such manipulation on one or more other variables.

Independent Variables and Dependent Variables

You probably noticed that the definition of *experiments* mentioned two kinds of variables: those that are manipulated and those that then are measured. In an experiment, researchers manipulate one variable at a time in order to observe possible changes in another variable. The variable that a researcher manipulates is called the **independent variable** (so named because it is free to change—it is independent). The variable that may change as a result is called the **dependent variable** (because its value *depends* on the independent variable). When the independent variable is changed, the accompanying changes in the dependent variable are the *effect*. A researcher might separately manipulate several independent variables (always keeping all else constant while a single variable is changed), hoping to discover which ones cause the greatest effect on the dependent variable.

Of course, researchers could not use an experimental design to investigate the specific question about helplessness during early loss and subsequent depression after a breakup. A researcher ethically cannot cause a person to have a major loss during childhood (or to feel helpless at the time). Participants in an experimental study come as they are—with particular neurological, psychological, and social histories that can't be changed.

This is why most of the research on causes of psychological disorders does not use an experimental design. For ethical reasons as well as practical ones, researchers cannot alter participants' genes, subject participants to high levels of stress, cause them to

Experiments
Research studies in which investigators intentionally manipulate one variable at a time, and measure the consequences of such manipulation on one or more other variables.

Independent variable
A variable that a researcher manipulates.

Dependent variable
A variable that is measured and that may change its values as a result of manipulating the independent variable.

have traumatic experiences, or create disruptive family events—all of which would involve intentionally manipulating independent variables. However, some aspects of psychopathology can be studied with an experimental design. For instance, Watson and Rayner's experiment with Little Albert (1920; see Chapter 2) used an experimental design to test a theory about the etiology of a phobia. In that study, the independent variable was whether or not the conditioned (that is, the initially neutral) stimulus had been paired with an aversive unconditioned stimulus. The dependent variable was the presence of fear-related behaviors—as measured by Albert's crying and trying to get away from the white rat. When the conditioned stimulus (CS) and the unconditioned stimulus (UCS) had not yet been paired, Albert was not afraid of the rodent. His fear-related behaviors (the dependent variable) depended on his exposure to the pairing of CS and UCS. (Note that the ethical guidelines that apply to research today had not yet been developed at the time of Watson and Rayner's study with Little Albert.)

Other examples of experimental designs in research on psychopathology include studies of people who have *panic attacks*—specific periods of intense dread or fear, accompanied by physical symptoms of fear; the independent variable is the situation or condition that may induce a panic attack (which is manipulated by presenting or removing such a situation or condition), and the dependent variable is the number of such attacks. Further examples include studies of people who have substance abuse problems, where the independent variable is the type of *cues*, or stimuli, that trigger cravings to take a drug or to drink alcohol, and the dependent variable may be intensity of cravings for the drug or alcohol or physiological measures of arousal.

If an experiment has not been carefully designed, some factors might inadvertently affect the variables of interest. These factors are called **confounding variables**, also referred to as *confounds*. For example, suppose that you conducted an experiment in which the independent variable was the type of movie viewed by two groups of participants, those who had experienced a loss during childhood and those who did not. One movie involved the death of a loved one and the other did not touch on the theme of loss, and the dependent variable was mood. Then suppose that for the "loss" group, the movie involving loss was always shown immediately after a serious drama, whereas for the "no loss" group, the movie that did not involve loss was always shown immediately after a comedy. It could be the type of movie shown first—drama or comedy—and not differences between the groups that produces the effects on the dependent variable; thus, the type of film first shown is a confounding variable. Confounds lead to ambiguous or uncertain results. To minimize the possibility of confounds, a researcher should try to ensure that the experimental manipulation alters only the independent variables (and does not inadvertently affect other variables, such as the order in which the movies are presented) and that only those changes in the independent variables affect the dependent variable.

Control Groups and Control Conditions

A common method for ruling out possible effects of confounds in an experiment is to create a control group. The experimental group (or groups) and the control group are treated identically throughout the experiment, except that the independent variable is not manipulated for the **control group**. For example, say that the participants who had suffered an early loss and experienced helplessness did in fact have a more negative mood after watching a movie with the theme of loss. But here's a potential confound: Maybe these people are just very sensitive to depressing movies in general, not to themes of loss specifically. To rule out this possibility, you would control for this factor by testing another group of these people, showing them a depressing movie that has nothing to do with loss. (This movie should be as similar as possible to the first one in every way, except that it does not have the theme of loss.) If the finding does not result from a confounding, then you should find a much larger drop in mood following the movie

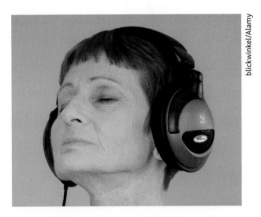

blickwinkel/Alamy

Some studies investigating psychopathology use an experimental design. Here the independent variable is different types of music, in major versus minor keys, and the dependent variable is participants' self-reported mood after listening to the two types of music.

Confounding variables
Factors that might inadvertently affect the variables of interest in an experiment.

Control group
A group of participants in an experiment for which the independent variable is not manipulated, but which is otherwise treated identically to the experimental group.

about loss than following the movie that was merely depressing—which would provide evidence that the theme of loss itself is important.

To use a control group appropriately, it must be as similar as possible to the experimental group. If the members of a control group differ from members of the experimental group in terms of age, education, cultural background, temperament, or any other characteristic, one or more confounding variables has been introduced. Such a confound would cloud the interpretation of the results because a difference in the dependent variable could be attributed to the confound instead of to the relationship you intended to test. Perhaps the control group responded less strongly to the depressing movie simply because most of the participants in that group happened to be temperamentally placid.

You can imagine how hard it can be to match a control group perfectly to an experimental group. This difficulty often leads researchers to match the experimental group to the most similar possible control group: the experimental group itself! Sometimes, rather than having two separate groups that are treated differently, researchers have all participants take part in different *conditions*, or circumstances, which correspond to the different ways that experimental and control groups would be treated in a study that had both types of groups. For example, the same people could watch a movie about loss and at a different time watch a movie that is depressing but not about loss. However, when the same group of people take part in more than one condition, you need to avoid a confound introduced by the order of presentation of the conditions. For instance, if the "loss" film was always presented first, it could be that the participants were more alert during that part of the study and that's why they responded differently. To avoid this, you would *counterbalance* the order of exposure to each condition: Half of the participants would watch the "loss" film first, and the other half would watch the "nonloss/depressing" film first. This procedure would ensure that each condition occurred equally often in each place in the order of presentation.

Possible Effects of Bias

The way a study is set up can affect the assignment of participants into groups or can inappropriately influence the outcome of the experiment. For instance, suppose that you have two groups: Members of one group see a "loss-and-depressing" film, and members of the other see a "nonloss-but-depressing" film. When you assign participants to the groups, you inadvertently assign the people who smile at you to the "non-loss-but-depressing" group. Whether or not it is conscious (intentional) or unconscious (unintentional), a tendency or influence that distorts data—which ends up producing a confound—is called **bias**. This is why researchers place participants in groups using **random assignment**, assigning participants to each group by a procedure that relies on chance.

Many sorts of biases exist. For example, a particularly important one is **sampling bias**, which occurs when the participants are not drawn randomly from the relevant population. Sampling bias needs to be avoided if you want to be able to *generalize* (i.e., extrapolate) from the people in your study to the population at large. This brings us to an important distinction: The **population** is the complete set of possible participants (e.g., all rats or all people, or, in certain cases, all people of a particular age, gender, or race). The **sample** is the small portion of the population that is examined in a study.

Internal and External Validity

A study has **internal validity** if it controls for possible confounding variables. Internal validity means that variations in the independent variable are in fact responsible for variations in the dependent variable (or variables, in studies in which more than one type of measurement is taken) and that the results are not a by-product of other, extraneous variables.

Bias
A tendency that distorts data.

Random assignment
Assigning participants to each group in a study using a procedure that relies on chance.

Sampling bias
The distortion that occurs when the participants in an experiment have not been drawn randomly from the relevant population under investigation.

Population
The complete set of possible relevant participants.

Sample
The small portion of a population that is examined in a study.

Internal validity
A characteristic of a study that indicates that it measures what it purports to measure because it has controlled for confounds.

A study is said to have **external validity** when (1) the results generalize from the sample (the particular participants who were tested) to the population from which it was drawn and (2) the conditions used in the study (such as the particular movies shown) generalize to similar conditions outside the study. If a study does not have internal validity, it cannot have external validity. In contrast, even if a study has internal validity (its results are not produced by confounds), it is not guaranteed to have external validity (that its results apply to other people and other similar situations).

Suppose researchers want to know what the prevalence is in the United States of the type of depression that results from seasonal changes in the amount of daylight (sometimes referred to as *seasonal affective disorder*). Researchers in Portland, Oregon, collaborated on a study with researchers in Boston, New York, Chicago, and Detroit. Participants in the study are drawn from those five cities. Do you see the sampling bias problem? All these cities are in the northern half of the United States and therefore have a different number of daylight hours than does the southern half. Whatever prevalence rate was calculated would not reflect the entire United States.

Quasi-Experimental Design

Ideally, the participants in a study are randomly assigned to groups. But in many cases, random assignment is not ethical, desirable, or possible. For instance, when trying to test hypotheses about why a disorder develops, researchers cannot "assign" one group to have a particular set of genes or brain functioning, a particular way of thinking, a particular type of traumatic experience, or particular friends or families. Therefore, in trying to understand possible causes of psychopathology, researchers often use *quasi-experimental designs*, which rely on groups that already exist. In fact, the "experiment" that we have been discussing is—like much research on psychopathology—a quasi-experiment: As in an experiment, an independent variable was manipulated and a dependent variable was measured, but participants were selected from preexisting groups, not randomly assigned.

To have made a true experiment, you would need to have assigned participants randomly to three groups (loss with helplessness, loss without helplessness, and no loss) *during childhood*. Obviously, this is undesirable and impossible. But in a quasi-experimental design, you can sort participants into groups—those who had a childhood loss and experienced helplessness, those who had a childhood loss but didn't experience helplessness, and those without a childhood loss. Then you might show people in all three groups a film that involves relationships breaking up. After viewing the film, participants in all three groups would rate their mood. Your hypothesis would be that participants who experienced early loss and helplessness (like Carlos) will report greater sadness after seeing the film than will those in the other two groups. With a quasi-experimental design, you still try to control as many variables—such as age, health, education, and economic level—as you can in order to make the groups as similar as possible.

Correlational Research

Experiments and quasi-experiments allow researchers to zero in on which variables cause which effects. In some cases, however, manipulating variables, even in a quasi-experiment, can be unethical or difficult. When independent variables can't or shouldn't be manipulated, researchers can study the relationships among variables by looking for a **correlation**, a relationship between the measurements of two variables in which a change in the value of one variable is associated with a change in the value of the other variable. Much of the research on defining and understanding psychopathology is correlational.

External validity
A characteristic of a study that indicates that the results generalize from the sample to the population from which it was drawn and from the conditions used in the study to relevant conditions outside the study.

Correlation
The relationship between the measurements of two variables in which a change in the value of one variable is associated with a change in the value of the other variable.

A correlational study found that suicide is more likely to be the cause of death in high-altitude states, such as Colorado, than in lower-altitude states (D. Cheng, 2002). This relationship may arise for a number of reasons, such as decreased levels of oxygen from the higher altitude (McCook, 2002), the challenges of mountain living, differences in the age and education levels of the populations, or perhaps the fact that depressed people seek a type of solitude more often found in high-altitude states. One possible confound the study did not control for was the amount of time those who committed suicide had lived at the higher altitude: Those who were born in high-altitude states would have adapted to the lower oxygen level. Researchers could have investigated one possible explanation by examining this variable (McCook, 2002).

A correlation compares two measurements and indicates the amount of similarity in their variations; the stronger the correlation, the more closely related the two variables are. There are no independent and dependent variables in *correlational research*: Nothing is manipulated; instead, naturally occurring variations among measurements of different variables are compared. These comparisons can involve measures from different individuals or groups, or measures from the same participants at different times. For example, if your study were correlational, your two variables of interest might be the extent to which a child experienced helplessness during a loss (perhaps rated by relatives who were present at the time or by the person's memory of how severe the feeling of helplessness was) and the number of symptoms of depression experienced as an adult, after a breakup. Twin studies (discussed in Chapter 2) often involve correlational research.

Correlation Does Not Imply Causation

A major disadvantage of correlational methods is that they only indicate that two variables are related. A correlation between variables *does not demonstrate causation*—that is, it does not mean that either variable caused the other to change. In an experiment or in a quasi-experiment, the point is to show that changes in the independent variable cause changes in the dependent variable. In contrast, in a correlational research study, the point is only to show that the values of two variables are related. For example, although the degree of helplessness felt during childhood loss and the amount of depression after an adult relationship breaks up may be correlated, the loss experienced after the breakup may not be the cause of the depression. As discussed earlier, it could be that depression comes first, and it causes the breakup! Simple correlations do not control for possible confounding variables.

Measuring a Correlation

The strength of the correlation between any two variables is quantified by a number called a **correlation coefficient** (most typically symbolized by r). When this number is positive, it signifies that the variables change in the same direction; both variables either increase or decrease in the same general pattern. A *positive relationship* is indicated by any correlation coefficient between 0 and +1. When the correlation coefficient is negative, it signifies that the variables change in opposite directions in the same general pattern; one goes up while the other goes down. A *negative relationship* is indicated by a correlation coefficient between 0 and −1. In either case, positive or negative, the stronger the relationship, the closer the coefficient is to +1 or −1, which would indicate a perfect correspondence.

If the variables do not have any relationship at all, the correlation coefficient is 0. If you plot two variables on a graph, putting one variable on each axis, you can see whether or not the variables change together. The closer the data points are to a straight line that has a slope (either up, for positive correlations, or down for negative ones), the stronger the correlation. Figure 4.2 illustrates five correlations.

Statistical Significance

Even when variables are completely independent, they might vary in the same pattern simply by chance. In fact, the correlation coefficient between any two randomly selected sets of data is very seldom exactly 0. A correlation coefficient—or the result of performing any other statistical test (such as a "t-test," which assesses the difference between means)—is **statistically significant** when it is greater than what would be

Correlation coefficient
A number that quantifies the strength of the correlation between two variables; the correlation coefficient is most typically symbolized by *r*.

Statistically significant
The condition in which the value of a statistical test is greater than what would be expected by chance alone.

Epidemiology
The type of correlational research that investigates the rate of occurrence, the possible causes and risk factors, and the course of diseases or disorders.

expected by chance alone. Statistical significance is not the same thing as "importance." It simply means that the observed result is unlikely to be a quirk of random variation in the data. Suppose that, for your participants, you calculated the correlation between age when experiencing a loss during childhood and symptoms of depression after an adult breakup, and the result was $r = -0.31$. This means the younger a person was when a loss occurred, the more symptoms of depression he or she is likely to have after a breakup as an adult. However, this relationship may not hold for every participant. Researchers want to know not only the correlation coefficient but also the value of p (which stands for *probability*) that is associated with that coefficient; the value of p indicates how likely it is that the correlation could have arisen due to chance. For instance, your correlation coefficient of -0.31 was tied to $p < .01$. This means that the probability that the correlation is due to chance is less than 1 in 100. Similarly, a value of $p < .05$ means that the probability that the correlation is due to chance is less than 5 in 100. In fact, $p < .05$ is usually considered the cutoff for statistical significance. As a rule, the more participants that were tested, the lower the correlation can be and be statistically significant.

Using Correlational Methods

Correlational research in psychopathology is designed to discover whether one variable (which often taps a characteristic of a disorder) is linked to other variables (which often tap a symptom or associated factor, such as alterations in neural activity, irrational thoughts, or family functioning). **Epidemiology** is a type of correlational research that investigates the rate of occurrence, the possible causes and risk factors, and the course of diseases or disorders. Thus, in epidemiological studies of psychopathology, researchers identify people with one (or more) disorder and correlate the presence or severity of the disorder with other variables, such as the age of onset of the disorder, the number of people in the family who have had symptoms of the disorder, or socioeconomic status.

Note that certain factors (such as having a relative with a disorder) can be *risk factors*, which increase the likelihood of developing a disorder. However, by definition, risk factors are simply that—risks, not destiny. How are such risks identified? Studies often use correlational data to determine whether people who have a psychological disorder are different in some way from people who don't have the disorder. Some of these studies are **longitudinal studies**, which are designed to determine whether a given variable is a risk factor by using data collected from

FIGURE 4.2 • Five Values of Correlation

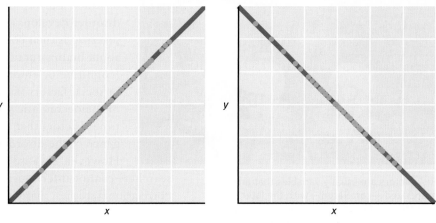

Perfect-positive correlation (1.0)　　　Perfect-negative correlation (−1.0)

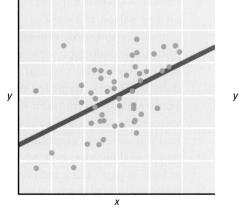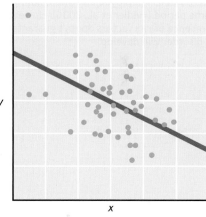

Moderate-positive correlation (.5)　　　Moderate-negative correlation (−.5)

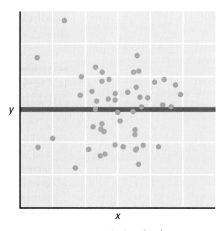

No correlation (0.0)

Longitudinal studies (in studies of psychopathology)
Research studies that are designed to determine whether a given variable is a risk factor by using data collected from the same participants at various points in time.

Risk factors are usually variables that are associated—correlated—with the later emergence of psychological disorders. For instance, soldiers who fought in the Gulf War in 1991 were more likely to develop psychological disorders in the next year than were soldiers deployed elsewhere during that time period (Fiedler et al., 2006). However, the presence of risk factors doesn't guarantee that a disorder will develop.

the same participants at multiple points in time. Specifically, such studies track a group of children or adults over time and observe whether a disorder develops. The presence or absence of the disorder (or its level of severity) is then correlated with neurological factors (perhaps information about brain structure or function or hormone levels), psychological factors (cognitive or emotional functioning, beliefs, or personality traits), and/or social factors (family and other intimate relations, school performance, or socioeconomic status) that typically were assessed at an earlier point in time. Factors that are significantly correlated with the subsequent emergence of the disorder are taken to signal risk for developing that disorder. However, because such longitudinal studies are usually correlational, researchers cannot infer causality on the basis of the findings. As with virtually all correlational studies, many factors can explain differences observed in longitudinal studies.

Case Studies

Research on psychopathology may also rely on **case studies**, which focus in detail on one person and the factors that underlie his or her psychological disorder or disorders. For instance, someone noticed that a young patient had a very bad sore throat prior to developing symptoms of *obsessive-compulsive disorder* (OCD)—a disorder that is characterized by frequent and intrusive unwanted thoughts and behaviors that the individual feels compelled to engage in (we will say more about this in Chapter 7). Studies that were inspired by this observation found that OCD may sometimes develop from a particular type of streptococcal infection (Swedo et al., 1998), and eventually researchers identified *pediatric autoimmune neuropsychiatric disorder associated with streptococcal infection*, or PANDAS (Giulino et al., 2002). PANDAS appears to arise, at least in part, when antibodies that attack the strep bacteria also attack a part of the brain known as the basal ganglia. Antibiotics that treat the strep infection (leading to lower levels of antibodies) end up decreasing the OCD symptoms. The discovery of PANDAS began from a case study. Case 4.1 discusses a case of a young woman with *autism spectrum disorder*—a disorder that is diagnosed in childhood and involves significant problems with communication and social interactions. (We'll discuss this disorder in more detail in Chapter 14.)

Case studies (in studies of psychopathology)
A research method that focuses in detail on one individual and the factors that underlie that person's psychological disorder or disorders.

CASE 4.1 • FROM THE OUTSIDE: Menstruation-Related Exacerbation of Autism Symptoms

A 19-year-old nonverbal girl [with autism spectrum disorder and severe intellectual disability (previously called mental retardation)] was referred for treatment of aggression and SIB [self-injurious behavior]. At onset of menarche at age 12, agitation dramatically increased. Her mother recorded cyclical behavioral changes along with her menses. Before each menses, she became withdrawn, apathetic, quiet, irritable, and easily agitated with increased tantrums and appeared anxious. She also had a cyclical amplification of baseline autistic behaviors: stereotypies (rocking), sensitivity to changes, and sensitivity to noise. New-onset cyclical handbiting was so intense that scarring resulted, and cyclical aggression directed at objects and others occurred several times daily. Teacher reports recorded and corroborated aggression and SIB that corresponded to the days before the onset of her menstrual period. Within 1 day of menstrual onset, mood symptoms and SIB abated. Neither behavioral therapy with positive or negative reinforcement nor treatment with acetaminophen or ibuprofen yielded improvement. Treatment with paroxetine [Paxil, an SSRI medication] 20 mg every morning resulted in improvement of premenstrual mood symptoms and premenstrual exacerbated SIB. On discontinuation of paroxetine on two distinct occasions, cyclical mood symptoms, aggression, and SIB returned.

(Lee, 2004, p. 1193)

Uses and Limits of Case Studies

A case study focuses on a particular individual in detail, often describing neurological, psychological, and social factors: Such a study often provides information about a person's medical and family history, as well as his or her culture and the context of the problem. Mental health professionals use case studies for a variety of reasons:

- to demonstrate some aspect of diagnosis, etiology, or treatment;
- to provide support for (or evidence against) a particular hypothesis or theory; and
- to train other mental health professionals, who are given case studies and must then propose diagnoses and appropriate treatments.

Mental health clinicians and researchers must resist the temptation to generalize from a single case: Don't assume that the findings from a case study necessarily can be extended to other similar cases, let alone to the population at large. Sometimes the findings can be generalized, but sometimes they cannot be; every individual is unique, and a person's particular history presents many possible confounding factors. In addition, if a case study relies on correlations among variables, this method—as usual—prevents us from drawing conclusions about causality.

Single-Participant Experiments

Case studies are not necessarily limited to *describing* the values of variables and relations among them. In some situations, clinicians and researchers can actually perform experiments with only a single case. For instance, a researcher could treat someone suspected of having PANDAS-related OCD with antibiotics and determine whether the OCD symptoms improved. Experiments with only a single case are called **single-participant experiments**.

Single-participant experiments may rely on an *ABAB design*, which is often used to measure change in target behaviors as a result of some treatment. In many cases, a single participant receives both conditions: a baseline condition with no treatment (the first phase A of the ABAB design) and the treatment (phase B of the ABAB design) (Drotar, 2006). The data for the target behavior in the baseline phase (A) are compared to the data for that behavior in the next phase (B). In the second A phase, the treatment in phase B is withdrawn, and researchers can determine whether, or how quickly, the person's targeted behavior returns to baseline (for example, withdrawing behavior modification treatment and observing what happens with extinction). This second A phase addresses the question "Will any behavior change from the previous phase persist once treatment is withdrawn?" The treatment is then presented again in the second B phase, which essentially should obtain an effect related to the effect the first time the treatment was presented.

Like case studies, single-participant experiments consider only one individual, so the results can be specific to that individual and based on neurological, psychological, or social factors that may not apply to others, or at least not in the same combination. When researchers publish the results of single-participant experiments, they often wish to inform clinicians about possible interventions that might work for patients with the same problem and in similar circumstances.

Meta-Analysis

Despite the best efforts of researchers to minimize confounds, the results of any one study must be taken with a grain of salt; it's not clear whether researchers would obtain comparable results if the study were undertaken in somewhat different circumstances. Moreover, if a study's results are not statistically significant, it may simply indicate that not enough participants were tested. **Meta-analysis**

Single-participant experiments
Experiments with only a single participant.

Meta-analysis
A research method that statistically combines the results of a number of studies that address the same question to determine the overall effect.

TABLE **4.1** • Research Methods in Psychopathology

Research method	Important feature(s)	Drawback(s)
Experimental design	Use of independent and dependent variables and random assignment allows researchers to infer cause and effect	Most etiological factors that contribute to psychopathology cannot be studied with experiments (but experiments are often used to study the effects of treatment).
Quasi-experiments	Used when it is possible to identify independent and dependent variables, but random assignment of participants to groups is not possible; researchers can still infer cause and effect	Because random assignment isn't possible, possible confounds are difficult to eliminate.
Correlational research	Used when it is not possible to manipulate independent variables such as etiological factors; researchers can examine relationships between variables	Results indicate only *related* factors, not *causal* factors.
Case studies	Often descriptive, but can use various research methods applied to a single participant	Caution must be exercised in generalizing from the sole participant to others; there are many possible confounding factors.
Single-participant experiments	An experiment with one participant (and so random assignment isn't possible); cause and effect can be inferred	Caution must be exercised in generalizing from the sole participant to others; there are many possible confounding factors.
Meta-analysis	A statistical analysis that combines the results of a number of studies that examine the same general question to determine the overall effect	It is difficult to estimate the number of studies that failed to find an effect and thus were not published and not included in the analysis; the studies analyzed are often not of equal quality but their results are nevertheless weighted equally in the analysis.

TABLE **4.2** • Information Provided for Obtaining Informed Consent

When obtaining informed consent from participants, a researcher must give participants the following information:

(1) the purpose of the research, expected duration, and procedures;

(2) their right to decline to participate and to withdraw from the research once participation has begun;

(3) the foreseeable consequences of declining or withdrawing;

(4) reasonably foreseeable factors that may be expected to influence their willingness to participate such as potential risks, discomfort, or adverse effects;

(5) any prospective research benefits;

(6) limits of confidentiality;

(7) incentives for participation; and

(8) whom to contact for questions about the research and research participants' rights.

is a research method that statistically combines the results of a number of studies that address the same question. This strategy can be especially valuable when some studies show an effect but others do not (Rosenthal, 1991). Because a meta-analysis increases the size of the overall data set, it can help to determine whether or not certain variables are related; a meta-analysis can uncover a relationship that is not apparent in any single study, which considers only a single sample from a particular population. In many cases, when studies are considered together in a single meta-analysis, the effect emerges loud and clear. However, a meta-analysis is only as good as the quality of the studies that go into it; if studies are poorly designed or conducted, the conclusions from a meta-analysis of them will be shaky. Table 4.1 provides a summary of the different research methods we've discussed.

Ethical Guidelines for Research

We've mentioned several times that it would not be ethical to conduct certain kinds of experiments, but how do researchers decide which research studies are ethical and which are not? To address this question, psychologists have developed ethical guidelines for research, which are part of the overall ethical code for psychologists. For instance, before someone participates in a study, the investigator must provide information describing the study, as outlined in Table 4.2. If a person decides to participate after reading the information, he or she signs an *informed consent* form. By signing, the person acknowledges that he or she understands what is involved in the study and agrees to participate, knowing that he or she can withdraw from the study at any point (American Psychological Association, 2002).

GETTING THE PICTURE

If a researcher wanted to determine the extent to which being in a bar leads former alcoholics (who have stopped drinking) to relapse, which of the following designs (conveyed in the corresponding photos) would likely be considered unethical by an IRB—the bartender offers the participant a non-alcoholic drink (the photo on the left), or the bartender offers the participant an alcoholic drink (the photo on the right)? Answer: The photo on right: Offering the participant an alcoholic drink rather than soft drink needlessly increases the likelihood that the participant would relapse and creates too great a risk of harm.

Another ethical guideline for research is that investigators must *debrief* participants after a study is over. They must ask each participant about his or her experience, particularly about any negative aspects of the experience (in part so that the study can be adjusted to minimize possible negative experiences for future participants). Investigators must also clear up any misconceptions that the participant may have about the study (American Psychological Association, 2002).

In addition, agencies that fund research on psychopathology and treatment require that the study be reviewed and approved by an institutional review board (IRB) in the setting that hosts the study (e.g., hospital, university, or clinic). The IRB is composed of scientists, clinicians, and members of the community at large. The board evaluates each study's possible risks and benefits, and then decides whether the study should be approved. This serves as another check on any ethical issues that might arise while a study is being conducted or afterward.

Thinking Like A Clinician

Dr. Xavier treats people with compulsive gambling; she also conducts research on people with this disorder. Based on her experience, she believes that people who begin gambling compulsively in their teens and early 20s have a different type of problem than those who begin gambling compulsively in their 40s or later. What type of research design would you suggest she use (experimental, quasi-experimental, or correlational) to evaluate her hypothesis, and why? What might be some confounding variables she should try to control? What types of information would you want to know before generalizing from her results to other people with compulsive gambling?

☐ Research Challenges in Understanding Abnormality

Let's now examine the hypothesis about the relationship between experiencing a childhood loss and feeling depressed after a breakup in adulthood. How can we use the neuropsychosocial approach to understand why breaking up might lead some people to become depressed?

- We could investigate neurological mechanisms by which early loss, associated with helplessness, might make people more vulnerable to later depression.
- We could investigate psychological effects resulting from early loss, such as problems with emotional regulation.
- We could investigate social mechanisms, such as how economic hardships arising from the early loss created a higher baseline of response to daily stress.
- And, crucially, we could propose ways in which these possible factors might interact with one another. For example, perhaps daily financial stress not only increases the degree of worrying about money but such worrying in turn changes neurological functioning as well as social functioning (as preoccupying financial worries alter social interactions).

Whatever type of factors researchers investigate, each type comes with its own challenges, which affect the way a study is undertaken and which limit the conclusions that can be drawn from a study's results (Slavich et al., 2011). In what follows, we examine the major types of challenges to research on the nature and causes of abnormality from the neuropsychosocial perspective.

Challenges in Researching Neurological Factors

DSM-5 does not generally consider neurological factors when assigning diagnoses, but many researchers are exploring the possible role of neurological factors in causing psychological disorders. In fact, current findings about neurological factors are coming to play an increasingly large role in treatment.

With the exception of genetics, almost all techniques that assess neurological factors identify abnormalities in the structure or function of the brain. This assessment is done directly (e.g., with neuroimaging) or indirectly (e.g., with neuropsychological testing or measurements of the level of stress hormones in the bloodstream). Such abnormalities are associated (correlated) with specific disorders or symptoms. For instance, people with schizophrenia have larger-than-normal ventricles (the fluid-containing cavities in the brain), and other areas of the brain are correspondingly smaller (Vita et al., 2006). Like all other correlational studies, the studies that revealed the enlarged ventricles cannot establish causation; for example, this finding does not specify whether schizophrenia arises because of the effects of this brain abnormality, whether schizophrenia creates these abnormalities, or whether some third variable is responsible for the brain abnormality and for the mental disorder. Another limitation of research using neuroimaging is that we do not yet have a complete understanding of what different parts of the brain do. Thus, researchers cannot be sure about the implications of abnormalities in the structure or the functioning of any specific brain structure.

Nevertheless, the outlook is encouraging. Researchers do know a considerable amount about what specific parts of the brain do, and they are learning more every day. Also, they can use other techniques in combination with neuroimaging to learn which brain areas may play a role in causing or contributing to certain disorders. We will have more to say about neuroimaging research in subsequent chapters.

Challenges in Researching Psychological Factors

Scientists who study neurological factors examine the difficulties with the biological *mechanisms* that process information or that give rise to emotion. In contrast, scientists who study psychological factors examine specific mental contents, mental processes, behaviors, or emotions. Information about psychological factors typically is obtained from patients' self-reports, from reports by others close to patients, or from direct observations.

Biases in Mental Processes That Affect Assessment

Assessing mental contents, emotions, and behaviors via self-report or report by others can yield inaccurate information because of biases in what people pay attention to, remember, and report. Sometimes beliefs, expectations, or habits bias how participants respond, consciously or unconsciously. For instance, people who have anxiety disorders are more likely than others to be extremely attentive to stimuli that might be perceived as a threat (Cloitre et al., 1994; Mogg et al., 2000). In contrast, people with depression do not have this particular bias but tend to be biased in what they recall; they are more likely than people who are not depressed to recall unpleasant events (Watkins, 2002; Wisco & Nolen-Hoecksema, 2009). In fact, researchers have found that people in general are more likely to recall information consistent with their current mood than information that is inconsistent with their current mood (referred to as *mood-congruent memory bias*; Teasdale, 1983).

Research Challenges with Clinical Interviews

Patients' responses can be affected by whether they are asked questions by an interviewer or receive them in writing (see Figure 4.3). Consider a study in which participants were asked questions about their symptoms of either OCD or social phobia. When the questions were first asked by a clinician as part of an interview, participants tended not to report certain avoidance-related symptoms that they later did report on a questionnaire. In contrast, when participants completed the questionnaire first, they reported these symptoms both on the questionnaire and in the subsequent interview (Dell'Osso et al., 2002).

FIGURE **4.3 • How the Question Is Asked Affects the Answer** Patients may respond differently to a question, depending on whether they read it or are asked it by an interviewer (Dell'Osso et al., 2002).

Moreover, when interviewing family members or friends about a patient's behavior, researchers must keep in mind that these people may have their own biases. They may pay more attention to, and so be more likely to remember, particular aspects of a patient's behavior, and they may have their own views about the causes of the patient's behavior (Achenbach, 2008; Kirk & Hsieh, 2004). For example, when assessing children, researchers sometimes rely heavily on reports from others, such as parents and teachers; however, these individuals often do not agree on the nature or cause of a child's problems (De Los Reyes & Kazdin, 2004).

Research Challenges with Questionnaires

In psychopathology research, administering questionnaires is a relatively inexpensive way to collect a lot of data quickly. However, questionnaires must be designed carefully in order to avoid various biases. For example, one sort of bias arises when a range of alternative responses are presented. Some questionnaires provide only two choices in response to an item ("yes" or "no"), whereas other questionnaires give participants more than two choices (such as, "all the time," "frequently," "sometimes," "infrequently," or "never"). With more choices come more opportunities for bias: Twice a week might be interpreted as frequent by one person and infrequent by another. To reduce the effects of such bias, some questionnaires—such as the Posttraumatic Diagnostic Scale (Foa et al., 1997)—define the frequency choices in terms of specific numerical values (such as having "frequently" defined as three times a week).

In addition, the range of values on a scale is important. For example, consider the findings obtained when people were asked to rate how successful they have been in life. When asked to respond on a rating scale with numbers from −5 to +5, like this:

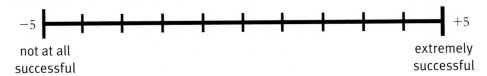

34% reported having been highly successful in life. When asked to respond on a scale with numbers from 0 to 10, like this:

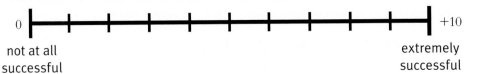

only 13% reported having been highly successful in life (Schwarz et al., 1991).

Response bias is another problem to avoid when designing questionnaires. **Response bias** refers to a tendency to respond in a particular way, regardless of what is being asked by the questions. For instance, some people, and members of some cultures in general, are more likely to check "agree" than "disagree," regardless of the content of the statement (Javeline, 1999; Welkenhuysen-Gybels et al., 2003). This type of response bias, called *acquiescence*, can be reduced by wording half the items negatively. Thus, if you were interested in assessing self-reported shyness in a questionnaire, you might include both the item "I often feel shy when meeting new people" and the item "I don't usually feel shy when meeting new people," which is simply a negative rewording of the first item.

Another type of response bias is **social desirability**: answering questions in a way that the respondent thinks makes him or her look good in a way that he or she thinks is socially desirable, even if the answer is not true. For instance, some people might not agree with the statement "It is better to be honest, even if others don't like you for it." However, they may think that they *should* agree and respond accordingly. In contrast to a social desirability bias, some people answer questions in a way that they think makes them "look bad" or look worse than they actually are. To compensate for these biases, many personality inventories have a scale that assesses the participant's tendency to answer in a socially desirable or falsely symptomatic manner. This scale is then used to adjust (or, in the language of testing, to "correct") the scores on the part of the inventory that measures traits.

Challenges in Researching Social Factors

Information obtained from and about people always has a context. For research on psychopathology, a crucial part of the context is defined by other people. Social factors arise from and characterize the setting (such as a home, hospital, outpatient clinic,

Response bias
The tendency to respond in a particular way, regardless of what is being asked by the question.

Social desirability
A bias toward answering questions in a way that respondents think makes them appear socially desirable, even if the responses are not true.

or university), the people administering the study, and the cultural context writ large. Challenges to conducting research on social factors that affect psychopathology include the ways that the presence or behavior of the investigator and the beliefs and assumptions of a particular culture can influence participants' responses.

Investigator-Influenced Biases

Like psychological factors, social factors are often assessed by self-report (such as patient's reports of financial problems), reports by others (such as family members' descriptions of family interactions or of a patient's behavior), and direct observation. Along with the biases we've already mentioned, the social interaction between investigator and participant can affect these kinds of data.

Experimenter Expectancy Effects

Experimenter expectancy effect refers to the investigator's intentionally or unintentionally treating participants in ways that encourage particular types of responses. The experimenter expectancy effect is slightly misnamed: It applies not only to experiments but to all psychological investigations in which an investigator interacts with participants. For instance, suppose that you are interviewing patients about their symptoms. It's possible that you might ask certain types of questions (such as about their social lives) with a particular tone of voice or facial expression, unintentionally suggesting the type of answer you hope to hear. Participants might, consciously or unconsciously, try to respond as they think you would like, perhaps exaggerating certain symptoms a bit. Such a social interaction can undermine the validity of the study.

To minimize the likelihood of experimenter expectancy effects, researchers often use a **double-blind design**: Neither the participants nor the investigator's assistant (who has contact with the participants) know the group to which each participant has been assigned or the predicted results of the study. Moreover, instructions given to participants or questions asked of them are standardized, so that all participants are treated in the same way.

Reactivity

Have you ever noticed that you were being watched while you were doing something? Did you find that you behaved somewhat differently simply because you knew that you were being observed? If so, then you have experienced **reactivity**—a behavior change that occurs when one becomes aware of being observed. When participants in a study know that they are observed, they may subtly (or not so subtly) change their behavior, leading the study to have results that may not be valid. One way to counter such an effect is to use hidden cameras, but this may raise ethical issues—many people (rightfully) object to being "spied on."

Cultural Differences in Evaluating Symptoms

Some researchers compare and contrast a given disorder in different cultures, trying to distinguish universal symptoms from symptoms that are found only in certain cultures. But assessing psychological and social factors in other cultures can be challenging. For one thing, many words and concepts do not have exact equivalents across languages, making full translation impossible. And even when two cultures share a language, the meaning of a word may be different in each culture. For example, when a comprehensive set of interview questions was translated into Spanish and administered to residents of Puerto Rico and Mexico, 67% of the questions had to be changed because the meanings of some

Experimenter expectancy effect
The investigator's intentionally or unintentionally treating participants in ways that encourage particular types of responses.

Double-blind design
A research design in which neither the participant nor the investigator's assistant knows the group to which specific participants have been assigned or the predicted results of the study.

Reactivity
A behavior change that occurs when one becomes aware of being observed.

Although reactivity may be decreased by observing participants via video camera, they can still be aware that they are being observed by others and modify their behavior accordingly.

of the Spanish words were understood differently by the two populations (Kihlstrom, 2002b).

In addition, members of different cultures may have different response biases. For instance, the Japanese consider it rude to say, "No," so we must be suspect of results from Japanese surveys that require Yes/No responses. Sampling biases may also vary across cultures. For example, women may be underrepresented in samples from certain countries in the Middle East.

Thinking Like A Clinician

Suppose you are reading about a psychologist who conducts research that is aimed at better understanding people who have pyromania—the intense urge to start fires—and why they start fires. The participants can come from two groups: those who've been arrested for arson and those who have interacted in a chat room for people with urges to start fires. To collect data, the researcher could either have participants complete an anonymous survey online or arrange to interview them over the phone. What biases might uniquely affect each method, and what biases might affect both? How could a researcher try to minimize these biases? Suppose some participants agree to have their brains scanned while they imagined lighting fires: How might an investigator use such neuroimaging information?

☐ Researching Treatment

Let's say that your interest in depression that follows breakups, plus your experiences at the counseling center helping students like Carlos, have led you to develop a new short-term treatment. In this treatment, which you have named "grief box therapy," you encourage patients to create "grief boxes"—boxes into which they place reminders of their recently ended relationships and objects that symbolize their feelings of loss and hopelessness. You—and others—will want to know whether your treatment is effective; is using grief boxes better for treating depression (specifically the sort following a breakup) than doing nothing? Is it better than other treatments?

Research on treatment has challenges above and beyond those we've already discussed for research on psychopathology. And such research faces different challenges, depending on whether the target of treatment is neurological, psychological, or social factors.

Researching Treatments That Target Neurological Factors

Researchers and clinicians want to answer several questions when a new medication is developed, when an existing medication is used in a new way (to treat different symptoms), or when a new biomedical procedure is developed:

- Is the new treatment more effective than no treatment?

- If a treatment is effective, is it because of its actual properties (such as a medication's particular ingredients) or because of patients' expectations about what the treatment will do?

- Is the treatment more effective than other treatments currently used for those symptoms or problems?

- What are the treatment's side effects, and are they troubling enough that patients tend to stop the treatment? How does this dropout rate compare to that for the other treatments?

To assess a treatment, researchers first need to determine what specific variables should be measured and to define what it means to be "effective." Research on treatment frequently relies on an experimental or quasi-experimental design; in such studies, the independent variables might be the type of treatment, a specific technique, or type or dose of medication. And the dependent variables (the things measured) might be any of several variables, such as neural activity, specific mental contents, behavior, or family functioning. These variables are often related to the symptoms listed in the DSM-5 criteria for the disorder under investigation.

Drug Effect or Placebo Effect?

One way to determine whether a treatment is effective is to compare it to no treatment. If people receiving the treatment are better off than those who don't receive any treatment, the treatment may have made the difference. But perhaps patients improve after taking a medication not because of the properties of the medication itself but because they expect to improve after taking it. In fact, many studies have confirmed that expecting a treatment to be helpful leads to improvement, even if the patients don't receive any actual treatment (Colloca & Miller, 2011; Kirsch, 2010; Kirsch & Lynn, 1999).

The best way to discover whether a medication is effective is to give a group of participants a *placebo*, an inert substance or a procedure that itself has no direct medical value. Often, a placebo is simply a sugar pill. A positive effect of such a medically inert substance or procedure is called a **placebo effect**. If patients who are given a sugar pill show the same improvement as patients who are given the pill with active ingredients, then a researcher can infer that the medication itself is not effective and that its apparent benefit is a result of the placebo effect.

The fact that people who suffer from certain disorders, including depression, sometimes improve following a placebo treatment (Kirsch, 2010; Kirsch et al., 2002) does not mean that their problem was imaginary or that they should throw away their medication. Rather, it seems that—for some people and for some disorders—the hope and positive expectations that go along with taking a medication (or undergoing a procedure) allow the body to mobilize its own resources to function better (Benedetti, 2009, 2010; Kirsch & Lynn, 1999; Scott et al., 2008).

Dropouts

On average, more than half of those who begin a treatment that is part of a research study do not complete the treatment—they drop out of the study (Kazdin, 1994; West, 2009); this reduction in the number of research participants during a study is called **attrition**. When attrition in a research study is different for different demographic groups (such as men versus women, younger people versus older ones, or people of different races), researchers can't easily draw definitive conclusions about how well the treatment would have worked for members of all the groups (Kendall et al., 2004; Lambert & Ogles, 2004).

Researching Treatments That Target Psychological Factors

Many of the research issues that arise with biomedical treatments also arise in research on treatments that target psychological factors. In addition, as shown in Table 4.3, research on treatments that target psychological factors may be designed to investigate which aspects of therapy in general, or of particular types of therapy—such as the grief box therapy—are most helpful. In this section we consider factors that influence research on treatments.

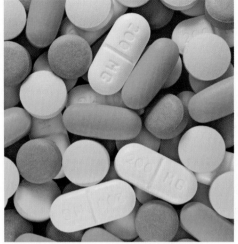

The placebo effect can be strengthened or weakened by the outward qualities of the placebo: Taking more placebo pills generally has a greater effect; capsules do a better job than pills; and injections do better than capsules. And (placebo) pills that are reported to be more expensive are more effective than "less expensive" ones (Waber et al., 2008).

Placebo effect
A positive effect of a medically inert substance or procedure.

Attrition
The reduction in the number of participants during a research study.

TABLE 4.3 • Treatment-Related Variables

Therapy variables	Patient variables	Therapist variables	Patient–therapist interaction variables
• Theoretical orientation • Specific techniques used	• Level of motivation and ability to change • Belief in the ability of treatment to help • Community resources available (social and financial support) • Preferred style of coping and relating to others • Preferred treatment focus: on symptoms or their meaning • Personality traits	• Enthusiasm for and belief in the treatment • Usual style of interacting (such as supportive or challenging) • Treatment focus: on symptoms or on their meaning • Empathic ability • Personality traits • Experience with the particular type of treatment	• Structure of the relationship (therapist as expert vs. therapist as coach) • Fit between patient's and therapist's personalities • Fit between patient's and therapist's treatment focus (symptoms vs. their meaning) • Sense of alliance between patient and therapist

Common Factors and Specific Factors

Just as placebos can provide relief even though they lack medically beneficial ingredients, the very act of seeing a therapist or counselor—or even setting up a meeting with one—may provide relief for some disorders (regardless of the specific techniques or theoretical approach of the therapist or counselor). Such relief may result from, at least in part, **common factors**, which are helpful aspects of therapy that are shared by virtually all types of psychotherapy. According to results from numerous studies (Lambert & Ogles, 2004; Wampold, 2010), common factors can include:

- opportunities to express problems;
- some explanation and understanding of the problems;
- an opportunity to obtain support, feedback, and advice;
- encouragement to take (appropriate) risks and achieve a sense of mastery;
- hope; and
- a positive relationship with the therapist.

Common factors, and certain patient characteristics—such as being motivated to change (Bohart & Tallman, 2010; Clarkin & Levy, 2004)—can contribute more to having a positive outcome from therapy than the specific techniques used. If the grief box therapy were effective, it might be because of such common factors and not something unique to your particular method.

The existence of common factors creates a challenge for researchers who are interested in determining the benefits of a particular type of treatment or technique. The characteristics that give rise to these unique benefits of a specific type of treatment are known as **specific factors**. For instance, when researching grief box therapy, you might want to investigate whether the process of creating the grief box provides benefits above and beyond the common factors that any therapy provides.

In fact, research has shown that common factors alone may not be *sufficient* to produce benefits in therapy for some disorders (Elliott et al., 2004; Kirschenbaum & Jourdan, 2005; Lambert, 2004); at least for some disorders, specific factors play a key role in treatment. The leftmost column in Table 4.3 notes specific factors—the therapy variables—that are the subject of research targeting psychological treatments. (In subsequent chapters, we will discuss research on treatments for specific disorders; such studies typically examine specific factors.)

Common factors
Helpful aspects of therapy that are shared by virtually all types of psychotherapy.

Specific factors
The characteristics of a particular treatment or technique that lead it to have unique benefits, above and beyond those conferred by common factors.

Is Therapy Better Than No Treatment?

Researchers have questioned whether people actually improve more by receiving therapy than they would have improved if they hadn't received any treatment. To address this question, researchers randomly assign participants to one of two groups: "treatment" and "no treatment." However, participants in the "no treatment" group are often assigned to a waiting list for treatment (which is ethically preferable to not providing any treatment at all), and thus this group is often called a *wait-list control group* (Kendall et al., 2004, Lambert & Bergin, 1994). Researchers usually assess the dependent variable, such as level of symptoms, in both groups at the beginning of the study, before treatment begins—this is their *baseline assessment*. Then, researchers assess the same variables again after the treatment period (for the wait-list control group, this means assessing symptom level after the same duration of time as that over which the treatment group received treatment); this is called the *outcome assessment*. Researchers then compare the results of the two groups, and may also assess the variables at a later follow-up point, called a *follow-up assessment* (see Figure 4.4).

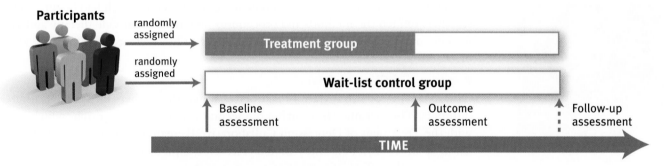

FIGURE **4.4 • Comparing a Treatment Group to a Wait-List Control Group** Participants are randomly assigned to one of two groups, a treatment group and a wait-list control group (although a study could have more than two groups). Generally, the dependent variables, such as intensity of symptoms, are assessed before the treatment period begins, to obtain a baseline. After treatment ends (or after the equivalent number of weeks for the wait-list control group), the dependent variables are again assessed (and may also be assessed later for follow-up) and the data from the two groups are compared.

Alternatively, instead of (or in addition to) a "no treatment" or wait-list control group, researchers may use a *placebo control group*, the members of which meet with a "therapist" with the same frequency as the members of the treatment group. The "placebo therapist" refrains from using any of the active treatment techniques employed in the treatment group, but patients still receive attention and some level of support. For a study of your grief box therapy, a placebo control group might consist of patients who meet with therapists who listen to their concerns or complaints—without grief boxes, social support, or any other specific interventions.

With either type of control group—wait-list or placebo—the symptoms of members of the control group might diminish simply with the passage of time. Thus, the crucial comparison is not whether people in the treatment group got better but rather how much more they improved than did the people in the control group.

Researchers have conducted such studies for over half a century. How did they answer the question of whether therapy works? With a resounding "yes." Therapy really does make a difference (Lambert & Ogles, 2004; Wampold, 2010). And, not surprisingly, treatment shows a larger effect when a treatment group is compared to a wait-list control group than when a treatment group is compared to a placebo group, which highlights the beneficial effects of common factors (Lambert & Ogles, 2004; Roth & Fonagy, 2005; Wampold, 2010).

But what does it really mean to say that therapy works? The results must have *clinical significance*, which means that they change a person's life in meaningful, practical ways. Assessments of clinical significance may be based on the patients' own perceptions, on observations of friends and family members of the patients, or on the therapists' judgment.

Is One Type of Therapy Generally More Effective Than Another?

With the advent of behavior therapy in the 1960s, some researchers asked whether one type of therapy is generally more effective than another. The initial results of such research were surprising: No type of therapy appeared to be more effective than another. This first generation of research on specific treatments found that, in general, any type of the treatments of psychological disorders led to better outcomes than no treatment, and no single treatment was superior to others. The latter finding became referred to as the *Dodo bird verdict* of psychotherapy (Luborsky et al., 1975), after the character in the book *Alice's Adventures in Wonderland* who states: "Everybody has won, and all must have prizes."

However, by the 1980s, a second generation of such research had begun, and researchers refined the methods and procedures they used to provide therapy and assess its outcome. Let's briefly consider key advances in how researchers study the effects of various psychotherapies.

Randomized Clinical Trials

Different types of therapy are in fact better suited than others for treating different disorders. This became clear during the second generation of research, which began with the Treatment of Depression Collaborative Research Program study (TDCRP; Elkin et al., 1985). This study used a research design analogous to the design used to measure the effect of a medication on symptoms of a medical disorder; this research design is referred to as a **randomized clinical trial** (**RCT**; also referred to as *randomized controlled trial*). RCTs have at least two groups—a treatment group and a control group (usually a placebo control)—and participants are randomly assigned to the groups (Kendall et al., 2004). RCTs may also involve patients and therapists at multiple sites in a number of cities.

RCTs are the best way to evaluate therapies because they use the scientific method to identify the specific factors that underlie a beneficial treatment. The independent variable is often the type of treatment or technique, as it was in the TDCRP, but it can be any other variable listed in Table 4.3. The dependent variable is usually some aspect of patients' symptoms—such as frequency or intensity—or quality of life.

RCTs generally require therapists to base their treatments on detailed manuals that provide session-by-session guidance and specify techniques to be used with patients. RCTs provide brief therapy, typically from 6 to 16 sessions. *Manual-based treatment* ensures that all therapists who use one particular approach provide similar therapy that is distinct from other types of therapy (Kendall et al., 2004; Nathan, Skinstad, & Dolan, 2000).

The TDCRP was designed to compare the benefits of four kinds of treatment for depression given over 16 weeks: interpersonal therapy (IPT, *interpersonal therapy,* a time-limited therapy that focuses on relationships; we will discuss this treatment in more detail in Chapter 5), cognitive-behavioral therapy (CBT), the antidepressant medication *imipramine* (which was widely used at the time of the study) together with supportive sessions with a psychiatrist, and a placebo medication together with supportive sessions with a psychiatrist. Various

Mary Evans Picture Library/Alamy

THE DODO SOLEMNLY PRESENTED THE THIMBLE, SAYING, "WE BEG YOUR ACCEPTANCE OF THIS ELEGANT THIMBLE."

Initially, studies designed to test the overall superiority of one form of psychotherapy over another did not find any one type of therapy to be more effective than any other. This finding has been called the *Dodo bird verdict*, in reference to the Dodo bird's proclamation in *Alice's Adventures in Wonderland*: "Everybody has won, and all must have prizes." However, the Dodo bird verdict was based on research of particular therapies available at that time, using less rigorous research methods than are generally used today (Beutler, 2000).

Randomized clinical trial (RCT)
A research design that has at least two groups—a treatment group and a control group (usually a placebo control)—to which participants are randomly assigned.

dependent variables were measured. The main results told an interesting story: At the 18-month follow-up assessment, the CBT group had a larger sustained effect and fewer relapses, especially compared with the imipramine group (Elkin, 1994; Shea et al., 1992). But when the most severely depressed patients in each group were compared, IPT and imipramine were found to have been more effective than CBT (Elkin et al., 1995). However, most important in this study, the quality of the "collaborative bond" between therapist and patient (which was assessed by independent raters who viewed videotapes of sessions) had an even stronger influence on treatment outcome than did the type of treatment (Krupnick et al., 1996).

The Importance of Follow-up Assessment

It's one thing for a type of therapy to have an immediate effect, but another—and usually more important—thing for it to produce enduring change. The TDCRP study followed patients for over 18 months after treatment ended, but some studies—because of financial or logistical constraints—do not make any follow-up assessment. This is unfortunate because one type of treatment may be more beneficial at the end of therapy, but those patients may have a higher rate of relapse a year later, leaving the patients in another treatment group better off in the long run (Kendall et al., 2004).

Allegiance Effect

Another issue in RCT research is the **allegiance effect**, in which studies conducted by investigators who prefer a particular theoretical orientation tend to obtain data that support that particular orientation (Luborsky et al., 1999). Specifically, RCT investigators who support one type of treatment tend to have patients who do better with that type of treatment, whereas patients in the same study (using the same manuals) whose investigators support a different type of treatment tend to do better with that treatment. This means that even the use of manuals is not enough to control all types of confounds completely.

Different Therapies for Different Disorders

The bottom line is that a specific type or types of therapy are in general best suited for treating specific types of disorders. We will discuss which types of therapy are best for which specific disorders in later chapters of this book. In fact, enough is now known about the effectiveness of particular types of therapy for particular disorders that clinicians should have an *evidence-based practice*; that is, for each patient, they should pick a treatment or set of techniques that research has shown to be effective for that patient's problem. (Such a judgment should also take into account sociocultural factors, as well as the therapist's preference for—and training in—a particular method.)

The Therapy Dose–Response Relationship

Is more treatment related to greater improvement? In other words, is a higher "dose" of therapy (more sessions) associated with a better "response"? This association between dose and response is referred to as the **dose–response relationship**, and research suggests that the general answer to this question is yes. More sessions are associated with a better outcome (Hansen, Lambert, & Forman, 2002; Shadish et al., 2000). In general, patients improve the most during the early phase of treatment (see Figure 4.5), and they continue to improve, but at diminishing rates, over time (Lutz et al., 2002). There are individual exceptions to this general pattern; people with more severe or entrenched problems, such as schizophrenia or personality disorders, may not show as much benefit in the early stages of therapy but rather may only improve over a longer period of time.

Russell Sadur/Getty Images

Should a therapist use aromatherapy— having patients smell certain plant-based essential oils—to treat psychological disorders? Aromatherapy is not an empirically supported treatment for psychological disorders (Louis & Kowalski, 2002). This technique is in the realm of pseudopsychology, where claims are supported primarily by case studies or poorly designed studies with few participants, often without an appropriate control group.

Allegiance effect
A pattern in which studies conducted by investigators who prefer a particular theoretical orientation tend to obtain data that supports that particular orientation.

Dose–response relationship
The association between more treatment (a higher dose) and greater improvement (a better response).

FIGURE **4.5 • The Dose–Response Relationship** Comparing a more stringent definition of "improvement" (Figure 4.5a) to a more liberal one (Figure 4.5b) makes it clear that the exact criteria for improvement determine the particular height and shape of the curve for the dose–response relationship. Source: Lambert et al., 2001.

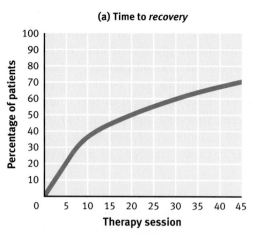

(a) Time to *recovery*

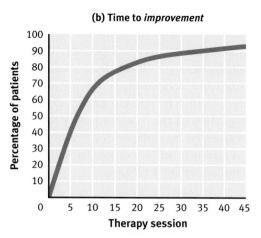

(b) Time to *improvement*

Among 10,000 patients with various psychological disorders, half attained clinically significant improvement (that is, recovery) by the 21st session. Another 25% attained clinically significant improvement by the 40th session. However, most people in RCTs, or in therapy in general, receive far fewer than 40 sessions.

Examining data using a lower standard of improvement—any positive change that was stable over time—and including patients who started out able to function reasonably well despite their disorder, yields different results: Half the patients attained this lower standard of improvement by the 7th session, with another 25% "improved" by the 14th session (Lambert, Hansen, & Finch, 2001).

The dose–response relationship is correlational; it does not indicate whether the increased number of sessions *causes* the increased response. It is possible that people who are feeling better during the course of treatment are more eager or more willing to attend additional sessions than those who are not responding as well. If this were the case, the response would be "causing" the increased dose (increased number of sessions) (Otto, 2002; Tang & DeRubeis, 1999). Alternatively, both dose and response could be affected by some other factor. As noted earlier in this chapter, correlation does not imply causation.

A curious finding invites speculation: People in the eastern part of the United States remain in treatment longer than those in the western part ("Fee, Practice, and Managed Care Survey," 2000). This is merely a correlation. One possible explanation is that people in the eastern part have a different definition of "improvement"; that is, they continue in treatment until their symptoms have improved more than those of their counterparts in the western part of the country. However, there are other possible explanations; perhaps you can think of some.

Researching Treatments That Target Social Factors

Research on treatment also may investigate the possible benefits of targeting social factors or the ways in which treatment may be affected by the larger social context.

Gender and Ethnicity of Patient and Therapist

All types of psychotherapy involve a relationship between two (or more) people. Therapists and patients may be similar with regard to racial or ethnic background and gender, or they may be different. Does such a difference matter? Research suggests not: Differences between patient and therapist in ethnicity, gender, and age do not systematically alter how effective therapy is (Fiorentine & Hillhouse, 1999; Lam & Sue, 2001; Maramba & Hall, 2002). However, with regard to gender, one study found that women and men are both less likely to drop out of treatment if they have a female therapist (Flaherty & Adams, 1998).

Nevertheless, some people prefer a therapist with a similar ethnic or racial background to their own. For those with a strong preference, such as some Asian Americans, matching the ethnicity of the patient and therapist may lead to better outcomes (Sue et al., 1994), and it can result in lower dropout rates among non-Whites (Fiorentine & Hillhouse, 1999; Sue et al., 1999).

Research on matching by ethnicity usually involves broad categories, such as patient and therapist who are both Asian American. However, when patients prefer a therapist from their own ethnic group, matching them with a therapist from a broadly similar group may not suffice. A Korean American patient, for instance, may prefer a Korean American therapist, but if such a therapist is not available, that patient may not prefer a Chinese American therapist over a therapist of any other background (Karlsson, 2005).

Some patients prefer a therapist who shares their ethnic background, and this common background may make a patient less likely to drop out of treatment. However, such matching does not appear to produce better treatment outcomes (Beutler et al., 1994; Garfield, 1994; Lam & Sue, 2001).

Culturally Sanctioned Placebo Effects

We've seen that placebos can be very powerful. It turns out that different products and practices may operate as placebos in different cultures. Throughout time and across cultures, people in the role of healer have used different methods to treat abnormality—and at least some of these methods may have relied on the placebo effect. For instance, among the Shona people of Africa, those who have psychological problems often visit a *n'anga* (healer), who may recommend herbal remedies or steam baths, or may throw bones to determine the source of a person's "bewitchment." Once the source is determined, the ill person's family is told how to mend community tensions that may have been caused by a family member's transgressing in some way (Linde, 2002). These *n'anga*'s treatments, if effective, may work because of the placebo effect and the common factors that arise from any treatment (even a placebo): hope, support, and a framework for understanding the problem and its resolution.

But members of nonindustrialized societies are not the only ones who are susceptible to such cultural forces. In Western cultures over the past two decades, people diagnosed with depression who are enrolled in studies to evaluate various medications have responded progressively more strongly to placebos (Walsh, Seidman, et al., 2002). Over that same two decades, pharmaceutical companies have increasingly advertised their medications directly to potential consumers, informing them about the possible benefits of the drugs. It is possible that the participants in these studies became more likely to believe that medication will be helpful than were participants 30 years ago, before direct advertising to consumers. And, in fact, research suggests that expectations that symptoms will improve may account for the lion's share of the positive response to an antidepressant among people with depression (Kirsch, 2010; Kirsch & Lynn, 1999; Walach & Maidhof, 1999).

TABLE 4.4 • Ethical Guidelines for Research on Experimental Treatments

Psychologists conducting research on experimental treatments must clarify to participants at the outset of the research:

(1) the experimental nature of the treatment;

(2) the services that will or will not be available to the control group(s) if appropriate;

(3) the means by which assignment to treatment and control groups will be made;

(4) available treatment alternatives if an individual does not wish to participate in the research or wishes to withdraw once a study has begun; and

(5) compensation for or monetary costs of participating.

Ethical Research on Experimental Treatments

Any research on treatment conducted by a psychologist is bound by the ethical guidelines for research and usually must be approved by an IRB, discussed earlier in the chapter. As shown in Table 4.4, research on a new type of treatment—an *experimental* treatment such as your grief box therapy—is subject to additional guidelines because the researchers may not be aware of some of the risks and benefits of the new treatment at the outset of the study.

Thinking Like A Clinician

Based on a survey, County Community College has found that 23% of its first-year students have anxiety or depression severe enough to meet the DSM-5 criteria. The college would like to institute a treatment program for these students. In fact, the staff at the counseling center plans to conduct a research study and offer several different types of treatment: medication (if appropriate), CBT with an individual therapist, and CBT in group therapy. Students can sign up for whichever type of treatment they prefer and can even receive more than one type of treatment. The results will be recorded and used to guide how treatment is provided in the future. Is this study a randomized clinical trial? Why or why not? What are some potential problems with the research design of this study? To learn whether each of the treatments is helpful to students, what questions should be asked of the students before and after the study?

▢ SUMMING UP

Using the Scientific Method to Understand Abnormality

• Researchers use the scientific method to understand and study psychopathology. In doing so, they observe relevant phenomena, identify a question to be answered, develop and test hypotheses that might answer the question, draw on the evidence to formulate a reasonable theory, and test the theory.

• Researchers systematically manipulate one or more independent variables (changing one at a time) and observe possible changes in the dependent variable(s). Researchers note how changes in the independent variable(s) are accompanied by changes in the dependent variable(s). In addition, researchers examine the possible contribution of confounds by using control groups or control conditions. To minimize unintentional bias, they randomly assign participants to groups and choose stimulus items to minimize confoundings. Experiments should have both internal and external validity.

• When random assignment is not ethical, desirable, or possible, the researchers may use a quasi-experimental design.

• Correlational research is used when independent variables cannot or should not be manipulated. Such studies allow researchers to investigate the relationship between two variables and note whether a change in one variable is associated with a change in the other. However, a correlation does not imply causation; it only indicates that the two variables are related.

• Case studies allow clinicians and researchers to examine one individual in detail. However, information from a particular case may not generalize to others.

• Meta-analysis allows researchers to aggregate the results of a number of related studies in order to determine the relations among certain variables.

• Psychologists have developed an ethical code of conduct that lays out guidelines for research, including that the research must be approved by an IRB, informed consent must be obtained from participants, and participants must be debriefed after a study is over.

Research Challenges in Understanding Abnormality

• Many studies that focus on neurological factors are correlational and so do not reveal how neurological factors may cause psychological disorders.

• Researchers must take care in phrasing questions in order to minimize various types of biases.

• Challenges in studying social factors can create challenges in studying other types of factors. Such challenges include experimenter-influenced biases, such as experimenter expectancy effects and reactivity.

Researching Treatment

• When studying medication, a placebo effect—rather than a true drug effect—may influence the results. Attrition rates can also distort the apparent effects of a treatment.

• A treatment may be effective because of common factors, as well as because of specific factors unique to that treatment. Control groups can allow researchers to examine specific factors and to rule out possible effects of some confounding variables. In general, therapy is more helpful than no treatment, but some specific therapies are better than others for some particular disorders.

• Some studies use a randomized clinical trial (RCT) design, which allows researchers to investigate the efficacy of specific factors or treatments; a RCT typically involves manual-based treatment. The results of such research generally suggest a dose–response relationship.

• Research on treatments that target social factors reveals that matching patients and therapists by ethnicity, gender, or age does not systematically alter the effectiveness of therapy. For patients with a strong preference, however, matching may lead to a better outcome.

Key Terms

Scientific method (p. 88)

Data (p. 88)

Replication (p. 88)

Hypothesis (p. 89)

Theory (p. 89)

Predictions (p. 89)

Experiments (p. 90)

Independent variable (p. 90)

Dependent variable (p. 90)

Confounding variables (p. 91)

Control group (p. 91)

Bias (p. 92)

Random assignment (p. 92)

Sampling bias (p. 92)

Population (p. 92)

Sample (p. 92)

Internal validity (p. 92)

External validity (p. 93)

Correlation (p. 93)

Correlation coefficient (p. 94)

Statistically significant (p. 94)

Epidemiology (p. 94)

Longitudinal studies (in studies of psychopathology) (p. 95)

Case studies (in studies of psychopathology) (p. 96)

Single-participant experiments (p. 97)

Meta-analysis (p. 97)

Response bias (p. 102)

Social desirability (p. 102)

Experimenter expectancy effect (p. 103)

Double-blind design (p. 103)

Reactivity (p. 105)

Placebo effect (p. 105)

Attrition (p. 105)

Common factors (p. 106)

Specific factors (p. 106)

Randomized clinical trial (RCT) (p. 108)

Allegiance effect (p. 109)

Dose–response relationship (p. 109)

More Study Aids

For additional study aids related to this chapter, including quizzes to make sure you've retained everything you've learned and a Student Video Activity exploring how researchers conducted an experiment on the placebo effect, go to: www.worthpublishers.com/launchpad/rkabpsych2e.

Masterfile

CHAPTER 5

Mood Disorders and Suicide

Kay Redfield Jamison, a psychologist who studies mood disorders, is uniquely qualified to report and reflect on such disorders. Not only has she made mood disorders her area of professional expertise, but she has also lived with such a disorder. In her memoir, *An Unquiet Mind* (1995), Jamison recounts her experiences. The youngest of three children in a military family, she and her siblings attended four different elementary schools—some in foreign countries—by the time she was in 5th grade. She describes her father, a meteorologist and Air Force officer, as enthusiastic, with infectious good moods, and impulsive, often giving the children gifts. However, he also suffered periods when he was immobilized by depression, and he generally had trouble regulating his emotions.

As we'll see in this chapter, Jamison herself developed difficulties regulating her emotions. She recounts that when she was a senior in high school, her mood became so dark that her thinking

> . . . was torturous. I would read the same passage over and over again only to realize that I had no memory at all for what I had just read. Each book or poem I picked up was the same way. Incomprehensible . . . I could not begin to follow the material presented in my classes. . . . It was very frightening . . . [my mind] no longer found anything interesting or enjoyable or worthwhile. It was incapable of concentrated thought and turned time and time again to the subject of death: I was going to die, what difference did anything make? Life's run was only a short and meaningless one, why live? . . . I dreaded having to talk with people, avoided my friends whenever possible. . . . (Jamison, 1995, pp. 37–38)

IN THIS PASSAGE, Jamison describes problems arising from her *mood*, a persistent emotion lurking in the background, regardless of what is occurring. The general category of psychological disorders referred to as **mood disorders** encompasses prolonged and marked disturbances in mood that affect how people feel, what they believe and expect, how they think and talk, and how they interact with others. In any particular year, about 9% of Americans experience a mood disorder (Centers for Disease Control and Prevention [CDC],

Mood disorders
Psychological disorders characterized by prolonged and marked disturbances in mood that affect how people feel, what they believe and expect, how they think and talk, and how they interact with others.

Psychologist Kay Redfield Jamison described being depressed as being intruded on by visual and auditory images related to death.

TABLE 5.1 • Three Types of Mood Disorder Episodes

- A *major depressive episode* involves symptoms of depression.

- A *manic episode* involves elated, irritable, or *euphoric* mood (mood that is extremely positive and may not necessarily be appropriate to the situation).

- A *hypomanic episode* involves elated, irritable, or euphoric mood that is less distressing or severe than mania and is different from the person's nondepressed state. That is, how a person behaves during a hypomanic episode is different from his or her usual state.

Major depressive episode (MDE)
A mood episode characterized by severe depression that lasts at least 2 weeks.

Anhedonia
A difficulty or inability to experience pleasure.

Psychomotor agitation
An inability to sit still, evidenced by pacing, hand wringing, or rubbing or pulling the skin, clothes, or other objects.

2010a). Mood disorders are among the leading causes of disability worldwide (World Health Organization [WHO], 2008).

DSM-5 distinguishes between two categories of mood disorders: depressive disorders and bipolar and related disorders. *Depressive disorders* are mood disorders in which someone's mood is consistently low; in contrast, *bipolar disorders* are mood disorders in which a person's mood is sometimes decidedly upbeat, perhaps to the point of being manic, and sometimes may be low. Mood disturbances that are part of depressive disorders and bipolar disorders are not the normal ups and downs that we all experience; they are more intense and longer lasting than just feeling "blue" or "happy."

DSM-5 defines three types of mood episodes as the foundations of mood disorders: *major depressive episode*, *manic episode*, and *hypomanic episode* (see Table 5.1). If a patient experiences different types of mood episodes over time (or a different mixture of such episodes), his or her diagnosis may change. We will first examine depressive disorders—what they are and their causes and treatments—and then consider bipolar and related disorders. Once we know more about mood disorders, we'll examine what is known about suicide and how to prevent it.

☐ Depressive Disorders

Most people who read Jamison's description of her senior year in high school would think that she was depressed during that time. But what, exactly, does it mean to say that someone is *depressed*? The diagnoses of depressive disorders are based on the presence of *building blocks*, which are episodes of specific types of abnormal mood. For depressive disorders, the building block that leads to a diagnosis is a *major depressive episode*; people whose symptoms have met the criteria for a major depressive episode (see Table 5.2) are diagnosed with *major depressive disorder*.

Major Depressive Episode

A **major depressive episode (MDE)** is characterized by severe depression that lasts at least 2 weeks. MDE is not itself a diagnosis but a set of symptoms that support making a diagnosis. Mood (which is a type of *affect*) is not the only symptom of a major depressive episode. As noted in Table 5.2, specific types of behavior and cognition also characterize depression.

Affect: The Mood Symptoms of Depression

During an MDE, a person can feel unremitting sadness, hopelessness, or numbness. Some people also suffer from a loss of pleasure, referred to as **anhedonia**, a state in which activities and intellectual pursuits that were once enjoyable no longer are, or at least are not nearly as enjoyable as they once were. Someone who liked to go to the movies, for instance, may no longer find it so interesting or fun and may feel that it is not worth the effort. Anhedonia can thus lead to social withdrawal. Other mood-related symptoms of depression include weepiness—crying at the drop of a hat or for no apparent reason—and decreased sexual interest or desire.

Behavioral and Physical Symptoms of Depression

People who are depressed make more negative comments, make less eye contact, are less responsive, speak more softly, and speak in shorter sentences than people who are not depressed (Gotlib & Robinson, 1982; Segrin & Abramson, 1994). Depression may also be evident behaviorally in one of two ways: *psychomotor agitation* or *psychomotor retardation*. **Psychomotor agitation** is an inability to sit still, evidenced by pacing, hand wringing, or rubbing or pulling the skin, clothes, or other objects. In contrast, **psychomotor retardation** is a slowing of motor functions indicated by slowed bodily movements and speech (in particular, longer pauses in answering) and lower volume, variety, or amount of speech. Psychomotor retardation, along with changes in appetite, weight, and sleep, are classified as *vegetative signs* of depression. Sleep changes can involve insomnia or, less commonly, **hypersomnia**, which is sleeping more hours each day than normal. In addition, people who are depressed may feel less energetic than usual or feel tired or fatigued even when they don't physically exert themselves.

Cognitive Symptoms of Depression

When in the grip of depression, people often feel worthless or guilt-ridden, may evaluate themselves negatively for no objective reason, and tend to ruminate over their past failings (which they may exaggerate). They may misinterpret ambiguous statements made by other people as evidence of their worthlessness. For instance, a depressed man, Tyrone, might hear a colleague's question "How are you?" as an indication that he is incompetent and infer that the colleague is asking the question because Tyrone's incompetence is so obvious. Depressed patients can also feel unwarranted responsibility for negative events, to the point of having delusions that revolve around a strong sense of guilt, deserved punishment, worthlessness, or personal responsibility for problems in the world. They blame themselves for their depression and for the fact that they cannot function well. During a depressive episode, people may also report difficulty thinking, remembering, concentrating, and making decisions, as author William Styron describes in Case 5.1. To others, the depressed person may appear distracted.

TABLE 5.2 • DSM-5 Criteria for Major Depressive Episode

A. Five (or more) of the following symptoms have been present during the same 2-week period and represent a change from previous functioning; at least one of the symptoms is either (1) depressed mood or (2) loss of interest or pleasure.

Note: Do not include symptoms that are clearly attributable to another medical condition.

1. Depressed mood most of the day, nearly every day, as indicated by either subjective report (e.g., feels sad, empty, or hopeless) or observation made by others (e.g., appears tearful). (**Note:** In children and adolescents, can be irritable mood.)

2. Markedly diminished interest or pleasure in all, or almost all, activities most of the day, nearly every day (as indicated by either subjective account or observation).

3. Significant weight loss when not dieting or weight gain (e.g., a change of more than 5% of body weight in a month), or decrease or increase in appetite nearly every day. (**Note:** In children, consider failure to make expected weight gain.)

4. Insomnia or hypersomnia nearly every day.

5. Psychomotor agitation or retardation nearly every day (observable by others; not merely subjective feelings of restlessness or being slowed down).

6. Fatigue or loss of energy nearly every day.

7. Feelings of worthlessness or excessive or inappropriate guilt (which may be delusional) nearly every day (not merely self-reproach or guilt about being sick).

8. Diminished ability to think or concentrate, or indecisiveness, nearly every day (either by subjective account or as observed by others).

9. Recurrent thoughts of death (not just fear of dying), recurrent suicidal ideation without a specific plan, or a suicide attempt or a specific plan for committing suicide.

B. The symptoms cause clinically significant distress or impairment in social, occupational, or other important areas of functioning.

C. The episode is not attributable to the physiological effects of a substance or another medical condition.

Reprinted with permission from the Diagnostic and Statistical Manual of Mental Disorders, Fifth Edition, (Copyright ©2013). American Psychiatric Association. All Rights Reserved.

CASE 5.1 • FROM THE INSIDE: Major Depressive Episode

Another experience of depression was captured by the writer William Styron in his memoir, *Darkness Visible*:

> In depression this faith in deliverance, in ultimate restoration, is absent. The pain is unrelenting, and what makes the condition intolerable is the foreknowledge that no remedy will come—not in a day, an hour, a month, or a minute. If there is mild relief, one knows that it is only temporary; more pain will follow. It is hopelessness even more than pain that crushes the soul. So the decision making of daily life involves not, as in normal affairs, shifting from one annoying situation to another less annoying—or from discomfort to relative comfort, or from boredom to activity—but moving from pain to pain. One does not abandon, even briefly, one's bed of nails, but is attached to it wherever one goes.
>
> (Styron, 1990, p. 62)

Note, however, that depression is *heterogeneous*, which means that people with depression experience these symptoms in different combinations. No single set of symptoms is shared by all people with depression (Hasler et al., 2004). Moreover, researchers distinguish two types of depression: Whereas with *typical* depression, people develop insomnia,

Psychomotor retardation
A slowing of motor functions indicated by slowed bodily movements and speech and lower volume, variety, or amount of speech.

Hypersomnia
Sleeping more hours each day than normal.

Normal bereavement has characteristics that are similar to symptoms of a major depressive episode: sad thoughts and feelings, problems concentrating, and changes in appetite and sleep. However, according to DSM-5, bereaved people are not generally overcome with feelings of hopelessness or anhedonia.

lose weight, and their poor mood persists throughout the day, with *atypical* depression, people sleep more, gain weight, and their mood brightens in response to positive events.

The symptoms of MDE develop over days and weeks. A **prodrome** is the early symptoms of a disorder or an episode, and the prodrome of an MDE may include anxiety or mild depressive symptoms that last weeks to months before fully emerging as a major depressive episode. An untreated MDE typically lasts approximately 4 months or longer (American Psychiatric Association, 2000). The more severe the depression, the longer the episode is likely to last (Melartin et al., 2004). About two thirds of people who have an MDE eventually recover from the episode completely and return to their previous level of functioning—referred to as the **premorbid** level of functioning. About 20–30% of people who have an MDE find that their symptoms lessen over time, to the point where they no longer meet the criteria for an MDE, but their depression doesn't completely resolve and may persist for years.

What distinguishes depression from simply "having the blues"? One distinguishing feature is the number of symptoms. People who are sad or blue generally have fewer than five of the symptoms listed in the DSM-5 diagnostic criteria for a major depressive episode (see Table 5.2). In addition, someone who is truly depressed has severe symptoms for a relatively long period of time and is unable to function effectively at home, school, or work.

One possible exception is grief—which can mimic most or even all symptoms of depression. In the previous edition of DSM (DSM-IV), people were not considered to have an MDE if the symptoms could have occurred because of the loss of a loved one; this was called the "bereavement exclusion." With this exclusion, if someone has symptoms of depression within a couple months after the loss of a loved one and isn't suffering from significantly impaired functioning, thoughts of suicide, or psychotic behavior, that person shouldn't be considered to have an MDE.

However, in DSM-5 this exception has been removed, and that change is controversial. On the one hand, those who support removing this exception claim that bereavement-related depression, unlike grief, is similar to an MDE unrelated to bereavement (Kendler et al., 2008; Lamb et al., 2010; Zisook et al., 2007). They claim that the hallmark of grief is waves of loss and emptiness and thoughts of the deceased, whereas the hallmark of depression is persistent and sad or depressed thoughts that are not solely focused on one thing. They stress that, left untreated, depression related to bereavement can be as harmful and debilitating as other forms of depression.

On the other hand, removing the bereavement exclusion may lead to overdiagnosis of—and rush to treat with medication or psychotherapy—people who are merely grieving (Wakefield & First, 2012). Training and careful evaluation are required to distinguish normal grieving from an MDE (Pies, 2013), but not every clinician will have that training nor the time to make the careful evaluation. This is particularly likely for family doctors or internists, who are at the forefront of diagnosing and treating depression (Katz, 2012; Montano, 1994).

Prodrome
Early symptoms of a disorder.

Premorbid
Referring to the period of time prior to a patient's illness.

Major depressive disorder (MDD)
A mood disorder marked by five or more symptoms of an MDE lasting more than 2 weeks.

Major Depressive Disorder

According to DSM-5, once someone's symptoms meet the criteria for a major depressive episode, he or she is diagnosed as having **major depressive disorder (MDD)**—five or more symptoms of an MDE lasting more than 2 weeks. Moreover, the clinician specifies whether *mixed features* characterize the mood episode—whether the person has some symptoms of mania or hypomania (to be discussed later) but not enough of these sorts of symptoms to meet the criteria for those mood episodes. The mental health professional also specifies whether this is the first or a recurrent episode. Thus, for example, after Kay Jamison had her first major depressive episode, she had the diagnosis of MDD, *single episode*. More than half of those who have had a single depressive episode go on to have at least one additional episode, noted as *recurrent depression*. Some people have increasingly frequent episodes over time, others have clusters of episodes, and still others have isolated depressive episodes followed by several years without symptoms (American Psychiatric Association, 2000; McGrath et al., 2006). DSM-5 allows mental health professionals to rate the patient's depression as mild, moderate, or severe.

Major depressive disorder leads to lowered productivity at work—both from missing days on the job and from *presenteeism*, being present but being less productive than normal (Adler et al., 2006; Druss et al., 2001; Stewart et al., 2003). For people whose jobs require high levels of cognitive effort, even mild memory or attentional difficulties may disrupt their ability to function adequately at work.

Sometimes recurrent depression follows a seasonal pattern, occurring at a particular time of year. Previously referred to as *seasonal affective disorder*, this variant of MDD commonly is characterized by recurrent depressive episodes, hypersomnia, increased appetite (particularly for carbohydrates), weight gain, and irritability. These symptoms usually begin in autumn and continue through the winter months. The symptoms either disappear or are much less severe in the summer. Surveys find that approximately 4–6% of the general population experiences a winter depression, and the average age of onset is 23 years. The disorder is four times more common in women than in men (American Psychiatric Association, 2000). Winter depression often can be treated effectively with **phototherapy** (also called *light-box therapy*), in which full-spectrum lights are used as a treatment (Golden et al., 2005).

MDD is common in the United States: Up to 20% of Americans will experience it at some point during their lives (Kessler et al., 2003). The documented rate of depression in the United States is increasing (Lewinsohn et al., 1993; Rhode et al., 2013), perhaps because of increased stressors in modern life or decreased social support; in addition, at least part of this increase may simply reflect higher reporting rates. Depression is currently associated with more than $30 billion of lost productivity among U.S. workers annually (Stewart et al., 2003).

Evidence also suggests that the risk of developing depression is increasing for each **age cohort**, a group of people born in a particular range of years. The risk of developing depression is higher among people born more recently than those born during earlier parts of the previous century. In addition, if someone born more recently does develop depression, that person probably will first experience it earlier in life than someone in an older cohort. Table 5.3 provides more facts about MDD.

In some cases, such as that of Marie Osmond in Case 5.2, depression emerges during pregnancy or within 4 weeks of giving birth; depression in this context is designated as having a *peripartum onset* (Wisner et al., 2013). Those most at risk for peripartum depression are women who have had recurrent depression before giving birth (Forty et al., 2006).

Phototherapy can be helpful to people who have winter depression. Typically, a person using phototherapy sits near special lights for an average of 30 minutes per day.

Phototherapy
Treatment for depression that uses full-spectrum lights; also called *light-box therapy*.

Age cohort
A group of people born in a particular range of years.

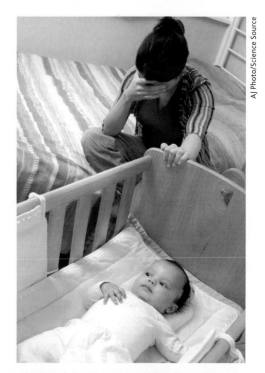

Although depression can arise after giving birth, for many women "postpartum" depression may actually begin during pregnancy, particularly the latter half, and persist after the birth.

Persistent depressive disorder (dysthymia)
A depressive disorder that involves as few as two symptoms of a major depressive episode but in which the symptoms persist for at least 2 years.

Disruptive mood dysregulation disorder (DMDD)
A depressive disorder in children characterized by persistent irritability and frequent episodes of out-of-control behavior.

CASE 5.2 • FROM THE INSIDE: Peripartum Onset of Depression

After the birth of her seventh child, Marie Osmond developed peripartum depression:

I'm collapsed in a pile of shoes on my closet floor. . . . I sit with my knees pulled up to my chest. I barely move. It's not that I want to be still. I am numb. I can tell I'm crying, but it's not like tears I've shed before. My eyes feel as though they have moved deep into the back of my head. There is only hollow space in front of them. Dark, hollow space. I am as empty as the clothing hanging above me. Despite my outward appearance, I feel like a lifeless form.

I can hear the breathing of my sleeping newborn son in his bassinet next to the bed. My ten-year-old daughter, Rachael, opens the bedroom door and whispers, "Mom?" into the room, trying not to wake the baby. Not seeing me, she leaves. She doesn't even consider looking in the closet on the floor. Her mother would never be there. She's right. This person sitting on the closet floor is nothing like her mother. I can't believe I'm here myself. I'm convinced that I'm losing my mind. This is not me.

I feel like I'm playing hide-and-seek from my own life, except that I just want to hide and never be found. I want to escape my body. I don't recognize it anymore. I have lost any resemblance to my former self. I can't laugh, enjoy food, sleep, concentrate on work, or even carry on a conversation. I don't know how to go on feeling like this: the emptiness, the endless loneliness. Who am I? I can't go on.

(Osmond et al., 2001)

Depression often occurs along with another disorder. In fact, depression and anxiety disorders co-occur about 50% of the time. Because of this high comorbidity, researchers propose that the two types of disorders have a common cause, presently unknown. In addition, although not common, depression can occur with *psychotic features*—hallucinations (e.g., in which a patient can feel that his or her body is decaying) or delusions (e.g., in which the patient believes that he or she is evil and living in hell).

Depression in Children and Adolescents

In a given 6-month period, 1–3% of elementary-school children and 5–8% of teenagers are depressed (Garber & Horowitz, 2002; Lewinsohn & Essau, 2002). Moreover, some clinicians and researchers are reporting depression among preschool children, evidenced by avoidance, decreased enthusiasm, and increased anhedonia (Luby et al., 2006). Younger children who are depressed are not generally considered to be at high risk of developing depression in adulthood. However, those who first become depressed as teenagers are considered to be at high risk for being depressed as adults (Lewinsohn, Rohde, et al., 1999; Rhode et al., 2013; Weissman, Wolk, Wickramaratne, et al., 1999; Weissman, Wickramaratne, et al., 2006). Teenage depression has far-reaching effects: Depressed teens are more likely than their nondepressed peers to drop out of school or to have unplanned pregnancies (Waslick et al., 2002).

Persistent Depressive Disorder

When symptoms of major depressive disorder persist for a long period of time, the person may be diagnosed with **persistent depressive disorder (dysthymia)**, characterized by depressed mood and as few as two

---

TABLE 5.3 • Major Depressive Disorder Facts at a Glance

Prevalence

- Approximately 10–25% of women and 5–12% of men will develop MDD over their lifetimes, although some studies find even higher rates (Rhode et al., 2013). Before puberty, however, boys and girls develop MDD in equal numbers (Kessler et al., 2003).

- People with different ethnic backgrounds, education levels, incomes, and marital statuses are generally afflicted equally (Kessler et al., 2003; Weissman et al., 1991).

Comorbidity

- Most people with MDD also have an additional psychological disorder (Rush et al., 2005), such as an anxiety disorder (Barbee, 1998; Kessler et al., 2003) or substance use disorder (Rush et al., 2005).

Onset

- MDD can begin at any age, with the average age of onset in the mid-20s, although people are developing MDD at increasingly younger ages (Rhode et al., 2013).

Course

- Among people who have had a single MDE, approximately 50–65% will go on to have a second episode (Angst et al., 1999; Solomon et al., 2000).

- Those who have had two episodes have a 70% chance of having a third, and those who have had three episodes have a 90% chance of having a fourth.

Gender Differences

- Women are approximately twice as likely as men to develop MDD (Kessler, 2003; Rhode et al., 2013).

- Some women report that depressive symptoms become more severe premenstrually.

Unless otherwise noted above, the source for information is American Psychiatric Association, 2013.

Disruptive Mood Dysregulation Disorder: Overlabeling of Tantrums?

Disruptive mood dysregulation disorder (DMDD) is a depressive disorder in children characterized by persistent irritability and frequent episodes of out-of-control behavior. It is supposed to be a more accurate description of kids who have out-of-control rage episodes and were incorrectly labeled as having bipolar disorder and then were (inappropriately) treated for that disorder. The criteria for using this diagnosis, which is brand new in DSM-5, include:

- Severe, recurrent temper outbursts, including verbal or physical aggression, with a duration or intensity that is out of proportion to the situation and inconsistent with the child's developmental level.
- These outbursts occur at least three times a week, on average.
- Even between outbursts, mood is persistently irritable or angry.
- This pattern starts between ages 6 and 10, occurs in at least two settings, continues for at least 1 year without letting up for 3 months, and is not exclusively the result of another mental disorder.

On the one hand, just as a diagnosis of bipolar disorder was overused to describe children with out-of-control rage episodes, a diagnosis of DMDD might label as mentally ill children who merely have a lot of tantrums, perhaps simply as a way to gain attention. Moreover, diagnosing a child with DMDD might focus on—and lead to treatment of—the child when the real problem is in the family.

On the other hand, the specifics of the criteria (e.g., severity, frequency, duration) should prevent diagnosing children who merely are sometimes grumpy or throw occasional tantrums. To apply this diagnosis, the child's irritable mood must be *persistent* and daily, even when there is no reinforcement (such as attention) for a tantrum. The rages must occur in at least two settings (e.g., school and home) and not be an expected response to a home or school situation. This diagnosis might lead to fewer such children being put on bipolar medication because they will no longer be considered to have bipolar disorder.

CRITICAL THINKING Even with narrow criteria designed to prevent inappropriate diagnosis of bipolar disorder, won't some clinicians apply (and overuse) this diagnosis to children who are merely "difficult" attention seekers? How can we prevent this?

(James Foley, College of Wooster)

other depressive symptoms that last for at least 2 years and that do not recede for longer than 2 months at any time during that period (see Table 5.4). Note that people can come to be diagnosed with this disorder if they have fewer symptoms of depression than necessary for MDD but have these symptoms for at least 2 years or they have MDD that lasts for at least 2 years (also referred to as *chronic* depression).

Because symptoms are chronic, people with persistent depressive disorder often incorporate the symptoms into their enduring self-assessment, seeing themselves as incompetent or uninteresting. Whereas people with shorter-lasting MDD see their symptoms as happening *to* them, people with persistent depressive disorder often view their symptoms as an integral part *of* themselves ("This is just how I am"), like Mr. A, in Case 5.3. Moreover, people with persistent depressive disorder are less likely to experience the vegetative signs associated with an MDE (psychomotor retardation and changes in sleep, appetite, and weight; American Psychiatric Association, 2000). In addition, people who have persistent depressive disorder are generally younger than those with MDD. See Table 5.5 for more facts about persistent depressive disorder.

TABLE 5.4 • DSM-5 Diagnostic Criteria for Persistent Depressive Disorder (Dysthymia)

A. Depressed mood for most of the day, for more days than not, as indicated by either subjective account or observation by others, for at least 2 years.

Note: In children and adolescents, mood can be irritable and duration must be at least 1 year.

B. Presence, while depressed, of two (or more) of the following:

1. Poor appetite or overeating.
2. Insomnia or hypersomnia.
3. Low energy or fatigue.
4. Low self-esteem.
5. Poor concentration or difficulty making decisions.
6. Feelings of hopelessness.

C. During the 2-year period (1 year for children and adolescents) of the disturbance, the individual has never been without the symptoms in Criteria A and B for more than 2 months at a time.

D. Criteria for a major depressive disorder may be continuously present for 2 years.

E. There has never been a manic episode or a hypomanic episode, and criteria have never been met for cyclothymic disorder.

F. The disturbance is not better explained by a persistent schizoaffective disorder, schizophrenia, delusional disorder, or other specified or unspecified schizophrenia spectrum and other psychotic disorder.

G. The symptoms are not attributable to the physiological effects of a substance (e.g., a drug of abuse, a medication) or another medical condition (e.g., hypothyroidism).

H. The symptoms cause clinically significant distress of impairment in social, occupational or other important areas of functioning.

TABLE 5.5 • Persistent Depressive Disorder Facts at a Glance

Prevalence

- In a given year, 2% of Americans have persistent depressive disorder.

Comorbidity

- Compared to people with MDD, those with persistent depressive disorder are more likely to have at least one other psychological disorder, particularly an anxiety disorder or substance use disorder.

Onset

- This disorder tends to emerge earlier than MDD.

Course

- The course of persistent depressive disorder is, by its nature, chronic; symptoms are less likely to fully resolve than with an MDE.

Gender Differences

- Boys and girls are equally likely to develop persistent depressive disorder.
- In adulthood, women are two to three times more likely than men to develop persistent depressive disorder.

Source: The source for information is American Psychiatric Association, 2013.

CASE 5.3 • FROM THE INSIDE: Persistent Depressive Disorder

Mr. A, a 28-year-old, single accountant, sought consultation because, he said, "I feel I am going nowhere with my life." Problems at work included a recent critical job review because of low productivity, conflicts with his boss, and poor management skills. His fiancée recently postponed their wedding because she has doubts about their relationship, especially his remoteness, critical comments, and lack of interest in sex.

Describing himself as a pessimist who has difficulty experiencing pleasure or happiness, Mr. A has long felt a sense of hopelessness—of life not being worth living. His mother was hospitalized with [peripartum] depression after the birth of his younger sister; his father had a drinking problem. His high school classmates found him gloomy and "not fun."

Although not troubled by thoughts of suicide nor significant vegetative signs of depression, Mr. A. does have months when his concentration is impaired, his energy level is lowered, and his interest in sex wanes. At such times, he withdraws from other people (although he always goes to work), staying in bed on weekends.

(Adapted from Frances & Ross, 1996, pp. 123–124)

Understanding Depressive Disorders

How do depressive disorders arise? Why do some people, but not others, suffer from them? Like all other psychological disorders, depressive disorders are best understood as arising from neurological, psychological, and social factors and the feedback loops among them. However, we must note that many of the factors that have been identified are correlational. As you know, correlation does not imply causation. In some cases, there is evidence for causal factors, but in most cases we cannot know whether a specific factor gives rise to depression or vice versa—or whether some third factor gives rise to both.

Neurological Factors

Neurological factors that contribute to depressive disorders can be classified into three categories: brain systems, neural communication, and genetics. Stress-related hormones—which underlie a specific kind of neural communication—are particularly important in understanding depressive disorders.

Brain Systems

Studies of depressed people have shown that they have unusually low activity in a part of the frontal lobe that has direct connections to the amygdala (a brain structure that is involved in fear and other strong emotions) and to other brain areas involved in emotion (Kennedy et al., 1997). The frontal lobe plays a key role in regulating other brain areas, and signals from it can inhibit activity in the amygdala. This finding hints that the depressed brain is not as able as the normal brain to regulate emotion. Moreover, this part of the frontal lobe has connections to the brain areas that produce the neurotransmitters dopamine, serotonin, and norepinephrine. Thus, this part of the frontal lobe may be involved in regulating the amounts of such neurotransmitters. This is important because these substances are involved in reward and emotion, which again hints that the brains of these people are not regulating emotion normally. Researchers have refined this general observation and reported that one aspect of depression—lack of motivated behavior—is specifically related to reduced activity in the frontal and parietal lobes (Milak et al., 2005).

Neural Communication

Researchers have long known that the symptoms of depression can be alleviated by medications that alter the activity of serotonin or norepinephrine (Arana & Rosenbaum, 2000). Indeed, when this fact was first discovered, some researchers thought that the puzzle of depression was nearly solved. However, we now know that the story is not so simple: Depression is not caused by too much or too little of any one specific neurotransmitter. Instead, the disorder arises in part from complex interactions among numerous neurotransmitters and depends on how much of each is released into the synapses, how long each neurotransmitter lingers in the synapses, and how the neurotransmitters interact with receptors in other areas of the brain that are involved in the symptoms of depression (Nemeroff, 1998).

Stress-Related Hormones

The chemical story doesn't end with neurotransmitters. Nemeroff (1998, 2008) formulated the *stress–diathesis model* of depression (which is to be distinguished from the general *diathesis–stress model*, discussed in Chapter 1). The stress–diathesis model of depression focuses on a part of the brain involved in the fight-or-flight response, the hypothalamic–pituitary–adrenal axis (HPA axis). The HPA axis is particularly important because it governs the production of the hormone cortisol, which is secreted in larger amounts when a person experiences stress (see Figure 5.1). According to the stress–diathesis model, people with depression have an excess of cortisol circulating in their blood, which makes their brains prone to overreacting when they experience stress.

Moreover, this stress reaction, in turn, alters the serotonin and norepinephrine systems, which underlie at least some of the symptoms of depression. Antidepressant medications can lower people's cortisol levels and also decrease their depressive symptoms (Deuschle et al., 2003; Werstiuk et al., 1996).

FIGURE **5.1** • **The HPA Axis** Stress activates the hypothalamus, which releases corticotropin-releasing factor (CRF), which in turn stimulates the pituitary gland to release adrenocorticotropic hormone (ACTH), which then leads the adrenal glands to release cortisol. According to the stress–diathesis model of depression, people who become depressed have high levels of cortisol, which leads to heightened reactivity to stress and increased serotonin levels.

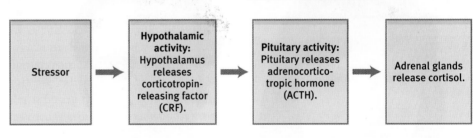

The stress–diathesis model of depression receives support from several sources (Nemeroff, 2008). For instance, higher levels of cortisol are associated with decreases in the size of the hippocampus, which thereby impairs the ability to form new memories (of the sort that later can be voluntarily recalled)—which in turn may contribute to the decreased cognitive abilities that characterize depression. And, in fact, researchers have reported that parts of this brain structure are smaller in depressed people than in people who are not depressed (Neumeister et al., 2005; Neumeister et al., 2005), which suggests that stress affects the symptoms of depression in part by altering levels of cortisol, which in turn impairs the functioning of the hippocampus.

Genetics

Twin studies show that when one twin of a monozygotic (identical) pair has MDD, the other twin has a risk of also developing the disorder that is four times higher than when the twins are dizygotic [(fraternal) (Bowman & Nurnberger, 1993; Kendler et al., 1999a)]. Because monozygotic twins basically share all of their genes but dizygotic twins share only half of their genes, these results point to a role for genetics in this disorder. One possibility is that genes influence how a person responds to stressful events (Costello et al., 2002; Kendler et al., 2005). If a person is sensitive to stressful events, the sensitivity could lead to increased HPA axis activation (Hasler et al., 2004), which in turn could contribute to depression.

However, genes are not destiny. The environment clearly plays an important role in whether a person will develop depression (Hasler et al., 2004; Rice et al., 2002). Even with identical twins, if one twin is depressed, this does not guarantee that the co-twin will also be depressed—despite their having basically the same genes. Whether a person becomes depressed depends partly on his or her life experiences, including the presence of hardships and the extent of social support.

Psychological Factors

Particular ways that people think about themselves and events, in concert with stressful or negative life experiences, are associated with an increased risk of depression. In the following sections we consider psychological factors that can influence whether a person develops depression; these factors range from biases in attention to the effects of different ways of thinking to the results of learning.

Attentional Biases

People who are depressed are more likely to pay attention to sad or angry stimuli. For instance, they will pay more attention to sad or angry faces than to faces that display positive emotions (Gotlib, Kasch, et al., 2004; Gotlib, Krasnoperova, et al., 2004; Leyman et al., 2007); people who do not have this psychological disorder spend equal time looking at faces that express different emotions. This attentional bias has also been found for negative words and scenes, as well as for remembering depression-related—versus neutral—stimuli (Caseras et al., 2007; Gotlib, Kasch, et al., 2004; Mogg et al., 1995). Such an attentional bias may leave depressed people more sensitive to other people's sad moods and to negative feedback from others, compounding their depressive thoughts and feelings.

Dysfunctional Thoughts

As discussed in Chapter 2, Aaron Beck proposed that *cognitive distortions* are the root cause of many disorders. Beck (1967) has suggested that people with depression tend to have overly negative views about: (1) the world, (2) the self, and (3) the future, referred to as the *negative triad of depression*. These distorted views can cause and maintain chronically depressed feelings and depression-related behaviors. For instance, a man who doesn't get the big raise he hoped for might respond with cognitive distortions that give rise to dysfunctional thoughts. He might think that he isn't "successful" because he didn't get the raise and therefore that he must be worthless (notice the circular reasoning). This man is more likely to become depressed than he would be if he didn't have such dysfunctional thoughts (Gibb et al., 2007).

Rumination and Attributional Style

While experiencing negative emotions, some people reflect on these emotions and the events that led to them; during such *ruminations*, they might say to themselves: "Why do bad things always happen to me?" or "Why did they say those hurtful things about me? Is it something I did?" (Nolen-Hoeksema & Morrow, 1991). Such ruminative thinking has been linked to depression (Just & Alloy, 1997; Nolen-Hoeksema, 2000; Nolen-Hoeksema & Morrow, 1991, 1993).

◎ GETTING THE PICTURE

In contrast to people who are not depressed, depressed people are more likely to pay attention to which of these two photos? Answer: The photo on the right; paying attention to sad or angry faces will also make such faces more likely to be remembered than happy faces.

People who consistently attribute negative events to their own qualities—called an *internal attributional style*—are more likely to become depressed. In one study, mothers-to-be who had an internal attributional style were more likely to be depressed 3 months after childbirth than were mothers-to-be who had an *external attributional style*—blaming negative events on qualities of others or on the environment (Peterson & Seligman, 1984). Similarly, college students who tended to blame themselves (rather than external factors) for negative events were more likely than those who did not to become depressed after receiving a bad grade (Metalsky et al., 1993).

Three particular aspects of attributions are related to depression: whether the attributions are *internal* or *external*, *stable* (enduring causes) or *unstable* (local, transient causes), and *global* (general, overall causes) or *specific* (particular, precise causes). People who tend to attribute negative events to internal, stable, and global factors have a *negative attributional style*. These people not only make negative predictions about the future (e.g., "Even if I find another girlfriend, she'll dump me too," Abramson et al., 1999) but also are vulnerable to becoming depressed when negative events occur (Abramson et al., 1978).

In fact, people who consistently make stable and global attributions for negative events—whether to internal or external causes—are more likely to feel hopeless in the face of negative events and come to experience *hopelessness depression*, a form of depression in which hopelessness is a central element (Abramson et al., 1989).

⬡ GETTING THE PICTURE

People with a negative attributional style are likely to attribute which adverse situation to negative and enduring aspects of themselves? Answer: People in a car accident, because they are more likely to blame the accident on enduring qualities such as poor driving or lack of attention to the road. In contrast, people who have a negative attributional style are less likely to blame themselves for a natural disaster.

Learned Helplessness

Hopelessness depression is not always based on incorrect attributions. It can arise from situations in which undesirable outcomes *do* occur and the person *is* helpless to change the situation, such as may occur when children are subjected to physical abuse or neglect (Widom et al., 2007). Such circumstances lead to *learned helplessness*, in which a person gives up trying to change or escape from a negative situation (Overmier & Seligman, 1967; see Chapter 2 for a more detailed discussion). For example, people in abusive relationships might become depressed if they feel that they cannot escape the relationship and that no matter what they do, the situation will not improve.

Social Factors

Depression is also associated with a variety of social factors, including stressful life events (including in personal relationships), social exclusion, and social interactions (which are affected by culture). These social factors can affect whether depression develops or persists.

Stressful Life Events

In approximately 70% of cases, an MDE occurs after a significant life stressor, such as getting fired from a job or losing an important relationship. Such events are particularly likely to contribute to a first or second depressive episode (Lewinsohn, Allen, et al., 1999; Tennant, 2002).

It might seem obvious that negative life events can lead to depression, but separating possible confounding factors and trying to establish causality have challenged researchers. For instance, people who are depressed (or have symptoms of depression) may have difficulty doing their job effectively; they may experience stressors such as problems with their coworkers and supervisors, job insecurity, or financial worries. In such cases, the depressive symptoms may *cause* the stressful life events, not be caused by them. Alternatively, some people, by virtue of their temperament, may seek out situations or experiences that are stressful; for example, some soldiers volunteer to go to the front line (Foley et al., 1996; Lyons et al., 1993). The point is that the relationship between stressful life events and depression may not be as straightforward as it might seem.

Social Exclusion

Feeling the chronic sting of social exclusion—being pushed toward the margins of society—is also associated with depression. For instance, those who are the targets of prejudice are more likely than others to become depressed. Such groups include homosexuals who experience community alienation or violence (Mills et al., 2004), those from lower socioeconomic groups (Field et al., 2006; Henderson et al., 2005; Inaba et al., 2005), and, in some cases, the elderly (Hybels et al., 2006; Sachs-Ericsson et al., 2005).

Some studies find that Latinos and African Americans experience more depression than other ethnic groups in the United States; a closer look at the data, however, suggests that socioeconomic status, rather than ethnic or racial background per se, is the variable associated with depression (Bromberger et al., 2004; Gilmer et al., 2005).

Social Interactions

To a certain extent, emotions can be contagious: People can develop depression, sadness, anxiety, or anger by spending time with someone who is already in such a state (Coyne, 1976; Segrin & Dillard, 1992). For instance, one study found that roommates developed symptoms of depression after 3 weeks of living with someone who was depressed (Joiner, 1994), and other studies find similar results (Haeffel & Hames, in press).

Another factor associated with depression is a person's *attachment style* in infancy, which can affect the way adults typically interact in their personal relationships (Ainsworth et al., 1978; Bowlby, 1973, 1979). Adults tend to display one of the following three patterns:

1. *Secure attachment.* Adults with this style generally display a positive relationship style.

2. *Avoidant attachment.* Adults with this style are emotionally distant from others.

3. *Anxious-ambivalent attachment.* Adults with this style chronically worry about their relationships.

The quality of the bond between elderly partners can buffer against the negative effects of stressful life events (Kraaij & Garnefski, 2002).

© OJO Images Ltd/Alamy

Adults who are characterized by the second and third forms of attachment are more vulnerable to depression: Those with anxious-ambivalent attachment are the most likely to experience episodes of depression, followed by those with avoidant attachment. Adults with secure attachment are least likely to do so (Bifulco et al., 2002; Cooper et al., 1998; Fonagy et al., 1996).

Culture

A person's culture and context can influence how the person experiences and expresses depressive symptoms (Lam et al., 2005). For instance, in Asian and Latin cultures, people with depression may not mention mood but may instead talk about "nerves" or describe headaches. Similarly, depressed people in Zimbabwe tend to complain about fatigue and headaches (Patel et al., 2001). In contrast, some depressed people from Middle Eastern cultures may describe problems with their heart, and depressed Native Americans of the Hopi people may report feeling heartbroken (American Psychiatric Association, 2000).

The influence of culture doesn't end with the way symptoms are described. Each culture—and subculture—also leads its members to take particular symptoms more or less seriously. For instance, in cultures that have strong prohibitions against suicide, having suicidal thoughts is a key symptom; in cultures that emphasize being productive at work, having difficulty functioning well at work is considered a key symptom (Young, 2001).

A particular culture can also be influenced by another culture and change accordingly. Consider that depressed people in China have typically reported mostly physical symptoms of depression, but these reports are changing as China becomes increasingly exposed to Western views of depression (Parker et al., 2001).

Gender Difference

In North America, women are about twice as likely as men to be diagnosed with depression (Marcus et al., 2005), and studies in Europe find a similar gender difference (Angst et al., 2002; Dalgard et al., 2006). Research results indicate that the gender difference arises at puberty and continues into adulthood (Alloy & Abramson, 2007; Jose & Brown, 2008).

One explanation for the gender difference in rates of depression is that girls' socialization into female roles can lead them to experience more body dissatisfaction, which in turn can make them more vulnerable to automatic negative thoughts that lead to depression (Cyranowski et al., 2000; Nolen-Hoeksema & Girgus, 1994).

Another explanation for this difference focuses on a ruminative response to stress: Women are more likely than men to mull over a stressful situation, whereas men more often respond by distracting themselves and taking action (Nolen-Hoeksema, 1987; Nolen-Hoeksema & Morrow, 1993; Vajk et al., 1997). A ruminative pattern can be unlearned: College students who learned to use distraction more and rumination less improved their depressed mood (Nolen-Hoeksema & Morrow, 1993).

An additional consideration is that women may be more likely than men to *report* symptoms of depression, perhaps because they are less concerned about appearing "strong"; thus, women may not necessarily *experience* more of these symptoms than men (Sigmon et al., 2005).

Furthermore, biological differences—such as specific female hormonal changes involved in puberty—may contribute to this gender difference (Halbreich & Kahn, 2001; Steiner et al., 2003). A role for this biological factor is consistent with the finding that before puberty, boys and girls have similar rates of depression (Cohen et al., 1993). Additional evidence that hormones influence depression is the fact that women and men have similar rates of the disorder after women have reached menopause (and hence their levels of female hormone are greatly reduced) (Hyde et al., 2008).

Girls typically are encouraged to cope with stressors by ruminating. In contrast, boys typically are encouraged to use activity and distraction. This gender difference may contribute to the higher rate of depression among women than among men (Nolen-Hoeksema, 1987, 2001).

The different explanations for the gender difference are not mutually exclusive, and these factors may interact with one another (Hyde et al., 2008). For instance, girls who enter puberty early are more likely to become depressed (Kaltiala-Heino et al., 2003), perhaps in part because their early physical development makes them more likely to be noticed and teased about their changing bodies, which in turn can lead to dissatisfaction with and rumination about their bodies. Let's examine more broadly how feedback loops contribute to depression.

Feedback Loops in Understanding Depressive Disorders

How do neurological, psychological, and social factors interact through feedback loops to produce depression? As we noted in the section on genetics, some people are more vulnerable than others to stress. For these people, the HPA axis is highly responsive to stress (and often the stress is related to social factors). For example, abuse or neglect at an early age, with accompanying frequent or chronic increase in the activity of the HPA axis, can lead cortisol-releasing cells to over respond to any stressor—even a mild one (Nemeroff, 1998). In fact, college students with a history of MDD reported feeling more tension and responded less well after a stressful cognitive task (one that, unknown to these participants, was impossible to solve) than college students with no history of MDD (Ilgen & Hutchison, 2005). These results support the notion that people who are vulnerable to MDD are affected by stressors differently than are people without such a vulnerability (Hasler et al., 2004).

A cognitive factor that makes a person vulnerable to depression, such as a negative attributional style, ruminative thinking, or dysfunctional thoughts (all psychological factors), can amplify the negative effects of a stressor. In fact, such cognitive factors can lead people to be hypervigilant for stressors or to interpret neutral events as stressors, which in turn activates the HPA axis. This neurological response then can lead such people to interact differently with others (social factor)—making less eye contact, being less responsive, and becoming more withdrawn.

Researchers have identified other ways that neurological, psychological, and social factors create feedback loops in depression. According to James Coyne's interactional theory of depression (Coyne, 1976; Coyne & Downey, 1991; Joiner et al., 1999), someone who is neurologically vulnerable to depression (perhaps because of genes or neurotransmitter abnormalities) may, through verbal and nonverbal behaviors (psychological factor), alienate people who would otherwise be supportive (social factor; Nolan & Mineka, 1997). For example, researchers have found that depressed undergraduates are more likely than nondepressed undergraduates to solicit negative information from happy people—which in turn can lead happier people to reject the depressed questioner (Wenzlaff & Beevers, 1998). And soliciting negative information (and similar behaviors) could arise from negative attributions and views about self and the environment (psychological factors), which in turn could arise from group interactions (social factors), such as being teased or ridiculed, or modeling the behavior of someone else.

In short, people's psychological characteristics affect how they interpret events and how they behave, which in turn influences how they are treated in social interactions, which then influences their beliefs about themselves and others (Casbon et al., 2005). And all this is modulated by whether the person is neurologically vulnerable to depression. Figure 5.2 illustrates the feedback loops.

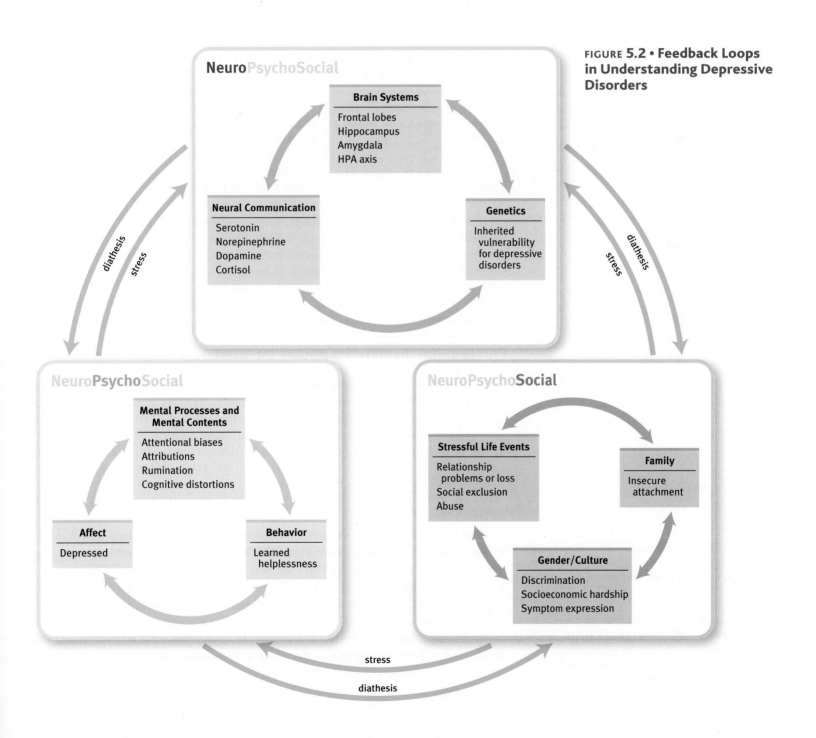

FIGURE **5.2 • Feedback Loops in Understanding Depressive Disorders**

Treating Depressive Disorders

Different treatments target different factors that contribute to depression. However, successful treatment of any one factor will affect the others. For example, improving disrupted brain functioning will alter a person's thoughts, mood, and behavior, and interactions with others.

Targeting Neurological Factors

In treating depressive disorders, clinicians rely on two major types of treatment that directly target neurological factors: medication and brain stimulation.

Medication

Several types of medications are commonly prescribed for depression, but it can take weeks for one of these medications to improve depressed mood. Antidepressant medications include the following:

- **Selective serotonin reuptake inhibitors (SSRIs)**, such as *fluoxetine* (Prozac), *paroxetine* (Paxil), and *sertraline* (Zoloft). SSRIs slow the reuptake of serotonin from synapses. Because these antidepressants affect only certain receptors, they have fewer side effects than other types of antidepressant medications, which can make people less likely to stop taking them (Anderson, 2000; Beasley et al., 2000). However, SSRIs are the only type of antidepressant to have the side effect of decreased sexual interest, which can lead some patients to stop taking them (Brambilla et al., 2005). Many patients also find that the same dose of an SSRI brings less benefit over time (Arana & Rosenbaum, 2000).

- **Tricyclic antidepressants (TCAs),** such as *amitriptyline* (Elavil). TCAs are named after the three rings of atoms in their molecular structure. These medications have been used since the 1950s to treat depression and, until SSRIs became available, were the most common medication to treat this disorder. TCAs are generally as effective as Prozac for depression (Agency for Health Care Policy and Research, 1999). The side effects of TCAs differ from those of SSRIs: The most common side effects include low blood pressure, blurred vision, dry mouth, and constipation (Arana & Rosenbaum, 2000).

- **Monoamine oxidase inhibitors (MAOIs)**, such as phenelzine (Nardil). Some neurotransmitters, such as serotonin, dopamine, and norepinephrine, are classified as monoamines; monoamine oxidase is a naturally produced enzyme that breaks down monoamines in the synapse. MAOIs inhibit this chemical breakdown, so the net effect is to increase the amount of neurotransmitter in the synapse. MAOIs are more effective for treating atypical depression (Cipriani et al., 2007) than typical depression. An MAOI is now available as a skin patch, which avoids absorption via the gastrointestinal tract; this method reduces the medical risks of oral MAOIs, including potentially fatal blood pressure changes that are associated with eating tyramine-rich foods such as cheese and wine (Patkar et al., 2006).

SSRIs have been the most popular antidepressants, in part because they have the fewest side effects. By 2004, however, mental health professionals and laypeople were raising concerns about whether SSRI use was associated with increased suicide rates. Studies comparing SSRIs to other antidepressants did, in fact, find a greater risk for suicidal thoughts and suicide attempts in children and adolescents taking such medications (Martinez et al., 2005); these findings led to a warning label indicating that the medications may increase the risk of suicide in children who take them and that the children should be closely monitored for suicidal thoughts or behaviors or for an increase in depressive symptoms. Since the warning label was mandated, additional research suggests that the benefits of SSRI antidepressants for youngsters outweigh

Selective serotonin reuptake inhibitors (SSRIs)
Medications that slow the reuptake of serotonin from synapses.

Tricyclic antidepressants (TCAs)
Older antidepressants named after the three rings of atoms in their molecular structure.

Monoamine oxidase inhibitors (MAOIs)
Antidepressant medications that increase the amount of monoamine neurotransmitter in synapses.

any risk of suicide, although people taking them should continue to be carefully monitored (Bridge et al., 2007).

Some newer antidepressants, such as *venlafaxine* (Effexor) and *duloxetine* (Cymbalta), affect neurons that respond both to serotonin and norepinephrine; such medications are sometimes referred to as *serotonin/ norepinephrine reuptake inhibitors (SNRIs)*. Other new antidepressants affect noradrenaline (the alternative term for norepinephrine) and serotonin and are referred to as *noradrenergic and specific serotonergic antidepressants* (NaSSAs, where *Na* stands for "noradrenergic"). The antidepressant *mirtazapine* (Remeron) is a NaSSA. These new medications can help some patients who do not respond to the earlier medications.

Some people with depression who do not want to take prescription medication have successfully used an extract from a flowering plant called St. John's wort (*Hypericum perforatum*). Results of meta-analytic studies comparing St. John's wort to prescription antidepressants and placebos indicate that the herbal medication can help patients with mild to moderate depression, and sometimes—but less commonly—even those with severe depression (Linde et al., 2005; Linde et al., 2008). Patients taking St. John's wort report fewer side effects than do patients taking prescription medications (Linde et al., 2008); the most common side effect is dry mouth or dizziness.

St. John's wort, shown here as the plant and in capsule form, may reduce mild to moderate depression but may not be as effective as antidepressant medication for those with severe MDD (Linde et al., 2005).

Brain Stimulation: ECT and TMS

When patients with depression are not helped by medication or by other commonly employed treatments, they may receive **electroconvulsive therapy (ECT)**, which consists of electrical pulses that are sent into the brain to cause a controlled brain seizure. This seizure may reduce or eliminate the symptoms of certain psychological disorders, most notably some forms of depression. ECT may be used when a patient: (1) has severe depression that has not improved significantly with either medication or psychotherapy, (2) cannot take medication because of side effects or other medical reasons, or (3) has a psychotic depression (depression with psychotic features) that does not respond to medication (Fink, 2001; Lam et al., 1999).

In the ECT procedure, electrical pulses are delivered via electrodes placed on the scalp. Just before ECT treatment, the patient receives a muscle relaxant, and the treatment occurs while the patient is under anesthesia. Because of the risks associated with anesthesia, ECT is performed in a hospital and may require a hospital stay. ECT for depression is usually administered 2 to 3 times a week over several weeks, for a total of 6 to 12 sessions (Shapira et al., 1998; Vieweg & Shawcross, 1998). Depressive symptoms typically decrease a few weeks after the treatment begins, although scientists don't yet understand exactly how ECT provides relief (Pagnin et al., 2004). Some people receiving ECT suffer memory loss for events that occurred during a brief period of time before the procedure (Semkovska & McLoughlin, 2010).

Depressed patients who did not respond to antidepressants commonly relapse after receiving ECT: At least half of these patients experience another episode of depression over the following 2 years (Gagne et al., 2000; Sackheim et al., 2001). To minimize the risk of a relapse, patients usually begin taking antidepressant medication after ECT ends.

Electroconvulsive therapy (ECT)
A procedure that sends electrical pulses into the brain to cause a controlled brain seizure, in an effort to reduce or eliminate the symptoms of certain psychological disorders.

Transcranial magnetic stimulation is a relatively recent technique that has some advantages over ECT for treating depression.

Some patients with depression benefit from *transcranial magnetic stimulation*. In contrast to ECT, which relies on electrical impulses, **transcranial magnetic stimulation (TMS)** uses sequences of short, strong magnetic pulses sent into the brain via a coil placed on the scalp. Each pulse lasts only 100–200 microseconds. TMS has varying effects on the brain, depending on the exact location of the coil and the frequency of the pulses, and researchers are still working to understand how the magnetic field affects brain chemistry and brain activity (George et al., 1999; Wassermann et al., 2008). In some encouraging studies, about half of the depressed patients who did not improve with medication were treated successfully enough with TMS that they did not need to receive ECT (Epstein et al., 1998; Figiel et al., 1998; Klein et al., 1999). Nevertheless, ECT generally is more effective than TMS (Slotema et al., 2010), but TMS is easier to administer and causes fewer side effects than ECT. However, unlike with ECT, researchers have yet to establish definitive guidelines for TMS that govern critical features of the treatment, such as the positioning of the coils that deliver magnetic pulses and how often the treatment should be administered (Holtzheimer & Avery, 2005). In 2008, the Federal Drug Administration approved TMS as a treatment for depression to be used when medication treatments have failed.

Targeting Psychological Factors

Biomedical treatments are not the only treatments available for depression. A variety of treatments are designed to alter psychological factors—changing the patient's behaviors, thoughts, and feelings.

Behavioral Therapy and Methods

Behavior therapy rests on two ideas: (1) Maladaptive behaviors stem from previous learning, and (2) new learning can allow patients to develop more adaptive behaviors, which in turn can change cognitions and emotions. Behavioral methods focus on identifying depressive behaviors and then changing them; such methods focus on the *ABCs* of an unwanted behavior pattern:

- the *antecedents* of the behavior (the stimuli that trigger the behavior),
- the *behavior* itself, and
- the *consequences* of the behavior (which may reinforce the behavior).

For instance, being socially isolated or avoiding daily activities can lead to depressive thoughts and feelings or can help maintain them (Emmelkamp, 1994). Changing these behaviors can, in turn, increase the opportunities to receive positive reinforcement (Lewinsohn, 1974).

Specific techniques to change such behaviors are collectively referred to as *behavioral activation* (Gortner et al., 1998). These techniques include *self-monitoring* (keeping logs of activities, thoughts, or behaviors), scheduling daily activities that lead to pleasure or a sense of mastery, and identifying and decreasing avoidant behaviors. Behavioral activation may also include problem solving—identifying obstacles that interfere with achieving a goal and then developing solutions to circumvent or eliminate those obstacles. For instance, a depressed college student may feel overwhelmed at the thought of asking for an extension for an overdue paper. The student and therapist work together to solve the problem of how to go about asking for the extension; they come up with a realistic timetable to complete the paper and discuss how to talk with the professor.

Behavioral activation techniques may initially be aversive to a person with depression because they require more energy than the person feels able to summon;

Transcranial magnetic stimulation (TMS)
A procedure that sends sequences of short, strong magnetic pulses into the brain via a coil placed on the scalp, which is used to reduce or eliminate the symptoms of certain psychological disorders.

Behavior therapy
The form of treatment that rests on the ideas that: (1) maladaptive behaviors stem from previous learning, and (2) new learning can allow patients to develop more adaptive behaviors, which in turn can change cognitions and emotions.

however, mood improves in the long term. In fact, behavioral activation is superior to cognitive therapy techniques in treating both moderate and severe depression (Dimidjian et al., 2006).

Cognitive Therapy and Methods

In contrast to behavior therapy, **cognitive therapy** rests on these ideas: (1) Mental contents—in particular, conscious thoughts—influence a person's feelings and behavior; (2) irrational thoughts and incorrect beliefs contribute to mood and behavior problems; and (3) correcting such thoughts and beliefs, sometimes referred to as *cognitive restructuring*, leads to more rational thoughts and accurate beliefs and therefore will lead to better mood and more adaptive behavior.

The methods of cognitive therapy often require patients to collect data to assess the accuracy of their beliefs, which are often irrational and untrue (Hollon & Beck, 1994). This process can relieve some patients' depression and can prevent or minimize further episodes of depression (Teasdale & Barnard, 1993; Teasdale et al., 2002).

Consider Kay Jamison: She felt that she was a burden to her friends and family and that they would all be better off if she were dead. In cognitive therapy, the therapist would explore the accuracy of these beliefs: Why did she think she was a burden? What evidence did she have to support this conclusion? How might friends or family react if she told them that they'd be better off if she were dead? A cognitive therapist might even suggest that she talk to them about her beliefs and listen to their responses to determine whether her beliefs were accurate. Most likely, her friends and family would *not* agree that they'd be better off if she were dead.

Cognitive-Behavior Therapy

Although cognitive and behavior therapies began separately, their approaches are complementary and are frequently combined; when methods from cognitive and behavior therapies are implemented in the same treatment, it is called **cognitive-behavior therapy (CBT)**. CBT, particularly when it includes behavioral activation, is often about as successful as medication (Sava et al., 2009; Spielmans et al., 2011, TADS Team, 2007). In some ways, CBT may be better than medication. For example, the side effects of medication may lead patients to stop taking it: Various studies have found that about 75% of patients either stop taking their antidepressant medication within the first 3 months or take less than an optimal dose (Mitchell, 2007). And when patients stop taking medication, a high proportion of them relapse. Furthermore, even when medication is successful, research suggests that people at risk for further episodes should continue to take the medication for the rest of their lives to prevent relapses (Hirschfield et al., 1997). In contrast, the beneficial effects of CBT can persist after treatment ends (Hollon et al., 2005); CBT is an alternative that need not be administered for life.

As usual, CBT and medication can be used together. In fact, studies have shown that a combination of CBT and medication is more effective than medication alone— even for severely depressed adolescents and adults (TADS Team, 2007; Thase et al., 1997). In addition, after treatment with antidepressants has ended, a patient's residual symptoms of depression can be reduced through CBT; this supplemental CBT can reduce the relapse rate (Fava et al., 1998a, 1998b).

Targeting Social Factors

Treatment for depression can also directly target a social factor—personal relationships. Such treatment is designed to increase the patient's positive interactions with others and minimize the negative interactions.

Cognitive therapy
The form of treatment that rests on the ideas that: (1) mental contents influence feelings and behavior; (2) irrational thoughts and incorrect beliefs lead to psychological problems; and (3) correcting such thoughts and beliefs will therefore lead to better mood and more adaptive behavior.

Cognitive-behavior therapy (CBT)
The form of treatment that combines methods from cognitive and behavior therapies.

Interpersonal Therapy

Interpersonal therapy (IPT) emphasizes the links between mood and events in a patient's recent and current relationships (Klerman et al., 1984). The theory underlying IPT is that symptoms of psychological disorders such as depression become exacerbated when a patient's relationships aren't functioning well. The goal of IPT is thus to improve the patient's skills in relationships so that they become more satisfying; as relationships improve, so do the patient's thoughts and feelings, and the symptom of depression lessen. IPT addresses four general aspects of relationships, generally in about 16 sessions:

Interpersonal therapy seeks to improve patients' relationships and thereby alleviate depression.

- a deficiency in social skills or communication skills, which results in unsatisfying social relationships;

- persistent, significant conflicts in a relationship;

- grief about a loss; and

- changes in interpersonal roles (for example, a partner with a new job may have become less emotionally available).

IPT is effective in a wide range of circumstances and settings (Cuijpers et al., 2011). For example, in an innovative study of depressed people in 30 Ugandan rural villages, researchers randomly assigned depressed residents from 15 villages to group IPT, consisting of 16 weeks of 90-minute sessions. The depressed residents from the other 15 villages received no treatment (the control group). Those who received group IPT had a significant decrease in their depressive symptoms (and were better able to provide for their families and participate in community activities) than those in the control group (Bolton et al., 2003).

IPT has also successfully reduced the occurrence of peripartum depression in pregnant women at high risk for the disorder (Zlotnick et al., 2006). In addition to alleviating depressive symptoms, occasional additional "maintenance" sessions of IPT—either alone or in combination with CBT—may prevent relapse (Frank et al., 2007; Klein et al., 2004).

Systems Therapy: A Focus on the Family

A family's functioning also may be a target of treatment; this usually occurs when a family member's depression is related either to a maladaptive pattern of interaction within the family or to a conflict that arose within the family. For example, conflicts—particularly over values—may arise within families that have immigrated to the United States; immigrant parents and their children who grow up in the United States may experience tension because what the parents want for their children conflicts with what the children (as they become adults) want for themselves. Immigrant parents from Mexico, for instance, may want to be very involved in their children's lives, just as they would be in their native hometown. But their children, growing up in the United States, may come to resent what the children perceive as their parents' intrusive and controlling behavior (compared to the parents of their non-immigrant peers) (Santisteban et al., 2002). The parents, in turn, may think that their children are rejecting both their Mexican heritage and the parents themselves. Caught between two cultures—the old and the new—and wanting to maintain aspects of their heritage but also feel "American," the resulting conflict can contribute to depression (Hovey, 1998, 2000).

Such problems in families may be treated with *systems therapy*, which is designed to change the communication or behavior patterns of one or more family members. According to this approach, the family is a system that strives to maintain *homeostasis*, a state of equilibrium, so that change in one member affects other family members. Systems therapy is guided by the view that when one member changes (perhaps through therapy),

Interpersonal therapy (IPT)
The form of treatment that is intended to improve the patient's skills in relationships so that they become more satisfying.

change is forced on the rest of the system (Bowen, 1978; Minuchin, 1974). To a family systems therapist, the "patient" is the family; systems therapy focuses on communication and power within the family. The symptoms of a particular family member are understood to be a result of that person's intentional or unintentional attempts to maintain or change a pattern within the family or to convey a message to family members.

Feedback Loops in Treating Depressive Disorders

The goals of any treatment for depressive disorders are ultimately the same:

- to reduce symptoms of distress and depressed mood as well as negative or unrealistic thoughts about the self (psychological factors),

- to reduce problems related to social interactions—such as social withdrawal—and to make social interactions more satisfying and less stressful (social factors), and

- to correct imbalances in the brain associated with some of the symptoms, such as by normalizing neurotransmitter functioning or hormone levels (neurological factors).

Treatments that target one type of factor also affect other factors. CBT, for instance, not only can reduce psychological symptoms but can also change brain activity (Goldapple et al., 2004), improve physical symptoms (including disrupted sleep, appetite, and psychomotor symptoms), and improve social relations. Moreover, medication for depression works both through its effects on neurological functioning and through the placebo effect (see Chapter 4 for a discussion about the placebo effect). Thus, a depressed patient's beliefs (psychological factor) can account for much of the effect of antidepressant medication. Figure 5.3 illustrates the various treatments discussed, the targets of treatments for depressive disorders, and the feedback loops that arise with successful treatment.

Note that Figure 5.3 lists the various types of treatment for depressive disorders, sorted into the three types of factors; in two cases, we go one step further and list

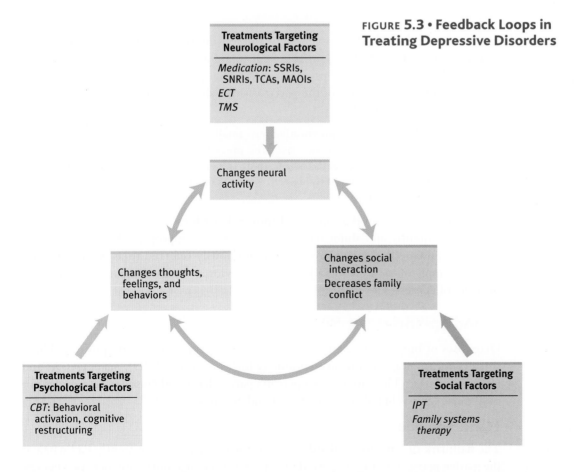

FIGURE 5.3 • Feedback Loops in Treating Depressive Disorders

Treatments Targeting Neurological Factors

Medication: SSRIs, SNRIs, TCAs, MAOIs
ECT
TMS

Changes neural activity

Changes thoughts, feelings, and behaviors

Changes social interaction
Decreases family conflict

Treatments Targeting Psychological Factors

CBT: Behavioral activation, cognitive restructuring

Treatments Targeting Social Factors

IPT
Family systems therapy

specific types of drugs and specific CBT methods. Why are we specific with only these two forms of treatment? Because these forms of treatment have been studied the most extensively, and hence more is known about which specific medications and CBT methods are most likely to reduce symptoms and improve quality of life. Rigorous studies of other types of treatments are less common, and hence less is known about the specific methods that are most likely to be effective. You will find this same disparity in knowledge reflected in subsequent figures that illustrate feedback loops of treatments for other disorders (most of these types of figures can be found on the book's website).

Now that we've discussed depressive disorders, let's look back at what we know about Kay Jamison thus far and see whether MDD is the diagnosis that best fits her symptoms. She experienced depressed moods, anhedonia, fatigue, and feelings of worthlessness. She also had recurrent thoughts of death, as well as difficulty concentrating. Taken together, these symptoms seem to meet the criteria for MDD. However, she also has symptoms that may support the diagnosis of another mood disorder. We examine those building blocks in the following section.

Thinking Like A Clinician

Suppose that a friend began to sleep through morning classes, seemed uninterested in going out and doing things, and became quiet and withdrawn. What could you conclude or not conclude based on these observations? If you were concerned that these were symptoms of depression, what other symptoms would you look for? If your friend's symptoms did not appear to meet the criteria for an MDE, what could you conclude or not conclude? If your friend was, in fact, suffering from depression, how might the three types of factors explain the depressive episode? What treatments might be appropriate?

☐ Bipolar Disorders

After receiving her Ph.D. in psychology and joining the faculty of the Department of Psychiatry at UCLA, Kay Jamison went to a garden party for faculty. The man who would later become her psychiatrist was there, and years later they discussed the party. Jamison's memory of the party was that she was confident and alluring; in contrast, he remembered her as:

> . . . dressed in a remarkably provocative way, totally unlike the conservative manner in which he had seen me dressed over the preceding year. I had on much more makeup than usual and seemed, to him, to be frenetic and far too talkative. He says he remembers having thought to himself, Kay looks manic. I, on the other hand, had thought I was splendid. (p. 71)

The other set of mood disorders is **bipolar disorders**—in which a person's mood is often persistently and abnormally upbeat or shifts inappropriately from upbeat to markedly down. (Bipolar disorders were previously referred to as *manic-depressive illness* or simply *manic depression*.) Jamison's behavior at the garden party indicates the opposite of depression—mania.

Mood Episodes for Bipolar Disorders

Diagnoses of bipolar disorders are based on three types of mood episodes. These three types are major depressive episode (which underlies MDD), *manic episode*, and *hypomanic episode*. The patterns of a person's particular mood episodes determines not only the diagnosis but also the treatment and prognosis.

Manic Episode

The hallmark of a **manic episode**, such as the one Jamison apparently had when at the garden party, is a discrete period of at least 1 week of abnormally increased energy

Bipolar disorders
Mood disorders in which a person's mood is often persistently and abnormally upbeat or shifts inappropriately from upbeat to markedly down.

or activity and abnormally euphoric feelings, intense irritability, or an *expansive mood*. During an **expansive mood**, the person exhibits unceasing, indiscriminate enthusiasm for interpersonal or sexual interactions or for projects. The expansive mood and related behaviors contrast with the person's usual state. For instance, a normally shy person may have extensive intimate conversations with strangers in public places during a manic episode. For some, though, the predominant mood during a manic episode may be irritability. Alternatively, during a manic episode, a person's mood can shift between abnormal and persistent euphoria and irritability, as it did for Jamison:

> When you're high, it's tremendous. The ideas and feelings are fast and frequent like shooting stars, and you follow them until you find better and brighter ones. Shyness goes, the right words and gestures are suddenly there, the power to captivate others a felt certainty . . . Sensuality is pervasive and the desire to seduce and be seduced irresistible. Feelings of ease, intensity, power, well-being, financial omnipotence, and euphoria pervade one's marrow. But, somewhere, this changes. The fast ideas are far too fast, and there are far too many; overwhelming confusion replaces clarity. Memory goes. Humor and absorption on friends' faces are replaced by fear and concerns. Everything previously moving with the grain is now against—you are irritable, angry, frightened, uncontrollable, and enmeshed totally in the blackest caves of the mind . . . It will never end, for madness carves its own reality.
>
> (1995, p. 67)

Table 5.6 lists the criteria for a manic episode.

As noted in Table 5.6, during a manic episode, a person may begin projects that he or she doesn't have the special knowledge or training to complete; for instance, the person might try to install a dishwasher, despite knowing nothing about plumbing. Moreover, when manic, some people are uncritically grandiose—often believing themselves to have superior abilities or a special relationship to political or entertainment figures; these beliefs may reach delusional proportions, to the point where a person may stalk a celebrity, believing that he or she is destined to marry that famous person.

TABLE 5.6 • DSM-5 Criteria for Manic Episode

A. A distinct period of abnormally and persistently elevated, expansive, or irritable mood and abnormally and persistently increased goal-directed activity or energy, lasting at least 1 week and present most of the day, nearly every day (or any duration if hospitalization is necessary).

B. During the period of mood disturbance and increased energy or activity, three (or more) of the following symptoms (four if the mood is only irritable) are present to a significant degree and represent a noticeable change from usual behavior:

1. Inflated self-esteem or grandiosity.

2. Decreased need for sleep (e.g., feels rested after only 3 hours of sleep).

3. More talkative than usual or pressure to keep talking.

4. Flight of ideas or subjective experience that thoughts are racing.

5. Distractibility (i.e., attention too easily drawn to unimportant or irrelevant external stimuli), as reported or observed.

6. Increase in goal-directed activity (either socially, at work or school, or sexually) or psychomotor agitation (i.e., purposeless non-goal-directed activity).

7. Excessive involvement in activities that have a high potential for painful consequences (e.g., engaging in unrestrained buying sprees, sexual indiscretions, or foolish business investments).

C. The mood disturbance is sufficiently severe to cause marked impairment in social or occupational functioning or to necessitate hospitalization to prevent harm to self or others, or there are psychotic features.

D. The episode is not attributable to the physiological effects of a substance (e.g., a drug of abuse, a medication, other treatment) or to another medical condition.

Manic episode
A period of at least 1 week characterized by abnormally increased energy or activity and abnormal and persistent euphoria or expansive mood or irritability.

Expansive mood
A mood that involves unceasing, indiscriminate enthusiasm for interpersonal or sexual interactions or for projects.

Manic episodes can lead to the reckless pursuit of pleasurable activities, including uncharacteristic risqué or indiscriminant sexual behavior.

Flight of ideas
Thoughts that race faster than they can be said.

During a manic episode, a person needs much less sleep—so much less that he or she may be able to go days without it, or sleep only a few hours nightly, yet not feel tired. Similarly, when manic, the affected person may speak rapidly or loudly and may be difficult to interrupt; he or she may talk nonstop for hours on end, not letting anyone else get a word in edgewise. Moreover, when manic, the person rarely sits still (Cassano et al., 2009). Another symptom of mania is a **flight of ideas**—thoughts that race faster than they can be said. When speaking while in this state of mind, the person may flit from topic to topic; flight of ideas has commonly been described by patients as something like watching two or three television programs simultaneously.

During a manic episode, the person may also be highly distractible and unable to screen out irrelevant details in the environment or in conversations. Another symptom of a manic episode is excessive planning of, and participation in, multiple activities. A college student with this symptom might participate in eight time-intensive extracurricular activities, including a theatrical production, a musical performance, a community service group, and a leadership position in a campus political group. The expansiveness, unwarranted optimism, grandiosity, and poor judgment of a manic episode can lead to the reckless pursuit of pleasurable activities, such as spending sprees or unusual sexual behavior (such as infidelity or indiscriminate sexual encounters with strangers). These activities often lead to adverse consequences: credit card debt from the spending sprees or sexually transmitted diseases, including HIV, from unprotected sex.

People who have had a manic episode report afterward that they felt as if their senses were sharper during the episode—that their ability to smell or hear was better. People often don't recognize that they're ill during a manic phase; this was the case with Jamison, who, for many years, resisted getting treatment.

Typically, a manic episode begins suddenly, with symptoms escalating rapidly over a few days; symptoms can last from a few weeks to several months. Compared to an MDE, a manic episode is briefer and ends more abruptly.

Hypomanic Episode

The last type of mood episode associated with bipolar disorders is a *hypomanic episode*, which has the same criteria as a manic episode, with two significant differences: The symptoms (1) don't impair functioning, require hospitalization, or have psychotic features; and (2) they last a minimum of 4 days, not 1 week. Hypomania rarely includes the flight of ideas that bedevils someone in the grips of mania (American Psychiatric Association, 2013). In contrast to the grandiose thoughts people have about themselves during manic episodes, during hypomanic episodes people are uncritically self-confident but not grandiose. When hypomanic, some people may be more efficient and creative than they typically are (American Psychiatric Association, 2013). During a hypomanic episode, people may tend to talk loudly and rapidly, but, unlike when people are manic, it is possible to interrupt them.

During a hypomanic episode, which is less impairing than a manic episode, a person may go on spending sprees or make foolish investments.

The Two Types of Bipolar Disorder

The presence of different types of mood episodes leads to different diagnoses. According to DSM-5, there are two types of bipolar disorder: bipolar I disorder and bipolar II disorder. Another disorder—cyclothymia (discussed shortly)—is characterized by symptoms of hypomania and depression that do not meet the criteria for either of the two types of bipolar disorder.

The presence of manic *symptoms*—but not a manic episode—is the common element of the two types of bipolar disorder. The types differ in the severity of the manic symptoms. To receive the diagnosis of the more severe *bipolar I disorder*, a person must have a manic episode; an MDE may also occur with bipolar I. Thus, just as an MDE automatically leads to a diagnosis of MDD, having a manic episode automatically leads to a diagnosis of bipolar I. Writer and actor Carrie Fisher, who suffers from bipolar disorder I, describes her experience in Case 5.4.

Ryan Miller/Getty Images

Are people with bipolar disorders more creative? Although actress, author, and screenwriter Carrie Fisher has a bipolar disorder, many people with such a disorder are not exceptionally creative, and many creative people do not have such a disorder. Research suggests that the two variables—the presence of bipolar disorder and creativity—may be unrelated (Rothenberg, 2001).

CASE 5.4 • FROM THE INSIDE: Bipolar Disorder

"I never shut up," she says of the times her mania would start to take over. "I could be brilliant. I never had to look long for a word, a thought, a connection, a joke, anything." Such heady feelings never lasted, though.

"I'd keep people on the phone for eight hours. When my mania is going strong, it's sort of a clear path. You know, I'm flying high up onto the mountain, but it starts going too fast."

"I stop being able to connect. My sentences don't make sense. I'm not tracking anymore and I can't sleep and I'm not reliable."

(Staba, 2004)

In contrast, to be diagnosed with *bipolar II disorder*, a person must alternate between hypomanic episodes and MDEs (see Table 5.7); bipolar II can be thought of as less severe because of the absence of manic episodes; however, the unpredictable changes in mood and the depressive episodes can impair a person's functioning. Table 5.8 provides additional facts about bipolar disorders.

TABLE 5.7 • DSM-5 Diagnostic Criteria for Bipolar II Disorder

- Presence (or history) of at least one major depressive episode (MDE)
- Presence (or history) of at least one hypomanic episode
- No history of manic episodes
- These symptoms (either the depression or the cycling between the depression and the hypomania) are creating problems with functioning or significant distress.

Source: Diagnostic and Statistical Manual of Mental Disorders, Fifth Edition, American Psychiatric Publishing, 2013.

Both types of bipolar disorder can include **rapid cycling** of moods, defined as having four or more of any type of mood episode within 1 year (American Psychiatric Association, 2013). Rapid cycling is most common with bipolar II disorder and in women (Papadimitriou et al., 2005). Rapid cycling of either type of bipolar disorder is associated with difficulty finding an effective treatment (Ozcan et al., 2006). As with MDD, people with bipolar disorders may experience psychotic symptoms. People of different races and ethnicities are equally likely to be afflicted with bipolar disorders, just as with depression. Some mental health clinicians, however, tend to diagnose schizophrenia instead of a bipolar disorder when evaluating Black patients (Neighbors et al., 2003).

From Jamison's descriptions, some of her experiences, such as those at the faculty garden party, appear to have been manic episodes. Because she had at least one manic episode, Jamison would be diagnosed with bipolar I disorder, thus changing from the tentative diagnosis of MDD proposed earlier in the chapter.

Rapid cycling (of moods)
Having four or more episodes that meet the criteria for any type of mood episode within 1 year.

TABLE **5.8** • Bipolar Disorders Facts at a Glance

Prevalence

• Between 0.4% and 1.6% of Americans suffer from bipolar I disorder; worldwide the prevalence is 0.6% (Merikangas et al., 2011).

• Approximately 0.5–1% of Americans will develop bipolar II disorder in their lifetimes (Merikangas et al., 2007); worldwide the prevalence is 0.4% (Merikangas et al., 2011).

Onset

• Both men and women begin to have symptoms of bipolar I and II disorder by age 20, on average, although the symptoms do not necessarily include full-blown manic attacks.

Comorbidity

• Up to 75% of those with any bipolar disorder are also diagnosed with another mental disorder, such as anxiety disorders and eating disorders (Merikangas et al., 2011).

Course

• People who have had one manic episode have a 90% chance of having at least one further manic episode.

• Bipolar II disorder typically has a more chronic, though less severe, course than bipolar I disorder (Judd et al., 2003).

• People with either type of bipolar disorder have MDEs that are more severe and lead to more lost work days than do people with depressive disorders (Kessler, Akiskal, et al., 2006).

• Between 5 and 15% of people with bipolar II will have a manic episode at some point, thereby changing the diagnosis to bipolar I.

Gender Differences

• Bipolar I disorder is equally common among males and females; research indicates that bipolar II disorder may be more common among females than among males.

• Almost half of men with bipolar I disorder have their first full-blown manic episode by age 25; in contrast, only one third of women have their first manic episode by that age (Kennedy et al., 2005).

• In males, the number of manic episodes (or hypomanic, in the case of bipolar II disorder) often equals or exceeds the number of MDEs, whereas in women, MDEs predominate (Altshuler et al., 2010).

• For women, having a bipolar disorder boosts the risk of developing mood episodes (of any kind) immediately after giving birth; women are also more likely to have rapid mood cycling.

Cultural Differences

• In one international study, the United States has the highest rate of bipolar disorders, with up to 4.4% of Americans having the disorder in their lifetimes (Merikangas et al., 2011).

Source: Unless otherwise noted, the source for information is American Psychiatric Association, 2013.

Cyclothymic Disorder

Just as persistent depressive disorder is a more chronic but typically less intense version of MDD, *cyclothymia* is a more chronic but less intense version of bipolar II disorder. The main feature of **cyclothymic disorder** is a chronic, fluctuating mood disturbance with numerous periods of hypomanic symptoms that alternate with depressive symptoms, each of which does not meet the criteria for its respective mood episodes. These symptoms have been present for at least half of the time within a 2-year period and have not completely disappeared for more than 2 consecutive months (see Table 5.9). Cyclothymia has a lifetime prevalence of 0.4–1.0% and affects men and women equally often (American Psychiatric Association, 2013). Some people may function particularly well during the hypomanic periods of cyclothymic disorder but be impaired during depressive periods; this diagnosis is given only if the person's depressed mood leads him or her to be distressed or impaired. Thus, someone with cyclothymic disorder may feel upbeat and energetic when having symptoms of hypomania and may begin several projects at work or complete projects ahead of schedule. However, when having

Cyclothymic disorder
A mood disorder characterized by chronic, fluctuating mood disturbance with numerous periods of hypomanic symptoms alternating with depressive symptoms, each of which does not meet the criteria for its respective mood episodes.

TABLE 5.9 • DSM-5 Diagnostic Criteria for Cyclothymic Disorder

A. For at least 2 years (at least 1 year in children and adolescents) there have been numerous periods with hypomanic symptoms that do not meet criteria for a hypomanic episode and numerous periods with depressive symptoms that do not meet criteria for a major depressive episode.

B. During the above 2-year period (1 year in children and adolescents), the hypomanic and depressive periods have been present for at least half the time and the individual has not been without the symptoms for more than 2 months at a time.

C. Criteria for a major depressive, manic, or hypomanic episode have never been met.

D. The symptoms in Criterion A are not better explained by schizoaffective disorder, schizophrenia, schizophreniform disorder, delusional disorder, or other specified or unspecified schizophrenia spectrum or other psychotic disorder.

E. The symptoms are not attributable to the physiological effects of a substance (e.g., a drug of abuse, a medication, other treatment) or to another medical condition.

F. The symptoms cause clinically significant distress or impairment in social, occupational, or other important areas of functioning.

symptoms of depression, he or she may have difficulty concentrating or mustering the energy to work on the projects and so may fall behind on the deadlines.

Cyclothymia usually unfolds slowly during early adolescence or young adulthood, and it has a chronic course, as Mr. F's history reveals (see Case 5.5). Approximately 15–50% of people with cyclothymia go on to develop bipolar disorder (American Psychiatric Association, 2013).

CASE 5.5 • FROM THE OUTSIDE: Cyclothymic Disorder

At his girlfriend's insistence, Mr. F., a 27-year-old single man, goes for a psychiatric evaluation. Mr. F. reports that he is excessively energetic, unable to sleep, and irritable, and he isn't satisfied with the humdrum nature of his work and personal life. He is often dissatisfied and irritable for periods of time ranging from a few days to a few weeks. These periods alternate with longer periods of feeling dejected, hopeless, worn out, and wanting to die; his moods can shift up to 20–30 times each year, and he describes himself as on an "emotional roller-coaster" and has been for as long as he can remember. He twice impulsively tried to commit suicide with alcohol and sleeping pills, although he has never had prominent vegetative symptoms, nor has he had psychotic symptoms.

(Adapted from Frances & Ross, 1996, p. 140)

Because Jamison had both MDEs and manic episodes, her symptoms do not meet the criteria for cyclothymic disorder. Figure 5.4 identifies the various mood episodes and the corresponding mood disorders.

Understanding Bipolar Disorders

Kay Jamison made her professional life into a quest to understand mood disorders and why some people develop them. In the following sections we examine what is known about bipolar disorders using the neuropsychosocial approach.

Neurological Factors

As with depressive disorders, both distinctive brain functioning and genetics are associated with bipolar disorders.

Brain Systems

One hint about a neurological factor that may contribute to bipolar disorders is the finding that the amygdala is enlarged in people who have been diagnosed with a bipolar disorder (Altshuler et al., 1998). This finding is pertinent because the amygdala is involved in expressing emotion, as well as in governing mood and accessing emotional memories (LeDoux, 1996). Researchers have also found that the amygdala is more active in people who are experiencing a manic

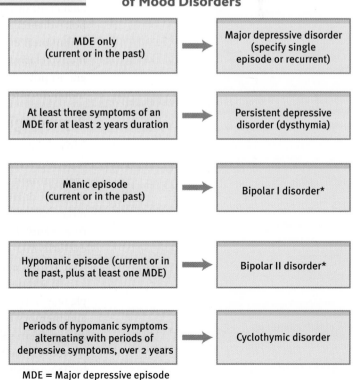

FIGURE 5.4 • Differential Diagnosis of Mood Disorders

MDE = Major depressive episode

* According to DSM-5, once this diagnosis is made, the clinician should also note what type of mood episode is current or most recent.

episode than it is in a control group of people who are not manic (Altshuler et al., 2005). The more reactive the amygdala, the more readily it triggers strong emotional reactions—and hence the fact that it is especially active during a manic episode makes sense.

Neural Communication

As we've discussed earlier in this chapter and in Chapter 2, imbalances in the levels of certain chemicals in the brain can contribute to psychological disorders. There's reason to believe that serotonin (Goodwin & Jamison, 1990) and norepinephrine have roles in bipolar disorders. For example, treatment with lithium (discussed shortly) not only lowers norepinephrine levels but also reduces the symptoms of a bipolar disorder (Rosenbaum, Arana, et al., 2005). Serotonin is an inhibitory neurotransmitter, and low levels of it have been associated with depression (Mundo, Walker, et al., 2000). However, glitches in neural communication contribute to psychological disorders in complex ways; the problem rarely (if ever) is limited to an imbalance of a single substance but rather typically involves complex interactions among substances. In fact, researchers have also reported that the left frontal lobes of patients with mania produce too much of the excitatory neurotransmitter glutamate (Michael et al., 2003), so at least three neurotransmitters—serotonin, norepinephrine, and glutamate—are involved in bipolar disorders.

Genetics

Twin and adoption studies suggest that genes influence who will develop bipolar disorders. If one monozygotic twin has a bipolar disorder, the co-twin has a 40–70% chance of developing the disorder; if one dizygotic twin has the disorder, the co-twin has only about a 5% chance of developing the disorder, which is still over twice the prevalence in the population (Fridman et al., 2003; Kieseppä et al., 2004; McGuffin et al., 2003). In general, if you have a first-degree relative who has bipolar disorder, you have a 4–24% risk of developing the disorder (American Psychiatric Association, 2013).

Depressive disorders and bipolar disorders—even though they now are considered distinct disorders—in fact may be different manifestations of the same genetic vulnerability. When a dizygotic twin has a bipolar disorder, the other twin has an 80% chance of developing any mood disorder (MDD, persistent depressive disorder, a bipolar disorder, or cyclothymia) (Karkowski & Kendler, 1997; McGuffin et al., 2003; Vehmanen et al., 1995). Given such findings, it's not surprising that Jamison had many relatives (on her father's side) who had mood disorders. However, researchers do not yet know how specific genes contribute to an inherited vulnerability for mood disorders.

Psychological Factors: Thoughts and Attributions

Most research on the contribution of psychological factors to bipolar disorders focuses on cognitive distortions and automatic negative thoughts, which not only are common among people with depression but also plague people with a bipolar disorder during MDEs. In fact, research suggests that when depressed, people with either MDD or a bipolar disorder have a similar internal attributional style for negative events (Lyon et al., 1999; Scott et al., 2000). Mirroring these results, people with cyclothymia or persistent depressive disorder have a similar negative attributional style (Alloy et al., 1999).

In addition, even after a manic episode is completely resolved, up to one third of people may have residual cognitive deficits, ranging from difficulties with attention, learning, and memory to problems with executive functioning (planning and decision making) and problem solving (Kolur et al., 2006; Thompson et al., 2005; Zubieta et al., 2001). Moreover, the more mood episodes a person has, the more severe these deficits tend to be. Researchers propose that the persistent cognitive deficits associated with mania should become part of the diagnostic criteria for bipolar disorders, in addition to criteria on mood-related behaviors (Phillips & Frank, 2006).

Social Factors: Social and Environmental Stressors

Social factors such as starting a new job or moving to a different city can also affect the course of bipolar disorders (Goodwin & Jamison, 1990; Malkoff-Schwartz et al., 1998). Stress appears to be part of the process that leads to a first episode (Kessing et al., 2004); people who develop a bipolar disorder often experience significant stressors in their lives before their first episode (Goodwin & Ghaemi, 1998; Tsuchiya, Agerbo, et al., 2005). Stress can also worsen the course of the disorder (Johnson & Miller, 1997). In addition, stress—in particular, family-related stress—may contribute to relapse; people who live with family members who are critical of them are more likely to relapse than those whose family members are not critical (Honig et al., 1997; Miklowitz et al., 1988).

Social factors can also have indirect effects, such as occurs when a new job disrupts a person's sleep pattern, which in turn triggers neurological factors that can lead to a mood episode.

Stressful life events, such as moving, can affect the course of bipolar disorder.

Yellow Dog Productions/Getty Images

Feedback Loops in Understanding Bipolar Disorders

Bipolar disorders have a clear genetic and neurological basis, but feedback loops nevertheless operate among the neurological, psychological, and social factors associated with these disorders. Consider the effects of sleep deprivation. It may directly or indirectly affect neurological functioning, making the person more vulnerable to a manic or depressive episode. Moreover, like people with depression, people with a bipolar disorder tend to have an attributional style (psychological factor) that may make them more vulnerable to becoming depressed. In turn, their attributional style may affect how these people interact with others (social factor), such as in the way they respond to problems in relationships. Even after a mood episode is over, residual problems with cognitive functioning—which affect problem solving, planning, or decision making—can adversely influence the work and social life of a person with a bipolar disorder.

ONLINE

We can now understand Jamison's bipolar disorder as arising from a confluence of neuropsychosocial factors and feedback loops. Her family history provided a strong genetic component to her illness, which has a clear neurological basis (neurological factors). Her struggle against recognizing that she had an illness (psychological factors) meant that she didn't do as good a job as she could have done in protecting herself from overwork (social factor), making her more vulnerable to a mood episode.

Treating Bipolar Disorders

As with depressive disorders, treatment for bipolar disorders can directly target any of the three types of factors—neurological, psychological, and social. Keep in mind, though, that the effects of any successful treatment extend to all the types of factors. Jamison describes the subtle ways that feedback loops operated on her disorder and treatment:

> My temperament, moods, and illness clearly, and deeply, affected the relationships I had with others and the fabric of my work. But my moods were themselves powerfully shaped by the same relationships and work. The challenge was in learning to understand the complexity of this mutual beholdenness and in learning to distinguish the roles of [the medication] lithium, will, and insight in getting well and in leading a meaningful life. It was the task and gift of psychotherapy.
> (1995, p. 88)

Targeting Neurological Factors: Medication

People diagnosed with a bipolar disorder usually take some type of **mood stabilizer**—a medication that minimizes mood swings—for the rest of their lives. (The term *mood stabilizer* is sometimes used more broadly to include medications that decrease impulsive behavior and violent aggression.) Mood stabilizers can reduce recurrences of both manic and depressive episodes (Arana & Rosenbaum, 2000). The oldest mood stabilizer is **lithium**; technically the medication is called *lithium carbonate*, a type of salt. Jamison describes her response to the drug: "I took [lithium] faithfully and found that life was a much stabler and more predictable place than I had ever reckoned. My moods were still intense and my temperament rather quick to the boil, but I could make plans with far more certainty and the periods of absolute blackness were fewer and less extreme" (1995, p. 153). Lithium apparently affects several different neurotransmitters (Lenox & Hahn, 2000) and thereby alters the inner workings of neurons (Friedrich, 2005). However, too high a dose of lithium can produce severe side effects, including coordination problems, vomiting, muscular weakness, blurred vision, and ringing in the ears; thus, patients must have their blood levels of lithium checked regularly to ensure that they are taking an appropriate dosage (Arana & Rosenbaum, 2000).

Lithium is not an effective treatment for all patients. In fact, up to half of patients who are prescribed lithium either cannot tolerate the side effects or do not show significant improvement, especially patients who have rapid cycling (Burgess et al., 2001; Keck & McElroy, 2003; Montgomery et al., 2001). In such cases, other mood stabilizers may help to prevent extreme mood shifts, especially recurring manic episodes. These include antiepileptic medications (also called *anticonvulsants*) such as *divalproex* (Depakote), *carbamazepine* (Tegretol), *lamotrigine* (Lamictal), and *gabapentin* (Neurontin).

Some people with bipolar disorders stop taking mood stabilizers not because of the common side effects (such as thirst, frequent urination, and diarrhea) but rather because the medication does what it's supposed to do—evens out their moods (Arana & Rosenbaum, 2000; Rosa et al., 2007). Some of these people report that they miss aspects of their manic episodes and feel that the medication blunts their emotions.

Mood stabilizers aren't the only medications given for bipolar disorders. Patients with a bipolar disorder may be given antidepressant medication for depression, but such medications can induce mania and so should be taken along with a mood stabilizer; in addition, patients with a bipolar disorder who take antidepressant medication should take it for as brief a period as possible (Rosenbaum, Arana, et al., 2005). For a manic episode, the person may be given an antipsychotic medication such as *olanzapine* (Zyprexa) or *aripiprazole* (Abilify) or a high dose of a benzodiazepine—a class of medications commonly known as tranquilizers (Keck et al., 2009; Yildiz et al., 2011).

Despite the number of medications available to treat bipolar disorders, mood episodes still recur; in one study, half of the participants developed a subsequent mood episode within 2 years of recovery from an earlier episode (Perlis, Ostacher, et al., 2006).

Targeting Psychological Factors: Thoughts, Moods, and Relapse Prevention

Medication can be an effective component of treatment for bipolar disorders, but often it isn't the only component. Treatment that targets psychological factors focuses on helping patients develop patterns of thought and behavior that minimize the risk of relapse (Fava, Bartolucci, et al., 2001; Jones, 2004; Scott & Gutierrez, 2004). CBT can help patients stick with their medication schedules, develop better sleeping strategies, and recognize early signs of mood episodes, such as needing less sleep (Frank et al., 2005; Miklowitz, 2008; Miklowitz et al., 2007).

Targeting Social Factors: Interacting with Others

Treatments that target social factors are designed to help patients minimize disruptions in their social patterns and develop strategies for better social interactions (Lam et al., 2000), which can reduce the rate of relapse. One such treatment, adapted from IPT, is called *interpersonal and social rhythm therapy* (IPSRT; Frank et al., 1999). As in IPT, IPSRT sessions focus on identifying themes of social stressors, such as a relationship conflict that arises because partners have different expectations of the relationship. Treatment can then focus on developing effective ways for the patient to minimize such social stressors. In addition, IPSRT focuses on the timing of events (such as arranging weekend activities so that the patient wakes up at the same time each morning and goes to sleep at the same time each night—weekend and weekday), increasing overall regularity in daily life (such as having meals at relatively fixed times during the day), and helping the patient *want* to maintain regularity. IPSRT plus medication is more effective than medication alone (Miklowitz, 2008; Miklowitz et al., 2007).

📷 GETTING THE PICTURE

For someone making use of interpersonal social and rhythm therapy, which of the wakeup times shown in the photos would be best on a weekend, assuming that the person wakes up at 6:00 A.M. during the week? Answer: 6:00 A.M. (the photo on the left); keeping a regular sleep–wake schedule 7 days per week can help reduce the risk of relapse.

Other treatments that target social factors focus on the family: educating family members about bipolar disorder and providing emergency counseling during crises (Miklowitz et al., 2000, 2003, 2007). Also, family therapy that leads family members to be less critical of the patient can reduce relapses (Honig et al., 1997). Another treatment with a social focus is group therapy or a self-help group, either of which can decrease the sense of isolation or shame that people with a bipolar disorder may experience; group members support each other as they try to make positive changes.

Feedback Loops in Treating Bipolar Disorder

Both Jamison and her psychiatrist understood that treatment could affect multiple factors. She recognized that medication might help her, but she had to *want* to take the medication. Similarly, she recognized that psychotherapy alone could not prevent her mood episodes. She needed them both.

We have seen that successful treatments for bipolar disorders can address multiple factors—for example, CBT can result in more consistent medication use, and IPSRT can reduce the frequency of events that might trigger relapse. Successful treatment can also affect interpersonal relationships, leading patients to interact differently with others, develop a more regular schedule, and come to view themselves differently. Moreover, such therapy leads patients to change the attributions they make about events and even change how reliably they take medication for the disorder.

ONLINE

Jamison's treatment involved interactions among the factors: Her therapy helped her to recognize and accept her illness and encouraged her to take care of herself more appropriately (psychological and social factors), including sticking with a daily regimen of lithium (neurological factor). Furthermore, the successful lithium treatment allowed her to have better relationships with others (social factor), which led to a positive change in how she saw herself (psychological factor).

Thinking Like A Clinician

You get in touch with a friend from high school who tells you that she recently had experiences that you realize are symptoms of hypomania. What are two possible DSM-5 diagnoses that might apply to her? (Be specific.) What will determine which diagnosis is most appropriate? What are a few of the symptoms that are hallmarks of hypomania? What would be the difference in symptoms if your friend instead experienced a manic episode? Would her diagnosis change or stay the same? Explain. What would be the most appropriate ways to treat bipolar disorders?

▫ Suicide

On more than one occasion, Kay Jamison seriously contemplated suicide. One day, when deeply depressed, she did more than think about it—she attempted suicide. She was seeking relief from her pain and for the pain she felt she was inflicting on her family and friends:

> In a perverse linking with my mind I thought that . . . I was doing the only fair thing for the people I cared about; it was also the only sensible thing to do for myself. One would put an animal to death for far less suffering.
> (p. 115)

When Jamison attempted suicide, she was already receiving treatment for her disorder; in contrast, a majority of people who die by suicide have an untreated mental disorder, most commonly depression. Jamison's attempt was foiled. She later describes being grateful that she continued living. The hopelessness that she had felt went away, and she was able to enjoy life again.

Past research suggested that suicide rates peak in the spring for both men and women (Meares et al., 1981). However, more recent research suggests that such a relationship may be weakening over time (Yip et al., 1998, 2000, 2006), perhaps because the effects of seasonal differences are minimized by modern artificial environments (Simkins et al., 2003).

Suicidal Thoughts and Suicide Risks

In the United States and Canada, suicide is ranked 10th among causes of death (CDC, 2010a; Statistics Canada, 2005). Approximately 32,000 people die by suicide each year in the United States (CDC, 2005), which constitutes about 1% of all deaths per year (McIntosh, 2003). Worldwide, suicide is the second most frequent cause of death among women under 45 years old (tuberculosis ranks first), and it is the fourth most frequent cause among men under 45 (after road accidents, tuberculosis, and violence; WHO, 1999). Table 5.10 lists more facts about suicide.

Thinking About, Planning, and Attempting Suicide

When suffering from a mood disorder, people may have thoughts of death or thoughts about committing suicide, known as **suicidal ideation** (Rihmer, 2007). But suicidal ideation does not necessarily indicate the presence of a psychological disorder or an actual suicide risk. Approximately 10–18% of the general population—including both those with and without disorders—has at some point had suicidal thoughts (Weissman, Bland, et al., 1999). One study found that 6% of people who were healthy and had never been depressed occasionally thought about suicide (Farmer et al., 2001). Suicidal thoughts may range from believing that others would

Suicidal ideation
Thoughts of suicide.

© Craig Tuttle/Corbis

TABLE 5.10 · Suicide Facts at a Glance

Prevalence

- Approximately 1.3% of all deaths in the United States are considered to be suicides—more than 32,000 people annually (CDC, 2005).

- Worldwide, the elderly (65 and older) are three times as likely to commit suicide as are those under 25 years old (WHO, 1999).

- In the United States, suicide is most likely to occur among the middle aged (45–54), particularly White men; young people (under 26) are the next most likely to commit suicide (CDC, 2000, 2005, 2013; Miniño et al., 2002).

- From 1950 to 1995, worldwide suicide rates increased by 60%, particularly among young men (WHO, 1999), making it the third leading cause of death for teenagers, particularly males (Waters, 2000).

Gender Differences

- Worldwide, women are more likely to attempt suicide than are men (Nock et al., 2008).

- In the United States, although women are more likely to attempt suicide, men are four times more likely to die from an attempt (CDC, 2005).

Cultural Differences

- Hanging is the most common method of suicide worldwide, but guns are the most common method in the United States (particularly among men), undoubtedly because access to them is easier than in other countries (De Leo, 2002a; Moscicki, 1995; Romero & Wintemute, 2002).

- Internationally, Eastern European countries, as a region, have the highest rates of suicide; examples are Belarus (41.5 per 100,000) and Lithuania (51.6 per 100,000). Latin American countries tend to have the lowest rates; examples are Paraguay (4.2 per 100,000) and Colombia (4.5 per 100,000) (WHO, 2002).

be better off if the person were dead (which Jamison had) to specific plans to commit suicide.

Approximately 30% of those who have thoughts of suicide have also conceived of a plan (Kessler, Borges, et al., 1999). Even having a plan does not by itself indicate that a person is at risk for suicide. However, certain behaviors can suggest serious suicidal intent and can serve as warning signs (Packman et al., 2004):

- giving away possessions,

- saying goodbye to friends or family members,

- talking about death or suicide generally or about specific plans to commit suicide,

- threatening to commit suicide, and

- rehearsing a plan for suicide.

Not everyone who plans or is about to commit suicide displays such warning signs.

For some people, suicidal thoughts or plans do turn into actions. Certain methods of suicide are more lethal than others, and the more lethal the method, the more likely it is that the suicide attempt will result in death or serious medical problems. For instance, shooting, hanging, and jumping from a high place are more lethal than taking pills and cutting a vein. In the latter situations, the person often has at least a few minutes to seek help after having acted. Some people may be very ambivalent about suicide and so may attempt suicide with a less lethal method or try to ensure that they are found by others before any lasting damage is done. Unfortunately, these suicide attempts may still end in death because the help the person had anticipated may not materialize. Other people who attempt suicide do not appear to be ambivalent; they may or may not display warning signs

family

I'm so sorry for what I've put you through I never meant to hurt all of you so much and I don't blame any one of you for disowning me I just cant be a burden to you and my friends any longer you are all better off with out me. I'm so sorry for this.

I've just snapped I cant take this meaningless existence anymore I've been a constant disappointment and that trend would have only continued. just remember the good times we had together

I love you mommy
I love you dad
I love you Kira
I love you Valancia
I love you Cynthia
I love you Zach
I love you Cayle
I love you Mark. (ps. I'm really sorry)

Researchers have examined suicide notes to evaluate what leads some people to try to kill themselves. Any conclusions drawn from such data, however, are limited. Fewer than 40% of the people who commit suicide leave notes, and there may be important differences between those who leave notes and those who don't (Leenaars, 1988; O'Connor et al., 1999). Moreover, suicide notes are subject to various self-report biases, including the desire to leave a particular impression and to elicit a particular reaction from the readers (Leenaars, 2003).

but will follow through unless someone or something intervenes (Maris, 2002).

Not all acts associated with suicide—such as certain types of skin cutting—are, in fact, suicide attempts. Such deliberate but nonlethal self-harming is sometimes referred to as *parasuicidal behavior*. People may harm themselves without any suicidal impulse because they feel numb or because such self-harming behaviors allow them to "feel something" (Linehan, 1981). Alternatively, some people deliberately harm themselves to elicit particular reactions from others. Parasuicidal behavior is discussed in more detail in Chapter 13.

Risk and Protective Factors for Suicide

The risk of suicide is higher for people who have a psychological disorder—whether officially diagnosed or not—than for those who do not have a disorder. The three most common types of disorders among those who commit suicide are (Brown et al., 2000; Duberstein & Conwell, 1997; Isometsä, 2000; Moscicki, 2001):

- major depressive disorder (50%),
- personality disorders (40%), and
- substance-related disorders (up to 50% of those who commit suicide are intoxicated by alcohol at the time of their death).

People who commit suicide may have more than one of these disorders. Recognizing that people with disorders other than mood disorders may contemplate suicide, DSM-5 includes a question about suicidal ideation in its cross-cutting symptoms assessment (described in Chapter 3) (American Psychiatric Association, 2013).

Substance use or abuse plays a pivotal role in many suicide attempts because drugs and alcohol can cloud a person's judgment and ability to reason. A history of being impulsive is another significant risk factor for suicide (Sánchez, 2001). Impulsive people may not exhibit warning signs of serious suicidal intent.

Beyond the presence of specific psychological disorders or impulsivity, another strong predictor of completed suicide is a history of past suicide attempts (Moscicki, 1997; Oquendo et al., 2007). Specifically, people who previously made serious attempts are more likely subsequently to die by suicide than are those who did not make serious attempts (Ivarsson et al., 1998; Stephens et al., 1999). Additional risk factors are listed in Table 5.11. Those at risk may benefit from early evaluation and treatment.

One group at increased risk for suicide is gays and lesbians, particularly during adolescence (Ramafedi, 1999). The increased risk, however, stems primarily from the social exclusion and discrimination experienced by these people (Igartua et al., 2003). Among homosexuals, suicide is most likely during the period when disclosing their homosexuality to immediate family members (Igartua et al., 2003). In addition, military personnel in certain settings are at high risk for committing suicide, probably because of the strain on family relationships caused by long and repeated tours of duty, combat-related stress, substance abuse, and legal and financial problems.

Despite such risks, most people who are depressed or have thoughts of suicide do not actually try to kill themselves. Even when in the blackest suicidal despair, specific factors can reduce the risk of a suicide attempt: receiving support from family and friends, holding religious or cultural beliefs that discourage suicide, and getting

TABLE 5.11 • Risk and Protective Factors for Suicide

Risk Factors
• Mental disorder associated with suicidal behavior (e.g., depression, substance abuse, or personality disorder)
• Feeling hopeless
• Being male (in the United States)
• Prior suicidal behavior (suicide threats, suicide attempts)
• Specific behaviors that suggest suicide planning (giving away possessions, saying goodbye to friends, talking about death or suicide, talking about specific plans to commit suicide, rehearsing a suicidal act, and/or accumulating medications)
• Family history of suicidal behavior
• Chronic impulsivity or aggression and low stress tolerance
• Poor coping and problem-solving skills
• Poor judgment and rigid, distorted thinking
• Major life stressors (physical or sexual assault, threats against life, diagnosis of serious medical problem, dissolution of a significant relationship, or sexual identity issues)
• Breakdown of support systems or social isolation
• Changes in mental status (acute deterioration in mental functioning, onset of major mental illness, extreme anxiety, paranoia, or severe depression)
• Unsatisfying relationship history (never married, separated, divorced, or lack of significant relationships)
• Poor work history (spotty work history or chronic unemployment)
• Childhood abuse
• History of violent behavior

Protective Factors
• Married (or having a significant relationship)
• Employed or involved in a structured program (educational or vocational training program)
• Presence of a support system (family, friends, church, and/or social clubs)
• Having children who are under 18 years of age
• Constructive use of leisure time (enjoyable activities)
• General purpose for living (including religious conviction)
• Involved in mental health treatment
• Effective problem-solving skills

Source: Adapted from Sánchez, 2001, Appendix A.

prompt and appropriate treatment for any depression or substance abuse. Additional protective factors are listed in Table 5.11.

Understanding Suicide

To understand why some people commit suicide, we now turn to examine relevant neurological, psychological, and social factors and their feedback loops.

Neurological Factors

Because the main risk factors for suicide are associated with depression and impulsivity (as well as past suicide attempts), it is difficult to identify neurological factors that uniquely contribute to suicide as distinct from factors that contribute to depression and impulsivity. Nevertheless, neurological factors that contribute to suicide per se are beginning to be identified.

Guided by the finding that mood disorders reflect, at least in part, levels of the neurotransmitter serotonin, Bielau and colleagues (2005) reported a suggestive trend: People who committed suicide tended to have fewer neurons in the part of the brain that produces serotonin than did people who died of other causes. In addition, researchers have found that people who commit suicide may have had fewer serotonin receptors in their brains (Boldrini et al., 2005). Notably, impulsivity is also associated with low serotonin levels.

Suicide seems to "run in families" (Correa et al., 2004), but it is difficult to discern a *specific* role of genes in influencing people to commit suicide. Depression has a genetic component, which may account for the higher rates of suicide among both twins in monozygotic pairs (13%) compared to dizygotic pairs (<1%) (Zalsman et al., 2002).

Psychological Factors: Hopelessness and Impulsivity

A number of the risk factors in Table 5.11 are psychological factors, such as poor coping skills (e.g., behaving impulsively) and poor problem-solving skills (e.g., difficulty identifying obstacles that interfere with meeting goals or failing to develop ways to work around obstacles), distorted and rigid thinking (thought patterns associated with depression), and hopelessness. Hopelessness, with its bleak thoughts of the future, is especially associated with suicide (Beck et al., 1985, 1990).

Cultural norms and customs can influence suicide rates. Among the Yuit Eskimos of St. Lawrence, when someone requests suicide three times, relatives are supposed to help the person kill himself or herself (Leighton & Hughes, 1955). In contrast, among the Tiv of Nigeria, suicide reportedly never occurs (Evans & Farberow, 1988). Such cultural norms about suicide can affect a person's beliefs and expectations about suicide.

© Natalie Forbes/Corbis

Social Factors: Alienation and Cultural Stress

Suicide rates vary across countries (De Leo, 2002a; Vijayakumar et al., 2005; WHO, 1999), which suggests that social and cultural factors affect these rates. In some developing countries, the presence or history of a psychological disorder poses less of a risk for suicide than it does in developed countries (Vijayakumar et al., 2005).

One important social factor that influences suicidal behavior is religion. Countries where the citizens are more religious tend to have lower suicide rates than do countries where citizens are less religious. Countries with a large Muslim population are among those with the lowest suicide rates in the world, followed by countries with a large Roman Catholic population; the tenets of both of these religions forbid suicide (De Leo, 2002a; Simpson & Conklin, 1989).

ONLINE

Feedback Loops in Understanding Suicide

Suicide can best be understood as arising from the confluence of neurological, psychological, and social factors. A neurological vulnerability, such as abnormal neurotransmitter functioning, serves as the backdrop. Add to that the psychological factors: depression or feelings of hopelessness, beliefs about suicide, poor coping skills, and perhaps impulsive or violent personality traits. In turn, these factors affect, and are affected by, social and cultural forces—such as economic realities, wars, cultural beliefs and norms about suicide, religion, stressful life events, and social support. The dynamic balance among all these factors can influence a person's suicidal ideation, plans, and behavior (Sánchez, 2001; Wenzel et al., 2009).

Preventing Suicide

Suicide prevention efforts can focus on immediate safety or longer-term prevention.

Crisis Intervention

For a person who is actively suicidal, the first aim of suicide prevention is to make sure that the person is safe. After this, crisis intervention helps the person see past the hopelessness and rigidity that pervades his or her thinking, identifies whatever stressors have brought the person to this point, helps him or her develop new solutions to the problems, and enhances his or her ability to cope.

In addition, a clinician tries to discover whether the person is depressed or abusing substances; if so, these problems, which may lead to suicidal thoughts or behaviors, should be treated (Reifman & Windle, 1995). Because most people who die by suicide had untreated depression, treatment for depression that targets psychological factors—typically CBT—can play a key role in suicide prevention. Medications may also be prescribed to reduce depressive symptoms.

Long-Term Prevention

Ideally, long-term prevention programs decrease risk factors and increase protective factors, which should decrease the suicide rate. Thus, programs to prevent child abuse, to provide affordable access to mental health care (and so make it easier to obtain treatment for psychological disorders, in particular depression), to decrease substance abuse, and to increase employment may all help prevent suicides in the long term.

Part of the national suicide prevention plan in the United States is to increase awareness about suicide (Satcher, 1999), both among people who may feel suicidal and among the friends and family of someone feeling suicidal. The hope is that suicidal people will receive appropriate help before they commit suicide (see Table 5.12).

In 2012 the number of suicides among U.S. Army soldiers was greater than in previous years, having risen sharply since 2005 (Williams, 2012). The Army's suicide prevention efforts include hiring additional mental health providers and instituting a program to teach junior Army leaders how to recognize signs of suicide intention in their troops and how to then intervene (Tyson, 2008).

TABLE 5.12 • Suicide Prevention: What to Do

What can you do if someone you know seems to be suicidal? According to the National Institute of Mental Health (Goldsmith et al., 2002):

• don't leave the person alone;

• get help by calling 911 or other trained emergency professionals;

• try to make sure that potential means for committing suicide, such as firearms or poisons, are not easily accessible; and

• let the person know that you are concerned and try not to be judgmental.

If you, or someone you know, are at risk for suicide, the following organizations can help:

• National Suicide Prevention Lifeline
  Phone: 800-273-TALK (8255). This will connect you with a crisis center in your area.
  Website: **www.suicidepreventionlifeline.org**

• American Foundation for Suicide Prevention
  Phone: 212-363-3500
  Website: **www.afsp.org**

• Suicide Prevention Resource Center
  Phone: 617-438-7772
  Website: **www.sprc.org**

Thinking Like A Clinician

Based on what you have learned about suicide, explain Kay Jamison's suicide attempt in terms of the three types of factors. Identify how the neurological, psychological and social factors might have influenced each other via feedback loops. From what you know of her, what were Jamison's risk and protective factors?

☐ SUMMING UP

Depressive Disorders

- A major depressive episode (MDE) is a mood episode upon which a diagnosis of major depressive disorder (MDD) is based. Symptoms of an MDE can arise in three areas: affect, behavior, and cognition. Most people who have an MDE return to their premorbid level of functioning after the episode, but some people will have symptoms that do not completely resolve, even after several years.

- Depression is becoming increasingly prevalent in younger cohorts. Depression and anxiety disorders have a high comorbidity—around 50%.

- MDD may arise with psychotic features.

- In some cases, depression is related to pregnancy and giving birth (peripartum onset) or to seasonal changes in light.

- A diagnosis of persistent depressive disorder requires fewer symptoms than does a diagnosis of MDD; however, the symptoms of persistent depressive disorder must persist for at least 2 years.

- Neurological factors related to depression include low levels of activity in the frontal lobes, and abnormal functioning of various neurotransmitters (dopamine, serotonin, and norepinephrine). The stress–diathesis model of depression highlights the role of increased activity of the HPA axis and of excess cortisol in the blood. Genes can play a role in depression, perhaps by influencing how a person responds to stressful events, which in turn affects the activity of the HPA axis.

- Psychological factors that are associated with depression include a bias toward paying attention to negative stimuli, dysfunctional thoughts, rumination, a negative attributional style, and learned helplessness.

- Social factors that are associated with depression include stressful life events, social exclusion, and problems with social interactions or relationships. Culture and gender can influence the specific ways that symptoms of depression are expressed.

- Neurological, psychological, and social factors can affect each other through feedback loops, as outlined by the stress–diathesis model and Coyne's interactional theory of depression. According to the stress–diathesis model, abuse or neglect during childhood (a stressor) and increased activity in the HPA axis can lead to overreactive cortisol-releasing cells (a diathesis), which respond strongly to even mild stressors. Psychological factors can create a cognitive vulnerability to depression, which in turn can amplify the negative effects of a stressor and change social interactions. Coyne's theory proposes that among neurologically vulnerable people, their depression-related behaviors may alienate other people, producing social stressors.

- Biomedical treatments that target neurological factors for depressive disorders are medications (SSRIs, TCAs, MAOIs, SNRIs, NaSSAs) and St. John's wort, and brain stimulation (ECT or TMS).

- Treatments for depression that target psychological factors include CBT (particularly with behavioral activation).

- Treatments that target social factors include IPT and systems therapy.

Bipolar Disorders

- The three types of mood episode that underlie bipolar disorders are major depressive episode (MDE), manic episode, and hypomanic episode. Symptoms of a manic episode include grandiosity, pressured speech, flight of ideas, distractibility, poor judgment, decreased need for sleep, and psychomotor agitation. A hypomanic episode involves mood that is persistently elated, irritable, or euphoric; unlike other mood episodes, hypomanic episodes do not impair functioning.

- There are two types of bipolar disorder: Bipolar I disorder—usually more severe—requires only a manic episode; an MDE may occur but is not necessary for this diagnosis. Bipolar II disorder requires alternating hypomanic episodes and MDEs and no history of manic episodes. Cyclothymic disorder is a more chronic but less intense version of bipolar II disorder.

- Neurological factors that are associated with bipolar disorders include an enlarged and more active amygdala. Norepinephrine, serotonin, and glutamate are also involved. Bipolar disorders are influenced by genetic factors, which may affect mood disorders in general.

- Psychological factors that are associated with bipolar disorders include the cognitive distortions and negative thinking associated with depression.

- Social factors that are associated with bipolar disorders include disruptive life changes and social and environmental stressors. The different factors create feedback loops that can lead to a bipolar disorder or make the patient more likely to relapse.

- Treatments that target neurological factors include medications that act as mood stabilizers, such as lithium and anticonvulsants. When manic, patients may receive an antipsychotic medication or a benzodiazepine. Patients with a bipolar disorder who have MDEs may receive an antidepressant along with a mood stabilizer.

- Treatment that targets psychological factors—particularly CBT—helps patients recognize warning signs of mood episodes, develop better sleeping strategies, and, when appropriate, stay on medication.

- Treatments that target social factors include interpersonal and social rhythm therapy (IPSRT), family therapy, and group therapy or a self-help group.

Suicide

- Suicide is ranked 10th among causes of death in North America. Having thoughts of suicide or making a plan to carry it out may indicate a risk for suicide; certain behavioral changes (such as giving away possessions) may indicate a more serious risk. However, not everyone who attempts or commits suicide displays warning signs. In addition, certain types of self-harm may be parasuicidal behaviors rather than suicide attempts. The presence of certain psychological disorders, such as MDD, and a history of previous serious suicide attempts increase a person's risk for suicide.

- Neurological factors that are associated with suicide include altered serotonin activity and a genetic predisposition. Psychological risk factors for suicide include poor coping and problem-solving skills, distorted and rigid thinking, and a sense of hopelessness. Variations in suicide rates across countries point to a relationship between social factors and suicide.

- Crisis intervention efforts to prevent suicide first ensure that the suicidal person is safe and then help the person see past the hopelessness and rigidity that pervade his or her thinking. Longer-term suicide prevention may also help the patient to identify the stressors that led him or her to feel suicidal and develop new solutions to the problems.

Key Terms

Mood disorders (p. 115)

Major depressive episode (MDE) (p. 116)

Anhedonia (p. 116)

Psychomotor agitation (p. 116)

Psychomotor retardation (p. 117)

Hypersomnia (p. 117)

Prodrome (p. 118)

Premorbid (p. 118)

Major depressive disorder (MDD) (p. 118)

Phototherapy (p. 119)

Age cohort (p. 119)

Persistent depressive disorder (dysthymia) (p. 120)

Disruptive mood dysregulation disorder (DMDD) (p. 120)

Selective serotonin reuptake inhibitors (SSRIs) (p. 130)

Tricyclic antidepressants (TCAs) (p. 130)

Monoamine oxidase inhibitors (MAOIs) (p. 130)

Electroconvulsive therapy (ECT) (p. 131)

Transcranial magnetic stimulation (TMS) (p. 132)

Behavior therapy (p. 132)

Cognitive therapy (p. 133)

Cognitive-behavior therapy (CBT) (p. 133)

Interpersonal therapy (IPT) (p. 134)

Bipolar disorders (p. 136)

Manic episode (p. 137)

Expansive mood (p. 137)

Flight of ideas (p. 138)

Rapid cycling (of moods) (p. 139)

Cyclothymic disorder (p. 140)

Mood stabilizer (p. 144)

Lithium (p. 144)

Suicidal ideation (p. 146)

More Study Aids

For additional study aids related to this chapter, including quizzes to make sure you've retained everything you've learned and a Student Video Activity exploring one man's struggle with persistent depressive disorder, go to: www.worthpublishers.com/launchpad/rkabpsych2e.

Photodisc

CHAPTER **6**

Anxiety Disorders

Earl Campbell, born in 1955, gained fame as a National Football League (NFL) running back from 1978 to 1985. Campbell was such an outstanding athlete that he was voted most valuable player for each of his first 3 years in the NFL. He was later inducted into the Football Hall of Fame and went on to achieve in other areas of life: He became a food manufacturer, restaurateur, and businessman.

Campbell possessed remarkable talents and abilities and an unusually strong drive to achieve. But he also suffered from symptoms of anxiety disorders. *Anxiety disorders* involve significant fear, agitation, and nervousness and can impair functioning in any or all spheres of life, including school, work, and interpersonal relationships. Campbell developed such severe anxiety symptoms that he became unable to work effectively.

IN THIS CHAPTER, we discuss six types of anxiety disorders that are described in DSM-5: generalized anxiety disorder, panic disorder, agoraphobia, social anxiety disorder, specific phobia, and separation anxiety disorder. We'll start with a general discussion of what anxiety is and identify some of the common features of the different anxiety disorders. In the process, we'll examine how Earl Campbell responded to and handled his anxieties.

▢ Common Features of Anxiety Disorders

Earl Campbell played high school football and, after graduating, became a star running back on the University of Texas–Austin football team. From there, he went on to play for the Houston Oilers in the NFL. At age 24, he married Reuna, a woman from his hometown whom he had been dating for 10 years. Five years later, they had their first child, and 2 years after that, at the age of 31, Campbell retired from football.

In his 30s, former NFL player Earl Campbell suddenly developed symptoms of anxiety—racing heart and trouble breathing—which frightened him, as they would most people.

Campbell went on to work for the University of Texas–Austin as a goodwill ambassador, representing the school at various functions, and helping student-athletes commit to their studies. One day, as Campbell was driving from Austin to Dallas, he stopped at a traffic light and had an unusual experience:

> Out of the blue, my heart started racing. I felt my chest. Then I broke into a cold sweat, began hyperventilating, and became convinced I was having a heart attack. The people in the car next to mine seemed totally unaware that anything was wrong. My heart just kept racing. I couldn't stop it. I was going to die. How could I stop it? It was getting worse. I was dying! The driver behind me started blowing his horn. The light had turned green. I needed help. I couldn't get out of the car. "God help me!" I prayed. Then it stopped—just like that, my heart stopped racing. I put my hand to my heart again. It felt normal. My hands and arms were covered with a cold clammy sweat. I wiped the perspiration from my face and look[ed] at myself in the rearview mirror. For the first time in my life, I caught sight of a frightened Earl Campbell and I didn't like it. . . .
> (Campbell & Ruane, 1999, pp. 83–84)

Not only did Campbell have frightening bodily sensations, but he also developed worries about "the little details that most people don't even think about. They weigh on me and tie up my mind. I am continually inundated with intrusive thoughts related to everything I say or do. Do I look okay? Am I walking right? Did I do this right? That right? Why is everyone looking at me? Is it because I'm Earl Campbell, or is it because there's something wrong with me?" (Campbell & Ruane, 1999, p. 199). Campbell's experiences involve anxiety.

What Is Anxiety?

Like the term *depression*, the words *anxiety* and *anxious* are used in everyday speech. But what do mental health professionals and researchers mean when they use these terms? **Anxiety** refers to a sense of agitation or nervousness, which is often focused on an upcoming potential danger.

We all feel afraid and anxious from time to time. These feelings can be adaptive, signaling the presence of a dangerous stimulus, which in turn leads us to be more alert—which then heightens our senses. For instance, if you are walking alone down a dark, quiet street late at night, you might feel anxious, which makes you alert; you might then be able to hear particularly well or be more sensitive to another person's presence behind you. Such heightened senses can be adaptive on a dark street. Should you hear or sense someone, you may choose to head quickly to a well-lit and busier street. Similarly, a moderate level of anxiety before a test or presentation can enhance your performance (Deshpande & Kawane, 1982)—and, in fact, the absence of anxiety can lead to lackluster performance, even if you know the material well. Thus, feeling afraid or anxious can be normal and adaptive.

Extreme anxiety, however, is a persistent, vague sense of dread or foreboding even when not in the presence of a feared stimulus (such as a snake or a plane trip). An **anxiety disorder** involves fear, extreme anxiety, intense arousal, and extreme attempts to avoid stimuli that lead to fear and anxiety. These emotions, or the efforts to avoid experiencing them, can create a high level of distress, which can interfere with normal functioning.

The Fight-or-Flight Response Gone Awry

Campbell describes some of the frightening physical sensations he experienced in this way: "Visualize yourself just sitting back in a chair, relaxing. Suddenly, your heart starts racing as if you had just run a hundred-yard dash. You break into a cold sweat. You have trouble breathing. You feel there is nothing you can do to stop all

Anxiety
A sense of agitation or nervousness, which is often focused on an upcoming possible danger.

Anxiety disorder
A category of psychological disorders in which the primary symptoms involve fear, extreme anxiety, intense arousal, and/or extreme attempts to avoid stimuli that lead to fear and anxiety.

AP Photo

of these things from happening" (Campbell & Ruane, 1999, p. i). Campbell was describing the effects of the **fight-or-flight response**, also called the *stress response* (see Chapter 2), which occurs when a person perceives a threat. Suppose you think you see a mugger lurking on a dark doorstep as you are hurrying home, alone, late at night. Your brain and body respond as if you must either fight or take flight, primarily by activating the sympathetic branch of the autonomic nervous system. The stress response prepares your body to exert physical energy for an action, either fighting the threat or running away from it. It does not matter whether there is an actual threat. Your body automatically responds because you *perceive* a threat. Your body responds in a number of ways, most notably by:

- increasing your heart rate and breathing rate (in order to provide more oxygen to your muscles and brain),
- increasing the sweat on your palms (a small amount, which helps you grip better—yet not so much as to make your palms become slippery), and
- dilating your pupils (in order to let in more light and help you to see better).

Your body responds this way even to threats that do not require a lot of physical energy, such as—for many people—speaking in front of a group (or even *thinking* about speaking in front of them) or taking a pop quiz. In such cases, your body gets prepared, but most of the physical preparations aren't really necessary.

This fight-or-flight (stress) response underlies the fear and anxiety involved in almost all anxiety disorders. Some people have an overactive stress response—they have higher levels of arousal during this response. Other people may not have an overactive stress response, but they may misinterpret their arousal during this response and attribute the bodily sensations to a physical ailment. They might, for instance, interpret an increased heart rate as a heart attack. In either case, some people come to feel afraid or anxious about the physical sensations of the fight-or-flight response or the conditions that seem to have caused it. When their arousal feels as if it is getting out of control, they may start to feel **panic**, which is an extreme sense (or fear) of imminent doom, together with an extreme stress response (Bouton et al., 2001)—what Campbell experienced sitting in his car at a stoplight. Some people who become panicked develop a **phobia**, which is an exaggerated fear of an object or a situation, together with an extreme avoidance of that object or situation. Such avoidance can interfere with everyday life. For instance, at one point, Campbell avoided crowded rooms because he thought that they might bring on the uncomfortable physical sensations he'd experienced.

Significant anxiety and phobias are not unusual or rare. In the United States, anxiety disorders are the most common kind of mental disorder (Barlow, 2002a); approximately 15% of people will have some type of anxiety disorder in their lifetimes (Somers et al., 2006). Women are twice as likely as men to be diagnosed with an anxiety disorder (Somers et al., 2006). Some explanations of this gender difference rest on biological factors, such as the hormonal shifts that occur during a woman's childbearing years (Ginsberg, 2004); the possible role of hormones is consistent with the fact that the gender difference in anxiety disorders coincides with the onset of puberty (as is the case with depression; see Chapter 5). Other explanations for the gender difference rest on cultural factors (Pigott, 1999): Unlike Campbell, many men tend to be reluctant to acknowledge symptoms of anxiety because they fear that admitting such feelings might undercut the masculine image they project to others.

Comorbidity of Anxiety Disorders

As you'll see throughout this text, symptoms of anxiety or avoidance may occur in many psychological disorders, including *mood disorders* (Chapter 5), *body dysmorphic*

Fight-or-flight response
The automatic neurological and bodily response to a perceived threat; also called the *stress response*.

Panic
An extreme sense (or fear) of imminent doom, together with an extreme stress response.

Phobia
An exaggerated fear of an object or a situation, together with an extreme avoidance of the object or situation.

People with phobias, such as musicians with performance anxiety (stage fright), may use alcohol to relieve their anxiety symptoms. However, using alcohol in this way can lead to alcoholism, as was the case in the early days of Sheryl Crow's career.

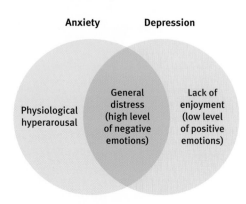

FIGURE **6.1 • Tripartite Model of Anxiety and Depression** Anxiety and depression have in common a high level of negative emotions, but each has unique elements: Anxiety generally involves a very high level of physiological arousal, whereas depression involves a low level of positive emotions.

Generalized anxiety disorder (GAD)
An anxiety disorder characterized by uncontrollable worry and anxiety about a number of events or activities, which are not solely the result of another disorder.

disorder (Chapter 7), and *anorexia nervosa* (Chapter 10). Clinicians must determine whether the anxiety and avoidance symptoms are the *primary* cause of the disturbance or a by-product of another type of problem. In the case of anorexia nervosa, for example, when someone gets anxious about eating high-calorie foods, the anxiety is *secondary* to larger concerns about food, weight, and appearance.

Anxiety and depression often occur together; approximately 50% of people with an anxiety disorder are also depressed (Brown et al., 2001). Researchers and clinicians are trying to discover why there is such high comorbidity between anxiety disorders and depression. Some researchers have proposed a three-part model of anxiety and depression that specifies the ways in which the two kinds of disorders overlap and the ways in which they are distinct (Clark & Watson, 1991; Mineka, Watson, & Clark, 1998). This model has been supported by research (Joiner, 1996; Olino et al., 2008). The three parts of the model are depicted in Figure 6.1. Another disorder that commonly co-occurs with an anxiety disorder is substance use disorder, and approximately 10–25% of people who have anxiety disorders also abuse alcohol (Bibb & Chambless, 1986; Otto et al., 1992).

Thinking Like A Clinician

What is the difference between fear and anxiety? Why (or when) might the fight-or-flight response become a problem? If people can have symptoms of anxiety when they have other types of disorders, what determines whether an anxiety disorder should be the diagnosis?

Generalized Anxiety Disorder

Earl Campbell became a worrier—even during the best of times:

> On a day when life seems absolutely wonderful—say, a beautiful fall Saturday or Sunday when I'm watching one of my boys play football—I'll often be overcome by the fear that it will all come to an end somehow. It's just too good. Something bad is going to ruin it for me. This past year was the most difficult one I've had. . . . Tyler [his son] was in the fifth grade, and I worried the entire year. I was in the fifth grade when my father died, and I thought my fate was sealed. I was scared I would die and my boys would have to go through life without a father, the way I did.
> (Campbell & Ruane, 1999, p. 204)

Worrying is a normal part of life, and some people worry more than others. But how much is "too much" worrying?

What Is Generalized Anxiety Disorder?

Generalized anxiety disorder (GAD) is characterized by excessive and persistent worry and anxiety about a number of events or activities (which are not solely the focus of another disorder, such as worrying about having a panic attack) (see Table 6.1; American Psychiatric Association, 2013). For people suffering from GAD, the worry and anxiety focus primarily on family, finances, work, and illness (Sanderson & Barlow, 1990), and—given the actual extent of the problem with family, finances, work, or illness—the person's worries are excessive (as determined by the mental health clinician). Earl Campbell worried mostly about family and illness; other people may worry about minor matters (Craske et al., 1989). In contrast to most other people, people with GAD worry even when things are going well. Moreover, their worries intrude into their awareness when they are trying to focus on other thoughts, and they lead people to feel on edge or have muscle tension (American Psychiatric Association, 2013). Like A. H., discussed in Case 6.1, people with GAD feel a chronic, low level of anxiety or worry about many things. Moreover, the fact that they constantly worry in itself causes them distress.

CASE 6.1 • FROM THE OUTSIDE: Generalized Anxiety Disorder

A. H. was a 39-year-old divorced mother of two (son aged 12, daughter aged 7) who worked as a bank manager. However, she had become concerned about her ability to concentrate on and remember information while at work. A. H. had made some "financially disastrous" mistakes and was now—at the suggestion of her supervisor—taking some vacation time to "get her head together." Because of her concentration and memory problems, it had been taking her longer to complete her work, so she had been arriving at work 30 minutes early each day, and she often took work home. She reported being unable to relax, even outside of work, and at work it was hard to make decisions because she ruminated endlessly ("Is this the right decision, or should I do that?") and hence tried to avoid making decisions altogether. Her concentration and memory problems were worst when she was worried about some aspect of life, which was most of the time. She reported that 75% of her waking life each day was spent in a state of anxiety and worry. In addition to worrying about her performance at work, she worried about her children's well-being (whether they had been hurt or killed while out playing in the neighborhood). She also worried about her relationships with men and minor things such as getting to work on time, keeping her house clean, and maintaining regular contact with friends and family. A. H. recognized that her fears were both excessive and uncontrollable, but she couldn't dismiss any worry that came to mind. She was irritable, had insomnia, had frequent muscle tension and headaches, and felt generally on edge.

(Adapted from Brown & Barlow, 1997, pp. 1–3)

Because the symptoms are chronic (lasting at least 6 months) and because many people with GAD can usually function adequately in some areas of their daily lives, they come to see their worrying and anxiety as a part of themselves, not as a disorder. However, the intrusive worrying can lead to problems in work and social life. See Table 6.2 for more facts about GAD.

As noted in Table 6.2, GAD and depression have an extremely high comorbidity. Among people who have both disorders at the same time, only 27% eventually experience remission, compared to 48% of those who have only GAD and 41% of those who have only depression (Schoevers et al., 2005). People with both disorders are also likely to have had their symptoms arise at a younger age, to have more severe symptoms of each disorder, and to function less well than those who have only one of the two disorders (Moffitt et al., 2007; Zimmerman & Chelminski, 2003). The high comorbidity also suggests that GAD and depression may reflect different facets of the same underlying problem, which is rooted in distress, worry, and the continued intrusion of negative thoughts (Ruscio et al., 2011; Schoevers et al., 2003).

Understanding Generalized Anxiety Disorder

GAD can be best understood by using the neuropsychosocial approach to examine its etiology—by considering neurological, psychological, and social factors and the feedback loops among them. Each type of factor, by itself, seems to be

---

TABLE 6.1 • DSM-5 Diagnostic Criteria for Generalized Anxiety Disorder (GAD)

A. Excessive anxiety and worry (apprehensive expectation), occurring more days than not for at least 6 months, about a number of events or activities (such as work or school performance).

B. The individual finds it difficult to control the worry.

C. The anxiety and worry are associated with three (or more) of the following six symptoms (with at least some symptoms having been present for more days than not for the past 6 months):

Note: Only one item is required in children.

1. Restlessness or feeling keyed up or on edge.
2. Being easily fatigued.
3. Difficulty concentrating or mind going blank.
4. Irritability.
5. Muscle tension.
6. Sleep disturbance (difficulty falling or staying asleep, or restless, unsatisfying sleep).

D. The anxiety, worry, or physical symptoms cause clinically significant distress or impairment in social, occupational, or other important areas of functioning.

E. The disturbance is not attributable to the physiological effects of a substance (e.g., a drug of abuse, a medication) or another medical condition (e.g., hyperthyroidism).

F. The disturbance is not better explained by another mental disorder (e.g., anxiety or worry about having panic attacks in panic disorder, negative evaluation in social anxiety disorder [social phobia], contamination or other obsessions in obsessive-compulsive disorder, separation from attachment figures in separation anxiety disorder, reminders of traumatic events in posttraumatic stress disorder, gaining weight in anorexia nervosa, physical complaints in somatic symptom disorder, perceived appearance flaws in body dysmorphic disorder, having a serious illness in illness anxiety disorder, or the content of delusional beliefs in schizophrenia or delusional disorder).

TABLE 6.2 • Generalized Anxiety Disorder Facts at a Glance

Prevalence

• Approximately 9% of people will develop GAD in their lifetime.

Comorbidity

• GAD occurs very frequently with depression, with up to 80% of those having GAD also experiencing depression at some point (Judd et al., 1998).

Onset

• Approximately half the people with GAD develop the disorder before the age of 30.

Course

• People diagnosed with GAD report that they have felt nervous and anxious all their lives.

• Once someone has GAD, its course is likely to be chronic, with symptoms fluctuating in response to stress.

Gender Differences

• Twice as many women as men are diagnosed with GAD.

Cultural Differences

• The content of the worries of people with GAD is shaped by their culture, their personal experiences, and the environment in which they live. Some people worry about catastrophic events, such as natural disasters; others worry about human-caused calamities, such as nuclear war or terrorist acts.

Source: Unless otherwise noted, the source for information is American Psychiatric Association, 2013

Hypervigilance
A heightened search for threats.

A construction forewoman talks with a member of her crew. If one of her employees were to have GAD, he might be hypervigilant for possible threats in his environment—for example, constantly scanning the boss's face for possible signs of displeasure or glancing at the figure in the background to make sure he wasn't a threat.

necessary but not sufficient to give rise to this disorder. It may be best to conceive of neurological and psychological factors as setting the stage, and social factors as triggering the symptoms.

Neurological Factors

The parasympathetic nervous system appears to play a special role in GAD, a complex mix of neurotransmitters is involved in the disorder, and genetics can predispose someone to develop GAD.

Brain Systems

Unlike most other types of anxiety disorders, GAD isn't associated with the cranked-up sympathetic nervous system activity that underlies the fight-or-flight response (Marten et al., 1993). Instead, GAD is associated with decreased arousal that arises from an unusually responsive parasympathetic nervous system. The parasympathetic nervous system tends to cause effects opposite those caused by the sympathetic nervous system. So, for instance, heightened parasympathetic activity slows heart rate, stimulates digestion and the bladder, and causes pupils to contract (Barlow, 2002a). When a person with GAD perceives a threatening stimulus, his or her subsequent worry temporarily *reduces* arousal (Borkovec & Hu, 1990), suppresses negative emotions (see Figure 6.1), and produces muscle tension (Barlow, 2002a; Pluess et al., 2009). These facts are in stark contrast to Earl Campbell's symptoms, which suggest that he did not have GAD.

Neural Communication

Although the frontal lobes of patients with GAD are normal in size, the dopamine in the frontal lobes of these patients does not function normally (Stein, Westenberg, & Liebowitz, 2002). In fact, numerous studies suggest that a wide range of neurotransmitters, including gamma-aminobutyric acid (GABA), serotonin, and norepinephrine, may not function properly in people with GAD (Nutt, 2001). These neurotransmitters affect, among other things, people's response to reward, their motivation, and how effectively they can pay attention to stimuli and events.

Genetics

Studies of the genetics of GAD have produced solid evidence that GAD has a genetic component, and the disorder is equally heritable for men and women (Hettema, Prescott, & Kendler, 2001). However, if one family member has GAD, other family members are likely to have GAD or depression, which suggests a common underlying genetic vulnerability (Gorwood, 2004; Kendler et al., 2007).

Psychological Factors: Hypervigilance and the Illusion of Control

Psychological factors that contribute to GAD generally involve three characteristic modes of thinking and behaving:

1. People with GAD pay a lot of attention to stimuli in their environment, searching for possible threats. This heightened search for threats is called **hypervigilance**.

Dana White/Photo Edit

2. People with GAD typically feel that their worries are out of control and that they can't stop or alter the pattern of their thoughts, no matter what they do.

3. The mere act of worrying prevents anxiety from becoming panic (Craske, 1999), and thus the act of worrying is negatively reinforcing (Borkovec, 1994a; Borkovec et al., 1999). The worrying does not help the person to cope with the problem at hand, but it does give him or her the *illusion* of coping, which temporarily decreases anxiety about the perceived threat. Some people think that if they worry, they are actively addressing a problem. But they are not—worrying is not the same thing as effective problem solving; the original concern isn't reduced by the worrying, and it remains a problem, along with the additional problem of chronic worrying.

The content of the worries of people with GAD is influenced by their culture and the types of catastrophic events most likely to occur in their locale. Those who live along the Gulf Coast of the United States may worry about hurricanes; those who reside in California may worry about earthquakes; and those who reside in the Midwest may worry about tornadoes.

Social Factors: Stressors

Stressful life events—such as a death in the family, friction in a close relationship, or trouble on the job—can trigger symptoms of GAD in someone who is neurologically and psychologically vulnerable to developing it. For people who develop GAD after age 40, the disorder often arises after the person experiences a significant stressor.

GAD also appears to be related more directly to relationships. People with GAD may experience increased stress if they view themselves as having serious problems in relationships. Increased stress, in turn, can lead to distress and negative emotions that can be difficult to manage and regulate (Mennin et al., 2004).

Feedback Loops in Understanding Generalized Anxiety Disorder

Stressful life experiences (typically social factors) can trigger the onset of GAD, but most people who experience stressful periods in their lives—even extreme stress—never develop this disorder. Moreover, people who develop GAD often report that they were afraid and avoidant as children (American Psychiatric Association, 2013), which may be explained by abnormal neurological functioning. However, such abnormal functioning in childhood could arise from genes, might develop in childhood because of early life experiences, or could be caused by some combination of the two. To develop GAD, a person probably must have abnormal neurological functioning (which may reflect abnormal levels of GABA or another neurotransmitter), have learned certain kinds of worry-related behaviors such as hypervigilance for threats, and have experienced a highly stressful event or set of events such as a death in the family. Any one of these alone—and probably any two of these—will not cause GAD.

ONLINE

Treating Generalized Anxiety Disorder

Treatment for GAD can target neurological, psychological, or social factors, but neurological or psychological factors are the predominant focus of treatments. As usual, interventions targeting any one type of factor have ripple effects that in turn alter the other types of factors.

Targeting Neurological Factors: Medication

The antianxiety medication *buspirone* (Buspar) effectively reduces the symptoms of GAD, probably by decreasing serotonin release. Serotonin facilitates changes in the amygdala that underlie learning to fear objects or situations (Huang & Kandel, 2007); thus, reducing serotonin may impair learning to fear or worry about specific objects or situations.

Biofeedback
A technique in which a person is trained to bring normally involuntary or unconscious bodily activity, such as heart rate or muscle tension, under voluntary control.

Habituation
The process by which the emotional response to a stimulus that elicits fear or anxiety is reduced by exposing the patient to the stimulus repeatedly.

Exposure
A behavioral technique that involves repeated contact with a feared or arousing stimulus in a controlled setting, bringing about habituation.

Most people with GAD are also depressed, but buspirone only helps anxiety symptoms (Davidson, 2001). In contrast, the serotonin/norepinephrine reuptake inhibitor (SNRI) *venlafaxine* (Effexor) and certain selective serotonin reuptake inhibitors (SSRIs), such as *paroxetine* (Paxil) and *escitalopram* (Lexapro), appear to relieve both anxiety and depressive symptoms (Baldwin & Polkinghorn, 2005; Davidson, 2001). This is why an SNRI is considered the "first-line medication" for people with both GAD and depression, meaning that it is the medication that clinicians try first with these patients (unless there is a reason not to use it).

Targeting Psychological Factors

Psychological treatments for GAD generally have several aims:

• to increase the person's sense of control over thoughts and worries,

• to allow the person to assess more accurately how likely and dangerous perceived threats actually are, and

• to decrease muscle tension.

Psychotherapy for GAD generally consists of behavioral and cognitive methods, which can successfully decrease symptoms (Cottraux, 2004; Durham et al., 2003; Hanrahan et al., 2013).

Behavioral Methods

Behavioral methods to treat GAD focus on three main areas (Barlow, 2002a):

• awareness and control of breathing,

• awareness and control of muscle tension and relaxation, and

• elimination, reduction, or prevention of worries and behaviors associated with worries.

Breathing retraining requires patients to become aware of their breathing and to try to control it by taking deep, relaxing breaths. Such breathing can help induce relaxation and provide a sense of coping—of doing something positive in response to worry.

Similarly, *muscle relaxation training* requires patients to become aware of early signs of muscle tension, a symptom of GAD in some people, and then to relax those muscles.

This woman is learning how to control the muscle tension in her face through biofeedback.

Patients can learn how to identify tense muscles and then relax them through standard relaxation techniques or **biofeedback**, a technique in which a person is trained to bring normally involuntary or unconscious bodily activity, such as heart rate or muscle tension, under voluntary control. Typically, electrodes are attached to a targeted muscle or group of muscles, and the patient can see on a monitor or hear from a speaker signals that indicate whether the monitored muscles are tense or relaxed. This feedback helps the patient learn how to detect and reduce the tension, eventually without relying on the feedback.

A common treatment for anxiety disorders, including GAD, is based on the principle of **habituation**: The emotional response to a stimulus that elicits fear or anxiety is reduced by exposing the patient to the stimulus repeatedly. The technique of **exposure** involves such repeated contact with the (feared or arousing) stimulus in a controlled setting, and usually in a gradual way, bringing about habituation. Exposure, and therefore habituation, to fear- or anxiety-related stimuli does not normally occur outside of therapy because people avoid the object or situation, thereby making exposure (and habituation) unlikely. In exposure-based treatment, the patient first creates a hierarchy of feared events, arranging them from least to most feared, and then begins the exposure process by having contact with the least-feared item on the hierarchy. With GAD, that might be addressing worries about possibly bouncing a check (lower in the hierarchy) to worries that if a spouse is late it is because he or she was in a car accident. With sustained exposure, the symptoms diminish within 20 to 30 minutes or less; that is, habituation to the fear- or anxiety-inducing stimuli occurs. Over multiple sessions, this process is repeated with items higher in the hierarchy (i.e., those that are more feared), until all items no longer elicit significant symptoms. Patients in therapy can experience exposure in three ways:

- *imaginal exposure*, which relies on forming mental images of the stimulus;

- *virtual reality exposure*, which consists of exposure to a computer-generated (often very realistic) representation of the stimulus; and

- **in vivo exposure**, which is direct exposure to the actual stimulus.

People with GAD often develop behaviors that are associated with their worries. For instance, a patient who worries that "something bad" may happen to her family may call home several times each day. By calling home and finding out that everyone is fine, she temporarily reduces her anxiety, thus (negatively) reinforcing the calling behavior. People with GAD do not naturally habituate to such anxiety; as they worry about one set of concerns, they get increasingly anxious until they shift the focus of their worry to another set of concerns, never becoming habituated to any specific set of concerns.

Using exposure to treat GAD, patients are asked to think about only one specific worry (this is the exposure) and to imagine their worst possible fears about the subject of that worry, such as the possible deaths of family members. Patients are asked to think about their worry continuously for about 30 minutes. After this half-hour of exposure, patients then list their rational responses to the worst outcomes they imagined. Patients' anxiety and level of worry should decrease both over the course of the session and across sessions. When patients can think about one set of concerns without much worry or anxiety, they move on to use the same procedure with another set of concerns (see Figure 6.2, on the next page).

Cognitive Methods

Cognitive methods for treating GAD focus on first helping patients to identify the thought patterns that are associated with their worries and anxieties and then helping them to use cognitive restructuring and other methods to prevent these thought patterns from spiraling out of control. The methods can also decrease the *intensity* of patients' responses to their thought patterns, so that they are less likely to develop symptoms. Specific cognitive methods include the following:

- *Psychoeducation*, which is the process of educating patients about research findings and therapy procedures relevant to their situation. For patients with GAD, this means educating them about the nature of worrying and GAD symptoms and about available treatment options and their possible advantages and disadvantages.

- *Meditation*, which helps patients learn to "let go" of thoughts and reduce the time spent thinking about worries (Evans et al., 2008; Lehrer & Woolfolk, 1994; Miller et al., 1995).

- *Self-monitoring*, which helps patients become aware of cues that lead to anxiety and worry. For instance, patients may be asked to complete a daily log about their worries, identifying events or stimuli that lead them to worry more or worry less.

- *Problem solving*, which involves teaching the patient to think about worries in very specific terms—rather than global ones—so that they can be addressed through cognitive restructuring.

- *Cognitive restructuring*, which involves helping patients learn to identify and shift automatic, irrational thoughts related to worries (see the third panel in Figure 6.2).

Targeting Social Factors

The neuropsychosocial approach leads us to notice whether certain kinds of treatments are available for particular disorders. For instance, at present, there are very few treatments for GAD that specifically target social factors, and none of them have been successful enough to summarize here.

In vivo exposure
A behavioral therapy method that consists of direct exposure to a feared or avoided situation or stimulus.

Psychoeducation
The process of educating patients about research findings and therapy procedures relevant to their situation.

Worry exposure first involves evoking a particular worry as vividly as possible and trying to imagine the worst-case scenario related to that worry.

The patient then tries to stay focused on the single worry for about a half-hour; the patient should habituate to the anxiety caused by the worry.

Once the patient has habituated somewhat to the worry, the patient and therapist generate possible rational alternatives to the worst-case scenario.

After the patient has habituated to and developed a rational response to a particular worry, he or she is ready go through the same process with a new, specific worry.

FIGURE 6.2 • Worry Exposure

Feedback Loops in Treating Generalized Anxiety Disorder

When behavioral methods and cognitive methods are successful, the person develops a sense of mastery of and control over worries and anxiety (which decreases the worries and anxiety even further), and social interactions reinforce new behaviors. Similarly, medication directly targets neurological factors, which in turn reduces the person's worries and anxiety; he or she becomes less preoccupied with these concerns, which increases the ability to focus at work and in relationships.

Did Earl Campbell develop GAD? Although his worries may seem excessive and uncontrollable at times, they do not appear to have had the effects necessary for the diagnosis, such as muscle tension, irritability, or difficulty sleeping. Any irritability or sleep problems he had are better explained as symptoms of another anxiety disorder—panic disorder, which we discuss in the following section.

Panic attack
A specific period of intense fear or discomfort, accompanied by physical symptoms, such as a pounding heart, shortness of breath, shakiness, and sweating, or cognitive symptoms, such as a fear of losing control.

Thinking Like A Clinician

Based on what you have read, what differentiates a "worrywart"—someone who worries a lot—from someone with GAD? If having GAD is distressing, why don't patients simply stop worrying? What factors maintain the disorder? If someone you know with GAD asked you for advice about what kind of treatment to get, what would you recommend (based on what you have read) and why?

⬜ Panic Disorder and Agoraphobia

Earl Campbell's uncomfortable episodes of anxiety didn't stop:

> The second night we were in the [new] house, I had my third episode. It felt just like the second one had. I was lying in bed watching television, and Reuna was sound asleep next to me. I was trying to relax and not think about my problem, but my problem was all I could think about. All of a sudden, my heart went crazy—pounding, pounding harder and harder. I thought it was going to leap right out of my chest. I sat up, struggling to regain my composure. It got worse. I couldn't breathe again.
> (Campbell & Ruane, 1999, p. 92)

Campbell again thought he was having a heart attack and that his life was ending. He was not; instead, Campbell was having a panic attack. A **panic attack** is a specific period of intense fear or discomfort, accompanied by physical symptoms, such as a pounding heart, shortness of breath, shakiness, and sweating, or cognitive symptoms, such as a fear of losing control.

The Panic Attack—A Key Ingredient of Panic Disorder

Some of the physical symptoms of a panic attack may resemble those associated with a heart attack—heart palpitations, shortness of breath, chest pain, and a feeling of choking or being smothered (see Table 6.3), which is why Earl Campbell mistook his panic attacks for heart attacks. In fact, emergency room staff have learned to look for evidence of a panic attack when a patient who purportedly has had a heart attack arrives. During a panic attack, the symptoms generally begin quickly, peak after a few minutes, and disappear within an hour.

In some cases, panic attacks are *cued*—that is, associated with particular objects, situations, or sensations. Although panic attacks are occasionally cued by a particular external stimulus (such as seeing a snake), they are more frequently cued by situations that are associated with internal sensations similar to panic, such as breaking out into a sweat (when overheated). In other cases, panic attacks are *uncued*—that is, spontaneous and feel as though they come out of the blue—and are not associated with a particular object or situation. Panic attacks can occur at any time, even while sleeping (referred to as *nocturnal panic attacks*, which Campbell experienced). Infrequent panic attacks are not unusual; they affect 30% of adults at some point in their lives.

Recurrent panic attacks may interfere with daily life (for example, if they occur on a bus or at work) and may cause the person to leave the situation to return home or seek medical help. The symptoms of a panic attack are so unpleasant that people who suffer from this disorder may try to prevent another attack by avoiding environments and activities that increase their heart rates (hot places, crowded rooms, elevators, exercise, sex, mass transportation, or sporting events). They might even avoid leaving home (Bouton et al., 2001).

TABLE 6.3 • DSM-5 Criteria for a Panic Attack

A discrete period of intense fear or discomfort, in which at least four of the following symptoms develop abruptly and reach a peak within minutes:

- palpitations, pounding heart, or accelerated heart rate
- sweating
- trembling or shaking
- sensations of shortness of breath or smothering
- feeling of choking
- chest pain or discomfort
- nausea or abdominal distress
- feeling dizzy, unsteady, lightheaded, or faint
- chills or heat sensations
- paresthesias (numbness or tingling sensations)
- derealization (feelings of unreality) or depersonalization (being detached from oneself)
- fear of losing control or going crazy
- fear of dying

Chip East/Reuters/Landov

People who suffer from panic attacks may try to prevent another attack by avoiding crowded environments such as commuter trains or public transportation altogether. Some may even avoid leaving their homes.

Panic disorder
An anxiety disorder characterized by frequent, unexpected panic attacks, along with fear of further attacks and possible restrictions of behavior in order to prevent such attacks.

What Is Panic Disorder?

Campbell describes *panic disorder*: ". . . the fear of having another panic attack, because the last thing in the world you want to face is one more of those horrible, frightening experiences. And the last thing you want to accept is the idea of living the rest of your life with panic. This condition caused me to shut myself up in the my house, where I would sit in the dark, frustrated, crying, afraid to go out. At one point, I even considered suicide" (Campbell & Ruane, 1999, p. ii).

To mental health clinicians, **panic disorder** is marked by frequent, unexpected panic attacks, along with worry about further attacks or their consequences (such as potentially losing control) and restrictions of behavior in order to prevent such attacks, lasting at least 1 month (see Table 6.4). Note, however, that having panic attacks doesn't necessarily indicate a panic disorder. Panic attacks are distinguished from panic disorder by the frequency and unpredictability of the attacks and the person's reaction to the attacks. Research suggests that among people with panic disorder, panic attacks aren't as out of the blue as they feel: Changes in breathing and heart rate occur over 30 minutes before the onset of a panic attack (Meuret et al., 2011). Table 6.5 lists additional facts about panic disorder, and Case 6.2 provides a glimpse of a woman who suffers from panic attacks.

CASE 6.2 • FROM THE OUTSIDE: Panic Disorder

S was a 28-year-old married woman with two children, aged 3 and 5 years. S had experienced her first panic attack approximately 1 year prior to the time of the initial assessment. Her father had died 3 months before her first panic attack; his death was unexpected, the result of a stroke. In addition to grieving for her father, S became extremely concerned about the possibility of herself having a stroke. S reported [that before her father's death, she'd never had a panic attack nor been concerned about her health.] Apparently, the loss of her father produced an abrupt change in the focus of her attention, and a cycle of anxiety began [which led to a heightened] awareness of the imminence of her own death, given that "nothing in life was predictable." . . . S became increasingly aware of different bodily sensations. Following her first panic attack, S was highly vigilant for tingling sensations in her scalp, pain around her eyes, and numbness in her arms and legs. She interpreted all of these symptoms as indicative of impending stroke. Moreover, because her concerns became more generalized, she began to fear any signs of impending panic, such as shortness of breath and palpitations.

Her concerns led to significant changes in her lifestyle [and she avoided] unstructured time in the event she might dwell on "how she felt" and, by so doing, panic. . . . S felt that her life revolved around preventing the experience of panic and stroke.

(Craske et al., 2000, pp. 45–46)

TABLE 6.4 • DSM-5 Diagnostic Criteria for Panic Disorder

A. Recurrent unexpected panic attacks.

B. At least one of the attacks has been followed by 1 month (or more) of one or both of the following:

1. Persistent concern or worry about additional panic attacks or their consequences (e.g., losing control, having a heart attack, "going crazy").

2. A significant maladaptive change in behavior related to the attacks (e.g., behaviors designed to avoid having panic attacks, such as avoidance of exercise or unfamiliar situations).

C. The disturbance is not attributable to the physiological effects of a substance (e.g., a drug of abuse, a medication) or another medical condition (e.g., hyperthyroidism, cardiopulmonary disorders).

D. The disturbance is not better explained by another mental disorder (e.g., the panic attacks do not occur only in response to feared social situations, as in social anxiety disorder; in response to circumscribed phobic objects or situations, as in specific phobia; in response to obsessions, as in obsessive-compulsive disorder; in response to reminders of traumatic events, as in posttraumatic stress disorder; or in response to separation from attachment figures, as in separation anxiety disorder).

Symptoms of panic disorder are similar across cultures, but in some cultures the symptoms focus on fear of magic or witchcraft (American Psychiatric Association, 2000); in other cultures, the physical symptoms may be expressed differently. For example, among Cambodian refugees, symptoms of panic disorder include a fear that "wind-and-blood pressure" (referred to as *wind overload*) may increase to the point of bursting the neck area, and patients may complain of a sore neck, along with headache, blurry vision, and dizziness (Hinton et al., 2001).

In some cultures, people experience symptoms that are similar—but not identical—to the classic symptoms of a panic attack. In the Caribbean, Puerto Rico, and some areas of Latin America, an anxiety-related problem called *ataque de nervios* can occur, usually in women. The most common symptoms are uncontrollable screaming and crying attacks, together with palpitations, shaking, and numbness. An *ataque de nervios* differs from a panic attack not only in the specific symptoms experienced but also because it usually is triggered by a specific upsetting event, such as a funeral or a family conflict. Panic attacks that are part of panic disorder tend not to have such an obvious situational trigger. Furthermore, people who have had an *ataque de nervios* are usually not worried about recurrences (Guarnaccia, 1997b; Salmán et al., 1997).

Panic disorder, as well as *ataque de nervios* and other anxiety disorders, is diagnosed at least twice as often in women as in men (American Psychiatric Association, 2013). A cultural explanation for this gender difference is that men may be less likely to report symptoms of anxiety or panic because they perceive them as inconsistent with how men are "supposed" to behave in their culture (Ginsburg & Silverman, 2000).

In short, panic disorder has a core of common symptoms across the world, centering on frequent, unexpected panic attacks and fear of further attacks, but culture does affect the specifics.

What Is Agoraphobia?

After Campbell's first panic attack, he refused to go out:

> I knew I could not set foot outside my house. Until I learned what was wrong with me, the only place I would go was to a doctor's office or a hospital. . . . Reuna thought that was part of my problem. I was shutting myself off from the world. . . . What if I had another attack? What if it happened while I was in church? Or while I was walking down the aisle of a crowded grocery store? What would I do? How could I deal with the humiliation that such a loss of control would bring?
> (Campbell & Ruane, 1999, pp. 93–94)

Campbell had developed *agoraphobia*.

Agoraphobia (which literally means "fear of the marketplace") refers to the persistent avoidance of situations that might trigger panic symptoms or from which escape would be difficult or help would not be available. For these reasons, public transportation, tunnels, bridges, crowded places, or even being home alone are typically avoided or entered with difficulty by people with agoraphobia.

TABLE 6.5 · Panic Disorder Facts at a Glance

Prevalence

- Up to 3% of people worldwide will experience panic disorder at some point in their lives (Somers et al., 2006). However, 30% of people will experience at least one panic attack in their lives. Up to 60% of people seen by cardiologists have panic disorder.

Comorbidity

- About 80% of people with panic disorder will have an additional disorder (Ozkan & Altindag, 2005). The three disorders mostly commonly associated with panic disorder are depression (up to 65% of cases), agoraphobia (up to 50% of cases), and substance abuse (up to 30% of cases) (Keller & Hanks, 1994; Magee et al., 1996).
- Approximately 15–30% of those with panic disorder also have social anxiety disorder or GAD, and 2–20% have some other type of anxiety disorder (Goisman et al., 1995).

Onset

- Panic disorder is most likely to arise during young adulthood.

Course

- The frequency of panic attacks varies from person to person: some people get panic attacks once a week for months, others have attacks every day for a week.
- The frequency of panic attacks can vary over time.

Gender Differences

- Women are two times more likely than men to be diagnosed with panic disorder.

Cultural Differences

- Symptoms of panic disorder are generally similar across cultures, although people in some cultures may experience or explain the symptoms differently, such as "wind overload" among the Khmer (Hinton et al., 2002, 2003).

Source: Unless otherwise noted, information in the table is from American Psychiatric Association, 2013.

Agoraphobia
An anxiety disorder characterized by persistent avoidance of situations that might trigger panic symptoms or from which help would be difficult to obtain.

TABLE 6.6 • DSM-5 Diagnostic Criteria for Agoraphobia

A. Marked fear or anxiety about two (or more) of the following five situations:

1. Using public transportation (e.g., automobiles, buses, trains, ships, planes).

2. Being in open spaces (e.g., parking lots, marketplaces, bridges).

3. Being in enclosed places (e.g., shops, theaters, cinemas).

4. Standing in line or being in a crowd.

5. Being outside of the home alone.

B. The individual fears or avoids these situations because of thoughts that escape might be difficult or help might not be available in the event of developing panic-like symptoms or other incapacitating or embarrassing symptoms (e.g., fear of falling in the elderly; fear of incontinence).

C. The agoraphobic situations almost always provoke fear or anxiety.

D. The agoraphobic situations are actively avoided, require the presence of a companion, or are endured with intense fear or anxiety.

E. The fear or anxiety is out of proportion to the actual danger posed by the agoraphobic situations and to the sociocultural context.

F. The fear, anxiety, or avoidance is persistent, typically lasting for 6 months or more.

G. The fear, anxiety or avoidance causes clinically significant distress or impairment in social, occupational or other important areas of functioning.

H. If another medical condition (e.g., inflammatory bowel disease, Parkinson's disease) is present, the fear, anxiety or avoidance is clearly excessive.

I. The fear, anxiety or avoidance is not better explained by the symptoms of another mental disorder—for example, the symptoms are not confined to specific phobia, situational type; do not involve only social situations (as in social anxiety disorder); and are not related exclusively to obsessions (as in obsessive-compulsive disorder); perceived defects or flaws in physical appearance (as in body dysmorphic disorder), reminders of traumatic events (as in posttraumatic stress disorder), or fear of separation (as in separation anxiety disorder).

About half of the people with agoraphobia also have panic disorder, and most of the other half experience panic symptoms (but the symptoms are not strong or frequent enough to meet the criteria for panic disorder); a patient with agoraphobia can also be diagnosed with panic disorder if he or she has symptoms that meet the criteria for panic disorder. The avoidance that is a part of agoraphobia is typically a (maladaptive) attempt not to enter situations that could lead to panic symptoms. These people avoid situations in which they fear they might panic or lose control of themselves. However, people who only avoid particular kinds of stimuli (*only* bridges or *only* parties) are not diagnosed with agoraphobia, which is a more general pattern of avoiding many kinds of environments or situations. Table 6.6 lists the criteria for agoraphobia. Table 6.7 lists additional facts about agoraphobia, Shirley B., in Case 6.3, suffered from symptoms of agoraphobia.

CASE 6.3 • FROM THE OUTSIDE: Agoraphobia

"The Story of an Agoraphobic" by Shirley B.:

There isn't much I can say about how I became agoraphobic. I just slipped a little day by day. . . . My daughter Nadeen was always by my side on those rare occasions when I ventured outside, forced to leave my home when I needed medical attention. In the past my fear kept me at home with all sorts of physical pains and ailments, as horrific as the pain was, the pain of facing the outside world was greater. When I had two abscessed teeth and my jaw was swollen to twice its normal size I was in such excruciating pain that I had to go to the dentist. So with my legs wobbling, my heart pounding, my hands sweating, and my throat choking, to the dentist I went. After examining my x-rays, the dentist said he wouldn't be able to do anything with my teeth because they were so infected, he prescribed medication for the pain and infection and said that I must return in ten days, not in two years. I felt as though those ten days were a countdown to my own execution. Each day passed at lightning speed—like a clock ticking away. The fear grew stronger and stronger. I had to walk around with my hand on my heart to keep it from jumping so hard, as if I were pledging allegiance, which I was—to my fears and phobia. I asked God to please give me strength to go back to the dentist. When the day came, I knew that my preparations would take me a little over four hours. I had to leave time, not just to bathe and dress, but to debate with myself about going.

(Anxiety Disorders Association of America)

People with extreme agoraphobia cannot function normally in daily life. Some are totally housebound, too crippled by anxiety and fear to go to work, the supermarket, or the doctor. Others with agoraphobia are able to function better than Shirley B. and can enter many situations without triggering panic or marked fear or anxiety. Relying on a friend or family member, often referred to as a "safe" person (for Shirley it was her daughter Nadeen), can help the sufferer enter feared situations that otherwise might be avoided.

People with agoraphobia who also have panic symptoms or panic attacks avoid situations that are associated with past panic; thus, they do not have the opportunity to learn that they can be in such situations and not have a panic attack.

Understanding Panic Disorder and Agoraphobia

"I still don't know what triggers a panic attack, but I can tell anyone reading this who has never experienced one that it is a devastating experience. . . . An attack may hit me on a day when I'm feeling relaxed and happy. That's when I think, 'Why me?' 'Why today?'" (Campbell & Ruane, 1999, p. 151). The neuropsychosocial approach allows us to address Campbell's question about why panic disorder and agoraphobia occur and are maintained. Because agoraphobia typically develops as a way to avoid panic symptoms, in what follows we will focus more on panic disorder. Each type of factor makes an important and unique contribution.

Neurological Factors

Brain systems, neural communication, and genetics contribute to panic disorder and agoraphobia. Specifically, these three types of neurological factors appear to give rise to a heightened sensitivity to breathing changes.

Brain Systems

One key to explaining panic attacks came after researchers discovered that they could induce such attacks in the laboratory. Patients who had had panic attacks volunteered to hyperventilate (that is, to breathe in rapid, short pants, decreasing carbon dioxide levels in the blood), which triggered panic attacks. Moreover, researchers found that injections of some medically safe substances, such as sodium lactate (a salt produced in sweat) and caffeine, also produced attacks—but only in people who have panic disorder (Nutt & Lawson, 1992; Pitts & McClure, 1967). Why do these substances induce panic attacks? One possibility is that the brains of people who experience panic attacks have a low threshold for detecting decreased oxygen in the blood, which triggers a brain mechanism that warns us when we are suffocating (Beck et al., 1999; Papp et al., 1993, 1997). As predicted by this theory, patients with panic disorder cannot hold their breath as long as control participants can (Asmundson & Stein, 1994). When triggered, the neural mechanism not only produces panic but also leads to hyperventilation and a strong sense of needing to escape.

Neural Communication

Researchers also have been investigating the role of neurotransmitters in giving rise to panic disorder. One key neurotransmitter is norepinephrine, too much of which is apparently produced in people who have anxiety disorders (Nutt & Lawson, 1992). The *locus coeruleus* is a small structure in the brainstem that produces norepinephrine, and some researchers have theorized that it is too sensitive in people with panic disorder (Gorman et al., 1989)—and thus may produce too much norepinephrine. The locus coeruleus and norepinephrine are important because they are central to the body's "alarm system," which causes the fight-or-flight response (including faster breathing, increased heart rate, and sweating), which often occurs at times of panic.

Finally, we note that SSRIs can reduce the frequency and intensity of panic attacks (DeVane, 1997); SSRIs reduce the effects of serotonin, which affects the locus coeruleus in complex ways (Bell & Nutt, 1998).

Genetics

Genetic factors appear to play a role in the emergence of panic disorder. In fact, first-degree biological relatives of people with panic disorder are up to eight times more likely to develop the disorder than are control participants, and up to 20 times more likely to do so if the relative developed it before 20 years of age (Crowe et al., 1983; Torgersen, 1983; van den Heuvel et al., 2000). Twin studies have yielded similar results by examining concordance rates; a **concordance rate** is the probability that both twins will have a characteristic or disorder, given that one of them has it. The concordance rate in pairs of female identical (monozygotic) twins is approximately 24%, in contrast to 11% for pairs of fraternal (dizygotic) twins (Kendler et al., 1993). Thus, the more genes in common, the higher the concordance rates.

TABLE 6.7 • Agoraphobia Facts at a Glance

Prevalence
• Up to 2% of people worldwide will develop agoraphobia at some point in their lives (Somers et al., 2006).

Comorbidity
• About half of people with agoraphobia will also have another anxiety disorder (including panic disorder), the symptoms of which predate the agoraphobia.
• Depression and substance use disorders are also common comorbid disorders, but unlike with other anxiety disorders, these disorders tend to emerge after the agoraphobia.

Onset
• Two-thirds of people with agoraphobia develop it before age 35.
• About half of people with agoraphobia report having had panic attacks or panic disorder before developing agoraphobia.

Course
• Agoraphobia is a chronic mental disorder, persisting over time unless treated.
• More than one-third of people with this disorder are completely housebound.

Gender Differences
• Women are twice as likely as men to be diagnosed with agoraphobia.

Cultural Differences
• People with agoraphobia in Hong Kong also have a fear of being a burden to others or making others worry (Hui et al., 2012).

Source: Unless otherwise noted, information in the table is from American Psychiatric Association, 2013.

Concordance rate
The probability that both twins will have a characteristic or disorder, given that one of them has it.

Psychological Factors

Not all cases of panic disorder are related to a person's threshold for detecting suffocation; some cases of panic disorder arise from learning. Thus, behavioral and cognitive theories can also help us understand how panic disorder and agoraphobia arise and are perpetuated: People come to associate certain stimuli with the sensations of panic and then develop maladaptive beliefs and behaviors with regard to those stimuli and the sensations that are related to anxiety and panic.

Learning: An Alarm Going Off

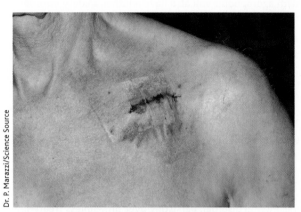

People whose hearts sometimes beat too quickly can be treated with a device implanted under the skin that shocks the heart, which causes it to beat at a normal speed again. However, the shocks can be uncomfortable and alarming. Research suggests that people who receive more frequent and intense shocks are more likely to develop panic disorder, which arises as a conditioned fear in response to the automatic shocks (Godemann et al., 2001).

Learning theory offers one possible explanation for at least some cases of panic disorder. Initially, a person may have had a first panic attack in response to a stressful or dangerous life event (*a true alarm*). This experience produces conditioning, whereby the initial bodily sensations of panic (such as increased heart rate or sweaty palms) become *false alarms* associated with panic attacks. As the normal sensations that are part of the fight-or-flight response come to be associated with subsequent panic attacks, the bodily sensations of arousal themselves come to *elicit* panic attacks (*learned alarms*). The person then develops a *fear of fear*—a fear that the arousal symptoms of fear will lead to a panic attack (Goldstein & Chambless, 1978), much as S did in Case 6.2. After developing this fear of fear, the person tries to avoid behaviors or situations where such sensations might occur (Mowrer, 1947; White & Barlow, 2002).

Cognitive Explanations: Catastrophic Thinking and Anxiety Sensitivity

Cognitive theories, which focus on how a person *interprets* and then responds to alarm signals from the body, offer other possible reasons why panic disorder could arise. People with panic disorder may misinterpret normal bodily sensations as indicating catastrophic effects (Salkovskis, 1988), which is referred to as *catastrophic thinking*. Catastrophic thinking can arise in part from *anxiety sensitivity*, which is a tendency to fear bodily sensations that are related to anxiety along with the belief that such sensations indicate that harmful consequences will follow (McNally, 1994; Reiss, 1991; Schmidt et al., 1997). For example, a person with high anxiety sensitivity is likely to believe—or fear—that an irregular heartbeat indicates a heart problem or that shortness of breath signals being suffocated. People with high anxiety sensitivity tend to know what has caused their bodily symptoms—for instance, that exercise caused a faster heart rate—but they become afraid anyway, believing that danger is indicated, even if it is not an immediate danger (Bouton et al., 2001; Brown et al., 2003).

Social Factors: Stressors, a Sign of the Times, and "Safe People"

Evidence suggests that social stressors contribute to panic disorder: People with panic disorder tend to have had a higher-than-average number of such stressful events during childhood and adolescence (Horesh et al., 1997). Moreover, 80% of people with panic disorder reported that the disorder developed after a stressful life event.

Researchers have shown that the mental stressors of basic military training are more challenging to people with preexisting anxiety sensitivity than they are to others.

In addition, cultural factors can influence whether people develop panic disorder, perhaps through culture's influence on personality traits. For example, over the past five decades, increasing numbers of Americans have developed the personality trait of anxiety-proneness (Spielberger & Rickman, 1990). The average child today scores higher on measures of this trait than did children who received psychiatric diagnoses in the 1950s (Twenge, 2000)! The higher baseline level of anxiety in the United States may be a result of greater dangers in the environment—such as higher crime rates, new threats of terrorism, and new concerns about food safety—or greater media exposure of such dangers.

Dr. P. Marazzi/Science Source

Robert Nickelsberg/Getty Images

Social factors are also often related to the ways patients cope with agoraphobia. As with GAD, the presence of a close relative or friend—a "safe person" or companion—can help the patient temporarily cope with agoraphobia. In this case, the presence of a safe person can decrease catastrophic thinking and panicking, as well as the sufferer's arousal. Although a safe person can make it possible for the patient with agoraphobia to go into situations that he or she wouldn't enter alone, reliance on a safe person can end up perpetuating the disorder: By venturing into anxiety-inducing situations only when a safe person is around, the patient never habituates to the anxiety symptoms experienced when alone and in the situation.

Feedback Loops in Understanding Panic Disorder and Agoraphobia

Cognitive explanations of panic disorder can help show how a few panic attacks can progress to panic disorder, but not everyone who has panic attacks develops panic disorder. It is only when neurological and psychological factors interact with bodily states that panic disorder develops (Bouton et al., 2001). For example, a man's argument with his wife (social factor) might arouse his anger and increase his breathing rate. Breathing faster results in a lower carbon dioxide level in the blood, which then leads the blood vessels to constrict—which means less oxygen throughout the brain and body (neurological factor); the ensuing physical sensations (such as light-headedness) may be misinterpreted (psychological factor) as the early stages of suffocation, leading the man to panic (Coplan et al., 1998). This is how such physical changes can serve as a false alarm (Beck, 1976). After many false alarms, the associated sensations may become learned alarms and trigger panic in the absence of a social stressor (Barlow, 1988). Also, this man may become hypervigilant for alarm signals of panic attacks, leading to anticipatory anxiety. In turn, this anxiety increases activity in his sympathetic nervous system, which causes the breathing and heart rate changes that he feared. In this way, the man may trigger his own panic attack. Figure 6.3, on the next page, illustrates these three factors and their feedback loops.

Treating Panic Disorder and Agoraphobia

Earl Campbell received treatment for his panic disorder—medication, cognitive-behavior therapy (CBT), and social support—which targeted all three types of neuropsychosocial factors. Treatment for agoraphobia also addresses panic symptoms because fear of having panic symptoms drives sufferers to narrow their lives.

Targeting Neurological Factors: Medication

To treat panic disorder, a psychiatrist or another type of health care provider licensed to prescribe medication may recommend an antidepressant or a benzodiazepine. Benzodiazepines are prescribed as a short-term remedy; the benzodiazepines *alprazolam* (Xanax) and *clonazepam* (Klonapin) affect the targeted symptoms within 36 hours, and they need not be taken regularly. One of these drugs might be prescribed during a short but especially stressful period. Side effects of benzodiazepines include drowsiness and slowed reaction times, and patients can suffer withdrawal or need to take increasingly larger doses when these drugs are taken for an extended period of time. For these reasons, antidepressants such as an SNRI, an SSRI, or TCAs (tricyclic antidepressants), such as *clomipramine* (Anafranil), are better long-term medications and are now considered "first-line" medications for panic disorder (Batelaan et al., 2012). However, these medications can take up to 10 days

FIGURE 6.3 • Feedback Loops in Understanding Panic Disorder and Agoraphobia

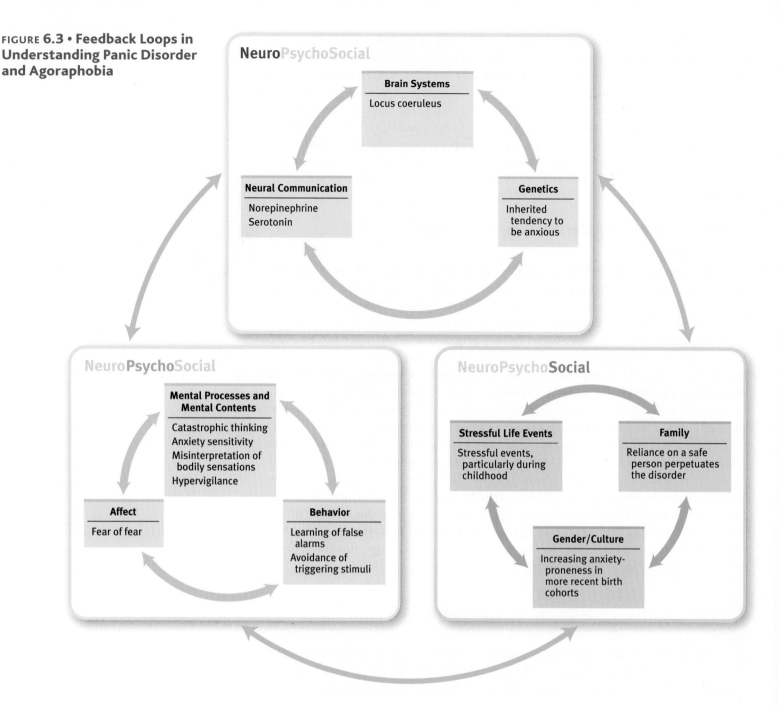

to have an effect (Kasper & Resinger, 2001). After Campbell's panic attacks were diagnosed, he initially relied on such medications as his sole treatment; like most people, though, when he stopped taking the medication or forgot to take a pill, his symptoms returned. Such recurrences motivated him to make use of other types of treatments.

Targeting Psychological Factors

CBT is the first-line treatment for panic disorder because it has the most enduring beneficial effects of any treatment (Cloos, 2005; DiMauro et al., 2013). Effective CBT methods can emphasize either the behavioral or the cognitive aspects of change.

Behavioral Methods: Relaxation Training, Breathing Retraining, and Exposure

For people with panic disorder, any bodily arousal can lead to a fight-or-flight response. Therapists may teach patients breathing retraining and relaxation techniques, which stop the progression from bodily arousal to panic attack and increase a sense of control over bodily sensations. Campbell reported how he learned to take "long deep breaths and relax my body completely when panic struck. . . . I somehow had to convince myself that the attack was not really happening. I had to fight it off by relaxing myself" (Campbell & Ruane, 1999, p. 119).

Other behavioral methods include exposure. To decrease a patient's reaction to bodily sensations associated with panic, behavioral therapists may use **interoceptive exposure**: They have the patient intentionally elicit the bodily sensations associated with panic so that he or she can habituate to those sensations and not respond with fear. During exposure to interoceptive cues, patients are asked to behave in ways that induce the long-feared sensation, such as spinning around to the point of dizziness or intentionally hyperventilating (see Table 6.8 for a more extensive list). Within approximately 30 minutes, the bodily arousal subsides. This procedure allows patients to learn that the bodily sensations pass and no harm befalls them. For people with agoraphobia symptoms, exposure addresses the patient's tendency to avoid activities and situations associated with panic attacks (such as exercise or crowded theaters, respectively).

Cognitive Methods: Psychoeducation and Cognitive Restructuring

Cognitive methods for panic disorder help the patient recognize misappraisals of bodily symptoms and learn to correct mistaken inferences about such symptoms. First, psychoeducation for people with panic disorder involves

This man might just be casually spinning in his office chair, but this same action is part of interoceptive exposure: The therapist intentionally tries to elicit from the patient the bodily sensations associated with panic so that he or she can habituate to those sensations and not respond with fear. Dizziness, for example, is associated with panic, so a therapist may have a patient repeatedly spin around to experience, and thus habituate to, dizziness in a safe, controlled environment.

Andersen Ross/Getty Images

TABLE 6.8 • Interoceptive Exposure Exercises for Treatment of Panic Disorder

Exercise	Duration (seconds)	Sensation intensity (0–8)	Anxiety (0–8)	Similarity (0–8)
Shake head from side to side	30			
Place head between legs and then lift	30			
Run on spot	60			
Hold breath	30, or as long as possible			
Completely tense body muscles	60, or as long as possible			
Spin in swivel chair	60			
Hyperventilate	60			
Breathe through narrow straw	120			
Stare at spot on wall or own mirror image	90			

Source: Craske & Barlow, 1993, Table 1.4, p. 36. For more information see the Permissions section.

People receiving interoceptive exposure perform each of the exercises listed in this table for the indicated duration; such exercises are likely to elicit sensations typically associated with panic. After each exercise, they rate how intense the sensations were, their level of anxiety while doing the exercise, and how similar the sensations were to panic symptoms.

Interoceptive exposure
A behavioral therapy method in which patients intentionally elicit the bodily sensations associated with panic so that they can habituate to those sensations and not respond with fear.

helping them understand both how their physical sensations are symptoms of panic—not of a heart attack or some other harmful medical situation—and the role of catastrophic thinking. Campbell read a pamphlet about panic disorder that described his symptoms perfectly. Having learned about the disorder in this way, he was better able to handle future panic attacks: "One of the most important things I have learned about my panic disorder over the years is that although my heart may be racing and I may feel like I'm having a heart attack, I know that I'm not. And I know it's going to stop" (Campbell & Ruane, 1999, p. 204).

Second, cognitive restructuring is then used to transform the patient's initial frightened thoughts of a medical crisis into more realistic thoughts, identifying the symptoms of panic, which may be uncomfortable but do not indicate danger (Beck et al., 1979). For instance, a therapist may help a patient identify the automatic negative thought about bodily arousal ("I won't be able to breathe . . . I'll pass out") and then challenges the patient about the belief: Was the patient truly unable to breathe, or was breathing only difficult? Has the patient fainted before? In this way, each of the patient's automatic negative thoughts related to panic sensations are challenged and thereby reduced. Learning to interpret correctly both internal and external events can play a key role in preventing panic attacks that occur when a person experiences symptoms of suffocation (Clark, 1986; Taylor & Rachman, 1994).

Targeting Social Factors: Group and Couples Therapy

Therapy groups (either self-help or conducted by a therapist) that focus specifically on panic disorder and agoraphobia can be a helpful component of a treatment program (Galassi et al., 2007). Meeting with others who have similar difficulties and sharing experiences can help to decrease a patient's sense of isolation and shame. Moreover, couples therapy or family therapy may be appropriate when a partner or other family member has been the safe person; as the patient gets better, he or she may rely less on that person, which can affect their relationship. In some cases, the patient's increasing independence is satisfying for everyone; but if the safe person has found satisfaction in tending to the patient, the patient's increased independence can be a stressful transition for that person.

Feedback Loops in Treating Panic Disorder and Agoraphobia

Because agoraphobia frequently co-occurs with panic disorder, we discuss treatments for both here. Invariably, medication—which changes neurological functioning—stops being beneficial when the patient stops taking it. The positive changes in neural communication and brain activity and the associated changes in thoughts, feelings, and behaviors do not endure; the symptoms of panic disorder return. However, for some patients, medication is a valuable first step, providing enough relief from symptoms that these patients are motivated to obtain CBT, which can change their reactions (psychological factor) to perceived bodily sensations (neurological factor). When a patient receives both medication and CBT, the medication should be at a low enough dose that the patient can still feel the sensations that led to panic in the past (Taylor, 2000). In fact, the dose should be gradually decreased so that the patient can experience enough anxiety to be increasingly able to make use of cognitive-behavioral methods. It is the CBT that leads to enduring changes. Successful treatment will probably lead the patient, especially if he or she also has agoraphobia, to become more independent—which in turn can change the person's relationships, particularly with their safe people (social factor). These factors and their feedback loops are summarized in Figure 6.4.

These women may just be affectionately crossing the street, but a person with agoraphobia may rely on a friend or family member, often referred to as a "safe" person, who can help the sufferer enter feared situations that otherwise might be avoided.

Voisin/Phanie/Superstock

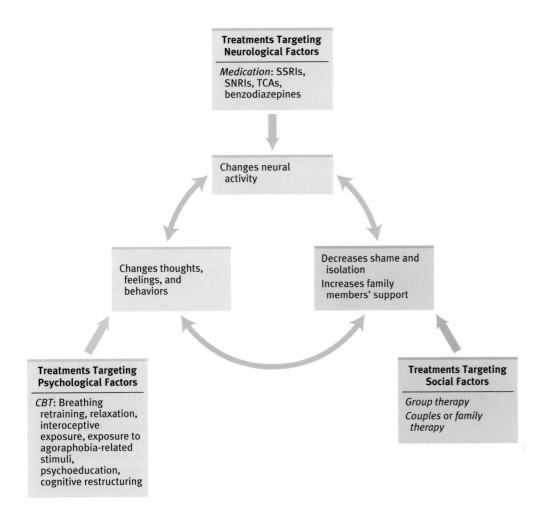

FIGURE **6.4 • Feedback Loops in Treating Panic Disorder and Agoraphobia**

Thinking Like A Clinician

All you know about Fiona is that she has had about 10 panic attacks. Is this enough information to determine whether she has panic disorder? If it is, does she have the disorder? If this isn't enough information, what else would you want to know, and why? Now suppose that Fiona starts missing Monday classes because of panic attacks on those days. She also stops going to parties on weekends because she had a couple of panic attacks at parties. Would you change or maintain your answer about whether she has panic disorder? Why or why not? Suppose Fiona does have panic disorder. Explain how she might have developed the disorder. By the end of the semester, Fiona no longer goes out of her apartment for fear of getting a panic attack. What might be appropriate treatments for Fiona?

□ Social Anxiety Disorder (Social Phobia)

As Earl Campbell's anxiety increased, he became concerned about what other people might think of him if they knew about his problem. As noted earlier, he was very aware of when people were looking at him. He also avoided crowds. Could Campbell have developed *social anxiety disorder*?

TABLE 6.9 • DSM-5 Diagnostic Criteria for Social Anxiety Disorder

A. Marked fear or anxiety about one or more social situations in which the individual is exposed to possible scrutiny by others. Examples include social interactions (e.g., having a conversation, meeting unfamiliar people), being observed (e.g., eating or drinking), and performing in front of others (e.g., giving a speech).

   Note: In children, the anxiety must occur in peer settings and not just during interactions with adults.

B. The individual fears that he or she will act in a way or show anxiety symptoms that will be negatively evaluated (i.e., will be humiliating or embarrassing; will lead to rejection or offend others).

C. The social situations almost always provoke fear or anxiety.

   Note: In children, the fear or anxiety may be expressed by crying, tantrums, freezing, clinging, shrinking, or falling to speak in social situations.

D. The social situations are avoided or endured with intense fear or anxiety.

E. The fear or anxiety is out of proportion to the actual threat posed by the social situation and to the sociocultural context.

F. The fear, anxiety, or avoidance is persistent, typically lasting for 6 months or more.

G. The fear, anxiety, or avoidance causes clinically significant distress or impairment in social, occupational, or other important areas of functioning.

H. The fear, anxiety or avoidance is not attributable to the physiological effects of a substance (e.g., a drug of abuse, a medication) or another medical condition.

I. The fear, anxiety or avoidance is not better explained by the symptoms of another mental disorder, such as panic disorder, body dysmorphic disorder, or autism spectrum disorder.

J. If another medical condition (e.g., Parkinson's disease, obesity, disfigurement from burns or injury) is present, the fear, anxiety or avoidance is clearly unrelated or is excessive.

Reprinted with permission from the Diagnostic and Statistical Manual of Mental Disorders, Fifth Edition, (Copyright ©2013). American Psychiatric Association. All Rights Reserved.

Social anxiety disorder
An anxiety disorder characterized by intense fear of public humiliation or embarrassment; also called *social phobia*.

What Is Social Anxiety Disorder?

Social anxiety disorder, also called *social phobia*, is an intense fear of or anxiety about being scrutinized by others when in social situations, (see Table 6.9; American Psychiatric Association, 2013). Such social situations fall into three types: social interactions (such as a conversation); being observed (such as when eating or using public restrooms); and performing (such as giving a speech). People with social anxiety disorder may avoid making eye contact and avoid their feared social situations whenever possible. As noted in Table 6.9, a DSM-5 criterion is that the fear or anxiety is disproportional to the danger actually posed.

When a social situation cannot be avoided and must be endured, the person with social anxiety disorder experiences fear or anxiety, sometimes including symptoms of upset stomach, diarrhea, sweating, muscle tension, and heart palpitations. DSM-5 distinguishes between a social phobia that is limited to specific social performances where the person is the center of attention—such as making a presentation—and a more generalized social phobia, which leads a person to fear and avoid all social situations, as does Rachel in Case 6.4. Table 6.10 lists additional facts about social anxiety disorder.

CASE 6.4 • FROM THE OUTSIDE: Social Anxiety Disorder

Rachel was a twenty-six-year-old woman who worked as an assistant manager of a small bookstore. [She sought treatment] for her intense anxiety about her upcoming wedding. Rachel wasn't afraid of being married (i.e., the commitment, living with her spouse, etc.); she was terrified of the wedding itself. The idea of being on display in front of such a large audience was almost unthinkable. In fact, she had postponed her wedding on two previous occasions because of her performance fears. . . .

She reported being shy from the time she was very young. When she was in high school, her anxiety around people had become increasingly intense and had affected her school life. She was convinced that her classmates would find her dull or boring or that they would notice her anxiety and assume that she was incompetent. Typically, she avoided doing oral reports at school and didn't take any classes where she felt her performance might be observed or judged by her classmates (e.g., gym). On a few occasions, she even went out of her way to obtain special permission to hand in a written essay instead of doing an oral report.

Throughout college, Rachel had difficulty making new friends. Although people liked her company and often invited her to parties and other social events, she rarely accepted. She had a long list of excuses to get out of socializing with other people. She was comfortable only with her family and several longtime friends but aside from those, she tended to avoid significant contact with other people.

(Antony & Swinson, 2000b, pp. 5–6)

People who have social anxiety disorder also tend to be very sensitive to criticism and rejection and to worry about not living up to the perceived expectations of others. Thus, they often dread being evaluated or taking tests, and they may not perform up to their potential at school or work. Their diminished performance challenges their self-esteem, increasing their anxiety during subsequent performances or tests. Similarly, achievement at work may suffer because they avoid social situations that are important for advancement on the job, such as making presentations. People with social anxiety disorder are less likely to marry or have a partner than people who do not have this disorder.

Sometimes, a clinician or researcher cannot easily distinguish whether a person's symptoms indicate that he or she has social anxiety or agoraphobia. However, there are two key features that distinguish these disorders:

1. People with social anxiety disorder fear other people's scrutiny.

2. People with social anxiety disorder rarely have panic attacks when alone.

In contrast, people who have agoraphobia do not exhibit these features.

TABLE **6.10** • Social Anxiety Disorder Facts at a Glance

Prevalence
• Social anxiety disorder is one of the most common anxiety disorders, with prevalence estimates ranging from 3% to 13%.
• A fear of public speaking or public performance is the most common symptom, followed by a fear of talking to strangers or meeting new people.
Comorbidity
• Among those with social anxiety disorder, over half will also have one other psychological disorder at some point in their lives, and 27% will have three or more disorders during their lives (Chartier et al., 2003). Approximately 20–44% will have a mood disorder (Chartier et al., 2003; Roth & Fonagy, 2005).
Onset
• Most people with social anxiety disorder were shy as children, and they developed the disorder during childhood, with broader symptoms generally appearing during adolescence.
Course
• Social anxiety disorder may develop gradually or it may begin suddenly after a humiliating or stressful social experience.
• Symptoms typically are chronic, although they may lessen for some adolescents as they enter adulthood.
• Only half the people with this disorder seek treatment for it—usually after 15 years of symptoms.
• For some people, symptoms can improve over the course of time.
Gender Differences
• Social anxiety disorder is approximately twice as common in females as in males.
Cultural Differences
• Culture can influence the specific form of social anxiety disorder symptoms; for instance, in Japan, some people with social anxiety disorder may fear that their body odor will offend others (Dinnel et al., 2002), whereas people with social anxiety disorder in Hong Kong are more likely to be afraid of talking to people who have a higher social status (Lee et al., 2009).

Source: Unless otherwise noted, information in the table is from American Psychiatric Association, 2013.

Understanding Social Anxiety Disorder

Because of the very nature of this disorder, social factors are prominent contributors to it. Neveretheless, as we'll see, all three types of factors play a role and contributed to Campbell's problems.

Neurological Factors

Why does social anxiety disorder exist at all? Evolutionary psychologists speculate that social anxiety disorder may have its origins in behaviors of animals that are lower on a dominance hierarchy: Less powerful animals fear aggressive action from those more dominant and therefore behave submissively toward them. It is possible that social phobias arise when this innate mechanism becomes too sensitive or otherwise responds improperly (Hofmann et al., 2002). Key facts about the brains of people with social anxiety disorder are consistent with this conjecture, as we see in the following section.

Brain Systems and Neural Communication

Social anxiety disorder involves fear, and researchers have shown repeatedly that the amygdala is strongly activated when animals—including humans—are afraid (Rosen & Donley, 2006). Thus, it's no surprise that the amygdala is more strongly activated when people with social anxiety disorder see faces with negative expressions (such as anger) than when they see happy faces and that this difference is greater than observed in control participants who do not have the disorder (Del Casale et al., 2012; Phan et al., 2006). Indeed, the more symptoms of social anxiety disorder a

What is your amygdala doing when you see this negative facial expression? The amygdalae of people with social anxiety disorder are more active when seeing negative facial expressions, such as this one here, compared to people without the disorder.

Jonathan Kirn/Getty Images

person has, the more strongly the amygdala is activated when the person views faces with negative expressions.

In addition, neurotransmitters may function abnormally in people who have social anxiety disorder (Li, Lindenberger, & Sikström, 2001). In particular, researchers have found that patients with social anxiety disorder show less activation in brain areas that rely on dopamine than do control participants. Furthermore, people with social anxiety disorder have too little serotonin, which may suggest why SSRIs have sometimes helped these patients (Gorman & Kent, 1999; Lykouras, 1999).

Genetics

As is the norm for anxiety disorders, social anxiety disorder appears to arise from both genetic factors and environmental factors (Mathew et al., 2001; Stein, Jang, & Livesly, 2002). The heritability of social anxiety disorder is about 37% on average (Beatty et al., 2002; Fyer, 2000; Li et al., 2001; Neale et al., 1994).

We noted earlier that some people with social anxiety disorder were extremely shy as children; they had what is called a shy temperament, or *behavioral inhibition* (Biederman et al., 2001; Kagan, 1989), which has a genetic component. These patients cannot really be said to have *developed* a phobia, since they always had a basic level of discomfort in particular social situations (Coupland, 2001).

📷 GETTING THE PICTURE

Which one of these children is more likely to be diagnosed with social anxiety disorder as an adult? Answer: The child on the right, who seems shy and may have a behaviorally inhibited temperament.

Psychological Factors

Three types of psychological factors influence the emergence and maintenance of social anxiety disorder: cognitive biases and distortions, classical conditioning, and operant conditioning.

Cognitive Biases and Distortions

People who have social anxiety disorder have particular biases in attention and memory (Ledley & Heimberg, 2006; Lundh & Öst, 1996; Wenzel & Cochran, 2006). In particular, people with social anxiety disorder tend to pay more attention to—and hence better remember—faces that they perceive as critical, which in turn feeds into their fears about being evaluated.

Similarly, cognitive distortions about the world can lead people with social anxiety disorder to see it as a very dangerous place; they then become chronically hypervigilant for potential social threats and negative evaluations by others (Beck & Emery, 1985; Joorman & Gotlib, 2006; Rapee & Heimberg, 1997). People with social anxiety disorder also use distorted *emotional reasoning* as proof that they will be judged negatively: They evaluate the impression they made on others based on how anxious they became during the interaction, regardless of what actually transpired. Furthermore, people with social anxiety disorder interpret ambiguous cues as negative, which becomes proof that they were correct in their concerns. For instance, an anxious woman giving a talk may interpret the fact that some audience members in the front row are leaning forward in their seats during her talk as proof that they are "waiting for me to falter or make a jerk out of myself" rather than that they might be leaning in to hear her better or might be stretching their backs.

Classical and Operant Conditioning

In some cases, classical conditioning can contribute to the development of social anxiety disorder: A social situation (the conditioned stimulus) becomes paired with a negative social experience (such as public humiliation) to produce a conditioned emotional response (Mineka & Zinbarg, 1995). The conditioned response (fear or anxiety) may generalize to other, or even all, types of social situations.

Operant conditioning principles apply to social anxiety disorder as well: Like a person with agoraphobia, a person with social anxiety disorder might avoid social situations in order to decrease the probability of an uncomfortable experience. The avoidant behavior does decrease anxiety and is thus reinforced (Mowrer, 1939). Campbell's avoidance of crowds does not appear to have been related to social anxiety but rather to his attempting to avoid places where he might have a panic attack.

Social Factors

Extreme overprotection by parents is associated with childhood anxiety (Hudson & Rapee, 2001; Wiborg & Dahl, 1997); such overprotection may lead children to avoid certain situations to cope with their anxiety (Barrett et al., 1996).

In addition, different cultures emphasize different concerns about social interactions, and these concerns influence the specific nature of social anxiety disorder. For example, in certain Asian cultures, such as those of Korea and Japan, a person with social anxiety disorder may be especially afraid of offending others; in particular, he or she may fear that his or her body odor or blushing will be offensive. In Japan, this fear is known as *taijin kyofusho* (Dinnel et al., 2002; Guarnaccia, 1997a). This contrasts with a fear among North Americans and Europeans of being humiliated by something they say or do (Lee & Oh, 1999). This difference in type of social fears is consistent with the collectivist orientation of Asian countries compared to the individualist orientation of Western countries (Norasakkunit et al., 2012). The results from one study suggest that social phobias are becoming more common over time, and a higher proportion of people in more recent birth cohorts will develop the disorder (Heimberg et al., 2000).

Culture can influence the nature of the symptoms of social anxiety disorder. In Korea, for example, social fears called *taijin kyofusho* involve the possibility of offending others, perhaps through body odor or blushing. The social anxieties of Westerners, in contrast, involve fears of being humiliated by their own actions.

Chung Sung-Jun/Getty Images

Feedback Loops in Understanding Social Anxiety Disorder

ONLINE

A genetic or other neurological vulnerability, such as a shy temperament, can predispose people to developing social anxiety disorder (Bienvenu et al., 2007). The neurological vulnerability both contributes to and is affected by distorted thinking and conditioning to social situations (psychological factors). In addition, the anxiety and cognitive distortions may be triggered by a negative social event (social factor) and are then perpetuated by negative self-evaluations and avoidance of the feared social interactions (Antony & Barlow, 2002). Based on these psychological factors, people with social anxiety disorder may interact with others in ways that lead other people to rebuff them (Taylor & Alden, 2006), confirming their own negative view of themselves and of social interactions.

Treating Social Anxiety Disorder

Various forms of treatment are effective for social anxiety disorder; although these treatments typically target a single type of factor, as usual, they indirectly affect the other types of factors.

Targeting Neurological Factors: Medication

For people whose social fears are limited to periodic performances—such as a business presentation, a class presentation, or an onstage performance—a beta-blocker, such as *propranolol* (Inderal), is the medication of choice (Rosenbaum et al., 2005). Beta-blockers bind to some of the brain's receptors for epinephrine and norepinephrine and hence make these receptors less sensitive. Both of these neurotransmitters are released during the fight-or-flight response. Thus, if the person perceives a "threat" and more epinephrine or norepinephrine is released as part of the fight-or-flight response, he or she will not experience its physical effects, such as increased heart rate, as strongly after taking a beta-blocker.

For those whose social anxiety arises in a wider and more frequent set of circumstances, the medication of choice is the SSRI *paroxetine* (Paxil) or *sertraline* (Zoloft). Other SSRIs and SNRIs, such as *venlafaxine* (Effexor) and *nefazodone* (Serzone), and NaSSAs, such as *mirtazapine* (Remeron), can also help treat social anxiety disorder (Rivas-Vazques, 2001; Van der Linden, Stein, & van Balkom, 2000). These medications affect the amygdala and the locus coeruleus, decreasing their activation. As with panic disorder, medication may be effective in treating social anxiety disorder in the short run (Federoff & Taylor, 2001), but symptoms generally return when medication is discontinued; thus, CBT is often also appropriate.

Targeting Psychological Factors: Exposure and Cognitive Restructuring

The cognitive aspects of CBT help people to identify irrational thoughts about social situations, develop more realistic thoughts and expectations, and test predictions about the consequences of engaging in specific behaviors (Antony & Barlow, 2002;

📷 GETTING THE PICTURE

© Ocean/Corbis

© Steve Hix/Somos/Corbis

Which photo best captures the type of situation that would be part of exposure treatment for social fears about public speaking? Answer: The photo on the left.

Clark et al., 2006). In addition, the behavioral method of exposure can be very effective in treating people with social anxiety disorder: When people put themselves in social situations in order to habituate to their anxiety symptoms, their anxiety diminishes (Taylor, 1996).

Targeting Social Factors: Group Interactions

Because the anxiety symptoms relate to social interactions, group therapy is the preferred mode of exposure treatment. Such therapy immerses people in the very type of experience that is associated with anxiety. *Cognitive-behavioral group therapy* uses exposure and cognitive restructuring in a group setting. This setting allows patients to try out their new skills immediately (Heimberg et al., 1990, 1998). Moreover, the exposure involved in group therapy helps to extinguish the conditioned bodily arousal (learned alarm) that arises in social situations. Cognitive-behavioral group therapy is as effective as medication (Davidson et al., 2004) and has the added benefit that the positive effects continue after treatment ends (Aderka et al., 2011; Furukawa et al., 2013).

In addition to therapy groups, there are self-help organizations for people who are afraid of speaking in public, such as Toastmasters, which give people an opportunity to practice making both spontaneous speeches and planned ones. (For more information, go to www.toastmasters.org.)

Feedback Loops in Treating Social Anxiety Disorder

ONLINE

Research indicates that CBT has effects on the brain that are comparable to those of some medications; both sorts of treatments actually reduce the activity in certain key brain areas. For example, one study investigated two kinds of treatments with participants who had untreated social anxiety disorder (Furmark et al., 2002). The study began by scanning the participants' brains as they performed a public speaking task—which made them all anxious. Each participant was then randomly assigned to one of three groups: After the first scan, members of one group received the SSRI *citalopram*, members of another received CBT, and members of the third group were placed on a waiting list.

Nine weeks after the first scan, patients in the two treatment groups had improved by the same amount; however, patients in the waiting list group had not improved. At this point, all participants received a second brain scan, again while they performed the public speaking task. Comparison of the before and after brain scans revealed that a host of brain areas had less activity after treatment, particularly those involved in fear (and related emotions) and memory. Specifically, the amygdala, the hippocampus, and related areas were activated less strongly during the second scan, and the activation decreased comparably for the participants in the two treatment groups. The patients who responded best to treatment showed the greatest decrease in activation. And perhaps most striking, 1 year later the people who had the greatest reduction in activation from the first scan to the second scan were the most improved clinically. This means that the brain scans indicated how well the treatment worked for people with social anxiety disorder.

However, when medication is discontinued, symptoms of social anxiety disorder often recur. Such relapse is less likely after CBT. From a neuropsychosocial approach, CBT changes the way a patient thinks about and behaves in social situations (psychological factors). Viewing these situations more realistically and with less anxiety means that the patient does not get as physically aroused (neurological factor). This lowered arousal, along with positive or neutral expectations about the previously feared social situations, leads the patient to enter more willingly into a social situation (social factor), with less negative expectations. When such social experiences are positive, the patient feels increasing mastery (psychological factor) and less arousal (neurological factor) and perhaps receives reinforcement from others (social factor) for these changes.

TABLE 6.11 • DSM-5 Diagnostic Criteria for Specific Phobia

A. Marked fear or anxiety about a specific object or situation (e.g., flying, heights, animals, receiving an injection, seeing blood).

   Note: In children, the fear or anxiety may be expressed by crying, tantrums, freezing, or clinging.

B. The phobic object or situation almost always provokes immediate fear or anxiety.

C. The phobic object or situation is actively avoided or endured with intense fear or anxiety.

D. The fear or anxiety is out of proportion to the actual danger posed by the specific object or situation and to the sociocultural context.

E. The fear, anxiety, or avoidance is persistent, typically lasting for 6 months or more.

F. The fear, anxiety, or avoidance causes clinically significant distress or impairment in social, occupational, or other important areas of functioning.

G. The disturbance is not better explained by the symptoms of another mental disorder, including fear, anxiety and avoidance of situations associated with panic-like symptoms or other incapacitating symptoms (as in agoraphobia); objects or situations related to obsessions (as in obsessive-compulsive disorder); separation from home or attachment figures (as in separation anxiety disorder); or social situations (as in social anxiety disorder).

Reprinted with permission from the Diagnostic and Statistical Manual of Mental Disorders, Fifth Edition, (Copyright ©2013). American Psychiatric Association. All Rights Reserved.

Specific phobia
An anxiety disorder characterized by excessive or unreasonable anxiety about or fear related to a specific situation or object.

Specific Phobia

Another type of anxiety disorder—one that does not seem to apply to Campbell—is *specific phobia*. To understand why this diagnosis would not apply to him, we need to learn what specific phobia is.

What Is Specific Phobia?

What distinguishes normal fear and avoidance of an object or situation from its "abnormal" counterpart? DSM-5 describes the central element of **specific phobia** as a marked anxiety or fear of a specific situation or object that is disproportional to the actual danger posed (see Table 6.11; American Psychiatric Association, 2013). A person with a specific phobia works hard to avoid the feared stimulus, often significantly restricting his or her activity in the process (see Case 6.5). A person with an elevator phobia, for example, will choose to walk up many flights of stairs rather than take the elevator. A specific phobia you might recognize include claustrophobia (fear of small spaces), arachnophobia (spiders), hydrophobia (water), and acrophobia (heights).

CASE 6.5 • FROM THE OUTSIDE: A Specific Phobia (Hydrophobia)

Kevin described an experience in which he almost drowned when he was 11. He and his parents were swimming in the Gulf of Mexico, in a place where there were underwater canyons with currents that would often pull a swimmer out to sea. He remembered the experience very distinctly. He was standing in water up to his neck, trying to see where his parents were. Suddenly, a large wave hit him and dragged him into one of the underwater canyons. Fortunately, someone on shore saw what had happened and rescued him. After the experience, he became very much afraid of the ocean, and the fear generalized to lakes, rivers, and large swimming pools. He avoided them all.

(McMullin, 1986, p. 165)

DSM-5 lists five types or categories of specific phobia: *animal, natural environment, blood-injection-injury, situational,* and *"other"* (American Psychiatric Association, 2013):

- The *animal type* of specific phobia pertains to an extreme fear or avoidance of a kind of animal; commonly feared animals include snakes and spiders. Symptoms of the animal type of specific phobia usually emerge in childhood. People with a phobia for one kind of animal often also have a phobia for another kind of animal.

- The *natural environment* type of specific phobia typically focuses on heights, water, or storms. Phobias about the natural environment typically emerge during childhood.

- The *blood-injection-injury type* of specific phobia produces a strong response to seeing blood, having injections, sustaining bodily injuries, or watching surgery. This type of phobia runs in families and emerges in early childhood. A unique response of this specific phobia involves first an increased arousal, then a rapid decrease in heart rate and blood pressure, which often causes fainting. Among people with this type of phobia, over half report having fainted in response to a feared stimulus (Öst, 1992).

- A *situational type* of specific phobia involves a fear of a particular situation, such as being in an airplane, elevator, or other enclosed space, or of driving a car. Some people develop this type of phobia in childhood, but in general it has a later onset, often in the mid-20s. People with this type of phobia tend to experience more panic attacks than do people with other types of specific phobia (Lipsitz et al., 2002). Situational phobia has a gender ratio, age of onset, and family history similar to those of panic disorder or agoraphobia.

- *Other type* of specific phobia includes any such phobia that does not fall into the other four categories. Examples of specific phobias that would be classified as "other" are a fear of costumed characters (such as clowns at a circus) and a phobic avoidance of situations that may lead to choking or vomiting.

Specifics About Specific Phobia

As noted in Table 6.12, the majority of people who have one sort of specific phobia are likely to have at least one more. This high comorbidity among types of specific phobia has led some researchers to suggest that, like social anxiety disorder, specific phobia may take two forms: a focused type that is limited to a specific stimulus and a more generalized type that involves fear of various stimuli (Stinson et al., 2007).

The unrealistic fears and extreme anxiety of a specific phobia occur in the presence of the feared stimulus but may even occur when simply thinking about it. Often, people with a specific phobia fear that something bad will happen as a result of contact with the stimulus: "What if I get stuck in the tunnel, and it cracks open and floods?" "What if the spider bites me, and I get a deadly disease?" People may also be afraid of the consequences of their reaction to the phobic stimulus, such as losing control of themselves or not being able to get help: "What if I faint or have a heart attack while I'm in the tunnel?" or, "What if I mess my pants after the spider bites me?" In this sense, the fear of somehow losing control is similar to that in panic disorder (Horwath et al., 1993).

There is a very long list of stimuli to which people have developed phobias (see www.phobialist .com), but people do not seem to develop specific phobias toward all kinds of stimuli; for example, a phobia of flowers is extremely unusual. Humans, like other animals, have a natural readiness for certain stimuli to produce certain conditioned responses. This *preparedness* means that less learning from experience is needed to produce the conditioning (Öhman et al., 1976). Some psychologists (Menzies & Parker, 2001; Öhman, 1986) propose that such preparedness has an evolutionary advantage: People are more readily afraid of objects or situations that could lead to death, such as being too close to the edge of a cliff (and falling off) or being bitten by a poisonous snake or spider. According to this view, those among our early ancestors who were afraid of these stimuli and avoided them were more likely to survive and reproduce—and thus passed on genes that led their descendants to be prepared to fear these stimuli.

TABLE 6.12 • Specific Phobia Facts at a Glance

Prevalence

- Approximately 10% of Americans will experience in their lifetime a fear severe enough to meet the criteria for specific phobia (Stinson et al., 2007).

Comorbidity

- Only a quarter of those with a diagnosis of specific phobia have a single specific phobia; 50% have three or more phobias. In addition, the more phobias a person has, the more likely he or she is to have another type of anxiety disorder (Curtis et al., 1998; Stinson et al., 2007).

Onset

- There are different ages of onset for the various types of specific phobia, although they typically begin in childhood; the average age is approximately 10 years (Stinson et al., 2007).
- Specific phobia that arises after trauma can occur at any age.

Course

- Specific phobia that arises during childhood and persists through adulthood is less likely to improve without treatment.

Gender Differences

- Twice as many women are diagnosed with specific phobia as men, although this ratio varies across type of specific phobia (Stinson et al., 2007).

Cultural Differences

- The prevalence rates of the various types of specific phobia vary across countries, suggesting that cultural factors, such as the likelihood of coming into contact with various stimuli, affect the form that specific phobia takes (Chambers et al., 1986).

Source: Unless otherwise noted, information in the table is from American Psychiatric Association, 2013.

Although many people fear some kind of animal, such as spiders or snakes, the fear and avoidance of that type of animal do not constitute a specific phobia unless they cause marked distress or significantly interfere with normal functioning.

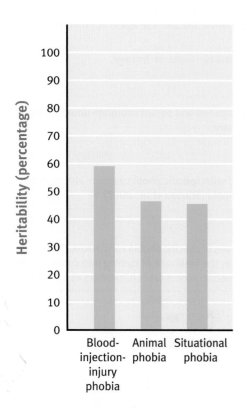

FIGURE **6.5 • Heritabilities of Specific Phobia**
Source: From Kendler, Karkowski, & Prescott, 1999b. Copyright 1999 by Cambridge University Press.

Understanding Specific Phobia

As we see in the following sections, neurological and psychological factors appear to contribute to specific phobia more heavily than do social factors.

Neurological Factors

Researchers are making good headway in understanding the neurological factors that underlie specific phobia.

Brain Systems and Neural Communication

Perhaps not surprisingly, our old friend the amygdala is again implicated in an anxiety disorder. In fact, the amygdala appears to have a hair-trigger in patients with specific phobia. For example, in one fMRI study, patients who were phobic of spiders and control participants were asked to match geometric figures. In this study, the trick was that in the background behind each figure—which was completely irrelevant to the task of matching the figures—was a picture of either a spider or a mushroom (because no one in the study was afraid of mushrooms). Even in this task, where the participants were not paying attention to the background pictures, the amygdala of the patients with the phobia was more strongly activated in response to the spiders than the mushrooms; this was not true for the control participants (Straube et al., 2006).

In addition, the sort of anxiety evoked by specific phobia is associated with too little of the inhibitory neurotransmitter GABA (File et al., 1999). When a benzodiazepine (such as *diazepam*, or Valium) binds to the appropriate receptors, it facilitates the functioning of GABA—and the drug thereby ultimately produces a calming effect.

Genetics

Researchers have discovered that some genes predispose people to develop a particular specific phobia, whereas other genes predispose people to develop some sort of specific phobia but do not affect which particular type it will be (Kendler et al., 2001; Lichtenstein & Annas, 2000). According to one theory, genetic differences may cause parts of the brain related to fear (in particular, the amygdala) to be too reactive to specific stimuli; that is, the amygdala is "prepared" to overreact to a specific stimulus, which leads to a specific phobia of that stimulus. In addition, some people's brains may generally be more prepared in this way than others', and so they are more likely to develop a specific phobia although not any particular one (LeDoux, 1996).

Furthermore, genes do not have equal effects for all types of specific phobia: The different types of specific phobia appear to be influenced to different degrees by genetics and the environment (see Figure 6.5 for the heritabilities of types of specific phobia). However, genetics cannot be all there is to it: If it were, then when one identical twin has specific phobia, so would the other twin, but this is not always the case. As we've noted before, the genes predispose, but rarely determine. Rather, certain environmental events are necessary to trigger the disorder. For example, family environment has proven to be an important risk factor for specific phobia (Kendler et al., 2001).

The sum of the research findings about neurological factors suggests that particular life experiences can lead to a particular specific phobia for people who—through genes or other life experiences—are neurologically vulnerable (Antony & Barlow, 2002).

Psychological Factors

Life experiences always have their impact via how a person perceives and interprets them. Thus, psychological factors play a key role in whether a person will develop a specific phobia. Three primary psychological factors contribute to a specific phobia: a tendency to overestimate the probability of a negative event's occurring based on contact with the feared stimuli, classical conditioning, and operant conditioning.

Faulty Estimations

Similarly to what we saw with social anxiety disorder, people who have a specific phobia have a particular cognitive bias—they believe strongly that something bad will happen when they encounter the feared stimulus (Tomarken et al., 1989). They also overestimate the probability that an unpleasant event, such as falling from a high place or an airplane's crashing into a tall building, will occur (Pauli et al., 1998). People who have a specific phobia may also have perceptual distortions related to their feared stimulus. For example, a person with a spider phobia may perceive that a spider is moving straight toward him or her when it isn't (Riskind et al., 1995).

People with specific phobia may have perceptional distortions that heighten their fears. For instance, someone with a fear of flying may misperceive the normal downward tilt of a plane during landing as a greater tilt than it is and think the plane is about to crash.

Conditioning: Classical and Operant

From a learning perspective, classical conditioning and operant conditioning could account for the development and maintenance of a specific phobia. Watson and Rayner's conditioning of Little Albert's fear of rats was the first experimental induction of a classically conditioned phobia (see Chapter 2). However, some recent research has questioned the importance of classical conditioning in the development of specific phobia. In studies of people with a phobia of water, heights, or spiders, researchers usually have not found evidence that classical conditioning played the role that had been predicted (Menzies & Clarke, 1993a, 1993b, 1995a, 1995b; Poulton et al., 1999). Further evidence for a limited role of classical conditioning comes from everyday observations: Many people experience the pairing of conditioned and unconditioned stimuli but do not become phobic.

Regardless of the extent of the role of classical conditioning, operant conditioning clearly plays a key role in maintaining a specific phobia: By avoiding the feared stimulus, a person can decrease the fear and anxiety that he or she would experience in the presence of it, which reinforces the avoidance.

Social Factors: Modeling and Culture

Sometimes, simply seeing other people being afraid of a particular stimulus is enough to make the observer become afraid of that stimulus (Mineka et al., 1984). For example, if as a young child, you saw your older cousin become agitated and anxious when a dog approached, you might well learn to do the same. Similarly, repeated warnings about the dangers of a stimulus can increase the risk of developing a specific phobia of that stimulus (Antony & Barlow, 2002).

Modeling is not the only way that culture can exert an effect on the content of specific phobia. Consider the fact that people in India are twice as likely as people in England to have a phobia of animals, darkness, or bad weather but are only half as likely to have social anxiety disorder or agoraphobia (Chambers et al., 1986). One explanation for this finding is that people in India are apt to spend more time at home than their English counterparts, so they have less opportunity to encounter feared social situations. Similarly, dangerous and predatory animals are more likely to roam free in India than in England.

ONLINE

Feedback Loops in Understanding Specific Phobia

A person may be neurologically vulnerable to developing a specific phobia in part because of his or her genes, which may make his or her amygdala "prepared" to react too strongly to certain stimuli. Through observing others' fear of a specific stimulus (social factor), the person can become afraid and develop faulty cognitions, which can lead to distorted thinking and the conditioning of false alarms to the feared stimulus (psychological factors). And, once the person begins to avoid the stimulus, the avoidance behavior is negatively reinforced. This behavior in turn affects not only the person's beliefs but also his or her social interactions (social factors).

Treating Specific Phobia

Treatment for specific phobia generally targets one type of factor, although the beneficial changes affect all the factors.

Targeting Neurological Factors: Medication

Medication, such as a benzodiazepine, may be prescribed for a specific phobia (alone or in combination with CBT), but this is generally not recommended. Medication is usually unnecessary because CBT treatment—even a single session—is highly effective in treating a specific phobia (Ellison & McCarter, 2002).

Targeting Psychological Factors

If you had to choose an anxiety disorder to have, specific phobia probably should be your choice. This is the anxiety disorder most treatable by CBT, with up to 90% lasting improvement rates even after only one session (Gitin et al., 1996; Öst, Salkovskis, & Hellström, 1991).

Behavioral Method: Exposure

The behavioral method of *graded exposure* has proven effective in treating specific phobia (Vansteenwegen et al., 2007), and is considered a first-line treatment. With this method, the patient and therapist progress through an individualized hierarchy of anxiety-producing stimuli or events as fast as the patient can tolerate; this process is like that used in exposure treatment for social anxiety discussed earlier in the chapter, but in this case substituting the specific feared stimulus for the feared social situation or interaction. Moreover, recent research on treating phobias with exposure suggests that virtual reality exposure works as well as in vivo exposure, at least for certain phobias (Pull, 2005), such as of flying and heights (Coelho et al., 2009; Emmelkamp et al., 2001, 2002), and this technique is part of many treatment programs for fear of flying.

Cognitive Methods

Cognitive methods for treating a specific phobia are similar to those used to treat other anxiety disorders, such as panic disorder, agoraphobia, and social anxiety disorder. The therapist and patient identify illogical thoughts pertaining to the feared stimulus, and the therapist helps highlight discrepant information and challenges the patient to see the irrationality of his or her thoughts and expectations. Table 6.13 provides an example of thoughts that someone with claustrophobia—a fear of enclosed spaces—might have.

In addition, group CBT may be appropriate for some kinds of phobias, such as fear of flying or of spiders (Rothbaum et al., 2006; Van Gerwen et al., 2006). However, unlike group CBT for social anxiety disorder, group treatment for specific phobia does not directly *target* social factors; rather, group CBT is a cost-effective way to teach patients behavioral and cognitive methods to overcome their fears.

TABLE 6.13 • Fearful Thoughts Related to Claustrophobia

- Many closed-in places, e.g., elevators, small rooms, do not have enough air.
- I will faint.
- If I go into a closed-in space, e.g., elevator or cave, I will not be able to get out.
- I will not be able to cope if I get stuck in a closed-in place.
- If I get too nervous, I may hurt myself.
- I will embarrass myself.
- I will lose control.
- I cannot think straight in enclosed places.
- I will go crazy.
- I will die.

Source: Antony, Craske, & Barlow, 1995, p. 105. For more information see the Permissions section.

Targeting Social Factors: A Limited Role for Observational Learning

Observational learning may play a role in the development of a specific phobia, but to many researchers' surprise, seeing others model how to interact normally with the feared stimulus generally is not an effective treatment for specific phobia. Perhaps observational learning is not effective because patients' cognitive distortions are powerful enough to negate any positive effects modeling might provide. For instance, someone with a spider phobia who observes someone else handling a spider might think, "Well, that person isn't harmed by the spider, but there's no guarantee that I'll be so lucky!"

Feedback Loops in Treating Specific Phobia

ONLINE

When treatment is effective in creating lasting change in one type of factor, it causes changes in the other factors. Consider dental phobia and its treatment. Over 16% of people between the ages of 18 and 26 have significant dental anxiety, according to one survey (Locker et al., 2001). One study examined the effect of a single session of CBT on dental phobia (Thom et al., 2000). The treatment group was given stress management training and imaginal exposure to dental surgery 1 week prior to the surgery; these patients were asked to review the stress management techniques and visualize dental surgery daily during the intervening week. Another group of people with dental phobia was only given a benzodiazepine 30 minutes before surgery. A third group was given nothing; this was the control group. Both types of treatment led to less anxiety during the dental surgery than was reported by the control group. However, those in the CBT group continued to maintain and show further improvement at a 2-month follow-up: 70% of them went on to have subsequent dental work, whereas only 20% of those in the benzodiazepine group and 10% of the control group did so.

The neuropsychosocial approach leads us to consider how the factors and their feedback loops interact to treat such a specific phobia: The medication, although temporarily decreasing anxiety (neurological factor), did not lead to sustained change either in brain functioning or in thoughts about dental procedures. The CBT, in contrast, targeted psychological factors and also led to changes in a neurological factor—brain functioning associated with decreased anxiety and arousal related to dental surgery. In turn, these changes led to social changes—additional dental work. And the added dental visits presumably led to better health, which in turn affected the participants' view of themselves and their interactions with others. Indeed, if the visits had cosmetic effects (such as a nicer smile), their social benefits would be even more evident. Such feedback loops underlie the treatment of all types of specific phobia.

Separation anxiety disorder
A disorder that typically arises in childhood and is characterized by excessive anxiety about separation from home or from someone to whom the person is strongly attached.

Thinking Like A Clinician

Iqbal is horribly afraid of tarantulas, refusing to enter insect houses at zoos. Do you need any more information before determining whether Iqbal has a specific phobia of tarantulas? If so, what would you need to know? If not, do you think he has a specific phobia? Explain. How might Iqbal have developed his fear of tarantulas? What factors are likely to have been involved in its emergence and maintenance? Suppose Iqbal decides that he wants to "get rid of" his fear of tarantulas. What treatments are likely to be effective, and what are the advantages and disadvantages of each?

Separation Anxiety Disorder

Separation anxiety disorder is characterized by excessive anxiety about separation from home or from someone to whom the person is strongly attached. This disorder occurs most commonly in children but can also affect adults. In what follows, we examine separation anxiety disorder in detail and then turn to its causes and treatment.

What Is Separation Anxiety Disorder?

During different phases of development, an infant or a toddler will normally become distressed on separating (or even thinking about separating) from a parent. (In this section the word *parent* refers to the person from whom the child fears separation; that person may be the mother, father, some other family member, caretaker, or another person involved in the child's life.) An adult may become distressed about leaving his or her partner the morning after a big fight, or if the partner is sick. To qualify for a diagnosis of separation anxiety disorder, the anxiety, distress, or impaired functioning must be excessive and typically is exhibited over a period of at least 6 months for adults (see Table 6.14).

TABLE 6.14 • DSM-5 Diagnostic Criteria for Separation Anxiety Disorder

A. Developmentally inappropriate and excessive fear or anxiety concerning separation from those to whom the individual is attached, as evidenced by at least three of the following:

1. Recurrent excessive distress when anticipating or experiencing separation from home or from major attachment figures.

2. Persistent and excessive worry about losing major attachment figures or about possible harm to them, such as illness, injury, disasters, or death.

3. Persistent and excessive worry about experiencing an untoward event (e.g., getting lost, being kidnapped, having an accident, becoming ill) that causes separation from a major attachment figure.

4. Persistent reluctance or refusal to go out, away from home, to school, to work, or elsewhere because of fear of separation.

5. Persistent and excessive fear of or reluctance about being alone or without major attachment figures at home or in other settings.

6. Persistent reluctance or refusal to sleep away from home or to go to sleep without being near a major attachment figure.

7. Repeated nightmares involving the theme of separation.

8. Repeated complaints of physical symptoms (e.g., headaches, stomachaches, nausea, vomiting) when separation from major attachment figures occurs or is anticipated.

B. The fear, anxiety, or avoidance is persistent, lasting at least 4 weeks in children and adolescents and typically 6 months or more in adults.

C. The disturbance causes clinically significant distress or impairment in social, academic, occupational, or other important areas of functioning.

D. The disturbance is not better explained by another mental disorder, such as refusing to leave home because of excessive resistance to change in autism spectrum disorder; delusions or hallucinations concerning separation in psychotic disorders; refusal to go outside without a trusted companion in agoraphobia; worries about ill health or other harm befalling significant others in generalized anxiety disorder; or concerns about having an illness in illness anxiety disorder.

Separation anxiety is more than a child's getting upset about temporarily saying goodbye to a parent. Children with separation anxiety disorder may become so homesick when away from home that activities—such as a sleepover at a friend's or a stay at overnight camp—are interrupted in order to return home. Or these children may want to know the parent's whereabouts at all times, using a cell phone to make frequent contact during any physical separation. And when away from the parent, they may also have physical symptoms of anxiety: dizziness, stomachaches, nausea and vomiting, and feeling faint (American Psychiatric Association, 2013).

Some children with separation anxiety disorder fear that they will get permanently "lost" from their parents, and their dreams have similar themes. And like people with agoraphobia, they may be unable to leave the house alone (at an age when it would be appropriate to do so) or even to be in their room alone. Such children often try to stay within a few feet of the parent, moving from room to room as the parent moves from room to room. At bedtime, they may be unable to fall asleep unless someone else is in the room with them, and during the night, they may crawl into bed with parents or a sibling. If parents lock their bedroom door at night, the child may sleep on the floor right outside the door. If children with this disorder are separated from their parent, they may have persistent fantasies about reuniting. Also, like people with generalized anxiety disorder, they may have recurrent fears about harm befalling their parent or themselves, as JC did, in Case 6.6. Table 6.15 lists additional facts about separation anxiety disorder.

This little girl might just be looking for something in the laundry basket, but a child with separation anxiety may want to know where his or her parent is at all times—even following the parent from room to room.

Commercial Eye/Getty Images

CASE 6.6 • FROM THE OUTSIDE: Separation Anxiety Disorder

JC is a 9-year-old boy who lives with his mother and attends the third grade, where he is an A student. During the last 2 weeks, he has refused to go to school and has missed 6 school days. He is awake almost all night worrying about going to school. As the start of the school day approaches, he cries and screams that he cannot go, chews holes in his shirt, pulls his hair, digs at his face, punches the wall, throws himself on the floor, and experiences headaches, stomachaches, and vomiting. If he attends school, he is less anxious until bedtime. As his separation anxiety has increased, he has become gloomy, has stopped reading for fun, and frequently worries about his mother's tachycardia [rapid heart rate].

JC was seen once by a psychiatrist at age 3 years for problems with separation anxiety. He did well in preschool and kindergarten. He was seen at a community mental health center during the first grade for school refusal, but did well again during the second grade. In addition to having recurrent symptoms of separation anxiety disorder, he is phobic of dogs, avoids speaking and writing in public, and has symptoms of generalized anxiety disorder and obsessive-compulsive disorder. His mother has a history of panic disorder.

(Hanna, Fischer, & Fluent, 2006, pp. 56–57)

Adults who have this disorder may worry about the loss of a loved one through an accident or illness or may not be able to fall sleep away from home unless the loved one is with them. The diagnosis of separation anxiety disorder is only made when another disorder, such as agoraphobia or generalized anxiety disorder, does not better account for the symptoms.

TABLE 6.15 • Separation Anxiety Disorder Facts at a Glance

Prevalence

- About 4% of adults had separation anxiety disorder in childhood (Shear et al., 2006).
- Separation anxiety disorder is the most prevalent anxiety disorder among children, particularly those younger than 12 years old.

Onset

- The disorder can begin as early as the preschool years.
- Separation anxiety disorder may emerge after some type of stressful event, such as a move, the death of a pet, or the illness of a relative.

Comorbidity

- Children with separation anxiety disorder are more likely to experience other anxiety disorders—especially generalized anxiety disorder—than are children in the general population (Brückl et al., 2006; Verduin & Kendall, 2003).

Course

- Symptoms often wax and wane.
- As the child gets older, symptoms tend to lessen; at some point before adulthood, most people no longer meet the criteria for the disorder (Foley, Pickles et al., 2004; Shear et al., 2006).

Gender Differences

- In the general population, more females than males have this disorder; however, comparable numbers of males and females with this disorder are treated as outpatients.

Cultural Differences

- Different ethnic groups and cultures have different norms about what constitutes appropriate responses to separation in children, which can affect parents' inclination to perceive a separation problem and create different thresholds for diagnosis across cultures.

Source: Unless otherwise noted, the source for information is American Psychiatric Association, 2013.

CURRENT CONTROVERSY

Separation Anxiety Disorder: Anxiety Disorder or Developmental Difference?

DSM-5 has chapters of disorders that are loosely organized based on when the disorders tend to emerge over the lifespan. Separation anxiety disorder, an extreme case of fear and worry related to current or potential separation from others, can occur across the lifespan but tends to emerge first in childhood. However, it is grouped with anxiety disorders, not with neurodevelopmental disorders (see Chapter 14). Is separation anxiety disorder in the most appropriate place in the DSM-5?

On the one hand, grouping the disorder with anxiety disorders makes sense because it shares symptoms with other anxiety disorders, including the pattern of fear out of proportion to danger, worry about possible future events, and physical symptoms triggered by anxiety. Treatment for this disorder is similar to treatment for other anxiety disorders.

Separation anxiety does *not* share the types of symptoms related to executive and intellectual functioning that are found in neurodevelopmental disorders.

On the other hand, separation anxiety disorder, like the neurodevelopmental disorders, typically starts in early childhood and can occur throughout the lifespan. Separation anxiety itself is a normal developmental process; what makes this a *disorder* is the range and severity of symptoms and the appearance of symptoms at a later age than would be expected. This could be seen as a divergence from the normal path of development.

CRITICAL THINKING When a disorder "fits" in more than one category of disorders, as does separation anxiety disorder, would it be better if such disorders were cross-listed in the relevant categories)? What would be the advantages and disadvantages to doing this?

(James Foley, College of Wooster)

Understanding and Treating Separation Anxiety Disorder

Separation anxiety disorder is more common among first-degree relatives (parents and siblings) than in the general population, and the disorder is considered to be moderately heritable (Roberson-Nay et al., 2012). However, the heritability probably reflects a heritability of anxiety in general: Separation anxiety is more common among children whose mothers have panic disorder than among children whose mothers don't have that disorder, as was true of JC in Case 6.6 (Cronk et al., 2004).

But other factors create feedback loops: Overprotective family members may reinforce behaviors associated with anxiety about separation and may punish behaviors associated with actual separation. If so, then children in such families who have temperaments that are high in harm avoidance and reward dependence (see Chapter 2) may be especially vulnerable because they will be relatively responsive to reward and punishment. Moreover, separation anxiety disorder is more common in children whose fathers are absent (Cronk et al., 2004), perhaps because that absence leads the child to have a heightened fear of losing the remaining parent.

As with other anxiety disorders, treatment of separation anxiety disorder may involve CBT (with exposure and cognitive restructuring; Schneider et al., 2011). Family therapy is included in treatment; the therapist identifies any family patterns that maintain the disorder and helps parents change their interaction patterns to encourage and reinforce their child to engage in appropriate separation behaviors (Siqueland et al., 2005).

Thinking Like A Clinician

Nia is 12 years old and going through puberty. Lately she's been coming home right after school and staying home during the weekend, no longer hanging out with her friends. In fact, Nia is unhappy when her mother (her parents are divorced) leaves her alone to go shopping or to go out in the evening; sometimes she tearfully begs her mother not to leave but won't—or can't—explain why she feels so upset. Based on what you have learned, how do you think Nia—and her mother—should proceed? Should they wait and hope the symptoms pass or try to find out more? Explain your answer in detail.

☐ Follow-up on Earl Campbell

The most appropriate diagnoses for Campbell appears to be both panic disorder and agoraphobia. Despite using medication, Campbell continues to have some panic symptoms, but he makes good use of cognitive and behavioral methods and of social support. He acknowledged his continuing efforts: "Even though crowds and noise bother me, I'll push myself to tolerate them for as long as I can. I know I must keep trying to get past the fear. It takes far more discipline for me to get through an average day with panic than it took for me to perform as a top running back in the NFL. The challenges of panic are greater" (Campbell & Ruane, 1999, p. 199).

◻ SUMMING UP

Common Features of Anxiety Disorders

- The key symptoms of anxiety disorders are fear, extreme anxiety, intense arousal, and attempts to avoid stimuli that lead to fear and anxiety.

- The fight-or-flight response (also called the stress response) arises when people perceive a threat; when the arousal feels out of control—either because the person has an overactive stress response or because he or she misinterprets the arousal—the person may experience panic. In response to the panic, some people develop a phobia of stimuli related to their panic and anxiety symptoms.

- Anxiety disorders frequently co-occur with other psychological disorders, such as depression or substance-use disorders. Mental health clinicians must determine whether the anxiety symptoms are the primary cause of the problem or are the by-product of another type of disorder.

- The high comorbidity of depression and anxiety disorders suggests that the two disorders share some of the same features, specifically high levels of negative emotions and distress—which can lead to concentration and sleep problems and irritability.

Generalized Anxiety Disorder

- Generalized anxiety disorder is marked by persistent and excessive worry about a number of events or activities that are not solely the focus of another disorder. Most people with GAD also have comorbid depression.

- Neurological factors associated with GAD include:

  - *decreased* arousal because the parasympathetic nervous system is extremely responsive (this is unlike most other anxiety disorders).

  - abnormal activity of serotonin, dopamine, and other neurotransmitters, which in turn influences motivation, response to reward, and attention.

  - a genetic predisposition to become anxious and/or depressed. This predisposition, however, is not specific to GAD.

- Psychological factors that contribute to GAD include being hypervigilant for possible threats, a sense that the worrying is out of control, and the reinforcing experience that worrying prevents panic.

- Social factors that contribute to GAD include stressful life events, which can trigger the disorder.

- Treatments for GAD include:

  - medication (which targets neurological factors), such as buspirone or an SNRI or SSRI when depression is present as a comorbid disorder.

  - CBT (which targets psychological factors), which may include breathing retraining, muscle relaxation training, worry exposure, cognitive restructuring, self-monitoring, problem solving, psychoeducation, and/or meditation.

Panic Disorder and Agoraphobia

- The hallmark of panic disorder is recurrent panic attacks—periods of fear and discomfort along with physical arousal symptoms or cognitive symptoms. Panic attacks may be cued by particular stimuli (usually internal sensations), or they may arise without any clear cue. Panic disorder also involves fear of further attacks and, in some cases, restricted behavior in an effort to prevent further attacks.

- People in different cultures may have similar—but not identical—constellations of panic symptoms, such as *ataque de nervios* and wind-and-blood pressure.

- About half of people with panic disorder also develop agoraphobia—avoiding situations that might trigger a panic attack or from which escape would be difficult, such as crowded locations or tunnels.

- Neurological factors that contribute to panic disorder and agoraphobia include:

  - A heightened sensitivity to breathing changes, which in turn leads to hyperventilation, panic, and a sense of needing to escape.

  - Too much norepinephrine (produced by an over-reactive locus coeruleus), which increases heart and respiration rates and other aspects of the fight-or-flight response.

  - A genetic predisposition to anxiety disorders, which makes some people vulnerable to panic disorder and agoraphobia.

- Psychological factors that contribute to panic disorder and agoraphobia include:

  - Conditioning of the initial bodily sensations of panic (interoceptive cues) or of external cues related to panic attacks, which leads them to become learned alarms and elicit panic symptoms. Some

people then develop a fear of fear and avoid panic-related cues.

  - Heightened anxiety sensitivity and misinterpretation of bodily symptoms of arousal as symptoms of a more serious problem, such as a heart attack, which can, in turn, lead to hypervigilance for—and fear of—further sensations and cause increased arousal, creating a vicious cycle.

- Social factors related to panic disorder and agoraphobia include:

  - greater-than-average number of social stressors during childhood and adolescence.

  - cultural factors, which can influence whether people develop panic disorder.

  - the presence of a safe person, which can decrease catastrophic thinking and panic.

- The treatment that targets neurological factors is medication, specifically benzodiazepines for short-term relief and antidepressants for long-term use.

- CBT is the first-line treatment for panic disorder and targets psychological factors. Behavioral methods focus on the bodily signals of arousal, panic, and agoraphobic avoidance. Cognitive methods (psychoeducation and cognitive restructuring) focus on the misappraisal of bodily sensations and on mistaken inferences about them.

- Treatments that target social factors include group therapy focused on panic disorder, and couples or family therapy, particularly when a family member is a safe person.

Social Anxiety Disorder (Social Phobia)

- Social anxiety disorder is an intense fear of or anxiety about being in any of three types of social situations: social interactions (such as a conversation); being observed (such as when eating or using public restrooms); and performing (such as giving a speech). When such social situations cannot be avoided, they trigger panic or anxiety.

- The anxiety about performing poorly and being evaluated by others can, in turn, impair a person's performance, creating a vicious cycle. The symptoms of social anxiety disorder may lead people with this disorder to be less successful than they could otherwise be because they avoid job-related social interactions that are required for advancement.

- Neurological factors that give rise to social anxiety disorder include an amygdala that is more easily activated in response to social stimuli, too little dopamine and serotonin, and a genetic predisposition toward a shy temperament (behavioral inhibition).

- Psychological factors that give rise to social anxiety disorder include cognitive distortions and hypervigilance for social threats—particularly about being negatively evaluated. Classical conditioning of a fear response in social situations may contribute to social anxiety disorder; avoiding feared social situations is then negatively reinforced (operant conditioning).

- Social factors that give rise to social anxiety disorder include parents' encouraging a child to avoid anxiety-inducing social interactions. Moreover, people in different cultures may express their social fears somewhat differently (e.g., *taijin kyofusho*). The rate of social anxiety disorder appears to be increasing in more recent birth cohorts.

- Medication is the treatment that targets neurological factors, specifically beta-blockers for periodic performance anxiety and SSRIs or SNRIs for more generalized social anxiety disorder. CBT is the treatment that targets psychological factors, specifically exposure and cognitive restructuring. Group CBT and exposure to feared social stimuli are the treatments that target social factors.

Specific Phobia

- Specific phobia involves (a) marked anxiety or fear related to a specific stimulus that (b) is disproportional to the actual danger posed, and (c) leads to attempts to avoid that feared stimulus. DSM-5 specifies five types of specific phobia: animal, natural environment, blood-injection-injury, situational, and other.

- People are biologically prepared to develop specific phobia to certain stimuli as well as to resist developing phobias to certain other stimuli.

- Neurological factors, such as an overly reactive amygdala, appear to contribute to specific phobia. GABA is one neurotransmitter that is involved in specific phobia. Research also suggests that some genes are associated with specific phobia generally, whereas other genes are associated with particular types of specific phobia.

- Psychological factors that give rise to specific phobia may include classical conditioning (but rarely), operant conditioning (negative reinforcement of avoiding the feared stimulus), and cognitive biases related to the stimulus (such as overestimating the probability that a negative event will occur following contact with the feared stimulus).

- Observational learning—a social factor—can influence what particular stimulus a person comes to fear.

- Treatment for specific phobia can include medication (targeting neurological factors), specifically a benzodiazepine. However, medication is usually not necessary because CBT—the treatment of choice for specific phobia—is extremely effective (targeting psychological factors). CBT—particularly when exposure is part of the treatment—can be effective after just one session.

Separation Anxiety Disorder

- Separation anxiety disorder is characterized by excessive anxiety about separation from home or from someone to whom the person is strongly attached.

- Separation anxiety disorder is most common in children but also can occur in adults.

- Separation anxiety disorder is moderately heritable; overprotective family members may inadvertently reinforce behaviors associated with separation anxiety and punish behaviors associated with appropriate separation.

- Separation anxiety disorder is treated with methods used to treat other anxiety disorders: CBT that includes exposure and cognitive restructuring, along with family therapy.

Key Terms

More Study Aids

Photodisc

For additional study aids related to this chapter, including quizzes to make sure you've retained everything you've learned and a Student Video Activity exploring how a 10-year-old boy struggles to overcome his phobia of dogs, go to: www.worthpublishers.com/launchpad/rkabpsych2e.

CHAPTER  **7**

Obsessive-Compulsive-Related and Trauma-Related Disorders

Howard Hughes is famous for many things: He was an industrialist, creating Hughes Aircraft Company and designing the planes his company built; he was an aviator who broke flying records; he was the owner of hotels and casinos; he was a reclusive billionaire who directed an Academy Award–winning film. During his lifetime, people around the world recognized his name and his accomplishments.

Hughes grew up in Texas, an only child in a wealthy family. As a child and teenager, Hughes was shy and had only one friend; he was "supersensitive"—he didn't seem to take teasing in stride as other children did—and he preferred to be alone or spend time with his mother. When he was almost 17, his mother, a homemaker, died unexpectedly of complications from a minor surgical procedure. Two years later, his father died unexpectedly of a heart attack. Hughes was independent and rich at the age of 19. Within the next 6 years, he'd have triumphs and disasters: He'd win an Academy Award and survive a horrific airplane crash that crushed his cheekbone. Four years later, he would found Hughes Aircraft Company, and 3 years after that, he'd set a world record for flight. As Hughes became more successful, he also became reclusive, seeing fewer and fewer people. But it wasn't simply that he became a hermit. He went through periods of time when he would do nothing but watch films, 24 hours a day, naked, moving only from bed to chair and back, with occasional forays to the bathroom. And Hughes was deathly afraid of being exposed to germs—and so he developed elaborate precautions to avoid contact with them (Barlett & Steele, 1979).

CLEARLY, HUGHES'S BEHAVIOR wasn't normal. Hughes suffered from symptoms of psychological disorders—to the point where he wasn't able to function adequately in any sphere of life. But what was the matter with him? The symptoms from which Hughes suffered involve anxiety (in fact, he appears to have suffered from social anxiety disorder). In this chapter, we explore two categories of disorder that involve anxiety: obsessive-compulsive-related disorders and trauma-related disorders.

Howard Hughes in his youth was vibrant and industrious; however, mental illness took a toll on him as he aged. In the later years of his life, he became a recluse. Few people saw him, and there are almost no known photographs of him from that period.

© Everett Collection, Inc./Alamy

195

▢ Obsessive-Compulsive Disorder and Related Disorders

After his parents' deaths, Hughes's health concerns increased, and his profound fear of germs—and the rituals and behaviors that he used to limit what he believed were possible routes of contamination—came to restrict his life severely. But the protective rituals and behaviors extended beyond himself (and beyond rational thinking); he made his aides and associates undertake similar extreme precautions even though that did not, in fact, decrease his risk:

> He viewed anyone who came near as a potential germ carrier. Those whose movements he could control—his aides, drivers, and message clerks—were required to wash their hands and slip on thin white cotton gloves . . . before handing him documents or other objects. Aides who bought newspapers or magazines were instructed to buy three copies—Hughes took the one in the middle. To escape dust, he ordered unused windows and doors of houses and cars sealed with masking tape.
> (Barlett & Steele, 1979, p. 175)

And it wasn't only exposure to germs that Hughes tried to control. Throughout his life, he'd been overly preoccupied with details; at one time or another, he concerned himself with every aspect of his companies—even demanding that employees conduct a detailed study of the vending machines at the Hughes Aircraft Company. Hughes's preoccupations and ritualistic behaviors were symptoms of obsessive-compulsive disorder.

People with OCD can spend hours dealing with their compulsions, such as repeatedly checking whether they turned off the stove in response to doubts about whether they did it properly the last time.

Obsessions
Intrusive and unwanted thoughts, urges, or images that persist or recur and usually cause distress or anxiety.

Compulsions
Repetitive behaviors or mental acts that a person feels driven to carry out and that usually must be performed according to rigid "rules" or correspond thematically to an obsession.

Obsessive-compulsive disorder (OCD)
A disorder characterized by one or more obsessions or compulsions.

What Is Obsessive-Compulsive Disorder?

Howard Hughes had obsessions and compulsions. **Obsessions** are intrusive and unwanted thoughts, urges, or images that persist or recur and usually cause distress or anxiety; people try to ignore, suppress, or neutralize these thoughts, urges, or images (American Psychiatric Association, 2013). For instance, Hughes had obsessions about germs; his preoccupations about them were intrusive and persistent. Worries about actual problems (such as, "How can I pay my bills this month?" or, "I don't think I can finish this project by the deadline") are not considered obsessions.

Whereas obsessions involve thoughts, urges, and images, compulsions involve behaviors. A **compulsion** is an excessive repetitive behavior (such as avoiding stepping on sidewalk cracks) or mental act (such as silently counting to 10) that a person feels driven to carry out; a compulsion usually must be performed according to rigid "rules" or corresponds thematically to an obsession and serves to "neutralize" the obsession and decrease anxiety or distress. For instance, Howard Hughes was obsessed by the possibility that he might be exposed to germs and was compelled to behave in ways that he believed would protect him from such germs.

The key element of **obsessive-compulsive disorder (OCD)** is characterized by having one or more obsessions or compulsions (See Table 7.1; American Psychiatric Association, 2013). The obsession can cause great distress and anxiety, despite a person's attempts to ignore or drive out the intrusive thoughts. Most people with OCD recognize that the beliefs that underlie their obsessions and compulsions are not valid in all situations. In a minority of cases, though, people may believe that their OCD-related beliefs are rational, and in DSM-5 such people might be considered to have reduced insight into their condition (American Psychiatric Association, 2013).

Table 7.2 identifies common types of obsessions and compulsions. Obsessions (listed on the left side of Table 7.2) include preoccupations with *contamination, order, fear of losing control,* and *doubts about whether the patient performed an action.* As noted earlier, compulsive behaviors are usually related to an obsession or anxiety associated with a particular situation or stimulus (also listed in Table 7.2) and include *washing, ordering, counting,* and *checking* (Mataix-Cols et al., 2005). Performing the behavior prevents or relieves the anxiety, but only temporarily. However, compulsions that relieve anxiety can take significant amounts of time to complete—sometimes more than an hour—and often create distress or impair functioning. Hughes clearly had compulsive symptoms of the contamination-washing type and had ordering types of obsessions and compulsions.

Like the other anxiety disorders we've discussed, OCD often involves an unrealistic or disproportionate fear—in this case, of adverse consequences if the compulsive behavior is not completed. For instance, people with an obsession about contamination, like Hughes, fear that if all germs aren't washed off, they will die of some disease. Additional facts about OCD are provided in Table 7.3, and Case 7.1 describes one woman's experience with OCD.

TABLE 7.1 • DSM-5 Diagnostic Criteria for Obsessive-Compulsive Disorder

A. Presence of obsessions, compulsions, or both:

Obsessions are defined by (1) and (2):

1. Recurrent and persistent thoughts, urges, or images that are experienced, at some time during the disturbance, as intrusive and unwanted, and that in most individuals cause marked anxiety or distress.

2. The individual attempts to ignore or suppress such thoughts, urges, or images, or to neutralize them with some other thought or action (i.e., by performing a compulsion).

Compulsions are defined by (1) and (2):

1. Repetitive behaviors (e.g., hand washing, ordering, checking) or mental acts (e.g., praying, counting, repeating words silently) that the individual feels driven to perform in response to an obsession or according to rules that must be applied rigidly.

2. The behaviors or mental acts are aimed at preventing or reducing anxiety or distress, or preventing some dreaded event or situation; however, these behaviors or mental acts are not connected in a realistic way with what they are designed to neutralize or prevent, or are clearly excessive.

Note: Young children may not be able to articulate the aims of these behaviors or mental acts.

B. The obsessions or compulsions are time-consuming (e.g., take more than 1 hour per day) or cause clinically significant distress or impairment in social, occupational, or other important areas of functioning.

C. The obsessive-compulsive symptoms are not attributable to the physiological effects of a substance (e.g., a drug of abuse, a medication) or another medical condition.

D. The disturbance is not better explained by the symptoms of another mental disorder (e.g., excessive worries, as in generalized anxiety disorder; preoccupation with appearance, as in body dysmorphic disorder; difficulty discarding or parting with possessions, as in hoarding disorder; hair pulling, as in trichotillomania [hair-pulling disorder]; skin picking, as in excoriation [skin-picking] disorder; sterotypies, as in stereotypic movement disorder; ritualized eating behavior, as in eating disorders; preoccupation with substances or gambling, as in substance-related and addictive disorders; preoccupation with having an illness, as in illness anxiety disorder; sexual urges or fantasies, as in paraphillic disorders; impulses, as in disruptive, impulse-control, and conduct disorders; guilty ruminations, as in major depressive disorder; thought insertion or delusional preoccupations, as in schizophrenia spectrum and other psychotic disorders; or repetitive patterns of behavior, as in autism spectrum disorder).

CASE 7.1 • FROM THE INSIDE: Obsessive-Compulsive Disorder

For someone with OCD, just getting up in the morning and getting dressed can be fraught with trials and tribulations:

Should I get up? It's 6:15. No, I better wait till 6:16, it's an even number. OK, 6:16, now I better get up, before it turns to 6:17, then I'd have to wait till 6:22.

OK, I'll get up, OK, I'm up, WAIT! I better do that again. One foot back in bed, one foot on the floor, now the other foot in bed and the opposite on the floor. OK. Let's take a shower, WAIT! That shoe on the floor is pointing in the wrong direction, better fix it. Oops, there's a piece of lint there, I better not set the shoe on top of it. . . . OH, JUST TOUCH THE SHOE TWICE AND GET OUTTA HERE!

All right, I got to the bedroom door without touching anything else, but I better step through and out again, just to be sure nothing bad will happen. THERE, THAT WAS EASY! Now to the bathroom. I better turn that light on, NO, off, NO, on, NO, off, NO, on, KNOCK IT OFF! All right, I'm done using the toilet, better flush it. OK, now spin around, wait for the toilet to finish a flush, now touch the handle, now touch the seat, remember you have to look at every screw on the toilet seat before you turn around again. OK, now turn around and touch the seat again, look at all the screws again. OK, now close the cover.

OK, let's get some underwear. I want to wear the green ones because they fit the best, but they're lying on top of the T-shirt my grandmother gave me, and her husband (my grandfather) died last year, so I better wash those again before I wear them. If I wear them, something bad might happen.

(Steketee & White, 1990, pp. 4–5)

TABLE 7.2 • Common Types of Obsessions and Compulsions

Type of obsession	Examples of obsessions: People with OCD may be preoccupied with anxiety-inducing thoughts about . . .	Type of compulsion	Examples of compulsions: In order to decrease anxiety associated with an obsession, people may repeatedly be driven to . . .
Contamination	germs, dirt	Washing	wash themselves or objects in order to minimize any imagined contamination
Order	objects being disorganized, or a consuming desire to have objects or situations conform to a particular order or alignment	Ordering	order objects, such as canned goods in the cupboard, so that everything in the environment is "just so" (and often making family members and friends maintain this order)
Losing control	the possibility of behaving impulsively or aggressively, such as yelling during a funeral	Counting	count in response to an unwanted thought, which leads to a sense that the unwanted thought is neutralized (for instance, after each thought of blurting out an obscenity, methodically counting to 50)
Doubt	whether an action, such as turning off the stove, was performed	Checking	check that they did, in fact, perform a behavior about which they had doubts (such as repeatedly checking that the stove is turned off)

OCD clearly involves fears and anxieties; it also often involves compulsive behaviors over which patients feel they have no control. A number of other disorders, such as *hair-pulling disorder* (also referred to as trichotillomania), *skin-picking disorder* (also referred to as excoriation disorder), *hoarding disorder*, and *body dysmorphic disorder*

TABLE 7.3 • Obsessive-Compulsive Disorder Facts at a Glance

Prevalence

• Approximately 2–3% of Americans will develop OCD at some point in their lives (Burke & Regier, 1994), with generally similar prevalence rates worldwide (Horwath & Weissman, 2000).

Comorbidity

• Over 90% of those with OCD have another disorder, with the most frequent categories of comorbid disorders being mood disorders (63%) and anxiety disorders (76%).

Onset

• Among males with OCD, symptoms typically begin to emerge between the ages of 6 and 15.
• Among females, symptoms typically emerge between the ages of 20 and 29.

Course

• Symptoms typically build gradually until they reach a level that meets the diagnostic criteria. Over the course of a lifetime, symptoms wax and wane, becoming particularly evident in response to stress but typically are chronic.

Gender Differences

• Men and women have an equal risk of developing OCD.

Cultural Differences

• Although the prevalence rates of OCD and the types of symptoms are about the same across cultures, the particular content of symptoms may reflect cultural or religious prohibitions (Matsunaga et al., 2007; Millet et al., 2000).

Source: Unless otherwise noted, information in the table is from American Psychiatric Association, 2000, 2013.

share some of these features and are considered to be related to obsessive-compulsive disorder:

- *Hair-pulling disorder* is characterized by the persistent compulsion to pull one's hair, leading to hair loss and distress or impaired functioning.

- *Skin-picking disorder* is characterized by compulsive skin picking to the point that lesions emerge on the skin.

- **Hoarding disorder** is characterized by persistent difficulty throwing away or otherwise parting with possessions—to the point that the possessions impair daily life, regardless of the value of those possessions.

- *Body dysmorphic disorder*, discussed in detail below, is characterized by preoccupations with a perceived defect in appearance and repetitive behaviors to hide the perceived defect.

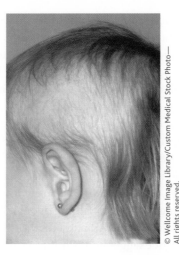

What these four disorders have in common with OCD is either or both of the following: preoccupations that arise from beliefs that are out of proportion to actual danger and/or compulsive behaviors that reduce tension or anxiety.

What Is Body Dysmorphic Disorder?

It's a common experience to believe that a pimple on your forehead appears like a red beacon for others to see; many people will try to cover up or hide a pimple. It's also common for people with a receding hairline to change their hairstyle to make the hair loss less noticeable. What isn't common—and, in fact, signals a psychological disorder—is when a slight imperfection in appearance, even an imagined defect, causes significant distress (Lambrou et al., 2011) or takes up so much time and energy that daily functioning is impaired. These are the signs of **body dysmorphic disorder**. The specific DSM-5 diagnostic criteria for this disorder (Table 7.4) indicate why body dysmorphic disorder is considered to fall on the spectrum of OCD-related disorders: It involves

Two disorders that are part of the OCD spectrum are hair-pulling disorder (left photo) and hoarding (right photo). People with hair-pulling disorder may feel so persistently compelled to pull their hair that they develop noticeable bald patches. Similarly, people who hoard feel unable to throw away objects even when the clutter is potentially life-threatening. Some people who compulsively hoard have died in fires in their homes because the hoarded objects took up so much space that it was difficult to leave once a fire started, or firefighters had to spend too much time trying to get into the house (Kaplan, 2007a). The woman in this photo found a cat amongst the clutter.

Hoarding disorder
An obsessive-compulsive-related disorder characterized by persistent difficulty throwing away or otherwise parting with possessions—to the point that the possessions impair daily life, regardless of the value of those possessions.

Body dysmorphic disorder
A disorder characterized by excessive preoccupation with a perceived defect or defects in appearance and repetitive behaviors to hide the perceived defect.

📷 GETTING THE PICTURE

Which of these people is more likely to have body dysmorphic disorder? Answer: Statistically, neither. Body dysmorphic disorder affects both genders equally often, but men and women tend to differ with regard to the specific body parts they view as defective.

TABLE 7.4 • DSM-5 Diagnostic Criteria for Body Dysmorphic Disorder

A. Preoccupation with one or more perceived defects or flaws in physical appearance that are not observable or appear slight to others.

B. At some point during the course of the disorder, the individual has performed repetitive behaviors (e.g., mirror checking, excessive grooming, skin picking, reassurance seeking) or mental acts (e.g., comparing his or her appearance with that of others) in response to the appearance concerns.

C. The preoccupation causes clinically significant distress or impairment in social, occupational, or other important areas of functioning.

D. The appearance preoccupation is not better explained by concerns with body fat or weight in an individual whose symptoms meet diagnostic criteria for an eating disorder.

preoccupations (some might say obsessions) about a perceived defect and, at some point, repetitive mental acts or behaviors (that might be compulsive) related to these preoccupations. The person might repeatedly compare his or her appearance to other people's (mental act) or repeatedly groom himself or herself or seek reassurance from others about appearance (behavior). As with OCD, the behaviors can consume hours.

Common preoccupations for people with body dysmorphic disorder are thinning or excessive hair, acne, wrinkles, scars, complexion (too pale, too dark, too red, and so on), facial asymmetry, or the shape or size of some part of the face or body. Some people are preoccupied with the belief that they aren't muscular enough or that their body build is too slight. The "defect" (or "defects") may change over the course of the illness (K. A. Phillips, 2001). People with body dysmorphic disorder may think that others are staring at them or talking about a "defect." Up to half of those with body dysmorphic disorder are delusional—that is, they believe their perception of a "defect" is accurate and not exaggerated (Phillips et al., 1994). Although Howard Hughes had beliefs about his body (related to germs), they do not appear to have been beliefs about bodily *defects*.

People with body dysmorphic disorder may compulsively exercise, diet, shop for beauty aids, pick at their skin, try to hide perceived defects, or spend hours looking in the mirror (like Ms. A., described in Case 7.2, who believed that she had multiple defects). A person with body dysmorphic disorder may seek reassurance ("How do I look?"), but any positive effects of reassurance are transient; a half-hour later, the person with body dysmorphic disorder may ask the same question—even of the same person! These behaviors, which are intended to decrease anxiety about appearance, actually end up increasing anxiety.

CASE 7.2 • FROM THE OUTSIDE: Body Dysmorphic Disorder

Ms. A was an attractive 27-year-old single white female who presented with a chief complaint of "I look deformed." She had been convinced since she was a child that she was ugly, and her mother reported that she had "constantly been in the mirror" since she was a toddler. Ms. A was obsessed with many aspects of her appearance, including her "crooked" ears, "ugly" eyes, "broken out" skin, "huge" nose, and "bushy" facial hair. She estimated that she thought about her appearance for 16 hours a day and checked mirrors for 5 hours a day. She compulsively compared herself with other people, repeatedly sought reassurance about her appearance . . ., applied and reapplied makeup for hours a day, excessively washed her face, covered her face with her hand, and tweezed and cut her facial hair. As a result of her appearance concerns, she had dropped out of high school. . . . She avoided friends and most social interactions. Ms. A felt chronically suicidal and had attempted suicide twice because, as she stated, "I'm too ugly to go on living."

(K. A. Phillips, 2001, pp. 75–76)

Deceased pop star Michael Jackson's face changed repeatedly over time, particularly his nose, chin, and cheeks, although he said that he only had surgery on his nose to help his singing. Might Michael Jackson have suffered from body dysmorphic disorder?

People who have body dysmorphic disorder may feel so self-conscious about a perceived defect that they avoid social situations (American Psychiatric Association, 2013), which results in their having few (or no) friends and no romantic partner. Some try to eliminate a "defect" through medical or surgical treatment such as plastic surgery, dental work, or dermatological treatment. But surgery often does not help; in fact, the symptoms of the disorder can actually be worse after surgery (Veale et al., 2003). In extreme cases, when some people with body dysmorphic disorder can't find a doctor to perform the treatment they think they need, they may try to do it themselves (so-called DIY, or do-it-yourself, surgery). Table 7.5 presents additional facts about body dysmorphic disorder.

TABLE 7.5 • Body Dysmorphic Disorder Facts at a Glance

Prevalence

- Approximately 2.4% of the general population of the United States has body dysmorphic disorder at any given time.
- Among people having plastic surgery or dermatological treatment, prevalence rates range from 7% to 8% (American Psychiatric Association, 2013).

Comorbidity

- Up to 60% of people with body dysmorphic disorder are also depressed; body dysmorphic disorder usually emerges first (Otto et al., 2001; K. A. Phillips, 2001).
- Thirty-eight percent of people with body dysmorphic disorder may also have social phobia (Coles et al., 2006).
- Up to 30% of people with body dysmorphic disorder also have OCD (K. A. Phillips, 2001).
- In one survey, almost half of those with body dysmorphic disorder had (at the time or previously) a substance-use disorder (Grant et al., 2005).
- Almost one third of those with body dysmorphic disorder will also develop an eating disorder (Ruffolo et al., 2006).

Onset

- Body dysmorphic disorder usually begins in childhood or adolescence (Bjornsson et al., in press; Phillips, Menard, et al., 2005).

Course

- Body dysmorphic disorder is generally chronic if left untreated.
- Over 25% of adults with body dysmorphic disorder have been housebound for at least 1 week; 8% are unable to work and receive disability payments (Albertini & Phillips, 1999; Phillips et al., 1994).
- Two surveys found that approximately 30% of people with body dysmorphic disorder had attempted suicide (Phillips et al., 1994; Phillips, Coles, et al., 2005).

Gender Differences

- Body dysmorphic disorder affects both genders with approximately equal frequency, but men and women tend to differ with regard to the specific body parts they view as defective (Phillips, Menard, & Fay, 2006): Women are preoccupied with body weight, hips, breasts, and legs and are more likely to pick their skin compulsively. In contrast, men are preoccupied with body build, genitals, height, excessive body hair, and thinning scalp hair.

Cultural Differences

- Generally, symptoms of body dysmorphic disorder are similar across cultures, although certain body attributes may be more likely to be the focus of concern, depending on what physical attributes are valued in a given culture (Pope et al., 1997; Pope, Gruber, et al., 2000).

Patients with body dysmorphic disorder exhibit a variety of cognitive biases. Such patients tend to focus their attention on isolated body parts and are hyper-vigilant for any possible bodily imperfections (Grocholewski et al., 2012). They also engage in *catastrophic thinking*, believing that bodily imperfections will lead to dire consequences; for example, the person might believe that having a pimple will lead others to think he or she is deformed (Buhlmann et al., 2008; Lambrou et al., 2012).

In addition, people with body dysmorphic disorder often engage in behaviors that temporarily reduce their anxiety. For example, they might try to avoid mirrors (and possibly people) or develop new ways to hide a "defect"—with painstakingly applied makeup or contrived use of clothing or hats (K. A. Phillips, 2001). If you think that some of the descriptions of the symptoms of body dysmorphic disorder resemble those of anxiety-related disorders, not just OCD, you're right. Like phobia disorders (agora-phobia, social anxiety disorder, and specific phobias), body dysmorphic disorder can lead the person to avoid anxiety-causing stimuli. Like social anxiety disorder, it involves an excessive fear of being evaluated negatively. And like OCD, it involves persistent preoccupations and compulsive behaviors. Because body dysmorphic disorder is related to OCD, in order to understand the former, we look to research on the latter.

Understanding Obsessive-Compulsive Disorder

Howard Hughes had neurological and psychological vulnerabilities for OCD that may have been exacerbated by psychological and social factors. However, with OCD, social factors have less influence than do neurological and psychological factors.

Neurological Factors

Researchers have made much progress in understanding the neurological underpinnings of OCD.

Brain Systems and Neural Communication

In general, when the frontal lobes trigger an action, there is feedback from the basal ganglia, in part via the thalamus (a brain structure involved in attention). Sometimes this feedback sets up a loop of repetitive activity, as shown in Figure 7.1 (Breiter et al., 1996;

FIGURE 7.1 • The Neural Loop That May Underlie Obsessive Thoughts The basal ganglia, the thalamus, and the frontal lobes are part of a neural loop of repeating brain activity associated with OCD.

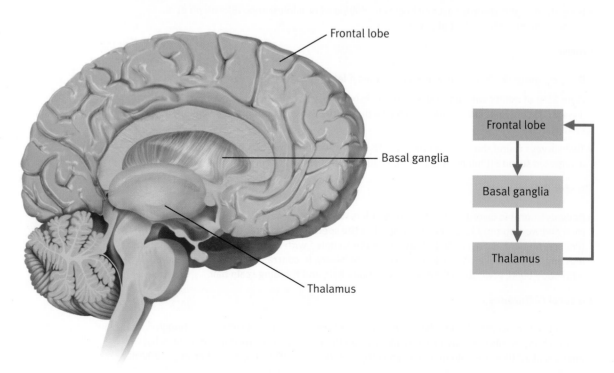

Frontal lobe

Basal ganglia

Thalamus

Rapoport, 1991; Rauch et al., 1994, 2001). Many researchers now believe that this neural loop plays a key role in obsessive thoughts, which intrude and cannot be stopped easily. Performing a compulsion might temporarily stop the obsessive thoughts by reducing the repetitive neural activity (Insel, 1992; Jenike, 1984; Modell et al., 1989). (But soon after the compulsive behavior stops, the obsessions typically resume.)

Much research has focused on whether OCD arises from abnormalities in the basal ganglia and frontal lobes in particular (Pigott et al., 1996; Saxena & Rauch, 2000). In fact, neuroimaging studies have revealed that both a part of the frontal cortex and the basal ganglia function abnormally in OCD patients (Baxter, 1992; Berthier et al., 2001; Saxena et al., 1998). This abnormal functioning could well prevent the frontal lobe from cutting off the loop of repetitive neural activity, as it appears to do in people who do not have this disorder.

OCD appears to arise in large part because brain circuits don't operate normally, but why don't they do so? One reason may be that people with OCD have too little of the neurotransmitter serotonin, which allows unusual brain activity to occur (Mundo, Richter, et al., 2000). And, in fact, medications that increase the effects of serotonin (such as Prozac), often by preventing reuptake of this neurotransmitter at the synapse (see Chapter 5), can help to treat OCD symptoms (Micallef & Blin, 2001; Thomsen, et al., 2001).

Genetics

Twin studies have shown that if one monozygotic (identical) twin has OCD, the other is very likely (65%) to have it. As expected if this high rate reflects common genes, the rate is lower (only 15%) for dizygotic twins (Pauls et al., 1991). Moreover, as you would expect from the results of the twin studies, OCD is more common among relatives of OCD patients (10% of whom also have OCD) than among relatives of control participants (of whom only 2% also have OCD) (Pauls et al., 1995).

However, although such studies have documented a genetic contribution to OCD, the link is neither simple nor straightforward: Members of the family of a person with OCD are more likely than other people to have an anxiety disorder, not OCD specifically (Black et al., 1992; Smoller et al., 2000).

When many people first learn about OCD, they recognize tendencies they've noticed in themselves. If you've had this reaction while reading this section, you shouldn't worry: OCD may reflect extreme functioning of brain systems that function the same way in each of us to produce milder forms of such thinking.

Psychological Factors

Psychological factors that help to explain OCD focus primarily on the way that operant conditioning affects compulsions and on the process by which normal obsessional thoughts become pathological.

Behavioral Explanations: Operant Conditioning and Compulsions

Compulsive behavior can provide short-term relief from anxiety that is produced by an obsession. Operant conditioning occurs when the behavior is negatively reinforced: Because the behavior (temporarily) relieves the anxiety, the behavior is more likely to recur when the thoughts arise again. All of Howard Hughes's various eccentric behaviors—his washing, his precautions against germs, his hoarding of newspapers and magazines—temporarily relieved his anxiety.

Former soccer star David Beckham suffers from OCD. His symptoms focus on ordering: "I have to have everything in a straight line or everything has to be in pairs. . . . I'll go into a hotel room. Before I can relax I have to move all the leaflets and all the books and put them in a drawer. Everything has to be perfect." (Dolan, 2006).

AP Photo/Matt Dunham

Cognitive Explanations: Obsessional Thinking

If you've ever had a crush on someone or been in love, you may have spent a lot of time thinking about the person—it may have even felt like an obsession. Such obsessions are surprisingly frequent (Weissman et al., 1994), but they don't usually develop into a disorder. One theory about how a normal obsession becomes part of OCD is that the person decides that his or her thoughts refer to something unacceptable, such as killing someone or, as was the case with Howard Hughes, catching someone else's illness (Salkovskis, 1985). These obsessive thoughts, which the person believes imply some kind of danger, lead to very uncomfortable feelings. Mental or behavioral rituals arise in order to reduce these feelings.

Consistent with this view, researchers have found that some mental processes function differently in people with OCD than in people without the disorder. In particular, such patients are more likely to pay attention to and remember threat-relevant stimuli, and they have impaired processing of complex visual stimuli (as, for example, is necessary to decide whether an object has been touched by a dirty or clean tissue among people with contamination fears; Muller & Roberts, 2005; Radomsky et al., 2001). Such processing may make threatening stimuli easier to remember and harder to ignore, which keeps them in the patients' awareness longer than normal (Muller & Roberts, 2005) and makes the irrational fears seem more plausible (Giele et al., 2011).

Social Factors

Two types of social factors can contribute to OCD: stress and culture.

Stress

The onset of OCD often follows a stressor, and the severity of the symptoms is often proportional to the severity of the stressor (Turner & Beidel, 1988). However, such findings are not always easy to interpret. For example, one study found that people with more severe OCD tend to have more kinds of family stress and are more likely to be rejected by their families (Calvocoressi et al., 1995). Note, however, that the direction of causation is not clear: Although stress in the family may cause the greater severity of symptoms, it is also possible that the more severe symptoms led the families to reject the patients.

Stress greatly affected the course of Hughes's symptoms. For much of his 20s, 30s, and early 40s, he was able to function relatively well, given the freedom his wealth and position provided. However, during one particularly stressful period in his late 30s, "Hughes began repeating himself at work and in casual conversations. In a series of memoranda on the importance of letter writing, he dictated, over and over again, 'a good letter should be immediately understandable . . . a good letter should be immediately understandable . . . a good letter should be immediately understandable . . .'" (Barlett & Steele, 1979, p. 132).

By the time Hughes was in his 50s, the stressors increased, and his functioning diminished. There were periods when he was so preoccupied with his germ phobia that he couldn't pay attention to anything else.

Culture

Different countries have about the same prevalence rates of OCD, although culture and religion can help determine the particular content of some obsessions or compulsions (Weissman et al., 1994). For instance, religious obsessions and praying compulsions are more common among Turkish men than French men (Millet et al., 2000) and more common among Brazilians than Americans or Europeans (Fontenelle et al., 2004). And a devoutly religious patient's symptoms can relate to the specific tenets and practices of his or her religion (Shooka et al., 1998): Someone who is Catholic may have obsessional worries about having impure thoughts or feel a compulsion to go to confession multiple times each day. In contrast, devout Jews or Muslims may have symptoms that focus on extreme adherence to religious dietary laws.

Feedback Loops in Understanding Obsessive-Compulsive Disorder

ONLINE

One neurological factor that contributes to OCD appears to be a tendency toward increased activity in the neural loop that connects the frontal lobes and the basal ganglia (neurological factor). A person with such a neurological vulnerability might learn early in life to regard certain thoughts as dangerous because they can lead to obsessions. When these thoughts appear later in life at a time of stress, someone who is vulnerable may become distressed and anxious about the thoughts and try to suppress them. But a conscious attempt to suppress unwanted thoughts often has the opposite effect: The unwanted thoughts become more likely to persist (Salkovkis & Campbell, 1994; Wegner et al., 1987). Thus, the intrusive thoughts cause additional distress, and so the person tries harder to suppress them, creating a vicious cycle (psychological factor).

The content of a person's unwanted thoughts determines the extent to which those thoughts are unacceptable. When a person wants to suppress the unwanted thoughts, he or she develops rituals and avoidance behaviors to increase a sense of control and decrease anxiety; these behaviors temporarily reduce anxiety and are thus reinforced. But the thoughts cannot be fully controlled and become obsessive; the obsessions and compulsions impair functioning and can affect relationships. The person with OCD may expect family members and friends to conform to compulsive guidelines; these people and others can become frustrated and dismayed at the patient's rituals and obsessions—which in turn can produce more stress for the patient (social factors).

Treating Obsessive-Compulsive Disorder

The primary targets of treatment for OCD are usually either neurological or psychological factors.

Targeting Neurological Factors: Medication

An SSRI is usually the type of medication used first to treat OCD: *paroxetine* (Paxil), *sertraline* (Zoloft), *fluoxetine* (Prozac), *fluvoxamine* (Luvox), or *citalopram* (Celexa) (Soomro et al., 2008). OCD can also be treated effectively with the TCA *clomipramine* (Anafranil), although a higher dose is required than that prescribed for depression or other anxiety disorders (Rosenbaum, Arana et al., 2005). People who develop OCD in childhood are less likely to respond well to clomipramine or to other antidepressants (Rosario-Campos et al., 2001).

Hughes's use of codeine and Valium did not appear to diminish his obsessions and compulsions significantly; in fact, such medications are not routinely prescribed for OCD. In any case, medication alone is not as effective as medication combined with behavioral treatment, such as exposure with response prevention (discussed in the following section). As with other anxiety disorders, when the medication is discontinued, OCD symptoms usually return (Foa et al., 2005).

Targeting Psychological Factors

Treatment that targets psychological factors focuses on decreasing the compulsive behaviors and obsessional thoughts. Both behavioral and cognitive methods are effective (Cottraux et al., 2001; Prazeres et al., 2013), and treatment may combine both types of methods (Franklin et al., 2002).

Exposure with response prevention
A behavioral technique in which a patient is carefully prevented from engaging in his or her usual maladaptive response after being exposed to a stimulus that usually elicits the response.

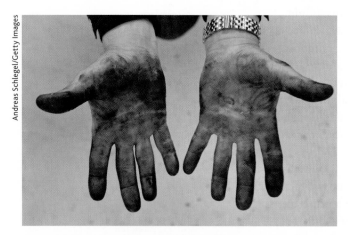

Patients with OCD often undertake exposure with response prevention. For instance, if someone were afraid of touching dirt, he would touch dirt but would not then wash his hands for a while. By not being able to respond to the dirt, the patient learns that nothing bad happens if compulsive behaviors aren't performed.

Behavioral Methods: Exposure With Response Prevention

Patients with OCD often undertake **exposure with response prevention**. For the *exposure* part, the patient is exposed to the feared stimulus (such as touching dirt) or the obsessive thought (such as the idea that the stove was left on) and, for the *response prevention* part, the patient is prevented from engaging in the usual compulsion or ritual. For instance, if someone were afraid of touching dirt, she would touch dirt but would not then wash her hands for a while. Through exposure with response prevention, patients learn that nothing bad happens if they don't perform their compulsive behavior; the fear and arousal subside without resorting to the compulsion, and they experience mastery. They survive the anxiety and in doing so exert control over the compulsion. When patients successfully respond differently to a feared stimulus, this mastery over the compulsion gives them hope and motivates them to continue to perform the new behaviors. Exposure with response prevention is also a technique used to treat body dysmorphic disorder.

Cognitive Methods: Cognitive Restructuring

The goal of cognitive methods is to reduce the irrationality and frequency of the patient's intrusive thoughts and obsessions (Clark, 2005). Cognitive restructuring focuses on assessing the accuracy of these thoughts, making predictions based on them ("If I don't go back to check the locks, I will be robbed"), and testing whether these predictions come to pass.

Although CBT for OCD hadn't been sufficiently developed during Hughes's lifetime, consider how it might have been used: There were periods when Hughes daily and "painstakingly used Kleenex to wipe 'dust and germs' from his chair, ottoman, side table, and telephone [for hours]." (Barlett & Steele, 1979, p. 233). During the same period of time, he didn't have his sheets changed for months at a time; to make the sheets last longer, he laid paper towels over them and slept on those. Moreover, he bathed only a few times a year. Clearly, such behavior was at odds with rational attempts to protect against germs. CBT would have, in part, focused on his overestimation of the probability of contracting an illness and the irrationality of his precautions.

Targeting Social Factors: Family Therapy

Although psychological and neurological factors are the primary targets of treatment for OCD, in some cases, social factors may also be addressed—for example, through family therapy or consultation with family members. This aspect of treatment educates family members about the patient's treatment and its goals and helps the family function in a more normal way. Family members and friends may have spent years conforming their behavior to the patient's illness (e.g., using clean tissues when handing an object to the patient), and they may be afraid to change their own behavior as the patient gets better, for fear of causing a relapse.

Feedback Loops in Treating Obsessive-Compulsive Disorder

ONLINE

As we've seen, medication can be effective in treating the symptoms of OCD (at least as long as the patient continues to take it). Medication works by changing neurochemistry, which in turn affects thoughts, feelings, and behaviors. We've also seen that CBT is effective. How does CBT have its effects? Could it be that therapy changes brain functioning in the same way that medication does? Researchers set out to answer this question.

In one study, researchers used PET scans to assess brain functioning in two groups of OCD patients. One group received behavior therapy, and the other group received the SSRI fluoxetine (Prozac) to reduce OCD symptoms. Both behavior therapy and Prozac decreased activity in a part of the basal ganglia that is involved in automatic behaviors. Prozac also affected activity in two parts of the brain involved in attention: the thalamus and the anterior cingulate (Baxter et al., 1992). Later research replicated the effects of behavior therapy on the brain (Schwartz et al., 1996). Although the altered brain areas overlapped, CBT changed fewer brain areas than did medication—which may reflect the fact that medication may have side effects, whereas CBT does not.

In short, behavior therapy or CBT changes the brain (neurological factor). As the patient improves, personal relationships change (social factor): The time and energy that once went into the compulsions can be diverted to other areas of life, including relationships. Moreover, the patient experiences mastery over the symptoms and develops hope and a new view of himself or herself (psychological factors). In turn, this makes the patient more willing to continue therapy, which further changes the brain, and so on, in a happy cycle of mutual feedback loops among neurological, psychological, and social factors.

Thinking Like A Clinician

You visit a new friend. When you use her bathroom, you notice that all her toiletries seem very organized. Her kitchen is also neatly ordered. The next day, you notice that her classwork is unusually well organized—arranged neatly in color-coded folders and notebooks. You don't think twice about it until she drops her open backpack and all her stuff falls out, spilling all over the floor. She starts to cry. Based on what you have learned, do you think she has OCD? Why or why not? What else would you want to know before reaching a conclusion? If she has OCD, is it because she has inherited the disorder? Explain your answer. If she does have OCD, what sorts of treatments should she consider?

Trauma-Related Disorders

Within a 15-year span, Howard Hughes suffered more than his share of brushes with death—of his own and other people's. He ran over and killed a pedestrian. He was the pilot in three plane accidents: In the first one, his cheekbone was crushed; in the second, two of his copilots died; in the third, he sustained such extensive injuries to his chest that his heart was pushed to the other side of his chest cavity, and he wasn't expected to live through the night. Hughes did survive, but he clearly had endured a highly traumatic event.

Some people who experience a traumatic or very stressful event go on to develop a disorder in the DSM-5 category *trauma- and stressor-related disorders*. According to DSM-5 (American Psychiatric Association, 2013), a trauma-related disorder is marked by four general types of persistent symptoms after exposure to the traumatic event:

- *Intrusive re-experiencing of the traumatic event.* Intrusion may involve flashbacks that can include illusions, hallucinations, or a sense of reliving the experience, as well as intrusive and distressing memories, dreams, or nightmares of the event.

- *Avoidance.* The person avoids anything related to the trauma.

- *Negative thoughts and mood, and dissociation.* Symptoms include persistent negative thoughts about oneself or others ("no one can be trusted"), persistent negative mood (fear, for instance, and

Howard Hughes survived several plane crashes, including the one shown above, and he ran over and killed a pedestrian (Fowler, 1986); any of these events would have been traumatic for most people. Some people who experience a traumatic event develop a trauma-related disorder: acute stress disorder or posttraumatic stress disorder.

©Bettmann/Corbis

difficulty experiencing positive emotions), and dissociation (a sense of feeling disconnected or detached from experiences).

- *Increased arousal and reactivity.* Arousal and reactivity symptoms include difficulty sleeping, hypervigilance, irritable behavior, angry outbursts, and a tendency to be easily startled (referred to as a heightened startle response).

What Are the Trauma-Related Disorders?

Among the trauma-related disorders in DSM-5 are:

- *acute stress disorder*, which is the diagnosis when some of the above symptoms emerge immediately after a traumatic event and last between 3 days and 1 month;

- *posttraumatic stress disorder (PTSD)*, which requires a certain number of symptoms from each of the four groups mentioned above, and the symptoms last more than 1 month.

Most people would agree that Hughes experienced a traumatic event when his airplane crashed and he was severely injured. But what constitutes a traumatic event? The answer, according to DSM-5, is an event that involves:

- directly experiencing actual or threatened serious injury, sexual violation, or death;

- witnessing (in person) actual or threatened serious injury, sexual violation, or death;

- learning of a violent or accidental death or threatened death of a close family member or friend; or

- experiencing extreme exposure to aversive details about the traumatic event (as might occur for first responders).

During times of political unrest, violence, or terrorism, rates of trauma-related disorders are likely to increase.

Traumatic events are more severe than the normal stressful events we all regularly encounter. Examples of traumatic events range from large-scale catastrophes with multiple victims (such as disasters and wars) to unintended acts or situations involving fewer people (such as motor vehicle accidents and life-threatening illnesses) to events that involve intentional and personal violence, such as rape and assault (Briere, 2004). Traumatic events are relatively common: Up to 30% of people will experience some type of disaster in their lifetime, 25% have experienced a serious car accident (Briere & Elliott, 2000), and 20% of women report having been raped during their lifetimes (most frequently by someone they know; Black et al., 2011). Note that according to the DSM-5 definition, emotional abuse is not a traumatic event because it does not involve actual or threatened physical injury or death.

Several factors can affect whether a trauma-related disorder will develop following a traumatic event:

- *The kind of trauma.* Trauma involving violence—particularly intended personal violence—is more likely to lead to a stress disorder than are natural disasters (Breslau et al., 1998; Briere & Elliott, 2000; Copeland et al., 2007; Dikel et al., 2005).

- *The severity of the traumatic event, its duration, and its proximity.* Depending on the specifics of the traumatic event, those physically closer to it—nearer to the primary area struck by a tornado, for example—are more likely to develop a stress disorder (Blanchard et al., 2004; Middleton et al., 2002), as are those who have experienced multiple traumatic events (Copeland et al., 2007). For instance, Vietnam veterans were more likely to develop PTSD if they had been wounded or if they had spent more time in combat (Gallers et al., 1988; King et al., 1999). The same is true of veterans who returned from Iraq and Afghanistan: Soldiers who were involved in combat were up to three times more likely to develop PTSD than soldiers who were not exposed to combat (Levin, 2007; Smith et al., 2008).

Being exposed to a traumatic event is one component of a trauma-related disorder. The second component is the person's response to the traumatic event. Although certain types of traumatic events are more likely than others to lead to such disorders, people differ in how they perceive the same traumatic event and how they respond to it. These differences will be based, in part, on previous experience with related events, appraisal of the stressors, and coping style.

What Is Posttraumatic Stress Disorder?

Posttraumatic stress disorder (PTSD) is diagnosed when people who have experienced a trauma persistently (a) have intrusive re-experiences the traumatic event, (b) avoid stimuli related to the event, (c) have negative changes in thoughts and mood associated with the traumatic event, and (d) have symptoms of reactivity and hyperarousal; all of these symptoms must persist for at least a month (American Psychiatric Association, 2013). These four types of symptoms form the *posttrauma* criteria for PTSD, as shown in Table 7.6, but symptoms may not emerge until months or years after the traumatic event. (Note that Table 7.6 applies to adults and children over the age of 6; DSM-5 contains separate criteria for children 6 and younger.)

Some people with PTSD may be diagnosed with a subtype that includes symptoms of *dissociation*: an altered sense of reality of surroundings or oneself (such as feeling in daze, a sense of the environment's or one's body being distorted or "not quite right," or a sense of time slowing down) (American Psychiatric Association, 2013; Stein et al., 2013). Table 7.7 presents additional information about PTSD. Case 7.3 describes the experiences of a man with PTSD.

CASE 7.3 • FROM THE OUTSIDE: Posttraumatic Stress Disorder

A. C. was a 42-year-old single man, a recent immigrant who, one year before his appearance at the clinic, had walked into his place of work while an armed robbery was taking place. Two men armed with guns hit him over the head, threatened to kill him, tied him up and locked him in a closet with four other employees. He was released from the closet 4 hours later when another employee came in to work. The police were notified and A. C. was taken to the hospital where his head wound was sutured and he was released. For two weeks after the robbery A. C. continued to function as he had before the robbery with no increase in anxiety.

One day while waiting to meet someone on the street he was struck by the thought that he might meet his assailants again. He began to shiver, felt his heart race, felt dizzy, started to sweat and felt that he might pass out. He was brought to an emergency room, examined and released with a referral to victims' services. His anxiety increased so much that he was unable to return to work because it reminded him of the robbery. He started to have sleep difficulties, waking in the middle of the night to check the front door lock at home. He quit his job and dropped out of school due to his anxiety. He would have flashbacks of the guns that were used in the robbery and started to avoid people on the street who reminded him of the robbers. He began to feel guilty that he had entered the office while the robbery was in progress feeling that he somehow should have known what was occurring. His avoidance extended to the subway, exercising and socializing with friends.

(New York Psychiatric Institute, 2006)

Posttraumatic stress disorder (PTSD) A traumatic stress disorder that involves persistent (a) intrusive re-experiencing of the traumatic event, (b) avoidance of stimuli related to the event, (c) negative changes in thoughts and mood, and (d) hyperarousal and reactivity that persist for at least a month.

TABLE 7.6 • DSM-5 Diagnostic Criteria for Posttraumatic Stress Disorder

Note: The following criteria apply to adults, adolescents, and children older than 6 years.

A. Exposure to actual or threatened death, serious injury, or sexual violence in one (or more) of the following ways:

1. Directly experiencing the traumatic event(s).

2. Witnessing, in person, the event(s) as it occurred to others.

3. Learning that the traumatic event(s) occurred to a close family member or close friend. In cases of actual or threatened death of a family member or friend, the event(s) must have been violent or accidental.

4. Experiencing repeated or extreme exposure to aversive details of the traumatic event(s) (e.g., first responders collecting human remains; police officers repeatedly exposed to details of child abuse).

   Note: Criterion A4 does not apply to exposure through electronic media, television, movies, or pictures, unless this exposure is work related.

B. Presence of one (or more) of the following intrusion symptoms associated with the traumatic event(s), beginning after the traumatic event(s) occurred:

1. Recurrent, involuntary, and intrusive distressing memories of the traumatic event(s).

   Note: In children older than 6 years, repetitive play may occur in which themes or aspects of the traumatic event(s) are expressed.

2. Recurrent distressing dreams in which the content and/or affect of the dream are related to the traumatic event(s).

   Note: In children, there may be frightening dreams without recognizable content.

3. Dissociative reactions (e.g., flashbacks) in which the individual feels or acts as if the traumatic event(s) were recurring. (Such reactions may occur on a continuum, with the most extreme expression being a complete loss of awareness of present surroundings.)

   Note: In children, trauma-specific reenactment may occur in play.

4. Intense or prolonged psychological distress at exposure to internal or external cues that symbolize or resemble an aspect of the traumatic event(s).

5. Marked physiological reactions to internal or external cues that symbolize or resemble an aspect of the traumatic event(s).

C. Persistent avoidance of stimuli associated with the traumatic event(s), beginning after the traumatic event(s) occurred, as evidenced by one or both of the following:

1. Avoidance of or efforts to avoid distressing memories, thoughts, or feelings about or closely associated with the traumatic event(s).

2. Avoidance of or efforts to avoid external reminders (people, places, conversations, activities, objects, situations) that arouse distressing memories, thoughts, or feelings about or closely associated with the traumatic event(s).

D. Negative alterations in cognitions and mood associated with the traumatic event(s), beginning or worsening after the traumatic event(s) occurred, as evidenced by two (or more) of the following:

1. Inability to remember an important aspect of the traumatic event(s) (typically due to dissociative amnesia and not to other factors such as head injury, alcohol, or drugs).

2. Persistent and exaggerated negative beliefs or expectations about oneself, others, or the world (e.g., "I am bad," "No one can be trusted," "The world is completely dangerous," "My whole nervous system is permanently ruined").

3. Persistent, distorted cognitions about the cause or consequences of the traumatic event(s) that lead the individual to blame himself/herself or others.

4. Persistent negative emotional state (e.g., fear, horror, anger, guilt, or shame).

5. Markedly diminished interest or participation in significant activities.

6. Feelings of detachment or estrangement from others.

7. Persistent inability to experience positive emotions (e.g., inability to experience happiness, satisfaction, or loving feelings).

E. Marked alterations in arousal and reactivity associated with the traumatic event(s), beginning or worsening after the traumatic event(s) occurred, as evidenced by two (or more) of the following:

1. Irritable behavior and angry outbursts (with little or no provocation) typically expressed as verbal or physical aggression toward people or objects.

2. Reckless or self-destructive behavior.

3. Hypervigilance.

4. Exaggerated startle response.

5. Problems with concentration.

6. Sleep disturbance (e.g., difficulty falling or staying asleep or restless sleep).

F. Duration of the disturbance (Criteria B, C, D, and E) is more than 1 month.

G. The disturbance causes clinically significant distress or impairment in social, occupational or other important areas of functioning.

H. The disturbance is not attributable to the physiological effects of a substance (e.g., medication, alcohol) or another medical condition.

TABLE **7.7** • PTSD Facts at a Glance

Prevalence
• Among adults in the United States, approximately 8% develop PTSD, although this number varies in part on large scale events. For instance, among members of the U.S. military returning from Iraq and Afghanistan, rates of PTSD ranged from 5–20% (Packnett et al., 2012).
Comorbidity
• About 80% of those with PTSD also have another psychological disorder, most commonly a mood disorder, substance use disorder, or an anxiety disorder.
Onset
• Symptoms usually begin within 3 months of the traumatic event, although some people may go months or years before symptoms appear.
• However, people who develop PTSD usually show symptoms in the immediate aftermath of the trauma, although not necessarily all the symptoms required for the diagnosis.
• Approximately 80% of people with acute stress disorder go on to develop PTSD (Harvey & Bryant, 2002).
Course
• Duration of the symptoms varies. About half of those with PTSD recover within 3 months, whereas others continue to have persistent symptoms for more than a year after the traumatic event. Still others have symptoms that wax and wane.
Gender Differences
• Women who have been exposed to trauma develop PTSD more often than do men, although males are more likely be victims of trauma (Tolin & Foa, 2006).
Cultural Differences
• Across cultures, people with PTSD may differ in the particular symptoms they express (e.g., more intrusive symptoms versus more arousal symptoms), depending on the coping styles that are encouraged in a given culture.

Source: Unless otherwise noted, information in the table is from American Psychiatric Association, 2013.

What Is Acute Stress Disorder?

If A. C.'s symptoms had lasted for less than 1 month or if he had sought help from a mental health clinician within a month of the event, A. C. might have been diagnosed with acute stress disorder. **Acute stress disorder** involves at least 9 of 14 symptoms that fall into five clusters: intrusively re-experiencing the traumatic event, avoiding stimuli related to the event, hyperarousal, negative mood, and dissociation.

As noted in Table 7.8, the symptoms occur within 1 month of the trauma (as A. C.'s did), must last at least 3 days but no more than 1 month, and must cause significant distress or impair functioning. Approximately 80% of those with acute stress disorder have symptoms that persist for more than a month, at which point for most people the diagnosis then changes to PTSD (Harvey & Bryant, 2002). Unlike A. C., though, most people who experience trauma do not develop PTSD (National Collaborating Centre for Mental Health, 2005; Shalev et al., 1998).

PTSD and acute stress disorder clearly involve intrusive re-experiencing, avoidance, negative mood, and hyperarousal. But unlike the other disorders we've reviewed in this chapter, PTSD and acute stress disorder arise from a clear and consistent cause: a traumatic event. A number of other disorders—one of which we will discuss in the next chapter—appear to share this feature.

Acute stress disorder
A traumatic stress disorder that involves (a) intrusive re-experiencing of the traumatic event, (b) avoidance of stimuli related to the event, (c) negative changes in thought and mood, (d) dissociation, and (e) hyperarousal and reactivity, with these symptoms lasting for less than a month.

TABLE 7.8 · DSM-5 Diagnostic Criteria for Acute Stress Disorder

A. Exposure to actual or threatened death, serious injury, or sexual violation in one (or more) of the following ways:

  1. Directly experiencing the traumatic event(s).

  2. Witnessing, in person, the event(s) as it occurred to others.

  3. Learning that the event(s) occurred to a close family member or close friend. **Note:** In cases of actual or threatened death of a family member or friend, the event(s) must have been violent or accidental.

  4. Experiencing repeated or extreme exposure to aversive details of the traumatic event(s) (e.g., first responders collecting human remains, police officers repeatedly exposed to details of child abuse).

  Note: This does not apply to exposure through electronic media, television, movies, or pictures, unless this exposure is work related.

B. Presence of nine (or more) of the following symptoms from any of the five categories of intrusion, negative mood, dissociation, avoidance, and arousal, beginning or worsening after the traumatic event(s) occurred:

Intrusion Symptoms

  1. Recurrent, involuntary, and intrusive distressing memories of the traumatic event(s). **Note:** In children, repetitive play may occur in which themes or aspects of the traumatic event(s) are expressed.

  2. Recurrent distressing dreams in which the content and/or affect of the dream are related to the event(s). **Note:** In children, there may be frightening dreams without recognizable content.

  3. Dissociative reactions (e.g., flashbacks) in which the individual feels or acts as if the traumatic event(s) were recurring. (Such reactions may occur on a continuum, with the most extreme expression being a complete loss of awareness of present surroundings.) **Note:** In children, trauma-specific reenactment may occur in play.

  4. Intense or prolonged psychological distress or marked physiological reactions in response to internal or external cues that symbolize or resemble an aspect of the traumatic event(s).

Negative Mood

  5. Persistent inability to experience positive emotions (e.g., inability to experience happiness, satisfaction, or loving feelings).

Dissociative Symptoms

  6. An altered sense of the reality of one's surroundings or oneself (e.g., seeing oneself from another's perspective, being in a daze, time slowing).

  7. Inability to remember an important aspect of the traumatic event(s) (typically due to dissociative amnesia and not to other factors such as head injury, alcohol, or drugs).

Avoidance Symptoms

  8. Efforts to avoid distressing memories, thoughts, or feelings about or closely associated with the traumatic event(s).

  9. Efforts to avoid external reminders (people, places, conversations, activities, objects, situations) that arouse distressing memories, thoughts, or feelings about or closely associated with the traumatic event(s).

Arousal Symptoms

  10. Sleep disturbance (e.g., difficulty falling or staying asleep, restless sleep).

  11. Irritable behavior and angry outbursts (with little or no provocation), typically expressed as verbal or physical aggression toward people or objects.

  12. Hypervigilance.

  13. Problems with concentration.

  14. Exaggerated startle response.

C. Duration of the disturbance (symptoms in Criterion B) is 3 days to 1 month after trauma exposure.

  Note: Symptoms typically begin immediately after the trauma, but persistence for at least 3 days and up to a month is needed to meet disorder criteria.

D. The disturbance causes clinically significant distress or impairment in social, occupational or other important areas of functioning.

E. The disturbance is not attributable to the physiological effects of a substance (e.g., medication or alcohol) or another medical condition (e.g., mild traumatic brain injury) and is not better explained by brief psychotic disorder.

Could Howard Hughes's problems have been related to an undiagnosed post-traumatic stress disorder? We don't know whether Hughes intrusively re-experienced any of his traumatic events or whether he had negative thoughts ormoods related to the traumas, but he did not appear to have obvious avoidance symptoms related to the traumatic experiences: He continued flying after each of his plane accidents. He did have symptoms of increased arousal, such as irritability, hypervigilance, difficulty concentrating, and sleep problems, but these symptoms are better explained by his OCD and drug use. There is no clear evidence that Hughes suffered from PTSD.

Understanding Trauma-Related Disorders: PTSD

We focus here on PTSD because more than three-quarters of people with acute stress disorder go on to develop PTSD (see Table 7.7), the symptoms of PTSD—almost by definition—last longer than those of acute stress disorder, and most research on trauma-related disorders focuses on PTSD.

Neurological Factors

The neurological factors that contribute to PTSD include overly strong sympathetic nervous system reactions and abnormal hippocampi. In addition, the neurotransmitters norepinephrine and serotonin have been implicated in the disorder, and there is evidence that genes contribute to (but by no means determine) the likelihood that experiencing trauma will result in PTSD.

Brain Systems

Research has often shown that people who suffer from PTSD have sympathetic nervous systems that react unusually strongly to cues associated with their traumatic experience. The cues can cause sweating or a racing heart (Orr et al., 1993, 2002; Prins et al., 1995). Furthermore, the changes in heart rate are distinct from the changes found in control participants who have been asked to pretend to have PTSD (Orr & Pitman, 1993); thus, PTSD patients react more strongly to the relevant cues than would be expected if they did not have a disorder.

In addition, the hippocampus apparently must work harder than normal in PTSD patients when they try to remember information, as shown by the fact that this brain structure is more strongly activated in these patients during memory tasks than in control participants (Shin et al., 2004). This is important because this brain structure plays a crucial role in storing information in memory (Squire & Kandel, 2000), and thus an impaired hippocampus should impair memory. And, in fact, as expected, PTSD patients have trouble recalling autobiographical memories (McNally et al., 1995).

Note that correlation does not imply causation; perhaps the brain abnormality predisposes people to PTSD, or perhaps PTSD leads to the brain abnormality (McEwen, 2001; Pitman et al., 2001). A twin study provides an important hint about what causes what: In this study, researchers compared the sizes of the hippocampi in veterans who had served in combat and had PTSD with the sizes of hippocampi in their identical twins who had not served in combat and did not have PTSD. The results were clear: In both twins, the hippocampi were smaller than normal (Gilbertson et al., 2002). This finding implies that the trauma did not cause the hippocampi to become smaller, but rather the smaller size is a risk factor (or is correlated with some other factor that produces the risk) that makes a person vulnerable to the disorder.

Neural Communication and Genetics

The neurotransmitter norepinephrine appears to be involved in PTSD. For example, Southwick and colleagues (1993) gave volunteers with and without PTSD a drug that allows norepinephrine levels to surge. When norepinephrine levels became very high, 70% of the PTSD patients had a panic attack, and 40% of them had a flashback to the traumatic event that precipitated their disorder; the volunteers who did not have PTSD exhibited minimal effects. Moreover, this drug resulted in more extreme biochemical and cardiovascular effects for the PTSD patients than for the controls.

Various types of evidence indicate that serotonin also plays a role in PTSD. For one, SSRIs can help treat the disorder, and they apparently do so in part by allowing serotonin to moderate the effects of stress (Corchs et al., 2009). In addition, people who have certain alleles of genes that produce serotonin are susceptible to developing the disorder following trauma (Adamec et al., 2008; Grabe et al., 2009).

However, research has shown that the effects of such genes may depend on a combination of factors, such as stressful environmental events in combination with low social support—and the same factors that affect whether people develop PTSD also affect whether they develop major depressive disorder (Kilpatrick et al., 2007; Sartor et al., 2012). Moreover, genes appear either to play a smaller role than the environment in predicting PTSD (McLeod et al., 2001) or are relevant only in the context of complex interactions between genes and environment (Broekman et al., 2007).

Psychological Factors: History of Trauma, Comorbidity, and Conditioning

Psychological factors that exist before a traumatic event occurs affect whether a person will develop PTSD. Such factors include the beliefs the person has about himself or herself and the world. Two specific beliefs that can make a person vulnerable to developing PTSD are considering yourself unable to control stressors (Heinrichs et al., 2005; Joseph et al., 1995) and the conviction that the world is a dangerous place (Keane, Zimering, & Caddell, 1985; Kushner et al., 1992).

People can be vulnerable to developing PTSD for a variety of other reasons. For example:

- by coping with a traumatic event by dissociating (disrupting the normal processes of perception, awareness, and memory; Shalev et al., 1996);

- by having severe mental disorders such as bipolar disorder (see Chapter 5) or schizophrenia (Chapter 12);

- by having some type of anxiety disorder (Copeland et al., 2007), perhaps because most anxiety disorders involve hyperarousal and hypervigilance—which may lead people to respond to traumatic events in ways that promote a stress disorder; and

- by having experienced a prior traumatic event (for example, having been assaulted and then, years later, living through a hurricane).

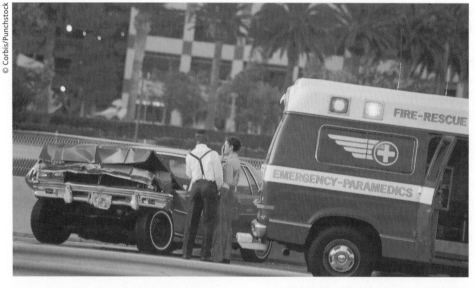

Among people who experienced a common type of traumatic event—a car accident—those who coped during the accident by dissociating were more likely to go on to develop PTSD than those who did not (Shalev et al., 1996). Other factors that increase the likelihood of PTSD's developing after a car accident are ruminating about the accident afterward, consciously trying to suppress thoughts about it, and having intrusive, unwanted thoughts and memories about it (Ehlers, Mayou, & Bryant, 1998).

After the traumatic event, classical conditioning and operant conditioning may help to explain how the person learns to avoid triggering PTSD attacks; such explanations parallel those for such behavior in anxiety disorders (Mowrer, 1939; see Chapter 6). In terms of classical conditioning, the traumatic stress is the unconditioned stimulus, and both internal sensations and external objects or situations can become conditioned stimuli, which in turn can come to induce powerful and aversive conditioned emotional responses (Keane, Zimmering, & Caddell, 1985). Thus, when a situation is similar to the traumatic one, it induces reactions that are aversive, leading the person to avoid the situation. In terms of operant conditioning, behaving in ways that avoid triggering PTSD symptoms is negatively reinforced. In addition, drugs and alcohol can temporarily alleviate symptoms; such substance use is also negatively reinforced, which explains why people with PTSD have a higher incidence of substance use disorders than do people who experienced a trauma but did not go on to develop PTSD (Chilcoat & Breslau, 1998; Jacobsen et al., 2001).

Social Factors: Socioeconomic Factors, Social Support, and Culture

Social factors—both before a traumatic event and afterward—also help determine whether a person will develop PTSD after a trauma. As with other stressors in life, socioeconomic factors can influence a person's ability to cope. People who face severe financial challenges—who aren't sure whether they'll be able to feed, clothe, and house themselves or their families—have fewer emotional resources available to cope with a traumatic event and so are more likely than more financially fortunate people to develop PTSD after a trauma (Mezey & Robbins, 2001).

In addition, socioeconomically disadvantaged people may be more likely to experience trauma (Breslau et al., 1998; Himle et al., 2009). For instance, poorer people are more likely to live in high-crime areas and are therefore more likely to witness crimes or become crime victims (Norris et al., 2003).

On a more hopeful note, people who receive support from others after a trauma have a lower risk of developing PTSD (Kaniasty & Norris, 1992; Kaniasty et al., 1990). For example, military servicemen and women who have experienced trauma during their service have a lower risk of developing PTSD if they have strong social support upon returning home (Jakupcak et al., 2006; King et al., 1999).

Finally, even when a person does develop PTSD, his or her surrounding culture can help determine which PTSD symptoms are more prominent. Cultural patterns might "teach" one coping style rather than another (Marsella et al., 1996). For example, Hurricane Paulina in Mexico and Hurricane Andrew in the United States were about equal in force, but the people who developed PTSD afterward did so in different ways (after controlling for the severity of a person's trauma): Mexicans were more likely to have intrusive symptoms, such as flashbacks about the hurricane and its devastation, whereas Americans were more likely to have arousal symptoms, such as an exaggerated startle response or hypervigilance (Norris et al., 2001). A similar finding was obtained from a study comparing Hispanic Americans to European Americans after Hurricane Andrew (Perilla et al., 2002).

Feedback Loops in Understanding Posttraumatic Stress Disorder

Neurological factors can make some people more vulnerable to developing PTSD after a trauma (van Zuiden et al., 2011). For example, in a study of people who were training to be firefighters, trainees who had a larger startle response to loud bursts of noise (which indicates a very reactive sympathetic nervous system) at the beginning of training were more likely to develop PTSD after a subsequent fire-related trauma (Guthrie & Bryant, 2005). In another study, researchers found that willingness to volunteer for combat and to accept riskier assignments is partly heritable (neurological factor; Lyons et al., 1993). This heritability may involve the dimension of temperament called *novelty seeking* (see Chapter 2). Someone high in novelty seeking pursues activities that are exciting and very stimulating, and a person with this characteristic may be more likely to volunteer for risky assignments (psychological factor), increasing the chance of encountering certain kinds of trauma. This means that neurological factors can influence both psychological and social factors, which in turn can increase the risk of trauma. At the same time, when a traumatic event is more severe (social factor), other types of factors are less important in influencing the onset of PTSD (Keane & Barlow, 2002).

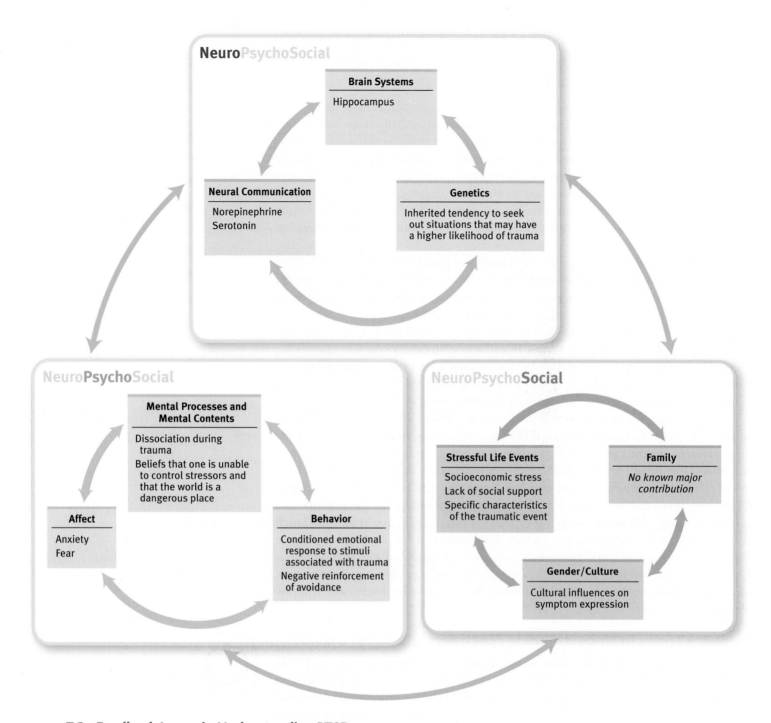

FIGURE **7.2 • Feedback Loops in Understanding PTSD**

Furthermore, ways of viewing the world and other personality traits (psychological factors) can influence the level of social support that is available to a person after suffering trauma (social factor). Figure 7.2 illustrates these factors and their feedback loops.

Treating Posttraumatic Stress Disorder

As usual, when a treatment is successful, changes in one factor affect the other factors.

Targeting Neurological Factors: Medication

The SSRIs *sertraline* (Zoloft) and *paroxetine* (Paxil) are the first-line medications for treating the symptoms of PTSD (Brady et al., 2000; Stein, Seedat, et al., 2000). An advantage of SSRIs is that these medications can also help reduce comorbid symptoms of depression (Hidalgo & Davidson, 2000)—which is important because many people with PTSD also have depression. However, as with anxiety disorders, when people discontinue the medication, the symptoms may return. This is why medication is not usually the sole treatment for PTSD but rather is combined with treatment that directly addresses psychological and social factors (Rosenbaum, Arana et al., 2005).

Targeting Psychological Factors

Treatments that target psychological factors generally employ a combination of behavioral methods and cognitive methods, which—separately or in combination—are about equally effective (Keane & Barlow, 2002; Schnurr et al., 2007; Tarrier et al., 1999).

Behavioral Methods: Exposure, Relaxation, and Breathing Retraining

Someone who has PTSD may go to unreasonable lengths to avoid stimuli associated with the trauma. This is why treatment aims to increase a sense of control over PTSD symptoms and to decrease avoidance. Just as exposure is used to decrease avoidance associated with anxiety disorders, it is used to treat PTSD: Exposure aims to induce habituation and to reduce the avoidance of internal and external cues associated with the trauma (Bryant & Harvey, 2000; Keane & Barlow, 2002). In this case, the specific stimuli in an exposure hierarchy are those associated with the trauma. As the person becomes less aroused and fearful of these stimuli and avoids them less, mastery

---

CURRENT CONTROVERSY

Eye Movement Desensitization and Reprocessing (EMDR) Treatment for Posttraumatic Stress Disorder

Eye movement desensitization and reprocessing (EMDR) is a widely used but debated psychological treatment for posttraumatic stress disorder (PTSD). The treatment rests on the idea that the symptoms of PTSD arise from the inability to process adequately the images and cognitions that arise when a person experiences a traumatic event (Shapiro, 2001). The treatment contains elements of both psychodynamic and cognitive-behavior therapy, and it was originally designed to help decrease negative emotions associated with traumatic memories (Shapiro & Maxfield, 2002). The phase of the treatment most similar to exposure therapy has the client think about the disturbing visual images or beliefs about the trauma while "moving the eyes from side to side for 15 or more seconds" as the therapist moves his or her fingers back and forth (Shapiro & Maxfield, 2002, p. 937).

On the one hand, EMDR has received enough research support to be considered one of a handful of treatments for PTSD that research suggests is effective (Perkins & Rouanzoin, 2002). However, what remains controversial is whether EMDR imparts any benefit above and beyond standard exposure therapy. Randomized trials comparing EMDR to exposure therapies have found little to no differences in outcomes for the two treatments (Ironson et al., 2002; Lee et al., 2002; Power et al., 2002; Taylor et al., 2003). From the perspective of a patient, the data suggest that the treatment works. But thinking about it from an ethical perspective, if EMDR does not lead to a better outcome than CBT, is the expensive training and certification required to practice the treatment warranted? In addition, some might argue that the eye movements increase the public's positive perception of the procedure as a medical treatment, even though there is no good evidence that eye movements enhance the benefit.

CRITICAL THINKING As a consumer, would you be concerned about undergoing a treatment if no one completely understood why all the components are helpful? What about taking a medication when we know that the medication helps the disorder but not exactly how it works?

(Randy Arnau, University of Southern Mississippi)

and control increase. To help with anxiety and reduce arousal symptoms, relaxation and breathing retraining are often included in treatment. Exposure can also be useful in preventing PTSD for people who, in the days following a trauma, have some symptoms of PTSD (Shalev et al., 2012).

Howard Hughes apparently used exposure with himself, which helped him resist developing PTSD. Before his near-fatal plane crash, he loved to fly. During his convalescence after that plane crash, he grew concerned that he'd become afraid of flying—perhaps because he was worried that stimuli associated with the crash (e.g., things related to planes) would lead to anxiety and flashbacks. Although Howard Hughes was worried about developing a fear of flying, the anxiety about flying—and an avoidance of it—didn't materialize. Because of his passion for the activity, he pushed himself to get back in the cockpit as soon as he was physically able (Barlett & Steele, 1979), and then he flew repeatedly, successfully undergoing a self-imposed in vivo exposure treatment.

Cognitive Methods: Psychoeducation and Cognitive Restructuring

To reduce the difficult emotions that occur with PTSD, educating patients about the nature of their symptoms (psychoeducation) can be a first step. As patients learn about PTSD, they realize that their symptoms don't arise totally out of the blue; their experiences become more understandable and less frightening.

In addition, cognitive methods can help patients understand the meaning of their traumatic experiences and the (mis)attributions they make about these experiences and the aftermath (Duffy et al., 2007, Foa et al., 1991, 1999), such as "I deserved this happening to me because I should have walked down a different street."

Studies have shown that CBT can significantly reduce the number of people who, with time, would have had their diagnosis change from acute stress disorder to PTSD (Bryant et al., 2005, 2006, 2008) and can decrease the risk of PTSD in people who, in the days after a traumatic event, exhibit enough symptoms to meet the criteria for PTSD (Shalev et al., 2012).

CBT conducted online helped people who developed PTSD as a result of the September 11, 2001, terrorist attack on the Pentagon (Litz et al., 2007).

Targeting Social Factors: Safety, Support, and Family Education

Because a traumatic event is almost always a social stressor, the early focus of treatment for PTSD is to ensure that the traumatized person is as safe as possible (Baranowsky et al., 2005; Herman, 1992). For instance, in a case that involves a woman with PTSD that arose from domestic abuse, the therapist and patient will spend time reviewing whether the woman is safe from further abuse, and if not, how to make her as safe as possible. For some types of traumatic events (such as combat-related trauma), group therapy—of any theoretical orientation—can provide support and diminish the sense of isolation, guilt, or shame about the trauma or the symptoms of PTSD (Schnurr et al., 2003). Moreover, family or couples therapy can help to educate family members and friends about PTSD and about ways in which they can support their loved one (Goff & Smith, 2005; Sherman et al., 2005).

Feedback Loops in Treating Posttraumatic Stress Disorder

To appreciate the interactive aspects of the neuropsychosocial approach, consider a study of people who developed PTSD after being in traffic accidents (as the driver, passenger, or pedestrian; Taylor et al., 2001). Prior to beginning the treatment, 15 of the 50 participants were taking an SSRI, a TCA, or a benzodiazepine. Treatment

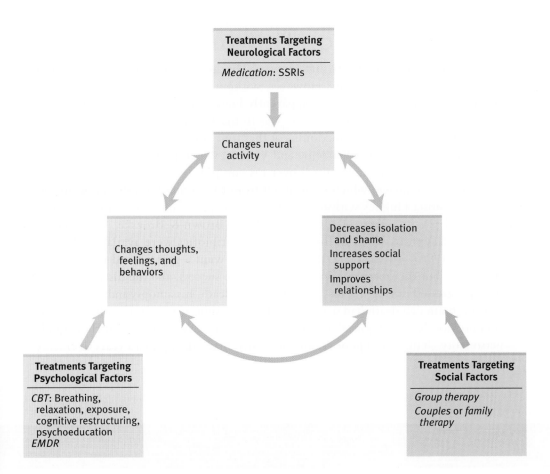

FIGURE 7.3 • Feedback Loops in Treating PTSD

consisted of 12 weeks of group CBT that involved psychoeducation about traffic accidents, their aftereffects, and PTSD; cognitive restructuring focused on faulty thoughts (such as overrating the dangerousness of road travel); relaxation training; and imaginal and in vivo exposure. After treatment, participants reported that they experienced less sympathetic nervous system reactivity, such as having fewer "hair-trigger" startle responses. In addition, they avoided the trauma–inducing stimuli less often and had fewer intrusive re-experiences of the trauma. These gains were maintained at the 3-month follow-up. So, an intervention that targets both social factors (group therapy with exposure to external trauma-related stimuli) and psychological factors (cognitive and behavioral interventions to change thinking and behavior) also apparently changed neurological functioning, as indicated by the reports of decreased hyperarousal. This change in turn affected both the person's thoughts and social interactions. Successful treatments for PTSD that target one or two factors ultimately affect all three. Figure 7.3 illustrates these feedback loops in treatment.

Thinking Like A Clinician

Two friends, Farah and Michelle, came back from winter break. Each had been devastated by personal experiences that occurred during the break. Farah's house burned down after the boiler exploded; fortunately, everyone was safe. Michelle's house had also been destroyed in a fire, but the police believed it was set by an "enemy" of her father's. Months pass, and by the time they go home for summer vacation, one of the friends has developed PTSD. Based on what you have read, which friend do you think developed PTSD, and why? What symptoms might she have and why? Based on what you have read, what do you think would be appropriate treatment for her?

▢ Follow-up on Howard Hughes

Despite the traumatic events that Howard Hughes experienced, he does not appear to have developed PTSD. However, without a doubt, he suffered from OCD. Although some of his symptoms apparently began in childhood, his OCD symptoms worsened significantly when he was in his 40s. There are several reasons for his progressively impaired functioning at that time. First, he used increasingly larger and more frequent doses of codeine and Valium, which probably led to diminished cognitive functioning and control over his compulsions. Second, he had by then suffered brain damage, which came about from two sources: (1) the 14 occurrences of head trauma Hughes withstood from various plane and car accidents (Fowler, 1986) and (2) the effects of advanced syphilis (Brown & Broeske, 1996). Hughes contracted syphilis when in his 30s, before antibiotics were available (Brown & Broeske, 1996). To treat the disease, he underwent a painful and risky mercury treatment, but the treatment was not a complete success, and the disease appears to have progressed during his 40s. After Hughes's death, his autopsy indicated that significant brain cell death had occurred, which is a sign of advanced syphilis (a condition previously called *general paresis*; see Chapter 1). Symptoms can include gradual personality changes and poor judgment, which may take up to 15 years to emerge.

▢ SUMMING UP

Obsessive-Compulsive Disorder and Related Disorders

- OCD is marked by persistent and intrusive obsessions or repetitive compulsions that usually correspond to the obsessions. People with OCD feel driven to engage in the compulsive behaviors, which provide only brief respite from the obsessions.

- Common obsessions include anxiety about contamination, order, losing control, and doubts. Common compulsions include washing, ordering, counting, and checking.

- Body dysmorphic disorder is characterized by an excessive preoccupation with a perceived defect in appearance that is either imagined or slight, and mental acts or behaviors related to the preoccupation. Body dysmorphic disorder shares features with OCD: preoccupations that arise from beliefs that are disproportional to the situation and time-consuming corresponding compulsive behaviors.

- Neurological factors associated with OCD include disruptions in the normal activity of the frontal lobes, the thalamus, and the basal ganglia; the frontal lobes do not turn off activity in the neural loop among these three brain areas, which may lead to the persistent

obsessions. Lower-than-normal levels of serotonin also appear to play a role. And genes appear to make some people more vulnerable to anxiety-related disorders in general—not necessarily to OCD specifically.

- Psychological factors that may underlie OCD include negative reinforcement of the compulsive behavior. In addition, normal preoccupying thoughts may become obsessions when the thoughts are deemed "unacceptable" and hence require controlling. In turn, the thoughts lead to anxiety, which is then relieved by a mental or behavioral ritual. People with OCD have cognitive biases related to their feared stimuli—in this case, regarding the theme of their obsessions.

- Social factors related to OCD include socially induced stress, which can influence the onset and course of the disorder, and culture, which can influence the particular content of obsessions and compulsions.

- Medication (such as an SSRI or clomipramine) directly targets neurological factors that underlie OCD. The primary treatment for OCD—exposure with response prevention—directly targets psychological factors. Family education or therapy, targeting social factors, may be used as an additional treatment.

Trauma-Related Disorders

- Trauma-related disorders are characterized by four types of persistent symptoms: intrusive re-experiencing of the trauma, avoidance of stimuli related to the event, negative thoughts and mood and dissociation, and increased arousal and reactivity.

- DSM-5 includes two types of trauma-related disorders: acute stress disorder and posttraumatic stress disorder (PTSD). Acute stress disorder is diagnosed when symptoms arise soon after the traumatic event and have lasted for at least 3 days but not more than 1 month; when symptoms last more than 1 month, the diagnosis can shift to PTSD. The diagnostic criteria for acute stress disorder also include symptoms of dissociation.

- An event is considered traumatic if the person experienced or witnessed an actual or threatened death, serious injury, or sexual violation. Types of traumatic events are large-scale events with multiple victims, unintended acts involving smaller numbers of people, and interpersonal violence.

- An unusually small hippocampus is a risk factor for PTSD. Patients with PTSD respond to high levels of norepinephrine by having panic attacks or flashbacks; they also have abnormal serotonin function. Although genes—through their influence on temperament—may affect a person's tendency to enter risky situations, characteristics of a traumatic event itself are more important in determining whether the person will develop PTSD.

- Psychological factors that exist before a traumatic event contribute to PTSD; these factors include a history of depression or other psychological disorders, a belief in being unable to control stressors, and the conviction that the world is a dangerous place. After a traumatic event, classical and operant conditioning contribute to the avoidance symptoms.

- Social factors that contribute to PTSD include the stress of low socioeconomic status and a relative lack of social support for the trauma victim. Culture can influence the ways that people cope with traumatic stress.

- Medication, specifically an SSRI, is the treatment that directly targets neurological factors. Treatments that target psychological factors include EMDR and CBT, specifically psychoeducation, exposure, relaxation, breathing retraining, and cognitive restructuring. Treatments that target social factors are designed to ensure that the person is as safe as possible from future trauma and to increase social support through group therapy or family therapy.

Key Terms

Obsessions (p. 196)
Compulsions (p. 196)
Obsessive-compulsive disorder (OCD) (p. 196)

Hoarding disorder (p. 199)
Body dysmorphic disorder (p. 199)
Exposure with response prevention (p. 206)

Posttraumatic stress disorder (PTSD) (p. 209)
Acute stress disorder (p. 211)

More Study Aids

For additional study aids related to this chapter, including quizzes to make sure you've retained everything you've learned and a Student Video Activity exploring one woman's struggle with body dysmorphic disorder, go to: www.worthpublishers.com/launchpad/rkabpsych2e.

Image Source

Dissociative and Somatic Symptom Disorders

Anna O., a well-to-do 21-year-old woman living in Austria in the late 19th century, had been caring for her ill father for weeks. Anna and her mother alternated shifts, Anna taking the night shift, staying awake by his bedside. Her father was dying of tuberculosis, and Anna also began to feel sick. Her symptoms included severe vision problems, headaches, a persistent cough, paralysis (in her neck, right arm, and both legs), lack of sensation in her elbows, and daily periods of a state of consciousness similar to sleep-walking. Anna was diagnosed with **hysteria**, an emotional condition marked by extreme excitability and bodily symptoms for which there is no medical explanation (hysteria is not a DSM-5 disorder).

For 2 years, Anna was treated by Dr. Joseph Breuer, a Viennese neurologist. Breuer became a colleague of Sigmund Freud and told Freud about Anna and her treatment, later described in *Studies in Hysteria* (Breuer & Freud, 1895/1955). Prior to Breuer's treatment of Anna, hypnosis was often used to treat hysteria. The physician hypnotized the patient (usually a woman) and then gave her a suggestion that the symptoms would go away. However, for some unknown reason, Breuer did not give Anna any suggestions, although he did hypnotize her. Instead, he asked her about her symptoms, and over time she told him about them. Anna and Breuer often met daily for treatment, sometimes twice a day. Anna's treatment usually involved Breuer's hypnotizing her and then asking her to tell him what she remembered about the origins of her symptoms. At other times, after being hypnotized, she simply told him what was on her mind. Anna referred to this process as the "talking cure." Freud was fascinated by Breuer's account of Anna's illness and her treatment; this "talking cure" was a precursor to psychoanalysis, and Freud's thoughts about Breuer and Anna led to the beginnings of his psychoanalytic theory (Freeman, 1980; see also Chapter 1).

Hysteria
An emotional condition marked by extreme excitability and bodily symptoms for which there is no medical explanation.

Anna O. was diagnosed with hysteria, which is a vague condition that is not in the DSM-5 classification system. Symptoms that were seen as part of hysteria are now generally considered to be symptoms of either dissociative disorders or somatic symptom disorders.

ANNA WAS DIAGNOSED WITH HYSTERIA—a common diagnosis at the time, particularly for women—but this term is a vague label for a condition that includes a wide range of symptoms. In DSM-5, symptoms that were once considered signs of hysteria are now part of the diagnostic criteria for two categories of disorders: dissociative disorders and somatic symptom disorders. The central feature of *dissociative disorders* is **dissociation**, the separation of mental processes—such as perception, memory, and self-awareness—and behavior that are normally integrated (Spiegel et al., 2011). Generally, each individual mental process is not disturbed, but their normal integrated functioning is disturbed. (With schizophrenia, in contrast, it is the mental processes themselves, such as the form or pattern of thoughts, that are disturbed; see Chapter 12.) *Somatic symptom and related disorders* (which we will refer to in this book simply as *somatic symptom disorders*) are characterized by complaints about physical well-being along with cognitive distortions about those bodily symptoms and their meaning; the focus on these bodily symptoms causes significant distress or impaired functioning. In this chapter we explore dissociative and somatic symptom disorders—their diagnostic criteria, criticisms of those criteria, the causes of the disorders, and treatments for them.

Dissociative Disorders

Breuer reported that Anna O. was an extremely bright young woman, prone to "systematic day-dreaming, which she described as her 'private theatre.'" Anna lived "through fairy tales in her imagination; but she was always on the spot when spoken to, so that no one was aware of it. She pursued this activity almost continuously while she was engaged in her household duties" (Breuer & Freud, 1895/1955, p. 22). These dissociative states, or "absences," began in earnest when Anna became too weak to care for her father, and they became more prominent after his death in April 1881. In what follows we examine dissociative disorders in more detail and then consider whether Anna's symptoms would meet the criteria for any of these disorders.

Dissociative Disorders: An Overview

Dissociation may arise suddenly or gradually, and it can be brief or chronic (Steinberg, 1994, 2001). Dissociative symptoms include:

- **amnesia**, or memory loss, which is usually temporary in dissociative disorders but, in rare cases, may be permanent;

- **identity problems**, in which a person isn't sure who he or she is or may assume a new identity;

- **derealization**, in which the external world is perceived or experienced as strange or unreal, and the person feels "detached from the environment" or as if viewing the world through "invisible filters" or "a big pane of glass" (Simeon et al., 2000); and

- **depersonalization**, in which the perception or experience of self—either one's body or one's mental processes—is altered to the point where the person feels like an observer, as though seeing oneself from the "outside." People experiencing depersonalization may describe it as feeling is if "under water" or "floating," "like a dead person," "as if I'm here but not here," "detached from my body," or "like a robot" (Simeon et al., 2000).

You may notice that some of these symptoms sound familiar. That's because all but identity problems are listed among the criteria for PTSD or acute stress disorder

Dissociation
The separation of mental processes—such as perception, memory, and self-awareness—that are normally integrated.

Amnesia
Memory loss, which in dissociative disorders is usually temporary but, in rare cases, may be permanent.

Identity problem
A dissociative symptom in which a person is not sure who he or she is or may assume a new identity.

Derealization
A dissociative symptom in which the external world is perceived or experienced as strange or unreal.

Depersonalization
A dissociative symptom in which the perception or experience of self—either one's body or one's mental processes—is altered to the point that the person feels like an observer, as though seeing oneself from the "outside."

(Chapter 7). In fact, as we'll discuss later in the chapter, trauma is thought to play a major role in dissociative disorders.

Anna O. appeared to experience derealization. After her father died, she recounted "that the walls of the room seemed to be falling over" (Breuer & Freud, 1895/1955, p. 23). She also reported having trouble recognizing faces and needing to make a deliberate effort to do so: "'this person's nose is such-and-such, his hair is such-and-such, so he must be so-and-so.' All the people she saw seemed like wax figures without any connection with her" (Breuer & Freud, 1895/1955, p. 26).

Normal Versus Abnormal Dissociation

Experiencing symptoms of dissociation is not necessarily abnormal; occasional dissociating is a part of everyday life (Seedat et al., 2003). For instance, you may find yourself in a class but not remember walking to the classroom. Or, on hearing bad news, you may feel detached from yourself, as if you're watching yourself from the outside.

In some cases, periods of dissociation are part of religious or cultural rituals (Boddy, 1992). Consider the phenomenon of *possession trance* observed in some societies: During a hypnotic trance, a kind of spirit is believed to assume control of the person's body. Later, the person has amnesia for the experience, and is otherwise normal. Moreover, people in different cultures may express dissociative symptoms differently. For example, *latah*, experienced by people—mostly women—in Indonesia and Malaysia (Bartholomew, 1994), involves fleeting episodes in which the person uses profanity and experiences amnesia and trancelike states. Unlike the typical course with psychosis, the "possessed" person returns to normal after the trance is over.

This woman is experiencing possession trance, a culturally sanctioned form of dissociation.

In some instances, dissociative experiences do indicate a disorder, but not necessarily a *dissociative* disorder; other psychiatric disorders can involve dissociative symptoms, such as when depersonalization or derealization occurs during a panic attack. DSM-5 reserves the category of **dissociative disorders** for cases in which consciousness, memory, emotion, perception, body representation, motor control, or identity are dissociated to the point where the symptoms are pervasive, cause significant distress, and interfere with daily functioning. Research findings suggest that pathological dissociation is qualitatively different from everyday types of dissociation, such as "spacing out" (Rodewald et al., 2011; Seedat et al., 2003). Only about 2% of the U.S. population reports having experienced dissociation to the extent that would be considered abnormal (Seedat et al., 2003).

Anna's dissociative symptoms do appear to have been abnormal; she had dissociations in perception, consciousness, memory, and identity:

> Two entirely distinct states of consciousness were present which alternated very frequently and without warning and which became more and more differentiated in the course of the illness. In one of these states she recognized her surroundings; she was melancholy and anxious, but relatively normal. In the other state she hallucinated and was "naughty"—that is to say, she was abusive, used to throw the cushions at people, . . . tore buttons off her bedclothes and linen with those of her fingers which she could move, and so on. At this stage of her illness if something had been moved in the room or someone had entered or left it [during her other state of consciousness] she would complain of having "lost" some time and would remark upon the gap in her train of conscious thoughts.

Dissociative disorders
A category of psychological disorders in which consciousness, memory, emotion, perception, body representation, motor control, or identity are dissociated to the point where the symptoms are pervasive, cause significant distress, and interfere with daily functioning.

Dissociative amnesia
A dissociative disorder in which the sufferer has significantly impaired memory for important experiences or personal information that cannot be explained by ordinary forgetfulness.

Soldiers with dissociative amnesia may forget combat experiences that were particularly troubling or traumatic. Although we don't know anything about this soldier, many soldiers encounter traumatic, and frequently mortal, events on their tours of duty. This soldier is attending a memorial service in Iraq for three of his comrades who were killed in a convoy attack.

TABLE 8.1 • DSM-5 Diagnostic Criteria for Dissociative Amnesia

A. An inability to recall important autobiographical information, usually of a traumatic or stressful nature, that is inconsistent with ordinary forgetting.

B. The symptoms cause clinically significant distress or impairment in social, occupational, or other important areas of functioning.

C. The disturbance is not attributable to the physiological effects of a substance (e.g., alcohol or other drug of abuse, a medication) or a neurological or other medical condition (e.g., partial complex seizures, transient global amnesia, sequelae of a closed head injury/traumatic brain injury, other neurological condition).

D. The disturbance is not better explained by dissociative identity disorder, posttraumatic stress disorder, acute stress disorder, somatic symptom disorder, or major or mild neurocognitive disorder.

These "absences" had already been observed before she took to her bed; she [would] stop in the middle of a sentence, repeat her last words and after a short pause go on talking. These interruptions gradually increased till they reached the dimensions that have just been described. . . . At the moments when her mind was quite clear she would complain of the profound darkness in her head, of not being able to think, . . . of having two selves, a real one and an evil one which forced her to behave badly, and so on.
(Breuer & Freud, 1895/1955, p. 24)

Anna's dissociative experiences were clearly beyond normal: They were pervasive and interfered with her daily functioning.

Types of Dissociative Disorders

DSM-5 defines three types of specific dissociative disorders, described in the following sections: *dissociative amnesia*, *depersonalization-derealization disorder*, and *dissociative identity disorder*.

Dissociative Amnesia

Anna's native language was German, but as her condition began to worsen while she was nursing her father, she started to speak only English (a language in which she was also fluent). She developed complete amnesia for speaking the German language. Let's examine why her amnesia for speaking in her native language might be considered dissociative.

What Is Dissociative Amnesia?

Dissociative amnesia is a dissociative disorder in which the sufferer has significantly impaired memory for autobiographical information—important experiences or personal information—that is not consistent with ordinary forgetfulness (see Table 8.1). The experiences or information typically involve traumatic or stressful events, such as occasions when the patient has been violent or tried to hurt herself or himself; the amnesia can come on suddenly. For example, soon after a bloody and dangerous battlefield situation, a soldier may not be able to remember what happened.

To qualify as dissociative amnesia, the memory problem cannot be explained by a medical disorder, substance use, or other disorders that have dissociation as a key symptom; as with all other dissociative disorders, it must also significantly impair functioning or cause distress (American Psychiatric Association, 2013). In Anna's case, her amnesia for speaking German could not really be considered as the loss of personal information but conceivably could be construed as the loss of an important experience and couldn't be explained by another disorder—and her father's illness and declining health had been extremely stressful for her.

The memory problems in dissociative amnesia can take any of several forms:

- *Localized amnesia*, in which the person has a memory gap for a specific period of time, often a period of time just prior to the stressful event, as did Mrs. Y in Case 8.1. This is the most common form of dissociative amnesia (American Psychiatric Association, 2013).

- *Selective amnesia*, in which the person can remember only some of what happened in an otherwise forgotten period of time. For instance, a soldier may forget about a particularly traumatic battlefield skirmish but remember what he and another person spoke about between phases of this skirmish.

- *Generalized amnesia*, in which the person can't remember his or her entire life. Although common in television shows and films, this type of amnesia is, in fact, extremely rare (Spiegel et al., 2011).

CASE 8.1 • FROM THE OUTSIDE: Dissociative Amnesia

Mrs. Y, a 51-year-old married woman . . . had a two-year history of severe depressive episodes with suicidal ideation, and reported total loss of memory for 12 years of her life . . . from the age of 37 to 49. [The amnesia began at age 49 when] she had had a car accident from which she sustained a very minor injury, but no loss of consciousness [nor any] posttraumatic stress symptoms. . . . She remembered what happened in the accident, and immediately preceding it, but suddenly had total loss of memory for the previous 12 years.

Mrs. Y had no problems recalling events which had occurred since the accident. She also had good autobiographical memory for her life events up to the age of 37.

Her parents and her grown-up children had told her that the . . . 12 years were painful for her. They would not tell her why, because they thought it would distress her even more. She was not only amnesic for these reputedly painful events, [but was unable] to recognize any of the friends she had made during that time. This included her present man friend, who was the passenger in her car at the time of the accident. Her family had told Mrs. Y that this gentleman (Mr. C) had been courting her for six years prior to the accident.

(Adapted from Degun-Mather, 2002, pp. 34–35)

In addition, some people with dissociative amnesia may have a subtype: *dissociative fugue*, which involves sudden, unplanned travel and difficulty remembering the past—which in turn can lead sufferers to be confused about who they are and sometimes to take on a new identity. Such a fugue typically involves generalized amnesia. In some cultures, people can develop a related set of symptoms referred to as a *running syndrome*. Although this condition has some symptoms that are similar to those of a dissociative fugue, it typically involves a sudden onset of a trancelike state and behavior such as running or fleeing, which leads to exhaustion, sleep, and subsequent amnesia for the experience. Running syndromes include (American Psychiatric Association, 2000):

- *pibloktoq* among native Arctic people,
- *grisi siknis* among the Miskito of Nicaragua and Honduras, and
- *amok* in Western Pacific cultures.

These syndromes have in common with dissociative fugue the symptom of unexpected travel, but amnesia occurs after the running episode is over, so the person doesn't remember that it happened. In contrast, with dissociative fugue, the memory problem arises during the fugue state, and the person can't remember his or her past. In addition, other criteria for dissociative amnesia do not necessarily apply to running syndromes. Additional facts about dissociative amnesia are listed in Table 8.2.

TABLE 8.2 • Dissociative Amnesia Facts at a Glance

Prevalence

- Dissociative amnesia is rare, and its lifetime prevalence is unknown.

Comorbidity

- Depression, anxiety, and substance-related disorders may be present along with dissociative amnesia. (Note: If the amnesia is a result of substance use, dissociative amnesia will not be the diagnosis.)

Onset

- Children or adults can develop this disorder.

Course

- Patients may have one or multiple episodes of amnesia.
- In some cases, the episode of amnesia resolves quickly; in other cases it persists.

Gender Differences

- No gender differences in the prevalence of dissociative amnesia have been reported.

Cultural Differences

- Dissociative amnesia may be a culture-related diagnosis; there are no reported cases of this disorder (due to a traumatic event by itself, in the absence of brain damage resulting from the trauma) prior to 1800 (Pope et al., 2007).

Source: Unless otherwise noted, the source is American Psychiatric Association, 2013. For more information see the Permissions section.

Some cultures have syndromes that are similar to dissociative fugue, such as *grisi siknis*, which shares with dissociative fugue a sudden flight from home and problems with memory. This photo shows local healers of an indigenous Miskito community in Nicaragua treating people with grisi siknis.

People with dissociative amnesia typically are unaware—or only minimally aware—of their memory problems (American Psychiatric Association, 2013). Some people may spontaneously remember forgotten experiences or information, particularly if their amnesia developed in response to a traumatic event and they leave the traumatic situation behind (such as occurs when a soldier with combat-related localized amnesia leaves the battlefield). Anna O. recovered her ability to speak German at the end of her treatment with Dr. Breuer, after she reenacted a traumatic nightmare that she'd had at her father's sickbed (and that marked the start of her problems).

Understanding Dissociative Amnesia

The following sections apply the neuropsychosocial approach as a framework for understanding the nature of dissociative amnesia. However, because the disorder is so rare, not much is known about either the specific factors that give rise to it or how those factors might influence each other.

Neurological Factors: Brain Trauma?

Neurological factors are clearly involved in cases of amnesia that arise following brain injury, such as that suffered in a car accident (Piper & Merskey, 2004a). However, when amnesia follows brain injury, it is not considered to be *dissociative* amnesia. Neurological factors that may contribute to dissociative amnesia are less clear-cut.

Some researchers have suggested that dissociative amnesia may result in part from damage to the hippocampus, which is critically involved in storing new information about events in memory. These researchers assume that periods of prolonged stress affect the hippocampus so that it does not operate well when the person is highly aroused (Joseph, 1999). The arousal—which typically accompanies a traumatic event—will impair the ability to store new information about that event. Later, this process would lead to the symptoms of dissociative amnesia for that event.

However, the idea that damage to the hippocampus underlies dissociative amnesia cannot explain all cases of the disorder. Because such damage would prevent information from being stored in the first place, the subsequent amnesia would not be reversible: There would be no way to retrieve the memories later because the memories would not exist (Allen et al., 1999). That is, the hippocampus is a critical gate-keeper of memory; without it, new information about facts cannot be stored. If damage to the hippocampus prevents new information from being stored, then such information is not available for later retrieval (even if the hippocampus itself recovers). Given that many cases of dissociative amnesia are characterized by "recovered" memories, it is not clear which brain systems would be involved.

Psychological Factors: Disconnected Mental Processes

The earliest theory of the origins of dissociative amnesia was dubbed the *dissociation theory* (Janet, 1907). Dissociation theory posits that very strong emotions (which may occur in response to a traumatic stressor) narrow the focus of attention and also disorganize cognitive processes, which prevent them from being integrated normally. According to this theory, the poorly integrated cognitive processes allow memory to be dissociated from other aspects of cognitive functioning, leading to dissociative amnesia. At best, the theory provides only a broad explanation for dissociative amnesia; it does not outline specific mechanisms to account for the dissociation and possible later reintegration of memory.

In contrast, *neodissociation theory* (Hilgard, 1994; Woody & Bowers, 1994) proposes that an "executive monitoring system" in the brain (specifically, the frontal lobes) normally coordinates various cognitive systems, much like a chief executive officer coordinates the various departments of a large company. However, in some circumstances (such as while a person is experiencing a traumatic event), the various cognitive systems can operate independently of the executive monitoring system. When this occurs, the executive system no longer has access to the information stored or processed by the separate cognitive systems. Memory thus operates as an independent cognitive system, and an "amnestic barrier" arises between memory and the executive system. This barrier causes the information in memory to be cut off from conscious awareness—that is, dissociated. Aspects of both dissociation and neodissociation theories have received some support from research (Green & Lynn, 1995; Hilgard, 1994; Kirsch & Lynn, 1998).

Social Factors: Indirect Effects

Many traumatic events result from social interactions, such as combat and abuse. These kinds of social traumas are likely to contribute to dissociative disorders, particularly dissociative amnesia. In fact, people with a dissociative disorder report childhood physical or sexual abuse almost three times more often than do people without a dissociative disorder (Foote et al., 2006). However, some researchers point out that traumatic events can also induce anxiety, which can lead people to have dissociative symptoms. Thus, traumatic events may not *directly* cause dissociative symptoms such as amnesia; rather, such events may indirectly lead to such symptoms by triggering anxiety (Cardeña & Spiegel, 1993; Kihlstrom, 2001).

As noted in Table 8.2, some researchers propose that dissociative amnesia is a disorder of modern times because there are no written accounts of its occurring before 1800 in any culture (Pope et al., 2007).

In sum, dissociative amnesia in the absence of physical trauma to the brain is extremely rare, which makes research on etiology and treatment similarly rare. Although researchers have proposed theories about why and how dissociative amnesia arises, these theories address dissociation generally; dissociative amnesia as a disorder is not well understood. These same deficiencies—a scarcity of research and vague theories that do not adequately characterize the specific mechanisms—also limit our understanding of the other dissociative disorders.

Depersonalization-Derealization Disorder

Like many other people, you may have experienced depersonalization or derealization. This does not mean that you have depersonalization-derealization disorder. A *persistent* feeling of being detached from one's mental processes, body, or surroundings is the key symptom of **depersonalization-derealization disorder**; people who have this disorder may experience depersonalization only, derealization only, or they may have both dissociative symptoms.

What Is Depersonalization-Derealization Disorder?

People afflicted with depersonalization-derealization disorder may *feel* "detached from my body" or "like a robot," or their surroundings may feel surreal, but they do not *believe* that they are truly detached, that they are actually a robot, or that their surroundings have actually become surreal. They still recognize reality. (In contrast, people who have a psychotic disorder may feel and believe such things; see Chapter 12.) In addition, people with depersonalization-derealization disorder may not react emotionally to events; they may feel that they don't control their behavior and are just being swept along by what is happening around them. These symptoms may lead sufferers to feel that they are "going crazy." Table 8.3 presents the DSM-5 diagnostic criteria; symptoms meet the criteria for the disorder

TABLE 8.3 • DSM-5 Diagnostic Criteria for Depersonalization-Derealization Disorder

A. The presence of persistent or recurrent experiences of depersonalization, derealization, or both;

1. **Depersonalization:** Experiences of unreality, detachment, or being an outside observer with respect to one's thoughts, feelings, sensations, body, or actions (e.g., perceptual alterations, distorted sense of time, unreal or absent self, emotional and/or physical numbing).

2. **Derealization:** Experiences of unreality or detachment with respect to surroundings (e.g., individuals or objects are experienced as unreal, dreamlike, foggy, life-less, or visually distorted).

B. During the depersonalization or derealization experiences, reality testing remains intact.

C. The symptoms cause clinically significant distress or impairment in social, occupational, or other important areas of functioning.

D. The disturbance is not attributable to the physiological effects of a substance (e.g., a drug of abuse, medication) or another medical condition (e.g., seizures).

E. The disturbance is not better explained by another mental disorder, such as schizophrenia, panic disorder, major depressive disorder, acute stress disorder, posttraumatic stress disorder, or another dissociative disorder.

Depersonalization-derealization disorder
A dissociative disorder, the primary symptom of which is a persistent feeling of being detached from one's mental processes, body, or surroundings.

TABLE 8.4 • Depersonalization-Derealization Disorder Facts at a Glance

Prevalence

• The prevalence of depersonalization-derealization disorder is unknown but thought to be from extremely low to 2.8% (Sar et al., 2007; Spiegel et al., 2011).

Comorbidity

• People with depersonalization-derealization disorder may also have symptoms of anxiety (Bremner et al., 1998; Marshall et al., 2000; Segui et al., 2000). In one sample of 204 people with depersonalization-derealization disorder, almost three quarters had an anxiety disorder at the time or previously (Baker et al., 2003).

• Major depressive disorder is also a common comorbid disorder.

Onset

• The average age of onset of depersonalization-derealization disorder is 16 years old; it is very rare for it to develop after age 40.

• Episodes can be triggered by a wide range of events, including trauma, extreme stress, depression, panic, and the ingestion of a psychoactive drug such as marijuana or alcohol (Raimo et al., 1999; Simeon, Knutelska, et al., 2003).

Course

• Episodes of depersonalization or derealization can last from hours to years.

• The course is often persistent, with a third of people with the disorder having discrete episodes, a third with continuous symptoms after onset, and a third with symptoms initially episodic but eventually becoming continuous.

Gender Differences

• Equal numbers of males and females have this disorder.

Source: Unless otherwise noted, the source is American Psychiatric Association, 2013.

only when they occur independently of anxiety symptoms and when they impair functioning or cause significant distress. Table 8.4 provides more facts about depersonalization–derealization disorder, and Case 8.2 shares the story of Mr. E, who has the disorder.

CASE 8.2 • FROM THE OUTSIDE: Depersonalization-Derealization Disorder

[Mr. E] was a 29-year-old, single man, employed as a journalist, who reported a 12-year history of [depersonalization-derealization] disorder. He described feeling detached from the world as though he was living "inside a bubble" and found it difficult to concentrate since he felt as though his brain had been "switched off." His body no longer felt solid and he could not feel himself walking on the ground. The world appeared two-dimensional and he reported his sense of direction and spatial awareness to be impaired. He described himself as having lost his "sense of himself" and felt that he was acting on "auto-pilot." He also reported symptoms of depression and some symptoms of OCD, which took the form of counting and stepping on cracks in the pavement, although he did not report the latter as a problem.

Prior to the onset of his [depersonalization-derealization disorder], he experienced transient [depersonalization] symptoms when intoxicated with cannabis. At the age of 17, he started at a new school and felt very anxious and experienced [depersonalization] symptoms when not under the influence of cannabis. . . . He described the first time this happened as "terrifying" since he felt he had "gone into another world." He reported difficulty with breathing and believed he may have a brain tumor or that his "brain was traumatized into a state of panic." From the age of 17 to 19, the episodes of [depersonalization] became more frequent until they became constantly present. He reports the symptoms as "enormously restricting" his life in that he felt frustrated since he has been "unable to express or enjoy myself."

(Hunter et al., 2003, Appendix A, pp. 1462–1463)

Understanding Depersonalization-Derealization Disorder

Researchers are beginning to chart the factors that contribute to depersonalization-derealization disorder—but again, because the disorder is so rare, there are relatively few studies of it.

Neurological Factors

Studies converge in providing evidence that depersonalization-derealization disorder arises, at least in part, from disruptions of emotional processing (Sierra et al., 2002). For example, when patients with this disorder viewed faces with highly emotional expressions, activity in the limbic system decreased rather than increased, as it does for most people—and this occurred in response to both very happy and very sad expressions (Lemche et al., 2007). This study also showed that the patients had unusually high levels of activity in the frontal lobes when viewing such facial expressions. This is important because the frontal lobes can suppress emotional responses, which might produce the sense of emotional detachment that such patients report. Such an effect might also explain why brain areas involved in emotion are not activated when patients with depersonalization-derealization disorder try to remember words that name emotions, whereas these brain areas are activated when normal control participants perform this task (Medford et al., 2006).

A PET study of patients with depersonalization-derealization disorder found unusual levels of activation (either too high or too low) in parts of the brain specifically involved in various phases of perception—the temporal and parietal lobes (Simeon et al., 2000). The researchers noted that these findings are consistent with the idea that depersonalization-derealization disorder involves dissociations in perception.

In addition, patients with depersonalization-derealization disorder do not produce normal amounts of norepinephrine. In fact, the more strongly they exhibit symptoms of the disorder, the less norepinephrine they apparently produce (as measured in their urine; Simeon, Guralnick, et al., 2003). Norepinephrine is associated with activity of the autonomic nervous system, and thus this finding is consistent with the idea that these patients have blunted responses to emotion.

Psychological Factors: Cognitive Deficits

Patients with depersonalization-derealization disorder have cognitive deficits that range from problems with short-term memory to impaired spatial reasoning, but the root cause of these difficulties appears to lie with attention: These patients cannot easily focus and sustain their attention (Guralnik et al., 2000, 2007). This is consistent with neuroimaging studies that reveal decreased activity in parts of the brain involved in perception. However, it is not clear whether the attentional problems are a cause or an effect of the disorder: On one hand, if a person were feeling disconnected from the world, he or she would not pay normal attention to objects and events; on the other hand, if a person had such attentional problems, this could contribute to feeling disconnected from the world. Moreover, given that many patients with depersonalization-derealization disorder also have depression or an anxiety disorder (Baker et al., 2003), it is not clear whether the problems with attention are specifically related to depersonalization-derealization disorder or arise from the comorbid disorder.

Social Factors: Childhood Emotional Abuse

We noted earlier that stressful events (often a result of social interactions) can trigger depersonalization-derealization disorder. Moreover, a specific type of social stressor—severe and chronic emotional abuse experienced during childhood—seems to play a particularly important role in triggering depersonalization-derealization disorder (Simeon et al., 2001), although it is not clear why such abuse might lead to depersonalization-derealization disorder only in some cases. Once the disorder develops, the perception of threatening social interactions and new environments can exacerbate its symptoms (Simeon, Knuteska, et al., 2003). For instance, if Mr. E in Case 8.2 had a fight with a friend, his depersonalization symptoms would probably become worse during the fight.

ONLINE

Feedback Loops in Understanding Depersonalization-Derealization Disorder

One hypothesis for how depersonalization-derealization disorder arises is as follows: First, a significant stressor (often a social factor) elicits neurological events (partly in the frontal lobes) that suppress normal emotional responses (Hunter et al., 2003; Sierra & Berrios, 1998; Simeon, Knutelska, et al., 2003). Following this, the disconnection between the intensity of the perceived stress and the lack of arousal may lead these patients to feel "unreal" or that their surroundings are unreal, which they may then attribute (a psychological factor) to being mentally ill (Baker, Earle, et al., 2007; Hunter et al., 2003). And, in turn, the incorrect and catastrophic attributions that the patients make about their symptoms can lead to further anxiety (as occurs with panic disorder). The attributions can also lead to further depersonalization or derealization symptoms. Patients then become extremely sensitive to and hypervigilant for possible symptoms of "unreality" and come to fear that the symptoms indicate that they are "going crazy." They may also avoid situations likely to elicit the symptoms.

Dissociative Identity Disorder

Dissociative identity disorder, once known as *multiple personality disorder*, may be the most controversial of all DSM-5 disorders. First we examine what dissociative identity disorder is, then some criticisms of the DSM-5 diagnostic criteria, and then factors that may contribute to the disorder. In the process of examining these factors, we delve into the controversy about the disorder.

What Is Dissociative Identity Disorder?

The central feature of **dissociative identity disorder (DID)** is the presence of two or more distinct "personality states" (sometimes referred to as *alters*) or an experience of being "possessed," which leads to a discontinuity in the person's sense of self and ability to control his or her functioning. Such a discontinuity can affect any aspect of functioning, including mood, behavior, consciousness, memory, perception, thoughts, and sensory-motor functioning.

In some cases, these personality states have separate characteristics and history, and they take turns controlling the person's behavior. For example, a person with this disorder might have an "adult" personality state that is very responsible, thoughtful, and considerate and a "child" personality state that is irresponsible, impulsive, and obnoxious. Each personality state can have its own name, mannerisms, speaking style, and vocal pitch that distinguish it from others. Some personality states report being unaware of the existence of others, and thus they experience amnesia (because the memory gaps are longer than ordinary forgetting).

Perhaps the most compelling characteristic of personality states is that, for some patients, each personality state can have unique medical problems and histories: One

Dissociative identity disorder (DID)
A dissociative disorder characterized by the presence of two or more distinct personality states, or an experience of possession trance, which gives rise to a discontinuity in the person's sense of self and agency.

TABLE 8.5 • DSM-5 Diagnostic Criteria for Dissociative Identity Disorder

A. Disruption of identity characterized by two or more distinct personality states, which may be described in some cultures as an experience of possession. The disruption in identity involves marked discontinuity in sense of self and sense of agency, accompanied by related alterations in affect, behavior, consciousness, memory, perception, cognition, and/or sensory-motor functioning. These signs and symptoms may be observed by others or reported by the individual.

B. Recurrent gaps in the recall of everyday events, important personal information, and/or traumatic events that are inconsistent with ordinary forgetting.

C. The symptoms cause clinically significant distress or impairment in social, occupational, or other important areas of functioning.

D. The disturbance is not a normal part of a broadly accepted cultural or religious practice.

Note: In children, the symptoms are not better explained by imaginary playmates or other fantasy play.

E. The symptoms are not attributable to the physiological effects of a substance (e.g., blackouts or chaotic behavior during alcohol intoxication) or another medical condition (e.g., complex partial seizures).

Reprinted with permission from the Diagnostic and Statistical Manual of Mental Disorders, Fifth Edition, (Copyright ©2013). American Psychiatric Association. All Rights Reserved.

might have allergies, medical conditions, or even EEG patterns that the others do not have (American Psychiatric Association, 2000). Stressful events can trigger a switch of personality states, whereby the one that was dominant at one moment recedes and another becomes the dominant. Although the number of personality states that have been reported ranges from 2 to 100, most people diagnosed with DID have 10 or fewer (American Psychiatric Association, 2000).

In other cases, the personality states may be less obvious and other personality states only emerge for brief periods of time. Such patients may report feeling detached from themselves (as if they were observing themselves), hearing voices (such as children crying), or having waves of strong emotion—out of the blue—over which they have no control. Table 8.5 lists the DSM-5 diagnostic criteria for DID, and Table 8.6 provides further information about the disorder.

People with DID may not be able to remember periods of time in the past (such as getting married) or skills they learned (such as how to drive a car or aspects of their job), or they may discover "evidence" of actions they don't remember performing, such as finding new clothes in their closet or furniture moved. Moreover, they may find themselves somewhere and not know how they got there (American Psychiatric Association, 2013).

For some people, a personality state takes the form of "possession" by a spirit, ghost, or another person who has taken control. In such cases, patients may act and speak as if they were the entity who has "taken over," such as the spirit of someone in the community who died. (However, when possession is part of a spiritual practice, these symptoms would be considered normal, and a diagnosis of DID would not be made.) To qualify for a diagnosis of DID, the additional personality states must impair functioning or be significantly distressing; in fact, 70% of people with this disorder attempt suicide (American Psychiatric Association, 2013). Case 8.3 presents the personality states of someone with DID, which was previously called *multiple personality disorder* (MPD).

TABLE 8.6 • Dissociative Identity Disorder Facts at a Glance

Prevalence

• The prevalence rate for DID is difficult to determine, although several surveys estimate it to be about 1% (Johnson, Cohen, et al., 2006a; Loewenstein, 1994). However, some researchers view this figure as a significant overestimate (Rifkin et al., 1998).

Comorbidity

• People with DID may also be diagnosed with a mood disorder, an anxiety disorder, a substance-related disorder, PTSD, or a personality disorder (to be discussed in Chapter 13). DID may be difficult to distinguish from schizophrenia or bipolar disorder.

Onset

• It can take years to make the diagnosis of DID from the time that symptoms first emerge. Because of this long lag time and the rarity of the disorder, there is no accurate information about the usual age of onset.

Course

• DID is usually chronic.

Gender Differences

• This disorder is equally prevalent in males and females.

Cultural Differences

• DID is observed only in some Western cultures and was extremely uncommon before the 1976 television movie *Sybil*, which was about a "true case" of what was then called multiple personality disorder (Kihlstrom, 2001; Lilienfeld et al., 1999).

Source: Unless otherwise noted, the source is American Psychiatric Association, 2013.

CASE 8.3 • FROM THE INSIDE: Dissociative Identity Disorder

In Robert B. Oxnam's memoir, *A Fractured Mind*, his various personality states (11 in all) tell their stories. The following excerpts present recollections from 2 of the alters, beginning with Robert:

> This is Robert speaking. Today, I'm the only personality who is strongly visible inside and outside. . . . Fifteen years ago, I rarely appeared on the outside, though I had considerable influence on the inside; back then, I was what one might call a "recessive personality."
>
> Although [Bob, another alter] was the dominant MPD personality for thirty years, [he] did not have a clue that he was afflicted by multiple personality disorder until 1990, the very last year of his dominance. That was the fateful moment when Bob first heard that he had an "angry boy named Tommy" inside of him.
>
> (Oxnam, 2005, p. 11)

Another alter, Bob, recounts:

> There were blank spots in my memory where I could not recall anything that happened for blocks of time. Sometimes when a luncheon appointment was canceled, I would go out at noon and come back at 3 P.M. with no knowledge of where I had been or what I had done. I returned tired, a bit sweaty, but I quickly showered and got back to work. Once, on a trip to Taiwan, a whole series of meetings was canceled because of a national holiday; I had zero memory of what I did for almost three days, but I do recall that, after the blank spot disappeared, I had a severe headache and what seemed to be cigarette burns on my arm.
>
> (Oxnam, 2005, p. 31)

Criticisms of the DSM-5 Criteria

Significant problems plague the DSM-5 diagnostic criteria for DID, including the following (Piper & Merskey, 2004b):

- DSM-5 does not define the separate "personality states"; accordingly, a normal emotional state that emerges episodically—such as periodic angry outbursts—could be considered a "personality state" that is different than the person's "usual" state. Thus, the criteria permit possibility that normal emotional fluctuations could be considered pathological.

- DID—which is easy to role-play—can be difficult to distinguish from malingering (Labott & Wallach, 2002; Stafford & Lynn, 2002). When people can easily fake symptoms of a disorder, the validity of the disorder as a diagnostic entity can be questioned.

- DID can be difficult to distinguish from rapid-cycling bipolar disorder because both involve sudden changes in mood and demeanor. However, appropriate treatments for bipolar disorder differ from those for DID, which is why accurate diagnosis is important (Piper & Merskey, 2004b).

Some of Anna O.'s dissociative experiences seem similar to those of patients with DID, such as her "naughty" states (for which she had amnesia) and her feeling that she had two selves, a real one and an evil one, which would "take control."

Understanding Dissociative Identity Disorder

Research findings on various factors associated with DID can be at odds with each other, which only fuels the controversy over the validity of the diagnosis itself. As we shall see, much of the research on, and theorizing about, factors that may contribute to DID hinge on the fact that many people with this disorder report having been severely and chronically abused as children (Lewis et al., 1997; Ross et al., 1991).

Neurological Factors: Alters in the Brain?

One hallmark of DID is that memories acquired by one personality state are not directly accessible to others. However, studies suggest that although alters may report the subjective experience of amnesia, they do, in fact, have access to memories of other alters (Huntjens et al., 2005, 2006, 2007; Kong et al., 2008). Consistent with these findings, researchers have used changes in electrical activity on the scalp

© Ramin Talaie/Corbis

Simply being sensitive to context or responding differently when in different emotional states does not mean that you have "personality states." For example, one study found that people who are bilingual responded differently to a personality test, depending on which language was used for the test (Ramírez-Esparza et al., 2006). Can you think of reasons for this result that do not involve personality states?

to show that the brain responds as if the patient with DID recognizes previously learned words, even when the learning took place when one alter was dominant and the testing occurred when another alter was dominant (Allen & Movius, 2000).

Perhaps the key characteristic of DID is that each alter has a different "sense of self." To the person with DID, it feels as if different personalities "take over" in turn. To explore the neural bases of this phenomenon, Reinders and colleagues (2003) asked 11 DID patients to listen to stories about their personal traumatic history while their brains were scanned using PET. Each patient was scanned once when an alter who was aware of the past trauma was dominant and once when an alter who was not aware of the past trauma was dominant. Two results are of particular interest: First, and most basic, the brain responded differently for the two alters. This alone is evidence that something was neurologically different when the person was in the two states. Second, the traumatic history activated brain areas known to be activated by autobiographical information—but only when the alter that was aware of that information was dominant during the PET scanning.

However, it is difficult to interpret the results of many studies that investigate neurological differences among alters because the studies do not include an appropriate control group (Merckelbach et al., 2002). Researchers have found that hypnosis can alter brain activity (Kosslyn et al., 2000), so it is possible that at least some of the neurological differences between alters reflect a form of self-hypnosis. That is, the person with DID—perhaps unconsciously—hypnotizes himself or herself, which produces different neurological states when different alters come to the fore.

Researchers have also investigated what role genetics might play in DID. Using a questionnaire, a team of researchers assessed the capacity for dissociative experiences in monozygotic and dizygotic twins in the general population (Jang et al., 1998). This questionnaire did not address DID directly, but it did assess the capacity for both "normal" dissociations (such as becoming very absorbed in a television show or a movie) and "abnormal" dissociations (such as not recognizing your face in a mirror). These researchers found that almost half the variation in abnormal dissociations could be attributed to genes.

Psychological Factors

The primary psychological factor associated with DID is hypnotizability: Patients with this diagnosis are highly hypnotizable and can easily dissociate (Bliss, 1984; Frischholz et al., 1990, 1992). That is, they can spontaneously enter a trance state and frequently experience symptoms of dissociation, such as depersonalization or derealization. These abilities play a critical role in a psychologically based theory of DID, described in the upcoming section on feedback loops.

Social Factors: A Cultural Disorder?

Social factors have apparently affected the frequency of diagnosis of DID. DID was rarely diagnosed until 1976 (Kihlstrom, 2001; Lilienfeld et al., 1999; Spanos, 1994). What happened in 1976? The television movie *Sybil* was aired and received widespread attention. This movie portrayed the "true story" of a woman with DID. The movie apparently affected either patients (who became able to express their distress in this popularized way) or therapists (who became more willing to make the diagnosis) or both. However, years later, it was revealed that the patient who was known as Sybil did not have alters but rather had been encouraged by her therapist to "name" her different feelings as if they were alters; thus, what Sybil's therapist wrote about the alters was not based on Sybil's actual experiences (Borch-Jacobsen, 1997; Rieber, 1999).

Courtesy Everett Collection

Some researchers attribute the increased prevalence of DID since 1976 to the movie *Sybil*, which claimed to portray the "true story" of a woman with DID. In a scene near the end of the movie, Sybil (played by Sally Field, lying down) and her psychiatrist (Joanne Woodward) work to "integrate" the different alters. In fact, it was later revealed that the real-life "Sybil" had been explicitly encouraged to give names to different aspects of her personality but did not actually dissociate, as her psychiatrist had claimed she did.

Consistent with the view that DID is a disorder induced by social factors present in some cultures, many countries, such as India and China, have an extremely low or zero prevalence rate of DID (Adityanjee et al., 1989; Draijer & Friedl, 1999; Xiao et al., 2006). In other countries, such as Uganda, people with DID symptoms are considered to be experiencing the culturally sanctioned possession trance, not suffering from DID (van Dujil et al., 2005).

ONLINE

Feedback Loops in Understanding Dissociative Identity Disorder: Two Models for the Emergence of Alters

Two models of dissociative identity disorder—the posttraumatic model and the sociocognitive model—are based on the existence of feedback loops among neurological, psychological, and social factors. However, the two models emphasize the roles of different factors and have different accounts of how the factors influence each other.

The Posttraumatic Model In addition to dissociating or entering hypnotic trances easily, most DID patients have at least one alter that reports having suffered severe, often recurring, physical abuse when young (which would imply a stress response; neurological factor) (Lewis et al., 1997; Ross et al., 1991). This trauma, induced by others (social factor), may increase the ease of dissociating (psychological factor). In fact, children who experienced severe physical abuse later report that during the traumatic events, their minds temporarily left their bodies (which presumably was a way of coping); that is, they dissociated. Putting these observations together, the *posttraumatic model* proposes that after frequent episodes of abuse with accompanying dissociation, the child's dissociated state can develop its own memories, identity, and way of interacting with the world, thereby becoming an "alter" (Bremner, 2010; Gleaves, 1996; Putnam, 1989).

Several studies support some aspects of the posttraumatic model. As would be expected from this model, some people with DID do have documented histories of severe physical abuse in childhood (Lewis et al., 1997; Putnam, 1989; Swica et al., 1996) and also report having displayed signs of dissociation in childhood (Lewis et al., 1997). Moreover, these patients report that they either don't remember being abused or remember very little of it (Lewis et al., 1997; Swica et al., 1996). In addition, girls who were easy to hypnotize *and* able to dissociate readily were found to be the ones most likely to have been abused physically or sexually (Putnam et al., 1995).

In addition, research on sleep and dissociation may shed light on how DID emerges (Lynn et al., 2012). Specifically, when healthy volunteers are deprived of sleep, they are more likely to experience dissociative symptoms (Giesbrecht et al., 2007). And when patients with dissociative symptoms receive treatment to help improve their sleep, their dissociative symptoms diminish (van der Kloet, Giesbrecht, et al., 2012). When someone's sleep cycle is altered—perhaps because of a traumatic experience—he or she may become more likely to dissociate or experience vivid dreams when falling asleep or waking up (van der Kloet, Giesbrecht, et al., 2012; van der Kloet, Merckelbach, et al., 2012). In turn, continued sleep deprivation leads to cognitive deficits, such as difficulties with memory and attention, which are aspects of symptoms of DID.

However, if the posttraumatic model is correct, there should be a significant number of cases of childhood DID. In fact, very few such cases have been documented (Giesbrecht et al., 2008, 2010; Boysen, 2011), and most studies of abused children have found only a great ability to dissociate, *not the presence of alters* (Piper & Merskey, 2004a). Moreover, most studies of adults with DID who experienced childhood abuse have not obtained independent corroborating evidence of abuse or trauma but rather rely solely on the patient's—or an alter's—report of abuse during childhood (Piper & Merskey, 2004a, 2004b).

The Sociocognitive Model In contrast to the posttraumatic model of DID, the *sociocognitive model* proposes that social interactions between therapist and patient (social factor) foster DID by influencing the beliefs and expectations of the patient (psychological factor). According to the sociocognitive model, the therapist unintentionally causes the patient to act in ways that are consistent with the symptoms of DID (Lilienfeld et al., 1999; Lynn et al., 2012; Sarbin, 1995; Spanos, 1994). This explanation is plausible in part because hypnosis was commonly used to bring forth alters, and researchers have pointed out that suggestible patients can unconsciously develop alters (and ensuing neurological changes) in response to the therapist's promptings (Spanos, 1994). For instance, a therapist may encourage a patient to develop alters by asking leading questions ("Have people come up to you who seem to know you, but they are strangers to you?") and then showing special interest when the patient answers "yes" to any such question. One finding that supports the sociocognitive model is that many people who have been diagnosed with DID had no notion of the existence of any alters before they entered therapy (Lilienfeld et al., 1999). In fact, in reviewing published studies on DID, no documented cases of DID occurring outside of therapy could be found (Boysen & VanBergen, 2013). In addition, cultural cues regarding DID (such as in portrayals in movies and memoirs or interviews of people with the disorder) may influence a patient's behavior.

Dissociative identity disorder is described or portrayed in various memoirs and films, such as the popular 1999 film *Fight Club*. According to the sociocognitive model of this disorder, such media portrayals can help create expectations in both patients and therapists about how people with the disorder behave. Therapists, in turn, unintentionally reinforce patients for behaving in ways consistent with such portrayals.

The Debate About Dissociative Identity Disorder

The phenomenon of people presenting in treatment with different personality states exists. The issue debated is how it arises and continues in a given patient. Proponents of the sociocognitive model recognize that childhood trauma—at least in some cases—can indirectly be associated with DID: Childhood trauma may lead people to become more suggestible or more able to fantasize, which can magnify the effects on their behavior of social interactions with a therapist (Lilienfeld et al., 1999; Lynn et al., 2012). In other words, dissociation and DID symptoms may be *indirect* results of childhood trauma rather than direct posttraumatic results.

GETTING THE PICTURE

Which of these photos best captures the explanation for DID proposed by the sociocognitive model? Answer: The photo on the right, in which the therapist's actions (such as using hypnosis to bring forth alters) inadvertently lead the patient to behave in ways that are consistent with DID.

Proponents of the sociocognitive model also point out that cultural influences, such as the airing of the movie *Sybil*, may have led therapists to ask leading questions regarding DID—and may have led highly suggestible patients to follow these leads unconsciously; such influences would account for the great variability in the number of cases over time. Proponents of the posttraumatic model counter that the increased prevalence of DID after 1976 simply reflects improved procedures for assessment and diagnosis.

In sum, we do know that severe trauma can lead to dissociative disorders and can have other adverse effects (Putnam, 1989; Putnam et al., 1995). However, we do not know whether all of the people who are diagnosed with DID have actually experienced traumatic events, nor even how severe an event must be in order to be considered "traumatic." Similarly, experiencing a traumatic event does not *specifically* cause DID (Kihlstrom, 2005); some people respond by developing depression or an anxiety disorder. Further, as noted in Chapter 7, many people who experience a traumatic event do not develop any psychological disorder.

Treating Dissociative Disorders

In general, dissociative amnesia improves spontaneously, without treatment. However, clinicians who encounter people with other dissociative disorders have used some of the treatments discussed below. Because dissociative disorders are so rare, few systematic studies of treatments have been conducted—and none have attempted to determine which treatments are most effective for a particular dissociative disorder. Thus, we consider treatments for dissociative disorders in general.

Targeting Neurological Factors: Medication

In general, medication is not used to treat the symptoms of dissociative disorders because research suggests that it is not helpful for dissociative symptoms (Sierra et al., 2003; Simeon et al., 1998). However, people with dissociative disorders may receive medication for a comorbid disorder or for anxiety or mood symptoms that arise in response to the dissociative symptoms.

Targeting Psychological and Social Factors: Coping and Integration

Treatments that target the psychological factors underlying dissociative disorders focus on three elements: (1) reinterpreting the symptoms so that they don't create stress or lead the patient to avoid certain situations; (2) learning additional coping strategies to manage stress (Hunter et al., 2005); and (3) for DID patients, addressing the presence of alters and dissociated aspects of their memories or identities. The first two foci are similar to aspects of treatment for PTSD (Kluft, 1999; see Chapter 7).

When addressing the presence of alters in patients with DID, the type of treatment a clinician employs depends on which theory he or she accepts and thus uses to guide treatment. Proponents of the posttraumatic model advise clinicians to identify in detail (or to "map") each alter's personality, recover memories of possible abuse, and then help the patient to integrate the different alters (Chu & International Society for the Study of Dissociation, 2005). In contrast, proponents of the sociocognitive model advise *against* mapping alters or trying to recover possible memories of abuse (Gee et al., 2003). Instead, they recommend that the therapist use learning principles to extinguish patients' mention of alters: Alters are to be ignored, and the therapist doesn't discuss multiple identities. Alters are interpreted as creations inspired by the patient's desire for attention, and treatment focuses on current problems rather than on past traumas (Fahy et al., 1989; McHugh, 1993).

In addition, hypnosis has sometimes been used as part of treatment, particularly by therapists who treat DID according to the posttraumatic model; in this case, hypnosis might be used to help the patient learn about his or her different alters and integrate them into a single, functional whole (Boyd, 1997; Kluft, 1999). Using hypnosis is, by its very nature, a social event: The therapist helps the patient achieve a hypnotic state through suggestions and bears witness to whatever the patient shares about the dissociated experience. However, using hypnosis to treat DID is controversial because the patient will be more suggestible when in a hypnotic trance, and the therapist may inadvertently make statements that the patient interprets as suggestions to produce more DID symptoms.

Treatment may also focus on reducing the traumatic stress that can induce dissociative disorders. For instance, soldiers who experience dissociation during combat may be removed from the battlefield, which can then reduce the dissociation.

When using hypnosis to treat dissociative symptoms, the therapist may make suggestions such as "You will feel yourself becoming relaxed . . . you will notice yourself going into a state of trance . . . you will find yourself about to remember whatever was pushed aside." One goal is to help (re)integrate whatever has been dissociated, such as specific memories.

Feedback Loops in Treating Dissociative Disorders

When Breuer was treating Anna O., he relied on the "talking cure"—having her talk about relevant material, at first while in a hypnotic trance and later while not in a trance. This use of hypnosis continues today and is often part of a treatment program for people with dissociative disorders (Butler et al., 1996), including dissociative amnesia and DID (Putnam & Loewenstein, 1993). Here we examine hypnotic treatment for DID as it has been used from the perspective of the posttraumatic model, and we see how it leads to feedback loops among neurological, psychological, and social factors.

ONLINE

Researchers have investigated the neurological changes that occur as a result of hypnosis and established that hypnosis alters brain events (Crawford et al., 1993; Kosslyn et al., 2000; Spiegel et al., 1985). The specific brain changes vary, however, depending on the task being performed during the hypnotic trance. When hypnotized, patients may be able to retrieve information that was previously dissociated; in turn, this may allow them to experience perceptions and memories in a more normal way (psychological factor).

In addition, hypnosis can be induced only when patients are willing to be hypnotized, and the beneficial effects of hypnosis occur when patients go along with the therapist's hypnotic suggestions (social factor). In turn, the hypnotic state brings about changes in brain activity (neurological factor), which ultimately might play a role in integrating the stored information that was previously dissociated.

Thinking Like A Clinician

The leading story of the evening news was that a 17-year-old young man murdered his stepfather. The boy said that his stepfather brutally abused him as a child, and local medical and emergency room records indicate numerous "accidents" that were consistent with such abuse. The young man also said that he has no memory of killing his stepfather; his defense attorney and several psychiatrists claim that he has DID and that an alter killed the stepfather. Based on what you have read in this chapter, how might this young man have developed this disorder? (Mention neurological, psychological, and social factors and possible feedback loops.) What would be appropriate treatments for him, and why? Do think it is fair to punish a patient with DID for what an alter did? Why or why not?

Somatic symptom disorders
A category of psychological disorders characterized by symptoms about physical well-being along with cognitive distortions about bodily symptoms and their meaning; the focus on these bodily symptoms causes significant distress or impaired functioning.

TABLE 8.7 • Common Bodily Complaints of Patients with Somatic Symptom Disorders

- Muscle and joint pain
- Palpitations
- Lower back pain
- Irritable bowel
- Tension headache
- Dizziness
- Atypical facial pain
- Insomnia
- Chronic fatigue
- Non-ulcer dyspepsia (indigestion)
- Non-cardiac chest pain

Source: Mayou & Farmer, 2002. For more information see the Permissions section.

University Library, Leipzig, Germany/Archives Charmet/The Bridgeman Art Library

Symptoms of somatic symptom disorders have existed for millennia and were written about in the *Papyrus Ebers*, an ancient Egyptian medical document dating to 1600 B.C.E. However, the Egyptians believed that these symptoms had an underlying medical cause.

Somatic Symptom Disorders

During the course of her illness, Anna O. developed medical symptoms that her doctors could not explain. For instance, she saw an eye doctor for problems with her vision, but he was unable to identify the cause (Breuer & Freud, 1895/1955). Similarly, doctors were unable to find a medical explanation for her chronic cough. How might persistent medically unexplained physical symptoms such as these arise? How should they best be treated? Such bodily symptoms (also called *somatic* symptoms) may fall under the category of *somatic symptom disorders* in DSM-5.

Somatic Symptom Disorders: An Overview

The hallmark of **somatic symptom disorders** is complaints about physical well-being along with cognitive distortions about bodily symptoms and their meaning; the focus on these bodily symptoms causes significant distress or impaired functioning. With these disorders, it is the person's response to bodily symptoms that is notable and excessive. Common bodily complaints of patients with somatic symptom disorders are listed in Table 8.7.

Somatic symptom disorders are relatively rare in the general population but are the most common type of psychological disorder in medical settings (Bass et al., 2001). The medical costs of caring for patients with somatic symptom disorders are substantial; according to one estimate, these costs come to over $250 billion each year in the United States alone (Barsky et al., 2005).

Somatic symptom disorders are not new phenomena; they have a long history, although different labels have been given to them over time. They were described by the ancient Greek philosopher Hippocrates, who thought that somatic symptoms—generally reported by women—were caused by a wandering uterus, from which the term *hysteria* is derived (*hystera* is Greek for "uterus"; Phillips, 2001). *Hysteria* was often used to refer to bodily symptoms that lack a medical explanation, as was true of Anna O.; in addition, patients with hysteria typically describe their symptoms dramatically.

One somatic symptom disorder that must be distinguished from the others is *factitious disorder*, mentioned in Chapter 3, in which people *intentionally* induce symptoms or falsely report symptoms that they do not in fact have in order to receive attention from others. People who have any of the other somatic symptom disorders neither pretend to have symptoms nor intentionally induce physical symptoms for any type of gain. (However, in DSM-5, factitious disorder is considered a somatic symptom disorder because bodily symptoms may be among those feigned.)

Putting aside factitious disorder, somatic symptom disorders share two common features (Looper & Kirmayer, 2002):

1. *bodily preoccupation*, which is similar to the heightened awareness of panic-related bodily sensations experienced by people with panic disorder (see Chapter 6), except that with somatic symptom disorders, the patient can be preoccupied with any aspect of bodily functioning; and

2. *symptom amplification*, or directing attention to bodily symptoms such as those in Table 8.7, which in turn intensifies the symptoms (Kirmayer & Looper, 2006; Looper & Kirmayer, 2002). A common example of symptom amplification occurs when someone with a headache pays attention to the headache—and, invariably, the pain worsens.

In the following sections, we focus on three of these disorders in turn—*somatic symptom disorder*, *conversion disorder*, and *illness anxiety disorder*.

Somatic Symptom Disorder

The hallmark of **somatic symptom disorder (SSD)** is at least one somatic symptom that is distressing or disrupts daily life, about which the person has excessive thoughts, feelings, or behaviors (American Psychiatric Association, 2013). For example, Anna O.'s eye problems and her cough were both physical symptoms that disrupted her daily life. Because the name of the disorder and this category of disorders are so similar (the former is singular and the latter plural), we will abbreviate the disorder as SSD.

What Is Somatic Symptom Disorder?

To be diagnosed with SSD according to DSM-5 criteria, the person must have at least one distressing or impairing bodily symptom and respond excessively to it. Examples of an excessive response are unrealistic thoughts about the seriousness of the symptoms, significant anxiety about the symptoms or health in general, or devoting excessive amount of time and energy to it—such as seeing multiple doctors when such visits aren't necessary. For instance, a man who had a heart attack might become preoccupied with his heart rate and be afraid to go up and down stairs, lest he increase his heart rate and have another heart attack—despite his doctor's assuring him that walking on stairs would be okay. Sometimes the single bodily symptom is pain (American Psychiatric Association, 2013). Table 8.8 lists the DSM-5 diagnostic criteria for SSD.

A clinician diagnoses SSD only if the person's response to the symptoms is more extreme than what would be expected based on the medical assessment. SSD must be distinguished from various other disorders, including anxiety disorders. Many laboratory tests and visits to doctors may be required to rule out other medical and psychological diagnoses, which is necessary before a diagnosis of SSD can be made (Hilty et al., 2001). Table 8.9 lists additional facts about SSD.

People with SSD may avoid certain activities that they believe are associated with their bodily symptoms, such as any type of exercise. In so doing, patients attempt to minimize the physical sensations associated with the disorder. As a result, they may become so out of shape that even normal daily activities, such as walking to a store from the parking lot, may lead them to experience bodily symptoms—which creates a vicious cycle of avoidance and increased bodily symptoms, impairing daily life. For people with SSD, these symptoms impair daily life, which is what happened to Edward in Case 8.4.

TABLE 8.8 • DSM-5 Diagnostic Criteria for Somatic Symptom Disorder

A. One or more somatic symptoms that are distressing or result in significant disruption of daily life.

B. Excessive thoughts, feelings, or behaviors related to the somatic symptoms or associated health concerns as manifested by at least one of the following:

1. Disproportionate and persistent thoughts about the seriousness of one's symptoms.

2. Persistently high level of anxiety about health or symptoms.

3. Excessive time and energy devoted to these symptoms or health concerns.

C. Although any one somatic symptom may not be continuously present, the state of being symptomatic is persistent (typically more than 6 months).

Reprinted with permission from the Diagnostic and Statistical Manual of Mental Disorders, Fifth Edition, (Copyright ©2013). American Psychiatric Association. All Rights Reserved.

CASE 8.4 • FROM THE OUTSIDE: Somatic Symptom Disorder

As an infant, Edward had scarlet fever and a mild form of epilepsy, from which he recovered. By school age, he was complaining of stomachaches and joint pain and often missed school. There were many doctors, but no dire diagnosis: Edward was healthy, but many commented, a somewhat lonely and serious little boy.

Through high school and college Edward capitalized on those traits, achieving high grades and going into the insurance business. At forty-five, he is plagued by mysterious symptoms—heart palpitations, dizziness, indigestion, pain in his shoulders, back, and neck, and fatigue—and lives with his parents. His physical disabilities have made it impossible for Edward to hold a job, and his engagement was broken off. He remains on disability and spends much of his time in and out of hospitals undergoing various tests and procedures.

(Cantor, 1996, p. 54)

Somatic symptom disorder (SSD)
A somatic symptom disorder characterized by at least one somatic symptom that is distressing or disrupts daily life, about which the person has excessive thoughts, feelings, or behaviors.

TABLE 8.9 • Somatic Symptom Disorder Facts at a Glance

Prevalence

- About 5–7% of the general population is estimated to have somatic symptom disorder (SSD).

- SSD is a serious problem in medical settings; patients with this disorder use at least three times as many outpatient medical services and cost at least nine times more to treat than people who do not have this disorder (Hollifield et al., 1999).

Comorbidity

- People with SSD often have other psychological disorders, most frequently an anxiety disorder (particularly panic disorder) or depression.

- Patients with SSD who take benzodiazepines or narcotics for relief of bodily symptoms are at increased risk for developing a substance-related disorder (Holder-Perkins & Wise, 2001).

Onset

- Initial symptoms of SSD can emerge any time between childhood and old age.

Course

- Symptoms may fluctuate in location or in intensity (so that the criteria for SSD are no longer met), but symptoms usually never completely disappear.

- Patients with SSD often take many medications and receive numerous medical tests and diagnoses (Holder-Perkins & Wise, 2001), and they can be extremely sensitive to medication side effects.

Gender Differences

- Women are more likely to have this disorder, or at least are more likely to report bodily symptoms than are men.

Cultural Differences

- The specific symptoms of patients with SSD vary across cultures, and some ethnic groups have a higher prevalence of this disorder than others.

Source: Unless otherwise noted, the source is American Psychiatric Association, 2013.

In an effort to minimize their bodily symptoms, people with somatic symptom disorder may restrict their activities. If this model were suffering from somatic symptom disorder, his inactivity could create additional symptoms (such as back pain) or make existing symptoms worse (such as increased heart rate or difficulty breathing).

Understanding Somatic Symptom Disorder

SSD can be fully understood only by considering multiple factors, including genetics, bodily preoccupation, symptom amplification and catastrophic thinking, and other people's responses to illness.

Neurological Factors: Genetics

Most of the progress in understanding the neurological factors that underlie SSD has been in the area of genetics. For example, in a large-scale twin study, researchers found that genetic effects may account for as much as half of the variability in SSD (Kendler, Walters, et al., 1995). Note, however, that this finding does not imply that the disorder itself is necessarily inherited; it could be that temperament or other characteristics that are influenced by genetics predispose a person to develop the disorder in certain environments. (This same point can be made about most findings that link genes to disorders.) Kendler and colleagues (1995) also reported that characteristics of families have no consistent effect on whether members of the family develop this disorder. This finding suggests that, in addition to genes, specific experiences of a particular person—not shared experiences among members of a family—affect whether a person develops the disorder.

Psychological Factors: Misinterpretation of Bodily Signals and Coping

Like all other somatic symptom disorders, SSD involves bodily preoccupation and symptom amplification, as well as catastrophic thinking—in this case, about physical sensations or fears of illness. These patients may believe, for example, that headaches indicate a brain tumor. Their mental processes—particularly attention—focus on bodily sensations, including the beating of their hearts (Barsky, Cleary, et al., 1993, 1994), leading to symptom amplification and catastrophic thinking. These effects also arise in part from faulty beliefs about their bodies and bodily sensations. For example, people with SSD may erroneously believe that health is the absence of *any* uncomfortable physical sensations (Rief & Nanke, 1999). People who do not have a somatic symptom disorder do not habitually develop catastrophic misinterpretations of such sensations.

Somatic symptoms can also serve as a coping strategy, leading the person to focus attention away from a stressor and onto a bodily sensation. This observation can help to explain why somatic symptom disorders, including SSD, sometimes develop after the death of a loved one (as happened to Anna O. after her father died) or after another significant stressor (Hiller et al., 2002).

Social Factors: Observational Learning and Culture

Observational learning may also play a role in SSD. Such learning can explain the finding that people with SSD are more likely than those without the disorder to have had an ill parent (Bass & Murphy, 1995; Craig et al., 1993).

In these cases, an ill parent may have inadvertently modeled illness behavior. Moreover, operant conditioning can also be at work, when people reinforce a person's illness behavior: During the patient's childhood, family members may have unintentionally reinforced illness behavior by paying extra attention to the child or buying special treats for the child when he or she was ill (Craig et al., 2004; Holder-Perkins & Wise, 2001). Similarly, adults with SSD may be reinforced for their symptoms by the attention of medical personnel, family, friends, or coworkers (Maldonado & Spiegel, 2001).

In addition, in many cultures—including in the United States—somatic symptoms may be regarded as an acceptable way to express helplessness, such as by those who experienced abuse during childhood (Walling et al., 1994). The use of somatic symptoms to express helplessness may explain the bodily symptoms of Anna O. and other upper-middle-class women of the Victorian era, whose lives were severely restricted by societal conventions. However, although symptoms of SSD occur around the globe, the nature of the symptoms differs across cultures. For instance, symptoms of burning hands or feet are more common in Africa and South Asia than in Europe or North America (American Psychiatric Association, 2000).

Children whose parents have chronic pain may be more likely to report pain themselves.

Feedback Loops in Understanding Somatic Symptom Disorder

It is common for people with SSD to have had a disease, an illness, an accident, or another form of trauma prior to developing the disorder. In fact, people with this disorder are more likely to report a history of childhood abuse than are other medical patients (Brown et al., 2005). People who are genetically predisposed to SSD (neurological factor), interpret the bodily sensations caused by an illness or accident as signaling a catastrophic illness (psychological factor). In turn, this misinterpretation may cause the person to change his or her behavior in a way that ultimately becomes dysfunctional, restricting activities and straining relationships.

Such misinterpretations may initially grow out of modeling. For example, children whose parents have chronic pain are more likely to report abdominal pain themselves

FIGURE 8.1 • Feedback Loops in Understanding Somatic Symptom Disorder

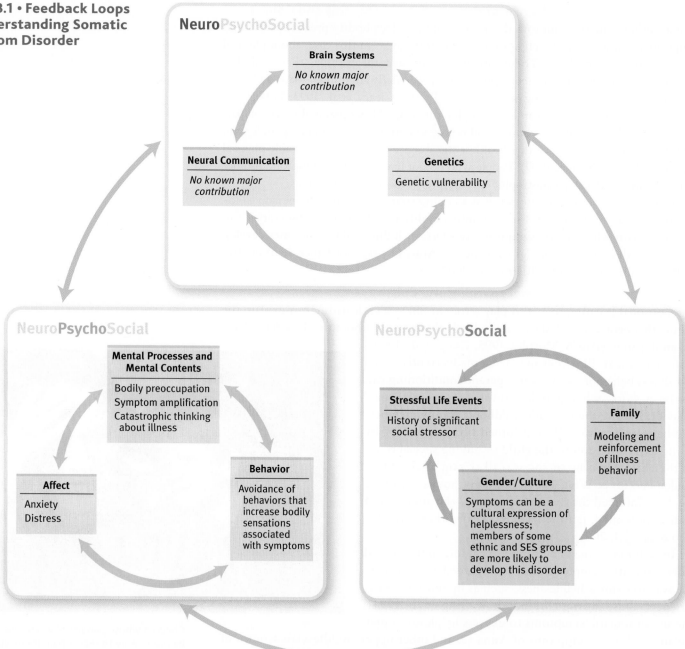

and to use more pain relievers than a comparison group of children (Jamison & Walker, 1992). These children's experiences with their ill parent (social factor) may influence their body via their brains (perhaps they have more stomach acid because they are more anxious and stressed; neurological factor), their attention to and attributions for bodily sensations (psychological factors), and their reporting of pain (social factor).

Moreover, a patient's symptoms may have been unintentionally reinforced by friends and family members (social factor). And, as with panic disorder (see Chapter 6), the arousal that occurs in response to stress can increase troubling bodily sensations that then become the focus of preoccupations (see Figure 8.1).

Conversion Disorder

Conversion disorder involves sensory or motor symptoms that are incompatible or inconsistent with known neurological or medical conditions.

Conversion disorder
A somatic symptom disorder that involves sensory or motor symptoms that are incompatible with known neurological and medical conditions.

What Is Conversion Disorder?

Patients who have conversion disorder do not consciously produce the symptoms they experience (as in factitious disorder or malingering), and these patients are significantly distressed or their functioning is impaired by the symptoms (see Table 8.10). Conversion disorder is similar to SSD in that both involve physical symptoms; however, conversion disorder is limited to sensory and motor symptoms that appear to be neurological (that is, related to the nervous system) but, on closer examination, are inconsistent with the effects of known neurological or medical disorders (see Figure 8.2). A diagnosis of conversion disorder can be made only after physicians rule out all possible medical causes—and this process can take years. Conversion disorder is sometimes referred to as *functional neurological symptom disorder* because the neurological symptom relates to the *functioning* of some aspect of the nervous system but not to an underlying medical cause of the symptom.

Conversion disorder is characterized by one or more of three types of symptoms (American Psychiatric Association, 2000; Maldonado & Speigel, 2001):

- *Motor symptoms.* Examples include tremors that become worse when the person pays attention to them, tics or jerks, muscle spasms, swallowing problems, staggering, and paralysis (sometimes referred to as *pseudoparalysis*, which may also involve significant muscle weakness).

- *Sensory symptoms.* Examples include blindness, double vision, deafness, auditory hallucinations, and lack of feeling on the skin that doesn't correspond to what is produced by malfunctioning of an actual nerve path.

- *Seizures.* Examples include not only the motor symptoms of twitching or jerking of some part of the body but also loss of consciousness with uncontrollable spasms of the large muscles in the body, causing the person to writhe on the floor. These seizures are often referred to as *nonepileptic seizures* because they do not have a neurological origin and are not usually affected by medication for seizures. The nonepileptic seizures are likely to occur when other people are present.

Anna O. had both motor conversion symptoms (paralysis of her neck, arm, and legs) and sensory conversion symptoms (problems with vision, a lack of sensation in her elbows). Breuer did not report any seizure-like symptoms.

In conversion disorder, symptoms do not correspond to what would be produced by the relevant nerve pathways, but rather they arise from the patients' (perhaps unconscious) *ideas about* what would happen if certain nerve pathways were disrupted. Thus, a patient may not be able to write but can scratch an itch, which would be impossible with true paralysis of the hand muscles. Similarly, when the sensory symptom of blindness occurs in conversion disorder, medical tests reveal that all parts of the visual system function normally, as was true for Mary, described in Case 8.5.

CASE 8.5 • FROM THE INSIDE: Conversion Disorder

On graduating from high school, Mary decided to enter a convent, and by the age of 21 had taken her vows of poverty, chastity, and obedience. This came as a shock to her family, who, although they were practicing Catholics, had been far from religious. "I had a great need to help people and do something spiritual and good," Mary recalls. . . .

For the first decade she enjoyed the sense of community and the studious aspect of convent life. . . . But as time went on she became disenchanted with the church, which she felt was "out of touch with real people. . . . The church required blind obedience and no disagreement."

Mary began feeling nervous and anxious. She was rarely sick, but one day [when she was 36 years old] developed soreness in the back of her eye. Every time she moved it, she'd feel pins and needles. . . . By the fourth day she couldn't see out of one eye. A neurologist said it was optic neuritis, a diagnosis of nerve inflammation of unknown origin. She was hospitalized and given cortisone, but her sight didn't improve.

TABLE 8.10 • DSM-5 Diagnostic Criteria for Conversion Disorder (Functional Neurological Symptom Disorder)

A. One or more symptoms of altered voluntary motor or sensory function.

B. Clinical findings provide evidence of incompatibility between the symptom and recognized neurological or medical conditions.

C. The symptom or deficit is not better explained by another medical or mental disorder.

D. The symptom or deficit causes clinically significant distress or impairment in social, occupational, or other important areas of functioning or warrants medical evaluation.

Reprinted with permission from the Diagnostic and Statistical Manual of Mental Disorders, Fifth Edition, (Copyright ©2013). American Psychiatric Association. All Rights Reserved.

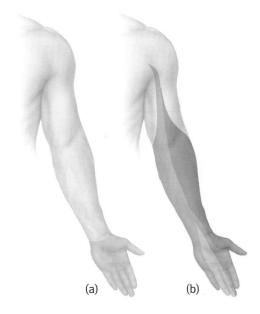

(a)   (b)

FIGURE 8.2 • Conversion Disorder: Glove Anesthesia Patients who suffer from conversion disorder have sensory or motor symptoms that at first may appear to be neurological but on further investigation do not correspond to true neurological damage. One example is glove anesthesia, in which the person reports that his or her hand—and only the hand—has no sensation, as shown in (a). However, the neural pathways that would create such an anesthesia in the hand would also create a lack of sensation in the arm (b); the color-coded regions show the areas served by different nerves. Thus, conversion disorder may be the appropriate diagnosis when a patient reports glove anesthesia in the absence of anesthesia of the arm.

> . . . Mary took a leave of absence and spent the good part of a year at a less stressful convent in the countryside. She began meeting regularly with a psychologist. . . . "I discovered I was a perfectionist, overworking to avoid my growing doubts.". . . Her eyesight gradually came back, and shortly after that she left the church.
>
> . . . "During that period in my life I was undergoing deep psychological trauma. I was so unhappy, and I literally didn't want to see," she says. "I believed then, as I do today, that the body was telling me something, and I had to listen to it."
>
> (Cantor, 1996, pp. 57–58)

People with conversion disorder may react in radically different ways to their symptoms and to what they might imply: Some seem indifferent whereas others respond dramatically. Anna O.'s response was "a slight exaggeration, alike of cheerfulness and gloom; hence she was sometimes subject to moods" (Breuer & Freud, 1895/1955, p. 21). Table 8.11 provides more facts about conversion disorder.

TABLE 8.11 • Conversion Disorder Facts at a Glance

Prevalence

- Persistent conversion disorder is very rare, with prevalence estimates from 0.001% to 0.005% in the general population and up to 5% of those who are referred to neurologists.

Comorbidity

- Studies have found that up to 85% of people with conversion disorder also have major depressive disorder (Roy, 1980; Ziegler et al., 1960); comorbid anxiety disorders are also common.
- Patients with conversion disorder may also have a neurological disorder, such as multiple sclerosis or a condition that produces seizures (Maldonado & Spiegel, 2001).
- A history of sexual or physical abuse is common among patients with conversion disorder (Bowman, 1993).

Onset

- This disorder can arise throughout life.
- Symptoms typically emerge suddenly after a significant stressor, such as the loss of a loved one, or a physical injury (Stone et al., 2009).
- For men, the disorder is most likely to develop in the context of the military or industrial accidents (American Psychiatric Association, 2000; Maldonado & Spiegel, 2001).

Course

- Symptoms typically last only a brief period of time.
- Between 25% and 67% of those with the disorder have a recurrence up to 4 years later (Maldonado & Spiegel, 2001).

Gender Differences

- Conversion disorder is two to three times more common among women than men.

Cultural Differences

- Conversion disorder is more common in rural populations, among those from lower SES backgrounds, and among those less knowledgeable about psychological and medical concepts.
- It is also more common in developing countries than in industrialized countries, and as a country becomes industrialized, the prevalence of conversion disorder decreases.
- Small "epidemics" of conversion disorder have been reported in countries undergoing cultural change or significant stress (Piñeros et al., 1998; Cassady et al., 2005).

Source: Unless otherwise noted, the source is American Psychiatric Association, 2000, 2013.

Criticisms of the DSM-5 Criteria

Both the diagnosis of conversion disorder and its placement among the somatic symptom disorders are controversial (Brown & Lewis-Fernández, 2011). Some researchers have suggested that conversion disorder is not a distinct disorder but rather a variant of SSD; these researchers point out that both disorders may involve the bodily expression of psychological distress (Bourgeois et al., 2002). Other researchers believe that conversion symptoms in general, and nonepileptic seizures in particular, are more like dissociative symptoms than like symptoms of other somatic symptom disorders (Kihlstrom, 2001; Mayou et al., 2005). As they note, dissociation can not only affect memory and the sense of self but also can disrupt the integration of sensory or motor functioning.

Understanding Conversion Disorder

Research on neurological factors in conversion disorder focuses on how brain systems operate differently in people with the disorder than in other people.

Neurological Factors: Not Faking It

When considering making a diagnosis of conversion disorder, clinicians must rule out simple malingering, or faking of symptoms, which is difficult to do (Stone et al., 2010). Could all cases of conversion disorder just be faking? Neuroimaging findings suggest that muscle weakness arising from conversion disorder is not the same as consciously simulated muscle weakness. For example, Stone and colleagues (2007) scanned the brains of patients with conversion disorder and of healthy control participants while their ankles were flexed. The patients with conversion disorder all reported weakness in the manipulated ankle prior to the study; during the study, participants in the control group were asked to pretend that their ankles were weak. The results were clear: Some brain areas were more activated in the patients than in the controls (such as the insula, which is involved in registering bodily sensations), and some brain areas (including areas in the frontal lobes) were less activated in the patients than in the controls. These findings are good evidence that the patients in this study were not simply faking their disorder.

In addition, some patients with chronic pain develop sensory deficits, a kind of "psychological" anesthesia. In one study, researchers scanned the brains of four such patients, using fMRI, while sharp plastic fibers were pressed into the skin (Mailis-Gagnon et al., 2003). These patients had apparent sensory deficits in only one limb, and thus the researchers could directly compare stimulation of the normal and affected limbs. When the researchers stimulated the normal limb, the sharp plastic fibers activated a brain network that registers pain, as is normal. In contrast, this network was not activated when the researchers stimulated the affected limb, as is shown in Figure 8.3. These findings indicate that the "psychological" anesthesia actually affected the brain and inhibited activation in the brain areas that register sensation and pain.

Other studies have shown that conversion disorder is not a direct consequence of abnormal functioning of brain areas that *register* peripheral sensations but rather reflects abnormal functioning of brain areas that *interpret* sensations and *manage* other brain areas (that is, areas that are involved in "executive functions") (Hoechstetter et al., 2002; Lorenz et al., 1998). At least in some cases, abnormal processing in brain areas responsible for executive functions might inhibit brain areas that process sensation and pain or that produce movements, which in turn causes them to fail to function properly.

Psychological Factors: Self-Hypnosis?

There is no generally accepted explanation for how psychological factors might produce the selective bodily symptoms in conversion disorder (Halligan, Athwal, et al., 2000). But self-hypnosis offers one possible explanation—that the disorder is the

FIGURE 8.3 • Brain Activation in Conversion Disorder: Healthy Limb Versus Affected Limb Brain areas activated when the skin of the healthy, nonaffected limb was stimulated (top row) compared to those activated when the skin of the affected limb was stimulated (bottom row); arrows show the key areas of activation (Mailis-Gagnon et al., 2003). It's clear that the scans in the bottom row show much less activation.

Source: A. Mailis-Gagnon, M.D., et al., *Neurology* 2003;60:1501–1507. © 2003 American Academy of Neurology.

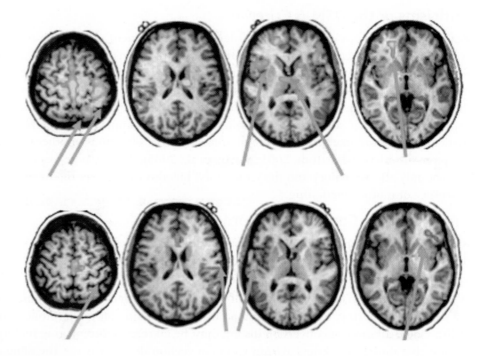

Symptoms of conversion disorder may be more common after significant psychological stressors, such as military combat. This soldier is displaying muscular spasms as part of his conversion disorder. Such symptoms among soldiers are thought to resolve a conflict between their loyalty to comrades and their fear of battle: Soldiers with such symptoms are unable to fight (Spiegel, 1974).

Illness anxiety disorder
A somatic symptom disorder marked by a preoccupation with a fear or belief of having a serious disease in the face of either no or minor medical symptoms and excessive behaviors related to this belief.

result of unintended self-hypnotic suggestion. According to this theory, patients have, consciously or unconsciously, "suggested" to themselves that they have symptoms (Kozlowska, 2005); that is, particular sensations have become dissociated. This theory receives support from the fact that people with conversion disorder are unusually hypnotizable (Roelofs, Hoogduin, et al., 2002) and from the finding that areas of the brain activated by hypnotically induced paralysis are similar to those activated by paralysis in patients with conversion disorder (Halligan, Bass, & Wade, 2000; Oakley, 1999).

Social Factors: Stress Response

Life stressors, such as combat, can trigger conversion disorder. Moreover, the greater the severity or number of stressors, the more severe the conversion symptoms (Roelofs et al., 2005). As we saw with SSD, somatic symptoms can be a culturally accepted way to express feelings of helplessness (Celani, 1976), which may explain why some soldiers develop conversion disorder in combat. Conversion disorder can also be a way to obtain the attention associated with being sick. This was certainly true for Anna O., as well as for many other women of the Victorian era.

Illness Anxiety Disorder

People who are diagnosed with **illness anxiety disorder** have either no or minor medical symptoms but nonetheless are preoccupied with a fear or belief that they have a serious disease; they engage in excessive behaviors related to this belief, such as repeatedly checking their bodies for sign of an illness or avoiding medical care. Despite the fact that physicians cannot identify a medical problem, patients with illness anxiety disorder persist in clinging strongly to their conviction that they have a serious disease. This diagnosis is in some ways similar to the DSM-IV diagnosis of *hypochondriasis*. However, in DSM-IV the disorder hypochondriasis included two groups of people—those without any significant medical symptoms (now classified as illness anxiety disorder) and those with at least one medical symptom but whose psychological response to the symptom is excessive (now classified as somatic symptom disorder). Although people with SSD and those with illness anxiety disorder share a

Omission of Hypochondriasis from DSM-5: Appropriate or Overreaction?

The previous edition of the DSM, DSM-IV, included the diagnosis of *hypochondriasis*, which pertained to people who worry excessively about their physical symptoms or about potential illnesses. This term was not included in DSM-5, partly because the DSM-5 team felt it had become pejorative (e.g., "acting like a hypochondriac") (American Psychiatric Association, 2013). As noted in this chapter, people previously diagnosed with hypochondriasis are now diagnosed either with *somatic symptom disorder* (in which the response to physical symptoms is greater than would be expected) or *illness anxiety disorder* (in which patients worry persistently about potentially having or developing a medical condition). Is this change warranted?

On one hand, it is not clear that the new categories make sense. If illness anxiety is so different from worries about actual symptoms, then why isn't it grouped with anxiety disorders (Frances, 2013)? If the difference is about the presence of actual bodily symptoms, maybe instead of two separate categories, we might have two traits that each fall on a spectrum of intensity of physical symptoms and levels of anxiety.

On the other hand, the new, separate diagnoses are useful because they may lead more people to appropriate treatment; both disorders apply to people who are more likely to go, at least initially, to a medical doctor's office rather than a mental health clinician's office. And physicians may be more likely to use the new labels because they feel the new labels are less pejorative—at least for now.

CRITICAL THINKING Which of these three diagnoses—hypochondriasis, SSD, or illness anxiety disorder—do you think is most pejorative, and which do you think is least stigmatizing? Why? How would you explain each of these diagnoses to patients?

(James Foley, College of Wooster)

---

focus on bodily symptoms, only people with illness anxiety disorder believe that they have a serious illness, despite reassurance from doctors and minimal physical symptoms, if any.

What Is Illness Anxiety Disorder?

Patients with illness anxiety disorder may or may not realize that their worries are excessive for the situation; when they do not, they are said to have *poor insight* into their condition. Consider a man who sees floating "spots" and does not believe his eye doctor when told that such *floaters* are normal and nothing to worry about. The man probably doesn't think that the doctor is lying about the spots, but he may believe that the doctor didn't do a thorough enough eye examination; he may think that the floaters indicate that he is going blind or that he has a tumor. His worries about this problem are distressing and preoccupying to the point that he functions less well at work—not because of the floaters but because of his frequent thoughts about the floaters.

People with this disorder may spend hours on the Internet, searching for illness-related information to reassure themselves, only to become more anxious or worried (Starcevic & Berle, 2013). To be diagnosed with this disorder, this kind of preoccupation with a perceived health problem must cause significant distress or impair the person's functioning and must have continued for at least 6 months (see Table 8.12). Because illness anxiety disorder is a newly defined disorder and most people (75%) previously diagnosed with hypochondriasis would now be diagnosed with somatic symptom disorder, additional facts about illness anxiety disorder, such as prevalence and course, are not known at this time. However, two thirds of people with this disorder are estimated to have at least one other psychological disorder, commonly anxiety or depressive disorders, and the disorder typically begins in early to middle adulthood (American Psychiatric Association, 2013).

TABLE 8.12 • DSM-5 Diagnostic Criteria for Illness Anxiety Disorder

A. Preoccupation with having or acquiring a serious illness.

B. Somatic symptoms are not present or, if present, are only mild in intensity. If another medical condition is present or there is a high risk for developing a medical condition (e.g., strong family history is present), the preoccupation is clearly excessive or disproportionate.

C. There is a high level of anxiety about health, and the individual is easily alarmed about personal health status.

D. The individual performs excessive health-related behaviors (e.g., repeatedly checks his or her body for signs of illness) or exhibits maladaptive avoidance (e.g., avoids doctor appointments and hospitals).

E. Illness preoccupation has been present for at least 6 months, but the specific illness that is feared may change over that period of time.

F. The illness-related preoccupation is not better explained by another mental disorder, such as somatic symptom disorder, panic disorder, generalized anxiety disorder, body dysmorphic disorder, obsessive compulsive disorder, or delusional disorder, somatic type.

Like people with SSD, those with illness anxiety disorder don't understand that even healthy people sometimes have aches and pains and other bodily discomforts. Instead, like the woman in Case 8.6, they unrealistically believe that having "good health" implies not having any unpleasant bodily symptoms (Barsky, Coeytaux, et al., 1993).

CASE 8.6 • FROM THE INSIDE: Illness Anxiety Disorder

I attended graduate school, held jobs, was married, had children. But my existence was peppered with episodes of illness. When the going got tough, I'd get sick. Or just the opposite: when things seemed to be going well, I'd come down with a symptom, or at least what I interpreted as one. It might be stomach pain, dizziness, black and blue marks, swollen glands, an achy heel. Anything. Whatever the symptoms, I always interpreted it as a precursor of some crippling illness: leukemia, Lou Gehrig's disease, scleroderma. I knew just enough about most diseases to cause trouble. Eventually I'd get past each episode, but it always took time—the cure a mysterious concoction of enough negative tests, a lessening of symptoms, some positive change in my life. And when the event was over, the realization that I was healthy and wasn't going to die, at least not immediately, was like a high, a reprieve, a new lease on life. That is, until the next time.

(Cantor, 1996, pp. 9–10)

Illness Anxiety Disorder, Anxiety Disorders, and OCD: Shared Features

Illness anxiety disorder has many features in common with anxiety disorders. In fact, certain forms of illness anxiety disorder and anxiety disorders are so similar that some researchers have advocated moving illness anxiety disorder from the category of somatic symptom disorders to the category of anxiety disorders (Mayou et al., 2005). Illness anxiety disorder, phobias, and panic disorder are all characterized by high levels of fear and anxiety, as well as a faulty belief of harm or danger. However, with illness anxiety disorder and panic disorder, the perceived danger is from an internal event that is thought to be producing a bodily sensation, whereas with phobias, it is from an external object (such as a snake) or a situation (such as giving a speech; Fava, Mangelli, & Ruini, 2001). People with panic disorder, phobias, and illness anxiety disorder all may try to avoid certain stimuli or situations; with panic disorder and illness anxiety disorder, what is avoided may be an elevated heart rate (Hiller et al., 2002).

In addition, both patients with illness anxiety disorder and those with obsessive-compulsive disorder (OCD) have obsessions and compulsions (Abramowitz & Braddock, 2006). In particular, patients with illness anxiety disorder obsess about possible illnesses or diseases they believe they might have. They may compulsively ask doctors, friends, or family members for reassurance or compulsively "check" their body for particular sensations. People with some forms of illness anxiety disorder spend hours compulsively consulting medical websites. It's important to keep in mind that some medically related Internet chat rooms or websites can spread false or misleading information.

Understanding Illness Anxiety Disorder

Because illness anxiety disorder is a diagnosis new to DSM-5, most research related to this disorder studied people diagnosed with hypochondriasis. Hence we use the term hypochondriasis when discussing studies of people with that diagnosis, and the term illness anxiety disorder when discussing experiences and symptoms that clearly apply to the new disorder. Most research has examined psychological factors, and not enough is known about neurological and social factors to understand the feedback loops among the types of factors.

Neurological Factors

Some researchers have suggested that the neurotransmitter serotonin does not function properly in at least some cases (King, 1990). As we'll see in the section on treatment, there is some indirect support for this hypothesis, based on the observation that SSRIs (which selectively affect serotonin reuptake) appear to improve the disorder. That is, the mere fact that SSRIs can improve the symptoms is evidence that the symptoms arise, at least in part, from disruption of the activity of serotonin. In addition, results from one twin study suggest that genetic differences contribute to hypochondriasis (Gillespie et al., 2000).

Psychological Factors: Catastrophic Thinking About the Body

People with hypochondriasis have specific biases in their reasoning: Not surprisingly, given their disorder, they both tend to seek evidence of health threats and also may fail to consider evidence that such threats are minimal or nonexistent (Salkovskis, 1996; Smeets et al., 2000). For instance, a man with illness anxiety disorder who notices a bruise on his leg might interpret it as evidence that he has leukemia rather than try to remember whether he recently bumped into something that could cause a black-and-blue mark.

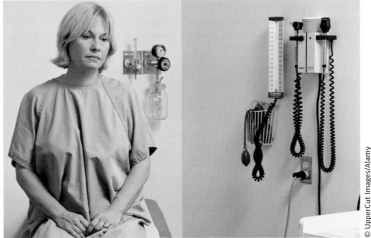

In addition, people afflicted with illness anxiety disorder focus attention closely on unpleasant sensations. They commonly focus on the functioning of body parts (such as the stomach or the heart), minor physical problems (such as a sore throat), and ambiguous physical sensations (such as "aching veins"). Moreover, they interpret bodily sensations as abnormal, pathological, and symptomatic of disease (Barsky, 1992; Barsky et al., 2000). In fact, like patients with SSD, patients with hypochondriasis (and likely with illness anxiety disorder) may engage in *catastrophic thinking* about their physical sensations or fears of illness, just as the woman in Case 8.6 did when she interpreted physical sensations as signs of "crippling illness."

As is the case with many anxiety disorders, people with illness anxiety disorder may engage in behaviors that temporarily reduce their anxiety. For example, they may repeatedly take their blood pressure, perform urine dipstick tests, feel body parts for cancerous lumps, or call their doctor about new symptoms. Such behaviors maintain their faulty beliefs and can, through negative reinforcement, sustain their anxiety in the long term.

Concern for one's health is normal. How do we begin to assess when the concern is excessive?

Social Factors: Stress Response

As with other somatic symptom disorders, research has shown that stressful events can precipitate hypochondriasis (Fallon & Feinstein, 2001). In addition, such people are more likely than people without the disorder to report having experienced traumatic sexual contact, physical violence, or major familial upheaval (such as their parents' divorce) (Barsky, Wool, et al., 1994). Moreover, through their attention and concern, relatives and friends may unintentionally reinforce patients' symptoms.

Treating Somatic Symptom Disorders

When treating any of the three somatic symptom disorders (SSD, conversion disorder, or illness anxiety disorder), clinicians target neurological, psychological, and social factors—individually or in combination. As we discuss below, cognitive-behavior therapy is generally the treatment of choice for somatic symptom disorders.

Targeting Neurological Factors

There has not been much rigorous research on neurologically-based treatments for somatic symptom disorders in general; the studies that have been reported have rarely included appropriate control groups, such as a placebo group or a wait-list control group to determine whether the disorder spontaneously improves with time. Some treatments target specific symptoms. For instance, medications, such as an SSRI, or St. John's wort may be used to treat some anxiety-related symptoms of somatic symptom disorders. As with anxiety disorders, however, when the medication is stopped, the anxiety-related symptoms usually return. Other types of treatments, such as biofeedback, target muscle tension.

Were Anna O. to be treated by a mental health clinician today, she might receive medication. Anxiety or depression may have contributed to her symptoms, and if medication for these disorders did not alleviate her hallucinations, the clinician might recommend an antipsychotic medication (Martorano, 1984). Note that Anna O. *was* given medications frequently used at that time: morphine (typically given for pain relief) and chloral hydrate (a narcotic used to induce sleep). She became addicted to both of these substances, and after her "talking cure" with Breuer ended, she needed inpatient treatment to end her addiction.

Targeting Psychological Factors: Cognitive-Behavior Therapy

Research indicates that the treatment of choice for most somatic symptom disorders is cognitive-behavior therapy (CBT). As shown in Table 8.13, the cognitive and behavioral methods used to treat each of the disorders vary because each disorder has different symptoms. Cognitive methods focus on identifying and then modifying irrational thoughts and shifting attention away from the body and bodily symptoms (Gropalis et al., 2013). Behavioral methods focus on decreasing compulsive behaviors and avoidance.

Targeting Social Factors: Support and Family Education

Patients with any of the somatic symptom disorders can be helped, in part, merely by feeling that someone understands the pain and distress they feel (Looper & Kirmayer, 2002). For SSD and conversion disorder, the therapist strives to understand the context of the symptoms and of their emergence and the way the symptoms affect the patient's

Perhaps the most effective treatment for leg paralysis due to conversion disorder may be the simplest: Educate the patient about the nature of the symptoms. At least for three patients in one study, simply showing them their normal test results and contradictions from their physical exam did the trick. These patients walked out of the hospital unaided immediately after these results were given to them (Letonoff et al., 2002).

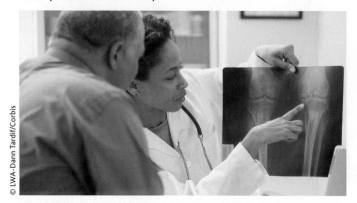

© LWA-Dann Tardif/Corbis

TABLE 8.13 • Cognitive-Behavior Therapy for Somatic Symptom Disorders

Disorder	Cognitive focus	Behavioral focus	Comment
Somatic symptom disorder (SSD)	Psychoeducation; cognitive restructuring to modify faulty or irrational beliefs about bodily sensations; teach patients not to amplify the sensations	Identify and then decrease avoidant behaviors, sensations, and activities that lead to physical or psychological discomfort or restriction of activities[a]; assertiveness training; relaxation to decrease physical tension	CBT is generally the most effective treatment for somatic symptom disorder.[b]
Conversion disorder	Psychoeducation; identify stressors or conflicts associated with the emergence of symptoms; develop alternative ways to resolve the conflict or cope with stressors (problem solving)[c]	Assertiveness training; to decrease symptoms, use paradoxical intention (suggest that the patient continue to have the symptom), as appropriate[d]	Insight-oriented treatment is sometimes used to help patients with conversion disorder understand the meaning of the symptoms. Once the meaning is understood, the symptoms may improve spontaneously.[e]
Illness anxiety disorder	Identify and modify faulty or irrational beliefs about health worries and bodily sensations (cognitive restructuring); teach patients not to amplify these sensations; decrease catastrophic attributions about sensations and illness worries	Identify sensations and activities that lead to discomfort; identify avoidant behaviors and decrease avoidance; use exposure with response prevention for compulsive behaviors such as checking the body, seeking reassurance, or visiting doctors frequently	CBT is the most effective treatment for illness anxiety disorder.[f] Pilot studies have adapted interpersonal therapy to treat illness anxiety disorder, and initial results are promising.[g]

[a]Mayou & Farmer, 2002; O'Malley et al., 1999; [b]Allen et al., 2006; Bass et al., 2001; [c]Maldonado & Spiegel, 2001; [d]Ataoglu et al., 2003; [e]Maldonado & Spiegel, 2001; [f]Barsky & Ahern, 2004; Taylor et al., 2005; Wattar et al., 2005; [g]Stuart & Noyes, 2005; Stuart et al., 2008.

interactions with others (Holder-Perkins & Wise, 2001); with these two disorders, treatment may focus on helping the patient communicate more assertively—which can help to relieve the social stressors that contribute to the disorders.

Treatment may also focus on the family—educating family members about the disorder and the ways they may have inadvertently contributed to or reinforced the patient's symptoms. The therapist may teach family members how to reinforce positive change and to extinguish behavior related to the symptoms (Looper & Kirmayer, 2002; Maldonado & Spiegel, 2001). For instance, if the patient has SSD, family members may be asked *not* to inquire about the patient's bodily symptoms. In addition, support groups may help patients feel less alone and isolated (Looper & Kirmayer, 2002).

Feedback Loops in Treating Somatic Symptom Disorders

CBT can provide new skills and new ways to interpret the sensations and modify the preoccupying thoughts, which in turn can decrease the bodily symptoms (neurological factor) and the attention paid to them (psychological factor). Similarly, although biofeedback and medication primarily target neurological factors, these techniques can in turn affect the type and quality of attention paid to bodily sensations and can change the meaning made of bodily sensations (psychological factors). In addition, the relationship with a therapist (social factor) can provide reassurance and support; as family members change how they respond to the patient's symptoms (social factor), positive change can be enhanced. Figure 8.4 shows how successful treatment of somatic symptom disorders affects the different types of factors directly and through their feedback loops.

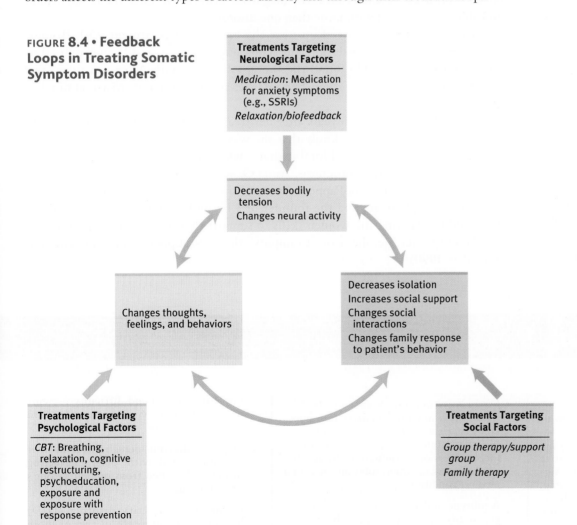

FIGURE **8.4 • Feedback Loops in Treating Somatic Symptom Disorders**

Treatments Targeting Neurological Factors

Medication: Medication for anxiety symptoms (e.g., SSRIs)
Relaxation/biofeedback

Decreases bodily tension
Changes neural activity

Changes thoughts, feelings, and behaviors

Decreases isolation
Increases social support
Changes social interactions
Changes family response to patient's behavior

Treatments Targeting Psychological Factors

CBT: Breathing, relaxation, cognitive restructuring, psychoeducation, exposure and exposure with response prevention

Treatments Targeting Social Factors

Group therapy/support group
Family therapy

Thinking Like A Clinician

Now 57 years old, Mr. Andre left his native Haiti 5 years ago and moved to the United States. Unemployment rates in the United States were high at the time of his arrival, and Mr. Andre had a hard time finding a job; he felt that he was being discriminated against. His wife supported the family for 2 years by cleaning houses. After 2 years of looking, Mr. Andre did get a job. However, within 4 months of starting this job, he had a bout of the flu, and he continued to feel tired even after he recovered from it. He began to worry that he might be developing cancer. (His father had died of cancer.) He went to see his doctor and had a variety of tests that were all negative. Nonetheless, Mr. Andre thinks that the doctors may have "missed something" or not given him the right test. He worries about this, and frequent visits to the doctor mean that he must rearrange his work schedule or miss work. What factors should (and shouldn't) clinicians take into account when evaluating Mr. Andre for some type of somatic symptom disorder? If they do think he has such a disorder, which one do you think it might be, and why? What treatment(s) should be recommended to Mr. Andre if you are correct? On what basis could some of the somatic symptom disorders be ruled out?

Despite Breuer's poor prognosis for Anna's future, she went on to live a full life, becoming an accomplished advocate for and benefactor of poor women and children. In Anna's time, having a psychological disorder was neither a personal disaster nor a signal that life had to become constrained and unrewarding. This is still the case.

Follow-up on Anna O.

Anna O.'s symptoms do not fit neatly into any single one of the disorders discussed in this chapter. She had hallucinations, dissociative symptoms, and bodily symptoms—but they probably wouldn't meet the diagnostic criteria for SSD. Today, she would probably be diagnosed with more than one disorder.

Anna's symptoms cleared up near the end of her treatment with Breuer. However, after their final session, she had a major relapse, and Breuer refused to continue to treat her. He found the therapy sessions with Anna too time- and energy-consuming, and, given her relapse, he was not optimistic about her prognosis.

Anna's history for the 6 years after her treatment with Breuer remains largely unknown, although we do know that she was hospitalized several times for her addiction to morphine and chloral hydrate, which Breuer had prescribed for her. Despite Breuer's negative prognosis, Anna O. went on to accomplish great things. Her real name was Bertha Pappenheim, and she became a social worker, the director of an orphanage, and the founder of a home for unwed mothers that was dedicated to teaching the women skills to support themselves and their children. For the rest of her life, she strove to improve the lives of poor women and children (Freeman, 1990).

SUMMING UP

Dissociative Disorders

- Dissociation involves a separation of mental processes that are normally integrated—such as consciousness, memory, emotion, or identity. To qualify as a dissociative disorder, this separation must cause significant distress or impair functioning. Specific symptoms of dissociative disorders include amnesia, identity problems, derealization, and depersonalization.

- Dissociative amnesia is characterized by significantly impaired memory for important experiences or for personal information that cannot be explained as ordinary forgetfulness or accounted for by another psychological disorder, substance use, or a medical condition.

- A subtype of dissociation amnesia, dissociative fugue, is characterized by sudden, unplanned travel and difficulty remembering the past, which in turn leads to identity confusion.

- Depersonalization-derealization disorder is characterized by the persistent feeling of being detached from oneself or one's surroundings.

- Dissociative identity disorder (DID) hinges on the presence of two or more distinct personality states, which gives rise to a discontinuity in the person's sense of self and agency.

- Although neuroimaging studies of patients with DID find that their brains function differently when different alters are dominant, such studies generally have not used appropriate control groups. People with this disorder are more hypnotizable and dissociate more readily than do people who do not have this disorder.

- Two models have been formulated to explain DID. The posttraumatic model proposes that DID is caused by severe, chronic physical abuse during childhood, which leads to dissociation during the abuse; the dissociated states come to constitute alters, with their own memories and personality traits. The sociocognitive model proposes that DID arises as the result of interactions between a therapist and a suggestible patient, during which the therapist inadvertently encourages the patient to behave in ways consistent with the diagnosis. Both

interpretations are consistent with the finding that severe childhood trauma is associated with the disorder.

- The goal of treatment for dissociative disorders is to reduce the symptoms themselves and lower the stress they induce.

Somatic Symptom Disorders

- Somatic symptom disorders center on complaints about physical well-being along with cognitive distortions about those bodily symptoms and their meaning; the focus on these symptoms causes significant distress or impairs functioning. All somatic symptom disorders involve bodily preoccupation and symptom amplification.

- Somatic symptom disorder (SSD) is characterized by at least one somatic symptom about which the person has excessive thoughts, feelings, or behaviors, and that is distressing or disrupts daily life.

- Factors that contribute to SSD include genes, catastrophic thinking about illness,

symptom amplification, bodily preoccupation, other people's responses to illness, and the way symptoms function as a means of expressing helplessness.

- Conversion disorder centers on sensory systems, motor symptoms, and seizures that may initially appear to have neurological causes but in fact are inconsistent with a neurological or medical condition.

- Illness anxiety disorder is characterized by misinterpretation of or worry about bodily sensations and symptoms, which leads to a belief that the person has a serious illness—despite the absence of evidence of a medical problem and reassurance from health care personnel.

- CBT is generally the treatment of choice for somatic symptom disorders; medications, when used, target anxiety-related symptoms. Group and family therapy are generally used as supplementary treatments.

Key Terms

Hysteria (p. 223)

Dissociation (p. 224)

Amnesia (p. 224)

Identity problem (p. 224)

Derealization (p. 224)

Depersonalization (p. 224)

Dissociative disorders (p. 225)

Dissociative amnesia (p. 226)

Depersonalization-derealization disorder (p. 229)

Dissociative identity disorder (DID) (p. 232)

Somatic symptom disorders (p. 240)

Somatic symptom disorder (SSD) (p. 241)

Conversion disorder (p. 244)

Illness anxiety disorder (p. 248)

More Study Aids

For additional study aids related to this chapter, including quizzes to make sure you've retained everything you've learned and a Student Video Activity exploring methods for treating and coping with pain, go to: www.worthpublishers.com/launchpad/rkabpsych2e.

Image Source

CHAPTER **9**

Substance Use Disorders

The musical group the Beatles were so famous that the four members—John Lennon, Paul McCartney, George Harrison, and Ringo Starr—found that they were essentially prisoners in their hotel rooms when on tour. Frenzied fans would try to steal into the rooms, going so far as to lower themselves down from the hotel roof! Sick of it all, the Beatles stopped touring and just recorded music in the studio. Many of their songs broke all the conventions of rock-and-roll music, and the Beatles developed the first themed rock album, with *Sgt. Pepper's Lonely Hearts Club Band*. The album practically reeked of drug use, and the band members became famous both for their music and for their lifestyles—setting a model for a generation that experimented with mind-altering drugs. Beneath the musical history of the Beatles is a story of substance use and use disorders that illustrates the focus of this chapter.

⬚ Substance Use: When Use Becomes a Disorder

The Beatles used some drugs because that was what their peers did. For instance, almost all boys—and some girls—their age in Liverpool, England, smoked cigarettes. It was simply what was done. Similarly, the young band members drank alcohol; again, doing so was the norm. Sometimes they used a drug specifically for the effect it brought, such as when they took "uppers" (stimulants) to stay awake when performing late at night. When they toured in the early 1960s, they took drugs to relieve the monotony of life on the road; they would swallow a pill, "just to see what would happen" (Norman, 1997, p. 244). A few years later, they took "acid" (LSD) to help them understand the meaning of life and attain enlightenment and peace. All four members of the Beatles tried various psychoactive substances. **Psychoactive substances**, commonly called *drugs*, are chemicals that alter mental ability, mood, or behavior. Frequent use of a psychoactive substance can develop into a substance use disorder.

Psychoactive substance
A chemical that alters mental ability, mood, or behavior.

Michael Ochs Archives/Getty Images

Sgt. Pepper's Lonely Hearts Club Band was the Beatles' first album that incorporated many references to drug use. The album's drug theme also reflects the band members increasing use of mind-altering substances in their personal lives.

According to DSM-5, **substance use disorders** are characterized by a loss of control over urges to use a psychoactive substance, even though such use may impair functioning or cause distress. With substance use disorders, the psychoactive substance is taken repeatedly either because of its effect on mood, behavior, or cognition or because it prevents uncomfortable symptoms if the person stops taking the drug (American Psychiatric Association, 2013). The DSM-5 set of substance use disorders includes specific disorders for each substance. We first discuss substance use disorders in general and then focus on specific substances.

Substance Use Versus Intoxication

The Beatles, individually and collectively, experimented with numerous drugs. Paul McCartney is generally described as having been the most cautious about drugs, whereas John Lennon used them regularly, sometimes continually. At one time or another, each Beatle could have been diagnosed with **substance intoxication**: reversible dysfunctional effects on thoughts, feelings, and behavior that arise from the use of a psychoactive substance (see Table 9.1). The specific effects of substance intoxication depend on the substance and whether a person uses it only occasionally (e.g., getting drunk on Saturday night) or chronically (e.g., drinking to excess every night).

In contrast to substance intoxication, *substance use* is a general term that indicates simply that a person has used a substance—via smoking, swallowing, snorting, injecting, or otherwise absorbing it. This term does not indicate the extent or effect of the exposure to the substance.

TABLE 9.1 • DSM-5 Diagnostic Criteria for Substance Intoxication

- The development of a reversible substance-specific syndrome attributable to recent ingestion of (or exposure to) a substance that is not listed elsewhere or is unknown.
- Clinically significant problematic behavioral or psychological changes that are attributable to the effect of the substance on the central nervous system (e.g., impaired motor coordination, psychomotor agitation or retardation, euphoria, anxiety, belligerence, mood lability, cognitive impairment, impaired judgment, social withdrawal) and develop during, or shortly after, use of the substance.
- The signs or symptoms are not attributable to another medical condition and are not better explained by another mental disorder, including substance intoxication with another substance.

Reprinted with permission from the Diagnostic and Statistical Manual of Mental Disorders, Fifth Edition, (Copyright ©2013). American Psychiatric Association. All Rights Reserved.

Substance use disorders
Psychological disorders that are characterized by loss of control over urges to use a psychoactive substance, even though such use may impair functioning or cause distress.

Substance intoxication
The reversible dysfunctional effects on thoughts, feelings, and behavior that arise from the use of a psychoactive substance.

Substance Use Disorders

The Beatles used stimulants nightly when performing in Germany, but does that mean they were abusing the drugs or had a substance use disorder? Were they addicted? Some mental health clinicians and researchers have avoided using the term *addiction*, partly because of its negative moral connotations. However, other clinicians and researchers are in favor of using the term addiction (O'Brien et al., 2006). Those clinicians and researchers define *addiction* as the compulsion to seek and then use a psychoactive substance either for its pleasurable effects or, with continued use, for relief from negative emotions such as anxiety or sadness. These compulsive behaviors persist, despite negative consequences (American Society of Addiction Medicine, 2011).

Like this definition of addiction, the DSM-5 definition of substance use disorders focuses on the behaviors related to obtaining and using a drug, as well as the consequences of that use. Whereas *intoxication* refers to the direct results of using a substance, the criteria of a *substance use disorder* focus both on the indirect effects of repeated use, such as unmet obligations or risky behavior while using the substance (for instance, driving while under the influence), and the cravings and biological changes

TABLE 9.2 • DSM-5 Diagnostic Criteria for Substance Use Disorders

A. A problematic pattern of use of an intoxicating substance leading to clinically significant impairment or distress, as manifested by at least two of the following, occurring within a 12-month period:

1. The substance is often taken in larger amounts or over a longer period than was intended.

2. There is a persistent desire or unsuccessful efforts to cut down or control use of the substance.

3. A great deal of time is spent in activities necessary to obtain the substance, use the substance, or recover from its effects.

4. Craving, or a strong desire or urge to use the substance.

5. Recurrent use of the substance resulting in a failure to fulfill major role obligations at work, school, or home.

6. Continued use of the substance despite having persistent or recurrent social or interpersonal problems caused or exacerbated by the effects of its use.

7. Important social, occupational, or recreational activities are given up or reduced because of use of the substance.

8. Recurrent use of the substance in situations in which it is physically hazardous.

9. Use of the substance is continued despite knowledge of having a persistent or recurrent physical or psychological problem that is likely to have been caused or exacerbated by the substance.

10. Tolerance, as defined by either of the following:

    a. A need for markedly increased amounts of the substance to achieve intoxication or desired effect.

    b. A markedly diminished effect with continued use of the same amount of the substance.

11. Withdrawal, as manifested by either of the following:

    a. The characteristic withdrawal syndrome for other (or unknown) substance.

    b. The substance (or a closely related substance) is taken to relieve or avoid withdrawal symptoms.

Reprinted with permission from the Diagnostic and Statistical Manual of Mental Disorders, Fifth Edition, (Copyright ©2013). American Psychiatric Association. All Rights Reserved.

"I abuse chocolate."

DSM-5 uses the term *use disorder* rather than *addiction*, in part because the word *addiction* has been overused. However, *use disorder* may come to be similarly overused.

that can occur with repeated use or stopping use. DSM-5 defines *craving* as a strong desire or urge to use the substance. Table 9.2 lists the DSM-5 diagnostic criteria.

Two neurologically based symptoms of substance use disorders can contribute to the diagnosis: *tolerance* and *withdrawal* (American Psychiatric Association, 2013). **Tolerance** occurs when, with repeated use, more of the substance is required to obtain the same effect. For instance, someone who drinks alcohol regularly is likely to develop tolerance to alcohol and find that it takes more drinks to obtain a "buzz" and even more drinks to get drunk. With regular use of alcohol and some drugs, the body adapts and tries to compensate for the repeated influx of the substance (see Figure 9.1). People who have been given certain medications for medical problems, such as some pain relievers, may develop tolerance even when taking the medications as prescribed; in such cases, tolerance would not be considered a symptom of a substance use disorder.

Withdrawal refers to the set of symptoms that arises when a regular substance user decreases intake of the substance. As shown in Figure 9.1, withdrawal arises because the body has compensated for the repeated influx of a drug, and the neurological compensatory mechanisms are still in place when the person stops taking the drug, but the drug is no longer there to compensate for them. Withdrawal symptoms

Tolerance
The biological response that arises from repeated use of a substance such that more of it is required to obtain the same effect.

Withdrawal
The set of symptoms that arises when a regular substance user decreases or stops intake of an abused substance.

(a) Normal

(b) Drug effect

(c) Adaptation (tolerance)

(d) Drug effect overcomes tolerance

(e) Tolerance; condition apparently normal, dependence masked

(f) Withdrawal

Note: BCR stands for "body's compensatory response." Source: Adapted from Goldstein, 1994.

FIGURE **9.1 • Tolerance and Withdrawal** Using a see-saw as a metaphor for the body's response to repeated drug use, this figure illustrates the progression to tolerance and withdrawal: (a) no drug use; (b) an imbalance arises from drug use; (c) the brain and body adapt to the drug, and tolerance begins; (d) more of the drug is taken to overcome tolerance; (e) the brain and body adapt to this higher level of drug use; (f) because of the adaptation, when drug use is discontinued (or reduced) that adaptation creates withdrawal symptoms.

can make it difficult for habitual users of some substances to cut back or stop their use: As they cut back, they may experience uncomfortable or even life-threatening symptoms that are temporarily alleviated by resuming use of the substance. In most cases, substances that can lead to tolerance with regular use are also likely to produce withdrawal symptoms if stopped or taken at lower doses. As with tolerance, people taking certain medications for a medical problem may experience withdrawal symptoms if the medication is stopped or the dosage lowered. In such cases, withdrawal would not be considered a symptom of a substance use disorder.

Substance Use Disorder as a Category or on a Continuum?

According to DSM-5, a habitual drug user either is or is not diagnosed with a substance use disorder; this is a categorical decision. However, research suggests that a more meaningful way to conceptualize harmful substance use, at least of alcohol, is on a continuum of severity (Heath et al., 2003; Langenbucher et al., 2004; Sher et al., 2005). According to this view, a substance use disorder anchors one end of a continuum, and unproblematic substance use anchors the other end. This continuum can be defined by the frequency, quantity, and duration of use, as well as the effects of use on daily functioning. The more frequent the use, the larger the quantity, or the longer the use has been going on, the more likely the use is to become a substance use disorder.

According to the continuum approach, we would determine whether any of the Beatles had a stimulant use disorder based on how much, how often, and for how long each of them took the stimulant, and the extent to which such use impaired their daily functioning.

📷 **GETTING THE PICTURE**

Can you match each of these photos to each corresponding pathway by which substance use can become a use disorder? The three pathways are: (1) the psychoactive component is a side effect of a medication taken to treat a medical problem; (2) through environmental exposure; (3) setting out to use a substance for its psychoactive effects. Answer: Matching the photos to the pathway, from left to right: A-2, B-1, C-3.

Use Becomes a Problem

People can develop substance use disorders in three general ways. First, substance use disorders can arise unintentionally, as can occur through environmental exposure. Second, substance use disorders can develop when the psychoactive element is a side effect, and the substance is taken for medicinal reasons unrelated to the psychoactive effect. Third, substance use disorders can develop as a result of the intentional use of a substance for its psychoactive effect. In this third path toward substance use disorders, someone may know the risks of using the substance but nonetheless underestimate his or her own level of risk (Weinstein, 1984, 1993). It is this third path toward developing substance use disorders that has been the target of most research, and two main models have been proposed to explain this type of slide from use to disorder.

Common Liabilities Model

The **common liabilities model** (also called *problem behavior theory*; Donovan & Jessor, 1985) explains how neurological, psychological, and social factors make a person vulnerable to developing a variety of problematic behaviors. It was developed in response to the results from a study that followed students from grades 7–9 into adulthood; the researchers found that adolescents who exhibited "problem behaviors," such as drug and alcohol use, early sexual intercourse, and delinquent behaviors (e.g., stealing and gambling), were likely later in life to develop a substance use disorder. The researchers proposed that these various problem behaviors at different ages may stem from the same underlying factors, called *common liabilities*. Subsequent studies have supported this explanation (Agrawal et al., 2004; Ellickson et al., 2004; Windle & Windle, 2012). One particularly important common liability is a problem with impulsivity—especially with difficulty restraining urges to engage in potentially harmful behaviors—which also underlies a variety of other disorders that involve compulsive behaviors, such as gambling.

Gateway Hypothesis

Another model that researchers have used to a explain the progression from use to a substance use disorder is the gateway hypothesis and the related *stage theory* (Kandel, 2002; Kandel & Logan, 1984). According to the **gateway hypothesis**, "entry" drugs such as cigarettes and alcohol serve as a gateway to (or the first stage in a progression to) use of "harder" drugs, such as cocaine, or illegal use of prescription medication. Researchers have found that some, but not all, adolescent users of entry drugs did go on to use marijuana (White et al., 2007), and some of these marijuana users moved on to harder drugs and hard liquor (Kandel, 2002; Kandel & Logan, 1984). Teens are unlikely to experiment with marijuana unless they first experimented with legal—but restricted—substances such as alcohol. Similarly, adolescents and young adults don't generally try other illegal substances without having used marijuana (see Figure 9.2).

This general pattern of progression has been found in various countries and among different ethnic groups (Kandel & Yamaguchi, 1985). Moreover, people who develop a substance use disorder often passed through a particular progression of stages of drug use: initiation, experimentation, casual use, regular use, and then substance use disorder (Clayton, 1992; Werch & Anzalone, 1995). Of course, not everybody progresses to the end of this sequence. In fact, the gateway hypothesis is not a blueprint for all users; rather, it is a way to understand how people who use substances can end up having a substance use disorder.

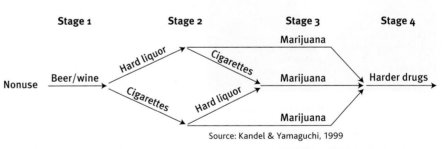

Source: Kandel & Yamaguchi, 1999

FIGURE 9.2 • Stages of Drug Use

Comorbidity

As we've noted in earlier chapters, many people with psychological disorders abuse substances—that is, they develop one or more symptoms of a substance use disorder—particularly alcohol, marijuana, cocaine, and opiates (Lingford-Hughes & Nutt, 2000). Studies have found that almost half of people with alcohol use disorder (the name for the substance use disorder when the substance is alcohol) also had another psychological disorder—and almost three-quarters of those with a different type of substance use disorder had another psychological disorder (Conway et al., 2006; Regier et al., 1993). Common comorbid disorders include mood disorders (most frequently depression), posttraumatic stress disorder (PTSD), schizophrenia, and *attention-deficit/hyperactivity disorder* (ADHD, discussed in Chapter 13), a disorder marked by problems sustaining attention or by physical hyperactivity (Brady & Sinha, 2005). People who have a non-substance-related psychological disorder have a greater risk of substance use turning into a use disorder (Lev-Ran et al., 2013). When substance use disorder develops after another psychological disorder has developed, clinicians may infer that the person is using substances in an attempt to alleviate symptoms of the other disorder—to self-medicate.

Polysubstance Abuse

As was true of the Beatles, some people abuse more than one substance, a behavior pattern that is called **polysubstance abuse**. One study found that among alcoholics, 64% also had an additional type of substance use disorder (Staines et al., 2001). Polysubstance abuse is dangerous because of the ways that drugs can interact: One lethal combination occurs when someone takes a drug that slows down breathing, such as barbiturates (which are often used as sleeping pills), along with alcohol. A form of polysubstance abuse that is seldom recognized is the combination of alcohol and cigarettes (nicotine): Cigarettes are the biggest killer of all drugs, and this is particularly true among alcoholics. Most alcoholics are more likely to die from nicotine-related medical consequences, such as cardiovascular disease, than from alcohol-related ones (Hurt et al., 1996).

Prevalence and Costs

The various types of substance use disorders are among the most common psychological disorders. In 2009, an estimated 9% of Americans aged 12 and older, or 22.5 million people, had a substance use disorder (Substance Abuse and Mental Health Services Administration [SAMHSA], 2010). Generally, men are more likely than women to be diagnosed with a substance use disorder, although women are more likely to be diagnosed with a substance use disorder related to legally obtained prescription medications (Simoni-Wastila et al., 2004).

The prevalence of drug use and substance use disorders varies across ethnic and racial groups in the United States. However, significant variations occur within each broad ethnic or racial category. For example, among Americans of Hispanic descent, the 1-month prevalence rate of heavy drinking (five or more drinks in a sitting) for Cuban Americans is 1.7%, whereas it is 7.4% for Mexican Americans (NIDA, 2003). Therefore, prevalence rates of racial and ethnic groups provide only a general overview, and they do so only at a particular moment in time.

A substance use disorder affects not only the user but also family members and friends, coworkers, and colleagues. Substance use disorders are associated with violence toward family members and neglect of children (Easton et al., 2000; Stuart et al., 2003). Parents who abuse substances may feel guilty and ashamed about their substance abuse, which ironically may lead them to increase their substance use to cope with these feelings (Gruber & Taylor, 2006). Children may find themselves

Using or abusing more than one substance can increase the risk of accidental overdose; actor Heath Ledger died in 2008 from taking a combination of drugs, reportedly for his chronic insomnia. The autopsy results indicated that he'd taken pain killers, several benzodiazepines (used to decrease anxiety), and an over-the-counter antihistamine that can induce drowsiness. He may have developed tolerance to standard doses of these medications; in combination, they caused his heart or breathing to slow down so much that he died (Falco, 2008).

Polysubstance abuse
A behavior pattern of abusing more than one substance.

Kevin Winter/Getty Images

shouldering adult tasks and responsibilities (Haber, 2000). Children of parents who abuse substances are at increased risk of developing emotional and behavioral problems (Grant, 2000; Kelley & Fals-Stewart, 2002).

Culture and Context

The line between use and abuse shifts over time and across cultures and ethnic groups. For example, cocaine was used legally as a remedy for many ills in the second half of the 19th century, but it has now been illegal for decades. And, during the Prohibition era (1920–1933) in the United States, alcohol use was illegal.

Various cultures use psychoactive substances for different purposes. Some Native American tribes, for example, use peyote or psilocybin mushrooms (which, when eaten, produce vivid hallucinations) as part of sacred rituals. Such cultural use of psychoactive substances is strongly regulated, and there are penalties for abusing those substances, including being put to death (Trimble, 1994).

In the remaining sections of this chapter we discuss specific substances that can develop into use disorders. We first describe what they are and consider the ways in which they have their effects. Because treatments for various types of substance use disorders are similar, we consider treatment for all types of substance use disorders in the final section of the chapter.

Jaime Razuri/AFP/Getty Images

Cultures may promote substance use in some contexts and not others. These Brazilian women are followers of Santo Daime, a spiritual practice that involves drinking *hoasca*, a tea made of plant-based hallucinogens. *Hoasca* is legal in Brazil and the United States when it is used as part of a religious practice.

Thinking Like A Clinician

Jorge and his friend Rick worked hard and played hard in high school. On weekend evenings, usually their only free time, they'd binge drink, along with others in their group. They went to different colleges. Jorge kept up his "study hard, party hard" lifestyle; Rick didn't do much binge drinking in college, but he started smoking marijuana in the evenings when he was done studying and he'd go dancing on Saturday nights and sometimes take stimulants. What information would you want to know in order to determine whether Jorge or Rick had a substance use disorder?

Stimulants

Stimulants are named for their effect on the central nervous system: They *stimulate* it, causing increased activity and arousal. Stimulants include nicotine and amphetamines (including Ritalin), which are restricted, as well as cocaine, crack, and MDMA (Ecstasy, or "e"), which are illegal. At low doses, a stimulant can make the user feel alert, less hungry, and more energetic, mentally and physically.

In 1960, when the Beatles first started playing in Germany, they got through their performances by taking a legal stimulant, Preludin. A bouncer at the club simply handed pills to the boys and suggested that they take them. The pills had their effect: The musicians played for hours and then stayed up for hours afterward, going to other clubs (Spitz, 2005). And Preludin wasn't the only stimulant that they took; they also drank coffee and tea and smoked cigarettes, all of which are legal stimulants.

What Are Stimulants?

In this section we first consider the illegal drugs cocaine and crack, and then we consider drugs that have both legal and illegal uses—amphetamines, methamphetamines, Ritalin, and MDMA.

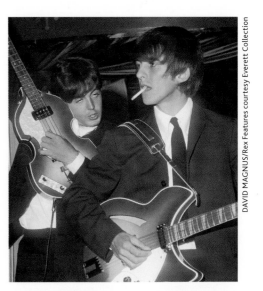

DAVID MAGNUS/Rex Features courtesy Everett Collection

Although all the Beatles smoked cigarettes during their teenage years, some of them continued to smoke. George Harrison (at right) smoked heavily for almost all of his adult life, up to the point where he was diagnosed with throat cancer, in 1998. He also developed lung cancer, which led to his death in 2001.

Cocaine and Crack

Derived from the coca leaf, cocaine was a popular medicine for various ailments in 18th-century Europe and North America. Its use was declared illegal at the beginning of the 20th century, after it became clear that the drug was being abused and leading to tolerance and withdrawal (Rebec, 2000). Cocaine that is obtained in the form of a powder is typically inhaled, or "snorted"; as *crack*, a crystalline form, it is smoked.

Cocaine acts as a local anesthetic. Thus, when snorted, it leaves the user's nose feeling numb; repeated snorting can lead to diminished sense of smell and difficulty swallowing (NIDA, 2007b). Although the first few experiences of cocaine use may provide a heightened sense of well-being that can last for up to an hour, this positive state becomes increasingly harder to attain as tolerance develops (NIDA, 2007b).

Higher doses of cocaine bring many negative effects: paranoia, to the point of delusions; hallucinations, such as feeling insects crawling on the body when there are none; compulsive, repetitive behaviors such as teeth grinding; and increased heart rate and blood pressure, with the accompanying risk of heart attack and sudden death. (The hallucinations occur because cocaine causes sensory neurons to fire spontaneously.) Users also lose their appetite, so people who have cocaine use disorder may develop malnutrition. Table 9.3 lists these and additional effects of regular cocaine use. People with cocaine use disorder often also have alcohol use disorder (Brady et al., 1995; Carroll et al., 1993; Regier et al., 1990); when these two substances are used at the same time, the risk of sudden death increases (NIDA, 2007b).

Smoked crack acts more quickly than snorted cocaine and has more intense effects. Like snorting cocaine, smoking crack leads to a sense of well-being, energy, and mental clarity. However, this "high" usually lasts only minutes (NIDA, 2007b). As with other stimulants, when the high from crack is over, it leaves in its wake a sense of depression and craving for more of the drug, as related by Mr. R. in Case 9.1. These aftereffects may lead the user to take more of the drug and may lead to tolerance or withdrawal. Moreover, whereas tolerance of or withdrawal from cocaine may take months or even years of use to develop, such symptoms can develop extremely rapidly when people take crack—within weeks (NIDA, 2004; Rebec, 2000).

TABLE 9.3 • Effects of Cocaine Abuse

Long-term effects of cocaine	Medical consequences of cocaine abuse
• Addiction • Irritability and mood disturbances • Restlessness • Paranoia • Hallucinations	Cardiovascular effects: • disturbances in heart rhythm • heart attacks Respiratory effects: • chest pain • respiratory failure Neurological effects: • strokes • seizures and headaches Gastrointestinal complications: • abdominal pain • nausea

Source: NIDA, 2004, p. 5.

CASE 9.1 • FROM THE INSIDE: Cocaine Use Disorder—Crack

Mr. R, a 28-year-old man, describes his abuse of crack:

> I first started using cocaine about 4 years ago. I don't remember the first time I smoked the crack cocaine. It puts you in another world. I can't explain this euphoric feeling that it gives you, but it's a feeling I had never experienced before. I just want to sit there and enjoy the feeling and not think about anything or do anything. I have to keep doing it constantly to keep up the high.
>
> I actually started staying out all night. I was smoking about five times a week and lost my apartment, lost everything. Everything was falling apart with my relationship, and I was starting to miss work a lot. But I just couldn't control it. You know, it overtook me. That's all I thought about and all I wanted to do was to keep smoking. Everything else was secondary.
>
> An intense craving for me is when my heart starts beating fast—actually, I get a little sweaty—and all I think about doing is just going to smoke. That's it. Nothing else—everything that's on my mind just kind of disappears.
>
> (Hyman, 2001, pp. 25–87)

As often happens when people develop a substance use disorder, Mr. R.'s life became focused on obtaining and using crack, and his intense cravings made it difficult for him to stop using the drug.

Amphetamines

Amphetamines typically produce the same effects as does cocaine, although these effects last longer. Common amphetamines include *Benzedrine*, *Dexedrine*, and *Adderall*. Amphetamines are usually available as pills, which typically are swallowed, although the contents of the pills may be snorted or diluted and injected. Amphetamines are legally used to treat some disorders, particularly ADHD and the sleep disorder *narcolepsy*, in which the sufferer spontaneously falls asleep for brief periods of time.

With repeated use of amphetamines, people may become hostile toward others, develop a sense of grandiosity, or exhibit disorganized thinking or behavior (Krystal et al., 2005). Because tolerance develops, repeat users may take high doses, which can cause *amphetamine psychosis*, a condition characterized by paranoid delusions and hallucinations (symptoms similar to those of paranoid schizophrenia; see Chapter 12). An amphetamine use disorder can have irreversible effects—including problems with memory and physical coordination—that arise from enduring changes in neurons (Volkow et al., 2001a), as well as reversible effects of irritability and violent behavior (Leccese, 1991; Wright & Klee, 2001). Withdrawal symptoms may include depression, fatigue, anxiety, and irritability.

Methamphetamine

Methamphetamine ("meth" or "speed") is chemically similar to amphetamines but has a greater and longer-lasting effect on the central nervous system. It can be inhaled, swallowed, smoked, or injected, in all cases leading to an intense "rush" of pleasure. Use rapidly becomes use disorder.

In addition to causing irritability, heart problems, hallucinations and paranoia at high doses (McKetin et al., 2013; NIDA, 2007e), methamphetamine use can adversely affect the functioning of the neurotransmitters dopamine and serotonin, which leads to motor problems, impaired memory, and emotional dysregulation. Moreover, the increased blood pressure that results from taking the drug can cause strokes (NIDA, 2007e; Thompson et al., 2004). Table 9.4 summarizes the effects of long-term methamphetamine abuse. Some—but not all—of the brain damage inflicted by methamphetamine abuse is reversible with long-term abstinence (Salo et al., 2011; Volkow et al., 2001a).

Ritalin

Ritalin (methylphenidate hydrochloride) is frequently prescribed for ADHD. Its neurological effect is similar to, but slower than, that of cocaine. People who abuse Ritalin take the stimulant in any of three ways:

- swallowing pills, which does not usually lead to use disorder;
- inhaling or snorting crushed pills, which leads to a quicker "high" and causes lung problems; or
- injecting the drug in liquid form, which produces an effect similar to that of cocaine.

Both inhaling and injecting Ritalin can lead to use disorder. People who do not have ADHD may occasionally swallow Ritalin pills for the stimulant effects—heightened alertness, increased attention, and decreased appetite. Although such casual use does not meet the criteria for a use disorder, it still carries the risk of adverse medical side effects, including heart problems and stroke.

MDMA (Ecstasy)

Methylenedioxymethamphetamine (MDMA), commonly called Ecstasy or simply "e," is usually taken in tablet form. It is chemically similar both to methamphetamine and to the hallucinogen mescaline, and it has the effects of both types of drugs: the stimulant effect of increased energy and the hallucinogenic effect of distorted perceptions. When first using it, people report heightened feelings of well-being, empathy, and warmth toward others, and a greater sensitivity to touch. This experience is less pervasive with subsequent use. Other effects are reduced anxiety and distorted time perception (NIDA, 2007e). Abuse can result in poor mood and difficulty regulating emotions, as well as anxiety and aggression, sleep problems, and decreased appetite (NIDA, 2008b).

TABLE 9.4 • Long-Term Effects of Methamphetamine Abuse

- Dependence
- Psychosis, including:
  - Paranoia
  - Hallucinations
- Repetitive motor activity
- Changes in brain structure and function
- Memory loss
- Aggressive or violent behavior
- Mood disturbances
- Severe dental problems
- Weight loss
- Increased blood pressure and possible stroke

Source: Adapted from NIDA, 2008c.

In addition, MDMA users can develop impaired cognitive functioning, especially problems with memory, after the drug wears off. These cognitive deficits become more severe when the drug is abused (Verkes et al., 2001). One survey of MDMA users found that almost 60% reported withdrawal symptoms that included poor concentration, depression, decreased appetite, and fatigue; moreover, almost half of these users developed MDMA use disorder (NIDA, 2007e; Stone et al., 2006). Frequent users of MDMA may experience tolerance and withdrawal symptoms (Leung & Cottler, 2008). Lynn Smith, in Case 9.2, recounts her experience of MDMA use disorder.

CASE 9.2 FROM THE INSIDE: MDMA Use Disorder

Sometimes I stopped eating and sleeping. I worked only two days a week to support my habit. The rest of the time was spent getting high, almost always on Ecstasy. The utter bliss of my first Ecstasy experience was a distant memory. Of course, I never could recapture that first high, no matter how much Ecstasy I took.

In five months, I went from living somewhat responsibly while pursuing my dream to a person who didn't care about a thing—and the higher I got, the deeper I sank into a dark, lonely place. When I did sleep, I had nightmares and the shakes. I had pasty skin, a throbbing head and the beginnings of feeling paranoid.(Partnership for a Drug-Free America, 2007)

MDMA's side effects are similar to those of other stimulants, including increased blood pressure and heart rate. Excessive sweating, another side effect, can cause acute dehydration and hyperthermia (abnormally high body temperature). The effects of MDMA may be difficult to predict in part because the tablets often contain other drugs, such as ketamine, cocaine, or other stimulants (Green, 2004).

"Bath Salts"

Another type of stimulant is commonly known as *bath salts*. These drugs are not to be confused with traditional bath salts, such as Epsom salts, which are used to enhance the experience of soaking in a bathtub; those bath salts are not psychoactive substances. Stimulant bath salts are a family of drugs that contains a chemical related to cathinone, which is found in the khat plant; it is chemically similar to amphetamines and Ecstasy. However, the exact composition of each packet of bath salts varies, and packets typically contain at least one other type of drug, such as MDMA. Bath salts may lead some users to feel more outgoing and happy, but other users become agitated and paranoid and even hallucinate or become violent (Penders et al., 2012). Users—even those who have had an unpleasant experience—report intense cravings for more of the substance (Slomski, 2012). Bath salts are typically sold as a powder, which is swallowed, inhaled, or injected; adverse effects occur most often when bath salts are snorted or injected (NIDA, 2012).

Bath salts increase the activation of dopamine and may kill neurons (Slomski, 2012). Users of bath salts may need to go to a hospital emergency room because of medical symptoms such as chest pains or racing heart or because of psychological symptoms such as hallucinations, paranoia, or panic attacks. Some people have died as a result of the side effects of using bath salts.

© Mills, Andy/Star Ledger/Corbis

The psychoactive substance known as "bath salts" is not used for soaking in the tub. Rather it is a type of stimulant. Users typically report intense craving for more.

Understanding Stimulants

For the most part, use disorders of the different stimulants arise for similar reasons; thus, in what follows we will consider the roles of the three kinds of factors in leading to use disorders of all stimulants.

Brain Systems and Neural Communication: Dopamine and Abuse

Dopamine plays a key role in both the pleasurable experience of taking stimulants and the abuse of stimulants (Kalivas & Volkow, 2005). To see how, we need to consider the neural circuits that rely on dopamine. To begin, let's consider one classic study. Researchers placed tiny electrodes in parts of rats' brains; when the rats pressed a lever, they got a small jolt of electricity, which activated neurons near the electrodes (Olds & Milner, 1954). The researchers discovered that the animals worked hard to receive electrical stimulation to certain parts of the brain. In fact, they sometimes seemed to prefer such stimulation to food or drink! (This cannot help but remind us of some forms of drug abuse, in which users sacrifice food and drink for the drug.) This sort of finding eventually led researchers to define a "reward system" in the brain. This reward system includes the ventral tegmental area, which in turn activates the nucleus accumbens (see Figure 9.3). The neurons in this system rely on the neurotransmitter dopamine. In fact, if animals are given a drug that blocks the effects of dopamine, they will not work as hard to receive electrical stimulation in these areas (Fibiger & Phillips, 1988). For this reason, the reward system is usually referred to as the **dopamine reward system**. A wide range of pleasurable activities, such as eating and having sex, activate the dopamine reward system.

All stimulant drugs affect the dopamine reward system *directly* (Tomkins & Sellers, 2001). Many other substances (e.g., alcohol) also activate the dopamine system directly, and still other types of substances activate it indirectly by altering other brain areas or neurotransmitters that, in turn, affect dopamine (Leone et al., 1991). Researchers have thus proposed the *dopaminergic hypothesis* of substance abuse: The rewarding effects of a drug arise from the dopamine reward system (Koob & Le Moal, 2008; Robbins & Everitt, 1999a, 1999b; Tomkins & Sellers, 2001).

Because of the neural changes that occur with continued abuse, after a while, the person needs the substance to feel "normal" and experiences cravings when not using the drug. Moreover, larger doses of the drug are necessary to experience pleasure. For example, consider how cocaine affects neurons in the dopamine reward system: Cocaine binds to dopamine transporters—the molecules that take excess dopamine from the synapse and bring it back to dopamine-containing sacs within the terminal buttons of the transmitting neuron (see Figure 9.4). When cocaine binds to these transporter molecules, the transporters don't operate as effectively to remove dopamine from the synapses—and thus more dopamine lingers there, which causes the receptors on the receiving neuron to become less sensitive. Thus, larger doses of the drug are needed to produce more dopamine before it produces pleasurable sensations.

A similar mechanism is at work when someone takes methamphetamine. Again, the drug binds to the molecules that transport excess dopamine back to the terminal buttons and prevents reuptake from operating effectively—thereby leaving more dopamine in the synapse, which in turn leads the dopamine receptors eventually to become desensitized. Moreover, as shown in Figure 9.5, not all of the damage inflicted on the brain by long-term methamphetamine use is reversible. The images in the figure show the distribution of dopamine transporters in the brain of a person who abused methamphetamine. As is evident, even 2 years after the person stopped using methamphetamine, the neurological effects of chronic abuse are not totally reversed.

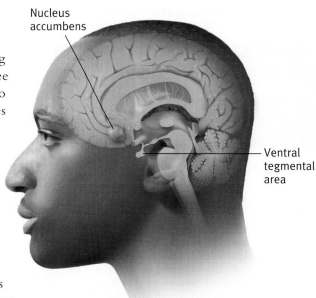

FIGURE 9.3 • The Dopamine Reward System Key brain areas of the dopamine reward system.

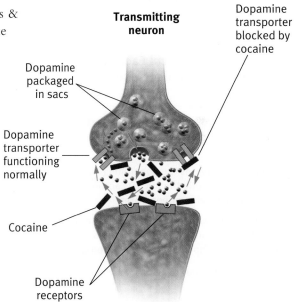

FIGURE 9.4 • Cocaine Use and Dopamine This schematic illustrates how cocaine binds to dopamine transporters, which prevents normal reuptake of dopamine back into the transmitting neuron and increases the amount of dopamine in the synapse—which thereby desensitizes the receptors and requires more dopamine to have an effect.

Dopamine reward system
The system of neurons, primarily in the nucleus accumbens and ventral tegmental area, that relies on dopamine and gives rise to pleasant feelings.

(a) No history of methamphetamine use
(b) 1 month after abuse stops
(c) 1 year after abuse stops

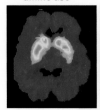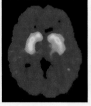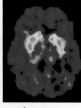

Source: Nora D. Volkow et al., *The Journal of Neuroscience*, December 1, 2001, 21(23):9414–9418.

FIGURE 9.5 • Long-Term Methamphetamine Use : Reversible and Irreversible Brain Damage
(a) This scan shows the distribution of dopamine transporters in a normal brain. (b) This scan shows the brain of a person who had used methamphetamine over a period of years; as is evident, even 1 month after this person stopped using the drug, the dopamine transporters are still in short supply. (c) This scan shows the brain of the same abuser more than a year after stopping the use of methamphetamine; although there is some recovery of function, the effects of chronic abuse are not completely reversed.

TABLE 9.5 • Neurological Factors That Contribute to Stimulant Use Disorders

- Stimulants bind to dopamine transporters, leading to increased dopamine in the synapse.
- Substance activates the dopamine reward system, specifically the nucleus accumbens and ventral tegmental area.*
- Associations between drug-related stimuli and drug use can activate the limbic system (and the dopamine reward system).*

*This factor is not unique to *stimulant* use disorders.

Reward craving
The desire for the gratifying effects of using a substance.

Relief craving
The desire for the temporary emotional relief that can arise from using a substance.

As researchers have come to understand the dopamine reward system in more detail, they have begun to gain insight into an age-old puzzle: Are some people more susceptible to developing a use disorder because they have less "character" or a weak "moral compass"? No. In fact, at least part of the answer is that the dopamine reward system is more sensitive and responsive in some people. For example, in one study, participants were given an injection of the stimulant Ritalin; participants who rated the experience as pleasant had fewer dopamine receptors in their brains than those who found it unpleasant (Volkow et al., 1999). Such findings support the hypothesis that people with fewer dopamine receptors may be more vulnerable to drug use (and use disorders); the smaller quantity of receptors means they have reduced activation in the reward system, which is boosted by substance use (Swanson & Volkow, 2002).

However, we want to end this section with an observation: As we've noted previously, brain areas work together in systems and often more than one system is involved in producing a particular behavior. This is true of use disorders of stimulants in particular and substance use disorders in general. Although the dopamine reward system plays a crucial role in leading people to abuse drugs, many other neurotransmitters and their related brain systems have been implicated in drug abuse, particularly gamma-aminobutyric acid (GABA), glutamate, and serotonin. Table 9.5 lists the neurological factors that contribute to use disorders of stimulants.

Psychological Factors: From Learning to Coping

Various psychological factors contribute to use disorders of stimulants and to substance use disorders in general. In what follows we examine these psychological factors in more detail.

Operant Conditioning

Operant conditioning influences stimulant use and whether a person will develop a substance use disorder in several ways. First, if stimulant use is followed by pleasant consequences, those consequences act as positive reinforcement (which leads to recurrent use). Research on the dopamine reward system shows that aspects of this type of learning have neurological underpinnings. In fact, the dopamine reward system begins to be activated with the *expectation* of a drug's positive effects (that is, the expectation of reinforcement), which leads to a specific type of craving, **reward craving**—the desire for the gratifying effects of using a substance (Verheul et al., 1999).

Second, using stimulants can independently lead to negative reinforcement— alleviating a negative state, thereby producing a desirable experience. (Remember that negative reinforcement is not the same as punishment.) In fact, such negatively reinforcing effects contribute to substance use disorders among people trying to manage the psychological aftereffects of physical or emotional abuse (Bean, 1992; Catanzaro & Laurent, 2004; Ireland & Widom, 1994); in particular, using drugs may (temporarily) distract them from painful memories or their present circumstances and hence be reinforcing.

The temporary emotional relief provided by substance use can create cravings for the drug when a person experiences negative emotions; this type of craving is sometimes referred to as **relief craving** (Verheul et al., 1999). Both reward craving and relief craving can cause people to use drugs compulsively, even when they would like to quit. Thus, cravings of both types are thought to play a primary role in maintaining substance use disorders, and having such cravings is one of the criteria for this category of disorders (American Psychiatric Association, 2013; Torrens & Martín-Santos, 2000).

A third way that operant conditioning contributes to substance use disorders also involves negative reinforcement, but in this case it occurs because using the substance can eliminate withdrawal symptoms, which can range from mildly unpleasant to extremely unpleasant and potentially lethal. Substance use eliminates the unpleasant withdrawal state, which increases the likelihood of subsequent use.

Classical Conditioning

Stimuli associated with drug use (such as drug paraphernalia or the music and crowds at a club) are referred to as **drug cues**, and they come to elicit conditioned responses through their repeated pairings with drug use. Connections among different brain areas, such as the amygdala and hippocampus, store such associations between drug use and the stimuli related to drug use. The drug cues are then associated with the reinforcing (positive or negative) effects of the drug; once such associations are established, these drug-related stimuli themselves can trigger the dopamine reward system (Tomkins & Sellers, 2001). That is, classical and operant conditioning interact: When the consequences (effects) of drug use are rewarding, the person is likely to use drugs again and again. Repeated drug use, in turn, can produce classical conditioning, whereby stimuli associated with drug use, such as the vial containing crack, elicit a *craving* for the drug (Epstein et al., 2009). Such factors affect each other and can become feedback loops that create a spiral of a substance use disorder. For example, people often handle money when buying cocaine and then use the cocaine shortly afterward; handling money can then become a conditioned stimulus. Thus, a person addicted to cocaine can come to crave it after handling money (Hamilton et al., 1998).

Moreover, simply imagining drug cues can activate structures in the limbic system (Dackis & O'Brien, 2001), which is tightly tied to the dopamine reward system, and lead to drug cravings (Hyman, 2005; Stewart et al., 1984). Even after successful treatment for substance use disorders, being exposed to drug cues can lead a former abuser to experience powerful cravings and can increase the risk of relapse (Hyman, 2005; Torrens & Martín-Santos, 2000). Cravings do not last indefinitely, however. When a person craves a substance but does not use it, the craving normally disappears within an hour (Wertz & Sayette, 2001). Researchers have found that a person is more likely to feel the craving when he or she expects to be able to take the drug.

Table 9.6 summarizes the psychological factors that contribute to use disorders of stimulants.

Social Factors

Various social factors can promote substance use disorders, such as patterns of family interactions and perceived social norms. Moreover, sociocultural factors increase the vulnerability of some people for developing use disorders of stimulants and substance use disorders in general.

Family Relations and Peers

Research grounded in the stage theory (introduced earlier in this chapter) found that teenagers whose drug use progressed from marijuana to other illegal substances did not have close relationships with their parents (Andrews et al., 1991). However, this finding is only a correlation; it could be that the factors that led to a use disorder also soured relationships between teenager and parents or that bad relationships contributed to drug abuse—or that some third factor, such as a particular temperament, contributed to both factors. In addition, many studies have found that adolescents who have dysfunctional family interactions (for example, have experienced child abuse, violence in the household, or parental substance abuse) are more likely to use and abuse substances (Becoña et al., 2012; Hawkins et al., 1992; Kilpatrick et al., 2000).

TABLE 9.6 • Psychological Factors That Contribute to Stimulant Use Disorders

- Observational learning: People observe models using substances as a coping strategy and develop expectations about drug use.*

- Operant conditioning:
  - Positive reinforcement leads to subsequent expectations of reward, which in turn lead to reward craving.*
  - Substance use alleviates a negative state, which provides negative reinforcement and leads to relief craving; substance use can become a chronic coping strategy.*

- Classical conditioning: Drug cues elicit a craving*

*This factor is not unique to *stimulant* use disorders.

Drug cues
The stimuli associated with drug use that come to elicit conditioned responses through their repeated pairings with use of the drug.

A person's family members can affect whether he or she comes to use or abuse substances. For instance, when older siblings use drugs, their closer-in-age younger siblings are more likely to do the same than are their further-apart-in-age younger siblings. And within the first year of when a spouse registers with a drug problem, his or her partner is at increased risk of abusing drugs (Kendler, Ohlsson, et al., 2013).

Another social factor involves peers. Friends do things together; they often have common views or activities they enjoy. It's not surprising, then, that peers' substance use can influence a friend's use and abuse of psychotropic substances (Brewer et al., 1998; Keyes et al., 2012). Studies have found that if a person's peers use or abuse substances, that person is likely to do the same (Dishion & Medici Skaggs, 2000; Fergusson et al., 2002). The influence of peers can also help explain findings that support the gateway hypothesis about increasing drug use. Once a (susceptible) person repeatedly uses an illicit entry drug, such as marijuana, he or she is then more likely to spend time with peers who also use this drug and become socialized into a subculture favorable to drug use.

Norms and Perceived Norms

Societies specify norms of behavior, which include the degree to which psychoactive substances can be taken without being considered a use disorder. The Beatles changed the social norms, at least for a while, of some portions of the population through their public association with drugs: Their arrests for possession of illegal drugs, Paul McCartney's admission that he used LSD, and song lyrics referring to drug use (such as, "I get high with a little help from my friends"). Many fans perceived that drug use was "in" and that they would not be "cool" unless they used drugs, too.

This observation highlights an important fact about social norms: It's a person's *perception* of the norms, not the actual social norms, that is the key. That is, when people think that "everyone" in their school, neighborhood, social class, or clique uses drugs, they are more likely to use drugs themselves. In contrast, people who think that only a minority of their classmates, neighbors, or friends use drugs will be less likely to use drugs. In fact, just watching movies can be enough to shift perceptions of social norms. For example, teenagers who watch movies in which the characters drink are more likely to binge drink themselves (Hanewinkel et al., 2012). The extent of the group's actual drug use is less important than what the person *perceives* it to be.

📷 GETTING THE PICTURE

Terry Harris/Alamy

Jenkedco/Shutterstock

Which photo shows a group of people more likely to have a social norm of frequent drug use? Answer: You may have guessed the photo on the left. However, from the perspective of perceived social norms, it doesn't matter which group actually does more drugs. People behave according to the *perceived* social norms of the social group with which they identify.

Sociocultural Factors

In addition to family and friends, other social forces can nudge individuals closer to or further away from a stimulant use disorder as well as substance use disorders in general. People who are experiencing economic hardship and are unemployed are at increased risk of developing substance use disorders (Reid et al., 2001; SAMHSA, 2000). Consider that children who grow up in economically disadvantaged neighborhoods are more likely to be exposed to ads for legal psychoactive substances (alcohol and cigarettes) and to have easier access to these legal psychoactive substances as well as to illegal ones. Children who live in such neighborhoods may also observe more abuse of substances among family members, peers, or adults; as noted earlier, such modeling can have an adverse effect. Moreover, these children are also more likely to experience or witness traumatic events and develop PTSD (see Chapter 7), which is associated with substance use disorders (Johnson, 2008; Stewart, 1996).

Society at large also influences substance use by establishing legal consequences (Torrens & Martín-Santos, 2000). Society's influence is also seen in how access to drug treatment centers is regulated and in the national policies that direct resources toward effective prevention and treatment programs. Table 9.7 summarizes the social factors associated with stimulant use disorder.

As noted by the asterisks in Tables 9.5, 9.6, and 9.7, most of the factors that contribute to use disorders of stimulants also contribute to use disorders of other substances; the one exception is the specific neurological effects of stimulant drugs. Because most of the factors contribute to substance use disorders generally, we do not examine the feedback loops among the factors until after we review all types of substance use disorders.

TABLE 9.7 • Social Factors That Contribute to Stimulant Use Disorders

- Dysfunctional family interactions are correlated with the presence of substance use disorders.*
- An individual's substance use is related to that of his or her peers.*
- Norms and perceived norms influence substance use.*
- Substance use disorders are correlated with economic hardship and unemployment.*

*This factor is not unique to *stimulant* use disorders.

Thinking Like A Clinician

One night before a major class project was due, Sierra had hours of work left to do, and she'd had all the coffee she could stand. She took one of her roommate's Ritalin pills and stayed up all night, completing the project by morning. Sierra gradually got in the habit of using amphetamines to help her stay up late and do course work. After college, Sierra took a job with lots of deadlines and lots of late hours. She continued to use stimulants to help her work, sometimes taking cocaine when she could get it.

At what point would Sierra's use of stimulants become a use disorder? What would be some specific symptoms that would indicate that she had cocaine use disorder? What symptoms would you expect to see if Sierra were taking a high dose of stimulants? According to the neuropsychosocial approach, what factors might have led Sierra to abuse stimulants, if she were abusing them?

☐ Depressants

Two members of the Beatles, Ringo Starr and John Lennon, both had long periods when they had alcohol use disorder. Starr reported that he "wasted" some years on alcohol, initially feeling that drinking gave him confidence but realizing later that it really didn't (Graff, 1989). And Lennon was frequently drunk during his 18-month separation from his wife, Yoko Ono.

What Are Depressants?

Alcohol is a depressant. Other depressants are opiates, barbiturates, and benzodiazepines such as *diazepam* (Valium). In contrast to stimulants, depressants tend to slow a person down, decreasing behavioral activity and level of awareness. Regular use of depressants tends to lead to tolerance, and discontinuing the use of depressants or cutting back on the dosage or frequency can produce withdrawal symptoms. In this section, we will discuss the effects of use and use disorders of three types of depressants: alcohol, barbiturates, and benzodiazepines.

Alcohol

Approximately 6% of Americans aged 12 or older (15 million people) are considered to have alcohol use disorder. Those who start to drink alcohol earlier in life are more likely to develop the disorder (SAMHSA, 2010).

Blood Alcohol Concentration

The crucial variable that determines intoxication is blood alcohol concentration, which is affected by the number of drinks consumed, the period of time over which they were consumed, the time since the person has last eaten, the person's body weight, and the person's gender. Different concentrations of alcohol in the blood are associated with different neurological and psychological states (see Figure 9.6). In the United States, Canada, and Mexico, 0.08% is the legal limit of blood alcohol concentration for driving.

The same amount of alcohol will have a slightly greater effect on a woman than a man of the same size and weight because men and women metabolize the drug differently (Frezza et al., 1990). This sex difference arises in part because women have, on average, less total water content in their bodies than do men, which means that ingested alcohol is less diluted (Greenfield, 2002; Van Thiel et al., 1988).

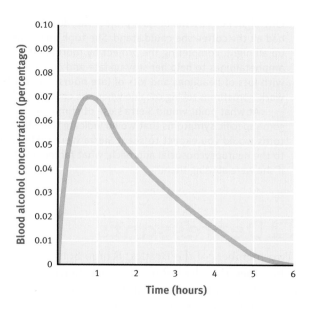

Blood alcohol concentration (percentage)	Changes in thoughts, feelings, and behavior	Impaired functions and activities (continuum)
0.01 – 0.05	Relaxation Sense of well-being Loss of inhibition	Alertness Judgment

0.06 – 0.10	Pleasure
	Numbing of feelings
	Nausea
	Sleepiness
	Emotional arousal
		Coordination
		  (especially fine motor skills)
		Visual tracking
		Reasoning and
		  depth perception

0.11 – 0.20	Mood swings Anger Sadness Mania	Social behavior (e.g., obnoxiousness)
0.21 – 0.30	Aggression Reduced sensations Depression Stupor	Speech (slurred) Balance Temperature regulation
0.31 – 0.40	Unconsciousness Death possible Coma	Bladder control Breathing
0.41 and greater	Death	Heart rate (slowed)

FIGURE 9.6 • Blood Alcohol Concentration and Its Effects
Different blood alcohol concentrations are, on average, associated with different effects. People may be motivated to drink alcohol because of the way it can affect thoughts, feelings, and behavior, but the same effects can impair functioning and, with repeated use, lead to alcohol use disorder. As shown in the graph on the right, alcohol's effects—both desirable and undesirable—may be experienced within a few minutes and last a number of hours. The more someone has had to drink, the more impaired he or she will be for a longer period of time.

📷 GETTING THE PICTURE

Which of these two people is likely to experience greater effects of alcohol? Answer: The female. Men and women metabolize alcohol differently, in part, because women have, on average, less total water content in their bodies than do men, and hence the alcohol is less diluted in women's blood.

Not only do the effects of a given amount of alcohol differ by gender, but there are also individual differences. Some people have a more intense response to alcohol than do others. This variability appears to be mediated in part by genes (Webb et al., 2011), but it is also related to the level of tolerance a person has acquired.

Binge Drinking

Binge drinking, or *heavy episodic drinking*, occurs when a person drinks until his or her blood alcohol concentration reaches at least 0.08% in a 2-hour period (which generally translates into four or more drinks for women, five or more for men; one drink is equivalent to 12 ounces of beer, 5 ounces of wine, or 1.5 ounces of 80-proof liquor) (National Institute on Alcohol Abuse and Alcoholism National Advisory Council, 2004). Binge drinking is likely to occur when a person sets out to get drunk (Schulenberg et al., 1996). Repetitive binge drinking can lead to alcohol use disorder.

Alcohol Use Disorder

Chronic drinking leads to tolerance and withdrawal, thus fulfilling the minimum two criteria for alcohol use disorder (sometimes referred to as *alcoholism*). According to the National Institute on Alcohol Abuse and Alcoholism (2012), alcoholism is marked by four symptoms:

- *craving*, which is a strong need, or urge, to drink;
- *loss of control*, which consists of an episode of drinking during which the person finds it difficult to stop compulsively drinking;
- *physical dependence*, which brings withdrawal symptoms, such as nausea, sweating, shakiness, and anxiety after stopping drinking; and
- *tolerance*, which causes a person to need to drink greater amounts of alcohol to get "high."

CASE 9.3 • FROM THE INSIDE: Alcohol Use Disorder

Caroline Knapp describes her alcohol use disorder in her memoir *Drinking: A Love Story* (1997):

By that point I don't even think the alcohol worked anymore. Certainly drinking was no longer fun. It had long ago ceased to be fun. A few glasses of wine with a friend after work could still feel reassuring and familiar, but drinking was so need driven by the end, so visceral and compulsive, that the pleasure was almost accidental. Pleasure just wasn't the point. At the end I didn't even feel like myself until I had a drink or two, and I remember that scared me a little: alcohol had become something I felt I needed in order to return to a sense of normalcy, in order to think straight. After one or two drinks I'd feel like I'd come back into my own skin—more clearheaded, more relaxed—but the feeling would last for only half an hour or so. Another few drinks and I'd be gone again, headed toward oblivion. (p. 231)

In Case 9.3, Knapp describes the four elements of alcoholism: craving ("need driven"), loss of control (she would continue to drink until she was "headed toward oblivion"), physical dependence ("something I felt I needed in order to return to normalcy"), and tolerance (the alcohol didn't have as strong an effect as it had initially).

Alcohol use disorder is also associated with memory problems, in particular, *blackouts*, periods of time during which the drinker cannot later remember what transpired while he or she was intoxicated. Knapp (1997) described her blackouts: "Sometimes I'd wake up at Sam's [a friend's] house, in his bed, wearing one of his T-shirts. I don't think we ever had sex but I can't say for sure" (p. 154).

Sedative-Hypnotic Drugs

Sedative-hypnotic drugs reduce pain and anxiety, relax muscles, lower blood pressure, slow breathing and heart rate, and induce sedation and sleep. In general, drugs in this class cause disinhibiting and depressant effects similar to those of alcohol (impaired physical coordination and mental judgment and increased aggressive or sexual behavior). Although these psychoactive substances can lower inhibitions and bring a sense of well-being, they also can cause memory problems, confusion, poor concentration, fatigue, and even respiratory arrest (NIDA, 2008e). When sedative-hypnotic drugs are mixed with another depressant, such as alcohol, the combined effect can be lethal: The person's breathing and heart rate can slow to the point where the person dies. Chronic use of these drugs can lead to tolerance. Two general types of drugs are in this class: *barbiturates* and *benzodiazepines*.

Barbiturates

Barbiturates, which include *amobarbital* (Amytal), *pentobarbital* (Nembutal), and *secobarbital* (Seconal), are usually prescribed to treat sleep problems. Although use of a barbiturate is legal with a prescription, this type of medication is commonly abused by both those with a prescription and those who obtain the drug illegally. As with other depressants, repeated barbiturate use leads to tolerance, so the person takes ever larger doses to get to sleep or reduce anxiety. Repeated barbiturate use can also lead to withdrawal symptoms, including agitation and restlessness, hallucinations, confusion, and, in some cases, seizures (NIDA, 2005c). People with barbiturate use disorder who want to discontinue or decrease their intake of the drug should do so with care; they should first consult a knowledgeable physician to determine an appropriate schedule for tapering off without inducing dangerous withdrawal symptoms. If they discontinue the drug abruptly, they risk having convulsions and could even die.

Benzodiazepines

Benzodiazepines are usually prescribed to alleviate muscle pain, to aid sleep, or as a short-term treatment for anxiety (see Chapter 6); however, long-term use leads to tolerance and withdrawal. Examples of benzodiazepines include *lorazepam* (Ativan), *triazolam* (Halcion), *clonazepam* (Klonopin), *diazapam* (Valium), and *alprazolam* (Xanax). As with barbiturate use disorder, a person with benzodiazepine use disorder should gradually taper off of the drug, in consultation with a physician; abruptly stopping use can lead to seizures and psychosis. A benzodiazepine-like class of sedative drugs, referred to as *nonbenzodiazepines*, can also be abused and have similar effects, side effects, and risks. Examples include *zolpidem* (Ambien), *eszopiclone* (Lunesta), and *zaleplon* (Sonata).

Understanding Depressants

In what follows, we will first discuss how brain systems and neural communication are affected by depressants in general and then turn to the effects of alcohol in particular.

Neurological Factors

In this section, we consider a set of closely related topics: the effects of depressants on the brain systems and neural communication, biological by-products of alcohol use disorder, and the genetics of alcoholism.

Brain Systems and Neural Communication

Benzodiazepines (such as Xanax), barbiturates, and alcohol directly affect the GABAnergic system, which is widespread in the brain and primarily activates inhibitory neurons. The resulting inhibition affects neurons in brain structures that are involved in anxiety, such as the amygdala. As we've noted before, the amygdala plays a key role in fear, and hence inhibiting it dulls the sense of fear and the related feeling of anxiety. Thus, it is not surprising that people who experience anxiety, for whatever reasons, find the use of depressants particularly reinforcing.

Although alcohol consumption induces the production of dopamine, which is rewarding, chronic use of alcohol stimulates the production of a type of neurotransmitter called *endogenous opioids*, sometimes referred to as "pleasure chemicals." (There is a class of drugs referred to as *opioids* or *opiates*, which we'll discuss later in the chapter. The word *endogenous*—which means *arises from an inside source*—is used to distinguish the neurotransmitter opioids from the drugs of the same name.) Endogenous opioids are responsible for "runner's high," the feeling that occurs when someone has pushed herself or himself to a physical limit and experiences a sense of deep pleasure. In chronic drinkers, the activity of endogenous opioids occurs only in response to alcohol; when they stop drinking, their bodies no longer produce endogenous opioids. Thus, when a chronic drinker isn't consuming alcohol, he or she may experience symptoms related to opioid withdrawal, which are unpleasant. This experience in turn may induce the person to consume more alcohol to produce more opioids (Gianoulakis, 2001). In addition, a single drink releases more opioids in heavy drinkers than in light drinkers (Mitchell et al., 2012). This is only a correlation, but one possible explanation for it is that some people may become heavy drinkers, in part, because their brains release more opioids in response to alcohol, thus activating the dopamine reward system.

Biological By-products of Alcohol Use Disorder

People who frequently drink a lot of alcohol may become malnourished when the calories in alcohol substitute for calories from food (Mehta et al., 2006). Such malnourishment can include a deficiency in vitamin B1, which eventually causes several key parts of the brain to atrophy—including brain structures important for storing new information in memory. Thus, drinking a lot of alcohol can indirectly lead to chronic memory problems (which produces a condition called *Korsakoff's syndrome*). Figure 9.7 shows a result of such brain atrophy: the increased size of the fluid-filled hollow areas, the ventricles, in the center of the brain.

For people with alcohol use disorder, a hangover indicates that their bodies are going through alcohol withdrawal as the alcohol leaves the system (Cicero, 1978); drinking more alcohol can temporarily diminish the discomfort of the withdrawal symptoms.

FIGURE 9.7 • Alcohol Use Disorder: Effects on the Brain One of the effects of long-term alcohol use disorder—alcoholism—is enlarged ventricles (the cavities in the brain filled with cerebrospinal fluid). (a) The ventricles in this MRI scan are normal size; (b) the enlarged ventricles in this MRI scan are those of a man with alcohol use disorder. The enlargement of the ventricles reflects the reduced size of a number of brain areas. These neurological changes may explain some of the memory problems associated with alcohol use disorder.

Source: Rosenbloom et al. (2003). *Alcohol Research & Health* 27(2):146–152.

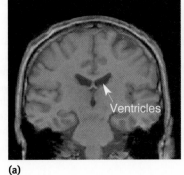

(a)

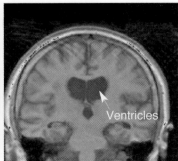

(b)

Delirium tremens (DTs)
The symptoms of alcohol withdrawal that include uncontrollable shaking, confusion, convulsions, visual hallucinations, and fever.

For a heavy drinker, withdrawal symptoms include headaches, weakness, tremors, anxiety, higher blood pressure, seizures, and increased heart and breathing rates. An extremely heavy drinker can also experience fever, agitation, and irritability, as well as more severe symptoms such as uncontrollable shaking, confusion, convulsions, and visual hallucinations. All these alcohol withdrawal symptoms are collectively referred to as **delirium tremens** (also simply called "the DTs"). Such withdrawal symptoms normally begin within 4 days after the person last drank alcohol (Romach & Sellers, 1991). Delirium tremens can be potentially lethal; when people with alcohol use disorder are ready to stop drinking, they should have a physician supervise the process.

Genetics of Alcoholism

The tendency to abuse drugs is affected by genes (Palmer et al., 2012). One sign of this is the fact that substance use disorders tend to run in families. However, only the genetics of alcoholism has been studied in depth. Researchers have found that biological offspring of alcoholics are about twice as likely to become alcoholics as people without such a family history (Nurnberger et al., 2004; Russell, 1990). Twin studies have also provided evidence for a genetic contribution to alcoholism (Carmelli et al., 1993). In addition, sometimes the offspring of alcoholics are adopted by parents who are not alcoholics, and researchers have studied some of these children after they've become adults. One striking finding is that even when they were raised by nonalcoholic parents, children whose biological parents were alcoholics are much more likely to abuse alcohol as adults than are those whose biological parents were not alcoholics (Kendler, Sundquist, et al., 2013). Table 9.8 summarizes the neurological factors that contribute to use disorders of depressants.

TABLE 9.8 • Neurological Factors That Contribute to Depressant Use Disorders

- Increased activity of the GABAnergic system leads to increased inhibition of anxiety-related brain structures.
- Depressants indirectly activate the dopamine reward system.
- Depressants generally cause the nervous system to be less responsive.
- Some substances directly activate the dopamine reward system, including the nucleus accumbens and the ventral tegmental area.*
- Associations between drug-related stimuli and drug use can activate the limbic system (and the dopamine reward system).*

*This factor is not unique to *depressant* use disorder.

Psychological Factors

Many of the psychological factors that contribute to use disorders of stimulants also contribute to use disorders of depressants (see the starred items in Table 9.6); in particular:

- observational learning of depressant use, which promotes expectations about experiences from such use and promotes such use as a coping strategy;
- operant conditioning, in which
  - positive reinforcement leads to positive expectations of depressant use and to reward craving;
  - negative reinforcement can lead to relief craving and to depressant use becoming a chronic coping strategy; and
- classical conditioning, whereby drug cues elicit cravings.

Let's examine in a bit more detail the role of coping strategies and expectations in alcohol use. Some people use alcohol as a way to cope with their problems. Consider Charles's experience in Case 9.4.

> **CASE 9.4 • FROM THE OUTSIDE:** Alcohol Use Disorder as a Coping Strategy
>
> Charles, a high-school teacher with a long-standing problem of alcohol [use disorder], identified boredom and anger as key high-risk relapse factors. His problem with anger involved a pattern of avoiding interpersonal conflicts and letting his anger build up. Over time, Charles would reach a point of total frustration and use his angry thoughts and feelings to justify drinking binges. [He had perceived his anger to be a] "bad feeling that could only be expressed through drinking" . . . he often became upset and angry because of certain beliefs he held about how others "should" treat him.
>
> (Daley & Salloum, 1999, p. 258)

Like Charles, other people use alcohol to try to cope with particular emotions. In Charles's case, it was anger; for other people, the emotions might be sadness, anxiety, fear, shame, or any of a range of other emotions (Gaher et al., 2006). Particular factors lead some people to have a higher risk of using alcohol to cope. One such factor relates to the trait of anxiety sensitivity (see Chapter 6): People who are high in this trait find alcohol to be very calming, which explains why an anxiety disorder frequently precedes an alcohol use disorder in people who have both kinds of disorders (Robinson et al., 2011; Stewart et al., 2001).

Finally, even when they are not related to a coping strategy, expectations of what will happen as a result of drinking can also affect behavior after drinking (Kirsch & Lynn, 1999): People who drink to get "wasted" are in fact more likely to feel and act more drunk than are people who drink while having dinner with friends in a restaurant, even when people in both situations end up with the same blood alcohol concentration.

Social Factors

A variety of social factors can contribute to substance use disorders (see the starred items in Table 9.7). For depressants, including alcohol, such factors include:

- dysfunctional family interactions (such as child abuse or neglect);

- peers' use of depressants;

- norms or perceived norms about depressant use (as in a subculture where drinking is the norm or is perceived to be so); and

- economic hardship and unemployment.

Another social factor is culture: Culture affects both the degree of alcohol abuse and the ways in which alcohol is used (Abbott & Chase, 2008). For example, the rate of alcohol use disorder among American women has increased over time. Historically, women in the United States had much lower rates of alcoholism than did men, but as social mores and roles for women changed, the incidence of alcoholism among women has come to approach that of men (Greenfield, 2002).

Cultures also create social norms for appropriate and inappropriate use of alcohol, such as allowing "fiesta" drunkenness on certain occasions (Finch, 2001; Room & Makela, 2000). Moreover, the media influence norms and perceived norms. One correlational study found that adolescents and young adults who saw more ads for alcohol drank more alcohol (Snyder et al., 2006), possibly because seeing more ads for alcohol led them to perceive the norm for alcohol use to be greater than it was.

The rate of alcohol use disorder among American women has increased over time—so, too, has the number of images of women drinking in TV shows, movies, and advertisements.

© Warner Bros/Courtesy Everett Collection

Thinking Like A Clinician

When you see your neighbor in the hallway in the evenings, she sometimes can't seem to walk in a straight line, her speech is slurred, and she reeks of alcohol. She frequently misses when she tries to put her key in the lock and begins giggling. Once you saw her vomit after such an incident. On a few occasions, she hasn't been so obviously "wasted" and has turned to you and roughly said, "What are you staring at?" One time, when you smirked as she tried to put her key in the lock, she came over to you and threatened to "kick your butt." Even during the daytime, though, she's not very nice or friendly.

Do you think this neighbor has a problem with alcohol, and if so, does it reach the level to be considered alcohol use disorder? Why or why not? What supports or refutes the conclusion that she has an alcohol problem? What information would you want to know before making a confident decision? According to the neuropsychosocial approach, what factors might underlie this neighbor's use of alcohol?

Other Abused Substances

This chapter has focused so far on stimulants and depressants because they are the most commonly abused substances. However, they are not the only substances that people abuse. In this section we briefly review three classes of other substances that are often abused: opioids (such as codeine and heroin), hallucinogens (such as marijuana), and dissociative anesthetics (such as ketamine).

What Are Other Abused Substances?

By 1969, the Beatles had not performed for 3 years. In that year, they agreed to perform and have their rehearsals filmed. They spent a month in a recording studio, composing and arranging songs, learning their parts, and rehearsing the songs. Rather than a true concert, however, the project culminated in a live, rooftop performance that was filmed. Some of this arduous process and the final concert were captured in the film *Let It Be*, which shows glimpses of the effects of John Lennon's heroin use. Lennon had difficulty remembering song lyrics from hour to hour and day to day, had trouble getting up each morning and arriving at the sessions on time, and had difficulty concentrating on writing and finishing songs (Spitz, 2005; Sulpy & Schweighardt, 1994). Such problems are typical of heroin use in particular and of the use of opioids more generally.

Opioids: Narcotic Analgesics

Opioids—also called *opiates* or *narcotic analgesics*—are derived from the opium poppy plant or chemically related substances. These substances are perhaps best characterized as *exogenous opioids* (*exogenous* means "arising from an outside source"). Exogenous opioids include methadone and heroin (to be discussed in more detail shortly), as well as codeine, morphine, and synthetic derivatives found in prescription pain relief medications such as *oxycodone* (OxyContin), *hydrocodone* (Vicodin), and others. Legal but restricted narcotic analgesics are generally prescribed for persistent coughing, severe diarrhea, and severe pain. These drugs can be injected, snorted, or taken by mouth.

All analgesics relieve pain, and people who take analgesics for recreational purposes may temporarily experience pleasant, relaxing effects. However, this category of drugs is highly addictive: Their use rapidly leads to tolerance and withdrawal and compulsive behavior related to procuring and taking the drug. Although users may experience euphoria after taking such a drug, that mood fades to apathy, unhappiness, impaired judgment, and psychomotor agitation (the "fidgets") or psychomotor retardation (sluggishness). Users may also experience confusion—as happened to John Lennon—as well as slurred speech, sedation, or unconsciousness. Narcotics depress the central nervous system and can cause drowsiness and slower breathing, which can lead to death if an opioid is taken with a depressant.

Withdrawal from an opioid typically begins within 8 hours after the drug was last used and peaks within several days. Physical symptoms of withdrawal include nausea and vomiting, muscle aches, dilated pupils, sweating, fever, and diarrhea; many of the symptoms are similar to those of a bad case of the flu. Depressed mood, irritability, and a sense of restlessness are also common during withdrawal.

Heroin is one of the stronger opioids and is very addictive. The contrast between the euphoria that the drug induces and the letdown that comes when its effects wear off can drive some people to crave the euphoria, and so they take the drug, again and again—which in turn leads to tolerance. Tolerance makes the same dose of heroin fall short: Instead of causing euphoria, it often causes irritability (NIDA, 2007c).

Although some narcotic analgesics are derived from the opium poppy plant, others are synthetic derivatives. Repeated use of any type of narcotic analgesic rapidly leads to tolerance and withdrawal—signs of a use disorder.

Surveys of people who have used heroin find that the typical user starts out snorting heroin (as Lennon did), progresses to injecting heroin under the skin but not into blood vessels (termed *skin popping*), and then ends up injecting into blood vessels (termed *mainlining*). Injecting heroin causes a more intense experience—a "rush," a feeling of immediate intensity. Most users proceed from occasional use to daily use, and their primary motivation in life becomes obtaining enough money to procure the next dose, or "fix." Because users become tolerant to the drug, they must increase the amount they use in order to get an effect.

Heroin use disorder is associated with a variety of medical problems, such as pneumonia and liver disease. In addition, heroin users who inject the drug are at risk of contracting HIV and hepatitis as well as collapsed veins—and an overdose can be fatal (NIDA, 2007c).

Hallucinogens

Hallucinogens are substances that induce sensory or perceptual distortions— hallucinations in any of the senses. That is, users think they see, hear, taste, or feel something that is not actually present or not present in the way it is perceived. Some hallucinogens also can induce mood swings. Hallucinogens frequently taken for recreational purposes include the following:

- *LSD* (a synthetic hallucinogen, also called *acid*),
- *mescaline* (a psychoactive substance produced by certain kinds of cacti),
- *psilocybin* (a psychoactive substance present in psilocybin mushrooms, commonly referred to as "magic mushrooms"), and
- *marijuana* (the dried leaves and flowers of the hemp plant, *cannabis sativa*).

The first three of these drugs are chemically similar to the neurotransmitter serotonin. A single moderate dose of any of these drugs (or a very high dose of marijuana) is enough to induce visual hallucinations. In what follows we examine the use disorders that can arise when people take LSD or marijuana.

LSD

All of the Beatles used LSD at one point or another, but John Lennon reported that he took LSD thousands of times—which surely would constitute abusing the drug. LSD is a hallucinogen because it alters the user's visual or auditory sensations and perceptions; it also induces shifting emotions. LSD normally has an effect within 30 to 90 minutes of being ingested, and the effects last up to 12 hours (NIDA, 2001).

The effects of LSD can be unpredictable. A "bad trip" (that is, an adverse reaction to LSD) can include intense anxiety, fear, and dread; a user may feel as if he or she is totally losing control, going crazy, or dying. People who are alone when experiencing a bad trip may get hurt or kill themselves as they respond to the hallucinations.

Two aftereffects can occur from LSD use, even after the pharmacological effects of the drug have worn off: psychosis (hallucinations and visual disturbances) and "flashbacks" (involuntary and vivid memories of sensory distortions that occurred while under the influence of the drug). Such aftereffects are rare, although LSD abuse can induce enduring psychotic symptoms in a small number of people (NIDA, 2007d).

Marijuana

The Beatles also smoked marijuana. The resin from the hemp plant's flowering tops is made into another, more potent drug, *hashish*. The active ingredient of marijuana and hashish is *tetrahydrocannabinol* (THC). Both marijuana and hashish can be either smoked or ingested.

Marijuana's effects are subtler than those of other hallucinogens, creating minor perceptual distortions that lead a person to experience more vivid sensations and to feel that time has slowed down (NIDA, 2005b). The user's cognitive and motor abilities are also slowed or temporarily impaired, which produces poor driving skills (Ramaekers et al., 2006). THC ultimately activates the dopamine reward system (NIDA, 2000). Not everyone who uses marijuana develops a use disorder, but some people do develop such a disorder. If a person develops *cannabis use disorder* (as is it is called in DSM-5), he or she will experience withdrawal symptoms after he or she stops using marijuana; such symptoms include irritability, anxiety, depression, decreased appetite, and disturbed sleep (Allsop et al., 2012; Kouri & Pope, 2000). Studies have found that chronic marijuana use adversely affects learning, memory, and motivation—even when the user has not taken the drug recently and is not under its direct influence (Lane et al., 2005; Pope et al., 2001; Pope & Yurgelin-Todd, 1996). These effects are particularly likely to occur if the person started to use marijuana heavily during adolescence (Meier et al., 2012).

Dissociative Anesthetics

A *dissociative anesthetic* produces a sense of detachment from the user's surroundings—a *dissociation*. The word *anesthetic* in the name reflects the fact that many of these drugs were originally developed as anesthetics to be used during surgery. Dissociative anesthetics act like depressants and also affect glutamate activity (Kapur & Seeman, 2002). These drugs can distort visual and auditory perception. Drugs of this type are included in the term "club drugs" because they tend to be taken before or during an evening of dancing at a nightclub. The most commonly abused members of this class of drugs are phencyclidine and ketamine, which we discuss in the following sections.

Phencyclidine (PCP)

Phencyclidine (PCP, also known as "angel dust" and "rocket fuel") became a street drug in the 1960s. It can be snorted, ingested, or smoked, and users can quickly begin to take it compulsively. PCP abusers may report feeling powerful and invulnerable while the drug is in their system, but they may become violent or suicidal (NIDA, 2007f).

PCP has deleterious effects even when taken at low to moderate doses. Medical effects include increased blood pressure, heart rate, and sweating, coordination problems, and numbness in the hands and feet. At higher doses, PCP users may experience hallucinations, delusions, paranoia, disordered thinking, and memory problems as well as speech and cognitive problems (as did the man in Case 9.5)—even up to a year after last use (NIDA, 2007f).

CASE 9.5 • FROM THE OUTSIDE: Phencyclidine Use Disorder

The patient is a 20-year-old man who was brought to the hospital, trussed in ropes, by his four brothers. This is his seventh hospitalization in the last 2 years, each for similar behavior. One of his brothers reports that he "came home crazy," threw a chair through a window, tore a gas heater off the wall, and ran into the street. The family called the police, who apprehended him shortly thereafter as he stood, naked, directing traffic at a busy intersection. He assaulted the arresting officers, escaped from them, and ran home screaming threats at his family. There his brothers were able to subdue him.

On admission, the patient was observed to be agitated, with his mood fluctuating between anger and fear. He had slurred speech and staggered when he walked. He remained extremely violent and disorganized for the first several days of his hospitalization, then began having longer and longer lucid intervals, still interspersed with sudden, unpredictable periods in which he displayed great suspiciousness, a fierce expression, slurred speech, and clenched fists.

After calming down, the patient denied ever having been violent or acting in an unusual way ("I'm a peaceable man") and said he could not remember how he got to the hospital. He admitted using alcohol and marijuana socially, but denied phencyclidine (PCP) use except for once, experimentally, 3 years previously. Nevertheless, blood and urine tests were positive for phencyclidine, and his brother believes "he gets dusted every day."

(Spitzer et al., 2002, pp. 121–122)

Ketamine

Ketamine ("Special K" or "vitamin K") induces anesthesia and hallucinations and can be injected or snorted. Ketamine is chemically similar to PCP but is shorter acting and has less intense effects. With high doses, some users experience a sense of dissociation so severe that they feel as if they are dying (NIDA, 2001). Ketamine use and abuse are associated with temporary memory loss, impaired thinking, a loss of contact with reality, violent behavior, and breathing and heart problems that are potentially lethal (Krystal et al., 2005; White & Ryan, 1996). Regular users of ketamine may develop tolerance and cravings (Jansen & Darracot-Cankovic, 2001).

Understanding Other Abused Substances

In what follows, we first consider neurological factors for each class of substances and then turn to psychological and social factors.

Neurological Factors

Depending on the abused substance, different brain systems and neural communication processes are critical.

Opioids

Among the narcotic analgesics, researchers have focused most of their attention on heroin—in large part because it poses the greatest problem. Like other opioids, heroin slows down activity in the central nervous system. It directly affects the part of the brain involved in breathing and coughing—the brainstem—and thus historically was used to suppress persistent coughs. In addition, heroin binds to opioid receptors in the brain, which has the effect of decreasing pain, and indirectly activates the dopamine reward system (NIDA, 2000). Continued heroin use also decreases the production of endorphins, a class of neurotransmitters that act as natural painkillers. Thus, over time heroin abuse reduces the body's natural pain-relieving ability. In fact, someone with heroin use disorder has his or her endorphin production reduced to the point that, when withdrawal symptoms arise, endorphins that would have kicked in to reduce pain are not able to do so, making the symptoms feel even worse than they otherwise would be.

Hallucinogens

THC, the active ingredient in marijuana, is chemically similar to the type of neurotransmitters known as *cannabinoids*, and it activates the dopamine reward system. People who began abusing marijuana at an early age have atrophy of brain areas that contain many receptors for cannabinoids (De Bellis et al., 2000; Ernst & Chefer, 2001; Wilson et al., 2000), especially the hippocampus and the cerebellum. Atrophy of the hippocampus can explain why chronic marijuana users develop memory problems, and atrophy of the cerebellum can explain why they develop balance and coordination problems. Cannabinoids also modulate other neurotransmitters and affect pain and appetite (Wilson & Nicoll, 2001).

The genetic bases of abuse of most types of substances have not been studied in depth. However, one twin study of cannabis use disorder (Lynskey et al., 2002) estimated that genes account for 45% of the variance in vulnerability to cannabis use disorder, shared environmental factors account for 20%, and nonshared environmental factors account for the remaining 35%.

Dissociative Anesthetics

PCP and ketamine increase the level of glutamate, a fast-acting excitatory neurotransmitter. Glutamate can be toxic; it actually kills neurons if too much is present. Thus, by increasing levels of glutamate, dissociative anesthetics may, eventually, lead to cell death in brain areas that have receptors for this neurotransmitter—which would explain the memory and other cognitive deficits observed in people who abuse these drugs.

Psychological Factors

Abuse of these other types of substances is affected by most of the same psychological factors that influence abuse of stimulants and depressants (see the starred items in Table 9.6): observational learning, operant conditioning, and classical conditioning all contribute to substance use disorders as a maladaptive coping strategy. We examine here the unique aspects of classical conditioning that are associated with heroin use disorder.

Classical conditioning can help explain how some accidental heroin "overdoses" occur (Siegel, 1988; Siegel et al., 2000). The quotation marks around the word *overdoses* are meant to convey that, in fact, the user often has not taken more than usual. Rather, he or she has taken a usual dose in the presence of novel stimuli (Siegel & Ramos, 2002). If a user normally takes heroin in a particular place, such as the basement of the house, he or she develops a conditioned response to being in that place: The brain triggers biological changes to get ready for the influx of heroin, activating compensatory mechanisms to dampen the effect of the about-to-be-taken drug (see Figure 9.1). This response creates a tolerance for the drug, but—and here's the most important point—only in that situation. The stimuli in a "neutral" setting (not associated with use of the drug), such as a bedroom, have not yet become paired with taking heroin—and hence the brain does not trigger these compensatory mechanisms before the person takes the drug. If the conditioned stimulus (e.g., the basement) is not present to elicit the compensatory response, the same dose of heroin can have a greater effect—causing an "overdose."

Social Factors

The social factors that are commonly associated with use disorders of stimulants and depressants also apply to opioids, hallucinogens, and dissociative anesthetics (see the starred items in Table 9.7). These include dysfunctional family interactions and a higher proportion of substance-abusing peers, which in turn affects the perceived norms of substance use and abuse (Kuntsche et al., 2009). Moreover, economic hardship and unemployment are associated with substance use disorders, perhaps because of chronic stress that arises from economic adversity as well as increased exposure to substance abuse.

Feedback Loops in Understanding Substance Use Disorders

The neurological, psychological, and social factors that contribute to substance use disorders in general do not act in isolation but affect each other through various feedback loops (see Figure 9.8).

Clearly, neurological factors play a key role, but can do so in different ways. Some neurological factors tend to have a direct relationship with substance use disorders: The effects that a given substance produces in the brain can be directly influenced by specific genes and a person's prior exposure to the drug—either in the mother's womb or after birth. Neurological factors, such as genes and their influence on temperament, can also have indirect effects: For example, some people have

FIGURE 9.8 • Feedback Loops in Understanding Substance Use Disorders

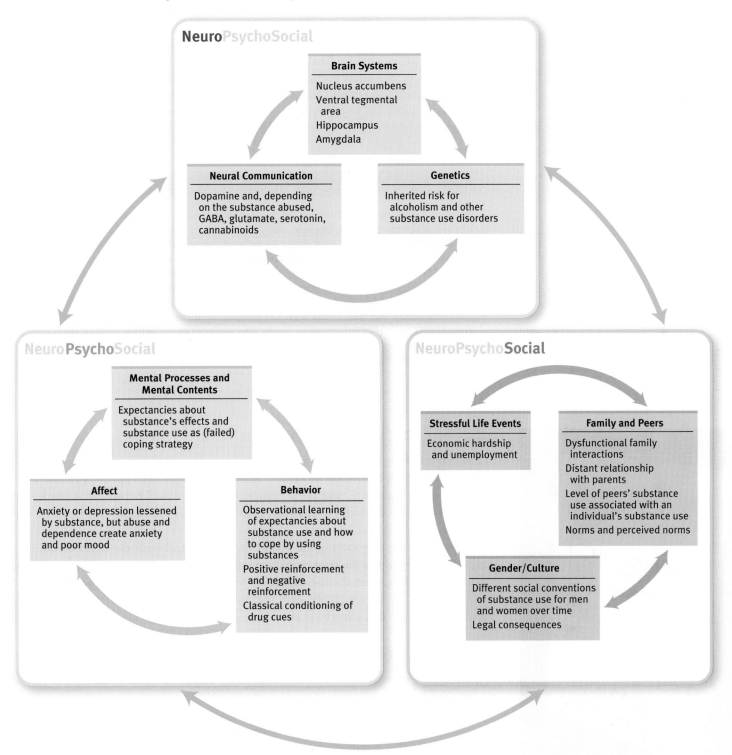

a temperament that leads them to be more responsive to reward (and to a drug's rewarding effects) than others are.

Psychological factors and social factors also play a role in the development of substance use disorders. Experiencing child abuse, neglect, or another significant social stressor increases the risk for substance use disorders (Compton et al., 2005).

Moreover, as we saw for alcohol use, peer and family interactions and culture (social factors) help determine perceived social norms, which in turn alter a person's expectations about the effects of taking a substance and his or her willingness to try the substance or continue to use it (psychological factor) (Kendler, Sundquist, et al., 2013). And once a person has tried a drug, its specific neurological effects and other consequences of its use—such as whether the experience of taking the drug is reinforced and how friends respond to the drug use (psychological and social factors)—will affect how likely the person is to continue using it.

Thinking Like A Clinician

Nat didn't care much for drinking; his drugs of choice were ketamine and LSD. His friends worried about him, though, because every weekend he'd either be clubbing (and taking ketamine) or tripping on LSD. What might be some of the sensations and perceptions that each drug induced in Nat, and why might his friends be concerned about him? Suppose he stopped using LSD but started smoking marijuana daily. What symptoms might he experience, and why might his friends become concerned? If he switched from taking ketamine to snorting heroin before clubbing, what difference might it make in the long term?

How would you determine whether Nat's substance use should be considered a use disorder? What other information might you want to know before making such a judgment? Do you think he might develop withdrawal symptoms? Why or why not? If so, which ones? According to the neuropsychosocial approach, what factors might underlie Nat's use of drugs?

☐ Treating Substance Use Disorders

Three of the four Beatles were known to have at least one type of substance use disorder: George Harrison, on nicotine (cigarettes), Ringo Starr on alcohol (for which he received treatment), and John Lennon on alcohol and heroin. It is not known whether any of the Beatles (other than Starr) received professional treatment for their use disorder.

We begin by considering the goals of treatment and what the best outcomes can be. Then we examine the treatments that target each of the three types of factors, and, when appropriate, note the use of specific treatments for particular types of substance use disorders. However, as we shall see, many treatments that target psychological and social factors can effectively treat more than one type of substance use disorder.

Goals of Treatment

Treatments for substance use disorders can have two competing ultimate goals. One goal is abstinence—leading the person to stop taking the substance entirely. When this is the goal of treatment, relapse rates tend to be high (up to 60%, by some estimates), particularly among patients with comorbid disorders (Brown & D'Amico, 2001; Curran et al., 2000; NIDA, 1999, 2008f). To help patients achieve abstinence, pharmaceutical companies have focused their efforts on developing two types of medications: (1) those that minimize withdrawal symptoms and (2) those that block the "high" if the substance is used, thereby leading to extinction of the conditioned responses arising from substance use disorders.

Given that abstinence-focused treatments have not been as successful as hoped, an alternative goal of treatment has emerged, which focuses on *harm reduction*—trying to reduce the harm to the individual and society that may come from substance use disorders. For example, needle exchange programs give users a clean needle for each

Two competing, alternate goals guide treatments for substance use disorders: One is abstinence (completely stopping the use of the substance), and the other is harm reduction (reducing the harmful effects related to the substance use, such as lowering the incidence of HIV/AIDS among heroin users by discouraging needle sharing).

Once an Alcoholic, Always an Alcoholic?

Most substance abuse treatment programs, especially those based on the Twelve-Step approach, insist that clients abstain from alcohol for the rest of their lives. With this approach, the assumption is that someone who has developed an alcohol use disorder will never again be able to drink without relapsing. This position is often summarized as, "Once an alcoholic, always an alcoholic." But is this true?

Many who advocate for an abstinence-only position do so based on both personal anecdotes of problem drinkers who tried to moderate their drinking and on treatment outcome studies in which relatively small proportions of former patients were able to moderate their drinking. (Unfortunately, only small proportions manage to abstain consistently.) The abstinence-only position is also grounded in the assumption that it is safer to counsel those with a drinking problem to quit completely because it's not possible to predict who will be able to moderate their drinking.

However, for the past 50 years, there has been growing support for the alternative position that at least some problem drinkers are able to moderate or control their drinking (Sobell & Sobell, 2006). Successful controlled drinking is typically defined as a reduction in the amount or frequency of consumption and the experience of fewer if any negative substance-related consequences associated with that consumption (e.g., Rosenberg, 2002). Research reviews suggest that problem drinkers are more likely to moderate their drinking if they have not adopted an "alcoholic identity," have selected controlled drinking as their outcome goal, are more psychologically and socially stable, and have a supportive posttreatment environment (Rosenberg, 1993). One advantage of offering controlled drinking is that it could attract and retain in treatment those problem drinkers who are ambivalent about abstaining for the rest of their lives (Ambrogne, 2002). Furthermore, behavioral techniques such as exposure to drinking cues have helped some problem drinkers moderate their consumption (Saladin & Santa Ana, 2004). Nonetheless, most treatment services in the United States and Canada do not offer controlled drinking training, even though acceptance of controlled drinking as an outcome goal is widespread in Australia and many Western Europe countries (Davis & Rosenberg, in press).

CRITICAL THINKING Based on what you have read, if a friend or family member who had a drinking problem wanted to control or moderate their drinking, on what basis would you support or resist their outcome goal? Why?

(Harold Rosenberg, Bowling Green State University)

---

heroin injection, which decreases the transmission of HIV/AIDS because users don't need to share needles that may be contaminated. In some cases, harm reduction programs may also seek to find a middle ground between use disorders and abstinence: controlled drinking or drug use. In the United States, most treatment programs have the goal of abstinence.

Targeting Neurological Factors

Many treatments of substance use disorders are directed toward neurological factors.

Detoxification

Detoxification (also referred to as *detox*) is medically supervised discontinuation of substance use. Detoxification may involve a gradual decrease in dosage over a period of time to prevent potentially lethal withdrawal symptoms, such as seizures. People with use disorders of alcohol, benzodiazepine, barbiturate, or opioids should be medically supervised when they stop taking the substance, particularly if they were using high doses. Use of other drugs, such as nicotine, cocaine, marijuana, and other hallucinogens, can be stopped abruptly without fear of medical problems, although the withdrawal symptoms may be unpleasant. John Lennon was not medically supervised when he stopped using heroin, and he described his disturbing withdrawal experience in his song "Cold Turkey": "Thirty-six hours/ Rolling in pain/Praying to someone/Free me again." Because substance use

Detoxification
Medically supervised discontinuation of substances for those with substance use disorders; also referred to as *detox*.

disorders can cause permanent brain changes (which are evident even years after withdrawal symptoms have ceased; Hyman, 2005), O'Brien (2005) proposed that treatment for substance use disorders should not end with detox but rather should be a long-term venture, similar to long-term treatment for chronic diseases such as diabetes and hypertension.

Medications

Medications that treat substance use disorders operate in any of several ways: (1) They interfere with the pleasant effects of drug use; (2) they reduce the unpleasant effects of withdrawal; or (3) they help maintain abstinence. Because of the high relapse rate among those with substance use disorders, however, medications should be supplemented with the sorts of relapse prevention strategies we describe later, in the sections on treatments targeting psychological and social factors (O'Brien, 2005). We now turn to consider medications that are used to treat substance-related disorders of various specific types of drugs.

Stimulants

Of all drugs, stimulants have the most direct effects on the dopamine reward system, but medications that modify the action of dopamine receptors in this system have not yet been developed. However, some medications do affect the functioning of dopamine. For example, a medication that helps people stop smoking is *bupropion* (marketed as Zyban), which alters the functioning of several neurotransmitters—including dopamine. Bupropion can help to decrease cravings for methamphetamines (Killen et al., 2006; Newton et al., 2006).

Depressants

Medication for use disorders of depressants (such as alcohol use disorder) minimizes withdrawal symptoms by substituting a less harmful drug in the same category for the more harmful one. For example, longer-acting benzodiazepines, such as Valium, may be substituted for alcohol or other depressants.

Disulfiram (**Antabuse**), a medication for treating alcohol use disorder, relies on a different approach. Antabuse causes violent nausea and vomiting when it is mixed with alcohol. When an alcoholic takes Antabuse and then drinks alcohol, the resulting nausea and vomiting should condition the person to have negative associations with drinking alcohol. When Antabuse is taken consistently, it leads people with alcohol use disorder to drink less frequently (Fuller et al., 1986; Sereny et al., 1986). However, many patients choose to stop taking Antabuse instead of giving up drinking alcohol (Suh et al., 2006).

Naltrexone (reVia and Vivitrol) is another medication used to treat alcohol use disorder; after detox, it can help maintain abstinence. Naltrexone indirectly reduces activity in the dopamine reward system, making drinking alcohol less rewarding; it is the most widely used medication to treat alcoholism in the United States, and it has minimal side effects.

Finally, people with alcohol use disorder who are undergoing detox may develop seizures; to prevent seizures and decrease symptoms of DTs, patients may be given benzodiazepines, along with the beta-blocker *atenolol*. However, a patient with DTs should be hospitalized (Arana & Rosenbaum, 2000).

Opioids

Medications that are used to treat opioid use disorder are generally chemically similar to the drugs but reduce or eliminate the "high"; treatments with these medications seek harm reduction because the medications are a safer substitute. For instance, heroin users may be given *methadone*, a synthetic opiate that binds to the same receptors as heroin. For about 24 hours after a current or former heroin user has taken

Antabuse
A medication for treating alcohol use disorder that induces violent nausea and vomiting when it is mixed with alcohol.

methadone, taking heroin will not lead to a high because methadone prevents the heroin molecules from binding to the receptors. Methadone also prevents heroin withdrawal symptoms and cravings (NIDA, 2007c). Treatment of opioid use disorder with substitution medications, such as methadone, is generally more successful than promoting abstinence (D'Ippoliti et al., 1998; Strain et al., 1999; United Nations International Drug Control Programme, 1997).

Because methadone can produce a mild high and is effective for only 24 hours, patients on methadone maintenance treatment generally must go to a clinic to receive a daily oral dose, a procedure that minimizes the sale of methadone on the black market. Methadone blocks only the effects of heroin, so those taking it might still use cocaine or other drugs to experience a high (El-Bassel et al., 1993). Another medication, LAAM (*levo-alpha-acetyl-methadol*), blocks the effects of opioids for up to 72 hours and does not produce a high. However, LAAM can cause heart problems and so is prescribed only for patients with opioid use disorder when other treatments have proven inadequate.

Methadone and LAAM are generally available only in drug treatment clinics. However, people seeking medication to treat opioid use disorder can receive a prescription for *buprenorphine* (Subutex) in a doctor's office. Buprenorphine is also available in combination with *naloxone* (Suboxone). In either preparation, buprenorphine has less potential for being abused than methadone because it does not produce a high.

Naltrexone is also used to treat alcohol use disorder and, in combination with buprenorphine, to treat opioid use disorder (Amass et al., 2004). Naltrexone is generally most effective for those who are highly motivated and willing to take medication that blocks the reinforcing effects of alcohol or opioids (Tomkins & Sellers, 2001).

Finally, the beta-blocker *clonidine* (Catapres) may help with withdrawal symptoms (Arana & Rosenbaum, 2000). A summary of medications used to treat substance use disorders is found in Table 9.9.

TABLE 9.9 • Medications Used to Treat Withdrawal and Promote Maintenance in People with Substance Use Disorders

Class of drugs	To treat withdrawal	To promote maintenance
Depressants	Longer-acting *depressants* (such as Valium) that block withdrawal symptoms	*Antabuse, naltrexone*
Narcotic analgesics	*Methadone, buprenorphine, clonidine*	*Methadone, buprenorphine, LAAM, naltrexone*

Hallucinogens

People who abuse LSD and want to quit can generally do so without withdrawal symptoms or significant cravings. Thus, marijuana is the only substance in this category that has been the focus of research on treatment, which generally targets psychological factors and social factors, not neurological ones (McRae et al., 2003).

Targeting Psychological Factors

Treatments that target psychological factors focus on four elements: (1) increasing a user's motivation to cease or decrease substance use, (2) changing the user's expectations of the drug experience, (3) increasing the user's involvement in treatment, and

(4) decreasing the (classically and operantly) conditioned behaviors associated with use of the drug. We first consider motivation, and then see how CBT and Twelve-Step Facilitation address other aspects of treatment.

Motivation

For people with substance use disorders, stopping or decreasing use is at best unpleasant and at worst is very painful and extremely aversive. Therefore, the user's motivation to stop or decrease strongly affects the ultimate success of any treatment.

Stages of Change

Extensive research has led to a theory of treatment that posits different stages of readiness for changing problematic behaviors. Research on this theory of **stages of change** has also led to methods that promote readiness for the next stage (Prochaska et al., 2007). Whereas most other treatments rely on a dichotomous view of substance use—users are either abstinent or not—this approach rests on the idea of intermediate states between these two extremes; the five stages of readiness to change are as follows:

1. *Precontemplation.* The user does not admit that there is a problem and doesn't intend to change. A temporary decrease in use in response to pressure from others will be followed by a relapse when the pressure is lifted.

2. *Contemplation.* The user admits that there is a problem and may contemplate taking action. However, no actual behavioral change occurs at this stage; behavior change is considered for the future.

3. *Preparation.* The user is prepared to change. He or she has a specific commitment to change, a plan for change, and the ability to adjust the plan of action and intends to start changing the substance use within a month. The user is very aware of the abuse, how it reached its current level, and available solutions. Although users in this stage are prepared to change, some are more ambivalent than others and may revert to the contemplation stage.

4. *Action.* The user actually changes his or her substance use behavior and environment. At this stage, others most clearly perceive the user's intentions to stop or decrease substance use; it is during this stage that family members and friends generally offer the most help and support.

5. *Maintenance.* The user builds on gains already made in stopping or decreasing substance use and tries to prevent relapses. Former substance users who do not devote significant amounts of energy and attention to relapse prevention are likely to relapse all the way back to the contemplation—or even the precontemplation—stage. Friends and family members often mistakenly think that because the substance abuse has stopped or diminished, the former user is finished taking action. In fact, the former user must *actively* prevent relapses, and help and support from friends and family members is very important in this stage.

This description of the five steps suggests a lock-step process: Each stage has discrete tasks that lead to the next stage in a linear progression. Research, however, suggests that the stages are not mutually exclusive (Littell & Girvin, 2002). For example, most people in the stage of action have occasional relapses and engage in the unwanted behavior, but they do not totally relapse into the old patterns. Also, uninterrupted forward progress is not the most typical path. People often regress before moving forward again. For example, only 5% of smokers who think about quitting

Stages of change
A series of five stages that characterizes how ready a person is to change problematic behaviors: precontemplation, contemplation, preparation, action, and maintenance.

go through all the stages of change within 2 years without a relapse (Prochaska, Velicer, et al., 1994).

Motivational Enhancement Therapy

Motivational enhancement therapy (also referred to as *motivational interviewing*) is specifically designed to boost patients' motivation to decrease or stop substance use (Bagøien et al., 2013; Hettema et al., 2005; Miller & Rollnick 1992). In this therapy, the patient sets his or her own goals regarding substance use, and the therapist points out discrepancies between the user's stated personal goals and his or her current behavior. The therapist then draws on the user's desire to meet the goals, helping him or her to override the rewarding effects of drug use. Therapists using motivational enhancement therapy do not dispense advice or seek to increase any specific skills; rather, they focus on increasing the motivation to change drug use, discussing both positive and negative aspects of drug use, reasons to quit, and how change might begin (Miller, 2001).

Studies have shown that this treatment is more successful when patients have a positive relationship with their therapist and are at the outset strongly motivated to obtain treatment (Etheridge et al., 1999; Joe et al., 1999). The beneficial effects of motivational enhancement therapy tend to fade over the course of a year (Hettema et al., 2005).

Cognitive-Behavior Therapy

Cognitive-behavior therapy (CBT) for substance use disorders has three general foci:

1. understanding and changing thoughts, feelings, and behaviors that lead to substance use;

2. understanding and changing the consequences of the substance use; and

3. developing alternative behaviors to substitute for substance use (Carroll, 1998; Marlatt & Gordon, 1985).

CBT treatment may focus in particular on decreasing the positive consequences of drug use and on increasing the positive consequences of abstaining from drug use (referred to as *abstinence reinforcement*). As patients are able to change these consequences, they should be less motivated to abuse the substance. CBT may be used more generally for *contingency management*, in which reinforcement is contingent on the desired behavior's occurring, or the undesired behavior's not occurring (Stitzer & Petry, 2006).

CBT has been used to treat a variety of types of substances, including heroin and cocaine (Higgins et al., 1993; Higgins & Silverman, 1999; Petry et al., 2011). The desired behavior (such as attendance at treatment sessions or abstinence from using cocaine, as assessed by urine tests) is reinforced with one or more of these consequences:

• monetary vouchers, the value of which increases with continued abstinence (Jones et al., 2004; Silverman et al., 1999, 2001, 2004);

• decreasing the frequency of mandatory counseling sessions if treatment has been court ordered;

• more convenient appointment times; or

• being allowed to take home a small supply of methadone (requiring fewer trips to the clinic) for people being treated for heroin use disorder.

Positive incentives (obtaining reinforcement for a desired behavior) are more effective than negative consequences (i.e., punishment, such as taking away

Motivational enhancement therapy
A form of treatment specifically designed to boost a patient's motivation to decrease or stop substance use by highlighting discrepancies between stated personal goals related to substance use and current behavior; also referred to as *motivational interviewing*.

privileges) in helping patients to stay in treatment and to decrease substance use (Carroll & Onken, 2005). The cost of providing such rewards can be high, and relapse often increases once rewards are discontinued, which limits the practicality and effectiveness of abstinence reinforcement as a long-term treatment (Carroll & Onken, 2005).

Once the patient has stopped abusing the substance, CBT may focus on preventing relapse by extinguishing the conditioned response (including cravings) to drug-related cues. Treatment may also focus on decreasing the frequency or intensity of emotional distress, which can contribute to relapse (Vuchinich & Tucker, 1996). One way treatment can help patients regulate emotional distress is by helping them to develop healthier coping skills, which will then increase self-control. Thus, many of the CBT methods used to treat depression and anxiety also can be effective here; such methods include self-monitoring, cognitive restructuring, problem solving, and various relaxation techniques.

Twelve-Step Facilitation (TSF)

Twelve-Step Facilitation (TSF) is based on the 12 steps or principles that form the basis of Alcoholics Anonymous (AA) (see Table 9.10). AA views alcohol abuse as a disease that can never be cured, although alcohol-related behaviors can be modified by the alcoholic's recognizing that he or she has lost control and is powerless over alcohol, turning to a higher power for help, and seeking abstinence. Research suggests that the AA approach can help people who are trying to stop their substance abuse (Laffaye et al., 2008).

TABLE 9.10 • Twelve Steps of Alcoholics Anonymous

(1) We admitted we were powerless over alcohol—that our lives had become unmanageable.
(2) Came to believe that a Power greater than ourselves could restore us to sanity.
(3) Made a decision to turn our will and our lives over to the care of God as we understood Him.
(4) Made a searching and fearless moral inventory of ourselves.
(5) Admitted to God, to ourselves and to another human being the exact nature of our wrongs.
(6) Were entirely ready to have God remove all these defects of character.
(7) Humbly asked Him to remove our shortcomings.
(8) Made a list of all persons we had harmed, and became willing to make amends to them all.
(9) Made direct amends to such people wherever possible, except when to do so would injure them or others.
(10) Continued to take personal inventory and when we were wrong promptly admitted it.
(11) Sought through prayer and meditation to improve our conscious contact with God as we understood Him, praying only for knowledge of His will for us and the power to carry that out.
(12) Having had a spiritual awakening as the result of these steps, we tried to carry this message to alcoholics, and to practice these principles in all our affairs.

Source: www.aa.org/en_pdfs/smf-121_en.pdf.

AA's groups are leaderless, whereas TSF's groups are led by mental health professionals, whose goal is to help group members become ready to follow the 12 steps of AA. The Twelve-Step model has been used by people who abuse narcotics (Narcotics Anonymous [NA]) and in numerous inpatient and outpatient treatment programs run by mental health professionals (Ries et al., 2008). TSF targets *motivation* to adhere to the steps. In essence, its goals are like those of motivational enhancement therapy, but the enhanced motivation focuses on sticking with a specific type of treatment.

Targeting Social Factors

Treatments that target social factors aim to change interpersonal and community *antecedents* (i.e., the events that lead up to) and *consequences* of substance abstinence and use. Antecedents might be addressed by decreasing family tensions, increasing summer employment among teens, and decreasing community violence. Consequences might be addressed by increasing community support for abstinence and providing improved housing or employment opportunities for reduced use or for abstinence.

Residential Treatment

Some people who seek treatment for substance use disorders may need more intensive help, such as the assistance that can be found in *residential treatment* (also called *inpatient treatment* or *psychiatric hospitalization*), which provides a round-the-clock therapeutic environment (such as the Betty Ford Center in California). Because it is so intensive, residential treatment can help a person more rapidly change how he or she thinks, feels, and behaves. Some residential treatment programs have a spiritual component. Depending on the philosophy of the program, various combinations of methods—targeting neurological, psychological, and social factors—may be available.

Group-Based Treatment

Treatments that target social factors are usually provided in groups. One approach focuses on providing group therapy, which typically takes place in residential treatment programs, methadone clinics, drug counseling centers, and *day-treatment programs* (to which patients come during the day to attend groups and receive individual therapy but do not stay overnight—also called partial hospitalization or intensive outpatient treatment). In addition, there are a number of self-help groups for people with substance use disorders.

Group Therapy

CBT may be used in a group format to help people with substance use disorders. The group provides peer pressure and support for abstinence (Crits-Christoph et al., 1999). Moreover, members may use role-playing to try out new skills, such as saying "no" to friends who offer drugs. Other types of groups include social-skills training groups, where members learn ways to communicate their feelings and desires more effectively, and general support groups to decrease shame and isolation as members change their substance abuse patterns.

Self-Help Groups

Self-help groups (sometimes called *support groups*), such as those that adopt the Twelve-Step programs of Alcoholics Anonymous and Narcotics Anonymous, hold regular meetings. Attending such a group might supplement other treatment or might be the only treatment a person pursues. As noted earlier, such groups often view belief in a "higher power" as crucial to

Various types of treatment for substance use disorders can be offered in the community, including day-treatment programs, methadone clinics (such as the one shown here), group therapy, and self-help groups.

Steven L. Raymer/National Geographic/Getty Images

recovery, and even people who are not religious can improve through such meetings (Humphreys & Moos, 2007; Moos & Timko, 2008). AA also provides social support, both from other group members and from a *sponsor*—a person with years of sobriety who serves as a mentor and can be called up when the newer member experiences cravings or temptations to drink again. A variety of other self-help groups and organizations address recovery from substance use disorders without a Twelve-Step religious or spiritual component.

A meta-analysis showed that attending a self-help group at least once a week is associated with drug or alcohol abstinence (Fiorentine, 1999). Other research confirms that longer participation in AA is associated with better outcomes (Moos & Moos, 2004). Just like group therapy, a self-help group can be invaluable in decreasing feelings of isolation and shame. In general, self-help groups can be valuable sources of information and support, not only for the person with a substance use disorder but also for his or her relatives.

Family Therapy

Family therapy is a treatment that involves an entire family or some portion of a family. Family therapy can be performed using any theoretical approach; the main focus is on the family rather than the individual. The goals of this type of therapy are tailored to the specific problems and needs of each family, but such therapy typically addresses issues related to communication, power, and control (Hogue et al., 2006). To the extent that family interactions lead to or help sustain abuse of a substance, changing the patterns of interaction in a family can modify these factors (Saatcioglu et al., 2006; Stanton & Shadish, 1997). Among adolescents treated for substance use disorders, outpatient family therapy can help them to abstain (Smith et al., 2006; Szapocznik et al., 2003), which suggests that changes in how parents and adolescents interact can promote and maintain abstinence. In fact, family therapy is usually a standard component of treatment for adolescents with substance use disorders (Austin et al., 2005).

Feedback Loops in Treating Substance Use Disorders

The following considerations help determine whether an intervention was successful. Did the person:

- complete the treatment, or is he or she still using or abusing the substance? (Is he or she abstinent—yes or no?)

- experience fewer harmful effects from the substance? (Is he or she using clean needles or no longer drinking to the point of passing out?)

- decrease use of the substance? (How much is the person using after treatment?)

- come to behave more responsibly? (Does he or she attend regular AA meetings or get to work on time?)

- feel better? (Is the person less depressed, anxious, "strung out," or are drug cravings less intense?)

- come to conform to societal norms? (Has he or she stayed out of jail?)

The treatments we've discussed can lead to improvement according to these considerations, but different types of treatments provide different paths toward improvement. Moreover, many people with substance use disorders may quit multiple times. In addition, like studies of treatments for other types of disorders, studies of treatments for substance use disorders have found a dose-response relationship: Longer treatment produces better outcomes than shorter treatment

Family therapy
A treatment that involves an entire family or some portion of a family.

(Hubbard et al., 1989; Simpson et al., 2002). And for those people who abuse more than one type of substance, treatment is most effective when it addresses the entire set of substances.

Ultimately, all successful treatments address all three types of factors that are identified in the neuropsychosocial approach. When people with a substance use disorder first stop abusing the substance, they will experience changes that are, at minimum, uncomfortable (neurological and psychological factors). Moreover, how they think and feel about themselves will change (psychological factor)—from "abuser" or "addict" to "ex-abuser" or "in recovery." Their interactions with others will change (social factors): Perhaps they will make new friends who don't use drugs, avoid friends who abuse drugs, behave differently with family members (who in turn may behave differently toward them), perform better at work, or have fewer run-ins with the law. Other people's responses to them will also affect their motivation to continue to avoid using the substance and endure the uncomfortable withdrawal effects and ignore their cravings. Thus, as usual, treatment ultimately relies on feedback loops among the three types of factors (see Figure 9.9).

FIGURE 9.9 • Feedback Loops in Treating Substance Use Disorders

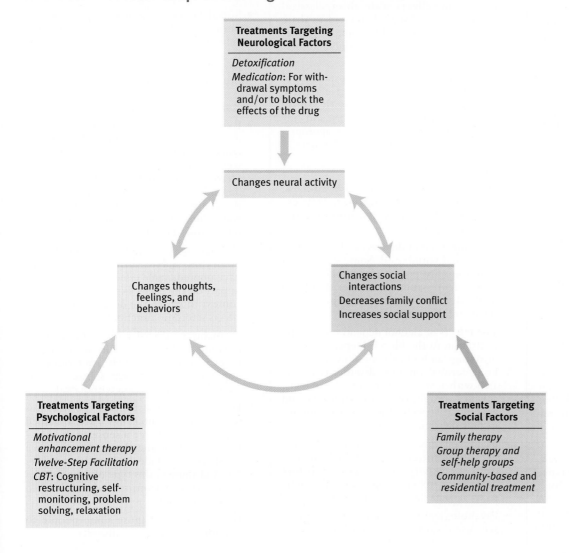

Thinking Like A Clinician

Karl has been binge drinking and smoking marijuana every weekend for the past couple of years. He's been able to maintain his job, but Monday mornings he's in rough shape, and sometimes he's had blackouts when he drinks. He's decided that he wants to quit drinking and smoking marijuana, but he feels that he needs some help to do so. Based on what you've read in this chapter, what would you advise for Karl, and why? What wouldn't you suggest to him as an appropriate treatment, and why? How would your answer change if he'd been using cocaine frequently?

▢ SUMMING UP

Substance Use: When Use Becomes a Disorder

- The hallmark of substance use disorders is loss of control over urges to use a psychoactive substance, even though such use might lead to significant problems.

- The term *addiction* focuses on the compulsive behaviors related to regular drug taking but is not used in DSM-5.

- Tolerance and withdrawal are symptoms of substance use disorders.

- The common liabilities model focuses on underlying factors that may contribute to a variety of problem behaviors, including substance use disorders. The gateway hypothesis focuses on factors that lead individuals to progress from using entry drugs to using harder drugs.

- Substance use disorders frequently co-occur with mood disorders (particularly depression), PTSD, schizophrenia, and ADHD. Many people with substance use disorders engage in polysubstance abuse.

- Cultures can promote or regulate substance use through the use of rituals and penalties.

Stimulants

- Stimulants, which increase arousal and brain activity, are the psychoactive substances in which use is most likely to lead to a use disorder. Unlike many other types of drugs, they act directly—rather than indirectly—on the dopamine reward system by binding to dopamine transporters in the synapse.

- Stimulants include cocaine and crack, amphetamines, methamphetamine, Ritalin, MDMA, and nicotine. In high doses, most of these stimulants can cause paranoia and hallucinations. With continued use, stimulants lead to tolerance and withdrawal.

- A neurological factor that contributes to substance use disorders is activation of the dopamine reward system.

- Psychological factors related to substance use disorders include operant reinforcement of the effects of the drug, classical conditioning of stimuli related to drug use, and observational learning of expectancies about the effects of drugs and their use of them.

- Social factors related to substance use disorders include the specific nature of a person's relationships with family members, socioeconomic factors, and cultural and perceived norms about appropriate and inappropriate uses of substances.

Depressants

- Depressants decrease arousal, awareness, and nervous system activity. Depressants include alcohol, barbiturates, and benzodiazepines.

- Continued use of depressants leads to tolerance and withdrawal. Some withdrawal symptoms are potentially lethal; people with a depressant use disorder should be medically supervised while tapering off the use of the drug.

- The effects of alcohol depend on its concentration in the blood. Repeated binge drinking can lead to alcohol use disorder. Long-term alcohol use disorder is associated with a variety of cognitive problems, as well as atrophy of certain brain areas and enlarged ventricles. Withdrawal symptoms include delirium tremens.

- Depressants directly affect the GABAnergic neurotransmitter system, which in turn dampens activity in key brain areas that give rise to anxiety. Depressants also indirectly activate the dopamine reward system.

- Psychological factors related to depressant use disorders include observational learning to expect specific effects from depressant use and to use depressants as a coping strategy, positive and negative reinforcement of the effects of the drug, and classical conditioning of drug cues that leads to cravings.

- Social factors related to depressant use disorders include the nature of a person's relationships with family members, peers' use of depressants, and norms and perceived norms about appropriate and inappropriate use of depressants.

Other Abused Substances

- Exogenous opioids can dull pain and decrease awareness. Continued opioid use quickly leads to tolerance and withdrawal, as well as compulsive drug-related behaviors. Heroin is an opioid. Opioids activate the dopamine reward system. They also depress the central nervous system and decrease endorphin production, thereby reducing the body's inherent ability to relieve pain.

- Hallucinogens include LSD, mescaline, psilocybin, and marijuana. Hallucinogens have unpredictable effects, which depend in part on the user's expectations and the context in which the drug is taken. LSD affects serotonin functioning.

- Cannabis use disorder affects motivation, learning, and memory. The active ingredient in marijuana, THC, activates the dopamine reward system. Chronic marijuana users may develop withdrawal.

- Dissociative anesthetics (sometimes referred to as "club drugs") are so named because they induce a sense of dissociation and cause anesthesia. Dissociative anesthetics include PCP and ketamine. Use and abuse of this type of drug impairs cognitive functioning and can lead to violent behavior.

- Genes may predispose some people to develop a substance use disorder.

- Psychological factors related to other substance use disorders include observational learning of what to expect from taking the drugs and of using the drugs as a coping strategy. Classical conditioning of stimuli related to drug use can lead to cravings and can play a role in building tolerance. In addition, the disorders may arise in part from operant conditioning.

- Social factors related to other substance use disorders include the person's relationships with family members, peers' use of substances, cultural norms and perceived norms about appropriate and inappropriate use of substances, and socioeconomic factors.

Treating Substance Use Disorders

- A treatment that focuses on neurological factors is detox to help reduce symptoms of withdrawal that come from substance use disorders. Medications may reduce unpleasant withdrawal symptoms or block the pleasant effects of using the substance, which can help maintain abstinence.

- Treatments that target psychological factors, such as motivational enhancement therapy, are designed to motivate people to decrease substance use. CBT addresses antecedents, consequences, and specific behaviors related to substance use. Twelve-Step Facilitation provides structure and support to help patients abstain.

- Social factors are targeted by residential treatment and other types of community-based treatment (group therapy and self-help groups), as well as family therapy to address issues of communication, power, and control.

Key Terms

Psychoactive substance (p. 257)
Substance use disorders (p. 258)
Substance intoxication (p. 258)
Tolerance (p. 259)
Withdrawal (p. 259)
Common liabilities model (p. 261)

Gateway hypothesis (p. 261)
Polysubstance abuse (p. 262)
Dopamine reward system (p. 267)
Reward craving (p. 268)
Relief craving (p. 268)
Drug cues (p. 269)

Delirium tremens (DTs) (p. 276)
Detoxification (p. 285)
Antabuse (p. 286)
Stages of change (p. 288)
Motivational enhancement therapy (p. 289)
Family therapy (p. 292)

More Study Aids

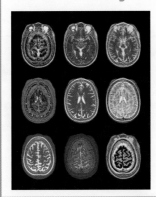

For additional study aids related to this chapter, including quizzes to make sure you've retained everything you've learned and a Student Video Activity exploring how hallucinogens affect brain activity, go to: www.worthpublishers.com/launchpad/rkabpsych2e.

Don Farrall/Digital Vision/Getty Images

CHAPTER **10**

Eating Disorders

By the time she was 9 years old, Marya Hornbacher had developed **bulimia nervosa**, which is an eating disorder characterized by binge eating along with vomiting or other behaviors to compensate for the large number of calories ingested. This was an unusually young age to develop an eating disorder. By the time she reached 15, she had **anorexia nervosa**, an eating disorder characterized by significantly low body weight along with an intense fear of gaining weight or using various methods to prevent weight gain. For the next 5 years, she careened from one eating disorder to another. By Hornbacher's own account, she had "been hospitalized six times, institutionalized once, had endless hours of therapy, been tested and observed and diagnosed . . . and fed and weighed for so long that I have begun to feel like a laboratory rat" (Hornbacher, 1998, p. 3). At the age of 23, Hornbacher wrote *Wasted: A Memoir of Anorexia and Bulimia* about her experiences with eating disorders, in which she observes that an eating disorder:

> . . . is an attempt to find an identity, but ultimately it strips you of any sense of yourself, save the sorry identity of "sick." It is a grotesque mockery of cultural standards of beauty that winds up mocking no one more than you. It is a protest against cultural stereotypes of women that in the end makes you seem the weakest, the most needy and neurotic of all women. It is the thing you believe is keeping you safe, alive, contained—and in the end, of course, you find it's doing quite the opposite. (1998, p. 6)

An **eating disorder** is characterized by abnormal eating and a preoccupation with body image. Approximately 90% of the people diagnosed with eating disorders are females, and so in this chapter, we will refer to a person with an eating disorder as "she" or "her"; however, the number of males with eating disorders has been slowly increasing (Hudson et al., 2007).

IN THIS CHAPTER, we discuss three disorders from the DSM-5 category of *feeding and eating disorders*: *anorexia nervosa*, *bulimia nervosa*, and *binge eating disorder*. We examine the criteria for and the medical effects of these disorders and discuss research findings that can illuminate why eating disorders develop and the various methods used to treat them.

Bulimia nervosa
An eating disorder characterized by binge eating along with vomiting or other behaviors to compensate for the large number of calories ingested.

Anorexia nervosa
An eating disorder characterized by significantly low body weight along with an intense fear of gaining weight or using various methods to prevent weight gain.

Eating disorder
A category of psychological disorders characterized by abnormal eating and a preoccupation with body image.

Anorexia Nervosa

After years of struggling with bulimia, Marya Hornbacher began "inching" toward anorexia; she gradually became significantly underweight by severely restricting her food intake, refusing to eat enough to obtain a healthy weight:

> Anorexia started slowly. It took time to work myself into the frenzy that the disease demands. There were an incredible number of painfully thin girls at [school], dancers mostly. The obsession with weight seemed nearly universal. Whispers and longing stares followed the ones who were visibly anorexic. We sat at our cafeteria tables, passionately discussing the calories of lettuce, celery, a dinner roll, rice. (Hornbacher, 1998, p. 102)

Hornbacher wanted to be thin, to be in control of her eating, and to feel more in control of herself generally. She began to eat less and less, to the point where she began to pass out at school.

Marya Hornbacher

People who have anorexia nervosa have a very low weight and, despite medical consequences, refuse to maintain a healthy weight. This young woman had been on her college swim team when she suffered a heart attack; her anorexia persisted, and she was considered to be a danger to herself and banned from campus.

What Is Anorexia Nervosa?

Key features of *anorexia nervosa* (often referred to simply as *anorexia*) are that the person will not maintain at least a low normal weight and employs various methods to prevent weight gain (American Psychiatric Association, 2013). Despite medical and psychological consequences of a low weight, people who have anorexia nervosa continue to pursue extreme thinness. Anorexia has a high risk of death: About 10–15% of people hospitalized with anorexia eventually die as a direct or indirect consequence of the disorder (Zipfel et al., 2000).

Anorexia Nervosa According to DSM-5

To be diagnosed with anorexia nervosa according to DSM-5, symptoms must meet three criteria (American Psychiatric Association, 2013):

1. *A significantly low body weight for the person's age and sex*, which results from not ingesting enough calories relative to the calories burned. Being slightly underweight is not enough.

2. *An intense fear of becoming fat or gaining weight, or behaving in ways that interfere with weight gain*, despite being significantly underweight. This fear is often the primary reason that the person refuses to attain a healthy weight. A person who has anorexia is obsessed with her body and food, and her thoughts and beliefs about these topics are usually illogical or irrational, such as imagining that wearing a certain clothing size is "worse than death." Moreover, her feelings about herself rise and fall with her caloric intake, weight, or how her clothes seem to fit. If someone with anorexia eats 50 more calories (for comparison, a single pat of butter provides about 35 calories) than she had allotted for her daily intake, she may experience intense feelings of worthlessness. People who suffer from anorexia often deny that they have a problem and do not see their low weight as a source of concern.

3. *Distortions of body image (the person's view of her body)*. People with anorexia often feel that their bodies are bigger and "fatter" than they actually are and overly value their body's weight or shape (see Figure 10.1). Note that people who have anorexia and people who have body dysmorphic disorder both have a distorted body image (Chapter 7); however, people with anorexia focus on overall body shape and weight, whereas people with body dysmorphic disorder typically focus on the face or a single body part. Moreover, the former typically have an actual physical problem with their body (that is—they are in fact significantly underweight) that they typically do not want to improve, whereas the latter have no or only a minimal "defect" but perceive it to be significant and want to hide it or minimize it in other ways (Hrabosky et al., 2009).

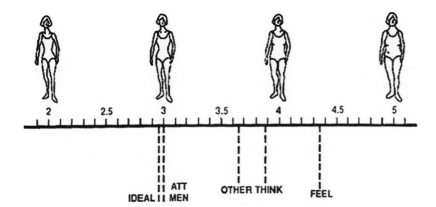

FIGURE **10.1 • Body Image Distortion** With respect to body image, women with anorexia may simply represent an extreme end of "normal" distortions; many other women do not assess their bodies accurately (Thompson, 1990). Here IDEAL is the average figure that women rated as ideal. ATT MEN ("attractive to men") shows the average figure that women rated as most attractive to men, whereas OTHER illustrates the average figure that men selected as most attractive. THINK depicts the average figure that women *thought* of as best matching their own, and FEEL depicts the average figure that women *felt* best matches their own.

Source: Larry Pasman, J. Kevin Thompson, International Journal of Eating Disorders Copyright © 1988 Wiley Periodicals, Inc., A Wiley Company.

Research suggests that people with anorexia also have distorted perceptions of the size of their meal portions, overestimating how much food is in a portion (Milos et al., 2013). Table 10.1 lists the DSM-5 diagnostic criteria for anorexia; additional facts about anorexia are provided in Table 10.2, and Caroline Knapp, Case 10.1, provides a glimpse of life with anorexia.

TABLE **10.2 • Anorexia Nervosa Facts at a Glance**

Prevalence

- In the course of a lifetime, about 1% of females and up to 0.3% of males will develop anorexia (Hoek & van Hoeken, 2003; Hudson et al., 2007).

Comorbidity

- Most studies find that at least half—but as high as 90%—of patients with anorexia have at least one comorbid psychological disorder. The most common types of comorbid disorders are depression, anxiety disorders, personality disorders, and body dysmorphic disorder (Cassin & van Ranson, 2005; Dingemans et al., 2012; Godart et al., 2003; Lucka, 2006; Sansone & Sansone, 2011).

Onset

- Anorexia typically emerges during adolescence or young adulthood, although the disorder can make its first appearance at an earlier or a later age (American Psychiatric Association, 2013).

Course

- Anorexia has the highest mortality rate of any psychological disorder—up to 15% (Zipfel et al., 2000). Half of the deaths are from suicide, and the others are from medical complications of the disorder. People with anorexia who also abuse substances have an even higher risk of death (Keel et al., 2003).

- According to some studies, fewer than 50% of people who survive fully recover (Keel et al., 2005; Von Holle et al., 2008), about 33% improve but do not recover, and 20% develop chronic anorexia (Fichter et al., 2006; Steinhausen, 2002); other studies have found higher rates of full recovery (Johnson et al., 2003; Keski-Rahkonen et al., 2007).

Gender Differences

- Approximately 75–90% of people with anorexia nervosa are female (Hoek & van Hoeken, 2003; Hudson et al., 2007).

Cultural Differences

- In the United States, females of Black, Hispanic, or Asian background are less likely to be diagnosed with anorexia nervosa than are White females (Alegría et al., 2007; Nicdao et al., 2007; Taylor et al., 2007).

TABLE **10.1 • DSM-5 Diagnostic Criteria for Anorexia Nervosa**

A. Restriction of energy intake relative to requirements, leading to a significantly low body weight in the context of age, sex, developmental trajectory, and physical health. *Significantly low weight* is defined as a weight that is less than minimally normal or, for children and adolescents, less than that minimally expected.

B. Intense fear of gaining weight or of becoming fat, or persistent behavior that interferes with weight gain, even though at a significantly low weight.

C. Disturbance in the way in which one's body weight or shape is experienced, undue influence of body weight or shape on self-evaluation, or persistent lack of recognition of the seriousness of the current low body weight.

CASE 10.1 · FROM THE INSIDE: Anorexia Nervosa

Caroline Knapp suffered from both anorexia and alcohol use disorder (see the excerpt from her book, *Drinking: A Love Story*, in Chapter 9, Case 9.3). In describing her relationship with food, she noted that people with anorexia nervosa develop bizarre eating habits and a kind of tunnel vision—focusing on food, on eating, and on not eating:

> When you're starving . . . it's hard to think about anything else [except eating or not eating. It's] very hard to see the larger picture of options that is your life, very hard to consider what else you might need or want or fear were you not so intently focused on one crushing passion. I sat in my room every night, with rare exceptions, for three-and-a-half years. In secret, and with painstaking deliberation, I carved an apple and one-inch square of cheddar cheese into tiny bits, sixteen individual slivers, each one so translucently thin you could see the light shine through it if you held it up to a lamp. Then I lined up the apple slices on a tiny china saucer and placed a square of cheese on each. And then I ate them one by one, nibbled at them like a rabbit, edge by tiny edge, so slowly and with such concentrated precision the meal took two hours to consume. I planned for this ritual all day, yearned for it, carried it out with the utmost focus and care.

(Knapp, 2003, pp. 48–49)

If, as you read Knapp's description of her eating ritual, you were reminded of symptoms of obsessive-compulsive disorder (OCD, see Chapter 7), you're on to something. Some symptoms of anorexia overlap with symptoms of OCD and related disorders: obsessions about symmetry, compulsions to order objects precisely, and hoarding. However, other symptoms of OCD—such as obsessions about contamination and checking and cleaning compulsions—do not overlap with those of anorexia (Halmi et al., 2003).

Two Types of Anorexia Nervosa: Restricting and Binge Eating/Purging

People with anorexia become extremely thin and maintain their very low weight by using one of two methods: restricting what they eat or binge eating and then purging. DSM-5 categorizes two types of anorexia, based on which method is used:

- *Restricting type.* Low weight is achieved and maintained through severe undereating or excessive exercise. (Mental health clinicians consider exercise to be excessive if the person feels high levels of guilt when she postpones or misses a workout; Mond et al., 2006.) There is no binge eating or purging. This is the classic type of anorexia, and Knapp's description in Case 10.1 illustrates the pattern of eating that is common among people with the restricting type.

- *Binge eating/purging type.* Some people with anorexia may engage in **binge eating**—eating much more food at one time than most people would eat in the same period of time or context. People often feel out of control while binge eating. For example, a "snack" might consist of a pint or two of ice cream with a whole jar of hot fudge sauce, and the person feels unable to stop at just one scoop. Among people with anorexia, binge eating is followed by **purging**, which is an attempt to reduce the ingested calories by vomiting or by using diuretics, laxatives, or enemas.

Medical, Psychological, and Social Effects of Anorexia Nervosa

Anorexia has serious negative effects on many aspects of bodily functioning. Because of the daily deficit between calories needed for normal functioning and calories taken in, the body tries to make do with less. However, this process comes at a high cost.

Binge eating
Eating much more food at one time than most people would eat in the same period of time or context.

Purging
Attempting to reduce calories that have already been consumed by vomiting or using diuretics, laxatives, or enemas.

Medical Effects of Anorexia

One possible effect of anorexia is that the heart muscle becomes thinner as the body, using available energy sources to meet its caloric demands, cannibalizes muscle generally and the heart muscle in particular. *Muscle wasting* is the term used when the body breaks down muscle in order to obtain needed calories. When people with anorexia exercise, they are not building muscle but *losing* it, especially heart muscle—which can be fatal. Excessive exercise is actively discouraged in people with anorexia, and even modest exercise may be discouraged, depending on the person's weight and medical status.

A physical examination and lab tests are likely to reveal other medical effects of anorexia, as the body adjusts to conserve energy. These include low heart rate and blood pressure, abdominal bloating or discomfort, constipation, loss of bone density (leading to osteoporosis and easily fractured bones), and a slower metabolism (which leads to lower body temperature, difficulty tolerating cold temperatures, and downy hairs forming on the body to provide insulation) (Mascolo et al., 2012). More visible effects include dry and yellow-orange skin, brittle nails, and loss of hair on the scalp. Symptoms that may not be as obvious to others include irritability, fatigue, and headaches (Mehler, 2003; Pomeroy, 2004). People with anorexia may also appear hyperactive or restless, which is probably a by-product of starvation, given that such behavior also occurs in starved animals (Klein & Walsh, 2005).

People with anorexia who purge may believe that they are getting rid of all the calories they've eaten, but they're wrong. In a starved state, the body so desperately needs calories that once food is in the mouth, the digestive process begins more rapidly than normal, and calories may begin to be absorbed before the food reaches the stomach; even if vomiting occurs, some calories are still absorbed, although water the body needs is lost. Diuretics (i.e., substances that force the body to excrete water) decrease only water in the body, not body fat or muscle, and laxatives and enemas simply get rid of water and the body's waste before it would otherwise be eliminated.

All four methods of purging—vomiting, diuretics, laxatives, and enemas—can result in dehydration because they all deprive the body of needed fluids. In turn, dehydration can create an imbalance in the body's *electrolytes*—salts that are critical for neural transmission and muscle contractions, including those of the heart muscle. When dehydration remains untreated, it can lead to death. In addition, recent studies of the long-term consequences of starvation during puberty indicate an increased risk of heart disease (Sparén et al., 2004).

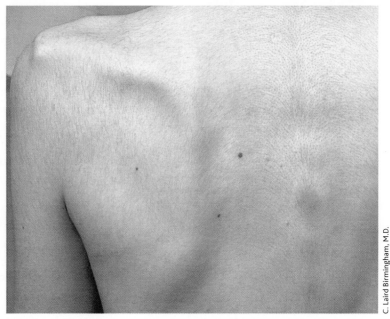

Like this woman, underweight people may develop lanugo hair—fine downy hair similar to that of newborns—on the abdomen, back, and face. Lanugo hair disappears when normal weight is attained.

C. Laird Birmingham, M.D.

Psychological and Social Effects of Starvation

Researchers in the 1940s documented a number of unexpected psychological and social effects of extreme caloric restriction, which were first discovered in what is sometimes called the *starvation study* (Keys et al., 1950). When healthy young men were given half their usual caloric intake for 6 months, they lost 25% of their original weight and suffered other changes: They became more sensitive to the sensations of light, cold, and noise; they slept less; they lost their sex drive; and their mood worsened. The men lost their sense of humor, argued with one another, and showed symptoms of depression and anxiety. They also became obsessed with food—talking

In the starvation study (Keys et al., 1950), men ate half their usual daily calories for 6 months. In this short amount of time, participants became preoccupied with food, as frequently occurs among people with anorexia. They also developed symptoms of depression and anxiety, which are often comorbid with anorexia. This photo shows a researcher obtaining information about a participant's body before the participant began to restrict his caloric intake.

and dreaming about food and collecting and sharing recipes. They began to hoard food and random items such as old books and knick-knacks. These striking effects persisted for months after the men returned to their normal diets, and abnormal eating and ruminations about food continued even 50 years later (Crow & Eckert, 2000). Such findings have since been substantiated by other researchers (Favaro et al., 2000; Polivy, 1996). It is sobering that, even on this diet, the participants in the starvation study still ate more each day than do many people with anorexia.

The participants in the starvation study were psychologically healthy adult men, and they developed the noticeable symptoms after less than 6 months on what would now be considered a relatively strict diet. Most people (females) with anorexia develop the disorder when they are younger than were the men in the study and maintain unhealthy eating patterns for a longer time than the 6 months of the study; the consequences of restricting eating at a young age may be more severe than those noted in the starvation study.

Moreover, some people with anorexia may have such distorted thinking about their weight and body that they may come to believe that there's really nothing wrong with their weight or restricted food intake (Csipke & Horne, 2007; Gavin et al., 2008). A minority may come to view anorexia as a lifestyle choice rather than a disorder. Unfortunately, anorexia has serious physical and mental health consequences, which are swept under the rug by such positive views of the condition.

Thinking Like A Clinician

Since the age of 12, Chris has been very thin, in part because of hours of soccer practice weekly. Now, at the age of 17, Chris eats very little (particularly staying away from foods high in fat), continues exercising, and gets angry when people comment about weight. What would you need to know to determine whether Chris has anorexia nervosa? If Chris does have anorexia, what would be some possible medical problems that might arise? What if Chris were male—would it change what you'd need to know to make the diagnosis? Explain your answer.

Bulimia Nervosa

Marya Hornbacher describes her descent into bulimia nervosa:

> I woke up one morning with a body that seemed to fill the room. Long since having decided I was fat, it was a complete crisis when my body, like all girls' bodies, acquired a significantly greater number of actual fat cells than it had ever possessed. At puberty, what had been a nagging, underlying discomfort with my body became a full-blown, constant obsession. . . . When I returned [from the bathroom after throwing up], everything was different. Everything was calm, and I felt very clean. Everything was in order. Everything was as it should be.
> (1998, pp. 40–44)

For Hornbacher, as for many other people with bulimia, the maladaptive eating behaviors started as an attempt to cope with negative feelings about weight, appearance, or eating "too much." In this section we examine the criteria for bulimia nervosa and the medical effects of the disorder.

What Is Bulimia Nervosa?

A key feature of *bulimia nervosa* (often simply referred to as *bulimia*) is repeated episodes of binge eating followed by inappropriate efforts to prevent weight gain. Such inappropriate efforts to prevent weight gain can include vomiting or using diuretics, laxatives, enemas, or engaging in other behaviors to prevent weight gain, such as fasting or excessive exercise.

As noted earlier, some people with anorexia may purge or fast. In those cases, according to DSM-5, the symptom that distinguishes the two disorders is that people with anorexia have significantly low weight whereas those with bulimia do not. Bulimia is two to three times more prevalent than anorexia and, like anorexia, is much more prevalent among females than among males (American Psychiatric Association, 2013). Like people with anorexia, people with bulimia typically overvalue their appearance and body image (Crowther & Williams, 2011; Delinsky et al., 2011). The DSM-5 criteria for bulimia nervosa are presented in Table 10.3, and additional facts about the disorder are listed in Table 10.4.

Often, people with bulimia don't simply eat normally at meals and then binge between meals (Walsh, 1993). Rather, they try to control what they eat, restricting their caloric intake at meals (trying to be "good" and eat less), but later they become ravenous, and their hunger feels out of control. They then binge eat, which in turn makes them feel physically and emotionally "bad" because they "lost control" of themselves. As a result of such feelings, they

TABLE 10.3 • DSM-5 Diagnostic Criteria for Bulimia Nervosa

A. Recurrent episodes of binge eating. An episode of binge eating is characterized by both of the following:

  1. Eating, in a discrete period of time (e.g., within any 2-hour period), an amount of food that is definitely larger than what most individuals would eat in a similar period of time under similar circumstances.

  2. A sense of lack of control over eating during the episode (e.g., a feeling that one cannot stop eating or control what or how much one is eating).

B. Recurrent inappropriate compensatory behaviors in order to prevent weight gain, such as self-induced vomiting; misuse of laxatives, diuretics, or other medications; fasting; or excessive exercise.

C. The binge eating and inappropriate compensatory behaviors both occur, on average, at least once a week for 3 months.

D. Self-evaluation is unduly influenced by body shape and weight.

E. The disturbance does not occur exclusively during episodes of anorexia nervosa.

TABLE 10.4 • Bulimia Nervosa Facts at a Glance

Prevalence
• Over the course of a lifetime, 1–2% of women and 0.1–0.5% of men develop the disorder (Hoek & van Hoeken, 2003; Hudson et al., 2007).

Comorbidity
• Up to 75% of people with bulimia have at least one other disorder, often an anxiety disorder or depression (Godart et al., 2003).

Onset
• Bulimia usually begins in late adolescence or early adulthood.
• People in more recent birth cohorts (that is, those born more recently) have a higher risk for developing bulimia (Hudson et al., 2007).

Course
• At a 15-month follow-up, almost one third of people diagnosed with bulimia still met the criteria for the diagnosis; at a 5-year follow-up, that proportion dropped to 15% (Fairburn et al., 2000); other studies find similar results (Zeeck et al., 2011). However, people who no longer meet the DSM-5 criteria for the disorder may nevertheless continue to have persistent symptoms of bulimia, although not the number, frequency, or intensity specified by the criteria (Ben-Tovim, 2003; Keel et al., 1999).
• People who have less intense negative attitudes about their bodies and who function better in daily life are more likely to have a healthier outcome (Ben-Tovim, 2003; Keel et al., 1999).

Gender Differences
• Approximately 75–90% of people who have bulimia nervosa are female (Hoek & van Hoeken, 2003; Hudson et al., 2007).

Cultural Differences
• Some studies find significant differences in prevalence, frequency, and symptoms of eating disorders across ethnic groups within the United States. Specifically, Black and Hispanic American women are less likely to be diagnosed with bulimia than are Asian American or White American women (Alegría et al., 2007; Nicdao et al., 2007; Taylor et al., 2007).

Source: Unless otherwise noted, the source for information is American Psychiatric Association, 2013.

may purge and subsequently strive to eat less, restricting their caloric intake at meals and creating a vicious cycle of restricting, bingeing, and usually purging (Fitzgibbon & Stolley, 2000). In Case 10.2, Gabriella presents a similar story.

CASE 10.2 • FROM THE OUTSIDE: Bulimia Nervosa

[Gabriella is] a young Mexican woman whose parents moved to the U.S. when she was just a child. While her mother and father continue to speak Spanish at home and place a high value on maintaining their Mexican traditions, Gabriella wants nothing more than to fit in with her friends at school. She chooses to speak only English, looks to mainstream fashion magazines to guide her clothing and make-up choices, and wants desperately to have a fashion-model figure. In an attempt to lose weight, Gabriella has made a vow to herself to eat only one meal a day—dinner—but on her return home from school, she is rarely able to endure her hunger until dinnertime. She often loses control and ends up "eating whatever I can get my hands on." Frantic to keep her problem hidden from her family, she races to the store to replace all the food she has eaten.

(Fitzgibbon & Stolley, 2000)

Medical Effects of Bulimia Nervosa

Like anorexia, bulimia can lead to significant physical changes and medical problems. For instance, chronic vomiting, a purging method used by Marya Hornbacher, can cause the parotid and salivary glands (in the jaw area) to swell (creating a kind of "chipmunk" look) and can erode dental enamel, making teeth more vulnerable to cavities and other problems. People who use syrup of ipecac to induce vomiting may develop heart and muscle problems (Pomeroy, 2004; Silber, 2004).

Furthermore, many people with bulimia use laxatives regularly, which can lead to a permanent loss of intestinal functioning as the body comes to depend on the chemical laxatives to digest food and eliminate waste. In such cases, the malfunctioning intestinal section must be surgically removed (Pomeroy, 2004). Bulimia can also produce constipation, abdominal bloating and discomfort, fatigue, and irregular menstruation (Mascolo et al., 2012; Pomeroy, 2004). As noted earlier, in the section on anorexia, all forms of purging can cause dehydration and an imbalance of the body's electrolytes, which disrupt normal neural transmission and heart contractions. The medical effects of bulimia can create significant—and enduring—problems, as they did for the woman in Case 10.3.

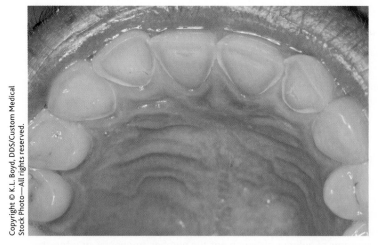

Frequent vomiting can permanently erode dental enamel, shown here, and lead to cavities and related problems.

CASE 10.3 • FROM THE INSIDE: Bulimia Nervosa

A 32-year-old woman describes how bulimia nervosa has affected her:

My life revolves around food and exercise. Because of my abuse of diet pills and purging, I had a stroke when I was 23. I now have headaches. I am at risk of having another stroke, and this time I have a high chance of not coming out of it. Emotionally, it's a daily battle. I'm depressed because I want to eat, and I'm depressed because I know if I do eat, I'll get fat and gain all the weight back that I have lost.

Everyone around me is terrified that I may die from this, and it has put a lot of stress on my marriage. I have no bedroom life anymore because I refuse to let my husband touch me or even look at my body. My kids are affected greatly by it because I usually have no energy to do anything with them, and when I do have energy, I am staying busy to burn the calories I have put in my body.

(Anonymous, 2003, p. 382)

Is Bulimia Distinct From Anorexia?

About half of people with anorexia go on to develop bulimia (Bulik et al., 1997; Tozzi et al., 2005), which may indicate that anorexia and bulimia are not distinct but rather represent phases of the same eating disorder, with the symptoms shifting over time. Some researchers have argued that a person's diagnosis may better reflect where she is in the course of the eating disorder at the time she is diagnosed (Fairburn & Cooper, 2011). In fact, the characteristics of the binge eating/purging type of anorexia have more in common with bulimia than with the restricting type of anorexia (Gleaves, Lowe, Snow, et al., 2000; Peterson et al., 2011). All that distinguishes the binge eating/purging type of anorexia from bulimia is the low weight.

Binge eating disorder
An eating disorder characterized by binge eating without subsequent purging.

Binge Eating Disorder and "Other" Eating Disorders

Like most other people, you've probably had occasions when you've eaten too much—when you felt stuffed and uncomfortable. You may even have felt as if you "binged." Odds are, though, that you don't have **binge eating disorder**, which is characterized by a pattern of binge eating without subsequent purging (American Psychiatric Association, 2013). Or perhaps you—or people you know—have a pattern of eating that is disordered but doesn't quite meet the criteria for anorexia, bulimia, or binge eating disorder. In what follows, we discuss binge eating disorder and disordered eating.

What Is Binge Eating Disorder?

As noted in Table 10.5, binge eating disorder is marked by a specific pattern of out-of-control binge eating in which the person must have at least three of the following symptoms: eat faster than normal, eat until uncomfortably full, eat a lot even when not hungry, eat alone because of being embarrassed by the quantity eaten, or have significant negative feelings about himself or herself about the amount eaten. People with this disorder do not typically fantasize about food or enjoy eating (either when bingeing or when not bingeing), and the bingeing causes distress. Note that binge eating disorder involves out-of-control binge eating and not weight per se; being overweight is not a psychological disorder.

Binge eating disorder is different from bulimia in two main ways:

- People with binge eating disorder do not persistently try to compensate for the binges; for instance, they don't purge or compulsively exercise.

- Most people with binge eating disorder are obese; people with bulimia generally range in weight from somewhat underweight to overweight but are not generally obese (Grucza et al., 2007; Hudson et al., 2007).

People with binge eating disorder are also more likely to develop medical problems as a result of their nutritional intake, such as diabetes, high blood pressure, high cholesterol, and heart disease. (Binges are typically high in fats, sugars, and/or salt, as was the case for the woman in Case 10.4.) Research suggests that the gender difference typical of other eating disorders

TABLE 10.5 • DSM-5 Diagnostic Criteria for Binge Eating Disorder

A. Recurrent episodes of binge eating. An episode of binge eating is characterized by both of the following:

1. Eating, in a discrete period of time (e.g., within any 2-hour period), an amount of food that is definitely larger than what most people would eat in a similar period of time under similar circumstances.

2. A sense of lack of control over eating during the episode (e.g., a feeling that one cannot stop eating or control what or how much one is eating).

B. The binge-eating episodes are associated with three (or more) of the following:

1. Eating much more rapidly than normal.

2. Eating until feeling uncomfortably full.

3. Eating large amounts of food when not feeling physically hungry.

4. Eating alone because of feeling embarrassed by how much one is eating.

5. Feeling disgusted with oneself, depressed, or very guilty afterward.

C. Marked distress regarding binge eating is present.

D. The binge eating occurs, on average, at least once a week for 3 months.

E. The binge eating is not associated with the recurrent use of inappropriate compensatory behavior as in bulimia nervosa and does not occur exclusively during the course of bulimia nervosa or anorexia nervosa.

is less pronounced with binge eating disorder. This disorder is more common than anorexia nervosa and bulimia nervosa combined (Grucza et al., 2007; Hudson et al., 2007). Table 10.6 contains additional facts about binge eating disorder.

CASE 10.4 • FROM THE OUTSIDE: Binge Eating Disorder

The 48-year-old African-American woman described below sought treatment for her binge eating disorder.

> The patient reported an onset of "eating binges" at approximately age 16. The binge eating began soon after she began babysitting for neighborhood children. [. . .] During those times she would "load up on junk food" that the family had provided. She recalled that she would eat chips, cookies, and brownies "non-stop," and that these eating episodes often lasted throughout the evening. She recalled feeling a loss of control during these episodes and stated that she would continue to eat despite not feeling physically hungry and that she would not stop until feeling physically ill. She reported that she was very embarrassed and secretive about these eating behaviors. [. . .] She denied any history of extreme inappropriate weight control or purging behaviors such as self-inducing vomiting or misusing laxatives.
>
> Around 6 months ago her binge eating increased in frequency to three to four times per week during her mother's illness, and increased to six to seven times per week following her mother's death [. . .] The patient described her typical binge episode as starting with an evening meal and extending for several hours [. . . when] she would then eat the "leftovers" while cleaning up after the meal, such that overall she would have consumed the equivalent of two full meals. She would then eat various foods throughout the rest of the evening until bedtime. During these episodes, she would alternate between salty and sweet snacks.
>
> (White et al., 2010, p. 12)

TABLE 10.6 • Binge Eating Facts at a Glance

Prevalence

- During their lifetime, 4–5% of Americans will develop binge eating disorder; it is more prevalent than anorexia and bulimia combined.
- Up to 30% of people seeking weight loss treatments have binge eating disorder (Hudson et al., 2007).

Comorbidity

- Almost 80% of people with binge eating disorder also have another psychological disorder (Hudson et al., 2007).

Onset

- Binge eating disorder typically begins when people are in their 20s (Kessler et al., 2013).
- The onset of binge eating is often followed by strenuous dieting.

Course

- Left untreated, people with binge eating disorder may cycle through periods of dieting followed by bingeing and weight gain.

Gender Differences

- Almost twice as many women as men will be diagnosed with binge eating disorder.

Cultural Differences

- In the United States, binge eating disorder is more common among Latinos and African-Americans than Whites (Marques et al., 2011).

Source: Unless otherwise noted, the source for information is American Psychiatric Association, 2013.

Is Binge Eating Disorder Diagnosis a Good Idea?

When using DSM-IV, clinicians and researchers ended up evaluating a significant number of people who had disordered eating but whose symptoms did not fully meet the necessary criteria for bulimia or anorexia—the only two eating disorders in that edition. But because the symptoms nonetheless caused significant distress or impaired functioning, such patients received the diagnosis *eating disorder not otherwise specified,* which was the nonspecific "other" diagnosis for the eating disorders category. In fact, more people received this "other" diagnosis than were diagnosed with anorexia or bulimia combined.

To address this problem, DSM-5 added the disorder *binge eating disorder,* which fit a subset of people with the "not otherwise specified" diagnosis. As noted in Table 10.5, the criteria for binge eating disorder involve more than simply overeating occasionally. But adding what is, in essence, out-of-control eating without "inappropriate" attempts to compensate for the calories is controversial.

On the one hand, some (Frances, 2013) criticize including this set of symptoms as a disorder. Although this type of overeating may feel bad—both physically and psychologically—it shouldn't be its own disorder. If such behavior constitutes a disorder, then any other form of self-control problem that makes the person feel bad should be considered a psychological disorder.

On the other hand, if the binge eating were accompanied by purging, it would be considered to be bulimia. So purging—or the absence of it—should not be the key determinant of whether disordered eating is considered an eating disorder. Moreover, making binge eating disorder a "disorder" allows treatment to be eligible for payment by insurance companies.

CRITICAL THINKING Even if the pattern of symptoms in binge eating disorder sounds disordered, is it really enough to be considered a valid diagnosis? Should we call something a disorder just because being out of control in some way is distressing?

(James Foley, College of Wooster)

Disordered Eating: "Other" Eating Disorders

Many adolescents and adults with significantly disturbed eating don't meet all the criteria for anorexia, bulimia, or binge eating disorder; those people may be diagnosed with a nonspecific "other" eating disorder. In one study, one quarter of patients with an eating disorder had this type of diagnosis (Fairburn & Cooper, 2011).

Because this "other" type does not specify particular criteria, people who are given this diagnosis have a wide range in number, frequency, and duration of symptoms. Nevertheless, people with this "other" diagnosis often fall into one of two groups. One group consists of people with **partial cases**, meaning that their symptoms meet some of the diagnostic criteria for a specific disorder but not enough to justify the diagnosis of that disorder. An example of a partial case of binge eating disorder would be someone whose symptoms meet all the other criteria for the disorder but who does not eat quickly, eat alone, or eat when not hungry; she would thus be diagnosed with the nonspecific "other" eating disorder.

Another group consists of people with **subthreshold cases**; they have symptoms that fit all the diagnostic criteria for a specific disorder but at levels lower than required for the diagnosis of that disorder. For instance, such people may have had anorexia or bulimia but then improved to the point where their symptoms no longer meet the criteria for either disorder. Nevertheless, these people still have clinically significant symptoms of an eating disorder. This was true of Marya Hornbacher: As the symptoms of her eating disorder abated, she no longer met the criteria for either anorexia or bulimia, and her diagnosis would be changed to "other" eating disorder.

Partial cases
Cases in which patients have symptoms that meet only some of the necessary criteria but not enough symptoms to meet all the necessary criteria for the diagnosis of a disorder.

Subthreshold cases
Cases in which patients have symptoms that fit all the necessary criteria, but at levels lower than required for the diagnosis of a disorder.

📷 **GETTING THE PICTURE**

Imagine that you know that both of these women are afraid of getting fat and believe themselves to be overweight. If you had to guess based on their appearance, which of these models would you think didn't meet all the criteria for anorexia nervosa and instead had a partial case? The woman on the right is more likely to have a partial case because, based on these photos, she does not appear to be significantly underweight.

Thinking Like A Clinician

Tanya had been dieting, but after a month or so, she began to pig out toward bedtime. After the first few of these gorging sessions, she felt both physically uncomfortable and ashamed of herself, and she would make herself vomit. After about a week, though, she stopped throwing up; instead, she began exercising for about an hour each day. This pattern of daily exercising and pigging out in the evening has persisted for about 6 months. Does Tanya have bulimia nervosa, binge eating disorder, the nonspecific "other" eating disorder, or just disordered eating but no DSM-5 diagnosis? What were the key factors that determined your answer?

☐ Understanding Eating Disorders

In the sections that follow, we focus on the two eating disorders that are best understood and for which treatments have been researched most extensively: anorexia and bulimia. Moreover, given that up to half of the people who have anorexia or bulimia have had or will have another of these disorders, it makes sense to examine the etiology of these disorders collectively rather than individually.

Why do these eating disorders arise? Marya Hornbacher asked this question and ventured the following response:

> While depression may play a role in eating disorders, either as cause or effect, it cannot always be pinpointed directly, and therefore you never know quite what you're dealing with. Are you trying to treat depression as a cause, as the thing that has screwed up your life and altered your behaviors, or as an effect? Or simply *depressing*? Will drug therapy help, or is that a Band–Aid cure? How big a role do your upbringing and family play? Does the culture have anything to do with it? Is your personality just problematic

Arun Nevader/FilmMagic/Getty Images

© PhotoAlto sas/Alamy

by nature, or is there, in fact, a faulty chemical pathway in your brain? If so, was it there before you started starving yourself, or did the starving put it there? . . . All of the above?

(1998, pp. 195–196)

In this passage, Hornbacher is trying to understand how, or why, some people—but not others—develop an eating disorder. Note that she mentions explanations that involve all three of the types of factors in the neuropsychosocial approach, although she does not consider ways in which such factors might interact.

Once an eating disorder has developed, it is difficult to disentangle the *causes* of the eating disorder from the widespread *effects* of an eating disorder on neurological (and, more generally, biological), psychological, and social functioning. This difficulty in untangling cause and effect means that researchers do not know which of the neuropsychosocial factors that are *associated* with eating disorders actually produce the disorders. All that can be said at this time is that a number of factors are associated with the emergence and maintenance of eating disorders (Dolan-Sewall & Insel, 2005; Jacobi et al., 2004; Striegel-Moore & Cachelin, 2001).

An additional challenge to researchers is the high rate of comorbidity of other psychological and medical disorders with eating disorders, which makes it difficult to determine the degree to which risk factors uniquely lead to eating disorders rather than being associated more generally with the comorbid disorders (Jacobi et al., 2004).

Neurological Factors: Setting the Stage

We've already noted that the excessive caloric restriction in anorexia leads to specific medical effects, notably changes in metabolism, and body functioning. The eating changes and purging involved in bulimia (and anorexia, if purging occurs) bring their own medical effects and biological changes.

Brain Systems

Neuroimaging studies have revealed many differences between the brains of people with eating disorders and those of control participants (Frank et al., 2004; Kaye, Frank et al., 2005). Most notably, people who have anorexia have unusually low activity in two key areas of the brain: (1) the frontal lobes, which are involved in inhibiting responses and in regulating behavior more generally (a deficit in such processing may contribute to eating too much or eating too little), and (2) the portions of the temporal lobes that include the amygdala, which is involved in fear and other strong emotions (fear helps prevent people from putting themselves in danger, and dampening this emotion may contribute to eating disorders).

Neuroimaging studies not only have documented abnormalities in the functioning of different parts of the brain in people who have eating disorders but also have shown that the structure of the brain itself changes with these disorders. In fact, anorexia is associated with loss of both gray matter (cell bodies of neurons) and white matter (myelinated axons of the neurons) in the brain (Addolorato et al., 1997; Frank et al., 2004; Herholz, 1996). The gray matter carries out various sorts of cognitive and emotion-related processes, such as those involved in learning and in fear responses. Deficits in white matter may imply that different parts of the brain are not communicating appropriately, which could contribute to the problems patients with anorexia have when they try to convert an intellectual

This student is trying to learn. Anorexia affects the brain's structure and function, including the ability to learn (and engage in various other cognitive processes).

understanding of their disorder into changes in their behavior. Many of these structural deficits improve when the patient recovers, although they do not necessary disappear completely (Frank et al., 2004; Herholz, 1996). Thus, an eating disorder may have long-term consequences for a person's neural functioning, which in turn affects cognitive abilities and emotional responses.

Neural Communication: Serotonin

Losing large amounts of weight (as occurs in anorexia) and the associated malnutrition clearly change the amounts of serotonin and other neurotransmitters. We will focus here on serotonin because it is involved in regulating a wide variety of behaviors and characteristics that are associated with eating disorders, including binge eating and irritability (Hollander & Rosen, 2000; McElroy et al., 2000).

Neuroimaging research has shown that serotonin receptors function abnormally in patients with anorexia and bulimia (Kaye, Bailer et al., 2005; Kaye, Frank et al., 2005). However, evidence seems to imply that the serotonin receptors are abnormal before patients develop anorexia. As discussed in Chapters 5 and 6, serotonin is related to mood and anxiety. Prior to developing anorexia, patients tend to be anxious and obsessional, and these traits persist even after recovery, which suggests a biologically based anxious temperament; this temperament may be related to serotonin levels or functioning (Kaye et al., 2003).

Consistent with this view, researchers have found that people with anorexia (Kaye, Bailer et al., 2005) and bulimia (Kaye et al., 2000; Smith et al., 1999) are less responsive to serotonin than normal. In fact, the worse the symptoms of bulimia, the less responsive to serotonin the patient generally is (Jimerson et al., 1992).

Genetics

When Marya Hornbacher told her parents that she had been making herself throw up, her mother admitted, "I used to do that." Did Hornbacher's genes predispose her to developing bulimia? As is true for people with mood disorders and anxiety disorders, people with an eating disorder are more likely than average to have family members with an eating disorder—but not necessarily the same disorder that they themselves have (Lilenfeld & Kaye, 1998; Strober et al., 2000).

Like genetic studies of other types of disorders, such studies of eating disorders compare identical twins to fraternal twins. The research findings indicate that anorexia has a substantial heritability, but estimates range from as low as 33% to as high as 88% (Bulik, 2005; Jacobi et al., 2004). Twin studies of bulimia also indicate that the disorder is influenced by genes and also yield a wide range of estimates of heritability, from 28% to 83% (Bulik 2005; Jacobi et al., 2004). Given that many people with bulimia previously had anorexia, it isn't surprising that both disorders have the same wide range of heritabilities; there is significant overlap in the two populations. The large variation in heritabilities may simply indicate, once again, that genes aren't destiny; the way the environment interacts with the genes is also important.

These identical twins both suffered from anorexia. Eating disorders may have a genetic component, but genes are only one of a variety of factors associated with developing an eating disorder.

REX USA/Tony Kerrigan/Newspix/Rex

Psychological Factors: Thoughts of and Feelings About Food

Eating and breathing are both essential to life, but eating can also evoke powerful feelings, memories, and thoughts. Hornbacher recalls her associations to eating:

> My memories of childhood are almost all related to food. . . . I was my father's darling, and the way he showed love was through food. I would give away my lunch at school, then hop in my father's car, and we'd drive to a fast-food place and, essentially, binge.

My mother was another story altogether. She ate, some. She would pick at cottage cheese, nibble at cucumbers, scarf down See's Candies. But she, like my father, and like me, associated food with love, and love with need.

(1998, p. 27)

Many psychological risk factors are not uniquely associated with eating disorders. Factors such as negative self-evaluation, sexual abuse and other adverse experiences, the presence of comorbid disorders (e.g., depression and anxiety disorders; Jacobi et al., 2004), and using avoidant strategies to cope with problems (Pallister & Waller, 2008; Spoor et al., 2007) are also associated with psychological disorders more generally. Thus, many researchers have focused on factors that are specifically related to symptoms of eating disorders—factors associated with food, weight, appearance, and eating. In the following sections we examine research findings about these factors.

Thinking About Weight, Appearance, and Food

People with eating disorders have automatic, irrational, and illogical thoughts about weight, appearance, and food (Garfinkel et al., 1992; Striegel-Moore, 1993). We consider two kinds of such thoughts in the following sections.

Excessive Concern With Weight and Appearance

Some people with eating disorders have excessive concern with—and tend to overvalue—their weight, body shape, and eating (Fairburn, 1997; Fairburn & Cooper, 2011). For instance, they may weigh themselves multiple times a day and feel bad about themselves when the scale indicates that they've gained half a pound. Some people are so concerned with weight and appearance that their food intake, weight, and body shape come to define their self-worth.

The two characteristics that are the most consistent predictors of the onset of an eating disorder are dieting and being dissatisfied with one's body (Neumark-Sztainer et al., 2011; Thompson & Smolak, 2001). Such concerns help maintain bulimia because people with these characteristics believe that their compensatory behaviors reduce their overall caloric intake (Fairburn et al., 2003).

Abstinence Violation Effect

Many people who have an eating disorder engage in automatic, illogical, black-or-white thinking about food: Vegetables are "good," whereas desserts are "bad." They may come to view themselves in the same way: They are "good" when acting to lose weight and "bad" when eating a "bad" food or when they feel that their eating is out of control. The **abstinence violation effect** (Polivy & Herman, 1993) occurs when the violation of a self-imposed rule about food restriction leads to feeling out of control with food, which then leads to overeating. For instance, having taken a taste of a friend's ice cream, a person thinks, "I shouldn't have had any ice cream; I've blown it for the day, so I might was well have my own ice cream—in fact, I'll get a pint and eat the whole thing." Then, after she eats the ice cream, she tries to negate the calories ingested during the binge by purging or using some other compensatory behavior. Thus, the abstinence violation effect explains bingeing that occurs after the person has "transgressed."

Operant Conditioning: Reinforcing Disordered Eating

As with many disorders, operant conditioning plays a role in the development and maintenance of symptoms—in this case, as we explain below, symptoms of disordered eating.

People with eating disorders often (mistakenly) categorize each type of food as "good" or "bad." According to the abstinence violation effect, if someone with bulimia eats even a small amount of a "bad" food, she feels she has transgressed, gives up trying to "be good," and binges on the tempting food.

© Stuart Corlett/Design Pics/Corbis

Abstinence violation effect
The result of violating a self-imposed rule about food restriction, which leads to feeling out of control with food, which then leads to overeating.

First, the symptoms of most eating disorders—anorexia, bulimia, or binge eating disorder—may inadvertently be reinforced through operant conditioning. For instance, preoccupations with food and weight or bingeing and purging can provide distractions from work pressures, family conflicts, or social problems. The never-ending preoccupations with food, weight, and body are negatively reinforced because they provide relief from what the person might otherwise be preoccupied about. (Remember that negative *reinforcement* is still reinforcement, but it occurs when something aversive is removed, which is not the same as punishment.)

Second, operant conditioning occurs when restricting behaviors are positively reinforced by the person's sense of power and mastery over her appetite, although such feelings of mastery are often short-lived as the disease takes over (Garner, 1997). Hornbacher noted: "The anorexic body seems to say: I do not need. It says: Power over the self" (1998, p. 85).

A third way in which operant conditioning affects eating disorders occurs when people are positively reinforced for "losing control" of their appetite and bingeing. How can losing control be positively reinforcing? Easy: They've set up the rules so that they get to eat certain foods they enjoy (positive reinforcement) only when they let themselves lose control of their food intake. That is, during a binge, people eat foods that they normally don't eat at all or eat only in small quantities—typically fats, sweets, or carbohydrates. This means that the only way some people can eat foods they may enjoy—such as ice cream, cake, candy, or fried foods—is by being "out of control."

Fourth, bingeing can also induce an endorphin rush, which creates a pleasant feeling much like a "runner's high," which is positively reinforcing. And, fifth, operant conditioning may occur because purging can be negatively reinforcing by relieving the anxiety and fullness that are created by overeating.

Personality Traits as Risk Factors

Particular personality traits are associated with—and are considered risk factors for—eating disorders: perfectionism and low self-esteem. *Perfectionism* is a persistent striving to attain perfection and excessive self-criticism about mistakes (Antony & Swinson, 1998; Franco-Paredes et al., 2005). Numerous studies find that people with eating disorders have higher levels of perfectionism than do people who do not have these disorders (Forbush et al., 2007). High perfectionism may lead to an intense drive to attain a desired weight or body shape and thus may contribute to the thoughts and behaviors that underlie an eating disorder. As illustrated in Figure 10.2, perfectionists are painfully aware of their imperfections, which is aversive for them. This heightened awareness of personal flaws—real or imagined—is called *aversive self-awareness* and leads to significant emotional distress, which may temporarily be dulled by focusing on immediate aspects of the environment, such as occurs with bingeing. Thus, bingeing may provide an escape

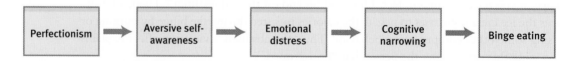

FIGURE **10.2 • Bingeing as Escape** For perfectionists, bingeing can be an escape from aversive feelings. Being aware of imperfections (referred to as aversive self-awareness) causes emotional distress. People high in perfectionism try to decrease this emotional distress by focusing on immediate aspects of the environment (referred to as cognitive narrowing), which they attain through bingeing (Blackburn et al., 2006; Heatherton & Baumeister, 1991).

from the emotional distress associated with perfectionism (Blackburn et al., 2006; Heatherton & Baumeister, 1991).

In addition, people who have low self-esteem may try to raise their self-esteem by controlling their food intake, weight, and shape, believing that such changes will increase their self-worth (Geller et al., 2000). For instance, they may think, "If I restrict my calories, that'll prove that I'm in control of myself and worthy of respect." However, efforts to increase self-worth in this way end up having a paradoxical effect: To the extent that the person fails to control food intake, weight, and shape, her self-esteem falls even lower—she feels that she's failed, yet again, to achieve something she wanted.

Dieting, Restrained Eating, and Disinhibited Eating

Frequently restricting specific foods—such as "fattening" foods—or overall caloric intake (as occurs when dieting or trying to maintain one's current weight) is referred to as **restrained eating**. If you've ever been on some type of diet, you know that continuing to adhere to such restrictions can be challenging. And at times the diet may feel so constraining that you get discouraged and frustrated and simply give up—which can lead to a bout of *disinhibited eating*, bingeing on a restricted type of food or simply eating more of a nonrestricted type of food (Polivy & Herman, 1985). In fact, dieters and people with eating disorders often alternate restrictive eating with disinhibited eating (Fairburn et al., 2005; Polivy & Herman, 1993, 2002).

Restrained eaters can become insensitive to internal cues of hunger and fullness. In order to maintain restricted eating, they may stop eating before they get a normal feeling of fullness and so end up trying to tune out sensations of hunger. If they binge, they may eat past the point of normal fullness. They therefore need to rely on external guides, such as portion size or elapsed time since their last meal, to control their food intake (Polivy & Herman, 1993). However, using external guides to direct food intake requires cognitive effort—to monitor the clock or to calculate how much food was last eaten and how much food should be eaten next. When a person is thinking about other tasks (such as a job or homework assignment), she may temporarily stop using external guides and simply eat, which in turn may lead to disinhibited or binge eating (Baumeister et al., 1998; Kahan et al., 2003).

Other Psychological Disorders as Risk Factors

Another factor associated with the subsequent development of an eating disorder is the presence of a psychological disorder in early adolescence (see Figure 10.3), particularly depression. A longitudinal study of 726 adolescents found that having a depressive disorder during early adolescence was associated with an increased risk for later dietary restriction, purging, recurrent weight fluctuations, and the emergence of an eating disorder. This was the case even when researchers statistically controlled for other disorders or eating problems before adulthood (Johnson, Cohen, Kotler, et al., 2002).

Social Factors: The Body in Context

Various social factors contribute to eating disorders. One social factor is the influence of family and friends, and another social factor is culture, which can contribute to eating disorders by promoting an ideal body shape. In this section we discuss these social factors as well as explanations of why so many more females than males develop eating disorders.

Restrained eating can lead people to rely on external cues, such as eating only at very specific times of day, rather than on the body's internal hunger cues.

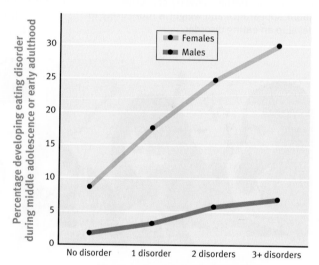

FIGURE 10.3 • Psychological Disorders and the Risk of Developing an Eating Disorder The more psychological disorders an adolescent—particularly a female adolescent—has, the more likely he or she is to develop an eating disorder (Johnson, Cohen, Kasen, & Brook, 2002).

Restrained eating
Restricting intake of specific foods or overall number of calories.

Fabrice Lerouge/Getty Images

A girl whose mother is overly concerned about appearance and weight is more likely to develop an eating disorder.

M Nader/Getty Images

For a teenage girl, her friends' comments can have a lasting influence on how she feels about her body, her willingness to diet, and her self-esteem.

The Role of Family and Peers

Researchers have had trouble disentangling the influences of genes on eating disorders from the influences of the family for two main reasons:

1. Family members provide a model for eating, body image, and appearance concerns through their own behaviors (Stein, Wooley, Cooper, et al., 2006). For example, parents who spend a lot of time on their appearance before leaving the house model that behavior for their children.

2. Family members affect a child's concerns through their responses to the child's body shape, weight, and food intake (Stein, Wooley, Senior, et al., 2006; Tantleff-Dunn et al., 2004; Thompson et al., 1999). For example, if a parent inquires daily about how much food his or her child ate at lunch (or weighs the child daily), the child learns to pay close attention to caloric intake and daily fluctuations in weight.

Children whose parents are overly concerned about these matters are more likely to develop an eating disorder (Strober, 1995). But this finding could also reflect shared genes.

Peers can shape a person's relationship to eating, food, and body, especially if they tease or criticize a person concerning her weight, appearance, or food intake; such comments can have a lasting influence on her (dis)satisfaction with her body, her willingness to diet, and her self-esteem. Such influences can make a person more vulnerable to developing an eating disorder (Cash, 1995; Keery et al., 2005).

Unfortunately, many girls and women feel that symptoms of eating disorders—particularly preoccupations with food and weight—are "normal" and that talking about these topics is a way to bond with others. Hornbacher was aware of this social facet of eating disorders and its underlying drawback:

> Women use their obsession with weight and food as a point of connection with one another, a commonality even between strangers. Instead of talking about *why* we use food and weight control as a means of handling emotional stress, we talk ad nauseum about the fact that we don't like our bodies. (1998, p. 283)

The Role of Culture

Some researchers believe that eating disorders have become more common and pervasive in recent decades. However, a meta-analysis of the incidence of eating disorders across cultures over the 20th century found only a small increase in the number of cases of anorexia. In contrast, the incidence of bulimia substantially increased from 1970 to 1990 (Keel & Klump, 2003)—which suggests a cultural influence—because bulimia arises only in the context of concerns about weight (Striegel-Moore & Cachelin, 2001).

Three elements come together to create the engine driving the culturally induced increase in eating disorders (Becker et al., 2002):

1. a cultural ideal of thinness,

2. repeated media exposure to this thinness ideal, and

3. a person's assimilation of the thinness ideal.

In order to examine the cultural ideal of thinness, David Garner and colleagues (1980) conducted an innovative study: They tracked the measurements of Miss America contestants and *Playboy* centerfold playmates over time and found that their waists and hips gradually became smaller. Other studies have found similar results (Andersen & DiDomenico, 1992; Field et al., 1999; Nemeroff et al., 1994). In fact, while the size of playmates' bodies has decreased over time (as assessed by the body mass index, or BMI, an adjusted ratio of weight to height), the average BMI of women age 20–29 has increased (see Figure 10.4; Ogden et al., 2004, Gammon, 2009). During the same period studied by Garner and colleagues, the prevalence of eating disorders increased in the United States. It is not clear whether the contestants and playmates were creating or following a cultural trend in ideal body shape. What is clear is that society's pressure to be thin increases women's—and girls'—dissatisfaction with their bodies, which is a risk factor for eating disorders (Grabe & Hyde, 2006; Lynch et al., 2008).

The cultural influence on weight and appearance isn't limited to women: Men who regularly engage in activities such as modeling and wrestling, which draw attention to their appearance and weight, are increasingly likely to develop eating disorders (Garner et al., 1998; Sundgot-Borgen, 1999). Similarly, men who have a heightened awareness of appearance (Ousley et al., 2008), such as some in the gay community, are also more likely to develop eating disorders (Russell & Keel, 2002).

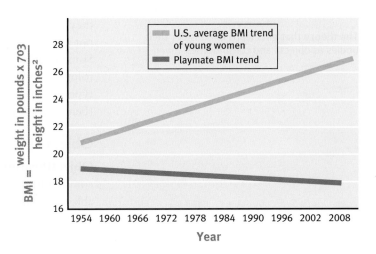

Eating Disorders Across Cultures

Eating disorders occur throughout the world but are found mainly in industrialized Western or Westernized countries (Lee et al., 1992; Pike & Walsh, 1996). Immigration to a Western country and internalization of Western norms increase the risk of developing symptoms of an eating disorder, as occurs among people who immigrate from China and Egypt to Western countries (Lee & Lee, 1996; Perez et al., 2002). Westernization (or modernization) of a culture similarly increases dieting (Gunewardene et al., 2001), which is a risk factor for eating disorders. In addition, as girls and women move into a higher socioeconomic bracket, they are increasingly likely to develop an eating disorder (Polivy & Herman, 2002).

Within the United States, prevalence rates of eating disorders vary across ethnic groups, based on different ideals of beauty and femininity: Native Americans have a higher risk for eating disorders than do other ethnic groups (Crago et al., 1996), and Black Americans have had the lowest risk (Striegel-Moore et al., 2003). However, prevalence rates are increasing among Black and Latina women (Franko et al., 2007; Gentile et al., 2007; Shaw et al., 2004; Taylor et al., 2007), perhaps because of the growing number of ethnic models in mainstream ads who are as thin as their White counterparts (Brodey, 2005).

The Power of the Media

The power of the media to influence cultural ideals of beauty and femininity is illustrated by the results of an innovative study in Fiji (a group of islands in the South Pacific) by Anne Becker and colleagues (2002). Prior to 1995, there was no television in Fiji. Traditional Fijian culture promoted robust body shapes and appetites, and there were no cultural pressures for thinness or dieting. Researchers collected data from adolescent girls shortly after the introduction of television in 1995 and again 3 years later. At the beginning of the study, when a large body size was the cultural ideal, they found almost no one who felt they were "too big or fat." After 3 years of watching television (primarily shows from Western countries), however, 75% reported that they felt "too big or fat" at least some of the time. In addition, feeling too big was associated with dieting to lose weight, which had become very prevalent: 62% of the girls had dieted within the prior 4 weeks.

A similar process might be occurring in industrialized societies, where ideals of thinness saturate the environment through television, movies, magazines, advertisements, books, and even cartoons. Numerous studies have documented associations between media exposure and disordered eating (Bissell & Zhou, 2004; Kim & Lennon, 2007); for instance, the more time adolescent girls spent watching television, the more likely

FIGURE 10.4 • Women's Body Size Over Time: Playmates and Average Young Women Over the past five decades, the size (specifically, the body mass index [BMI]) of the average young woman's body has become larger (orange line). Over the same period of time, the body size of Playboy playmates has become smaller (purple line), presenting an increasingly unattainable ideal.

When females move from a non-Western country to a Western country, their risk of developing an eating disorder increases.

Objectification theory
The theory that girls learn to consider their bodies as objects and commodities.

they were to report disordered eating a year later (Harrison & Hefner, 2006). However, not all girls and women who view these media images end up with an eating disorder. Some people are more affected than others, perhaps because of a combination of neurological, psychological, and social risk factors. For them, chronic exposure to these types of images may tip the scales and set them on a course toward an eating disorder (Ferguson et al., 2011; Levine & Harrison, 2004).

Objectification Theory: Explaining the Gender Difference

Objectification theory posits that girls learn to consider their bodies as objects and commodities, which explains how the cultural ideal of thinness makes women vulnerable to eating disorders (Fredrickson & Roberts, 1997). Western culture promotes the view of male bodies as agents—instruments that perform tasks—and of female bodies as objects mainly to be looked at and evaluated in terms of appearance (see Figure 10.5). Marya Hornbacher recounted her sense of being objectified:

> I remember the body from the outside in. . . . There will be copious research on the habit of women with eating disorders perceiving themselves through other eyes, as if there were some Great Observer looking over their shoulder. Looking, in particular, at their bodies and finding, more and more often as they get older, countless flaws.
> (1998, p. 14)

Implicit in Hornbacher's musings about her perceptions of her body is the sense of her body as an object—to be looked at and evaluated and, all too frequently, found defective.

According to the theory, objectification encourages eating disorders because female bodies are evaluated according to the cultural ideal, and girls and women strive to have their bodies conform so that they will be positively evaluated. As they internalize the ideal of thinness, they increase their risk for eating disorders (Calogero et al., 2005; Thompson & Stice, 2001)—especially in combination with learning to see their bodies as objects from the outside: If they hold an ideal of thinness and see their bodies as objects, they become more likely to pay attention to their flaws and to feel ashamed of their bodies, and these feelings motivate restrained eating (Fredrickson & Roberts, 1997; Moradi et al., 2005). Even preschool children attribute more negative qualities to fat women than to fat men (Turnbull et al., 2000).

Another possible explanation for the gender difference in prevalence rates of eating disorders focuses on the politics of a cultural ideal of thinness for women. Some researchers note that as women's economic and political power has increased, female models have become thinner and less curvaceous, creating a physical ideal of womanhood that is harder—if not impossible—to meet. Women then spend significant

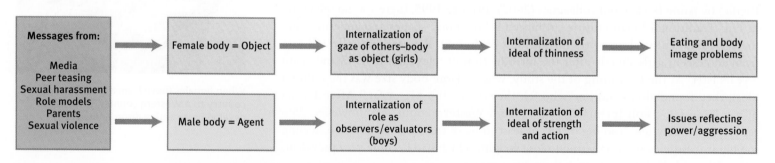

FIGURE 10.5 • Objectification and Eating Problems Objectification theory helps to explain the large gender difference in the prevalence of eating disorders. This theory proposes that whereas boys are encouraged to view their bodies as instruments that can perform tasks (agents), girls are encouraged to consider their bodies as objects and commodities to be evaluated (objects)—which makes girls more vulnerable to developing an eating disorder.

Source: Adapted from Smolak & Murmen, 2004.

time, energy, and money trying to emulate this thinner ideal through exercise, diet, medications, and even surgery, which in turn dissipates their economic and political power (Barber, 1998; Bordo, 1993).

Although today males are much less likely to develop any type of eating disorder than are women, this large gender discrepancy may not last. Data suggest that male physical ideals are increasingly unrealistic: Male film stars and Mr. Universe winners are increasingly muscular (Pope, Phillips, & Olivardia, 2000), paralleling the changes in women's bodies in the media. Just as females covet bodies similar to those promoted in the media, so do males (Ricciardelli et al., 2006): Two thirds of men want their bodies to be more similar to cultural ideals of the male body (McCabe & Ricciardelli, 2001a, 2001b; Ricciardelli & McCabe, 2001). However, rather than suffer from the specific sets of symptoms for anorexia or bulimia, males are more likely to develop a form of "other" eating disorder, with symptoms that focus on muscle building, either through excessive exercise or steroid use (Weltzin et al., 2005). Sam, in Case 10.5, is preoccupied with losing muscle mass.

Many female dolls have unattainable physical proportions; this is increasingly also becoming true of male dolls. As seen in this comparison of a 1970 G. I. Joe action figure (left) with one from 2010 (right), male action figures have become more muscular over this 40-year span (Baghurst et al., 2006).

CASE 10.5 · FROM THE INSIDE: An "Other" Eating Disorder

Forty-year-old Sam recounts his preoccupations with his muscles:

> I would get up in the morning and already wonder whether I lost muscle overnight while sleeping. I would rather be thinking about the day and who I was going to see, et cetera. But instead, the thoughts always centered on my body. Throughout the day, I would think about everything I ate, every physical movement I did, and whether it contributed to muscle loss in any way. I would go to bed and pray that I would wake up and think about something else the next day. It's a treadmill I can't get off of.

(Olivardia, 2007, pp. 125–126)

Feedback Loops in Understanding Eating Disorders

As we have seen, many neurological, psychological, and social factors are associated with the development and maintenance of eating disorders. In what follows we look at some theories about how these factors interact through feedback loops.

Most females in Western societies are exposed to images of thin women as ideals in the media, but only some women develop an eating disorder. Why? Neurological factors (such as a genetic vulnerability) may make some people more susceptible to the psychological and social factors related to eating disorders (Bulik, 2005). For instance, researchers hypothesize that young women who are prone to anxiety (neuroticism)—which is both a psychological factor and a neurological factor—are more susceptible to the effects of a familial focus on appearance, a social factor (Davis et al., 2004). Indeed, after statistically controlling for body size, researchers found that young women who were preoccupied with weight were more prone to anxiety and were more likely to have families that focused on appearance. This preoccupation both could result from anxiety and familial focus on appearance and could cause these effects. A preoccupation with weight can also lead to dieting, which can create its own neurochemical changes (neurological factor) that may lead to eating disorders (Walsh et al., 1995). In addition, the stringent rules that people may set for a diet can lead them to feel out of control with eating if they "violate" those rules (psychological factor). Further, people with higher levels of perfectionism and body dissatisfaction (psychological factors) may elicit comments about their appearance (social factor) or pay more attention to appearance-related comments (psychological factor) (Halmi et al., 2000). Figure 10.6 illustrates the feedback loops for eating disorders.

FIGURE **10.6 • Feedback Loops in Understanding Eating Disorders**

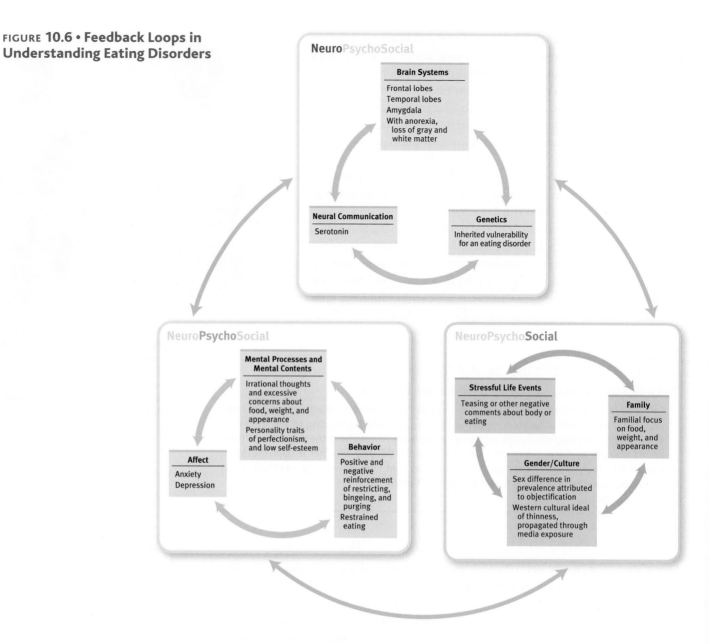

Thinking Like A Clinician

Suppose scientists discover genes that are associated with eating disorders. What could—and couldn't—you infer about the role of genetics in eating disorders? How could genes contribute to eating disorders if bulimia is a relatively recent phenomenon? In what ways does the environment influence the development of eating disorders? Why do only some people who are exposed to familial and cultural emphases on weight, food, and appearance develop an eating disorder?

Treating Eating Disorders

One important goal when treating a patient with anorexia is to help her attain a medically safe weight by helping her to eat more and/or purge less often; if that safe weight cannot be reached with outpatient treatment (treatment that does not involve an overnight stay in a hospital), then inpatient treatment becomes imperative. *Inpatient* treatment occurs in a psychiatric hospital or psychiatric unit of a general hospital; inpatient treatment for eating disorders may also take place at special stand-alone facilities.

When someone with an eating disorder *isn't* underweight enough to require inpatient treatment, many different factors can be the initial targets of treatment. In this section we examine specific treatments that target neurological (and biological, more broadly), psychological, and social factors and the role of hospitalization.

As with treatment for other disorders, the intensity of treatment for eating disorders can range from hospitalization, to day or evening programs, to *residential treatment* (staffed facilities in which patients sleep, take breakfast and dinner, and perhaps participate in evening groups), to weekly visits with a therapist. In all these forms of treatment, cognitive-behavior therapy (CBT) is generally considered the method of choice. Regardless of the severity of the eating disorder, frequent visits with an internist or a family doctor are an important additional component of treatment. The physician determines whether a patient should be medically hospitalized and, if not, whether she is medically stable enough to partake in daily activities. In what follows, we examine treatment options from the neuropsychosocial perspective.

Targeting Neurological and Biological Factors: Nourishing the Body

Neurologically and biologically focused treatments are designed to create a pattern of normal healthy eating and to stabilize medical problems that arise from the eating disorder. Treatments that focus specifically on these goals include nutritional counseling to improve eating, medical hospitalization to address significant medical problems, and medication to diminish some symptoms of the eating disorder as well as symptoms of comorbid anxiety and depression.

A Focus on Nutrition

For people with any type of eating disorder, increasing the nutrition and variety of foods eaten—and not purged—is critical. A nutritionist will help develop meal plans for increasing caloric intake at a reasonable pace. In the process of nutritional counseling, the nutritionist may identify a patient's mistaken beliefs about food and weight; the nutritionist then seeks to educate the patient and thus help her correct such beliefs. As people with anorexia begin to eat more, they may experience gastrointestinal discomfort: Because of a lack of body fat, having more food in the gastrointestinal system may compress a section of the duodenum (a part of the intestine) that is on top of an important artery (Adson et al., 1997). The discomfort goes away as she recovers.

Medical Hospitalization

The bodily effects of eating disorders—particularly anorexia—can be directly life-threatening. When medical problems related to eating disorders become severe, a *medical* hospitalization rather than a psychiatric hospitalization may be necessary. Medical hospitalization generally occurs in response to a medical crisis, such as a heart problem, gastrointestinal bleeding, or significant dehydration. The goal of medical hospitalization is to treat the specific medical problem and stabilize the patient's health.

Medication

Generally, medications do not help people with anorexia gain weight (Crow et al., 2009; Walsh et al., 2006). However, once the patient's normal weight is restored, selective serotonin reuptake inhibitors (SSRIs) may help prevent the person from developing anorexia again (Barbarich et al., 2004).

For bulimia, antidepressants—particularly SSRIs—may reduce some symptoms of the eating disorder. Compared to placebos, SSRIs can help decrease bingeing, vomiting, and weight and shape concerns, although other symptoms may still persist—including a fear of normal eating (Bacaltchuk et al., 2000; Mitchell et al., 2001). SSRIs may also reduce symptoms of comorbid depression. The SSRI Prozac (*fluoxetine*) is the most widely studied medication for bulimia, and the FDA has approved it to treat this disorder. Studies of the effects of Prozac on bulimia typically last no longer than 16 weeks, however, so it isn't clear how long the medication should be taken (de Zwaan et al., 2004). Moreover, as with other disorders, the beneficial effects of medication used to treat eating disorders typically stop soon after the medication is discontinued.

Targeting Psychological Factors: Cognitive-Behavior Therapy

CBT is the most widely studied treatment of eating disorders that directly targets psychological factors, and it is considered the treatment of choice (Pike et al., 2004). CBT for eating disorders focuses primarily on changes in thoughts, feelings, and behaviors that are related to eating, food, and the body, at least in the initial stages. At the outset of treatment, the patient and therapist discuss who monitors the patient's weight and at what point inpatient treatment would be recommended and pursued (Pike et al., 2004).

CBT for Anorexia

CBT can be effective in reducing symptoms of anorexia and has been shown to prevent relapses (Pike et al., 2003). CBT for anorexia focuses on identifying and changing thoughts and behaviors that impede normal eating and that maintain the symptoms of the disorder. Cognitive restructuring can decrease the patient's irrational thoughts (such as the belief that starving means having self-control) and help the patient to develop more realistic thoughts (for example, that appropriate eating indicates the ability to care for herself). The therapist also helps the patient to develop more adaptive coping strategies (Bowers & Ansher, 2008; Garner et al., 1997; Wilson & Fairburn, 2007), such as expressing anger or disappointment directly to other people rather than hiding or denying such "negative" feelings. Treatment may also involve psychoeducation (about the disorder and its effects), training in self-monitoring (to notice hunger cues and become aware of problematic behaviors), and relaxation training (to decrease anxiety that arises with increased eating). Because low weight can affect cognitive functioning, irrational thoughts may not change substantially until the patient's weight increases (McIntosh et al., 2005).

CBT for Bulimia

The benefits of CBT for bulimia are well documented (Agras, Crow, et al., 2000; Ghaderi, 2006; Walsh et al., 1997). When used as a treatment for bulimia, CBT focuses on the thoughts, feelings, and behaviors that: (1) prevent normal eating; and (2) promote bingeing, purging, and other behaviors that are intended to offset the calories eaten during a binge. CBT also addresses thoughts, feelings, and behaviors that are related to body image and appearance and that maintain the symptoms of bulimia. In addition to focusing on symptoms of the disorder, CBT may address issues associated with perfectionism, low self-esteem, and mood (Wilson & Fairburn, 2007). CBT for bulimia uses many of the same methods as CBT for anorexia: psychoeducation, cognitive restructuring, self-monitoring, and relaxation. In addition, treatment may employ a method used to treat obsessive-compulsive disorder (OCD): *exposure with response prevention* (discussed in Chapter 7). For bulimia, this method generally involves exposing the patient to anxiety-provoking stimuli, such as foods she would typically eat only during a binge. Patients are asked to consume a moderate amount of the binge food during a therapy session (the exposure), and the response prevention involves *not purging* or responding in another usual way to compensate for the calories taken in.

For people with bulimia, exposure with response prevention might involve foods normally eaten only during a binge but eating them in controlled portions in a normal way.

Tom Grill/Getty Images

Efficacy of CBT for Treating Eating Disorders

Most people with eating disorders who improve significantly with CBT do so within the first month of treatment (Agras, Crow, et al., 2000). However, although CBT helps decrease their bingeing, purging, and dieting behaviors, up to 50% of patients retain some symptoms after the treatment ends (Lundgren et al., 2004). One study of 48 patients who completely abstained from bingeing and purging after CBT found that 44% had relapsed 4 months later (Halmi et al., 2002). Various factors predicted which people relapsed, including more eating rituals, more food-related thoughts, and less motivation to change; stressful life events can also precipitate relapses (Grilo et al., 2012). Although CBT may be the treatment of choice and helps many people with eating disorders, it clearly isn't a panacea.

Targeting Social Factors

Given the important role that social factors play in contributing to eating disorders, it is not surprising that various effective treatments directly target these factors. Treatments that target social factors include interpersonal therapy, family therapy, group-based inpatient treatment programs, and prevention programs.

Interpersonal Therapy

A manual-based form of interpersonal therapy (IPT) has been applied to eating disorders; this version of IPT includes 4 to 6 months of weekly therapy (Fairburn, 1998; Wilfley et al., 2012). In any form of IPT, the focus is on problems in relationships that contribute to the onset, maintenance, and relapse of the disorder (Frank & Spanier, 1995; Klerman & Weissman, 1993). Although IPT was originally developed to treat depression, the central idea behind IPT for eating disorders is that as problems with relationships resolve, symptoms decrease, even though the symptoms are not addressed directly by the treatment (Tantleff-Dunn et al., 2004).

How does IPT work to treat eating disorders? The hypothesized mechanism is as follows: (1) IPT reduces longstanding interpersonal problems; (2) the resulting improvement of relationships makes people feel hopeful and empowered and increases their self-esteem; and, (3) these changes lead people to change other aspects of their lives, such as disordered eating; moreover, they lead to less concern about appearance and weight and, therefore, less dieting and bingeing (Fairburn, 1997).

Although IPT for anorexia has not yet been well researched, many studies have shown that IPT is an effective alternative to CBT for bulimia (Apple, 1999; Fairburn, 1997, 2005; Tanofsky-Kraff & Wilfley, 2010).

Family Therapy

The most widely used family-oriented treatment for anorexia is called the *Maudsley approach* (Dare & Eisler, 1997; le Grange & Eisler, 2009; Lock, Le Grange, et al., 2001), named after the hospital in which the treatment originated. This approach, most effective for young women and girls who live with their parents, does not view the family as responsible for causing problems and in fact makes no assumptions about the causes of the disorder. Instead, the **Maudsley approach** focuses on: (1) helping parents view the patient as distinct from her illness; and (2) supporting the parents as *they* figure out how to lead their daughter to eat appropriately. The therapist asks the parents to unite to feed their daughter, despite her anxiety and protests. Once her weight is normal and she eats without a struggle, they gradually return control to her, and other family issues—including general ones of adolescent development—become the focus (Lock, 2004). The initial phase of treatment requires an enormous commitment on the part of the family: A parent must be home continuously to monitor the daughter's eating. Clearly, the Maudsley approach is not feasible for all families.

Maudsley approach
A family treatment for anorexia nervosa that focuses on supporting parents as they determine how to lead their child to eat appropriately.

This mother is serving dinner to her daughter; in a type of family treatment for people with anorexia known as the Maudsley approach, the first step is to empower the parents to figure out how best to lead their daughter to resume normal eating.

Altrendo/Getty Images

But research results indicate that it is perhaps the most effective treatment for adolescents and young adults with anorexia (Keel & Haedt, 2008).

In addition, *systems therapy* is one type of family therapy provided to young women and girls with eating disorders. In this therapy, the family is viewed as a system; when one member changes, change is forced on the rest of the system (Bowen, 1978; Minuchin, 1974). Maladaptive family interactional patterns and structures are seen as the problem and are the focus of change. With family systems therapy, the therapist may not specifically address the patient's eating and food issues.

Psychiatric Hospitalization

In contrast to medical hospitalizations, psychiatric hospitalizations (also called inpatient treatment) for eating disorders are often planned in advance, and they usually take place in units or free-standing facilities that specialize in treating people with eating disorders. Psychiatric hospitalization is recommended when less intensive treatments have failed to change disordered eating behaviors sufficiently. The hospital environment is a 24-hour community in which patients attend many different types of group therapy, including groups focused on body image, coping strategies, and relationships with food. These groups can decrease the isolation and shame patients may feel and give patients an opportunity to try out new ways of relating. Hospitalized patients also receive individual therapy and usually some type of family therapy; patients may also receive medication.

The short-term goals of psychiatric hospitalization for anorexia and bulimia include increasing the person's weight to the normal range, establishing a normal eating pattern (three full meals and two snacks per day), curbing excessive exercise, and beginning to change irrational, maladaptive thoughts about food, weight, and body shape. For people who purge or otherwise try to compensate for their caloric intake, an additional goal is to stop or at least reduce such compensatory behaviors.

Psychiatric hospitalization can improve eating and help to change distorted thoughts about food, weight, and body. But, in many cases, these positive changes are not enduring. Twelve months after discharge from a psychiatric hospital, 30–50% of patients relapse (Helverskov et al., 2010; Pike, 1998). Consider that in 1 year, Marya Hornbacher was hospitalized three times.

Various explanations have been proposed for the high relapse rate. One is that some patients only accept the intensive treatment for health reasons or because of pressure from family members—and once out of the hospital, they are not willing to continue the changes they began.

A second reason for the high relapse rate after psychiatric hospitalization is that some patients do not receive appropriate outpatient care after they leave the hospital. This lack of care makes it more difficult for them to learn how to sustain their changed eating, weight, and views about their bodies when they are not in a supervised therapeutic environment.

A third reason for the high relapse rate focuses on economic pressures from insurance companies, which have cut the approved length of hospital stays for people with eating disorders (and for people with psychological disorders in general). Psychiatric

◉ GETTING THE PICTURE

Which tray of food is most typical of the type of lunch that would be served to someone who is receiving intensive treatment for an eating disorder? Answer: The photo on the left; the goal is for the person to learn to eat three "normal" nutritionally sound meals per day, plus snacks.

hospitalizations have become increasingly short, which reduces the amount of enduring change that can realistically be accomplished during a stay.

Prevention Programs

Many mental health clinicians and researchers seek to *prevent* eating disorders, particularly for people most at risk (Coughlin & Kalodner, 2006; Shaw et al., 2009): namely, people who have some symptoms of an eating disorder but do not meet all the diagnostic criteria. Prevention programs often seek to challenge maladaptive beliefs about appearance and food and to decrease overeating, fasting, and avoidance of some types of foods (Stice et al., 2013). Prevention programs may take place in a single session or in multiple sessions, may take the form of presentations or workshops, or may even be provided via the Internet (Zabinski et al., 2001, 2004).

Feedback Loops in Treating Eating Disorders

With all eating disorders, successful treatment should resolve medical crises and normalize eating and nutrition, directly or indirectly. For a person with anorexia, this means increasing her eating. Better nutrition leads to improved brain functioning (neurological factor) and cognitive functioning (psychological factor). For a person with bulimia, it means normalizing her meals—making sure that she is not only eating adequately throughout the day but also getting enough of the various food groups. Eating in this way will decrease the likelihood of extreme hunger, binges, or eating that feels out of control (psychological factor) (Shah et al., 2005).

FIGURE **10.7 • Feedback Loops in Treating Eating Disorders**

Treatments Targeting Neurological and Other Biological Factors

Nutritional counseling
Medical hospitalization
Medication: SSRIs

Changes weight, nutrition, medical functioning, and neural activity

Changes thoughts, feelings, and behaviors

Decreases shame and isolation
Decreases familial focus on appearance
Improves social and family interactions

Treatments Targeting Psychological Factors

CBT: Psychoeducation, cognitive restructuring, self-monitoring, relaxation, exposure with response prevention

Treatments Targeting Social Factors

IPT
Family therapy (including Maudsley approach for anorexia)
Group therapy
Psychiatric hospitalization

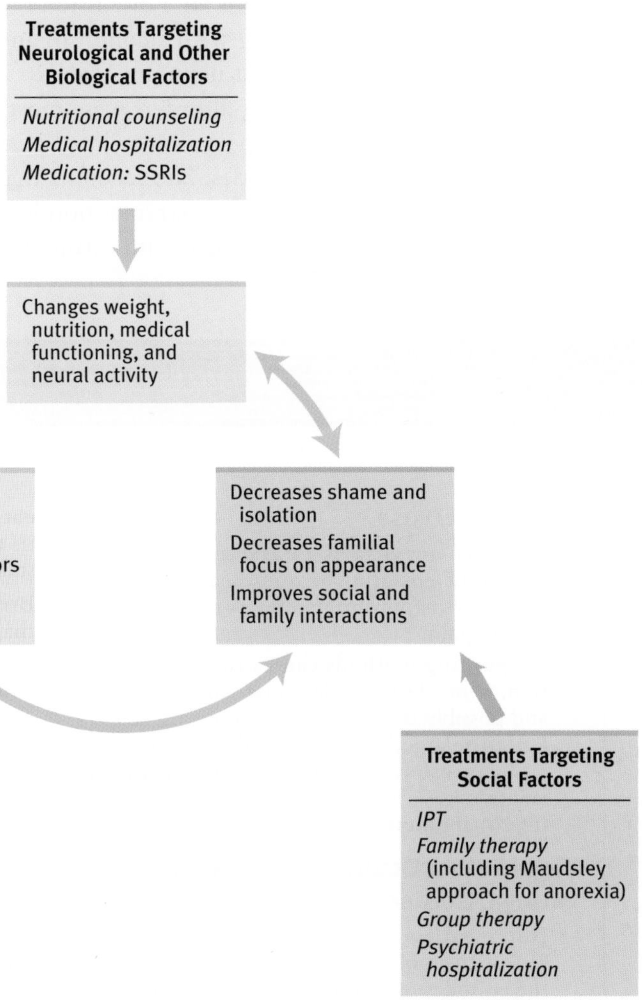

In most cases, enduring changes in eating result from changes in the way the person thinks about food and her beliefs about weight, appearance, femininity, and control. CBT may contribute to these enduring changes (psychological factor). In addition, the support of family and friends and the improved quality of these relationships, which may come from IPT or family therapy (social factor), can help the patient more realistically evaluate her appearance, weight, and body shape. Improved family interaction patterns can increase mood and satisfaction with relationships, which can decrease the level of attention that the person pays to cultural pressures toward an ideal body shape (psychological factor). The feedback loops involved in treating eating disorders are shown in Figure 10.7.

Thinking Like A Clinician

Suppose your local hospital establishes an eating disorders treatment program. Based on what you have learned in this chapter, what services should it offer, and why? If your friend, who has bulimia nervosa, asked your advice about what type of treatment she should get, how would you respond, and why?

Follow-up on Marya Hornbacher

Marya Hornbacher wrote her first memoir, *Wasted*, when she was 23 years old. Within a year of its publication, she was diagnosed with a rapid-cycling form of bipolar disorder. (See Chapter 5 for a discussion of bipolar disorder.) Hornbacher spent the next 10 years struggling with alcoholism and bipolar disorder; her struggles are recounted in her subsequent memoir, *Madness: A Bipolar Life* (2008). Although the flagrant symptoms of eating disorders were mostly behind her at the close of *Wasted*, in her later memoir, she reported occasional periods of restricting or purging as she struggled with manic episodes. She recounts that these periods of disordered eating were attempts to regulate her extreme moods. Her experiences highlight the frequent comorbidity among people with eating disorders.

SUMMING UP

Anorexia Nervosa

- The hallmark of anorexia nervosa is a significantly low body weight along with an intense fear of gaining weight or using various methods to prevent weight gain, plus distortions in body image. DSM-5 specifies two types of anorexia: restricting and binge eating/purging.

- Anorexia can lead to significant medical problems: muscle wasting (particularly of heart muscle), low heart rate, low blood pressure, loss of bone density, and decreased metabolism. Other symptoms include irritability, headaches, fatigue, and restlessness. All methods of purging—vomiting, diuretics, laxatives, and enemas—can cause dehydration because they primarily eliminate water, not calories, from the body.

Bulimia Nervosa

- Bulimia nervosa is characterized by recurrent episodes of binge eating followed by inappropriate efforts to prevent weight gain.

- All purging methods can cause dehydration, which leads to electrolyte imbalances and possibly death. Chronic vomiting can lead to enlarged parotid and salivary glands and can erode dental enamel. Chronic laxative use can lead to permanent loss of intestinal functioning.

Binge Eating Disorder and "Other" Eating Disorders

- Binge eating disorder is characterized by a pattern of feeling out of control during episodes of eating in which the person eats more than most people would eat in the same period of time and circumstances, without subsequent purging.

- Binge eating disorder is more common that anorexia and bulimia combined.

- People with significantly disturbed eating who do not meet the criteria for the other eating disorders may be diagnosed with a nonspecific "other" eating disorder.

Understanding Eating Disorders

- Cause-and-effect relationships among the factors associated with eating disorders are difficult to establish. This difficulty arises because the behaviors and their immediate consequences create neurological (and other biological), psychological, and social changes.

- Neurological factors associated with eating disorders include:
  - unusually low activity in the frontal and temporal lobes as well as reduced gray and white matter;
  - reduced responsiveness to serotonin, a neurotransmitter involved in mood, anxiety, and binge eating; and
  - a tendency for eating disorders to run in families, as well as evidence of substantial heritability, which indicates that genes play a role.
- Psychological factors related to eating disorders include:
  - irrational thoughts and excessive concerns about weight, appearance, and food;
  - binge eating as a result of the abstinence violation effect;
  - positive and negative reinforcement of symptoms of eating disorders;
  - certain personality traits, such as perfectionism and low self-esteem;
  - disinhibited eating, especially in restrained eaters; and
  - comorbid psychological disorders in female adolescents, particularly depression.

- Social factors related to eating disorders include:
  - family members and friends who provide a model for eating, concerns about weight, and focus on appearance through their own behaviors;
  - cultural factors, which play a key role, as evidenced by the increased prevalence over time of bulimia and concern about weight that is part of anorexia; and
  - conflicting gender roles in Western societies and a tendency to view women's bodies as objects and search for bodily flaws (objectification theory).

Treating Eating Disorders

- The treatments that target neurological and other biological factors include:
  - nutritional counseling to improve eating (and correct erroneous information about food and weight);
  - medical hospitalization for significant medical problems related to the disorder; and
  - medication, in particular SSRIs, to address some symptoms of the eating disorder and of anxiety and depression.

- The primary treatment that targets psychological factors is CBT, which is the treatment of choice for eating disorders. CBT addresses maladaptive thoughts, feelings, and behaviors that impede normal eating, promote bingeing and purging, and lead to body image dissatisfaction. CBT may include exposure with response prevention and help patients develop new coping strategies.
- Treatments that target social factors include:
  - interpersonal therapy, which is designed to improve the patient's relationships;
  - family therapy, particularly the Maudsley approach, which can be helpful for adolescents with anorexia who live at home;
  - psychiatric hospitalization, which provides supervised mealtimes to increase normal eating, and a range of therapeutic groups to address various psychological and social factors, plus individual therapy and possibly medication;
  - prevention programs.

Key Terms

Bulimia nervosa (p. 297)
Anorexia nervosa (p. 297)
Eating disorders (p. 297)
Binge eating (p. 300)
Purging (p. 300)
Binge eating disorder (p. 305)
Partial cases (p. 307)

Subthreshold cases (p. 307)
Abstinence violation effect (p. 311)
Restrained eating (p. 313)

Objectification theory (p. 316)
Maudsley approach (p. 321)

More Study Aids

Photodisc

For additional study aids related to this chapter, including quizzes to make sure you've retained everything you've learned and a Student Video Activity exploring one young woman's struggle with bulimia nervosa, go to: www.worthpublishers.com/launchpad/rkabpsych2e.

CHAPTER **11**

Gender and Sexual Disorders

Laura and Mike have been married for a couple of years. They generally get along well, but lately their relationship has been strained. They both work long hours and are tired when they get home. They spend weekends doing household chores or sitting in front of the television or their computers. Laura and Mike aren't spending much quality time together, and their sex life has become nonexistent. Their relationship has changed so much since they first started dating, when they were attracted to each other and enjoyed sexual relations. What went wrong, and what can they do to improve their relationship?

By its very nature, human sexuality emerges from a confluence of neuropsychosocial factors. Neurologically, sexuality relies on the actions of hormones and brain activity. Psychologically, sexuality arises from the desire to be sexual with a particular person, in a certain situation, at a specific moment. Fantasies and thoughts, body image, the subjective sense of being male or female—all these factors and others influence sexuality. Similarly, concerns about reproduction, infertility, or sexually transmitted diseases and past experiences related to sex, such as sexual abuse or rape, also affect a person's sexuality.

Moreover, sexuality is ultimately social: It involves relationships. In fact, even during solitary masturbation someone's thoughts and fantasies usually involve other people. Sexuality is influenced by general emotional satisfaction with a partner, moral and religious teachings about sexuality, and cultural views of appropriate sexual behavior (Malatesta & Adams, 2001). Such conditions and circumstances are ultimately rooted in social factors.

ABNORMALITIES IN SEXUALITY AND SEXUAL BEHAVIOR are influenced by all these neuropsychosocial factors. For instance, a person's brain (and, as a result, his or her body) may not respond to sexual stimuli in the usual way or may respond sexually to stimuli that are not generally considered to be sexual in nature (such as shoes). Similarly, some people may have sexual fantasies that disturb them, or they may have difficulties with sexual functioning that lead to distress or problems in their

Richard B. Levine/Newscom

John Eastcott & Yva Momatiuk/National Geographic/Getty Images

What is viewed as normal and abnormal sexuality is partly based on the cultural views of appropriate sexual behavior.

relationships. In addition, families, communities, and cultures determine which sexual fantasies, urges, and behaviors are considered "deviant" or "abnormal." These socially defined sexual "abnormalities" differ across cultures and shift over time. For example, masturbation and oral sex were once considered to be deviant. More recently, homosexuality was considered a psychological disorder until 1973, when it was removed from the DSM. Moreover, like most other psychological problems and disorders, normal and abnormal sexuality and sexual behavior fall on a continuum. However, DSM-5 relies on the categorical approach to define sex-related and sexual disorders; that is, according to DSM-5, sexual fantasies, urges, and behaviors are either normal or not normal.

As we'll see in this chapter, the diagnosis of most—although not all—gender or sexually related disorders in DSM-5 hinges on the patient's experience of distress (or, in some cases, impaired functioning) as a result of the symptoms (First & Frances, 2008). Simply having unusual or "deviant" sexual fantasies or engaging in unusual sexual behaviors is not generally sufficient for a diagnosis. Moreover, some disorders (specifically, some of the *sexual dysfunctions*) have predominantly neurological and other biological criteria, whereas others (the *paraphilic disorders* and *gender dysphoria*) have primarily psychological and social criteria. We examine these disorders in the following sections.

Gender Dysphoria

Last year, Mike got a Facebook status update from Sam, his friend since high school. Sam announced that he'd become Samantha; he had begun to dress and live as a woman. The news, and Samantha's new Facebook photo, took Mike by surprise. Sam had dated girls occasionally in high school—they'd even gone out on double dates together—and Sam seemed so "normal." In the Facebook photo, Mike found Samantha only vaguely recognizable as having been Sam. Mike didn't know how to make sense of Sam's change. Mike told Laura about Sam's change to Samantha, and Mike found himself wondering what life—and sex—had been like for Sam, and what it was like now for Samantha. What had happened, or would happen, to Sam's genitals? What in the world could have driven Sam to want to make such a drastic change? Mike surfed the Internet for reputable information about Sam's condition and discovered that it is called *gender dysphoria*.

What Is Gender Dysphoria?

Gender identity
The subjective sense of being male or female (or having the sense of a more fluid identity, outside the binary categories of male and female), as these categories are defined by a person's culture.

Like Sam, a small percentage of people at birth are (usually based on their observable sex organs) assigned one gender (either female or male) but do not feel comfortable with the corresponding gender identity. **Gender identity** is the subjective sense of being male or female (or having the sense of a more fluid identity, outside the binary categories of male and female), as these categories are defined by a person's culture. For instance, people like Sam, who have male sexual anatomy and have been labeled male since birth, may *feel* as if they are female. Conversely, some people have been labeled as female since birth but feel as if they are male. (The gender that a person is assigned at birth is referred to as the *natal* gender.) People who feel that their gender identity does not correspond to their natal gender thus experience *cross-gender identification*.

Transgender is a broad term sometimes used to describe people whose identification and behavior may be at odds with their natal gender but who do not necessarily seek medical treatment to change their sexual characteristics (Riley et al., 2013). If such people live as the "opposite gender" (e.g., a natal male dresses in daily life and is known by others as a female), they are referred to as *transsexuals*. Transsexuals may seek medical treatment to attain sexual characteristics that match their experienced gender. **Gender dysphoria** is an incongruence between a person's assigned gender (usually based on his or her natal gender) and the subjective experience of his or her gender, and that incongruence causes distress (American Psychiatric Association, 2013).

Gender dysphoria typically begins in childhood; children who are diagnosed with gender dysphoria usually strongly desire to be the opposite gender of their assigned one, preferring to dress or play with toys in ways that are typical of children of the other gender. That is, they wish to behave in accordance with the prototypical gender role of their experienced gender, not their assigned, natal gender; **gender role** refers to the outward behaviors, attitudes, and traits that a culture deems masculine or feminine. For instance, gender roles for females often allow a wider variety of emotions (anger, tears, and fear) to be displayed in public than do gender roles for males; in contrast, gender roles for males often allow more overtly aggressive or assertive behaviors than do gender roles for females. A person with gender dysphoria wants to adopt the gender role of the opposite gender not because of perceived cultural advantages of becoming the other gender but because the opposite gender role is more consistent with the person's sense of self.

In children, gender dysphoria is not simply "tomboyishness" in girls or "sissy" behavior in boys. Rather, gender dysphoria reflects a profound sense of identifying with the other gender, to the point of denying one's own sexual organs. For instance, natal girls with gender dysphoria report that they don't want to develop breasts or menstruate. However, long-term studies of children who have been diagnosed with gender dysphoria find that most of the children did not continue to have the disorder into adulthood (American Psychiatric Association, 2013; Drummond et al., 2008; Zucker, 2005).

Table 11.1 lists the criteria for gender dysphoria in children, and Table 11.2 lists the criteria for the disorder in adolescents and adults. Adolescents and adults may feel uncomfortable living publicly as their assigned, natal gender. In fact, these people may be preoccupied by the wish to *be* the other gender. They may take that wish further and live, at least some of the time, as someone of the other gender— dressing and behaving accordingly, whether at home or in public. Like Sam, some adults with gender dysphoria have medical and surgical treatments to assume the appearance of the other sex; such surgical procedures are called *sex reassignment surgery* (discussed in the section on treatment).

Gender dysphoria
A psychological disorder characterized by an incongruence between a person's assigned gender at birth and the subjective experience of his or her gender, and that incongruence causes distress.

Gender role
The outward behaviors, attitudes, and traits that a culture deems masculine or feminine.

TABLE 11.1 • DSM-5 Diagnostic Criteria for Gender Dysphoria in Children

A. A marked incongruence between one's experienced/expressed gender and assigned gender, of at least 6 months' duration, as manifested by at least six of the following (one of which must be Criterion A1):

1. A strong desire to be of the other gender or an insistence that one is the other gender (or some alternative gender different from one's assigned gender).

2. In boys (assigned gender), a strong preference for cross-dressing or simulating female attire; or in girls (assigned gender), a strong preference for wearing only typical masculine clothing and a strong resistance to the wearing of typical feminine clothing.

3. A strong preference for cross-gender roles in make-believe play or fantasy play.

4. A strong preference for the toys, games, or activities stereotypically used or engaged in by the other gender.

5. A strong preference for playmates of the other gender.

6. In boys (assigned gender), a strong rejection of typically masculine toys, games, and activities and a strong avoidance of rough-and-tumble play; or in girls (assigned gender), a strong rejection of typically feminine toys, games, and activities.

7. A strong dislike of one's sexual anatomy.

8. A strong desire for the primary and/or secondary sex characteristics that match one's experienced gender.

B. The condition is associated with clinically significant distress or impairment in social, school, or other important areas of functioning.

Reprinted with permission from the Diagnostic and Statistical Manual of Mental Disorders, Fifth Edition, (Copyright ©2013). American Psychiatric Association. All Rights Reserved.

TABLE **11.2** • DSM-5 Diagnostic Criteria for Gender Dysphoria in Adolescents and Adults

A. A marked incongruence between one's experienced/expressed gender and assigned gender, of at least 6 months' duration, as manifested by at least two of the following:

1. A marked incongruence between one's experienced/expressed gender and primary and/or secondary sex characteristics (or in young adolescents, the anticipated secondary sex characteristics).

2. A strong desire to be rid of one's primary and/or secondary sex characteristics because of a marked incongruence with one's experienced/expressed gender (or in young adolescents, a desire to prevent the development of the anticipated secondary sex characteristics).

3. A strong desire for the primary and/or secondary sex characteristics of the other gender.

4. A strong desire to be of the other gender (or some alternative gender different from one's assigned gender).

5. A strong desire to be treated as the other gender (or some alternative gender different from one's assigned gender).

6. A strong conviction that one has the typical feelings and reactions of the other gender (or some alternative gender different from one's assigned gender).

B. The condition is associated with clinically significant distress or impairment in social, occupational, or other important areas of functioning.

Reprinted with permission from the Diagnostic and Statistical Manual of Mental Disorders, Fifth Edition, (Copyright ©2013). American Psychiatric Association. All Rights Reserved.

In order for a person to be diagnosed with gender dysphoria, DSM-5 requires that the symptoms cause significant distress or impair functioning. However, the distress experienced by someone with gender dysphoria often arises because of *other people's responses* to the cross-gender behaviors (Nuttbrock et al., 2010; Roberts et al., 2012). For instance, a natal male child with gender dysphoria may be ostracized or made fun of by children or even teachers for consistently "playing girl games"—and thus the child feels distress because of the reactions of others. In contrast, for most disorders in DSM-5, the distress that the person feels arises directly from the symptoms themselves (e.g., distress that is caused by feeling hopeless or being afraid in social situations).

Like the person in Case 11.1, most adolescents and adults with gender dysphoria report having had symptoms of the disorder in childhood—even though most people who had gender dysphoria in childhood do not have it later in life.

Teena Brandon was born female, yet felt like a male on the inside and came to live as a man, though without having sex reassignment surgery. As an adult, Brandon was raped and later killed by young men after they discovered that Brandon was biologically female. Brandon's life was the subject of the documentary film *The Brandon Teena Story* and the feature film *Boys Don't Cry*.

CASE **11.1** • FROM THE INSIDE: Gender Dysphoria

In her memoir *She's Not There: A Life in Two Genders* (2003), novelist and English professor Jenny Finney Boylan (who was born male) describes her experiences of feeling, since the age of 3, as if she were a female in a male body:

Since then, the awareness that I was in the wrong body, living the wrong life, was never out of my conscious mind—never, although my understanding of what it meant to be a boy, or a girl, was something that changed over time. Still, this conviction was present during my piano lesson with Mr. Hockenberry, and it was there when my father and I shot off model rockets, and it was there years later when I took the SAT, and it was there in the middle of the night when I woke in my dormitory at Wesleyan. And at every moment I lived my life, I countered this awareness with an exasperated companion thought, namely, Don't be an idiot. You're not a girl. Get over it.

But I never got over it.

(pp. 19–21)

TABLE 11.3 · Gender Dysphoria Facts at a Glance

Prevalence
• The prevalence of gender dysphoria is very low, estimated at 0.014% or lower.

Comorbidity
• In one survey of 31 patients who were diagnosed with gender dysphoria and had not yet begun the process of sex reassignment surgery, almost 75% had another psychiatric disorder at some point in their lives, most often either a mood disorder or a substance-related disorder (Hepp et al., 2005). However, only 39% had another psychological disorder after they began the sex reassignment process; this finding suggests that the previous high comorbidity was at least partly related to living as a gender that did not correspond to a person's gender identity.

Onset
• Symptoms of cross-gender identity typically begin in childhood.

Course
• If symptoms persist into adulthood, they are likely to remain stable, leading many people with this disorder to seek sex reassignment surgery.

Gender Differences
• The ratio of natal males to natal females ranges from 2:1 to 6:1.

Cultural Differences
• Cross-gender identification is not considered pathological in all cultures; in some Native American and traditional African cultures, such people have high status and are seen as especially spiritual (Jacobs et al., 1997; Langer & Martin, 2004; Roscoe, 1993).

Source: Unless otherwise noted, information is from American Psychiatric Association, 2013.

Most commonly, people with gender dysphoria are heterosexual relative to their gender identification. For instance, natal men who see themselves as women tend to be attracted to men and thus feel as if they are heterosexual (Blanchard, 1989, 1990; Zucker & Bradley, 1995). However, some are homosexual relative to their gender identification; a natal woman who sees herself as a man may be sexually attracted to men. And some people with gender dysphoria are bisexual and some are asexual—they have little or no interest in any type of sex.

As noted in Table 11.3 (along with other facts about gender dysphoria), gender dysphoria is about three times more common among natal males than among natal females. One explanation for this difference is that in Western cultures, females have a relatively wide range of acceptable "masculine" behavior and dress (think of Diane Keaton's character in the move *Annie Hall*), whereas males have a relatively narrow range of acceptable "feminine" behavior and dress. A woman dressed in "men's" clothes might not even get a second look, but a man dressed in "women's" clothes will likely be subjected to ridicule.

United Artists/Photofest

Bob Barkany/Getty Images

Females have a wider range of acceptable "masculine" behavior and dress than males have of acceptable "feminine" behavior and dress. Women can wear men's clothes without risk of being labeled as deviant, whereas men who wear women's clothes (when not as part of a performance) are often considered to have something wrong with them.

Understanding Gender Dysphoria

As summarized in the following sections, we now know that various neurological, psychological, and social factors are associated with gender dysphoria.

Neurological Factors

Researchers have begun to document differences in specific brain structures in people who have gender dysphoria versus those who do not. In addition, evidence shows that hormones during fetal development play a role in producing this disorder. Genes can also play a large role in contributing to this disorder.

Brain Systems and Neural Communication

The brains of transsexuals differ from typical brains in ways consistent with their gender identity. In particular, Kruijver and colleagues (2000) examined a specific type of neuron in a brain structure called the *bed nucleus of the stria terminalis* (which is often regarded as an extension of the amygdala). Typically, males have almost twice as many of these neurons as females do. In this study, the number of these neurons in the brains of male-to-female transsexuals was in the range typically found in female brains, and the number in the brains of female-to-male transsexuals was in the range typically found in male brains.

How might such brain alterations arise? Research suggests that prenatal exposure to hormones may affect later gender identity (Bradley & Zucker, 1997; Wallien et al., 2008; Zucker & Bradley, 1995). In particular, maternal stress during pregnancy can produce hormones that alter brain structure and thereby predispose a person to gender dysphoria (Zucker & Bradley, 1995). In addition, fetal levels of testosterone—measured from amniotic fluid—are positively associated with later stereotypical "male" play behavior in girls and, to a lesser extent, in boys; the higher the level of testosterone in the fluid, the more "male" play the children exhibited when they were between 6 and 10 years old (Auyeung et al., 2009).

Genetics

Coolidge and colleagues (2002) studied 314 children who were either identical or fraternal twins and concluded that as much as 62% of the variance in gender dysphoria can arise from genes! If this result is replicated, it will provide strong support for these researchers' view that the disorder "may be much less a matter of choice and much more a matter of biology" (p. 251). However, even in this study, almost 40% of the variance was ascribed to the effects of nonshared environment, and thus genes—once again—are not destiny.

In short, neurological factors—brain differences, prenatal hormones, and genetic predispositions—may contribute to gender dysphoria, but the presence of any one of these factors does not appear to be sufficient to cause this disorder (Di Ceglie, 2000).

Psychological Factors: A Correlation with Play Activities?

In general, studies have found that boys engage in more rough-and-tumble play and have a higher activity level than do girls. Natal boys with gender dysphoria, however, do not have as high an activity level as their counterparts without the disorder. Similarly, natal girls with gender dysphoria are more likely to engage in rough-and-tumble play than are other girls (Bates et al., 1973, 1979; Zucker & Bradley, 1995). Both natal boys and natal girls with gender dysphoria are less likely to play with same-sex peers; instead, they seek out, feel more comfortable with, and feel themselves to be more similar to children of the other sex (Green, 1974, 1987).

However, such findings should be interpreted with caution, for two reasons: (1) These very characteristics are part of the diagnostic criteria for gender dysphoria in children, so it is not at all surprising that these behaviors are correlated with having the disorder; (2) a diagnosis of gender dysphoria in childhood does not usually persist into adulthood. Thus, beyond symptoms that are part of the criteria for gender dysphoria, no psychological factors are clearly associated with the disorder.

Social Factors: Responses From Others

Social factors may be associated with gender dysphoria, but such factors are unlikely to *cause* the disorder (Bradley & Zucker, 1997; Di Ceglie, 2000).

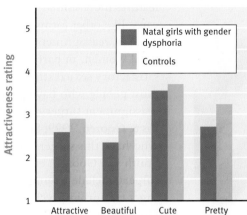

(a) Physical attractiveness of boys

(b) Physical attractiveness of girls

FIGURE **11.1 • Physical Attractiveness Ratings of Children With Gender Dysphoria**
(a) Viewing photographs, college students rated natal boys with gender dysphoria as more attractive than boys
without this disorder. (b) Similarly, natal girls with gender dysphoria were considered to be less attractive than girls
who did not have the disorder (Zucker et al., 1993).

Source: Adapted from Zucker & Bradley, 1995.

As shown in Figure 11.1(a), college students rated photographs of natal boys with
gender dysphoria as cuter and prettier than photos of boys without the disorder;
in contrast, Figure 11.1(b) shows that natal girls with gender dysphoria were rated
as less attractive than girls who did not have the disorder (Zucker et al., 1993).
These contrasting ratings of physical appearance may reflect the prenatal influence of hormones: Natal boys may have been exposed to more female hormones
in the womb, leading to the feminization of their facial features; conversely, natal
girls may have been exposed to more male hormones in the womb, leading to
the masculinization of their facial features. In turn, the feminized or masculin-
ized facial features may lead others to interact differently with people who then
develop this disorder.

Given how little is known about the factors that contribute to gender dysphoria,
we cannot comment on the nature of any feedback loops among them.

Treating Gender Dysphoria

Treatments for gender dysphoria may target all three types of factors.

Targeting Neurological and Other Biological Factors: Altered Appearance

One way for people with gender dysphoria to achieve greater congruence
between the gender they feel themselves to be and their natal gender is to alter
some or all of their biological sexual characteristics. This sort of treatment may
involve taking hormones. In natal women, taking male sex hormones will lower
the voice, stop menstruation, and begin facial hair growth. In natal men, taking female sex hormones will enlarge breasts and redistribute fat to the hips and
buttocks.

Some people with gender dysphoria go a step further and have **sex reassignment
surgery**, a procedure in which the genitals and breasts are surgically altered to appear
like those of the other gender. Sex reassignment surgery for natal males involves creating breasts and removing most of the penis and testes and then creating a clitoris and
vagina. For natal females, surgery involves removing breasts, ovaries, and uterus and

Sex reassignment surgery
A procedure in which a person's genitals (and
breasts) are surgically altered to appear like
those of the other sex.

Caroline Cossey, born Barry Cossey, increasingly felt during adolescence that although she had a male body, she was a female inside. When 20 years old, after a couple of years of taking female hormones and living as a woman, Cossey had sex reassignment surgery and later became a model and actress.

then creating a penis. Patients may also have subsequent surgeries to make their facial features more similar to those of the other gender. However, these surgical treatments can—like other forms of surgery—be risky and prohibitively expensive.

Sex reassignment surgery is technically more effective for natal men than for natal women, in part because it is difficult to create an artificial penis that provides satisfactory sexual stimulation (Steiner, 1985). Regardless of natal gender, however, most people who have gender dysphoria are satisfied with the outcome of their sex reassignment surgery, despite possible difficulty in attaining orgasm (Cohen-Kettenis & Gooren, 1999; Smith, van Goozen, et al., 2005). However, up to 10% of people who have this surgery (depending on the study) later regret it (Landen et al., 1998; Smith van Goozen, et al., 2001). Factors associated with a less positive outcome after surgery include having unsupportive family members (Landen et al., 1998) and having a comorbid psychological disorder (Midence & Hargreaves, 1997; Smith, van Goozen, et al., 2005).

In an effort to reduce the proportion of people who come to regret having sex reassignment surgery, those contemplating it are usually carefully evaluated beforehand regarding their emotional stability and their expectations of what the surgery will accomplish. A careful diagnostic evaluation and a long period of cross-dressing are required by most facilities before sex reassignment surgery.

Targeting Psychological Factors: Understanding the Choices

Treatment that targets psychological factors helps people with gender dysphoria not only to understand themselves and their situation but also to be aware of their options and goals regarding living publicly as the other gender; treatment also provides information about medical and surgical options. Such treatment is typically provided by mental health clinicians specially trained in diagnosing and helping people with gender dysphoria. These clinicians also help patients identify and obtain treatment for any other mental health issues, such as depression or anxiety (Carroll, 2000). For those who choose to live part time or full time as the other gender, the clinician helps them discover whether doing so is in fact more consistent with how they feel and how they see themselves. Moreover, the clinician helps the patient with problem solving related to living as the other gender—such as by identifying and developing possible solutions to issues that might arise regarding other people's responses to their changed gender.

Targeting Social Factors: Family Support

Family members of people with gender dysphoria may not understand the disorder or know how to be supportive; family therapy techniques that focus on communication and educating the family about gender dysphoria can help family members develop more effective ways to discuss problems.

In addition, groups for people with gender dysphoria can provide support and information. Group therapy may also focus on difficulties in relationships or problems that arise as a result of living as the other gender, such as experiencing sexual harassment for those newly living as a woman or taunting by men for those newly living as a man (Di Ceglie, 2000).

Treatment for gender dysphoria typically first targets psychological factors—helping people to determine whether they want to live as the other gender. If they decide to do so, then treatment targeting social factors comes into play, to address problems with family members and interactions with other people in general. Following this, treatment targeting neurological and other biological factors is provided when a person wishes to have medical or surgical procedures. After such treatment, clinicians may provide additional treatment that targets psychological and social factors.

Thinking Like A Clinician

When Nico was a boy, he hated playing with the other boys; he detested sports and loved playing "house" and "dress up" with the girls—except when the girls made him dress up as "the man" of the group. Sometimes he got to be the princess, and that thrilled him. As a teenager, Nico's closest friends continued to be females. Although Nico shied away from playing with boys, he felt himself sexually attracted to them. To determine whether Nico had gender dysphoria, what information would a clinician want? What specific information would count heavily? Should the fact that Nico is attracted to males affect the assessment? Why or why not?

Paraphilic Disorders

Mike found that he was disturbed about Sam's transformation into Samantha in part because it reminded Mike of his very private pastime during his teenage years: He had secretly "borrowed" some of his older sister's clothes from her room, dressed up in them, and admired himself in front of the mirror. He'd found this extremely erotic but also terrifying. He had worried that he'd get caught and felt that it somehow wasn't "right." Throughout his adulthood, Mike had struggled to overcome his urge to dress in women's clothes, usually successfully. During most of his marriage to Laura, he'd managed to keep this urge at bay, and he'd never told her about it. However, once he heard about Sam, he felt jealous because Samantha dressed as a woman. His urge to dress in women's clothes became stronger, which affected his relationship with Laura: He thought it best to avoid sexual relations with her until he felt more in control of himself.

Mike had felt alone in his worries and concerns until he discovered online chat rooms in which people discussed cross-dressing. Now he's spending a lot of time "chatting" with other men who like to cross-dress; he bought some women's clothes (which he keeps hidden) and puts them on and masturbates when Laura is out. What's going on with Mike? To find out, we need to consider another category of sexual disorders, called *paraphilic disorders*.

What Are Paraphilic Disorders?

Some people have unusual sexual interests—paraphilias. Specifically, they are sexually aroused and have fantasies about objects or activities that are not normally associated with sexual interests, such as women's shoes or spying on other people when they take off their clothes. A **paraphilia** (from the Greek *para-*, meaning "beside" or "beyond," and *philos*, meaning "fondness" or "love") is an intense and persistent sexual interest that is different than the usual fondling or genital stimulation with "normal physically mature consenting human partners" (American Psychiatric Association, 2013, p. 685).

Although paraphilias may be unusual, they are not necessarily considered to be mental disorders. In contrast, according to DSM-5, **paraphilic disorders** are paraphilias that lead to distress, impaired functioning, or harm—or risk of harm—to the person or to others. According to DSM-5, the sexual aspect of a paraphilic disorder is characterized by unusual preferences either in (1) sexual *activity* (such as activities involving pain and suffering or an odd variation of what might be considered "courtship"—such as exhibitionistic behavior) or (2) the *target* of the activity (such as children or objects).

This way of classifying paraphilic disorders misses an important element that some of these disorders share—that they involve partners who do not consent to

Paraphilia
An intense and persistent sexual interest that is different than the usual fondling or genital stimulation with "normal physically mature consenting human partners."

Paraphilic disorder
A category of disorders characterized by paraphilias that lead to distress, impaired functioning, or harm—or risk of harm—to the person or to others.

the activity. Other paraphilic disorders have pain and humiliation as the primary activity. Thus, in this section, we classify paraphilic disorders according to whether they involve:

- nonconsenting adults or children,
- nonhuman objects (such as women's shoes) or body parts, or
- suffering or humiliating oneself or one's partner; the diagnosis of a paraphilic disorder would apply only when such experiences are not part of sexual role-playing.

These fantasies, urges, or behaviors together form a predictable pattern of arousal that is consistent for the person. In addition, the diagnostic criteria for all paraphilic disorders require that the pattern of arousal (sometimes referred to as an *arousal pattern*) has been present for at least 6 months (American Psychiatric Association, 2013). However, the arousal pattern doesn't necessarily affect all areas of functioning; people with a paraphilic disorder may not be impaired at work or even necessarily in their family life.

Because DSM-5 uses a categorical approach, it must draw a line to separate "normal" from "abnormal." For some paraphilic disorders, DSM-5 draws the line at the point where the sexual arousal pattern causes significant distress or impairs functioning. Someone who becomes aroused in response to violent pornography or in response to particular items of clothing, for instance, would not be diagnosed as having a paraphilic disorder unless this arousal pattern caused significant distress, impaired functioning, or led to harm or a risk of harm. Thus, having a paraphilia is necessary, but not sufficient, to be diagnosed as having a paraphilic disorder. For instance, someone might have *exhibitionism* but not *exhibitionistic disorder*.

The specific arousal patterns of the types of paraphilic disorders are listed in Table 11.4, along with their DSM-5 diagnostic criteria. Paraphilias and paraphilic disorders are almost exclusively diagnosed in men; the only paraphilic disorder observed in a significant percentage of women is *sexual sadism disorder*. Because the vast majority of people who have the other paraphilic disorders are men, in this section we use the masculine pronouns (e.g., *him*) when discussing patients with these disorders. (In the section on understanding paraphilic disorders, we will examine possible reasons for this gender difference.)

Mental health researchers believe that, based on the number of websites and online chat rooms, the prevalence of paraphilic disorders is higher than had been previously thought, but the actual prevalence is unknown. Most research on paraphilic disorders has been conducted with men whose disorders involve nonconsenting people (such as child molesters, rapists, and exhibitionists) and who have come to the attention of mental health clinicians and researchers through the criminal justice system or at the urging of family members. We examine that type of paraphilic disorder first and then consider other types of paraphilic disorders.

Paraphilic Disorders Involving Nonconsenting People

The common feature of the paraphilic disorders discussed in this section is that the person with the disorder has recurrent sexual fantasies, urges, or behaviors that involve nonconsenting people of any age. Specifically, if the patient has recurrent fantasies or urges that involve a nonconsenting person *but does not act on them*, a diagnosis of the paraphilic disorder is given only if the fantasies and urges cause significant distress or impair functioning in some area of life (such as leading to difficulties in relationships). In contrast, if the man did act on those recurrent fantasies and urges with a nonconsenting person, the diagnosis would be made, even if the patient did not experience distress or impaired functioning. For instance, someone who "flashes"

TABLE 11.4 • Paraphilic Disorders: An Overview and the DSM-5 Diagnostic Criteria

Disorder	Specific Sexual Thoughts (Fantasies, or Urges) or Activities to Enhance Sexual Arousal	Digest of DSM-5 Diagnostic Criteria
Exhibitionistic disorder	Exposing genitals to an nonconsenting stranger	• Repeated and significant sexual arousal from thoughts or deeds related to showing one's private parts to a nonconsenting person. Must have occurred over at least 6 months. • The person has either acted on these thoughts or these thoughts impair normal functioning in some area of life.
Voyeuristic disorder	Watching someone who is taking their clothes off or having sex	• Repeated and significant sexual arousal from thoughts or deeds related to watching a person who is unclothed, in the process of removing clothing, or having sex; the person being observed is unaware of this fact. Must have occurred over at least 6 months. • The person with this arousal pattern is 18 or older. • The person has either acted on these thoughts or these thoughts impair normal functioning in some area of life.
Frotteuristic disorder	Non-violent physical contact with a nonconsenting person	• Repeated and significant sexual arousal from thoughts or deeds related to non-violent physical contact with a nonconsenting person. Must have occurred over at least 6 months. • The person has either acted on these thoughts or these thoughts impair normal functioning in some area of life.
Pedophilic disorder	Sexual activity with a child who has not reached puberty	• Repeated and significant sexual arousal from thoughts or deeds related to sexual activity involving a child who has not yet reached puberty (typically under age 13). Must have occurred over at least 6 months. • The person has either acted on these thoughts or these thoughts impair normal functioning in some area of life. • The person is at least 5 years older than the object of the sexual fantasy or activity and is at least 16.
Sexual Sadism Disorder	Sexual arousal from giving psychological or physical pain	• Repeated and significant sexual arousal from thoughts or deeds related to the physical or emotional suffering of another person. Must have occurred over at least 6 months. • The person has either acted on these thoughts or these thoughts impair normal functioning in some area of life.
Sexual Masochism Disorder	Sexual arousal from being made to suffer	• Repeated sexual arousal from thoughts or deeds related to being hurt, humiliated, or suffering in some other way. Must have occurred over at least 6 months. • These thoughts or activities impair normal functioning in some area of life.
Fetishistic Disorder	Sexual arousal from an object (shoes, underwear)	• Repeated and significant sexual arousal from an object(s) or a specific nongenital body part. Can be demonstrated either in imagination, desire or action. Must have occurred over at least 6 months. • The fetish items are not limited to objects used in cross-dressing or self-stimulation (such as vibrators). • These thoughts or activities impair normal functioning in some area of life.
Transvestic Disorder	Sexual arousal from dressing in the clothes of the opposite gender	• Repeated and significant sexual arousal from thoughts or deeds related to cross-dressing. Must have occurred over at least 6 months. • These thoughts or activities impair normal functioning in some area of life.

Paraphilic disorders include unusual sexual fantasies, urges, and activities that can be classified into three types: Those that involve nonconsenting partners or children (in **blue**); those that involve suffering or humiliating oneself or a partner (in **red**); and those that involve nonhuman animals or objects (in **green**). Note that sexual sadism involves nonconsenting people; nevertheless, DSM-5 groups sexual sadism disorder with sexual masochism disorder, rather than with the other paraphilic disorders that involve nonconsenting people. Note also that the specifics of the criterion related to distress, impaired functioning, or acting on the sexual thoughts vary across the paraphilic disorders, depending in part on whether the disorder involves nonconsenting individuals.

Source: Diagnostic and Statistical Manual of Mental Disorders, Fifth Edition, American Psychiatric Publishing, 2013.

others, who molests children, or who sadistically sexually assaults victims would be diagnosed with a paraphilic disorder if the duration criterion—at least 6 months—for the behavior were met.

Thus, men who engage in criminal sexual behaviors could qualify for the diagnosis of a paraphilic disorder, which creates confusion about what constitutes criminal behavior versus mental illness. However, some psychiatrists point out that paraphilic disorders should not be diagnosed *solely* on the basis of sexual behaviors because doing so "blurs the distinction between mental disorder and ordinary criminality" (First & Frances, 2008, p. 1240). In short, some people with this diagnosis might commit crimes, but not all people with this diagnosis do so.

Exhibitionistic Disorder: Physically Exposing Oneself

The paraphilic disorder **exhibitionistic disorder** is characterized by sexual fantasies, urges, or behaviors that involve a person's exposing his genitals to an unsuspecting person (see Table 11.4). To be considered a disorder, the man must either experience distress or impaired functioning as a result of the fantasies and urges—or must have actually exposed himself to someone who was not a willing observer. People who expose themselves for money (such as nude dancers or artists' models) are not considered exhibitionists because they do so for compensation, not for sexual arousal (McAnulty et al., 2001).

A man with exhibitionistic disorder typically gets an erection and may masturbate while exposing himself. Men with this disorder commonly report that they don't intend to frighten or shock strangers but hope that strangers will enjoy or be aroused by seeing their genitals (Lang et al., 1987; Langevin et al., 1979). Men with exhibitionistic disorder may rehearse beforehand; they may achieve orgasm during the exhibitionistic episode or later, when they think about it. One study found that, over the course of his life, the typical man with this disorder had "flashed" 514 people (Abel et al., 1987). (However, some very active men skew the average; the median number of people flashed is 34.) Between 2 and 4% of males are thought to have this disorder (American Psychiatric Association, 2013).

Voyeuristic Disorder: Watching Others

Voyeuristic disorder is a paraphilic disorder characterized by sexual fantasies, urges, or behaviors that involves *observing* someone who is in the process of undressing, is nude, or is engaged in sexual activity. The person being watched has neither consented to nor is aware of being observed (see Table 11.4). As with exhibitionistic disorder, for voyeuristic disorder to be classified as a disorder, the person's urges and fantasies must cause distress or impair functioning, or the person must have acted on those fantasies and urges.

A voyeur rarely has physical contact with the observed person. Moreover, voyeuristic disorder is distinguished from looking at pornography or watching nude dancing; voyeuristic disorder involves observing someone *who does not know that he or she is being observed*. A man with this disorder might use binoculars to "spy" on a woman, masturbating while observing her through her window as she undresses, or might plant hidden cameras and watch the video later or via an Internet feed. According to DSM-5, this disorder can only be diagnosed in people who are 18 years old or older, in order not to pathologize what is viewed as a "normal" sexual curiosity during puberty and adolescence.

© Krissi Lundgren/Alamy

People who are paid to disrobe—either partially, as is the case with these men, or fully—are not considered to have exhibitionistic disorder.

Exhibitionistic disorder
A paraphilic disorder in which sexual fantasies, urges, or behaviors involve exposing one's genitals to an unsuspecting person.

Voyeuristic disorder
A paraphilic disorder in which sexual fantasies, urges, or behaviors involve observing someone who is in the process of undressing, is nude, or is engaged in sexual activity, when the person being observed has neither consented to nor is aware of being observed.

Frotteuristic Disorder: Touching a Stranger

Frotteuristic disorder (from the French *frotter*, "to rub") is characterized by recurrent, intense, sexually arousing fantasies, sexual urges, or behaviors that involve touching or rubbing against a nonconsenting person (see Table 11.4). As with exhibitionistic disorder and voyeuristic disorder, the urges and fantasies must cause distress or problems in relationships, or the man must have acted on those fantasies and urges. This diagnosis has two types: men who like to rub and men who like to touch ("touchers"). On crowded public transportation, men with frotteuristic disorder try to stand or sit next to attractive females and rub their genitals against the victims' buttocks, thighs, or crotch, often while fantasizing that they are having consensual sex, as Charles, in Case 11.2, did. When discovered, men with frotteuristic disorder typically flee from the train or bus.

These two photos illustrate the key difference between voyeuristic disorder and frotteuristic disorder: physical contact. This man on the left may just be birdwatching, but some people with voyeuristic disorder may use binoculars to spy on people who are naked or engaged in sex. In contrast, frotteuristic disorder involves physical contact, and a crowded subway car is the kind of place where someone with frotteuristic disorder may find opportunity for physical contact.

CASE 11.2 • FROM THE OUTSIDE: Frotteuristic Disorder

Charles was 45 when he was referred for psychiatric consultation by his parole officer following his second arrest for rubbing up against a woman in the subway. According to Charles, he had a "good" sexual relationship with his wife of 15 years when he began, 10 years ago, to touch women in the subway. A typical episode would begin with his decision to go into the subway to rub against a woman, usually in her 20s. He would select the woman as he walked into the subway station, move in behind her, and wait for the train to arrive at the station. He would be wearing plastic wrap around his penis so as not to stain his pants after ejaculating while rubbing up against his victim. As riders moved on to the train, he would follow the woman he had selected. When the door closed, he would begin to push his penis up against her buttocks, fantasizing that they were having intercourse in a normal, noncoercive manner. In about half the episodes, he would ejaculate and then go on to work. If he failed to ejaculate, he would either give up for that day or change trains and select another victim. According to Charles, he felt guilty immediately after each episode, but would soon find himself ruminating about and anticipating the next encounter. He estimated that he had done this about twice a week for the last 10 years and thus had probably rubbed up against approximately a thousand women.

(Spitzer et al., 2002, pp. 164–165)

Pedophilic Disorder: Sexually Abusing Children

Child sexual abuse is a crime, but the DSM-5 diagnosis for those who fantasize about, have urges, or actually engage in sexual activity with a child (typically one who has not yet gone through puberty) is **pedophilic disorder** (previously called *pedophilia*)(see Table 11.4). To be diagnosed with this disorder, the person must be at least 16 years old and at least 5 years older than the child. Thus, someone is diagnosed with pedophilic disorder if he has had sexual activity with a child (and so would also be considered a *child molester*) *or* if he has related sexual fantasies or impulses that cause distress or significantly impair his relationships. Someone with pedophilic disorder may or may not sexually molest children; a child molester may or may not be diagnosed with pedophilic disorder, if his related fantasies, urges, or behaviors have occurred for less than 6 months (Camilleri & Quinsey, 2008).

People who have this disorder may engage in sexual behaviors that range from fondling to oral–genital contact to penetration. Approximately 25% of victims

Frotteuristic disorder
A paraphilic disorder in which recurrent, intense, sexually arousing fantasies, sexual urges, or behaviors involve touching or rubbing against a nonconsenting person.

Pedophilic disorder
A paraphilic disorder in which recurrent sexually arousing fantasies, sexual urges, or behaviors involve a child who has not yet gone through puberty.

(who are more likely to be girls than boys; McAnulty et al., 2001) are under 6 years of age, 25% are between 6 and 10 years old, and 50% are between 11 and 13 (Erickson et al., 1988). People with pedophilic disorder often say that they believe that adult sexual contact with children has positive effects for the child. In fact, some child molesters with pedophilic disorder report that they didn't think they were harming the children they molested but were "sharing pleasure" (Spitzer et al., 2002). Compared to rapists, people with pedophilic disorder who have molested children view themselves as less responsible for the abuse and view the child as more responsible (Stermac & Segal, 1989)—claiming that the child "seduced" them. Studies suggest that men with pedophilic disorder who are sex offenders are likely to have at least one other paraphilic disorder (Heil & Simons, 2008; Raymond et al., 1999).

Howard Kingsnorth/Getty Images

People who are sexually aroused by sadistic or masochistic fantasies, urges, or acts with consenting adults and who are neither distressed nor impaired by it would not be considered to have sexual sadism disorder or sexual masochism disorder.

Sexual sadism disorder
A paraphilic disorder in which recurrent sexually arousing fantasies, urges, and behaviors inflict, or would inflict, physical or psychological suffering on a nonconsenting person.

Sexual Sadism Disorder and Sexual Masochism Disorder: Pain and Humiliation

Sexual sadism disorder and sexual masochism disorder are two complementary sides of a mode of sexual interaction in which actual pain, suffering, or humiliation creates or enhances sexual excitement. People who do not experience significant distress or impaired functioning because of their sadistic or masochistic sexual fantasies, urges, and behavior and whose sexual partners are consenting adults would not be diagnosed with either of these disorders. That is, consensual, non-impairing, and nondistressing BDSM (bondage and discipline, dominance and submission, sadism and masochism) fantasies, urges, or behaviors would not be considered to be a paraphilic disorder (Shindel & Moser, 2011). In what follows we examine the DSM-5 criteria for these two disorders.

Sexual Sadism Disorder: Inflicting Pain

A person who becomes sexually aroused by fantasies, urges, and behaviors that inflict physical or psychological suffering on a nonconsenting person is said to have **sexual sadism disorder** (see Table 11.4). Note that sexual sadism disorder involves acts that actually do, or actually could (in the case of urges and fantasies) cause someone else to suffer (versus simulated acts, where no real suffering occurs). There are two sets of circumstances in which someone would be diagnosed with sexual sadism disorder: (1) The recurrent sadistic fantasies or urges cause the person significant distress, as occurs when a man is horrified to discover that he is consistently aroused when fantasizing about hurting his partner; or (2) the person has repeatedly subjected a nonconsenting partner to sexually sadistic acts, as occurs with sadistic rape, which is also a criminal act.

Any type of rape is a criminal act, and sadistic rape is also a type of sexual sadism disorder defined in DSM-5. What distinguishes sadistic rape from other forms of rape is that in the former, the offender becomes sexually aroused by gratuitous violence or the victim's suffering or humiliation (Heil & Simons, 2008). In contrast, nonsadistic rape occurs when the rapist uses force in order to get his victim to "comply" but not because such force is a critical element of his sexual arousal pattern (Yates et al., 2008).

For people diagnosed with sexual sadism disorder, the sadistic sexual fantasies often were present in childhood, and the sadistic behavior commonly began in early adulthood—as occurred with the man in Case 11.3. Sexual sadism disorder is usually chronic, and the severity of the sadistic behaviors increases over time (American Psychiatric Association, 2013).

CASE 11.3 • FROM THE OUTSIDE: Sexual Sadism Disorder

A physician, raised alone by his widowed mother since age 2, has been preoccupied with spanking's erotic charge for him since age 6. Socially awkward during adolescence and his 20s, he married the first woman he dated and gradually introduced her to his secret arousal pattern of imagining himself spanking women. Although horrified, she episodically agreed to indulge him on an infrequent schedule to supplement their frequent ordinary sexual behavior. He ejaculated only when imagining spanking [. . .] After 20 years of marriage, her psychologist instructed her to tell him, "No more." He fell into despair, was diagnosed with a major depressive disorder, and wrote a long letter to her about why he was entitled to spank her. He claimed to have had little idea that her participation in this humiliation was negatively affecting her mental health ("She even had orgasms sometimes after I spanked her!"). He became suicidal as a solution to the dilemma of choosing between his or her happiness and becoming conscious that what he was asking was abusive. He was shocked to discover that she had long considered suicide as a solution to her marital trap of loving an otherwise good husband and father who had an unexplained sick sexual need.

(Sadock & Sadock, 2007, pp. 709–710)

Sexual Masochism Disorder: Receiving Pain

Whereas sexual sadism disorder involves hurting others, **sexual masochism disorder** is characterized by recurrent sexual arousal in response to fantasies, urges, or behaviors related to being hurt oneself—specifically, being humiliated or made to suffer in other ways (see Table 11.4; American Psychiatric Association, 2013). For a diagnosis of sexual masochism disorder, the sexual fantasies, urges, and behavior must cause significant distress or impair functioning.

Sexual masochism disorder is diagnosed in both men and women and is, in fact, the only paraphilic disorder that occurs at measurable rates among women (Levitt et al., 1994). One study found that about one quarter of women who engage in sexually masochistic *behavior* reported a history of sexual abuse during childhood, which may suggest that the abuse made them more likely to be aroused by masochistic acts (Nordling et al., 2000). However, these women did not necessarily have sexual masochism disorder because they did not report that their sexual preferences caused distress or impaired functioning.

Paraphilic Disorders Involving Nonhuman Objects

Two paraphilic disorders—fetishistic disorder and transvestic disorder—are characterized by persistent sexual fantasies, urges, and behaviors that focus on nonhuman animals or objects, such as clothing, which lead to significant distress or impair functioning.

Fetishistic Disorder: Sexually Arousing Objects

Fetishistic disorder is the paraphilic disorder characterized by the repeated use of nonliving objects (such as women's shoes or undergarments) or nongenital body parts (such as feet) in sexual fantasies, urges, or behaviors, which in turn leads to distress or impaired functioning (see Table 11.4). The object or body part—termed a *fetish*—may be used to achieve sexual arousal or to maintain an erection with a partner or alone. For instance, a man with a shoe fetish will become aroused by seeing or smelling women's footwear. He may steal women's shoes and use them to masturbate (Shiah et al., 2006). When fetishistic disorder is severe, he may be unable to have sexual relations with a partner unless the fetish is part of the sexual experience. People with fetishistic disorder generally come to the attention of mental health professionals only after being apprehended for the theft of their fetish. As usual, in the absence of distress or impaired functioning, a diagnosis of a disorder should not be made. The man in Case 11.4 gets sexually excited about women's underwear.

Sexual masochism disorder
A paraphilic disorder in which the person repeatedly becomes sexually aroused by fantasies, urges, or behaviors related to being hurt—specifically, being humiliated or made to suffer in other ways—and this arousal pattern causes significant distress or impairs functioning.

Fetishistic disorder
A paraphilic disorder in which the person repeatedly uses nonliving objects or nongenital body parts to achieve or maintain sexual arousal and such an arousal pattern causes significant distress or impairs functioning.

The hallmark of fetishistic disorder is being sexually aroused by inanimate objects, such as footwear or mannequins—or nongenital body parts.

The man in this photograph doesn't seem distressed, so he probably wouldn't qualify for a diagnosis of transvestic disorder, which describes men who dress as women to become sexually aroused but also are distressed or impaired by doing so.

© Murray Sanders/Daily Mail/ZUMA Press

Transvestic disorder
A paraphilic disorder in which the person cross-dresses for sexual arousal and experiences distress or impaired functioning because of the cross-dressing.

CASE 11.4 • FROM THE OUTSIDE: Fetishistic Disorder

A single, 32-year-old male freelance photographer presented with the chief complaint of "abnormal sex drive." The patient related that although he was somewhat sexually attracted by women, he was far more attracted by "their panties" . . . His first ejaculation occurred at 12 via masturbation to fantasies of women wearing panties. He masturbated into his older sister's panties, which he had stolen without her knowledge. Subsequently he stole panties from her friends and other women he met socially. He found pretexts to "wander" into bedrooms of women during social occasions, and would quickly rummage through their possessions until he found a pair of panties to his satisfaction. He later used these to masturbate into and then "saved them" in a "private cache." The pattern of masturbating into women's underwear had been his preferred method of achieving sexual excitement and orgasm from adolescence until the present consultation . . . he felt anxious and depressed because his social life was limited by his sexual preference.

(Spitzer et al., 2002, p. 247)

Transvestic Disorder: Cross-Dressing for Sexual Arousal

Transvestic disorder is the diagnosis given to people (almost always men) who experience sexual arousal when they dress in clothes appropriate for people opposite to the person's assigned gender, and experience distress or impaired functioning because of it (Table 11.4), as Mike did. (Note that this is in contrast to people with gender dysphoria, who cross-dress *not* for sexual arousal but to make their outward appearance more congruent with their internal experience; see Table 11.5.) Moreover, men with transvestic disorder use female clothing differently than those with a nontransvestic fetish that involves female apparel, such as an underwear fetish. Men with a nontransvestic fetish may wear female clothes to achieve sexual arousal, but only if the clothes were previously worn by a woman; they do not try to appear female, as did Jenny Boylan, in Case 11.1. In contrast, men with transvestic disorder prefer to wear *new* female clothes and try to appear as female, as Mike did.

Transvestic disorder usually begins before age 10 and may involve only one or two items of clothing, or may involve dressing entirely as the other sex, including wearing wigs and cross-gender outer clothes (such as coats). Some men who experience distress may periodically throw away their women's clothes in the hopes that their urges and fantasies will subside.

As adults, the cross-dressing typically is not limited to the privacy of the home: Almost three quarters of men with this disorder who were surveyed reported that they had appeared in public while dressed as women. Almost two thirds are married, often with children; you may assume that they hide their fetish from their wives, but as with Mr. A. in Case 11.5, the wives often know about the cross-dressing. Most wives are ambivalent about it, and fewer than one third accept it (Docter & Prince, 1997).

TABLE 11.5 • Transvestic Disorder Versus Gender Dysphoria

Transvestic disorder	Gender dysphoria
Gender identity same as natal gender	Gender identity different from natal gender
Comfortable with own natal gender	Want to be the other gender
Cross-dress for sexual arousal or to feel "calmer"	Cross-dress for congruence between appearance and gender identity

---

CASE 11.5 • FROM THE OUTSIDE: Transvestic Disorder

Mr. A., [is] a 65-year-old security guard [married and with grown children], formerly a fishing-boat captain. . . . His first recollection of an interest in female clothing was putting on his sister's [underwear] at age 12, an act accompanied by sexual excitement. He continued periodically to put on women's underpants—an activity that invariably resulted in an erection, sometimes a spontaneous emission, and sometimes masturbation, but was never accompanied by fantasy. Although he occasionally wished to be a girl, he never fantasized himself as one. He was competitive and aggressive with other boys and always acted "masculine." During his single years he was always attracted to girls, but was shy about sex. Following his marriage at age 22, he had his first heterosexual intercourse.

His involvement with female clothes was of the same intensity even after his marriage. Beginning at age 45, after a chance exposure to a magazine called *Transvestia*, he began to increase his cross-dressing activity. He learned there were other men like himself, and he became more and more preoccupied with female clothing in fantasy and progressed to periodically dressing completely as a woman. . . . Over time [his cross-dressing] has become less eroticized and more an end in itself, but it still is a source of some sexual excitement. He always has an increased urge to dress as a woman when under stress; it has a tranquilizing effect. If particular circumstances prevent him from cross-dressing, he feels extremely frustrated.

(Spitzer et al., 2002, pp. 257–258)

Assessing Paraphilic Disorders

The paraphilic disorders are usually assessed by examining the now-familiar three types of factors: neurological (sometimes reflected by bodily responses), psychological, and social.

From a neurological perspective, sexual arousal in men can be measured by a *penile plethysmograph*, which is an indirect measure of neurological events. The device is placed on a man's penis and measures penile rigidity. The man is then shown "normal" and "deviant" stimuli (such as photos of footwear or whips), and the rigidity of the penis is measured after each stimulus is presented. If the plethysmograph registers unusual amounts of arousal when the man views deviant stimuli, compared to stimuli that induce arousal in men without a paraphilia, this response suggests that he has a paraphilia or paraphilic disorder.

From a psychological perspective, self-reports of arousal are used to assess paraphilic disorders: Men describe what they find sexually arousing, either to a mental health clinician or in response to a questionnaire.

Finally, from a social perspective, assessment of paraphilic disorders may rely on reports from partners or the criminal justice system, after men are apprehended for engaging in illegal sexual activity such as secretly observing nonconsenting people as they disrobe or having inappropriate sexual relations with children (McAnulty et al., 2001).

Criticisms of the DSM-5 Paraphilic Disorders

Critics of the set of paraphilic disorders identified in DSM-5 point out that what counts as "deviant" (or, the flip-side, "normal") has changed over time. The paraphilic disorders are, in essence, behaviors and fantasies that Western culture currently labels as deviant—and such deviance is relative to the current cultural concept of "normal" sexual behavior or fantasies (Moser & Kleinplatz, 2005). Normal sexual behavior typically has been defined by the church, the government, or the medical community (McAnulty et al., 2001; Moser, 2001). In addition, widely different types of attraction are grouped together (e.g., pedophilic disorder and fetishistic disorder), creating an overly broad category.

Understanding Paraphilic Disorders

Researchers are only just beginning to learn why paraphilic disorders emerge and persist, and not enough is known to understand how feedback loops might arise among neurological, psychological, and social factors.

Neurological Factors

Many theorists who have considered the neurological underpinnings of paraphilic disorders have noted the apparent similarities between these disorders and OCD, both of which involve obsessions and compulsions. As discussed in Chapter 7, OCD appears to result from abnormal functioning in a neural system that includes the basal ganglia (which play a central role in producing automatic, repetitive behaviors) and the frontal lobes (which normally inhibit such behaviors). In fact, researchers found that people with pedophilic disorder have very specific cognitive deficits when performing tasks that rely on this neural system (Tost et al., 2004). For example, these patients were strikingly impaired in inhibiting responses and in working memory—both of which rely heavily on the frontal lobes (Smith & Kosslyn, 2006).

In addition, evidence suggests that the neurotransmitters that are used in this neural system, such as dopamine and serotonin, do not function properly in people who have paraphilic disorders (Kafka, 2003). Indeed, SSRIs decrease the sexual fantasies and behaviors related to paraphilic disorders, which is consistent with the view that neural interactions involved in OCD are also involved in the paraphilic disorders (Bradford, 2001; Kafka & Hennen, 2000; Roesler & Witztum, 2000).

Psychological Factors: Conditioned Arousal

Both psychodynamic and cognitive-behavioral theories have been invoked to explain paraphilias in general and paraphilic disorders in particular, but research to date does not generally support either type of explanation (Osborne & Wise, 2005). However, behavioral theory can answer one intriguing question about paraphilias: Why are almost all people with paraphilias male? An answer may lie in principles of classical conditioning, which can contribute to paraphilias in part because of the nature of the male body: The position of the penis and testicles on the body can easily lead to their being inadvertently stimulated (Munroe & Gauvain, 2001). This is important because classical conditioning can occur if the genitals are stimulated right after or at the same time as seeing or feeling an object (Domjan et al., 2004; Köksal et al., 2004). Consider this example: A fetish for objects such as women's shoes can develop when an unconditioned stimulus that led to sexual arousal became paired with a conditioned stimulus (women's shoes). Thus, a boy who coincidentally saw his mother's shoes before—intentionally or accidentally—touching his penis may come to have a conditioned response of sexual arousal to women's shoes in the future. In fact, humans—or at least human males—may be biologically prepared to develop classically conditioned sexual arousal to some situations or objects (Osborne & Wise, 2005), which would explain why a pillow fetish is not common.

Classical conditioning may be amplified by the *Zeigarnik effect* (Deutsch, 1968), which makes people more likely both to recall interrupted activities than ones that they finished and to try to complete interrupted activities when later allowed to do so. Applied to paraphilias and paraphilic disorders, sexual arousal that has been associated with an object or situation may be such an interrupted activity: Sexual arousal at a young age that isn't allowed expression becomes "interrupted"; the person is later driven to "complete" the interrupted activity (Munroe & Gauvain, 2001).

Hulton Archive/Getty Images

Some men who fought in World War II, who were in their formative years during the war, spent time with women who wore gas masks, and such attire became a sexual turn-on for the men (Kaplan, 1991). If any of these men experienced significant distress or impaired functioning as a result of their unusual object of arousal, they might be considered to have a fetishistic disorder.

Social Factors: More Erotica?

The Zeigarnik effect can also help explain why fewer males in traditional, nonindustrialized societies have paraphilias than do males in Western societies: Western societies provide many erotic stimuli—in magazines, in movies, on billboards and television—to which males can become aroused. In turn, males, particularly boys, are thus more likely to be "interrupted," leading to a desire to complete the task (Munroe & Gauvain, 2001).

Treating Paraphilic Disorders

Only some people who have paraphilic disorders receive treatment—typically those who were caught engaging in predatory paraphilic behavior with nonconsenting people and so were brought into the criminal justice system (where they were classified as *sex offenders*). The goal of treatment, which may be ordered by a judge, is to decrease paraphilic impulses and behaviors by targeting neurological, psychological, and social factors; research on treatments for paraphilic disorders is not yet advanced enough to indicate how feedback loops arise as a result of treatment.

Targeting Neurological and Other Biological Factors: Medication

One goal of treatment for men who have engaged in predatory paraphilic behaviors with nonconsenting people is to decrease or eliminate their sex drive. *Chemical castration* refers to the use of medications to achieve this goal. Such medications include antiandrogen drugs such as *medroxyprogesterone acetate* (Depo-Provera) and *cyprotereone acetate* (Androcur), which decrease testosterone levels. Decreased testosterone levels lead to decreased sexual urges, fantasies, and behaviors in sex offenders (Bradford, 2000; Gijs & Gooren, 1996; Robinson & Valcour, 1995). However, these medications don't necessarily diminish men's paraphilic *interests* along with their sex drive. Moreover, within a few weeks of stopping the medication, the men again experience the urges and may engage in the predatory behaviors (Bradford, 2000; Gijs & Gooren, 1996).

In addition, as noted earlier, SSRIs may help decrease the sexual fantasies, urges, and behaviors in men whose paraphilic disorder has obsessive-compulsive elements. Thus, a treatment that targets neurological factors can affect thoughts (fantasies), which are psychological factors.

Most men who receive treatment for a paraphilic disorder do so after coming to the attention of the criminal justice system, as did this man.

AP Photo/via Immigration and Customs Enforcement agency

CURRENT CONTROVERSY

Sex Offenders: Is Surgical Castration an Ethical Solution?

For some, the surgical castration of sex offenders conjures thoughts of draconian medieval punishment, whereas for others it reflects a treatment approach maximally likely to decrease the chances of recidivism. In the Czech Republic and Slovakia, the procedure is offered on a voluntary basis to repeat sex offenders who have been diagnosed with a paraphilic disorder (such as pedophilic disorder). Each year about 10 men in the Czech Republic undergo the procedure, a 1-hour operation that involves removal of the tissue that produces testosterone (Bilefsky, 2009). However, The Committee for the Prevention of Torture of the Council of Europe has called for an immediate stop to this procedure, on the basis that it "amounts to degrading treatment" (Pfäfflin, 2010).

Proponents of castration from the Czech Republic argue that the procedure is medically safe and done only with the offender's consent and after an extensive approval process conducted by an independent committee of psychiatric and legal experts. Further, evidence suggests that the procedure reduces recidivism rates from 20% (with therapy alone) to between 2 and 5% (Hoy, 2007). One treated sex offender said that having his testicles removed "was like draining the gasoline from a car hard-wired to crash" (Bilefsky, 2009). In other words, surgical castration has the potential to benefit both society and the offender.

Opponents of the procedure, by contrast, focus on its being invasive, irreversible, mutilating, and motivated by revenge. Ales Butala, a Slovenian human rights lawyer, has argued that surgical castration is unethical because it is not medically necessary and deprives castrated men of the right to reproduce (Bilefsky, 2009). The Council of Europe has raised doubts about the voluntary nature of the intervention, noting that it may be offered to offenders as an alternative to life in prison. As one critic noted, "Is that really free and informed consent?" (Bifelsky, 2009).

CRITICAL THINKING Based on what you've read in this chapter, do you think that surgical castration would be an effective and ethical treatment for those suffering from a chronic paraphilic disorder with nonconsenting partners? Should it be extended to other paraphilic disorders such as sexual sadism disorder or frotteuristic disorder? Why or why not?

(Ken Abrams, Carleton College)

Targeting Psychological Factors: Cognitive-Behavior Therapy

CBT may be used to treat paraphilic disorders in several ways. For one, it can decrease cognitive distortions that promote paraphilic fantasies, urges, and behaviors. For example, such distortions might include the belief that sexual actions directed toward nonconsenting people are not harmful. In addition, behavioral methods, such as extinction, may decrease sexual arousal to paraphilic stimuli while increasing arousal to normal stimuli (Akins, 2004). Treatment for sex offenders may involve both medication and CBT (Heilbrun et al., 1998); both types of interventions, when effective, ultimately reduce problematic arousal patterns, sexual fantasies and urges, and sexual behaviors toward nonconsenting people.

In addition, treatment may sometimes include *relapse prevention training*, which teaches men to identify and recognize high-risk situations and learn strategies to avoid them. Such training also involves learning new coping skills, such as anger management or assertiveness (Pithers, 1990). However, such treatments tend not to reduce subsequent offenses among those sex offenders who are also *psychopaths*—people who lack empathy, show little remorse or guilt about hurting others, and shirk responsibility for their actions (Barbaree, 2005; Langton et al., 2006).

Targeting Social Factors

Some treatments for sex offenders target social factors, for example, by training these men to empathize with victims in the hopes that they will be less likely to reoffend in the future (Marshall et al., 1996). However, many offenders do not complete psychosocial treatments (Hanson et al., 2004; Langevin, 2006). Furthermore, such treatments typically are not very successful (Hanson et al., 2004).

Thinking Like A Clinician

Ben was getting distracted at work because he kept fantasizing about having sexual relations with young boys. He'd think about a neighbor's son or a boy in an advertisement. He hadn't *done* anything about his fantasies, but they were getting increasingly hard to ignore. According to DSM-5, which paraphilic disorder, if any, does Ben have? On what is your decision based? If Ben wasn't getting distracted by his fantasies, would your diagnosis change or stay the same, and why? Do you think that illegal acts (such as child sex abuse or sexual acts with nonconsenting people generally) should be part of the DSM criteria, as they presently are? Explain your answer. What treatment options are available to Ben?

Sexual Dysfunctions

Let's return to Laura and Mike, the married couple whose relationship—and sex life—had become strained. Laura found that she didn't particularly miss having sexual relations with Mike. In fact, Laura didn't have any sex drive, and the past few times she and Mike had made love, nothing had "happened" for her—she hadn't had an orgasm or even found herself aroused. She couldn't pinpoint where things had gone astray; she'd like to feel desire, to *want* to have sexual relations with her husband, but she just didn't know where to start or how to get herself worked up about it. Was there something wrong with their relationship, or with her? Or is such lack of interest "normal"?

An Overview of Sexual Functioning and Sexual Dysfunctions

People engage in sexual relations for two general reasons: to create babies (reproductive sex) and for pleasure (recreational sex). The vast majority of sexual acts are for pleasure, as opposed to procreation. Researchers have defined the "normal" progression of sexual pleasure as the *human sexual response cycle*, discussed in what follows. **Sexual dysfunctions** are characterized by problems in the sexual response cycle. We first examine this cycle and then consider various ways in which it can go awry for men and women.

The Normal Sexual Response Cycle

What is a normal sexual response? In the 1950s and 1960s, researchers William Masters and Virginia Johnson sought to answer this question by measuring the sexual responses of thousands of volunteers. Based on their research, Masters and Johnson (1966) outlined the **sexual response cycle** for both women and men as consisting of four stages (see Figure 11.2):

1. *Excitement.* Excitement occurs in response to sensory-motor, cognitive, and emotional stimulation that leads to erotic sensations or feelings. Such arousal includes muscle tension throughout the body and engorged blood vessels, especially in the genital area. In men, this means that the penis swells; in women, this means that the clitoris and external genital area swell, and vaginal lubrication occurs.

2. *Plateau.* Bodily changes that began in the excitement phase become more intense and then level off when the person reaches the highest level of arousal.

3. *Orgasm.* The arousal triggers involuntary contractions of internal genital organs, followed by ejaculation in men. In women, responses range from extended or multiple orgasms (without falling below the plateau level) to resolution.

4. *Resolution.* Following orgasm is a period of relaxation, of release from tension. For men, this period is often referred to as a *refractory period*, during which it is impossible to have an additional orgasm. Women rarely have such limitations and can often return to the excitement phase with effective sexual stimulation.

Although it is convenient to organize these events into stages, the boundaries between the stages are not clear-cut (Levin, 1994). In addition, other researchers have noted that before the excitement phase, the person must first experience sexual attraction, which should lead to sexual desire, which in turn leads to the first stage of the sexual response cycle: excitement (Kaplan, 1981). *Desire* consists of fantasies and thoughts about sexual activity along with an inclination or interest in being sexual. Sexual problems can occur when people experience a diminished—or even a lack of—sexual desire, or when they have difficulties related to sexual arousal or performance (the last three stages of sexual response). Laura appears to lack any sexual desire.

Disorders of sexual dysfunction are often divided into four categories: *sexual desire disorders, sexual arousal disorders, orgasmic disorders,* and *sexual pain disorders.* Many, if not most, problems in the sexual response cycle have psychological causes rather than physical causes relating to sex organs. These disorders can arise in people of various sexual orientations, such as heterosexuals, lesbians, gay men, or bisexuals.

Sexual dysfunctions
Sexual disorders that are characterized by problems in the sexual response cycle.

Sexual response cycle
The four stages of sexual response—excitement, plateau, orgasm, and resolution—outlined by Masters and Johnson.

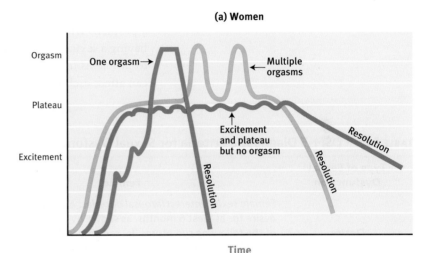

(a) Women

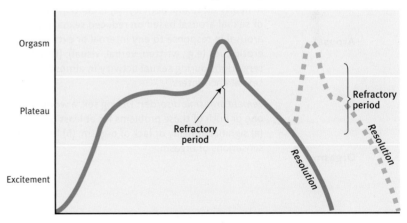

(b) Men

FIGURE 11.2 • The Human Sexual Response Cycle According to Masters and Johnson (1966), during the normal sexual response cycle, women and men go through four stages: excitement, plateau, orgasm, and resolution. However, women can experience multiple orgasms without a refractory period (a), whereas men must experience a refractory period before a subsequent orgasm (b).

Source: Masters & Johnson, 1966. For more information see the Permissions section.

Sexual Dysfunctions According to DSM-5

A person can have more than one kind of sexual dysfunction, such as occurs when a man with premature ejaculation becomes nervous about having sexual relations and so develops a dysfunction of desire or arousal. Moreover, a sexual dysfunction may have existed for a person's entire adult life (*lifelong*) or may have been acquired after a period of normal sexual functioning (*acquired*), as happened to Laura. In addition, the dysfunction may occur in all circumstances (*generalized*) or only in certain situations, with specific partners or types of stimulation (*situational*). Table 11.6 lists the DSM-5 sexual dysfunctions and their diagnostic criteria.

As noted in Table 11.6, for a sexual dysfunction to be considered a disorder, the sexual symptoms must cause significant distress or problems in relationships (American Psychiatric Association, 2013). This means that even though a person has a problem with an aspect of sexual response, he or she would not be diagnosed as having a sexual dysfunction disorder unless the problem caused marked distress or led to problems in his or her relationships. Case 11.6 illustrates how sexual dysfunctions can affect each member of a couple.

TABLE 11.6 • DSM-5 Diagnostic Criteria for Sexual Dysfunctions

Type of Sexual Dysfunction	Female	Male
Desire **Arousal**	*Female sexual interest/arousal disorder:* A lack of sexual desire for at least 6 months, as shown by at least three of the following symptoms: (a) reduction of interest in sex; (b) reduction of sexual thoughts; (c) reduction of initiating sex and of receptivity to partner's initiation of sex; (d) reduction or elimination of sexual enjoyment in nearly all sexual activity; (e) reduction or elimination of sexual arousal based on reduced sexual interest/arousal in response to any internal or external sexual/erotic cues (e.g., written, verbal, visual); (f) reduced sensations during sexual activity in almost all or all sexual encounters.	*Male hypoactive sexual desire disorder:* A lack of sexual desire and activity for at least 6 months; this diagnosis is based on clinical judgment, which takes into consideration the patient's age and social context. *Erectile disorder:* At least one of these symptoms must be apparent for at least 6 months during most sexual activity: (a) challenges in getting an erection; (b) challenges maintaining erection; (c) significant decrease in hardness of the erection.
Orgasm	*Female orgasmic disorder:* During sex, a woman has one or both of these problems for at least 6 months: (a) significant delay or lack of orgasm; (b) lessening in the sensations of orgasm.	*Delayed ejaculation:* During sex, a man has one or both of these symptoms for at least 6 months, without intention: (a) significant delay before ejaculation; (b) significantly infrequent or lack of ejaculation. *Premature (early) ejaculation:* A condition that occurs for at least 6 months in which ejaculation occurs less than a minute after penetration.
Pain	*Genito-pelvic pain/penetration disorder:* Frequent problems with one or more of the following symptoms: (a) vaginal pain during intercourse; (b) pelvic and/or vulvar pain during attempts at intercourse; (c) significant anxiety about pain during intercourse; (d) inability to relax pelvic floor muscles during penetration.	
General Criteria	These symptoms cause distress. The symptoms are not caused by another disorder, medical concern, and are not caused by problems in the relationship or other stressors.	

Note: To be diagnosed with a sexual dysfunction, the person must meet both the criteria for the specific sexual dysfunction and the general criteria.

Source: Diagnostic and Statistical Manual of Mental Disorders, Fifth Edition, American Psychiatric Publishing, 2013.

In the following sections, we examine sexual dysfunctions.

Sexual Desire Disorders and Sexual Arousal Disorders

Sexual desire can be thought of as having three major components: (1) a neurological and other biological component (related to hormones and brain activity, which lead to a genital response); (2) a cognitive component (related to an inclination or desire to be sexual); and (3) an emotional and relational component (related to being willing to engage in sex with a particular person at a specific place and time) (Levine, 1988). Difficulty in any of these components can lead to a sexual desire disorder. However, a discrepancy in the level of desire between someone and his or her partner does not, in and of itself, constitute a disorder in sexual desire.

Sexual arousal disorders occur when a person persistently cannot become aroused or cannot maintain arousal during a sexual encounter. These disorders can arise when a person has difficulty progressing from desire to excitement. This difficulty can occur when any of the following persistently interfere: (1) when *the pleasurable stimulation gets interrupted* (e.g., when a couple stops their sexual behavior because their young child enters their bedroom), (2) when *other external stimuli interfere* (e.g., when a car alarm goes off outside), or (3) when *internal stimuli interfere* (e.g., when the person becomes anxious, afraid, sad, or angry or has thoughts that intrude) (Malatesta & Adams, 2001).

Like sexual desire, sexual arousal involves neurological and other biological components (responses to stimuli and stimulation), cognitive components (thoughts), and emotional components (Rosen & Beck, 1988). And any, or any combination, of these components can contribute to a problem. For example, a man can have an adequate erection but think that he is inadequate because he believes that his penis is not hard enough. Similarly, a woman may respond to the biological sensations of sexual arousal by being afraid of losing control (Malatesta & Adams, 2001).

Male Hypoactive Sexual Desire Disorder

As specified in DSM-5, one type of problem of desire is **male hypoactive sexual desire disorder**, the hallmark of which is a persistent or recurrent lack of erotic or sexual fantasies or an absence of desire for sexual activity (see Table 11.6). This lack of desire may or may not be lifelong, and it may occur in all situations (generalized) or only in particular situations (such as with a specific person), but it must cause distress. Hypoactive sexual desire focuses primarily on a man's cognitive (fantasies) and emotional/relational (desire) state (Malatesta & Adams, 2001). Men with hypoactive sexual desire disorder may or may not still be willing to engage in sexual behavior with a partner.

However, a man who is depressed and, as part of the depression, has little or no sexual desire (a symptom of depression) is not considered to have hypoactive sexual desire disorder because the low desire is caused by another disorder.

Sexual desire is a multifaceted experience involving the body, thoughts, emotions, and another person.

Compassionate Eye Foundation/Monashee Frantz/Getty Images

Male hypoactive sexual desire disorder A sexual dysfunction characterized by a persistent or recurrent lack of erotic or sexual fantasies or an absence of desire for sexual activity.

Erectile Disorder

Erectile disorder (*impotence*, in nontechnical language) is an arousal disorder characterized by a persistent difficulty obtaining or maintaining an adequate erection until the end of sexual activity, or a decrease in erectile rigidity (see Table 11.6; American Psychiatric Association, 2013). Some men with erectile disorder are able to have erections during foreplay but not during actual penetration. Others are not able to obtain a full erection with a new partner or in some situations; still others, such as Harry, in Case 11.7, have the problem during any type of sexual activity. If the man is able to have a full erection during masturbation, biological causes are unlikely. More than half of men over 40 years old have at least some problems in attaining or maintaining an erection (Feldman et al., 1994), and thus erectile disorder can be seen as a normal by-product of aging. It is estimated that 300 million men worldwide will develop erectile disorder by the year 2025, in part because of the increased aging of the population (cited in Shabsigh et al., 2003). However, psychological factors can contribute to erectile disorder; it is not always a neurological or other biological problem or a consequence of normal aging.

> **CASE 11.7 • FROM THE OUTSIDE: Erectile Disorder**
>
> Harry [had been married for 2 years when] he found out his wife had been involved in numerous extramarital affairs and divorced her. He said his friends all knew but were reluctant to tell him. Following the divorce he encountered erectile problems with all partners—even those to whom he felt close.
>
> (Althof, 2000, p. 261)

Female Sexual Interest/Arousal Disorder

Women who have problems with sexual desire often also have problems with arousal, and hence DSM-5 groups these desire and arousal problems together in a single disorder: **female sexual interest/arousal disorder** (formerly known as *frigidity*), which is a persistent or recurrent lack of or reduced sexual interest or arousal.

Problems regarding interest or arousal may include no interest in any sexual activity, no erotic or sexual thoughts, hesitation either to respond to a partner's sexual invitations or to initiate sexual activity, reduced or no pleasure during most sexual encounters, or a lack of physical arousal. Any three of these six symptoms (see Table 11.6) are necessary for this diagnosis. As with all other sexual dysfunctions, the diagnosis of sexual interest/arousal disorder requires that the problem causes distress or difficulties in relationships and does not arise exclusively from another psychological or medical disorder.

Laura seems to have such a lack of sexual desire—a lack of any interest in sexual relations with Mike—and it bothers her that she doesn't feel desire. As women age, decreased interest in sex is normal and is probably related to women's hormonal shift with menopause: Women who have gone through menopause tend to report diminished desire (Eplov et al., 2007). In fact, women who enter menopause abruptly and at an early age because of the surgical removal of their uterus and ovaries are more likely to report low sexual desire than are their same-age counterparts who have not yet entered menopause (Dennerstein et al., 2006). In addition, psychological and social factors account for a given woman's *distress* about decreased desire, and women in different European countries report different levels of distress in response to decreased desire (Graziottin, 2007).

Orgasmic Disorders

An *orgasmic disorder* is diagnosed when a clinician determines that a man or woman has experienced normal excitement and adequate stimulation for orgasm in normal circumstances (based on the person's age and other factors)—but fails to have an

---

Erectile disorder
A sexual dysfunction characterized by a man's persistent difficulty obtaining or maintaining an adequate erection until the end of sexual activity, or a decrease in erectile rigidity; sometimes referred to as *impotence*.

Female sexual interest/arousal disorder
A sexual dysfunction characterized by a woman's persistent or recurrent lack of or reduced sexual interest or arousal; formerly referred to as *frigidity*.

orgasm. If a man or woman cannot achieve orgasm with intercourse but can do so through other types of sexual stimulation, the person is not necessarily considered to have an orgasmic disorder. Moreover, if orgasmic problems arise as a side effect from medications (such as SSRIs), a diagnosis of an orgasmic disorder should not be made. Disorders in this category may have neurological (and other biological), cognitive, and emotional elements.

Female Orgasmic Disorder

Female orgasmic disorder is diagnosed when a woman's normal sexual excitement does not lead to orgasm or her orgasms are significantly less intense (see Table 11.6). Women who experience occasional difficulty achieving orgasm do not have this disorder; the problem with achieving orgasm must be persistent and must exceed what would be expected based on the woman's age and sexual experience. Moreover, to be diagnosed with this disorder, the problem with orgasm should not be caused by inadequate sexual stimulation. If a woman experiences orgasm through clitoral stimulation but not through vaginal intercourse, a diagnosis would not be made; most women require clitoral stimulation to have an orgasm. As with all other sexual dysfunctions, female orgasmic disorder is diagnosed only if the problem concerning orgasm causes distress; many women who rarely or never have orgasms report being satisfied sexually (American Psychiatric Association, 2013). Approximately 5–24% of women have female orgasmic disorder (Laumann et al., 1994; Spector & Carey, 1990).

Clinicians distinguish between two types of female orgasmic disorder: generalized and situational. If female orgasmic disorder is *generalized*, the woman does not have an orgasm in any circumstance. If female orgasmic disorder is *situational*, the woman may have an orgasm but only in certain circumstances, for example, when masturbating. Lola, described in Case 11.8, has the generalized type of female orgasmic disorder.

CASE 11.8 • FROM THE OUTSIDE: Female Orgasmic Disorder

Lola, a 25-year-old laboratory technician, has been married to a 32-year-old cabdriver for 5 years. The couple has a 2-year-old son, and the marriage appears harmonious.

The presenting complaint is Lola's lifelong inability to experience orgasm. She has never achieved orgasm, although during sexual activity she has received what should have been sufficient stimulation. She has tried to masturbate, and on many occasions her husband has manually stimulated her patiently for lengthy periods of time. Although she does not reach climax, she is strongly attached to her husband, feels erotic pleasure during lovemaking, and lubricates copiously. According to both of them, the husband has no sexual difficulty.

Exploration of her thoughts as she nears orgasm reveals a vague sense of dread of some undefined disaster. More generally, she is anxious about losing control over her emotions, which she normally keeps closely in check.

(Spitzer et al., 2002, pp. 238–239)

Delayed Ejaculation

Delayed ejaculation is a delay or absence of ejaculation in males; Table 11.6 lists the specific criteria. Delayed ejaculation is different from female orgasmic disorder in several respects: (1) Delayed ejaculation typically involves problems ejaculating with a partner, even though the man can easily ejaculate during masturbation (Apfelbaum, 1989, 2000); (2) delayed ejaculation typically involves problems ejaculating only during vaginal intercourse (some men, however, cannot ever ejaculate); and (3) its prevalence (less than 10% of the general male population) is lower than that of female orgasmic disorder (Spector & Carey, 1990). There is no set definition of what constitutes a "delay," and the diagnosis should be made only if the man experiences adequate sexual stimulation.

Female orgasmic disorder
A sexual dysfunction characterized by a woman's normal sexual excitement not leading to orgasm or to her having diminished intensity of sensations of orgasm.

Delayed ejaculation
A sexual dysfunction characterized by a man's delay or absence of orgasm.

Premature (Early) Ejaculation

A second type of orgasm-related problem for men is **premature ejaculation**, which is characterized by ejaculation that occurs within a minute of vaginal penetration and before the male wishes it (Table 11.6; American Psychiatric Association, 2013). Men with premature ejaculation report not feeling a sense of control over their ejaculation and thus become apprehensive about future sexual encounters. (According to DSM-5, a man with "early" ejaculation that occurs without vaginal intercourse—such as with oral sex or anal intercourse—could not be diagnosed with this disorder.)

Premature ejaculation is considered by some to be a *couple's* problem, as with Mr. and Mrs. Albert in Case 11.9. That is, it is a problem only insofar as the couple prefers the man to ejaculate in a particular phase of his partner's sexual response cycle: Some couples try to have both partners achieve orgasm at around the same time, but this is difficult with premature ejaculation. Other couples do not find early ejaculation a problem; the partner is sexually stimulated to orgasm in other ways after the man ejaculates (Malatesta & Adams, 2001).

CASE 11.9 • FROM THE OUTSIDE: Premature Ejaculation

Mr. and Ms. Albert are an attractive, gregarious couple, married for 15 years, who [are in] the midst of a crisis over their sexual problems. Mr. Albert, a successful restaurateur, is 38. Ms. Albert, who since marriage has devoted herself to child rearing and managing the home, is 35. She reports that throughout their marriage she has been extremely frustrated because sex has "always been hopeless for us." She is now seriously considering leaving her husband.

The difficulty is the husband's rapid ejaculation. Whenever any lovemaking is attempted, Mr. Albert becomes anxious, moves quickly toward intercourse, and reaches orgasm either immediately upon entering his wife's vagina or within one or two strokes. He then feels humiliated and recognizes his wife's dissatisfaction, and they both lapse into silent suffering. He has severe feelings of inadequacy and guilt, and she experiences a mixture of frustration and resentment toward his "ineptness and lack of concern." Recently, they have developed a pattern of avoiding sex, which leaves them both frustrated, but which keeps overt hostility to a minimum. . . . [Mr. Albert's] inability to control his ejaculation is a source of intense shame, and he finds himself unable to talk to his wife about his sexual "failures." Ms. Albert is highly sexual and easily aroused in foreplay but has always felt that intercourse is the only "acceptable" way to reach orgasm.

In other areas of their marriage, including rearing of their two children, managing the family restaurant, and socializing with friends, the Alberts are highly compatible. Despite these strong points, however, they are near separation because of the tension produced by their mutual sexual disappointment.

(Spitzer et al., 2002, pp. 266–267)

Sexual Pain Disorder: Genito-Pelvic Pain/Penetration Disorder

Some women experience significant pain with sexual activity, particularly with sexual intercourse. A sexual dysfunction related to consistent pain associated with sexual intercourse for women is **genito-pelvic pain/penetration disorder**, which is characterized by pain, fear, or anxiety related to the vaginal penetration of intercourse (see Table 11.6). *Vaginismus*, recurrent or persistent involuntary spasms of the musculature of the outer third of the vagina that interfere with sexual intercourse, may occur with genito-pelvic pain/penetration disorder. These spasms may be so strong that it is impossible to insert the penis into the vagina, or at least not without significant discomfort.

Up to 10–20% of women report recurrent pain with intercourse, though not necessarily to the degree required for a diagnosis of genito-pelvic pain/penetration disorder (American Psychiatric Association, 2013; Laumann et al., 1999; Rosen et al., 1993). When the pain persists, it can lead to problems with desire or excitement. This disorder is not diagnosed if the problem is caused exclusively by a lack of lubrication. Lynn in Case 11.10 has genito-pelvic pain/penetration disorder. Table 11.7 provides more information about the sexual dysfunctions.

Premature (early) ejaculation
A sexual dysfunction characterized by ejaculation that occurs within a minute of vaginal penetration and before the man wishes it, usually before, immediately during, or shortly after penetration.

Genito-pelvic pain/penetration disorder
A sexual dysfunction in women characterized by pain, fear, or anxiety related to the vaginal penetration of intercourse.

CASE 11.10 • FROM THE INSIDE: Genito-Pelvic Pain/Penetration Disorder

Lynn talks about her experience with symptoms of genito-pelvic pain/penetration disorder.

We've been married for nine years and have two great kids. Unfortunately, family responsibilities and high stress jobs really cut into our together time. Exhaustion makes sex seem like an extra chore—just one more thing to do that we don't have time to enjoy and now can't. I don't know if it's from the busy, stressful lifestyle or not, or from being "out of practice," but about a year ago intercourse began to really hurt. It started with a burning sensation some of the time during sex. I found myself getting more anxious that it would hurt again and it usually did. Trips to the doctor revealed little besides the standard "do more foreplay or use more lubricant" advice. Now it seems like my body just "tightens up" and we can hardly have sex at all. Entry is painful and besides burning I feel tightness, spasms, discomfort and anxiety. The pleasure is gone, and there is only the expectation of discomfort and frustration. Our marriage is suffering and it feels like a deep chasm is growing between us as sex has become impossible. My husband and I fight a lot more and I know he is growing impatient. I don't want my children to be another statistic of divorce because of this. I just don't know what to do.

(Vaginismus.com, 2007)

TABLE 11.7 • Sexual Dysfunctions Facts at a Glance

Prevalence

• According to one survey of 1065 female and 447 male patients in a general medical practice, 22% of the men and 40% of the women had a "sexual dysfunction" in the preceding 4 weeks (Nazareth et al., 2003), and other studies find similar results (Shifren et al., 2008). However, the true prevalence of sexual dysfunctions is difficult to determine: Many surveys either equate sexual dissatisfaction—for any reason—with sexual dysfunction or use criteria that are different from those in DSM-5.

Comorbidity

• People with sexual dysfunctions may also have a co-occurring mood or anxiety disorder (Atlantis & Sullivan, 2012; Fabre & Smith, 2012) or medical disorder (Tan et al., 2012).

Onset

• A sexual dysfunction may arise from specific circumstances, or it may be lifelong.

Course

• As women age, sexual problems other than desire problems tend to decrease, except for hormonally induced lubrication problems.

• The opposite is true for men: As they age, their sexual problems tend to increase, usually because of erectile difficulties that are associated with prostate problems, cardiovascular problems, or other medical causes (Hackett, 2008; Heiman, 2002b).

Gender Differences

• In one study, the most common problems among men were lack of interest, premature ejaculation, and performance anxiety. Among women the most common problems were failure to achieve orgasm and painful intercourse.

Cultural Differences

• Cultural norms about sexuality affect the extent to which a sexual problem leads to enough distress or relationship difficulties for it to be considered a disorder (Hartley, 2006). For example, Japanese women have a low prevalence of problems with sexual desire, perhaps because Japanese women do not consider no or little sexual desire to be a problem (Kameya, 2001).

Source: Unless otherwise noted, the source for the table material is American Psychiatric Association, 2013.

FIGURE 11.3 • An Alternative Female Sexual Response Cycle An alternative model of the female sexual response cycle (Basson, 2001)—in the context of relationships—is analogous to a circle. The cycle starts with sexual neutrality: not feeling very sexual, but with an openness to seek or be receptive to sexual stimuli. In turn, such sexual stimuli may, depending on neurological (and other biological), psychological, and social factors operating at that moment, lead to sexual arousal, which in turn leads to a sense of desire and further arousal. The desire creates positive feedback loops (++) that lead to heightened arousal, which then leads to emotional and physical satisfaction. This satisfaction in turn produces a sense of emotional intimacy with her partner, making her more likely to be receptive to or seek out sexual stimuli in the future. She may also feel spontaneous sexual desire, which leads to positive feedback loops among the first three phases. Orgasm is not necessary for satisfaction.

Source: Adapted from Basson, 2001.

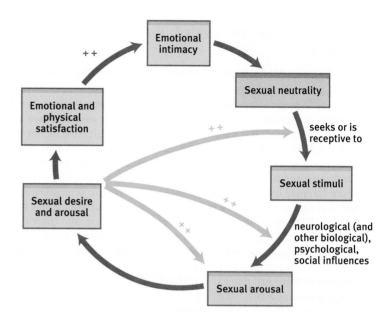

Criticisms of the Sexual Dysfunctions in DSM-5

Criticisms of the DSM-5 classification of and criteria for sexual dysfunctions focus on many issues, some of which carry over from the previous edition of DSM (Balon, 2008).In what follows we briefly consider three of these issues:

- The sexual dysfunctions are implicitly based on the progression in Masters and Johnson's model of the sexual response cycle. However, this may not be the best model for understanding sexual dysfunctions in women. As illustrated in the alternative female sexual response cycle (Figure 11.3), emotional and physical satisfaction may include orgasm but not all women need to have an orgasm to feel satisfied.

- The emphasis is on orgasm—in both men and women—as the conclusion of sexual activity (Tiefer, 1991). Sexual activity that does not end in orgasm is implicitly considered not satisfying (Kleinplatz, 2001).

- The DSM-5 criteria rest on a cultural definition of "normal" to define abnormal sexual functioning (Moynihan, 2003). Critics note that the norm promoted by American culture is that of an adolescent male, ever ready for sexual encounters and able to have erections on demand (Kleinplatz, 2001). As women and men age, they are more likely to meet the criteria for a sexual dysfunction even when there is no real "dysfunction"—only the body's growing older (Tiefer, 1987, 1991).

Understanding Sexual Dysfunctions

We can view Laura's lack of sexual desire as being related, at least in part, to Mike's sexual difficulties: As Mike became more distant, Laura's desire for sexual intimacy with Mike waned. Their experiences highlight the fact that sexuality and any problems related to it develop through feedback loops among neurological (and other biological), psychological, and social factors.

Neurological and Other Biological Factors

In this section, we first consider how disease, illness, surgery, and medication can, directly and indirectly, disrupt normal sexuality. We then turn to the effects of normal aging, which can produce sexual difficulties.

Sexual Side Effects: Disease, Illness, Surgery, and Medication

Disease or illness can produce sexual dysfunction directly, as occurs with prostate or cervical cancer, and indirectly, as occurs with diabetes or circulation problems that

Prolonged bike riding can sometimes crush the nerves and arteries to the penis or clitoris, leading to arousal problems.

Richard Price/Getty Images

limit blood flow to genital areas. In addition, surgery can lead to sexual problems: Half of women who survive major surgeries for gynecological-related cancer develop sexual difficulties that do not improve over time (Andersen et al., 1989).

Some medications can interfere with normal sexual response, including:

- SSRIs and dopamine-blocking medications such as traditional antipsychotics,
- beta-blockers and other medications that treat high blood pressure,
- anti-seizure medication,
- estrogen and progesterone medications,
- HIV medications, and
- narcotics and sedative-hypnotics.

Alcohol can also disrupt the normal sexual response cycle.

Aging

Researchers have found that normal aging can affect sexual functioning among older people (George & Weiler, 1981). For instance, older women often produce less vaginal lubrication after menopause; when this dryness is not addressed (for instance, with an over-the-counter lubricant such as Astroglide or K-Y Jelly), the dryness can cause intercourse to be painful and lead to genito-pelvic pain/penetration disorder.

In addition, as men age, their testosterone levels decrease significantly, which may lead them to require prolonged tactile stimulation before they can attain an erection. Older men are likely to experience reduced penile hardness, decreased urgency to reach orgasm, and a longer refractory period (Butler & Lewis, 2002; Masters & Johnson, 1966).

In addition to the normal biological changes that arise with age, older people of both sexes may develop illnesses or diseases that make sexual activity physically more challenging. They also may take medications that have side effects that interfere with their sexual response. However, most older people report that they continue to enjoy sex.

Men and women often experience changes in aspects of sexual performance as they get older, which may disrupt sexual activity. However, most will still experience pleasure from sexual activities (Leiblum & Seagraves, 2000).

Nick Daly/Getty Images

Psychological Factors in Sexual Dysfunctions

Certain beliefs and experiences can *predispose* people to develop sexual dysfunctions (see Table 11.8). In addition, a woman may believe that women in general lose their sexual desire as they age, and a man may believe that "real men" have intercourse at least twice a day and that only rock-hard erections will satisfy women (Nobre & Pinto-Gouveia, 2006). Such beliefs can lead to a self-fulfilling prophecy if they produce the perception of a dysfunction and that perception in turn leads to a real dysfunction. For example, a man who believes that women are only satisfied by very hard erections may develop a problem as he ages: He may notice that his erections are not as hard as they were when he was younger and then become self-conscious and preoccupied during sex, which does in fact lead him to fail to satisfy his partner.

Having been sexually abused as a child also predisposes a person to develop sexual dysfunctions. Consider the fact that male victims of childhood sexual abuse are three times more likely to have problems with their erections and twice as likely to have problems of desire and premature ejaculation as their peers who did not experience childhood sexual abuse (Laumann et al., 1999). Similarly, women who were

TABLE 11.8 • Predisposing Events for Sexual Dysfunctions

Event	Effect
The view that sex is dirty and sinful	Early learning of such negative attitudes toward sex and misinformation leads to fears and inhibitions, which can lead to problems of desire, arousal, orgasm, and pain.
Early negative conditioning experiences	In men, premature ejaculation can develop after hurrying to have an orgasm quickly for fear of being "caught." In women, a fear of pregnancy or being "caught" can lead to anxiety that contributes to sexual dysfunction.
Sexual trauma	Sexual trauma can produce negative conditioning and can lead to a fear of sex, as well as arousal and desire problems.

Sources: Bartoi & Kinder, 1998; Becker & Kaplan, 1991; Kaplan, 1981; Laumann et al., 1999; LoPiccolo & Friedman, 1988; Masters & Johnson, 1970; Silverstein, 1989.

victims of childhood sexual abuse are more likely than women who were not abused to report sexual problems (although not necessarily problems that meet the DSM-5 criteria for sexual dysfunctions; Staples et al., 2012).

Psychological factors that *precipitate*, or trigger, sexual dysfunctions generally involve the following sorts of preoccupations:

- focusing attention on sex-related fears and worries, which distract and detract during a sexual encounter;
- feeling uncomfortable with how one's body may look or feel to a partner (Berman & Berman, 2001); and
- worrying about nonsexual matters, such as work or family problems.

Once someone has a problem with desire, arousal, orgasm, or pain, he or she may become anxious that it will happen again, which sets up a self-fulfilling prophecy and becomes a *maintaining factor*. For instance, when a single sexual experience was perceived as a "failure," a person may become anxious during subsequent sexual experiences, monitoring his or her responsiveness (and so *thinking* about the sexual response rather than *experiencing* it)—which in turn can interfere with a normal sexual response and create a sexual dysfunction (Bach et al., 1999; Quinta Gomes & Nobre, 2012).

These young people might just be getting ready for a special occasion. But being chronically preoccupied and anxious about something—including how your body might look or feel to a partner—while engaged in sexual activity can interfere with the normal sexual response cycle and lead to a sexual dysfunction.

Social Factors

Although sexuality involves how we see ourselves, it usually also involves other people. (Woody Allen once said that his favorite part of masturbation was the cuddling afterwards. Think about why this is funny.) The sexual relations of a couple are influenced by how the partners relate to each other, specifically: (1) how they express and resolve a conflict, (2) how they communicate their needs and desires, their likes and dislikes, (3) how they handle stress, and (4) how strongly attracted they each are to each other (Tiefer, 2001). For women in particular, satisfaction with their relationship plays a big part in sexual desire, arousal, and orgasm (Burri et al., in press). For example, Mike's sexual secret led him to pull away from Laura sexually, which led her to think that he wasn't interested in sex. From her vantage point, he appeared to have a sexual desire problem, and she herself then lost interest.

Feedback Loops in Understanding Sexual Dysfunctions

Just as neurological, psychological, and social factors influence each other and contribute to a normal sexual response, feedback loops among these factors can contribute to sexual dysfunctions (see Figure 11.4). Such feedback loops best explain why some people, and not others, develop sexual dysfunctions. For instance, people's sexual beliefs ("I won't be able to have an orgasm"; psychological factor) can influence other factors: The beliefs create fears and anxieties that can lead to high levels of sympathetic nervous system activity (neurological factor), which then interfere with sexual arousal and orgasm (Apfelbaum, 2001; Kaplan, 1981; Masters & Johnson, 1970). Current problems in a relationship (social factor) similarly affect sexual functioning, as can having been sexually abused (Bartoi & Kinder, 1998; DiLillo, 2001; Laumann et al., 1999). And the influences also run in the opposite direction: If the body does not respond appropriately, this will affect not only a person's beliefs but also his or her relationships.

FIGURE **11.4 • Feedback Loops in Action: Sexual Dysfunctions**

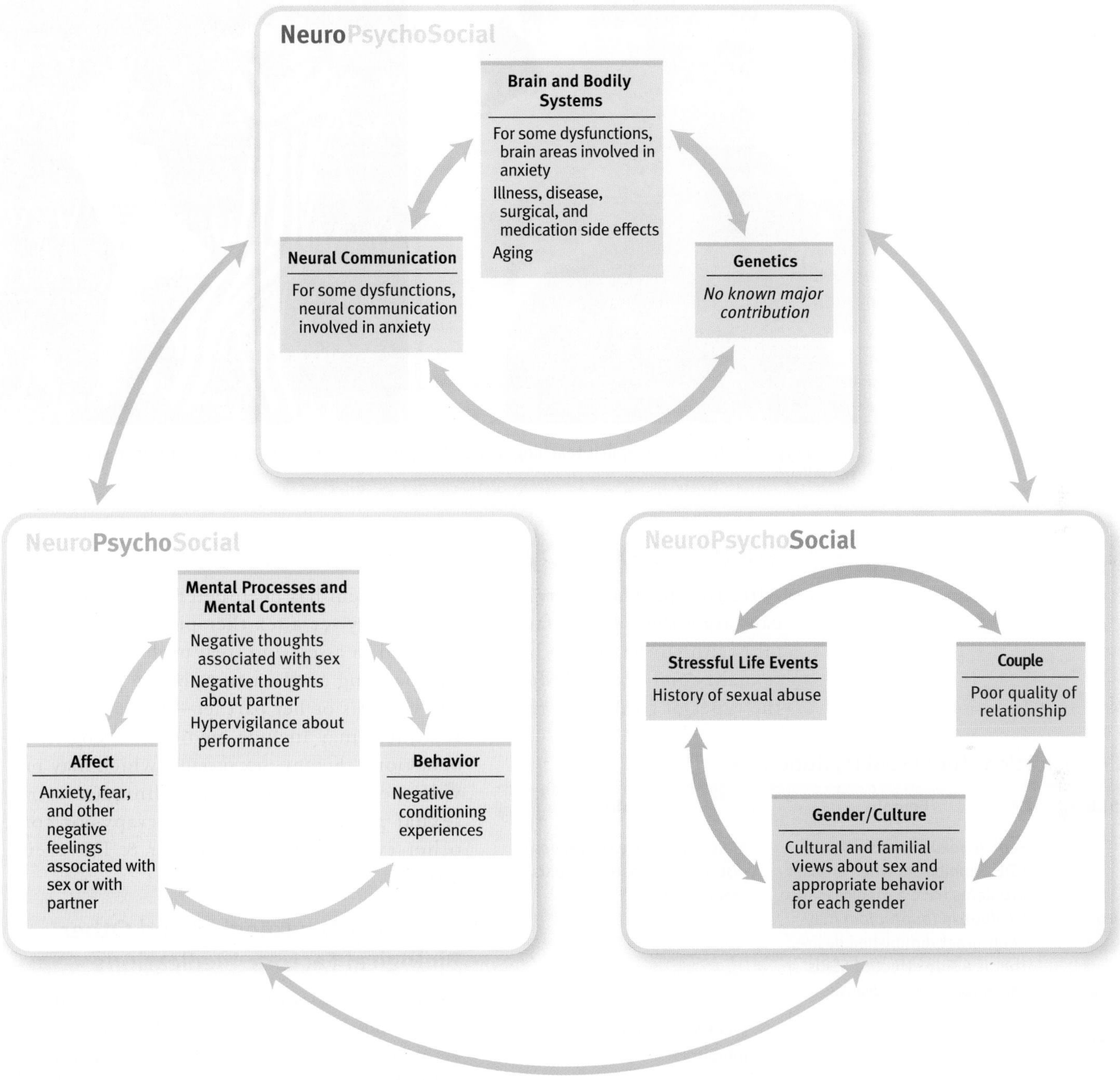

NeuroPsychoSocial

Brain and Bodily Systems

For some dysfunctions, brain areas involved in anxiety

Illness, disease, surgical, and medication side effects

Aging

Neural Communication

For some dysfunctions, neural communication involved in anxiety

Genetics

No known major contribution

Neuro**Psycho**Social

Mental Processes and Mental Contents

Negative thoughts associated with sex

Negative thoughts about partner

Hypervigilance about performance

Affect

Anxiety, fear, and other negative feelings associated with sex or with partner

Behavior

Negative conditioning experiences

NeuroPsycho**Social**

Stressful Life Events

History of sexual abuse

Couple

Poor quality of relationship

Gender/Culture

Cultural and familial views about sex and appropriate behavior for each gender

Familial and cultural views of sexuality (social factors) can also influence sexual functioning: We are all taught about sexuality both directly (what our parents, teachers, religious leaders, and peers tell us) and indirectly (through observations of family members or friends and from television, movies, books, and the Internet). Some people are taught that sexual relations outside of marriage are wrong, whereas other people are taught that sexual experimentation before marriage is a good thing. Such direct and indirect lessons help shape each person's concepts of appropriate or normal sexuality. Depending on what a person learns about sex, he or she may be primed to have sexual difficulties in some situations.

Thus, neurological, psychological, and social factors influence each other in ways that predispose some people to develop a sexual dysfunction, and that precipitate and maintain it once it develops.

LEMOINE/BSIP/SuperStock

Kevin Mazur/WireImage for MTV/Getty Images

Which type of influence—explicit teaching or watching in the media—played a larger role in shaping your sexuality?

Treating Sexual Dysfunctions

After the specific nature of a sexual problem has been determined, treatment can target the relevant factors. Patients may see a sex therapist, usually a mental health clinician who has been trained to assess and treat problems related to sexuality and sexual dysfunction. Depending on the nature of the problem and the types of treatments the patient—and his or her partner—are interested in, treatment may include medication, cognitive-behavioral therapy, *sex therapy* (which may provide specific guidance and techniques to treat sexual problems), couples therapy, or some other type of therapy (Moser & Devereux, 2012).

Targeting Neurological and Other Biological Factors: Medications

There has been an increasing trend toward the *medicalization* of sex therapy, a tendency to target neurological and other biological factors (see Table 11.9) and pay less attention to psychological and social factors. In the 1990s, medical treatments for erectile dysfunction began in earnest, with the advent of the drug Viagra and the marketing campaign for it, which brought the topic of erectile dysfunction from a rarely discussed but relatively common problem among older men to a topic of everyday conversation. Viagra (*sildenafil citrate*) is one of the class of drugs called *phosphodiesterase type 5 inhibitors*, or *PDE-5 inhibitors*. Viagra doesn't cause an erection directly; instead, the drug operates by increasing the flow of blood to the penis only when

TABLE 11.9 • Medications for Sexual Dysfunctions

Sexual phase	Female	Male
Desire	*Female sexual arousal disorder:* PDE-5 inhibitors when arousal problems have a medical cause. Wellbutrin (*bupropion*) may counteract diminished desire that is a side effect of SSRIs taken for another disorder	*Male hypoactive sexual desire disorder:* Testosterone pills or cream.
Arousal		*Erectile disorder:* PDE-5 inhibitors
Orgasm	*Female orgasmic disorder:* (Medications have not reliably proved effective in studies that include a placebo group.)	*Delayed ejaculation:* (Medications have not reliably proved effective in studies that include a placebo group.) *Premature ejaculation:* SSRIs
Pain	*Genito-pelvic pain/penetration disorder:* Estrogen cream for menopause related dryness; anti-anxiety medication for anticipatory anxiety about penetration.	

a man is sexually excited. Viagra (and its competitors, such as Cialis) is not a cure but a treatment for erectile dysfunction, and it is effective only if the man takes a pill before sexual activity.

Some women with arousal disorders use PDE-5 inhibitors because these medications can have an analogous effect on the clitoris. However, PDE-5 inhibitors are most effective with women who—for medical reasons—have reduced blood flow to the clitoral area, which leads to decreased physical arousal (Berman et al., 2001). Critics point out that prescribing this type of medication for a woman will not improve sexual functioning when the problem is with her relationship, not her anatomy (Bancroft, 2002).

Targeting Psychological Factors: Shifting Thoughts, Learning Behaviors

Two types of treatments directly target psychological factors: Sex therapy and psychological therapies—such as CBT or psychodynamic therapy—that address feelings and thoughts about oneself and others and how they may relate to sexual problems.

One of the goals of treatments that directly target psychological factors related to sexual dysfunctions is to educate patients about sexuality and the human sexual response. Another goal is to help patients develop strategies to counter negative thoughts, beliefs, or attitudes that may interfere with sexual desire, arousal, or orgasm (Carey & Gordon, 1995). For instance, during sexual activity, some people are preoccupied with nonsexual thoughts that prevent them from reaching full arousal or orgasm. These nonsexual thoughts might be work-related worries, thoughts about household tasks that need to be done, or being alert for someone who would interrupt the sexual encounter. Cognitive treatment may involve teaching a patient how to filter out such thoughts and (re)focus on the sexual interaction. The therapist might teach the patient to apply standard cognitive methods to sexual encounters, such as problem solving ("You could turn the phone off") or cognitive restructuring ("Are you likely to think of a solution to your work problem while making love? If not, you can let your mind focus on the physical sensations you are experiencing").

In addition to addressing very specific sex-related thoughts and feelings, the treatment may also address the patient's view of himself or herself. Sometimes the sense of being dysfunctional or inadequate generalizes from the sexual realm to the whole self, and the person with a sexual dysfunction comes to have low self-esteem and self-doubts generally. In such cases, the therapy may use cognitive and behavioral methods to address such dysfunctional thoughts and feelings.

Treatment that relies on CBT typically involves "homework." Depending on the nature of the problem, the homework may be completed by the patient or by the patient and his or her partner together. Homework for women with female orgasmic disorder (as well as other sexual dysfunctions) may include masturbation in order to learn more about which sensations and fantasies facilitate arousal and orgasm (Meston et al., 2004). For many patients, a first step is to begin to (re)discover pleasurable sensations through specific homework exercises. At the beginning of behavioral treatment, homework may include **sensate focus exercises**, which increase awareness of pleasurable sensations while prohibiting genital touching, intercourse, or orgasm; rather, partners take turns touching other parts of each other's bodies so that each can discover what kinds of stimulation feel most enjoyable (Baucom et al., 1998; LoPiccolo & Stock, 1986).

Sensate focus exercises
A behavioral technique that is assigned as homework in sex therapy, in which a person or couple seeks to increase awareness of pleasurable sensations that do not involve genital touching, intercourse, or orgasm.

⬚ GETTING THE PICTURE

Which of the two photos best captures the goal of the first step of sensate focus exercises—the relaxing bath or a vibrator? Answer: The relaxing bath because the vibrator is most likely to be used for genital stimulation.

The goals of behavioral techniques are to help patients develop a more relaxed awareness of their bodies and increase their orgasmic responses and control. Treatment may also involve a realistic look at a person's or couple's daily work schedule, followed by a discussion of how to have sexual encounters during which the partners are not too tired or distracted.

Targeting Social Factors: Couples Therapy

The sex therapy techniques discussed in the previous section may be implemented alone (by the person with a sexual dysfunction) or with a partner. Sex therapy may involve teaching couples specific cognitive and behavioral techniques. However, implementing such techniques with a partner requires motivation and willingness to be open with the partner about sexual matters and to experiment sexually. Moreover, how a couple interacts sexually occurs against the backdrop of their overall relationship. Treatment may focus on the issues in the couple's relationship (couples therapy, rather than sex therapy per se) and include teaching communication, intimacy, and relationship skills (Baucom et al., 1998; Beck, 1995; Heiman, 2002b); such skills include assertiveness, problem solving, negotiation, and conflict management. Couples therapy may also address issues of power, control, and lifestyle as they relate to the sexual dysfunction; for example, the therapist may employ techniques from systems therapy to focus on assertiveness within the sexual aspects of the relationship. Treatment for a partner's sexual dysfunction in a lesbian or gay couple may also address special issues that affect their sexual relationship, such as living "in the closet" or sexual intimacy when one partner is HIV positive (Nichols, 2000).

Feedback Loops in Treating Sexual Dysfunctions

Like successful treatment for any other psychological disorder, successful treatment of sexual dysfunctions ultimately affects all the neuropsychosocial factors (see Figure 11.5). For instance, CBT for female orgasmic disorder targets psychological factors (the thoughts, beliefs, and feelings related to sex or orgasm and behaviors such as masturbation) (Frühauf et al., in press; Heiman, 2002a). In turn, changes in psychological factors lead, through feedback loops, to changes in neurological and other biological factors (which underlie arousal and orgasm) as well as social factors (the meaning for both partners of a sexual interaction or an orgasm and the changes in their relationship). A similar set of feedback loops occurs with CBT for genito-pelvic pain/penetration disorder (ter Kuile et al., 2007): CBT changes thoughts and feelings

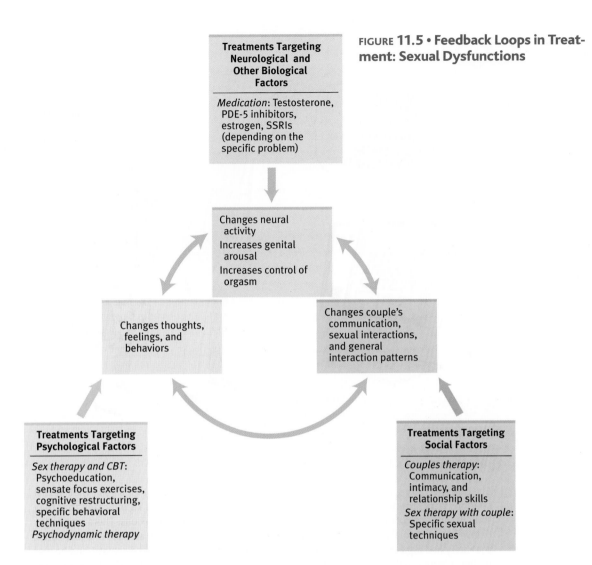

FIGURE **11.5 • Feedback Loops in Treatment: Sexual Dysfunctions**

about penetration, which in turn changes the responses of the vaginal muscles, making vaginal intercourse with a partner possible—which then affects the nature of the relationship.

Although all the techniques mentioned may alleviate sexual dysfunctions, the definition of "success" is less clear-cut than for treatments of most other psychological disorders. As we noted at the beginning of this chapter, sexuality and sexual dysfunctions typically involve other people, and a treatment that the patient views as successful may not be perceived that way by the partner. Consider an older man whose erectile dysfunction was treated with Viagra. He may have been pleased by his response to the drug treatment, only to discover that his wife was now unhappy about his sustained erections and more frequent desire for intercourse (Althof et al., 2006). She, then, might be diagnosed with a sexual desire problem. However, she might explain that when her husband had difficulty with his erections, he was much more affectionate, sexually attentive to her, and creative in their sexual interactions. Now he is goal-directed, focusing almost exclusively on intercourse; solving his erectile dysfunction led to changes in the couple's sexual relations that were not viewed as positive by his wife. Treatments—such as medication—that directly target only one type of factor may seem to resolve the problem for the patient but instead can (via feedback loops among the three types of factors) have unexpected negative consequences for the couple.

Targeting only a neurological (or other biological) factor in one partner may not improve the overall sexual functioning and satisfaction of the couple.

Thinking Like A Clinician

Chi-Ling and Yinong were in their 30s and had been trying to have a baby for a year. Their sexual relations were strained: They had sex when the ovulation predictor test kit indicated that they should, and each month's attempt and subsequent failure made them anxious. There was no joy or love in their sexual relations, and most of the time Chi-Ling was barely aroused and lubricated; she rarely had orgasms anymore. She just wanted Yinong to hurry up and ejaculate, and he was finding it increasingly difficult to do so. Based on what you have read, do you think that Chi-Ling or Yinong has a sexual dysfunction, and if so, which one(s)? Support your position. If you could obtain additional information before you decide, what would you want to know, and why?

▢ SUMMING UP

Gender Dysphoria

- Gender dysphoria is characterized by persistent cross-gender identification that leads to chronic discomfort with one's natal sex. Symptoms of gender dysphoria often emerge in childhood, but most children diagnosed with the disorder no longer have it when they become adults.

- In children, symptoms of gender dysphoria include cross-dressing and otherwise behaving in ways typical of the other gender, such as engaging in other-gender types of play, choosing other-gender playmates, and even claiming to be the other gender. In adults, symptoms

include persistent and extreme discomfort from living publicly as their natal gender, which leads many to live (at least some of the time) as someone of the other gender.

- Some brain areas in adults with gender dysphoria are more similar to the corresponding brain areas of members of their desired gender than they are to those of people who have their natal gender.

- Treatments that target neurological (and other biological) factors include hormone treatments and sex reassignment surgery. Treatments that target psychological factors include psychoeducation, helping the patient choose among gender-related lifestyle

options, and problem solving about potential difficulties. Treatments that target social factors include family education, support groups, and group therapy.

Paraphilic Disorders

- Paraphilic disorders are characterized by a predictable sexual arousal pattern regarding "deviant" fantasies, objects, or behaviors. Paraphilic disorders can involve (1) nonconsenting adults or children (exhibitionistic disorder, voyeuristic disorder, frotteuristic disorder, and pedophilic disorder), (2) suffering or humiliating oneself or one's partner (sexual masochism disorder and sexual sadism disorder), or

(3) arousal by nonhuman objects (fetishistic disorder and transvestic disorder). To be diagnosed with a paraphilic disorder, either the person must have acted on these sexual urges and fantasies or these arousal patterns must cause the patient significant distress or impair functioning.

- Critics of the DSM-5 paraphilic disorders classification note that what is determined to be sexually "deviant" varies across cultures and over time.

- Research shows that paraphilic disorders share similarities with OCD. Additional possible contributing factors include classically conditioned arousal and the Zeigarnik effect.

- Most frequently, men who receive treatment for paraphilic disorders are ordered to do so by the criminal justice system. Treatments that target neurological factors decrease paraphilic behaviors through medication; however, although the behaviors may decrease, the interests often do not. Treatments that target psychological factors are designed to change cognitive distortions about the predatory sexual behaviors.

Sexual Dysfunctions

- Sexual dysfunctions are psychological disorders characterized by problems in the human sexual response cycle. The response cycle traditionally has been regarded as having four phases: excitement, plateau, orgasm, and resolution—but it is now commonly regarded as beginning with sexual attraction and desire.

- Sexual dysfunctions fall into one of four categories: disorders of desire, arousal, orgasm, and pain. To be classified as dysfunctions, they must cause significant distress or problems in the person's relationships.

- Sexual desire and arousal disorders involve three components: cognitive, emotional, and neurological (and other biological). Problems with any of these components can lead to male hypoactive sexual desire disorder, erectile disorder, or female sexual interest/arousal disorder.

- Sexual orgasmic disorders are characterized by persistent problems with the orgasmic response after experiencing a normal excitement phase and adequate stimulation. DSM-5 includes in this category: female orgasmic disorder, delayed ejaculation, and premature ejaculation.

- Genito-pelvic pain/penetration disorder is characterized by pain with sexual intercourse and occurs only in women.

- Criticisms of the way DSM-5 classifies sexual dysfunction disorders include: (1) The sexual response cycle may not apply equally well to women; (2) the end goal is orgasm, not satisfaction; (3) the criteria rest on a particular definition of normal sexual functioning that doesn't encompass normal aging.

- Various factors contribute to sexual dysfunctions. Neurological (and other biological) factors include disease, illness, surgery or medications, and the normal aging process.

- Psychological factors include: predisposing factors (such as negative attitudes toward sex), negative conditioning experiences, and a history of sexual abuse; precipitating factors, such as anxiety about sex and distraction because of sexual or nonsexual matters; and maintaining factors, such as worrying about future sexual problems.

- Social factors include the quality of the partners' relationship, the partner's sexual functioning, a history of abuse, and sexual mores in the person's subculture.

- Treatments that target neurological (and other biological) factors are medications for erectile dysfunction and for analogous arousal problems in women.

- Treatments that target psychological factors include psychoeducation, sensate focus exercises, and CBT to counter negative thoughts, beliefs, and behaviors associated with sexual dysfunction.

- Treatments that target social factors address problematic issues in a couple's relationship as well as teach the couple specific sex-related cognitive or behavioral strategies.

- Treatments that focus on one type of factor for a given patient can create complex feedback loops, which sometimes have unexpected—and perhaps negative—consequences for the couple.

Key Terms

Gender identity (p. 328)

Gender dysphoria (p. 329)

Gender role (p. 329)

Sex reassignment surgery (p. 333)

Paraphilia (p. 335)

Paraphilic disorders (p. 335)

Exhibitionistic disorder (p. 338)

Voyeuristic disorder (p. 338)

Frotteuristic disorder (p. 339)

Pedophilic disorder (p. 339)

Sexual sadism disorder (p. 340)

Sexual masochism disorder (p. 341)

Fetishistic disorder (p. 341)

Transvestic disorder (p. 342)

Sexual dysfunctions (p. 347)

Sexual response cycle (p. 347)

Male hypoactive sexual desire disorder (p. 349)

Erectile disorder (p. 350)

Female sexual interest/arousal disorder (p. 350)

Female orgasmic disorder (p. 351)

Delayed ejaculation (p. 351)

Premature (early) ejaculation (p. 352)

Genito-pelvic pain/penetration disorder (p. 352)

Sensate focus exercises (p. 359)

More Study Aids

For additional study aids related to this chapter, including quizzes to make sure you've retained everything you've learned and a Student Video Activity exploring how men's and women's attitudes toward sex may relate to sexual dysfunctions, go to: www.worthpublishers.com/launchpad/rkabpsych2e.

Fancy Collection/SuperStock

Schizophrenia and Other Psychotic Disorders

In 1930, female quadruplets were born in a small midwestern city. All four survived, which at that time was remarkable. This set of quadruplets (or quads) was also remarkable in two other ways: All four developed from a single fertilized egg and so basically were genetically identical. In addition, all four went on to develop symptoms of schizophrenia as young adults. In the psychological literature, the quadruplets came to be known by pseudonyms they were given to protect their privacy: Nora, Iris, Myra, and Hester Genain.

The quads were born to parents of limited financial means. Their father, Henry, was abusive, violent, and alcoholic. He also exhibited some symptoms of schizophrenia. Their mother, Maud, had been a nurse. Maud was very strict with the girls, but she was a better parent than Henry.

By the time the quads were in their early 20s, three had been hospitalized for schizophrenia at least once, and the fourth had symptoms of schizophrenia. Also around that time, Mrs. Genain was recovering from bladder surgery, and it was becoming increasingly difficult for her to care for the young women. The family's problems were brought to the attention of researchers at the National Institute of Mental Health (NIMH), and the family was invited to move to a research and treatment facility in Washington, DC. At the facility, the sisters were treated, studied, and written about extensively. In fact, the pseudonyms the quads were given related to the initials of NIMH: Nora, Iris, Myra, and Hester. Their false last name, Genain, means "dire birth" in Greek.

THE FACT THAT ALL FOUR OF THE GENAIN SISTERS developed symptoms of schizophrenia was by no means an inevitable result. For identical twins, the chance of both twins developing schizophrenia is about 48%. For identical quads, the odds of all four developing schizophrenia are about one in six, or 16% (Rosenthal, 1963). The quads' story offers possible clues about why all four of them developed schizophrenia and can help us understand what causes the disorder. In this chapter, we discuss the symptoms of schizophrenia, what is known about its causes, and current treatments for this disorder.

Nora, Iris, Myra, and Hester Genain were identical quadruplets. All four suffered from schizophrenia, although this outcome is statistically unlikely. The symptoms and course of the disorder were different for each sister, illustrating the range of ways that this disorder can affect people.

AP Photo

Jason Jaroslav Cook/age fotostock. Photo for illustrative purposes only; any individual depicted is a model.

Schizophrenia
A psychological disorder characterized by psychotic symptoms that significantly affect emotions, behavior, and mental processes and mental contents.

Positive symptoms
Symptoms of schizophrenia that are characterized by the *presence* of abnormal or distorted mental processes, mental contents, or behaviors.

▢ What Are Schizophrenia and Other Psychotic Disorders?

Schizophrenia is a psychological disorder characterized by psychotic symptoms—hallucinations and delusions—that significantly affect emotions, behavior, and, most notably, mental processes and mental contents. The symptoms of schizophrenia can interfere with a person's abilities to comprehend and respond to the world in a normal way. DSM-5 lists schizophrenia as a single disorder (see Table 12.1), but in its chapter titled *Schizophrenia Spectrum and Psychotic Disorders*, it describes a group of disorders related to and including schizophrenia; research suggests that schizophrenia itself is not a unitary disorder (Blanchard et al., 2005; Turetsky et al., 2002). Instead, schizophrenia is a set of related disorders. Research findings suggest that each variant of schizophrenia has different symptoms, causes, course of development, and, possibly, response to treatments. In the following sections we examine in more detail the symptoms of schizophrenia and other related psychotic disorders.

The Symptoms of Schizophrenia

The criteria for schizophrenia in DSM-5 fall into two clusters:

* *positive symptoms*, which consist of delusions and hallucinations and disorganized speech and behavior; and

* *negative symptoms*, which consist of the absence or reduction of normal mental processes, mental contents, feelings, or behaviors, including speech, emotional expressiveness, and/or movement.

Table 12.1 lists the DSM-5 criteria for schizophrenia. After considering these criteria, we discuss criticisms of these criteria and an alternative way to diagnose schizophrenia.

Positive Symptoms

Positive symptoms are so named because they are marked by the *presence* of abnormal or distorted mental processes, mental contents, or behaviors. Positive symptoms of schizophrenia are

* hallucinations (distortions of perception),

* delusions (distortions of thought),

* disorganized speech, and

* disorganized behavior.

These symptoms are extreme. From time to time, we all have hallucinations, such as thinking we hear the doorbell ring when it didn't. But the hallucinations experienced by people with schizophrenia are intrusive—they may be voices that talk constantly or scream at the patient. Similarly, the delusions of someone with schizophrenia aren't isolated, one-time false beliefs (e.g., "My roommate took my sweater, and that's why it's missing"). With schizophrenia and other psychotic disorders, the delusions are extensive, although they often focus on one topic (e.g., "My roommate is out to get me, and the fact that she has taken my sweater is just one more example").

The positive symptoms of disorganized speech and disorganized behavior are apparent from watching or talking to a person who has them; it's difficult, if not impossible, to understand what's being said, and the person's behavior is clearly odd (wearing a coat during a heat wave, for example). We next examine the four positive symptoms in more detail.

TABLE 12.1 • DSM-5 Diagnostic Criteria for Schizophrenia

A. Two (or more) of the following, each present for a significant portion of time during a 1-month period (or less if successfully treated). At least one of these must be (1), (2), or (3):

1. Delusions.

2. Hallucinations.

3. Disorganized speech (e.g., frequent derailment or incoherence).

4. Grossly disorganized or catatonic behavior.

5. Negative symptoms (i.e., diminished emotional expression or avolition).

B. For a significant portion of the time since the onset of the disturbance, level of functioning in one or more major areas, such as work, interpersonal relations, or self-care, is markedly below the level achieved prior to the onset (or when the onset is in childhood or adolescence, there is failure to achieve expected level of interpersonal, academic, or occupational functioning).

C. Continuous signs of the disturbance persist for at least 6 months. This 6-month period must include at least 1 month of symptoms (or less if successfully treated) that meet Criterion A (i.e., active-phase symptoms) and may include periods of prodromal or residual symptoms. During these prodromal or residual periods, the signs of the disturbance may be manifested by only negative symptoms or by two or more symptoms listed in Criterion A present in an attenuated form (e.g., odd beliefs, unusual perceptual experiences).

D. Schizoaffective disorder and depressive or bipolar disorder with psychotic features have been ruled out because either 1) no major depressive or manic episodes have occurred concurrently with the active-phase symptoms, or 2) if mood episodes have occurred during active-phase symptoms, they have been present for a minority of the total duration of the active and residual periods of the illness.

E. The disturbance is not attributable to the physiological effects of a substance (e.g., a drug of abuse, a medication) or another medical condition.

F. If there is a history of autism spectrum disorder or a communication disorder of childhood, the additional diagnosis of schizophrenia is made only if prominent delusions or hallucinations, in addition to the other required symptoms of schizophrenia, are also present for at least 1 month (or less if successfully treated).

Hallucinations

As discussed in Chapter 1, **hallucinations** are sensations so vivid that the perceived objects or events seem real even though they are not. Any of the five senses can be involved in a hallucination, although auditory hallucinations—specifically, hearing voices—are the most common type experienced by people with schizophrenia. Pamela Spiro Wagner describes one of her experiences with auditory hallucinations:

> [The voices] have returned with a vengeance, bringing hell to my nights and days. With scathing criticism and a constant scornful commentary on everything I do, they sometimes order me to do things I shouldn't. So far, I've stopped myself, but I might not always be able to. . . .
>
> (Wagner & Spiro, 2005, p. 2)

Research that investigates possible underlying causes of auditory hallucinations finds that people with schizophrenia, and to a lesser extent their unaffected siblings, have difficulty distinguishing between verbal information that is internally generated (as when imagining a conversation or talking to oneself) and verbal information that is externally generated (as when another person is actually talking) (Brunelin et al., 2007). People with schizophrenia are also more likely to (mis)attribute their own internal conversations to another person (Brunelin, Combris, et al., 2006); this misattribution apparently contributes to the experience of auditory hallucinations.

Delusions

People with schizophrenia may also experience **delusions**—incorrect beliefs that persist, despite evidence to the contrary. Delusions often focus on a particular theme, and several types of themes are common among these patients. *Persecutory delusions* involve the theme of being persecuted by others. Pamela Spiro Wagner's persecutory delusions involved extraterrestrials:

> I barricade the door each night for fear of beings from the higher dimensions coming to spirit me away, useless as any physical barrier would be against them. I don't mention the NSA, DIA, or Interpol surveillance I've detected in my walls or how intercepted conversations among these agencies have intruded into TV shows.
>
> (Wagner & Spiro, 2005, p. 2)

In contrast, *delusions of control* revolve around the belief that the person is being controlled by other people (or aliens), who literally put thoughts into his or her head, called *thought insertion*:

> I came to believe that a local pharmacist was tormenting me by inserting his thoughts into my head, stealing mine, and inducing me to buy things I had no use for. The only way I could escape the influence of his deadly radiation was to walk a circuit a mile in diameter around his drugstore, and then I felt terrified and in terrible danger.
>
> (Wagner, 1996, p. 400)

Another delusional theme is believing oneself to be significantly more powerful, knowledgeable, or capable than is actually the case, referred to as *grandiose delusions*. Someone with this type of delusion may believe that he or she has invented a new type of computer when such an achievement by that person is clearly impossible. Grandiose delusions may also include the mistaken belief that the person is a different—often famous and powerful—person, such as the president or a prominent religious figure.

Yet another delusional theme is present in *referential delusions*: the belief that external events have special meaning for the person. Someone who believes that a song playing in a movie is in some kind of code that has special meaning *just for* him or her, for instance, is having a referential delusion.

Hallucinations
Sensations that are so vivid that the perceived objects or events seem real, although they are not. Hallucinations can occur in any of the five senses.

Delusions
Persistent false beliefs that are held despite evidence that the beliefs are incorrect or exaggerate reality.

Nobel Laureate John Nash (portrayed in the film, *A Beautiful Mind*) had entrenched delusions.

© Reuters/Corbis

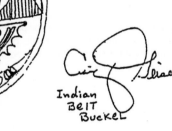

Drawing by Craig Geiser from *Living with Schizophrenia* by Stuart Emmons, Craig Geiser, Kalman J. Kaplan, Martin Harrow. Taylor & Francis, 1997

The man who made this drawing said, "This belt buckle symbolized safety for me in my stay in the hospital. I felt no harm would come to me while I wore it. I also left it visible to me on my nightstand next to my bed at night. I thought several times the belt buckle saved me from whatever was going on. My belt buckle seemed as though it was wearing thinner, using up its strength a little at a time in helping me" (Emmons et al., 1997, p. 183). Although many people have a good luck charm, the fact that this man believed that his belt buckle was getting thinner because it was "using up its strength" suggests that he had a delusional belief about it.

Grunnitus Studio/Science Source

This woman suffers from catatonia, in which people assume odd postures or poses for hours at a time. When catatonic, people cannot care for themselves and require constant attention.

Catatonia
A condition in which a person does not respond to the environment or remains in an odd posture or position, with rigid muscles, for hours.

Disorganized Speech

People with schizophrenia can sometimes speak incoherently, although they may not necessarily be aware that other people cannot understand what they are saying. Speech can be disorganized in a variety of different ways. One type of disorganized speech is *word salad*, which is a random stream of seemingly unconnected words. For example, a patient might say something like, "Pots dog small is tabled." Another type of disorganized speech involves many *neologisms*, or words that the patient makes up:

> That's *wish-bell*. Double vision. It's like walking across a person's eye and reflecting personality. It works on you, like dying and going to the spiritual world, but landing in the *Vella* world.
>
> (Marengo et al., 1985, p. 423)

In this case, "wish-bell" is the neologism; it doesn't exist, nor does it have an obvious meaning or function as a metaphor.

Grossly Disorganized Psychomotor Behavior

Another positive symptom (and recall that *positive* in this context means "present," not "good") of schizophrenia is *grossly disorganized or abnormal psychomotor behavior*; the term *psychomotor* refers to intentional movements, and in this case such behavior is so unfocused and disconnected from a goal that the person cannot successfully accomplish a basic task, or the behavior is inappropriate in the situation. Disorganized behavior can range from laughing inappropriately in response to a serious matter or masturbating in front of others, to being unable to perform normal daily tasks such as washing oneself, putting together a simple meal, or even selecting appropriate clothes to wear.

The category of grossly disorganized psychomotor behavior also includes **catatonia** (also referred to as *catatonic behavior*), which occurs when a person does not respond to the environment or remains in an odd posture or position, with rigid muscles, for hours. For example, during her early 20s, Iris Genain's symptoms included standing in the same position for hours each day.

These positive symptoms—hallucinations, delusions, disorganized speech, and grossly disorganized psychomotor behavior—constitute four of the five DSM-5 symptom criteria for schizophrenia; the fifth criterion is any negative symptom (discussed in the following section). Emilio, in Case 12.1, has positive symptoms of schizophrenia.

CASE 12.1 • FROM THE OUTSIDE: Schizophrenia

Emilio is a 40-year-old man who looks 10 years younger. He is brought to the hospital, his twelfth hospitalization, by his mother because she is afraid of him. He is dressed in a ragged overcoat, bedroom slippers, and a baseball cap and wears several medals around his neck. His affect ranges from anger at his mother ("She feeds me shit . . . what comes out of other people's rectums") to a giggling, obsequious seductiveness toward the interviewer. His speech and manner have a childlike quality, and he walks with a mincing step and exaggerated hip movements. His mother reports that he stopped taking his medication about a month ago and has since begun to hear voices and to look and act more bizarrely. When asked what he has been doing, he says, "eating wires and lighting fires." His spontaneous speech is often incoherent and marked by frequent rhyming and clang associations [speech in which sounds, rather than meaningful relationships, govern word choice].

Emilio's first hospitalization occurred after he dropped out of school at age 16, and since that time he has never been able to attend school or hold a job. He has been treated with neuroleptics [antipsychotic medications] during his hospitalizations but doesn't continue to take medication when he leaves, so he quickly becomes disorganized again. He lives with his elderly mother, but sometimes disappears for several months at a time and is eventually picked up by the police as he wanders in the streets. There is no known history of drug or alcohol abuse.

(Spitzer et al., 2002, pp. 189–190)

Negative Symptoms

In contrast to positive symptoms, **negative symptoms** are characterized by the *absence* or reduction of normal mental processes, mental contents, or behaviors. DSM-5 specifies a number of negative symptoms: diminished emotional expression and avolition.

Diminished Emotional Expression: Muted Expression

Some people with schizophrenia exhibit *diminished emotional expression* (sometimes referred to as **flat affect**), which occurs when a person does not display a large range of emotion, sometimes speaking robotically and seeming emotionally neutral. Such people may not express or convey much information through their facial expressions, body language, tone of voice, and they tend to refrain from making eye contact (although they may smile somewhat and do not necessarily come off as "cold").

Avolition: Difficulty Initiating or Following Through

In movies that portray people with schizophrenia, hospitalized patients are often shown sitting in chairs apparently doing nothing all day, not even talking to others. This portrayal suggests **avolition**, which consists of difficulty initiating or following through with activities. For example, Hester Genain would often sit for hours, staring into space, and had difficulty beginning her chores.

Other negative symptoms that are less prominent in schizophrenia are:

- *Alogia*—speaking less than do most other people. A person with alogia will take a while to muster the mental effort necessary to respond to a question.
- *Anhedonia*—a diminished ability to experience pleasure (see Chapter 5).
- *Asociality*—disinterest in social interactions.

The sets of positive and negative symptoms in DSM-5 grew out of decades of clinical observations of patients with schizophrenia; these symptoms can generally be observed or can be inferred by a trained researcher or clinician. According to DSM-5, to be diagnosed with schizophrenia, the person must have two out of five symptoms (and at least one symptom must be hallucinations, delusions, or disorganized speech); these symptoms must be present for at least 1 month continuously and at least one symptom must have been present for 6 months; the symptoms must significantly impair functioning. However, research has revealed that cognitive deficits—which are not as easily observed and are not part of the DSM-5 criteria—also play a crucial role in schizophrenia, as we discuss below.

Cognitive Deficits: The Specifics

Research has revealed that cognitive deficits (also called *neurocognitive deficits*) often accompany schizophrenia (Barch, 2005; Green, 2001). It is not clear whether these deficits cause the disorder, are a necessary or common precondition that makes the disorder more likely to develop, or are a result of the disorder. Specific deficits are found in attention, memory, and executive functioning, and they arise in most people with schizophrenia (Keefe et al., 2005; Wilk et al., 2005).

Deficits in Attention

Cognitive deficits include difficulties in sustaining and focusing attention, which can involve distinguishing relevant from irrelevant stimuli (Gur et al., 2007). One person with schizophrenia recounted: "If I am talking to someone they only need to cross their legs or scratch their heads and I am distracted and forget what I was saying" (Torrey, 2001, p. 29).

Deficits in Working Memory

Another area of cognitive functioning adversely affected in people with schizophrenia is *working memory*, which organizes, temporarily retains, and transforms incoming information during reasoning and related mental activities (Baddeley, 1986). For

Negative symptoms
Symptoms of schizophrenia that are characterized by the absence or reduction of normal mental processes, mental contents, or behaviors.

Flat affect
A lack of, or considerably diminished, emotional expression, such as occurs when someone speaks robotically and shows little facial expression.

Avolition
A negative symptom of schizophrenia marked by difficulty initiating or following through with activities.

example, if you are trying to remember items you need to buy at the store, you will probably use working memory to organize the items into easy-to-recall categories. People with schizophrenia do not organize information effectively, which indicates that their working memories are impaired.

Deficits in Executive Functioning

Deficits in working memory contribute to problems that people with schizophrenia have with **executive functions**, which are mental processes involved in planning, organizing, problem solving, abstract thinking, and exercising good judgment (Cornblatt et al., 1997; Erlenmeyer-Kimling et al., 2000; Kim et al., 2004). The problems with executive functioning have far-reaching consequences for cognition in general. For instance, Hester had the most severe symptoms of the Genain quads, and her deficits in executive functioning were prominent much of the time. She had difficulty performing household chores that required multiple steps—such as making mashed potatoes by herself, which required peeling the potatoes, then boiling them, knowing when to take them out of the water, and mashing them with other (measured) ingredients. Obviously, deficits in executive functioning can impair a person's overall ability to function.

Cognitive Deficits Endure Over Time

Neurocognitive deficits do not necessarily make their first appearance at the same time that the positive and negative symptoms of schizophrenia first emerge. For many people who develop schizophrenia, cognitive deficits exist in childhood, well before a first episode of schizophrenia (Cannon et al., 1999; Ott et al., 2002; Torrey, 2002). In addition to predating symptoms of schizophrenia, cognitive deficits often persist after the positive and negative symptoms improve (Hoff & Kremen, 2003; Rund et al., 2004). Thus, at least some of the time these deficits "set the stage" for the disorder but do not actually cause it. However, as we discuss shortly, in some cases such deficits may directly contribute to specific symptoms.

The lives of Genain sisters illustrate both the importance of cognitive deficits and their variety. Hester had the most difficulty academically and was held back in 5th grade because of her poor performance. In contrast, Myra did not exhibit any significant cognitive deficits, and she graduated from high school, held a job, married, and had two children. Nora and Iris had moderate levels of cognitive deficits; they could perform full-time work for periods of time but could not function independently for long stretches (Mirsky & Quinn, 1988; Mirsky et al., 1987, 2000).

Limitations of DSM-5 Criteria

Although the DSM-5 criteria provide a relatively reliable way to diagnose schizophrenia, a number of researchers point to drawbacks of those criteria—both of the specific criteria and of the grouping of positive and negative symptoms (Fauman, 2006; Green, 2001). A more diagnostically and prognostically relevant set of symptoms, these researchers suggest, would focus on the extent of cognitive deficits and the breadth and severity of the DSM-5 symptoms.

Absence of Focus on Cognitive Deficits

Cognitive deficits are not specifically addressed in the DSM-5 criteria, despite their importance. Although the DSM-5 set of positive symptoms includes disorganized speech and grossly disorganized psychomotor behavior (see Table 12.1), research suggests that these two symptoms together form an important cluster, independent of hallucinations and delusions. This cluster apparently reflects specific types of underlying cognitive deficits, which clearly contribute to disorganized thinking. For instance, cognitive deficits can cause thoughts to skip from one topic to another,

Executive functions
Mental processes involved in planning, organizing, problem solving, abstract thinking, and exercising good judgment.

topics that are related to each other only tangentially if at all. (This process is referred to as a *loosening of associations*.) Thus, disorganized speech arises from disorganized thinking. Similarly, grossly disorganized psychomotor behavior, such as laughing at a funeral or putting on four pairs of underwear, can occur because the person's cognitive deficits prevent him or her from organizing social experiences into categories covered by general rules of behavior or conventions.

Cognitive deficits can also lead to unusual social behavior or asociality. As we'll discuss in more detail later, people with schizophrenia may be socially isolated and avoid contact with others because such interactions can be overwhelming or confusing. People with schizophrenia can have difficulty understanding the usual, unspoken rules of social convention. Also, even after an episode of schizophrenia has abated, they may not understand when someone is irritated because they do not notice or correctly interpret the other person's facial expression or tone of voice (which are types of cognitive deficits; Clark et al., 2013). When irritation erupts into anger, it can seem to come out of the blue, frightening and overwhelming people with schizophrenia. So, they may try to tread a safer path and avoid others as much as possible. In turn, the poor social skills and social isolation are related to an impaired ability to work (Dickinson et al., 2007). The disorganized behavior, asociality, and poor social skills, and perhaps avolition, all are indicators of underlying cognitive deficits (Farrow et al., 2005).

Deficit/Nondeficit Subtypes

Researchers make a distinction between patients diagnosed with schizophrenia who have significant cognitive deficits and those who do not (Horan & Blanchard, 2003). To be considered to have the *deficit subtype*, a patient must have severe neurocognitive deficits in attention, memory, and executive functioning, as well as the positive and negative symptoms that are manifestations of these deficits, such as disorganized speech and grossly disorganized psychomotor behavior. Such patients are generally more impaired than are other patients with schizophrenia, and their symptoms are less likely to improve with currently available treatments. They may be more impaired, at least in part, because parts of their brains do not work together normally; neuroimaging results show that people with the deficit subtype of schizophrenia (but not those who have the nondeficit subtype) have abnormalities in their "white matter tracts"—sets of axons that connect neurons (Voineskos et al., 2013). (They are white because they are covered with the fatty insulator substance myelin.)

To be considered to have the *nondeficit subtype*, a patient must have positive symptoms, such as hallucinations and delusions, in conjunction with relatively intact cognitive functioning. People with this subtype are generally less impaired, and they have a better prognosis (McGlashan & Fenton, 1993).

Distinguishing Between Schizophrenia and Other Disorders

Positive or negative symptoms may arise in schizophrenia or in the context of other disorders. Clinicians and researchers must determine whether the positive or negative symptoms reflect schizophrenia, another disorder, or, in some cases, schizophrenia *and* another disorder.

Psychotic Symptoms in Schizophrenia, Mood Disorders, and Substance-Related Disorders

Other psychological disorders, most notably mood disorders and substance-related disorders, may involve symptoms such as hallucinations and delusions. (Mood disorders with psychotic features are discussed in Chapter 5, and substance-induced hallucinations and delusions are discussed in Chapter 9.) The content of these psychotic symptoms is usually consistent with the characteristics of the mood disorder or substance-related disorder, and the psychotic symptoms only arise during a mood episode or with substance use or withdrawal.

For example, people with mania may become psychotic, developing grandiose delusions about their abilities. Psychotic mania is distinguished from schizophrenia by the presence of other symptoms of mania—such as pressured speech or little need for sleep.

Similarly, psychotically depressed people may have delusions or hallucinations; the delusions usually involve themes of the depressed person's worthlessness or the "badness" of certain body parts (e.g., "My intestines are rotting"). Some negative symptoms of schizophrenia can be difficult to distinguish from symptoms of depression: People with schizophrenia or depression may show little interest in activities, hardly speak at all, give minimal replies to questions, and avoid social situations. As noted in Table 12.2, although both of these disorders may involve similar outward behaviors, the behaviors arise from different causes. In general, people with schizophrenia but not depression do not have other symptoms of depression, such as changes in weight or sleep or feelings of worthlessness and inappropriate guilt (American Psychiatric Association, 2013). Of course, people with schizophrenia may develop comorbid disorders, such as depression.

TABLE **12.2** • Behavioral Symptoms Common to Depression and Schizophrenia

Behavioral symptoms	Causes in depression	Causes in schizophrenia
Little or no interest in activities, staring into space for long periods of time	Lack of pleasure in activities (anhedonia), difficulty making decisions	Difficulty initiating behavior (avolition)
Short or "empty" replies to questions	Lack of energy	Difficulty organizing thoughts to speak
Social isolation	Lack of energy, anhedonia, feeling undeserving of companionship	Feeling overwhelmed by social situations, lack of social skills

Finally, substance-related disorders can lead to delusions (see Chapter 9), such as the persecutory delusions that arise from chronic use of stimulants. Substances (and withdrawal from them) can also induce hallucinations, such as the tactile hallucinations that can arise with cocaine use (e.g., the feeling that bugs are crawling over a person's arms). Determining the correct diagnosis can be particularly challenging when a person has more than one disorder and the symptoms of those disorders appear similar.

Other Psychotic Disorders

Although mood disorders and substance-related disorders may involve psychotic symptoms, the diagnostic criteria for these two categories of disorders do not specifically require the presence of psychotic symptoms. In contrast, the criteria for the disorders collectively referred to as *psychotic disorders* specifically require the presence of symptoms related to psychosis; these disorders are part of a spectrum, related to each other in their symptoms and risk factors but differing in their specific constellations of symptoms, duration, and severity.

Schizophreniform and Brief Psychotic Disorders

In some cases, a person's symptoms may meet most, but not all, of the criteria for a diagnosis of schizophrenia. The person clearly suffers from some psychotic symptoms and has significant difficulty in functioning as a result of his or her psychological problems. However, the impaired functioning hasn't been present for the minimum 6-month duration required for a diagnosis of schizophrenia. Two disorders fall into this class, depending on the specifics of the symptoms and their duration.

Schizophreniform disorder is the diagnosis given when a person's symptoms meet all the criteria for schizophrenia *except* that symptoms have been present for between 1 and 6 months (American Psychiatric Association, 2013). In addition, daily functioning may or may not have declined over that period of time. If the symptoms persist for more than 6 months (and daily functioning has significantly declined), the diagnosis shifts to schizophrenia.

In contrast, **brief psychotic disorder** refers to the sudden onset of hallucinations, delusions, or disorganized speech or behavior that last between 1 day and 1 month and are followed by full recovery (American Psychiatric Association, 2013). For this diagnosis, no negative symptoms should be present during the episode. Rather, brief psychotic disorder is characterized by intense emotional episodes and confusion, during which the person may be so disorganized that he or she cannot function safely and independently; he or she also has an increased risk of suicide during the episode. Once recovered, people who had this disorder have a good prognosis for full recovery (Pillman et al., 2002).

Schizoaffective Disorder

Schizoaffective disorder is characterized by the presence of both schizophrenia *and* a depressive or manic episode (see Chapter 5). For this diagnosis, the mood episode must be present during most of the period when the symptoms of schizophrenia are present; in addition, delusions or hallucinations must be present for at least 2 weeks when there is no mood episode. Because schizoaffective disorder involves mood episodes, negative symptoms such as flat affect are less common, and the diagnosis is likely to be made solely on the basis of positive symptoms. Because of their mood episodes, people with schizoaffective disorder are at greater risk for committing suicide than are people with schizophrenia (Bhatia et al., 2006; De Hert et al., 2001). The prognosis for recovery from schizoaffective disorder is somewhat better than that for recovery from schizophrenia, particularly when stressors or events clearly contribute to the disorder (American Psychiatric Association, 2013).

Delusional Disorder

A person is diagnosed with **delusional disorder** when the sole symptom is delusional beliefs—such as believing that someone is following you when they actually are at work on the other side of town—that have persisted for at least 1 month. Clinicians and researchers have identified the following types of delusions in delusional disorder (American Psychiatric Association, 2013):

- *Erotomanic.* The belief that another person is in love with the patient. This delusion usually focuses on romantic or spiritual union rather than sexual attraction.

- *Grandiose.* The belief that the patient has a great (but unrecognized) ability, talent, or achievement.

- *Persecutory.* The belief that the patient is being spied on, drugged, harassed, or otherwise conspired against.

Schizophreniform disorder
A psychotic disorder characterized by symptoms that meet all the criteria for schizophrenia *except* that the symptoms have been present for only 1–6 months, and daily functioning may or may not have declined over that period of time.

Brief psychotic disorder
A psychotic disorder characterized by the sudden onset of positive or disorganized symptoms that last between 1 day and 1 month and are followed by full recovery.

Schizoaffective disorder
A psychotic disorder characterized by the presence of both schizophrenia *and* a depressive or manic episode.

Delusional disorder
A psychotic disorder characterized by the presence of delusions that have persisted for more than 1 month.

Diana Napolis suffered from persecutory delusions about filmmaker Stephen Spielberg and singer and actress Jennifer Love Hewitt; she believed that both were controlling her brain (Soto, 2003).

Jeff Kravitz/FilmMagic/Getty Images

Jon Kopaloff/Film Magic/Getty Images

- *Somatic.* The false belief that something is wrong with the body (such as insects on the skin) and these delusions are not considered a symptom of another psychological disorder, such as obsessive-compulsive disorder (Chapter 7) or body dysmorphic disorder (Chapter 7).

- *Jealous.* The belief that the patient's romantic partner is unfaithful. This belief is based on tiny amounts of "evidence," such as the partner's arriving home a few minutes late.

People with delusional disorder may appear normal when they are not talking about their delusions. Their behavior may not be particularly odd nor their functioning otherwise impaired. Henry Genain, the quads' father, exhibited some signs of delusional disorder of the jealous type: Soon after he met Maud, the Genains' mother, he asked her to marry him, but she refused. He pestered her for months, threatening that if she didn't marry him, neither of them would live to marry anyone else. On multiple occasions, he threatened to kill himself or her. After she consented to marry him (because his family begged her to), he didn't want her to socialize with anyone else, including her family. His jealousy was so extreme that he didn't want her to go out of the house because people walking down the street might smile at her. When the quads were 7 years old, Mrs. Genain thought of leaving Henry, but he told her, "If you leave me, I will find you where you go and I'll kill you" (Rosenthal, 1963, p. 69). She believed him and stayed with him.

One extremely unusual and rare presentation of delusional symptoms involves a shared delusion among two or more people (sometimes referred to as *folie à deux*, which is French for "paired madness"). (Technically, this is an "other" psychotic disorder because it doesn't meet the criteria for any specific disorder in the category of psychotic disorders.) With this variant, a person develops delusions as a result of his or her close relationship with another person who has delusions as part of a psychotic disorder. The person who had the disorder at the outset is referred to as the *primary person* and is usually diagnosed with schizophrenia or delusional disorder. The delusions of the primary person may be shared by more than one other person, as can occur in families when the primary person is a parent. When the primary person's delusions subside, the other person's shared delusions may or may not also subside.

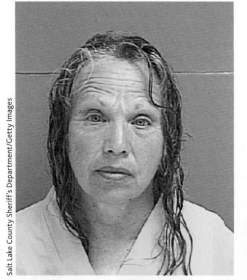
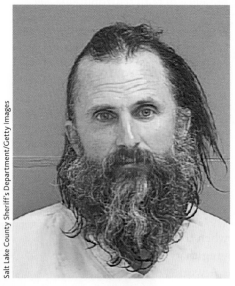

Wanda Barzee and her husband, Brian David Mitchell, kidnapped 14-year-old Elizabeth Smart in 2002. Mitchell believed he was God, and Barzee apparently came to share his belief. Although diagnosing Barzee was difficult, some doctors who examined her believed that she suffered from a shared delusion.

Schizotypal Personality Disorder

Eccentric behaviors and difficulty with relationships are the hallmarks of *schizotypal personality disorder*, discussed in more detail with the other personality disorders in Chapter 13. A person with schizotypal personality disorder may have very few if any close friends, may feel that he or she doesn't fit in, and may experience social anxiety. Schizotypal personality disorder, unlike schizophrenia, does not involve psychotic symptoms. Although schizotypal personality disorder is thus not technically a psychotic disorder, some research suggests that it may in fact be a milder form of schizophrenia (Dickey et al., 2002); for this reason, in DSM-5 the disorder is placed within the schizophrenia spectrum as

TABLE **12.3** • Overview of Schizophrenia Spectrum and Psychotic Disorders

Psychotic disorder	Features
Schizophrenia	At least two symptoms—one of which must be delusions, hallucinations, or disorganized speech—for a minimum of 1 month; continuous symptoms for at least 6 months, during which time the person has impaired functioning in some area(s) of life. *Note: Criteria are listed in Table 12.1.*
Schizophreniform disorder	Symptoms meet all the criteria for schizophrenia *except* that the symptoms have been present for only 1–6 months; daily functioning may or may not have declined over that period of time.
Brief psychotic disorder	The sudden onset of positive symptoms, which persist between a day and a month, followed by a full recovery. No negative symptoms are present during the episode.
Schizoaffective disorder	Symptoms meet the criteria for both schizophrenia and mood disorder, with symptoms of schizophrenia present for at least 2 weeks without symptoms of a mood disorder, and a mood episode present during most of the period when the symptoms of schizophrenia are present. Negative symptoms of schizophrenia are less common with this disorder.
Delusional disorder	The presence of delusions that persist for at least 1 month, without a diagnosis of schizophrenia.

The various psychotic disorders have in common the presence of hallucinations and/or delusions. Although schizotypal personality disorder is not a psychotic disorder (because hallucinations and delusions are absent), this personality disorder is considered to be on the spectrum of schizophrenia-related disorders.

well as within the personality disorders; we have listed its criteria in Chapter 13 (American Psychiatric Association, 2013). With this personality disorder, problems in relationships may become evident by early adulthood, marked by discomfort when relating to others as well as by being stiff or inappropriate in relationships. Table 12.3 summarizes the key features of schizophrenia spectrum and psychotic disorders.

CURRENT CONTROVERSY

Attenuated Psychosis Syndrome: The Diagnosis That Wasn't

Attenuated psychosis syndrome is a diagnosis that was proposed for inclusion in DSM-5 but that did not make it in. This condition is defined by "attenuated" (that is, reduced or weakened) psychotic symptoms of psychosis. For example, rather than paranoid delusions, someone may be generally mistrustful, and rather than hearing voices, someone may hear rumblings or murmurs.

On the one hand, proponents of adding this diagnosis thought it would help detect and treat cases of psychotic disorders before they became full blown; therefore, the alternative name for this disorder was *psychotic risk syndrome* (McFarlane et al., 2012; McGorry, 2010, 2012). Psychotic episodes can create long-lasting disturbances in brain activation, cognitive functioning, and social relations; the proponents of this diagnosis hoped that identifying and intervening earlier might reduce the likelihood that "at risk" cases would become full-blown schizophrenia (McGorry et al., 2002; Wade et al., 2006).

On the other hand, critics charge that identifying people whose symptoms don't meet the criteria for positive symptoms of schizophrenia labels them as "psychotic" when they aren't and might never become so (Frances, 2013; Schultze-Lutter et al., 2013; Tsuang et al., in press). Furthermore, critics argue that treating such people with antipsychotic medications—which have significant and serious side effects—when the symptoms don't warrant it would be inappropriate.

CRITICAL THINKING If this diagnosis—or some version of it—is adopted in the future, how can we reduce the likelihood that this diagnosis will be used to overlabel and overtreat people with attenuated symptoms?

(James Foley, College of Wooster)

Schizophrenia Facts in Detail

In this section we discuss additional facts about schizophrenia.

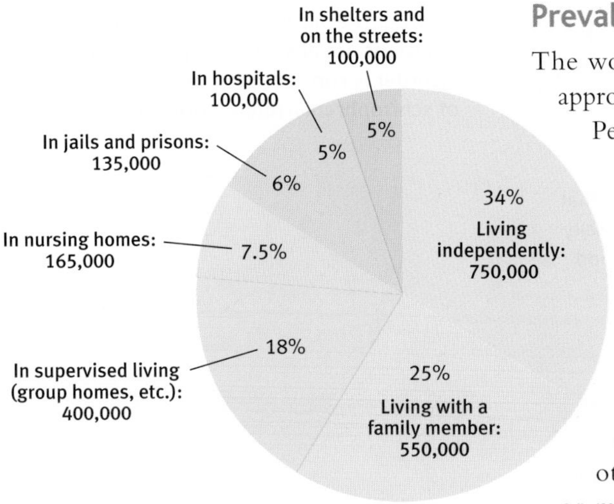

Prevalence

The world over—from China or Finland to the United States or New Guinea—approximately 1% of the population will develop schizophrenia (Gottesman, 1991; Perälä et al., 2007).

Schizophrenia is one of the top five causes of disability among adults in developed nations, ranking with heart disease, arthritis, drug use, and HIV (Murray & Lopez, 1996). In the United States, about 5% of people with schizophrenia (about 100,000 people) are homeless, 5% are in hospitals, and 6% are in jail or prison (Torrey, 2001). In contrast, 34% of people with this disorder live independently (see Figure 12.1).

Comorbidity

Over 90% of people with schizophrenia also suffer from at least one other psychological disorder (and, as the numbers below suggest, often two or more other disorders; Sands & Harrow, 1999). Substance-related disorders, mood disorders, and anxiety disorders are the most common comorbid disorders:

- *Mood disorders.* Approximately 50% of people with schizophrenia also have some type of mood disorder, most commonly depression (Buckley et al., 2009; Sands & Harrow, 1999). As noted earlier, according to DSM-5, some of these people may have *schizoaffective disorder.*

- *Anxiety disorder.* Almost half of people with schizophrenia also have panic attacks (Goodwin et al., 2002) and anxiety disorders (Cosoff & Hafner, 1998).

- *Substance use disorders.* Up to 60% of people with schizophrenia have a substance abuse problem that is not related to tobacco (Swartz et al., 2006). Moreover, 90% of those with schizophrenia smoke cigarettes (Regier et al., 1990), and they tend to inhale more deeply than do other smokers (Tidey et al., 2005).

Researchers have also noted that even before their positive symptoms emerged, some people with schizophrenia abused drugs, particularly nicotine (cigarettes), marijuana, amphetamines, phencyclidine (PCP), mescaline, and lysergic acid diethylamide (LSD) (Bowers et al., 2001; Weiser et al., 2004). For example, a study of Swedish males found that those who used marijuana in adolescence were more likely later to develop schizophrenia. The more a person used marijuana, the more likely he or she was to develop schizophrenia, particularly if the drug was used more than 50 times (Moore et al., 2007; Zammit et al., 2002).

However, keep in mind that the correlation between using marijuana and subsequent schizophrenia does not show that the drug *causes* schizophrenia. For example, perhaps marijuana use leads to schizophrenic symptoms only in those who were likely to develop the disorder anyway, or a predisposition to develop schizophrenia also might make drug use attractive (Kahn et al., 2011). It is also possible that marijuana "tips the scales" in those who are vulnerable but who would not develop schizophrenia if they did not use the drug (Large et al., 2011). Or perhaps some other factor affects both substance abuse and subsequent schizophrenia

FIGURE **12.1 • Distribution of the 2.2 Million Americans With Schizophrenia**

In shelters and on the streets: 100,000 — 5%
In hospitals: 100,000 — 5%
In jails and prisons: 135,000 — 6%
In nursing homes: 165,000 — 7.5%
In supervised living (group homes, etc.): 400,000 — 18%
Living independently: 750,000 — 34%
Living with a family member: 550,000 — 25%

Guitarist Peter Green (lying down), cofounder of the rock group Fleetwood Mac, developed schizophrenia after using LSD frequently. Although Green attributes his illness to his drug abuse, researchers cannot yet definitively state that such abuse causes schizophrenia in people who might not otherwise develop the disorder.

Araldo Di Crollalanza/Rex Features, Courtesy Everett Collection

(Bowers et al., 2001). Researchers do not yet know enough to be able to choose among these possibilities, and true experiments designed to investigate them would obviously be unethical.

Course

Typically, schizophrenia develops in phases. In the *premorbid phase*, before symptoms develop, some people may display personality characteristics or cognitive deficits that later evolve into negative symptoms (MacCabe et al., 2013). However, it is important to note that the vast majority of people who are odd or have eccentric tendencies do not develop schizophrenia. During the **prodromal phase**, which is between the onset of symptoms and the time when the minimum criteria for a disorder are met. In the **active phase**, a person has full-blown positive (and possibly negative) symptoms that meet the criteria for the disorder. If the positive symptoms have subsided but negative symptoms persist, the full criteria for schizophrenia are no longer met; the person can be said to be in the *residual phase,* which indicates that there is a residue of (negative) symptoms but the pronounced positive symptoms have faded away. As shown in Table 12.4, over time, the person may fully recover, may have intermittent episodes, or may develop chronic symptoms that interfere with normal functioning.

Although most of the Genain sisters were not able to live independently, like many other people with schizophrenia (Levine et al., 2011), the symptoms of the Genain sisters generally improved (Mirsky et al., 2000). Iris and Nora were able to work part time as volunteers; in their 40s and beyond, these two sisters were able to live outside a hospital setting (Mirsky et al., 2000; Rosenthal, 1963).

TABLE 12.4 • 10-Year and 30-Year Course of Schizophrenia

	10 years later	30 years later
Completely recovered	25%	25%
Much improved, relatively independent	25%	35%
Improved but requiring extensive support network	25%	15%
Hospitalized, unimproved	15%	10%
Dead, mostly by suicide	10%	15%

Source: Torrey, 2001, p. 130.

Gender Differences

Men are more likely to develop schizophrenia than are women; 1.4 men develop the disorder for every woman (McGrath, 2006). Moreover, men are more likely to develop the disorder in their early 20s whereas women are more likely to develop the disorder in their late 20s or later. Compared to men, women usually have fewer negative symptoms (American Psychiatric Association, 2013; Maric et al., 2003) and more mood symptoms (Maurer, 2001), and they are less likely to have substance abuse problems or to exhibit suicidal or violent behavior (Seeman, 2000). Moreover, women generally function at higher levels before their illness develops.

Culture

Two findings bear on the role of culture and schizophrenia. First, across various countries, schizophrenia is more common among people in urban areas and lower socioeconomic classes than among people in rural areas and higher socioeconomic classes (Freeman, 1994; Mortensen et al., 1999), as we'll discuss in more detail later in this chapter. Moreover, there are ethnic differences in prevalence rates in the United States: Blacks are twice as likely as Whites or Latinos to be diagnosed with schizophrenia (Dassori et al., 1995; Keith et al., 1991). These prevalence differences may reflect the influence of a variety of moderating variables, such as biases in the use of certain diagnostic categories for different ethnic groups.

Second, people with schizophrenia in non-Western countries are generally better able to function in their societies than are their Western counterparts, and thus they have a better prognosis. We'll discuss possible reasons for this finding in the *Understanding Schizophrenia* section on social factors.

Table 12.5 provides a summary of facts about schizophrenia.

Prodromal phase
The phase that is between the onset of symptoms and the time when the minimum criteria for a disorder are met.

Active phase
The phase of a psychological disorder (such as schizophrenia) in which the person exhibits symptoms that meet the criteria for the disorder.

Table 12.5 • Schizophrenia Facts at a Glance

Prevalence

• Approximately 1% of people worldwide have schizophrenia (Gottesman, 1991; Tandon et al., 2008).

Comorbidity

• Over 90% of people with schizophrenia also have at least one other disorder. The most frequent comorbid disorders are mood, anxiety, and substance use disorders.

Onset

• Men are more likely to develop the disorder in their early 20s, whereas women are more likely to develop it in their late 20s or later.

Course

• About two thirds of people who have had one episode will go on to have subsequent episodes.

• About one third of people with schizophrenia become chronically ill, without much reduction of symptoms; for most others, the symptoms subside.

Gender Differences

• Schizophrenia affects men more frequently than women (1.4 : 1 male-to-female ratio; McGrath, 2006), and—as noted above—women tend to develop the disorder at older ages than do men.

• Women have fewer negative symptoms than do men.

Cultural Differences

• Schizophrenia is more common among people in urban areas and in lower socioeconomic groups (Freeman, 1994; Saha et al., 2005).

• In non-Western countries, people with schizophrenia generally function better in society than do those in Western countries (Hopper et al., 2007).

• In a given country, immigrants are almost twice as likely to develop schizophrenia as are native-born residents (Saha et al., 2005).

• Within the United States, Latinos and Whites are less likely to be diagnosed with schizophrenia than are Blacks (Zhang & Snowden, 1999).

Source: Unless otherwise noted, citations for above table are: American Psychiatric Association, 2000, 2013.

📷 GETTING THE PICTURE

Tips Images/SuperStock

JL Images/Alamy

Does one of the two countries shown in these photos (China and the United States) have a higher prevalence of schizophrenia, and if so, which one? Answer: These two countries, and other countries worldwide, have the same general prevalence rate—about 1%.

Prognosis

In general, the long-term prognosis for schizophrenia follows the rule of thirds:

- one third of patients improve significantly;

- one third basically stay the same, having episodic relapses and some permanent deficits in functioning, but are able to hold a "sheltered" job—a job designed for people with mild to moderate disabilities; and

- one third become chronically and severely disabled by their illness.

Table 12.6 summarizes factors associated with a better prognosis in Western countries. However, this table does not indicate a crucial fact about the prognosis for people with schizophrenia: Over the course of their lives, people with schizophrenia are more likely than others to die by suicide or to be victims of violence. In what follows we examine these risks in greater detail.

Suicide

People with schizophrenia have a higher risk of dying by suicide than do other people: As Table 12.4 shows, as many as 10–15% of people with schizophrenia commit suicide (Caldwell & Gottesman, 1990; Siris, 2001). Those with paranoid symptoms are at the highest risk for suicide. Perhaps paradoxically, patients at risk for committing suicide are those who are most likely to be aware of their symptoms: They have relatively few negative symptoms but pronounced positive symptoms; they tend to be highly intelligent, have career goals, are aware of their deterioration, and have a pattern of relapsing and then getting better, with many episodes; and—like other people who die by suicide—they are more likely to be male than female (Fenton, 2000; Funahashi et al., 2000; Siris, 2001). Ironically, some of these factors—a high level of premorbid functioning, few negative symptoms, and an awareness of the symptoms and their effects—are associated with a better prognosis (see Table 12.6). As researchers have identified these risk factors, they have used them to focus suicide prevention efforts.

Violence

A small percentage of people with schizophrenia commit violent acts. Risk factors associated with violent behavior include being male, having comorbid substance abuse, not taking medication, and having engaged in criminal behavior or having had psychopathic tendencies before schizophrenia developed (Hunt et al., 2006; Monahan et al., 2001; Skeem & Mulvey, 2001; Tengström et al., 2001).

Rather than being violent, people with schizophrenia are much more likely to be victims of violence. One survey found that almost 20% of people with a psychotic disorder had been victims of violence in the previous 12 months. Those who were more disorganized and functioned less well were more likely to have been victimized (Chapple et al., 2004), perhaps because their impaired functioning made them easier "marks" for perpetrators.

TABLE 12.6 • Factors Associated With a Better Prognosis for People With Schizophrenia

People with schizophrenia who significantly improve often have one or more of the following characteristics:

- They functioned at a relatively high level before their first episode.
- The symptoms had a sudden onset.
- They developed symptoms later in life.
- They have a family history of mood disorders, not schizophrenia.
- They have symptoms of paranoia or the nondeficit subtype, with relatively good cognitive functioning.
- They have fewer negative symptoms.
- They are aware of their symptoms and recognize that the symptoms are caused by an illness.
- They are women.

Sources: 1991; Fenton & McGlashan, 1994; Green, 2001.

Thinking Like A Clinician

Suppose you are a mental health clinician working in a hospital emergency room in the summer; a woman is brought in for you to evaluate. She's wearing a winter coat, and in the waiting room, she talks—or shouts—to herself or an imaginary person. You think that she may be suffering from schizophrenia. What information would you need in order to make that diagnosis? What other psychological disorders could, with only brief observation, appear similar to schizophrenia?

□ Understanding Schizophrenia

Despite the low odds that all four of the Genain quads would develop schizophrenia, it did happen. Why? The neuropsychosocial approach helps us to understand the factors that lead to schizophrenia and how these factors influence each other. As we shall see, although neurological factors (including genes) can make a person vulnerable to the disorder, psychological and social factors also play key roles—which may help explain not only why all four Genain quads ended up with schizophrenia but also why the disorder affected them differently.

The quads shared virtually all the same genes, looked alike, and, at least in their early years, were generally treated similarly, especially by Mrs. Genain. However, Hester was smaller and frailer than the others; she weighed only 3 pounds at birth and could not always keep up with her sisters. Because of Hester's difficulties, it wasn't always possible to treat the four girls the same, and so Mr. and Mrs. Genain sometimes treated them as two pairs of twins: Nora and Myra were paired together (they were seen as most competent), and Iris—who in fact was almost as competent as Nora and Myra—was paired with Hester.

In the following we will examine the specific neurological, psychological, and social factors that give rise to schizophrenia and then examine how these factors affect one another.

Neurological Factors in Schizophrenia

Perhaps more than for any other psychological disorder, neurological factors play a crucial role in the development of schizophrenia. These factors involve brain systems, neural communication, and genetics.

Brain Systems

People who have schizophrenia have abnormalities in the structure and function of their brains. The most striking example of a structural abnormality in the brains of people with schizophrenia is enlarged ventricles, which are cavities in the center of the brain that are filled with cerebrospinal fluid (Vita et al., 2006). Larger ventricles means that the size of the brain itself is reduced. Thus, people who later develop schizophrenia have brains that are smaller than normal even before they develop the disorder. This occurs, in part, because their brains never grew to "full" size. In addition, research suggests that schizophrenia causes parts of the brain to shrink (DeLisi et al., 1997; Gur et al., 1997; Rapoport et al., 1999).

In 1981, the Genain sisters, then 51 years old, returned to NIMH for a 3-month evaluation; during that time, they were taken off their medications. CT scans of the quads showed similar brain abnormalities in all four sisters (Mirsky & Quinn, 1988). However, even though they were basically genetically identical, their performance on neuropsychological tests varied: Nora and Hester showed more evidence of neurological difficulties, and they were more impaired in their daily functioning when not taking medication. Thus, once again, we see that genes are not destiny and that brain function cannot be considered in isolation. The brain is a mechanism, but how it performs depends in part on how it is "programmed" by learning and experience—which are psychological factors.

In the following sections, we consider the likely role of specific brain abnormalities and possible causes of such abnormalities, and then we examine telltale neurological, bodily, or behavioral signs that may indirectly reveal that a person is vulnerable to developing the disorder.

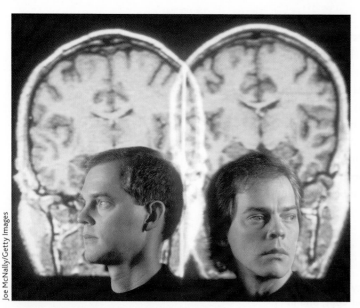

Joe McNally/Getty Images

These brain scans of identical twins show, for one of them, the enlarged ventricles that typically are associated with schizophrenia. The twin on the right has schizophrenia, and the twin on the left does not.

A Frontal Lobe Defect?

Based on the specific cognitive deficits exhibited by people with schizophrenia, many researchers have hypothesized that such people have impaired frontal lobe functioning. The root of this impairment may lie in the fact that the human brain has too many connections among neurons at birth, and part of normal maturation is the elimination, or *pruning*, of unneeded connections (Huttenlocher, 2002). Research results suggest that an excess of such pruning takes place during adolescence for people who develop schizophrenia: Too many of the neural connections in the frontal lobes are eliminated, which may account for some of the neurocognitive deficits that typically accompany this disorder (Pantelis et al., 2003; Walker et al., 2004).

Impaired Temporal Lobe and Thalamus?

Enlarged ventricles are associated with decreased size of the temporal lobes. This is significant for people with schizophrenia because the temporal lobes process auditory information, some aspects of language, and visual recognition (Levitan et al., 1999; Sanfilipo et al., 2002). Abnormal functioning of the temporal lobes may underlie some positive symptoms, notably auditory hallucinations, in people with schizophrenia. The thalamus, which transmits sensory information to other parts of the brain, also appears to be smaller and to function abnormally in people with schizophrenia (Andrews et al., 2006; Guller et al., 2012). Abnormal functioning of the thalamus is associated with difficulties in focusing attention, in distinguishing relevant from irrelevant stimuli, and in particular types of memory difficulties, all of which are cognitive deficits that can arise with schizophrenia.

Abnormal Hippocampus?

The hippocampus—a subcortical brain structure crucially involved in storing new information in memory—is smaller in people with schizophrenia and their first-degree relatives (parents and siblings) than in control participants (Seidman et al., 2002; Vita et al., 2006). This abnormal characteristic may contribute to the deficits in memory experienced by people with schizophrenia (Olson et al., 2006; Yoon et al., 2008).

Interactions Among Brain Areas

Some researchers propose that schizophrenia arises from disrupted interactions among the frontal lobes, the thalamus, and the cerebellum—which may act as a time-keeper, synchronizing and coordinating signals from many brain areas (Andreasen, 2001; Andreasen et al., 1999). According to this theory, the thalamus fails to screen out sensory information, which overwhelms subsequent processing—and thus the form and content of the person's thoughts become confused.

Possible Causes of Brain Abnormalities

How might these brain abnormalities arise? Researchers have identified several possible causes, some of which could affect the developing brain of a fetus or a newborn:

* *maternal malnourishment* during pregnancy, particularly during the first trimester (Brown, van Os, et al., 1999; Wahlbeck et al., 2001).

* *maternal illness* during the 6th month of pregnancy. During fetal development, neurons travel to their final destination in the brain and establish connections with other neurons (in a process called *cell migration*). If the mother catches the flu or another viral infection in the second trimester, this may disrupt cell migration in the developing fetus's brain, which causes some neurons to fall short of their intended destinations. Because the neurons are not properly positioned, they form different connections than they would have formed if they had been in the correct locations—leading to abnormal neural communication (Brown, Begg, et al., 2004; Green, 2001; McGlashan & Hoffman, 2000). In general, an immune challenge to

Biological marker
A neurological, bodily, or behavioral characteristic that distinguishes people with a psychological disorder (or a first-degree relative with the disorder) from those without the disorder.

the developing fetus in turn can affect brain development (Meyer, 2013; Watanabe et al., 2010).

- *oxygen deprivation*, which can arise from prenatal or birth-related medical complications (McNeil et al., 2000; Zornberg et al., 2000). Studies have shown that people with schizophrenia who did not receive enough oxygen at specific periods before birth have smaller hippocampi than do people with schizophrenia who were not deprived of oxygen during or before birth (van Erp et al., 2002)—which may be related to memory problems.

Biological Markers

When a neurological, bodily, or behavioral characteristic distinguishes people with a psychological disorder (or people with a first-degree relative with the disorder) from people who do not have the disorder, it is said to be a **biological marker** for the disorder. One biological marker for schizophrenia, but not other non-psychotic psychological disorders, is difficulty maintaining smooth, continuous eye movements when tracking a light as it moves across the visual field; such tracking is called *smooth pursuit eye movements* (Holzman et al., 1984; Iacono et al., 1992). This difficulty reflects underlying neurological factors and is associated with irregularities in brain activation while people visually track moving objects (Hong et al., 2005). Although it is not clear exactly why people with schizophrenia and their family members have this specific difficulty, researchers believe that it can help to identify people who are at risk to develop schizophrenia. Figure 12.2 shows the results of smooth pursuit eye movement recordings for the Genain sisters.

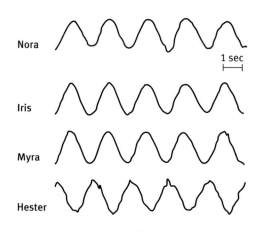

FIGURE 12.2 • Genain Sisters' Smooth Pursuit Eye Movements The Genain sisters completed this test in 1981. The results show that Nora and Hester had more irregularities in their eye movements, and they also performed more poorly on some of the neuropsychological tests, which indicates that they were more neurologically impaired.

Source: Courtesy of Dr. Deborah Levy, McLean Hospital, Belmont, MA.

Another biological marker for schizophrenia is *sensory gating* (Freedman et al., 1996), which is assessed as follows: Participants hear two clicks, one immediately after the other. Normally, the brain responds less strongly to the second click than to the first. However, people with schizophrenia and their first-degree relatives don't show the normal large drop in the brain's response to the second click. This has been interpreted as a manifestation of the difficulties that people with schizophrenia can have in filtering out unimportant stimuli.

A third type of biological marker for schizophrenia has been reported by researchers who performed careful analyses of home movies of children who were later diagnosed with schizophrenia (Grimes & Walker, 1994; Walker et al., 1993). They found that children who went on to develop schizophrenia were different from their siblings: They made more involuntary movements, such as writhing or excessive movements of the tongue, lips, or arms. This tendency for involuntary movement was particularly evident from birth to age 2 but could be seen even through adolescence in people who later developed the disorder (Walker et al., 1994). Moreover, those who displayed more severe movements of this type later developed more severe symptoms of schizophrenia (Neumann & Walker, 1996).

The child in this photo went on to develop schizophrenia. Notice the child's unusual hand postures (indicating involuntary movement). Studies of home movies of children who later developed schizophrenia revealed many such involuntary movements, particularly of the tongue, lips, or arms.

Walker © 1994. Used by permission of Oxford University Press.

Neural Communication

Schizophrenia is likely to involve a complex interplay of many brain systems, neurotransmitters, and hormones.

Dopamine

One neurotransmitter that is clearly involved in schizophrenia is dopamine. The *dopamine hypothesis* proposes that an overproduction of dopamine or an increase in the number or sensitivity of dopamine receptors is responsible for schizophrenia. According to this hypothesis, the excess dopamine or extra sensitivity to this neurotransmitter triggers a flood of unrelated thoughts, feelings, and perceptions. Delusions are then attempts to organize these disconnected events into a coherent, understandable experience (Kapur, 2003).

Consistent with the dopamine hypothesis, neuroimaging studies of people with schizophrenia have found abnormally low numbers of dopamine receptors in their frontal lobes (Okubo et al., 1997), as well as increased production of dopamine (possibly to compensate for the reduced numbers of receptors in the frontal lobes) in the striatum (parts of the basal ganglia that produce dopamine; Heinz, 2000). Nevertheless, research has definitively documented that the dopamine hypothesis was an oversimplification (McDermott & de Silva, 2005). Dopamine affects, and is affected by, other neurotransmitters that, in combination with the structural and functional abnormalities of various brain areas, give rise to some of the symptoms of schizophrenia (Vogel et al., 2006; Walker & Diforio, 1997).

Serotonin and Glutamate

Medications that affect serotonin levels can decrease both positive and negative symptoms in people with schizophrenia. However, this finding does not imply that serotonin levels per se are the culprit. Research studies suggest complex interactions among serotonin, dopamine, and glutamate (Andreasen, 2001). For example, serotonin has been shown to enhance the effect of glutamate, which is the most common fast-acting excitatory neurotransmitter in the brain (Aghajanian & Marek, 2000). Studies have found unusually high levels of glutamate in people with schizophrenia, particularly in the frontal lobe (Abbott & Bustillo, 2006; van Elst et al., 2005); such an excess of glutamate may disrupt the timing of neural activation in the frontal lobe, which in turn may impair cognitive activities (Lewis & Moghaddam, 2006).

Stress and Cortisol

Research findings suggest that stress can contribute to schizophrenia because stress affects the production of the hormone cortisol, which in turn affects the brain. In fact, children who are at risk for developing schizophrenia react more strongly to stress, and their baseline levels of cortisol are higher than those of other children (Walker et al., 1999). The relationship between stress, cortisol, and symptoms of schizophrenia has also been noted during adolescence, the time when prodromal symptoms often emerge: A 2-year longitudinal study of adolescents with schizotypal personality disorder found that cortisol levels—and symptoms of schizophrenia—increased over the 2 years (Walker et al., 2001). Even after adolescence, people with schizophrenia have higher levels of stress-related hormones, including cortisol (Zhang et al., 2005).

Thus, people who develop schizophrenia appear to be unusually biologically reactive to stressful events. A hypothesized mechanism for this relationship is that the biological changes and stressors of adolescence promote higher levels of cortisol, which may then affect dopamine activity. The relationship between cortisol and schizophrenia is supported by research indicating that anti-inflammatory medications (such as aspirin or other types of drugs referred to as *COX-2 inhibitors*), which indirectly reduce the levels of cortisol, reduce the symptoms of schizophrenia (Keller et al., 2013).

Effects of Estrogen

We noted earlier that when women develop schizophrenia, they often have different symptoms than men do, and they tend to function better. Such findings have led to the *estrogen protection hypothesis* (Seeman & Lang, 1990). According to this hypothesis, the hormone estrogen, which is present at higher levels in women than in men, protects against

Which of the two women pictured would have a lower risk of developing schizophrenia (or have less severe symptoms if she had the disorder), assuming all the factors are the same for both of them except age? Answer: The younger woman, because her estrogen levels are higher, which is a protective factor.

symptoms of schizophrenia via its effects on serotonin and dopamine. This protection may explain why women typically develop the disorder later in life than do men. Evidence for the estrogen protection hypothesis comes from two sources. One is the finding that women with schizophrenia who had higher levels of estrogen also had better cognitive functioning (Hoff et al., 2001). The other is the finding that constant doses of estrogen provided by a skin patch (in addition to antipsychotic medication) reduced the positive symptoms of women with severe schizophrenia more than did antipsychotic medication without supplementary estrogen (Kulkarni et al., 2008).

Genetics

Various twin, family, and adoption studies indicate that genes play a role in schizophrenia (Aberg et al., 2013; Tienari et al., 2006; Wicks et al., 2010; Wynne et al., 2006). The more genes a person shares with a relative who has schizophrenia, the higher the risk that that person will also develop schizophrenia (see Table 12.7). However, even for those who have a close relative with schizophrenia, the chance of developing the disorder is still relatively low: More than 85% of people who have one parent or one sibling (who is not a twin) with the disorder *do not* go on to develop it themselves (Gottesman & Moldin, 1998)—and this percentage is even higher for people with a grandparent, aunt, or uncle (second-degree relatives) with the disorder (Gottesman & Erlenmeyer-Kimling, 2001). Nonetheless, a family history of schizophrenia is still the strongest known risk factor for developing the disorder (Hallmayer, 2000).

If the cause of schizophrenia were entirely genetic, then when one identical twin developed the disorder, the co-twin would also develop the disorder; that is, the co-twin's risk of developing schizophrenia would be 100%. But this is not what happens; the actual risk of a co-twin's developing schizophrenia ranges from 46 to 53% (in different studies), as shown in Table 12.7.

TABLE 12.7 • Degree of Relatedness and Risk of Developing Schizophrenia

Family member(s) with schizophrenia	Risk of developing schizophrenia
First cousin	2%
Half-sibling	6%
Full sibling	9%
One parent	13%
Two parents	46%
Fraternal twin	14–17%
Identical twin	46–53%

Sources: Gottesman, 1991; Kendler, 1983.

However, identical twins have the same *predisposition* for developing schizophrenia, although only one of them may develop it. This means that even if only one twin in a pair develops the disorder, the children of both twins (the one with the disorder and the one without) have the same genetic risk of developing it. That is, both the affected and the unaffected twin transmit the same genetic vulnerability to their offspring (Gottesman & Bertelsen, 1989).

As evident from the studies of twins, genes alone do not determine whether someone will develop schizophrenia; rather, the interaction between genes and environment is crucial (Owen et al., 2011). For example, in one illustrative study, researchers tracked two groups of adopted children: those whose biological mothers had schizophrenia and those whose biological mothers did not (considered the control group). None of the adoptive parents of these children had schizophrenia, but some adoptive families were dysfunctional—and the children often experienced stress (Tienari et al., 1994, 2006). In the control group, the incidence of schizophrenia was no higher than in the general population, regardless of the characteristics of the adoptive families. In contrast, the children whose biological mothers had schizophrenia and whose adoptive families were dysfunctional were much more likely to develop schizophrenia than were the children whose biological mothers had schizophrenia but whose adoptive families were not dysfunctional. Thus, better parenting appeared to protect children who were genetically at risk for developing schizophrenia.

Psychological Factors in Schizophrenia

We have seen that schizophrenia is not entirely a consequence of brain structure, brain function, or genetics. As the neuropsychosocial approach implies, schizophrenia arises from a combination of different sorts of factors. For example, the neurocognitive deficits that plague people with schizophrenia also affect how they perceive the social world, and their perceptions affect their ability to function in that world (Sergi et al., 2006). If we understand their experiences, their behaviors may not appear so bizarre. However, not every person with schizophrenia experiences each type of difficulty we discuss in the following sections (Walker et al., 2004).

Mental Processes and Cognitive Difficulties: Attention, Memory, and Executive Functions

We've already noted problems with attention, working memory, and executive function in schizophrenia. Let's now consider how such problems may contribute to the disorder.

The difficulties with attention—specifically in being able to focus on relevant stimuli and ignore irrelevant stimuli—occur even when the person is taking medication and isn't psychotic (Cornblatt et al., 1997). This attentional problem can make it hard for people with schizophrenia to discern which stimuli are important and which aren't; such people may feel overwhelmed by a barrage of stimuli. This leads to problems in organizing what they perceive and experience, which would contribute to their difficulties with perception and memory (Sergi et al., 2006).

Another cognitive problem common to people with schizophrenia is that they often don't realize that they are having unusual experiences or behaving abnormally; this inability is referred to as a *lack of insight*. Thus, they are unaware of their disorder or the specific problems it creates for themselves and others (Amador & Gorman, 1998) and see no need for treatment (Buckley et al., 2007). In Case 12.2, psychologist Fred Frese discusses his lack of insight into his own schizophrenia and its effects.

Courtesy of Fred Frese

Psychologist Fred Frese was diagnosed with paranoid schizophrenia in 1965 when he was a Marine Corps security officer. He was hospitalized many times over the next 10 years but was able to earn a Ph.D. in psychology in 1978. Over the past 35 years, he has written about mental illness from both sides of the experience, been an advocate for the mentally ill, and served as Director of Psychology at Western Reserve Psychiatric Hospital.

CASE **12.2** • FROM THE INSIDE: Schizophrenia

Psychologist Fred Frese describes his history with schizophrenia:

I was 25 years old, and I was in the Marine Corps at the time, and served two back to back tours in the Far East, mostly in Japan. And when I came back I was a security officer in charge of a Marine Corps barracks with 144 men. And we had responsibilities for security for atomic weapons . . . and a few other duties. About 6 months into that assignment, I made a discovery—to me it was a discovery—that somehow the enemy had developed a new weapon by which they could psychologically hypnotize certain high-ranking officials. And I became very confident that I had stumbled onto this discovery. And because it was a psychological sort of thing I would share this with a person who would be likely to know most about this kind of stuff and that was the base psychiatrist. So I called him up and he agreed to see me right away, and I went down and told him about my discovery, and he listened very politely and when I got finished to get up and leave there were these two gentlemen in white coats on either side of me—either shoulder. And I often say I think one of them looked like he might be elected governor of Minnesota somewhere along the way. But they escorted me down into a seclusion padded room [sic]. And within a day or two I discovered that they had me labeled as paranoid schizophrenic. Of course I immediately recognized that the psychiatrist was under the control of the enemies with their new weapons. I spent about 5 months mostly in Bethesda, which is the Navy's major hospital, and was discharged with a psychiatric condition. However, that was my discovery that I was diagnosed with . . . schizophrenia. The way the disorder works is, I didn't have a disorder, I had "made this discovery". So it was a number of years before I came to this conclusion that there was something wrong here and I was hospitalized about ten times, almost always involuntarily . . . over about a 10-year period of time.
(WCPN, 2003).

To develop a sense of the consequences of having such cognitive difficulties, imagine the experience of a man with these deficits who tries to go shopping for ingredients for dinner. He may find himself in the supermarket, surrounded by hundreds of food items; because of his attentional problems, each item on a shelf may capture the same degree of his attention. Because of deficits in executive functioning, he loses track of why he is there—what was he supposed to buy? And if he remembers why he is there ("I need to get chicken, rice, and vegetables"), he may not be able to exercise good judgment about how much chicken to buy or which vegetables. Or, because of the combination of his cognitive deficits, he may find the whole task too taxing and leave without the dinner ingredients.

Beliefs and Attributions

Cognitive deficits that are present before symptoms occur affect what the person comes to believe. For example, because children with such cognitive deficits may do poorly in school and often are socially odd, they may be ostracized or teased by their classmates; they may then come to believe that they are inferior and proceed to act in accordance with that belief, perhaps by withdrawing from others (Beck & Rector, 2005).

In addition, if people with schizophrenia have delusional beliefs, the delusions almost always relate to themselves and their extreme cognitive distortions (e.g., "The FBI is out to get me"). These distortions influence what they pay attention to and what beliefs go unchallenged. People with schizophrenia may be inflexible in their beliefs or may jump to conclusions, and their actions based on their beliefs can be extreme (Garety et al., 2005). Moreover, they may be very confident that their (false) beliefs are true (Moritz & Woodward, 2006). For example, a man with paranoid schizophrenia might attribute a bad connection on a cell phone call to interference by FBI agents or aliens; he searches for and finds "confirming evidence" of such interference ("There's a bad connection when I call my friend and they want to listen in, but there's no static when I call for a weather report and there's no need for them to listen in"). Disconfirming evidence—that cell phone service is weak in the spot where he was standing when he made the call to his friend—is ignored (Beck & Rector, 2005).

Similarly, people with schizophrenia who have auditory hallucinations do not generally try to discover where the sounds of the hallucinations are coming from. For example, they don't check whether the radio is on or whether people are talking in the hallway. They are less likely to question the reality of an unusual experience (that is, whether it arises from something outside themselves) and so do not correct their distorted beliefs (Johns et al., 2002).

Negative symptoms can also give rise to unfounded beliefs; specifically, people who have negative symptoms generally overestimate the extent of their deficits and are particularly likely to have low expectations of themselves. Although such low expectations could indicate an accurate assessment of their abilities, research suggests that this is generally not the case. When cognitive therapy successfully addresses the negative self-appraisals of people with schizophrenia, their functioning subsequently improves (Rector et al., 2003). This finding suggests that the negative self-appraisals are distorted beliefs that became self-fulfilling prophecies (Beck & Rector, 2005).

Emotional Expression

Another psychological factor is the facial expressions of people with schizophrenia, which are less pronounced than those of people who do not have the disorder (Brozgold et al., 1998). Moreover, people with schizophrenia are less accurate than control participants in labeling the emotions expressed by faces they are shown (Penn & Combs, 2000; Schneider-Axmann et al., 2006). Part of the explanation for problems related to emotional expression may be the cognitive deficits. Because they cannot "read" nonverbal communication well, they are confused when someone's words and subsequent behavior are at odds; people with schizophrenia are likely to miss the nonverbal communication that helps most people make sense of the apparent inconsistency between what others say and what they do (Greig et al., 2004). In fact, even biological relatives of people with schizophrenia tend to have problems understanding other people's nonverbal communication (Janssen et al., 2003), which suggests that neurological factors are involved.

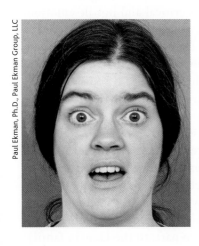   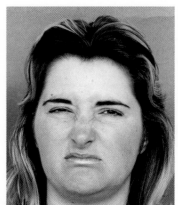

Social Factors in Schizophrenia

We've seen that schizophrenia often includes difficulty in understanding and navigating the social world. We'll now examine this difficulty in more detail and also consider the ways that economic circumstances and cultural factors can influence schizophrenia.

How do you interpret these facial expressions? Do you see surprise, anger, fear and disgust? People with schizophrenia may have difficulty accurately "reading" other people's emotional expressions, which can make social interactions confusing and lead them to respond inappropriately.

Understanding the Social World

Each of us develops a **theory of mind**—a theory about other people's mental states (their beliefs, desires, feelings) that allows us to predict how they will behave in a given situation. People with schizophrenia have difficulty with tasks that require an accurate theory of mind (Russell et al., 2006) and may thus find relating to others confusing. Because people with schizophrenia have difficulty interpreting emotional expression in others, they don't fully understand the messages people convey. The symptoms of paranoia and social withdrawal in people with schizophrenia may directly result from this social confusion (Frith, 1992). To a person with schizophrenia, other people can seem to behave in random and unpredictable ways. Thus, it makes sense that such a person tries to explain other people's seemingly odd behavior (persecutory delusion) or else tries to minimize contact with others because their behavior seems inexplicable.

Despite the fact that they were basically genetically identical, the Genain quads did not have the same level of social skills or ability to navigate the social world. For instance, Myra had markedly better social skills and social desires than her sisters, and was able to work as a secretary for most of her life—a job that requires social awareness and social skills (Mirsky et al., 2000).

Stressful Environments

Orphanages are notoriously stressful environments, which may be one reason why being raised in an orphanage increases the likelihood of later developing schizophrenia in those who are genetically vulnerable. In fact, children born to a parent with schizophrenia are more likely to develop schizophrenia as adults if they were raised in an institution than if they were raised by the parent with schizophrenia (Mednick et al., 1998).

Stress also contributes to whether someone who recovered from schizophrenia will relapse (Gottesman, 1991). Almost two thirds of people hospitalized with schizophrenia live with their families after leaving the hospital. These families can create a stressful environment for a person with schizophrenia, especially if the family is high in expressed emotion. The concept of **high expressed emotion (high EE)** is not aptly named: It's not just that the family with this characteristic expresses emotion in general but rather that family members express critical and hostile emotions and are overinvolved (for example, by frequently criticizing or nagging the patient to change his or her behavior; Wuerker et al., 2002). In fact, hospitalized patients who return to live with a family high in EE are more likely to relapse than patients who do not return to live with such a family (Butzlaff & Hooley, 1998; Kavanagh, 1992). The Genain quads certainly experienced significant stress, and their family would be considered high in EE.

The relationship between high EE and relapse of schizophrenia is a correlation. High EE probably does not cause schizophrenia in the first place, but it may contribute to a relapse. However, it is also possible that the causality goes the other way—that people whose symptoms of schizophrenia are more severe between episodes elicit more attempts by their family members to try to minimize the positive or negative symptoms. And then these behaviors lead the family to be classified as high in EE. This explanation may apply, in part, to the Genain family: Among the four sisters, Hester's symptoms were the most chronic and debilitating. She received the most physical punishment, including being whipped and having her head dunked in water, often in response to behaviors that her father wanted her to stop.

Researchers have also discovered ethnic differences in how patients perceive critical and intrusive family behaviors. Among Black American families, for instance,

Theory of mind
A theory about other people's mental states (their beliefs, desires, and feelings) that allows a person to predict how other people will react in a given situation.

High expressed emotion (high EE)
A family interaction style characterized by hostility, unnecessary criticism, or emotional overinvolvement.

behaviors by family members that focus on problem solving are associated with a better outcome for the person with schizophrenia, perhaps because such behaviors are interpreted as reflecting caring and concern (Rosenfarb et al., 2006). Thus, what is important is not the family behavior *in and of itself* but how such behavior is perceived and interpreted by family members.

Immigration

A well-replicated finding is that schizophrenia is more common among immigrants than among people who stayed in the immigrants' original country and people who are natives in the immigrants' adopted country (Cantor-Graae & Selten, 2005; Lundberg et al., 2007; Veling et al., 2012). This higher rate of schizophrenia among immigrants occurs among people who have left a wide range of countries and among people who find new homes in a range of European countries. In fact, one meta-analysis found that being an immigrant was the second largest risk factor for schizophrenia, after a family history of this disorder (Cantor-Graae & Selten, 2005). Both first-generation immigrants—that is, those who left their native country and moved to another country—and their children have relatively high rates of schizophrenia; this is especially true for immigrants and their children who have darker skin color than the natives of the adopted country, which is consistent with the role of social stressors (discrimination in particular) in schizophrenia (Selten et al., 2007). For instance, the increased rate of schizophrenia among African-Caribbean immigrants to Britain (compared to British and Caribbean residents who are not immigrants) may arise from the stresses of immigration, socioeconomic disadvantage, and racism (Jarvis, 1998). Researchers have sought to rule out potential confounds such as illness or nutrition, and have found that such factors do not explain the higher risk of schizophrenia among immigrants. Case 12.3 describes the symptoms of schizophrenia of an immigrant from Haiti to the United States.

Schizophrenia occurs more frequently among immigrants and their children than among people who live in their native country. The various stresses of the immigration process, including financial problems and discrimination, may account, at least in part, for this increased risk. The people in this photo are beginning the process of becoming legal immigrants.

CASE 12.3 • FROM THE OUTSIDE: Schizophrenia

Within a year after immigrating to the United States, a 21-year-old Haitian woman was referred to a psychiatrist by her schoolteacher because of hallucinations and withdrawn behavior. The patient was fluent in English, although her first language was Creole. Her history revealed that she had seen an ear, nose, and throat specialist in Haiti after her family doctor could not find any medical pathology other than a mild sinus infection. No hearing problems were noted and no treatment was offered. Examination revealed extensive auditory hallucinations, flat affect, and peculiar delusional references to voodoo. The psychiatrist wondered if symptoms of hearing voices and references to voodoo could be explained by her Haitian background, although the negative symptoms seem unrelated. As a result, he consulted with a Creole-speaking, Haitian psychiatrist.

The Haitian psychiatrist interviewed the patient in English, French, and Creole. Communication was not a problem in any language. He discovered that in Haiti, the patient was considered "odd" by both peers and family, as she frequently talked to herself and did not work or participate in school activities. He felt that culture may have influenced the content of her hallucinations and delusions (i.e., references to voodoo) but that the bizarre content of the delusions, extensive hallucinations, and associated negative symptoms were consistent with the diagnosis of schizophrenia.

(Takeshita, 1997, pp. 124–125)

In Case 12.3, notice that, although the women had odd and prodromal behaviors in Haiti, her full-blown symptoms did not emerge until she immigrated to the United States. These symptoms could have emerged when she got older even if she had stayed in Haiti. As compelling as single cases can be, full-scale studies—with adequate controls—must play a central role in helping us understand psychological disorders.

Economic Factors

Another social factor associated with schizophrenia is socioeconomic status. A disproportionately large number of people with schizophrenia live in urban areas and among lower economic classes (Hudson, 2005; Mortensen et al., 1999). As discussed in Chapter 2, researchers have offered two possible explanations for this association between the disorder and economic status: social selection and social causation (Dauncey et al., 1993). The **social selection hypothesis** proposes that people who are mentally ill "drift" to a lower socioeconomic level because of their impairments (and hence social selection is sometimes called *social drift*). Consider a young woman who grows up in a middle-class family and moves to a distant city after college, and where, after she graduates, she supports herself reasonably well working full time. She subsequently develops schizophrenia but refuses to return home to her family, who cannot afford to send her much money. Her income now consists primarily of meager checks from governmental programs—barely enough to cover food and housing in a poor section of town where rent is cheapest. She has drifted from the middle class to a lower class.

Another possible explanation is the **social causation hypothesis**: The daily stressors of urban life, especially for the poor, trigger mental illness in people who are vulnerable (Freeman, 1994; Hudson, 2005). Social causation would explain cases of schizophrenia in people who grew up in a lower social class. The stressors these people experience include poverty or financial insecurity, as well as living in neighborhoods with higher crime rates. Both hypotheses—social selection and social causation—may be correct.

Cultural Factors: Recovery in Different Countries

Although the prevalence of schizophrenia is remarkably similar across countries and cultures, the same cannot be said about recovery rates. Some studies report that people in developing countries have higher recovery rates than do people in industrialized countries (Kulhara & Chakrabarti, 2001), although this was not found in all earlier studies (Edgerton & Cohen, 1994; von Zerssen et al., 1990).

If the results from the more recent studies can be replicated, what might account for this cultural difference? The important distinction may not be the level of industrial and technological development of a country but how individualist its culture is. *Individualist cultures* stress values of individual autonomy and independence. In contrast, *collectivist cultures* emphasize the needs of the group, group cohesion, and interdependence. Collectivist cultures may more readily help people with schizophrenia be a part of the community at whatever level is possible. And in fact, people with schizophrenia in collectivist cultures, such as those of Japan, Hong Kong, and Singapore, have a more favorable course and prognosis than people with schizophrenia in individualist cultures such as the United States (Lee et al., 1991; Tsoi & Wong, 1991).

Social selection hypothesis
The hypothesis that people who are mentally ill "drift" to a lower socioeconomic level because of their impairments; also referred to as *social drift*.

Social causation hypothesis
The hypothesis that the daily stressors of urban life, especially as experienced by people in a lower socioeconomic class, trigger mental illness in those who are vulnerable.

The collectivist characteristics of a culture may help a patient to recover for several reasons. Consider that people in collectivist countries may:

• be more tolerant of people with schizophrenia and therefore less likely to be critical, hostile, and controlling toward them. In particular, the families of patients with schizophrenia may be more likely to have lower levels of expressed emotion, decreasing the risk of relapse and leading to better recoveries (El-Islam, 1991).

• elevate the importance of community and, in so doing, provide a social norm that creates more support for people with schizophrenia and their families.

• have higher expectations of people with schizophrenia—believing that such people can play a functional role in society—and these expectations become a self-fulfilling prophecy (Mathews et al., 2006).

Thus, collectivism—and the strong family values that usually accompany it—may best explain the better recovery rates in less developed countries, which are generally more collectivist (Weisman, 1997). In fact, for Latino patients, increasing their perception of the cohesiveness of the family is associated with fewer psychiatric symptoms and less distress (Weisman et al., 2005).

Feedback Loops in Understanding Schizophrenia

No individual risk factor by itself accounts for a high percentage of the cases of schizophrenia. Genetics, prenatal environmental events (such as maternal malnutrition and maternal illness), and birth complications that affect fetal development (neurological factors) can increase the likelihood that a person will develop schizophrenia. But many people who have these risk factors do not develop the disorder. Similarly, cognitive deficits (psychological factors) can contribute to the disorder because they create cognitive distortions, but such factors do not actually cause schizophrenia. And a dysfunctional family or another type of stressful environment (social factors), again, can contribute to, but do not cause, schizophrenia.

As usual, in determining the origins of psychopathology, no one factor reigns supreme in producing schizophrenia; instead, the feedback loops among the three types of factors provide the best explanation (Mednick et al., 1998; Tienari et al., 2006). To get a more concrete sense of the effects of the feedback loops, consider the fact that economic factors (which are social) can influence whether a pregnant woman is likely to be malnourished, which in turn affects the developing fetus (and his or her brain). And various social factors create stress (and not simply among immigrants or among children raised in an orphanage—but for all of us). The degree of stress a person experiences (a psychological factor) in turn can trigger factors that affect brain function, including increased cortisol levels. Coming full circle, as shown in Figure 12.3, these psychological and neurological factors are affected by culture (a social factor), which influences the prognosis, how people with schizophrenia are viewed, and how they come to view themselves (psychological factors).

The Genain quads illustrate the effects of these feedback loops. A family history of schizophrenia as well as prenatal complications made the quads neurologically vulnerable to developing schizophrenia. They were socially isolated, were teased by other children, and experienced physical and emotional abuse. Had the Genain quads grown up in a different home environment, with parents who treated them differently, it is possible that some of them might not have developed schizophrenia, and those who did might have suffered fewer relapses.

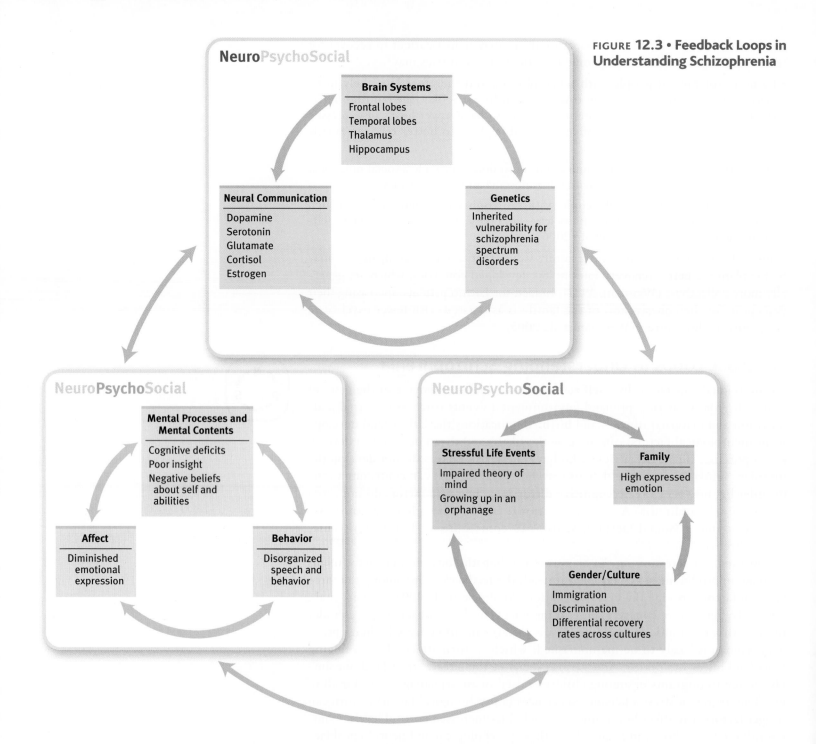

FIGURE **12.3 • Feedback Loops in Understanding Schizophrenia**

Thinking Like A Clinician

Using the neuropsychosocial approach, explain in detail how the three types of factors and their feedback loops may have led all four Genain sisters to develop schizophrenia—and formulate a hypothesis to explain why they had some different symptoms.

Treating Schizophrenia

The Genain sisters were treated at NIMH and then subsequently in hospitals, residential settings, and community mental health centers. During the early years of the quads' illness, antipsychotic medications were only just beginning to be used, and treatments that target psychological and social factors have changed substantially since then. Today, treatment for schizophrenia occurs in steps, with different symptoms and problems targeted in each step (Green, 2001):

STEP 1: When the patient is actively psychotic, first reduce the positive symptoms.

STEP 2: Reduce the negative symptoms.

STEP 3: Improve neurocognitive functioning.

STEP 4: Reduce the person's disability and increase his or her ability to function in the world.

As we'll see, the last step is the most challenging.

Targeting Neurological Factors in Treating Schizophrenia

At present, interventions targeting neurological factors generally focus on the first two steps of treatment: reducing positive and negative symptoms. However, some such treatments address on the third step: improving cognitive function.

Medication

Doctors began to use medication to treat symptoms of schizophrenia in the 1950s, with the development of the first antipsychotic (also called *neuroleptic*) medication, thorazine. Since then, various antipsychotic medications have been developed, and two general types of these medications are now used widely, each with its own set of side effects.

Traditional Antipsychotics

Thorazine (chlorpromazine) and other similar antipsychotics are dopamine antagonists, which effectively block the action of dopamine. Positive symptoms—hallucinations and delusions—diminish in approximately 75–80% of people with schizophrenia who take such antipsychotic medications (Green, 2001). Since their development, traditional antipsychotics have been the first step in treating schizophrenia. When taken regularly, they can reduce the risk of relapse: Only 25% of those who took antipsychotic medication for 1 year had a relapse, compared to 65–80% of those not on medication for a year (Rosenbaum et al., 2005). Traditional antipsychotics quickly sedate patients; above and beyond such sedation, psychotic symptoms start to improve anywhere from 5 days to 6 weeks after the patient begins to take the medication (Rosenbaum et al., 2005).

Some of the side effects of traditional antipsychotics create problems when a person takes them regularly for an extended period of time. For example, patients can develop **tardive dyskinesia**, an enduring side effect that produces involuntary lip smacking and odd facial contortions as well as other movement-related symptoms. Although tardive dyskinesia typically does not go away even when traditional antipsychotics are discontinued, its symptoms can be reduced with another type of medication. Other side effects of traditional antipsychotics include tremors, weight gain, and a sense of physical restlessness.

Atypical Antipsychotics: A New Generation

More recently, doctors have been able to use a different class of medications to treat schizophrenia: **Atypical antipsychotics** (also referred to as *second-generation antipsychotics*) affect dopamine and serotonin. Examples of atypical antipsychotics include *Risperdal* (risperidone), *Zyprexa* (olanzapine), and *Seroquel* (quetiapine). Atypical antipsychotics also can reduce comorbid symptoms of anxiety and depression (Marder et al., 1997). Like traditional antipsychotics, they decrease the likelihood of relapse, at least for 1 year (which is the longest period studied; Csernansky et al., 2002; Lauriello & Bustillo, 2001). However, any benefits of newer antipsychotics must be weighed against medical costs: Side effects include changes in metabolism that cause significant weight gain and increased risk of heart problems, and these side effects can become so severe or problematic that some people won't or shouldn't continue to use these medications (McEvoy et al., 2007). In addition, atypical antipsychotics, like traditional antipsychotics, sometimes cause tardive dyskinesia (Woods et al., 2010).

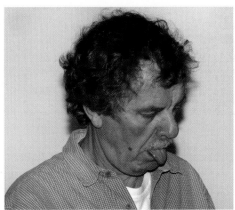

© Art Directors & TRIP/Alamy

This man is exhibiting signs of tardive dyskinesia—involuntary lip smacking and odd facial grimaces that can be an enduring side effect of long-term use of antipsychotic medication.

Tardive dyskinesia
An enduring side effect of traditional antipsychotic medications that produces involuntary lip smacking and odd facial contortions as well as other movement-related symptoms.

Atypical antipsychotics
A relatively new class of antipsychotic medications that affects dopamine and serotonin activity; also referred to as *second-generation antipsychotics*.

Either type of antipsychotic medication is considered "successful" when it significantly reduces symptoms and the side effects can be tolerated. However, sometimes medication is not successful because it isn't really given a fighting chance: Patients often stop taking their prescribed medication without consulting their doctor, which is referred to as *noncompliance*. Many people who stop taking their medication—whether in consultation with their doctor or not—cite significant unpleasant side effects as the main reason (Lieberman et al., 2005).

Discontinuing Medication

Given how often patients stop taking their medication (up to two thirds in one study; Lieberman et al., 2005), we need to understand the effects of discontinuing medication: When people with schizophrenia discontinue their medication, they are more likely to relapse. One study found that among those who were stable for over 1 year and then stopped taking their medication, 78% had symptoms return within 1 year after that, and 96% had symptoms return after 2 years (Gitlin et al., 2001). And even up to 5 years after discharge, patients who had been hospitalized for schizophrenia and then discontinued their medication were five times as likely to relapse as those who didn't (Robinson et al., 1999).

Brain Stimulation: ECT

Electroconvulsive therapy (ECT) was originally used to treat schizophrenia but generally was not successful. Although currently used only infrequently to treat this disorder, a course of ECT may be administered to people with active schizophrenia who are not helped by medications. ECT may reduce symptoms, but its effects are short lived; furthermore, "maintenance" ECT—that is, regular although less frequent treatments—may be necessary for long-term improvement (Keuneman et al., 2002). Three of the Genain sisters—Nora, Iris, and Hester—received numerous sessions of ECT before antipsychotic medication was available. After ECT, their symptoms improved at least somewhat but, usually within months, if not weeks, worsened again until the symptoms were so bad that a course of ECT was again administered (Mirsky et al., 1987; Rosenthal, 1963).

In experimental studies with small numbers of patients, transcranial magnetic stimulation (TMS) appears to decrease hallucinations, at least in the short term (Brunelin, Poulet et al., 2006; Poulet et al., 2005). However, not all studies have found this positive effect (McNamara et al., 2001; Saba et al., 2006). The specifics of ECT and TMS administration are discussed in Chapter 5.

Targeting Psychological Factors in Treating Schizophrenia

Treatments for schizophrenia that target psychological factors address three of the four general treatment steps; they (1) reduce psychotic symptoms through cognitive-behavior therapy (CBT); (2) reduce negative symptoms of schizophrenia through CBT; and (3) improve neurocognitive functioning (and quality of life) through psychoeducation and motivational enhancement (Tarrier & Bobes, 2000).

Cognitive-Behavior Therapy

CBT addresses the patient's symptoms and the distress they cause. Treatment may initially focus on understanding and managing symptoms, by helping patients to:

• learn to distinguish hallucinatory voices from people actually speaking,

• highlight the importance of taking effective medications,

• address issues that interfere with compliance, and

• develop more effective coping strategies.

When a therapist uses CBT to address problems arising from delusions, he or she does not try to challenge the delusions themselves but instead tries to help the patient move forward in life, despite these beliefs. For instance, if a man believes that the CIA is after him, the CBT therapist might focus on the effects of that belief: What if the CIA were following him? How can he live his life more fully, even if this were the case?

Patient and therapist work together to implement new coping strategies and monitor medication compliance. In fact, such uses of CBT not only improve overall functioning (Step 4) but also can decrease positive (Pfammatter et al., 2006; Rector & Beck, 2002a, 2002b) and negative symptoms (Grant et al., 2012; Turkington et al., 2006).

Treating Comorbid Substance Abuse: Motivational Enhancement

Because many people with schizophrenia also abuse drugs or alcohol, recent research has focused on developing treatments for people with both schizophrenia and substance use disorders; motivational enhancement is one facet of such treatment. As we discussed in Chapter 10, patients who receive motivational enhancement therapy develop their own goals, and then clinicians help them meet those goals. For people who have both schizophrenia and substance use disorders, one goal might be to take medication regularly (Lehman et al., 1998). For people who have two disorders, treatment that targets both of them appears to be more effective than treatment that targets one or the other alone (Barrowclough et al., 2001).

Targeting Social Factors in Treating Schizophrenia

Treatments that target social factors address three of the four general treatment steps: They identify early warning signs of positive and negative symptoms through family education and therapy; when necessary, such treatments involve hospitalizing people who cannot care for themselves or are at high risk of harming themselves or others. These treatments also reduce certain negative symptoms through social skills training and improve overall functioning (and quality of life) through community-based interventions. Community-based interventions include work-related and residential programs (Tarrier & Bobes, 2000).

Family Education and Therapy

By the time a person is diagnosed with schizophrenia, family members typically have struggled for months—or even years—to understand and help their loved one. Psychoeducation for family members can provide practical information about the illness and its consequences, how to recognize early signs of relapse, how to recognize side effects of medications, and how to manage crises that may arise. Such education can decrease relapse rates (McWilliams et al., 2012; Pfammatter et al., 2006). In addition, family-based treatments may provide emotional support for family members (Dixon et al., 2000). Moreover, family therapy can create more adaptive family interaction patterns:

> In 1989, my older sister and I joined Mom in her attempts to learn more about managing symptoms of her illness. Mom's caseworkers met with us every 6 to 8 weeks for over 8 years. Mom, who had never been able to admit she had an illness, now told us that she did not want to die a psychotic. This was one of the many positive steps that we observed in her recovery. Over the years, other family members have joined our group. . . . With the help of the treatment team, we can now respond *effectively* to Mom's symptoms and identify stress-producing situations that, if left unaddressed, can lead to episodes of hospitalization. With Mom's help we have identified the different stages of her illness. In the first stage, we listed withdrawal, confusions, depression, and sleeping disorder. Fifteen years ago when mom reported her symptoms to me, I just told her everything would be okay. Today we respond immediately. For 8 years she has maintained a low dosage of medications, with increases during times of stress.
> (Sundquist, 1999, p. 620)

Family therapy can also help high EE families change their pattern of interaction, so that family members are less critical of the patient, which can lower the relapse rate from 75% to 40% (Leff et al., 1990).

Group Therapy: Social Skills Training

Given the prominence of social deficits in many people with schizophrenia, clinicians often try to improve a patient's social skills. Social skills training usually occurs in a group setting, and its goals include learning to "read" other people's behaviors, learning

Substance abuse is a common problem for people with schizophrenia. In such cases, motivational enhancement may be part of a treatment program.

Community care
Programs that allow mental health care providers to visit patients in their homes at any time of the day or night; also known as *assertive community treatment.*

what behaviors are expected in particular situations, and responding to others in a more adaptive way. Social skills training teaches these skills by breaking complex social behaviors into their components: maintaining eye contact when speaking to others, taking turns speaking, learning to adjust how loudly or softly to speak in different situations, and learning how to behave when meeting someone new. The leader and members of a group take turns role-playing these different elements of social interaction.

In contrast to techniques that focus specifically on behaviors, cognitive techniques focus on group members' irrational beliefs about themselves, their knowledge of social conventions, the beliefs that underlie their interactions with other people, and their ideas about what others may think; such beliefs often prevent people with schizophrenia from attempting to interact with others. Each element of the training is repeated several times, to help patients overcome their neurocognitive problems when learning new material.

Inpatient Treatment

Short-term or long-term hospitalization is sometimes necessary for people with schizophrenia. A short-term hospital stay may be required when someone is having an acute schizophrenic episode (that is, is actively psychotic, extremely disorganized, or otherwise unable to care for himself or herself) or is suicidal or violent. The goal is to reduce symptoms and stabilize the patient. Once hospitalized, the patient will probably receive medication and therapy. The patient may participate in various therapy groups, such as a group to discuss side effects of medications. Once the symptoms are reduced to the point where appropriate self-care is possible and the risk of harm is minimized, the patient will probably be discharged. Long-term hospitalization may occur only when treatments have not significantly reduced symptoms and the patient needs full-time intensive care.

Legal measures have made it difficult to hospitalize people against their will (Torrey, 2001). Although these tougher standards protect people from being hospitalized simply because they do not conform to common social conventions (see Chapter 1), they also have downsides: People who have a disorder that *by its very nature* limits their ability to comprehend that they have an illness may not receive appropriate help until their symptoms have become so severe that they are dangerous to themselves or others, or they are unable to take care of themselves adequately. Early intervention for ill adults who do not want help but do not realize that they are ill is legally almost impossible today. This issue will be discussed in more detail in Chapter 16.

Minimizing Hospitalizations: Community-Based Interventions

In Chapter 1 we noted that asylums and other forms of 24-hour care, treatment, and containment for those with severe mental illness have met with mixed success over the past several hundred years. Traditionally, people with chronic schizophrenia were likely to end up in such institutions. However, beginning in the 1960s, with the widespread use of antipsychotic medications, the U.S. government established the social policy of *deinstitutionalization*—trying to help those with severe mental illness live in their communities rather than remain in the hospital. Not everyone thinks that deinstitutionalization is a good idea, at least not in the way it has been implemented. The main problem is that the patients were sent out into communities without adequate social, medical, or financial support. It is now common in many U.S. cities to see such people on street corners, begging for money or loitering, with no obvious social safety net.

The good news is that some communities have adequately funded programs to help people with chronic schizophrenia (and other chronic and debilitating psychological disorders) live outside institutions. **Community care** (also known as *assertive community treatment*) programs allow mental health staff to visit patients in their homes at any time of the day or night (Mueser, Bond, et al., 1998). Patients who receive such community care report greater satisfaction with their care; however, such treatment may not necessarily lead to better outcomes (Killaspy et al., 2006).

© America/Alamy

Deinstitutionalization was mandated without adequate funding for communities to take care of people with schizophrenia and other serious mental illnesses. One result has been increased poverty and homelessness among people with such disorders.

Residential Settings

Some people with schizophrenia may be well enough not to need hospitalization but are still sufficiently impaired that they cannot live independently or with family members. Alternative housing for such people includes a variety of supervised residential settings. Some of these patients live in highly supervised housing, in which a small number of people live with a staff member. Residents take turns shopping for and making meals. They also have household chores and attend house meetings to work out the normal annoyances of group living. Those able to handle somewhat more responsibility may live in an apartment building filled with people of similar abilities, with a staff member available to supervise any difficulties that arise. As patients improve, they transition to less supervised settings.

Vocational Rehabilitation

Various types of programs assist people with schizophrenia to acquire job skills; such programs are specifically aimed at helping patients who are relatively high functioning but have residual symptoms that interfere with functioning at, or near, a normal level. For instance, patients who are relatively less impaired may be part of *supported employment* programs, which place people in regular work settings and provide an onsite job coach to help them adjust to the demands of the job itself and the social interactions involved in having a job (Bustillo et al., 2001). Examples of supported employment jobs might include work in a warehouse, packaging items for shipment or restocking items in an office or a store ("Project search," 2006). Those who are more impaired may participate in *sheltered employment*, working in settings that are specifically designed for people with emotional or intellectual problems who cannot hold a regular job. For example, people in such programs may work in a hospital coffee shop or create craft items that are sold in shops.

What predicts how well a patient with schizophrenia can live and work in the world? Researchers have found that a person's ability to live and perhaps work outside a hospital is associated with a specific cognitive function: his or her ability to use working memory (Dickinson & Coursey, 2002).

Details of the treatment that the Genain sisters received are only available for their time at NIMH in the 1950s, when less was known about the disorder and how to treat it effectively. During the sisters' stay at NIMH, therapists tried to reduce the parents' level of emotional expressiveness and criticism; however, such attempts do not appear to have been effective. After their departure from NIMH, the sisters lived in a variety of settings: Nora lived first with Mrs. Genain and subsequently in a supervised apartment with Hester. Iris was less able to live independently and lived in the hospital, in supervised residential settings, or at home with Mrs. Genain; she died in 2002. Myra, long divorced, generally lived independently; after Mrs. Genain died in 1983, Myra moved into her mother's house with her older son. Like Iris, Hester spent many years in the hospital and then with Mrs. Genain. She lived with Nora in a supervised apartment until she died in 2003 (Mirsky & Quinn, 1988; Mirsky et al., 1987, 2000).

Feedback Loops in Treating Schizophrenia

To be effective, treatment for people with schizophrenia must employ interventions that induce interactions among neurological, psychological, and social factors (see Figure 12.4). When successful, medication (treatment targeting neurological factors) can reduce the positive and negative symptoms and even help improve cognitive functioning. These changes in neurological and psychological factors, in turn, make it possible for social treatments, such as social skills training and vocational rehabilitation, to be effective. If patients are not psychotic and have improved cognitive abilities, they can better learn social and vocational skills that allow them to function more effectively and independently. Moreover, to the extent that the patients function more effectively, they may experience less stress, which reduces cortisol levels—which in turn affects neurological functioning. And such improved neurological functioning can further facilitate cognitive functioning, which helps the patients live in the social world.

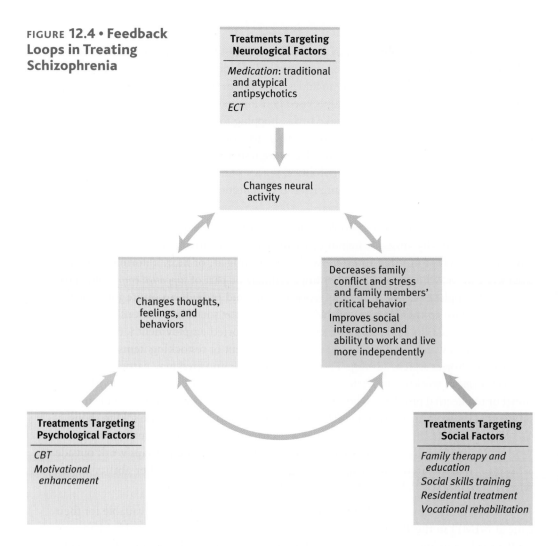

FIGURE **12.4 • Feedback Loops in Treating Schizophrenia**

Thinking Like A Clinician

Suppose you are designing a comprehensive treatment program for people with schizophrenia. Although you'd like to provide each program participant with many types of services, budgetary constraints mean that you have to limit the types of treatments your program offers. Based on what you have read about the treatment of schizophrenia, what would you definitely include in your treatment program, and why? Also list the types of treatment you'd like to include if you had a bigger budget.

☐ SUMMING UP

What Are Schizophrenia and Other Psychotic Disorders?

- According to DSM-5, schizophrenia is characterized by two or more positive and negative symptoms, at least one of which must be hallucinations, delusions, or disorganized speech; these symptoms must be present for a minimum of 6 months and must significantly impair functioning.

- Positive symptoms are delusions, hallucinations, disorganized speech, and disorganized behavior.

- Negative symptoms include diminished emotional expression, avolition, alogia, anhedonia, and asociality.

- Research studies have indicated that cognitive deficits accompany symptoms of schizophrenia. Such deficits include

problems with attention, working memory, and executive functioning.

- Symptoms of schizophrenia can appear to overlap with those of other disorders, notably mood disorders and substance use disorders.

- Schizophrenia, schizophreniform disorder, brief psychotic disorder, schizoaffective disorder, and delusional disorder, along with schizotypal personality disorder, are part of a spectrum of schizophrenia-related disorders.

- Schizophrenia occurs in approximately 1% of the population worldwide. Men have an earlier onset of the disorder than do women.

- Up to 15% of people with schizophrenia commit suicide. People with this disorder who behave violently are most likely to have a comorbid disorder that is associated with violent behavior, such as a substance use disorder. People with schizophrenia are more likely than other people to be victims of violence.

Understanding Schizophrenia

- Various neurological factors are associated with schizophrenia:
  - Abnormalities in brain structure and function have been found in the frontal and temporal lobes, the thalamus, and the hippocampus. Moreover, certain brain areas do not appear to interact with each other properly. People with schizophrenia are likely to have enlarged ventricles.
  - These brain abnormalities appear to be a result of, at least in some cases, maternal malnourishment, illness during pregnancy, and/or fetal oxygen deprivation.

  - Schizophrenia is associated with abnormalities in dopamine, serotonin, and glutamate activity, as well as a heightened stress response and increased cortisol production.
  - Genetics is still the strongest predictor that a given person will develop schizophrenia. Genetics alone, though, cannot explain why a given person develops the disorder.

- Psychological factors that are associated with schizophrenia and shape the symptoms of the disorder include:
  - cognitive deficits (in attention, working memory, and executive functioning);
  - dysfunctional beliefs and attributions;
  - difficulty conveying and recognizing emotions.

- Various social factors are also associated with schizophrenia:
  - an impaired theory of mind, which makes it difficult to understand other people's behavior, which in turn means that other people's behavior appears to be unpredictable;
  - a stressful home environment, such as being raised in an orphanage or by a parent with schizophrenia;

  - the stresses of immigration—particularly for people likely to encounter discrimination—and economic hardship; and
  - the individualist nature of the culture, which is associated with lower recovery rates for people with schizophrenia.

Treating Schizophrenia

- Treatments that target neurological factors include traditional and atypical antipsychotics:
  - When these medications do not significantly decrease positive symptoms, ECT may be used;
  - Many patients discontinue medication because of side effects. People who stop taking medication are much more likely to relapse.

- Treatments that target psychological factors include CBT to help patients better manage their psychotic symptoms and motivational enhancement to decrease comorbid substance abuse.

- Treatments that target social factors include family education, family therapy to improve the interaction pattern among family members, and group therapy to improve social skills.

Key Terms

Schizophrenia (p. 366)

Positive symptoms (p. 366)

Hallucinations (p. 367)

Delusions (p. 367)

Catatonia (p. 368)

Negative symptoms (p. 369)

Flat affect (p. 369)

Avolition (p. 369)

Executive functions (p. 370)

Schizophreniform disorder (p. 373)

Brief psychotic disorder (p. 373)

Schizoaffective disorder (p. 373)

Delusional disorder (p. 373)

Prodromal phase (p. 377)

Active phase (p. 377)

Biological marker (p. 382)

Theory of mind (p. 388)

High expressed emotion (high EE) (p. 388)

Social selection hypothesis (p. 390)

Social causation hypothesis (p. 390)

Tardive dyskinesia (p. 393)

Atypical antipsychotics (p. 393)

Community care (p. 396)

More Study Aids

For additional study aids related to this chapter, including quizzes to make sure you've retained everything you've learned and a Student Video Activity exploring one woman's struggle with hallucinations due to schizophrenia, go to: www.worthpublishers.com/launchpad/rkabpsych2e.

Barbara Chase/Creatas/Jupiter Images/Getty Images

CHAPTER **13**

Personality Disorders

achel Reiland wrote a memoir called *Get Me Out of Here*, about living with a personality disorder. In the opening of the book, Reiland remembers Cindy, the golden-haired grade-school classmate who was their teacher's favorite. At the end of a painting class, Cindy's painting was beautiful, with distinctive trees. Rachel's painting looked like a "putrid blob." Rachel then recounts:

> I seethed with jealousy as Mrs. Schwarzheuser showered Cindy with compliments. Suddenly, rage overwhelmed me. I seized a cup of brown paint and dumped half of it over my picture. Glaring at Cindy, I leaned across the table and dumped the other half over her drawing. I felt a surge of relief. Now Cindy's picture looked as awful as mine.
>
> "Rachel!" Mrs. Schwarzheuser yelled. "You've completely destroyed Cindy's beautiful trees. Shame on you. You are a *horrible* little girl. The paint is everywhere—look at your jeans. . . ."
>
> I felt my body go numb. My legs, arms, and head were weightless. Floating. It was the same way I felt when Daddy pulled off his belt and snapped it. Anticipation of worse things to come—things I had brought on myself because I was different.
>
> "In all my years, I've never seen a child like you. You are the *worst* little girl I've ever taught. Go sit in the corner, immediately."
>
> Shame on Rachel. That language I understood. And deserved. . . .
> Mrs. Schwarzheuser was right. I was horrible.

(2004, pp. 1–2)

REILAND'S ACTIONS TOWARD CINDY that day were troublesome and troubling, but many children have episodes of feeling intensely jealous and angry toward others and then "act out" those feelings. Such episodes don't necessarily indicate that a child, or the adult he or she grows up to be, has a disorder.

But some children and teenagers exhibit problems with relationships that persist into adulthood—problems that interfere with an aspect of daily life, such as work or family life. These problems have existed for so long that they seem to be a part of who the person is, a part of his or her personality. Such persistent problems are central to **personality disorders**, a category of psychological disorders characterized by an enduring pattern of inflexible and maladaptive thoughts, emotional responses, interpersonal functioning, and impulse control problems that arise across a range of situations and lead to distress or dysfunction.

Diagnosing Personality Disorders
What Are Personality Disorders?
Understanding Personality Disorders in General
Treating Personality Disorders: General Issues

Odd/Eccentric Personality Disorders
Paranoid Personality Disorder
Schizoid Personality Disorder
Schizotypal Personality Disorder
Treating Odd/Eccentric Personality Disorders

Dramatic/Erratic Personality Disorders
Antisocial Personality Disorder
Borderline Personality Disorder
Understanding Borderline Personality Disorder
Histrionic Personality Disorder
Narcissistic Personality Disorder

Fearful/Anxious Personality Disorders
Avoidant Personality Disorder
Dependent Personality Disorder
Obsessive-Compulsive Personality Disorder
Understanding Fearful/Anxious Personality Disorders
Treating Fearful/Anxious Personality Disorders

Follow-up on Rachel Reiland

Personality disorders
A category of psychological disorders characterized by an enduring pattern of inflexible and maladaptive thoughts, emotional responses, interpersonal functioning, and impulse control problems that arise across a range of situations and lead to distress or dysfunction.

Tiziana Nanni/Getty Images. Photo for illustrative purposes only; any individual depicted is a model.   **401**

Rachel Reiland

Diagnosing Personality Disorders

It's not unusual for children to act out in school, as Rachel Reiland did. But as children get older, they mature. In Reiland's case, she went on to do well academically in high school and college, but in the nonacademic areas of her life, things didn't go as well. While in high school, she developed anorexia nervosa. In high school and college, she frequently got drunk and had numerous casual sexual encounters. Moreover, she hadn't yet grown out of the maladaptive childhood patterns of behavior that got her into so much trouble.

In her mid-20s, Reiland unintentionally became pregnant when dating a man named Tim. They decided to marry and did so, even though she had a miscarriage before the wedding. They then had two children, first Jeffrey and 2 years later, Melissa. It seemed that Reiland had straightened out her life and that her childhood problems were behind her.

She temporarily stopped working while the children were young. When they were 2 and 4 years old, Reiland found herself overwhelmed—alternately angry and needy. One day during this period of her life, her husband called to say he'd be late at work and wouldn't be home until 6 or 7 P.M. She responded by asking whether his coming home late was her fault. Reiland recounts their ensuing exchange:

> "I didn't say it's your fault, honey. It's just that . . . well, I've got to get some stuff done." I began to twist the phone cord around my finger, tempted to wrap it around my neck.
>
> "I'm a real pain in the ass, aren't I? You're pissed, aren't you?" Tim tried to keep his patience, but I could still hear him sigh.
>
> "Please, Rachel. I've got to make a living."
>
> "Like I don't do anything around here? Is that it? Like I'm some kind of stupid housewife who doesn't do a god-damned thing? Is that what you're getting at?" Another sigh.
>
> "Okay. Look, sweetheart, I've got to do this presentation this afternoon because it's too late to cancel. But I'll see if I can reschedule the annuity guy for tomorrow. I'll be home by four o'clock, and I'll help you clean up the house."
>
> "No, no, no!"
>
> I was beginning to cry.
>
> "What now?"
>
> "God, Tim. I'm such an idiot. Such a baby. I don't do a thing around this house, and here I am, wanting you to help me clean. I must make you sick."
>
> "You don't make me sick, sweetheart. Okay? You don't. Look, I'm really sorry, but I've got to go."
>
> The tears reached full strength. The cry became a moan that turned to piercing screams. *Why in the hell can't I control myself? The man has to make a living. He's such a good guy; he doesn't deserve me—no one should have to put up with me!*
>
> "Rachel? Rachel? Please calm down. Please! Come on. You're gonna wake up the kids; the neighbors are gonna wonder what in the hell is going on. Rachel?"
>
> "[Screw you!] Is that all you care about, what the *neighbors* think? [Screw] you, then. I don't need you home. I don't want you home. Let this [damn] house rot; let the [damn] kids starve. I don't give a shit. And I don't need your shit!"
>
> (2004, pp. 11–12)

When Tim responds by saying he's going to cancel all his appointments and can be home in a few minutes, she sobs, "You must really hate me . . . you really hate me, don't you?" (Reiland, 2004, p. 12).

Reiland's behavior seems extreme, but is it so extreme that it indicates a personality disorder, or is it just an emotional outburst from a mother of young children who is feeling overwhelmed? In order to understand the nature of Reiland's problems and see how a clinician determines whether a person's problems merit a diagnosis of personality disorder, we must focus on *personality*, and contrast normal versus abnormal variations of personality.

When you describe your roommate or new friends to your parents, you usually describe his or her **personality**—enduring characteristics that lead a person to behave in relatively predictable ways across a range of situations. Similarly, when you imagine how family members will react to bad news you're going to tell them, you are probably basing your predictions of their reactions on your sense of their personality characteristics. Such characteristics—or *personality traits*—are generally thought of as being on a continuum, with a trait's name, such as "interpersonal warmth," at one end of the continuum and its opposite, such as "standoffishness," at other end of the continuum. Each person is unique in terms of the combination of his or her particular personality traits—and how those traits affect his or her behavior in various situations.

In this section we examine in more detail the DSM-5 category of personality disorders and then the specific personality disorders that it contains.

What Are Personality Disorders?

Some people consistently and persistently exhibit extreme versions of personality traits, such as being overly conscientious and rule-bound or, like Reiland, being overly emotional and quick to anger. In some cases, extreme traits are also inflexible—the person cannot easily control or modulate them. Such extreme and inflexible traits can become maladaptive and cause distress or dysfunction—characteristics of a personality disorder. In the following we examine the definition of personality disorders more closely.

As Table 13.1 notes, personality disorders reflect persistent thoughts, feelings, and behaviors that are significantly different from the norms in the person's culture. Specifically, these differences involve the ABCs of psychological functioning:

- *affect*, which refers to the range, intensity, and changeability of emotions and emotional responsiveness and the ability to regulate emotions;

- *behavior*, which refers to the ability to control impulses and interactions with others; and

- *cognition* (mental processes and mental contents), which refers to the perceptions and interpretations of events, other people, and oneself.

The differences in the ABCs of psychological functioning are relatively inflexible and persist across a range of situations, which highlights how central these maladaptive personality traits are to the way the person functions. This rigidity across situations in turn leads to distress or impaired functioning, as it did for Sarah, in Case 13.1. To be diagnosed with a personality disorder, the maladaptive traits typically should date back at least to early adulthood and should not primarily arise from a substance-related or medical disorder or another psychological disorder (American Psychiatric Association, 2013).

We can now answer the question of whether Reiland's difficulties were more than those of an overwhelmed mother of young children: Her problems indicate that she has a personality disorder.

Personality disorders are characterized by a pattern of inflexible and maladaptive thoughts, feelings, and behaviors that arise across a range of situations. This woman might be diagnosed with a personality disorder if she consistently got angry with little provocation and had difficulty controlling her anger in a variety of settings.

TABLE 13.1 • DSM-5 General Diagnostic Criteria for a Personality Disorder

A. An enduring pattern of inner experience and behavior that deviates markedly from the expectations of the individual's culture. This pattern is manifested in two (or more) of the following areas:

  1. Cognition (i.e., ways of perceiving and interpreting self, other people, and events).

  2. Affectivity (i.e., the range, intensity, lability, and appropriateness of emotional response).

  3. Interpersonal functioning.

  4. Impulse control.

B. The enduring pattern is inflexible and pervasive across a broad range of personal and social situations.

C. The enduring pattern leads to clinically significant distress or impairment in social, occupational, or other important areas of functioning.

D. The pattern is stable and of long duration, and its onset can be traced back at least to adolescence or early adulthood.

E. The enduring pattern is not better explained as a manifestation of consequence of another mental disorder.

F. The enduring pattern is not attributable to the physiological effects of a substance (e.g., a drug of abuse, a medication) or another medical condition (e.g., head trauma).

Personality
Enduring characteristics that lead a person to behave in relatively predictable ways across a range of situations.

CASE 13.1 • FROM THE OUTSIDE: Personality Disorder

Sarah, a 39-year-old single female, originally requested therapy at . . . an outpatient clinic, to help her deal with chronic depression and inability to maintain employment. She had been unemployed for over a year and had been surviving on her rapidly dwindling savings. She was becoming increasingly despondent and apprehensive about her future. She acknowledged during the intake interview that her attitude toward work was negative and that she had easily become bored and resentful in all of her previous jobs. She believed that she might somehow be conveying her negative work attitudes to prospective employers and that this was preventing them from hiring her. She also volunteered that she detested dealing with people in general. . . .

Sarah had a checkered employment history. She had been a journalist, a computer technician, a night watch person, and a receptionist. In all of these jobs she had experienced her supervisors as being overly critical and demanding, which she felt caused her to become resentful and inefficient. The end result was always her dismissal or her departure in anger. Sarah generally perceived her co-workers as being hostile, unfair, and rejecting. However, she would herself actively avoid them, complaining that they were being unreasonable and coercive when they tried to persuade her to join them for activities outside of work. For example, she would believe that she was being asked to go for drinks purely because her co-workers wanted her to get drunk and act foolishly. Sarah would eventually begin to take "mental health" days off from work simply to avoid her supervisors and colleagues.

(Thomas, 1994, p. 211)

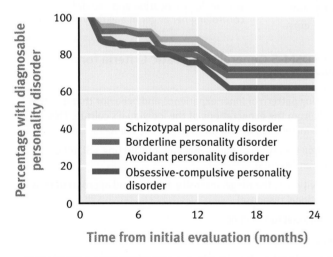

FIGURE 13.1 • Stability of Personality Disorders Within 2 years of being diagnosed with a personality disorder, around one quarter to one third of the people in one study no longer met the diagnostic criteria for 12 consecutive months (Grilo et al., 2004). This finding indicates that personality disorders are not as stable as once thought.

Source: Grilo et al., 2004. For more information see the Permissions section.

Although personality disorders are considered to be relatively stable, at least from adolescence into adulthood, research suggests that (as shown in Figure 13.1) these disorders are not as enduring as once thought (Clark, 2009; Zanarini et al., 2005); rather, symptoms can improve over time for some people (Grilo et al., 2004; Johnson et al., 2000).

As a group, people with personality disorders obtain less education (Torgersen et al., 2001) and are more likely never to have married or to be separated or divorced (Torgersen, 2005) than people who don't have such disorders. Personality disorders are associated with suicide: Among people who die by suicide, about 30% apparently had a personality disorder; among people who attempt suicide, about 40% apparently have a personality disorder (American Psychiatric Association Work Group on Suicidal Behaviors, 2003).

Assessing Personality Disorders

Personality disorders can be difficult to diagnose in a first interview, largely because patients may not be aware of the symptoms. In many cases, people who have a personality disorder are so familiar with their lifelong pattern of emotional responses, behavioral tendencies, and mental processes and contents that the ways in which this pattern is maladaptive may not be apparent to them. In fact, most people with a personality disorder identify *other* people or situations as being the problem, not something about themselves.

Given that many people with personality disorders are not aware of the nature of their problems, clinicians may diagnose a patient with a personality disorder based both on what the patient says and on patterns in the way he or she says it (Skodol, 2005). For instance, Sarah, in Case 13.1, probably had specific complaints about her coworkers, but the key information lies in the *pattern of her complaints*—in her claim that most of her coworkers, in various companies, were hostile and rejecting. Multiple patient visits may be required to identify such a pattern and to diagnose a personality disorder, more such visits than is usually needed to diagnose other types of disorders. And more than with other diagnoses, clinicians must make inferences about the patient in order to diagnose a personality disorder. However, clinicians

must be careful not to assume that their inferences are correct without further corroboration (Skodol, 2005).

To help assess personality disorders, clinicians and researchers may interview the patient and also have patients complete personality inventories or questionnaires. To diagnose a personality disorder, the clinician may also talk with someone in the patient's life, such as a family member—who often describes the patient very differently than does the patient (Clark, 2007; Clifton et al., 2004). The picture that emerges of someone with a personality disorder is a pattern of chronic *interpersonal* difficulties or chronic problems with *self*, such as a feeling of emptiness (Livesley, 2001).

According to DSM-5, when clinicians assess personality disorders, they should take into account the person's culture, ethnicity, and social background. For instance, a woman who appears to be unable to make any decisions independently (even about what to make for dinner) and constantly defers to family members might have a personality disorder. However, for some immigrants, this pattern of behavior may be within a normal range for their ethnic or religious group. When immigrants have problems that are related to the challenges of adapting to a new culture or that involve behaviors or a worldview that is typical of people with their background, a personality disorder shouldn't be diagnosed. A clinician who isn't familiar with a patient's background should get more information from other sources.

Although a person may exhibit a pattern of problems that indicates a personality disorder, clinicians should take into consideration the person's ethnicity, social background, and culture. If the person's patterns of thoughts, feelings, and behaviors are characteristic of people from his or her background, a diagnosis of a personality disorder is not warranted.

DSM-5 Personality Clusters

DSM-5 lists 10 personality disorders, grouped into three clusters. Each cluster of personality disorders shares a common feature. **Cluster A personality disorders** are characterized by odd or eccentric behaviors that have elements related to those of schizophrenia. **Cluster B personality disorders** are characterized by emotional, dramatic, or erratic behaviors that involve problems with emotional regulation. **Cluster C personality disorders** are characterized by anxious or fearful behaviors. We will discuss the specific disorders in each cluster as we progress through this chapter. Table 13.2 provides an overview of facts about personality disorders in general.

In the subsequent discussions of individual personality disorders, you may notice that adding the prevalence rates for the various disorders gives a higher total than the overall prevalence rate of 14% listed in Table 13.2 on the next page. This mathematical discrepancy is explained by the high comorbidity, also noted in the table: Half of people who have a personality disorder will be diagnosed with at least one other personality disorder (and, in some cases, with more than one other personality disorder).

Criticisms of the DSM-5 Category of Personality Disorders

The category of personality disorders, as defined in DSM-5 (and in DSM-IV), has been criticized on numerous grounds. One criticism is that DSM-5 treats personality disorders as categorically distinct from normal personality (Widiger & Lowe, 2008). In contrast, most psychological researchers currently view normal personality and personality disorders as being on continua. In DSM-5 terms, two people might differ only slightly in the degree to which they exhibit a personality trait, but one person would be considered to have a personality disorder and the other person would not. A related criticism is that the DSM-5 criteria for personality disorders create an arbitrary cutoff on the continuum between normal and abnormal (Morey et al., 2012; Widiger & Trull, 2007). In part to address this point, newly created for DSM-5 is an alternative model of personality disorders that allows mental health professionals to rate how impaired patients are in terms of various dimensions (American Psychiatric Association, 2013).

Cluster A personality disorders
Personality disorders characterized by odd or eccentric behaviors that have elements related to those of schizophrenia.

Cluster B personality disorders
Personality disorders characterized by emotional, dramatic, or erratic behaviors that involve problems with emotional regulation.

Cluster C personality disorders
Personality disorders characterized by anxious or fearful behaviors.

TABLE **13.2** • An Overview: Personality Disorder Facts at a Glance

Prevalence

- Researchers estimate that up to 14% of Americans will have at least one personality disorder over the course of their lives (Grant, Hasin, et al., 2004; Lenzenweger, 2006).

Comorbidity

- Up to 75% of those with a personality disorder will also be diagnosed with another type of psychological disorder (Dolan-Sewell et al., 2001; Lenzenweger, 2006). Common comorbid disorders are mood disorders, anxiety disorders, and substance use disorders (Grant, Stinson et al., 2004; Johnson et al., 2006b; Lenzenweger, 2006).
- Approximately 50% of people with a personality disorder will be diagnosed with at least one other personality disorder (Skodol, 2005).

Onset

- The DSM-5 diagnostic criteria require that symptoms are present by young adulthood.
- For one personality disorder—antisocial personality disorder—a diagnostic criterion requires that symptoms are present before age 15.

Course

- Symptoms of personality disorders are often relatively stable, but they may fluctuate or improve as people go through adulthood.

Gender Differences

- Specific personality disorders have gender differences in prevalence, but there is no such difference across all personality disorders.

Source: Unless otherwise noted, American Psychiatric Association, 2000.

Another criticism pertains to the clusters, which were organized by superficial commonalities. Research does not necessarily support the organization of personality disorders into these clusters (Sheets & Craighead, 2007). Moreover, some of the specific personality disorders are not clearly distinct from each other (Trull et al., 2012).

In addition, some personality disorders are not clearly distinct from other disorders in DSM (Harford et al., 2013; Widiger & Trull, 2007). The diagnostic criteria for avoidant personality disorder, for example, overlap considerably with those for social phobia, as we'll discuss in the section on avoidant personality disorder. Similarly, critics point out that the general criteria for personality disorders (see Table 13.1) could apply to other disorders, such as persistent depressive disorder and schizophrenia (Oldham, 2005).

The process by which the DSM-IV/DSM-5 criteria were determined is another target of criticism. The minimum number of symptoms needed to make a diagnosis, as well as the specific criteria, aren't necessarily supported by research results (Widiger & Trull, 2007). Moreover, different personality disorders require different numbers of symptoms and different levels of impairment (Livesley, 2001; Skodol, 2005; Westen & Shedler, 2000).

The high comorbidity among personality disorders invites another criticism: that the specific personality disorders do not capture the appropriate underlying problems, and so clinicians must use more than one diagnosis to describe the types of problems exhibited by patients (Widiger & Mullins-Sweatt, 2005). In fact, the most frequently diagnosed personality disorder is a nonspecific personality disorder that we'll call *other personality disorder* in this chapter; this disorder is often diagnosed along with an additional personality disorder (Hopwood et al., 2012; Verheul et al., 2007; Verheul & Widiger, 2004). As with other categories of disorders, the nonspecific "other" diagnosis is used when a patient's symptoms cause distress or impair functioning but do not fit the criteria for any of the disorders within the relevant category—in this case, one of the 10 specific personality disorders.

Understanding Personality Disorders in General

At one point, Reiland became impatient with her 4-year-old son Jeffrey and "lost it." She slapped and then cursed him. As he cried, she commanded him to stop crying. He didn't, and she proceeded to spank him so hard that it hurt her hand:

> The reality slowly sunk in. I had beaten my child. Just as my father had beaten his. Just as I swore I never ever would. A wave of nausea rose within me. *I was just like my father.* Even my children would be better off without me. There was no longer any reason to stay alive. (Reiland, 2004, p. 19)

Reiland's realization was relatively unusual for someone with a personality disorder: She recognized in this instance that *she* had created a problem—*she* had done something wrong, although her father never recognized his responsibility. He too was quick to anger and hit her and her siblings. Do personality disorders run in families? If so, to what extent do genes and environment lead to personality disorders? How might personality disorders arise?

Neurological Factors in Personality Disorders: Genes and Temperament

Perhaps the most influential neurological factor associated with personality disorders is genes (Cloninger, 2005; Paris, 2005). Researchers have not produced evidence that genes underlie specific personality disorders, but they have shown that genes clearly influence *temperament*, which is the aspect of personality that reflects a person's typical affective state and emotional reactivity (see Chapter 2). Temperament, in turn, plays a major role in personality disorders. Genes influence temperament via their effects on brain structure and function, including neurotransmitter activity.

It is possible that the genes that affect personality traits can predispose some people to develop a personality disorder (South & DeYoung, 2013). For instance, some people are genetically predisposed to seek out novel and exciting stimuli, such as those associated with stock trading, race car driving, or bungee jumping, whereas other people are predisposed to become easily overstimulated and habitually prefer low-key, quiet activities, such as reading, writing, or walking in the woods. Such differences in temperament are the foundation on which different personality traits are built—and, at their extremes, temperaments can give rise to inflexible personality traits that are associated with personality disorders. Examples include a novelty seeker (temperament) who compulsively seeks out ever more exciting activities (inflexible behavior pattern), regardless of the consequences, and a person who avoids overstimulation (temperament) and turns down promotions because the new position would require too many activities that would be overstimulating (inflexible behavior pattern).

Reiland may well have inherited a tendency to develop certain aspects of temperament, which increased the likelihood of her behaving like her father in certain types of situations. However, her genes and her temperament don't paint the whole picture; psychological and social factors also influenced how she thought, felt, and behaved.

🅾 GETTING THE PICTURE

Temperament—which is partly genetic—can make a person vulnerable to specific personality disorders. Which of these two situations—driving a motorcycle fast in traffic or being nervous about being in a room full of strangers—is more likely to signal a personality disorder associated with novelty seeking? Answer: Driving a motorcycle fast in traffic.

Psychological Factors in Personality Disorders: Temperament and the Consequences of Behavior

Although an infant may be born with a genetic bias to develop certain temperamental characteristics, these characteristics—and personality traits—evolve through experience in interacting with the world. Personality traits involve sets of learned behaviors and emotional reactions to specific stimuli; what is learned is in part shaped by the consequences of behavior, including how other people respond to the behavior. The mechanisms of operant conditioning are at work whenever a person experiences consequences of behaving in a certain way: If the consequences are positive, the behavior is reinforced (and hence likely to recur); if the consequences are negative, the behavior is punished (and hence likely to be dampened down).

The consequences of behaving in a specific way not only affect how temperament develops but also influence a person's expectations, views of others, and views of self (Bandura, 1986; Farmer & Nelson-Gray, 2005). Based on what they have learned, people can develop maladaptive and faulty beliefs, which in turn lead them to misinterpret other people's words and actions. These (mis)interpretations reinforce their views of themselves and the world in a pervasive self-fulfilling cycle, biasing what they pay attention to and remember, which in turn reinforces their views of self and others (Beck et al., 2004; Linehan, 1993; Pretzer & Beck, 2005). The consequences of behavior can thereby lead to pervasive dysfunctional beliefs—which can form the foundation for some types of personality disorders. For instance, at one point Rachel Reiland states her belief that her husband "doesn't deserve me—no one should have to put up with me!" (Reiland, 2004, p. 11). This belief leads her to be hypervigilant for any annoyance her husband expresses or implies. She's likely to misinterpret his actions and comments as confirming her belief that she is undeserving, and she then alternates lashing out in anger with groveling in grief.

Social Factors in Personality Disorders: Insecurely Attached

Another factor that influences whether a person will develop a personality disorder is *attachment style*—the child's emotional bond and way of interacting with (and thinking about) his or her primary caretaker (Bowlby, 1969; see Chapter 1). The attachment style established during childhood often continues into adulthood, affecting how the person relates to others (Waller & Shaver, 1994). Most children develop a *secure attachment style* (Schmitt et al., 2004), which is characterized by a positive view of their own worth and of the availability of others. However, a significant minority of children develop an *insecure attachment style*, which can involve a negative view of their own worth, the expectation that others will be unavailable, or both (Bretherton, 1991). People with personality disorders are more likely to have an insecure attachment style (Crawford et al., 2006; Lahti et al., 2012).

People can develop an insecure attachment style for a variety of reasons, such as childhood abuse (sexual, physical, or verbal), neglect, or inconsistent discipline (Johnson et al., 2005; Johnson, Cohen, et al., 2006; Paris, 2001). Reiland's father abused her physically and verbally, alternating the abuse with bouts of neglect. However, such social risk factors may lead to psychopathology in general, not personality disorders in particular (Kendler et al., 2000). A single traumatic event does not generally lead to a personality disorder (Rutter, 1999).

Feedback Loops in Understanding Personality Disorders

As with other kinds of psychological disorders, no one factor reigns supreme as the underlying basis of personality disorders. People must have several adverse factors—neurological, psychological, or social—to develop a personality disorder, and social adversity will have the biggest effect on those who are neurologically vulnerable (Paris, 2005).

© plainpicture /Martin Langer

Insecure attachment to a parent can make a child vulnerable to developing a personality disorder. Insecure attachment can arise from abuse, neglect, or inconsistent discipline. For instance, the adult in this photo is neglecting the child by not getting up to help him/her.

ONLINE

Consider the fact that people with personality disorders tend to have parents with psychological disorders (Bandelow et al., 2005; Siever & Davis, 1991). The parents' dysfunctional behavior clearly creates a stressful social environment for children, and the children may model some of their parents' behavior (psychological factor). Moreover, they may also inherit a predisposition toward a specific temperament (neurological factor). Similarly, chronic stress and abuse, such as Reiland experienced, affects brain structure and function (neurological factor; Teicher et al., 2003), which in turn affects mental processes (psychological factor).

The specific personality disorder a person develops depends on his or her temperament and family members' reactions to that temperament (Linehan, 1993; Rutter & Maughan, 1997). For instance, children with difficult temperaments—such as those that lead a person to be extremely passive—tend to have more conflict with their parents and peers (Millon, 1981; Rutter & Quinton, 1984), which leads them to experience a higher incidence of physical abuse and social rejection. These children may then come to expect (psychological factor) to be treated poorly by others (social factor). Thus, social factors can amplify underlying temperaments and traits so that they subsequently form the foundation for a personality disorder (Caspi et al., 2002; Paris, 1996, 2005).

Treating Personality Disorders: General Issues

People with disorders other than personality disorders often say that their problems "happened" to them—the problems are overlaid on their "usual" self. They want the problems to get better so that they can go back to being that usual self, and thus they seek treatment. In contrast, people with personality disorders don't see the problem as overlaid on their usual self; by its very nature, a personality disorder is integral to the way such people function in the world. And so people with these disorders are less likely to seek treatment unless they also have another type of disorder—in which case, they typically seek help for the other disorder.

Addressing and reducing the symptoms of a personality disorder can be challenging because patients' entrenched maladaptive beliefs and behaviors can lead them to be poorly motivated during treatment and not inclined to collaborate with the therapist. Treatment for personality disorders generally lasts longer than does treatment for other psychological disorders. However, there is little research on treatment for most personality disorders. The next section summarizes what is known about treating personality disorders in general; later in the chapter we discuss treatments for the specific personality disorders for which there are substantial research results.

We don't know why this couple has ended up on this couch, but we do know that treating people who have personality disorders can be challenging because patients may not see themselves as having a problem.

Targeting Neurological Factors in Personality Disorders

Treatments for personality disorders that target neurological factors include antipsychotics, antidepressants, mood stabilizers, or other medications. Generally, however, such medications are only effective for symptoms of certain other disorders (such as anxiety) and are not very helpful for symptoms of personality disorders per se (Paris, 2005, 2008). Nevertheless, some of these medications may reduce temporarily some symptoms (Paris, 2003; Soloff, 2000).

Targeting Psychological Factors in Personality Disorders

Both cognitive-behavior therapy (CBT) and psychodynamic therapy have been used to treat personality disorders. Both therapies focus on core issues that are theorized to give rise to the disorders; they differ in terms of the inferred core issues. Psychodynamic therapy addresses unconscious drives and motivations, whereas CBT addresses maladaptive views of self and others and negative beliefs that give rise to the problematic feelings, thoughts, and behaviors of the personality disorder (Beck et al., 2004). CBT is intended to increase the patient's sense of self-efficacy and mastery and to modify the negative, unrealistic beliefs that lead to maladaptive behaviors.

In addition, because people with personality disorders may not be motivated to address the problems associated with the disorder, treatment may employ motivational enhancement strategies to help patients identify goals and become willing to work with the therapist. Treatment that targets psychological factors has been studied in depth only for borderline personality disorder; we examine such treatment in the section discussing that personality disorder.

Targeting Social Factors in Personality Disorders

Guidelines for treating personality disorders also stress the importance of the relationship between therapist and patient, who must collaborate on the goals and methods of therapy (Critchfield & Benjamin, 2006). In fact, the relationship between patient and therapist may often become a focus of treatment as the patient's typical style of interacting with others plays out in the therapy relationship. This relationship often provides an opportunity for the patient to become aware of his or her interaction style and to develop new ways to interact with others (Beck et al., 2004).

In addition, family education, family therapy, or couples therapy can provide a forum for family members to learn about the patient's personality disorder and to receive practical advice about how to help the patient—for example, how to respond when the patient gets agitated or upset. Family therapy can provide support for families as they strive to change their responses to the patient's behavior, thereby changing the reinforcement contingencies (Ruiz-Sancho et al., 2001).

Moreover, interpersonal or group therapy can highlight and address the maladaptive ways in which patients relate to others. Therapy groups also provide a forum for patients to try out new ways of interacting (Piper & Ogrodniczuk, 2005). For example, if a man thinks and acts as if he is better than others, the comments and responses of other group members can help him understand how his haughty and condescending way of interacting creates problems for him.

Thinking Like A Clinician

V.J. was 50 years old, never married, and had never been very successful professionally. He was a salesman and changed companies every few years, either because he was passed over for a promotion and quit or because he didn't like the new rules—or the way that the rules were enforced—at the job. He'd been in love a few times, but it had never worked out. He chalked it up to difficulty finding the right woman. He had some "friends" who were really people he'd known over the years and saw occasionally. Most of his positive social interactions happened in chat rooms or texts.

Is there anything about the information presented that would lead you to wonder whether V.J. might have a personality disorder? If so, what was the information? (And if not, why not?) Based on what you have read, how should mental health clinicians go about determining whether V.J. might have a personality disorder or whether his personality traits are in the normal range?

▢ Odd/Eccentric Personality Disorders

Cluster A personality disorders involve odd or eccentric behaviors and ways of thinking. Patients who have a Cluster A personality disorder are also likely to develop another psychological disorder that involves psychosis, such as schizophrenia or delusional disorder (Oldham et al., 1995; see Chapter 12). The three personality disorders in this cluster—paranoid, schizoid, and schizotypal personality disorders—are on the less severe end of the spectrum of schizophrenia-related disorders; of these three, only schizotypal personality disorder is considered to be on the *schizophrenia spectrum* in DSM-5. We'll examine each of the three Cluster A personality disorders in turn and then discuss what is known about the factors that give rise to them and about how to treat them. Rachel Reiland did not exhibit symptoms characteristic of this group of personality disorders.

Paranoid Personality Disorder

The essential feature of **paranoid personality disorder** is persistent and pervasive mistrust and suspiciousness, accompanied by a bias to interpret other people's motives as hostile (see Table 13.3). Someone with this personality disorder may distrust coworkers and family members and may even (incorrectly) believe that his or her partner is having an affair, despite the partner's denials. The patient's accusations create a difficult situation for the partner who is not having an affair but can't "prove" it to the patient's satisfaction.

People with paranoid personality disorder are better able to evaluate whether their suspicions are based on reality than are people with paranoid schizophrenia. Moreover, the sources of their perceived threats are not likely to be strangers or bizarre types of signals (such as radio waves), as is the case with paranoid schizophrenia, but rather known individuals (Skodol, 2005). If the symptoms arise while a person is using substances or during a psychotic episode of schizophrenia or a mood disorder, then paranoid personality disorder is not diagnosed. As you'll see in Case 13.2, about Ms. X., it may not be immediately apparent from a patient's report what is "true" and what is a paranoid belief.

TABLE 13.3 • DSM-5 Diagnostic Criteria for Paranoid Personality Disorder

A. A pervasive distrust and suspiciousness of others such that their motives are interpreted as malevolent, beginning by early adulthood and present in a variety of contexts, as indicated by four (or more) of the following:

1. Suspects, without sufficient basis, that others are exploiting, harming, or deceiving him or her.

2. Is preoccupied with unjustified doubts about the loyalty or trustworthiness of friends or associates.

3. Is reluctant to confide in others because of unwarranted fear that the information will be used maliciously against him or her.

4. Reads hidden demeaning or threatening meanings into benign remarks or events.

5. Persistently bears grudges (i.e., is unforgiving of insults, injuries, or slights).

6. Perceives attacks on his or her character or reputation that are not apparent to others and is quick to react angrily or to counterattack.

7. Has recurrent suspicions, without justification, regarding fidelity of spouse or sexual partner.

B. Does not occur exclusively during the course of schizophrenia, a bipolar disorder or depressive disorder with psychotic features, or another psychotic disorder and is not attributable to the physiological effects of another medical condition.

Reprinted with permission from the Diagnostic and Statistical Manual of Mental Disorders, Fifth Edition, (Copyright ©2013). American Psychiatric Association. All Rights Reserved.

CASE 13.2 • FROM THE OUTSIDE: Paranoid Personality Disorder

Ms. X. is a middle-aged African-American woman who has lived in the area all of her life. She began seeking treatment . . . after her family members had noted that, to them, she was acting strangely. Ms. X. stated that she believed that her family members were out to make her crazy and convince her neighbors of the same. She stated the reason for this was because she was the "darkest one" in her family. Ms. X. was a fair-skinned black woman. She was born to a dark-skinned black mother and a white father. She was the darkest sibling of her family. Because of this, she felt that her family had treated her and her mother unjustly. She stated that as a child, she was instructed to look after her lighter-skinned older sisters, whom the family held in high regard. She stated that she did not complete high school because she had to care for her older sister's children. She described that she would be instructed to "cook and clean" for them, as though she were their slave, and be available to them whenever they needed her. . . . Because of this, [she claimed] she was not able to have a social life. After Ms. X. married, she continued to receive the same treatment from her sisters. She stated that her children were treated unfairly, because of their darker skin as well. . . . As she got older, Ms. X. stated that her sisters, who were part of the elite society, would "embarrass" her while around their socialite friends. She believed this to be due to her darker skin color. She stated that her sisters convinced her neighbors that she was a "bad" person, and because of this, her neighbors would do "evil" things to spite her.

Ms. X. met with her sisters to discuss this issue. When confronted, the sisters denied that they were treating her negatively. They acknowledged that their skin was fairer than hers but denied that they were treating her in such a way. They believed that their sister was "delusional." Ms. X. refused to believe her sisters, and when confronted with the idea that her family was not in any way harming her, she would shift the conversation to another topic.

(Paniagua, 2001, pp. 135–136)

Paranoid personality disorder
A personality disorder characterized by persistent and pervasive mistrust and suspiciousness, accompanied by a bias to interpret other people's motives as hostile.

For most people, this kitchen scene would be an unpleasant but infrequent conflict between parent and child. But for people with paranoid personality disorder, such conflict may not be occasional. People with paranoid personality disorder distrust others and tend to interpret other people's remarks or behaviors as having malevolent intent. They are likely to maintain these interpretations despite evidence to the contrary.

As was the case with Ms. X.'s refusal to believe her sisters, people with paranoid personality disorder cannot readily be persuaded that their paranoid beliefs do not reflect reality. However, such people can recognize that there are multiple ways to interpret other people's reactions and behaviors.

Although less obvious in the case of Ms. X., other common characteristics of people with this personality disorder include a strong desire to be self-sufficient and in control, which stems from a distrust of others, and a tendency to be critical of others and blame them for problems that arise. People with this disorder may also be unable to accept criticism *from* others. In response to stress, they may become briefly psychotic, with their paranoid beliefs reaching delusional proportions.

In addition, people with paranoid personality disorder tend to be difficult to get along with because their suspiciousness frequently leads them to be secretive or "cold," argumentative, complaining, or to bear a grudge. These behaviors often elicit hostility or anger in others, which then confirms the person's suspicious beliefs. Table 13.4 provides additional information about paranoid personality disorder.

To summarize, paranoid personality disorder involves a chronic pattern of suspiciousness and mistrust that often creates interpersonal problems because of the guarded ways in which the patient interacts with others. Little is known about the specific factors that give rise to this personality disorder.

TABLE 13.4 • Paranoid Personality Disorder Facts at a Glance

Prevalence

• Between 2.3% and 4.5% of the general population is estimated to have paranoid personality disorder.

Comorbidity

• People with paranoid personality disorder may also have another personality disorder, usually another Cluster A (odd/eccentric) personality disorder (schizoid or schizotypal) or narcissistic, avoidant, or borderline personality disorder.

Onset

• Symptoms can first appear in childhood or adolescence, when the person appears hypersensitive, has difficulties with peers, and has odd thoughts or fantasies or uses language unconventionally.

Course

• The symptoms of paranoid personality disorder are relatively stable over time (Seivewright et al., 2002).

Gender Differences

• Based on surveys in the general population, there is no clear gender difference in the prevalence of paranoid personality disorder. However, among people with this disorder, men are more likely than women to come to the attention of mental health professionals (Morey, Alexander, & Boggs, 2005).

Source: Unless otherwise noted, the source is American Psychiatric Association, 2000, 2013.

Schizoid Personality Disorder

Schizoid personality disorder is characterized by a restricted range of emotions in social interactions and few—if any—close relationships (American Psychiatric Association, 2013). Table 13.5 lists the DSM-5 diagnostic criteria. People with schizoid personality disorder often lack social skills and may not pick up on or understand the normal social cues required for smooth social interactions—for instance, they may return someone's smile with a stare. Such difficulties with social cues can lead to problems in jobs that require interacting with others; people with this personality disorder generally are not interested in developing personal relationships.

In addition, people with schizoid personality disorder may react passively to adverse events. They may seem to lack initiative and drift through life. People with this disorder appear to be emotionless and often don't express anger, even when provoked. And, in fact, they often report that they rarely experience strong emotions such as joy and anger (Livesley, 2001). In contrast to those with paranoid personality disorder, people with schizoid personality disorder generally aren't suspicious and are indifferent to other people (Skodol, 2005). Case 13.3 on the next page describes one woman with schizoid personality disorder, and Table 13.6 presents some additional facts about schizoid personality disorder.

In sum, schizoid personality disorder involves a chronic pattern of limited emotional expression and diminished social understanding, few relationships, and little desire for relationships.

TABLE 13.5 • DSM-5 Diagnostic Criteria for Schizoid Personality Disorder

A. A pervasive pattern of detachment from social relationships and a restricted range of expression of emotions in interpersonal settings, beginning by early adulthood and present in a variety of contexts, as indicated by four (or more) of the following:

1. Neither desires nor enjoys close relationships, including being part of a family.
2. Almost always chooses solitary activities.
3. Has little, if any, interest in having sexual experiences with another person.
4. Takes pleasure in few, if any, activities.
5. Lacks close friends or confidants other than first-degree relatives.
6. Appears indifferent to the praise or criticism of others.
7. Shows emotional coldness, detachment, or flattened affectivity.

B. Does not occur exclusively during the course of schizophrenia, a bipolar disorder or depressive disorder with psychotic features, or another psychotic disorder and is not attributable to the physiological effects of another medical condition.

Reprinted with permission from the Diagnostic and Statistical Manual of Mental Disorders, Fifth Edition, (Copyright ©2013). American Psychiatric Association. All Rights Reserved.

TABLE 13.6 • Schizoid Personality Disorder Facts at a Glance

Prevalence

• Approximately 3% of the general population is estimated to have schizoid personality disorder (Grant, Hasin, et al., 2004).

Comorbidity

• Common comorbid personality disorders are the other Cluster A (odd/eccentric) personality disorders and avoidant personality disorder. Half of the people diagnosed with schizoid personality disorder will also be diagnosed with schizotypal personality disorder (McGlashan et al., 2000).

Onset

• Those who develop schizoid personality disorder were often socially isolated underachievers who were teased by their classmates as children and adolescents.

Course

• Schizoid personality disorder is relatively stable over time (Seivewright et al., 2002).

Gender Differences

• This personality disorder tends to be diagnosed more often in men than in women.
• Men with this personality disorder are often more impaired than their female counterparts.

Source: Unless otherwise noted, the source is American Psychiatric Association, 2013.

Schizoid personality disorder
A personality disorder characterized by a restricted range of emotions in social interactions and few—if any—close relationships.

Schizotypal personality disorder
A personality disorder characterized by eccentric thoughts, perceptions, and behaviors, in addition to having very few close relationships.

TABLE 13.7 • DSM-5 Diagnostic Criteria for Schizotypal Personality Disorder

A. A pervasive pattern of social and interpersonal deficits marked by acute discomfort with, and reduced capacity for, close relationships as well as by cognitive or perceptual distortions and eccentricities of behavior, beginning by early adulthood and present in a variety of contexts, as indicated by five (or more) of the following:

1. Ideas of reference (excluding delusions of reference).

2. Odd beliefs or magical thinking that influences behavior and is inconsistent with subcultural norms (e.g., superstitiousness, belief in clairvoyance, telepathy, or "sixth sense"; in children and adolescents, bizarre fantasies or preoccupations).

3. Unusual perceptual experiences, including bodily illusions.

4. Odd thinking and speech (e.g., vague, circumstantial, metaphorical, overelaborate, or stereotyped).

5. Suspiciousness or paranoid ideation.

6. Inappropriate or constricted affect.

7. Behavior or appearance that is odd, eccentric, or peculiar.

8. Lack of close friends or confidants other than first degree relatives.

9. Excessive social anxiety that does not diminish with familiarity and tends to be associated with paranoid fears rather than negative judgments about self.

B. Does not occur exclusively during the course of schizophrenia, a bipolar disorder or depressive disorder with psychotic features, another psychotic disorder, or autism spectrum disorder.

Note: Cognitive-perceptual symptoms are in green, interpersonal symptoms are in blue, and disorganized symptoms are in red.

CASE 13.3 • FROM THE OUTSIDE: Schizoid Personality Disorder

A 33-year-old woman with three children became a cause of concern to social services because of her limited caring abilities. Investigations led to two of her children being taken into [foster] care and, after a further period of 2 years, her third child was also taken away. At this time she was referred to psychiatric services because she was felt to be isolated from society and had such poor social function. It proved very difficult to engage her as she would go to great lengths to avoid contact and it was uncertain to what extent she required compulsory treatment. Eventually, she was admitted under a compulsory order after threatening a community worker. . . . After discharge from [the] hospital she was transferred to supportive housing but resented the frequent monitoring of her progress, which she perceived as intrusion and tried to avoid contact. . . . She functioned better with no contact and so a transfer was agreed to a supported [apartment] where she would be left undisturbed apart from one visit each week from a support worker and a full review every 6 months. After 2 years she remains well on no treatment and is very happy with her life, which despite little interaction with other people now includes regular contact with her family.

(Tyrer, 2002, p. 470)

Schizotypal Personality Disorder

People with **schizotypal personality disorder** have eccentric thoughts, perceptions, and behaviors, in addition to having very few close relationships, like those with schizoid personality disorder (American Psychiatric Association, 2013).

What Is Schizotypal Personality Disorder?

According to the DSM-5 diagnostic criteria, schizotypal personality disorder has nine symptoms (see Table 13.7). These symptoms can be organized into three distinct groups (Calkins et al., 2004; Raine, 2006; Reynolds et al., 2000) although DSM-5 does not do so:

- *Cognitive-perceptual*

  ○ (Criterion A1) *ideas of reference*, in which the person interprets ordinary events to have particular meaning for him or her (a milder form of referential delusions, described in Chapter 12);

  ○ (A2) odd beliefs or magical thinking, in which the person believes that he or she has control over external events, as occurs with superstitious beliefs;

  ○ (A3) unusual perceptual experiences, such as feeling "dislocated" from parts of one's body or hearing a voice on the radio murmuring one's name;

  ○ (A5) suspiciousness or paranoid ideation, which consists of paranoid beliefs that are less entrenched than paranoid delusions.

- *Interpersonal*

  ○ (A6) inappropriate or constricted affect, such as showing only a narrow range of emotions;

  ○ (A8) lack of close friends because of a preference for being alone;

  ○ (A9) excessive social anxiety that arises because of a general suspiciousness about other people.

- *Disorganized*

  ○ (A4) odd thinking and speech, such as being overly vague or elaborate or using words idiosyncratically (as in "My coworker isn't talkable");

  ○ (A7) behavior or appearance that is odd or eccentric, such as wearing mismatched or unkempt clothing, avoiding eye contact, or being unable to make conversation.

IK, in Case 13.4, had symptoms that represent all three groups highlighted in Table 13.7. This personality disorder is on the schizophrenia spectrum (see Chapter 12). Additional facts about schizotypal personality disorder are listed in Table 13.8.

CASE 13.4 • FROM THE OUTSIDE: Schizotypal Personality Disorder

IK is a 33-year-old man who had both schizotypal personality disorder and obsessive-compulsive disorder (OCD) for at least 17 years. His schizotypal symptoms included poor interpersonal relatedness, ideas of reference (not delusional), social anxiety, unusual perceptual experiences (such as seeing things in the periphery, but not there when viewed directly), constricted affect, and some paranoid ideation (in particular with regard to police officers, but his father reported that this was unrealistic).

IK's social skills deficits were primarily conversation skills, inappropriate affect, poor assertion skills, and lack of eye contact with the therapist and family members. He was also prone to aggressive outbursts in the home, often breaking objects due to frustration.

(McKay & Neziroglu, 1996, pp. 190–191)

TABLE 13.8 • Schizotypal Personality Disorder Facts at a Glance

Prevalence
• Approximately 0.6–4.6% of the general population has schizotypal personality disorder.

Comorbidity
• Common comorbid personality disorders include other Cluster A personality disorders (McGlashan et al., 2000), as well as borderline, avoidant, and obsessive-compulsive personality disorders (Raine, 2006).
• Common comorbid psychological disorders are major depressive disorder, social phobia, and panic disorder (Raine, 2006).

Onset
• Symptoms emerge by early adulthood.
• In childhood and adolescence, symptoms may include social isolation and social anxiety, academic underachievement, hypersensitivity, odd fantasies and thoughts, and idiosyncratic use of language.

Course
• Although schizotypal personality disorder most commonly is stable over time, symptoms may improve for some people (Fossati et al., 2003). In fact, for almost one quarter of patients, symptoms improve to the point where they no longer meet all the diagnostic criteria (Grilo et al., 2004).
• Among other patients with this disorder, the opposite is true: A small percentage go on to develop schizophrenia or another psychotic disorder (Grilo et al., 2004).

Gender Differences
• Schizotypal personality disorder is slightly more common among men than women.

Source: Unless otherwise noted, the source is American Psychiatric Association, 2013.

Schizotypal personality disorder differs from schizoid personality disorder in that the former includes cognitive-perceptual symptoms—such as IK's ideas of reference and seeing things with peripheral vision that could not be seen with a direct gaze—and odd behavior. Nevertheless, research suggests that these two disorders may not be distinct from each other; half of those with schizoid personality disorder are also diagnosed with schizotypal personality disorder (McGlashan et al., 2000). Some researchers propose that schizoid personality disorder may simply be a subtype of schizotypal personality disorder (Raine, 2006).

Understanding Schizotypal Personality Disorder

We focus on understanding schizotypal personality disorder, the most researched of the Cluster A personality disorders. As noted in Chapter 12, schizotypal personality disorder includes less intense manifestation of features of schizophrenia: delusions and unusual perceptions.

Neurological factors that are associated with schizophrenia are associated with schizotypal personality disorders, such as maternal illness or malnourishment during pregnancy.

AJ Photo/BSIP/SuperStock

Neurological Factors in Schizotypal Personality Disorder

Most of the neurological factors that contribute to schizophrenia have also been found to contribute to schizotypal personality disorder: genes and prenatal environment, such as maternal illness and malnourishment, and birth complications (Raine, 2006; Torgersen et al., 2000). In both disorders, researchers have documented similar abnormalities in brain structure and in neural function (activity of dopamine, serotonin, and glutamate). These abnormalities are generally not as severe in people with schizotypal personality disorder as in people with schizophrenia (Buchsbaum et al., 2002; Siever & Davis, 2004).

Genes also play a role: The rates of schizotypal personality disorder are higher among family members of people with schizophrenia than among the general population (Siever & Davis, 2004; Tienari et al., 2003).

Psychological Factors in Schizotypal Personality Disorder

Like people with schizophrenia, those with schizotypal personality disorder tend to have specific cognitive deficits. These include problems with attention (distinguishing relevant from irrelevant stimuli), memory, and executive function (used in problem solving, planning, and judgment) (Voglmaier et al., 2000). According to Beck and colleagues (2004), schizotypal personality disorder is unusual among the personality disorders in that the primary distortions are in mental processes (e.g., perceptions) rather than in mental contents. However, problems with social interactions can arise from the cognitive deficits: People with this personality disorder tend to have an impaired *theory of mind*—and thus have difficulty recognizing emotions in others (Waldeck & Miller, 2000) and in taking another's point of view or recognizing another's mental state (Langdon & Coltheart, 2001; Miller & Lenzenweger, 2012). Although people with schizotypal personality disorder have cognitive deficits, they generally have better cognitive skills than do people with schizophrenia (Trestman et al., 1995).

People with this personality disorder also often behave in unusual ways, which can make other people more likely to mistreat them, intentionally or not. Such mistreatment may thus confirm their beliefs about themselves and other people. People with this disorder also pay attention to, remember, and interpret stimuli in ways that are consistent with their beliefs—and that thus reinforce their isolation from, and avoidance of, other people.

Social Factors in Schizotypal Personality Disorder

Certain social factors appear to play a relatively large role in the onset of schizotypal personality disorder, in contrast to their lesser role in schizophrenia. These social factors include physical abuse or neglect, insecure attachment to parents, and discrimination (Berenbaum et al., 2008; Raine, 2006; Wilson & Constanzo, 1996)—all stressful events. In fact, some of these social factors may be related to each other: Insecure attachment may, at least in part, result from abuse or neglect. Children who develop schizotypal personality disorder are more likely to have experienced trauma, abuse, and neglect than are those who develop most other personality disorders (Yen et al., 2002). These negative childhood experiences influence patients' views of other people as untrustworthy and having malevolent motives.

Feedback Loops in Understanding Schizotypal Personality Disorder

With schizotypal personality disorder, as with schizophrenia, neuropsychosocial factors create feedback loops. For instance, early social stressors such as neglect and trauma can contribute to brain abnormalities, particularly if a genetic or other neurological vulnerability exists before birth. The neurological changes, in turn, contribute to disturbances in cognitive and emotional functioning (Raine, 2006). These cognitive and emotional disturbances then can lead to problems in social interactions, which in turn produces stress (Skodol, Gunderson et al., 2002)—and the stress can then affect neurological functioning. Moreover, trauma, neglect, and insecure attachment may give rise to a paranoid attributional style and discomfort with others (Raine, 2006).

Treating Odd/Eccentric Personality Disorders

Very little research has been conducted to evaluate treatments for odd/eccentric personality disorders. People with any of these sorts of personality disorders tend not to be interested in treatment and, if urged or coerced into it, are often reluctant participants at best. Treatment may create significant anxiety for the patient. Thus, the particular challenge of treating people with odd/eccentric personality disorders is their tendency not to collaborate with the therapist to develop goals for treatment (Beck et al., 2004; Farmer & Nelson-Gray, 2005).

Nevertheless, when such patients do participate in CBT, they can develop more adaptive strategies, such as improved social skills (which makes them less likely to be conspicuous and in turn leads them to feel safer with others). CBT may also employ relaxation techniques, exposure to avoided social situations, and cognitive restructuring of distorted views of self and others, and of dysfunctional beliefs (Beck et al., 2004; Farmer & Nelson-Gray, 2005).

Most of the medications that effectively treat symptoms of schizophrenia can also treat symptoms of schizotypal personality disorder, although the medications are often taken at lower doses (Koenigsberg et al., 2003; Raine, 2006; see Chapter 12).

Thinking Like A Clinician

Shawna has few friends; most of the time she's quiet and shy, avoiding eye contact. Occasionally, she mentions that her troubles—work, social, and financial—are because of the radiation coming out of the computer. She says it with a straight face, but it's hard to tell whether she's joking. When asked whether she's being serious, she reluctantly says that she's not, but it's not clear whether she's being honest. If you were asked to determine whether she has a personality disorder, what kinds of questions would you ask? Based on what you have read, what types of answers would distinguish quirky behavior from the truly odd behavior that characterizes a Cluster A personality disorder? If you determined that her behavior was odd enough to merit a diagnosis of a Cluster A (odd/eccentric) personality disorder, what would you look for in order to decide which of those disorders might be the best diagnosis?

▢ Dramatic/Erratic Personality Disorders

In her memoir, Rachel Reiland recalls an occasion when a minor matter set off an escalating fight between her and her husband. She raged at him until she realized that she might drive him away. So she decided to leave him before he had a chance to leave her. She ran out of the house barefoot and then ran for miles through the city. After several hours, her husband and children—who had been searching for her—pulled up their car beside her and brought her home (Reiland, 2004).

Reiland's response to this fight with her husband exemplifies the typical reactions of people with Cluster B personality disorders: impulsive, dramatic, and erratic behaviors. These disorders arise because of difficulty regulating emotions. This commonality can sometimes make it difficult to determine which specific Cluster B personality disorder a given patient has; many of the symptoms specified in the diagnostic criteria are not unique to a single personality disorder in the cluster (Blais et al., 1999; Zanarini & Gunderson, 1997). People with a dramatic/erratic personality disorder also tend to have certain additional psychological disorders: substance-related disorders, mood disorders, anxiety disorders, or eating disorders (Dolan-Sewell et al., 2001; McGlashan et al., 2000; Skodol et al., 1999; Zanarini et al., 1998).

Antisocial personality disorder
A personality disorder diagnosed in adulthood characterized by a persistent disregard for the rights of others.

Conduct disorder
A psychological disorder that typically arises in childhood and is characterized by the violation of the basic rights of others or of societal norms that are appropriate to the person's age.

Antisocial Personality Disorder

One day, Reiland was particularly angry, and she put the following note on the front door: *"You need to pick up the kids. I'm upstairs in the attic. Don't even think of going up there if you know what's good for you!"* Another note was on the attic door, which was locked: *"I might die anyway, but if you dare come in here, you might all be dead! You don't know what I have up here!"* (Reiland, 2004, p. 148).

Some might say that Reiland's behavior—and her apparent lack of concern for how her husband and children might respond to the notes—had elements of **antisocial personality disorder**, which involves a persistent disregard for the rights of others. As noted in Table 13.9, people with antisocial personality disorder may violate rules or laws (for example, by stealing) and may lie or act aggressively, hurting others, believing that they are entitled to break the rules (American Psychiatric Association, 2013). They may also act impulsively, putting themselves or others at risk of harm. In addition to these behaviors, people with antisocial personality disorder shirk their responsibilities—they don't pay their bills or show up for work on time, for instance. They may also exhibit a fundamental lack of regret for or guilt about their antisocial behaviors, seeming to lack a conscience, a moral sense, or a sense of empathy. In Reiland's case, though, holing up in the attic and writing the threatening notes probably resulted from uncontrollable emotions rather than from a disregard for others.

The diagnostic criteria for antisocial personality disorder are the most behaviorally specific of the criteria for personality disorders and even include overt criminal behaviors (Skodol, 2005). Because of this specificity, antisocial personality disorder is the most reliably diagnosed personality disorder (Skodol, 2005).

Like other personality disorders, antisocial personality disorder manifests itself in childhood or adolescence, but DSM-5 is again very specific about antisocial personality disorder: The symptoms must have arisen by age 15, although the diagnosis cannot be made until the person is at least 18 years old; this was true of John in Case 13.5. The diagnosis for people who exhibit a similar pattern of symptoms but are younger than 18 is **conduct disorder**, which is characterized by consistently violating the rights of others (through lying, threatening, and destructive and aggressive behaviors) or violating societal norms and typically diagnosed in children and adolescents. (In Chapter 14 we discuss conduct disorder in detail.) Table 13.10 provides additional facts about antisocial personality disorder.

> **CASE 13.5 • FROM THE OUTSIDE:** Antisocial Personality Disorder
>
> John and his sister were adopted by the same family when they were respectively 1.5 and 3 years of age. From the very beginning, John was severely physically abused by his adoptive father as a result of just minor misbehaviors. Furthermore, John felt that he and his sister were neglected (lack of warmth and attention) by his adoptive parents and that he and his sister were thought of much less highly by them than their only biological son. From age 10 John and his sister were sexually abused on a regular basis by his adoptive father, and John was forced to watch when his father raped his sister. He demonstrated more and more oppositional and angry behavior, and he became a notorious thief. John left junior secondary technical school prematurely and had many short-term jobs, but he was dismissed every time because of lack of motivation, disobedience, and/or theft. As a consequence of his deviant behavior, John was placed in a juvenile correctional and observation institute when he was 16 years of age. A psychiatric report from this episode described him as a socially, emotionally, morally, and sexually underdeveloped person who was very suspicious and angry. He projected his discomfort on the outside world. After his release from the juvenile correctional institute (when he was 18 years of age), John was arrested because of violent pedophilic rape, theft, and fraud. John was sentenced to forensic psychiatric treatment. But soon after his release, when he was 24, John was sentenced to life imprisonment because he committed an excessively violent sexual homicide on a 9-year-old boy.
> (Martens, 2005, pp. 117–118)

TABLE **13.10** • Antisocial Personality Disorder Facts at a Glance

Prevalence
• Between 1% and 4% of Americans are diagnosed with antisocial personality disorder (Grant, Hasin, et al., 2004).
• Approximately 60% of male prisoners in a number of countries have antisocial personality disorder (Moran, 1999).
Comorbidity
• The most common comorbid psychological disorders are anxiety disorders, mood disorders, substance use disorders, and somatization disorders (Compton, Conway, et al., 2005; Sareen et al., 2004).
• In a clinical setting, most patients who meet the criteria for antisocial personality disorder also are diagnosed with at least one other personality disorder, typically another dramatic/erratic personality disorder (Widiger & Corbitt, 1997).
Onset
• As required by the DSM-5 criteria, symptoms of conduct disorder emerge before age 15, and specific symptoms of antisocial behavior occur since age 15. The specific antisocial behaviors then continue into adulthood.
Course
• Antisocial personality disorder has a chronic course, but symptoms may improve as patients age, particularly in their 40s (Seivewright et al., 2002).
Gender Differences
• Antisocial personality disorder is diagnosed more often in men than in women.

Source: Unless otherwise noted, citations are to American Psychiatric Association, 2013.

Psychopathy
A set of emotional and interpersonal characteristics marked by a lack of empathy, an unmerited feeling of high self-worth, and a refusal to accept responsibility for one's actions.

The term *psychopath* (or *sociopath*, which was used in the first DSM) has often been used to refer to someone with symptoms of antisocial personality disorder. However, **psychopathy** emphasizes specific emotional and interpersonal characteristics, such as a lack of empathy, an unmerited feeling of high self-worth, and a refusal to accept responsibility for one's actions—as well as antisocial behaviors. The classification of psychopathy is narrower (i.e., more restrictive, because there are more criteria) than the diagnosis of antisocial personality disorder. In contrast, the diagnosis of antisocial personality disorder tends to focus more on *behaviors*—mostly criminal ones, such as stealing or breaking other laws—than on the personality traits that may underlie the behaviors. Only a minority of prisoners (15% of male prisoners, 7.5% of female prisoners) meet the specific criteria for psychopathy, but a majority of prisoners (50–80%) meet the broad behavioral criteria for antisocial personality disorder (Hare, 2003).

Psychopathy is generally considered to be a more universal concept than antisocial personality disorder; most cultures recognize a similar cluster of psychopathic characteristics (Cooke, 1998; Gacono et al., 2001).

Understanding Antisocial Personality Disorder and Psychopathy

The concept of psychopathy has been employed longer than the diagnosis of antisocial personality disorder. Hence, more research has addressed psychopathy and criminality than antisocial personality disorder—and the relative lack of research on antisocial personality disorder makes it difficult to identify the factors that contribute to the disorder (Ogloff, 2006). Moreover, most research that does examine factors that con-

Antisocial personality disorder is characterized by an emphasis on criminal behaviors, whereas psychopathy is more narrowly defined by personality traits that underlie the behaviors.

tribute to antisocial personality disorder has studied participants who are or have been in prisons or jails or who have comorbid substance abuse problems; hence, numerous confounds prevent us from conclusively identifying the factors that contribute solely to antisocial personality disorder. Therefore, the following sections examine neurological, psychological, and social factors—and the feedback loops among them—that contribute to antisocial personality disorder and/or psychopathy, keeping in mind the limitations of existing research.

Neurological Factors in Antisocial Personality Disorder and Psychopathy

People with antisocial personality disorder or psychopathy (and the groups have not been rigorously separated in most of this research) may have abnormal brain *structures* as well as abnormal brain *function* (Pridmore et al., 2005).

First, regarding brain structure, people with antisocial personality disorder or psychopathy tend to have unusually small frontal lobes (Raine et al, 2000). The smaller frontal lobes might suggest problems in inhibiting and planning behavior.

Second, regarding brain function, the frontal and temporal lobes of these patients tend to show less activation than normal during many tasks (Schneider et al., 2000; Smith, 2000; Völlum et al., 2004). Moreover, these patients exhibit deficits on tasks that rely on the frontal lobes, such as those requiring planning or discovering that a rule has been changed (Dolan & Park, 2002). Such deficits probably contribute to their problems in inhibiting and planning behavior.

Antisocial personality disorder has been linked to genes that regulate dopamine production (Prichard et al., 2007) and also to genes that regulate serotonin (Lyons–Ruth et al., 2007). Genes that affect dopamine and serotonin may influence temperament and have been linked to being highly motivated by the possibility of reward (Gray, 1987), not being strongly motivated by the threat of punishment (Cloninger et al., 1993; Gray, 1987; Lykken, 1995), and having low frustration tolerance—which often leads to impulsive behavior and a tendency to take shortcuts.

However, effects of genes are modulated by the environment. Adoption studies have found that the environment in which a child is raised influences the risk of criminal behavior or antisocial personality disorder only if the child is biologically vulnerable, as shown in Table 13.11. When a child's biological parents were not criminals, the child's later criminal behavior was unaffected by environmental influences, such as the number of foster placements before adoption or the adoptive parents' criminality (Caspi et al., 2002; Mednick et al., 1984).

TABLE 13.11 • Percentage of Children Who Later Committed Crimes: The Role of Biology and Family Environment in Criminality

Exposure to environmental forces associated with criminality	Biological parents' criminality	
	High	Low
High	40.0%	6.7%
Low	12.1%	2.9%

Note: Environmental forces associated with criminality include variables such as the number of foster placements before adoption and the adoptive father's socioeconomic status.

Source: Brock et al., 1996. For more information see the Permissions section.

Psychological Factors in Antisocial Personality Disorder and Psychopathy

Antisocial personality disorder and psychopathy appear to develop, in part, because of problems with classical and operant conditioning processes. Whereas classical conditioning and operant conditioning lead most people to learn to avoid encounters with a painful stimulus (such as a shock), criminals with psychopathic traits do not learn to avoid painful stimuli. Thus, they cannot easily learn from punishing experiences (Eysenck, 1957) and are likely to repeat behavior associated with negative consequence, despite receiving punishment, such as a prison sentence (Zuckerman, 1999). And because they are highly motivated by rewarding activities, they are less inclined to inhibit themselves to avoid punishment; they thus behave in ways that are impulsive, have difficulty delaying gratification, and have poor judgment (Silverstein, 2007).

Social Factors in Antisocial Personality Disorder and Psychopathy

One risk factor for conduct disorder and subsequent antisocial personality disorder is a child's relationship with his or her parents or primary caretakers. Each parent or other primary caretaker has a style of interacting with the child from infancy. Some parents abuse or neglect their children or are inconsistent in disciplining them, which can lead to an insecure attachment (Bowlby, 1969). These children have a relatively high risk of developing conduct disorder and later antisocial personality disorder (Levy & Orlans, 1999, 2000; Ogloff, 2006; Shi et al., 2012). Note, however, that this finding is simply a correlation and does not necessarily mean that attachment difficulties *cause* later antisocial behavior; it is possible that some other variable both interferes with a child's developing normal attachment *and* promotes antisocial behaviors.

Other childhood factors associated with the later development of antisocial personality disorder include poverty, family instability, and—in those who are genetically vulnerable—adoptive parents' criminality (Raine et al., 1996).

Feedback Loops in Understanding Antisocial Personality Disorder and Psychopathy

Various factors create feedback loops that ultimately produce psychopathy or antisocial personality disorder. Twin and adoption studies reveal that some people have a predisposition toward criminality or associated temperaments (neurological factor), but the environment in which children grow up (social factor) influences whether that predisposition is likely to lead to criminal behavior. One study found that children with conduct disorder who were punished for their offenses were less likely to develop antisocial personality disorder later in life, confirming the contribution of operant conditioning to the disorder (Black, 2001).

ONLINE

However, the types of temperaments that are associated with antisocial personality disorder and psychopathy can impede the types of classical and operant conditioning processes that promote empathy and discourage antisocial behaviors (psychological factor; Kagan & Reid, 1986; Martens, 2005; Pollock et al., 1990). Moreover, the experience of abuse or neglect by parents (social factor) may contribute to a tendency toward underarousal (Schore, 2003), which in turn leads people to seek out more arousing (and reckless) activities that may increase their risk of seeing or experiencing violence (Jang et al., 2001)—which they may find stimulating, and which then may reinforce such behavior.

Treating Antisocial Personality Disorder and Psychopathy

Most research on treatment involves people who are diagnosed with psychopathy, not antisocial personality disorder specifically. Some of the personality traits associated with psychopathy interfere with a therapeutic collaboration: problems in delaying gratification, lack of empathy, and low frustration tolerance. Psychopathy has a poor prognosis, and treatments developed thus far are not likely to alter behavior or reduce symptoms (Gacono et al., 2001; Rice et al., 1992; Serin, 1991). People with psychopathy who are in prison are likely to commit additional crimes after their release (Ogloff et al., 1990; Seto & Barbaree, 1999). When a person with psychopathy is violent, *managing* the patient may be more realistic and appropriate than *treating* the patient's personality problems (Ogloff, 2006).

Ultimately, a challenge in treating people with antisocial personality disorder is their lack of motivation. Because they aren't disturbed by their behavior, they are rarely genuinely motivated to change, which makes any real collaboration between therapist and patient unlikely; patients often will attend therapy only when required to do so. Treatment generally focuses on changing overt behaviors (Farmer & Nelson-Gray, 2005).

Treatments for people with antisocial personality disorder who are not psychopathic have some success—at least in the short term. These treatments focus on comorbid substance abuse and aggressive behavior (Henning & Frueh, 1996). The most effective treatments provide clear rules about behavior—including clear and consistent consequences for rule violations—and target behavior change and behavioral control, as is addressed with CBT.

CURRENT CONTROVERSY

Should Psychopaths Receive Treatment?

Psychopathy has a distinctive pattern of interpersonal, behavioral, and affective symptoms (Hare, 1997). According to Hare (1993, p. 25), "psychopaths can be described as intraspecies predators who use charm, manipulation, intimidation and violence to control others and to satisfy their own selfish needs." Psychopathy is a difficult disorder to treat, and individuals with psychopathy rarely seek treatment unless it is for self-serving purposes such as probation or parole (Hare, 1993). The question arises, then, as to whether psychopaths should receive treatment at all.

Studies on the efficacy of treatment in psychopathy have been mixed (Salekin et al., 2010), with some research reporting *higher* recidivism rates in psychopaths who *received* treatment (Rice et al., 1992). Others have suggested that psychopaths who complete treatment may merely be perfecting their interpersonal skills to manipulate others (Hare, 1997; Hart, 1998). For example, Rice et al. (1992) measured the effects of an intensive treatment program on violent psychopathic and nonpsychopathic forensic patients. After a 10-year

follow-up, the violent recidivism rate was 55% for untreated psychopaths, and 77% for treated psychopaths. Researchers have also noted that no effective treatments are available to treat psychopathy (O'Neill et al., 2003), regardless of the type of setting (e.g., community), and psychopaths tend to drop out of treatment programs early (Ogloff et al., 1990).

On the other hand, in a review of three studies designed to reduce violence and offending behaviors in psychopathic offenders, Wong et al. (2012) reported positive treatment outcomes. Olver and Wong (2009) found that psychopathic sex offenders who completed treatment were less likely to violently reoffend. Other researchers (D'Silva et al., 2004; Salekin, 2002), however, have pointed out several methodological flaws in many of the studies measuring treatment response in psychopathy.

CRITICAL THINKING If you were to treat a psychopath, what outcome measures could you assess to ensure that therapy was indeed effective? In your opinion, how should forensic psychologists treat psychopaths: as criminals or individuals with a mental illness? Why?

(Richard Conti, Kean University)

Borderline Personality Disorder

The term *borderline personality* originally was used by psychodynamic therapists to describe patients whose personality was on the border between neurosis and psychosis (Kernberg, 1967). Now, however, it is generally used to describe the DSM-5 personality disorder that includes some features of that type of personality: **borderline personality disorder** is characterized by volatile emotions, an unstable self-image, and impulsive behavior in relationships (American Psychiatric Association, 2013). The diagnostic criteria for borderline personality disorder are noted in Table 13.12. A key criterion is emotional dysregulation (also known as affective instability), which leads the person frequently to respond more emotionally than a situation warrants and to display quickly changing emotions—lability (Glenn & Klonsky, 2009). Another prominent criterion refers to a relationship pattern of idealizing the other person at the beginning of the relationship, spending a lot of time with the person and revealing much, thus creating an intense intimacy. But then positive feelings quickly switch to negative ones, which leads the person with this disorder to devalue the other person. Rachel Reiland's pattern of thoughts, feelings, and behaviors meet the criteria for borderline personality disorder. Reiland describes the switch in how she viewed other people:

> I saw people as either good or evil. When they were "good," I vaulted them to the top of a pedestal. They could do no wrong, and I loved them with all of my being. When they were "bad," they became objects of scorn and revenge.

Borderline personality disorder
A personality disorder characterized by volatile emotions, an unstable self-image, and impulsive behavior in relationships.

In relationships with those closest to me, the "good" and "bad" assessments could alternate wildly, sometimes from one hour to the next. The unrealistic expectations of perfection that came with the good-guy pedestal were destined to be unfulfilled, which led to disappointment and sense of betrayal.

(2004, p. 88)

The highly fluid and impulsive behaviors that are part of borderline personality disorder occur in part, because of the patient's strong responses to emotional stimuli, which may stem from difficulty understanding emotions (Peter et al., 2013). For example, if a patient with borderline personality disorder has to wait for someone who is late for an appointment, the patient often cannot understand and regulate the ensuing powerful feelings of anger, anxiety, or despair, which can last for days. The person with this personality disorder is extremely sensitive to any hint of being abandoned, which also can cause strong emotions that are then difficult to bring under control.

When not in the throes of intense emotions, people with borderline personality disorder may feel chronically empty, lonely, and isolated (Klonsky, 2008). When feeling empty, they may harm themselves in some nonlethal way—such as superficial cutting of skin—in order to feel "something"; such behavior has been called *parasuicidal* rather than suicidal because the intention is *not* to commit suicide but rather to gain relief from feeling emotionally numb. The parasuicidal behavior usually occurs when the person is in a dissociated state, often after he or she has felt rejected or abandoned (Livesley, 2001). More worrying to clinicians, family members, and friends is when self-harming behavior is a suicide attempt. People with borderline personality disorder may have comorbid depression, which frequently contributes to increased suicidal thoughts, plans, or attempts. When borderline personality disorder symptoms diminish—including a decrease in emotional sensitivity—depression is likely to improve (Gunderson et al., 2004). Table 13.13 provides additional facts about borderline personality disorder. Donna, in Case 13.6, exhibits extreme emotional sensitivity.

TABLE 13.12 • DSM-5 Diagnostic Criteria for Borderline Personality Disorder

A pervasive pattern of instability of interpersonal relationships, self-image, and affects, and marked impulsivity, beginning by early adulthood and present in a variety of contexts, as indicated by five (or more) of the following:

1. Frantic efforts to avoid real or imagined abandonment. (**Note:** Do not include suicidal or self-mutilating behavior covered in Criterion 5.)
2. A pattern of unstable and intense interpersonal relationships characterized by alternating between extremes of idealization and devaluation.
3. Identity disturbance: markedly and persistently unstable self-image or sense of self.
4. Impulsivity in at least two areas that are potentially self-damaging (e.g., spending, sex, substance abuse, reckless driving, binge eating). (**Note:** Do not include suicidal or self-mutilating behavior covered in Criterion 5.)
5. Recurrent suicidal behavior, gestures, or threats, or self-mutilating behavior.
6. Affective instability due to a marked reactivity of mood (e.g., intense episodic dysphoria, irritability, or anxiety usually lasting a few hours and only rarely more than a few days).
7. Chronic feelings of emptiness.
8. Inappropriate, intense anger or difficulty controlling anger (e.g., frequent displays of temper, constant anger, recurrent physical fights).
9. Transient, stress-related paranoid ideation or severe dissociative symptoms.

Reprinted with permission from the Diagnostic and Statistical Manual of Mental Disorders, Fifth Edition, (Copyright ©2013). American Psychiatric Association. All Rights Reserved.

People with borderline personality disorder may engage in parasuicidal behaviors, such as cutting their arms, to help regulate their emotions. These scars on a 50-year-old woman are a result of such parasuicidal behavior. Self-harming behavior may also occur in an attempt to commit suicide.

JOTI/Getty Images

CASE 13.6 • FROM THE OUTSIDE: Borderline Personality Disorder

[A woman, Donna, exhibited] episodes of explosive anger and bitter tirades, along with weekly (sometimes daily) expressions of bitterness and resentment. Frustrations and disappointments, which are inevitable within any relationship and would only be annoying inconveniences to most people, were perceived by Donna as outrageous mistreatments or exploitations. Even when she recognized that they did not warrant a strong reaction, she still had tremendous difficulty stifling her feelings of anger and resentment. Her tendency to misperceive innocent remarks as being intentionally inconsiderate (at times even malevolent) further exacerbated her propensity to anger. She acknowledged that she would often push, question, and test her friends and lovers so hard for signs of disaffection, reassurances of affection, or admissions of guilt, that they would become frustrated and exasperated and might eventually lash out against her. She would often find herself embroiled in fruitless arguments that she subsequently regretted. She had no long-standing relationships, but there were numerous people who remained embittered toward her. Three marriages had, in fact, all ended in acrimonious divorce.

(Widiger et al., 2002, p. 443)

Although online message boards may provide support for adolescent girls and young women, they may also encourage or normalize the self-harming behavior that is associated with borderline personality disorder (Whitlock et al., 2006).

TABLE 13.13 • Borderline Personality Disorder Facts at a Glance

Prevalence

- Borderline personality disorder occurs in about 2% of the general population, 10% of outpatients, and 20% of inpatients.
- Borderline personality disorder is the most common personality disorder: 30–60% of those diagnosed with a personality disorder have borderline personality disorder (Adams et al., 2001; Widiger & Trull, 1993).
- Borderline personality disorder is five times more common among first-degree relatives of someone with the disorder than in the general population.

Comorbidity

- Common comorbid disorders include mood disorders, substance use disorders, eating disorders (especially bulimia), and anxiety disorders (Grilo et al., 2004; Gunderson, Weinberg et al., 2006; Zanarini et al., 2004).

Onset

- As with all other personality disorders, symptoms for borderline personality disorder emerge in childhood or adolescence.

Course

- People with borderline personality disorder have a high suicide rate, with almost 10% dying by suicide (Linehan & Heard, 1999; Paris, 1993).
- The early adulthood years of people with this disorder are marked by mood episodes and serious impulse control problems, including suicide attempts; the risk of suicide peaks during early adulthood.
- Those who survive into their 20s and 30s are likely to improve within 10 years (Gunderson et al., 2011; Zanarini et al., 2010).

Gender Differences

- Approximately 75% of those diagnosed with borderline personality disorder are female.

Cultural Differences

- The diagnostic criteria for borderline personality disorder—and its conceptual underpinnings—may not apply equally well in all cultures, especially Asian cultures (Lee, 2008).

Source: Unless otherwise noted, citations should be for American Psychiatric Association, 2013.

Understanding Borderline Personality Disorder

The neuropsychosocial approach allows us to appreciate the complexity of borderline personality disorder. In fact, this approach underlies the most comprehensive analysis that has been made of the disorder and its treatment (Linehan, 1993).

Neurological Factors: Born to Be Wild?

Considerable research has been reported on the neurological bases of borderline personality disorder.

Brain Systems The frontal lobes, hippocampus, and amygdala are unusually small in people with borderline personality disorder (Driessen et al., 2000; Schmahl, Vermetten et al., 2003; Tebartz van Elst et al., 2003). These structures are part of a network of brain areas that functions abnormally in people with this disorder. The frontal lobes (which are involved in regulating emotions and formulating plans) are less strongly activated in these patients than is normal. Consistent with findings from neuroimaging studies, numerous studies have shown that people who have borderline personality disorder have difficulty performing tasks that rely on the frontal lobes (LeGris & van Reekum, 2006); specifically, people with this disorder also have difficulty focusing attention, organizing visual material, and making decisions (LeGris & van Reekum, 2006).

The amygdala (which is involved in the perception and production of strong emotions, notably fear) is *more* strongly activated than normal in these patients when they see faces with negative expressions (Donegan et al., 2003). This finding makes sense because the frontal lobes normally inhibit the amygdala (LeDoux, 1996); thus, if the frontal lobes are not working properly, they may fail to keep activation of the amygdala within a normal range.

In addition, consistent with the unusually small hippocampus, these patients have impaired visual and verbal memory (LeGris & van Reekum, 2006).

Neural Communication Relatively low levels of serotonin are related to impulsivity, which is characteristic of borderline personality disorder. Thus, it is not surprising that these patients have been shown to have abnormal serotonin functioning (Soloff et al., 2000); in particular, their serotonin receptors are less sensitive than normal, and thus the effects of serotonin are diminished (Hansenne et al., 2002). In addition, this dysfunction involving serotonin is apparently greater in women than in men with the disorder (New et al., 2003; Soloff, Kelly et al., 2003)—and many more women than men receive this diagnosis.

Thus, people with borderline personality disorder are likely to be neurologically vulnerable to emotional dysregulation. This vulnerability is usually expressed as a low threshold for emotional responding, with responses that are often extreme and intense. In addition, the brains of these people are relatively slow to return to a normal baseline of arousal.

Genetics Genetic studies reveal a genetic vulnerability to components of this disorder, such as impulsivity, emotional volatility, and anxiety (Adams et al., 2001; Heim & Westen, 2005; Skodol, Siever, et al., 2002).

Psychological Factors: Emotions on a Yo-Yo

The core feature of borderline personality disorder is dysregulation—of emotion, of sense of self, of cognition, and of behavior (Robins et al., 2001). The behaviors of people with this disorder can be extreme: In one instant, they will fly into a rage over some inconsequential thing, but in the next instant, they will break down in tears and beg for reassurance, as Reiland did. These behaviors may inadvertently be reinforced by family members' attention.

People with this disorder often engage in other behaviors that are more directly self-destructive—including substance use or abuse, binge eating, and parasuicidal behaviors; they may act in these ways to try to feel better after interpersonal stress (Paris, 1999). And, in fact, such maladaptive behaviors can be (negatively) reinforcing because they *do* temporarily relieve emotional pain. (Recall that negative reinforcement is different from punishment; removing something aversive is reinforcing.)

Social Factors: Invalidation

Borderline personality disorder also involves interpersonal dysregulation—relationships are typically intense, chaotic, and difficult (Robins et al., 2001). One explanation for the interpersonal problems suggests that they arose in childhood—that family members and friends were likely to *invalidate* the patient's experience (Linehan, 1993). For instance, a parent might tell a child, "You're too sensitive" or "You're overreacting." During childhood, such chronic dismissals may have led to fear of rejection and abandonment, if not actual rejection. Such experiences may have sensitized the child, leading him or her subsequently to overreact to the slightest hint of being invalidated.

In addition, this interpersonal dysregulation may arise in part because of patients' emotional and cognitive dysregulation (Fonagy & Bateman, 2008). When people with borderline personality disorder meet someone who is positive or helpful, they often begin by depending on that person to help calm their emotions, as Reiland

What do you see in this negative expression? People with borderline personality disorder tend to have stronger activation of their amygdalae (a brain structure notably involved in fear) when viewing faces with negative expressions. This finding may help explain why people who have this personality disorder are especially sensitive to being rejected by others.

© JGI/Blend Images/Corbis

did with her husband. But, paradoxically, once they feel dependent, they fear being abandoned—which leads them to behave in ways likely to lead to rejection. Friends and family members may come to respond with caring and concern only when the patient exhibits self-destructive behaviors (which, in turn, inadvertently reinforces those behaviors).

Feedback Loops in Understanding Borderline Personality Disorder

Linehan's (1993) model of borderline personality disorder rests on a series of feedback loops (like those illustrated in Figure 13.2): Some children have brain systems (neurological factor) that lead them to have extreme emotional reactions (psychological factor), and their parents may have difficulty soothing them (social factor) when they are emotionally aroused (Graybar & Boutelier, 2002; Linehan, 1993). Either

FIGURE 13.2 • Feedback Loops in Understanding Borderline Personality Disorder

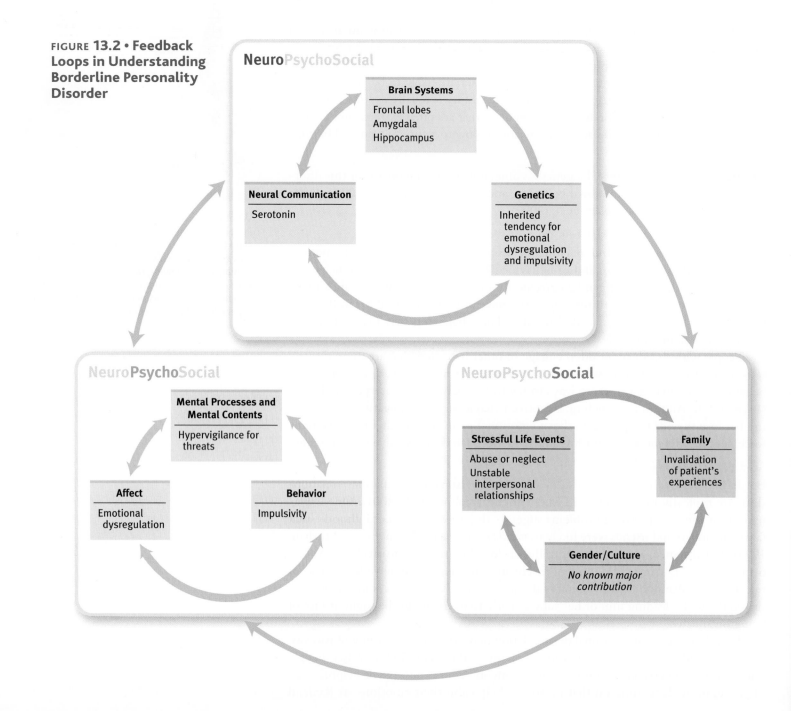

because the parents create an invalidating environment ("It's not as bad as you're making it out to be"; social factor) or because they engage in outright abuse or neglect (as occurred with Reiland), the children may become insecurely attached to their parents. In turn, the children don't learn to regulate their emotions or behaviors (and cognitions) and elicit untoward reactions from others, which then confirms their view of themselves and others.

This invalidating process, according to Linehan, leaves the person feeling punished for his or her thoughts, feelings, and behaviors—they are trivialized, dismissed, disrespected (Linehan & Kehrer, 1993). Such people therefore have a hard time identifying and labeling their emotions accurately and coming to trust their own experiences and perceptions as valid (psychological factor). They don't learn effective problem solving or ways to cope with distress.

Treating Borderline Personality Disorder: New Treatments

Borderline personality disorder is among the most challenging personality disorders to treat (Robins et al., 2001), in part, because of the patient's parasuicidal or suicidal thoughts and behaviors. It can also be challenging because of the intense anger that a patient may direct at the mental health clinician. In what follows we examine the various targets of treatment—neurological factors, psychological factors, and social factors—and pay particular attention to a comprehensive psychological treatment that is the treatment of choice: *dialectical behavior therapy.*

Targeting Neurological Factors: Medication

Various medications may be prescribed to people with borderline personality disorder for a comorbid non-personality disorder or to target certain symptoms, including quickly changing moods, anxiety, impulsive behavior, and psychotic symptoms (Lieb et al., 2004). An SSRI—compared to a placebo—may diminish symptoms of emotional lability and anxiety and help with anger management. In addition, antipsychotics can alleviate psychotic symptoms, and mood stabilizers may help some symptoms (Binks et al., 2006a). Although medications may reduce the intensity of some symptoms, medications have limited effect and should not be the only form of treatment for people with borderline personality disorder (Koenigsberg et al., 2007).

Targeting Psychological Factors: Dialectical Behavior Therapy

Marsha Linehan, a pioneer in the treatment of borderline personality disorder, initially treated such patients with CBT, which focuses on identifying and correcting irrational thoughts and faulty beliefs (Beck et al., 2004; Linehan, 1993)—but this led some people to drop out of treatment because they felt that the focus on changing their thoughts and beliefs implicitly criticized and invalidated them (Dimeff & Linehan, 2001). In response, Linehan (1993) developed a new treatment for people with borderline personality disorder. From CBT she incorporated skill development and cognitive restructuring. In addition, in her new therapy, she underscored the importance of a warm and collaborative bond between patient and therapist; to this mix she added the following elements:

- *An emphasis on validating the patient's experience.* That is, the patient's thoughts, feelings, and behaviors in a given situation make sense in the context of his or her life, past experiences, and strengths and weaknesses.

- *A Zen Buddhist approach.* Patients should see, and then without judgment, accept any painful realities of their lives. Patients are encouraged to "let go" of emotional attachments that cause them suffering. Mindfulness, or nonjudgmental awareness, is the goal (Perroud et al., 2012).

- *A dialectics component. Dialectics* refers to a synthesis of opposing elements; in this context, it refers to the patient's coming to accept the situation and aspects of it that he or she does not feel able to change (e.g., validating his or her experience) while at the same time recognizing that in order to feel better, change must occur (Robins et al., 2001).

Linehan called this treatment **dialectical behavior therapy (DBT)**, and it entails both group and individual therapy. The initial priority of DBT is to reduce self-harming behaviors such as burning or cutting oneself. As these behaviors are reduced, treatment focuses on other behaviors that interfere with therapy and with the quality of life. Therapy also helps patients develop skills to change what can be changed: their own behavior rather than the behavior of other people, such as family members. In addition, treatment helps patients to recognize aspects of their lives that they can't change: For instance, although patients can learn to change the way they behave toward their parents, they can't change the way their parents behave toward them. Treatment lasts about 1 year.

Researchers have conducted many studies to evaluate DBT and have noted impressive results for patients with borderline personality disorder: DBT does decrease suicidal thoughts and behaviors and leads to lower dropout and hospitalization rates—and it does so more effectively than other specialized treatments for this disorder (Binks et al., 2006b; Linehan et al., 2006). DBT has been adapted to treat people with other psychological disorders that involve impulsive symptoms, such as bulimia (Palmer et al., 2003).

Intensive forms of psychodynamically oriented psychotherapy have also been shown to be effective for patients with borderline personality disorder (Clarkin et al., 2007; Gregory & Remen, 2008). Similarly, research indicates that cognitive therapy and CBT can be effective (Davidson et al., 2006; Wenzel et al., 2006).

Targeting Social Factors: Interpersonal Therapy

Interpersonal therapy (IPT) has been adapted to treat borderline personality disorder. The goal of IPT for this personality disorder is to help the patient develop more adaptive interpersonal skills so that he or she feels and functions better. This therapy tries to help patients integrate their extreme but opposed feelings about a person: When they talk about feeling one way about someone ("He's perfect"), the therapist tries to discuss opposite feelings as well, underscoring that no individual is all good or all bad (Markowitz, 2005; Markowitz et al., 2006). A course of IPT for borderline personality disorder typically lasts about 8 months. Social interactions are also a focus of the group therapy component of DBT.

Feedback Loops in Treating Borderline Personality Disorder

Successful treatment of borderline personality disorder may target more than one factor; positive changes in any factor, though, affect other factors via feedback loops (see Figure 13.3). For example, one goal of DBT is to help patients regulate their emotions (psychological factor). When the therapy is successful, better emotional regulation allows patients to calm themselves more effectively when they are anxious or angry, which directly affects brain mechanisms (neurological factor) and in turn makes their relationships less volatile (social factors). Similarly, the honest and caring feedback from others within the therapeutic environment (part of DBT, IPT, CBT, and intensive psychodynamic therapy) challenges patients to alter their behaviors and ways of thinking about themselves and their relationships (psychological and social factors), which in turn decreases their emotional reactivity (neurological and psychological factors).

Dialectical behavior therapy involves both individual and group therapy; this treatment validates the patient's experience, encourages nonjudgmental awareness, and acceptance of opposing elements of life.

Dialectical behavior therapy (DBT)
A form of treatment that includes elements of CBT as well as an emphasis on validating the patient's experience, a Zen Buddhist approach, and a dialectics component.

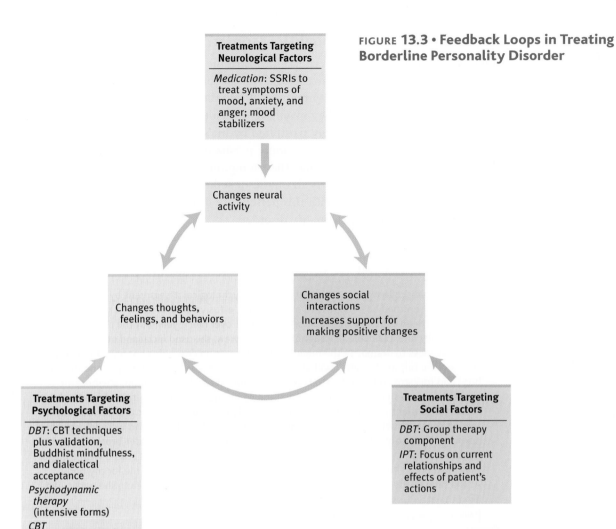

FIGURE **13.3 • Feedback Loops in Treating Borderline Personality Disorder**

Treatments Targeting Neurological Factors

Medication: SSRIs to treat symptoms of mood, anxiety, and anger; mood stabilizers

Changes neural activity

Changes thoughts, feelings, and behaviors

Changes social interactions
Increases support for making positive changes

Treatments Targeting Psychological Factors

DBT: CBT techniques plus validation, Buddhist mindfulness, and dialectical acceptance
Psychodynamic therapy (intensive forms)
CBT

Treatments Targeting Social Factors

DBT: Group therapy component
IPT: Focus on current relationships and effects of patient's actions

Histrionic Personality Disorder

You may know someone who initially seemed charming, open, enthusiastic—maybe even flirtatious. After a while, did he or she seem to go to great lengths to be the center of attention, behaving too dramatically? Did the person have temper tantrums, sobbing episodes, or other dramatic displays of emotion that appeared to turn on and off like a light switch? These are the qualities of people with **histrionic personality disorder**, who seek attention and exaggerate their emotions (American Psychiatric Association, 2013).

Rachel Reiland relates her desire to be the center of attention:

> I wanted to be the entire focus of any person I was obsessed with. My incessant hunger for attention had been a part of my life for as long as I could remember. The burning heartache of emptiness obsessed me even when my peers had been taken with Barbie dolls and coloring books. I knew even then that these constant feelings were not normal. . . .
>
> When the object of my longing—the teacher, the coach, the boss—was present in the room, I geared everything to that person. I contrived every word, action, inflection, and facial expression for him. *Does he see me laughing? Does he see how funny everybody thinks I am?*
>
> (2004, pp. 335–336)

Reiland's behavior involved some features of histrionic personality disorder; in what follows we examine the disorder in more detail.

Radius Images/Getty Images

We don't know why this woman is so upset. But in people with histrionic personality disorder, this type of exaggerated response is not unusual. Histrionic personality disorder is characterized by attention-seeking and dramatic emotions.

Histrionic personality disorder
A personality disorder characterized by attention-seeking behaviors and exaggerated and dramatic displays of emotion.

TABLE 13.14 • DSM-5 Diagnostic Criteria for Histrionic Personality Disorder

A pervasive pattern of excessive emotionality and attention seeking, beginning by early adulthood and present in a variety of contexts, as indicated by five (or more) of the following:

1. Is uncomfortable in situations in which he or she is not the center of attention.

2. Interaction with others is often characterized by inappropriate sexually seductive or provocative behavior.

3. Displays rapidly shifting and shallow expression of emotions.

4. Consistently uses physical appearance to draw attention to self.

5. Has a style of speech that is excessively impressionistic and lacking in detail.

6. Shows self-dramatization, theatricality, and exaggerated expression of emotion.

7. Is suggestible (i.e., easily influenced by others or circumstances).

8. Considers relationships to be more intimate than they actually are.

Reprinted with permission from the Diagnostic and Statistical Manual of Mental Disorders, Fifth Edition, (Copyright ©2013). American Psychiatric Association. All Rights Reserved.

What Is Histrionic Personality Disorder?

Table 13.14 lists the diagnostic criteria for histrionic personality disorder. Beyond the overt attention seeking and dramatic behavior, people with histrionic personality disorder may exhibit more subtle symptoms: When they feel bored or empty, they seek out novelty and excitement; they may have difficulty delaying gratification and tend to become easily and excessively frustrated by life's challenges. Being in long-term relationships with people with histrionic personality disorder can be challenging because they usually don't recognize their symptoms—they don't feel as though they are overreacting or being overly dramatic or seductive, although they clearly are. Case 13.7 presents a woman with this personality disorder and Table 13.15 provides additional facts about the personality disorder.

CASE 13.7 • FROM THE OUTSIDE: Histrionic Personality Disorder

A 23-year-old single woman was referred for a psychological assessment by her gynecologist. The patient had been described as "outgoing, effusive, and 'dressed to kill'."

She had been experiencing debilitating pain for over half a year, but the pain seemed to be medically unexplainable. Throughout the interview, she used facial and other nonverbal expressiveness to dramatize the meaning of her words. In describing her pain, for example, she said she felt as though "I will absolutely expire" as she closed her eyes and dropped her head forward to feign death. However, when asked about her pain, she became coquettish and was either unable or unwilling to provide details. She talked freely about topics tangential to the interview, skipping quickly from topic to topic and periodically inserting sexual double entendres. She described her family as happy and well-adjusted but acknowledged conflict with her mother and complained that her older brothers treated her like a baby. . . . She was not currently in a serious relationship, but stated with a giggle that most boys "find me very attractive," adding that they "just want me for my body." . . . At the time of the interview, she was working as a dancer at an adult club; she particularly liked the attention and the money that the job provided.

(Millon & Davis, 2000, p. 237; quoted in Horowitz, 2004, pp. 190–191)

TABLE 13.15 • Histrionic Personality Disorder Facts at a Glance

Prevalence

• Approximately 2% of the general population will have histrionic personality disorder at some point during their lives (Grant, Hasin, et al., 2004).

• Among people seeking treatment in inpatient and outpatient mental health settings, the prevalence of this disorder is 10–15%.

Comorbidity

• Common comorbid personality disorders are borderline, narcissistic, antisocial, and dependent personality disorders (Skodol, 2005).

• Common comorbid psychological disorders are somatic symptom disorders and major depressive disorder.

Onset

• As with other personality disorders, symptoms must emerge by young adulthood.

Course

• Symptoms of histrionic personality disorder may improve over time but rarely completely resolve (Seivewright et al., 2002).

Gender Differences

• Some studies find histrionic personality disorder to occur as frequently in men as in women, but others find that it is diagnosed more frequently in women.

• Men with histrionic personality disorder may appear "macho" and seek attention for their athletic skills, not their appearance.

Source: Unless otherwise noted, the source is American Psychiatric Association, 2000, 2013.

Distinguishing Between Histrionic Personality Disorder and Other Disorders

Although people with antisocial personality disorder, borderline personality disorder, and histrionic personality disorder are all manipulative and impulsive, their motivations differ: People with histrionic personality disorder desire frequent attention from others; people with antisocial personality disorder seek power or material gain; and people with borderline personality disorder want nurturance (Skodol, 2005). Moreover, although both histrionic and borderline personality disorders involve rapidly shifting emotions, only with the latter are the emotions usually related to anger.

Reiland's behavior fit some of the criteria for histrionic personality disorder, in that some of her dramatic displays seemed to be motivated by a desire for attention. She might be diagnosed with histrionic personality disorder as a comorbid disorder; however, the elements of her behavior that indicate borderline personality disorder overshadow the features of histrionic personality disorder. A clinician trying to make a definitive diagnosis (or diagnoses) would want to find out more about any thoughts, feelings, or behaviors that might indicate or rule out histrionic personality disorder. Little formal research has been conducted that illuminates factors that contribute to this personality disorder, and so we next focus on how to treat this personality disorder.

Treating Histrionic Personality Disorder

A goal of treatment for histrionic personality disorder is to help patients recognize and then modify their maladaptive beliefs and strategies. Specifically, using techniques from CBT or psychodynamic therapy, the therapist tries to help patients increase their capacity to cope with distress, develop more adaptive ways of responding to frustration, recognize the negative impact that their actions have on their relationships, and shift their view of themselves and other people (Beck et al., 2004; Farmer & Nelson-Gray, 2005). Like other patients with dramatic/erratic personality disorders, those with histrionic personality disorder often do not remain in treatment for long; they become bored or frustrated and continue to see other people as the primary problem.

Narcissistic Personality Disorder

Unlike antisocial and borderline personality disorders, narcissistic personality disorder does not involve impulsiveness or self-destructive tendencies but rather a sense of grandiosity.

What Is Narcissistic Personality Disorder?

People with **narcissistic personality disorder** have an inflated sense of their own importance; they expect—and demand—praise and admiration, and they lack empathy (American Psychiatric Association, 2013). This sense of self-importance, however, masks mixed feelings. On the one hand, they are preoccupied with their own concerns and expect others to be as well, and they get angry when other people don't defer to them. They overvalue themselves and undervalue other people, which is true of Patricia in Case 13.8. On the other hand, their self-esteem can be fragile, leading them to fish for compliments. They are relatively insensitive to others' feelings and points of view. Table 13.16 lists the diagnostic criteria for narcissistic personality disorder, and Table 13.17 presents additional information about this disorder.

Narcissistic personality disorder
A personality disorder characterized by an inflated sense of self-importance, an excessive desire to be admired, and a lack of empathy.

TABLE 13.16 • DSM-5 Diagnostic Criteria for Narcissistic Personality Disorder

A pervasive pattern of grandiosity (in fantasy or behavior), need for admiration, and lack of empathy, beginning by early adulthood and present in a variety of contexts, as indicated by five (or more) of the following:

1. Has a grandiose sense of self-importance (e.g., exaggerates achievements and talents, expects to be recognized as superior without commensurate achievements).

2. Is preoccupied with fantasies of unlimited success, power, brilliance, beauty, or ideal love.

3. Believes that he or she is "special" and unique and can only be understood by, or should associate with, other special or high-status people (or institutions).

4. Requires excessive admiration.

5. Has a sense of entitlement (i.e., unreasonable expectations of especially favorable treatment or automatic compliance with his or her expectations).

TABLE 13.17 • Narcissistic Personality Disorder Facts at a Glance

Prevalence

- Up to 1% of the general population will have narcissistic personality disorder at some point in their lifetimes.

Comorbidity

- Common comorbid personality disorders include paranoid personality disorder and the other Cluster B (dramatic/erratic) personality disorders.
- Common psychological comorbid disorders are substance use disorders and anorexia nervosa.

Onset

- As with other personality disorders, symptoms must emerge by early adulthood.

Course

- People with narcissistic personality disorder may have a hard time adjusting to physical or occupational limitations that arise with advancing age.

Gender Differences

- Between 50% and 75% of those diagnosed with narcissistic personality disorder are male.

Source: Unless otherwise noted, the source is American Psychiatric Association, 2013.

CASE 13.8 • FROM THE OUTSIDE: Narcissistic Personality Disorder

Patricia was a 41-year-old married woman who presented at an outpatient mental health clinic complaining of interpersonal difficulties at work and recurring bouts of depression. She described a series of jobs in which she had experienced considerable friction with coworkers, stating that people generally did not treat her with the respect she deserved. . . . Shortly before her entrance into treatment, Patricia was demoted from a supervisory capacity at her current job because of her inability to effectively interact with those she was supposed to supervise. She described herself as always feeling out of place with her coworkers and indicated that most of them failed to adequately appreciate her skill or the amount of time she put in at work. She reported that she was beginning to think that perhaps she had something to do with their apparent dislike of her. Patricia stated several times . . . that the tellers at the bank were jealous of her status and abilities as a loan officer and that this made them dislike her.

(Corbitt, 2002, pp. 294–295)

Note that Patricia, in Case 13.8, said that people didn't treat her with the respect that she felt she deserved and that she didn't feel adequately appreciated; people with narcissistic personality disorder often report such feelings. Reiland's symptoms do not meet the criteria for a diagnosis of narcissistic personality disorder; her problematic behaviors were often impulsive and self-destructive, and she did not have a stable, inflated sense of self.

As is true for histrionic personality disorder, very little research illuminates factors that contribute to narcissistic personality disorder—and so we move directly to examine ways to treat narcissistic personality disorder.

Treating Narcissistic Personality Disorder

Treatment for narcissistic personality disorder is basically the same as treatment for histrionic disorder: The therapist seeks to help patients recognize and then modify their maladaptive beliefs and strategies, using techniques of CBT or psychodynamic therapy. However, as for all patients with personality disorders, those with narcissistic personality disorder usually do not remain in treatment for long—and typically continue to see other people as the primary problem rather than their own beliefs or behaviors.

Avoidant personality disorder
A personality disorder characterized by extreme shyness that usually stems from feeling inadequate and being overly sensitive to negative evaluation.

Thinking Like A Clinician

In high school and college, Will acted in school plays. Now in his 30s, he travels a lot, making presentations for his job, and so has a lot of independence. He likes the freedom of not having a boss looking over his shoulder all the time, and he enjoys making presentations. Because no one really knows how many hours he works, he sometimes starts late in the morning or quits early; then he heads for a bar to down a few beers. Occasionally, he takes whole days off—after he's had too much to drink the night before. He's been through a series of girlfriends, never staying with one for more than 6 months. Lately, though, his single status has been bothering him, and he's been wondering why there don't seem to be any decent women out there.

In what ways does Will seem typical of someone with a Cluster B (dramatic/erratic) personality disorder? In what ways is he unusual? What would you need to know before you could decide whether he had a dramatic/erratic personality disorder? Which specific personality disorder seems most likely from the description of him, and why? Why is—or isn't—this information enough to make a diagnosis?

□ Fearful/Anxious Personality Disorders

The personality disorders in Cluster C—avoidant, dependent, and obsessive-compulsive personality disorders—share the feature of anxiety or fear. Although they have this superficial commonality, there is little overlap among the diagnostic criteria for these three disorders; this is in sharp contrast to the disorders within Cluster A (odd/eccentric) and those within Cluster B (dramatic/erratic), which have overlapping criteria. Nonetheless, people who have anxiety disorders and a comorbid personality disorder are most likely to have that personality disorder be from Cluster C (Friborg et al., 2013).

Avoidant Personality Disorder

The predominant characteristic of people with **avoidant personality disorder** is *social inhibition*—extreme shyness—that usually stems from feeling inadequate and being overly sensitive to negative evaluation (American Psychiatric Association, 2013). People with avoidant personality disorder are often characterized as shy, isolated, timid, or lonely.

What Is Avoidant Personality Disorder?

The diagnostic criteria for avoidant personality disorder (see Table 13.18) all relate to the person's predominant concern about embarrassing himself or herself during social interactions—perhaps by blushing or crying—and being socially rejected or humiliated. These fears, in turn, lead the person to limit social interactions.

People with avoidant personality disorder are so reluctant to engage in social interactions that they may turn down a promotion if the position requires increased social contact. And they are often hypervigilant for any indication of criticism or rejection. These fears and anxieties may cause them to behave in tense and fearful ways—for example, not talking about themselves for fear of what others might think—when they do interact with

TABLE 13.18 • DSM-5 Diagnostic Criteria for Avoidant Personality Disorder

A pervasive pattern of social inhibition, feelings of inadequacy, and hypersensitivity to negative evaluation, beginning by early adulthood and present in a variety of contexts, as indicated by four (or more) of the following:

1. Avoids occupational activities that involve significant interpersonal contact because of fears of criticism, disapproval, or rejection.

2. Is unwilling to get involved with people unless certain of being liked.

3. Shows restraint within intimate relationships because of the fear of being shamed or ridiculed.

4. Is preoccupied with being criticized or rejected in social situations.

5. Is inhibited in new interpersonal situations because of feelings of inadequacy.

6. Views self as socially inept, personally unappealing, or inferior to others.

7. Is unusually reluctant to take personal risks or to engage in any new activities because they may prove embarrassing.

TABLE 13.19 • Avoidant Personality Disorder Facts at a Glance

Prevalence
• Approximately 2.5% of the American population has avoidant personality disorder (Grant, Hasin, et al., 2004).
• Up to 10% of those seen in outpatient clinics have this disorder.

Comorbidity
• Because the diagnostic criteria overlap with those of social phobia, comorbidity between the two disorders is very high (Shea et al., 2004; Skodol, 2005; Skodol et al., 1995); in one study, 43% of people diagnosed with social phobia were also diagnosed with avoidant personality disorder (Faravelli et al., 2000).
• Common comorbid personality disorders are dependent personality disorder (because patients are dependent on the few friends they have), borderline personality disorder, and the Cluster A (odd/eccentric) personality disorders.
• Common comorbid psychological disorders are mood disorders and anxiety disorders.

Onset
• Based on the diagnostic criteria, symptoms such as shyness or a fear of strangers or new situations must emerge by early adulthood.

Course
• Two years after diagnosis, approximately 50% of people with avoidant personality disorder improve enough with treatment that their symptoms no longer meet the criteria (Grilo et al., 2004).

Gender Differences
• Men and women do not consistently differ in their prevalence rates for avoidant personality disorder (Torgersen, 2005).

Source: Unless specifically noted, citations are to American Psychiatric Association, 2000, 2013.

other people. This anxious way of relating to others may inadvertently elicit a mild version of the very reaction they fear—that others will evaluate them in a negative light. Among all people with personality disorders, those with avoidant personality disorder report the lowest quality of life (Cramer et al., 2003; Wilberg et al., 2009). Case 13.9 describes one person's experience, and Table 13.19 provides additional facts about this disorder.

CASE 13.9 • FROM THE OUTSIDE: Avoidant Personality Disorder

Marcus is a 33-year-old man who recently divorced.

His marriage deteriorated over several years and primarily as the result of his wife's increasing frustration with his unwillingness to do anything to improve his situation. He is employed as a warehouse manager and has held the same position for 9 years. He sees others doing more with their lives and wishes that he could as well. Although he hates that his wife chose to leave the marriage, he cannot blame her for doing so. Each evening after work he is filled with feelings of self-contempt and anguish. He would like to go out and be with other people, but he is certain that no one wants his company. He finds that drinking alcohol and watching television usually takes his mind off this unfulfilling life. Marcus thinks of committing suicide frequently.

(Rasmussen, 2005, p. 201)

Distinguishing Between Avoidant Personality Disorder and Other Disorders

If you're thinking that you've read about a disorder that seems similar to avoidant personality disorder earlier in this textbook, you're correct. Avoidant personality disorder has much in common with social phobia (Chapter 6), and the symptoms of the two disorders overlap (Chambless et al., 2008; Tillfors et al., 2004). However, the criteria for avoidant personality disorder are broader than those for social phobia, and the symptoms include a more pervasive sense of inadequacy or inferiority and a reluctance to take risks (Skodol, 2005), as was true of Marcus in Case 13.9.

When making the diagnosis of avoidant personality disorder, clinicians must take cultural factors into account (American Psychiatric Association, 2013). For example, recent immigrants may exhibit symptoms of this disorder, perhaps because of language barriers or concerns about safety, and so clinicians must be sure to ask whether the behavior predates immigration. Because the three fearful/anxious personality disorders have not been studied in depth, we will discuss the underlying bases for and treatment of all three disorders after we consider specific features of each of them separately.

Dependent Personality Disorder

Dependent personality disorder is characterized by submissive and clingy behaviors, based on fear of separation. The DSM-5 definition notes that the clingy behaviors are intended to elicit attention, reassurance, and decisive behaviors from other people (American Psychiatric Association, 2013). These behaviors are not a temporary bid for attention or reassurance (like the behaviors of those with borderline or histrionic personality disorder) but are part of a chronic pattern of helpless behavior.

People with dependent personality disorder are chronically plagued by self-doubt and consistently underestimate their abilities (see Table 13.20 for the list of diagnostic criteria). Thus, they have a hard time making all kinds of decisions, from life-altering ones about what career to pursue to mundane decisions about what clothes to wear. They prefer to have other people make such choices for them. And because they are quick to believe they are wrong, they are likely to see any criticism or disapproval as proof of their negative beliefs about themselves.

People with dependent personality disorder often don't learn the skills needed to function independently and so are, in fact, dependent on others; they have reason to be concerned about living on their own. When a relationship ends, they typically leap into another one in order to ensure that they are not alone. Even while in an intimate relationship, they are often preoccupied with the possibility that the relationship will end, and they will have to fend for themselves. People with dependent personality disorder are most comfortable in relationships with people who take the initiative—and take responsibility. Not surprisingly, then, they often choose overprotective and dominating people to be their friends and partners, becoming passive in those relationships.

Generally, people who have dependent personality disorder have a limited social circle, consisting of only a few people on whom they depend, as is true of Matthew in Case 13.10. Once they have established a relationship, people with dependent personality disorder are hesitant to disagree

This woman might just be bored, but meetings like the one shown in this photo make people with avoidant personality disorder uncomfortable. Symptoms of avoidant personality disorder and social phobia overlap, and people with either disorder are excessively concerned about being rejected by others or behaving in a way that leads them to feel humiliated. However, the social difficulties and feelings of inadequacy of people with avoidant personality disorder are generally more pervasive than those of people with other types of disorders.

Dependent personality disorder
A personality disorder characterized by submissive and clingy behaviors, based on fear of separation.

TABLE 13.20 • DSM-5 Diagnostic Criteria for Dependent Personality Disorder

A pervasive and excessive need to be taken care of that leads to submissive and clinging behavior and fears of separation, beginning by early adulthood and present in a variety of contexts, as indicated by five (or more) of the following:

1. Has difficulty making everyday decisions without an excessive amount of advice and reassurance from others.
2. Needs others to assume responsibility for most major areas of his or her life.
3. Has difficulty expressing disagreement with others because of fear of loss of support or approval. (**Note:** Do not include realistic fears of retribution.)
4. Has difficulty initiating projects or doing things on his or her own (because of a lack of self-confidence in judgment or abilities rather than a lack of motivation or energy).
5. Goes to excessive lengths to obtain nurturance and support from others, to the point of volunteering to do things that are unpleasant.
6. Feels uncomfortable or helpless when alone because of exaggerated fears of being unable to care for himself or herself.
7. Urgently seeks another relationship as a source of care and support when a close relationship ends.
8. Is unrealistically preoccupied with fears of being left to take care of himself or herself.

Reprinted with permission from the Diagnostic and Statistical Manual of Mental Disorders, Fifth Edition, (Copyright ©2013). American Psychiatric Association. All Rights Reserved.

TABLE **13.21** • Dependent Personality Disorder Facts at a Glance

Prevalence

- The prevalence of dependent personality disorder in the American population is less than 1% (Grant, Hasin, et al., 2004).

Comorbidity

- Common comorbid personality disorders are avoidant, borderline, and histrionic personality disorders.
- Common psychological disorders are mood disorders and anxiety disorders.

Onset

- As required by the diagnostic criteria, symptoms must emerge by young adulthood.

Course

- Symptoms may improve over time, to the point where the person no longer meets the criteria for the disorder (Markowitz et al., 2005).

Gender Differences

- In the general population, women tend to be diagnosed with dependent personality disorder more often than men (Torgersen, 2005).

Source: Unless otherwise noted, citations are to American Psychiatric Association, 2000, 2013.

Some people with obsessive-compulsive personality disorder may feel an urge to perfect a work-related task so strongly that they have difficulty stopping work.

Obsessive-compulsive personality disorder
A personality disorder characterized by preoccupations with perfectionism, orderliness, and self-control, as well as low levels of flexibility and efficiency.

with the other person for fear that he or she will withdraw emotional support. In fact, a person with this personality disorder may go to great lengths to maintain the support that the other person provides, even tolerating mental or physical abuse (American Psychiatric Association, 2013).

CASE **13.10** • FROM THE OUTSIDE: Dependent Personality Disorder

Matthew is a 34-year-old single man who lives with his mother and works as an accountant. He is seeking treatment because he is very unhappy after having just broken up with his girlfriend. His mother had disapproved of his marriage plans, ostensibly because the woman was of a different religion. Matthew felt trapped and forced to choose between his mother and his girl-friend, and because "blood is thicker than water," he had decided not to go against his mother's wishes.... Matthew is afraid of disagreeing with his mother for fear that she will not be supportive of him and he will then have to fend for himself. He criticizes himself for being weak, but also admires his mother and respects her judgment.... He feels that his own judgment is poor.

Matthew works at a job several grades below what his education and talent would permit. On several occasions he has turned down promotions because he didn't want the responsibility of having to supervise other people or make independent decisions. ... He has two very close friends whom he has had since early childhood. He has lunch with one of them every single workday and feels lost if his friend is sick and misses a day.

Matthew is the youngest of four children and the only boy. . . . He had considerable separation anxiety as a child—he had difficulty falling asleep unless his mother stayed in the room, mild school refusal, and unbearable homesickness when he occasionally tried "sleepovers." ... He has lived at home his whole life except for 1 year of college, from which he returned because of homesickness.

(Spitzer, Gibbon et al., 2002, pp. 179–180)

It is important to note that even if a person possesses enough of the characteristics to meet the diagnostic criteria in Table 13.20, he or she will not be diagnosed with dependent personality disorder unless these characteristics significantly impair functioning in major areas of life. Table 13.21 provides additional information about this disorder, although little is known about its etiology.

Obsessive-Compulsive Personality Disorder

Obsessive-compulsive personality disorder is characterized by preoccupations with perfectionism, orderliness, and self-control, as well as low levels of flexibility and efficiency (American Psychiatric Association, 2013). This personality disorder is associated with the least disability (Skodol, Gunderson et al., 2002) and the highest obtained educational level (Torgersen et al., 2001). Rachel Reiland describes her father as having some elements of obsessive-compulsive personality disorder: He was strict, "coveted control," and became enraged when events weren't to his liking. Reiland herself had some elements of this disorder: "Once upon a time perfectionism was my noble aspiration. My perfectionism extended beyond academics or career. I also aspired to be the perfect mother, lover, and friend, always appropriate in all my emotional expressions" (2004, p. 361).

What Is Obsessive-Compulsive Personality Disorder?

People with obsessive-compulsive personality disorder can get so bogged down in details that they leave the most important elements to the last minute (see Table 13.22). For instance, when preparing a presentation, people with this disorder might spend hours creating a single PowerPoint slide, trying to get it perfect, and end up running out of time for organizing their talk. They can't see the forest for the trees. For people with obsessive-compulsive personality disorder, decision making is a painful, long process; thus, once they've made a decision, they're not likely to change their minds—which can end up making them appear rigid and inflexible. And, like Reiland's father, when they are unable to control a situation, they may become angry, irritable, or upset.

Some (but not all) people who are workaholics may have obsessive-compulsive personality disorder—they may feel uncomfortable on vacations unless they take work along with them. And some with obsessive-compulsive personality disorder may spend excessive amounts of time on hobbies or household chores, striving for perfection and adhering to rules inflexibly. They may hold others to these same unrealistically stringent standards.

The relationships of people with obsessive-compulsive personality disorder are normally formal and serious; they are preoccupied with logic and intellect, are overly conscientious, and are intolerant of emotional or "illogical" behavior in others. Typically, people with obsessive-compulsive personality disorder feel uncomfortable with others who express emotions easily and openly. People with this disorder are not likely to express tender feelings or pay compliments. Other people often feel frustrated by their rigidity. In turn, people with obsessive-compulsive personality disorder have difficulty acknowledging the perspectives of others, as is true of Mr. V in Case 13.11. Table 13.23 provides additional information about this disorder.

CASE 13.11 • FROM THE OUTSIDE: Obsessive-Compulsive Personality Disorder

Mr. V, a 25-year-old philosophy graduate student, began twice-weekly psychotherapy. His presenting complaint was difficulty with completing work effectively, particularly writing tasks, due to excessive anxiety and obsessionality.... When he came for treatment, he was struggling to make progress on his master's thesis. Although Mr. V socialized quite a bit, he reported that intimate relationships often felt "wooden." He was usually overcommitted, with an endless list of "shoulds" that he would constantly mentally review and remind himself how much he was failing to satisfy his obligations. A central theme throughout treatment was his tendency to be self-denigrating, loathing himself as a person deserving of punishment in some way yet being extremely provocative.... He also held very strong political beliefs, sure that his way of viewing things was superior to others.

(Bender, 2005, p. 413)

TABLE 13.23 • Obsessive-Compulsive Personality Disorder Facts at a Glance

Prevalence

• Approximately 2–8% of the general population has obsessive-compulsive personality disorder, making it the most prevalent personality disorder (American Psychiatric Association, 2013; Grant, Hasin, et al., 2004).

Comorbidity

• Most people with obsessive-compulsive disorder (OCD) do not also have obsessive-compulsive personality disorder.

Onset

• The diagnostic criteria specify that symptoms must emerge by early adulthood.

Course

• Symptoms of up to one third of patients may improve over time to the point that they no longer meet the diagnostic criteria (Grilo et al., 2004).

Gender Differences

• Twice as many men as women are diagnosed with obsessive-compulsive personality disorder.

Source: Unless otherwise noted, citations should be American Psychiatric Association, 2013.

TABLE 13.22 • DSM-5 Diagnostic Criteria for Obsessive-Compulsive Personality Disorder

A pervasive pattern of preoccupation with orderliness, perfectionism, and mental and interpersonal control, at the expense of flexibility, openness, and efficiency, beginning by early adulthood and present in a variety of contexts, as indicated by four (or more) of the following:

1. Is preoccupied with details, rules, lists, order, organization, or schedules to the extent that the major point of the activity is lost.

2. Shows perfectionism that interferes with task completion (e.g., is unable to complete a project because his or her own overly strict standards are not met).

3. Is excessively devoted to work and productivity to the exclusion of leisure activities and friendships (not accounted for by obvious economic necessity).

4. Is overconscientious, scrupulous, and inflexible about matters of morality, ethics, or values (not accounted for by cultural or religious identification).

5. Is unable to discard worn-out or worthless objects even when they have no sentimental value.

6. Is reluctant to delegate tasks or to work with others unless they submit to exactly his or her way of doing things.

7. Adopts a miserly spending style toward both self and others; money is viewed as something to be hoarded for future catastrophes.

8. Shows rigidity and stubbornness.

Some workaholics have obsessive-compulsive personality disorder: They are perfectionistic and extremely orderly and organized. However, they can become so preoccupied with doing a job perfectly that they are inefficient or can't complete the task. Moreover, when problems arise, they can be rigid and inflexible.

Distinguishing Between Obsessive-Compulsive Personality Disorder and OCD

Obsessive-compulsive personality disorder is distinguished from OCD by the absence of true obsessions and compulsions. Rather, those with obsessive-compulsive personality disorder are preoccupied with details—as was Mr. V when writing his master's thesis—and are inflexible. Researchers are still trying to determine whether obsessive-compulsive personality disorder and OCD differ quantitatively or qualitatively. Research studies addressing this question have reported mixed findings (Eisen et al., 2006; Wu et al., 2006). Most people with one of the two disorders do not have the other (Mancebo et al., 2005).

Understanding Fearful/Anxious Personality Disorders

Virtually nothing is known about the neurological bases of fearful/anxious personality disorders, but the apparent similarity between these disorders and anxiety disorders might indicate that the amygdala is involved. In contrast, psychological factors associated with these disorders have been identified—fear and anxiety. Temperament can contribute to the development of any of these disorders, especially avoidant personality disorder (Joyce et al., 2003; Taylor et al., 2004). In fact, many of the factors related to social phobia are also associated with avoidant personality disorder, which makes sense, given the overlap in the symptoms of the two disorders. Moreover, people with both disorders have similar negative beliefs about themselves in relation to other people and avoid social situations for fear of embarrassing themselves (B. Meyer, 2002; Morey et al., 2003).

Cognitive and behavioral factors apparently contribute to all three fearful/anxious personality disorders. For all three, patients avoid situations that lead to discomfort and anxiety: With avoidant personality disorder, patients avoid social situations; with dependent personality disorder, they avoid making decisions and having responsibility; and with obsessive-compulsive personality disorder, they avoid making mistakes and experiencing strong emotions. The avoidance perpetuates the cognitive distortions because the patients' fears go unchallenged (Beck et al., 2004; Farmer & Nelson-Gray, 2005).

Social factors apparently also contribute to these personality disorders. These factors include anxious or avoidant attachment style, which may have arisen in childhood as a result of particular interaction patterns with parents (Gude et al., 2004; Pincus & Wilson, 2001).

Treating Fearful/Anxious Personality Disorders

As for most other personality disorders, there is little research on the treatment of fearful/anxious personality disorders, and what research there is has focused primarily on avoidant personality disorder. The findings suggest that the best treatment for social phobia can also help people with avoidant personality disorder—namely, CBT that uses exposure to avoided stimuli as well as cognitive restructuring of maladaptive beliefs and strategies (Beck et al., 2004; Emmelkamp et al., 2006; Farmer & Nelson-Gray, 2005; Reich, 2000). Treatment may also include family or couples therapy to help family members change their responses to—and thus the consequences of—the patient's maladaptive behaviors.

Table 13.24 summarizes the contrasting characteristics of the 10 personality disorders.

TABLE 13.24 • The Personality Disorders: A Summary

Personality disorder	Affect	Behavior	Cognition	Social functioning
Odd/eccentric: Cluster A				
Paranoid	Easily feels betrayed and angry	Hypervigilant for betrayal	Distrustful/suspicious of others; reads malevolent meaning into neutral remarks	Generally avoids relationships
Schizoid	Emotionally constricted, detached	Avoids people when possible	Views relationships as messy and undesirable	Indifferent to praise or criticism; generally avoids relationships
Schizotypal	Generally emotionally constricted but displays inappropriate affect and anxiety	Avoids people whenever possible	Perceptual distortions, ideas of reference, magical thinking	Generally avoids relationships
Dramatic/erratic: Cluster B				
Antisocial	Aggressive feelings toward others, lack of empathy	Generally poor impulse control	Believes that he or she is entitled to break rules	Dominant in relationships
Borderline	Emotionally expressive, with inappropriately strong and rapid reactions	Poor impulse control	Dramatic shifts between overvaluing and undervaluing others; may develop paranoid thinking under stress	Alternately dominant and submissive in relationships
Histrionic	Rapidly shifting but shallow emotions	Relatively poor impulse control; strives to be center of attention	Wants to be the center of attention	Dominant in relationships
Narcissistic	No empathy; haughty toward others	Manipulates others	Grandiosity	Dominant in relationships
Fearful/anxious: Cluster C				
Avoidant	Anxiety in social situations	Overcontrol of behavior	Excessively negative self-opinion; worries about being rejected or criticized	Submissive in relationships, but generally avoids them
Dependent	Anxiety about possible separation from others and having to function independently	Overcontrol of behavior	Believes that he or she is helpless and incompetent and so must rely on others	Submissive in relationships
Obsessive-compulsive	Constricted in expression of emotion to others	Overcontrol of behavior	Perfectionism; rigid thinking; preoccupation with details, rules, and lists	Dominant and relatively detached in relationships

Source: Pretzer & Beck, 2005; Skodol, 2005.

Thinking Like A Clinician

Juan and his wife, Beatriz, are from Argentina. They have been referred to mental health services by their family doctor. Beatriz always brings her husband with her to her doctor's appointments, and she always wants her husband in the room during the examination, although her English is more than sufficient to express herself and understand the doctor.

Beatriz happened to mention at her last medical visit that she never leaves the house if Juan isn't with her. She didn't see why she should because Juan is happy to go with her wherever she needs to go. She said that she likes it this way—that she doesn't feel "stuck" at home and that Juan pretty much takes care of whatever she doesn't feel able to do.

What specific areas of Beatriz's functioning would you want to know more about before making a diagnosis, and why? What other types of information would you want to have (for example, about cultural issues), and why? Might Beatriz be suffering from a comorbid psychological disorder that is not a personality disorder? If so, which one, and what would you need to know to be relatively certain of that?

◻ Follow-up on Rachel Reiland

We can say with certainty that Rachel Reiland suffered from borderline personality disorder. In addition, she displayed significant elements of two other personality disorders: histrionic personality disorder (her dramatic behaviors may have been motivated by excessive emotional reactivity and a desire for attention) and obsessive-compulsive personality disorder (her rigid thoughts and behaviors may have been motivated by perfectionism). However, it is difficult to determine whether these aspects of her personality met the criteria for the diagnosis of comorbid personality disorders. Her symptoms of borderline personality disorder were so pronounced that they might have masked additional personality disorders.

What happened to Reiland? In her memoir, she notes that she was hospitalized three times; the first time because of significant suicidal impulses. After discharge from that first hospitalization, she spent 4 years in intensive outpatient therapy with a psychiatrist—three times a week during the first 2 years of treatment. She was hospitalized twice more over the course of her therapy and again developed anorexia for a period of time. Her symptoms were sufficiently severe that her therapist imposed strict limits on their interactions; for instance, he banned physical contact of any kind. Although her therapist used psychodynamic therapy, he also incorporated elements of CBT and DBT into the treatment: The therapist addressed Reiland's black-and-white thinking and validated her experiences while trying to help her accept her feelings without judging herself. In addition to the hospitalizations and outpatient therapy, Reiland tried various medications, settling on antidepressants that she gradually stopped before her therapy ended.

Her treatment was successful. She wrote her memoir 8 years after her therapy ended; she developed and sustained the ability to regulate her moods, to control her impulses, and to have productive and enjoyable relationships.

◻ SUMMING UP

Diagnosing Personality Disorders

- A personality disorder is characterized by maladaptive personality traits that begin by young adulthood and continue through adulthood; these traits are relatively inflexible, are expressed across a wide range of situations, and lead to distress or impaired functioning. A personality disorder affects three areas of functioning: affect, behavior (including social behavior), and cognition.

- In DSM-5, personality disorders are grouped into three clusters: Cluster A, characterized by odd or eccentric behaviors related to features of schizophrenia; Cluster B, characterized by dramatic and erratic behaviors and problems with emotional regulation; and Cluster C, characterized by anxious or fearful behaviors.

- The category of personality disorders in DSM-5 has been criticized on numerous grounds.

- The neuropsychosocial approach explains how personality disorders develop by highlighting the interactions among three sorts of factors:

  ○ Neurological factors primarily involve the effects of genes on temperament.

  ○ Psychological factors include temperament, operant conditioning, and dysfunctional beliefs.

  ○ Social factors include insecure attachment that can result from childhood abuse or neglect.

- Treatments for personality disorders include medications for comorbid symptoms, CBT or psychodynamic therapy, and family education and therapy, as well as couples, interpersonal, and group therapy.

Odd/Eccentric Personality Disorders

- The essential feature of paranoid personality disorder is a persistent and pervasive mistrust and suspiciousness, which is accompanied by a bias to interpret other people's motives as hostile. Although paranoid personality disorder and paranoid schizophrenia both involve suspicious beliefs, people with the personality disorder have some capacity to evaluate whether their suspicions are based on reality.

- Schizoid personality disorder is characterized by a restricted range of emotions in social interactions and few—if any—close relationships; people with this disorder have poor social skills. They report rarely experiencing strong emotions, and they prefer to be—and function best when—isolated from others.

- Schizotypal personality disorder is characterized by eccentric thoughts, perceptions, and behaviors, as well as by having very few close relationships. This personality disorder has three groups of symptoms: cognitive-perceptual, interpersonal, and disorganized. Schizotypal personality disorder is viewed as a milder form of schizophrenia.

- Paranoid, schizoid, and schizotypal personality disorders are on the spectrum of schizophrenia-related disorders, and close relatives of people with any of these odd/eccentric personality disorders are more likely to have schizophrenia. Schizotypal personality disorder involves neurological abnormalities that are less severe than those associated with schizophrenia.

- People with odd/eccentric personality disorders are reluctant participants in treatment. Treatment may address fundamental issues, such as isolation and suspiciousness. Treatment for schizotypal personality disorder may include antipsychotic medication (although at lower doses than used for psychotic disorders), and CBT.

Dramatic/Erratic Personality Disorders

- The hallmark of antisocial personality disorder is a persistent disregard for the rights of others, which may lead these people to violate rules or laws or to act aggressively.

- The diagnostic criteria for antisocial personality disorder overlap with aspects of psychopathy. However, psychopathy is defined by a more restrictive set of criteria, which focus on emotional and interpersonal characteristics, such as a lack of empathy and antisocial behaviors.

- Psychopathy and antisocial personality disorder arise from feedback loops among various factors, including genes, lack of empathy, classical and operant conditioning, abuse or neglect or inconsistent discipline in childhood, parents' criminal behavior, and attachment style. Treatment for psychopathy has generally not been successful; treatment for antisocial personality disorder focuses on modifying specific behaviors and has some degree of success, at least temporarily, in motivated people.

- Borderline personality disorder is characterized by volatile emotions, an unstable self-image, and impulsive behavior in relationships. People with this disorder have problems with emotional regulation and may engage in self-harming behaviors or try to commit suicide.

- Factors that contribute to borderline personality disorder include the genetic and neurological underpinnings of emotional dysregulation, a relatively low threshold for emotional responsiveness, an easily changeable sense of self, cognitive distortions, and a history of abuse, neglect, or feeling invalidated by others. Treatment for borderline personality may include medication, DBT, CBT, intensive psychodynamic therapy, and IPT.

- The hallmark of histrionic personality disorder is attention seeking, usually through exaggerated emotional displays. Symptoms may also include a sense of boredom or emptiness and a low tolerance for frustration.

- Narcissistic personality disorder is characterized by a grandiose sense of self-importance and a constant desire for praise and admiration. People with this disorder may also feel a sense of entitlement, behave arrogantly, and have difficulty understanding other people's points of view.

Fearful/Anxious Personality Disorders

- The hallmark of avoidant personality disorder is social inhibition, which usually stems from feeling inadequate and being overly sensitive to negative evaluation. Although similar to social phobia, the criteria for avoidant personality disorder are more pervasive and involve a more general reluctance to take risks. CBT methods that are used to treat social phobia can also be effective with avoidant personality disorder.

- Dependent personality disorder is characterized by submissive and clingy behaviors, based on fear of separation; these behaviors are intended to elicit attention and reassurance, and place responsibility for making decisions on other people. People with dependent personality disorder are chronically plagued by self-doubt and consistently underestimate their abilities; in fact, they may not know how to function independently.

- Obsessive-compulsive personality disorder is characterized by preoccupations with perfectionism, orderliness, and self-control and by low levels of flexibility and efficiency. These rigid personality traits may lead these people to have difficulty prioritizing and making decisions, and they are often intolerant of emotional or "illogical" behavior in others.

Key Terms

More Study Aids

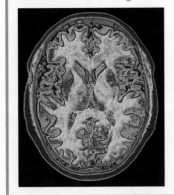

For additional study aids related to this chapter, including quizzes to make sure you've retained everything you've learned and a Student Video Activity exploring the possible connections between personality disorders and brain disorders, go to: www.worthpublishers.com/launchpad/rkabpsych2e.

Image Source Black/Alamy

CHAPTER **14**

Neurodevelopmental and Disruptive Behavior Disorders

Lela and Carlos Enriquez have three children: Javier, Pia, and Richie. It's been a very challenging year for the family, full of heartache; all three children have been having various difficulties at home or at school. Lela and Carlos are trying to figure out what, exactly, the problems are and what can be done about them.

The most troubling problem concerns their youngest son, Richie. He's almost 2 years old, but he has yet to smile at his parents—or anyone else. He's not talking, either, and although he seems to understand what people say to him, he is a bit slow to respond. Whereas most toddlers are talking in two- or three-word sentences, Richie doesn't say even single words. Richie also seems shy in the extreme; he doesn't even look people in the eye.

Richie's older siblings have also been having problems. Javier is 10 years old, and he's had both academic and social problems at school; his teacher suggested that he receive a thorough evaluation. And his 8-year-old sister, Pia, has been a bit of a puzzle. On her last report card, her teacher noted that she's very bright but doesn't seem to be working as hard as she could.

Like Richie, Pia, and Javier, many children achieve milestones, such as walking and talking, later than the average child or have problems socially or academically. When do such difficulties fall in the range of normal development, and when do they signal a larger problem? In this chapter we address this question by exploring two categories of DSM-5 disorders that typically arise in childhood: (1) *neurodevelopmental* disorders, which involve problems with the brain—the *neuro* part of the term—and are typically first diagnosed during infancy, childhood, or adolescence—the *developmental* part of the term, and (2) disruptive behavior disorders, also typically first diagnosed before adulthood. However, we must note that these are not the only disorders that can affect children; children can also be diagnosed with many of the disorders discussed in previous chapters.

Intellectual disability
A neurodevelopmental disorder characterized by cognitive abilities that are significantly below normal, along with impaired adaptive functioning in daily life; also called *intellectual developmental disorder* and previously referred to as *mental retardation*.

WE BEGIN THIS CHAPTER by examining intellectual disability—a disorder that can profoundly affect the lives of children and their families and that may require special schools or residential placements as well as other special services.

▢ Intellectual Disability (Intellectual Developmental Disorder)

When either Lela or Carlos calls Richie's name, he often seems to ignore it. They can tell that he's not deaf—he clearly notices street noises and other sounds, and he startles in response to loud noises. His cognitive abilities are noticeably less developed than Javier's and Pia's were when they were his age; Richie's intellectual functioning doesn't seem normal. Could he have intellectual developmental disorder?

What Is Intellectual Disability?

Intellectual disability (also called *intellectual developmental disorder* [IDD], and related to what was previously called *mental retardation*, a term that is generally no longer used) is characterized by deficits in cognitive abilities (significantly below normal), as determined both by standardized intelligence testing and by clinical assessment, along with impaired adaptive functioning in daily life. Specific deficits are in academic learning, in social understanding, and in "practical understanding" (such as knowing how to manage money) and involve a variety of cognitive abilities: reasoning and problem solving, planning, abstract thinking, judgment, and understanding complex ideas.

Although the DSM-5 criteria themselves do not specify a specific IQ score cutoff, the part of the manual that discusses the criteria in detail suggests that impaired intelligence would entail having an IQ score that is at least two standard deviations below average. On a standard IQ test where the mean is set at 100, an IQ approximately equal to or less than 70 (plus or minus 5 points) would be two standard deviations below average.

But DSM-5 is clear that a low IQ by itself is not enough to diagnose IDD; the child must also have impaired adaptive functioning in daily life as a result of the cognitive deficits. Adaptive functioning involves three domains, assessed relative to the person's age and background:

- *conceptual* (language, mathematical, reasoning used to solve problems, and judgments in novel situations),

- *social* (being aware of and having empathy for other people's experiences and emotions; the capacity for friendship and social judgment and communication), and

- *practical* (being able to care for oneself; manage money, school, and job responsibilities).

The deficits in intellectual ability and adaptive functioning (see Table 14.1) must have emerged during childhood and thus cannot be the result of brain trauma in adulthood.

Although a person's IQ score may serve as a rough guide to evaluating mental abilities, the most important criterion for determining the level of intellectual disability is the level of impaired adaptive functioning. DSM-5 specifies four levels of severity of these impairments—mild, moderate, severe, and profound—which reflect functioning in conceptual, social, and practical

TABLE 14.1 • DSM-5 Diagnostic Criteria for Intellectual Disability (Intellectual Developmental Disorder)

A. Deficits in intellectual functions, such as reasoning, problem solving, planning, abstract thinking, judgment, academic learning, and learning from experience, confirmed by both clinical assessment and individualized, standardized intelligence testing.

B. Deficits in adaptive functioning that result in failure to meet developmental and socio-cultural standards for personal independence and social responsibility. Without ongoing support, the adaptive deficits limit functioning in one or more activities of daily life, such as communication, social participation, and independent living, across multiple environments, such as home, school, work, and community.

C. Onset of intellectual and adaptive deficits during the developmental period.

domains. In general, the greater the severity, the more impaired the person is likely to be:

- *Mild intellectual disability.* Most people with intellectual disability fall into this group. People in this mild range may be able to function relatively independently with training but usually need additional help and support during stressful periods and seem "immature" in social interactions.

- *Moderate intellectual disability.* Although they are not able to function independently, with training and supervision, people in this group may be able to perform unskilled work and take basic care of themselves; although able to have relationships, people in this range may not accurately interpret social cues.

- *Severe intellectual disability.* A small number of people with intellectual disability fall into this group. Adults in this group are likely to live with their family or in a supervised setting and are able to perform simple tasks only with close supervision. They may be able to speak in simple phrases and do simple counting. During childhood, they may begin speaking later than other children.

- *Profound intellectual disability.* The smallest number of people with intellectual disability fall into this group. People in this group need constant supervision or help to perform simple tasks and may communicate only nonverbally; they are likely to have significant neurological problems.

Like Sean Penn's character in the movie *I Am Sam*, people with mild intellectual disability can, with training, learn to function independently. In this scene Penn is shown with Michelle Pfeiffer, who plays his lawyer in his fight to retain custody of his young daughter.

Information from parents and teachers may help the clinician to determine a person's ability to function. Depending on IQ and level of adaptive functioning, someone with IDD may require supervision, ranging from minimal to constant care. Like Larry in Case 14.1, many of these people have needs and abilities that fall somewhere in the middle.

CASE 14.1 • FROM THE OUTSIDE: Intellectual Disability

Larry, a 34-year-old man with moderate [intellectual disabilities]. . . had been referred for complaints of seeing "monsters," "scary faces," and "the bogeyman." He initially appeared paranoid and delusional, describing the feared bogeyman in detail. An assessment of possible neurochemical or physical factors that might help explain the recent onset of these symptoms yielded no significant diagnostic information. . . .

Larry's perception of monsters was specific to certain situations, such as being alone in a dark room. . . .

Specifically, when asked to go alone to any dark place [including the dark stairwell in his group home, where Larry must go to carry out his assigned chore of taking down the trash], he became agitated, resisted, and made loud statements about monsters and scary faces. . . .

Larry's monsters could be attributed to his limited means of communicating his fear of being alone in the dark. [It appears, then, that Larry has a phobic response to the dark.] . . .

(Nezu et al., 1992, pp. 78, 164)

Larry had two disorders: intellectual disability and a specific phobia. because of his intellectual disability, he had difficulty explaining his fears. He received CBT for his phobia, which was successful, and he was then able to go down to the basement without fear.

Like people of normal intelligence, people with intellectual disability exhibit a wide variety of personality characteristics: some are passive or easygoing, and others are impulsive or aggressive; some people with intellectual disability, like Larry, may have difficulty communicating verbally—which can heighten aggressive or impulsive tendencies. People with intellectual disability are more likely than average to be exploited or abused by others. Table 14.2 lists additional facts about IDD.

TABLE 14.2 • Intellectual Disability Facts at a Glance

Prevalence

• Approximately 1% of the general population has intellectual disability; however, prevalence estimates vary depending on the age, the survey method used, and the particular population studied.

Onset

• Severe and profound intellectual disability are generally identified at birth, although in some cases intellectual disability is caused by a medical condition later in childhood, such as head trauma.

• Mild intellectual disability is sometimes not diagnosed until relatively late in childhood, although the onset may have been earlier.

Comorbidity

• Compared to the general population, people with intellectual disability are three to four times more likely to have an additional psychological disorder, cerebral palsy, or epilepsy.

• Among the most common comorbid disorders are major depressive disorder, attention-deficit/hyperactivity disorder, and autism spectrum disorder.

Course

• The diagnosis is typically lifelong for moderate to severe intellectual disability, but beneficial environmental factors can improve adaptive functioning for those with mild intellectual disability to the point where they no longer meet all the criteria for the disorder.

• Educational opportunities, support, and stimulation can improve the level of functioning.

Gender Differences

• Intellectual disability occurs more frequently in males, with a male-to-female ratio of about 1.5 to 1.

Cultural Differences

• Although the criteria for intellectual disability used in many other countries are similar to those used in the United States, they are not always the same; such differences may account for the higher prevalence rates in some other countries, such as 4.5% in France (Oakland et al., 2003).

Source: Unless otherwise noted, the source for information is American Psychiatric Association, 2013.

 CURRENT CONTROVERSY

Changing *Mental Retardation* to *Intellectual Disability*: Will Such a Switch Be Beneficial?

People with intelligence levels low enough to affect their daily life have been labeled in various ways over the decades. The newest change in the DSM-5 is to replace the diagnosis of *mental retardation* with that of *intellectual disability*. However, this is not simply a change in label; the criteria have changed: The diagnosis and its severity are no longer a function of the assessed intelligence level. (Previously the diagnosis and its severity were anchored in IQ scores of various ranges.) Rather, the diagnosis and its severity are now based on levels of adaptive functioning—how well the person can adapt and function—in three domains: conceptual, social, and practical.

On the one hand, the new name more accurately describes the disorder in that it is not simply that mental abilities are *delayed* (that is "retarded"). Moreover, changing the criteria to deemphasize IQ scores and emphasize the three domains of functioning is ultimately more relevant to people's ability to function and their need for services.

On the other hand, if the name change has been made in order to reduce stigma, it could be just a matter of time before this new diagnosis becomes a stigmatizing label. The diagnosis may be more descriptive, but is the description accurate? If the emphasis is more on adaptive functioning than intellectual level, then using the diagnostic term "intellectual disability" could be confusing.

CRITICAL THINKING Do you think that the term *intellectual disability* will come to be as stigmatizing as *mental retardation*? Why or why not? Is there a better word than *intellectual*, given that the diagnosis focuses more on the ability to adapt and function than on intellect?

(James Foley, College of Wooster)

Understanding Intellectual Disability

Many neurological events can lead to intellectual disability, some of which reflect the fact that the fetus was exposed to certain types of substances (such as drugs or a virus) or to other stimuli (such as radiation); such harmful substances and stimuli are referred to as **teratogens**. Intellectual disability may also result from particular complications during labor (such as occurs when a newborn receives insufficient oxygen during birth) or from exposure to high levels of lead prenatally or during childhood.

Neurological Factors: Teratogens and Genes

One type of teratogen is environmental toxins, to which a fetus typically is exposed through the placenta after the toxin has entered the mother's bloodstream. Examples of environmental toxins include synthetic chemicals such as methyl mercury, polychlorinated biphenyls (PCBs), and pesticides. Exposure to these toxins in the first trimester of pregnancy can disrupt early developmental processes of the central nervous system (Lanphear et al., 2005). Intellectual disability may also arise because of a variety of genetic abnormalities, listed in Table 14.3.

The cognitive and behavioral deficits observed in people with intellectual disability occur because the brain does not process information appropriately, often because of abnormal brain structure. For example, *fetal alcohol syndrome* is a set of birth defects caused by the mother's alcohol use during pregnancy. (Alcohol is a teratogen.) People who have this syndrome have an unusually small head size, which occurs in part because the frontal lobes are smaller than normal—specifically the portions involved in planning, carrying out tasks, and controlling impulsive behavior (Riley & McGee, 2005). All of these activities are difficult for many children with fetal alcohol syndrome.

Although severe or profound intellectual disability often involves global abnormalities, each case of mild or moderate IDD may have a unique profile of specific impaired abilities, related to the particular cause of the disability.

Teratogens
Substances or other stimuli that are harmful to a fetus.

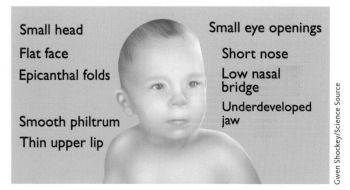

The characteristic facial features associated with fetal alcohol syndrome include small eyes; a smooth philtrum—the space between the upper lip and the nose; and a thin upper lip.

(image labels: Small head, Flat face, Epicanthal folds, Smooth philtrum, Thin upper lip, Small eye openings, Short nose, Low nasal bridge, Underdeveloped jaw)

Gwen Shockey/Science Source

TABLE 14.3 • Genetic Causes of Intellectual Disability

Cause of intellectual disability	Genetic abnormality
Down syndrome	Abnormality in chromosome 21
Rett's disorder (females only)	Abnormality in X chromosome (which is lethal for male fetuses)
Fragile X (the most common cause of inherited intellectual disability)	Repetition of a piece of genetic code on the X chromosome that becomes progressively more severe in each generation
Prader-Willi and *Angelman syndromes*	Deletion on chromosome 15 that has different consequences depending on which parent's genes contribute the deletion
Phenylketonuria (PKU)	A genetically based defect in an enzyme, *phenylalanine hydroxylase,* that leads to a failure to convert phenylalanine to tyrosine. Unconverted phenylalanine is toxic to brain cells, leading to intellectual disability, which can be prevented if PKU is identified (through a blood test at birth) and the person adheres to a diet that restricts phenylalanine.
Congenital hypothyroidism	Inadequate production of thyroid hormone caused by a genetic mutation. The fetus gets thyroid hormone from the mother, but after birth, the deficiency leads to defects in the developing brain. If hypothyroidism is not detected within the first 3 months of life, the damage cannot be reversed, even with thyroid hormone replacement.

Source: For more information see the Permissions section.

When this child gets excited, she engages in the stereotyped behavior of hand flapping. Other stereotyped behaviors exhibited by people with intellectual disability include rocking back and forth and repeatedly moving a finger.

Maria Platt-Evans/Science Source

Psychological Factors: Problem Behaviors

People with intellectual disability often engage in two types of problematic behaviors that are not specifically mentioned in the DSM-5 criteria: (1) **stereotyped behaviors** (also referred to as *stereotypies*), which are repetitive behaviors that don't serve a function, such as hand flapping, slight but fast finger and hand motions, and body rocking; and (2) *self-injurious behaviors*, such as hitting the head against something and hitting or biting oneself. People with intellectual disability who exhibit both stereotypic behaviors and self-injurious behaviors have greater deficits in nonverbal social skills than those with only one type of problematic behavior (Matson et al., 2006).

Other problematic behaviors that often go along with intellectual disability include consistently choosing to interact with objects rather than people, inappropriately touching others, and resisting physical contact or affection.

Social Factors: Understimulation

If an infant is severely understimulated (e.g., the child is not played with enough) or is undernourished, he or she may subsequently develop intellectual disability (Dennis, 1973; Dong & Greenough, 2004; Skeels & Dye, 1939). For example, children raised in orphanages where they are essentially warehoused, ignored and neglected, may develop this disorder.

In sum, most cases of intellectual disability arise primarily from neurological factors—teratogens or genes—that produce abnormal brain structure and function, which then cause cognitive deficits. Children with intellectual disability may exhibit stereotyped or self-injurious behaviors.

Treating Intellectual Disability

Intellectual disability cannot be "cured," but interventions can help people with IDD to function more independently in daily life. Such interventions are designed to improve specific skills and abilities, such as the person's ability to communicate. But more than that, clinicians try to prevent intellectual disability from arising in the first place. Prevention efforts seek to avert or reduce the factors that cause intellectual disability.

Targeting Neurological Factors: Prevention

Because the key causes of intellectual disability are neurological, this type of factor is the target of prevention efforts. For example, one successful prevention effort focuses on *phenylketonuria* (PKU). Since the 1950s, virtually all newborns in the United States have received a test to detect whether they have PKU, which addresses a problem metabolizing the enzyme phenylalanine hydroxylase. For newborns who test positive, lifelong dietary modifications can prevent any brain damage, thereby preventing intellectual disability.

Another successful prevention effort addresses childhood exposure to lead, which can trigger brain abnormalities. Lead was banned as an ingredient in paint in 1978; laws were passed that required landlords and homeowners to inform any prospective renters or buyers of any known lead paint on the property. Beginning in the 1970s, lead was also phased out as an additive to gasoline. As a result of these measures, lead exposure—and lead-induced intellectual disability—has decreased.

There are no neurological treatments for intellectual disability, although symptoms of comorbid disorders and some self-injurious behaviors may respond to medication (Unwin & Deb, 2011).

Stereotyped behaviors
Repetitive behaviors—such as body rocking—that do not serve a function; also referred to as *stereotypies*.

Targeting Psychological and Social Factors: Communication

Given the deficits and heterogeneous symptoms that accompany intellectual disability, no single symptom is the focus of all psychological and social treatments. Rather, psychological and social treatments depend on the person's specific constellation of symptoms and comorbid disorders. In some cases, treatment targets significant communication deficits. Such treatment may teach nonvocal communication, for example, using a technique called the Picture Exchange Communication System (PECS) (Bondy & Frost, 1994). With this system, children learn to give a picture of the desired item to someone in exchange for that item.

Targeting Social Factors: Accommodation in the Classroom—It's the Law

With the passage of the Americans with Disabilities Act in 1990 and the subsequent Individuals with Disabilities Education Act (IDEA) in 1997, eligible children with disabilities between the ages of 3 and 21 are guaranteed special education and related services that are individually tailored to the child's needs, at no cost to the parents. An *individualized education program* (IEP) specifies educational goals as well as supplementary services or products that should be used to help the student benefit from the regular curriculum. Each child with disabilities receives a comprehensive evaluation, and the child is placed in the least restrictive environment that responds to his or her needs.

For many children, one goal of the IEP is to facilitate **inclusion**—placing students with disabilities in a regular classroom, with guidelines for any accommodations that the regular classroom teacher or special education teacher should make. Note that *mainstreaming* is not the same as inclusion; mainstreaming simply refers to placing a child with disabilities into a regular classroom, with no curricular adjustments to accommodate the disability.

Legal mandates have brought people with intellectual disability (and other disabilities) out from the shadows of institutional living into society: Depending on the severity of their retardation, they live in communities, hold jobs, and have families.

Is intellectual disability an appropriate diagnosis for Richie Enriquez? It may well be, but in the next section, we'll examine a set of disorders that might better account for these problems.

With the Picture Exchange Communication System, a child who has intellectual disability with poor verbal communication skills can make his or her desires known: The child presents a card with the picture of the desired object to another person, who then may give the actual object to the child.

Used with permission of Pyramid Educational Consultants, Inc./www.pecs.com

Like this girl with Down syndrome, youngsters with mild to moderate intellectual disability may be placed in regular classrooms, either as part of inclusion (in which the teacher makes specific accommodations based on the child's special needs) or mainstreaming (in which the teacher doesn't make specific accommodations).

Paul Conklin/Photo Edit

Thinking Like A Clinician

Clare just graduated from college and started working in a center for adults with various intellectual disabilities. She is trying to get to know each client—his or her strengths and weaknesses. The clients with intellectual disability are classified in the moderate-to-severe range. Based on what you've learned, what can—and can't—you assume about those clients? Why might people with mild or profound intellectual disability not be at the center?

Autism Spectrum Disorder

Richie Enriquez exhibits some behaviors that are not typical of people diagnosed with intellectual disability: He avoids making eye contact, hardly smiles, and can spend hours playing with a glittery plastic ball. When his mother takes a toy away from him, perhaps because it's time for lunch, he has a nuclear-sized temper tantrum: "He screams, he cries, he hits his head against the wall. . . . I don't know what to

Inclusion

The placement of students with disabilities in a regular classroom, with guidelines for any accommodations that the regular classroom teacher or special education teacher should make.

Autism spectrum disorder (ASD)
A neurodevelopmental disorder characterized by deficits in communication and social interaction skills, as well as stereotyped behaviors and narrow interests.

do. When I try to hold him, to comfort him, it seems to make things even worse. I've never seen a child like him." His father notes that "if the evening routine—dinner, bath, three books, bed—varies, if I forget to read the third book, Richie freaks out, rocking himself and screaming. And he has no interest in playing with Javier and Pia—even though they try so hard to get him to play or to laugh." From these descriptions, Richie's behaviors sound like symptoms of autism spectrum disorder.

What Is Autism Spectrum Disorder?

Autism spectrum disorder (ASD) is characterized by deficits in communication and social interaction skills, as well as stereotyped behaviors and narrow interests. The term *spectrum* is used because people with the disorder may differ in the severity of the symptoms and in their developmental level relative to their chronological age. The term *autism* by itself does not capture the range of variations that can occur. As noted in Table 14.4, the DSM-5 criteria include problems with social communication and interaction: difficulty with normal back-and-forth conversations or even initiating social interaction, poor eye contact, difficulty using facial expressions and body language as a means of communication, difficulty understanding the social communication of others, and difficulty developing and maintaining age-appropriate relationships.

Like children with intellectual disability (but unlike other children), children with ASD (1) are much more or much less reactive to sensory stimuli, (2) engage in very repetitive play, and (3) often display stereotyped behaviors (such as flapping their hands). These children insist on repeating the same behaviors or activities for much longer periods than other children do. People with ASD also become distressed when certain routines are not carried out or completed, as was Richie when his father varied the evening activities in any way; to calm themselves down, they may rock themselves, as did Richie. To diagnose ASD, these symptoms must impair the ability to function on a daily basis.

ASD is caused primarily by neurological abnormalities and dysfunctions (Ecker et al., 2012; Kundert & Trimarchi, 2006). Symptoms of ASD usually become evident during infancy or early childhood, and many children also have comorbid intellectual disability, which may be true of Richie. Children for whom intellectual disability is the only psychological disorder usually look people in the eye, and they tend to respond when hearing their names and to smile at other people. In contrast, children with ASD—with or without intellectual disability—generally avoid eye contact and shy away from social interactions. (DSM-IV, the previous version of DSM, contained two separate disorders—*autistic disorder* and a milder form, *Asperger's disorder*—that have been combined in DSM-5, in part because research suggests that they have related symptoms and etiology; Towbin et al., 2002.)

People with ASD tend to be oblivious to—and so appear to ignore—others. Younger children with ASD appear to be uninterested in making friends. Some older children may want to make friends, but they don't understand the basic rules of social interaction; thus, their attempts are

TABLE 14.4 • DSM-5 Diagnostic Criteria for Autism Spectrum Disorder (ASD)

A. Persistent deficits in social communication and social interaction across multiple contexts, as manifested by the following, currently or by history (examples are illustrative, not exhaustive; see text):

1. Deficits in social-emotional reciprocity, ranging, for example, from abnormal social approach and failure of normal back-and-forth conversation; to reduced sharing of interests, emotions, or affect; to failure to initiate or respond to social interactions.

2. Deficits in nonverbal communicative behaviors used for social interaction, ranging, for example, from poorly integrated verbal and nonverbal communication; to abnormalities in eye contact and body language or deficits in understanding and use of gestures; to a total lack of facial expressions and nonverbal communication.

3. Deficits in developing, maintaining, and understanding relationships, ranging, for example, from difficulties adjusting behavior to suit various social contexts; to difficulties in sharing imaginative play or in making friends; to absence of interest in peers.

B. Restricted, repetitive patterns of behavior, interests, or activities, as manifested by at least two of the following, currently or by history (examples are illustrative, not exhaustive; see text):

1. Stereotyped or repetitive motor movements, use of objects, or speech (e.g., simple motor stereotypes, lining up toys or flipping objects, echolalia, idiosyncratic phrases).

2. Insistence on sameness, inflexible adherence to routines, or ritualized patterns of verbal or nonverbal behavior (e.g., extreme distress at small changes, difficulties with transitions, rigid thinking patterns, greeting rituals, need to take same route or eat same food every day).

3. Highly restricted, fixated interests that are abnormal in intensity or focus (e.g., strong attachment to or preoccupation with unusual objects, excessively circumscribed or perseverative interests).

4. Hyper- or hyporeactivity to sensory input or unusual interest in sensory aspects of the environment (e.g., apparent indifference to pain/temperature, adverse response to specific sounds or textures, excessive smelling or touching of objects, visual fascination with lights or movement).

C. Symptoms must be present in the early development period (but may not become fully manifest until social demands exceed limited capacities, or may be masked by learned strategies in later life).

unlikely to be successful. To understand how symptoms of ASD translate into daily life, consider the following list of "peculiarities" that a mother compiled about her 4-year-old son, George, before he was diagnosed with autism (Moore, 2006, pp. 94–95):

- He talks [by reciting] quotations and by imitating adult speech.
- Has poor social interaction. Doesn't know how to play with others.
- Avoids eye contact with strangers.
- He is very excitable (easily aroused, not easy to calm).
- He complains about strong stimuli, such as the sun, loud noises.
- Abnormalities of attention, including the ability to shut people out and be absorbed in something trivial for a long time.
- Loves nature, will stand and look at the moon for as long as he is allowed, despite freezing weather.
- Has a strong aversion to strangers, groups, and crowds.
- Obsessive.
- Ritualistic.
- Lines up [Lego bricks or matches them by color, but] doesn't build. Always destroys.
- Occasionally plays with feces.
- Doesn't dress or undress—just beginning to put on trousers and coat.
- Could recognize simple words at twenty months.
- Has a strong reaction to colors.
- Never asks questions except where is Mummy, Daddy, Sam.
- Only just starting to correlate facial expressions of others to emotion.

George, on the left, is the oldest of three boys and has ASD; his middle brother, Sam, also has ASD; his youngest brother does not. The brothers, and their mother, Charlotte, are shown here.

These behaviors might not be that unusual for a 1-year-old, but they are definitely not typical for a 4-year-old. The items on George's mother's list span the problem areas that are the hallmarks of ASD: impaired communication and social interactions and restricted and repetitive behaviors. Some of these problem areas—symptoms of ASD—overlap with symptoms of schizophrenia that arises during childhood: playing with feces, not dressing oneself, and becoming very upset in response to unwanted change. However, symptoms of ASD are present in early childhood (e.g., before age 3), as was true of George, and symptoms of childhood schizophrenia typically emerge later, after normal development.

DSM-5 also specifies three levels of severity of ASD, each of which is associated with different levels of required support. The least severe level requires some support, and the most severe level requires very substantial support.

When assessed with an intelligence test that measures both verbal and visual abilities, many people with ASD are also diagnosed as having intellectual disability. When researchers use an intelligence test that does not rely on verbal instructions or responses, however, intelligence scores of people with ASD are often significantly higher—in or above the average intelligence range (Dawson, Mottron, et al., 2005). Moreover, unlike people who have intellectual disability, people with ASD may not be impaired in all domains (although, as a rule, the impairments are general enough to be considered pervasive). In fact, about 20% of people with ASD have pockets of unique skills relating to art, music, numbers, or calendars, such as the ability to identify the day of the week on which a given date fell, even when the date is many years in the past (Hermelin, 2001); such people are sometimes referred to as *autistic savants*. James, the person described in Case 14.2, has a remarkable ability to remember information he has heard.

CASE 14.2 • FROM THE OUTSIDE: Autism Spectrum Disorder

James was the third of four children, born following an uncomplicated pregnancy and labor. His health during the first 3 months of life was good, but shortly thereafter his mother expressed concern because of his sensitivities to light and sound, his failure to make an anticipatory response to being picked up, his fluctuating moods between inconsolable crying and extreme passiveness, and his failure to look at her when she fed him. She reported that he preferred lying in his crib, staring at the mobile, to being held or played with. Because his motor milestones appeared at the appropriate times, James's pediatrician reassured his mother that his development was fine. By age 16 months, James had not begun to babble or say single words, and spent most of his time in a corner, repetitively moving toy cars back and forth. At 20 months, other symptoms emerged: he developed unusual hand movements and body postures; his obliviousness to people increased; he reacted to even the most subtle interruption in his routine or other changes in the world with extreme disorganization and panic; he developed a fascination with light switches and with studying tiny bits of paper and twigs.

At 4 years, James had not yet begun to speak socially to others, but could identify by name many numbers and all of the letters of the alphabet. . . He persisted in lining up objects in the most complex patterns, but could never use objects appropriately. . . At about the age of 4-1/2 years, he began to echo long and complicated sentences, some of which his mother reported he may have heard days or even weeks before. He was able to complete puzzles designed for 8- and 9-year olds quickly, but was unable to reproduce a line or circle.

At about age 5, James made his first spontaneous statement. His mother reported that he had been looking at the sky and said, "It looks like a flower." He did not speak again for 8 months, but then began talking in full sentences. . . When he met strangers, he mechanically introduced himself without ever establishing eye contact, and then rushed on to ask what the person's birthday, anniversary, and social security number were, often appearing to pause long enough to get the answers. Years later, upon re-meeting the person, he was able to recite back these facts.

(Caparulo & Cohen, 1977, pp. 623–624; case printed in Sattler, 1982, p. 474)

For the most part, people with ASD do not go through childhood milestones (language, social, or motor) in a normal fashion. They may speak with a monotone voice, and the rhythm of their speech may be odd. Moreover, they often have a variety of problems with attention and may be impulsive or aggressive. Typically, children with ASD have only one narrow interest, such as the names of subway stations. Richie probably has intellectual disability *and* ASD: intellectual disability best explains his general cognitive slowing, which is not limited to social interactions. His other odd behaviors—such as avoidance of eye contact, lack of social interest in his siblings, and extreme preoccupation with his ball—are best accounted for by ASD. Table 14.5 provides additional facts about ASD.

TABLE 14.5 • Autism Spectrum Disorder Facts at a Glance

Prevalence
• Up to 1% of the population has ASD, but among children and adolescents (which is a younger cohort), the estimate is closer to 2% (Blumberg et al., 2013).
• The reported prevalence of ASD is increasing (Atladóttir, 2007; Hertz-Picciotto & Delwiche, 2009), at least in part because of earlier diagnosis of the disorder (Parner et al., 2008).

Onset
• Symptoms usually arise during infancy (Ozonoff et al., 2008).
• However, symptoms may not be recognized until the second year of life (or earlier, if symptoms are severe).

Comorbidity
• Between 50% and 70% of people with ASD also have intellectual disability (Sigman et al., 2006). However, some researchers believe the high comorbidity is an overestimate (Edelson, 2006), particularly because people with ASD tend to have higher IQs when tested using nonverbal IQ tests.

Course
• Children with ASD often improve in some areas of functioning during the elementary school years (Shattuck et al., 2007).
• During adolescence, some children's symptoms worsen, whereas other children's symptoms improve (Fountain et al., 2012).

Gender Differences
• Males are four times more likely than females to develop ASD.

Source: Unless otherwise noted, the source for information is American Psychiatric Association, 2013.

Understanding Autism Spectrum Disorder

ASD appears to be rooted primarily in neurological factors, which interact with psychological and social factors. The symptoms themselves involve a range of psychological and social factors.

Neurological Factors

ASD is associated with significant abnormalities in brain structure and function.

Brain Systems

The connections among brain areas appear abnormal in ASD (Minshew & Williams, 2007). Moreover, brain areas in the same immediate region appear to communicate excessively, whereas distant areas appear not to communicate enough (Courchesne & Pierce, 2005); in particular, the frontal lobes apparently do not communicate effectively with other brain areas (Murias et al., 2006). In addition, parts of the frontal lobes often are less active than normal, which is consistent with the documented deficits in executive function in ASD (Silk et al., 2006).

Genetics

How might these abnormalities arise? Genes appear to play a role. Researchers have long observed that ASD tends to run in families; 8% of siblings of affected children will also have the disorder (compared to at most 0.2% of the general population; Muhle et al., 2004). Additional evidence comes from twin studies: Monozygotic twin pairs are up to nine times more likely to have the disorder than are dizygotic twin pairs (Bailey et al., 1995; Hallmayer et al., 2011; Le Couteur et al., 1996). However, researchers have not located a single gene that gives rise to ASD (Weiss et al., 2008). Instead, most forms of ASD probably result from interactions among genes—perhaps 15 or more of them (Santangelo & Tsatsanis, 2005).

Psychological Factors: Cognitive Deficits

Neurological factors produce psychological symptoms, particularly cognitive deficits in shifting attention and in mental flexibility (Chawarska et al., 2010; Ozonoff & Jensen, 1999). These deficits underlie the extreme difficulty in transitioning from one activity to another that people with more severe forms of ASD experience. These deficits also underlie a tendency to focus on details at the expense of the broader picture (Frith, 2003).

Another problem is difficulty recognizing facial expressions of emotions (Serra et al., 2003; Tye et al., 2013). For example, in one study researchers used EEG to assess 3- and 4-year-olds' brain activity while they were shown photographs of faces that either expressed fear or had neutral expressions. Children who did not have ASD had greater brain activity in response to the fear expressions than to the neutral expressions—but children with ASD responded to both types of facial expressions with the same pattern of brain activity (Dawson et al., 2004).

📷 GETTING THE PICTURE

Beastfromeast/Getty Images

What is a person with ASD most likely to focus on in this picture? Answer: People with ASD tend to focus on an object's details, such as the doors of the bus in this drawing, and can overlook the "big picture," such as the fact that this drawing is of a city.

People with ASD also have difficulty viewing the world from another person's perspective—with using a **theory of mind**, which is a theory about other people's mental states (their beliefs, desires, and feelings) that allows each of us to predict how others will react in a given situation (Tager-Flusberg, 1999). Because a theory of mind requires thinking about somebody else, by definition, this ability involves both psychological and social factors.

Social Factors: Communication Problems

The earliest indications of ASD arise in interactions with other people: Children with ASD don't respond to their own name or to parents' voices (Baranek, 1999); in addition, they pay attention to other people's mouths, not their eyes (Dawson, Webb, & McPartland, 2005). Moreover, their cognitive deficits in communication and in the ability to recognize faces and emotions, both in voices (Rutherford et al., 2002) and in facial expressions (Bölte & Poustka, 2003), make social interactions confusing and unpredictable.

Even older children with ASD who have developed some communication skills may still have deficits that prevent normal conversation. And, despite adequate verbal skills, adults with ASD often don't understand elements of conversation involving a back-and-forth exchange of information and interest in the other person, and so cannot interact normally.

Treating Autism Spectrum Disorder

There is no cure for ASD, and no one type of intervention is helpful for all those with the disorder. Treatment of ASD generally focuses on increasing communication skills and appropriate social behaviors. The treatments that are most effective are time intensive (at least 25 hours per week), require strong family involvement, are individualized for each child, and begin as early in the child's life as possible (Rogers, 1998). Early treatment depends on early diagnosis of the disorder; to ensure early diagnosis, the American Academy of Pediatrics recommends that all children receive screening tests for ASD before the age of 2 (Johnson et al., 2007).

Targeting Neurological Factors

No treatments successfully target the neurological factors that underlie autism spectrum disorders. Medication may help treat symptoms of comorbid disorders or of agitation or aggression. The medications most likely to be prescribed are antipsychotics and SSRIs (des Portes et al., 2003).

Targeting Psychological Factors: Applied Behavior Analysis

The technique most widely used to modify maladaptive behaviors associated with ASD is called **applied behavior analysis**, which uses *shaping* to help people learn complex behaviors. The key idea is that a complex behavior is broken down into short, simple actions that are reinforced and then ultimately strung together. For example, many children with ASD eat with their hands and resist eating with utensils, which can create problems when they eat with classmates or when the family goes out to eat. Thus, learning to use a spoon is one behavior that is often shaped via applied behavior analysis. Initially, the therapist looks for any spoon-related behavior—such as a glance at the spoon or the child's moving a hand near the spoon—and responds with verbal reinforcement ("That's right, there is the spoon, good job") and perhaps some concrete reward, such as a small candy. After a few successful attempts at approaching the spoon, the child is reinforced for picking up the spoon, then for putting the spoon in the mouth, and finally for using it with food. Parents of children with ASD are encouraged to use this method at home.

AP Photo/The Daily Messenger, Eric Sucar

Jason McElwain, at 17, was manager of his high school's basketball team. At the final home game, which his team was losing, with 4 minutes to go, he was allowed to play. Here he is being cheered by his teammates and the crowd after he went on to score 20 points and win the game. Jason was diagnosed with autism when he was 2 years old; he didn't begin speaking until he was 5 years old (Associated Press, 2006). As he grew older, his social skills improved (McElwain & Paisner, 2008).

Theory of mind
A theory about other people's mental states (their beliefs, desires, and feelings) that allows a person to predict how other people will react in a given situation.

Applied behavior analysis
A technique used to modify maladaptive behaviors by reinforcing new behaviors through shaping.

Targeting Social Factors: Communication

Treatment for ASD that addresses social factors often focuses, in one way or another, on facilitating communication and interpersonal interactions. For example, when a child with ASD has severe communication difficulties, treatment may include the use of PECS, a picture system for facilitating communication. For people who have high-functioning ASD, treatment may focus on training appropriate social behaviors through social skills groups or through individual instruction and modeling—observing others engaging in appropriate social behavior and then role-playing such behaviors (Bock, 2007). For instance, when Richie enters elementary school, he might attend a social skills group for selected kindergarteners and first-graders; the psychologist who leads such groups explicitly teaches the children appropriate social behavior—such as making eye contact and asking and answering questions—and has the children practice with each other. Parents are asked to continue social skills training at home by modeling desired social behaviors and reinforcing their children for improved behavior (Kransny et al., 2003).

In addition, various training programs have been developed to help people with ASD who do not also have intellectual disability; such programs help them perceive and interpret social cues—facial expressions and body language—more accurately. In fact, computer games have been developed to provide such training (Golan & Baron-Cohen, 2006).

Thinking Like A Clinician

The center where Clare works also has clients with ASD. Based on what you have learned, what is the most important information that Clare should know about people with this disorder and why? How might Clare use her knowledge about ASD when she is working with the center's clients?

▭ Specific Learning Disorder: Problems with the Three Rs

Richie Enriquez's older brother, Javier, is in the 4th grade. Javier's teacher has noted that his reading ability doesn't seem up to what it should be. Javier is a bright boy, but when the students take turns reading aloud, Javier isn't able to read as well as his classmates. Javier generally has things he wants to say in class—sometimes raising his hand so high and waving it so energetically that he practically hits the heads of nearby children. His comments often show a keen understanding of what the teacher has said, and his apparent reading problem seems to be at odds with his general intelligence. Could Javier have a learning disorder?

What Is Specific Learning Disorder?

Specific learning disorder is characterized by well below average skills in reading, writing, or math, based on the expected level of performance for the person's age, general intelligence, cultural group, gender, and education level. For the diagnosis to be made, the deficits must significantly interfere with school or work performance or daily living (when supports and services are not provided). Table 14.6 lists the DSM-5 criteria for specific learning disorders.

DSM-5 lists three categories of specific learning disorder (American Psychiatric Association, 2013):

- *Reading*, often referred to as **dyslexia**, characterized by difficulty with accuracy, speed, or comprehension when reading, to the point that the difficulty interferes with academic achievement or activities of daily functioning that involve reading.

Specific learning disorder
A neurodevelopmental disorder characterized by skills well below average in reading, writing, or math, based on the expected level of performance for the person's age, general intelligence, cultural group, gender, and education level.

Dyslexia
A learning disorder characterized by difficulty with reading accuracy, speed, or comprehension that interferes with academic achievement or activities of daily functioning that involve reading.

TABLE 14.6 • DSM-5 Diagnostic Criteria for Specific Learning Disorder

A. Difficulties learning and using academic skills, as indicated by the presence of at least one of the following symptoms that have persisted for at least 6 months, despite the provision of interventions that target those difficulties:

   1. Inaccurate or slow and effortful word reading (e.g., reads single words aloud incorrectly or slowly and hesitantly, frequently guesses words, has difficulty sounding out words).

   2. Difficulty understanding the meaning of what is read (e.g., may read text accurately but not understand the sequence, relationships, inferences, or deeper meanings of what is read).

   3. Difficulties with spelling (e.g., may add, omit, or substitute vowels or consonants).

   4. Difficulties with written expression (e.g., makes multiple grammatical or punctuation errors within sentences; employs poor paragraph organization; written expression of ideas lacks clarity).

   5. Difficulties mastering number sense, number facts, or calculation (e.g., has poor understanding of numbers, their magnitude, and relationships; counts on fingers to add single-digit numbers instead of recalling the math fact as peers do; gets lost in the midst of arithmetic computation and may switch procedures).

   6. Difficulties with mathematical reasoning (e.g., has severe difficulty applying mathematical concepts, facts, or procedures to solve quantitative problems).

B. The affected academic skills are substantially and quantifiably below those expected for the individual's chronological age, and cause significant interference with academic or occupational performance, or with activities of daily living, as confirmed by individually administered standardized achievement measures and comprehensive clinical assessment. For individuals age 17 years and older, a documented history of impairing learning difficulties may be substituted for the standardized assessment.

C. The learning difficulties begin during school-age years but may not become fully manifest until the demands for those affected academic skills exceed the individual's limited capacities (e.g., as in timed tests, reading or writing lengthy complex reports for a tight deadline, excessively heavy academic loads).

D. The learning difficulties are not better accounted for by intellectual disabilities, uncorrected visual or auditory acuity, other mental or neurological disorders, psychosocial adversity, lack of proficiency in the language of academic instruction, or inadequate educational instruction.

- *Written expression*, characterized by poor spelling, significant grammatical or punctuation mistakes, or problems with writing in a clear and organized manner.

- *Mathematics*, sometimes referred to as *dyscalculia*, characterized by difficulty understanding the relationships among numbers, memorizing arithmetic facts, accurately and fluently making calculations, and reasoning effectively about math problems.

Nancy, in Case 14.3, has a specific learning disorder that involves reading. Additional facts about specific learning disorder are presented in Table 14.7.

CASE 14.3 • FROM THE INSIDE: Specific Learning Disorder (Reading)

Nancy Lelewer, author of *Something's Not Right: One Family's Struggle With Learning Disabilities* (1994), describes what having a learning disorder was like for her:

I began public elementary school in the early 1940s. . . . Reading was taught exclusively by a whole-word method dubbed "Look, Say" because of its reliance on recognizing individual words as whole visual patterns, rather than focusing on letters or letter patterns. In first grade, I listened to my classmates, and when it was my turn, I read the pictures, not the words, "Oh Sally! See Spot. Run. Run. Run." When we were shown flash cards and responded in unison to them, I mouthed something.

Then came our first reading test. The teacher handed each student a sheet of paper, the top half of which was covered with writing. I looked at it and couldn't read a word. . . . The room grew quiet as the class began to read.

As I stared at the page, total panic gripped me. My insides churned, and I began to perspire as I wondered what I was going to do. As it happened, the boy who sat right in front of me was the most able reader in my class. Within a few minutes, he had completed the test and had pushed his paper to the front of his desk, which put it in my full view. . . . [I copied his answers and] passed the test and was off on a track of living by my wits rather than being able to read.

The "wits track" is a nerve-wracking one. I worried that the boy would be out sick on the day we had a reading test. I worried that the teacher might change the location of my desk. I worried that I would get caught copying another student's answers. I knew that something was wrong with me, but I didn't know what. Why couldn't I recognize words that my classmates read so easily?

(pp. 15–17)

TABLE **14.7** • Specific Learning Disorder Facts at a Glance

Prevalence

- Between 5% and 15% of school-age children in the United States are estimated to have this disorder.

Onset

- Symptoms of specific learning disorder and its diagnosis typically occur in elementary school, when the relevant academic skills are needed.

Comorbidity

- Common comorbid disorders include depressive disorders and attention-deficit/hyper-activity disorder.

Course

- With early identification and intervention, some children with dyslexia can overcome their difficulties; for others, difficulties in reading fluency, comprehension, and spelling may persist into adulthood.

Gender Differences

- Between 60% and 75% of people with dyslexia are male; however, it may be that males are more likely to be diagnosed because of their disruptive behavior, which calls attention to their difficulties.

Cultural Differences

- In the United States, Hispanic children are least likely to be diagnosed with a learning disorder, perhaps because language barriers make it more difficult to diagnose (Boyle et al., 2011).

Source: Unless otherwise noted, the source for information is American Psychiatric Association, 2013.

Specific learning disorder may cast a long shadow over many areas of life for many years. People with a learning disorder are 50% more likely to drop out of school than are people in the general population, and work and social relationships are more likely to suffer (American Psychiatric Association, 2000). These people are also more likely than average to suffer from poor self-esteem.

Understanding Specific Learning Disorder

Like intellectual disability and ASD, specific learning disorder is primarily caused by neurological factors. But psychological and social factors also play a role.

Neurological Factors

Among the three domains of specific learning disorder, dyslexia has been studied the most extensively. Evidence is growing that impaired brain systems underlie this disorder and that genes contribute to these impaired systems.

Brain Systems

In most forms of dyslexia, the brain systems involved in auditory processing do not function as well as they should (Marshall et al., 2008; Ramus et al., 2003). The results of many neuroimaging studies have converged to identify a set of brain areas that is disrupted in people who have dyslexia (Shaywitz et al., 2006). First, two rear areas in the left hemisphere are not as strongly activated during reading tasks in people with dyslexia as they are in people who read normally. One of these areas is involved in converting visual input to sounds (Friedman et al., 1993), and the other area, at the junction of the parietal and occipital lobes, appears to be used to recognize whole words, based on their visual forms (Cao et al., 2006; McCandliss et al., 2003). Second, two other brain areas are more strongly activated in people with dyslexia than in people who read normally. These areas appear to be used in carrying out compensatory strategies, which rely on stored information instead of the vision–sound conversion process.

Genetics

A specific learning disorder in reading is moderately to highly heritable (Hawke et al., 2006; Schulte-Körne, 2001), and at least four specific genes are thought to affect the development of this disorder (Fisher & Francks, 2006; Marino et al., 2007). Some of these genes affect how neurons become connected during brain development (Rosen et al., 2007), and some may affect the functioning of neurons or influence the activity of neurotransmitters (Grigorenko, 2001).

Psychological Factors

Some children with a specific learning disorder succeed in situations where others fail. For example, they might persevere in solving a difficult puzzle. Why? In order to address this question, researchers interviewed college students with a specific learning disorder and asked about their experiences as young children (Miller, 2002). These people reported a number of psychological factors that played important roles in shaping their *motivation* to overcome their disorder; these factors included self-determination, recognizing particular areas of strength, identifying the learning disability, and developing ways to cope with it.

Social Factors

Social factors play a role in shaping motivation to persist in the face of a learning disorder (Miller, 2002). Other people, such as parents and teachers, were important in supporting and encouraging children who later succeeded in overcoming their learning disabilities. In addition, certain social environments—such as attending a low-quality school or coming from a disadvantaged family—apparently can contribute to at least some forms of dyslexia (Shaywitz et al., 2006; Wadsworth et al., 2000).

Treating Dyslexia

As with the other childhood disorders discussed thus far in this chapter, neurological factors generally are not directly targeted for treatment (unless the treatment is for a comorbid disorder). Dyslexia has been the subject of the most research on treatment, and researchers have reported successful interventions for this disorder.

One technique for helping people with dyslexia is phonological practice, which consists of learning to divide words into individual sounds and to identify rhyming words. Another technique focuses on teaching children the *alphabetic principle*, which governs

What do (left to right) singer Jewel, TV star Patrick Dempsey, martial artist Billy Blanks, business mogul Richard Branson, and actress Keira Knightley have in common? They all have dyslexia, but it has not stopped them from attaining success in their fields.

the way in which letters signal elementary speech sounds (Shaywitz et al., 2004). In fact, various forms of training using these techniques have been shown not only to improve performance but also to improve the functioning of brain areas that were impaired prior to the training (Gaab et al., 2007; Simos et al., 2007; Temple et al., 2003).

Thinking Like A Clinician

Nikhil recently graduated from college and is about to start working in the *Teach for America* program. He's been assigned to teach at an inner-city school. Nikhil was a math major in college and doesn't know much about learning disabilities. However, he was a peer tutor in college and saw that some people had a *really* hard time understanding different elements of math. Based on what you've read, what information should Nikhil know (and hopefully will be taught as part of his training) about specific learning disorder before he walks into a classroom, and why should he learn this material?

Disorders of Disruptive Behavior and Attention

In addition to Javier Enriquez's apparent difficulties reading, his teacher has commented—not very positively—on Javier's high energy level. He doesn't always stay in his chair during class, and when he's working on a group project, other kids seem to get annoyed at him: "He can get 'in their face' a bit." Javier's mother, Lela, and his father, Carlos, acknowledge that Javier is a very active, energetic boy. But Carlos says, "I was that way when I was a kid, but I grew out of it as I got older." Javier's teacher recently mentioned the possibility of his having attention-deficit/hyperactivity disorder.

In contrast, Javier's sister, 8-year-old Pia, is definitely not energetic. Like her brother, Pia is clearly bright, but her teacher says she seems to "space out" in class. The teacher thinks that Pia simply does not apply herself, but her parents wonder whether she's underachieving because she's bored and understimulated in school. At home, Pia has defied her parents increasingly often—not doing her chores or performing simple tasks they ask her to do. At other times, Pia is off in her own world, "kind of like an absent-minded professor." Is Pia's behavior in the normal range, or does it signal a problem? If so, what might the problem be?

And what about Javier's behavior—is it in the normal range? Most children are disruptive some of the time. But in some cases, the disruptive behavior is much more frequent and obtrusive and becomes a cause for concern. Even if disruptive behaviors do not distress the children who perform them, they often distress other people or violate social norms (Christophersen & Mortweet, 2001). The most common reason that children are referred to a mental health clinician is because they engage in disruptive behavior at home, at school, or both (Frick & Silverthorn, 2001). The clinician must distinguish between normal behavior and pathologically disruptive behavior and, if the behavior falls outside the normal range, determine which disorder(s) might be the cause.

Three disorders are associated with disruptive behavior: *conduct disorder, oppositional defiant disorder*, and *attention deficit/hyperactivity disorder* (which is characterized mainly by problems with attention but sometimes by disruptive behavior as well). Although DSM-5 does not put attention-deficit/hyperactivity disorder in the category of disruptive disorders (but rather puts it in category of neurodevelopmental disorders), we discuss it here both because the symptoms can include disruptive behavior and because symptoms of these three disorders commonly—though not always—occur together.

Children with conduct disorder exhibit a pattern of violating the rights of others, such as frequently hurting other children, as is the girl in this photograph.

RubberBall/SuperStock

What Is Conduct Disorder?

The hallmark of **conduct disorder** is a violation of the basic rights of others or of societal norms that are appropriate to the person's age (American Psychiatric Association, 2013). As outlined in Table 14.8, 15 types of behaviors are listed in the diagnostic criteria for conduct disorder; these behaviors are sorted into four categories.

DSM-5 requires the presence of at least 3 out of the 15 types of behavior within the past 12 months and at least 1 type of such behavior must have occurred during the past 6 months. Although the diagnosis requires impaired functioning in some area of life, it does *not* require distress.

Just as the criteria for antisocial personality disorder (Chapter 13) focus almost exclusively on behavior that violates the rights of others, so do the criteria for conduct disorder. However, people diagnosed with conduct disorder also often have outbursts of anger, recklessness, and poor frustration tolerance. Most people diagnosed with conduct disorder are under 18 years old; if the behaviors persist into adulthood, the person usually meets the criteria for antisocial personality disorder.

Like people with antisocial personality disorder, people with conduct disorder appear to lack empathy and concern for others, and they don't exhibit genuine remorse for their misdeeds. In fact, when the intent of another person's behavior is

TABLE 14.8 • DSM-5 Criteria for Conduct Disorder

A. A repetitive and persistent pattern of behavior in which the basic rights of others or major age-appropriate societal norms or rules are violated, as manifested by the presence of at least three of the following 15 criteria in the past 12 months from any of the categories below, with at least one criterion present in the past 6 months:

Aggression to People and Animals

1. Often bullies, threatens, or intimidates others.

2. Often initiates physical fights.

3. Has used a weapon that can cause serious physical harm to others (e.g., a bat, brick, broken bottle, knife, gun).

4. Has been physically cruel to people.

5. Has been physically cruel to animals.

6. Has stolen while confronting a victim (e.g., mugging, purse snatching, extortion, armed robbery).

7. Has forced someone into sexual activity.

Destruction of Property

8. Has deliberately engaged in fire setting with the intention of causing serious damage.

9. Has deliberately destroyed others' property (other than by fire setting).

Deceitfulness or Theft

10. Has broken into someone else's house, building, or car.

11. Often lies to obtain goods or favors or to avoid obligations (i.e., "cons" others).

12. Has stolen items of nontrivial value without confronting a victim (e.g., shoplifting, but without breaking and entering; forgery).

Serious Violations of Rules

13. Often stays out at night despite parental prohibitions, beginning before age 13 years.

14. Has run away from home overnight at least twice while living in the parental or parental surrogate home, or once without returning for a lengthy period.

15. Is often truant from school, beginning before age 13 years.

B. The disturbance in behavior causes clinically significant impairment in social, academic, or occupational functioning.

C. If the individual is age 18 years or older, criteria are not met for antisocial personality disorder.

Conduct disorder
A psychological disorder that typically arises in childhood and is characterized by the violation of the basic rights of others or of societal norms that are appropriate to the person's age.

ambiguous, a person with conduct disorder is likely to misconstrue the other's motives as threatening or hostile and then feel justified in his or her own aggressive behavior. People with conduct disorder typically blame others for their inappropriate behaviors ("He made me do it").

DSM-5 specifies three levels of intensity for the symptoms of conduct disorder: *mild* (few behaviors or causing minimal harm), *moderate,* and *severe* (many behaviors or causing significant harm). Symptoms may progress from mildly disruptive to severely disruptive.

People with conduct disorder are also likely to use—and abuse—substances at an earlier age than are people without this disorder. Similarly, they are more likely to have problems in school (such as suspension or expulsion), legal problems, unplanned pregnancies and sexually transmitted diseases, and physical injuries that result from fights. Because of their behavioral problems, children with conduct disorder may live in foster homes or attend special schools. They may also have poor academic achievement and score lower than normal on verbal intelligence tests. Problems with relationships, financial woes, and other psychological disorders may persist into adulthood (Colman et al., 2009).

When clinicians assess whether conduct disorder might be an appropriate diagnosis for a person, they will of course talk with him or her; however, the nature of conduct disorder is such that a child or an adult patient may not provide complete information about his or her behavior. Thus, when diagnosing a child, clinicians try to obtain additional information from other sources, usually school officials or parents, although even these people may not know the full extent of a child's conduct problems. By the same token, when diagnosing adults, clinicians try to obtain additional information from family members, peers, or coworkers. Usually, the behaviors that characterize conduct disorder are not limited to one setting but occur in a variety of settings: in school or work, at home, in the neighborhood. This was true for Brad, as described in Case 14.4.

CASE 14.4 • FROM THE OUTSIDE: Conduct Disorder

Brad was [a teenager and] small for his age but big on fighting. For him, this had gone beyond schoolyard bullying. He had four assault charges during the previous 6 months, including threatening rape and beating up a much younger boy who was mentally challenged. The family was being asked to leave their apartment complex because of Brad's aggressive behavior and several stealing incidents. Other official arrests included burglaries and trespassing. Brad had participated in a number of outpatient services, including anger management classes in which he had done well, but obviously he was not applying what he had learned to everyday life. He was referred to [a treatment] program by the juvenile court judge.

Prior to placement, Brad had lived with his mother and older brother. Their family life had been characterized by many disruptions, including contact with several abusive father figures and frequent moves. Brad's older brother also had a record with the juvenile authorities, but his offenses were confined to property crimes and the use of alcohol. He had graduated from an inpatient substance abuse program. Brad and his brother had a history of physical fighting. Prior to the boys' births, Mrs. B had had two children removed from her custody by state protective services. Mrs. B was very protective of Brad. She felt that the police and schools had it "in for him" and regularly defended him as having been provoked or blamed falsely. Although she was devastated at having Brad removed from her home, Mrs. B reported that she could no longer deal with Brad's aggression.

(Chamberlain, 1996, pp. 485–486)

DSM-5 uses the timing of onset to define two types of conduct disorder, which typically have different courses and prognoses:

- *adolescent-onset type,* in which no symptoms were present before age 10; and

- *childhood-onset type,* which is more severe and in which the first symptoms appeared when the child was younger than 10 years old.

TABLE 14.9 • Conduct Disorder Facts at a Glance

Prevalence

- Studies find a wide range of prevalence rates in the general population (2–10%), depending on how the study was conducted and the exact composition of the population studied. Approximately 10% of Americans will be diagnosed with conduct disorder during their lives (Nock et al., 2006).

Onset

- According to DSM-5, when symptoms arise before age 10, the diagnosis is childhood-onset type; when there are no symptoms before age 10, it is adolescent-onset type.

Comorbidity

- With the childhood-onset type, common comorbid disorders include oppositional defiant disorder and attention-deficit/hyperactivity disorder (both discussed later) (Costello et al., 2003); some studies estimate that up to 90% of children with conduct disorder exhibit symptoms of attention-deficit/hyperactivity disorder (Frick & Muñoz, 2006).

Course

- The earlier the onset and the more severe the disruptive behaviors, the worse the prognosis (Barkley et al., 2002; Frick & Loney, 1999).
- People with childhood-onset conduct disorder are likely to develop additional symptoms of the disorder by puberty and continue to have the disorder through adolescence.
- People with the childhood-onset type are more likely than those with the adolescent-onset type to be diagnosed with antisocial personality disorder in adulthood.

Gender Differences

- During their lives, about 12% of American males and 7% of American females will have had symptoms that meet the criteria for conduct disorder (Nock et al., 2006). Although more males than females are diagnosed with this disorder (both types), the sex difference is more marked for the childhood-onset type, with 10 males diagnosed for each female (Moffitt & Caspi, 2001).
- Males with conduct disorder tend to be confrontationally aggressive (fighting, stealing, vandalism, and school-related problems); females tend to be nonconfrontational (lying, truancy, running away, substance use, and prostitution).

Source: Unless otherwise noted, the source for information is American Psychiatric Association, 2013.

As noted in Table 14.9, various characteristics of conduct disorder that develop in childhood are different from those of the conduct disorder that develops in adolescence. In the following sections we examine them in more detail.

Adolescent-Onset Type

For people with adolescent-onset type, the symptoms of conduct disorder emerge after—but not before—puberty, considered in DSM-5 to occur at 10 years of age. The disruptive behaviors are not likely to be violent and typically include minor theft, public drunkenness, and property offenses rather than violence against people and robbery, which are more likely with childhood-onset type (Moffitt et al., 2002). The behaviors associated with adolescent-onset type conduct disorder can be thought of as exaggerations of normal adolescent behaviors (Moffitt & Caspi, 2001). With this type, the disruptive behaviors are usually transient, and adolescents with this disorder are able to maintain relationships with peers. This type of conduct disorder has been found to have a small sex difference; the male to female ratio is 1.5 to 1 (Moffitt & Caspi, 2001).

Childhood-Onset Type

Research has shown that people with the childhood-onset type of conduct disorder can be further divided into two categories: Those who are *callous and/or unemotional* (Caputo et al., 1999; Frick et al., 2000), which are features of psychopathy (discussed in Chapter 13), and those who are not.

Childhood-Onset Type, Neither Callous nor Unemotional

People with childhood-onset conduct disorder who are not callous and display feelings of guilt or remorse for their deeds are less likely to be aggressive in general; when they are aggressive, it is usually as a *reaction* to a perceived or real threat—it is not premeditated (Frick et al., 2003). People with this sort of conduct disorder have difficulty regulating their negative emotions: They have high levels of emotional distress (Frick & Morris, 2004; Frick et al., 2003), and they react more strongly to other people's distress and to negative emotional stimuli generally (Loney et al., 2003; Pardini et al., 2003).

In addition, such people process social cues less accurately than normal and so are more likely to misperceive such cues and respond aggressively when (mis)perceiving threats (Dodge & Pettit, 2003). Because of their problems in regulating negative emotions, they are more likely to act aggressively and antisocially in *impulsive* ways when distressed. They often feel bad afterward but still can't control their behavior (Pardini et al., 2003). Children with this disorder may fall into a negative interaction pattern with their parents: When a parent brings up the child's past or present misconduct, the child becomes agitated and then doesn't appropriately process what the parent says, becomes more distressed, and impulsively behaves in an aggressive manner. The parent may respond with aggression (verbal or physical), creating a vicious cycle (Gauvain & Fagot, 1995).

Childhood-Onset Type, With Callous and Unemotional Traits

Although not consider a "subtype" in DSM-5, the manual allows mental health professionals to specify when someone with childhood-onset conduct disorder has callous and unemotional features (specified in DSM-5 as *with limited prosocial emotions*). This group of people has some unique characteristics: Like adults with psychopathy, these young people seek out exciting and dangerous activities, are relatively insensitive to threat of punishment, and are strongly oriented toward the possibility of reward (Frick et al., 2003; Pardini et al., 2003). Moreover, they react less strongly to threatening or distressing stimuli (Frick et al., 2003; Loney et al., 2003).

Researchers propose that the decreased sensitivity to punishment—associated with low levels of fear—underlies the unique constellation of callousness and increased aggression (Frick, 2006; Pardini et al., 2006). People with this sort of conduct disorder are not concerned about the negative consequences of their violent behaviors. And being insensitive to punishment, they don't learn to refrain from certain behaviors and thereby fail to internalize social norms or develop a conscience or empathy for others (Frick & Morris, 2004; Pardini, 2006; Pardini et al., 2003). In fact, people with conduct disorder with callous and unemotional traits are less likely to recognize emotional expressions of sadness (Blair et al., 2001). This variant of conduct disorder has the highest heritability and is associated with more severe symptoms (Viding et al., 2005).

What Is Oppositional Defiant Disorder?

The defining characteristics of **oppositional defiant disorder** are angry or irritable mood, defiance or argumentative behavior, or vindictiveness. As noted in Table 14.10, for a diagnosis of oppositional defiant disorder, DSM-5 requires that the person exhibit four out of eight symptoms, many of which are confrontational behaviors, such as arguing with authority figures, intentionally annoying others, and directly refusing to comply with an authority figure's or adult's request, which were true of Josh, in Case 14.5. (However, according to DSM-5, such behavior with a sibling is not grounds for diagnosing the disorder.) Young children with oppositional defiant disorder may have intense and frequent temper tantrums. Pia did not comply with her parents' requests to complete her chores or help with other tasks; her teacher has commented on a similar behavior pattern at school.

These behaviors must have occurred for at least 6 months, more frequently than would be expected for the person's age and developmental level, and must impair functioning.

TABLE 14.10 • DSM-5 Diagnostic Criteria for Oppositional Defiant Disorder

A. A pattern of angry/irritable mood, argumentative/defiant behavior, or vindictiveness lasting at least 6 months as evidenced by at least four symptoms from any of the following categories, and exhibited during interaction with at least one individual who is not a sibling.

Angry/Irritable Mood

1. Often loses temper.

2. Is often touchy or easily annoyed.

3. Is often angry and resentful.

Argumentative/Defiant Behavior

4. Often argues with authority figures or, for children and adolescents, with adults.

5. Often actively defies or refuses to comply with requests from authority figures or with rules.

6. Often deliberately annoys others.

7. Often blames others for his or her mistakes or misbehavior.

Vindictiveness

8. Has been spiteful or vindictive at least twice within the past 6 months.

B. The disturbance in behavior is associated with distress in the individual or others in his or her immediate social context (e.g., family, peer group, work colleagues), or it impacts negatively on social, educational, occupational, or other important areas of functioning.

C. The behaviors do not occur exclusively during the course of a psychotic, substance use, depressive, or bipolar disorder. Also, the criteria are not met for disruptive mood dysregulation disorder.

Reprinted with permission from the Diagnostic and Statistical Manual of Mental Disorders, Fifth Edition, (Copyright ©2013). American Psychiatric Association. All Rights Reserved.

CASE 14.5 • FROM THE OUTSIDE: Oppositional Defiant Disorder

At school and with friends, Josh behaves like a perfectly normal ten-year-old boy. At home, however, it's a very different story. Josh pushes every limit possible. He often swears at his parents and harasses his siblings. Forget about asking Josh to do things around the house—he refuses to do even the most routine chores without serious resistance toward his parents. Communication between Josh and his parents consists of a series of arguments, leaving them all exhausted, angry, and tense.

(Bernstein, 2006, p. 2)

Oppositional defiant disorder
A disorder that typically arises in childhood or adolescence and is characterized by angry or irritable mood, defiance or argumentative behavior, or vindictiveness.

Children with oppositional defiant disorder typically are verbally aggressive with authority figures but are not generally violent.

The disruptive behaviors of oppositional defiant disorder are different in several important ways from those characterizing conduct disorder. Oppositional defiant disorder involves only a subset of the symptoms of conduct disorder—the overtly defiant behaviors—and these are often verbal. The disruptive behaviors of oppositional defiant disorder are:

• generally directed toward authority figures;

• not usually violent and do not usually cause severe harm; and

• in children, often exhibited only in specific situations with parents or other adults the children know well (Christophersen & Mortweet, 2001).

The clinician must obtain information from others when assessing disruptive behaviors and must keep in mind any cultural factors that might influence which sorts of behaviors are deemed acceptable or unacceptable.

According to DSM-5, if a person meets the diagnostic criteria for both oppositional defiant disorder and conduct disorder, both disorders would be diagnosed. Table 14.11 lists additional facts about oppositional defiant disorder.

TABLE 14.11 • Oppositional Defiant Disorder Facts at a Glance

Prevalence

• Estimates of prevalence rates for this disorder vary widely, from 1% to 11%, depending on the specific population investigated and the specific research methods used.

Onset

• Symptoms usually emerge before 8 years of age, although they may become evident as late as 13.

• The onset progresses gradually, over months or even years, until the symptoms reach the point where the diagnostic criteria are met. Symptoms are typically observed at home before occurring in other contexts.

Comorbidity

• Up to 90% of children with oppositional defiant disorder also exhibit symptoms of attention-deficit/hyperactivity disorder (Frick & Muñoz, 2006).

Course

• Most people with the childhood-onset type of conduct disorder were previously diagnosed with oppositional defiant disorder (Whittinger et al., 2007); however, most people with oppositional defiant disorder do not go on to develop conduct disorder.

Gender Differences

• Before puberty, more males than females are diagnosed with oppositional defiant disorder. After puberty, there is no sex difference in prevalence.

• Males exhibit more persistent and more confrontational symptoms than females do.

Cultural Differences

• Different cultures may have different norms concerning what defiant behaviors are considered inappropriate or unacceptable.

Source: Unless otherwise noted, the source for information is American Psychiatric Association, 2013.

What Is Attention-Deficit/Hyperactivity Disorder?

People who have oppositional defiant disorder or conduct disorder intend to defy rules, authority figures, or social norms, and hence behave disruptively. But people may *unintentionally* behave disruptively because they have another disorder,

TABLE 14.12 • DSM-5 Diagnostic Criteria for Attention-Deficit/Hyperactivity Disorder

A. A persistent pattern of inattention and/or hyperactivity-impulsivity that interferes with functioning or development, as characterized by (1) and/or (2):

1. **Inattention:** Six (or more) of the following symptoms have persisted for at least 6 months to a degree that is inconsistent with developmental level and that negatively impacts directly on social and academic/occupational activities:

   Note: For older adolescents and adults (age 17 and older), at least five symptoms are required.

   a. Often fails to give close attention to details or makes careless mistakes in schoolwork, at work, or during other activities (e.g., overlooks or misses details, work is inaccurate).

   b. Often has difficulty sustaining attention in tasks or play activities (e.g., has difficulty remaining focused during lectures, conversations, or lengthy reading).

   c. Often does not seem to listen when spoken to directly (e.g., mind seems elsewhere, even in the absence of any obvious distraction).

   d. Often does not follow through on instructions and fails to finish schoolwork, chores, or duties in the workplace (e.g., starts tasks but quickly loses focus and is easily sidetracked).

   e. Often has difficulty organizing tasks and activities (e.g., difficulty managing sequential tasks; difficulty keeping materials and belongings in order; messy, disorganized work; has poor time management; fails to meet deadlines).

   f. Often avoids, dislikes, or is reluctant to engage in tasks that require sustained mental effort (e.g., schoolwork or homework; for older adolescents and adults, preparing reports, completing forms, reviewing lengthy papers).

   g. Often loses things necessary for tasks or activities (e.g., school materials, pencils, books, tools, wallets, keys, paperwork, eyeglasses, mobile telephones).

   h. Is often easily distracted by extraneous stimuli (for older adolescents and adults, may include unrelated thoughts).

   i. Is often forgetful in daily activities (e.g., doing chores, running errands; for older adolescents and adults, returning calls, paying bills, keeping appointments).

2. **Hyperactivity and impulsivity:** Six (or more) of the following symptoms have persisted for at least 6 months to a degree that is inconsistent with developmental level and that negatively impacts directly on social and academic/occupational activities:

   Note: For older adolescents and adults (age 17 and older), at least five symptoms are required.

   a. Often fidgets with or taps hands or feet or squirms in seat.

   b. Often leaves seat in situations when remaining seated is expected (e.g., leaves his or her place in the classroom, in the office or other workplace, or in other situations that require remaining in place).

   c. Often runs about or climbs in situations where it is inappropriate. (**Note:** In adolescents or adults, may be limited to feeling restless.)

   d. Often unable to play or engage in leisure activities quietly.

   e. Is often "on the go," acting as if "driven by a motor" (e.g., is unable to be or uncomfortable being still for extended time, as in restaurants, meetings; may be experienced by others as being restless or difficult to keep up with).

   f. Often talks excessively.

   g. Often blurts out an answer before a question has been completed (e.g., completes people's sentences; cannot wait for turn in conversation).

   h. Often has difficulty waiting his or her turn (e.g., while waiting in line).

   i. Often interrupts or intrudes on others (e.g., butts into conversations, games, or activities; may start using other people's things without asking or receiving permission; for adolescents and adults, may intrude into or take over what others are doing).

B. Several inattentive or hyperactive-impulsive symptoms were present prior to age 12 years.

C. Several inattentive or hyperactive-impulsive symptoms are present in two or more settings (e.g., at home, school, or work; with friends or relatives; in other activities).

D. There is clear evidence that the symptoms interfere with, or reduce the quality of, social, academic, or occupational functioning.

E. The symptoms do not occur exclusively during the course of schizophrenia or another psychotic disorder and are not better explained by another mental disorder (e.g., mood disorder, anxiety disorder, dissociative disorder, personality disorder, substance intoxication or withdrawal.

attention-deficit/hyperactivity disorder (ADHD), which is characterized by six or more symptoms of inattention, hyperactivity, and/or impulsivity (five or more in people 17 years old or greater). People diagnosed with this disorder vary in which set of symptoms is most dominant; some primarily have difficulty maintaining attention, whereas others primarily have difficulty with hyperactivity and impulsivity. Still others have all three types of symptoms. To meet the criteria for the diagnosis (see Table 14.12), the symptoms must impair functioning in at least two settings, such as at school *and* at work or at work *and* at home, and some symptoms must have been present by age 12. The impulsivity and hyperactivity are most noticeable and

Attention-deficit/hyperactivity disorder (ADHD)
A disorder that typically arises in childhood and is characterized by inattention, hyperactivity, and/or impulsivity.

disruptive in a classroom setting. Javier's difficulty staying in his chair at school, which disrupted the class, may have reflected this disorder. In Case 14.6, an adult recounts how he recognized his own ADHD.

CASE 14.6 • FROM THE INSIDE: Attention Deficit/Hyperactivity Disorder

Attention-deficit disorder (ADD) was the term used in the third edition of the DSM. In his book *Driven to Distraction: Recognizing and Coping with Attention Deficit Disorder from Childhood Through Adulthood*, psychiatrist Edward Hallowell recounts what happened when he learned about the disorder:

> I discovered I had ADD when I was thirty-one years old, near the end of my training in child psychiatry at the Massachusetts Mental Health Center in Boston. As my teacher in neuro-psychiatry began to describe ADD in a series of morning lectures during a steamy Boston summer, I had one of the great "Aha!" experiences of my life.
>
> "There are some children," she said, "who chronically daydream. They are often very bright, but they have trouble attending to any one topic for very long. They are full of energy and have trouble staying put. They can be quite impulsive in saying or doing whatever comes to mind, and they find distractions impossible to resist."
>
> So there's a name for what I am! I thought to myself with relief and mounting excitement. There's a term for it, a diagnosis, an actual condition, when all along I'd thought I was just slightly daft. . . . I wasn't all the names I'd been called in grade school—"a day-dreamer," "lazy," "an underachiever," "a spaceshot"—and I didn't have some repressed unconscious conflict that made me impatient and action-oriented.
>
> What I had was an inherited neurological syndrome characterized by easy distractibil-ity, low tolerance for frustration or boredom, a greater-than-average tendency to say or do whatever came to mind . . . and a predilection for situations of high intensity. Most of all, I had a name for the overflow of energy I so often felt—the highly charged, psyched-up feeling that infused many of my waking hours in both formative and frustrating ways.

(Hallowell & Ratey, 1994, pp. ix–x)

Symptoms of hyperactivity may be different in females than in males: Girls who have hyperactive symptoms may talk more than other girls or may be more emotionally reactive, rather than hyperactive with their bodies (Quinn, 2005). Some researchers propose that ADHD is underdiagnosed in girls, who are less likely to have behavioral problems at school and so are less likely to be referred for evaluation (Quinn, 2005). In fact, female teenagers with ADHD are likely to be diagnosed with and treated for depression before the ADHD is diagnosed (Harris International, 2002, cited in Quinn, 2005).

Because the sets of symptoms of ADHD vary, clinicians find it useful to classify ADHD into different forms ("presentations" to use the DSM-5 term). The predominantly *hyperactive/impulsive* form is associated with disruptive behaviors, accidents, and rejection by peers, whereas the *inattentive* form of ADHD is associated with academic problems that are typical of deficits in executive functions: difficulty remembering a sequence of behaviors, monitoring and shifting the direction of attention, organizing material to be memorized, and inhibiting interference during recall. Some patients may have a combination of the two types of symptoms.

However, symptoms may change over time; as some children get older, the particular set of symptoms they exhibit can shift, most frequently from hyperactive/impulsive to the type that has a combination of the two sets of symptoms (Lahey, Pelham, et al., 2005). Children with ADHD often have little tolerance for frustration, as was true of Edward Hallowell in Case 14.6; such children tend to have temper outbursts, changeable moods, and symptoms of depression. Once properly diagnosed and treated, such symptoms often decrease.

Problems with attention are likely to become more severe in group settings, where the person receives less attention or rewards, in settings when sustained attention is necessary, or when a task is thought to be boring—which is what

This girl may simply be in a talkative mood. But girls with the hyperactive form of ADHD tend to talk more than girls without the hyperactive form of ADHD.

© New Stock/Alamy

happened to Javier. Various psychological and social factors can reduce symptoms, including:

- frequent rewards for appropriate behavior;
- close supervision;
- being in a new situation or setting;
- doing something interesting; and
- having someone else's undivided attention.

Socially, people with ADHD may initiate frequent shifts in the topic of a conversation, either because they are not paying consistent attention to the conversation or because they are not following implicit social rules. People with symptoms of hyperactivity may talk so much that others can't get a word in edgewise, or they may inappropriately start conversations. These symptoms can make peer relationships difficult. In addition, symptoms of impulsivity can lead to increased risk of harm. As the child heads into adulthood, hyperactive and impulsive symptoms tend to decrease but not disappear. Symptoms of inattention, however, do not tend to decrease as much. Additional facts about ADHD are presented in Table 14.13.

TABLE 14.13 • Attention-Deficit/Hyperactivity Disorder Facts at a Glance

Prevalence

- The estimated prevalence of ADHD in school-aged children increased from 6% in 1997 to almost 10% in 2007 (National Center for Health Statistics, 2008; Visser et al., 2010).
- Prevalence among American adults is about 4% (Kessler, Adler, et al., 2006).

Comorbidity

- Common comorbid disorders include mood and anxiety disorders, learning disorders, and oppositional defiant disorder (American Psychiatric Association, 2013; Larson et al., 2011).
- Up to half of children with ADHD also have oppositional defiant disorder.
- Children with hyperactive and impulsive symptoms are more likely to be diagnosed with oppositional defiant disorder or conduct disorder than are those with inattentive symptoms (Christophersen & Mortweet, 2001).

Onset

- Children are not usually diagnosed before age 4 or 5 because the range of normal behavior for preschoolers is very wide.
- In younger children, the diagnosis is generally based more on hyperactive and impulsive symptoms than on inattention symptoms.

Course

- Symptoms of ADHD become obvious during the elementary school years, when attentional problems interfere with schoolwork.
- By early adolescence, the more noticeable signs of hyperactivity—difficulty sitting still, for example—typically diminish to a sense of restlessness or a tendency to fidget.
- Almost a third of childhood cases carry over into adulthood (Barbaresi et al., in press).

Gender Differences

- Males are more likely—in one survey, more than twice as likely—to be diagnosed with ADHD, particularly the hyperactive/impulsive type, although this gender difference may reflect a bias in referrals to mental health clinicians rather than any actual difference in prevalence (National Center for Health Statistics, 2008).

Cultural Differences

- In the United States, non-Hispanic White children are more likely to be diagnosed with ADHD than are Hispanic or Black children (Havey et al., 2005; Stevens et al., 2005).
- Worldwide, the prevalence of the disorder among children averages about 5% (Polanczyk & Rohde, 2007), although some studies find higher prevalence rates (Bird, 2002; Ofovwe et al., 2006); variability across countries can be explained by the different thresholds at which behaviors are judged as reaching a symptomatic level, as well as somewhat different diagnostic criteria (Bird, 2002).

Source: Unless otherwise noted, the source for information is American Psychiatric Association, 2000.

Understanding Disorders of Disruptive Behavior and Attention

Given the high comorbidity and overlap of symptoms among the three disorders—conduct disorder, oppositional defiant disorder, and ADHD—we'll focus on the disorder that is best understood, ADHD. Studies of factors related to oppositional defiant disorder and conduct disorder probably include participants who also have ADHD, which makes it difficult to determine which factors are uniquely associated with oppositional defiant disorder and conduct disorder and *not* ADHD.

Neurological Factors

Research has revealed that people who have ADHD have abnormal brain structure and function, and research also has begun to characterize the roles of neurotransmitters and genes in these brain abnormalities.

ADHD: Brain Systems and Neural Communication

The behavioral problems that characterize people with ADHD may arise in part from impaired frontal lobe functioning. This hypothesis is consistent with the fact that people with ADHD often cannot perform functions well that rely on the frontal lobes, such as various executive functions (e.g., formulating and following plans; Kiliç et al., 2007) and estimating time accurately, which affects their ability to plan and follow through on commitments (Barkley et al., 2001; McInerney & Kerns, 2003; Riccio et al., 2005).

Studies have shown that children and adolescents with this disorder have smaller brains than do children and adolescents without the disorder, and the deficit in size is particularly marked in the frontal lobes (Schneider, Retz et al., 2006; Sowell et al., 2003; Valera et al., 2007). Indeed, particular parts of the frontal lobes have been shown to be relatively small in adults with ADHD (Durston et al., 2004; Hesslinger et al., 2002).

Although research findings implicate the frontal lobes, they also indicate that it is not the sole culprit that underlies ADHD. In particular, people with ADHD also have smaller cerebellums, which is noteworthy because this brain structure is crucial to attention and timing; in fact, the smaller this structure, the worse the symptoms of ADHD are (Castellanos et al., 2002; Mackie et al., 2007).

Studies have also shown that ADHD is not a result of impaired functioning in any single brain area but rather emerges from how different areas interact. Neuroimaging studies have revealed many patterns of abnormal brain functioning in people who have ADHD (Rubia et al., 2007; Stevens et al., 2007; Vance et al., 2007). In general, neural structures involved in attention tend not to be activated as strongly (during relevant tasks) in people with this disorder as in people without it (Stevens et al., 2007; Schneider, Retz, et al., 2006; Vance et al., 2007). However, virtually every lobe in the brains of people with ADHD has been shown not to function normally during tasks that draw on their functions (Mulas et al., 2006; Vance et al., 2007).

Moreover, abnormal brain functioning can influence the autonomic nervous system (see Chapter 2): ADHD (and some types of conduct disorder) has been associated with unusually low arousal in response to normal levels of stimulation (Crowell et al., 2006), a response that could explain some of the stimulation-seeking behavior seen in people with this disorder. That is, these people could engage in stimulation-seeking behavior in order to obtain an optimal level of arousal.

People with ADHD have lower-than-normal levels of dopamine—which is a key neurotransmitter used in the frontal lobes and in many other brain areas. However, the overall pattern of difficulties that characterizes ADHD suggests problems with multiple neurotransmitters—including serotonin and norepinephrine—that are involved in

Bored in class? For a child with ADHD, it may be even worse than for these kids. ADHD is associated with low levels or arousal to normal levels of stimulation. For a child with ADHD, when a teacher or the material discussed isn't "exciting" or interesting, time in the classroom can feel particularly understimulating and boring.

© Caro/Alamy

coordinating and organizing cognition and behavior (Arnsten, 2006; Volkow et al., 2007). Given the number of brain areas that are involved, problems with multiple neurotransmitters are probably associated with the disorder.

ADHD and Genetics

Genes may be one reason why people with ADHD have abnormal brain systems and disrupted neural communication. Indeed, not only does this disorder run in families, but also parent and teacher reports indicate that it is highly correlated among monozygotic twins (with correlations ranging from 0.60 to 0.90). In addition, a large set of data reveals that this disorder is among the most heritable of psychological disorders (Martin et al., 2006; Stevenson et al., 2005; Waldman & Gizer, 2006).

However, as with most other psychological disorders that are influenced by genes, a combination of genes—not a single gene—probably contributes to it (Faraone et al., 2005). In fact, over a dozen different genes have so far been identified as possibly contributing to this disorder (Guan et al., 2009; Swanson et al., 2007; Waldman & Gizer, 2006).

Moreover, as usual, genes are not destiny: The effects of the genes depend in part on the environment. For example, children whose mothers smoked while pregnant are much more likely to develop ADHD than are children whose mothers did not smoke (Braun et al., 2006), and this relationship appears to be particularly strong for children who have a specific gene (Neuman et al., 2007).

Psychological Factors: Recognizing Facial Expressions, Low Self-Esteem

In addition to problems with attention and executive function, people with ADHD may have other, perhaps less obvious, difficulties. In particular, as with ASD, people with ADHD have difficulty recognizing emotions in facial expressions (Demopoulos et al., 2013)—but not all emotions; they have problems recognizing anger and sadness in particular. Why? The answer isn't known, but one suggestion is that these people might have had very negative experiences with others who are sad or angry, and these unpleasant experiences motivate them to tune out such expressions (Pelc et al., 2006).

In addition, children with ADHD appear to have an attributional style that leaves them vulnerable to low self-esteem. In one study (Milich, 1994), children with ADHD initially overestimated their ability to succeed in a challenging task, and—when confronted with failure—boys with ADHD became more frustrated and were less likely to persist with the challenging task than were boys in a control group. Moreover, in another study (Collett & Gimpel, 2004), children with ADHD attributed the cause of negative events to global and stable characteristics about themselves ("I am a failure") rather than external, situational factors ("That was a very hard task"). Conversely, children with ADHD were more likely than children without a psychological disorder to attribute positive events to external, situational causes. These attribution patterns were observed regardless of whether children were taking medication for ADHD. Such patterns are often seen in people who experience low self-esteem (Sweeney et al., 1986; Tennen & Herzberger, 1987).

Low self-esteem among those with ADHD isn't restricted to children. One study compared college students with and without ADHD and matched them to control participants who had comparable demographic variables and grade-point averages. Students with ADHD reported lower self-esteem and social skills than did students without ADHD (Shaw-Zirt et al., 2005). Other studies report lower self-esteem among adolescents with ADHD (Slomkowski et al., 1995).

Social Factors: Blame and Credit

The low self-esteem of children with ADHD may also be related to social factors, in particular to their parents' attributions: Although parents don't necessarily blame their children for ADHD-related behaviors, they don't give their children as much credit for positive behaviors as do parents of children without ADHD (Johnston &

What does this man's expression mean? For people with ADHD, it might not be clear that he's not happy to see a visitor. People with ADHD can have difficulty noticing and understanding certain social cues; specifically, they may not recognize the facial expressions that correspond to anger and sadness.

JupiterImages/Brand X/Alamy

Freeman, 1997). The parents of children with ADHD tend to attribute children's positive behaviors to random situational factors.

In addition, social factors can indirectly influence the development of this disorder. For example, children typically are raised in homes selected by their parents—based on various social factors, such as parents' financial status, proximity to extended family, and community resources. If children are raised in a house where lead paint has been applied, they may be more vulnerable to ADHD. In fact, children whose hair contains higher levels of lead (which is a measure of exposure to lead, perhaps from lead paint in one's home environment) are more likely to have ADHD than are children who have lower levels of lead in their hair (Tuthill, 1996). Even children who were exposed to very low levels of lead in their environment are more likely to develop ADHD than are children who were not exposed (Nigg, 2006b).

Feedback Loops in Understanding Attention-Deficit/Hyperactivity Disorder

In this section, we examine how the different factors related to ADHD create feedback loops (see Figure 14.1). Current research suggests that psychological and social factors contribute to the development of ADHD in people whose genes lead them to be neurologically vulnerable to the disorder.

Consider the finding that children with ADHD are less accurate at recognizing sad and angry facial expressions (Pelc et al., 2006). Such deficits, particularly difficulty in recognizing anger, are associated with more interpersonal problems. These results suggest that when peers or adults (typically parents or teachers) show—rather than tell—their displeasure to a child who has ADHD, that child is less likely to perceive (psychological factor) the social cue (social factor) than is a child who does not have the disorder. This difficulty in perceiving others' displeasure in turn creates additional tension for both the child and those who interact with him or her. In fact, children with ADHD are more likely than those without the disorder to be rejected by their peers (Mrug et al., 2009). Moreover, other people's responses to the child's behavior (social factor) in turn influence how the child comes to feel about himself or herself (psychological factor; Brook & Boaz, 2005).

Other research results suggest that the family environment is associated with ADHD. In particular, family conflict is higher in families that include a child with ADHD than in control families (Pressman et al., 2006). However, do family environments that are higher in conflict play a role in causing a child to develop ADHD? Or do the symptoms of the disorder—inattention, hyperactivity, or impulsivity—create more tension in the family? Or do difficulties associated with the disorder, such as difficulty in recognizing angry or sad facial expressions, increase family tension? It may be that all these possible influences occur.

Treating Disorders of Disruptive Behavior and Attention: Focus on ADHD

Treatments for disorders of disruptive behavior and attention are usually comprehensive, targeting more than one type of factor and sometimes all three types of factors. And children with ADHD may be legally entitled to special services and accommodations in school. Specific treatments for ADHD focus both on attentional symptoms and, when present, on hyperactivity/impulsivity symptoms.

Targeting Neurological Factors: Medication

Medication for ADHD often treats symptoms of both ADHD and also comorbid oppositional defiant disorder or conduct disorder. One type of medication for ADHD targets dopamine, which plays a key role in the functioning of the frontal lobes (Solanto, 2002). Many of these medications are stimulants, which may sound counterintuitive because people with ADHD don't seem to need more stimulation.

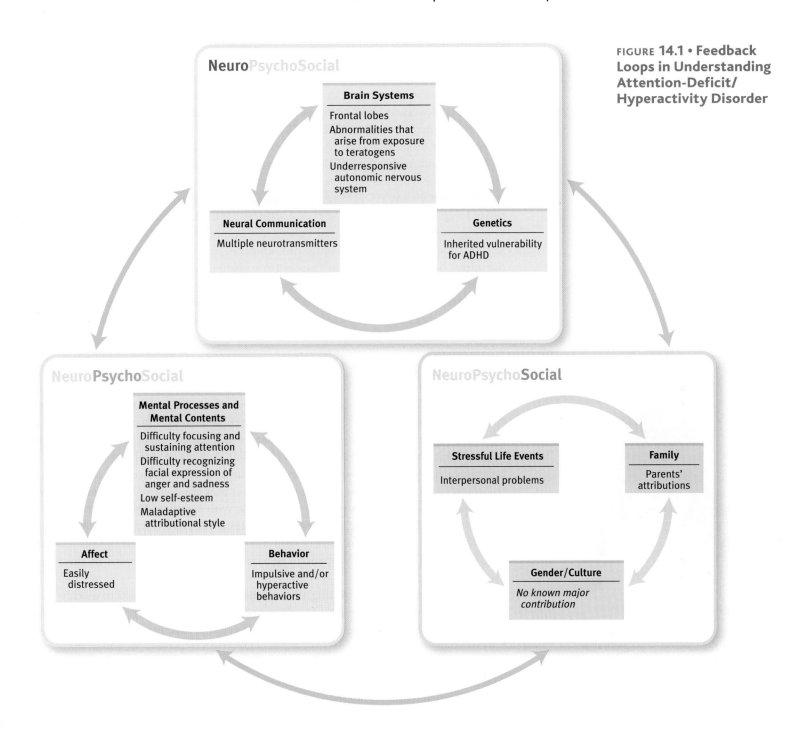

FIGURE **14.1 • Feedback Loops in Understanding Attention-Deficit/ Hyperactivity Disorder**

However, these stimulants increase attention and reduce general activity level and impulsive behavior. Although the mechanism that produces these effects is not entirely understood, the medications appear to have their effects by disrupting the reuptake of dopamine, leaving more dopamine in the synapse and thus correcting at least some of the imbalance in this neurotransmitter that has been observed in the brains of people with ADHD (Volkow et al., 2005). In addition, this disorder may arise in part because the person is understimulated and hence seeks additional stimulation; by providing stimulation internally, the medications reduce the need to seek it externally.

Stimulant medications for ADHD may contain *methylphenidate* (such as Ritalin, Concerta, and Focalin) or an amphetamine (such as Adderall) and are available in relatively short-acting formulas (requiring two or three daily doses) and in a timed-release formula (requiring only one dose per day). Methylphenidate is also available as a daily skin patch. About 65–75% of people with ADHD who receive stimulants improve (compared to 4–30% of controls who receive placebos), and the side effects are not severe for most people (Pliszka, 2007; Pliszka et al., 2006). In fact, stimulants have been shown to improve the functioning of various brain areas that are impaired in this disorder (Bush et al., 2008; Clarke et al., 2007; Epstein et al., 2007).

Another medication for ADHD is *atomoxetine* (Strattera); it is a noradrenaline reuptake inhibitor, not a stimulant. Atomoxetine has effects and side effects similar to those of the stimulant medications (Kratochvil et al., 2002) and currently is the medication of choice for people with both ADHD and substance abuse.

Medications for ADHD reduce impulsive behaviors, which seems to decrease related aggressive behaviors (Frick & Morris, 2004). This effect can have wideranging consequences. As noted earlier, the symptoms of ADHD can give rise to feedback loops with a child's family or with peers, and these feedback loops can cause disruptive behaviors to escalate. Successful treatment with medication disrupts these feedback loops, reducing the frequency and intensity of disruptive behaviors, which in turn leads family members and peers not to become as irritated and angry, which thereby reduces their undercutting the child's self-esteem (Frick & Muñoz, 2006; Hinshaw et al., 1993; Jensen et al., 2001).

Targeting Psychological Factors: Treating Disruptive Behavior

Treatments that target psychological factors have been developed for all three disruptive disorders. These treatments usually employ behavioral and cognitive methods to address disruptive behaviors. One reason for such behaviors is that children with any of these disorders tend to have low frustration tolerance and difficulty in working for delayed—rather than immediate—reward. Thus, behavioral methods may focus on helping such children restrain their behavior and accept a delayed reward. Specific techniques include a reinforcement program that uses concrete rewards, such as a toy, and social rewards, such as praise or special time with a parent. These methods slowly increase the delay until the child receives either a concrete reward ("Now you can have that toy") or a social reward ("You did a great job, I'm proud of you"), which should motivate the child to control behavior for a delayed reward in the future (Sonuga-Barke, 2006).

Behavioral methods for treating all three disorders may also be used to modify social behaviors, such as not responding to others aggressively or not interrupting others. For example, when children enter preschool or kindergarten, this may be the first time they have to sit quietly for a length of time and wait for a turn to participate. Often the teacher will ask children to raise a hand and wait until called on to answer a question. A child with ADHD will be more likely than other children to speak out of turn or to keep vigorously waving a raised hand, trying to get the teacher's attention. A program of rewarding the child for increasingly longer times of not speaking out or waving frantically can teach the child to behave with more restraint, which can ease relations with classmates.

Cognitive methods seek to enhance children's social problem-solving abilities. Specifically, the therapist helps the child interpret social cues in a more realistic way—for instance, acknowledging that the other person may not have hostile motives when he asked you to move your backpack—and develop more appropriate social goals and responses (Dodge & Pettit, 2003). Through skills-building, modeling, and roleplaying, the treatment also helps the child to learn how to inhibit angry or impulsive reactions and to learn more effective ways to respond to others. The therapist praises the child's successes in these areas. To enhance the generalizability of the new skills to life outside the therapy session, parents and teachers may be asked to help with role-playing and modeling and to use praise in their contacts with the child. CBT for adults with ADHD (which focuses on helping the person with planning, organization, and coping with distractions) is also effective (Safren et al., 2010).

To help increase a child's frustration tolerance—which is typically low in children with a disruptive disorder—parents may institute a reinforcement program that rewards the child for restraining himself or herself.

© HD57life/Alamy

Targeting Social Factors: Reinforcement in Relationships

Most of the treatments that target social factors are designed to help parents—and teachers, when necessary—to use operant conditioning principles to shape a child's prosocial behavior and decrease defiant or impulsive behavior.

Contingency Management: Changing Parents' Behavior

Contingency management is a procedure for modifying behavior by changing the conditions that lead to, or are produced by, the behavior. Treatment may target parents of children with ADHD to help them set up a contingency management program with their child—particularly in cases in which the parents have been inconsistent in their use of praise (and other reinforcers) or punishment (Frick & Muñoz, 2006).

The first step of contingency management training with parents is psychoeducation—teaching the parents that the symptoms are not the result of intentional misbehavior but part of a disorder (Barkley, 1997, 2000). The subsequent training then is intended to:

1. change parents' beliefs about the reasons for their child's behavior so that parents approach their child differently and develop realistic goals for their child's behavior;

2. help parents to institute behavior modification, which includes paying attention to desired behaviors, being consistent and clear about directions, and developing reward programs; and

3. teach parents to respond consistently to misbehavior.

Parent training targets social factors—interactions between parents and child. Changes in the way parents think about and interact with their child, in turn, change the child's ability to control behavior (psychological factor). Parent training may be the best treatment for families who have children with mild ADHD or preschoolers with ADHD (Kratochvil et al., 2004).

Parent Management Training

Parent management training is designed to combine contingency management techniques with additional techniques that focus on improving parent–child interactions generally—improving communication and facilitating real warmth and positive interest in the parent for his or her child (Kazdin, 1995).

Multisystemic Therapy

Multisystemic therapy (Henggeler et al., 1998) is based on family systems therapy and focuses on the context in which the child's behavior occurs: with peers, in school, in the neighborhood, and in the family. This comprehensive treatment may involve family and couples therapy, interventions with peers, CBT with the child, and an intervention in the school (such as meeting with the child's teacher or directly assisting in the classroom to help the child manage his or her behavior). The specific techniques employed are tailored to change systems in the child's life in order to manage his or her behavior better.

Feedback Loops in Treating Attention-Deficit/Hyperactivity Disorder

At first glance, medication might seem to have its effects solely through neurological mechanisms, but this isn't so. Taking medication (neurological factor) not only leads to increased control of attention and hyperactive or impulsive behaviors, but it is also associated with higher levels of self-esteem (psychological factor; Frankel et al., 1999), which can lead a child not to seek attention as vigorously. Moreover, such increased control of attention and behavior also improves social functioning (social factor; Chacko et al., 2005). And better social functioning feeds back to improve self-esteem.

Other feedback loops originate from programs for parents or the family (which target social factors); such interventions in turn create feedback loops with psychological factors—improving the child's thoughts, feelings, and behaviors. Figure 14.2 illustrates feedback loops among the various factors that are used to treat ADHD.

Contingency management
A procedure for modifying behavior by changing the conditions that led to, or are produced by, it.

Onoky/SuperStock

This little boy seems to be enjoying a leap on the couch, but is it inappropriate? Parents of children with ADHD are taught contingency management training to develop realistic goals for their child's behavior, to institute appropriate behavior modification plans, and to respond consistently to the child's misbehavior.

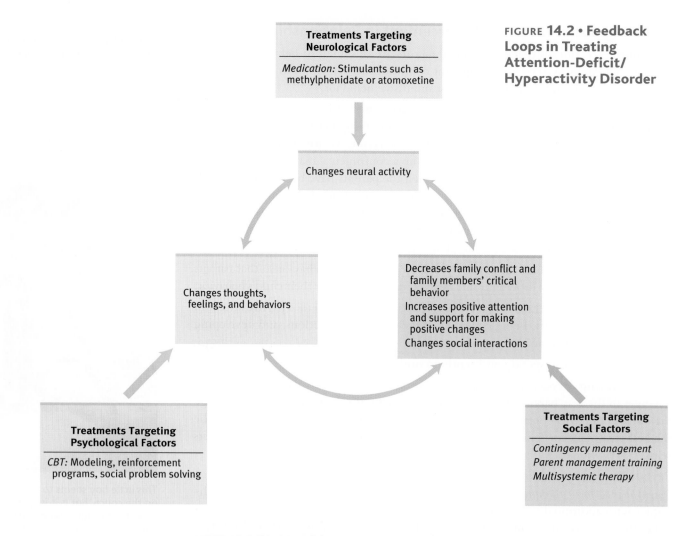

FIGURE **14.2 • Feedback Loops in Treating Attention-Deficit/ Hyperactivity Disorder**

Thinking Like A Clinician

Nikhil has some first-hand familiarity with oppositional defiant disorder and conduct disorder: He went to a large middle school and large high school, where some kids always acted up and got into trouble. And during high school and college, some of his friends and then one of his roommates had ADHD. Even though Nikhil may think he knows something about disruptive behavior disorders and ADHD, based on what you have read, what information about these disorders should he be given before he begins to teach, and why?

SUMMING UP

Intellectual Disability (Intellectual Developmental Disorder)

- The diagnosis of intellectual disability typically involves both cognitive deficits that are significantly below normal *and* impaired daily functioning in conceptual, social, and/or practical areas. Some people with intellectual disability—particularly at the severe or profound level—may have difficulty communicating verbally.

- Neurological factors are the primary direct cause of most cases of intellectual disability—usually a genetic abnormality or prenatal exposure to a teratogen, which in turn alters brain structure and function.

- Many types of intellectual disability can be prevented, such as those related to PKU and lead poisoning.

- Interventions are designed to improve the person's functioning by increasing his or her communication and daily living skills.

- Legally, children with an intellectual disability are entitled to special education and related services, tailored to their individual needs.

Autism Spectrum Disorder

- Autism spectrum disorder (ASD) involves two types of problems: (1) significant deficits in communication and social interaction skills and (2) stereotyped behaviors or narrow interests.

- Many people with ASD also have comorbid intellectual disability when tested with conventional intelligence tests; on tests that do not rely on verbal abilities, people with ASD tend to score in the average range or higher.

- Neurological factors that underlie ASD include abnormal connections and communication among different brain areas.

- Psychological symptoms of ASD include deficits in shifting attention, in mental flexibility, and an impaired theory of mind.

- Social symptoms of ASD include problems in recognizing emotion in the voices and faces of others and in understanding the give and take of social communication.

- Treatment for ASD that targets psychological factors includes applied behavior analysis to modify maladaptive behaviors. Treatments that target psychological and social factors focus on teaching the person to recognize conventional social cues, to read the emotional expressions of others, and to communicate, as well as how to initiate and respond in social situations.

Specific Learning Disorder: Problems with the Three Rs

- Specific learning disorder is characterized by well-below-average skills in reading, writing, or math, based on the expected level of performance for the person's age, general intelligence, cultural group, gender, and education level. DSM-5 includes three types of learning disorders related to: reading (dyslexia), written expression, and mathematics (dyscalculia).

- Dyslexia appears to result from disruptions in brain systems that process language and that process visual stimuli. Treatment for dyslexia may involve various cognitive techniques to compensate for reading difficulties.

Disorders of Disruptive Behavior and Attention

- Conduct disorder is characterized by a violation of the basic rights of others or of societal norms that are appropriate to the person's age. Conduct disorder involves four types of behavior: aggression to people and animals, destruction of property, deceitfulness or theft, and serious violation of rules. The disorder may begin in childhood or adolescence. Conduct disorder is commonly comorbid with attention-deficit/hyperactivity disorder.

- Childhood-onset conduct disorder with callous and unemotional traits has the highest heritability among the various types of conduct disorder; this variant is also associated with more severe symptoms.

- Oppositional defiant disorder is characterized by angry or irritable mood, defiance or argumentative behavior, or vindictiveness. The behaviors are usually not violent, nor do they cause severe harm, and they often occur only in certain contexts.

- Attention-deficit/hyperactivity disorder (ADHD) is characterized by inattention, hyperactivity, and/or impulsivity.

- Oppositional defiant disorder, conduct disorder, and ADHD are highly comorbid, making it difficult to sort out factors that contribute uniquely to one of the disorders.

- Neurological factors that contribute to ADHD include frontal lobe problems and genes. Too little dopamine and imbalances in other transmitters also play a role.

- Psychological factors associated with ADHD include low self-esteem and difficulty recognizing facial expressions of anger and sadness.

- Social factors that contribute to ADHD include parents' not giving children enough credit for their positive behaviors.

- Treatment targeting neurological factors in ADHD involves medication—typically methylphenidate or atomoxetine. Treatments targeting psychological factors include behavioral methods to increase a person's ability to tolerate frustration and to delay reward, and cognitive methods to enhance social problem-solving ability. Treatments that target social factors include group therapy and comprehensive treatments such as contingency management, parent management training, and multisystemic therapy.

Key Terms

More Study Aids

Photodisc

For additional study aids related to this chapter, including quizzes to make sure you've retained everything you've learned and a Student Video Activity exploring the case of one boy with autism spectrum disorder, go to: www.worthpublishers.com/launchpad/rkabpsych2e.

CHAPTER 15

Neurocognitive Disorders

Mrs. B. was an 87-year-old woman at the time that she was referred for neuropsychological testing. Mrs. B. wasn't always able to get to the toilet in time to urinate, her hearing and vision weren't as good as they had been and, because of an inner-ear problem, she sometimes lost her balance and fell. A neuropsychologist was asked to determine the nature of Mrs. B.'s problems—specifically the extent to which a neurocognitive disorder might account for at least some of her difficulties. The neuropsychologist noted that Mrs. B.:

> had moved from another state several months earlier at the urging of her daughter, who had been receiving reports from neighbors and relatives that she was unable to care for herself or her home and was increasingly suspicious and argumentative. Her first residence in her new community was . . . a nursing home, but it soon became apparent that she was functioning at a higher level than other residents and she moved to a small board-and-care home [a small residential facility for elders who need round-the-clock help with daily functioning and personal care]. With only a few persons in the home and a low resident-to-staff ratio, this seemed a good arrangement for an older person who needed an intermediate level of assistance. Mrs. B. apparently thought otherwise.
>
> She often refused to admit staff to her room or to accept assistance with activities such as bathing, despite an unsteady gait and several recent falls. She had arguments with other residents that sometimes escalated into shouting matches. A private-duty companion was hired to assist her for several hours a day and to take her on excursions outside of the home. This was helping somewhat, but accusations and arguments continued at an unsettling rate. Mrs. B. sometimes seemed to forget plans that she had agreed to and was occasionally tearful and sad.

(La Rue & Watson, 1998, pp. 6, 10)

WHAT MIGHT ACCOUNT FOR MRS. B.'S disruptive behavior and memory problems? One possibility is that she had a neurocognitive disorder. According to DSM-5, **neurocognitive disorders** are a category of psychological disorders in which the primary symptom is significantly reduced cognitive abilities relative to a prior level of functioning. These disorders are also referred to as *cognitive disorders*.

Neurocognitive disorders
A category of psychological disorders in which the primary symptom is significantly reduced cognitive abilities, relative to a prior level of functioning; also referred to as *cognitive disorders*.

Because such deficits reflect a *reduction* of a previous ability, they cannot be present at birth. (The neurodevelopmental disorders discussed in Chapter 14 involve deficits either since birth or at some point during childhood.)

Impaired cognitive abilities are not unique to neurocognitive disorders. Many of the disorders discussed in previous chapters involve a change in cognitive functioning: People who are depressed or anxious can have impaired attention, concentration, and memory; those with a psychotic disorder have impaired perception and judgment; and substance use disorder can lead to a wide variety of cognitive impairments (Balash et al., 2013). The cognitive changes associated with these other disorders, however, are secondary to the symptoms that characterize the disorders: depressed mood, anxiety and fear, psychotic symptoms, or behaviors related to substance abuse.

In contrast, with neurocognitive disorders, the changes in cognitive functioning—in mental processes—constitute the primary set of symptoms. Patients may (or may not) also have unusual behavior, mood, or mental contents. Usually, the undesired cognitive changes arise from a medical disease such as Parkinson's disease, a medical condition such as a *stroke*, or the use of or withdrawal from a psychoactive substance (which may include exposure to a toxic substance).

Neurocognitive disorders are almost exclusively caused by neurological factors (hence their name), and thus this chapter does not contain any *Feedback Loops* sections or figures. Although psychosocial treatments may buffer or delay the ways that the disorders impair functioning or cause distress, they do not generally feed back to affect the neurological factors that lead to the disorder.

In most cases, these disorders afflict older adults rather than younger adults. So, part of the job of diagnosing these disorders is to distinguish their symptoms from changes that occur with normal aging. In what follows we first examine the changes in cognitive functioning that occur during the normal aging process, which will allow us to contrast these effects with those described in subsequent sections.

This woman might just be thinking, but she also could be worrying. In fact, many older adults are concerned that they might have a neurocognitive disorder because these disorders more frequently afflict the elderly than the young. Clinicians need to be able to distinguish these disorders from the normal aging process.

Juanmonino/Getty Images

▢ Normal Versus Abnormal Aging and Cognitive Functioning

The neuropsychologist assessing Mrs. B. needed to determine whether her disturbances in memory, mood, and behavior were normal for an 87-year-old, particularly one with a variety of medical problems. And, if her memory, mood, and behavior weren't in the normal range, given her circumstances, what, specifically, were her difficulties? And what could account for them? The neuropsychologist initially assessed Mrs. B. using a clinical interview (discussed in Chapter 3), observing her as well as noting her responses to questions:

> Mrs. B. arrived promptly for her appointment, accompanied by her private-duty nurse. She was well-groomed and alert but ambulated slowly, leaning against the railing on the wall to maintain her balance; she was also unsteady on rising and standing from a chair. She was fluent and willing to talk at great length about her situation, although her speech was often repetitive and tangential. Mood was . . . positive during the interview. She denied hallucinations, delusions, or suicidal ideation but admitted to some depression, which she felt had improved somewhat on antidepressant medication. She was able to describe some aspects of her experience at the [nursing home] and gave several examples of the types of things that annoyed her at the current board-and-care home.
> (La Rue & Watson, 1998, p. 6)

Mrs. B. was able to remember aspects of her nursing home experience that she didn't like, but she forgot other types of information, such as her upcoming plans. In the normal course of events, however, various cognitive functions tend to decline with advancing age. Even healthy older adults have some cognitive deficits, compared to their younger selves, and these must be taken into account when attempting to determine whether an older person has a disorder. Thus, the neuropsychologist must assess whether Mrs. B.'s functioning has declined and, if so, whether this decline is beyond what occurs with the normal aging process. In this section, we examine what happens to cognitive functioning during normal aging and then examine the neurological factors that can disrupt cognitive functioning.

Cognitive Functioning in Normal Aging

Most—although not all—aspects of cognitive functioning remain relatively stable during older adulthood.

Intelligence

Let's first examine intelligence, which can be divided into two types (Cattell, 1971): **Crystallized intelligence** relies on using knowledge to reason in familiar ways; such knowledge has "crystallized" from previous experience. For example, an avid fisherman can use knowledge gleaned from prior experience to reason about where fish are likely to be lurking in a stream. Normally, crystallized intelligence remains stable or actually increases with age, even among older adults; crystallized intelligence is often assessed by tests that measure verbal ability, and these tests often allow ample time for people to respond to questions. In contrast, **fluid intelligence** relies on the ability to create novel strategies to solve new problems, without relying solely on familiar approaches. For example, fluid intelligence would be required to devise a new way to catch fish without a hook, line, and sinker—perhaps using a shirt or basket as a net. Fluid intelligence relies on *executive functions*, which include the abilities to think abstractly, to plan, and to exert good judgment. Fluid intelligence is typically assessed with tests of visual-motor skills, problem solving, and perceptual speed (Salthouse, 2005). As adults age, their scores on most measures of fluid intelligence decline.

Crystallized intelligence
A type of intelligence that relies on using knowledge to reason in familiar ways; such knowledge has "crystallized" from previous experience.

Fluid intelligence
A type of intelligence that relies on the ability to create novel strategies to solve new problems, without relying solely on familiar approaches.

📷 GETTING THE PICTURE

Which photo best illustrates crystallized intelligence? Answer: The photo on the left. If a person has been fishing for years, this knowledge would contribute to the crystalized intelligence used to decide where best to try to catch fish (with a pole). If a fishing pole were not available, reasoning about novel ways to catch fish—such as by using a basket as a net—would draw on fluid intelligence.

Normal cognitive decline must be judged in relation to each person's own base-line. An older adult who starts out with a high IQ and has functioned well will probably be able to continue to function well even with the normal decline of aging. In contrast, the functioning of someone who has a lower IQ initially (such as in the low normal range, an IQ between 85 and 100) will be affected more dramatically—perhaps to the point where his or her ability to function independently is curtailed (Harvey, 2005a).

Memory

Memory is not a single ability, and various aspects of it are affected in different ways by aging.

The elderly (generally considered to be people aged 65 and older; World Health Organization [WHO], 2009) tend to have problems recalling previously stored information. To *recall* information is to become aware of that information after voluntarily attempting to "look it up" in memory. In contrast, healthy older people often have little difficulty with recognition; to *recognize* information requires first perceiving it and then comparing it to information previously stored in memory to determine whether the perceived information matches the stored information.

For example, older people sometimes have trouble recalling the names of common objects on demand. Thus, they might say, "I went to the store to buy a 'thingamajig' this morning." Despite difficulty recalling the names of objects, cognitively healthy older people can describe the object or recognize the correct word when someone else says it, and may even recall the correct word a few minutes later when talking about something else (Nicholas et al., 1985).

However, in spite of these difficulties, healthy older people can often recall temporarily forgotten names of common things when given cues or hints. Moreover, with normal aging, the ability to recall personal information is preserved; people can recall important episodes from their past.

Andersen Ross/Iconica/Getty Images

This man may remember that the cabbage he's holding is called bok choi. But if he doesn't, he shouldn't worry about it. It isn't unusual for an older person to be unable to recall the name of a common object sometimes, but be able to recognize the name if someone else says it. This and other normal aging-related cognitive changes do not usually impair daily functioning.

Processing Speed, Attention, and Working Memory

People generally process information more slowly as they reach old age. One explanation for this slowed processing speed is that the myelin sheaths coating the axons of neurons degrade or disappear, which then causes the neurons' signals to dissipate—and hence communication among brain areas is impaired (Andrews-Hanna et al., 2007).

The slowed processing speed that occurs with advanced age affects many cognitive functions. For example, consider storing new information in memory: Older adults generally acquire new information at a slower rate and thus typically need more exposure to the to-be-stored material; they also need more practice in retrieving the information after they have stored it. For these reasons, elderly people may be impaired when carrying out tasks that require rapidly recalling and using stored information (Fillit et al., 2002; Salthouse, 2001).

Another cognitive function that often declines with age is attention. Attention involves selecting some information for more careful analysis: what a person pays attention to gets processed more fully than what he or she does not pay attention to. In part because processing slows down with aging, the ability to switch attention sequentially among multiple tasks (known as *multitasking*) is likely to decline as people age (Parasuraman et al., 1989). Thus, older adults may have a harder time performing tasks such as scanning e-mail while talking on the phone.

Elderly people typically have problems using *working memory* (De Beni & Palladino, 2004; Li, Lindenberger, & Sikström, 2001). Working memory requires keeping information activated (so that you are aware of it) while operating on it in a specific way; for example, holding the steps of a recipe in mind while cooking and progressing from one step to the next requires working memory. Working memory relies on executive functions that are implemented in the frontal lobes, which don't operate as effectively in elderly people as they do in younger people.

Psychological Disorders and Cognition

Most older adults don't have a psychological disorder; in fact, older adults have the lowest prevalence of psychological disorders and of significant psychological distress of any age group (Centers for Disease Control and Prevention, 2012; Karlin et al., 2008). But when an older person does have a psychological disorder, its symptoms can impair cognitive functioning. Thus, before assuming that an older person's deteriorated cognitive functioning is a result of a *neurocognitive* disorder, the clinician must first determine whether the deterioration could result from another sort of psychological disorder. For instance, Mrs. B. had a history of depression and described herself as having a "hot temper" even as a young adult. Mrs. B.'s daughter described her mother "as always somewhat self-centered and suspicious of the motives of others, but this had worsened noticeably in recent years, to the point where she had been isolated within her own home," which led to the move to the nursing home (La Rue & Watson, 1998, p. 6).

The neuropsychologist must determine whether Mrs. B.'s memory problems might reflect a psychological disorder—such as depression, an anxiety disorder, or schizophrenia.

Depression

Older adults are less likely than their younger counterparts to be diagnosed with depression. When they are depressed, however, the symptoms often differ from those of younger adults: Older depressed adults have more anxiety, agitation, and memory problems (Segal, 2003). Thus, cognitive functioning is affected by depression both directly (memory problems) and indirectly (anxiety and agitation affect attention, concentration, and other mental processes; see Table 15.1).

In addition, a mental health clinician must determine whether symptoms of depression in an older person could be *caused* by a neurocognitive disorder: Some symptoms of depression, such as fatigue, may be caused by brain changes associated with a neurocognitive disorder (Puente, 2003). Mrs. B. had a history of depression and was taking antidepressant medication. However, the neuropsychologist who assessed Mrs. B.'s cognitive functioning determined that the difficulties she was having were not a result of depression (La Rue & Watson, 1998). Mr. Rosen, in Case 15.1, had cognitive problems that may or may not have been related to his depression.

TABLE 15.1 • Common Cognitive Deficits in Late-Life Depression

Information Processing Speed

• Slow to respond or initiate behavior; incomplete grasp of complex information (because of a lag in processing)

Attention and Concentration

• Absentmindedness for daily activities, events, and appointments; tasks left incomplete; decreased attentiveness for reading or conversation

Executive Function

• Difficulty with calculating, sequencing, multitasking, and novel problem solving; inflexible behavior or thinking; perseverative or ruminative thinking; decline in organization and planning; indecisiveness, decreased initiation of behavior

Memory

• Forgetfulness and absentmindedness, but should improve with prompts, cues, or memory aids

Source: Potter & Steffens, 2007. For more information see the Permissions section.

CASE 15.1 • FROM THE OUTSIDE: Normal Aging or Something More?

Maurice Rosen was 69 when he made an appointment for a neurological evaluation. He had recently noticed that his memory was slipping and he had problems with concentration that were beginning to interfere with his work as a self-employed tax accountant. He complained of slowness and losing his train of thought. Recent changes in the tax laws were hard for him to learn, and his wife said he was becoming more withdrawn and reluctant to initiate activities. However, he was still able to take care of his personal finances and accompany his wife on visits to friends. Although mildly depressed about his disabilities, he denied other symptoms of depression, such as disturbed sleep or appetite, feelings of guilt, or suicidal ideation.

Mr. Rosen has a long history of treatment for episodes of depression, beginning in his 20s. He has taken a number of different antidepressants and once had a course of electroconvulsive therapy. As recently as 6 months before this evaluation, he had been taking an antidepressant.

(Spitzer et al., 2002, p. 70)

Anxiety Disorders

Like depression, anxiety disorders are less common among older adults than among younger adults. The anxiety disorder most prevalent among older adults is generalized anxiety disorder (Segal, 2003). About 5% of older adults have generalized anxiety disorder, most often along with depression; in about half the cases, the anxiety disorder only emerged when the person became older (Flint, 2005). The fears and worries that accompany generalized anxiety disorder can impair cognitive functioning, in part because the person may become preoccupied with fears and worries and have difficulty paying attention and concentrating.

Schizophrenia

About 15% of people with schizophrenia are older than 44 when they have their first psychotic episode (Cohen et al., 2000). Schizophrenia can involve both *positive* symptoms, such as delusions and hallucinations, and *negative* symptoms, such as an absence of initiative (avolition; see Chapter 12); these symptoms can also occur with neurocognitive disorders.

Medical Factors That Can Affect Cognition

In some cases, impaired cognitive functioning is not a result of a neurocognitive disorder but rather is caused by medical problems. We summarize some of these problems in the following sections.

Diseases and Illnesses

Various physical diseases and illnesses can affect cognition—directly or indirectly. Some medical illnesses, such as encephalitis (a viral infection of the brain) and brain tumors, directly affect the brain and, in doing so, affect cognition. The specific cognitive deficits that arise depend on the particular features of the illness, such as the size and location of a brain tumor.

Some chronic diseases or illnesses indirectly affect cognition by creating pain, which can disrupt attention, concentration, and other mental processes. For example, arthritis can cause chronic pain, and the aftermath of surgery can cause acute pain. In addition, pain can interfere with sleep, which

Many physical diseases and illnesses can affect cognitive functioning. One example is pain—such as that caused by arthritis. In such cases, the person would not be considered to have a neurocognitive disorder.

SelectStock/Getty Images

further impairs mental processes. These detrimental effects may be temporary, so that cognitive functioning improves as the symptoms resolve or the pain recedes. In other cases, however, the person may never return to his or her prior level of functioning.

In still other cases, an older adult may *appear* to have impaired cognitive functioning but actually has undiagnosed or uncorrected sensory problems, such as hearing loss or vision problems. If someone chronically mishears what is said, he or she will seem "not with it" or "senile" when, in fact, the problem is simply that the person thinks the topic of conversation is something other than what it actually is.

Stroke

A **stroke** (so named because it was originally assumed to be a "stroke of God") is the interruption of normal blood flow to or within the brain (often because of an obstruction—such as a blood clot—in a blood vessel). The result is that part of the brain fails to receive oxygen and nutrients, and the neurons in that area die. The cognitive, emotional, and behavioral consequences of a stroke depend crucially on which specific group of neurons is affected; depending on their location in the brain, different deficits are produced. The most common deficits are discussed below.

Aphasia

Aphasia is a problem in using language. (The word *aphasia* literally means "an absence of speech.") Traditionally, there are two main types of aphasia, each named after the neurologist who first characterized it in detail. **Broca's aphasia** is characterized by problems producing speech. Patients with Broca's aphasia speak haltingly, and their speech can be very telegraphic—consisting of only the main words. In contrast, **Wernicke's aphasia** is characterized by problems with both comprehending language and producing meaningful utterances. Although these patients may appear to speak fluently, they often order words incorrectly and sometimes make up nonsense words.

Agnosia

Patients who have *agnosia* have difficulty understanding what they perceive, although neither their sensory abilities nor their knowledge about objects is impaired. Many forms of agnosia can arise. For example, *prosopagnosia* is a particular type of agnosia in which the person cannot recognize faces—often including his or her own face in a mirror! Some forms of agnosia can lead to disorientation, which must be distinguished from disorientation that occurs with dementia (to be discussed shortly).

Apraxia

Another medical condition that can affect cognitive functioning is **apraxia** (Kosslyn & Koenig, 1995), which involves problems in organizing and carrying out voluntary movements even though the muscles themselves are not impaired. The problem is in the brain, not in the muscles. Apraxia can take a variety of forms. For example, some patients have trouble sequencing movements (such as the movements necessary to light a candle, that is, taking out a match, striking it, and holding the flame to the wick). Clinicians must distinguish between such problems with voluntary movements and the avolition (difficulty initiating or following through with activities) that may accompany schizophrenia (noted in Chapter 12).

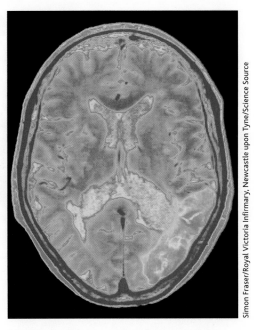

A stroke is an interruption of normal blood flow to the brain that causes neurons in that part of the brain to die. The effect of a stroke depends on its location in the brain and the size of the brain area that it affects. This image shows a colored MRI scan of the brain of a woman who had a stroke, with orange indicating dead brain tissue and green indicating healthy tissue.

Stroke
The interruption of normal blood flow to or within the brain, which results in neuronal death.

Aphasia
A neurological condition characterized by problems in producing or comprehending language.

Broca's aphasia
A neurological condition characterized by problems producing speech.

Wernicke's aphasia
A neurological condition characterized by problems comprehending language and producing meaningful utterances.

Apraxia
A neurological condition characterized by problems in organizing and carrying out voluntary movements even though the muscles themselves are not impaired.

Head injury—which might arise from playing football, soccer, or other sports, or from accidents that damage the brain—can lead to neurocognitive disorders.

Head Injury

Cognitive disorders may arise from head injuries—which may result from a car accident, from a fall, or in a variety of other ways. The specific cognitive deficits that develop depend on the exact nature of the head injury. The same kinds of deficits that follow a stroke can also occur after a head injury.

Substance-Induced Changes in Cognition

We saw in Chapter 9 that some people take substances (including prescribed medications) to alter their level of awareness or their emotional or cognitive state. But medications or exposure to toxic substances can produce unintended changes in attention, memory, judgment, or other cognitive functions, particularly when a person takes a high dose. In fact, older people are more sensitive than others to the effects of medications, and so a dose appropriate for a younger adult is more likely to have negative effects or side effects in an older adult (Mort & Aparasu, 2002). Even anesthesia for surgery can subsequently affect cognitive functioning (Thompson, 2003).

Thinking Like A Clinician

Evan is a first-year college student who lives with his grandmother because her home is near his school. Before he started living with her, he had spent only a few days at a time with her, usually on trips with his mother. Now that he's spending more time with his grandmother, he has noticed that she frequently tells him the same stories from her childhood. When she asks him to do an errand, she sometimes forgets the words of the objects she wants him to bring home or the shop she wants him to visit. And sometimes when he enters a room that she's in, she seems momentarily confused about who he is and why he's there. Evan is concerned that there is something "not right" with his grandmother, and is wondering whether he should suggest that she be evaluated by a doctor. Based on what you've learned about normal versus abnormal changes with aging, what specific advice would you give to Evan to help him determine whether his grandmother's cognitive problems are likely to be those of normal aging (and so Evan need not urgently suggest that she see her doctor)?

🔲 Delirium

Mrs. B.'s cognitive difficulties emerged gradually over time. Although she forgot appointments, she never forgot—and was never confused about—who and where she was. Moreover, she did not experience unusual or rapid changes in consciousness or in the ability to focus her attention. If she had, these symptoms might have indicated that she was delirious, as are many residents of nursing homes who are 85 years old or older (American Psychiatric Association, 2013).

What Is Delirium?

Delirium is characterized by a disturbance in attention and awareness as well as disruption of at least one other aspect of cognitive functioning (American Psychiatric Association, 2013). These symptoms develop rapidly—over hours to days—and fluctuate within a 24-hour period. The disturbance in attention is evidenced by difficulty directing, focusing, sustaining, and shifting attention, as well as a decreased awareness of the external environment; the person may appear "stoned" or seem to be focusing on internally generated stimuli, such as mental images. A delirious

Delirium
A neurocognitive disorder characterized by a relatively sudden disturbance in attention and awareness as well as disruption of at least one other aspect of cognitive functioning.

patient may have a hard time understanding a question, or may have trouble shifting attention to a new question and remain focused on the previous one. Alternatively, he or she may be distracted and unable to pay attention to any question. The DSM-5 diagnostic criteria are summarized in Table 15.2.

These attentional problems can make it difficult for a clinician to interview the delirious patient; the clinician must infer the patient's mental state from his or her behavior and unusual responses and then seek information from family members or friends. Case 15.2 describes one woman's experience with delirium.

CASE 15.2 • FROM THE OUTSIDE: Delirium

A 74-year-old African American woman, Ms. Richardson, was brought to a city hospital emergency room by the police. She is unkempt, dirty, and foul-smelling. She does not look at the interviewer and is apparently confused and unresponsive to most of his questions. She knows her name and address, but not the day or the month. She is unable to describe the events that led to her admission.

The police reported that they were called by neighbors because Ms. Richardson had been wandering around the neighborhood and not taking care of herself. The medical center mobile crisis unit went to her house twice but could not get in . . . they broke into the apartment . . . and then found Ms. Richardson hiding in the corner, wearing nothing but a bra. The apartment was filthy. . . .

[Ms. Richardson was diabetic, and her diabetes was out of control when she was admitted to the hospital. They begin to stabilize her medically and decided to transfer her the next day to a medical unit. Her mental state improved when the diabetes was treated.]

(Spitzer et al., 2002, pp. 13–14)

When delirious, people may also be disoriented, not knowing where they are or what the time, day, or year is; this was the case with Ms. Richardson in Case 15.2. Less frequently, when delirious, people may not know *who* they are. In addition, they may have difficulty speaking clearly, naming objects, or writing. The content of their speech may resemble that of someone in a manic episode: pressured and nonsensical, or flitting from topic to topic.

Delirious people may also experience perceptual alterations, including:

- *misinterpretations* (correctly perceiving sensory stimuli but incorrectly interpreting what they are, such as correctly identifying the smell of smoke but incorrectly attributing the smell to a roaring fire rather than to an extinguished match);
- *illusions* (misperceiving an object, as in perceiving the form of a pair of pants crumpled on the floor as a dog); and
- *hallucinations* (seeing—or hearing—someone or something that isn't actually there).

The perceptual disturbances are most frequently visual. Delirious people may believe that their perceptual experiences are real and behave accordingly. Hallucinations that are threatening may make them afraid, and they may respond by attacking others. Sometimes people in a delirious state are injured while responding to their altered perceptions, and their behavior can appear bizarre. Because of the perceptual difficulties, such patients may not consent to appropriate treatment.

Delirium is most common among the elderly and terminally ill, as well as patients who have just had surgery; it is not yet known why delirium is more likely among these groups, but neurological changes related to aging may make the elderly more vulnerable to developing delirium. Table 15.3 provides additional information about delirium.

TABLE 15.2 • DSM-5 General Diagnostic Criteria for Delirium

A. A disturbance in attention (i.e., reduced ability to direct, focus, sustain, and shift attention) and awareness (reduced orientation to the environment).

B. The disturbance develops over a short period of time (usually hours to a few days), represents a change from baseline attention and awareness, and tends to fluctuate in severity during the course of a day.

C. An additional disturbance in cognition (e.g., memory deficit, disorientation, language, visuospatial ability, or perception).

D. The disturbances in Criteria A and C are not better explained by another preexisting, established, or evolving neurocognitive disorder and do not occur in the context of a severely reduced level of arousal, such as coma.

E. There is evidence from the history, physical examination, or laboratory findings that the disturbance is a direct physiological consequence of another medical condition, substance intoxication or withdrawal (i.e., due to a drug of abuse or to a medication), or exposure to a toxin, or is due to multiple etiologies.

TABLE 15.3 • Delirium Facts at a Glance

Prevalence
• Older adults are more likely than others to develop delirium.
• Between 14% and 24% of patients admitted to a hospital are delirious.
• Approximately 70–87% of people in intensive care may become delirious.
• Delirium occurs in up to 60% of nursing home residents.
• Up to 80% of terminally ill patients will become delirious at the end of life (Brown & Boyle, 2002).
Comorbidity
• Delirium may occur along with another neurocognitive disorder or as a result of a substance-related disorder.
Onset
• When delirium arises after head trauma, symptoms often develop immediately.
Course
• Delirium typically resolves, and does so sooner, when the underlying problem is treated.
• Symptoms of delirium typically fluctuate over the course of the day.
• For most people, symptoms completely subside within a few hours or days; for others, especially the elderly, symptoms may persist for months or longer.
• People who had relatively good health and cognitive functioning before their delirium began are likely to make a better recovery than those with poor health and cognitive functioning.
• People with previous episodes of delirium are vulnerable to subsequent episodes.
Gender Differences
• Among elderly people, men are more likely than women to become delirious.
Cultural Differences
• Countries have different guidelines for diagnosing delirium, which can prohibit making meaningful comparisons across countries (Leentjens & Diefenbacher, 2006).

Source: Unless otherwise noted, the source for information is American Psychiatric Association, 2013.

Symptoms that appear similar to delirium can occur with other disorders, which may make it difficult to provide a definitive—or even a tentative—diagnosis. The following symptoms may appear similar to those of delirium:

• *Psychotic symptoms.* In schizophrenia or a mood disorder with psychotic features, the psychotic elements (i.e., delusions and hallucinations) are often consistent with other symptoms of the disorder. In contrast, in delirium, the symptoms that appear psychotic are not as consistent with the non-psychotic symptoms of schizophrenia and mood disorders.

• *Mood, anxiety, or dissociative symptoms.* With mood, anxiety, or dissociative disorders, the symptoms of fear, anxiety, or dissociation are relatively stable and tend not to vary with cognitive symptoms. In contrast, with delirium, symptoms of fear, anxiety, or dissociation tend to fluctuate along with the cognitive symptoms, and attentional problems are prominent.

If a clinician has reason to suspect that the symptoms arise because of a medical condition (such as untreated diabetes, infection, or substance use), delirium is a tentative diagnosis, pending physical or laboratory tests.

Understanding Delirium: A Side Effect?

Delirium can be a side effect of prescribed medication, substance use or exposure, or can result from a medical condition.

Delirium Caused by Substance Use

Delirium can arise from the effects of a psychoactive substance such as alcohol or a medication, or from withdrawal from such a substance. Intoxication and withdrawal are considered to give rise to delirium only when the symptoms are severe enough to require more than the usual clinical attention and treatment provided to someone who used the substance in question. If the symptoms are not severe enough to reach the level needed for a diagnosis of delirium, the appropriate diagnosis is a substance-related disorder, either intoxication or withdrawal (see Chapter 9).

Delirium Caused by a General Medical Condition

Like a fever, delirium can arise for a variety of medical reasons:

• infection,

• dehydration,

• electrolyte imbalance (which can arise from an eating disorder; see Chapter 10),

• stroke,

• brain tumor,

• pneumonia,

• heart attack,

• head trauma, or

• surgery (arising from anesthesia).

Some of these causes, such as dehydration, can be fatal if not treated (Brown & Boyle, 2002).

Clinicians determine the underlying cause of a person's delirium in several ways: from a physical examination, a consultation with someone who knows the patient and may know something about what led to the symptoms, results of laboratory tests, and a review of the patient's medical history.

Delirium can arise from a variety of medical problems, including dehydration, or after receiving anesthesia. Some surgery patients—particularly elderly ones—become temporarily delirious in response to anesthesia.

Treating Delirium: Rectify the Cause

Treatment for delirium usually targets neurological factors—treating the underlying medical condition or substance use that affects the brain and causes the delirium. In most cases, as the medical condition improves or the substance intoxication or withdrawal resolves, the delirium ends. In some cases, however, treatment for the underlying medical problem—for example, administering antibiotics to treat bacterial pneumonia—can take days to affect the delirium; in other cases, such as when people are close to death, doctors may not be able to treat the underlying cause of the delirium. For temporary relief, the patient may be given antipsychotic medication, usually haloperidol or risperidone (Leentjens & van der Mast, 2005). In fact, studies find that giving haloperidol preventatively to elderly patients about to undergo surgery can decrease the severity and duration of postoperative delirium (Kalisvaart et al., 2005).

Treatment may also target psychological and social factors. Such interventions for people with delirium include (Brown & Boyle, 2002):

• providing hearing aids or eyeglasses to eliminate sensory and perceptual impairments;

• teaching the person to focus on the here and now, by providing very visible clocks and calendars or other devices and encouraging the person to use them;

- creating an environment that optimizes stimulation, perhaps by providing adequate lighting and reducing unnecessary noise;
- ensuring that the person is fed and warm;
- making the environment safe by removing objects with which the patient could harm himself or herself or others; and
- educating the people who interact with the person (residential staff, friends, and family members) about delirium.

Thinking Like A Clinician

Drew is on his college's football team and had to have surgery on his knee. For the procedure, he had general anesthesia. His mom was with him right after the surgery, and Drew was delirious and remained so for hours. What can you assume, and what should you not assume, about Drew's emotions and his cognitive functions? What might be a likely cause of his delirium? What should be done, if anything, to help Drew?

▢ Dementia (and Mild Versus Major Neurocognitive Disorders)

Mrs. B. seemed to have memory problems. But memory was not the only aspect of her cognitive functioning that had declined. During neuropsychological testing, "the principal areas of difficulty on [certain] tests were in mental control, as evidenced by tangential and repetitive speech; psychomotor slowing [in this case, slow movements based on mental processes, not reflexes]; and reduced flexibility in thought and action" (La Rue & Watson, 1998, p. 9). Some of these difficulties are characteristic of *dementia*. Could Mrs. B. have dementia?

In this section we focus on dementia: what it is, what neurological factors give rise to it, and what treatments are available for it.

What Is Dementia?

Although not a DSM-5 disorder, **dementia** is the general term for a set of neurocognitive disorders characterized by deficits in learning new information or recalling information already learned *plus* at least one of the following types of impaired cognition:

- *Aphasia.* In dementia, problems with using language often appear as overuse of the words *thing* and *it* because of difficulty remembering the correct specific words.
- *Apraxia.* Problems with executing motor tasks (even though there isn't anything wrong with the appropriate muscles, limbs, or nerves). Such problems can lead to difficulties in dressing oneself and eating, at which point self-care becomes impossible.
- *Agnosia.* People with dementia may not recognize common objects—or friends, family members, or even their own face.
- *Executive function problems.* These patients may also have difficulties in planning, initiating, organizing, abstracting, and sequencing or even in recognizing that one has memory problems. (These problems arise primarily in dementia that affects the frontal lobes.) These deficits can make it impossible to meet the demands of daily life. Mrs. B. had difficulties in tasks that required executive functions.

We discussed aphasia, apraxia, and agnosia earlier, in the context of effects of brain damage on cognition. Unlike the effects caused by a stroke or a head injury, however, dementia is not caused by an isolated incident, nor do the deficits emerge quickly. Rather, they arise over a period of time, as brain functioning degrades; symptoms of dementia often change over time, typically becoming progressively worse (referred

Dementia
A set of neurocognitive disorders characterized by deficits in learning new information or recalling information already learned *plus* at least one other type of cognitive impairment.

to as a *progressive dementia*), but sometimes remaining static or in a minority of cases even reversing course. Dementia can arise as a result of a medical disease, such as Alzheimer's and Parkinson's diseases, but it is the dementia, not the medical disease itself, that is considered to be a neurocognitive disorder in DSM-5. In the United States, one estimate is that caring for people with dementia costs as much as caring for those with heart disease or cancer—up to $2.15 billion per year (Hurd et al., 2013). Most people with dementia are over 65 years old when symptoms emerge, termed *late onset*. When symptoms begin before age 65, the disorder is said to have *early onset*. Early onset, particularly before age 50, is rare and is usually hereditary (Ikeuchi et al., 2008).

Mild and Major Neurocognitive Disorders

In DSM-5, dementia is not a disorder; rather, people with dementia or other adult-onset cognitive deficits (such as difficulties with language) are diagnosed with either *mild* or *major neurocognitive disorder* (discussed below), depending on the person's symptoms and ability to function independently. Specifically, DSM-5 specifies six cognitive domains in which deficits may occur for these disorders:

- *Complex attention*—such as focusing and sustaining attention,
- *Executive functions*—such as planning and decision making,
- *Learning and memory*—such as learning new skills and remembering them,
- *Language*—such as speaking or understanding,
- *Perceptual-motor*—such as hand–eye coordination,
- *Social cognition*—such as recognizing emotions in others.

Impaired cognitive functioning can lead many patients to become easily overwhelmed or confused, causing them to be agitated. The confusion or agitation may then lead a patient to become violent, which can make it difficult or potentially dangerous for the patient to remain living at home with family members—and hence the patient may be moved to a residential care facility.

Depending on the specific cognitive processes that are impaired, a patient with dementia may:

- behave inappropriately (for instance, tell unsuitable jokes or be overly familiar with strangers);
- misperceive reality (for instance, think that a caretaker is an intruder); or
- wander away while trying to get "home" (a place he or she lived previously).

According to DSM-5, the hallmark of **mild neurocognitive disorder** is evidence of a *modest* decline from baseline in at least one of the six cognitive domains above, but that decline is *not* enough to interfere with daily functioning (see Table 15.4). In contrast, the hallmark of **major neurocognitive disorder** is evidence of a *substantial* decline in at least one cognitive domain, and impaired daily functioning that results from this decline (see Table 15.5) (American Psychiatric Association, 2013).

Mild neurocognitive disorder
A neurocognitive disorder characterized by a modest decline from baseline in at least one cognitive domain, but that decline is *not* enough to interfere with daily functioning.

Major neurocognitive disorder
A neurocognitive disorder characterized by evidence of a substantial decline in at least one cognitive domain, and impaired daily functioning.

TABLE 15.4 • DSM-5 Diagnostic Criteria for Mild Neurocognitive Disorder

A. Evidence of modest cognitive decline from a previous level of performance in one or more cognitive domains (complex attention, executive function, learning and memory, language, perceptual motor, or social cognition) based on:

1. Concern of the individual, a knowledgeable informant, or the clinician that there has been a mild decline in cognitive function; and

2. A modest impairment in cognitive performance, preferably documented by standardized neuropsychological testing or, in its absence, another quantified clinical assessment.

B. The cognitive deficits do not interfere with capacity for independence in everyday activities (i.e., complex instrumental activities of daily living such as paying bills or managing medications are preserved, but greater effort, compensatory strategies, accommodation may be required).

C. The cognitive deficits do not occur exclusively in the context of a delirium.

D. The cognitive deficits are not better explained by another mental disorder (e.g., major depressive disorder, schizophrenia).

Reprinted with permission from the Diagnostic and Statistical Manual of Mental Disorders, Fifth Edition, (Copyright ©2013). American Psychiatric Association. All Rights Reserved.

TABLE 15.5 • DSM-5 Diagnostic Criteria for Major Neurocognitive Disorder

A. Evidence of significant cognitive decline from a previous level of performance in one or more cognitive domains (complex attention, executive function, learning and memory, language, perceptual-motor, or social cognition) based on:

1. Concern of the individual, a knowledgeable informant, or the clinician that there has been a significant decline in cognitive function; and

2. A substantial impairment in cognitive performance, preferably documented by standardized neuropsychological testing or, in its absence, another quantified clinical assessment.

B. The cognitive deficits interfere with independence in everyday activities (i.e., at a minimum, requiring assistance with complex instrumental activities of daily living such as paying bills or managing medications).

C. The cognitive deficits do not occur exclusively in the context of delirium.

D. The cognitive deficits are not better explained by another mental disorder (e.g., major depressive disorder, schizophrenia).

Reprinted with permission from the Diagnostic and Statistical Manual of Mental Disorders, Fifth Edition, (Copyright ©2013). American Psychiatric Association. All Rights Reserved.

Alzheimer's disease
A medical condition in which the afflicted person initially has problems with both memory and executive function and which leads to progressive dementia.

The diagnosis of mild neurocognitive disorder was introduced in DSM-5. The inclusion of this diagnosis has been criticized as pathologizing normal aging, especially because daily functioning should not be impaired for this diagnosis. As we discussed earlier, as people get older, some of their cognitive abilities modestly decline relative to their baseline—without any significant problems in their daily life (Frances, 2013; Greenberg, 2013).

Mild and Major Neurocognitive Disorders

Among the new diagnoses in DSM-5 is the diagnosis of *mild neurocognitive disorder* (see Table 15.6). This diagnosis is controversial because only a "modest" cognitive decline is needed (one or two standard deviations below what would be expected for a given patient)—and unlike almost any other diagnosis in DSM-5, the symptoms do *not* need to cause distress or impair functioning. In fact, a requirement for the diagnosis is that functioning is not impaired!

On the one hand, this new diagnosis can focus the attention of researchers and clinicians on early signs of dementia (Geda & Nedelska, 2012; Gutierrez et al., 1994). The new diagnosis will make it easier for researchers to investigate factors related to faster or slower decline, and clinicians may

able to intervene earlier with new medications that delay or arrest further declines.

On the other hand, the new term can create confusion. The medical term for the level of cognitive ability that is in between normal functioning and dementia (or major neurocognitive disorder, in DSM-5 lingo) is *mild cognitive impairment*. This is the term neurologists use. So DSM-5 has created a different term, sowing confusion for mental health clinicians, patients, and their families. Patients will receive two diagnoses for the same condition (Siberski, 2013).

CRITICAL THINKING Given that neither distress nor impaired functioning are criteria, do you think mild neurocognitive disorder should be considered a "disorder"? Why or why not?

(James Foley, College of Wooster)

People whose cognitive functioning started out at a very high level may notice deficits in functioning that are mild symptoms of dementia, but neuropsychological testing is likely to show that the patient's abilities are within the normal range for his or her age. The early signs of dementia might otherwise go undiagnosed if current abilities aren't compared to previous abilities; with such early signs, the person might be diagnosed with mild neurocognitive disorder (American Psychiatric Association, 2013; Harvey, 2005a).

People with dementia can become confused about where they live and become lost.

Dementia and Alzheimer's Disease

The most common cause of dementia is **Alzheimer's disease** (also called simply *Alzheimer's*), in which the afflicted person initially has problems with both memory and executive function. As the disease advances, memory problems worsen, attention and language problems emerge, and spatial abilities may deteriorate; the patient may even develop psychotic symptoms, such as hallucinations and delusions (particularly persecutory delusions). In the final stage, the patient's memory loss is complete—he or she doesn't recognize family members and friends, can't communicate, and is completely dependent on others for care. In Case 15.3, Diana Friel McGowin describes her experience with dementia due to Alzheimer's disease; additional facts about dementia are provided in Table 15.6.

CASE 15.3 • FROM THE INSIDE: Dementia

Diana Friel McGowin was 45 years old when she became aware of memory problems. She got lost on the way home because no landmarks looked familiar; she was unable to remember her address or to recognize her cousin. After neuropsychological and neuroimaging tests, she was diagnosed with early-onset Alzheimer's disease (because the disorder emerged before age 65). In her memoir about the progressive nature of this disease, *Living in the Labyrinth* (1993), McGowin describes sharing with her neurologist some of the symptoms she was having:

> I showed him the burns on my wrists and arms sustained because I forgot to protect myself when inserting or removing food from the oven. I told him of becoming lost in the neighborhood grocery store where I had shopped for over twenty years. I showed him my scribbled notes and sketched maps of how to travel to the bank, the post office, the grocery, and work. (p. 41)

She describes other memory problems as the disease progressed:

> I sometimes lost my thread of thought in mid-sentence. Memories of childhood and long ago events were quite clear, yet I could not remember if I ate that day. On more than one occasion when my grandchildren were visiting, I forgot they were present and left them to their own devices. Moreover, on occasions when I had picked them up to come play at my house, the small children had to direct me home. (pp. 64–65)

Further into her memoir, she notes:

> As my grip upon the present slips, more and more comfort is found within my memories of the past. Childhood nostalgia is so keen I can actually smell the aroma of the small town library where I spent so many childhood hours. (p. 109)
>
> Painfully lonely, I still contrarily, deliberately, sit alone in my home. The radio and TV are silent. I am suspended. Somewhere there is that ever-present reminder list of what I am supposed to do today. But I cannot find it. (p. 112)

TABLE 15.6 • Dementia Facts at a Glance

Prevalence

- Approximately 5 million older Americans are estimated to have dementia (Alzheimer's Association, 2007).
- In 2010, more than 35 million people worldwide were estimated to have dementia (Prince et al., 2013).
- Approximately 1–2% of 65-year-olds are diagnosed with dementia, but as many as 30% of 85-year-olds are so diagnosed.

Comorbidity

- Depression (Kales et al., 2005; Snow et al., 2005) and psychotic symptoms such as hallucinations and delusions (Tractenberg et al., 2003) commonly co-occur with dementia.

Onset

- Onset usually occurs late in life.
- Cognitive deterioration can be rapid or gradual, depending on the cause of the dementia.
- Impaired learning and recall are early signs of some types of dementia.

Course

- People with dementia may be unable to perform complex tasks in new situations but may still be able to perform simple ones in familiar surroundings.
- Some types of dementia, such as that caused by Alzheimer's disease, get progressively worse; other types of dementia, such as that caused by HIV infection, can get better with treatment of the underlying cause. Still other types remain relatively unchanging.

Gender Differences

- Dementia is slightly more common in males than in females.

Cultural Differences

- Some cultures and ethnic groups—such as African Americans, Asian Americans, and Hispanic Americans—may be more tolerant of impaired memory and other cognitive dysfunctions that affect elderly people, in some cases viewing these changes as a normal part of aging. These family members thus may wait longer before seeking medical assistance for an older person with dementia (Cox, 2007).

Source: Unless otherwise noted, the source for information is American Psychiatric Association, 2000, 2013.

TABLE 15.7 • Symptoms Unique and Common to Delirium and Dementia

Unique to delirium	Unique to dementia	Common to both delirium and dementia
• Delirium has a rapid onset.	• Dementia has a gradual onset.	• Memory problems.
• Symptoms (including changes in consciousness) fluctuate within a 24-hour period.	• Symptoms typically do not fluctuate within a 24-hour period.	• Problems with other types of cognitive functioning.
• Hallucinations—frequently visual—are present.	• Hallucinations are often absent.	
• Symptoms often gradually improve.	• Symptoms rarely improve.	
• The person is not alert and focused.	• The person is consistently alert.	

In the early phases of a progressive dementia, when the person has relatively little decline in executive function, he or she may become so depressed about the diagnosis and its prognosis that he or she attempts suicide. Diana McGowin became acutely aware of her symptoms during the early phase of the disease and worked hard to try to compensate by making maps and lists. With some patients, mental health clinicians may have difficulty determining whether the particular symptoms reflect delirium, dementia, or both (see Table 15.7).

Understanding Dementia

Dementia is caused by a variety of neurological factors, and according to DSM-5, each of these factors corresponds to the diagnosis of a specific mild or major neurocognitive disorder. In what follows we review the most common types of dementia: dementia due to Alzheimer's disease, vascular dementia, and dementias that result from other medical conditions.

Alzheimer's Disease

Almost three quarters of dementia cases are caused by Alzheimer's disease (Plassman et al., 2007); in DSM-5, this form of dementia is referred to as *neurocognitive disorder due to Alzheimer's disease*. There is no routine lab test for diagnosing this disease at present, and so this type of dementia is diagnosed by ruling out other possible causes.

Artist William Utermohlen learned in 1995 that he had Alzheimer's disease—which causes a type of progressive dementia. He responded to the news by painting self-portraits. Alzheimer's can specifically affect brain areas involved in spatial abilities, which are crucial for painting. As his dementia progressed, Utermohlen's images became less distinct and more abstract; these three portraits were done in (left to right) 1998, 1999, and 2000. Although he recognized that his paintings weren't what he wanted, he said that he "could not figure out how to correct them" (Grady, 2006).

Courtesy of Galerie Beckel-Odille-Boicos, Paris

Courtesy of Galerie Beckel-Odille-Boicos, Paris

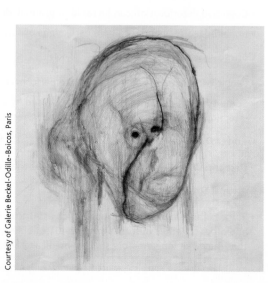

Courtesy of Galerie Beckel-Odille-Boicos, Paris

The Progression of Alzheimer's Disease

The onset of Alzheimer's disease is gradual, with symptoms becoming more severe over time. Often, the early signs of dementia of the Alzheimer's type involve difficulty remembering recent events or newly learned information. In the early stages of Alzheimer's, the memory problems are prominent (Petersen & O'Brien, 2006); it is only as the disease progresses that other sorts of deficits in cognitive processing emerge, such as aphasia, apraxia, agnosia, and deteriorated spatial abilities. (Such patients may often become lost when walking around their neighborhood.) Patients may also become irritable and their personality may change—and such changes may become more pronounced as cognitive functioning declines. In the final stage of the disease, perceptual-motor problems arise, creating difficulties with walking, talking, and self-care. Generally, these patients die about 8–10 years after the first symptoms emerge.

In some cases, people with dementia also have behavioral problems, such as those a woman reported about her husband:

> My husband used to be such an easy-going, calm person. Now, he suddenly lashes out at me and uses awful language. Last week, he got angry when our daughter and her family came over and we sat down to eat. I never know when it's going to happen. He's changed so much—it scares me sometimes.
>
> (National Institute on Aging, 2003, p. 47)

People with Alzheimer's who behave in unusual or disturbed ways are more likely to have greater declines in cognitive functioning and to need institutional care sooner than patients whose behavior causes less concern (Scarmeas et al., 2007). As noted in Table 15.8, slightly more females than males develop this form of dementia, and it accounts for progressively more cases of dementia in older age groups.

Brain Abnormalities Associated With Alzheimer's Disease: Neurofibrillary Tangles and Amyloid Plaques

Two brain abnormalities are associated with Alzheimer's disease: *neurofibrillary tangles* and *amyloid plaques*. The internal support structure of a neuron includes microtubules, which are tiny, hollow tubes that create tracks from the cell body to the end of the axon; nutrients are distributed within the cell via these microtubules. A protein, called *tau*, helps stabilize the structure of these tracks (see Figure 15.1).

TABLE 15.8 • Prevalence of Dementia Due to Alzheimer's From Age 65 On

Age (in years)	Prevalence among males	Prevalence among females
65	0.6%	0.8%
85	11%	14%
90	21%	25%
95	36%	41%

As people age beyond 65 years old, they are increasingly likely to develop Alzheimer's disease. About half the cases in each age group have moderate to severe cognitive impairment (American Psychiatric Association, 2000).

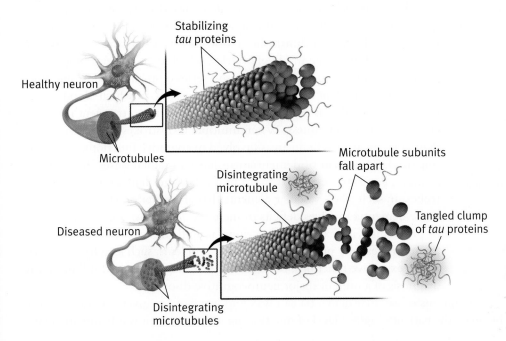

FIGURE 15.1 • Neurofibrillary Tangles in Alzheimer's Disease Tau proteins stabilize the structure of a neuron from the cell body through the end of the axon. With Alzheimer's disease, these proteins become entangled, destroying the structure of the neuron and disrupting its communication with other neurons.

Source: National Institute on Aging

Neurofibrillary tangles
The mass created by tau proteins that become twisted together and destroy microtubules, leaving the neuron without a distribution system for nutrients.

Amyloid plaques
Fragments of protein that accumulate on the outside surfaces of neurons, particularly neurons in the hippocampus.

Vascular dementia
A type of dementia caused by reduced or blocked blood supply to the brain, which arises from plaque buildup or blood clots.

With Alzheimer's disease, the tau proteins become twisted together into **neurofibrillary tangles**, and these proteins no longer hold together the microtubules—which thereby disrupts the neuron's distribution system for nutrients. In addition, the collapse of this support structure prevents normal communication with other neurons. This process may also contribute to the death of neurons. In fact, people with Alzheimer's have smaller brains than usual (Henneman et al., 2009).

The brains of people with Alzheimer's disease are abnormal in another way—they have **amyloid plaques**, which are fragments of proteins (one type of which is called *amyloid*) that accumulate on the outer surfaces of neurons, particularly neurons in the hippocampus—the brain area predominately involved in storing new information in memory.

Researchers have not yet determined whether the neurofibrillary tangles and plaques *cause* Alzheimer's disease or are a byproduct of some other process that causes the disease (National Institute on Aging, 2003; Schwitzer, 2012). However, neurofibrillary tangles and amyloid plaques are generally discovered during autopsies, and PET scanning that uses a particular chemical marker has been able to detect the amyloid plaques and neurofibrillary tangles that distinguish Alzheimer's disease from other causes of memory problems in living patients (Ikonomovic et al., 2008; Small et al., 2006; Snitz et al., 2013; Zhang et al., 2012).

Genetics

People who have a specific version of one gene, *apo E*, are more susceptible to late-onset Alzheimer's disease than people who don't have this particular gene. However, someone can have this version of the apo E gene and not develop Alzheimer's; conversely, someone can develop Alzheimer's and not have this version of the gene.

In contrast, early-onset Alzheimer's is caused by the mutation of one of three other genes, and two of these mutations lead to Alzheimer's disease in 100% of cases. However, the third type of mutation (a rare form called *presenilin 2*) does not always cause the disease (Williamson-Catania, 2007), which suggests that other neurological factors and/or psychosocial factors may play a role.

Vascular Dementia

Vascular refers to blood vessels, and *vascular diseases* refer to problems with blood vessels, such as high blood pressure or high cholesterol. Vascular disease can reduce or block blood supply to the brain, which in turn can cause **vascular dementia** (in DSM-5, referred to as *vascular neurocognitive disorder*). Blood vessels can be involved in dementia in two ways: (1) Plaque builds up on artery walls, making the arteries narrower, which then diminishes blood flow to the brain, or (2) bits of clotted blood block the inside of arteries, which then prevents blood from reaching the brain. Such clots can cause a series of small strokes (sometimes referred to as *transient ischemic attacks* or *ministrokes*), in which blood supply to parts of the brain is temporarily blocked, leading to transient impaired cognition or consciousness. When multiple ministrokes occur over time, dementia can arise as brain areas involved in cognitive functioning become impaired. This form of dementia can have a gradual onset. In contrast, a single, large stroke inflicts more brain damage than a series of ministrokes; in such cases, vascular dementia has an abrupt onset. Note that because dementia involves deficits in memory *and* aphasia, apraxia, agnosia, or problems with executive functions, not all strokes produce dementia: Some strokes only produce very specific problems, such as aphasia or deficits in executive functions, but the results of the stroke could still merit the diagnosis of a mild or major neurocognitive disorder.

Symptoms of vascular dementia can wax and wane over a given 24-hour period, but even the patient's highest level of functioning is lower than it was before dementia

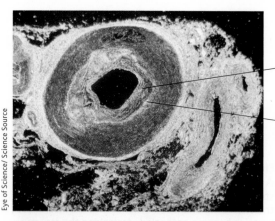

Eye of Science/ Science Source

Plaque

Arterial opening

A buildup of plaque in the arteries can lead to a narrowing of the artery and decreased blood supply to the brain, which in turn can cause vascular dementia.

set in (Puente, 2003). In addition, neuroimaging may reveal lesions ("dead" neurons) in particular brain areas. People with vascular dementia may also have Alzheimer's disease, particularly if they are very old (Kalaria & Ballard, 1999). Vascular dementia is more common in men than women.

The course of vascular dementia is variable, depending on the specific brain areas affected; when symptoms become more severe, they worsen in a stepwise fashion, with more deficits apparent after each instance of reduced blood supply to the brain. Aggressive treatment of the underlying vascular disease (typically via medication) may prevent additional strokes or reduced blood flow to brain areas.

Dementia Due to Other Medical Conditions

Dementia can also be caused by a variety of other medical conditions, including Parkinson's disease, late-stage HIV infection, and Huntington's disease. With these and certain other medical conditions, the onset can be gradual or sudden, the course can range from acute to chronic, and the patient may also develop behavioral disturbances.

Dementia Due to Parkinson's Disease

Parkinson's disease is characterized by a slow, progressive loss of motor function; typical symptoms are trembling hands, a shuffling walk, and muscular rigidity. About 1 million Americans have Parkinson's disease, and approximately 50% of people with Parkinson's disease develop dementia due to this disease, in DSM-5 referred to as *neurocognitive disorder due to Parkinson's disease*. People who develop this type of dementia are usually older (age of onset is about 65 years old) or are in a more advanced stage of the disease (Papapetropoulos et al., 2005). The dementia generally involves problems in memory and executive functions. Comorbid depression can cause additional cognitive deficits.

Parkinson's disease causes damage to dopamine-releasing neurons in an area of the brain known as the *substantia nigra*. As a consequence, the brains of these patients do not have normal amounts of this neurotransmitter, which is critically involved in motor functions as well as executive functions. Parkinson's disease is thought to arise from a combination of genetics and other neurological factors, such as brain damage caused by exposure to pesticides and other toxins.

Dementia Due to Lewy Bodies

Another type of progressive dementia is *dementia due to Lewy bodies*, in DSM-5 referred to as *neurocognitive disorder with Lewy bodies*. *Lewy bodies* consist of a type of protein that, in some people, builds up inside neurons that produce dopamine or acetylcholine and can eventually cause the neurons to die. The neurons most often affected are involved in memory and motor control. (Neurons associated with other functions can also be affected.)

Clinicians may have difficulty distinguishing this form of dementia from Alzheimer's, and autopsies have revealed that about 20% of people who were diagnosed with Alzheimer's also had abnormal Lewy bodies (Rabin et al., 2006). However, although people who have dementia due to Lewy bodies have characteristics in common with people who have Alzheimer's, they have more severe disruptions of:

• visuospatial ability, and

• executive functions (Kaufer, 2002; Knopman et al., 2003; Walker & Stevens, 2002).

Moreover, people who have dementia due solely to Lewy bodies have three features that are not shared by people who have dementia that arises from Alzheimer's disease:

• the presence of (visual) hallucinations early in the course of the disorder,

• a tendency to retain the ability to name objects, and

• stiff movements early in the course of the disorder, which are similar to that of people with Parkinson's disease (rigid muscles, tremors, slowed movements, and a shuffling style of walking).

Like patients with Alzheimer's disease, patients with dementia due to Lewy bodies progressively deteriorate until death, which on average occurs about 8–10 years after diagnosis.

Dementia Due to HIV Infection

The human immunodeficiency virus (HIV) can destroy white matter and subcortical brain areas, which then gives rise to a type of dementia referred to in DSM-5 as *neurocognitive disorder due to HIV infection*. The symptoms of this form of dementia include impaired memory, concentration, and problem solving, as well as cognitive slowing. Moreover, patients may exhibit signs of apathy, social withdrawal, delirium, delusions, or hallucinations. They may develop tremors or repetitive movements or have problems keeping their balance (McArthur et al., 2003; Price, 2003; Shor-Posner et al., 2000). Antiretroviral medications that treat HIV infection slow—and in some cases may actually reverse—the brain damage, improving cognitive functioning (Sacktor et al., 2006).

Dementia Due to Huntington's Disease

Huntington's disease is a progressive disease that kills neurons and affects cognition, emotion, and motor functions; it leads to dementia and eventually results in death. Early symptoms of Huntington's disease include bipolar-like mood swings between mania and depression, irritability, and hallucinations or delusions; in DSM-5 it is referred to as *neurocognitive disorder due to Huntington's disease*. Motor symptoms include slow or restless movements, and the cognitive symptoms include memory problems (which become severe as the disease progresses), impaired executive function, and poor judgment.

Huntington's disease is inherited and is based on a single gene. If a parent has Huntington's disease, his or her children each have a 50% chance of developing it. Genetic testing can assess whether the gene is present.

Dementia Due to Head Trauma

Head trauma can cause dementia or other impaired cognitive functioning, referred to as *neurocognitive disorder due to traumatic brain injury* in DSM-5. The precise deficits and their severity depend on which brain areas are affected and to what degree. A person with this form of dementia may also behave unusually, such as being agitated. Such a patient may have amnesia for events during and after the trauma, as well as other persistent memory problems. In addition, he or she may have sensory or motor problems and even personality changes (becoming increasingly aggressive or apathetic or suffering severe mood swings) (American Psychiatric Association, 2000).

This form of dementia is most common among young males, who are more likely than others to engage in risk-taking behaviors (such as reckless drinking) that may lead to a single trauma to the head (such as a car accident); when the dementia is caused by multiple traumas (as occurs with boxers), it may become worse over time (American Psychiatric Association, 2013).

Substance/Medication-Induced Neurocognitive Disorder

When the cognitive deficits of dementia are caused by substance use but persist beyond the period of intoxication or withdrawal, the clinician makes the DSM-5 diagnosis of *substance/medication-induced neurocognitive disorder*. A patient who receives this diagnosis usually has a long history of substance use, and symptoms rarely occur in patients younger than 20 years. The onset is slow, as is the progression of deficits; the first symptoms arise while the person has a substance use disorder. If the person is over age 50, the deficits often are not reversible and may even get worse when the substance use is discontinued (American Psychiatric Association, 2013).

As we've noted, dementia may be caused by a number of medical illnesses or conditions, and these causes are not mutually exclusive; a given person's dementia may have more than one cause. For example, someone may have both vascular dementia

Perhaps unique among the various types of dementias, dementia due to HIV infection can be reversed with antiretroviral medication for HIV such as Truvada.

AP Photo/Jeff Chiu

Huntington's disease
A progressive disease that kills neurons and affects cognition, emotion, and motor functions; it leads to dementia and eventually results in death.

TABLE 15.9 • Key Facts About Different Types of Dementia

Dementia due to . . .	Approximate percentage of all dementia cases	Prognosis/course	Onset	Gender difference
Alzheimer's disease	70%	Poor	Gradual, often after age 65; early onset is rare	Slightly more common among women than men
Vascular disease	15% (often comorbid with Alzheimer's type)	Cognitive loss may remain stable or worsen in a stepwise fashion.	Abrupt; earlier age of onset than Alzheimer's	More common among men
Lewy bodies	15% (can be comorbid with Alzheimer's type)	Poor	Gradual; age of onset is between 50 and 85	Slightly more common among men than women
HIV infection	Less than 10%	Poor unless treated with antiretroviral medication	Gradual; depends on age at which HIV infection is acquired	Estimates of sex ratios vary, depending in part on the sex difference in HIV prevalence and the availability of antiretroviral treatment at the time a study is undertaken
Parkinson's disease	Less than 10%; often comorbid with Alzheimer's type and/or vascular dementia; about 50% of patients with Parkinson's disease develop dementia	Poor	Gradual; typical age of onset is in the 70s	More men than women develop Parkinson's disease, and so men are more likely to develop this type of dementia
Huntington's disease	Less than 10%	Poor	Gradual; onset usually occurs in the 40s or 50s.	No sex difference
Head trauma	Unknown	Depends on the specific nature of the trauma	Usually abrupt, after the head injury	Unknown, but most common among young men
Substance-induced	Unknown	Variable, depends on the specific substance and deficits	Gradual; in the 30s and beyond	Unknown

Note: Most cases of dementia are caused by Alzheimer's disease. However, dementia in a given person can arise from more than one cause, and the percentages in the second column reflect these comorbidities; for this reason, the numbers add up to more than 100%.

and Alzheimer's disease. When this occurs, the clinician diagnoses each type (cause) separately. Table 15.9 summarizes key facts about the different types of dementia.

With a progressive dementia, such as occurs in Alzheimer's disease, a person's diagnosis may change over time from a mild neurocognitive disorder to major neurocognitive disorder; this changed diagnosis occurs after the disorder has advanced and the person's cognitive abilities are impaired to the point where he or she can't function effectively (e.g., can't remember to pay bills or take medication). In other cases, such as cognitive impairments that arise from head trauma, a person's deficits might remain relatively mild and stable, so that the person can functioning relatively well in daily life, with perhaps some reduced ability relative to his or her pervious baseline; in such cases, a mild neurocognitive disorder would not change to major neurocognitive disorder.

Treating Dementia

With most types of dementia, such as the Alzheimer's type and vascular dementia, treatments cannot return cognitive functioning to normal (HIV-induced dementia being the exception to the rule, as noted earlier), and instead consist of rehabilitation. Given the high proportion of dementia that is caused by Alzheimer's disease (see Table 15.9), in the following sections we focus on treatment for that type of dementia, unless otherwise noted.

Targeting Neurological Factors

Medications have been developed to delay the progression of cognitive difficulties in people with Alzheimer's disease. One class of drugs, *cholinesterase inhibitors*, such as *galantamine* (Razadyne) or *donepezil* (Aricept), is used for mild to moderate cognitive symptoms; these medications increase levels of acetylcholine (Lyle et al., 2008; Poewe et al., 2006). Another type of drug, *memantine* (Namenda), affects levels of glutamate (Tariot et al., 2004) and is used to treat moderate to severe Alzheimer's dementia (Kavirajan, 2009). Still other, experimental, medications are intravenous immunoglobulin (Relkin et al., 2012) and EVP-6124 (Hilts et al., 2012). Although each of these drugs may help some patients (Atri et al., 2008; Cummings et al., 2008; Homma et al., 2008), they are new, and few carefully controlled studies of these medications have been completed.

Antipsychotic medications are sometimes given for psychotic symptoms or behavioral disturbances, but the side effects of both traditional and atypical antipsychotics caution against their long-term use (Ballard & Howard, 2006; Schneider et al., 2006b). Patients with dementia due to Lewy bodies should not be given antipsychotic medication for behavioral disturbances because this type of medication makes their symptoms worse.

Targeting Psychological Factors

The American Association for Geriatric Psychiatry (2006) recommends that the first line of intervention for dementia should help patients maintain as high a quality of life as is possible, given the symptoms. Such interventions focus on psychological and social factors.

To target psychological factors, people in the early stages of dementia—and their friends and relatives—may be taught strategies and given devices to compensate for memory loss. Such strategies include ways of organizing information so that it can later be retrieved from memory more readily. One such strategy is the use of *mnemonics*, which may help people to remember simple information, such as where the car is parked at the mall. For example, someone might repeatedly visualize the location of the car in the parking lot, which will help him or her retain this information. In addition, structured and predictable daily activities can reduce patients' confusion (Gitlin et al., 2010; Spector et al., 2000).

Moreover, patients may be given a GPS tracking device to wear so that they can be found relatively quickly and easily if they get lost (Rabin et al., 2006).

People who are in the early stages of progressive dementias are often anxious and depressed (Porter et al., 2003; Ross et al., 1998). One type of treatment that may alleviate these comorbid conditions is *reality orientation therapy* (Giordano et al., 2010; Woods, 2004), which is designed to decrease a patient's confusion by focusing on the here and now. For example, the clinician may frequently repeat the patient's name ("Good morning, Mr. Rodrigues; how are you on this Monday morning, Mr. Rodrigues?") and remind the patient of the day and time; calendars and clocks are located where the patient can see them easily. Patients whose cognitive functioning is impaired to the point where they are in residential centers are encouraged to join in activities rather than isolate themselves.

Another method that may decrease the depression and anxiety that can accompany progressive cognitive decline is *reminiscence therapy*, which stimulates the patients' memories that are least affected by dementia—those of their early lives. When providing this treatment, the therapist focuses on patients' life histories and asks patients to explore and share their experiences with group members or with the therapist; patients may feel relief at being able to remember some information, and their anxiety decreases and their mood improves (Subramaniam & Woods, 2012).

People with dementia can wander off and become confused about who they are and where their home is. Some people with dementia wear small GPS tracking devices, like the one in this sneaker, so that if they wander off they can be found relatively quickly and easily.

Monitoring whereabouts

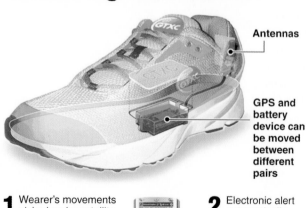

Antennas

GPS and battery device can be moved between different pairs

1 Wearer's movements picked up by satellite, relayed to monitoring center and made accessible to care takers by internet or phone

2 Electronic alert automatically issued if wearer enters or breaks a pre-defined area

© 2007 MCT
Source: Images: GTX Corporation   Graphic: Elsebeth Nielsen, Eeli Polli

Polli/MCT/Newscom

Caregivers—family members and paid caretakers—may be trained to treat behavioral disturbances, such as agitation and aggression that sometimes arise with dementia. Such training may lead them to first be asked to identify the antecedents and consequences of the problematic behavior (Ayalon et al., 2006; Spira & Edelstein, 2006). Following this, they are advised how to modify those aspects of the environment or personal interactions. For instance, if a patient becomes aggressive only at night after waking up to go to the bathroom, a night-light in his or her room may help reduce any anxiety that arises because the patient is confused upon awakening.

Targeting Social Factors

One way to reduce the cognitive load of someone with dementia is to enlist others to structure the patient's environment so that memory is less important. For instance, family members can place labels on the outside of cupboards and room doors at home or at a residential facility; each label identifies what is on the other side of the door (for example, "dishes," "kitchen," "Sally Johnson's room"). In some rehabilitation centers, the doors to bathrooms are painted a distinctive color, and arrows on the walls or floors show the direction to a bathroom, so patients don't need to rely as much on memory to get around the facility (Wilson, 2004).

As cognitive and physical functioning decline, patients with dementia may receive services that target social factors—such as *elder day care*, which is a day treatment program for older adults with cognitive or physical impairments. Such day treatment both allows the patient to interact with other people and provides a respite for family members who care for the patient. As the patient continues to decline, however, he or she may require live-in caretakers or full-time care in a nursing home or other residential facility.

Taking care of a family member who has Alzheimer's disease is often extremely stressful; for example, patients may need to be watched constantly and closely, for fear that they may inadvertently harm themselves or other people. This stress increases the caretaker's risk of developing a psychological or medical disorder. In recent years, clinicians who treat patients with dementia have also reached out to family members who act as caretakers to provide education, support, and, when needed, treatment to help these people develop less stressful ways of interacting with the patients. Such interventions help family members (and, indirectly, the patients themselves) function as well as possible under the circumstances.

Thinking Like A Clinician

Sixty-five-year-old Lucinda recently retired from her job as corporate vice-president of marketing. Lucinda lives alone but frequently visits her son, his wife, and their young daughter. She's noticed lately that she loses umbrellas and often forgets things—such as where her keys are, lunch dates with friends, and other appointments. She's chalked up these problems to her retirement and the resulting changes in her daily routines. At what point might losing and forgetting things indicate a neurocognitive disorder? If you knew only that Lucinda had dementia, what should and shouldn't you assume about its cause(s) and her prognosis?

▢ Diagnosing Mrs. B.'s Problems

Let's reconsider the specific nature of Mrs. B.'s problems. The neuropsychologist recounted that Mrs. B. knew who and where she was and understood test instructions. Results of tests of her ability to remember information both immediately after learning it and after a 30-minute delay were normal for her age, which indicated that she probably did not have Alzheimer's disease or another disease that involves significant memory impairment. Instead, the neuropsychologist suggested that Mrs. B.'s problems reflected a mild dementia (possibly a mild vascular neurocognitive disorder) combined with depression and chronic pain. The neuropsychologist wrote in her report:

> Feedback to Mrs. B. reinforced her belief that her current memory problems do not suggest [Alzheimer's disease]. She was asked about activities that she enjoys, and we explored ways of increasing her opportunities for these activities with her attendant (e.g., she has recently visited a senior day-care program and hopes to attend one or two days a week). She was encouraged to give her current living situation a longer try, working with her daughter and staff to improve the most bothersome aspects of the situation. Written reports were provided to the daughter (who is Mrs. B.'s legal guardian) and other medical professionals involved in her care. Feedback was also provided by telephone to the daughter and the referring psychiatrist to answer questions about results and to further discuss approaches to care. Recommendations included continuing psychotherapy and antidepressant medication, negotiating brief written contracts between Mrs. B. and staff members at the board-and-care home to clarify mutual expectations in problem areas, and considering low-dose antipsychotic medication in the event that aggressive and accusatory behaviors escalated despite behavioral intervention. Neither returning home nor moving into the daughter's home was recommended. . . .
>
> For Mrs. B., things got worse before they got better. Her "fit" in the board-and-care home continued to deteriorate, and after much discussion, she moved back to a nursing home. For a time, she was taking multiple psychoactive medications and her cognitive function deteriorated at a rapid rate [which might be considered a major medication-induced neurocognitive disorder]. [She was taken off her medications] and her [cognitive functioning] rebounded. A year later, after an intervening small stroke, her memory function is slightly worse, but her mood is brighter, she communicates well, and she has fewer complaints about staff and other residents than she did in the board-and-care home.
>
> (La Rue & Watson, 1998, p. 11)

☐ SUMMING UP

Normal Versus Abnormal Aging and Cognitive Functioning

- Most aspects of cognitive functioning remain stable during the normal course of aging. However, fluid intelligence, processing speed, recalling verbal information on demand, maintaining attention, and multitasking decline in older adults. But these declines do not generally impair daily functioning.

- The disorders that are most common among older adults are depression and generalized anxiety disorder. These disorders can lead to impaired cognitive functioning that may superficially resemble symptoms of a neurocognitive disorder.

- Brain injury, most commonly from a stroke, can produce various cognitive deficits. Among the deficits that may follow a stroke or a head injury are aphasia, agnosia, and apraxia.

- Legally prescribed medications or illegal substances can alter awareness, emotional states, and cognitive functioning.

Delirium

- According to DSM-5, delirium is characterized as a disturbance in attention and awareness as well as changes in another aspect of cognitive functioning. These symptoms develop rapidly and fluctuate over the course of a 24-hour period.

- Delirium most commonly occurs among the elderly, the terminally ill, and patients who have just had surgery.

- Delirium can arise from substance intoxication or withdrawal; delirium can also arise from a medical condition—such as an infection or head trauma—or as a result of anesthesia.

- Treatment for delirium that targets neurological factors often addresses the underlying physical cause, typically through medication.

- Treatments that target psychological and social factors include correcting sensory impairments, helping patients increase their awareness of the here and now, and educating people who interact with the delirious patient about the symptoms of the disorder.

Dementia (and Mild Versus Major Neurocognitive Disorders)

- Dementia is the umbrella term for a set of cognitive disorders that involve deficits in memory *and* aphasia, apraxia, agnosia, or problems with executive functions.

- Dementia can give rise to hallucinations and delusions.

- All types of dementia are caused by neurological factors. The most common type of dementia—that due to Alzheimer's disease—is a progressive disorder characterized by neurofibrillary tangles and amyloid plaques in the brain. Although symptoms may emerge before age 65, the late-onset form is much more common.

- Vascular dementia is caused by reduced or blocked blood flow to the brain, usually because of narrowed arteries or strokes.

- Other types of dementia are caused by medical conditions:
  - Parkinson's disease is a progressive disorder that affects motor functions.
  - Lewy bodies build up inside certain types of neurons and cause the neurons to die, leading to progressive, irreversible dementia.
  - HIV disease can eventually destroy white matter and subcortical brain areas; however, in some cases this type of dementia can be arrested and even reversed with antiretroviral medication.
  - Huntington's disease is a progressive disease that involves death of neurons in brain areas that are involved in cognition, emotion, and motor control.
  - Head trauma is caused by accidents or incurred as part of an athletic sport.
  - Substance use problems or medications can lead to temporary or persistent dementia.
- Mild neurocognitive disorder is characterized by evidence of a modest decline in cognitive function from baseline but people are able to function independently.

In contrast, major neurocognitive disorder is characterized by significant cognitive decline and impaired ability to function independently.

- Treatments for dementia that target neurological factors include medications that affect the levels of acetylcholine or glutamate.
- Psychological and social interventions for people with dementia are designed to improve the patients' quality of life. Methods include the use of memory aids, reality orientation therapy, reminiscence therapy, and restructuring of the environment.

Key Terms

Neurocognitive disorders (p. 477)

Crystallized intelligence (p. 479)

Fluid intelligence (p. 479)

Stroke (p. 483)

Aphasia (p. 483)

Broca's aphasia (p. 483)

Wernicke's aphasia (p. 483)

Apraxia (p. 483)

Delirium (p. 484)

Dementia (p. 488)

Mild neurocognitive disorder (p. 489)

Major neurocognitive disorder (p. 489)

Alzheimer's disease (p. 490)

Neurofibrillary tangles (p. 494)

Amyloid plaques (p. 494)

Vascular dementia (p. 494)

Huntington's disease (p. 496)

More Study Aids

Photodisc

For additional study aids related to this chapter, including quizzes to make sure you've retained everything you've learned and a Student Video Activity exploring the case of a man who has lost both his short-term and long-term memory, go to: www.worthpublishers.com/launchpad/rkabpsych2e.

CHAPTER 16

Ethical and Legal Issues

I t's the early evening rush hour in New York City in January 1998. People are waiting in a subway station for a train to take them home, to meet friends, or to go out to dinner. Kendra Webdale, a 32-year-old woman, is among the people waiting at the platform. Andrew Goldstein, a 29-year-old man, comes up from behind her and pushes her in front of an oncoming train as it enters the station. He murdered her, as many witnesses later testified. This might seem an open-and-shut criminal case, but it's not. Goldstein had a 10-year history of mental illness, had been in and out of psychiatric units and hospitals, and had been diagnosed with paranoid schizophrenia.

If Goldstein wasn't in his "right mind" when he pushed Webdale, should he face a trial? And if found guilty, should he go to jail, or perhaps be executed? Or should he be judged and treated as someone who is mentally ill—and if so, why? If the mentally ill commit criminal acts, should they be dealt with differently than people who are not mentally ill? Moreover, what if Goldstein had been seeing a psychotherapist and had mentioned that he might do something like this—should the therapist have reported his statement to the police? Mental health clinicians are bound by a code of ethics and by state and federal laws. What are the relevant ethical guidelines and laws that affect how mental health clinicians treat their patients? These are the types of questions that address the relationships among the law, ethics, and the reality of mental illness and its treatment.

IN THIS CHAPTER, we examine the legal and ethical issues that can affect mental health professionals and their patients, paying particular attention to criminal actions by people who are mentally ill—the circumstances under which they are considered insane, what happens to them when they are dangerous to themselves or others, and whether and when they receive treatment.

Yagi Studio/Taxi Japan/Getty Images. Photo for illustrative purposes only; any individual depicted is a model.

503

Andrew Goldstein (left) killed Kendra Webdale (right) by pushing her off a subway station platform into an oncoming train. Goldstein had a history of mental illness and had been diagnosed with paranoid schizophrenia. How do we determine whether he should be treated as a person suffering from a disease or as a cold-blooded murderer?

▢ Ethical Issues

Various mental health professionals had contact with Andrew Goldstein during the years that led up to his pushing Kendra Webdale to her death. Any mental health professional may at times have to balance ethical and legal obligations to a patient against the safety of others. Suppose Goldstein had confided to a mental health professional that he sometimes had impulses to hurt people—impulses that he felt he might not be able to control. How should the clinician treat such information? If Goldstein gave specifics about when, where, or with whom he was likely to become violent, would that affect how the clinician should treat such information? What is the clinician ethically bound to do in such instances? We address these questions in the following sections.

An Ethical Principle: The Role of Confidentiality

Different types of mental health professionals assess and provide treatment for psychological problems. Each profession has its own code of ethics, although all of the codes have some guidelines in common. (Websites containing the specific codes of ethics for the different types of mental health professionals are listed in Table 16.1.) The most important common feature is the ethical requirement to maintain **confidentiality**—not to disclose information about a patient (even whether someone *is* a patient) to others unless legally mandated to do so. The ethical principles and code of conduct of the American Psychological Association requires that mental health records remain confidential. In addition, the clinician must inform patients about the limits of confidentiality—that is, under what circumstances confidentiality may be broken.

TABLE 16.1 • Websites for the Ethical Codes of Various Mental Health Professions

Mental health profession	URL of website presenting ethical code
Psychologist	www.apa.org/ethics
Psychiatrist	www.psychiatry.org/practice/ethics/resources-standards
Social worker	www.socialworkers.org/pubs/code/code.asp
Psychiatric nurse	http://nursingworld.org/MainMenuCategories/EthicsStandards/CodeofEthicsforNurses/Code-of-Ethics.pdf
List of specific types of mental health clinicians	http://kspope.com/ethcodes/index.php

Confidentiality
The ethical requirement not to disclose information about a patient (even whether someone *is* a patient) to others unless legally compelled to do so.

Ambiguities Regarding Confidentiality

The principle of confidentiality appears to be straightforward, but some clinical situations are thorny and difficult to resolve. When a therapist is treating a couple, for instance, the therapist is bound by confidentiality, but each person in the couple is not; this means that each partner may tell other people about what transpires in therapy sessions. Similarly, in group therapy, although the therapist is bound by confidentiality, each member is not (although group members are asked not to talk about anything they hear from other members). However, when a patient is a minor (under 18 years of age), the clinician may inform the parents about information that the child has told the clinician. The clinician usually discusses the limits of confidentiality with a child old enough to understand them—or at least discusses possible circumstances in which the clinician may need to share information with parents or others.

A mental health clinician is bound by confidentiality, but each member of a couple participating in couples therapy is not.

In addition, the use of digital technology in therapy can lead to concerns about confidentiality (Klein, 2011; Van Allen & Roberts, 2011). For instance, the visits with a mental health clinician may also be part of a patient's electronic medical records (Steinfeld & Keys, 2011), which may be seen by other health providers. In addition, if a patient contacts his or her therapist via e-mail, even if the therapist's e-mail server is secure, the patient's e-mail server may not be (and if the patient e-mails from work, the e-mails may remain the "property" of the employer). In such cases, despite the therapist's best efforts to ensure confidentiality, their correspondence may not remain private. Similarly, when therapy is performed remotely—via the telephone, e-mail, or as a videoconference—the therapist cannot ensure confidentiality because at the patient's locale, other people might be able to listen in or access the communication.

Limits of Confidentiality: HIPAA in Action

Congress passed the Health Insurance Portability and Accountability Act in 2002 (HIPAA; U.S. Department of Health and Human Services, 2002), and in doing so widened the set of circumstances under which confidential information could be shared with other individuals and organizations participating in the care or monitoring of a patient in order to improve patient care. No longer was the patient's permission to share information with other health providers legally required. However, according to HIPAA, patients must provide specific written consent before clinicians can share separate notes from their psychotherapy sessions. Without such consent, the mental health clinician can share only limited information—such as the dates of treatment, the patient's diagnosis and prognosis, and the medications prescribed—with other people or organizations involved in the treatment or monitoring of the patient.

Thus, through HIPAA, patients lost some control over the distribution of their health records (Appelbaum, 2002). The circumstances under which health care information can be shared without a patient's consent (or even without the patient's being told about it) now include the following (U.S. Department of Health and Human Services, 2002):

1. *During litigation.* The opposing lawyer in a lawsuit can request health information from a provider and must only state that he or she made reasonable attempts to notify the patient about the request for information. During litigation, lawyers can even request the medical records of witnesses!

2. *When the person is a police suspect.* Police officers can request health information about a suspect without having a warrant or being under any judicial oversight.

3. *Marketing efforts by health providers (and their business associates) to patients.* For instance, if a community health center were initiating a therapy group for people with depression, the center would be able to send a brochure about the group to patients currently receiving treatment at the facility.

Privileged communication
Confidential information that is protected from being disclosed during legal proceedings.

4. *Research.* When investigators have approval for a study that uses patients' medical records, the investigators may have access to those records without the patients' explicit permission.

However, unless information is shared specifically to facilitate treatment, the law specifies that the provider should disclose only the minimum necessary information.

Legal Restrictions on Confidentiality

States usually have laws to protect confidentiality. However, most states have exceptions to those rules. Typically, confidentiality can be violated in certain situations:

- when a patient gives the clinician permission to violate confidentiality, for example by explicitly giving permission to a therapist to speak to the patient's spouse;

- when a clinician has reasonable cause to suspect abuse of children, of elderly people, or of disabled people. In such cases, the clinician usually must report the suspected abuse to the appropriate authorities so that steps can be taken to protect those who cannot otherwise protect themselves;

- when a clinician has reasonable cause to believe that a patient is likely to harm himself or herself significantly or to attempt suicide. In this situation, the clinician must take steps to protect the patient; and

- when a clinician has good reason to believe that a patient is likely to inflict significant harm on a specified other person. In this case, the clinician must take steps to protect that other person.

Thus, a clinician should not have violated Goldstein's confidentiality if he spoke in generalities about his violent urges. Even if Goldstein had said that he had violent impulses that he couldn't control when in subway stations or when around blond-haired women, such a statement would probably not be viewed as posing a specific enough danger to violate confidentiality. However, the clinician would have been legally compelled to violate Goldstein's confidentiality if he had specifically named Kendra Webdale as someone he planned to harm.

Privileged Communication

Confidentiality is an ethical term. A related *legal* term, **privileged communication**, refers to confidential information that is protected from being disclosed during legal proceedings. Just as a priest cannot legally be compelled to reveal what was said by a parishioner in the confessional, the Supreme Court has ruled that communication between a patient and a therapist is privileged (*Jaffee v. Redmond*, 1996; Mosher & Swire, 2002). However, not all confidential information is privileged and vice versa.

The person who shared information with the clinician is usually the one who decides whether it can be revealed, but others can make this decision in certain circumstances. For example, if a judge orders that a defendant must undergo a mental health evaluation, as happened to Goldstein after he was taken into custody, the communication between the mental health clinician(s) doing the evaluation and the defendant may not be considered privileged in some courts, depending on the jurisdiction (Meyer & Weaver, 2006; Myers, 1998). In such a circumstance, in order to comply with the law and behave ethically, the mental health clinician should explain to the defendant at the very beginning of the evaluation that anything said to the clinician may be disclosed to the judge. Whenever the law regarding privileged communication conflicts with the ethics of confidentiality, patients should be told of the limits of confidentiality as soon as possible (Meyer & Weaver, 2006).

Another type of exception to the laws governing privileged communication occurs when a patient (or former patient) initiates a civil lawsuit against another party and raises the issue of personal injury with mental health consequences as part

The term *confidentiality* refers to the ethical requirement not to disclose information about a patient; in contrast, *privileged communication* is a legal requirement that refers to confidential information that should not be disclosed during a legal proceeding. There are some circumstances in which mental health clinicians are legally obligated to violate confidentiality, and thus the communication is not privileged.

of the suit. An example of this type of case would be one in which a woman sues her employer for anguish that resulted from harassment at work. In these sorts of lawsuits for personal injury, the mental health clinician is legally bound to testify if his or her testimony is relevant to the case (Bartol & Bartol, 2004).

It is not always clear who owns a privileged communication about information revealed during group therapy. In this situation, the therapist may not be compelled to testify about what transpired, but group members may be. At present, judges decide on a case-by-case basis whether a therapist must testify, depending on the specific circumstances (Meyer & Weaver, 2006).

Informed Consent to Participate in Research on Mental Illness: Can Patients Truly Be Informed?

Can someone who is mentally ill give truly informed consent to participate in psychological research pertaining to his or her disorder? People who have anxiety disorders may be able to understand fully the research procedure and possible adverse effects, but what about people with schizophrenia? Are such patients' mental processes impaired to the extent that their consent isn't really informed? What about people who are having a first episode of psychosis and agree to participate in a study before the psychotic episode has abated?

The general rule of thumb for researchers is that potential participants must be capable of understanding and reasoning about what they are consenting to (Meyer & Weaver, 2006). Thus, the ability to understand and reason about the research procedure may be more important to informed consent than whether the person is psychotic at the time of consent (Kovnick et al., 2003; Misra & Ganzini, 2004).

Researchers are developing ways to ensure that patients who may be cognitively impaired by a psychological disorder adequately understand the benefits and risks of their participating in research. For instance, Wirshing and colleagues (2005) developed an educational video to increase awareness about informed consent among patients with schizophrenia. Among other points, the video explained that participants can withdraw from the study at any time. Researchers continue to develop and assess methods to ensure that participants give truly informed consent to participate in research (Eyler et al., 2005).

Thinking Like A Clinician

Rina is taking medication and seeing a therapist for depression. During one therapy session, she remarks, "Sometimes I think my family would be better off if I were dead." Based on what you have read, should Rina's therapist violate confidentiality and take steps to prevent Rina from hurting herself? Why or why not?

What if, instead, Rina had said about her multiply handicapped brother, "Sometimes I think my family would be better off if he were dead"? Would your view of whether Rina's therapist should violate confidentiality change—why or why not? What would Rina need to do or say to provide a *clear* indication that the therapist should violate confidentiality?

□ Criminal Actions and Insanity

After Andrew Goldstein pushed Kendra Webdale in front of the oncoming subway train, other passengers detained him until the police arrived. When taken to the police station, he explained in a signed statement why he pushed her: "I felt a sensation like something was entering me like a ghost or a spirit or something like that. . . . When I have the sensation that something is entering me, I get the urge to push, shove, or sidekick" (Rohde, 1999b).

Criminally responsible
The determination that a defendant's crime was the product of both an *action* or attempted action (the alleged criminal behavior) and his or her *intention* to perform that action.

M'Naghten test (or rule)
The legal test in which a person is considered insane if, because of a "defect of reason, from disease of the mind," he or she did not know what he or she was doing (at the time of committing the act) and did not know that it was wrong.

Irresistible impulse test
The legal test in which a person is considered insane if he or she knew that his or her criminal behavior was wrong but nonetheless performed it because of an irresistible impulse.

PORTRAIT OF DANIEL M'NAUGHTEN.

The earliest insanity defense case was that of Daniel M'Naghten, a Scottish man whose delusions about the British prime minister led him, in 1841, to commit murder. After M'Naghten was found not guilty by reason of insanity, the House of Lords narrowed the criteria for determining insanity; these criteria came to be known as the M'Naghten test.

Goldstein then said he "watched in 'horror'" as the train ran over Webdale, after which he is reported to have turned to the man next to him, "raised his arms in the air and said, 'I don't know'" (Rohde, 1999b). When police came, he told them he was a "'psychotic patient' who had suffered a 'psychotic attack'" (Rohde, 1999b) and asked to be taken to the hospital.

Goldstein was arraigned on the charge of second-degree murder and then, perhaps because he seemed to be mentally ill or because of his long psychiatric history, he was taken to a hospital rather than to jail. As we shall see, if someone who allegedly committed a crime was mentally ill during or after the criminal act, jail may not be the appropriate place for that person to be. Moreover, treatment—rather than detention—may be an appropriate goal for such a defendant's immediate future. In what follows we review the legal and clinical issues that arise after a crime has been committed by someone who is mentally ill.

As discussed in Chapter 1, the term *insanity* is a legal term and is not used in DSM-5. The legal concept of insanity addresses the question of whether a person was, at the time he or she committed a crime, *criminally responsible*—which involves both action and intention: To be **criminally responsible** means that a defendant's crime was the product of both an *action* or attempted action (the alleged criminal behavior) and his or her *intention* to perform that action (Greene et al., 2007; Meyer & Weaver, 2006).

After a crime has been committed and a person has been arrested, the legal system specifies two distinct periods when the defendant could have been suffering from a mental illness: (1) *At the time he or she (allegedly) committed the act*; might the insanity defense be appropriate? (2) *During the time of assessment, leading up to the trial*; can the person adequately assist in his or her own defense? Is the person competent to stand trial? We next discuss each of these circumstances in turn.

While Committing the Crime: Sane or Insane?

In the United States, the legal definition of insanity corresponds to a "test" that is used to determine whether a person is insane. The particular test used has changed over time.

From the M'Naghten Test to the Durham Test

In England in 1841, a Scottish man named Daniel M'Naghten believed that the British prime minister, Sir Robert Peel, was personally responsible for M'Naghten's woes. M'Naghten attempted to shoot Peel but missed him and killed Peel's secretary. During M'Naghten's trial, witnesses testified that he was insane, and the jury found him *not guilty by reason of insanity* (NGBI). This verdict did not sit well with many citizens, including Queen Victoria, the reigning monarch at the time. In response, the House of Lords narrowed the insanity defense by limiting the relevance of the defendant's mental state to the time the alleged crime was committed. In what came to be known as the **M'Naghten test (or rule)**, the question asked at a trial became whether, *at the time of committing the act*, the defendant knew what he or she was doing and, if so, knew that the act was wrong—and if he or she did not know this, it was because of "a defect of reason, from disease of the mind." With this narrower test, the judges reversed the verdict and found M'Naghten guilty.

The M'Naghten test of insanity was adopted in the United States and continued to be used until 1886, when the definition of insanity was widened. The new definition, specified by the **irresistible impulse test**, focused on whether the defendant knew that the criminal behavior was wrong but nonetheless performed it because of an irresistible impulse.

In 1954, the Supreme Court ruled on a case, *Durham v. U.S.*, and again broadened the test for the insanity defense. The **Durham test** was designed to determine whether the irresistible impulse was *due to mental defect or disorder* present at the time of the alleged crime. The Durham ruling shifted the insanity defense so that it hinged on evidence that the behavior did not arise entirely from free will. The Durham ruling moved away from consideration about morality (knowing "right from wrong") and into the realm of science (having a mental impairment).

However, the Durham ruling had a major drawback: It left unclear what constituted a mental defect or disorder. For instance, it is possible that someone who was drunk while committing a crime might be considered to have a mental defect. And what about someone with antisocial personality disorder (or psychopathy)? Might that disorder allow that person to use the insanity defense? Moreover, how could the court decide whether the criminal behavior was *caused by* the disorder or defect (Greene et al., 2007; Meyer & Weaver, 2006)? This drawback is so significant that most states use other definitions of insanity; only New Hampshire still uses the Durham test (Wrightsman & Fulero, 2005).

The American Legal Institute Test

To address some of the thorny issues that arose from the Durham test, the American Legal Institute (ALI) proposed two alternative criteria for insanity:

1. The person lacks a *substantial capacity* to appreciate that the behavior was wrong (versus has *no* capacity); or

2. the person has a diminished ability to make his or her behavior conform to the law, that is, an irresistible impulse.

The **American Legal Institute (ALI) test** consists of these criteria, which are sometimes referred to as *knowledge (cognition)* and *impulse (volition)* criteria. The ALI test broadened the test for insanity because it provided these two possible criteria (Greene et al., 2007; Meyer & Weaver, 2006). The ALI test also specified that if an individual's only defect or disorder is criminal behavior, the insanity defense cannot be used. This prevented people with antisocial personality disorder (or psychopathy) and people whose only crime is using illegal substances from using these problems as the basis for an insanity defense. The ALI test continues to be used by many states.

Insanity Defense Reform Acts

In federal courts, the insanity test changed again in 1984, as a result of John Hinckley's 1981 attempted assassination of then-President Ronald Reagan and Hinckley's subsequent acquittal as not guilty by reason of insanity. Hinckley was a young man with a history of mental illness; he reported that he shot the president in order to impress actress Jodie Foster, about whom he had obsessive delusions.

The jury found Hinckley insane on the basis of the impulse (volition) element of the ALI test. This means that the jury decided that Hinckley knew it was wrong to shoot the president but that he was not able to restrain himself. He was sent to a psychiatric hospital, not prison. The fact that Hinckley would serve no prison time greatly disturbed some lawmakers, who, through the Insanity Defense Reform Acts of 1984 and 1988, proceeded to restrict the test for insanity. The new test for insanity, used only in federal court, is most similar to the M'Naghten test—it asks whether the individual, because of a *severe* mental defect or

Durham test
The legal test in which a person is considered insane if an irresistible impulse to perform criminal behavior was due to a mental defect or disorder present at the time of the crime.

American Legal Institute (ALI) test
The legal test in which a defendant is considered insane if he or she either lacks a substantial capacity to appreciate that his or her behavior was wrong or has a diminished ability to make his or her behavior conform to the law.

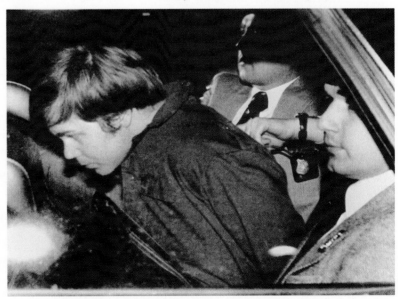

John Hinckley developed an obsessive preoccupation with actress Jodie Foster and repeatedly tried to communicate with her by phone and letter. After his attempts were rebuffed, he developed the delusional belief that assassinating President Ronald Reagan would impress Foster and induce her to pay attention to him. In 1981, he acted on that belief and shot the president and three other people.

AFP/Getty Images

disorder, has a diminished capacity to understand right from wrong (cognition). In an effort to make a plea of NGBI more difficult to enter, Congress also put an end to the irresistible impulse element (volition) in federal courts. Defendants with intellectual disability, psychotic disorders, or mood disorders may qualify for the insanity defense under these new rules, depending on the circumstances of the crime and the defendant's state of mind at the time, but having a disorder *in and of itself* is not enough for an insanity defense. Case 16.1 describes a woman who entered a plea of insanity in a murder case. Table 16.2 provides an overview of the various tests of insanity.

Andrea Yates, who was tried for murdering her five children, said she drowned them in order to save them from hell. Her lawyers used the insanity defense.

AP Photo/Steve Ueckert, Pool

CASE 16.1 • FROM THE OUTSIDE: The Insanity Defense

In 2001, Andrea Yates confessed to police that she drowned her five children, ages 6 months to 7 years old, in her bathtub. She reported that she believed Satan was inside her, and she drowned them to try to save them from hell. Yates's lawyers said that she had been psychotic at the time of the murders and that she did not know that her actions were wrong. (According to Texas state law, the key element of the insanity defense is knowing that the actions were wrong at the time of the crime.) Her lawyers pointed to her history of mental illness: two previous suicide attempts and four psychiatric hospitalizations for schizophrenia and postpartum depression.

During her trial, an expert witness for the prosecution, psychiatrist Dr. Park Dietz, agreed with previous witnesses that Yates had been psychotic at the time of the drownings, but testified that she was still able to know right from wrong and therefore not insane under Texas law. To support his position, Dr. Dietz brought up the television series *Law and Order*, which he had been told Yates had watched. Dietz, who also served as a consultant to the producers of that television series, testified that shortly before she drowned her children, an episode of *Law and Order* aired that involved a woman with postpartum depression who drowned her children in a bathtub and was declared insane. Prosecutors used Dietz's testimony about the television show to indicate that Yates knew her actions were wrong (Greene et al., 2007).

It turns out, however, that no such episode had been aired; this error was discovered after the jury convicted Yates of murder but before they began deliberating about her punishment. Rather than declare a mistrial, the judge simply told the jurors about the error. Yates was given a life sentence in prison. The appeals court ruled that a mistrial had occurred, and Yates was retried. She was ultimately found not guilty by reason of insanity and placed in a state mental hospital, where she will remain until she is no longer considered a danger to others or herself.

(Ewing & McCann, 2006).

TABLE 16.2 • Tests for the Insanity Defense Used Over Time

Test	Legal standard
M'Naghten (1843)	"Didn't know what he or she was doing or didn't know it was wrong"
Irresistible impulse (1886)	"Could not control conduct"
Durham (1954)	"Criminal act was caused by mental illness"
American Legal Institute (ALI; 1962)	"Lacks substantial capacity to appreciate the wrongfulness of the conduct *or* to control it" [emphasis added]
Present federal law (1984 and 1988)	"Lacks capacity to appreciate the wrongfulness of his or her conduct"

Source: Meyer & Weaver, 2006, p. 123, which was adapted in part from Morris, 1986.

The Insanity Defense: Current Issues

Use of the insanity defense is rare (only 1% of cases, according to one study), and *successful* use of the defense is exceptionally rare—only one quarter of the time it is used, or 0.25% of cases (Steadman et al., 1993). Despite its rarity, the federal requirements for the insanity defense have narrowed over time. However, the courts have yet to resolve two issues about how this defense can be applied:

- whether the person knew the act was *wrong* (a moral question) versus *illegal* (a legal question); and

- whether the person knew *in the abstract* that the act was wrong versus knew *that the specific behavior* was wrong in a particular circumstance. For instance, someone can know that killing people is wrong but, because of a mental illness, believe that killing a particular person for a specific reason is justified: "He was the devil, tempting me, so I had to kill him."

Let's examine how these issues about the insanity defense apply to Andrew Goldstein, who pleaded not guilty by reason of insanity. At the trial, an eyewitness to the murder, Ms. Lorenzino, who was standing nearby on the platform, testified that she:

> entered the subway station . . . just behind Mr. Goldstein and immediately noticed that he was acting strangely. "I saw a man walking in front of me walking oddly," Ms. Lorenzino said. She said Mr. Goldstein would take a few "baby steps" on his "tip toes" and then stumble. Mr. Goldstein then started walking normally, then paced furiously back and forth on the southern end of the platform. He mumbled to himself and eyed Ms. Lorenzino and Ms. Webdale, who was reading a magazine about six feet away from Ms. Lorenzino, each time he passed them. . . .
>
> As the wait for a train dragged on, Mr. Goldstein walked up to Ms. Lorenzino and stood beside her, she said. "I felt very uncomfortable that he was standing next to me. . . . I said, 'What are you looking at?' Then he backed off as if he was frustrated." Mr. Goldstein paced for a few more minutes, Ms. Lorenzino said, looked down the track as if checking for a train and then walked down the platform to Ms. Webdale. "Do you have the time?" he asked her. Ms. Webdale glanced at her watch and answered, "a little after five," Ms. Lorenzino said. Mr. Goldstein then positioned himself against the wall behind Ms. Webdale, who returned to her magazine, Ms. Lorenzino said.
>
> When the train sped into the station, she said, Mr. Goldstein "darted" off the wall and violently pushed Ms. Webdale. Ms. Lorenzino said she was struck by how well-planned the push seemed. It gave Ms. Webdale no time to escape. "It was perfect," she said, referring to the timing. Ms. Webdale's body never hit the rails, she said, "she just flew right under the train."
>
> Police Officer Raymond McLoughlin, who also testified . . . said he arrived at the station to find people shouting, "He's right here! He's right here!" He found Mr. Goldstein, who made no effort to escape, sitting on the platform with his legs crossed, surrounded by 20 enraged people who were berating him, he said.
> (Rohde, 1999c)

After the murder, during Goldstein's confession, the prosecutor tried to understand whether Goldstein understood what he was doing—that is, whether his

> mental illness caused him to lack a "substantial capacity" to know or appreciate "the nature and consequence" of the attack or know that it was wrong. On the video-tape, [the prosecutor] pointedly asks Mr. Goldstein if he thinks it was wrong to push Ms. Webdale. Mr. Goldstein nods and then appears confused. The prosecutor asks him if he understands. Mr. Goldstein says no, and then [the prosecutor] asks him again if he thinks the attack was wrong. "I wasn't thinking about anything when I pushed her," Mr. Goldstein said. "It's like an attack. You don't really think. . . . It's like whoosh, whoosh," he added, referring to what he repeatedly described during the confession as

the sensation of a "spirit" or "ghost" entering his body that gave him an overwhelming desire to push, kick or shove. Mr. Goldstein says that he pushed Ms. Webdale only "slightly," but then seems confused again. He blurts out that "I didn't push her thinking she would end up on tracks," and that he did not know in what direction he was pushing Ms. Webdale.

> Mr. Goldstein then says, "I wouldn't push anyone onto the tracks."
> "Because you know it's wrong?" [the prosecutor] asks.
> "Yes," Mr. Goldstein replies.

(Rohde, 1999a)

The prosecutor continues to try to clarify whether Goldstein understood that what he had done to Webdale was wrong:

> "But you knew," says the interrogator, "that if you pushed her off the platform, she might get . . ."
> "Killed, yeah," Mr. Goldstein says.
> "And you also knew that if you did that, it would be the wrong thing to do?"
> "Yeah, definitely," Mr. Goldstein says. "I would never do something like that."
> "Well, you did."
> "I know, but the thing is I would never do it on purpose."

Assessing Insanity for the Insanity Defense

How does a *jury* go about determining whether a defendant was insane at the time a crime was committed? The members of a jury rely on testimony about the defendant's mental state during the time leading up to the crime. Such testimony may come from friends and family members or from witnesses. In Goldstein's case, witnesses testified that he was acting strangely before pushing Ms. Webdale in front of the train. Jurors may hear about a defendant's history of mental illness prior to the crime (as occurred for both Goldstein and Hinckley). Expert witnesses who are mental health clinicians may give testimony or submit reports.

How do *mental health clinicians* determine whether a defendant was insane at the time a crime was committed? They may interview the defendant in jail and administer and interpret psychological tests (see Chapter 3). However, such after-the-fact assessments of the defendant's mental state should take into account events that occurred after the crime and before the clinician's evaluation. Specifically, the defendant's mental state may be affected by his or her experiences in jail, medications he or she may be taking, decision to plead NGBI, reactions to the crime, coaching from the defendant's lawyer or other inmates, and even responses to various assessment methods (Meyer & Weaver, 2006).

Past psychiatric history doesn't necessarily indicate a person's mental state at the time he or she committed a crime, but a history of mental illness can provide a context for evaluating the person at the time when the crime was committed. In Goldstein's case, symptoms of schizophrenia arose when he was 16 years old, and he was committed to a state psychiatric facility when he was in college. Following this stay, he had a lengthy history of mostly brief hospital stays, each one lasting only until he was "stabilized" (not actively psychotic); he was then released to outpatient treatment. However, because of a lack of state funds for mental health care, Goldstein's outpatient treatment usually consisted of almost no treatment. For most of the time he was ill, he did not have close supervision or monitoring and did not reliably take his medication (Kleinfield & Roane, 1999). He would eventually deteriorate to the point where he needed to be hospitalized, was stabilized and released again, and then the cycle would be repeated—a process often referred to as a "revolving door."

States' Rights: Doing Away with the Insanity Defense

Some states have abolished the insanity defense, replacing it with another type of defense that recognizes that a defendant did not have "free will" while committing a crime (Meyer & Weaver, 2006). Two alternative options are:

- *Diminished capacity*, whereby a person, due to mental illness or defect, was less able to understand that the criminal behavior was wrong or to formulate a specific intention. With this defense, the person is still considered guilty but receives a lesser sentence, is convicted of a lesser crime, or receives a modified form of punishment. This defense contains variations on the two elements of the ALI test of insanity.

- *Guilty but mentally ill*, whereby a convicted defendant is found to be "responsible" for the crime but often sent to a psychiatric facility and, if his or her mental state improves over time, may also serve time in prison; alternatively, the defendant may be sent to a prison immediately, where he or she may or may not receive psychiatric care. Note that with "guilty but mentally ill," the person isn't acquitted (that is, found not guilty of a crime), and there is no guarantee that mental health services will be provided (Meyer & Weaver, 2006; Ogundipe & Shankar, 2013). In fact, in many states, prisoners who have been found guilty but mentally ill receive no more psychological treatment than do other prisoners (Wrightsman & Fulero, 2005).

CURRENT CONTROVERSY

Criminal Behavior: Does Abnormal Neural Functioning Make It More Excusable?

With advances in medical technology and neuroimaging, a question of particular relevance to the justice system, clinical psychology, and neuroscience has emerged (Yang et al., 2008): Should individuals with abnormal neural functioning be held less responsible for their criminal behavior than people with normally functioning brains?

On one hand, neuropsychological evidence suggests that disruptions in brain structure and function may be associated with criminal behavior. For example, individuals who commit impulsive murders generally have reduced activity in the prefrontal cortex (Raine et al., 1998). The prefrontal cortex, along with other areas of the frontal lobe, is important for impulse control and plays a key role in regulating social behavior (Beer et al., 2006). Disruptions in the functions of these brain areas have been observed in individuals with antisocial personality disorder (see Chapter 13; Volkow et al., 1995; Raine et al., 1997). In one case, for example, a man's tumor in part of the frontal lobe is believed to have led to his criminal sexual behavior, which included reduced sexual impulse control and pedophilia. He claimed that before his tumor he'd never engaged in such behavior; when the tumor was removed, the aberrant sexual behavior stopped, but it resurfaced when the tumor regrew less than a year later (Burns & Swerdlow, 2003).

On the other hand, caution is needed when considering the relationship between brain structure and behavior. First, even seemingly simple behaviors are remarkably complex from a neurological and cognitive standpoint; as such, it is often difficult and even irresponsible to claim that abnormality of any single brain structure is the "cause" of abnormal behavior. Also, although the findings from some studies of individuals with antisocial personality disorder suggest an association between structure and function, association (that is, correlation) is not causation. This point is particularly striking when we consider that although we usually think that brain structure and function drive behavior, our behavior can impact brain structure and function as well. For example, drug abuse can produce harmful changes in neurochemistry and brain structure (Rosenbloom et al., 2003), just as cognitive and behavioral interventions can enhance neural function and lead to positive changes in brain structure (Olesen et al., 2003).

CRITICAL THINKING If it turns out that criminal behavior can be caused by disrupted neural functioning, how do you think society should deal with criminals who have abnormal brains? Should they be considered not guilty by reason of insanity?

(Meghana Karnik-Henry, Green Mountain College)

With the Insanity Defense, Do People Really "Get Away with Murder"?

After the Hinckley trial, some people perceived the insanity defense as a way to "get away with murder." But as noted earlier, this perception isn't very accurate. Consider a landmark study of 9,000 felony cases across eight states from 1976 to 1987 (Steadman et al., 1993). Among those cases, only one quarter of 1% of defendants were acquitted (that is, found not guilty of the crime). And of this 0.25%, only 7%—2 cases—were acquitted by a jury rather than a judge. This indicates that the defense of not guilty by reason of insanity was not very successful. Researchers have also compared the average time spent in jail by defendants who were found guilty (5 years) versus the average time spent in a mental hospital by those who were found NGBI (4.7 years) and concluded that when the insanity defense is used successfully, people do not "get away with murder" (Meyer & Weaver, 2006).

After Committing the Crime: Competent to Stand Trial?

Whereas the insanity defense refers to a defendant's mental state at the time the crime was committed, his or her **competency to stand trial** is based on an evaluation of mental state during the time leading up to the trial. That is, does a mental defect or disorder prevent the defendant from participating in his or her own defense? Competency to stand trial usually entails being able to:

- understand the proceedings that will take place,
- understand the facts in the case and the legal options available,
- consult with his or her "lawyer with a reasonable degree of rational understanding" (*Dusky v. United States*, 1960), and
- assist the lawyer in building the defense.

With this all-or-nothing standard, Goldstein was found competent to stand trial.

The same all-or-nothing standard is used to determine whether a defendant is *competent to plead guilty* as well as *competent to waive the right to an attorney* (*Godinez v. Moran*, 1993; Perlin, 2000a). If a person is found not competent to stand trial, he or she would also be considered to be not competent to plead guilty or to waive the right to an attorney. Someone who is found not competent is referred for mental health treatment (*Dusky v. United States*, 1960). Case 16.2 examines the issue of competency to stand trial and waive counsel.

CASE 16.2 • FROM THE OUTSIDE: Competent to Stand Trial and Waive Counsel

On December 7, 1993, Colin Ferguson intentionally killed 6 people and injured 19 others on a New York commuter train. After his arrest, Ferguson was diagnosed with paranoid personality disorder. Because he was assessed as rational and not delusional, he was deemed competent to stand trial; he fired his attorney when the attorney stated that he would propose an insanity defense. Ferguson then chose to represent himself but did not use the insanity defense. The legal system allowed a mentally ill man to be his own legal counsel, although he did not defend himself adequately. Those following the trial witnessed an intelligent but clearly mentally ill man state that he would call as a witness an exorcist who would testify that a microchip—supposedly planted by the governor of New York—had been lasered out of Ferguson's head by a remote control device (McQuiston, 1995; Perlin, 2000a). That witness was never called to the stand.

Ferguson was convicted on 6 counts of murder and 19 counts of attempted murder.

Competency to stand trial
The determination that a defendant's mental state during the time leading up to the trial enables him or her to participate in his or her own defense.

When defendants are found not competent to stand trial, they sometimes are medicated to reduce the symptoms of their mental illness and make them able to stand trial. Occasionally, defendants do not want to take the medication but are given it against their will, perhaps by injection. However, the Supreme Court ruled that mentally ill patients accused of nonviolent crimes could not be forced to take medication in order to become competent to stand trial (*Sell v. United States*, 2003). If it appears unlikely that a person will become competent to stand trial, he or she may be civilly committed to a psychiatric facility if deemed a danger to self or others.

In 2002, while suffering from delusions, Brian David Mitchell kidnapped young Elizabeth Smart. He was apprehended 9 months later (Smart was found alive and returned to her parents) and continued to have delusions. In 2009, he had yet to be found competent to stand trial. A judge had ruled against forcing Mitchell to take medication in order to be competent to stand trial because the judge did not believe that the treatment would succeed (Carlisle, 2009). In 2010, he was found guilty.

Thinking Like A Clinician

Jon has been arrested for disturbing the peace and destroying private property; at 2 A.M. last night, he was yelling and kicking over trash cans on Main Street, and he broke several store windows. His rant went on for 25 minutes, until the police arrived. Jon initially resisted arrest and then cooperated. It seemed to the police that Jon was behaving as if he were having a manic episode, and, in fact, he had a history of bipolar disorder. How might mental health clinicians and the legal system go about determining whether Jon was "insane" at the time of the crime? What information would you want to know in order to determine whether he was insane? What if, rather than a history of bipolar disorder, Jon had a history of alcohol use disorder and was drunk the night of the crime. Would that change your opinions? Why or why not?

Dangerousness: Legal Consequences

Andrew Goldstein's attack on Kendra Webdale wasn't the first time he had engaged in dangerous behavior, and his dangerous behavior wasn't a secret:

> In the two years before Kendra Webdale was instantly killed on the tracks, Andrew Goldstein attacked at least 13 other people. The hospital staff members who kept treating and discharging Goldstein knew that he repeatedly attacked strangers in public places.
>
> He was hospitalized after assaulting a psychiatrist at a Queens clinic. [The clinic note from November 14, 1997, reads]: "Suddenly, without any warning, patient springs up and attacks one of [the] doctors, pushing her into a door and then onto the floor. He was hospitalized after threatening a woman, [again] after attacking two strangers at a Burger King [and yet again] after fighting with an apartment mate." [A note from March 2, 1998, says]: "Broke down roommate's door because he could not control the impulse." And particularly chilling, six months before Kendra Webdale's death, he was hospitalized for striking another woman he did not know on a New York subway.
> (Winerip, 1999a)

Goldstein's history indicates that he had become dangerous. **Dangerousness**, a legal term, refers to someone's potential to harm self or others. Determining whether someone is dangerous, in this sense, rests on assessing threats of violence to self or to others, or establishing an inability to care for oneself. Dangerousness can be broken down into four components regarding the potential harm (Brooks, 1974; Perlin, 2000c):

1. *severity* (how much harm might the person inflict?),

2. *imminence* (how soon might the potential harm occur?),

3. *frequency* (how often is the person likely to be dangerous?), and

4. *probability* (how likely is the person to be dangerous?)

Dangerousness
The legal term that refers to someone's potential to harm self or others.

TABLE 16.3 • Major Risk Factors for a Patient to Act Violently

Patient's Prior Arrests

- More serious crimes
- Greater frequency of crimes

Patient Experienced Child Abuse

- Experienced more serious abuse
- Experienced greater frequency of abuse

Patient's Father . . .

- Used drugs
- Was absent during patient's childhood

Patient's Demographics

- Younger
- Male
- Unemployed

Patient's Diagnosis

- Antisocial personality disorder

Other Clinical Information About Patient

- Has substance abuse problems
- Has problems controlling anger
- Has violent fantasies
- Has had loss of consciousness
- Has been brought to the attention of mental health professionals involuntarily, through the legal system

Source: Monahan et al., 2001. For more information see the Permissions section.

Although some people with mental illness may create a public nuisance, like this man yelling at voices that only he can hear, such public displays are not dangerous and should not, in and of themselves, lead to hospitalization (Perlin, 2000c).

Evaluating Dangerousness

Clinicians are sometimes asked to evaluate how dangerous a patient may be—specifically, the severity, imminence, and likelihood of potential harm (McSherry & Keyzer, 2011; Meyer & Weaver, 2006). Such evaluations are either/or in nature—the individual is either deemed not to be dangerous (or at least not dangerous enough to violate confidentiality) or deemed to be dangerous, in which case, confidentiality is broken or the patient remains in a psychiatric facility in order to protect the individual from self-harm or to protect others (Otto, 2000; Quattrocchi & Schopp, 2005). Prior to each discharge from a hospital or psychiatric unit, Goldstein had to be evaluated for dangerousness; he was then discharged because he was deemed not dangerous, or not dangerous enough.

Researchers set out to determine the risk factors that could best identify which patients discharged from psychiatric facilities would subsequently act violently. A summary of the findings appears in Table 16.3.

Confining people who are deemed to be dangerous involves taking away their liberty—their freedom—and is not done lightly. Loitering or yelling at "voices" should not be considered legally dangerous. Rather, the legal system allows a person to be incarcerated or hospitalized, or to continue to be incarcerated or hospitalized, in only two types of situations:

1. when the person has not yet committed a violent crime but is perceived to be at imminent risk to do so, or

2. when the person has already served a prison term or received mandated treatment in a psychiatric hospital and is about to be released but is perceived to be at imminent risk of behaving violently.

To prevent such people from harming themselves or others, the law provides that they can be confined as long as they continue to pose a significant danger.

Actual Dangerousness

Although we have focused on the relationship between some forms of mental illness and violence, as occurred with Goldstein, most mentally ill people are *not* violent. Mentally ill people who engage in criminal acts receive a lot of media attention, which may give the impression that the mentally ill commit more crimes than they really do (Pescosolido et al., 1999). In fact, criminal behavior among the mentally ill population is no more common than it is in the general population (Fazel & Grann, 2006). Indeed, when mentally ill people are in jail or prison, it is usually for minor nonviolent offenses related either to trying to survive (e.g., stealing food) or to substance abuse—the mental illness usually is not a direct cause of the incarceration (Hiday & Wales, 2003).

However, two sets of circumstances related to mental illness do increase dangerousness: (1) when the mental illness involves psychosis, and the person may be a danger to self as well as others (Fazel & Grann, 2006; Wallace et al., 2004)—particularly when delusions lead the mentally ill person to be angry (Coid et al., 2013), and especially (2) when serious mental illness is combined with substance abuse (Howsepian, 2011; Maden et al., 2004). The relationship between various major mental illnesses, substance use disorders, and violence is shown in Figure 16.1.

Confidentiality and the Dangerous Patient: Duty to Warn and Duty to Protect

In the 1960s, University of California college student Prosenjit Poddar liked fellow student Tatiana Tarasoff. However, his interest in her was greater than was hers in him. He became depressed by her rejection and began treatment with a

Adam Sylvester/Photo Researchers, Inc.

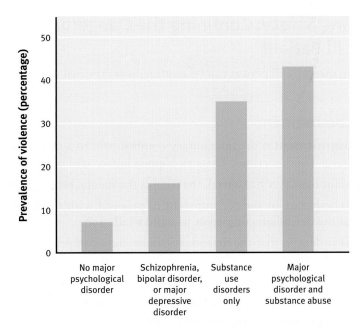

FIGURE 16.1 • Lifetime Prevalence of Violent Behavior Substance use disorders (with or without a comorbid major psychological disorder) are associated with a much higher rate of violent behaviors (such as the use of a weapon in a fight or coming to blows with another person) than is observed in the general population (Swanson, 1994).

Source: Monahan et al., 1994. For more information see the Permissions section.

psychologist. During the course of his treatment, his therapist became concerned that Mr. Poddar might hurt or kill Ms. Tarasoff. (Poddar had purchased a gun for that purpose.) The therapist informed campus police that Poddar might harm Tarasoff. The police briefly restrained him, but they determined that he was rational and not a threat to Tarasoff. Ms. Tarasoff was out of the country at the time, and neither she nor her parents were alerted to the potential danger. Two months later, Poddar killed Tarasoff.

Her parents sued the psychologist, saying that Tarasoff should have been protected either by warning her or by having Poddar committed to a psychiatric facility. In what has become known as the **Tarasoff rule**, the Supreme Court of California (and later courts in other states) ruled that psychologists have a duty to protect potential victims who are in imminent danger (*Tarasoff v. Regents of the University of California*, 1974, 1976). This rule has been extended to other mental health clinicians.

Mental health professionals who decide that a patient is about to harm a specific person can choose to do any of the following (Quattrocchi & Schopp, 2005):

• warn the intended victim or someone else who can warn the victim,

• notify law enforcement agencies, or

• take other reasonable steps to prevent harm (depending on the situation), such as having the patient voluntarily or involuntarily committed to a psychiatric facility for an extended evaluation (that is, have the patient confined).

The Tarasoff rule effectively extended a clinician's *duty to warn* of imminent harm to a *duty to protect* (Werth et al., 2009). The clinician must violate confidentiality in order to take reasonable care to protect an identifiable—or reasonably foreseeable—victim (*Brady v. Hopper*, 1983; *Cairl v. State*, 1982; Egley, 1991; *Emerich v. Philadelphia Center for Human Development*, 1998; Schopp, 1991; *Thompson v. County of Alameda*, 1980). Note, however, that potential danger to property is not sufficient to compel clinicians to violate confidentiality (Meyer & Weaver, 2006).

Tarasoff rule
A ruling by the Supreme Court of California (and later other courts) that psychologists have a duty to protect potential victims who are in imminent danger.

Maintaining Safety: Confining the Dangerously Mentally Ill Patient

A dangerously mentally ill person can be confined via criminal commitment or civil commitment.

Criminal Commitment

Criminal commitment is the involuntary commitment to a mental health facility of a person charged with a crime. This can happen before trial or after trial:

- If the defendant hasn't yet had a trial, the time at the mental health facility is used to

  - evaluate whether he or she is competent to proceed with the legal process (for instance, is the defendant competent to stand trial?) and

  - provide treatment so that the defendant can become competent to participate in the legal proceedings.

- If the defendant has had a trial and was acquitted due to insanity (Meyer & Weaver, 2006).

Based on a 1972 ruling (*Jackson v. Indiana*, 1972), it is illegal to confine someone indefinitely under a criminal commitment. Thus, a defendant found not competent to stand trial cannot remain in a mental health facility for life. But the law is unclear as to exactly how long is long enough. Judges have discretion about how long they can commit a defendant to a mental health facility to determine whether treatment may lead to competence to stand trial. Such treatment may last several years. If the defendant does not become competent, he or she may not remain committed for the original reason—to receive treatment in order to become competent. In this case, the process of deciding whether he or she should be released from the mental health facility proceeds just as it does for anyone who hasn't been criminally charged. If the individual is deemed to be dangerous, however, he or she may be civilly committed.

Civil Commitment

When an individual hasn't committed a crime but is deemed to be at significant risk of harming himself or herself, or of harming a specific other person, the judicial system can confine that individual in a mental health facility, which is referred to as a **civil commitment**. This is the more common type of commitment.

There are two types of civil commitment: (1) inpatient commitment to a 24-hour inpatient facility, and (2) outpatient commitment to some type of monitoring and/or treatment program (Meyer & Weaver, 2006). Civil commitment grows out of the idea that the government can act as a caregiver, functioning as a "parent" to people who are not able to care for themselves; this legal concept is called *parens patriae*.

Civil commitments can conflict with individual rights, so guidelines have been created to protect patients' rights by establishing the circumstances necessary for an involuntary commitment, the duration of such a commitment—and who decides when it ends—as well as the right to refuse a specific type of treatment or treatment in general (Meyer & Weaver, 2006). It may seem that civil commitments are always forced or coerced, but that is not so. Some civil commitments are voluntary (that is, the patient agrees to the hospitalization); however, some "voluntary" hospitalizations may occur only after substantial coercion (Meyer & Weaver, 2006).

Many people who are civilly committed belong to a subset of the mentally ill population—those who are overrepresented in the revolving door after their release that leads to jails or hospitals. This revolving door evolved because lawmakers and clinicians wanted a more humane approach to dealing with the mentally ill, by treating them in the least restrictive setting—before their condition deteriorates to the point where they harm themselves or others (Hiday, 2003).

Criminal commitment
The involuntary commitment to a mental health facility of a person charged with a crime.

Civil commitment
The involuntary commitment to a mental health facility of a person deemed to be at significant risk of harming himself or herself or a specific other person.

Mandated Outpatient Commitment

Mandated outpatient commitment developed in the 1960s and 1970s, along with increasing deinstitutionalization of patients from mental hospitals; the goal was to develop less restrictive alternatives to inpatient care (Hiday, 2003). Such outpatient commitment may consist of legally mandated treatment that includes some type of psychotherapy, medication, or periodic monitoring of the patient by a mental health clinician. The hope is that mandated outpatient commitment will preempt the "revolving door" cycle that occurs for many patients who have been committed: (1) getting discharged from inpatient care, (2) stopping their medication, (3) becoming dangerous, and (4) ending up back in the hospital through a criminal or civil commitment or landing in jail.

Researchers have investigated whether mandated outpatient commitment is effective: Are the patient and the public safer than if the patient was allowed to obtain voluntary treatment after discharge from inpatient care? Does mandated outpatient treatment result in less frequent hospitalizations or incarcerations for the patient? To address these questions, one study compared involuntarily hospitalized patients who either were invited to use psychosocial treatment and services voluntarily upon discharge or who were court-ordered to obtain outpatient treatment for 6 months— and made frequent use of services (between 3 and 10 visits/month) (Hiday, 2003; Swartz et al., 2001). The results indicated that those who received mandated outpatient treatment:

- went back into the hospital less frequently and for shorter periods of time,

- were less violent,

- were less likely to be victims of crime themselves, and

- were more likely to take their medication or obtain other treatment, even after the mandated treatment period ended.

Other studies have found similar benefits of mandated outpatient commitment (Hough & O'Brien, 2005). That said, it is also clear that mandated outpatient commitment is not effective without adequate funding for increased therapeutic services (Perlin, 2003; Rand Corporation, 2001). In what follows we examine what happens without adequate funding.

The Reality of Treatment for the Chronically Mentally Ill

Andrew Goldstein generally *wanted* to be hospitalized and repeatedly tried to make that happen:

> He signed himself in voluntarily for all 13 of his hospitalizations. His problem was what happened after discharge. The social workers assigned to plan his release knew he shouldn't have been living on his own, and so did Goldstein, but everywhere they looked they were turned down. They found waiting lists for long-term care at state hospitals, waiting lists for supervised housing at state-financed group homes, waiting lists for a state-financed intensive-case manager, who would have visited Goldstein daily at his apartment to make sure he was coping and taking his meds.
>
> More than once he requested long-term hospitalization at Creedmoor, the state hospital nearby. In 1997, he walked into the Creedmoor lobby, asking to be admitted. "I want to be hospitalized," he said. "I need a placement." But in a cost-cutting drive, New York [had] been pushing hard to reduce its patient census and to shut state hospitals. Goldstein was instead referred to an emergency room, where he stayed overnight and was released.
>
> Again, in July 1998, Goldstein cooperated with psychiatrists, this time during a month-long stay at Brookdale Hospital, in hopes of getting long-term care at Creedmoor. Brookdale psychiatrists had a well-documented case. In a month's time, Goldstein committed three violent acts: punching the young woman on the subway; attacking a Brookdale therapist, a psychiatrist, a social worker and a ward aide; striking a Brookdale nurse in the face. This time, Creedmoor officials agreed in principle to

take him, but explained that there was a waiting list, that they were under orders to give priority to mental patients from prison and that they did not know when they would have an opening. Days later, Goldstein was discharged from Brookdale. (Winerip, 1999a)

Not only was Goldstein underserved by the mental health system, but so was the public at large. When appropriate services were available to him, Goldstein made good use of them. He spent a year in a residential setting on the grounds of the state hospital—he did well, was cooperative and friendly, and regularly took his medications. But personnel at state hospitals are under pressure to move patients to less expensive programs, even if the patients aren't ready. Goldstein was considered too low-functioning to qualify for a program that provided less supervision, but he was discharged from the residential program nonetheless—to a home where he received almost no support. A year before the murder he tried, without success, to return to a supervised group but no spaces were available (Winerip, 1999a).

Goldstein's history with the mental health system in New York is not unique. People with severe mental illness generally don't receive the care they need (which is also in society's interest for them to receive) unless their families are wealthy and willing to pay for needed services—long-term hospitalization, supervised housing, or intensive daytime supervision. Even when a defendant is deemed to be mentally ill and ordered to be transferred to a psychiatric facility, space may not be available in such a facility; the options then are to hold the defendant in jail or to release him or her and provide a less intensive form of mental health treatment (Goodnough, 2006).

As discussed in Chapter 12, deinstitutionalization is a reasonable option for those who can benefit from newer, more effective treatments, and providing treatment in the least restrictive alternative setting is also a good idea. However, such community-based forms of care are not adequately funded, which forces facilities to prioritize and provide treatment only to the sickest, leaving everyone else to make their own way. Thus, most people with severe mental illness lack adequate supervision, care, or housing. They may be living on their own in tiny rented rooms, on the street, in homeless shelters that are not equipped to handle mentally ill people, or they may be in jail. The law may mandate treatment for severely mentally ill individuals, but that doesn't mean they receive it.

After the murder of Kendra Webdale, New York State passed *Kendra's law*, allowing family members, roommates, and mental health clinicians to request court-mandated outpatient treatment for a mentally ill person who refuses treatment; a judge makes the final decision about mandating treatment. The unfortunate irony is that Goldstein sought further treatment. In his case, the real culprit may have been the lack of resources to provide the type of support and services that he and others like him—such as David Tarloff, described in Case 16.3—need.

Eight months after David Tarloff committed murder, the judge hearing the case declared Tarloff unfit to stand trial. Tarloff was sent to a psychiatric facility (Eligon, 2008). His 2013 trial was declared a mistrial because the jury was deadlocked about whether he was not guilty by reason of insanity (Buettner & Goodman, 2013). In prison, he awaits a new trial.

James Keivom/NY Daily News Archive via Getty Images

CASE 16.3 • FROM THE OUTSIDE: A Failed Mandated Outpatient Treatment

On February 12, 2008, David Tarloff murdered psychologist Kathryn Faughey and injured psychiatrist Kent Shinbach in a delusional plan to steal money to fly to Hawaii with his elderly mother. Tarloff, who had been a patient of Shinbach, was hospitalized over a dozen times since 1991, when he was diagnosed with paranoid schizophrenia. In the year leading up to the murders, Tarloff received psychiatric care three times after violent or threatening behavior; he was stabilized on medication and released, despite his family's request for continued inpatient treatment. After release each time, he stopped taking his medication. His family even made use of Kendra's law, so that Tarloff was supposed to receive mandated outpatient treatment, but he avoided the periodic outpatient visits. He was released from a psychiatric unit 10 days before he murdered Faughey. (Konigsberg & Farmer, 2008).

Sexual Predator Laws

People who are repeat sexual offenders—often referred to as *sexual predators*—are clearly dangerous. How do they fit into the legal concept of dangerousness? Are they to be treated as mentally ill? How do the criminal justice and mental health systems view such individuals?

The answers to these questions have evolved over time. Before the 1930s, a sexual offense was viewed as a criminal offense: The perpetrator was seen as *able* to control the behavior although he or she didn't do so. In the 1930s, sexual offenses were viewed as related to mental illness (sexual psychopaths), and treatment programs for those who committed such offenses proliferated. Unfortunately, the treatments were not effective. By the 1980s, sexual offenses were again seen as crimes for which prison sentences were appropriate consequences. In the 1990s, after highly publicized cases of sexual mutilation and murder of children, some states passed additional laws to deal with sexually violent predators, who were seen as having no or poor ability to control their impulses. Rather than emphasizing treatment (which had not been effective), the new laws called for incarcerating these individuals as a preventative measure.

In 1997, the Supreme Court upheld the constitutionality of state laws regarding sexual predators (*Kansas v. Hendricks*, 1997); these laws are based on the concept of *parens patriae,* under which the government, as "parent," has the power to protect the public from threats, as well as the duty to care for those who cannot take care of themselves (Perlin, 2000c). These laws were intended to prevent sex offenders from committing similar offences, in some cases by ensuring that offenders do not reenter society while there is a significant risk that they will reoffend. At the end of a prison term, if a sexual predator was deemed likely to reoffend *and* was suffering from a mental abnormality or personality disorder, that person could be committed to a psychiatric hospital indefinitely (Tucker & Brakel, 2012; Winick, 2003). In 2010, the Supreme Court extended such civil commitments to sexually violent predators in federal custody (*United States v. Comstock*, 2010).

However, some people viewed such laws as too restrictive, and in 2002, the Supreme Court ruled that in order to commit a sexual offender indefinitely after a jail or prison sentence has been served, it must be demonstrated that the person has difficulty controlling the behavior (*Kansas v. Crane*, 2002; the Supreme Court did not say how to demonstrate this, other than pointing to the individual's past history). In prison, treatment is voluntary, whereas with commitment it is mandatory.

Thinking Like A Clinician

Tyrone was diagnosed with schizoaffective disorder when he was 25; his mother couldn't supervise and take care of him to the extent that he needed. Cutbacks in mental health services in his community meant that he couldn't receive adequate services outside of a hospital. By age 30, he was living on the streets or in jail for petty crimes such as stealing food from a grocery store, and he'd been treated for brief periods in a psychiatric facility. Based on what you have read, do you think Tyrone is dangerous—why or why not? Suppose, during psychotic episodes, he darts across busy streets—causing car accidents as drivers quickly brake to avoid hitting him. Would he legally be considered dangerous then—why or why not? What would be the advantages and disadvantages to him, and to society, of committing him to inpatient treatment? To outpatient treatment?

🖵 Legal Issues Related to Treatment

In the 1960s and 1970s, the courts decided several landmark cases regarding the rights of the mentally ill. These cases addressed the right to treatment and the right to refuse treatment.

Right to Treatment

In 1966, the Supreme Court ruled that people who are forced to receive treatment through civil commitment should be given the least restrictive alternative treatment available *(Lake v. Cameron)*. That is, they should have the type of treatment that infringes the least on their individual liberties. If a person doesn't need the 24-hour monitoring and care of an inpatient unit, that person should be treated in a less restrictive environment (such as in a residential setting and with outpatient treatment).

One year after this ruling, the Supreme Court ruled that civil commitment must entail more than warehousing or confining people; the Court ruled that appropriate treatment must also be provided, while recognizing that treatment might not necessarily be successful *(Rouse v. Cameron, 1967)*. In subsequent cases during the 1970s, courts in various jurisdictions outlined specific minimal criteria for such treatment—including the minimum staffing ratio (number of patients per care provider) and number of hours per week of treatment, as well as the need for each patient to have an individualized treatment plan *(Wyatt v. Stickney, 1971)*. The specifics of these requirements differ from jurisdiction to jurisdiction.

The Supreme Court also ruled that civil commitment may not be used simply to confine people against their will indefinitely (except as previously noted with some sexual predators). When patients no longer meet the criteria for commitment (that is, they are no longer dangerous) and can survive independently or with help from willing family members, then they must be discharged *(O'Connor v. Donaldson, 1975)*. The reasoning behind this ruling is that the purpose of the confinement is treatment, and so when inpatient treatment is no longer required, the person should be released.

Right to Refuse Treatment

A federal district court in New Jersey set another standard when it ruled that a civilly committed patient has the right to refuse treatment *(Rennie v. Klein, 1978)*. Generally, this ruling has been applied to a patient's right to refuse to take medications, most frequently traditional antipsychotics that carry the risk of a serious side effect called *tardive dyskinesia* (see Chapter 12) (Perlin, 2000b). However, the court did not establish the right to refuse treatment in all situations. As long as there has been a fair and adequate hearing of the issues involved for a given patient, his or her refusal can be overridden after weighing certain factors (Meyer & Weaver, 2006):

- the patient is physically threatening to others (which may include patients and staff members),
- the proposed treatment carries only a small risk of irreversible side effects,
- there are no less restrictive treatment alternatives available, and
- the patient has significantly diminished capacity to decide rationally about particular treatments

Competence to Refuse Treatment

One of the acceptable circumstances for overriding a committed patient's refusal of a treatment is that he or she does not have the capacity to decide rationally about treatment. Being competent to refuse treatment is different from being competent to stand trial, although both competencies involve some of the same mental processes and abilities. Does being mentally ill imply that a person cannot make rational decisions? One study that investigated the general question of competence to refuse treatment (Appelbaum & Grisso, 1995; Grisso & Appelbaum, 1995) found that about half of patients with schizophrenia performed reasonably well on several tasks assessing their ability to make decisions. Not surprisingly, the more severe the symptoms the less well they performed on the tasks. An even greater proportion of patients hospitalized for depression—about 75%—performed adequately on the tasks that assess decision making. Unlike the patients with more severe symptoms of schizophrenia, patients with more severe depression were generally competent to make decisions. Thus, having a severe mental illness did not routinely make these patients "not competent to refuse treatment." (Note though that while some individuals who receive outpatient commitment may be competent to refuse treatment, the law may not allow them to refuse.)

Mental Health and Drug Courts

Federal, state, and local court dockets are filled with cases awaiting a hearing or trial. In order to hasten the speed with which cases are resolved, municipalities have instituted specialized courts, such as divorce courts, to address particular types of problems. Two such special courts are particularly relevant to the mentally ill: drug courts and mental health courts.

Drug courts were developed in Miami in 1989 for first-time drug abusers—those whose substance abuse was viewed as the underlying motivation for their crime (Miethe et al., 2000). Soon after arrest, these people were offered an alternative to jail: They could attend a drug treatment program, submit to random and frequent drug testing by urinalysis, and meet with the drug court judge regularly. If they did not show up for a court hearing, a bench warrant would be issued within hours and they could be sent to jail.

The overall goal of drug courts is to help defendants reintegrate into society. Thus, drug courts not only promote intensive treatment for drug abuse and relapse prevention—they also encourage education and employment. Drug court programs do not simply aim to decrease substance abuse; they recognize the complex nature of the factors that contribute to such abuse.

Relapse rates are between 4% and 20% for those entering a program and even lower (less than 4%) for those who complete one. Many communities have extended drug court programs to include people who were previously jailed for substance abuse–related crimes, with equivalent success (Drug Court Clearinghouse and Technical Assistance Project, 1998).

The success of drug courts led to the development of mental health courts, which began in Florida and now exist in most states, but not necessarily in most districts (Council of State Governments, 2005). Mental health courts seek to treat, rather than incarcerate, mentally ill people who are charged with a misdemeanor. When mentally ill people receive treatment, they are subsequently less likely to become violent or to reoffend (Dirks-Lindhorst & Linhorst, 2012; Hiday & Ray, 2010).

Drug courts recognize that maintaining abstinence can depend on a complex interplay of factors, such as educational opportunities and employment.

John Sundlof/Alamy

Thinking Like A Clinician

Ella is in the throes of a psychotic episode and is in the hospital. At times, she feels bugs crawling under her skin, and so she viciously scratches herself until she bleeds. At other times, she thinks she has superpowers and can fly—if there were an open window, she'd jump out of it. Her psychiatrist has prescribed an antipsychotic medication, but she won't take it: "I don't like the way it makes me feel." Based on what you have read, do you think Ella has the right to refuse treatment? Why or why not?

▣ The Wheels of Justice: Follow-up on Andrew Goldstein

The jury that heard Andrew Goldstein's case was deadlocked—some jurors voted to convict and some voted him not guilty by reason of insanity. The deadlocked jury meant that another trial was necessary. This time, with Goldstein's permission, his lawyers took him off his medication several weeks before he was to testify so that jurors could see the extent of his mental illness. However, his mental state at the time of trial could not be used to determine his mental state at the time he committed the crime. This strategy was very controversial, and the judge allowed it, provided that Goldstein be asked daily whether he wanted to receive medication and that he be given medication forcibly if he appeared to become not competent to stand trial (Rohde, 2000). Goldstein hit his social worker within several weeks of stopping his medication, which meant that he resumed taking it and did not take the stand. The jury found Goldstein guilty, although they acknowledged that he was mentally ill. They decided that he knew what he was doing when he threw Kendra Webdale onto the tracks, and that he knew it was wrong.

After his trial, Goldstein was sent to prison, where he was evaluated to determine whether he needed to be admitted to a psychiatric hospital to become stable. If so, once stable, he would be returned to prison. In such cases, hospitalizations are brief, only long enough to get the defendant well enough to return to prison. In 2006, 8 years after the murder, Goldstein's conviction was overturned because of a technical misstep during the second trial. In a third trial, Goldstein's lawyers entered a plea of guilty, with the understanding that he would serve 23 years in prison, followed by 5 years of psychiatric oversight and supervision after his release.

▣ SUMMING UP

Ethical Issues

- Each type of mental health professional works under his or her discipline's ethical code; all disciplines include in their ethical code the principle of confidentiality, which applies to information that patients share with mental health professionals.

- Because of HIPAA, the limits of confidentiality have been redefined. Now limited information about a patient may be shared with the patient's other health providers in order to facilitate treatment.

- Although laws protect confidentiality, confidentiality may be violated against a patient's wishes when a clinician has reasonable cause to: (1) suspect abuse of children, the elderly, or the disabled, or (2) believe that a patient is likely to do significant harm to himself or herself or a specified other person.

- The legal counterpart of the ethical principle of confidentiality is privileged communication—the protection of confidential information from disclosure during legal proceedings.

Criminal Actions and Insanity

- Various tests have been used to determine whether a defendant is insane. The first was the M'Naghten test in 1843, followed by the irresistible impulse test. After almost 70 years came the Durham test. Many states presently use the American Legal Institute (ALI) test, which requires either impaired knowledge that the behavior was wrong (cognition) or impaired capacity to resist the impulse to act illegally (volition). The Insanity Defense Reform Acts of the 1980s did away with the volition element to determine insanity in federal courts.

- To assess insanity, a jury may rely on testimony about the defendant's mental state during the time leading up to the crime, the defendant's history of mental illness prior to the crime, and testimony or reports from expert witnesses about the defendant's mental state or mental illness.

- Mental health clinicians may assess a defendant's sanity through interviews with the person, psychological tests and questionnaires, and interviews with family members and friends. However, such measures may be affected by the defendant's experiences in jail, medications he or she may be taking, the decision to plead not guilty by reason of insanity, reactions to the crime, coaching from the defendant's lawyer or other inmates, and the way the defendant responds to various assessment methods. But none of this information necessarily indicates the defendant's mental state at the time of the crime.

- Research indicates that acquittal on the basis of the insanity defense is extremely rare, particularly when the decision is made by a jury rather than a judge.

- Competency to stand trial addresses the defendant's mental state before the trial and whether the defendant is competent to participate in his or her own defense; someone who is not competent to stand trial would also be deemed not competent to plead guilty and not competent to waive the right to an attorney.

Dangerousness: Legal Consequences

- Dangerousness has four components related to the potential harm the person may inflict: severity, imminence, frequency, and probability.

- Mental health clinicians have a legal duty to warn and to protect specified potential victims who are judged to be in imminent danger of being harmed by a patient. A clinician may warn the intended victim, notify law enforcement agencies, and/or take other reasonable steps, such as having the patient confined to a psychiatric facility. Clinicians may violate confidentiality to fulfill these duties.

- Criminal commitment may occur before a defendant's trial to evaluate his or her competence for upcoming legal proceedings or to obtain treatment for the defendant so that he or she can become competent to take part in legal proceedings. When criminal commitment occurs after a trial, it is because the defendant was acquitted for the reason of insanity.

- Civil commitments occur before a crime has been committed, in order to prevent harm to the patient or others deemed to be at significant risk of harm. Patients may be committed to inpatient or outpatient facilities.

Legal Issues Related to Treatment

- The Supreme Court has ruled that people who are civilly committed should be given the least restrictive alternative *treatment* available. Civil commitments may not be used solely to confine people against their will indefinitely.

- Patients usually have a right to refuse treatment, such as medication. However, patients who have physically threatened other people may be forced to take medication or receive other treatment, as long as there has been a fair and adequate hearing of the issues involved.

- Defendants may be sent to drug courts if their drug use was the underlying motivation for the crime; such courts have been successful in decreasing rates of relapse and reoffending.

- Mental health courts can mandate treatment for mentally ill defendants; such programs have been found to decrease violence and subsequent offences.

Key Terms

Confidentiality (p. 504)

Privileged communication (p. 506)

Criminally responsible (p. 508)

M'Naghten test (or rule) (p. 508)

Irresistible impulse test (p. 508)

Durham test (p. 509)

American Legal Institute test (ALI test) (p. 509)

Competency to stand trial (p. 514)

Dangerousness (p. 515)

Tarasoff rule (p. 517)

Criminal commitment (p. 518)

Civil commitment (p. 518)

More Study Aids

For additional study aids related to this chapter, including quizzes to make sure you've retained everything you've learned and a Student Video Activity exploring the ethical and legal dilemmas involved in the case of a man diagnosed with schizophrenia who is also convicted of murder, go to: www.worthpublishers.com/launchpad/rkabpsych2e.

Image Source

GLOSSARY

° A °

Abnormal psychology The subfield of psychology that addresses the causes and progression of psychological disorders; also referred to as *psychopathology*.

Abstinence violation effect The result of violating a self-imposed rule about food restriction, which leads to feeling out of control with food, which then leads to overeating.

Action potential The wave of chemical activity that moves from the cell body down the axon when a neuron fires.

Active phase The phase of a psychological disorder (such as schizophrenia) in which the person exhibits symptoms that meet the criteria for the disorder.

Acute stress disorder A traumatic stress disorder that involves (a) intrusive re-experiencing of the traumatic event, (b) avoidance of stimuli related to the event, (c) negative changes in thought and mood, (d) dissociation, and (e) hyperarousal and reactivity, with these symptoms lasting for less than a month.

Affect An emotion that is associated with a particular idea or behavior, similar to an attitude.

Age cohort A group of people born in a particular range of years.

Agoraphobia An anxiety disorder characterized by persistent avoidance of situations that might trigger panic symptoms or from which help would be difficult to obtain.

Allegiance effect A pattern in which studies conducted by investigators who prefer a particular theoretical orientation tend to obtain data that supports that particular orientation.

Alzheimer's disease A medical condition in which the afflicted person initially has problems with both memory and executive function and which leads to progressive dementia.

American Legal Institute (ALI) test The legal test in which a defendant is considered insane if he or she either lacks a substantial capacity to appreciate that his or her behavior was wrong or has a diminished ability to make his or her behavior conform to the law.

Amnesia Memory loss, which in dissociative disorders is usually temporary but, in rare cases, may be permanent.

Amyloid plaques Fragments of protein that accumulate on the outside surfaces of neurons, particularly neurons in the hippocampus.

Anhedonia A difficulty or inability to experience pleasure.

Anorexia nervosa An eating disorder characterized by significantly low body weight along with an intense fear of gaining weight or using various methods to prevent weight gain.

Antabuse A medication for treating alcohol use disorder that induces violent nausea and vomiting when it is mixed with alcohol.

Antisocial personality disorder A personality disorder diagnosed in adulthood characterized by a persistent disregard for the rights of others.

Anxiety A sense of agitation or nervousness, which is often focused on an upcoming possible danger.

Anxiety disorder A category of psychological disorders in which the primary symptoms involve fear, extreme anxiety, intense arousal, and/or extreme attempts to avoid stimuli that lead to fear and anxiety.

Aphasia A neurological condition characterized by problems in producing or comprehending language.

Applied behavior analysis A technique used to modify maladaptive behaviors by reinforcing new behaviors through shaping.

Apraxia A neurological condition characterized by problems in organizing and carrying out voluntary movements even though the muscles themselves are not impaired.

Asylums Institutions to house and care for people who are afflicted with mental illness.

Attention-deficit/hyperactivity disorder (ADHD) A disorder that typically arises in childhood and is characterized by inattention, hyperactivity, and/or impulsivity.

Attrition The reduction in the number of participants during a research study.

Atypical antipsychotics A relatively new class of antipsychotic medications that affects dopamine and serotonin activity; also referred to as *second-generation antipsychotics*.

Autism spectrum disorder (ASD) A neurodevelopmental disorder characterized by deficits in communication and social interaction skills, as well as stereotyped behaviors and narrow interests.

Avoidant personality disorder A personality disorder characterized by extreme shyness that usually stems from feeling inadequate and being overly sensitive to negative evaluation.

Avolition A negative symptom of schizophrenia marked by difficulty initiating or following through with activities.

° B °

Behavior therapy The form of treatment that rests on the ideas that: (1) maladaptive behaviors stem from previous learning, and (2) new learning can allow patients to develop more adaptive behaviors, which in turn can change cognitions and emotions.

Behavioral genetics The field that investigates the degree to which the variability of characteristics in a population arises from genetic versus environmental factors.

Behaviorism An approach to psychology that focuses on understanding directly observable behaviors in order to understand mental illness and other psychological phenomena.

Bias A tendency that distorts data.

Binge eating Eating much more food at one time than most people would eat in the same period of time or context.

Binge eating disorder An eating disorder characterized by binge eating without subsequent purging.

Biofeedback A technique in which a person is trained to bring normally involuntary or unconscious bodily activity, such as heart rate or muscle tension, under voluntary control.

Biological marker A neurological, bodily, or behavioral characteristic that distinguishes people with a psychological disorder (or a first-degree relative with the disorder) from those without the disorder.

Biopsychosocial approach The view that a psychological disorder arises from the combined influences of three types of factors—biological, psychological, and social.

Bipolar disorders Mood disorders in which a person's mood is often persistently and abnormally upbeat or shifts inappropriately from upbeat to markedly down.

Body dysmorphic disorder A disorder characterized by excessive preoccupation with a perceived defect or defects in appearance and repetitive behaviors to hide the perceived defect.

Borderline personality disorder A personality disorder characterized by volatile emotions, an unstable self-image, and impulsive behavior in relationships.

Brain circuits Sets of connected neurons that work together to accomplish a basic process.

Brain systems Sets of brain circuits that work together to accomplish a complex function.

Brief psychotic disorder A psychotic disorder characterized by the sudden onset of positive or disorganized symptoms that last between 1 day and 1 month and are followed by full recovery.

Broca's aphasia A neurological condition characterized by problems producing speech.

Bulimia nervosa An eating disorder characterized by binge eating along with vomiting or other behaviors to compensate for the large number of calories ingested.

° C °

Case studies (in studies of psychopathology) A research method that focuses in detail on one individual and the factors that underlie that person's psychological disorder or disorders.

Catatonia A condition in which a person does not respond to the environment or remains in an odd posture or position, with rigid muscles, for hours.

Cerebral cortex The outer layer of cells on the surface of the brain.

Civil commitment The involuntary commitment to a mental health facility of a person deemed to be at significant risk of harming himself or herself or a specific other person.

Classical conditioning A type of learning that occurs when two stimuli are paired so that a neutral stimulus becomes associated with another stimulus that elicits a reflexive behavior; also referred to as *Pavlovian conditioning*.

Clinical assessment The process of obtaining relevant information and making a judgment about mental illness based on the information.

Clinical interview A meeting between clinician and patient during which the clinician asks questions related to the patient's symptoms and functioning.

Clinical psychologist A mental health professional who has a doctoral degree that requires several years of related coursework and several years of treating patients while receiving supervision from experienced clinicians.

Cluster A personality disorders Personality disorders characterized by odd or eccentric behaviors that have elements related to those of schizophrenia.

Cluster B personality disorders Personality disorders characterized by emotional, dramatic, or erratic behaviors that involve problems with emotional regulation.

Cluster C personality disorders Personality disorders characterized by anxious or fearful behaviors.

Cognitive-behavior therapy (CBT) The form of treatment that combines methods from cognitive and behavior therapies.

Cognitive distortions Dysfunctional, maladaptive thoughts that are not accurate reflections of reality and contribute to psychological disorders.

Cognitive therapy The form of treatment that rests on the ideas that: (1) mental contents influence feelings and behavior; (2) irrational thoughts and incorrect beliefs lead to psychological problems; and (3) correcting such thoughts and beliefs will therefore lead to better mood and more adaptive behavior.

Common factors Helpful aspects of therapy that are shared by virtually all types of psychotherapy.

Common liabilities model The model that explains how neurological, psychological, and social factors make a person vulnerable to a variety of problematic behaviors, including substance use disorders; also called *problem behavior theory*.

Community care Programs that allow mental health care providers to visit patients in their homes at any time of the day or night; also known as *assertive community treatment*.

Comorbidity The presence of more than one disorder at the same time in a given patient.

Competency to stand trial The mental state during the time leading up to the trial enables him or her to participate in his or her own defense.

Complex inheritance The transmission of traits that are expressed along a continuum by the interaction of sets of genes.

Compulsions Repetitive behaviors or mental acts that a person feels driven to carry out and that usually must be performed according to rigid "rules" or correspond thematically to an obsession.

Computerized axial tomography (CT) A neuroimaging technique that uses X-rays to build a three-dimensional image (CT or CAT scan) of the brain.

Concordance rate The probability that both twins will have a characteristic or disorder, given that one of them has it.

Conditioned emotional responses Emotions and emotion-related behaviors that are classically conditioned.

Conditioned response (CR) A response that comes to be elicited by the previously neutral stimulus that has become a conditioned stimulus.

Conditioned stimulus (CS) A neutral stimulus that, when paired with an unconditioned stimulus, comes to elicit the reflexive behavior.

Conduct disorder A disorder that typically arises in childhood and is characterized by the violation of the basic rights of others or of societal norms that are appropriate to the person's age.

Confidentiality The ethical requirement not to disclose information about a patient (even whether someone *is* a patient) to others unless legally compelled to do so.

Confounding variables Factors that might inadvertently affect the variables of interest in an experiment.

Contingency management A procedure for modifying behavior by changing the conditions that led to, or are produced by, it.

Control group A group of participants in an experiment for which the independent variable is not manipulated, but which is otherwise treated identically to the experimental group.

Conversion disorder A somatic symptom disorder that involves sensory or motor symptoms that are incompatible with known neurological and medical conditions.

Correlation The relationship between the measurements of two variables in which a change in the value of one variable is associated with a change in the value of the other variable.

Correlation coefficient A number that quantifies the strength of the correlation between two variables; the correlation coefficient is most typically symbolized by r.

Counseling psychologist A mental health professional who has either a Ph.D. degree from a psychology program that focuses on counseling or an Ed.D. degree from a school of education.

Criminal commitment The involuntary commitment to a mental health facility of a person charged with a crime.

Criminally responsible The determination that a defendant's crime was the product of both an *action* or attempted action (the alleged criminal behavior) and his or her *intention* to perform that action.

Crystallized intelligence A type of intelligence that relies on using knowledge to reason in familiar ways; such knowledge has "crystallized" from previous experience.

Culture The shared norms and values of a society that are explicitly and implicitly conveyed to its members by example and through the use of reward and punishment.

Cyclothymic disorder A mood disorder characterized by chronic, fluctuating mood disturbance with numerous periods of hypomanic symptoms alternating with depressive symptoms, each of which does not meet the criteria for its respective mood episodes.

∘ **D** ∘

Dangerousness The legal term that refers to someone's potential to harm self or others.

Data Methodical observations, which include numerical measurements of phenomena.

Defense mechanisms Unconscious processes that work to transform psychological conflict in order to prevent unacceptable thoughts and feelings from reaching consciousness.

Delayed ejaculation A sexual dysfunction characterized by a man's delay or absence of orgasm.

Delirium A neurocognitive disorder characterized by a relatively sudden disturbance in attention and awareness as well as disruption of at least one other aspect of cognitive functioning.

Delirium tremens (DTs) The symptoms of alcohol withdrawal that include uncontrollable shaking, confusion, convulsions, visual hallucinations, and fever.

Delusional disorder A psychotic disorder characterized by the presence of delusions that have persisted for more than 1 month.

Delusions Persistent false beliefs that are held despite evidence that the beliefs are incorrect or exaggerate reality.

Dementia A set of neurocognitive disorders characterized by deficits in learning new information or recalling information already learned *plus* at least one other type of cognitive impairment.

Dependent personality disorder A personality disorder characterized by submissive and clingy behaviors, based on fear of separation.

Dependent variable A variable that is measured and that may change its values as a result of manipulating the independent variable.

Depersonalization A dissociative symptom in which the perception or experience of self—either one's body or one's mental processes—is altered to the point that the person feels like an observer, as though seeing oneself from the "outside."

Depersonalization-derealization disorder A dissociative disorder, the primary symptom of which is a persistent feeling of being detached from one's mental processes, body, or surroundings.

Derealization A dissociative symptom in which the external world is perceived or experienced as strange or unreal.

Detoxification Medically supervised discontinuation of substances for those with substance use disorders; also referred to as *detox*.

Diagnosis The identification of the nature of a disorder.

Diagnostic bias A systematic error in diagnosis.

Dialectical behavior therapy (DBT) A form of treatment that includes elements of CBT as well as an emphasis on validating the patient's experience, a Zen Buddhist approach, and a dialectics component.

Diathesis–stress model A model that rests on the idea that a psychological disorder is triggered when a person with a predisposition—a diathesis—for the particular disorder experiences an environmental event that causes significant stress.

Disruptive mood dysregulation disorder (DMDD) A depressive disorder in children characterized by persistent irritability and frequent episodes of out-of-control behavior.

Dissociation The separation of mental processes—such as perception, memory, and self-awareness—that are normally integrated.

Dissociative amnesia A dissociative disorder in which the sufferer has significantly impaired memory for important experiences or personal information that cannot be explained by ordinary forgetfulness.

Dissociative disorders A category of psychological disorders in which consciousness, memory, emotion, perception, body representation, motor control, or identity are dissociated to the point where the symptoms are pervasive, cause significant distress, and interfere with daily functioning.

Dissociative identity disorder (DID) A dissociative disorder characterized by the presence of two or more distinct personality states, or an experience of possession trance, which gives rise to a discontinuity in the person's sense of self and agency.

Dizygotic twins Twins who developed from two fertilized eggs and so have the same overlap in genes (50%) as do siblings not conceived at the same time; also referred to as *fraternal twins*.

Dopamine reward system The system of neurons, primarily in the nucleus accumbens and ventral tegmental area, that relies on dopamine and gives rise to pleasant feelings.

Dose–response relationship The association between more treatment (a higher dose) and greater improvement (a better response).

Double-blind design A research design in which neither the participant nor the investigator's assistant knows the group to which specific participants have been assigned or the predicted results of the study.

Drug cues The stimuli associated with drug use that come to elicit conditioned responses through their repeated pairings with use of the drug.

Durham test The legal test in which a person is considered insane if an irresistible impulse to perform criminal behavior was due to a mental defect or disorder present at the time of the crime.

Dyslexia A learning disorder characterized by difficulty with reading accuracy, speed, or comprehension that interferes with academic achievement or activities of daily functioning that involve reading.

◦ E ◦

Eating disorder A category of psychological disorders characterized by abnormal eating and a preoccupation with body image.

Ego According to Freud, the psychic structure that is charged with mediating between the id's demands for immediate gratification and the superego's high standards of morality, as well as the constraints of external reality.

Electroconvulsive therapy (ECT) A procedure that sends electrical pulses into the brain to cause a controlled brain seizure, in an effort to reduce or eliminate the symptoms of certain psychological disorders.

Emotion A short-lived experience evoked by a stimulus that produces a mental response, a typical behavior, and a positive or negative subjective feeling.

Epidemiology The type of correlational research that investigates the rate of occurrence, the possible causes and risk factors, and the course of diseases or disorders.

Erectile disorder A sexual dysfunction characterized by a man's persistent difficulty obtaining or maintaining an adequate erection until the end of sexual activity, or a decrease in erectile rigidity; sometimes referred to as *impotence*.

Etiology The factors that lead a person to develop a psychological disorder.

Executive functions Mental processes involved in planning, organizing, problem solving, abstract thinking, and exercising good judgment.

Exhibitionistic disorder A paraphilic disorder in which sexual fantasies, urges, or behaviors involve exposing one's genitals to an unsuspecting person.

Expansive mood A mood that involves unceasing, indiscriminate enthusiasm for interpersonal or sexual interactions or for projects.

Experimenter expectancy effect The investigator's intentionally or unintentionally treating participants in ways that encourage particular types of responses.

Experiments Research studies in which investigators intentionally manipulate one variable at a time, and measure the consequences of such manipulation on one or more other variables.

Exposure A behavioral technique that involves repeated contact with a feared or arousing stimulus in a controlled setting, bringing about habituation.

Exposure with response prevention A behavioral technique in which a patient is carefully prevented from engaging in his or her usual maladaptive response after being exposed to a stimulus that usually elicits the response.

External validity A characteristic of a study that indicates that the results generalize from the sample to the population from which it was drawn and from the conditions used in the study to relevant conditions outside the study.

◦ F ◦

Factitious disorder A psychological disorder marked by the false reporting or inducing of medical or psychological symptoms in order to receive attention.

Family therapy A treatment that involves an entire family or some portion of a family.

Female orgasmic disorder A sexual dysfunction characterized by a woman's normal sexual excitement not leading to orgasm or to her having diminished intensity of sensations of orgasm.

Female sexual interest/arousal disorder A sexual dysfunction characterized by a woman's persistent or recurrent lack of or reduced sexual interest or arousal; formerly referred to as *frigidity*.

Fetishistic disorder A paraphilic disorder in which the person repeatedly uses nonliving objects or nongenital body parts to achieve or maintain sexual arousal and such an arousal pattern causes significant distress or impairs functioning.

Fight-or-flight response The automatic neurological and bodily response to a perceived threat; also called the *stress response*.

Flat affect A lack of, or considerably diminished, emotional expression, such as occurs when someone speaks robotically and shows little facial expression.

Flight of ideas Thoughts that race faster than they can be said.

Fluid intelligence A type of intelligence that relies on the ability to create novel strategies to solve new problems, without relying solely on familiar approaches.

Frotteuristic disorder A paraphilic disorder in which recurrent, intense, sexually arousing fantasies, sexual urges, or behaviors involve touching or rubbing against a nonconsenting person.

Functional magnetic resonance imaging (fMRI) A neuroimaging technique that uses MRI to obtain images of brain functioning, which reveal the extent to which different brain areas are activated during particular tasks.

◦ **G** ◦

Gateway hypothesis The proposal that use can become a use disorder when "entry" drugs serve as a gateway to (or the first stage in a progression to) use of "harder" drugs.

Gender dysphoria A psychological disorder characterized by an incongruence between a person's assigned gender at birth and the subjective experience of his or her gender, and that incongruence causes distress.

Gender identity The subjective sense of being male or female (or having the sense of a more fluid identity, outside the binary categories of male and female), as these categories are defined by a person's culture.

Gender role The outward behaviors, attitudes, and traits that a culture deems masculine or feminine.

Generalized anxiety disorder (GAD) An anxiety disorder characterized by uncontrollable worry and anxiety about a number of events or activities, which are not solely the result of another disorder.

Genes Segments of DNA that control the production of particular proteins and other substances.

Genito-pelvic pain/penetration disorder A sexual dysfunction in women characterized by pain, fear, or anxiety related to the vaginal penetration of intercourse.

Genotype The sum of an organism's genes.

◦ **H** ◦

Habituation The process by which the emotional response to a stimulus that elicits fear or anxiety is reduced by exposing the patient to the stimulus repeatedly.

Hallucinations Sensations that are so vivid that the perceived objects or events seem real, although they are not. Hallucinations can occur in any of the five senses.

Heritability An estimate of how much of the variation in a characteristic within a population (in a specific environment) can be attributed to genetics.

High expressed emotion (high EE) A family interaction style characterized by hostility, unnecessary criticism, or emotional overinvolvement.

Histrionic personality disorder A personality disorder characterized by attention-seeking behaviors and exaggerated and dramatic displays of emotion.

Hoarding disorder An obsessive-compulsive-related disorder characterized by persistent difficulty throwing away or otherwise parting with possessions—to the point that the possessions impair daily life, regardless of the value of those possessions.

Hormones Chemicals that are released directly into the bloodstream that activate or alter the activity of neurons.

Huntington's disease A progressive disease that kills neurons and affects cognition, emotion, and motor functions; it leads to dementia and eventually results in death.

Hypersomnia Sleeping more hours than normal each day.

Hypervigilance A heightened search for threats.

Hypothesis A preliminary idea that is proposed to answer a question about a set of observations.

Hysteria An emotional condition marked by extreme excitability and bodily symptoms for which there is no medical explanation.

◦ **I** ◦

Id According to Freud, the seat of sexual and aggressive drives, as well as of the desire for immediate gratification of physical and psychological needs.

Identity problem A dissociative symptom in which a person is not sure who he or she is or may assume a new identity.

Illness anxiety disorder A somatic symptom disorder marked by a preoccupation with a fear or belief of having a serious disease in the face of either no or minor medical symptoms and excessive behaviors related to this belief.

Inappropriate affect An expression of emotion that is not appropriate to what a person is saying or to the situation.

Inclusion The placement of students with disabilities in a regular classroom, with guidelines for any accommodations that the regular classroom teacher or special education teacher should make.

Independent variable A variable that a researcher manipulates.

Intellectual disability A neurodevelopmental disorder characterized by cognitive abilities that are significantly below normal, along with impaired adaptive functioning in daily life; also called *intellectual developmental disorder* and previously referred to as *mental retardation*.

Internal validity A characteristic of a study that indicates that it measures what it purports to measure because it has controlled for confounds.

Interoceptive exposure A behavioral therapy method in which patients intentionally elicit the bodily sensations associated with panic so that they can habituate to those sensations and not respond with fear.

Interpersonal therapy (IPT) The form of treatment that is intended to improve the patient's skills in relationships so that they become more satisfying.

In vivo exposure A behavioral therapy method that consists of direct exposure to a feared or avoided situation or stimulus.

Irresistible impulse test The legal test in which a person is considered insane if he or she knew that his or her criminal behavior was wrong but nonetheless performed it because of an irresistible impulse.

◦ **L** ◦

Labile affect Affect that changes inappropriately rapidly.

Learned helplessness The state of "giving up" that arises when an animal or person is in an aversive situation where it seems that no action can be effective.

Lithium The oldest mood stabilizer.

Longitudinal studies (in studies of psychopathology) Research studies that are designed to determine whether a given variable is a risk factor by using data collected from the same participants at various points in time.

◦ **M** ◦

Magnetic resonance imaging (MRI) A neuroimaging technique that creates especially sharp images of the brain by measuring the magnetic properties of atoms in the brain.

Major depressive disorder (MDD) A mood disorder marked by five or more symptoms of an MDE lasting more than 2 weeks.

Major depressive episode (MDE) A mood episode characterized by severe depression that lasts at least 2 weeks.

Major neurocognitive disorder A neurocognitive disorder characterized by evidence of a substantial decline in at least one cognitive domain, and impaired daily functioning.

Male hypoactive sexual desire disorder A sexual dysfunction characterized by a persistent or recurrent lack of erotic or sexual fantasies or an absence of desire for sexual activity.

Malingering Intentional false reporting of symptoms or exaggeration of existing symptoms, either for material gain or to avoid unwanted events.

Manic episode A period of at least 1 week characterized by abnormally increased energy or activity and abnormal and persistent euphoria or expansive mood or irritability.

Maudsley approach A family treatment for anorexia nervosa that focuses on supporting parents as they determine how to lead their child to eat appropriately.

Mental contents The specific material that is stored in the mind and operated on by mental processes.

Mental processes The internal operations that underlie cognitive and emotional functions (such as perception, memory, and guilt feelings) and most human behavior.

Meta-analysis A research method that statistically combines the results of a number of studies that address the same question to determine the overall effect.

Mild neurocognitive disorder A neurocognitive disorder characterized by a modest decline from baseline in at least one cognitive domain, but that decline is *not* enough to interfere with daily functioning.

Monoamine oxidase inhibitors (MAOIs) Antidepressant medications that increase the amount of monoamine neurotransmitter in synapses.

Monozygotic twins Twins who have basically the same genetic makeup because they began life as a single fertilized egg (zygote), which then divided into two embryos; also referred to as *identical twins*.

Mood A persistent emotion that is not attached to a stimulus; it exists in the background and influences mental processes, mental contents, and behavior.

Mood disorders Psychological disorders characterized by prolonged and marked disturbances in mood that affect how people feel, what they believe and expect, how they think and talk, and how they interact with others.

Mood stabilizer A category of medication that minimizes mood swings.

Moral treatment Treatment of the mentally ill that involved providing an environment in which people with mental illness were treated with kindness and respect and functioned as part of a community.

Motivational enhancement therapy A form of treatment specifically designed to boost a patient's motivation to decrease or stop substance use by highlighting discrepancies between stated personal goals related to substance use and current behavior; also referred to as *motivational interviewing*.

M'Naghten test (or rule) The legal test in which a person is considered insane if, because of a "defect of reason, from disease of the mind," he or she did not know what he or she was doing (at the time of committing the act) and did not know that it was wrong.

∘ **N** ∘

Narcissistic personality disorder A personality disorder characterized by an inflated sense of self-importance, an excessive desire to be admired, and a lack of empathy.

Negative punishment The type of punishment that takes place when a behavior is followed by the *removal* of a pleasant or desired event or circumstance, which decreases the probability of that behavior's recurrence.

Negative reinforcement The type of reinforcement that occurs when an aversive or uncomfortable stimulus is *removed* after a behavior, which makes that behavior more likely to be produced again in the future.

Negative symptoms Symptoms of schizophrenia that are characterized by the absence or reduction of normal mental processes, mental contents, or behaviors.

Neurocognitive disorders A category of psychological disorders in which the primary symptom is significantly reduced cognitive abilities, relative to a prior level of functioning; also referred to as *cognitive disorders*.

Neurofibrillary tangles The mass created by tau proteins that become twisted together and destroy microtubules, leaving the neuron without a distribution system for nutrients.

Neurons Brain cells that process information related to physical, mental, and emotional functioning.

Neuropsychological testing The employment of assessment techniques that use behavioral responses to test items in order to draw inferences about brain functioning.

Neuropsychosocial approach The view that a psychological disorder arises from the combined influences of neurological, psychological, and social factors—which affect and are affected by one another through feedback loops.

Neurosis According to psychoanalytic theory, a pattern of thoughts, feelings, or behaviors that expresses an unresolved conflict between the ego and the id or between the ego and the superego.

Neurotransmitters Chemicals that are released by the terminal buttons and cross the synaptic cleft.

∘ **O** ∘

Objectification theory The theory that girls learn to consider their bodies as objects and commodities.

Observational learning The process of learning through watching what happens to others; also referred to as *modeling*.

Obsessions Intrusive and unwanted thoughts, urges, or images that persist or recur and usually cause distress or anxiety.

Obsessive-compulsive disorder (OCD) A disorder characterized by one or more obsessions or compulsions.

Obsessive-compulsive personality disorder A personality disorder characterized by preoccupations with perfectionism, orderliness, and self-control, as well as low levels of flexibility and efficiency.

Operant conditioning A type of learning in which the likelihood that a behavior will be repeated depends on the consequences associated with the behavior.

Oppositional defiant disorder A disorder that typically arises in childhood or adolescence and is characterized angry or irritable mood, defiance or argumentative behavior, or vindictiveness.

∘ **P** ∘

Panic An extreme sense (or fear) of imminent doom, together with an extreme stress response.

Panic attack A specific period of intense fear or discomfort, accompanied by physical symptoms, such as a pounding heart, shortness of breath, shakiness, and sweating, or cognitive symptoms, such as a fear of losing control.

Panic disorder An anxiety disorder characterized by frequent, unexpected panic attacks, along with fear of further attacks and possible restrictions of behavior in order to prevent such attacks.

Paranoid personality disorder A personality disorder characterized by persistent and pervasive mistrust and suspiciousness, accompanied by a bias to interpret other people's motives as hostile.

Paraphilia An intense and persistent sexual interest that is different than the usual fondling or genital stimulation with "normal physically mature consenting human partners."

Paraphilic disorder A category of disorders characterized by paraphilias that lead to distress, impaired functioning, or harm—or risk of harm—to the person or to others.

Partial cases Cases in which patients have symptoms that meet only some of the necessary criteria but not enough symptoms to meet all the necessary criteria for the diagnosis of a disorder.

Pedophilic disorder A paraphilic disorder in which recurrent sexually arousing fantasies, sexual urges, or behaviors involve a child who has not yet gone through puberty.

Persistent depressive disorder (dysthymia) A depressive disorder that involves as few as two symptoms of a major depressive episode but in which the symptoms persist for at least 2 years.

Personality Enduring characteristics that lead a person to behave in relatively predictable ways across a range of situations.

Personality disorders A category of psychological disorders characterized by an enduring pattern of inflexible and maladaptive thoughts, emotional responses, interpersonal functioning, and impulse control problems that arise across a range of situations and lead to distress or dysfunction.

Phenotype The sum of an organism's observable traits.

Phobia An exaggerated fear of an object or a situation, together with an extreme avoidance of the object or situation.

Phototherapy Treatment for depression that uses full-spectrum lights; also called *light-box therapy*.

Placebo effect A positive effect of a medically inert substance or procedure.

Polysubstance abuse A behavior pattern of abusing more than one substance.

Population The complete set of possible relevant participants.

Positive punishment The type of punishment that takes place when a behavior is followed by an undesirable consequence, which makes the behavior less likely to recur.

Positive reinforcement The type of reinforcement that occurs when a desired reinforcer is *received* after a behavior, which makes the behavior more likely to occur again in the future.

Positive symptoms Symptoms of schizophrenia that are characterized by the *presence* of abnormal or distorted mental processes, mental contents, or behaviors.

Positron emission tomography (PET) A neuroimaging technique that measures blood flow (or energy consumption) in the brain and requires introducing a very small amount of a radioactive substance into the bloodstream.

Posttraumatic stress disorder (PTSD) A traumatic stress disorder that involves persistent (a) intrusive re-experiencing of the traumatic event, (b) avoidance of stimuli related to the event, (c) negative changes in thoughts and mood, and (d) hyperarousal and reactivity that persist for at least a month.

Predictions Hypotheses that should be confirmed if a theory is correct.

Premature (early) ejaculation A sexual dysfunction characterized by ejaculation that occurs within a minute of vaginal penetration and before the man wishes it, usually before, immediately during, or shortly after penetration.

Premorbid Referring to the period of time prior to a patient's illness.

Prevalence The number of people who have a disorder in a given period of time.

Privileged communication Confidential information that is protected from being disclosed during legal proceedings.

Prodromal phase The phase that is between the onset of symptoms and the time when the minimum criteria for a disorder are met.

Prodrome Early symptoms of a disorder.

Prognosis The likely course and outcome of a disorder.

Projective test A tool for personality assessment in which the patient is presented with ambiguous stimuli (such as inkblots or stick figures) and is asked to make sense of and explain them.

Psychiatric nurse A mental health professional who has an M.S.N. degree, plus a C.S. certificate in psychiatric nursing.

Psychiatrist A mental health professional who has an M.D. degree and has completed a residency that focuses on mental disorders.

Psychoactive substance A chemical that alters mental ability, mood, or behavior.

Psychoanalytic theory The theory that thoughts, feelings, and behaviors are a result of conscious and unconscious forces continually interacting in the mind.

Psychoeducation The process of educating patients about research findings and therapy procedures relevant to their situation.

Psychological disorder A pattern of thoughts, feelings, or behaviors that causes significant personal *distress*, significant *impairment* in daily life, and/or significant *risk of harm*, any of which is unusual for the context and culture in which it arises.

Psychomotor agitation An inability to sit still, evidenced by pacing, hand wringing, or rubbing or pulling the skin, clothes or other objects.

Psychomotor retardation A slowing of motor functions indicated by slowed bodily movements and speech and lower volume, variety, or amount of speech.

Psychopathy A set of emotional and interpersonal characteristics marked by a lack of empathy, an unmerited feeling of high self-worth, and a refusal to accept responsibility for one's actions.

Psychosexual stages According to Freud, the sequence of five distinct stages of development (oral, anal, phallic, latency, and genital) through which children proceed from infancy to adulthood; each stage has a key task that must be completed successfully for healthy psychological development.

Psychosis An impaired ability to perceive reality to the extent that normal functioning is difficult or not possible. The two types of psychotic symptoms are hallucinations and delusions.

Punishment The process by which an event or object that is the consequence of a behavior *decreases* the likelihood that the behavior will occur again.

Purging Attempting to reduce calories that have already been consumed by vomiting or using diuretics, laxatives, or enemas.

◦ **R** ◦

Random assignment Assigning participants to each group in a study using a procedure that relies on chance.

Randomized clinical trial (RCT) A research design that has at least two groups—a treatment group and a control group (usually a placebo control)—to which participants are randomly assigned.

Rapid cycling (of moods) Having four or more episodes that meet the criteria for any type of mood episode within 1 year.

Reactivity A behavior change that occurs when one becomes aware of being observed.

Receptors Specialized sites on dendrites and cell bodies that respond only to specific molecules.

Reinforcement The process by which the consequence of a behavior *increases* the likelihood of the behavior's recurrence.

Reliable A property of classification systems (or measures) that consistently produce the same results.

Relief craving The desire for the temporary emotional relief that can arise from using a substance.

Replication The process of repeating a study using the same data collection methods under identical or nearly identical conditions to obtain data that should have the same characteristics as those from the original study.

Response bias The tendency to respond in a particular way, regardless of what is being asked by the question.

Restrained eating Restricting intake of specific foods or overall number of calories.

Reuptake The process of moving leftover neurotransmitter molecules in the synapse back into the sending neuron.

Reward craving The desire for the gratifying effects of using a substance.

◦ **S** ◦

Sample The small portion of a population that is examined in a study.

Sampling bias The distortion that occurs when the participants in an experiment have not been drawn randomly from the relevant population under investigation.

Schizoaffective disorder A psychotic disorder characterized by the presence of both schizophrenia *and* a depressive or manic episode.

Schizoid personality disorder A personality disorder characterized by a restricted range of emotions in social interactions and few—if any—close relationships.

Schizophrenia A psychological disorder characterized by psychotic symptoms that significantly affect emotions, behavior, and mental processes and mental contents.

Schizophreniform disorder A psychotic disorder characterized by symptoms that meet all the criteria for schizophrenia *except* that the symptoms have been present for only 1–6 months, and daily functioning may or may not have declined over that period of time.

Schizotypal personality disorder A personality disorder characterized by eccentric thoughts, perceptions, and behaviors, in addition to having very few close relationships.

Scientific method The process of gathering and interpreting facts that generally consists of collecting initial observations, identifying a question, developing a hypothesis that might answer the question, collecting relevant data, developing a theory, and testing the theory.

Selective serotonin reuptake inhibitors (SSRIs) Medications that slow the reuptake of serotonin from synapses.

Sensate focus exercises A behavioral technique that is assigned as homework in sex therapy, in which a person or couple seeks to increase awareness of pleasurable sensations that do not involve genital touching, intercourse, or orgasm.

Separation anxiety disorder A disorder that typically arises in childhood and is characterized by excessive anxiety about separation from home or from someone to whom the person is strongly attached.

Sex reassignment surgery A procedure in which a person's genitals (and breasts) are surgically altered to appear like those of the other sex.

Sexual dysfunctions Sexual disorders that are characterized by problems in the sexual response cycle.

Sexual masochism disorder A paraphilic disorder in which the person repeatedly becomes sexually aroused by fantasies, urges, or behaviors related to being hurt—specifically, being humiliated or made to suffer in other ways—and this arousal pattern causes significant distress or impairs functioning.

Sexual response cycle The four stages of sexual response—excitement, plateau, orgasm, and resolution—outlined by Masters and Johnson.

Sexual sadism disorder A paraphilic disorder in which recurrent sexually arousing fantasies, urges, and behaviors inflict, or would inflict, physical or psychological suffering on a nonconsenting person.

Single-participant experiments Experiments with only a single participant.

Social anxiety disorder An anxiety disorder characterized by intense fear of public humiliation or embarrassment; also called *social phobia*.

Social causation hypothesis The hypothesis that the daily stressors of urban life, especially as experienced by people in a lower socioeconomic class, trigger mental illness in those who are vulnerable.

Social desirability A bias toward answering questions in a way that respondents think makes them appear socially desirable, even if the responses are not true.

Social selection hypothesis The hypothesis that people who are mentally ill "drift" to a lower socioeconomic level because of their impairments; also referred to as *social drift*.

Social support The comfort and assistance that an individual receives through interactions with others.

Social worker A mental health professional who has an M.S.W. degree and may have had training to provide psychotherapy to help individuals and families.

Somatic symptom disorder (SSD) A somatic symptom disorder characterized by at least one somatic symptom that is distressing or disrupts daily life, about which the person has excessive thoughts, feelings, or behaviors.

Somatic symptom disorders A category of psychological disorders characterized by symptoms about physical well-being along with cognitive distortions about bodily symptoms and their meaning; the focus on these bodily symptoms causes significant distress or impaired functioning.

Specific factors The characteristics of a particular treatment or technique that lead it to have unique benefits, above and beyond those conferred by common factors.

Specific learning disorder A neurodevelopmental disorder characterized by skills well below average in reading, writing, or math, based on the expected level of performance for the person's age, general intelligence, cultural group, gender, and education level.

Specific phobia An anxiety disorder characterized by excessive or unreasonable anxiety about or fear related to a specific situation or object.

Stages of change A series of five stages that characterizes how ready a person is to change problematic behaviors: precontemplation, contemplation, preparation, action, and maintenance.

Statistically significant The condition in which the value of a statistical test is greater than what would be expected by chance alone.

Stereotyped behaviors Repetitive behaviors—such as body rocking—that do not serve a function; also referred to as *stereotypies*.

Stimulus generalization The process whereby responses come to be elicited by stimuli that are similar to the conditioned stimulus.

Stroke The interruption of normal blood flow to or within the brain, which results in neuronal death.

Substance intoxication The reversible dysfunctional effects on thoughts, feelings, and behavior that arise from the use of a psychoactive substance.

Substance use disorders Psychological disorders that are characterized by loss of control over urges to use a psychoactive substance, even though such use may impair functioning or cause distress.

Subthreshold cases Cases in which patients have symptoms that fit all the necessary criteria, but at levels lower than required for the diagnosis of a disorder.

Suicidal ideation Thoughts of suicide.

Superego According to Freud, the seat of the conscience, which works to impose morality.

Synapse The place where the tip of the axon of one neuron sends signals to another neuron.

° T °

Tarasoff rule A ruling by the Supreme Court of California (and later other courts) that psychologists have a duty to protect potential victims who are in imminent danger.

Tardive dyskinesia An enduring side effect of traditional antipsychotic medications that produces involuntary lip smacking and odd facial contortions as well as other movement-related symptoms.

Temperament The aspects of personality that reflect a person's typical emotional state and emotional reactivity (including the speed and strength of reactions to stimuli).

Teratogens Substances or other stimuli that are harmful to a fetus.

Theory A principle or set of principles that explains a set of data.

Theory of mind A theory about other people's mental states (their beliefs, desires, and feelings) that allows a person to predict how other people will react in a given situation.

Tolerance The biological response that arises from repeated use of a substance such that more of it is required to obtain the same effect.

Transcranial magnetic stimulation (TMS) A procedure that sends sequences of short, strong magnetic pulses into the brain via a coil placed on the scalp, which is used to reduce or eliminate the symptoms of certain psychological disorders.

Transvestic disorder A paraphilic disorder in which the person cross-dresses for sexual arousal and experiences distress or impaired functioning because of the cross-dressing.

Tricyclic antidepressants (TCAs) Older antidepressants named after the three rings of atoms in their molecular structure.

° U °

Unconditioned response (UCR) A behavior that is reflexively elicited by a stimulus.

Unconditioned stimulus (UCS) A stimulus that reflexively elicits a behavior.

° V °

Valid A property of classification systems (or measures) that actually characterize what they are supposed to characterize.

Vascular dementia A type of dementia caused by reduced or blocked blood supply to the brain, which arises from plaque buildup or blood clots.

Voyeuristic disorder A paraphilic disorder in which sexual fantasies, urges, or behaviors involve observing someone who is in the process of undressing, is nude, or is engaged in sexual activity, when the person being observed has neither consented to nor is aware of being observed.

° W °

Wernicke's aphasia A neurological condition characterized by problems comprehending language and producing meaningful utterances.

Withdrawal The set of symptoms that arises when a regular substance user decreases or stops intake of an abused substance.

Abbott, C., & Bustillo, J. (2006). What have we learned from proton magnetic resonance spectroscopy about schizophrenia? A critical update. *Current Opinion in Psychiatry, 19,* 135–139.

Abbott, M. J., & Rapee, R. M. (2004). Post-event rumination and negative self-appraisal in social phobia before and after treatment. *Journal of Abnormal Psychology, 113,* 136–144.

Abbott, P., & Chase, D. (2008). Culture and substance abuse: Impact of culture affects approach to treatment. *Psychiatric Times, 25.* Retrieved on November 7, 2013 from http://www.psychiatrictimes.com/articles/culture-and-substance-abuse-impact-culture-affects-approach-treatment.

Abel, G. G., Becker, J. V., Mittelman, M., Cunningham-Rathner, J., Rouleau, J. L., & Murphy, W. D. (1987). Self-reported sex crimes of nonincarcerated paraphiliacs. *Journal of Interpersonal Violence, 2,* 3–25.

Aberg, K. A., Liu, Y., Bukszar, J., McClay, J. L., Khachane, A. N., et al. (2013). A comprehensive family-based replication study of schizophrenia genes. *JAMA Psychiatry, 70,* 1–9.

Abouesh, A., & Clayton, A. (1999). Compulsive voyeurism and exhibitionism: A clinical response to paroxetine. *Archives of Sexual Behavior, 28,* 23–30.

Abraham, S. F., Brown, T., Boyd, C., Luscombe, G., & Russell, J. (2006). Quality of life: Eating disorders. *Australian and New Zealand Journal of Psychiatry, 40,* 150–155.

Abramowitz, J. S. (1997). Effectiveness of psychological and pharmacological treatments for obsessive-compulsive disorder: A quantitative review. *Journal of Consulting and Clinical Psychology, 65,* 44–52.

Abramowitz, J. S., & Braddock, A. E. (2006). Hypochondriasis: Conceptualization, treatment, and relationship to obsessive-compulsive disorder. *Psychiatric Clinics of North America, 29,* 503–519.

Abrams, K., Rassovsky, Y., & Kushner, M. G. (2006). Evidence for respiratory and nonrespiratory subtypes in panic disorder. *Depression and Anxiety, 23,* 474–481.

Abramson, L. Y., Alloy, L. B., Hogan, M. E., Whitehouse, W. G., Donovan, P., et al. (1999). Cognitive vulnerability to depression: Theory and evidence. *Journal of Cognitive Psychotherapy, 13,* 5–20.

Abramson, L. Y., Metalsky, G. I., & Alloy, L. B. (1989). Hopelessness depression: A theory-based subtype of depression. *Psychological Review, 96,* 358–372.

Abramson, L. Y., Seligman, M. E., & Teasdale, J. D. (1978). Learned helplessness in humans: Critique and reformulation. *Journal of Abnormal Psychology, 87,* 49–74.

Abreu, J. M. (1999). Conscious and nonconscious African American stereotypes: Impact on first impression and diagnostic ratings by therapists. *Journal of Consulting and Clinical Psychology, 67,* 387–393.

Achenbach, T. M. (2008). Multicultural perspectives on developmental psychopathology. In J. J. Hudziak (Ed.), *Developmental psychopathology and wellness: Genetic and environmental influences* (pp. 23–47). Arlington, VA: American Psychiatric Publishing.

Achenbach, T. M., Krukowski, R. A., Dumenci, L., & Ivanova, M. Y. (2005). Assessment of adult psychopathology: Meta-analyses and implications of cross-informant correlations. *Psychological Bulletin, 131,* 361–382.

Achenbach, T. M., McConaughy, S. H., & Howell, C. T. (1987). Child/adolescent behavioral and emotional problems: Implications of cross-informant correlations for situational specificity. *Psychological Bulletin, 101,* 213–232.

Acheson, D. T., Forsyth, J. P., Prenoveau, J. M., & Bouton, M. E. (2007). Interoceptive fear conditioning as a learning model of panic disorder: An experimental evaluation using 20% CO-enriched air in a non-clinical sample. *Behaviour Research and Therapy, 45,* 2280–2294.

Ackerman, N. J. (1980). The family with adolescents. In E. A. Carter & M. McGoldrick (Eds.), *The family life cycle* (p. 181). New York: Gardner Press.

Adamec, R., Holmes, A., & Blundell, J. (2008). Vulnerability to lasting anxiogenic effects of brief exposure to predator stimuli: sex, serotonin and other factors—relevance to PTSD. *Neuroscience and Biobehavioural Reviews, 32,* 1287–1292.

Adams, H. E., Bernat, J. A., & Luscher, K. A. (2001). Borderline personality disorder: An overview. In P. B. Sutker & H. E. Adams (Eds.), *Comprehensive handbook of psychopathology* (3rd ed., pp. 491–507). New York: Kluwer Academic/Plenum.

Addolorato, G., Taranto, C., De Rossi, G., & Gasbarrini, G. (1997). Neuroimaging of cerebral and cerebellar atrophy in anorexia nervosa. *Psychiatry Research: Neuroimaging, 76,* 139–141.

Aderka, I. M., Hermesh, H., Marom, S., Weizman, A., & Gilboa-Schechtman, E. (2011). Cognitive behavior therapy for social phobia in large groups. *International Journal of Cognitive Therapy, 4*(1), 92–103.

Adewuya, A. O. (2006). Early postpartum mood as a risk factor for postnatal depression in Nigerian women. *American Journal of Psychiatry, 163,* 1435–1437.

Adityanjee, Raju, G. S., & Khandelwal, S. K. (1989). Current status of multiple personality disorder in India. *American Journal of Psychiatry, 146,* 1607–1610.

Adler, C. M., McDonough-Ryan, P., Sax, K. W., Holland, S. K., Arndt, S., & Strakowski, S. M. (2000). fMRI of neuronal activation with symptom provocation in unmedicated patients with obsessive compulsive disorder. *Journal of Psychiatric Research, 34,* 317–324.

Adler, D. A., McLaughlin, T. J., Rogers, W. H., Chang, H., Lapitsky, L., & Lerner, D. (2006). Job performance deficits due to depression. *American Journal of Psychiatry, 163,* 1569–1576.

Adler, N. E., Epel, E. S., Castellazzo, G., & Ickovics, J. R. (2000). Relationship of subjective and objective social status with psychological and physiological functioning: Preliminary data in healthy white women. *Health Psychology, 19,* 586–592.

Adson, D. E., Mitchell, J. E., & Trenkner, S. W. (1997). The superior mesenteric artery syndrome and acute gastric dilatation in eating disorders: A report of two cases and a review of the literature. *International Journal of Eating Disorders, 21,* 103–114.

Afifi, T. O., Brownridge, D. A., Cox, B. J., & Sareen, J. (2006). Physical punishment, childhood abuse and psychiatric disorders. *Child Abuse & Neglect, 30,* 1093–1103.

Agency for Health Care Policy and Research. (1999). *Newer antidepressant drugs are equally as effective as older-generation drug treatments, research shows.* AHCPR Pub. No. 99-E013. Rockville, MD: Author.

Agency for Health Care Policy and Research. (2002). *S-adenosyl-L-methionine for treatment of depression, osteoarthritis, and liver disease.* AHRQ Publication No. 02-E033, August 2002. Rockville, MD: Author. Retrieved October 24, 2008, from www.ahrq.gov/clinic/epcsums/samesum.htm

Agerbo, E., Gunnell, D., Bonde, J. P., Mortensen, P. B., & Nordentoft, M. (2007). Suicide and occupation: The impact of socio-economic, demographic and psychiatric differences. *Psychological Medicine, 37,* 1131–1140.

Aghajanian, G. K., & Marek, G. J. (2000). Serotonin model of schizophrenia: Emerging role of glutamate mechanisms. *Brain Research Reviews, 31,* 302–312.

Aghevli, M. A., Blanchard, J. J., & Horan, W. P. (2003). The expression and experience of emotion in schizophrenia: A study of social interactions. *Psychiatry Research, 119,* 261–270.

Agliata, A. K., Tantleff-Dunn, S., & Renk, K. (2007). Interpretation of teasing during early adolescence. *Journal of Clinical Psychology, 63,* 23–30.

Agosti, V., & Levin, F. R. (2006). The effects of alcohol and drug dependence on the course of depression. *The American Journal on Addictions, 15,* 71–75.

Agras, W. S. (2001). The consequences and costs of the eating disorders. *Psychiatric Clinics of North America, 24,* 371–379.

Agras, W. S., & Apple, R. F. (1997). *Overcoming Eating Disorders—Therapist Guide.* Graywind/The Psychological Corporation.

Agras, W. S., & Apple, R. F. (2008). *Overcoming Eating Disorders—Therapist Guide.* 2nd edition. New York: Oxford University Press.

Agras, W. S., Crow, S. J., Halmi, K. A., Mitchell, J. E., Wilson, G. T., & Kraemer, H. C. (2000). Outcome predictors for the cognitive behavior treatment of bulimia nervosa: Data from a multisite study. *American Journal of Psychiatry, 157,* 1302–1308.

Agras, W. S., Walsh, B. T., Fairburn, C. G., Wilson, G. T., & Kraemer, H. C. (2000). A multicenter comparison of cognitive-behavioral therapy and interpersonal psychotherapy. *Archives of General Psychiatry, 54,* 459–465.

Agrawal, A., Neale, M. C., Prescott, C. A., & Kendler, K. S. (2004). A twin study of early cannabis use and subsequent use and abuse/dependence of other illicit drugs. *Psychological Medicine, 34,* 1227–1237.

Aikens, J. E., Nease Jr., D. E., & Klinkman, M. S. (2008). Explaining patients' beliefs about the necessity and harmfulness of antidepressants. *Annals of Family Medicine, 6,* 23–29.

Ainsworth, M. (1989), Attachments beyond infancy. *American Psychologist, 44,* 709–716.

Ainsworth, M. D. S., & Bell, S. M. (1970). Attachment, exploration, and separation: Illustrated by the behavior of one-year-olds in a strange situation. *Child Development, 41,* 49–67.

Ainsworth, M. D. S., Blehar, M. C., Waters, E., & Wall, S. (1978). *Patterns of attachment: A psychological study of the strange situation.* Hillsdale, NJ: Lawrence Erlbaum.

Ait-Daoud, N., Dameron, Z. C., III, Marzani-Nissen, G. R., Wells, L. T., & Johnson, B. A. (2006). Glutaminergic agents for the treatment of alcohol and substance abuse disorders. *Primary Psychiatry, 13,* 56–64.

Akins, C. K. (2004). The role of Pavlovian conditioning in sexual behavior: A comparative analysis of human and nonhuman animals. *International Journal of Comparative Psychology, 17,* 241–262.

Akiskal, H. S. (1996). The prevalent clinical spectrum of bipolar disorders: Beyond DSM-IV. *Journal of Clinical Psychopharmacology, 16*(Suppl. 1), 4S–14S.

Akiskal, H. S. (2003). Validating "hard" and "soft" phenotypes within the bipolar spectrum: Continuity or discontinuity? *Journal of Affective Disorder, 73,* 1–5.

Albert, U., Maina, G., Forner, F., & Bogetto, F. (2004). DSM-IV-TR obsessive-compulsive personality disorder: Prevalence in patients with anxiety disorders and in healthy comparison subjects. *Comprehensive Psychiatry, 45,* 325–332.

Albertini, R. S., & Phillips, K. A. (1999). Thirty-three cases of body dysmorphic disorder in children and adolescents. *Journal of the American Academy of Child & Adolescent Psychiatry, 38,* 453–459.

Aldao, A., & Nolen-Hoeksema, S. (2010). Specificity of cognitive emotion regulation strategies: A transdiagnostic examination. *Behaviour Research and Therapy, 48,* 974–983.

Alegría, M., Canino, G., Shrout, P. E., Woo, M., Duan, N., et al. (2008). Prevalence of mental illness in immigrant and non-immigrant U.S. Latino groups. *American Journal of Psychiatry, 165,* 359–369.

Alegría, M., Woo, M., Cao, Z., Torres, M., Meng, X., & Striegel-Moore, R. (2007). Prevalence and correlates of eating disorders in Latinos in the United States. *International Journal of Eating Disorders, 40,* S15–S21.

Alexander, F., & French, T. M. (1946). *Psychoanalytic therapy: Principles and application.* Oxford, England: Ronald Press.

Alexander, W. (1996). Strong relationship found between schizophrenia, mood disorders. *Psychiatric Times, 13,* n.p.

Alford, G. S., & Karns, L. (2000). Psychosis. In A. E. Kazdin (Ed.), *Encyclopedia of psychology* (Vol. 6, pp. 452–456). Washington, DC: American Psychological Association.

Allen, J. G., Console, D. A., & Lewis, L. (1999). Dissociative detachment and memory impairment: Reversible amnesia or encoding failure? *Comparative Psychiatry, 40,* 160–171.

Allen, J. J., & Movius, H. L., II (2000). The objective assessment of amnesia in dissociative identity disorder using event-related potentials. *International Journal of Psychophysiology, 38,* 21–41.

Allen, L. A., Woolfolk, R. L., Escobar, J. I., Gara, M. A., & Hamer, R. M. (2006). Cognitive-behavioral therapy for somatization disorder: A randomized controlled trial. *Archives of Internal Medicine, 166,* 1512–1518.

Allison, P. D., & Furstenberg, F. F., Jr. (1989). How marital dissolution affects children: Variations by age and sex. *Developmental Psychology, 25,* 540–549.

Alloy, L. B., & Abramson, L. Y. (2007). The adolescent surge in depression and emergence of gender differences: A biocognitive vulnerability-stress model in developmental context. In D. Romer & E. Walker (Eds.), *Adolescent psychopathology and the developing brain: Integrating brain and prevention science* (pp. 284–312). New York: Oxford University Press.

Alloy, L. B., Reilly-Harrington, N., Fresco, D. M., Whitehouse, W. G., & Zechmeister, J. S. (1999). Cognitive styles and life events in subsyndromal unipolar and bipolar disorders: Stability and prospective prediction of depressive and hypomanic mood swings. *Journal of Cognitive Psychotherapy, 13,* 21–40.

Allsop, D. J., Copeland, J., Norberg, M. M., Fu, S., Molnar, A., et al. (2012). Quantifying the clinical significance of cannabis withdrawal. *PLoS ONE, 15.* Retrieved June 10, 2013, from www.plosone.org/article/info%3Adoi%2F10.1371%2Fjournal.pone.0044864

Allyne, R. (2007, October 31). Man who had sex with bike in court. Telegraph. Retrieved April 17, 2009, from www.telegraph.co.uk/news/uknews/1567410/Man-who-had-sex-with-bike-in-court.html

Alonso, P., Pujol, J., Cardoner, N., Benlloch, L., Deus, J., et al. (2001). Right prefrontal repetitive transcranial magnetic stimulation in obsessive-compulsive disorder: A double- blind, placebo-controlled study. *American Journal of Psychiatry, 158,* 1143–1145.

Althof, S. E. (2000). Erectile dysfunction: Psychotherapy with men and couples. In S. R. Leiblum & R. C. Rosen (Eds.), *Principles and practice of sex therapy* (3rd ed., pp. 242–275). New York: Guilford Press.

Althof, S. E., O'Leary, M. P., Cappelleri, J. C., Glina, S., King, R., et al. (U.S. and International SEAR study group). (2006). Self-esteem, confidence, and relationships in men treated with sildenafil citrate for erectile dysfunction. *Journal of General Internal Medicine, 21,* 1069–1074.

Altshuler, L., Bookheimer, S., Proenza, M. A., Townsend, J., Sabb, F., et al. (2005). Increased amygdala activation during mania: A functional magnetic resonance imaging study. *American Journal of Psychiatry, 162,* 1211–1213.

Altshuler, L. L., Bartzokis, G., Grieder, T., Curran, J., & Mintz, J. (1998). Amygdala enlargement in bipolar disorder and hippocampal reduction in schizophrenia: An MRI study demonstrating neuroanatomic specificity. *Archives of General Psychiatry, 55,* 663–664.

Altshuler, L. L., Bauer, M., Frye, M. A., Gitlin, M. J., Mintz, J., et al. (2001). Does thyroid supplementation accelerate tricyclic antidepressant response? A review and meta-analysis of the literature. *American Journal of Psychiatry, 158,* 1617–1622.

Altshuler, L. L., Kupka, R. W., Hellemann, G., Frye, M. A., Sugar, C. A., et al. (2010). Gender and depressive symptoms in 711 patients with bipolar disorder evaluated prospectively in the Stanley Foundation bipolar treatment outcome network. *American Journal of Psychiatry, 167,* 708–715.

Alvarez, L. (2008, July 8). After the battle, fighting the bottle at home. *New York Times.* Retrieved November 12, 2008, from www.nytimes.com/2008/07/08/us/08vets.html?sq=ptsd%20AND%20Afghanistan%20AND%20 iraq&st=nyt&scp=1&pagewanted=all

Alvidrez, J., Azocar, F., & Miranda, J. (1996). Demystifying the concept of ethnicity for psychotherapy research. *Journal of Consulting and Clinical Psychology, 64,* 903–908.

Alzheimer's Association. (2007). *Alzheimer's disease facts and figures 2007.* Retrieved December 2, 2007, from www.alz.org/national/documents/report_alzfactsfigures2007.pdf

Amador, X. F., & Gorman, J. M. (1998). Psychopathologic domains and insight in schizophrenia. *Psychiatric Clinics of North America, 21,* 27–42.

Amador, X. F., Strauss, D. H., Yale, S. A., & Gorman, J. M. (1991). Awareness of illness in schizophrenia. *Schizophrenia Bulletin, 17,* 113–132.

Amass, L., Ling, W., Freese, T. E., Reiber, C., Annon, J. J., et al. (2004). Bringing buprenorphine-naloxone detoxification to community treatment providers: The NIDA Clinical Trials Network Field Experience. *American Journal on Addictions, 13,* S42–S66.

Amat, J., Matus-Amat, P., Watkins, L. R., & Maier, S. F. (1998). Escapable and inescapable stress differentially and selectively alter extracellular levels of 5-HT in the ventral hippocampus and dorsal periaqueductal gray of the rat. *Brain Research, 797,* 12–22.

Amat, J., Sparks, P. D., Matus-Amat, P., Griggs, J., Watkins, L. R., & Maier, S. F. (2001). The role of habenular complex in the elevation of dorsal raphe nucleus serotonin and the changes in the behavioral responses produced by uncontrollable stress. *Brain Research, 917*, 118–126.

Ambrogne, J. A. (2002). Reduced-risk drinking as a treatment goal: What clinicians need to know. *Journal of Substance Abuse Treatment, 22,* 45–53.

American Association for Geriatric Psychiatry. (2006). *American Journal of Geriatric Psychiatry, 14*, 561–572. Retrieved December 4, 2007, from www.aagponline.org/prof/position_caredmnalz.asp

American Psychiatric Association. (1952). *Diagnostic and Statistical Manual of Mental Disorders.* Washington, DC: Author.

American Psychiatric Association. (2000). *Diagnostic and statistical manual of mental disorders* (4th ed., text revision). Washington, DC: Author.

American Psychiatric Association. (2010). *DSM-5 proposed revisions includes new risk syndromes and suicide risk assessment tool. News Release.* February 10. Retrieved December 24, 2011, from www.dsm5.org/Newsroom/Documents/Suicide%20Scale-Risk%20Syndrome%20release%20FINAL%202.05.pdf

American Psychiatric Association. (2013). *Diagnostic and statistical manual, fifth edition.* Washington, DC: American Psychiatric Press, Inc.

American Psychiatric Association Work Group on Suicidal Behaviors (Jacobs, D. G., Baldessarini, R. J., Conwell, Y., Fawcett, J. A., Horton, L., Meltzer, H., Pfeffer, C. R., & Simon, R. I.). (2003). Practice guideline for the assessment and treatment of patients with suicidal behaviors. *American Journal of Psychiatry, 160*(Suppl.), 1–60.

American Psychological Association. (2002). *Ethical principles of psychologists and code of conduct.* Retrieved September 9, 2008, from www.apa.org/ethics/code2002.pdf

American Psychological Association, Working Group on the Older Adult. (1998). What practitioners should know about working with older adults. *Professional Psychology: Research and Practice, 29*, 413–427.

American Society of Addiction Medicine. (2011). Public Policy Statement: Definition of addiction. Retrieved March 6, 2012, from www.asam.org/docs/publicy-policy-statements/1definition_of_addiction_long_4–11.pdf?sfvrsn=2

Amir, R. E., Van den Veyver, I. B., Wan, M., Tran, C. Q., Francke, U., & Zoghbi, H. (1999). Rett syndrome is caused by mutations in X-linked MECP2, encoding methyl CpG binding protein 2. *Nature Genetics, 23*, 185–188.

Anastasi, A. (1988). *Psychological testing* (6th ed.). New York: Macmillan.

Andersen, A. E., & DiDomenico, L. (1992). Diet vs. shape content of popular male and female magazines: A dose-response relationship to the incidence of eating disorders? *International Journal of Eating Disorders, 11*, 283–287.

Andersen, A. E., & Hay, A. (1985). Racial and socioeconomic influences in anorexia nervosa and bulimia. *International Journal of Eating Disorders, 4*, 479–487.

Andersen, A. E., Bowers, W. A., & Watson, T. (2001). A slimming program for eating disorders not otherwise specified: Reconceptualizing a confusing, residual diagnostic category. *Psychiatric Clinics of North America, 24*, 271–280.

Andersen, B. L., Anderson, B., & DeProsse, C. (1989). Controlled prospective longitudinal study of women with cancer: I. Sexual functioning outcomes. *Journal of Consulting and Clinical Psychology, 57*, 683–691.

Anderson, I. M. (2000). Selective serotonin reuptake inhibitors versus tricyclic antidepressants: A meta-analysis of efficacy and tolerability. *Journal of Affective Disorders, 58*, 19–36.

Anderson, P. L., Zimand, E., Hodges, L. F., & Rothbaum, B. O. (2005). Cognitive behavioral therapy for public-speaking anxiety using virtual reality for exposure. *Depression and Anxiety, 22*, 156–158.

Andersson, G., Carlbring, P., Holmström, A., Sparthan, E., Furmark, T., et al. (2006). Internet-based self-help with therapist feedback and in vivo group exposure for social phobia: A randomized controlled trial. *Journal of Consulting and Clinical Psychology, 74*, 677–686.

Andreasen, N. C. (1979). Thought, language, and communication disorders: Clinical assessment, definition of terms, and assessment of their reliability. *Archives of General Psychiatry 36*, 1315–1321.

Andreasen, N. C. (2001). *Brave new brain: Conquering mental illness in the era of the genome.* New York: Oxford University Press.

Andreasen, N. C., Arndt, S., Swayze, V., Cizadlo, T., Flaum, M., et al. (1994). Thalamic abnormalities in schizophrenia visualized through magnetic resonance image averaging. *Science, 266*, 294–298.

Andreasen, N. C., Nopoulos, P., O'Leary, D. S., Miller, D. D., Wassink, T., & Flaum, M. (1999). Defining the phenotype of schizophrenia: Cognitive dysmetria and its neural mechanisms. *Biological Psychiatry, 46*, 908–920.

Andrews, J. A., Hops, H., Ary, D., Lichtenstein, E., & Tildesley, E. (1991). The construction, validation and use of the Guttman scale of adolescent substance use: An investigation of family relationships. *Journal of Drug Issues, 21*, 557–572.

Andrews, J., Wang, L., Csernansky, J. G., Gado, M. H., & Barch, D. M. (2006). Abnormalities of thalamic activation and cognition in schizophrenia. *American Journal of Psychiatry, 163*, 463–469.

Andrews-Hanna, J. R., Snyder, A. Z., Vincent, J. L., Lustig, C., Head, D., et al. (2007). Disruption of large-scale brain systems in advanced aging. *Neuron, 56*, 924–935.

Angell, M. (2011, June 23). The epidemic of mental illness: Why? *The New York Review*, retrieved on November 7, 2013 from http://www.nybooks.com/articles/archives/2011/jun/23/epidemic-mental-illness-why/?page=1

Angermeyer, M. C. (2000). Schizophrenia and violence. *Acta Psychiatrica Scandinavica, 102*, 63–67.

Angst, J. (1998). The emerging epidemiology of hypomania and bipolar II disorder. *Journal of Affective Disorders, 50*, 143–151.

Angst, J. (1999). Major depression in 1998: Are we providing optimal therapy? *Journal of Clinical Psychiatry, 60*, 5–9.

Angst, J., Angst, F., & Stassen H. H. (1999). Suicide risk in patients with major depressive disorder. *Journal of Clinical Psychiatry, 60*(Suppl 2), 57–62.

Angst, J., Gamma, A., Benazzi, B., Ajdacica, V., Eich, D., & Rössler, W. (2003). Toward a re-definition of subthreshold bipolarity: Epidemiology and proposed criteria for bipolar-II, minor bipolar disorders and hypomania. *Journal of Affective Disorders, 73*, 133–146.

Angst, J., Gamma, A., Gastpar, M., Lépine, J.-P., Mendlewicz, J., & Tylee, A. (2002). Gender differences in depression: Epidemiological findings from the European DEPRES I and II studies. *European Archives of Psychiatry and Clinical Neuroscience, 252*, 201–209.

Anonymous. (2003, August 16). Commentary. *British Medical Journal, 327*, 382–383.

Ansbacher, H. L., & Ansbacher, R. R. (Eds.). (1956). *The individual psychology of Alfred Adler: A systematic presentation of selections from his writings.* New York: Basic Books.

Ansseau, M., Fischler, B., Dierick, M., Mignon, A., & Leyman, S. (2005). Prevalence and impact of generalized anxiety disorder and major depression in primary care in Belgium and Luxemburg: The GADIS study. *European Psychiatry, 20*, 229–235.

Antonuccio, D. O., Burns, D., Danton, W. G., & O'Donohue, W. (2000). The rumble in Reno: The psychosocial perspective on depression. *Psychiatric Times, 17*, 24–28. www.mhsource.com/pt/p000824.html

Antonuccio, D. O., Burns, D. D., & Danton, W. G. (2002). Antidepressants: A triumph of marketing over science? *Prevention & Treatment, 5*, Article 25. www.journals.apa.org/prevention/volume5/pre0050025c.html

Antonuccio, D. O., Danton, W. G., & DeNelsky, G. Y. (1995). Psychotherapy versus medication for depression: Challenging the conventional wisdom with data. *Professional Psychology: Research & Practice, 26*, 574–585.

Antony, M. M., & Barlow, D. H. (Eds.). (2002). *Handbook of assessment and treatment planning for psychological disorders.* New York: Guilford Press.

Antony, M. M., Craske, M. G., & Barlow, D. H. (1995). *Mastery of your specific phobia.* New York: Graywind Publications.

Antony, M. M., & Swinson, R. P. (1998). *When perfect isn't good enough: Strategies for coping with perfectionism.* Oakland, CA: New Harbinger.

Antony, M. M., & Swinson, R. P. (2000a). *The shyness & social anxiety workbook: Proven techniques for overcoming your fears.* Oakland, CA: New Harbinger.

Antony, M. M., & Swinson, R. P. (2000b). Specific phobia. In M. M. Antony & R. P. Swinson (Eds.), *Phobic disorders and panic in adults: A guide to assessment and treatment* (pp. 79–104). Washington, DC: American Psychological Association.

Anxiety Disorders Association of America. Retrieved September 23, 2002, from www.adaa.org/GettingHelp/Articles/ShirlyB.asp

Apfelbaum, B. (1989). Retarded ejaculation: A much-misunderstood syndrome. In S. R., Leiblum & R. C. Rosen (Eds.), *Principles and practice of sex therapy: Update for the 1990s* (2nd ed., pp. 168–206). New York: Guilford Press.

Apfelbaum, B. (2000). Retarded ejaculation: A much misunderstood syndrome. In S. R. Leiblum & R. C. Rosen (Eds.), *Principles and practice of sex therapy* (3rd ed., pp. 205–241). New York: Guilford Press.

Apfelbaum, B. (2001). What the sex therapies tell us about sex. In P. J. Kleinplatz (Ed.), *New directions in sex therapy: Innovations and alternatives.* (pp. 5–28). Philadelphia: Taylor and Rutledge.

Appelbaum, P. S. (2002). Privacy in psychiatric treatment: Threats and responses. *American Journal of Psychiatry, 159,* 1809–1818.

Appelbaum, P. S., & Grisso, T. (1995). The MacArthur Treatment Competence Study: I. Mental illness and competence to consent to treatment. *Law and Human Behavior, 19,* 105–126.

Apple, R. F. (1999). Interpersonal therapy for bulimia nervosa. *Journal of Clinical Psychology, 55,* 715–725.

Arana, G. W., & Rosenbaum, J. F. (2000). *Handbook of psychiataric drug therapy.* Philadelphia: Lippincott Williams & Wilkins.

Arcia, E., Sánchez-LaCay, A., & Fernández, M. C. (2002). When worlds collide: Dominican mothers and their Latina clinicians. *Transcultural Psychiatry, 39,* 74–96.

Arnold, S. E., Hyman, B. T., Van Hoesen, G. W., & Damasio, A. R. (1991). Some cytoarchitectural abnormalities of the entorhinal cortex in schizophrenia. *Archives of General Psychiatry, 48,* 625–632.

Arnsten, A. F. (2006). Fundamentals of attention-deficit/hyperactivity disorder: Circuits and pathways. *Journal of Clinical Psychiatry, 67*(Suppl. 8), 7–12.

Aronson, S. C., Black, J. E., McDougle, C. J., Scanley B. E., Heninger, G. R., et al. (1995). Serotonergic mechanisms of cocaine effects in humans. *Psychopharmacology, 119,* 179–185.

Arriaza, C. A., & Mann, T. (2001). Ethnic differences in eating disorder symptoms among college students: The confounding role of body mass index. *Journal of American College Health, 49,* 309–315.

Arroll, B., Macgillivray, S., Ogston, S., Reid, I., Sullivan, F., et al. (2005). Efficacy and tolerability of tricyclic antidepressants and SSRIs compared with placebo for treatment of depression in primary care: A meta-analysis. *Annals of Family Medicine, 3,* 449–456.

Arseneault, L., Cannon, M., Poulton, R., Murray, R., Caspi, A., & Moffitt, T. E. (2002). Cannabis use in adolescence and risk for adult psychosis: Longitudinal prospective study. *British Medical Journal, 325,* 1195–1199.

Arseneault, L., Milne, B. J., Taylor, A., Adams, F., Delgado, K., et al. (2008). Being bullied as an environmentally mediated contributing factor to children's internalizing problems: A study of twins discordant for victimization. *Archives of Pediatric Adolescent Medicine, 162,* 145–150.

Artaloytia, J. F., Arango, C., Lahti, A., Sanz, J., Pascual, A., et al. (2006). Negative signs and symptoms secondary to antipsychotics: A double-blind, randomized trial of a single dose of placebo, haloperidol, and risperidone in healthy volunteers. *American Journal of Psychiatry, 163,* 488–493.

Asmundson, G. J. G., & Stein, M. B. (1994). Triggering the false suffocation alarm in panic disorder patients by using a voluntary breath-holding procedure. *American Journal of Psychiatry, 151,* 264–266.

Associated Press. (2006). Autistic hoops star going Hollywood. *MSNBC,* March 2. Retrieved December 30, 2006, from www.msnbc.msn.com/id/11526448/

Ataoglu, A., Ozcetin, A., Icmeli, C., & Ozbulut, O. (2003). Paradoxical therapy in conversion reaction. *Journal of Korean Medical Science, 18,* 581–584.

Atladóttir, H. O. (2007). Time trends in reported diagnoses of childhood neuropsychiatric disorders: A Danish cohort study. *Archives of Pediatric and Adolescent Medicine, 161,* 193–198.

Atlantis, E., & Sullivan, T. (2012). Bidirectional association between depression and sexual dysfunction: A systematic review and meta-analysis. *Journal of Sexual Medicine, 9*(6), 1497–1507.

Atri, A., Shaughnessy, L. W., Locascio, J. J., & Growdon, J. H. (2008). Long-term course and effectiveness of combination therapy in Alzheimer disease. *Alzheimer Disease & Associated Disorders, 22,* 209–221.

August, G. J., Bloomquist, M. L., Realmuto, G. M., & Hektner, J. M. (2007). The Early Risers "Skills for Success" Program: A targeted intervention for preventing conduct problems and substance abuse in aggressive elementary school children. In P. Tolan, J. Szapocznik, & S. Sambrano (Eds.), *Preventing youth substance abuse: Science-based programs for children and adolescents* (pp. 137–158). Washington, DC: American Psychological Association.

Aursnes, I., Tvete, I. F., Gaasemyr, J., & Natvig, B. (2005). Suicide attempts in clinical trials with paroxetine randomized against placebo. *BMC Medicine, 3,* 3–14.

Austin, A. M., Macgowan, M. J., & Wagner, E. F. (2005). Effective family-based interventions for adolescents with substance use problems: A systematic review. *Research on Social Work Practice, 15,* 67–83.

Auyeung, B., Baron-Cohen, S., Ashwin, E., Knickmeyer, R., Taylor, K., et al. (2009). Fetal testosterone predicts sexually differentiated childhood behavior in girls and in boys. *Psychological Science, 20,* 144–148.

Avery, D. H., Holtzheimer, P. E. III, Fawaz, W., Russo, J., Neumaier, J., et al. (2006). A controlled study of repetitive transcranial magnetic stimulation in medication-resistant major depression. *Biological Psychiatry, 59,* 187–194.

Ayalon, L., Gum, A., Feliciano, L., & Areán, P. A. (2006). Effectiveness of nonpharmacological interventions for the management of neuropsychiatric symptoms in patients with dementia: A systematic review. *Archives of Internal Medicine, 166,* 2182–2188.

Aziz, A. (2004). Sources of perceived stress among American medical doctors: A cross-cultural perspective. *Cross Cultural Management, 11,* 28–39.

Bacaltchuk, J., Hay, P., & Mari, J. J. (2000). Antidepressants versus placebo for the treatment of bulimia nervosa: A systematic review. *Australian and New Zealand Journal of Psychiatry, 34,* 310–317.

Bach, A. K., Brown, T. A., & Barlow, D. H. (1999). The effects of false negative feedback on efficacy expectancies and sexual arousal in sexually functional males. *Behavior Therapy, 30,* 79–95.

Baddeley, A. (1986). *Working memory.* New York: Clarendon Press/Oxford University Press.

Baden, A. L., & Wong, G. (2008). Assessment issues for working with diverse populations of elderly: Multiculturally sensitive perspectives. In L. A. Suzuki & J. G. Ponterotto (Eds.), *Handbook of multicultural assessment: Clinical, psychological, and educational applications* (pp. 594–623). San Francisco: Jossey-Bass.

Baer, J. C., & Martinez, C. D. (2006). Child maltreatment and insecure attachment: A meta-analysis. *Journal of Reproductive and Infant Psychology, 24,* 187–197.

Baghurst, T., Hollander, D. B., Nardella, B., & Haff, G. G. (2006). Change in sociocultural ideal male physique: An examination of past and present action figures. *Body Image, 3,* 87–91.

Bagøien, G., Bjørngaard, J. H., Østensen, C., Reitan, S. K., Romundstad, P., & Morken, G. (2013). The effects of motivational interviewing on patients with comorbid substance use admitted to a psychiatric emergency unit—A randomised controlled trial with two year follow-up. *BMC Psychiatry, 13,* Article ID 93.

Bailey, A., Le Couteur, A., Gottesman, I., & Bolton, P. (1995). Autism as a strongly genetic disorder: Evidence from a British twin study. *Psychological Medicine, 25,* 63–77.

Bailey, S. L. (1992). Adolescents' multisubstance use patterns: The role of heavy alcohol and cigarette use. *American Journal of Public Health, 82,* 1220–1224.

Baker, D., Earle, M., Medford, N., Sierra, M., Towell, A., & David, A. (2007). Illness perceptions in depersonalization disorder: Testing an illness attribution model. *Clinical Psychology & Psychotherapy, 14,* 105–116.

Baker, D., Hunter, E. C. M., Lawrence, E., Medford, N., Sierra, M., et al. (2003). Depersonalisation disorder: Clinical features of 204 cases. *British Journal of Psychiatry, 182,* 428–433.

Baker, J. R., Jatlow, P., & McCance-Katz, E. F. (2007). Disulfiram effects on responses to intravenous cocaine administration. *Drug and Alcohol Dependence, 87,* 202–209.

Baker, T. B., Brandon, T. H., & Chassin, L. (2004). Motivational influences on cigarette smoking. *Annual Review of Psychology, 55,* 463–491.

Balash, Y., Mordechovich, M., Shabtai, H., Giladi, N., Gurevich, T., & Korczyn, A. D. (2013). Subjective memory complaints in elders: Depression, anxiety, or cognitive decline? *ActaNeurologicaScandinavica, 127,* 344–350.

Baldwin, D. S., & Polkinghorn, C. (2005). Evidence-based pharmacotherapy of generalized anxiety disorder. *International Journal of Neuropsychopharmacology, 8,* 293–302.

Ball, J. R., Mitchell, P. B., Corry, J. C., Skillecorn, A., Smith, M., & Malhi, G. S. (2006). A randomized controlled trial of cognitive therapy for bipolar disorder: Focus on long-term change. *Journal of Clinical Psychiatry, 67,* 277–286.

Ball, S., Smolin, J., & Shekhar, A. (2002). A psychobiological approach to personality: Examination within anxious outpatients. *Journal of Psychiatric Research, 36,* 97–103.

Ballard, C., & Howard, R. (2006). Neuroleptic drugs in dementia benefits and harm. *Nature Reviews Neuroscience, 7,* 492–500.

Balon, R. (2008). The DSM criteria of sexual dysfunction: Need for a change. *Journal of Sex and Marital Therapy, 34,*186–197.

Balon, R., Segraves, R. T., Clayton, A. (2007). Issues for DSM-V: Sexual dysfunction, disorder, or variation along normal distribution: Toward rethinking DSM criteria of sexual dysfunctions. *American Journal of Psychiatry, 164,* 198–200.

Baltas, Z., & Steptoe, A. (2000). Migration, culture conflict and psychological well-being among Turkish-British married couples. *Ethnicity and Health, 5,* 173–180.

Bancroft, J. (1989). Man and his penis—a relationship under threat? *Journal of Psychology & Human Sexuality, 2,* 7–32.

Bancroft, J. (2002). The medicalization of female sexual dysfunction: The need for caution. *Archives of Sexual Behavior, 31,* 451–455.

Bandelow, B., Krause, J., Wedekind, D., Broocks, A., Hajak, G., & Rüther, E. (2005). Early traumatic life events, parental attitudes, family history, and birth risk factors in patients with borderline personality disorder and healthy controls. *Psychiatry Research, 134,* 169–179.

Bandini, S., Antonelli, G., Moretti, P., Pampanelli, S., Quartesan, R., & Perriello, G. (2006). Factors affecting dropout in outpatient eating disorder treatment. *Eating and Weight Disorders, 11,* 179–184.

Bandura, A. (1986). The explanatory and predictive scope of self-efficacy theory. *Journal of Social & Clinical Psychology, 4,* 359–373.

Bandura, A. (1997). *Self-efficacy: The exercise of control.* New York: W. H. Freeman/Times Books/Henry Holt & Co.

Bandura, A., Ross, D., & Ross, S. A. (1961). Transmission of aggression through imitation of aggressive models. *Journal of Abnormal and Social Psychology, 63,* 575–582.

Baranek, G. T. (1999). Autism during infancy: A retrospective video analysis of sensory-motor and social behaviors at 9–12 months of age. *Journal of Autism and Developmental Disorders, 29,* 213–224.

Baranowsky, A. B., Gentry, J. E., & Schultz, D. F. (2005). *Trauma practice: Tools for stabilization and recovery.* Ashland, OH: Hogrefe & Huber.

Barbaree, H. E. (2005). Psychopathy, treatment behavior, and recidivism: An extended follow-up of Seto and Barbaree. *Journal of Interpersonal Violence, 20,* 1115–1131.

Barbaresi, W. J., Colligan, R. C., Weaver, A. L., Voigt, R. G., Killian, J. M., & Katuic, S. K. (in press). Mortality, ADHD, social adversity in adults with childhood ADHD: A prospective study. *Pediatrics.*

Barbarich, N. C., McConaha, C. W., Halmi, K. A., Gendall, K., Sunday, S. R., et al. (2004). Use of nutritional supplements to increase the efficacy of fluoxetine in the treatment of anorexia nervosa. *International Journal of Eating Disorders, 35,* 10–15.

Barbee, J. G. (1998). Mixed symptoms and syndromes of anxiety and depression: Diagnostic, prognostic, and etiologic issues. *Annals of Clinical Psychiatry, 10,* 15–29.

Barber, C. (2008, February). The medicated Americans: Antidepressant prescriptions on the rise. *Scientific American.* Retrieved October 11, 2008, from www.sciam. com/article.cfm?id=the-medicated-americans

Barber, N. (1998). The slender ideal and eating disorders: An interdisciplinary "telescope" model. *International Journal of Eating Disorders, 23,* 295–307.

Barch, D. M. (2005). The cognitive neuroscience of schizophrenia. *Annual Review of Clinical Psychology, 1,* 321–353.

Barkham, M., & Shapiro, D. A. (1990). Brief psychotherapeutic interventions for job-related distress: A pilot study of prescriptive and explanatory therapy. *Counselling Psychology Quarterly, 3,* 133–147.

Barkley, R. A. (1997). *Defiant children: A clinician's manual for assessment and parent training* (2nd ed.). New York: Guilford Press.

Barkley, R. A. (2000). *Taking charge of ADHD: The complete authoritative guide for parents* (rev. ed.). New York: Guilford Press.

Barkley, R. A., Edwards, G., Laneri, M., Fletcher, K., & Metevia, L. (2001). Executive functioning, temporal discounting, and sense of time in adolescents with attention-deficit hyperactivity disorder (ADHD) and oppositional defiant disorder (ODD). *Journal of Abnormal Child Psychology, 29,* 541–556.

Barkley, R. A., Shelton, T. L., Crosswait, C., Moorehouse, M., Fletcher, K., et al. (2002). Preschool children with disruptive behavior: Three-year outcome as a function of adaptive disability. *Development and Psychopathology, 14,* 45–67.

Barlett, D. L., & Steele, J. B. (1979). *Howard Hughes: His life and madness.* New York: Norton.

Barlow, D. H. (1988). *Anxiety and its disorders: The nature and treatment of anxiety and panic.* New York: Guilford Press.

Barlow, D. H. (2002). *Anxiety and its disorders* (2nd ed.). New York: Guilford Press.

Barlow, D. H. (2002a). The experience of anxiety: Shadow of intelligence or specter of death? In D. H. Barlow (Ed.), *Anxiety and its disorders: The nature and treatment of anxiety and panic* (pp. 1–36). New York: Guilford Press.

Barlow, D. H. (2002b). True alarms, false alarms, and learned (conditioned) anxiety: The origins of panic and phobia. In D. H. Barlow (Ed.), *Anxiety and its disorders: The nature and treatment of anxiety and panic* (pp. 219–251). New York: Guilford Press.

Barlow, D. H. & Chorpita, B. F. (1998). The development of anxiety. *Psychological Bulletin, 124,* 3–21.

Barlow, D. H., Esler, J. L., & Vitali, A. E. (1998). Psychosocial treatments for panic disorders, phobias, and generalized anxiety disorder. In P. E. Nathan & J. M. Gorman (Eds.), *A guide to treatments that work* (pp. 288–318). New York: Oxford University Press.

Barnes, J. (2000a, March 25). Insanity defense fails for man who threw woman onto track. *The New York Times,* p. A1.

Barnes, J. (2000b, March 24). Subway killer to be treated in cell or in hospital, or both. *The New York Times,* p. B3.

Barnett, J. E., & Scheetz, K. (2003). Technological advances and telehealth: Ethics, law, and the practice of psychotherapy. *Psychotherapy: Theory, Research, Practice, Training, 40,* 86–93.

Baron-Cohen S., Leslie, A. M., & Frith, U. (1985). Does the autistic child have a "theory of mind"? *Cognition, 21,* 37–46.

Barraclough, B. M., & White, S. J. (1978a). Monthly variation of suicide and undetermined death compared. *British Journal of Psychiatry, 132,* 275–278.

Barraclough, B. M., & White, S. J. (1978b). Monthly variation of suicidal, accidental and undetermined poisoning deaths. *British Journal of Psychiatry, 132,* 279–282.

Barrett, P. M., Rapee, R. M., Dadds, M. R., & Ryan, S. M. (1996). Family enhancement of cognitive style in anxious and aggressive children. *Journal of Abnormal Child Psychology, 24,* 187–203.

Barrowclough, C., Haddock, G., Tarrier, N., Lewis, S. W., Moring, J., et al. (2001). Clinical outcome following neuroleptic discontinuation in patients with remitted recent-onset schizophrenia. *American Journal of Psychiatry, 158,* 1835–1842.

Barsky, A. J. (1992). Hypochondriasis and obsessive compulsive disorder. *Psychiatric Clinics of North America, 15*, 791–801.

Barsky, A. J., & Ahern, D. K. (2004). Cognitive behavior therapy for hypochondriasis: A randomized controlled trial. *JAMA: Journal of the American Medical Association, 291*, 1464–1470.

Barsky, A. J., Bailey, E. D., Fama, J. M., & Ahern, D. K. (2000). Predictors of remission in DSM hypochondriasis. *Comprehensive Psychiatry, 41*, 179–183.

Barsky, A. J., Cleary, P. D., Sarnie, M. K., & Klerman, G. L. (1993). The course of transient hypochondriasis. *American Journal of Psychiatry, 150*, 484–488.

Barsky, A. J., Cleary, P. D., Sarnie, M. K., & Ruskin, J. N. (1994). Panic disorder, palpitations, and the awareness of cardiac activity. *Journal of Nervous & Mental Disease, 182*, 63–71.

Barsky, A. J., Coeytaux, R. R., Sarnie, M. K., & Cleary, P. D. (1993). Hypochondriacal patients' beliefs about good health. *American Journal of Psychiatry 150*, 1085–1089.

Barsky, A. J., Orav, E. J., & Bates, D. W. (2005). Somatization increases medical utilization and costs independent of psychiatric and medical comorbidity. *Archives of General Psychiatry, 62*, 903–910.

Barsky, A. J., Wool, C., Barnett, M. C., & Cleary, P. D. (1994). Histories of childhood trauma in adult hypochondriacal patients. *American Journal of Psychiatry, 151*, 397–401.

Bartholomew, R. E. (1994). Disease, disorder, or deception? *Latah* as habit in a Malay extended family. *Journal of Nervous and Mental Disease, 182*, 331–338.

Bartholomew, R. E. (1998). The medicalization of exotic deviance: A sociological perspective on epidemic koro. *Transcultural Psychiatry, 35*, 5–38.

Bartoi, M. G., & Kinder, B. N. (1998). Effects of child and adult sexual abuse on adult sexuality. *Journal of Sex & Marital Therapy, 24*, 75–90.

Bartol, C. R., & Bartol, A. M. (2004). *Psychology and law: Theory, research, and application.* Belmont, CA: Thomson/Wadsworth.

Basic Behavioral Science Task Force of the National Advisory Mental Health Council. (1996). Basic behavioral science research for mental health, *American Psychologist, 51*, 722–731.

Bass, C., & Murphy, M. (1995). Somatoform and personality disorders: Syndromal comorbidity and overlapping developmental pathways. *Journal of Psychosomatic Research, 39*, 403–427.

Bass, C., Peveler, R., & House, A. (2001). Somatoform disorders: Severe psychiatric illnesses neglected by psychiatrists. *British Journal of Psychiatry, 179*, 11–14.

Basson, R. (2001). Using a different model for female sexual response to address women's problematic low sexual desire. *Journal of Sex & Marital Therapy, 27*, 395–403.

Basson, R. (2005). Women's sexual dysfunction: Revised and expanded definitions. *Canadian Medical Association Journal, 172*, 1327–1333.

Basson, R., Berman, J., Burnett, A., Derogatis, L., Ferguson, D., et al. (2001). Report of the International Consensus Development Conference on Female Sexual Dysfunction: Definitions and classifications. *Journal of Sex & Marital Therapy, 27*, 83–94.

Basson, R., Brotto, L. A., Laan, E., Redmond, G., & Utian, W. H. (2005). Assessment and management of women's sexual dysfunctions: Problematic desire and arousal. *Journal of Sexual Medicine, 2*, 291–300.

Basson, R., Leiblum, S., Brotto, L., Derogatis, L., Fourcroy, J., et al. (2004). Revised definitions of women's sexual dysfunction. *Journal of Sexual Medicine, 1*, 40–48.

Batelaan, N. M., Van Balkom, A. J. L. M., & Stein, D. J. (2012). Evidence-based pharmacotherapy of panic disorder: An update. *International Journal of Neuropsychopharmacology, 15*, 403–415.

Bateman, A. W., & Fonagy, P. (2004). *Psychotherapy for borderline personality disorder: Mentalization based treatment.* Oxford, England: Oxford University Press.

Bates, J. E., Bentler, P. M., & Thompson, S. K. (1973). Measurement of deviant gender development in boys. *Child Development, 44*, 591–598.

Bates, J. E., Bentler, P. M., & Thompson, S. K. (1979). Gender-deviant boys compared with normal and clinical control boys. *Journal of Abnormal Child Psychology, 7*, 243–259.

Battle, C. L., Shea, M. T., Johnson, D. M., Yen, S., Zlotnick, C., et al. (2004). Childhood maltreatment associated with adult personality disorders: Findings from the collaborative longitudinal personality disorders study. *Journal of Personality Disorders, 18*, 193–211.

Baucom, D. H., Shohan, V., Mueser, D. T., Daiuto, A. D., & Stickle, T. R. (1998). Empirically supported couple and family interventions for marital distress and adult mental health problems. *Journal of Consulting and Clinical Psychology, 66*, 53–88.

Baumeister, R. F., Bratslavsky, E., Muraven, M., & Tice, D. M. (1998). Ego depletion: Is the active self a limited resource? *Journal of Personality and Social Psychology, 74*, 1252–1265.

Baxter, L. R. (1992). Neuroimaging studies of obsessive compulsive disorder. *Psychiatric Clinics of North America, 15*, 871–884.

Baxter, L. R., Schwartz, J. M., Bergman, K. S., Szuba, M. P., Guze, B. H., et al. (1992). Caudate glucose metabolic rate changes with both drug and behavior therapy for obsessive-compulsive disorder. *Archives of General Psychiatry, 49*, 681–689.

Baxter, L. R., Schwartz, J. M., & Guze, B. H. (1991). Brain imaging: Toward a neuroanatomy of OCD. In J. Zohar, T. Insel, & S. Rasmussen (Eds.), *The psychobiology of obsessive-compulsive disorder.* New York: Springer.

Bean, N. M. (1992). Elucidating the path toward alcohol and substance abuse by adolescent victims of sexual abuse. *Journal of Applied Social Sciences, 17*, 57–94.

Beasley, C. M., Jr., Koke, S. C., Nilsson, M. E., & Gonzales, J. S. (2000). Adverse events and treatment discontinuations in clinical trials of fluoxetine in major depressive disorder: An updated meta-analysis. *Clinical Therapeutics: The International Journal of Drug Therapy, 22*, 1319–1330.

Beasley, C. M. Jr., Sutton, V. K., Taylor, C. C., Sethuraman, G., Dossenbach, M., & Naber, D. (2006). Is quality of life among minimally symptomatic patients with schizophrenia better following withdrawal or continuation of antipsychotic treatment? *Journal of Clinical Psychopharmacology, 26*, 40–44.

Beatty, M. J., Heisel, A. D., Hall, A. E., Levine, T. R., & La France, B. H. (2002). What can we learn from the study of twins about genetic and environmental influences on interpersonal affiliation, aggressiveness, and social anxiety? A meta-analytic study. *Communication Monographs, 69*, 1–18.

Beck, A., & Emery, G. (1985). *Anxiety disorders and phobias.* New York: Basic Books.

Beck, A. T. (1967). *Depression: Causes and treatment.* Philadelphia: University of Pennsylvania Press.

Beck, A. T. (1976). *Cognitive therapy and the emotional disorders.* Oxford, England: International Universities Press.

Beck, A. T. (1999, February). *From the president's corner: New research in cognitive therapy.* Bala Cynwyd, PA: Beck Institute for Cognitive Therapy and Research.

Beck, A. T. (2003). From the President: Synopsis of the Cognitive Model of Borderline Personality Disorder. The Beck Institute. Retrieved October 6th, 2009, from www.beckinstitute.org/ InfoID/56/RedirectPath/Add1/FolderID/165/ SessionID/{018DB423-1F38-4EBC-9156- 03D1A34B14E8}/InfoGroup/Main/InfoType/ Article/PageVars/Library/InfoManage/Zoom.htm

Beck, A. T. (2005). The current state of cognitive therapy: A 40-year retrospective. *Archives of General Psychiatry, 62*, 953–959.

Beck, A. T., Brown, G., Berchick, R. J., Stewart, B. L., & Steer, R. A. (1990). Relationship between hopelessness and ultimate suicide: A replication with psychiatric outpatients. *American Journal of Psychiatry, 147*, 190–195.

Beck, A. T., Butler, A. C., Brown, G. K., Dahlsgaard, K. K., Newman, C. F., & Beck, J. S. (2001). Dysfunctional beliefs discriminate personality disorders. *Behaviour Research and Therapy, 39*, 1213–1225.

Beck, A. T., Emery, G., & Greenberg, R. L. (2005). *Anxiety disorders and phobias: A cognitive perspective.* New York: Basic Books.

Beck, A. T., Freeman, A., & Davis, D. D. (2004). *Cognitive therapy of personality disorders* (2nd ed.). New York: Guilford Press.

Beck, A. T., & Rector, N. A. (2005). Cognitive approaches to schizophrenia: Theory and therapy. *Annual Review of Clinical Psychology, 1*, 577–606.

Beck, A. T., Rush, A. J., Shaw, B. F., & Emery, G. (1979). *Cognitive therapy of depression: A treatment manual.* New York: Guilford Press.

Beck, A. T., Steer, R. A., & Brown, G. K. (1996). *BDI–II: Beck Depression Inventory Manual*, (2nd ed.). San Antonio, TX: The Psychological Corporation.

Beck, A. T., Steer, R. A., Kovacs, M., & Garrison, B. (1985). Hopelessness and eventual suicide: A 10-year prospective study of patients hospitalized with suicidal ideation. *American Journal of Psychiatry, 142*, 559–563.

Beck, D., Casper, R., & Anderson, A. (1996). Truly late onset of eating disorders: A study of 11 cases averaging 60 years of age at presentation. *International Journal of Eating Disorders, 20*, 389–395.

Beck, J. G. (1995). Hypoactive sexual desire disorder: An overview. *Journal of Consulting and Clinical Psychology, 63*, 919–927.

Beck, J. G., Ohtake, P. J., & Shipherd, J. C. (1999). Exaggerated anxiety is not unique to CO_2 in panic disorder: A comparison of hypercapnic and hypoxic challenges. *Journal of Abnormal Psychology, 108*, 473–482.

Becker, A., & Hamburg, P. (1996). Culture, the media, and eating disorders. *Cross-Cultural Psychiatry, 4*, 163–167.

Becker, A. E. (1994). Nurturing and negligence: Working on others' bodies in Fiji. In T. J. Csordas (Ed.), *Embodiment and experience: The existential ground of culture and self* (pp. 100–115). New York: Cambridge University Press.

Becker, A. E., Burwell, R. A., Herzog, D. B., Hamburg, P., & Gilman, S. E. (2002). Eating behaviours and attitudes following prolonged exposure to television among ethnic Fijian adolescent girls. *British Journal of Psychiatry, 180*, 509–514.

Becker, D., & Lamb, S. (1994). Sex bias in the diagnosis of borderline personality disorder and posttraumatic stress disorder. *Professional Psychology: Research and Practice, 25*, 55–61.

Becker, J. V. (1989). Impact of sexual abuse on sexual functioning. In S. R. Leiblum & R. C. Rosen (Eds.), *Principles and practice of sex therapy: Update for the 1990s* (2nd ed., pp. 298–318). New York: Guilford Press.

Becker, J. V., & Kaplan, M. S. (1991). Rape victims: Issues, theories, and treatment. *Annual Review of Sex Research, 2*, 267–292.

Becoña, E., Martínez, Ú., Calafat, A., Juan, M., Fernández-Hermida, J. R., & Secades-Villa, R. (2012). Parental styles and drug use: A review. *Drugs: Education, Prevention & Policy, 19*(1), 1–10.

Beech, A., & Ford, H. (2006). The relationship between risk, deviance, treatment outcome and sexual reconviction in a sample of child sexual abusers completing residential treatment for their offending. *Psychology, Crime & Law, 12*, 685–701.

Beer, J. S., John, O. P., Scabini, D., & Knight, R. T. (2006). Orbitofrontal cortex and social behavior: I integrating self-monitoring and emotion-cognition interactions. *Journal of Cognitive Neuroscience, 18*(6), 871–879.

Bell, C. J., & Nutt, D. J. (1998). Serotonin and panic. *British Journal of Psychiatry, 172*, 465–471.

Bellgrove, M. A., Chambers, C. D., Vance, A., Hall, N., Karamitsios, M., & Bradshaw, J. L. (2006). Lateralized deficit of response inhibition in early-onset schizophrenia. *Psychological Medicine, 36*, 495–505.

Bellgrove, M. A., Hawi, Z., Lowe, N., Kirley, A., Robertson, I. H., & Gill, H. (2005). DRD4 gene variants and sustained attention in attention deficit hyperactivity disorder (ADHD): Effects of associated alleles at the VNTR and -521 SNP. *American Journal of Medical Genetics: Part B Neuropsychiatry Genetics, 136*, 81–86.

Bender, D. S. (2005). Therapeutic alliance. In J. M. Oldham, A. E. Skodol, & D. S. Bender (Eds.), *The American Psychiatric Publishing textbook of personality disorders* (pp. 405–420). Washington, DC: American Psychiatric Publishing.

Bender, L. (1963). *Bender visual motor Gestalt test*. New York: American Orthopsychiatric Corporation.

Benedetti, F. (2009). *Understanding the mechanisms in health and disease*. New York: Oxford University Press.

Benedetti, F. (2010). Conscious and unconscious placebo responses: How the ritual of the therapeutic act changes the patient's brain. In E. Perry, D. Collerton, F. LeBeau, & H. Ashton (Eds.), *Advances in consciousness research: New horizons in the neuroscience of consciousness* (pp. 259–268). Amsterdam: John Benjamins.

Benes, F. M. (2000). Emerging principles in panic disorder: A comparison of altered neural circuitry in schizophrenia. *Brain Research Reviews, 31*, 251–269.

Benony, H., Van Der Elst, D., Chahraoui, K., Benony, C., & Marnier, J. P. (2007). Link between depression and academic self-esteem in gifted children. *Encephale, 33*, 11–20.

Benton, A. L., Hamsher, N. R., Varney, N. R., & Spreen, O. (1983). *Contributions to neuropsychological assessment*. Oxford, UK: Oxford University Press.

Ben-Tovim, D. I. (2003). Eating disorders: Outcome, prevention and treatment of eating disorders. *Current Opinion in Psychiatry, 16*, 65–69.

Ben-Zeev, D., Young, M. A., & Corrigan, P. W. (2010). DSM-V and the stigma of mental illness. *Journal of Mental Health, 19*, 318–327.

Berenbaum, H., Thompson, R. J., Milanek, M. E., Boden, M. T., & Bredemeier, K. (2008). Psychological trauma and schizotypal personality disorder. *Journal of Abnormal Psychology, 117*, 502–519.

Berman, J., & Berman, L. (with Bumiller, E.). (2001). *For women only: A revolutionary guide to reclaiming your sex life*. New York: Holt.

Berman, L. A., Berman, J. R., Bruck, D., Pawar, R. V., & Goldstein, I. (2001). Pharmacotherapy or psychotherapy? Effective treatment for FSD related to unresolved childhood sexual abuse. *Journal of Sex & Marital Therapy, 27*, 421–425.

Bernal, G., & Scharró-del-Río, M. R. (2001). Are empirically supported treatments valid for ethnic minorities? Toward an alternative approach for treatment research. *Cultural Diversity and Ethnic Minority Psychology, 7*, 328–342.

Bernstein, J. (2006). *10 days to a less defiant child: The breakthrough program for overcoming your child's difficult behavior*. Cambridge, MA: Da Capo Press.

Berthier, M. L., Kulisevsky, J., Gironell, A., & López, O. L. (2001). Obsessive-compulsive disorder and traumatic brain injury: Behavioral, cognitive, and neuroimaging findings. *Neuropsychiatry, Neuropsychology, & Behavioral Neurology, 14*, 23–31.

Beutler, L. E. (2000). David and Goliath: When empirical and clinical standards of practice meet. *American Psychologist, 55*, 997–1007.

Beutler, L. E. (2002). The dodo bird is extinct. *Clinical Psychology: Science and Practice, 9*, 30–34.

Beutler, L. E., & Harwood, T. M. (2002). What is and can be attributed to the therapeutic relationship?. *Journal of Contemporary Psychotherapy, 32*, 25–33.

Beutler, L. E., Harwood, T. M., Alimohamed, S. & Malik, M. (2002). Functional impairment and coping style: Patient moderators of therapeutic relationships. In J. N. Norcross (Ed.), *Empirically supported therapeutic relationships* (pp. 145–170). New York: Oxford University Press.

Beutler, L. E. & Karno, M. (1999). Psychotherapy research: Basic or applied? *Journal of Clinical Psychology, 55*, 171–180.

Beutler, L. E., Machado, P. P. P., & Neufeldt, S. A. (1994). Therapist variables. In A. E. Bergin & S. L. Garfield (Eds.), *Handbook of psychotherapy and behavior change* (4th ed., pp. 229–269). Oxford, England: John Wiley & Sons.

Beutler, L. E., & Malik, M. L. (2002). *Rethinking the DSM: A psychological perspective*. Washington, DC: American Psychological Association.

Bhatia, T., Thomas, P., Semwal, P., Thelma, B. K., Nimgaonkar, V. L., & Deshpande, S. N. (2006). Differing correlates for suicide attempts among patients with schizophrenia or schizoaffective disorder in India and USA. *Schizophrenia Research, 86*, 208–214.

Bhugra, D., & Ayondrinde, O. (2001). Racism, racial life events and mental ill health. *Advances in Psychiatric Treatment, 7*, 343–349.

Bhui, K., Stansfeld, S., McKenzie, K., Karlsen, S., Nazroo, J., & Weich, S. (2005). Racial/ethnic discrimination and common mental disorders among workers: Findings from the EMPIRIC Study of Ethnic Minority Groups in the United Kingdom. *American Journal of Public Health, 95*, 496–501.

Bibb, J. L., & Chambless, D. L. (1986). Alcohol use and abuse among diagnosed agoraphobics. *Behaviour Research and Therapy, 24*, 49–58.

Bickel, W. K., & Marsch, L. A. (2001). Toward a behavioral economic understanding of drug dependence: Delay discounting processes. *Addiction, 96*, 73–86.

Bieberich, A. A., & Morgan, S. B. (1998). Affective expression in children with autism or Down syndrome. *Journal of Autism and Developmental Disorders, 28*, 333–338.

Bieberich, A. A., & Morgan, S. B. (2004). Self-regulation and affective expression during play in children with autism or Down syndrome: A short-term longitudinal study. *Journal of Autism and Developmental Disorders, 34,* 439–448.

Biederman, J., Faraone, S. V., Milberger, S., Jetton, J. G., Chen, L., et al. (1996). Is childhood oppositional defiant disorder a precursor to adolescent conduct disorder? Findings from a four-year follow-up study of children with ADHD. *Journal of the American Academy of Child & Adolescent Psychiatry, 35,* 1193–1204.

Biederman, J., Hirshfeld-Becker, D. R., Rosenbaum, J. F., Hérot, C., Friedman, D., et al. (2001). Further evidence of association between behavioral inhibition and social anxiety in children. *American Journal of Psychiatry, 158,* 1673–1679.

Biederman, J., Kwon, A., Aleardi, M., Chouinard, V., Marino, T., et al. (2005). Absence of gender effects on attention-deficit hyperactivity disorder: Findings in nonreferred subjects. *American Journal of Psychiatry, 162,* 1083–1089.

Biederman, J., Mick, E., & Faraone, S. V. (2000). Age-dependent decline of symptoms of attention-deficit hyperactivity disorder: Impact of remission definition and symptom type. *American Journal of Psychiatry, 157,* 816–818.

Biederman, J., Petty, C., Faraone, S. V., Hirshfeld-Becker, D. R., Henin, A., et al. (2005). Patterns of comorbidity in panic disorder and major depression: Findings from a nonreferred sample. *Depression and Anxiety, 21,* 55–60.

Bielau, H., Mawrin, C., Krell, D., Agelink, M. W., Trübner, K., et al. (2005). Differences in activation of the dorsal raphé nucleus depending on performance of suicide. *Brain Research, 1039,* 43–52.

Bienvenu, O. J., Hettema, J. M., Neale, M. C., Prescott, C. A., & Kendler, K. S. (2007). Low extraversion and high neuroticism as indices of genetic and environmental risk for social phobia, agoraphobia, and animal phobia. *American Journal of Psychiatry, 164,* 1714–1721.

Bienvenu, O. J., Nestadt, G., Samuels, J. F., Costa, P. T., Howard, W. T., & Eaton, W. W. (2001). Phobic, panic, and major depressive disorders and the five-factor model of personality. *Journal of Nervous and Mental Disease, 189,* 154–161.

Bienvenu, O. J., Onyike, C. U., Stein, M. B., Chen, L. S., Samuels, J., et al. (2006). Agoraphobia in adults: Incidence and longitudinal relationship with panic. *British Journal of Psychiatry, 188,* 432–438.

Bienvenu, O. J., Samuels, J. F., Riddle, M. A., Hoehn-Saric, R., Liang, K. Y., et al. (2000). The relationship of obsessive-compulsive disorder to possible spectrum disorders: Results from a family study. *Biological Psychiatry, 48,* 287–293.

Bierer, L. M., Yehuda, R., Schmeidler, J., Mitropoulou, V., New, A. S., et al. (2003). Abuse and neglect in childhood: Relationship to personality disorder diagnoses. *CNS Spectrums, 8,* 737–740, 749–754.

Bifulco, A., Moran, P. M., Ball, C., & Bernazzani, O. (2002). Adult attachment style.1: Its relation to clinical depression. *Social Psychiatry & Psychiatric Epidemiology, 37,* 50–59.

Bilefsky, D. (2009, March 11). Europeans debate castration of sex offenders. *The New York Times.* Retrieved April 17, 2013, from http://nytimes.com

Bilich, L. L., Deane, F. P., Phipps, A. B., Barisic, M., & Gould, G. (2008). Effectiveness of bibliotherapy self-help for depression with varying levels of telephone helpline support. *Clinical Psychology & Psychotherapy, 15,* 61–74.

Bilukha, O. O., & Utermohlen, V. (2002). Internalization of Western standards of appearance, body dissatisfaction and dieting in urban educated Ukrainian females. *European Eating Disorders Review, 10,* 120–137.

Binik, Y. M. (2005). Should dyspareunia be retained as a sexual dysfunction in DSM-V? A painful classification decision. *Archives of Sexual Behavior, 34,* 11–21.

Binik, Y. M., Reissing, E., Pukall, C., Flory, N., Payne, K. A., & Khalifé, S. (2002). The female sexual pain disorders: Genital pain or sexual dysfunction? *Archives of Sexual Behavior, 31,* 425–429.

Binks, C. A., Fenton, M., McCarthy, L., Lee, T., Adams, C. E., & Duggan, C. (2006a). Pharmacological interventions for people with borderline personality disorder. *Cochrane Database of Systematic Reviews, 25*(1): CD005653.

Binks, C. A., Fenton, M., McCarthy, L., Lee, T., Adams, C. E., & Duggan, C. (2006b). Psychological therapies for people with borderline personality disorder. *Cochrane Database of Systematic Reviews, 25*(1): CD005652.

Birchall, H. (1999). Interpersonal psychotherapy in the treatment of eating disorders. *European Eating Disorders Review, 7,* 315–320.

Bird, H. R. (2002). The diagnostic classification, epidemiology, and cross-cultural validity of ADHD. In P. S. Jensen & J. R. Cooper (Eds.), *Attention deficit hyperactivity disorder: State of the science—Best practices* (pp. 2-1–2-16). Kingston, NJ: Civic Research Institute.

Bird, T. D., Levy-Lahad, E., Poorkaj, P., Sharma, V., Nemens, E., et al. (1996). Wide range in age of onset for chromosome 1–related familial Alzheimer's disease. *Annals of Neurology, 40,* 932–936.

Bissell, K., & Zhou, P. (2004). Must-see TV or ESPN: Entertainment and sports media exposure and body-image distortion in college women. *Journal of Communication, 54,* 5–21.

Bjornsson, A. S., Didie, E. R., Grant, J. E., Menard, W., Stalker, E., & Phillips, K. A. (In press). Age at onset and clinical correlates in body dysmorphic disorder. *Comprehensive Psychiatry.* Advance online publication.

Black, D. W. (2001). Antisocial personality disorder: The forgotten patients of psychiatry. *Primary Psychiatry, 8,* 30–81.

Black, D. W., Noyes, R., Goldstein, R. B., & Blum, N. (1992). A family study of obsessive-compulsive disorder. *Archives of General Psychiatry, 49,* 362–368.

Black, M. C., Basile, K. C., Breiding, M. J., Smith, S. G., Walter, M. L., et al. (2011). The National Intimate Partner and Sexual Violence Survey (NISVS): 2010 Summary Report. Atlanta, GA: National Center for Injury Prevention and Control, Centers for Disease Control and Prevention. Access on January 7, 2012, from www.cdc.gov/ViolencePrevention/pdf/NISVS_Executive_Summary-a.pdf

Blackburn, S., Johnston, L., Blampied, N., Popp, D., & Kallen, R. (2006). An application of escape theory to binge eating. *European Eating Disorders Review, 14,* 23–31.

Blair, N. A., Yue, S. K., Singh, R., & Bernhardt, J. M. (2005). Depiction of substance use in reality television: A content analysis of *The Osbournes. British Medical Journal, 331,* 1517–1519.

Blair, R. J. R., Colledge, E., Murray, L. K., & Mitchell, D. G. V. (2001). Selective impairment in the processing of sad and fearful expressions by children with psychopathic tendencies. *Journal of Abnormal Child Psychology, 29,* 491–498.

Blais, M. A., Hilsenroth, M. J., & Fowler, J. C. (1999). Diagnostic efficiency and hierarchical functioning of the DSM-IV borderline personality disorder criteria. *Journal of Nervous and Mental Disease, 187,* 167–173.

Blais, M. A., McCann, J. T., Benedict, K. B., & Norman, D. K. (1997). Toward an empirical/theoretical grouping of the DSM-III-R personality disorders. *Journal of Personality Disorders, 11,* 191–198.

Blais, M. A., & Norman, D. K. (1997). A psychometric evaluation of the DSM-IV personality disorder criteria. *Journal of Personality Disorders, 11,* 168–176.

Blanchard, E. B. (2000). Biofeedback. In A. E. Kazdin (Ed.), *Encyclopedia of psychology* (Vol. 1, pp. 417–420). Washington, DC: American Psychological Association.

Blanchard, E. B., Kuhn, E., Rowell, D. L., Hickling, E. J., Wittrock, D., et al. (2004). Studies of the vicarious traumatization of college students by the September 11th attacks: Effects of proximity, exposure and connectedness. *Behaviour Research and Therapy, 42,* 191–205.

Blanchard, E. B., Lackner, J. M., Gusmano, R., Gudleski, G. D., Sanders, K., et al. (2006). Prediction of treatment outcome among patients with irritable bowel syndrome treated with group cognitive therapy. *Behaviour Research and Therapy, 44,* 317–337.

Blanchard, J. J., Horan, W. P., & Collins, L. M. (2005). Examining the latent structure of negative symptoms: Is there a distinct subtype of negative symptom schizophrenia? *Schizophrenia Research, 77,* 151–165.

Blanchard, R. (1989). The classification and labeling of nonhomosexual gender dysphorias. *Archives of Sexual Behavior, 18,* 315–334.

Blanchard, R. (1990). Gender identity disorders in adult men. In R. Blanchard & B. W. Steiner (Eds.), *Clinical management of gender identity disorders in children and adults* (pp. 47–76). Washington, DC: American Psychiatric Press.

Blaney, P. H. (1986). Affect and memory: A review. *Psychological Bulletin, 99,* 229–246.

Blatt, S. J., Sanislow, C. A., Zuroff, D. C., & Pilkonis, P. A. (1996). Characteristics of effective therapists: Further analyses of data from the National Institute of Mental Health Treatment of Depression Collaborative Research Program. *Journal of Consulting and Clinical Psychology, 64,* 1276–1284.

Blazer, D. G., Hybels, C. F., Simonsick, E. M., & Hanlon, J. T. (2000). Marked differences in antidepressant use by race in an elderly community sample: 1986–1996. *American Journal of Psychiatry, 157,* 1089–1094.

Blazer, D. G., Landerman, L. R., Hays, J. C., Simonsick, E. M., & Saunders, W. B. (1998). Symptoms of depression among community-dwelling elderly African-American adults. *Psychological Medicine, 28,* 1311–1320.

Bleiberg, K. L., & Markowitz, J. C. (2005). A pilot study of interpersonal psychotherapy for posttraumatic stress disorder. *American Journal of Psychiatry, 162,* 181–183.

Blinder, B. J., Cumella, E. J., & Sanathara, V. A. (2006). Psychiatric comorbidities of female inpatients with eating disorders. *Psychosomatic Medicine, 68,* 454–462.

Bliss, E. L. (1984). Spontaneous self-hypnosis in multiple personality disorder. *Psychiatric Clinics of North America, 7,* 135–148.

Block, J. J. (2008). Issues for DSM-V: Internet addiction. *American Journal of Psychiatry, 165,* 306–307.

Bloom, B. L. (1997). *Planned short-term psychotherapy: A clinical handbook* (2nd ed.). Boston: Allyn & Bacon.

Bloom, J. W. (1998). The ethical practice of Web counseling. *British Journal of Guidance & Counselling, 26,* 53–59.

Blum, K., Noble, E. P., Sheridan, P. J., Montgomery, A., Ritchie, T., et al. (1990). Allelic association of human dopamine D2 receptor gene in alcoholism. *Journal of the American Medical Association, 263,* 2055–2060.

Blumberg S. J., Bramlett, M. D., Kagan, M. D., Schieve, L. A., Jones, J. R., & Lu, M. C. (2013). Changes in prevalence of parent-reported autism spectrum disorder in school-aged U.S. children: 2007 to 2011–2012. *National Health Statistics Report, 65,* 1–12.

Bock, M. A. (2007). The impact of social-behavioral learning strategy training on the social interaction skills of four students with Asperger syndrome. *Focus on Autism and Other Developmental Disabilities, 22,* 88–95.

Boddy, J. (1992). Comment on the proposed DSM-IV criteria for trance and possession disorder. *Transcultural Psychiatric Research Review, 29,* 323–330.

Bodkin, J. A., Pope, H. G., Detke, M. J., & Hudson, J. I. (2007). Is PTSD caused by traumatic stress? *Journal of Anxiety Disorders, 21,* 176–182.

Bodlund, O., & Kullgren, G. (1996). Transsexualism—general outcome and prognostic factors: A five-year follow-up study of nineteen transsexuals in the process of changing sex. *Archives of Sexual Behavior, 25,* 303–316.

Bohart, A. C., & Tallman, K. (2010). Clients: The neglected common factor in psychotherapy. In B. L. Duncan, S. D. Miller, B. E. Wampold, & M. A. Hubble (Eds.), *The heart and soul of change: Delivering what works in therapy* (2nd ed.) (pp. 83–111). Washington DC: American Psychological Association.

Bohus, M., Haaf, B., Simms, T., Limberger, M. F., Schmahl, C., et al. (2004). Effectiveness of inpatient dialectical behavioral therapy for borderline personality disorder: A controlled trial. *Behaviour Research and Therapy, 42,* 487–499.

Bohus, M., Haaf, B., Stiglmayr, C., Pohl, U., Böhme, R., & Linehan, M. (2000). Evaluation of inpatient dialectical-behavioral therapy for borderline personality disorder—a prospective study. *Behaviour Research and Therapy, 38,* 875–887.

Boldrini, M., Underwood, M. D., Mann, J. J., & Arango, V. (2005). More tryptophan hydroxylase in the brainstem dorsal raphé nucleus in depressed suicides. *Brain Research, 1041,* 19–28.

Bölte, S., & Poustka, F. (2003). The recognition of facial affect in autistic and schizophrenic subjects and their first-degree relatives. *Psychological Medicine, 33,* 907–915.

Bolton, P., Bass, J., Neugebauer, R., Verdeli, H., Clougherty, K. F., et al. (2003). Group interpersonal psychotherapy for depression in rural Uganda: A randomized controlled trial. *JAMA: Journal of the American Medical Association, 289,* 3117–3124.

Bondy, A. S., & Frost, L. A. (1994). The Picture Exchange Communication System. *Focus on Autism and Other Developmental Disabilities, 9*(3), 1–19.

Booij, L., & Van der Does, A. J. W. (2007). Cognitive and serotonergic vulnerability to depression: Convergent findings. *Journal of Abnormal Psychology, 116,* 86–94.

Borch-Jacobsen, M. (1997), "Sybil: The making of a disease: An interview with Dr. Herbert Spiegel," *The New York Review,* April 27, 1997, p. 60.

Bordo, S. (1993). *Unbearable weight: Feminism, Western culture, and the body.* Berkeley: University of California Press.

Borkovec, T. D. (1994). The nature, functions, and origins of worry. In G. C. L. Davey & F. Tallis (Eds.), *Worrying: Perspectives on theory, assessment and treatment.* (pp. 5–33). Oxford, England: John Wiley & Sons.

Borkovec, T. D., & Castonguay, L. G. (1998). What is the scientific meaning of empirically supported therapy? *Journal of Consulting and Clinical Psychology, 66,* 136–142.

Borkovec, T. D., Hazlett-Stevens, J., & Diaz, M. L. (1999). The role of positive beliefs about worry in generalized anxiety disorder and its treatment. *Clinical Psychology and Psychotherapy, 6,* 126–138.

Borkovec, T. D., & Hu, S. (1990). The effect of worry on cardiovascular response to phobic imagery. *Behaviour Research and Therapy, 28,* 69–73.

Borkovec, T. D., & Miranda, J. (1999). Between-group psychotherapy outcome research and basic science. *Journal of Clinical Psychology, 55,* 147–158.

Borkovec, T. D., & Ruscio, A. M. (2001). Psychotherapy for generalized anxiety disorder. *Journal of Clinical Psychiatry, 62* (Suppl. 11), 37–42.

Bourgeois, J. A., Chang, C. H., Hilty, D. M., & Servis, M. E. (2002). Clinical manifestations and management of conversion disorders. *Current Treatment Options in Neurology, 4,* 487–497.

Bourguignon, E. (2004). Suffering and healing, subordination and power: Women and possession trance. *Ethos, 32,* 557–574.

Bouton, M. E., Mineka, S., & Barlow, D. H. (2001). A modern learning theory perspective on the etiology of panic disorder. *Psychological Review, 108,* 4–32.

Bowen, M. (1978). *Family therapy in clinical practice* (2nd ed.). Northvale, NJ: Jason Aronson.

Bower, G. H., & Forgas, J. P. (2000). Affect, memory, and social cognition. In E. Eich, J. F. Kihlstrom, G. H. Bower, J. P. Forgas, & P. M. Niedenthal (Eds.), *Cognition and emotion* (pp. 87–168). New York: Oxford University Press.

Bowers, M., Jr., Boutros, N., D'Souza, D. C., & Madonick, S. (2001). Substance abuse as a risk factor for schizophrenia and related disorders. *International Journal of Mental Health, 30,* 33–57.

Bowers, W. A., & Ansher, L. S. (2008). The effectiveness of cognitive behavioral therapy on changing eating disorder symptoms and psychopathy of 32 anorexia nervosa patients at hospital discharge and one year follow-up. *Annals of Clinical Psychiatry, 20,* 79–86.

Bowlby, J. (1969). *Attachment and loss: Vol. 1. Attachment.* New York: Basic Books.

Bowlby, J. (1973). *Attachment and loss: Vol. 2, Separation.* New York: Basic Books.

Bowlby, J. (1979). *The making and breaking of affectional bonds.* London: Tavistock.

Bowman, E. S. (1993). Etiology and clinical course of pseudoseizures: Relationship to trauma, depression, and dissociation. *Psychosomatics: Journal of Consultation and Liaison Psychiatry, 34,* 333–342.

Bowman, E. S., & Nurnberger, J. I. (1993). Genetics of psychiatry diagnosis and treatment. In D. L. Dunner (Ed.), *Current psychiatric therapy* (pp. 46–56). Philadelphia: Saunders.

Bowman, M. L. (1999). Individual differences in posttraumatic distress: Problems with the DSM-IV model. *The Canadian Journal of Psychiatry / La Revue canadienne de psychiatrie, 44,* 21–33.

Boyd, J. D. (1997). Clinical hypnosis for rapid recovery from dissociative identity disorder. *American Journal of Clinical Hypnosis, 40,* 97–110.

Boylan, J. F. (2003). *She's not there: A life in two genders.* New York: Broadway Books.

Boyle, C. A., Boulet, S., Schieve, L. A., Cohen, R. A., Blumberg, S. J., et al. (2011). Trends in the prevalence of developmental disabilities in US children, 1997–2008. *Pediatrics, 127*(6), 1034–1042.

Boyle, M. (2000). Kraepelin, Emil. In A. E. Kazdin (Ed.), *Encyclopedia of psychology* (Vol. 4, pp. 458–460). Washington, DC: American Psychological Association.

Boysen, G. A. (2011). The scientific status of childhood dissociative identity disorder: A review of published research. *Psychotherapy and Psychosomatics, 80*(6), 329–334.

Boysen, G. A., & VanBergen, A. (2013). A review of published research on adult dissociative identity disorder: 2000–2010. *Journal of Nervous and Mental Disease, 201*(1), 5–11.

Bradfield, J. W. B. (2006). A pathologist's perspective of the somatoform disorders. *Journal of Psychosomatic Research, 60,* 327–330.

Bradford, J. M. (2001). The neurobiology, neuropharmacology, and pharmacological treatment of the paraphilias and compulsive sexual behaviour. *Canadian Journal of Psychiatry, 46,* 24–25.

Bradford, J. M. W. (2000). The treatment of sexual deviation using a pharmacological approach. *Journal of Sex Research, 37,* 248–257.

Bradley, R., Greene, J., Russ, E., Dutra, L., & Westen, D. (2005). A multidimensional meta-analysis of psychotherapy for PTSD. *American Journal of Psychiatry, 162,* 214–227.

Bradley, S. J., & Zucker, K. J. (1997). Gender identity disorder: A review of the past 10 years. *Journal of the American Academy of Child & Adolescent Psychiatry, 36,* 872–880.

Brady v. Hopper, 570 F. Supp. 1333 (D. Colo. 1983).

Brady, K. (2005). *New pharmacological approaches to addiction.* Medscape. Retrieved February 15, 2006, from www.medscape.com/viewarticle/507191

Brady, K., Pearlstein, T., Asnis, G. M., Baker, D., Rothbaum, B., et al. (2000). Efficacy and safety of sertraline treatment of posttraumatic stress disorder: A randomized controlled trial. *JAMA: Journal of the American Medical Association, 283,* 1837–1844.

Brady, K., & Sinha, R. (2005). Co-occurring mental and substance use disorders: The neurobiological effects of chronic stress. *American Journal of Psychiatry, 162,* 1483–1493.

Brady, K. T., Sonne, E., Randall, C.L., Adinoff, B., & Malcolm, R. (1995). Features of cocaine dependence with concurrent alcohol abuse. *Drug and Alcohol Dependence, 39,* 69–71.

Brambilla, P., Cipriani, A., Hotopf, M., & Barbui, C. (2005). Side-effect profile of fluoxetine in comparison with other SSRIs, tricyclic and newer antidepressants: A meta-analysis of clinical trial data. *Pharmacopsychiatry, 38,* 69–77.

Brannigan, G. G., & Decker, S. L. (2003). *Bender visual-motor Gestalt test* (2nd ed.). Itasca, IL: Riverside Publishing.

Brannigan, G. G., & Decker, S. L. (2006). The Bender-Gestalt II. *American Journal of Orthopsychiatry, 76,* 10–12.

Braun, J., Kahn, R. S., Froehlich, T., Auinger, P., & Lanphear, B. P. (2006). Exposures to environmental toxicants and attention deficit hyperactivity disorder in US children. *Environmental Health Perspectives, 114,* 1904–1909.

Brauser, D. (2012). DSM-5 field trials generate mixed results. *Medscape,* May 8. Retrieved May 21, 2013, from www.medscape.com/viewarticle/763519

Breiter, H. C., Rauch, S. L., Kwong, K. K., Baker, J. R., Weisskoff, R. M., et al. (1996). Functional magnetic resonance imaging of symptom provocation in obsessive-compulsive disorder. *Archives of General Psychiatry, 53,* 595–606.

Breiter, H. C., & Rosen, B. R. (1999). Functional magnetic resonance imaging of brain reward circuitry in the human. In J. F. McGinty (Ed.), *Advancing from the ventral striatum to the extended amygdala: Implications for neuropsychiatry and drug use: In honor of Lennart Heimer* (pp. 523–547). New York: New York Academy of Sciences.

Bremner, J. D. (2010). Cognitive processes in dissociation: Comment on Giesbrecht et al. (2008). *Psychological Bulletin, 136*(1), 1–6.

Bremner, J. D., Krystal, J. H., Putnam, F. W., Southwick, S. M., Marmar, C., et al. (1998). Measurement of dissociative states with the Clinician-Administered Dissociative States Scale (CADSS). *Journal of Traumatic Stress, 11,* 125–136.

Bremner, J. D., Krystal, J. H., Southwick, S. M., & Charney, D. S. (1995). Functional neuroanatomical correlates of the effects of stress on memory. *Journal of Trauma and Stress, 8,* 527–553.

Bremner, J. D., Randall, P., Scott, T. M., Bronen, R. A., Seibyl, J. P., et al. (1995). MRI-based measurement of hippocampal volume in patients with combat-related posttraumatic stress disorder. *American Journal of Psychiatry, 152,* 973–981.

Bremner, J. D., Randall, P., Vermetten, E., Staib, L., Bronen, R. A., et al. (1997). Magnetic resonance imaging-based measurement of hippocampal volume in posttraumatic stress disorder related to childhood physical and sexual abuse: A preliminary report. *Biological Psychiatry, 41,* 23–32.

Bremner, J. D., Vermetten, E., Afzal, N., & Vythilingam, M. (2004). Deficits in verbal declarative memory function in women with childhood sexual abuse-related posttraumatic stress disorder. *Journal of Nervous and Mental Disease, 192,* 643–649.

Bremner, J. D., Vythilingam, M., Vermetten, E., Southwick, S. M., McGlashan, T., et al. (2003). MRI and PET study of deficits in hippocampal structure and function in women with childhood sexual abuse and posttraumatic stress disorder. *American Journal of Psychiatry, 160,* 924–932.

Breslau, J., Aguilar-Gaxiola, S., Kendler, K. S., Su, M., Williams, D., & Kessler, R. C. (2006). Specifying race-ethnic differences in risk for psychiatric disorder in a USA national sample. *Psychological Medicine, 36,* 57–68.

Breslau, J., Kendler, K. S., Su, M., Aguilar-Gaxiola, S., & Kessler, R. C. (2005). Lifetime risk and persistence of psychiatric disorders across ethnic groups in the United States. *Psychological Medicine, 35,* 317–327.

Breslau, N., Kessler, R. C., Chilcoat, H. D. Schultz, L. R., Davis, G. C., & Andreski, P. (1998). Trauma and posttraumatic stress disorder in the community: The 1996 Detroit Area Survey of Trauma. *Archives of General Psychiatry, 55,* 626–632.

Breslau, N., Lucia, V. C., & Alvarado, G. F. (2006). Intelligence and other predisposing factors in exposure to trauma and posttraumatic stress disorder. *Archives of General Psychiatry, 63,* 1238–1245.

Breslau, N., Peterson, E., & Schultz, L. R. (2008). A second look at prior trauma and the posttraumatic stress disorder effects of subsequent trauma: A prospective epidemiological study. *Archives of General Psychiatry, 65,* 431–437.

Bressan, R. A., & Crippa, J. A. (2005). The role of dopamine in reward and pleasure behaviour—review of data from preclinical research. *Acta Psychiatrica Scandinavica, 111,* 14–21.

Bretherton, I. (1991). The roots and growing points of attachment theory. In C. M. Parkes, J. Stevenson-Hinde, & P. Marris (Eds.), *Attachment across the life cycle* (pp. 9–32). New York: Tavistock/Routledge.

Bretlau, L. G., Lunde, M., Lindberg, L., Undén, M., Dissing, S., & Bech, P. (2008). Repetitive transcranial magnetic stimulation (rTMS) in combination with escitalopram in patients with treatment-resistant major depression. A double-blind, randomised, sham-controlled trial. *Pharmacopsychiatry, 41,* 41–47.

Breuer, J., & Freud, S. (1955). *Studies on hysteria* (Vol. 2). (J. Strachey, Trans.). London: Hogarth Press. (Original work published 1895.)

Brewer, D. D., Catalano, R. F., Haggerty, K., Gainey, R. R., & Fleming, C. B. (1998). A meta-analysis of predictors of continued drug use during and after treatment for opiate addiction. *Addiction, 93,* 73–92.

Brewer, K. R., & Wann, D. L. (1998). Observational learning effectiveness as a function of model characteristics: Investigating the importance of social power. *Social Behavior & Personality, 26,* 1–10.

Brewin, C. R., Andrews, B., & Valentine, J. D. (2000). Meta-analysis of risk factors for posttraumatic stress disorder in trauma-exposed adults. *Journal of Consulting and Clinical Psychology, 68,* 748–766.

Bridge, J. A., Iyengar S., Salary, C. B., Barbe, R. P., Birmaher, B., et al. (2007). Clinical response and risk for reported suicidal ideation and suicide attempts in pediatric antidepressant treatment: A meta-analysis of randomized controlled trials. *Journal of the American Medical Association, 297,* 1683–1696.

Briere, J. (2004). Trauma types and characteristics. In J. Briere (ed.), *Psychological assessment of adult posttraumatic states: Phenomenology, diagnosis, and measurement* (2nd ed., pp. 5–37). Washington, DC: American Psychological Association.

Briere, J., & Elliott, D. (2000). Prevalence, characteristics and long-term sequelae of natural disaster exposure in the general population. *Journal of Traumatic Stress, 13,* 661–679.

Briere, J., Scott, C., & Weathers, F. (2005). Peritraumatic and persistent dissociation in the presumed etiology of PTSD. *American Journal of Psychiatry, 162,* 2295–2301.

Brodey, D. (2005, September 20). Blacks join the eating-disorder mainstream. *New York Times.* Retrieved August 31, 2007, from www.nytimes .com/2005/09/20/health/psychology/20eat.html? ex=1188792000&en=07d24d3f858c7fc5&ei=5070

Brody, A. L., Saxena, S., Stoessel, P., Gillies, L. A., Fairbanks, L. A., et al. (2001). Regional brain metabolic changes in patients with major depression treated with either paroxetine or interpersonal therapy: Preliminary findings. *Archives of General Psychiatry, 58,* 631–640.

Broekman, B. F. P., Olff, M., & Boer, F. (2007). The genetic background to PTSD. *Neuroscience & Biobehavioral Reviews, 31,* 348–362.

Bromberg, W. (1937). *The mind of man: The story of man's conquest of mental illness.* New York: Harper.

Bromberger, J. T., Harlow, S., Avis, N., Kravitz, H. M., & Cordal, A. (2004). Racial/ethnic differences in the prevalence of depressive symptoms among middle-aged women: The Study of Women's Health Across the Nation (SWAN). *American Journal of Public Health, 94,* 1378–1385.

Brommelhoff, J. A., Conway, K., Merikangas, K., & Levy, B. R. (2004). Higher rates of depression in women: Role of gender bias within the family. *Journal of Women's Health, 13,* 69–76.

Brondolo, E., & Mas, F. (2001). Cognitive-behavioral strategies for improving medication adherence in patients with bipolar disorder. *Cognitive and Behavioral Practice, 8,* 137–147.

Brook, U., & Boaz, M. (2005). Attention-deficit and hyperactivity disorder (ADHD) and learning disabilities (LD): Adolescents' perspective. *Patient Education and Counseling, 58,* 187–191.

Brooks, A. (1974). *Law, psychiatry, and the mental health system.* Boston: Little, Brown.

Brooks, S., Prince, A., Stahl, D., Campbell, I. C., & Treasure, J. (2011). A systematic review and meta-analysis of cognitive bias to food stimuli in people with disordered eating. *Clinical Psychology Review, 31,* 37–51.

Brosvic, G. M., Dihoff, R. E., Epstein, M. L., & Cook, M. L. (2006). Feedback facilitates the acquisition and retention of numerical fact series by elementary school students with mathematics learning disabilities. *Psychological Record, 56,* 35–54.

Brown, A. S., Begg, M. D., Gravenstein, S., Schaefer, C. A., Wyatt, R. J., et al. (2004). Serologic evidence of prenatal influenza in the etiology of schizophrenia. *Archives of General Psychiatry, 61,* 774–780.

Brown, A. S., van Os, J., Driessens, C., Hoek, H. W., & Susser, E. S. (1999). Prenatal famine and the spectrum of psychosis. *Psychiatric Annals, 29,* 145–150.

Brown, G. K., Beck, A. T., Steer, R. A., & Grisham, J. R. (2000). Risk factors for suicide in psychiatric outpatients: A 20-year prospective study. *Journal of Consulting and Clinical Psychology, 68,* 371–377.

Brown, G. K., Newman, C. F., Charlesworth, S. E., Crits-Christoph, P., & Beck, A. T. (2004). An open clinical trial of cognitive therapy for borderline personality disorder. *Journal of Personality Disorders, 18,* 257–271.

Brown, H. D., Kosslyn, S. M., Delamater, B., Fama, J., & Barsky, A. J. (1999). Perceptual and memory biases for health-related information in hypochondriacal individuals. *Journal of Psychosomatic Research, 47,* 67–78.

Brown, M., Smits, J., Powers, M. B., & Telch, M. J. (2003). Differential factors in predicting panic disorder patients' subjective and behavioral hyperventilation challenge. *Journal of the Anxiety Disorders, 17,* 583–591.

Brown, P. H., & Broeske, P. H. (1996). *Howard Hughes: The untold story.* Cambridge, MA: Da Capo Press.

Brown, R. J., & Lewis-Fernández, R. (2011). Culture and conversion disorder: Implications for DSM-5. *Psychiatry: Interpersonal and Biological Processes, 74*(3), 187–206.

Brown, R. J., Schrag, A., & Trimble, M. R. (2005). Dissociation, childhood interpersonal trauma, and family functioning in patients with somatization disorder. *American Journal of Psychiatry, 162,* 899–905.

Brown, S. A., & D'Amico, E. J. (2001). Outcomes of alcohol treatment for adolescents. *Recent Developments in Alcoholism Research, 15,* 307–327.

Brown, S. A., Tate, S. R., Vik, P. W., Haas, A. L., & Aarons, G. A. (1999). Modeling of alcohol use mediates the effect of family history of alcoholism on adolescent alcohol expectancies. *Experimental and Clinical Psychopharmacology, 7,* 20–27.

Brown, T. A., & Barlow, D. H. (1997). *Casebook in abnormal psychology.* New York: Brooks/Cole.

Brown, T. A., & Barlow, D. H. (2002). Classification of anxiety and mood disorders. In D. H. Barlow (Ed.), *Anxiety and its disorders* (2nd ed., pp. 292–327). New York: Guilford Press.

Brown, T. A., Campbell, L. A., Lehman, C. L., Grisham, J. R., & Mancill, R. B. (2001). Current and lifetime comorbidity of the DSM-IV-TR anxiety and mood disorders in a large clinical sample. *Journal of Abnormal Psychology, 100,* 585–599.

Brown, T. A., O'Leary, T. A., & Barlow, D. H. (1993). Generalized anxiety disorder. In D. H. Barlow (Ed.), *Clinical handbook of psychological disorders: A step-by-step treatment manual* (2nd ed., pp. 137–188). New York: Guilford Press.

Brown, T. M., & Boyle, M. F. (2002). The ABC of psychological medicine: Delirium. *BMJ: British Medical Journal, 325,* 644–647.

Brown, W. A. (2002). Are antidepressants as ineffective as they look? *Prevention & Treatment, 5,* Article 26. www.journals.apa.org/prevention/volume5/pre0050026c.html

Brownell, K. D., & Rodin, J. (1992). Prevalence of eating disorders in athletes. In K. D. Brownell, J. Rodin, & J. H. Wilmore (Eds.), *Eating, body weight, and performance in athletes: Disorders of modern society* (pp. 128–145). Philadelphia: Lea & Febiger.

Brozgold, A. Z., Borod, J. C., Martin, C. C., Pick, L. H., Alpert, M., & Welkowitz, J. (1998). Social functioning and facial emotional expression in neurological and psychiatric disorders. *Applied Neuropsychology, 5,* 15–23.

Bruce, K. R., & Steiger, H. (2005). Treatment implications of Axis-II comorbidity in eating disorders. *Eating Disorders: Journal of Treatment & Prevention, 13,* 93–108.

Bruch, H. (1966). Anorexia nervosa and its differential diagnosis. *Journal of Nervous and Mental Disease, 141,* 555–566.

Brückl, T. M., Wittchen, H., Höfler, M., Pfister, H., Schneider, S., & Lieb, R. (2006). Childhood separation anxiety and the risk of subsequent psychopathology: Results from a community study. *Psychotherapy and Psychosomatics, 76,* 47–56.

Bruder, C. E., Piotrowski, A., Gijsbers, A. A., Andersson, R., Erickson, S., et al. (2008). Phenotypically concordant and discordant monozygotic twins display different DNA copy-number-variation profiles. *American Journal of Human Genetics, 82,* 763–771.

Brunelin, J., Combris, M., Poulet, E., Kallel, L., d'Amato, T., et al. (2006). Source monitoring deficits in hallucinating compared to non-hallucinating patients with schizophrenia. *European Psychiatry, 21,* 259–261.

Brunelin, J., d'Amato, T., Brun, P., Bediou, B., Kallel, L., et al. (2007). Impaired verbal source monitoring in schizophrenia: An intermediate trait vulnerability marker? *Schizophrenia Research, 89,* 287–292.

Brunelin, J., d'Amato, T., van Os, J., Cochet, A., Suaud-Chagny, M., & Saoud, M. (2008). Effects of acute metabolic stress on the dopaminergic and pituitary-adrenal axis activity in patients with schizophrenia, their unaffected siblings and controls. *Schizophrenia Research, 100,* 206–211.

Brunelin, J., Poulet, E., Bediou, B., Kallel, L., Dalery, J., et al. (2006). Low frequency repetitive transcranial magnetic stimulation improves source monitoring deficit in hallucinating patients with schizophrenia. *Schizophrenia Research, 81,* 41–45.

Brunello, N., & Racagni, G. (1998). Rationale for the development of noradrenaline reuptake inhibitors. *Human Psychopharmacology Clinical & Experimental, 13,* S13–S19.

Brunner, J., & Bronisch, T. (1999). Neurobiological correlates of suicidal behavior. *Facharzt für Psychiatrie und Psychotherapie, 67,* 391–412.

Bryant, R. A., Friedman, M. J., Spiegel, D., Ursano, R., & Strain, J. (2011). A review of acute stress disorder. *Depression and Anxiety, 28,* 802–817.

Bryant, R. A., & Harvey, A. G., (2000). *Acute stress disorder: A handbook of theory, assessment and treatment.* Washington, DC: American Psychological Association.

Bryant, R. A., Mastrodemenico, J., Felmingham, K. L., Hopwood, S., Kenny, L., et al. (2008). Treatment of acute stress disorder: A randomized controlled trial. *Archives of General Psychiatry, 65,* 659–667.

Bryant, R. A., Moulds, M. L., Guthrie, R. M., & Nixon, R. D. V. (2005). The additive benefit of hypnosis and cognitive-behavioral therapy in treating acute stress disorder. *Journal of Consulting and Clinical Psychology, 73,* 334–340.

Bryant, R. A., Moulds, M. L., Nixon, R. D. V., Mastrodomenico, J., Felmingham, K., & Hopwood, S. (2006). Hypnotherapy and cognitive behaviour therapy of acute stress disorder: A 3-year follow-up. *Behaviour Research and Therapy, 44,* 1331–1335.

Bryant-Waugh, R. (1993). Epidemiology. In B. Lask & R. Bryant-Waugh, (Eds.), *Childhood onset anorexia nervosa and related eating disorders* (pp. 55–68). Hillsdale, NJ: Lawrence Erlbaum.

Buchsbaum, M. S., Christian, B. T., Lehrer, D. S., Narayanan, T. K., Shi, B., et al. (2006). D2/D3 dopamine receptor binding with [F-18] fallypride in thalamus and cortex of patients with schizophrenia. *Schizophrenia Research, 85,* 232–244.

Buchsbaum, M. S., Nenadic, I., Hazlett, E. A., Spiegal-Cohen, J., Fleischman, M. B., et al. (2002). Differential metabolic rates in prefrontal and temporal Brodmann areas in schizophrenia and schizotypal personality disorder. *Schizophrenia Research, 54,* 141–150.

Buckalew, L. W., & Ross, S. (1981). Relationship of perceptual characteristics to efficacy of placebos. *Psychological Reports, 49,* 955–961.

Buckley, P. F., Miller, B. J., Lehrer, D. S., & Castle, D. J. (2009). Psychiatric comorbidities and schizophrenia. *Schizophrenia Bulletin, 35*(2), 383–402.

Buckley, P. F., Wirshing, D. A., Bhushan, P., Pierre, J. M., Resnick, S. A., & Wirshing, W. C. (2007). Lack of insight in schizophrenia: Impact on treatment adherence. *CNS Drugs, 21,* 129–141.

Budney, A. J., Hughes, J. R., Moore, B. A., & Vandrey, R. (2004). Review of the validity and significance of cannabis withdrawal syndrome. *American Journal of Psychiatry, 161,* 1967–1977.

Buettner, R. & Goodman, D. J. (2013, April 16). Mistrial declared in '08 killing of a psychiatrist. *The New York Times,* p. A18.

Buhlmann, U., Etcoff, N. L., & Wilhelm, S. (2006). Emotion recognition bias for contempt and anger in body dysmorphic disorder. *Journal of Psychiatric Research, 40,* 105–111.

Buhlmann, U., Etcoff, N. L., & Wilhelm, S. (2008). Facial attractiveness ratings and perfectionism in body dysmorphic disorder and obsessive-compulsive disorder. *Journal of Anxiety Disorders, 22,* 540–547.

Buhlmann, U., McNally, R. J., Wilhelm, S., & Florin, I. (2002). Selective processing of emotional information in body dysmorphic disorder. *Journal of Anxiety Disorders, 16,* 289–298.

Buka, S. L., Goldstein, J. M., Seidman, L. J., Zornberg, G. L., Donatelli, J. A., et al. (1999). Prenatal complications, genetic vulnerability and schizophrenia: The New England longitudinal studies of schizophrenia. *Psychiatric Annals, 29,* 151–156.

Bulik, C. M. (2004). Genetic and biological risk factors. In J. K. Thompson (Ed.), *Handbook of eating disorders and obesity* (pp. 3–16). Hoboken, NJ: John Wiley & Sons.

Bulik, C. M. (2005). Exploring the gene-environment nexus in eating disorders. *Journal of Psychiatry & Neuroscience, 30,* 335–339.

Bulik, C. M., Sullivan, P. F., Fear, J., & Pickering, A. (1997). Predictors of the development of bulimia nervosa in women with anorexia nervosa. *Journal of Nervous and Mental Disease, 185,* 704–707.

Burgess, S., Geddes, J., Hawton, K., Townsend, E., Jamison, K., & Goodwin, G. (2001). Lithium for maintenance treatment of mood disorders. *Cochrane Database System Review,* CD003013.

Burke, A. W. (1984). Racism and psychological disturbance among West Indians in Britain. *International Journal of Social Psychiatry, 30,* 50–68.

Burke, J. D., Jr., & Regier, D. A. (1994). Epidemiology of mental disorders. In R. E. Hales, S. C. Yudofsky, & J. A. Talbott (Eds.), *The American Psychiatric Press textbook of psychiatry* (2nd ed., pp. 81–104). Washington, DC: American Psychiatric Association.

Burnette, M. L., & Newman, D. L. (2005). The natural history of conduct disorder symptoms in female inmates: On the predictive utility of the syndrome in severely antisocial women. *American Journal of Orthopsychiatry, 75,* 421–430.

Burns, D. (1980). *Feeling good: The new mood therapy.* New York: Signet.

Burns, J. M., & Swerdlow, R. H. (2003). Right orbitofrontal tumor with pedophilia symptom and constructional apraxia sign. *Archives of Neurology, 60*(3), 437.

Burri, A., Spector, T., & Rahman, Q. (in press). A discordant monozygotic twin approach to testing environmental influences on sexual dysfunction in women. *Archives of Sexual Behavior.*

Bush, G., Spencer, T. J., Holmes, J., Shin, L. M., Valera, E. M., et al. (2008). Functional magnetic resonance imaging of methylphenidate and placebo in attention-deficit/hyperactivity disorder during the multi-source interference task. *Archives of General Psychiatry, 65,* 102–114.

Buss, A. H. (1995). *Personality: Temperament, social behavior, and the self.* Needham Heights, MA: Allyn & Bacon.

Bustillo, J. R., Lauriello, J., Horan, W. P., & Keith, S. J. (2001). The psychosocial treatment of schizophrenia: An update. *American Journal of Psychiatry, 158,* 163–175.

Butcher, J. N., Dahlstrom, W. G., Graham, J. R., Tellegen, A. & Kaemmer, B. (1989). *Manual for the restandardized Minnesota Multiphasic Personality Inventory: MMPI–2. An administrative and interpretive guide.* Minneapolis: University of Minnesota Press.

Butcher, J. N., & Rouse, S. V. (1996). Personality: Individual difference and clinical assessment. *Annual Review of Psychology, 47,* 87–111.

Butler, L. D., Duran, R. E. F., Jasiukaitis, P., Koopman, C., & Spiegel, D. (1996). Hypnotizability and traumatic experience: A diathesis-stress model of dissociative symptomatology. *American Journal of Psychiatry, 153,* 42–46.

Butler, R. N., & Lewis, M. I. (2002). *The new love and sex after 60.* New York: Ballantine Books.

Butzlaff, R. L., & Hooley, J. M. (1998). Expressed emotion and psychiatric relapse. *Archives of General Psychiatry, 55,* 547–552.

Cachelin, F. M., & Maher, B. A. (1998). Is amenorrhea a critical criterion for anorexia nervosa? *Journal of Psychosomatic Research, 44,* 435–440.

Cadoret, R. J. (1990). Genetics of alcoholism. In R. L. Collins, K. E. Leonard, & J. S. Searles (Eds.), *Alcohol and the family: Research and clinical perspectives* (pp. 39–78). New York: Guilford Press.

Cadoret, R. J., Yates, W. R., Troughton, E., Woodworth, G., & Stewart, M. A. (1995). Adoption study demonstrating two genetic pathways to drug abuse. *Archives of General Psychiatry, 52,* 42–52.

Cahn, W., Hulshoff Pol, H. E., Lems, E. B. T. E., van Haren, N. E. M., Schnack, H. G., et al. (2002). Brain volume changes in first-episode schizophrenia: A 1-year follow-up study. *Archives of General Psychiatry, 59,* 1002–1012.

Cairl v. State, 323 N. W.2d 20 (Minn. 1982).

Calderon, R., Vander Stoep, A., Collett, B., Garrison, M. M., & Toth, K. (2007). Inpatients with eating disorders: Demographic, diagnostic, and service characteristics from a nationwide pediatric sample. *International Journal of Eating Disorders, 40,* 622–628.

Caldwell, C., & Gottesman, I. (1990). Schizophrenics kill themselves too: A review of risk factors for suicide. *Schizophrenia Bulletin, 16,* 571–589.

Calkins, M. E., Curtis, C. E., Grove, W. M., & Iacono, W. G. (2004). Multiple dimensions of schizotypy in first degree biological relatives of schizophrenia patients. *Schizophrenia Bulletin, 30,* 317–325.

Callicott, J. H., Mattay, V. S., Verchinski, B. A., Marenco, S., Egan, M. F., & Weinberger, D. R. (2003). Complexity of prefrontal cortical dysfunction in schizophrenia: More than up or down. *American Journal of Psychiatry, 160,* 2209–2215.

Calogero, R. M., Davis, W. N., & Thompson, J. K. (2005). The role of self-objectification in the experience of women with eating disorders. *Sex Roles, 52,* 43–50.

Calvocoressi, L., Lewis, B., Harris, M., Trufan, S. J., Goodman, W. K., et al. (1995). Family accommodation in obsessive-compulsive disorder. *American Journal of Psychiatry, 152,* 441–443.

Camilleri, J. A., & Quinsey, V. L. (2008). Pedophilia: Assessment and treatment. In D. R. Laws & W. T. O'Donohue (Eds.), *Sexual deviance: Theory, assessment, and treatment* (2nd ed., pp. 183–212). New York: Guilford Press.

Campbell, E., & Ruane, J. (1999). *The Earl Campbell story.* Toronto: ECW Press.

Campbell, J. M., & Morgan, S. B. (1998). Asperger's disorder. In L. Phelps (Ed.), *Health-related disorders in children and adolescents: A guidebook for understanding and educating* (pp. 68–73). Washington, DC: American Psychological Association.

Campbell, L. F., & Smith, T. P. (2003). Integrating self-help books into psychotherapy. *Journal of Clinical Psychology/In Session, 59*(2), 177–186.

Campinha-Bacote, J. (1992). Voodoo illness. *Perspectives in Psychiatric Care, 28,* 11–17.

Canetto, S. S. (1992). Gender and suicide in the elderly. *Suicide and Life-Threatening Behavior, 22,* 80–97.

Canino, I. A., Rubio-Stipec, M., Canino, G. J., & Escobar, J. I. (1992). Functional somatic symptoms: A cross-ethnic comparison. *American Journal of Orthopsychiatry, 62,* 605–68.

Cannon, M., Jones, P., Huttunen, M. O., Tanskanen, A., Huttunen, T., et al. (1999). School performance in Finnish children and later development of schizophrenia: A population-based longitudinal study. *Archives of General Psychiatry, 56,* 457–463.

Cannon, T. D. (1997). On the nature and mechanisms of obstetric influences in schizophrenia: A review and synthesis of epidemiologic studies. *International Review of Psychiatry, 9,* 387–397.

Cannon, T. D. (1998). Neurodevelopmental influences in the genesis and epigenesis of schizophrenia: An overview. *Applied & Preventive Psychology, 7,* 47–62.

Cannon, T. D., Huttunen, M. O., Dahlstroem, M., Larmo, I., Raesaenen, P., & Juriloo, A. (2002). Antipsychotic drug treatment in the prodromal phase of schizophrenia. *American Journal of Psychiatry, 159,* 1230–1232.

Cantor, C. (1996). *Phantom illness: Shattering the myth of hypochondria.* Boston: Houghton Mifflin.

Cantor-Graae, E., & Selten, J. (2005). Schizophrenia and migration: A meta-analysis and review. *American Journal of Psychiatry, 162,* 12–24.

Cao, F., Bitan, T., Chou, T., Burman, D. D., & Booth, J. R. (2006). Deficient orthographic and phonological representations in children with dyslexia revealed by brain activation patterns. *Journal of Child Psychology and Psychiatry, 47,* 1041–1050.

Caparulo, B. K., & Cohen, D. J. (1977). Cognitive structures, language, and emerging social competence in autistic and aphasic children. *Journal of the American Academy of Child Psychiatry, 16,* 620–645.

Caplan, P. J. (1995). *They say you're crazy: How the world's most powerful psychiatrists decide who's normal.* Reading, MA: Addison Wesley Longman.

Caputo, A. A., Frick, P. J., & Brodsky, S. L. (1999). Family violence and juvenile sex offending: The potential mediating role of psychopathic traits and negative attitudes toward women. *Criminal Justice and Behavior, 26,* 338–356.

Cardeña, E., & Spiegel, D. (1993). Dissociative reactions to the San Francisco Bay Area earthquake of 1989. *American Journal of Psychiatry, 150,* 474–478.

Carey, M. P., & Gordon, C. M. (1995). Sexual dysfunction among heterosexual adults: Description, epidemiology, assessment, and treatment. In L. Diamant & R. D. McAnulty (Eds.), *The psychology of sexual orientation, behavior, and identity: A handbook* (pp. 165–196). New York: Greenwood.

Carlat, D. J., Camargo, C. A., Jr., & Herzog, D. B. (1997). Eating disorders in males: A report on 135 patients. *American Journal of Psychiatry, 154,* 1127–1132.

Carlbring, P., & Andersson, G. (2006). Internet and psychological treatment. How well can they be combined? *Computers in Human Behavior, 22,* 545–553.

Carlbring, P., Furmark, T., Steczkó, J., Ekselius, L., & Andersson, G. (2006). An open study of internet-based bibliotherapy with minimal therapist contact via email for social phobia. *Clinical Psychologist, 10,* 30–38.

Carlbring, P., Nilsson-Ihrfelt, E., Waara, J., Kollenstam, C., Buhrman, M., et al. (2005). Treatment of panic disorder: Live therapy vs. self-help via the Internet. *Behaviour Research and Therapy, 43,* 1321–1333.

Carlisle, N. (2009, February 13). Elizabeth Smart kidnap case: Mitchell booked into Salt Lake Country jail. *The Salt Lake Tribune.* Retrieved February 28, 2009, from www.sltrib.com/faith/ci_11697926

Carlson, N. R. (1994). *Physiology of behavior.* Needham Heights, MA: Allyn & Bacon.

Carmelli, D., Heath, R., & Robinette, D. (1993). Genetic analysis of drinking behavior in World War II veteran twins. *Genetic Epidemiology, 10,* 201–213.

Carr, J. E., & Chong, I. M. (2005). Habit reversal treatment of tic disorders: A methodological critique of the literature. *Behavior Modification, 29,* 858–875.

Carroll, K. M. (1998). *A cognitive-behavioral approach: Treating cocaine addiction.* National Institute on Drug Abuse. NIH Publication Number 98–4308. Retrieved October 6, 2009, from www.drugabuse.gov/TXManuals/CBT/CBT1.html

Carroll, K. M., & Onken, L. S. (2005). Behavioral therapies for drug abuse. *American Journal of Psychiatry, 162,* 1454–1460.

Carroll, K. M., Ball, S. A., Martino, S., Nich, C., Babuscio, T. A., et al. (2008). Computer-assisted delivery of cognitive-behavioral therapy for addiction: A randomized trial of CBT4CBT. *American Journal of Psychiatry, 165,* 881–888.

Carroll, K. M., Fenton, L. R., Ball, S. A., Nich, C., Frankforter, T. L., et al. (2004). Efficacy of disulfiram and cognitive behavior therapy in cocaine-dependent outpatients. *Archives of General Psychiatry, 61,* 264–272.

Carroll, K. M., Rounsaville, B. J., & Bryant, K. J. (1993). Alcoholism in treatment-seeking cocaine abusers: Clinical and prognostic significance. *Journal of Studies on Alcohol, 54,* 199–208.

Carroll, R. A. (2000). Gender dysphoria. In S. R. Leiblum & R. C. Rosen (Eds.), *Principles and practice of sex therapy* (3rd ed., pp. 368–397). New York: Guilford Press.

Carter, B., & McGoldrick, M. (1999). Overview: The expanded family life cycle: Individual, family, and social perspectives. In B. Carter & M. McGoldrick (Eds.), *The expanded family life cycle: Individual, family, and social perspectives* (3rd ed., pp. 1–26). Boston: Allyn & Bacon.

Carter, M. M., Hollon, S. D., Carson, R., & Shelton, R. C. (1995). Effects of a safe person on induced distress following a biological challenge in panic disorder with agoraphobia. *Journal of Abnormal Psychology, 104,* 156–163.

Casbon, T. S., Burns, A. B., Bradbury, T. N., & Joiner, T. E., Jr. (2005). Receipt of negative feedback is related to increased negative feedback seeking among individuals with depressive symptoms. *Behaviour Research and Therapy, 43,* 485–504.

Caseras, X., Garner, M., Bradley, B. P., & Mogg, K. (2007). Biases in visual orienting to negative and positive scenes in dysphoria: An eye movement study. *Journal of Abnormal Psychology, 116,* 491–497.

Cash, T. F. (1995). Developmental teasing about physical appearance: Retrospective descriptions and relationships with body image. *Social Behavior and Personality, 23,* 123–129.

Caspi, A., McClay, J., Moffitt, T. E., Mill, J., Martin, J., et al. (2002). Role of genotype in the cycle of violence in maltreated children. *Science, 297,* 851–854.

Caspi, A., Moffitt, T. E., Newman, D. L., & Silva, P. A. (1996). Behavioral observations at age 3 predict adult psychiatric disorders: Longitudinal evidence from a birth cohort. *Archives of General Psychiatry, 53,* 1033–1039.

Cassady, J. D., Kirschke, D. L., Jones, T. F., Craig, A. S., Bermudez, O. B., & Schaffner, W. (2005). Case series: Outbreak of conversion disorder among Amish adolescent girls. *Journal of the American Academy of Child & Adolescent Psychiatry, 44,* 291–297.

Cassano, G. B., Mula, M., Rucci, P., Miniati, M., Frank, E., et al. (2009). The structure of lifetime manic-hypomanic spectrum. *Journal of Affective Disorders, 112,* 59–70.

Cassin, S. E., & von Ranson, K. M. (2005). Personality and eating disorders: A decade in review. *Clinical Psychology Review, 25,* 895–916.

Castellanos, F. X., Lee, P. P., Sharp, W., Jeffries, N. O., Greenstein, D. K., et al. (2002). Developmental trajectories of brain volume abnormalities in children and adolescents with attention deficit/hyperactivity disorder. *Journal of the American Medical Association, 288,* 1740–1748.

Castillo, H. (2003). *Personality disorder: Temperament or trauma?* London: Jessica Kingsley.

Castillo, R. J. (1997). *Culture & mental illness: A client-centered approach.* Belmont, CA: Thomson/Brooks/Cole.

Castle, D. J., & Rossell, S. L. (2006). An update on body dysmorphic disorder. *Current Opinion in Psychiatry, 19,* 74–78.

Castonguay, L. G., Goldfried, M. R., Wiser, S., Raue, P. J., & Hayes, A. M. (1996). Predicting the effect of cognitive therapy for depression: A study of unique and common factors. *Journal of Consulting and Clinical Psychology, 64,* 497–504.

Catanzaro, S. J., & Laurent, J. (2004). Perceived family support, negative mood regulation expectancies, coping, and adolescent alcohol use: Evidence of mediation and moderation effects. *Addictive Behaviors, 29,* 1779–1797.

Cattell, R. B. (1971). *Abilities: Their structure, growth, and action.* New York: Houghton Mifflin.

Caudill, B. D., & Kong, F. H. (2001). Social approval and facilitation in predicting modeling effects in alcohol consumption. *Journal of Substance Abuse, 13,* 425–441.

Cederlund, M., & Gillberg, C. (2004). One hundred males with Asperger syndrome: A clinical study of background and associated factors. *Developmental Medicine & Child Neurology, 46,* 652–660.

Celani, D. (1976). An interpersonal approach to hysteria. *American Journal of Psychiatry, 133,* 1414–1418.

Centers for Disease Control and Prevention. (2010a). Current depression among adults—United States, 2006 and 2008. *Morbidity and Mortality Weekly Report, 59,* 1229–1235.

Centers for Disease Control and Prevention. (2010b). Web-based Injury Statistics Query and Reporting System (WISQARS) [Online]. National Center for Injury Prevention and Control, CDC (producer). Retrieved December 23, 2011, from www.cdc.gov/injury/wisqars/index.html

Centers for Disease Control and Prevention. (2012). Early release of selected estimates based on data from the 2011 National Health Interview Survey, Sample Adult Component. Figure 13.2. Retrieved September 12, 2012, from www.cdc.gov/nchs/data/nhis/earlyrelease/earlyrelease201206_13.pdf

Centers for Disease Control and Prevention. (2013). National Suicide Statistics at a Glance. National Center for Injury Prevention and Control, CDC (producer). Retrieved May 30, 2013, from www.cdc.gov/violenceprevention/suicide/statistics/trends05.html

Centers for Disease Control and Prevention, National Center for Health Statistics. (2000, July 24). Death and death rates for the 10 leading causes of death specified in age groups, by race and sex: United States, 1998. *Monthly Vital Statistics Reports, 48*(11), 26. Retrieved October, 6, 2002, from www.cdc.gov/nchs/fastats/suicide.htm

Centers for Disease Control and Prevention, National Center for Injury Prevention and Control. (2005). Web-based injury statistics query and reporting system (WISQARS) [Online]. Retrieved October 20, 2008, from www.cdc.gov/ncipc/wisqars/default.htm

Cervera, S., Lahortiga, F., Martinez-Gonzalez, M. A., Gual, P., Irala-Estevez, J. D., & Alonso, Y. (2003). Neuroticism and low self-esteem as risk factors for incident eating disorders in a prospective cohort study. *International Journal of Eating Disorders, 33,* 271–280.

Chacko, A., Pelham, W. E., Jr., Gnagy, E. M., Greiner, A., Vallano, G., et al. (2005). Stimulant medication effects in a summer treatment program among young children with attention-deficit/hyperactivity disorder. *Journal of the American Academy of Child & Adolescent Psychiatry, 44,* 249–257.

Chakraborty, A., & McKenzie, K. (2002). Does racial discrimination cause mental illness? *British Journal of Psychiatry, 180,* 475–477.

Chalkley, A. J., & Powell, G. E. (1983). The clinical description of forty-eight cases of sexual fetishism. *British Journal of Psychiatry, 142,* 292–295.

Chamberlain, P. (1996). Intensified foster care: Multi-level treatment for adolescents with conduct disorders in out-of-home care. In E. D. Hibbs & P. S. Jensen (Eds.), *Psychosocial treatments for child and adolescent disorders: Empirically based strategies for clinical practice* (pp. 475–495). Washington, DC: American Psychological Association.

Chambers, J., Yeragani, V. K., & Keshavan, M. S. (1986). Phobias in India and the United Kingdom: A trans-cultural study. *Acta Psychiatrica Scandinavica, 74,* 388–391.

Chambless, D. L. (2002a). Beware the dodo bird: The dangers of overgeneralization. *Clinical Psychology: Science & Practice, 9,* 13–16.

Chambless, D. L. (2002b). Identification of empirically supported counseling psychology interventions: Commentary. *Counseling Psychologist, 30,* 302–308.

Chambless, D. L., Fydrich, T., & Rodebaugh, T. L. (2008). Generalized social phobia and avoidant personality disorder: Meaningful distinction or useless duplication? *Depression and Anxiety, 25,* 8–19.

Chambless, D. L., & Gillis, M. M. (1994). A review of psychosocial treatments for panic disorder. In B. E. Wolfe & J. D. Maser (Eds.), *Treatment of panic disorder: A consensus development conference* (pp. 149–173). Washington, DC: American Psychiatric Association.

Chambless, D. L., & Hollon, S. D. (1998). Defining empirically supported therapies. *Journal of Consulting and Clinical Psychology, 66,* 7–18.

Chambless, D. L., & Ollendick, T. H. (2001). Empirically supported psychological interventions: Controversies and evidence. *Annual Review of Psychology, 52,* 685–716.

Chan, A. S., Kwok, I. C., Chiu, H., Lam, L., Pang, A., & Chow, L. (2000). Memory and organizational strategies in chronic and acute schizophrenic patients. *Schizophrenia Research, 41,* 431–445.

Chang, C., Chen, W. J., Liu, S. K., Cheng, J. J., Yang, W. O., et al. (2002). Morbidity risk of psychiatric disorders among the first degree relatives of schizophrenia patients in Taiwan. *Schizophrenia Bulletin, 28,* 379–392.

Chantarujikapong, S. I., Scherrer, J. F., Xian, H., Eisen, S. A., Lyons, M. J., et al. (2001). A twin study of generalized anxiety disorder symptoms, panic disorder symptoms and post-traumatic stress disorder in men. *Psychiatry Research, 103,* 133–146.

Chapple, B., Chant, D., Nolan, P., Cardy, S., Whiteford, H., & McGrath, J. (2004). Correlates of victimisation amongst people with psychosis. *Social Psychiatry and Psychiatric Epidemiology, 39,* 836–840.

Charney, D. S., Deutch, A. Y., Krystal, J. H., Southwick, S. M., & Davis M. (1993). Psychobiologic mechanisms of posttraumatic stress disorder. *Archives of General Psychiatry, 50,* 294–305.

Chartier, M. J., Walker, J. R., & Stein, M. B. (2003). Considering comorbidity in social phobia. *Social Psychiatry and Psychiatric Epidemiology, 38,* 728–734.

Chattopadhyay, S. (2005). Do schizophrenics experience emotion but differ in expression? *Internet Journal of Mental Health, 2,* 1–6.

Chaves, J. F. (2000). Hypnosis. In A. E. Kazdin (Ed.), *Encyclopedia of psychology* (Vol. 4, pp. 211–216). Washington, DC: American Psychological Association.

Chawarska, K., Volkmar, F., & Klin, A. (2010). Limited attentional bias for faces in toddlers with autism spectrum disorders. *Archives of General Psychiatry, 67,* 178–185.

Cheng, A. T. A. (2002). Expressed emotion: A cross-culturally valid concept? *British Journal of Psychiatry, 181,* 466–467.

Cheng, D. (2002, October 7). Moderate altitude increases suicide deaths. Poster presented at the Research Forum Educational Program, American College of Emergency Physicians, Seattle, Washington.

Chess, S., & Thomas, A. (1996). *Temperament: Theory and practice.* Philadelphia: Brunner/Mazel.

Cheung, V. Y., Bocking, A. D., & Dasilva, O. P. (1995). Preterm discordant twins: What birth weight difference is significant? *American Journal of Obstetrics & Gynecology, 172,* 955–959.

Chilcoat, H. D., & Breslau, N. (1998). Posttraumatic stress disorder and drug disorders: Testing causal pathways. *Archives of General Psychiatry, 55,* 913–917.

Christophersen, E. R. (1994). *Pediatric compliance: A guide for the primary care physician.* New York: Plenum Medical Book Co/Plenum Publishing Corp.

Christophersen, E. R., & Mortweet, S. L. (2001). Diagnosis and management of disruptive behavior disorders. In *Treatments that work with children: Empirically supported strategies for managing childhood problems* (pp. 11–48). Washington, DC: American Psychological Association.

Chu, J. A., & International Society for the Study of Dissociation. (2005). Guidelines for treating dissociative identity disorder in adults. *Journal of Trauma & Dissociation, 6,* 69–149.

Chung, H. (2002). The challenges of providing behavioral treatment for Asian Americans. *Western Journal of Medicine, 176*(4), 222–223.

Cicchetti, D., & Toth, S. L. (1991). *Internalizing and externalizing expressions of dysfunction.* Hillsdale, NJ: Lawrence Erlbaum.

Cicchetti, D., & Toth, S. L. (2005). Child maltreatment. *Annual Review of Clinical Psychology, 1,* 409–438.

Cicero, T. J. (1978). Tolerance to and physiological dependence on alcohol: Behavioral and neurobiological mechanisms. In M. A. Lipton, A. DiMascio, & K. F. Killman (Eds.), *Psychopharmacology.* New York: Raven.

Cipriani, A., Geddes, J. R., Furukawa, T. A., & Barbui, C. (2007). Meta-review on short-term effectiveness and safety of antidepressants for depression: An evidence-based approach to inform clinical practice. *The Canadian Journal of Psychiatry/La Revue canadienne de psychiatrie, 52,* 553–562.

Citron, M., Solomon, P., & Draine, J. (1999). Self-help groups for families of persons with mental illness: Perceived benefits of helpfulness. *Community Mental Health Journal, 35,* 15–30.

Claes, S. J. (2004). Corticotropin-releasing hormone (CRH) in psychiatry: From stress to psychopathology. *Annals of Medicine, 36,* 50–61.

Clark, C. M., Gosselin, F., & Goghari, V. M. (2013). Aberrant patterns of visual facial information usage in schizophrenia. *Journal of Abnormal Psychology, 122*(2), 513–519.

Clark, D. A. (2005). Focus on "cognition" in cognitive behavior therapy for OCD: Is it really necessary? *Cognitive Behaviour Therapy, 34,* 131–139.

Clark, D. M. (1986). A cognitive approach to panic. *Behaviour Research and Therapy, 24,* 461–470.

Clark, D. M., Ehlers, A., Hackmann, A., McManus, F., Fennell, M., et al. (2006). Cognitive therapy versus exposure and applied relaxation in social phobia: A randomized controlled trial. *Journal of Consulting and Clinical Psychology, 74,* 568–578.

Clark, D. M., Salkovskis, P. M., Gelder, M. G., Koehler, C., Martin, M., et al. (1988). Tests of a cognitive theory of panic. In I. Hand & H. U. Wittchen (Eds.), *Panic and phobias II.* New York: Springer-Verlag.

Clark, D. M., Salkovskis, P. M., Hackmann, A., Middleton, H., Anastasiades, P., & Gelder, M. (1994). A comparison of cognitive therapy, applied relaxation and imipramine in the treatment of panic disorder. *British Journal of Psychiatry, 164,* 759–769.

Clark, L. A. (2007). Assessment and diagnosis of personality disorder: Perennial issues and an emerging reconceptualization. *Annual Review of Psychology, 58,* 227–257.

Clark, L. A. (2009). Stability and change in personality disorder. *Current Directions in Psychological Science, 18,* 27–31.

Clark, L. A., & Watson, D. (1991). Tripartite model of anxiety and depression: Evidence and taxonomic implications. *Journal of Abnormal Psychology, 100,* 316–336.

Clarke, A. R., Barry, R. J., McCarthy, R., Selikowitz, M., & Johnstone, S. J. (2007). Effects of stimulant medications on the EEG of girls with attention-deficit/hyperactivity disorder. *Clinical Neurophysiology, 118,* 2700–2708.

Clarke, M. C., Harley, M., & Cannon, M. (2006). The role of obstetric events in schizophrenia. *Schizophrenia Bulletin, 32,* 3–8.

Clarkin, J. F., & Levy, K. N. (2004). The influence of client variables on psychotherapy. In M. J. Lambert (Ed.), *Bergin & Garfield's handbook of psychotherapy and behavior change* (5th ed., pp. 194–226). New York: John Wiley & Sons.

Clarkin, J. F., Levy, K. N., Lenzenweger, M. F., & Kernberg, O. F. (2007). Evaluating three treatments for borderline personality disorder: A multiwave study. *American Journal of Psychiatry, 164,* 922–928.

Clausius, N., Born, C., & Grunze H. (2009). The relevance of dopamine agonists in the treatment of depression. Neuropsychiatrie: Klinik, Diagnostik, Therapie und Rehabilitation: Organ der Gesellschaft Osterreichischer Nervenarzte und Psychiater, 23, 15–25.

Clayton, R. R. (1992). Transitions in drug use: Risk and protective factors. In M. Glantz & R. Pickens (Eds.), *Vulnerability to drug abuse* (pp. 15–51). Washington, DC: American Psychological Association.

Clementz, B. A., & Sweeney, J. A. (1990). Is eye movement dysfunction a biological marker for schizophrenia? A methodological review. *Psychological Bulletin, 108,* 77–92.

Clifton, A., Turkheimer, E., & Oltmanns, T. F. (2004). Contrasting perspectives on personality problems: Descriptions from the self and others. *Personality and Individual Differences, 36,* 1499–1514.

Cloitre, M., Shear, M. K., Cancienne, J., & Zeitlin, S. B. (1994). Implicit and explicit memory for catastrophic associations to bodily sensation words in panic disorder. *Cognitive Therapy & Research, 18,* 225–240.

Cloninger, C. R. (1987a). Neurogenetic adaptive mechanisms in alcoholism. *Science, 236,* 410–416.

Cloninger, C. R. (1987b). A systematic method for clinical description and classification of personality variants: A proposal. *Archives of General Psychiatry, 44,* 573–588.

Cloninger, C. R. (2005). Genetics. In J. M. Oldham, A. E. Skodol, & D. S. Bender (Eds.). *The American Psychiatric Publishing textbook of personality disorders* (pp. 143–154). Washington, DC: American Psychiatric Publishing.

Cloninger, C. R., Bohman, M., & Sigvardsson, S. (1981). Inheritance of alcohol abuse: Cross-fostering analysis of adopted men. *Archives of General Psychiatry, 38,* 861–868.

Cloninger, C. R., Svrakic, D. M., & Przybeck, T. R. (1993). A psychobiological model of temperament and character. *Archives of General Psychiatry, 50,* 975–990.

Cloos, J. (2005). The treatment of panic disorder. *Current Opinion in Psychiatry, 18,* 45–50.

Cobb, H. C., Reeve, R. E., Shealy, C. N., Norcross, J. C., Schare, M. L., et al. (2004). Overlap among clinical, counseling, and school psychology: Implications for the profession and combined-integrated training. *Journal of Clinical Psychology, 60,* 939–955.

Coelho, C. M., Waters, A. M., Hine, T. J., & Wallis, G. (2009). The use of virtual reality in acrophobia research and treatment. *Journal of Anxiety Disorders, 23,* 563–574.

Cohen, C. I., Cohen, G. D., Blank, K., Gaitz, C., Katz, I. R., et al. (2000). Schizophrenia and older adults: An overview: Directions for research and policy. *American Journal of Geriatric Psychiatry, 8,* 19–28.

Cohen, H., Kaplan, Z., Kotler, M., Kouperman, I., Moisa, R., & Grisaru, N. (2004). Repetitive transcranial magnetic stimulation of the right dorsolateral prefrontal cortex in posttraumatic stress disorder: A double-blind, placebo-controlled study. *American Journal of Psychiatry, 161,* 515–524.

Cohen, P., Cohen, J., Kasen, S., Velez, C., Hartmark, C., et al. (1993). An epidemiological study of disorders in late childhood and adolescence: I. Age- and gender-specific prevalence. *Journal of Child Psychology and Psychiatry, 34,* 851–867.

Cohen-Kettenis, P. T., & Gooren, L. J. G. (1999). Transsexualism: A review of etiology, diagnosis and treatment. *Journal of Psychosomatic Research, 46,* 315–333.

Coid, J. W., Ullrich, S., Kallis, C., Keers, R., Barker, D., et al. (2013). The relationship between delusions and violence: Findings from the East London first episode psychosis study. *JAMA Psychiatry, 70*(5), 465–471.

Colas, E. (1998). *Just checking: Scenes from the life of an obsessive-compulsive.* New York: Pocket Books.

Colder, C. R., Chassin, L., Stice, E. M., & Curran, P. J. (1997). Alcohol expectancies as potential mediators of parent alcoholism effects on the development of adolescent heavy drinking. *Journal of Research on Adolescence, 7,* 349–374.

Coles, J. (2007, March 9). Mechanic: I have sex with cars. *The Sun.* Retrieved April 17, 2009, from www.thesun.co.uk/sol/homepage/news/article21242.ece

Coles, M. E., Phillips, K. A., Menard, W., Pagano, M. E., Fay, C., et al. (2006). Body dysmorphic disorder and social phobia: Cross-sectional and prospective data. *Depression and Anxiety, 23*, 26–33.

Collett, B. R., & Gimpel, G. A. (2004). Maternal and child attributions in ADHD versus non-ADHD populations. *Journal of Attention Disorders, 7*, 187–196.

Collings, S., & King, M. (1994). Ten year follow-up of 50 patients with bulimia nervosa. *British Journal of Psychiatry, 164*, 80–87.

Colloca, L., & Miller, F. G. (2011). Role of expectations in health. *Current Opinion in Psychiatry, 24*(2), 149–155.

Colman, I., Murray, J., Abbott, R., Maughan, B, Kuh, D., et al. (2009). Outcomes of conduct problems in adolescence: 40 year follow-up of national cohort. *British Medical Journal, 338*, a2981.

Combs, D. R., Basso, M. R., Wanner, J. L., & Ledet, S. N. (2008). Schizophrenia. In M. Hersen & J. Rosqvist (Eds.), *Handbook of psychological assessment, case conceptualization, and treatment, Vol 1: Adults* (pp. 352–402). Hoboken, NJ: John Wiley & Sons.

Compton, W. M., Conway, K. P., Stinson, F. S., Colliver, J. D., & Grant, B. F. (2005). Prevalence, correlates, and comorbidity of DSM-IV-TR antisocial personality syndromes and alcohol and specific drug use disorders in the United States: Results from the National Epidemiologic Survey on Alcohol and Related Conditions. *Journal of Clinical Psychiatry, 66*, 677–685.

Compton, W. M., Thomas, Y. F., Conway, K. P., & Colliver, J. D. (2005). Developments in the epidemiology of drug use and drug use disorders. *American Journal of Psychiatry, 162*, 1494–1502.

Conger, R. D., & Donnellan, M. B. (2007). An interactionist perspective on the socioeconomic context of human development. *Annual Review of Psychology, 58*, 175–199.

Conrad, A., Isaac, L., & Roth, W. T. (2008). The psychophysiology of generalized anxiety disorder: 1. Pretreatment characteristics. *Psychophysiology, 45*, 366–376.

Constans, J. I., Foa, E. B., Franklin, M. E., & Mathews, A. (1995). Memory for actual and imagined events in OC checkers. *Behavior Research and Therapy, 33*, 665–671.

Conway, K. P., Compton, W., Stinson, F. S., & Grant, B, F. (2006). Lifetime comorbidity of DSM-IV mood and anxiety disorders and specific drug use disorders: Results from the National Epidemiologic Survey on Alcohol and Related Conditions. *Journal of Clinical Psychiatry, 67*, 247–257.

Cook, C. R., & Blacher, J. (2007). Evidence-based psychosocial treatments for tic disorders. *Clinical Psychology: Science and Practice, 14*, 252–267.

Cook-Darzens, S., Doyen, C., Falissard, B., & Mouren, M. (2005). Self-perceived family functioning in 40 French families of anorexic adolescents: Implications for therapy. *European Eating Disorders Review, 13*, 223–236.

Cooke, D. (1998). Psychopathy across cultures. In D. Cooke, A. Forth, & R. Hare (Eds.), *Psychopathy: Theory, research and implications for society* (pp. 13–45). NATO AS1 Series. Netherlands: Kluwer Academic.

Cooke, D. J., Hart, S. D., & Michie, C. (2004). Cross-national differences in the assessment of psychopathy: Do they reflect variations in raters' perceptions of symptoms? *Psychological Assessment, 16*, 335–339.

Coolidge, F. L., Thede, L. L., & Young, S. E. (2002). The heritability of gender identity disorder in a child and adolescent twin sample. *Behavior Genetics, 32*, 251–257.

Coons, P. M. (1998). The dissociative disorders. Rarely considered and underdiagnosed. *Psychiatric Clinics of North America, 21*, 637–648.

Cooper, M. L., Shaver, P. R., & Collins, N. L. (1998). Attachment styles, emotion regulation, and adjustment in adolescence. *Journal of Personality and Social Psychology, 74*, 1380–1397.

Cooperman, A. (2007, January 5). Sedative withdrawal made Rehnquist delusional in '81. *Washington Post*, p. A1.

Cooper-Patrick, L., Powe, N. R., Jenckes, M. W., Gonzales, J. J., Levine, D. M., & Ford, D. E. (1997). Identification of patient attitudes and preferences regarding treatment of depression. *Journal of General Internal Medicine, 12*, 431–438.

Copeland, W. E., Keeler, G., Angold, A., & Costello, E. J. (2007). Traumatic events and posttraumatic stress in childhood. *Archives of General Psychiatry, 64*, 577–584.

Copeland, W. E., Wolke, D., Angold, A., & Costello, E. J. (2013). Adult psychiatric patient outcomes of bullying and being bullied by peers in childhood and adolescence. *JAMA Psychiatry, 70*, 419–426.

Coplan, J. D., Goetz, R., Klein, D. F., Papp, L. A., Fyer, A. J., et al. (1998). Plasma cortisol concentrations preceding lactate-induced panic: Psychological, biochemical, and physiological correlates. *Archives of General Psychiatry, 55*, 130–136.

Corbitt, E. M. (2002). Narcissism from the perspective of the five-factor model. In P. T. Costa, Jr., & T. A. Widiger (Eds.), *Personality disorders and the five-factor model of personality* (2nd ed., pp. 293–298). Washington, DC: American Psychological Association.

Corchs, F., Nutt, D. J., Hood, S., & Bernik, M. (2009). Serotonin and sensitivity to trauma-related exposure in selective serotonin reuptake inhibitors-recovered posttraumatic stress disorder. *Biological Psychiatry, 66*, 17–24.

Cornblatt, B., & Obuchowski, M. (1997). Update of high-risk research: 1987–1997. *International Review of Psychiatry, 9*, 437–447.

Cornblatt, B., Lencz, T., & Obuchowski, M. (2002). The schizophrenia prodrome: Treatment and high-risk perspectives. *Schizophrenia Research, 54*, 177–186.

Cornblatt, B., Obuchowski, M., Schnur, D. B., & O'Brien, J. (1997). Attention and clinical symptoms in schizophrenia. *Psychiatric Quarterly, 68*, 343–359.

Cornblatt, B. A., & Correll, C. U. (2010). A new diagnostic entity in DSM-5? *Medscape*, September 3. Retrieved May 21, 2013, from www.medscape.com/viewarticle/727682

Cornblatt, B. A., Lenzenweger, M. F., Dworkin, R. H., & Erlenmeyer-Kimling, L. (1992). Childhood attentional dysfunctions predict social deficits in unaffected adults at risk for schizophrenia. *British Journal of Psychiatry, 161*, Suppl. 18, 59–64.

Correa, H., Campi-Azevedo, A. C., De Marco, L., Boson, W., Viana, M. M., et al. (2004). Familial suicide behaviour: Association with probands suicide attempt characteristics and 5-HTTLPR polymorphism. *Acta Psychiatrica Scandinavica, 110*, 459–464.

Corrigan, P. W., & Watson, A. C. (2001). Paradox of self-stigma and mental illness. *Clinical Psychological Science Practice, 9*, 35–53.

Coryell, W., Endicott, J., Andreasen, N. C., Keller, M. B., Clayton, P. J., et al. (1988). Depression and panic attacks: The significance of overlap as reflected in follow-up and family study data. *American Journal of Psychiatry, 145*, 293–300.

Cosoff, S. J., & Hafner, R. J. (1998). The prevalence of comorbid anxiety in schizophrenia, schizoaffective disorder and bipolar disorder. *Australian & New Zealand Journal of Psychiatry, 32*, 67–72.

Costello, A., Fletcher, P. C., Dolan, R. J., Frith, C. D., & Shallice, T. (1998). The origins of forgetting in a case of isolated retrograde amnesia following a haemorrhage: Evidence from functional imaging. *Neurocase, 4*, 437–446.

Costello, E. J., Angold, A., Burns, B. J., Stangl, D. K., Tweed, D. L., et al. (1996). The Great Smoky Mountains Study of youth: Goals, design, methods, and the prevalence of DSM-III-R disorders. *Archives of General Psychiatry, 53*, 1129–1136.

Costello, E. J., Compton, S. N., Keeler, G., & Angold, A. (2003). Relationships between poverty and psychopathology: A natural experiment. *JAMA: Journal of the American Medical Association, 290*, 2023–2029.

Costello, E. J., Mustillo, S., Erkanli, A., Keeler, G., & Angold, A. (2003). Prevalence and development of psychiatric disorders in childhood and adolescence. *Archives of General Psychiatry, 60*, 837–844.

Costello, E. J., Pine, D. S., Hammen, C., March, J. S., Plotsky, P. M., et al. (2002). Development and natural history of mood disorders. *Biological Psychiatry, 52*, 529–542.

Cottraux, J. (2004). Recent developments in the research on generalized anxiety disorder. *Current Opinion in Psychiatry, 17*, 49–52.

Cottraux, J., Note, I., Yao, S. N., Lafont, S., Note, B., et al. (2001). A randomized controlled trial of cognitive therapy versus intensive behavior therapy in obsessive compulsive disorder. *Psychotherapy & Psychosomatics, 70*, 288–297.

Coughlin, J. W., & Kalodner, C. (2006). Media literacy as a prevention intervention for college women at low- or high-risk for eating disorders. *Body Image, 3*, 35–43.

Coulston, C. M., Perdices, M., & Tennant, C. C. (2007). The neuropsychological correlates of cannabis use in schizophrenia: Lifetime abuse/dependence, frequency of use, and recency of use. *Schizophrenia Research, 96,* 169–184.

Coulter, D. (2007). Brothers and sisters and Asperger's syndrome. Retrieved October 23, 2007, from http://home.att.net/~coultervideo/assibessay.htm

Council of State Governments. (2005). Mental health courts: A national snapshot. Retrieved October 15, 2007, from www.ojp.usdoj.gov/BJA/pdf/MHC_National_Snapshot.pdf

Coupland, N. J. (2001). Social phobia: Etiology, neurobiology, and treatment. *Journal of Clinical Psychiatry, 62,* 25–35.

Courchesne, E., & Pierce, K. (2005). Why the frontal cortex in autism might be talking only to itself: Local over-connectivity but long-distance disconnection. *Current Opinion in Neurobiology, 15,* 225–230.

Cox, C. B. (2007). Culture and dementia. In C. B. Cox (Ed.), *Dementia and social work practice: Research and interventions* (pp. 173–187). New York: Springer.

Cox, T., Jack, N., Lofthouse, S., Watling, J., Haines, J., & Warren, M. (2005). King George III and porphyria: An elemental hypothesis and investigation. *The Lancet, 366,* 332–335.

Coyne, J. C. (1976). Toward an interactional description of depression. *Psychiatry: Journal for the Study of Interpersonal Processes, 39,* 28–40.

Coyne, J. C., & Downey, G. (1991). Social factors and psychopathology: Stress, social support, and coping processes. *Annual Review of Psychology, 42,* 401–425.

Crabtree, A. (2000). Mesmer, Franz Anton. In A. E. Kazdin (Ed.), *Encyclopedia of psychology* (Vol. 5, pp. 200–201). Washington, DC: American Psychological Association.

Craddock, N., & Owen, M. J. (2005). The beginning of the end for the Kraepelinian dichotomy. *British Journal of Psychiatry, 186,* 364–366.

Crago, M., Shisslak, C. M., & Estes, L. S. (1996). Eating disturbances among American minority groups: A review. *International Journal of Eating Disorders, 19,* 239–248.

Craig, K. (1978). Social modeling influences on pain. In R. Sternback (Ed.), *The psychology of pain* (pp. 67–95). New York: Raven Press.

Craig, T. K., Boardman, A. P., Mills, K., Daly-Jones, O., & Drake. H. (1993). The South London Somatisation Study. I: Longitudinal course and the influence of early life experiences. *British Journal of Psychiatry, 163,* 579–588.

Craig, T. K. J., Bialas, I., Hodson, S., & Cox, A. D. (2004). Intergenerational transmission of somatization behaviour: 2. Observations of joint attention and bids for attention. *Psychological Medicine, 34,* 199–209.

Cramer, V., Torgersen, S., & Kringlen, E. (2003). Personality disorders, prevalence, socio-demographic correlations, quality of life, dysfunction, and the question of continuity. *PTT: Persönlichkeitsstörungen Theorie und Therapie, 7,* 189–198.

Craske, M. G. (1999). *Anxiety disorders: Psychological approaches to theory and treatment.* Boulder, CO: Westview Press.

Craske, M. G., & Barlow, D. H. (1993). Panic disorder and agoraphobia. In D. H. Barlow (Ed.), *Clinical handbook of psychological disorders: A step-by-step treatment manual* (2nd ed., pp. 1–47). New York: Guilford Press.

Craske, M. G., Barlow, D. H., & Meadows, E. A. (2000). *Mastery of your anxiety and panic: Therapist guide for anxiety, panic, and agoraphobia* (3rd ed.). New York: Graywind Publications.

Craske, M. G., Rapee, R. M., Jackel, L., & Barlow, D. H. (1989). Qualitative dimensions of worry in DSM-III-R generalized anxiety disorder subjects and nonanxious controls. *Behaviour Research and Therapy, 27,* 397–402.

Craske, M. G., & Rowe, M. K. (1997). Nocturnal panic. *Clinical Psychology: Science and Practice, 4,* 153–174.

Crawford, H. J., Gur, R. C., Skolnick, B., Gur, R. E., & Benson, D. M. (1993). Effects of hypnosis on regional cerebral blood flow during ischemic pain with and without suggested hypnotic analgesia. *International Journal of Psychophysiology, 15,* 181–195.

Crawford, T. N., Shaver, P. R., Cohen, P., Pilkonis, P. A., Gillath, O., & Kasen, S. (2006). Self-reported attachment, interpersonal aggression, and personality disorder in a prospective community sample of adolescents and adults. *Journal of Personality Disorders, 20,* 331–351.

Creamer, M., Burgess, P., & McFarlane, A. C. (2001). Post-traumatic stress disorder: Findings from the Australian National Survey of Mental Health and Well-Being. *Psychological Medicine, 31,* 1237–1247.

Creed, F. (2006). Can DSM-V facilitate productive research into the somatoform disorders? *Journal of Psychosomatic Research, 60,* 331–334.

Creed, F., & Barsky, A. (2004). A systematic review of the epidemiology of somatisation disorder and hypochondriasis. *Journal of Psychosomatic Research, 56,* 391–408.

Crisp, A. H., Hsu, L. K., Harding, B., & Hartshorn, J. (1980). Clinical features of anorexia nervosa: A study of a consecutive series of 102 female patients. *Journal of Psychosomatic Research, 24,* 179–191.

Critchfield, K. L., & Benjamin, L. S. (2006). Principles for psychosocial treatment of personality disorder: Summary of the APA Division 12 Task Force/NASPR Review. *Journal of Clinical Psychology, 62,* 661–674.

Crits-Christoph, P., Siqueland, L., Blaine, J., Frank, A., Luborsky, L., et al. (1999). Psychosocial treatments for cocaine dependence: National Institute on Drug Abuse Collaborative Cocaine Treatment Study. *Archives of General Psychiatry, 56,* 493–502.

Croen, L. A., Najjar, D. V., Fireman, B., & Grether, J. K. (2007). Maternal and paternal age and risk of autism spectrum disorders. *Archives of Pediatric and Adolescent Medicine, 161,* 334–340.

Cronk, N. J., Slutske, W. S., Madden, P. A. F., Bucholz, K. K., & Heath, A. C. (2004). Risk for separation anxiety disorder among girls: Paternal absence, socioeconomic disadvantage, and genetic vulnerability. *Journal of Abnormal Psychology, 113,* 237–247.

Cross-Disorder Group of the Psychiatric Genomics Consortium. (2013). Identification of risk loci with shared effects on five major psychiatric disorders: A genome-wide analysis. *The Lancet, 381,* 1371–1379.

Crow, S., & Eckert, E. D. (2000, April). *Follow-up of the Minnesota Semi-Starvation Study Participants.* Paper presented at Ninth International Conference on Eating Disorders, New York.

Crow, S. J., Mitchell, J. E., Roerig, J. D., & Steffen, K. (2009). What potential role is there for medication treatment in anorexia nervosa? *International Journal of Eating Disorders, 42,* 1–8.

Crowe, R., Noyes, R., Pauls, D., & Slyman, D. (1983). A family study of panic disorder. *Archives of General Psychiatry, 40,* 1065–1069.

Crowell, S. E., Beauchaine, T. P., Gatzke-Kopp, L., Sylvers, P., Mead, H., & Chipman-Chacon, J. (2006). Autonomic correlates of attention-deficit/hyperactivity disorder and oppositional defiant disorder in preschool children. *Journal of Abnormal Psychology, 115,* 174–178.

Crowther, J. H., Kichler, J. C., Shewood, N. E., & Kuhnert, M. E. (2002). The role of familial factors in bulimia nervosa. *Eating Disorders: The Journal of Treatment & Prevention, 10,* 141–151.

Crowther, J. H., & Williams, N. M. (2011). Body image and bulimia nervosa. In T. F. Cash & L. Smolak (Eds.), *Body image: A handbook of science, practice, and prevention* (2nd ed.) (pp. 288–295). New York: Guilford Press.

Cryan, E. M., Butcher, G. J., and Webb, M. G. (1992). Obsessive-compulsive disorder and paraphilia in a monozygotic twin pair. *British Journal of Psychiatry, 161,* 694–698.

Csernansky, J. G., Mahmoud, R., & Brenner, R. (2002). A comparison of risperidone and haloperidol for the prevention of relapse in patients with schizophrenia. *New England Journal of Medicine, 346,* 16–22.

Csipke, E., & Horne, O. (2007). Pro-eating disorder websites: Users' opinions. *European Eating Disorders Review, 15,* 196–206.

Cuijpers, P. (1997). Bibliotherapy in unipolar depression: A meta-analysis. *Journal of Behavior Therapy and Experimental Psychiatry, 28,* 139–147.

Cuijpers, P. (1998). A psychoeducational approach to the treatment of depression: A meta-analysis of Lewinsohn's "Coping with depression" course. *Behavior Therapy, 29,* 521–533.

Cuijpers, P., Geraedts, A. S., van Oppen, P., Andersson, G., Markowitz, J. C., & van Straten, A. (2011). Interpersonal psychotherapy for depression: A meta-analysis. *American Journal of Psychiatry, 168,* 581–592.

Cukrowicz, K. C., White, B. A., Reitzel, L. R., Burns, A. B., Driscoll, K. A., et al. (2005). Improved treatment outcome associated with the shift to empirically supported treatments in a graduate training clinic. *Professional Psychology: Research and Practice, 36,* 330–337.

Cummings, J. L., Mackell, J., & Kaufer, D. (2008). Behavioral effects of current Alzheimer's disease treatments: A descriptive review. *Alzheimer's & Dementia, 4,* 49–60.

Cunningham Owens, D. G., Carroll, S., Fattah, Z., Clyde, Z., Coffey, I., & Johnstone, E. C. (2001). A randomized, controlled trial of a brief interventional package for schizophrenic outpatients. *Acta Psychiatrica Scandinavica, 103,* 362–371.

Curran, G. M., Flynn, H. A., Kirchner, J., & Booth, B. M. (2000). Depression after alcohol treatment as a risk factor for relapse among male veterans. *Journal of Substance Abuse Treatment, 19,* 259–265.

Curtis, G. C., Magee, W. J., Eaton, W. W., Wittchen, H. U., & Kessler, R. C. (1998). Specific fears and phobias: Epidemiology and classification. *British Journal of Psychiatry, 173,* 212–217.

Custace, J. (1952). *Wisdom, madness and folly.* New York: Pellegrini & Cudahy.

Cyranowski, J., Frank, E., Young, E., & Shear, K. (2000). Adolescent onset of the gender difference in lifetime rates of major depression: A theoretical model. *Archives of General Psychiatry, 57,* 21–27.

Czermak, C., Lehofer, M., Renger, H., Wagner, E. M., Lemonis, L, et al. (2004). Dopamine receptor D3 mRNA expression in human lymphocytes is negatively correlated with the personality trait of persistence. *Journal of Neuroimmunology, 150,* 145–149.

Dackis, C. A., & O'Brien, C. P. (2001). Cocaine dependence: A disease of the brain's reward centers. *Journal of Substance Abuse Treatment, 21,* 111–117.

Daley, D. C., & Salloum, I. (1999). Relapse prevention. In P. J. Ott, R. E. Tarter, & R. T. Ammerman (Eds.), *Sourcebook on substance abuse: Etiology, epidemiology, assessment, and treatment* (pp. 255–263). Needham Heights, MA: Allyn & Bacon.

d'Alfonso, A. A., Aleman, A., Kessels, R. P., Schouten, E. A., Postma, A., et al. (2002). Transcranial magnetic stimulation of left auditory cortex in patients with schizophrenia: Effects on hallucinations and neurocognition. *Journal of Neuropsychiatry and Clinical Neuroscience, 14,* 77–79.

Dalgard, O. S., Dowrick, C., Lehtinen, V., Vazquez-Barquero, J. L., Casey, P., et al. (The ODIN Group). (2006). Negative life events, social support and gender difference in depression: A multinational community survey with data from the ODIN study. *Social Psychiatry and Psychiatric Epidemiology, 41,* 444–451.

D'Amico, E. J., Metrik, J., McCarthy, D. M., Frissell, K. C., Applebaum, M., & Brown, S. A. (2001). Progression into and out of binge drinking among high school students. *Psychology of Addictive Behaviors, 15,* 341–349.

Dannon, P. N., Dolberg, O. T., Schreiber, S., & Grunhaus, L. (2002). Three- and six-month outcome following courses of either ECT or rTMS in a population of severely depressed individuals—preliminary report. *Biological Psychiatry, 51,* 687–690.

Dao, T. K., & Prevatt, F. (2006). A psychometric evaluation of the Rorschach Comprehensive System's Perceptual Thinking Index. *Journal of Personality Assessment, 86,* 180–189.

Dare, C., & Eisler, I. (1997). Family therapy for anorexia nervosa. In D. M. Garner & P. E. Garfinkel (Eds.), *Handbook of treatment for eating disorders* (2nd ed., pp. 307–324). New York: Guilford Press.

Dare, C., Eisler, I., Russell, G., Treasure, J., & Dodge, L. (2001). Psychological therapies for adults with anorexia nervosa: Randomised controlled trial of out-patient treatments. *British Journal of Psychiatry, 178,* 216–221.

Dassori, A. M., Miller, A. L., & Saldana, D. (1995). Schizophrenia among Hispanics: Epidemiology, phenomenology, course, and outcome. *Schizophrenia Bulletin, 21,* 303–312.

Dauncey, K., Giggs, J., Baker, K., & Harrison, K. (1993). Schizophrenia in Nottingham: Lifelong residential mobility of a cohort. *British Journal of Psychiatry, 163,* 613–619.

Davey, G. (Ed.). (1987). *Cognitive processes and Pavlovian conditioning in humans.* Oxford, England: John Wiley & Sons.

David, A. S. (1994). Schizophrenia and the corpus callosum: Developmental, structural and functional relationships. *Behavioural Brain Research, 64,* 203–211.

Davidovsky, A. S., Fleta, J. L. H., & Moreno, T. S. (2007). Neurosurgery and refractory obsessive-compulsive disease: A case report. *Actas Españolas de Psiquiatría, 35,* 336–337.

Davidson, J. R. T. (2001). Pharmacotherapy of generalized anxiety disorder. *Journal of Clinical Psychiatry, 62,* 46–50.

Davidson, J. R. T., DuPont, R. L., Hedges, D., & Haskins, J. T. (1999). Efficacy, safety, and tolerability of venlafaxine extended release and buspirone in outpatients with generalized anxiety disorder. *Journal of Clinical Psychiatry, 60,* 528–535.

Davidson, J. R. T., Foa, E. B., Huppert, J. D., Keefe, F. J., Franklin, M. E., et al. (2004). Fluoxetine, comprehensive cognitive behavioral therapy, and placebo in generalized social phobia. *Archives of General Psychiatry, 61,* 1005–1013.

Davidson, J. R. T., Landburg, P. D., Pearlstein, T., Weisler, R., Sikes, C., & Farfel, G. M. (1997). Double-blind comparison of sertraline and placebo in patients with posttraumatic stress disorder (PTSD). *Abstracts of the American College of Neuropsychopharmacology.* Paper presented at the 36th annual meeting, San Juan, Puerto Rico.

Davidson, K., Norrie, J., Tyrer, P., Gumley, A., Tata, P., et al. (2006). The effectiveness of cognitive behavior therapy for borderline personality disorder: Results from the borderline personality disorder study of cognitive therapy (BOSCOT) trial. *Journal of Personality Disorders, 20,* 450–465.

Davidson, R. J. (1992a). Emotion and affective style: Hemispheric substrates. *Psychological Science, 3,* 39–43.

Davidson, R. J. (1992b). A prolegomenon to the structure of emotion: Gleanings from neuropsychology. *Cognition and Emotion, 6,* 245–268.

Davidson, R. J. (1993). Parsing affective space: Perspectives from neuropsychology and psychophysiology. *Neuropsychology, 7,* 464–475.

Davidson, R. J. (1994). Honoring biology in the study of affective style. In P. Ekman & R. J. Davidson (Eds.), *The nature of emotion: Fundamental questions* (pp. 321–328). New York: Oxford University Press.

Davidson, R. J. (1998). Affective style and affective disorders: Perspectives from affective neuroscience. *Cognition and Emotion, 12,* 307–330.

Davidson, R. J. (2002). Anxiety and affective style: Role of prefrontal cortex and amygdala. *Biological Psychiatry, 51,* 68–80.

Davidson, R. J., Abercrombie, H., Nitschke, J. B., & Putnam, K. (1999). Regional brain function, emotion and disorders of emotion. *Current Opinion in Neurobiology, 9,* 228–234.

Davidson, R. J., Jackson, D. C., & Kalin, N. H. (2000). Emotion, plasticity, context, and regulation: Perspectives from affective neuroscience. *Psychological Bulletin, 126,* 890–909.

Davies, L., Stern, J. S., Agrawal, N., & Robertson, M. M. (2006). A case series of patients with Tourette's Syndrome in the United Kingdom treated with aripiprazole. *Human Psychopharmacology: Clinical and Experimental, 21,* 447–453.

Davis, A.K. & Rosenberg, H. (in press). Acceptability of non-abstinence by addiction professionals in the United States. *Psychology of Addictive Behaviors.*

Davis, C., Claridge, G., & Fox, J. (2000). Not just a pretty face: Physical attractiveness and perfectionism in the risk for eating disorders. *International Journal of Eating Disorders, 27,* 67–73.

Davis, C., Shuster, B., Blackmore, E., & Fox, J. (2004). Looking good—family focus on appearance and the risk for eating disorders. *International Journal of Eating Disorders, 35,* 136–144.

Davis, J. H. (1969). *The Bouviers: Portrait of an American family.* New York: Doubleday.

Davis, J. H. (1996). *Jacqueline Bouvier: An intimate memoir.* New York: Wiley.

Davison, G. C. (2005). Issues and nonissues in the gay-affirmative treatment of patients who are gay, lesbian, or bisexual. *Clinical Psychology: Science and Practice, 12,* 25–28.

Dawson, G., Webb, S. J., Carver, L., Panagiotides, H., & McPartland J. (2004). Young children with autism show atypical brain responses to fearful versus neutral facial expressions of emotion. *Developmental Science, 7,* 340–359.

Dawson, G., Webb, S. J., & McPartland, J. (2005). Understanding the nature of face processing impairment in autism: Insights from behavioral and electrophysiological studies. *Developmental Neuropsychology, 27,* 403–424.

Dawson, M., Mottron, L., Jelenic, P., & Soulières, I. (2005, May). Superior performance of autistics on RPM and PPVT relative to Wechsler scales provides evidence for the nature of autistic intelligence. Poster presented at the International Meeting for Autism Research, Boston, MA.

Dawson, M. E., Hazlett, E. A., Filion, D. L., Nuechterlein, K. H., & Schell, A. M. (1993). Attention and schizophrenia: Impaired modulation of the startle reflex. *Journal of Abnormal Psychology, 102,* 633–641.

De Bellis, M. D., Clark, D. B., Beers, S. R., Soloff, P. H., Boring, A. M., et al. (2000). Hippocampal volume in adolescent-onset alcohol use disorders. *American Journal of Psychiatry, 157,* 737–744.

De Bellis, M. D., Keshavan, M. S., Shifflett, H., Iyengar, S., Dahl, R. E., et al. (2002). Superior temporal gyrus volumes in pediatric generalized anxiety disorder. *Biological Psychiatry, 51,* 553–562.

De Beni, R., & Palladino, P. (2004). Decline in working memory updating through ageing: Intrusion error analyses. *Memory, 12,* 75–89.

de Beurs, E., van Balkom, A. J. L. M., Van Dyck, R., & Lange, A. (1999). Long-term outcome of pharmacological and psychological treatment for panic disorder with agoraphobia: A 1-year naturalistic follow-up. *Acta Psychiatrica Scandinavica, 99,* 59–67.

de Carufel, F., & Trudel, G. (2006). Effects of a new functional-sexological treatment for premature ejaculation. *Journal of Sex & Marital Therapy, 32,* 97–114.

De Hert, M., McKenzie, K., & Peuskens, J. (2001). Risk factors for suicide in young people suffering from schizophrenia: A long-term follow-up study. *Schizophrenia Research, 47,* 127–134.

De la Fuente, J. M., Goldman, S., Stanus, E., Vizuete, C., Morlan, I., et al. (1997). Brain glucose metabolism in borderline personality disorder. *Journal of Psychiatry Research, 31,* 531–541.

De Leo, D. (2002a). Struggling against suicide: The need for an integrative approach. *Crisis: The Journal of Crisis Intervention and Suicide Prevention, 23,* 23–31.

De Leo, D. (2002b). Why are we not getting any closer to preventing suicide? *British Journal of Psychiatry, 181,* 372–374.

De Los Reyes, A., & Kazdin, A. E. (2004). Measuring informant discrepancies in clinical child research. *Psychological Assessment, 16,* 330–334.

de Zwaan, M., Roerig, J. L., & Mitchell, J. E. (2004). Pharmacological treatment of anorexia nervosa, bulimia nervosa, and binge eating disorder. In J. K. Thompson (Ed.), *Handbook of eating disorders and obesity* (pp. 186–217). Hoboken, NJ: John Wiley & Sons.

Deckersbach, T., Rauch, S., Buhlmann, U., & Wilhelm, S. (2006). Habit reversal versus supportive psychotherapy in Tourette's disorder: A randomized controlled trial and predictors of treatment response. *Behaviour Research and Therapy, 44,* 1079–1090.

Degroot, A., & Treit, D. (2002). Dorsal and ventral hippocampal cholinergic systems modulate anxiety in the plus-maze and shock-probe tests. *Brain Research, 949,* 60–70.

Degun-Mather, M. (2002). Hypnosis in the treatment of a case of dissociative amnesia for a 12-year period. *Contemporary Hypnosis, 19,* 33–41.

DeJong, W. (2001). Finding common ground for effective campus-based prevention. *Psychology of Addictive Behaviors, 15,* 292–296.

Del Casale, A., Ferracuti, S., Rapinesi, C., Serata, D., Piccirilli, M., et al. (2012). Functional neuroimaging in specific phobia. *Psychiatry Research: Neuroimaging, 202,* 181–197.

Delgado, P. L., & Moreno, F. A. (1998). Different roles for serotonin in anti-obsessional drug action and the pathophysiology of obsessive-compulsive disorder. *British Journal of Psychiatry, 173,* 21–25.

Delinsky, S. S. (2011). Body image and anorexia nervosa. In T. F. Cash & L. Smolak (Eds.), *Body image: A handbook of science, practice, and prevention* (2nd ed.) (pp. 279–287). New York: Guilford Press.

DeLisi, L. E., Sakuma, M., Tew, W., Kushner, M., Hoff, A. L., & Grimson, R. (1997). Schizophrenia as a chronic active brain process: A study of progressive brain structural change subsequent to the onset of schizophrenia. *Psychiatry Research: Neuroimaging, 74,* 129–140.

Dell, P. F. (1988). Professional skepticism about multiple personality. *Journal of Nervous and Mental Disorders, 176,* 537–555.

Dell'Osso, L., Rucci, P., Cassano, G. B., Maser, J. D., Endicott, J., et al. (2002). Measuring social anxiety and obsessive-compulsive spectra: Comparison of interviews and self-report instruments. *Comprehensive Psychiatry, 43,* 81–87.

Demenescu, L. R., Kortekaas, R., den Boer, J. A., & Aleman, A. (2010). Impaired attribution of emotion to facial expressions in anxiety and major depression. *PLoS ONE, 5,* e15058.

Demopoulos, C., Hopkins, J., & Davis, A. (2013). A comparison of social cognitive profiles in children with autism spectrum disorders and attention-deficit/hyperactivity disorder: A matter of quantitative but not qualitative difference? *Journal of Autism and Developmental Disorders, 43*(5), 1157–1170.

Dennerstein, L., Koochaki, P., Barton, I., & Graziottin, A. (2006). Hypoactive sexual desire disorder in menopausal women: A survey of Western European women. *Journal of Sexual Medicine, 3,* 212–222.

Dennis, W. (1973). *Children of the creche.* New York: Appleton-Century-Crofts.

DeRubeis, R. J., Hollon, S. D., Amsterdam, J. D., Shelton, R. C., Young, P. R., et al. (2005). Cognitive therapy vs medications in the treatment of moderate to severe depression. *Archives of General Psychiatry, 62,* 409–416.

des Portes, V., Hagerman, R. J., & Hendren, R. L. (2003). Pharmacotherapy. In S. Ozonoff, S. J. Rogers, & R. L. Hendren (Eds.), *Autism spectrum disorders: A research review for practitioners.* (pp. 161–186). Washington, DC: American Psychiatric Publishing.

Deshpande, S. W., & Kawane, S. D. (1982). Anxiety and serial verbal learning: A test of the Yerkes-Dodson Law. *Asian Journal of Psychology & Education, 9,* 18–23.

Deuschle, M., Hamann, B., Meichel, C., Krumm, B., Lederbogen, F., et al. (2003). Antidepressive treatment with amitriptyline and paroxetine: Effects on saliva cortisol concentrations. *Journal of Clinical Psychopharmacology, 23,* 201–205.

Deutsch, M. (1968). Field theory in social psychology. In G. Lindzey & E. Aronson (Eds.), *Handbook of social psychology* (Vol. 1, pp. 412–487). Cambridge, MA: Addison-Wesley.

DeVane, C. L. (1997). The place of selective serotonin reuptake inhibitors in the treatment of panic disorder. *Pharmacotherapy, 17,* 282–292.

Deveson, A. (1991). *Tell me I'm here: One family's experience of schizophrenia.* New York: Penguin Books.

Devinsky, O., Mesad, S., & Alper, K. (2001). Nondominant hemisphere lesions and conversion nonepileptic seizures. *Journal of Neuropsychiatry and Clinical Neuroscience, 13,* 367–373.

Di Ceglie, D. (2000). Gender identity disorder in young people. *Advances in Psychiatric Treatment, 6,* 458–466.

Di Ceglie, D., Freedman, D., McPherson, S., & Richardson, P. (2002). Children and adolescents referred to a specialist gender identity development service: Clinical features and demographic characteristics. *International Journal of Transgenderism, 6,* n.p.

Dick, D. M., Viken, R. J., Kaprio, J., Pulkkinen, L., & Rose, R. J. (2005). Understanding the covariation among childhood externalizing symptoms: Genetic and environmental influences on conduct disorder, attention deficit hyperactivity disorder, and oppositional defiant disorder symptoms. *Journal of Abnormal Child Psychology, 33,* 219–229.

Dickerson, F. B. (2004). Update on cognitive behavioral psychotherapy for schizophrenia: Review of recent studies. *Journal of Cognitive Psychotherapy, 18,* 189–205.

Dickey, C. C., McCarley, R. W., & Shenton, M. E. (2002). The brain in schizotypal personality disorder: A review of structural MRI and CT findings. *Harvard Review of Psychiatry, 10,* 1–15.

Dickinson, D., & Coursey, R. D. (2002). Independence and overlap among neurocognitive correlates of community functioning in schizophrenia. *Schizophrenia Research, 56,* 161–170.

Dickinson, D., Bellack, A. S., & Gold, J. M. (2007). Social/communication skills, cognition, and vocational functioning in schizophrenia. *Schizophrenia Bulletin, 33,* 1213–1220.

Dickson, H., Laurens, K. R., Cullen, A. E., & Hodgins, S. (2012). Meta-analyses of cognitive and motor function in youth aged 16 years and younger who subsequently develop schizophrenia. *Psychological Medicine: A Journal of Research in Psychiatry and the Allied Sciences, 42,* 743–755.

Didic, M., Ali Chérif, A., Gambarelli, D., Poncet, M., & Boudouresques, J. (1998). A permanent pure amnestic syndrome of insidious onset related to Alzheimer's disease. *Annals of Neurology, 43*, 526–530.

Dikel, T. N., Engdahl, B., & Eberly, R. (2005). PTSD in former prisoners of war: Prewar, wartime, and postwar factors. *Journal of Traumatic Stress, 18*, 69–77.

DiLillo, D. (2001). Interpersonal functioning among women reporting a history of childhood sexual abuse: Empirical findings and methodological issues. *Clinical Psychology Review, 21*, 553–576.

DiMauro, J., Domingues, J., Fernandez, G., & Tolin, D. F. (2013). Long-term effectiveness of CBT for anxiety disorders in an adult outpatient clinic sample: A follow-up study. *Behaviour Research and Therapy, 51*(2), 82–86.

Dimeff, L., & Linehan, M. M. (2001). Dialectical behavior therapy in a nutshell. *The California Psychologist, 34*, 10–13.

Dimidjian, S., Hollon, S. D., Dobson, K. S., Schmaling, K. B., Kohlenberg, R. J., et al. (2006). Randomized trial of behavioral activation, cognitive therapy, and antidepressant medication in the acute treatment of adults with major depression. *Journal of Consulting and Clinical Psychology, 74*, 658–670.

Dingemans, A. E., van Rood, Y. R., de Groot, I., & van Furth, E. F. (2012). Body dysmorphic disorder in patients with an eating disorder: Prevalence and characteristics. *International Journal of Eating Disorders, 45*(4), 562–569.

Dinnel, D. L., Kleinknecht, R. A., & Tanaka-Matsumi, J. (2002). A cross-cultural comparison of social phobia symptoms. *Journal of Psychopathology & Behavioral Assessment, 24*, 75–84.

D'Ippoliti, D., Davoli, M., Perucci, C. A., Pasqualini, F., & Bargagli, A. M. (1998). Retention in treatment of heroin users in Italy: The role of treatment type and of methadone maintenance dosage. *Drug and Alcohol Dependence, 52*, 167–171.

Dirks-Linhorst, P. A., & Linhorst, D. M. (2012). Recidivism outcomes for suburban mental health court defendants. *American Journal of Criminal Justice, 37*(1), 76–91.

Dishion, T. J., & Medici Skaggs, N. (2000). An ecological analysis of monthly "bursts" in early adolescent substance use. *Applied Developmental Science, 4*, 89–97.

Dishion, T. J., & Stormshak, E. A. (2007). *Intervening in children's lives: An ecological, family-centered approach to mental health care.* Washington, DC: American Psychological Association.

Dixon, L., Adams, C., & Lucksted, A. (2000). Update on family psychoeducation for schizophrenia. *Schizophrenia Bulletin, 26*, 5–20.

Docter, R. F., & Prince, V. (1997). Transvestism: A survey of 1032 cross-dressers. *Archives of Sexual Behavior, 26*, 589–605.

Dodge, K. A., & Pettit, G. S. (2003). A biopsychosocial model of the development of chronic conduct problems in adolescence. *Developmental Psychology, 39*, 349–371.

Dodge, R., Sindelar, J., & Sinha, R. (2005). The role of depression symptoms in predicting drug abstinence in outpatient substance abuse treatment. *Journal of Substance Abuse Treatment, 28*, 189–196.

Doerfel-Baasen, D., & Rauh, H. (2001). Parents and teachers of young children under conditions of sociopolitical change. *American Behavioral Scientist, 44*, 1818–1842.

Dohrenwend, B. P., Levav, I., Shrout, P. E., Schwartz, S., Naveh, G., et al. (1992). Socioeconomic status and psychiatric disorders: The causation-selection issue. *Science, 255*, 946–952.

Dolan, A. (2006, April 3). The obsessive disorder that haunts my life. *Daily Mail.* Retrieved February 25 2009 from www.dailymail.co.uk/pages/live/articles/showbiz/showbiznews.html?in_article_id=381802&in_page_id=1773

Dolan, M., & Park, I. (2002). The neuropsychology of antisocial personality disorder. *Psychological Medicine, 32*, 417–427.

Dolan-Sewell, R., & Insel, T. R. (2005). Special issue on anorexia nervosa. *International Journal of Eating Disorders, 37*, S1–S9.

Dolan-Sewell, R. T., Krueger, R. F., & Shea, M. T. (2001). Co-occurrence with syndrome disorders. In J. W. Livesley (Ed.), *Handbook of personality disorders: Theory, research, and treatment* (pp. 84–104). New York: Guilford Press.

Domjan, M., Cusato, B., & Krause, M. (2004). Learning with arbitrary versus ecological conditioned stimuli: Evidence from sexual conditioning. *Psychonomic Bulletin & Review, 11*, 232–246.

Donegan, N. H., Sanislow, C. A., Blumberg, H. P., Fulbright, R. K., Lacadie, C., et al. (2003). Amygdala hyperreactivity in borderline personality disorder: Implications for emotional dysregulation. *Biological Psychiatry, 54*, 1284–1293.

Dong, W. K., & Greenough, W. T. (2004). Plasticity of nonneuronal brain tissue: Roles in developmental disorders. *Mental Retardation and Developmental Disabilities Research Reviews, 10*, 85–90.

Donovan, J., & Jessor, R. (1985). Structure of problem behavior in adolescence and young adulthood. *Journal of Consulting and Clinical Psychology, 53*, 890–904.

Dorcus, R. M., & Shaffer, G. W. (1945). Functional psychoses. In R. M. Dorcus & G. W. Shaffer, *Textbook of abnormal psychology* (3rd ed., pp. 304–330). Baltimore: Williams & Wilkins.

Dorr, D. (1998). Psychopathy in the pedophile. In T. Millon, E. Simonsen, M. Birket-Smith, & R. D. Davis (Eds.), *Psychopathy: Antisocial, criminal, and violent behavior* (pp. 304–320). New York: Guilford Press.

Dorris, L., Espie, C. A. E., Knott, F., & Salt, J. (2004). Mind-reading difficulties in the siblings of people with Asperger's syndrome: Evidence for a genetic influence in the abnormal development of a specific cognitive domain. *Journal of Child Psychology and Psychiatry, 45*, 412–418.

Double, D. (2002). The limits of psychiatry. *BMJ: British Medical Journal, 324*, 900–904.

Dowdall, G. W., Crawford, M., & Wechsler, H. (1998). Binge drinking among American college women: A comparison of single-sex and coeducational institutions. *Psychology of Women Quarterly, 22*, 705–715.

Dowling, J. E. (1992). *Neurons and networks: An introduction to neuroscience.* Cambridge, MA: Harvard University Press.

Draijer, N., & Friedl, M. (1999). The prevalence of dissociative disorders and DID among psychiatric inpatients: A meta-analysis of prevalence studies. In A. Aukamp, R. Blizard, J. Chu, G. Fair, & S. Gold (Eds.), *Proceedings of the 16th International Fall Conference of the International Society for the Study of Dissociation.*

Driessen, M., Herrmann J., Stahl, K., Zwaan, M., Meier, S., et al. (2000). Magnetic resonance imaging volumes of the hippocampus and the amygdala in women with borderline personality disorder and early traumatization. *Archives of General Psychiatry, 57*, 1115–1122.

Drotar, D. (2006). Research design considerations for psychological interventions. In D. Drotar, *Psychological interventions in childhood chronic illness* (pp. 59–83). Washington, DC: American Psychological Association.

Drug Court Clearinghouse and Technical Assistance Project. (1998, June). *Looking at a decade of drug courts* (Publication No. NCJ 171140).

Drummond, K. D., Bradley, S. J., Peterson-Badali, M., & Zucker, K. J. (2008). A follow-up study of girls with gender identity disorder. *Developmental Psychology, 44*, 34–45.

Druss, B. G., Schlesinger, M., & Allen, H. M., Jr. (2001). Depressive symptoms, satisfaction with health care, and 2-year work outcomes in an employed population, *American Journal of Psychiatry, 158*, 731–734.

D'Silva, K., Duggan, C., & McCarthy, L. (2004). Does treatment really make psychopaths worse? A review of the evidence. *Journal of Personality Disorders, 18*(2), 163–177.

Duberstein, P. R., & Conwell, Y. (1997). Personality disorders and completed suicide: A methodological and conceptual review. *Clinical Psychology: Science and Practice, 4*, 359–376.

Duffy, M., Gillespie, K., & Clark, D. M. (2007). Post-traumatic stress disorder in the context of terrorism and other civil conflict in Northern Ireland: Randomised controlled trial. *British Medical Journal, 334*, 1147.

Dugas, M. J., Ladouceur, R., Léger, E., Freeston, M. H., Langolis, F., et al. (2003). Group cognitive-behavioral therapy for generalized anxiety disorder: Treatment outcome and long-term follow-up. *Journal of Consulting and Clinical Psychology, 71*, 821–825.

Dukakis, K. (2002). *Kitty Dukakis Speaks Out About Shock Therapy.* CNN, airdate May 21, 2:21pm EST.

Dukakis, K., & Scovell, J. (1991). *Now you know.* New York: Simon and Shuster.

Dukakis, K., & Tye, L. (2006). *Shock.* New York: Avery.

Duncan, B. L. (2002). The Legacy of Saul Rosenzweig: The Profundity of the Dodo Bird. *Journal of Psychotherapy Integration, 12,* 32–57.

Dunner, D. L. (2001). Acute and maintenance treatment of chronic depression. *Journal of Clinical Psychiatry, 62,* 10–16.

Durbin, C. E., & Klein, D. N. (2006). Ten-year stability of personality disorders among outpatients with mood disorders. *Journal of Abnormal Psychology, 115,* 75–84.

Durham v. United States, 214 F. 2d 862 (1954).

Durham, R. C., Chambers, J. A., MacDonald R. R., Power, K. G., & Major, K. (2003). Does cognitive-behavioural therapy influence the long-term outcome of generalized anxiety disorder? An 8–14 year follow-up of two clinical trials. *Psychological Medicine, 33,* 499–509.

Durkheim, E. (1951). *Suicide: A study in sociology.* New York: Free Press. (Original work published 1897).

Durston, S., Hulshoff Pol, H. E., Schnack, H. G., Buitelaar, J. K., Steenhuis, M. P., et al. (2004) Magnetic resonance imaging of boys with attention-deficit/hyperactivity disorder and their unaffected siblings. *Journal of the American Academy of Child and Adolescent Psychiatry, 43,* 332–340.

Dusky v. United States, 362 U.S. 402 (1960), quoted in *Godinez,* 509 U.S. 398.

Dwight-Johnson, M., Sherbourne, C. D., Liao, D., & Wells, K. B. (2000). Treatment preferences among primary care patients. *Journal of General Internal Medicine, 15,* 527–534.

Dzokoto, V. A., & Adams, G. (2005). Understanding genital-shrinking epidemics in West Africa: Koro, juju, or mass psychogenic illness? *Culture, Medicine and Psychiatry, 29,* 53–78.

Eakin, E. (2000, January 15). Bigotry as mental illness or just another norm. *New York Times,* pp. 1, 31.

Easton, C. J., Swan, S., & Sinha, R. (2000). Prevalence of family violence in clients entering substance abuse treatment. *Journal of Substance Abuse Treatment, 18,* 23–28.

Eaton, W., & Kessler, L. (1985). The NIMH Epidemiologic Catchment Area Study. *Epidemiological Field Methods in Psychiatry.* New York: Academic Press.

Ecker, C., Suckling, J., Deoni, S. C., Lombardo, M. V., Bullmore, E. T., et al. (2012). Brain anatomy and its relationship to behavior in adults with autism spectrum disorder: A multicenter magnetic resonance imaging study. *Archives of General Psychiatry, 69,* 195–209.

Eddy, K. T., Dorer, D. J., Franko, D. L., Tahilani, K., Thompson-Brenner, H., & Herzog, D. B. (2007). Should bulimia nervosa be subtyped by history of anorexia nervosa? A longitudinal validation. *International Journal of Eating Disorders, 40,* S67–S71.

Eddy, K. T., Dorer, D. J., Franko, D. L., Tahilani, K., Thompson-Brenner, H., & Herzog, D. B. (2008). Diagnostic crossover in anorexia nervosa and bulimia nervosa: Implications for DSM-V. *American Journal of Psychiatry, 165,* 245–250.

Eddy, K. T., Keel, P. K., Dorer, D. J., Delinsky, S. S., Franko, D. L., & Herzog, D. B. (2002). Longitudinal comparison of anorexia nervosa subtypes. *International Journal of Eating Disorders, 31,* 191–201.

Edelson, M. G. (2006). Are the majority of children with autism mentally retarded? A systematic evaluation of the data. *Focus on Autism and Other Developmental Disabilities, 21,* 66–83.

Edgerton, R. B., & Cohen, A. (1994). Culture and schizophrenia: The DOSMD challenge. *British Journal of Psychiatry, 164,* 222–231.

Edwards, E., Kornrich, W., Houtten, P. V., & Henn, F. A. (1992). Presynaptic serotonin mechanisms in rats subjected to inescapable shock. *Neuropharmacology, 31,* 323–330.

Eger, E. I., II, Gong, D., Xing, Y., Raines, D. E., & Flood, P. (2002). Acetylcholine receptors and thresholds for convulsions from flurothyl and 1,2-dichlorohexafluorocyclobutane. *Anesthesia & Analgesia, 95,* 1611–1615.

Eggert, J., Levendosky, A., & Klump, K. (2007). Relationships among attachment styles, personality characteristics, and disordered eating. *International Journal of Eating Disorders, 40,* 149–155.

Egley, L. C. (1991). Defining the Tarasoff duty. *The Journal of Psychiatry and Law, 19,* 99–133.

Ehlers, A., Mayou, R. A., & Bryant, B. (1998). Psychological predictors of chronic posttraumatic stress disorder after motor vehicle accidents. *Journal of Abnormal Psychology, 107,* 508–519.

Eich, E., Macaulay, D., & Lam, R. W. (1997). Mania, depression, and mood dependent memory. *Cognition and Emotion, 11,* 607–618.

Eich, E., Macaulay, D., & Ryan, L. (1994). Mood dependent memory for events of the personal past. *Journal of Experimental Psychology: General, 123,* 201–215.

Eisen, J. L., Coles, M. E., Shea, M. T., Pagano, M. E., Stout, R. L., et al. (2006). Clarifying the convergence between obsessive compulsive personality disorder criteria and obsessive compulsive disorder. *Journal of Personality Disorders, 20,* 294–305.

Eisen, K. P., Allen, G. J., Bollash, M., & Pescatello, L. S. (2008). Stress management in the workplace: A comparison of a computer-based and an in-person stress-management intervention. *Computers in Human Behavior, 24,* 486–496.

Eisman, E. J., Dies, R. R., Finn, S. E., Eyde, L. D., Kay, G. G., et al. (2000). Problems and limitations in using psychological assessment in the contemporary health care delivery system. *Professional Psychology: Research and Practice, 31,* 131–140.

Ekman, P. (1984). Expression and the nature of emotion. In K. R. Scherer & P. Ekman (Eds.), *Approaches to emotion* (pp. 319–343). Hillsdale, NJ: Erlbaum.

El-Bassel, N., Schilling, R., Turnbull, J., & Su, K. (1993). Correlates of alcohol use among methadone patients. *Alcoholism, Clinical and Experimental Research, 17,* 681–686.

Eldredge, K. L., Agras, W. S., & Arnow, B. (1994). The last supper: Emotional determinants of pretreatment weight fluctuations in obese binge eaters. *International Journal of Eating Disorders, 16,* 83–88.

Eley, T. C., Deater-Deckard, K., Fombone, E., Fulker, D. W., & Plomin, R. (1998). An adoption study of depressive symptoms in middle childhood. *Journal of Child Psychology & Psychiatry & Allied Disciplines, 39,* 337–345.

Eligon, J. (2008, October 15). Suspect in therapist death is to be institutionalized. *The New York Times.* Retrieved March 2, 2009, from www.nytimes.com/2008/10/15/nyregion/15tarloff.html?pagewanted=print

El-Islam, M. F. (1991). Transcultural aspects of schizophrenia and ICD-10. *Psychiatria Danubina, 3,* 485–494.

Elkin, I. (1994). The NIMH Treatment of Depression Collaborative Research Program: Where we began and where we are. In A. E. Bergin & S. L. Garfield (Eds.), *Handbook of psychotherapy and behavior change* (4th ed., pp. 114–139). Oxford, England: John Wiley & Sons.

Elkin, I., Gibbons, R. D., Shea, M. T., Sotsky, S. M., Watkins, J. T., et al. (1995). Initial severity and differential treatment outcome in the National Institute of Mental Health Treatment of Depression Collaborative Research Program. *Journal of Consulting and Clinical Psychology, 63,* 841–847.

Elkin, I., Parloff, M. B., Hadley, S. W., & Autry, J. H. (1985). NIMH Treatment of Depression Collaborative Research Program: Background and research plan. *Archives of General Psychiatry, 42,* 305–316.

Elkins, I. J., McGue, M., Malone, S., & Iacono, W. G. (2004). The effect of parental alcohol and drug disorders on adolescent personality. *American Journal of Psychiatry, 161,* 670–676.

Ellickson, P. L., Tucker, J. S., Klein, D. J., & Saner, H. (2004). Antecedents and outcomes of marijuana use initiation during adolescence. *Preventive Medicine: An International Journal Devoted to Practice and Theory, 39,* 976–984.

Elliott, A. J., Pages, K. P., Russo, J., & Wilson, L. G. (1996). A profile of medically serious suicide attempts. *Journal of Clinical Psychiatry, 57,* 567–571.

Elliott, G. C., Cunningham, S. M., Linder, M., Colangelo, M., & Gross, M. (2005). Child physical abuse and self-perceived social isolation among adolescents. *Journal of Interpersonal Violence, 20,* 1663–1684.

Elliott, R., Greenberg, L. S., & Lietaer, G. (2004). Research on experiential psychotherapies. In M. J. Lambert (Ed.), *Bergin & Garfield's handbook of psychotherapy and behavior change* (5th ed., pp. 493–540). New York: John Wiley & Sons.

Ellis, A., & MacLaren, C. (1998). *Rational emotive behavior therapy: A therapist's guide.* Atascadero, CA: Impact Publishers.

Ellison, J. M., & McCarter, R. H. G. (2002). Combined treatment for anxiety disorders. In D. J. Stein & E. Holland (Eds.), *Textbook of anxiety disorders* (pp. 93–106). Washington DC: American Psychiatric Publishing.

Ellman, L. M. (2008). Pre and perinatal factors in the neurodevelopmental course of schizophrenia: Neurocognitive and clinical outcomes. *Dissertation Abstracts International: Section B: The Sciences and Engineering, 69(1),* 673B.

Elsass, P. (2001). Individual and collective traumatic memories: A qualitative study of post-traumatic stress disorder symptoms in two Latin American localities. *Transcultural Psychiatry, 38,* 306–316.

Elzinga, B. M., Phaf, R. H., Ardon, A. M., & van Dyck, R. (2003). Directed forgetting between, but not within, dissociative personality states. *Journal of Abnormal Psychology, 112,* 237–243.

EMDR Institute, Inc. website. Accessed April 28, 2013. www.emdr.com

Emerich v. Philadelphia Center for Human Development, 720 A.2d 1032 (Pa. 1998).

Emmelkamp, P. M. G. (1994). Behavior therapy with adults. In A. E. Bergin & S. L. Garfield (Eds.), *Handbook of psychotherapy and behavior change* (4th ed., pp. 379–427). Oxford, England: John Wiley & Sons.

Emmelkamp, P. M. G. (2004). Behavior therapy with adults. In M. J. Lambert (Ed.), *Bergin and Garfield's handbook of psychotherapy and behavior change* (5th ed., pp. 393–446). New York: John Wiley & Sons.

Emmelkamp, P. M. G., Benner, A., Kuipers, A., Feiertag, G. A., Koster, H. C., & van Apeldoorn, F. J. (2006). Comparison of brief dynamic and cognitive-behavioural therapies in avoidant personality disorder. *British Journal of Psychiatry, 189,* 60–64.

Emmelkamp, P. M. G., Bruynzeel, M., Drost, L., & Van Der Mast, C. A. P. G. (2001). Virtual reality treatment in acrophobia: A comparison with exposure in vivo. *CyberPsychology & Behavior, 4,* 335–339.

Emmelkamp, P. M. G., Krijn, M., Hulsbosch, A. M., de Vries, S., Schuemie, M. J., & van der Mast, C. A. P. G. (2002). Virtual reality treatment versus exposure in vivo: A comparative evaluation in acrophobia. *Behaviour Research & Therapy, 40,* 509–516.

Emmons, S., Geiser, C., Kaplan, K., & Harrow, M. (1997). *Living with schizophrenia.* Washington, DC: Taylor & Francis.

Eng, W., & Heimberg, R. G. (2006). Interpersonal correlates of generalized anxiety disorder: Self versus other perception. *Journal of Anxiety Disorders, 19,* 143–156.

Engel, G. L. (1977). The need for a new medical model: A challenge to biomedicine. *Science, 196,* 129–136.

Engel, G. L. (1980). The clinical application of the biopsychosocial model. *American Journal of Psychiatry, 137,* 535–544.

Entwisle, D. R. (1972). To dispel fantasies about fantasy-based measures of achievement motivation. *Psychological Bulletin, 77,* 377–391.

Eplov, L., Giraldi, A., Davidsen, M., Garde, K., & Kamper-Jorgensen, F. (2007). Sexual desire in a nationally representative Danish population. *Journal of Sexual Medicine, 4,* 47–56.

Epstein, C. M., Figiel, G. S., McDonald, W. M., Amazon-Leece, J., & Figiel, L. (1998). Rapid rate transcranial magnetic stimulation in young and middle-aged refractory depressed patients. *Psychiatric Annals, 28,* 36–39.

Epstein, D. H., Willner-Reid, J., Vahbzadeh, M., Mezghanni, M., Lin, J.-L., & Preston, K. L. (2009). Real-time electronic diary reports of cue exposure and mood in the hours before cocaine and heroin craving and use. *Archives of General Psychiatry, 66,* 88–94.

Epstein, J. N., Casey, B. J., Tonev, S. T., Davidson, M. C., Reiss, A. L., et al. (2007). ADHD- and medication-related brain activation effects in concordantly affected parent–child dyads with ADHD. *Journal of Child Psychology and Psychiatry, 48,* 899–913.

Ergene, T. (2003). Effective interventions on test anxiety reduction: A meta-analysis. *School Psychology International, 24,* 313–328.

Erickson, W. D., Walbeck, N. H., & Seely, R. K. (1988). Behavior patterns of child molesters. *Archives of Sexual Behavior, 17,* 77–87.

Eriksen, K., & Kress, V. E. (2005). *Beyond the DSM story: Ethical quandaries, challenges, and best practices.* Thousand Oaks, CA: Sage Publications.

Erkiran, M., Özünalan, H., Evren, C., Aytaçlar, S., Kirisci, L., & Tarter, R. (2006). Substance abuse amplifies the risk for violence in schizophrenia spectrum disorder. *Addictive Behaviors, 31,* 1797–1805.

Erlenmeyer-Kimling, L., Rock, D., Roberts, S. A., Janal, M., Kestenbaum, C., et al. (2000). Attention, memory, and motor skills as childhood predictors of schizophrenia-related psychoses: The New York High-Risk Project. *American Journal of Psychiatry, 157,* 1416–1422.

Ernst, A. M., & Chefer, S. (2001). Neuroimaging and substance abuse disorders in the year 2000. *Current Opinion in Psychiatry, 14,* 179–185.

Erzegovesi, S., Cavallini, M. C., Cavedini, P., Diaferia, G., Locatelli, M., & Bellodi, L. (2001). Clinical predictors of drug response in obsessive-compulsive disorder. *Journal of Clinical Psychopharmacology, 21,* 488–492.

Escobar, J. I. (1987). Cross-cultural aspects of the somatization trait. *Hospital and Community Psychiatry, 38,* 174–180.

Escobar, J. I. (1996). Pharmacological treatment of somatization/hypochondriasis. *Psychopharmacology Bulletin, 32,* 589–596.

Escobar, J. I., Nervi, C. H., & Gara, M. A. (2000). Immigration and mental health: Mexican Americans in the United States. *Harvard Review of Psychiatry, 8,* 64–72.

Espy, K. A., Molfese, D. L., Molfese, V. J., & Modglin, A. (2004). Development of auditory event-related potentials in young children and relations to word-level reading abilities at age 8 years. *Annals of Dyslexia, 54,* 9–38.

Etheridge, R. M., Craddock, S. G., Hubbard, R. L., & Rounds-Bryant, J. L. (1999). The relationship of counselling and self-help participation to patient outcomes in DATOS. *Drug and Alcohol Dependence, 57,* 99–112.

Eubanks-Carter, C., Burckell, L. A., & Goldfried, M. R. (2005). Enhancing therapeutic effectiveness with lesbian, gay, and bisexual clients. *Clinical Psychology: Science and Practice, 12,* 1–18.

Evans, G., & Farberow, N. L. (1988). *The encyclopedia of suicide.* New York: Facts on File.

Evans, G. W., & Stecker, R. (2004). Motivational consequences of environmental stress. *Journal of Environmental Psychology, 24,* 143–165.

Evans, J., Heron, J., Francomb, H., Oke, S., & Golding, J. (2001). Cohort study of depressed mood during pregnancy and after childbirth. *British Medical Journal, 323,* 257–260.

Evans, S., Ferrando, S., Findler, M., Stowell, C., Smart, C., & Haglin, D. (2008). Mindfulness-based cognitive therapy for generalized anxiety disorder. *Journal of Anxiety Disorders, 22,* 716–721.

Everly Jr., G. S., & Lating, J. M. (2004). The defining moment of psychological trauma: What makes a traumatic event traumatic? In G. S. Everly, Jr., & J. M. Lating (Eds.), *Personality-guided therapy for posttraumatic stress disorder* (pp. 33–51). Washington, DC: American Psychological Association.

Ewing, C. P., & McCann, J. T. (2006). *Minds on trial: Great cases in law and psychology.* New York: Oxford University Press.

Exner, J. E. (1974). *The Rorschach: A comprehensive system.* Oxford, UK: John Wiley.

Eyler, L. T., Mirzakhanian, H., & Jeste, D. V. (2005). A preliminary study of interactive questioning methods to assess and improve understanding of informed consent among patients with schizophrenia. *Schizophrenia Research, 75,* 193–198.

Eysenck, H. J. (1957). *The dynamics of anxiety and hysteria: An experimental application of modern learning theory topsychiatry.* Oxford, England: Praeger.

Eysenck, H. J. (1990). Genetic and environmental contributions to individual differences: The three major dimensions of personality. *Journal of Personality, 58,* 245–261.

Fabian, L. J., & Thompson, J. K. (1989). Body image and eating disturbance in young females. *International Journal of Eating Disorders, 8,* 63–74.

Fabiano, E., Robinson, D., & Porporino, F. (1990). *A preliminary assessment of the cognitive skills training program: A component of living skills programming: Program description, research findings and implementation strategy.* Ottawa: Correctional Service of Canada.

Fabre, L. F., & Smith, L. C. (2012). The effect of major depression on sexual function in women. *Journal of Sexual Medicine, 9(1),* 231–239.

Faces and Voices of Recovery. (2007a). Retrieved July 30, 2007 from www .facesandvoicesofrecovery.org/resources/story_ jamieson.php

Faces and Voices of Recovery. (2007b). Retrieved July 30, 2007 from www .facesandvoicesofrecovery.org/resources/story_ elaine.php

Faces and Voices of Recovery. (2007c). Retrieved July 30, 2007 from www .facesandvoicesofrecovery.org/resources/story_ brown.php

Fagan, P. J., Wise, T. N., Schmidt, C. W., Jr., & Berlin, F. S. (2002). Pedophilia. *JAMA: Journal of the American Medical Association, 288,* 2458–2465.

Fahy, T. A. (1988). The diagnosis of multiple personality disorder: A critical review. *British Journal of Psychiatry, 153,* 597–606.

Fahy, T. A., Abas, M., & Brown, J. C. (1989). Multiple personality: A symptom of psychiatric disorder. *British Journal of Psychiatry, 154,* 99–101.

Fairburn, C., Cooper, Z., Doll, H., Norman, P., & O'Conner, M. (2000). The natural course of bulimia nervosa and binge eating disorder in young women. *Archives of General Psychiatry, 57,* 659–665.

Fairburn, C. G. (1997). Interpersonal psychotherapy for bulimia nervosa. In D. M. Garner & P. E. Garfinkel (Eds.), *Handbook of treatment for eating disorders* (2nd ed., pp. 278–294). New York: Guilford Press.

Fairburn, C. G. (1998). Interpersonal psychotherapy for bulimia nervosa. In J. C. Markowitz (Ed.), *Interpersonal psychotherapy* (pp. w99–128). Washington, DC: American Psychiatric Association.

Fairburn, C. G. (2005). Evidence-based treatment of anorexia nervosa. *International Journal of Eating Disorders, 37,* S26–S30.

Fairburn, C. G., & Bohn, K. (2005). Eating disorder NOS (EDNOS): An example of the troublesome "not otherwise specified" (NOS) category in DSM-IV-TR. *Behaviour Research and Therapy, 43,* 691–701.

Fairburn, C. G., & Cooper, Z. (2011). Eating disorders, DSM-5, and clinical reality. *British Journal of Psychiatry, 198,* 8–10.

Fairburn, C. G., Cooper, Z., & Cooper, P. (1986). The clinical features and maintenance of bulimia nervosa. In K. D. Brownell & J. Foreyt (Eds.), *Physiology, psychology, and treatment of eating disorders* (pp. 389–404). New York: Basic Books.

Fairburn, C. G., Cooper, Z., Doll, H. A., & Davies, B. A. (2005). Identifying dieters who will develop an eating disorder: A prospective, population-based study. *American Journal of Psychiatry, 162,* 249–2255.

Fairburn, C. G., Jones, R., Peveler, R. C., Hope, R. A., & O'Connor, M. (1993). Psychotherapy and bulimia nervosa: Longer-term effects of interpersonal psychotherapy, behavior therapy, and cognitive behavior therapy. *Archives of General Psychiatry, 50,* 419–428.

Fairburn, C. G., Kirk, J., O'Connor, M., & Cooper, P. J. (1986). A comparison of two psychological treatments for bulimia nervosa. *Behaviour Research and Therapy, 24,* 629–643.

Fairburn, C. G., Marcus, M. D., & Wilson, G. T. (1993). Cognitive-behavioral therapy for binge eating and bulimia nervosa: A comprehensive treatment manual. In C. G. Fairburn & G. T. Wilson (Eds.), *Binge eating: Nature, assessment, and treatment* (pp. 361–404). New York: Guilford Press.

Fairburn, C. G., Norman, P. A., Welch, S. L., O'Connor, M., Doll, H., & Peveler, R. (1995). A prospective study of outcome in bulimia nervosa and the long-term effects of three psychological treatments. *Archives of General Psychiatry, 52,* 304–312.

Fairburn, C. G., Palmer, R. L., Bohn, K., Doll, H. A., & O'Connor, M. E. (in preparation). The clinical features of patients with Eating Disorders NOS.

Fairburn, C. G., Peveler, R. C., Jones, R., Hope, R. A., & Doll, H. A. (1993). Predictors of 12-month outcome in bulimia nervosa and the influence of attitudes to shape and weight. *Journal of Consulting and Clinical Psychology, 61,* 696–698.

Fairburn, C. G., Stice, E., Cooper, Z., Doll, H. A., Norman, P. A., & O'Connor, M. E. (2003). Understanding persistence of bulimia nervosa: A 5-year naturalistic study. *Journal of Consulting and Clinical Psychology, 71,* 103–109.

Fairburn, C. G., & Walsh, B. T. (2002). Atypical eating disorders (eating disorder not otherwise specified). In C. G. Fairburn & K. D. Brownell (Eds.), *Eating disorders and obesity* (2nd ed., pp. 171–182). New York: Guilford Press.

Falco, M. (2008, February 7). Sad lessons from Heath Ledger's death. CNN. Retrieved December 23, 2008, from www.cnn.com/ HEALTH/blogs/paging. dr.gupta/2008/02/ sad-lessons-from-heath-ledgers-death.html

Falicov, C. J. (1998). *Latino families in therapy: A guide to multicultural practice.* New York: Guilford Press.

Fallon, B. A. (2004). Pharmacotherapy of somatoform disorders. *Journal of Psychosomatic Research, 56,* 455–460.

Fallon, B. A., & Feinstein, S. (2001). Hypochondriasis. In K. A. Phillips (Ed.), *Somatoform and factitious disorders* (pp. 27–65). Washington, DC: American Psychiatric Association.

Fallon, B. A., Liebowitz, M. R., Salman, E. M., Schneier, F. R., Jusino, C., et al. (1993). Fluoxetine for hypochondriacal patients without major depression. *Journal of Clinical Psychopharmacology, 13,* 438–441.

Fallon, B. A., Qureshi, A. I., Laje, G., & Klein, B. (2000). Hypochondriasis and its relationship to obsessive-compulsive disorder. *Psychiatric Clinics of North America, 23,* 605–616.

Fallon, B. A., Qureshi, A. I., Schneier, F. R., Sanchez-Lacay, A., Vermes, D., et al. (2003). An open trial of fluvoxamine for hypochondriasis. *Psychosomatics: Journal of Consultation and Liaison Psychiatry, 44,* 298–303.

Fallon, B. A., Schneier, F. R., Marshall, R., Campeas, R., Vermes, D., et al. (1996). The pharmacotherapy of hypochondriasis. *Psychopharmacology Bulletin, 32,* 607–611.

Fan, A. P., & Eaton, W. W. (2001). Longitudinal study assessing the joint effects of socio-economic status and birth risks on adult emotional and nervous conditions. *British Journal of Psychiatry, 178,* s78–s83.

Farah, M. J. (2004). *Visual agnosia* (2nd ed.). Cambridge, MA: MIT Press/Bradford Books.

Faraone, S. V., Biederman, J., Spencer, T., Mick, E., Murray, K., et al. (2006). Diagnosing adult attention deficit hyperactivity disorder: Are late onset and subthreshold diagnoses valid? *American Journal of Psychiatry, 163,* 1720–1729.

Faraone, S. V., Perlis, R. H., Doyle, A. E., Smoller, J. W., Goralnick, J. J., et al. (2005). Molecular genetics of attention-deficit/ hyperactivity disorder. *Biological Psychiatry, 57,* 1313–1323.

Faraone, S. V., Tsuang, M. T., & Tsuang, D. W. (2001) *Genetics of mental disorders: What practitioners and students need to know.* New York: Guilford Press.

Faravelli, C., Zucchi, T., Viviani, B., Salmoria, R., Perone, A., et al. (2000). Epidemiology of social phobia: A clinical approach. *European Psychiatry, 15,* 17–24.

Farmer, A., Redman, K., Harris, T., Webb, R., Mahmood, A., et al. (2001). The Cardiff sib-pair study. *Crisis, 22,* 71–73.

Farmer, R. F., & Nelson-Gray, R. O. (2005). Behavioral treatment of personality disorders. In R. F. Farmer & R. O. Nelson-Gray, *Personality-guided behavior therapy* (pp. 203–243). Washington, DC: American Psychological Association.

Farrow, T. F. D., Hunter, M. D., Wilkinson, I. D., Green, R. D. J., & Spence, S. A. (2005). Structural brain correlates of unconstrained motor activity in people with schizophrenia. *British Journal of Psychiatry, 187,* 481–482.

Fauman, M. A. (2006). Defining a DSM infrastructure. *American Journal of Psychiatry, 163,* 1873–1874.

Fava, G. A., Bartolucci, G., Rafanelli, C., & Mangelli, L. (2001). Cognitive-behavioral management of patients with bipolar disorder who relapsed while on lithium prophylaxis. *Journal of Clinical Psychiatry, 62,* 556–559.

Fava, G. A., Mangelli, L., & Ruini, C. (2001). Assessment of psychological distress in the setting of medical disease. *Psychotherapy and Psychosomatics 70,* 171–175.

Fava, G. A., Rafanelli, C., Grandi, S., Canestrari, R., & Morphy, M. A. (1998b). Six-year outcome for cognitive behavioral treatment of residual symptoms in major depression. *American Journal of Psychiatry, 155,* 1443–1445.

Fava, G. A., Rafanelli, C., Grandi, S., Conti, S., & Belluardo, P. (1998a). Prevention of recurrent depression with cognitive behavioral therapy: Preliminary findings. *Archives of General Psychiatry, 55,* 816–820.

Favaro, A., Rodella, F. C., & Santonastaso, P. (2000). Binge eating and eating attitudes among Nazi concentration camp survivors. *Psychological Medicine, 30*, 463–466.

Favaro, A., Zanetti, T., Tenconi, E., Degortes, D., Ronzan, A., et al. (2005). The relationship between temperament and impulsive behaviors in eating disordered subjects. *Eating Disorders: The Journal of Treatment & Prevention, 13*, 61–70.

Fawcett, R. G. (2002). Olanzapine for the treatment of monosymptomatic hypochondriacal psychosis. *Journal of Clinical Psychiatry, 63*, 169.

Fazel, S., & Danesh, J. (2002). Serious mental disorder in 23000 prisoners: a systematic review of 62 surveys. *Lancet, 359*(9306), 545-550.

Fazel, S., & Grann, M. (2006). The population impact of severe mental illness on violent crime. *American Journal of Psychiatry, 163*, 1397–1403.

Federoff, I. C., & Taylor, S. (2001). Psychological and pharmacological treatments of social phobia: A meta-analysis. *Journal of Clinical Psychopharmacology, 21*, 311–324.

Fee, practice, and managed care survey. (2000). *Psychotherapy Finances, 10*(318), 10.

Feldman, H. A., Goldstein, I., Hatzichristou, D. G., Krane, R. J., &. McKinlay, J. B. (1994). Impotence and its medical and psychosocial correlates: Results of the Massachusetts Male Aging Study. *Journal of Urology, 151*, 54–61.

Fenton, W., & McGlashan, T. (1991). Natural history of schizophrenia subtypes: I. Longitudinal study of paranoid, hebephrenic, and undifferentiated schizophrenia. *Archives of General Psychiatry, 48*, 969–977.

Fenton, W. S. (2000). Depression, suicide, and suicide prevention in schizophrenia. *Suicide and Life-Threatening Behavior, 30*, 34–49.

Fenton, W. S., & McGlashan, T. H. (1994). Antecedent, symptoms progression, and long-term outcome of the deficit syndrome in schizophrenia. *American Journal of Psychiatry, 151*, 351–356.

Ferguson, C. J., Winegard, B., & Winegard, B. M. (2011). Who is the fairest one of all? How evolution guides peer and media influences on female body dissatisfaction. *Review of General Psychology, 15*, 11–28.

Fergusson, D., Doucette, S., Glass, K. C., Shapiro, S., Healy, D., et al. (2005). Association between suicide attempts and selective serotonin reuptake inhibitors: Systematic review of randomised controlled trials. *British Medical Journal, 330*, 396–369.

Fergusson, D. M., Swain-Campbell, N. R., & Horwood, L. J. (2002). Deviant peer affiliations, crime and substance use: A fixed effects regression analysis. *Journal of Abnormal Child Psychology, 30*, 419–430.

Fibiger, H. C., & Phillips, A. G. (1988). Mesocorticolimbic dopamine systems and reward. *Annals of the New York Academy of Sciences, 537*, 206–215.

Fichter, M. M., Quadflieg, N., & Hedlund, S. (2006). Twelve-year course and outcome predictors of anorexia nervosa. *International Journal of Eating Disorders, 39*, 87–100.

Fick, D. M., Cooper, J. W., Wade, W. E., Waller, J. L., Maclean, J. R., & Beers, M. H. (2003). Updating the Beers criteria for potentially inappropriate medication use in older adults: Results of a US consensus panel of experts. *Archives of Internal Medicine, 163*, 2716–2724.

Fiedler, N., Ozakinci, G., Hallman, W., Wartenberg, D., Brewer, N. T., et al. (2006). Military deployment to the Gulf War as a risk factor for psychiatric illness among US troops. *British Journal of Psychiatry, 188*, 453–459.

Field, A. E., Camargo, C. A., Jr., Taylor, C. B., Berkey, C. S., Frazier, L., et al. (1999). Overweight, weight concerns, and bulimic behaviors among girls and boys. *Journal of the American Academy of Child & Adolescent Psychiatry, 38*, 754–760.

Field, T., Hernandez-Reif, M., & Diego, M. (2006). Risk factors and stress variables that differentiate depressed from nondepressed pregnant women. *Infant Behavior & Development, 29*, 169–174.

Figiel, G. S., Epstein, C., McDonald, W. M., Amazon-Leece, J., Figiel, L., et al. (1998). The use of rapid-rate transcranial magnetic stimulation (rTMS) in refractory depressed patients. *Journal of Neuropsychiatry & Clinical Neurosciences, 10*, 20–25.

File, S. E., Gonzalez, L. E., & Gallant, R. (1999). Role of the dorsomedial hypothalamus in mediating the response to benzodiazepines on trial 2 in the elevated plus-maze test of anxiety. *Neuropsychopharmacology, 21*, 312–320.

File, S. E., Kenny, P. J., & Cheeta, S. (2000). The role of the dorsal hippocampal serotonergic and cholinergic systems in the modulation of anxiety. *Pharmacology, Biochemistry & Behavior, 66*, 65–72.

Fillit, H. M., Butler, R. N., O'Connel, A. W., Albert, M. S., Birren, J. E., et al. (2002). Achieving and maintaining cognitive vitality with aging. *Proceedings of the Mayo Clinic, 77*, 681–696.

Finch, A. E., Lambert, M. J., & Brown, G. (2000). Attacking anxiety: A naturalistic study of a multimedia self-help program. *Journal of Clinical Psychology, 56*, 11–21.

Finch, E. (2001). Social and transcultural aspects of substance misuse. *Current Opinion in Psychiatry, 14*, 173–177.

Fine, J. G., Semrud-Clikeman, M., Keith, T. Z., Stapleton, L. M., & Hynd, G. W. (2007). Reading and the corpus callosum: An MRI family study of volume and area. *Neuropsychology, 21*, 235–241.

Fink, M. (2001). Convulsive therapy: A review of the first 55 years. *Journal of Affective Disorders, 63*, 1–15.

Finn, J., & Banach, M. (2000). Victimization online: The down side of seeking services for women on the Internet. *CyberPsychology & Behavior, 3*, 243–254.

Finzi-Dottan, R., & Karu, T. (2006). From emotional abuse in childhood to psychopathology in adulthood: A path mediated by immature defense mechanisms and self-esteem. *Journal of Nervous and Mental Disease, 194*, 616–621.

Fiorentine, R. (1999). After drug treatment: Are 12-step programs effective in maintaining abstinence? *American Journal of Drug and Alcohol Abuse, 25*, 93–116.

Fiorentine, R., & Hillhouse, M. P. (1999). Drug treatment effectiveness and client–counselor empathy. *Journal of Drug Issues, 29*, 59–74.

First, M. B. (2006, July 26–28). *Dimensional approaches in diagnostic classification: A critical appraisal.* Dimensional Conference. Retrieved January 17, 2007, from http://dsm5.org/conference13.cfm

First, M. B., Bell, C. C., Cuthbert, B., Krystal, J. H., Malison, R., et al. (2002). Personality disorders and relational disorders: A research agenda for addressing crucial gaps in DSM. In D. J. Kupfer, M. B. First, & D. A. Regier (Eds.), *A research agenda for DSM-V* (pp. 123–199). Washington, DC: American Psychiatric Association.

First, M. B., & Frances, A. (2008). Issues for DSM-V: Unintended consequences of small changes: The case of paraphilias. *American Journal of Psychiatry, 165*, 1240–1241.

First, M. B., Spitzer, R. L., Gibbon, M., & Williams, J. B. W. (2002). *Structured clinical interview for DSM-IV Axis I disorders, research version, non-patient edition (SCID-I/NP).* New York: Biometrics Research, New York State Psychiatric Institute.

First, M. B., Spitzer, R. L., Williams, J. B. W., & Gibbon, M. (1997). *Structured clinical interview for DSM-IV Axis II personality disorders (SCID-II), user's guide and interview.* Washington, DC: American Psychiatric Press.

Fischer, S., Smith, G. T., & Anderson, K. G. (2003). Clarifying the role of impulsivity in bulimia nervosa. *International Journal of Eating Disorders, 33*, 406–410.

Fish, B., Marcus, B., Hans, S. L., Auerbach, J. G., & Perdue, S. (1992). Infants at risk for schizophrenia: Sequelae of a genetic neurointegrative defect. A review and replication analysis of pandysmaturation in the Jerusalem Infant Development Study. *Archives of General Psychiatry, 49*, 221–235.

Fishbain, D. A., Goldberg, M., Khalil, T. M., Asfour, S. S., Abdel-Moty, E., et al. (1988). The utility of electromyographic biofeedback in the treatment of conversion paralysis. *American Journal of Psychiatry, 145*, 1572–1575.

Fisher, S. E., & Francks, C. (2006). Genes, cognition and dyslexia: Learning to read the genome. *Trends in Cognitive Sciences, 10*, 250–257.

Fitzgibbon, M. L., & Stolley, M. R. (2000). Minority women: The untold story. *Nova: Dying to be thin.* Retrieved August 31, 2007, from www.pbs.org/wgbh/nova/thin/minorities.html

Flaherty, J., & Adams, S. (1998). Therapist–patient race and sex matching: Predictors of treatment duration. *Psychiatric Times, 15*, n.p. Retrieved March 12, 2008, from www.psychiatrictimes.com/display/article/10168/49886

Flaskerud, J. H. (1991). Effects of an Asian client-therapist language, ethnicity and gender match on utilization and outcome of therapy. *Community Mental Health Journal, 27*, 31–42.

Flaskerud, J. H., & Liu, P. Y. (1991). Effects of an Asian client-therapist language, ethnicity and gender match on utilization and outcome of therapy. *Community Mental Health Journal, 27,* 31–42.

Fleischman, D. A., Wilson, R. S., Gabrieli, J. D. E., Bienias, J. L., & Bennett, D. A. (2004). A longitudinal study of implicit and explicit memory in old persons. *Psychology and Aging, 19,* 617–625.

Flint, A. J. (2005). Generalised anxiety disorder in elderly patients: Epidemiology, diagnosis and treatment options. *Drugs and Aging, 22,* 101–114.

Foa, E. B., Cashman, L., Jaycox, L., & Perry, K. (1997). The validation of a self-report measure of posttraumatic stress disorder: The Posttraumatic Diagnostic Scale. *Psychological Assessment, 9,* 445–451.

Foa, E. B., Dancu, C. V., Hembree, E. A., Jaycox, L. H., Meadows, E. A., & Street, G. P. (1999). A comparison of exposure therapy, stress inoculation training, and their combination for reducing posttraumatic stress disorder in female assault victims. *Journal of Consulting and Clinical Psychology, 67,* 194–200.

Foa, E. B., Gilboa-Schechtman, E., Amir, N., & Freshman, M. (2000). Memory bias in generalized social phobia: Remembering negative emotional expressions. *Journal of Anxiety Disorders, 14,* 501–519.

Foa, E. B., & Goldstein, A. J. (1978). Continuous exposure and complete response prevention in the treatment of obsessive-compulsive neurosis. *Behavior Therapy, 9,* 821–829.

Foa, E. B., Liebowitz, M. R., Kozak, M. J., Davies, S., Campeas, R., et al. (2005). Randomized, placebo-controlled trial of exposure and ritual prevention, clomipramine, and their combination in the treatment of obsessive-compulsive disorder. *American Journal of Psychiatry, 162,* 151–161.

Foa, E. B., Rothbaum, B. O., Riggs, D. S., & Murdock, T. B. (1991). Treatment of posttraumatic stress disorder in rape victims: A comparison between cognitive-behavioral procedures and counseling. *Journal of Consulting and Clinical Psychology, 59,* 715–723.

Foa, E. B., Steketee, G., & Rothbaum, B. O. (1989). Behavioral/cognitive conceptualizations of post-traumatic stress disorder. *Behavior Therapy, 20,* 155–176.

Foley, D. L., Neale, M. C., & Kendler, K. S. (1996). A longitudinal study of stressful life events assessed at personal interview with an epidemiologic sample of adult twins: The basis of individual variation in event exposure. *Psychological Medicine, 26,* 1239–1252.

Foley, D. L., Pickles, A., Maes, H. M., Silberg, J. L., & Eaves, L. J. (2004). Course and short-term outcomes of separation anxiety disorder in a community sample of twins. *Journal of the American Academy of Child & Adolescent Psychiatry, 43,* 1107–1114.

Foley, D., Rutter, M., Pickles, A., Angold, A., Maes, H., et al. (2004). Informant disagreement for separation anxiety disorder. *Journal of the American Academy of Child & Adolescent Psychiatry, 43,* 452–460.

Folstein, S., & Rutter, M. (1977). Infantile autism: A genetic study of 21 twin pairs. *Journal of Child Psychology and Psychiatry, 18,* 297–321.

Folstein, S. E. (1989). *Huntington's disease: A disorder of families.* Baltimore: Johns Hopkins University Press.

Fombonne, E. (2005). The changing epidemiology of autism. *Journal of Applied Research in Intellectual Disabilities, 18,* 281–294.

Fonagy, P., & Bateman, A. (2008). The development of borderline personality disorder—a mentalizing model. *Journal of Personality Disorders, 22,* 4–21.

Fonagy, P., Leigh, T., Steele, M., Steele, H., Kennedy, R., et al. (1996). The relation of attachment status, psychiatric classification, and response to psychotherapy. *Journal of Consulting and Clinical Psychology, 64,* 22–31.

Fontenelle, L. F., Mendlowicz, M. V., Marques, C., & Versiani, M. (2004). Transcultural aspects of obsessive-compulsive disorder: A description of a Brazilian sample and a systematic review of international clinical studies. *Journal of Psychiatric Research, 38,* 403–411.

Foote, B., Smolin, Y., Kaplan, M., Legatt, M. E., & Lipschitz, D. (2006). Prevalence of dissociative disorders in psychiatric outpatients. *American Journal of Psychiatry, 163,* 623–629.

Forbush, K., Heatherton, T. F., & Keel, P. K. (2007). Relationships between perfectionism and specific disordered eating behaviors. *International Journal of Eating Disorders, 40,* 37–41.

Forgas, J. P. (1995). Strange couples: Mood effects on judgments and memory about prototypical and atypical relationships. *Personality and Social Psychology Bulletin, 21,* 747–765.

Forrest, K. A. (2001). Toward an etiology of dissociative identity disorder: A neurodevelopmental approach. *Consciousness and Cognition, 10,* 259–293.

Forty, L., Jones, L., Macgregor, S., Caesar, S., Cooper, C., et al. (2006). Familiality of postpartum depression in unipolar disorder: Results of a family study. *American Journal of Psychiatry, 163,* 1549–1553.

Fossati, A., Madeddu, F., & Maffei, C. (1999). Borderline personality disorder and childhood sexual abuse: A meta-analytic study. *Journal of Personality Disorders, 13,* 268–280.

Fossati, A., Raine, A., Carretta, I., Leonardi, B., & Maffei, C. (2003). The three-factor model of schizotypal personality: Invariance across age and gender. *Personality and Individual Differences, 35*(5), 1007–1019.

Fosse, G. K., & Holen, A. (2004). Cohabitation, education, and occupation of psychiatric outpatients bullied as children. *Journal of Nervous and Mental Disease, 192,* 385–388.

Fountain, C., Winter, A. S., & Bearman, P. S. (2012). Six developmental trajectories characterize children with autism. *Pediatrics, 129,* e1112–1120.

Fowler, R. D. (1986). Howard Hughes: A psychological autopsy. *Psychology Today, 20,* 22–33.

Fox, N. A., Nichols, K. E., Henderson, H. A., Rubin, K., Schmidt, L., et al. (2005). Evidence for a gene-environment interaction in predicting behavioral inhibition in middle childhood. *Psychological Science, 16,* 921–926.

Fraley, R. C., & Shaver, P. R. (1997). Adult attachment and the suppression of unwanted thoughts. *Journal of Personality and Social Psychology, 73,* 1080–1091.

Frances, A. (2013). *Saving normal: An insider's revolt against out-of-control psychiatric diagnoses, DSM-5, big pharma, and the medicalization of ordinary life.* New York: William Morrow.

Frances, A., First, M. B., & Pincus, H. A. (1995). *DSM-IV guidebook.* Washington, DC: American Psychiatric Association.

Frances, A., & Ross, R. (1996). *DSM-IV case studies: A clinical guide to differential diagnosis.* Washington, DC: American Psychiatric Press.

Franco-Paredes, K., Mancilla-Díaz, J. M., Vázquez-Arévalo, R., López-Aguilar, X., & Álvarez-Rayón, G. (2005). Perfectionism and eating disorders: A review of the literature. *European Eating Disorders Review, 13,* 61–70.

Frank, E., Gonzalez, J. M., & Fagiolini, A. (2006). The importance of routine for preventing recurrence in bipolar disorder. *American Journal of Psychiatry, 163,* 981–985.

Frank, E., Hlastala, S., Ritenour, A., Houck, P., Tu, X. M., et al. (1997). Inducing lifestyle regularity in recovering bipolar disorder patients: Results from the maintenance therapies in bipolar disorder protocol. *Biological Psychiatry, 41,* 1165–1173.

Frank, E., Kupfer, D. J., Buysse, D. J., Swartz, H. A., Pilkonis, P. A., et al. (2007). Randomized trial of weekly, twice-monthly, and monthly interpersonal psychotherapy as maintenance treatment for women with recurrent depression. *American Journal of Psychiatry, 164,* 761–767.

Frank, E., Kupfer, D. J., Thase, M. E., Mallinger, A. G., Swartz, H. A., et al. (2005). Two-year outcomes for interpersonal and social rhythm therapy in individuals with bipolar I disorder. *Archives of General Psychiatry, 62,* 996–1004.

Frank, E., & Spanier, C. (1995). Interpersonal psychotherapy for depression: Overview, clinical efficacy, and future directions. *Clinical Psychology: Science and Practice, 2,* 349–369.

Frank, E., Swartz, H. A., Mallinger, A. G., Thase, M. E., Weaver, E. V., & Kupfer, D. J. (1999). Adjunctive psychotherapy for bipolar disorder: Effects of changing treatment modality. *Journal of Abnormal Psychology, 108,* 579–587.

Frank, G. K., Bailer, U. F., Henry, S., Wagner, A., & Kaye, W. H. (2004). Neuroimaging studies in eating disorders. *CNS Spectrums, 9,* 539–548.

Frank, G. K., Kaye, W. H., Weltzin, T. E., Perel, J., Moss, H., et al. (2001). Altered response to meta-chlorophenylpiperazine in anorexia nervosa: Support for a persistent alteration of serotonin activity after short-term weight restoration. *International Journal of Eating Disorders, 30,* 57–68.

Frankel, F., Cantwell, D. P., Myatt, R., & Feinberg, D. T. (1999). Do stimulants improve self-esteem in children with ADHD and peer problems? *Journal of Child and Adolescent Psychopharmacology, 9*, 185–194.

Franklin, M. E., Abramowitz, J. S., Bux, D. A., Zoellner, L. A. & Feeny, N. C. (2002). Cognitive-behavioral therapy with and without medication in the treatment of obsessive-compulsive disorder. *Professional Psychology: Research and Practice, 33*, 162–168.

Franko, D. L., Becker, A. E., Thomas, J. J., & Herzog, D. B. (2007). Cross-ethnic differences in eating disorder symptoms and related distress. *International Journal of Eating Disorders, 40*, 156–164.

Franko, D. L., Wonderlich, S., Little, D., & Herzog, D. B. (2004). Diagnosis and classification of eating disorders: What's new? In J. K. Thompson (Ed.), *Handbook of eating disorders and obesity*. New York: Wiley.

Fraser, A. (2000). *The houses of Hanover and Saxe-Coburg*. Berkeley: University of California Press.

Fredrickson, B. L., & Roberts, T. (1997). Objectification theory: Toward understanding women's lived experiences and mental health risks. *Psychology of Women Quarterly, 21*, 173–206.

Fredrickson, B. L., Roberts, T.-A., Noll, S. M., Quinn, D. M., & Twenge, J. M. (1998). That swimsuit becomes you: Sex differences in self-objectification, restrained eating, and math performance. *Journal of Personality & Social Psychology, 75*, 269–284.

Fredrikson, M., Annas, P., Fischer, H., & Wik, G. (1996). Gender and age differences in the prevalence of specific fears and phobias. *Behaviour Research and Therapy, 34*, 33–39.

Freedman, R. (2008). Cannabis, inhibitory neurons, and the progressive course of schizophrenia. *American Journal of Psychiatry, 165*(4), 416–419.

Freedman, R., Adler, L. E., Myles-Worsley, M., Nagamoto, H. T., Miller, C., et al. (1996). Inhibitory gating of an evoked response to repeated auditory stimuli in schizophrenic and normal subjects: Human recordings, computer simulation, and an animal model. *Archives of General Psychiatry, 53*, 1114–1121.

Freels, S. A., Richman, J. A., & Rospenda, K. M. (2005). Gender differences in the causal direction between workplace harassment and drinking. *Addictive Behaviors, 30*, 1454–1458.

Freeman, H. (1994). Schizophrenia and city residence. *British Journal of Psychiatry, 164*, 39–50.

Freeman, L. (1980). *Freud rediscovered*. New York: Arbor House.

Freeman, L. (1990). *The story of Anna O.* New York: Paragon House.

Freemantle, N., Anderson, I. M., & Young, P. (2000). Predictive value of pharmacological activity for the relative efficacy of antidepressant drugs: Meta-regression analysis. *British Journal of Psychiatry, 177*, 292–302.

Frerikson, M., Annas, P., Fischer, H., & Wik, G. (1996). Gender and age differences in the prevalence of specific fears and phobias. *Behaviour Research and Therapy 34*, 33–39.

Freud, S. (1900/1958). *The interpretation of dreams.* New York: Basic Books.

Freud, S. (1905/1955). Three essays on the theory of sexuality. In J. Strachey (Ed. & Trans.), *The standard edition of the complete psychological works of Sigmund Freud* (Vol. 7, pp. 125–245). London: Hogarth Press.

Freud, S. (1920). Fear and anxiety. In S. Freud, *A general introduction to psychoanalysis* (pp. 340–355). New York: Liveright.

Freud, S. (1923/1961). *The ego and the id.* New York: W. W. Norton.

Freud, S. (1938). *Moses and monotheism.* New York: W. W. Norton.

Frezza, M., Di Padova, C., Pozzato, G., Terpin, M., Baraona, E., & Lieber, C. S. (1990). High blood alcohol levels in women. *New England Journal of Medicine, 322*, 95–99.

Friborg, O., Martinussen, M., Kaiser, S., Øvergård, K. T., & Jan, H. R. (2013). Comorbidity of personality disorders in anxiety disorders: A meta-analysis of 30 years of research. *Journal of Affective Disorders, 145*(2), 143–155.

Frick, P. J. (2006). Developmental pathways to conduct disorder. *Child and Adolescent Psychiatric Clinics of North America, 15*, 311–331.

Frick, P. J., & Loney, B. R. (1999). Outcomes of children and adolescents with oppositional defiant disorder and conduct disorder. In H. C. Quay & A. E. Hogan (Eds.), *Handbook of the disruptive behavior disorders* (pp. 507–524). New York: Kluwer Academic/Plenum.

Frick, P. J., & Morris, A. S. (2004). Temperament and developmental pathways to conduct problems. *Journal of Clinical Child and Adolescent Psychology, 33*, 54–68.

Frick, P. J., & Muñoz, L. (2006). Oppositional defiant disorder and conduct disorder. In C. A. Essau (Ed.), *Child and adolescent psychopathology: Theoretical and clinical implications* (pp. 26–51). New York: Routledge/Taylor & Francis.

Frick, P. J., & Silverthorn, P. (2001). Psychopathology in children. In P. B. Sutker & H. E. Adams (Eds.), *Comprehensive handbook of psychopathology* (3rd ed., pp. 881–920). New York: Kluwer Academic/Plenum.

Frick, P. J., Bodin, S. D., & Barry, C. T. (2000). Psychopathic traits and conduct problems in community and clinic-referred samples of children: Further development of the Psychopathy Screening Device. *Psychological Assessment, 12*, 382–393.

Frick, P. J., Cornell, A. H., Bodin, S. D., Dane, H. E., Barry, C. T., & Loney, B. R. (2003). Callous-unemotional traits and developmental pathways to severe conduct problems. *Developmental Psychology, 39*, 246–260.

Fridman, C., Ojopi, &. P. B., Gregório, S. P., Ikenaga, E. H., Moreno, D. H., Demetrio, F. N., Guimarães, P. E. M., Vallada, H. P., Gattaz, W. F., & Dias Neto, E. (2003). Association of a new polymorphism in ALOX12 gene with bipolar disorder. *European Archives of Psychiatry & Clinical Neuroscience, 253*, 40–43.

Friedman M. J., Resnick, P. A., Bryant, R. A., Strain, J., Horowitz, M., & Spiegel, D. (2011). Considering PTSD for DSM-5. *Depression & Anxiety, 28*, 750–769.

Friedman, R. F., Ween, J. E., & Albert, M. L. (1993). Alexia. In K. M. Heilman & E. Valenstein (Eds.), *Clinical neuropsychology* (3rd ed., pp. 37–62). New York: Oxford University Press.

Friedrich, M. J. (2005) Molecular studies probe bipolar disorder. *Journal of the American Medical Association, 293*, 545–546.

Frink, H. W. (1921). Psychology of the compulsion neurosis. In H. W. Frink (Ed.), *Morbid fears and compulsions: Their psychology and psychoanalytic treatment* (pp. 163–185). London: Kegan Paul.

Frischholz, E. J., Braun, B. G., Sachs, R. G., Hopkins, L., Shaeffer, D. M., et al. (1990). The Dissociative Experiences Scale: Further replication and validation. *Dissociation: Progress in the Dissociative Disorders, 3*, 151–153.

Frischholz, E. J., Lipman, L. S., Braun, B. G., & Sachs, R. G. (1992). Psychopathology, hypnotizability, and dissociation. *American Journal of Psychiatry, 149*, 1521–1525.

Frith, C. D. (1992). *The cognitive neuropsychology of schizophrenia.* Hillsdale, NJ: Lawrence Erlbaum Associates.

Frith, U. (2003). *Autism: Explaining the enigma* (2nd ed.). Malden, MA: Blackwell Publishing.

Frosch, A. (2002). Transference: Psychic reality and material reality. *Psychoanalytic Psychology, 19*, 603–633.

Frühauf, S., Gerger, H., Schmidt, H. M., Munder, T., & Barth, J. (in press). Efficacy of psychological interventions for sexual dysfunction: A systematic review and meta-analysis. *Archives of Sexual Behavior.*

Fuller, R. K., Branchey, L., Brightwell, D. R., Derman, R. M., Emrick, C. D., et al. (1986). Disulfiram treatment of alcoholism: A Veterans Administration cooperative study. *Journal of the American Medical Association 256*, 1449–1455.

Fuller, R., Nopoulos, P., Arndt, S., O'Leary, D., Ho, B.-C., & Andreasen, N. C. (2002). Longitudinal assessment of premorbid cognitive functioning in patients with schizophrenia through examination of standardized scholastic test performance. American Journal of Psychiatry, 159, 1183–1189.

Funahashi, T., Ibuki, Y., Domon, Y., Nishimura, T., Akehashi, D., & Sugiura, H. (2000). A clinical study on suicide among schizophrenics. Psychiatry and Clinical Neuroscience, 54, 173–179.

Furmark, T., Tillfors, M., Marteinsdottir, I., Fischer, H., Pissiota, A., et al. (2002). Common changes in cerebral blood flow in patients with social phobia treated with citalopram or cognitive-behavioral therapy. *Archives of General Psychiatry, 59*, 425–433.

Furukawa, T. A., Nakano, Y., Funayama, T., Ogawa, S., Ietsugu, T., et al. (2013). Cognitive–behavioral therapy modifies the naturalistic course of social anxiety disorder: Findings from an ABA design study in routine clinical practices. *Psychiatry and Clinical Neurosciences, 67*(3), 139–147.

Fyer, A. J. (2000). Heritability of social anxiety: A brief review. *Journal of Clinical Psychiatry, 54*, 10–12.

Gaab, N., Gabrieli, J. D. E., Deutsch, G. K., Tallal, P., & Temple, E. (2007). Neural correlates of rapid auditory processing are disrupted in children with developmental dyslexia and ameliorated with training: An fMRI study. *Restorative Neurology and Neuroscience, 25*, 295–310.

Gabbay, V., Asnis, G. M., Bello, J. A., Alonso, C. M., Serras, S. J., & O'Dowd, M. A. (2003) New onset of body dysmorphic disorder following frontotemporal lesion. *Neurology, 61*, 123–125.

Gabbott, P. L., Warner, T. A., Jays, P. R., Salway, P., & Busby, S. J. (2005). Prefrontal cortex in the rat: Projections to subcortical autonomic, motor, and limbic centers. *Journal of Comparative Neurology, 492*, 145–177.

Gacono, C. B., Nieberding, R. J., Owen, A., Rubel, J., & Bodholdt, R. (2001). Treating conduct disorder, antisocial, and psychopathic personalities. In J. B. Ashford, B. D. Sales, & W. H. Reid (Eds.), *Treating adult and juvenile offenders with special needs* (pp. 99–129). Washington, DC: American Psychological Association.

Gaffney, G. R., Lurie, S. F., & Berlin, F. S. (1984). Is there familial transmission of pedophilia? *Journal of Nervous and Mental Disease, 172*, 546–548.

Gagne, G. G., Furman, M. J., Carpenter, L. L., & Price, L. H. (2000). Efficacy of continuation ECT and antidepressant drugs compared to long-term antidepressants alone in depressed patients. *American Journal of Psychiatry, 157*, 1960–1965.

Gaher, R. M., Simons, J. S., Jacobs, G. A., Meyer, D., & Johnson-Jimenez, E. (2006). Coping motives and trait negative affect: Testing mediation and moderation models of alcohol problems among American Red Cross disaster workers who responded to the September 11, 2001 terrorist attacks. *Addictive Behaviors, 31*, 1319–1330.

Gainetdinov, R. R., Wetsel, W. C., Jones, S. R., Levin, E. D., Jaber, M., & Caron, M. G. (1999). Role of serotonin in the paradoxical calming effect of psychostimulants on hyperactivity. *Science, 283*, 397–401.

Galassi, F., Quercioli, S., Charismas, D., Niccolai, V., & Barciulli, E. (2007). Cognitive-behavioral group treatment for panic disorder with agoraphobia. *Journal of Clinical Psychology, 63*, 409–416.

Gallers, J., Foy, D. W., Donahoe, C. P., & Goldfarb, J. (1988). Post-traumatic stress disorder in Vietnam combat veterans: Effects of traumatic violence exposure with military adjustment. *Journal of Traumatic Stress, 1*, 181–192.

Gammon, K. (2009). Belle Curves. Wired, February, pp. 38–39. Retrieved on March 28, 2009 from http://www.wired.com/images/2009/.article/magazine/1702/WIRED_1702_Infoporn.pdf

Gara, M. A., Vega, W. A., Arndt, S., Escamilla, M., Fleck, D. E., et al. (2012). Influence of Patient race and ethnicity on clinical assessment in patients with affective disorders. *Archives of General Psychiatry, 69*, 593–600.

Garb, H. N. (1997). Race bias, social class bias, and gender bias in clinical judgment. *Clinical Psychology: Science & Practice, 4*, 99–120.

Garb, H. N., Wood, J. M., Lilienfeld, S. O., & Nezworski, M. T. (2005). Roots of the Rorschach controversy. *Clinical Psychology Review, 25*, 97–118.

Garber, J., & Horowitz, J. L. (2002). Depression in children. In I. H. Gotlib & C. L. Hammen (Eds.), *Handbook of depression* (pp. 510–540). New York: Guilford Press.

Garcia-Palacios, A., Botella, C., Hoffman, H., & Fabregat, S. (2007). Comparing acceptance and refusal rates of virtual reality exposure vs. in vivo exposure by patients with specific phobias. *CyberPsychology & Behavior, 10*, 722–724.

Garety, P. A., & Freeman, D. (1999). Cognitive approaches to delusions: A critical review of theories and evidence. British Journal of Clinical Psychology, 38, 113–154.

Garety, P. A., Freeman, D., Jolley, S., Dunn, G., Bebbington, P. E., Fowler, D. G., Kuipers, E., & Dudley, R. (2005). Reasoning, emotions, and delusional conviction in psychosis. *Journal of Abnormal Psychology, 114*, 373–384.

Garfield, S. L. (1994). Research on client variables in psychotherapy. In A. E. Bergin & S. L. Garfield (Eds.). *Handbook of psycho-therapy and behavior change* (4th ed.) (pp. 190–228). Oxford, England: John Wiley & Sons.

Garfield, S. L. (1998). Some comments on empirically supported treatments. *Journal of Consulting & Clinical Psychology, 66*, 121–125.

Garfield, S. L., & Bergin, A. E. (1994). Introduction and historical overview. In A. E. Bergin & S. L. Garfield (Eds.), *Handbook of psychotherapy and behavior change* (4th ed., pp. 3–18). Oxford, England: John Wiley & Sons.

Garfinkel, P. E., Goldbloom, D., Davis, R., Olmsted, M. P., Garner, D. M., & Halmi, K. A. (1992). Body dissatisfaction in bulimia nervosa: Relationship to weight and shape concerns and psychological functioning. *International Journal of Eating Disorders, 11*, 151–161.

Garfinkel, P. E., Kennedy, S. H., & Kaplan, A. S. (1995). Views on classification and diagnosis of eating disorders. *Canadian Journal of Psychiatry, 40*, 445–456.

Garfinkel, P. E., Lin, E., Goering, P., Spegg, C., Goldbloom, D., Kennedy, S., Kaplan, A. S., & Woodside, D. B. (1996). Should amenorrhoea be necessary for the diagnosis of anorexia nervosa? Evidence from a Canadian community sample. *British Journal of Psychiatry, 168*, 500–506.

Garner, D. M. (1997). Psychoeducational principles in treatment. In D. M. Garner & P. E. Garfinkel (Eds.), *Handbook of treatment for eating disorders* (2nd ed., pp. 147–177). New York: Guilford Press.

Garner, D. M., Garfinkel, P. E., Schwartz, D., & Thompson, M. (1980). Cultural expectations of thinness in women. *Psychological Reports, 47*, 483–491.

Garner, D. M., Rosen, L. W., & Barry, D. (1998). Eating disorders among athletes: Research and recommendations. *Child and Adolescent Psychiatric Clinics of North America, 7*, 839–857.

Garner, D. M., Vitousek, K. M., & Pike, K. M. (1997). Cognitive-behavioral therapy for anorexia nervosa. In Garner, David M. (Ed.); Garfinkel, Paul E. (Ed.), *Handbook of treatment for eating disorders (2nd ed.).* (pp. 94–144). New York, NY: Guilford Press.

Gaser, C., Nenadic, I., Buchsbaum, B. R., Hazlett, E. A., & Buchsbaum, M. S. (2004). Ventricular enlargement in schizophrenia related to volume reduction of the thalamus, striatum, and superior temporal cortex. *American Journal of Psychiatry, 161*, 154–156.

Gauvain, M., & Fagot, B. (1995). Child temperament as a mediator of mother-toddler problem solving. *Social Development, 4*, 257–276.

Gavin, J., Rodham, K., & Poyer, H. (2008). The presentation of "pro-anorexia" in online group interactions. *Qualitative Health Research, 18*, 325–333.

Geda, Y. E., & Nedelska, Z. (2012). Mild cognitive impairment: A subset of minor neurocognitive disorder? *The American Journal of Geriatric Psychiatry, 20*(10), 821–826.

Geddes, J. R., & Lawrie, S. M. (1995). Obstetric complications: A meta-analysis. British Journal of Psychiatry, 67, 786–793.

Geddes, J., Freemantle, N., Harrison, P., & Bebbington, P. (2000). Atypical antipsychotics in the treatment of schizophrenia: Systematic overview and meta-regression analysis. British Medical Journal, 321, 1372–1376.

Gee, T., Allen, K., & Powell, R. A. (2003). Questioning premorbid dissociative symptomatology in dissociative identity disorder: Comment on Gleaves, Hernandez, and Warner (1999). *Professional Psychology: Research and Practice, 34*, 114–116.

Geffken, G. R., Storch, E. A., Duke, D. C., Monaco, L., Lewin, A. B., & Goodman, W. K. (2006). Hope and coping in family members of patients with obsessive-compulsive disorder. *Journal of Anxiety Disorders, 20*, 614–629.

Gega, L., Marks, I., & Mataix-Cols, D. (2004). Computer-aided CBT self-help for anxiety and depressive disorders: Experience of a London clinic and future directions. *Journal of Clinical Psychology, 60*, 147–157.

Gelhorn, H., Stallings, M., Young, S., Corley, R., Rhee, S. H., Hopfer, C., & Hewitt, J. (2006). Common and specific genetic influences on aggressive and nonaggressive conduct disorder domains. *Journal of the American Academy of Child & Adolescent Psychiatry, 45,* 570–577.

Geller, J., Srikameswaran, S., Cockell, S. J., & Zaitsoff, S. L. (2000). Assessment of shape- and weight-based self-esteem in adolescents. *International Journal of Eating Disorders, 28,* 339–345.

Gentile, K., Raghavan, C., Rajah, V., & Gates, K. (2007). It doesn't happen here: Eating disorders in an ethnically diverse sample of economically disadvantaged, urban college students. *Eating Disorders: The Journal of Treatment & Prevention, 15,* 405–425.

George, L. K., & Weiler, S. J. (1981). Sexuality in middle and late life: The effects of age, cohort, and gender. *Archives of General Psychiatry, 38,* 919–923.

George, M. S., Lisanby, S. H., & Sackheim, H. A. (1999). Transcranial magnetic stimulation: Applications in neuropsychiatry. *Archives in General Psychiatry, 56,* 300–311.

George, S., & Moselhy, H. (2005). "Gateway hypothesis"—A preliminary evaluation of variables predicting non-conformity. *Addictive Disorders & Their Treatment, 4,* 39–40.

Geracioti, T. D., Jr., Carpenter, L. L., Owens, M. J., Baker, D. G., Ekhator, N. N., et al. (2006). Elevated cerebrospinal fluid substance p concentrations in posttraumatic stress disorder and major depression. *American Journal of Psychiatry, 163,* 637–643.

Ghaderi, A. (2006). Does individualization matter? A randomized trial of standardized (focused) versus individualized (broad) cognitive behavior therapy for bulimia nervosa. *Behaviour Research and Therapy, 44,* 273–288.

Ghaemi, N. (2012). DSM-5: Finding a middle ground. *Medscape,* June 1. Retrieved May 23, 2013, from www.medscape.com/viewarticle/764740

Ghashghaei, H. T., & Barbas, H. (2002). Pathways for emotion: Interactions of prefrontal and anterior temporal pathways in the amygdala of the rhesus monkey. *Neuroscience, 115,* 1261–1279.

Gianoulakis, C. (2001). Influence of the endogenous opioid system on high alcohol consumption and genetic predisposition to alcoholism. *Journal of Psychiatry & Neuroscience, 26,* 304–318.

Gibb, B. E., Alloy, L. B., Abramson, L. Y., Rose, D. T., Whitehouse, W. G., et al. (2001). History of childhood maltreatment, negative cognitive styles, and episodes of depression in adulthood. *Cognitive Therapy & Research, 25,* 425–446.

Gibb, B. E., Benas, J. S., Crosset, S. E., & Uhrlass, D. J. (2007). Emotional maltreatment and verbal victimization in childhood: Relation to adults' depressive cognitions and symptoms. *Journal of Emotional Abuse, 7,* 59–83.

Gick, M. L., & Thompson, W. G. (1997). Negative affect and the seeking of medical care in university students with irritable bowel syndrome. *Journal of Psychosomatic Research, 43,* 535–540.

Giele, C. L., van den Hout, M. A., Engelhard, I. M., Dek, E. C. P. & Hofmeijer, F. K. (2011). Obsessive-compulsive-like reasoning makes an unlikely catastrophe more credible. *Journal of Behavior Therapy and Experimental Psychiatry, 42,* 293–297.

Giesbrecht, T., Lynn, S. J., Lilienfeld, S. O., & Merckelbach, H. (2008). Cognitive processes in dissociation: An analysis of core theoretical assumptions. *Psychological Bulletin, 134,* 617–647.

Giesbrecht, T., Lynn, S. J., Lilienfeld, S. O., & Merckelbach, H. (2010). Cognitive processes, trauma, and dissociation—Misconceptions and misrepresentations: Reply to Bremner (2010). *Psychological Bulletin, 136*(1), 7–11.

Giesbrecht, T., Smeets, T., Leppink, J., Jelicic, M., & Merckelbach, H. (2007). Acute dissociation after 1 night of sleep loss. *Journal of Abnormal Psychology, 116*(3), 599–606.

Gijs, L., & Gooren, L. (1996). Hormonal and psychopharmacological interventions in the treatment of paraphilias: An update. *Journal of Sex Research, 33,* 273–290.

Gilbertson, M. W., Shenton, M. E., Ciszewski, A., Kasai, K., Lasko, N. B., et al. (2002). Smaller hippocampal volume predicts pathologic vulnerability to psychological trauma. *Nature Neuroscience, 5,* 1242–1247.

Gillespie, N. A., Cloninger, C. R., Heath, A. C., & Martin, N. G. (2003). The genetic and environmental relationship between Cloninger's dimensions of temperament and character. *Personality and Individual Differences, 35,* 1931–1946.

Gillespie, N. A., Zhu, G., Heath, A. C., Hickie, I. B., & Martin, N. G. (2000). The genetic aetiology of somatic distress. *Psychological Medicine, 30,* 1051–1061.

Gilmer, W. S., Trivedi, M. H., Rush, A. J., Wisniewski, S. R., Luther, J., et al. (2005). Factors associated with chronic depressive episodes: A preliminary report from the STAR-D project. *Acta Psychiatrica Scandinavica, 112,* 425–433.

Gilmour, H., Gibson, F., & Campbell, J. (2003). Living alone with dementia: A case study approach to understanding risk. *Dementia: The International Journal of Social Research and Practice, 2,* 403–420.

Ginsberg, D. L. (Ed.). (2004). Women and anxiety disorders: Implications for diagnosis and treatment. *CNS Spectrums, 9,* 1–16.

Ginsburg, G. S., & Silverman, W. K. (2000). Gender role orientation and fearfulness in children with anxiety disorders. *Journal of Anxiety Disorders, 14,* 5–67.

Ginzler, J. A., Cochran, B. N., Domenech-Rodríguez, M., Cauce, A. M., & Whitbeck, L. B. (2003). Sequential progression of substance use among homeless youth: An empirical investigation of the gateway theory. *Substance Use & Misuse, 38,* 725–758.

Giordano, M., Dominguez, L. J., Vitrano, T., Curatolo, M., Ferlisi, A., et al. (2010). Combination of intensive cognitive rehabilitation and donepezil therapy in Alzheimer's disease (AD). *Archives of Gerontology and Geriatrics, 51,* 245–249.

Giovanoli, E. J. (1988). ECT in a patient with conversion disorder. *Convulsive Therapy, 4,* 236–242.

Giraldi, A., & Levin, R. J. (2006). Vascular physiology of female sexual function. In: I. Goldstein, C. M. Meston, S. R. Davis, & A. M. Traish. (Eds.), *Women's Sexual Function and Dysfunction—Study, Diagnosis and Treatment.* London: Taylor and Francis. pp. 174–180.

Gitin, N. M., Herbert, J. D., & Schmidt, C. (1996, November). One-session in vivo exposure for odontophobia. Paper presented at the 30th annual convention of the Association for the Advancement of Behavior Therapy, New York.

Gitlin, M., Nuechterlein, K., Subotnik, K. L., Ventura, J., Mintz, J., et al. (2001). Clinical outcome following neuroleptic discontinuation in patients with remitted recent-onset schizophrenia. American Journal of Psychiatry, 158, 1835–1842.

Gitlin, L. N., Winter, L., Dennis, M. P., Hodgson, N., & Hauck, W. W. (2010). A biobehavioral home-based intervention and the well-being of patients with dementia and their caregivers. *JAMA, 304,* 983–991.

Giuffrida, A., Leweke, F. M., Gerth, C. W., Schreiber, D., Koethe, D., et al. (2004). Cerebrospinal anandamide levels are elevated in acute schizophrenia and are inversely correlated with psychotic symptoms. *Neuropsychopharmacology, 29,* 2108–2114.

Giulino, L., Gammon, P., Sullivan, K., Franklin, M., Foa, E., et al. (2002). Is parental report of upper respiratory infection at the onset of obsessive-compulsive disorder suggestive of pediatric autoimmune neuropsychiatric disorder associated with streptococcal infection? *Journal of Child & Adolescent Psychopharmacology, 12,* 157–164.

Givens, J. L., Houston, T. K., Van Voorhees, B. W., Ford, D. E., & Cooper, L. A. (2007). Ethnicity and preferences for depression treatment. *General Hospital Psychiatry, 29,* 182–191.

Gladis, M. M., Gosch, E. A., Dishuk, N. M., & Crits-Christoph, P. (1999). Quality of life: Expanding the scope of clinical significance. *Journal of Consulting and Clinical Psychology, 67,* 320–331.

Glass, R. M. (2001). Electroconvulsive therapy: Time to bring it out of the shadows. *JAMA: Journal of the American Medical Association, 285,* 1346–1348.

Gleaves, D. H. (1996). The sociocognitive model of dissociative identity disorder: A reexamination of the evidence. *Psychological Bulletin, 120,* 42–59.

Gleaves, D. H., Lowe, M. R., Green, B. A., Cororve, M. B., & Williams, T. L. (2000). Do anorexia and bulimia nervosa occur on a continuum? A taxometric analysis. *Behavior Therapy, 31,* 195–219.

Gleaves, D. H., Lowe, M. R., Snow, A. C., Green, B. A., & Murphy-Eberenz, K. P. (2000). Continuity and discontinuity models of bulimia nervosa: A taxometric investigation. *Journal of Abnormal Psychology, 109,* 56–68.

Glenn, C. R., & Klonsky, E. D. (2009). Emotion dysregulation as a core feature of borderline personality disorder. *Journal of Personality Disorders, 23,* 20–28.

Glisky, E. L., Ryan, L., Reminger, S., Hardt, O., Hayes, S. M., & Hupbach, A. (2004). A case of psychogenic fugue: I understand, aber ich verstehe nichts. *Neuropsychologia, 42,* 1132–1147.

Godart, N. T., Flament, M. F., Curt, F., Perdereau, F., Lang, F., et al. (2003). Anxiety disorders in subjects seeking treatment for eating disorders: A DSM-IV-TR controlled study. *Psychiatry Research, 117,* 245–258.

Goddard, A. W., Mason, G. F., Almai, A., Rothman, D. L., Behar, K. L., et al. (2001). Reductions in the occipital cortex GABA levels in panic disorder detected with 1H-magnetic resonance spectroscopy. *Archives of General Psychiatry 58,* 556–561.

Godemann, F., Ahrens, B., Behrens, S., Berthold, R., Gandor, C., et al. (2001). Classic conditioning and dysfunctional cognitions in patients with panic disorder and agoraphobia treated with an implantable cardioverter/defibrillator. *Psychosomatic Medicine, 63,* 231–238.

Godinez v. Moran, 509 U.S. 389 (1993).

Goff, B. S. N., & Smith, D. B. (2005). Systemic traumatic stress: The couple adaptation to traumatic stress model. *Journal of Marital & Family Therapy, 31,* 145–157.

Goisman, R. M., Goldenberg, I., Vasile, R. G., & Keller, M. B. (1995). Comorbidity of anxiety disorders in a multicenter anxiety study. *Comprehensive Psychiatry, 36,* 303–311.

Golan, O., & Baron-Cohen, S. (2006). Systemizing empathy: Teaching adults with Asperger syndrome or high-functioning autism to recognize complex emotions using interactive multimedia. *Development and Psychopathology, 18,* 591–617.

Goldapple, K., Segal, Z., Garson, C., Lau, M., Bieling, P., et al. (2004). Modulation of cortical-limbic pathways in major depression: Treatment-specific effects of cognitive behavior therapy. *Archives of General Psychiatry, 61,* 34–41.

Golden, C. J., Hammeke, T. A., & Purisch, A. D. (1980). *The Luria-Nebraska Neuropsychological Battery: manual.* Los Angeles: Western Psychological Services.

Golden, R. N., Gaynes, B. N., Ekstrom, R. D., Hamer, R. M., Jacobsen, F. M., et al. (2005). The efficacy of light therapy in the treatment of mood disorders: A review and meta-analysis of the evidence. *American Journal of Psychiatry, 162,* 656–662.

Goldfried, M. R., & Wolfe, B. E. (1998). Toward a more clinically valid approach to therapy research. *Journal of Consulting and Clinical Psychology, 66,* 143–150.

Goldkamp, J. S., & Irons-Guynn, C. (2000). Emerging judicial strategies for the mentally ill in the criminal caseload: Mental health courts in Fort Lauderdale, Seattle, San Bernardino, and Anchorage. U.S. Department of Justice, Office of Justice Programs; Bureau of Justice Assistance.

Goldsmith, S. K., Pellmar, T. C., Kleinman, A. M., & Bunney, W. E. (Eds.). (2002). *Reducing suicide: A national imperative.* Washington, DC: National Academies Press.

Goldstein, A. (1994) *Addiction: From Biology to Drug Policy.* New York: Freeman.

Goldstein, A. J., & Chambless, D. L. (1978). A reanalysis of agoraphobia. *Behavior Therapy, 9,* 47–59.

Goldstein, D. S. (2000). *The autonomic nervous system in health and disease.* New York: Marcel Dekker.

Goodnough, A. (2006, November 15). Officials clash over mentally ill in Florida jails. *The New York Times,* p. A1.

Goodwin, D. W., Schulsinger, F., Moller, N., Hermansen, L., Winokur, G., & Guze, S. B. (1974). Drinking problems in adopted and nonadopted sons of alcoholics. *Archives of General Psychiatry, 31,* 164–169.

Goodwin, F. K., & Ghaemi, S. N. (1998). Understanding manic-depressive illness. *Archives of General Psychiatry, 55,* 23–25.

Goodwin, F. K., & Jamison, K. R. (1990). *Manic-depressive illness.* New York: Oxford University Press.

Goodwin, J., Hill, S., & Attias, R. (1990). Historical and folk techniques of exorcism: Applications to the treatment of dissociative disorders. *Dissociation: Progress in the Dissociative Disorders, 3,* 94–101.

Goodwin, R., Lyons, J. S., & McNally, R. J. (2002). Panic attacks in schizophrenia. *Schizophrenia Research, 58,* 213–220.

Gordis, E. (1996). Alcohol research: At the cutting edge. *Archives of General Psychiatry, 53,* 199–201.

Gorman, J. M., & Kent, J. M. (1999). SSRIs and SNRIs: Broad spectrum of efficacy beyond major depression. *Journal of Clinical Psychiatry, 60,* 33–39.

Gorman, J. M., Liebowitz, M. R., Fyer, A. J., & Stein, J. (1989). A neuroanatomical hypothesis for panic disorder. *American Journal of Psychiatry, 146,* 148–161.

Gortner, E. T., Gollan, J. K., Dobson, K. S., & Jacobson, N. S. (1998). Cognitive-behavioral treatment for depression: Relapse prevention. *Journal of Consulting and Clinical Psychology, 66,* 377–384.

Gorwood, P. (2004). Generalized anxiety disorder and major depressive disorder comorbidity: An example of genetic pleiotropy? *European Psychiatry, 19,* 27–33.

Gosden, R. (2000). Prepsychotic treatment for schizophrenia: A rejoinder. Reply. Ethical Human Sciences & Services, 2, 211–214.

Götestam, K. G. (2002). One session group treatment of spider phobia by direct or modelled exposure. *Cognitive Behaviour Therapy, 31,* 18–24.

Gotlib, I. H., & Robinson, L. A. (1982). Responses to depressed individuals: Discrepancies between self-report and observer rated behavior. *Journal of Abnormal Psychology, 91,* 231–240.

Gotlib, I. H., Kasch, K. L., Traill, S., Joormann, J., Arnow, B. A., & Johnson, S. L. (2004). Coherence and specificity of information-processing biases in depression and social phobia. *Journal of Abnormal Psychology, 113,* 386–398.

Gotlib, I. H., Krasnoperova, E., Yue, D. N., & Joormann, J. (2004). Attentional biases for negative interpersonal stimuli in clinical depression. *Journal of Abnormal Psychology, 113,* 127–135.

Gottesman, I. I. (1991) *Schizophrenia genesis: The origin of madness.* New York: Freeman.

Gottesman, I. I., & Bertelsen, A. (1989). Confirming unexpressed genotypes for schizophrenia: Risks in the offspring of Fischer's Danish identical and fraternal discordant twins. *Archives of General Psychiatry, 46,* 867–872.

Gottesman, I. I., & Erlenmeyer-Kimling, L. (2001). Family and twin strategies as a head start in defining prodromes and endophenotypes for hypothetical early interventions in schizophrenia. *Schizophrenia Research, 51,* 93–102.

Gottesman, I. I., & Moldin, S. O. (1998). Genotypes, genes, genesis, and pathogenesis in schizophrenia. In M. F. Lenzenweger & R. H. Dworkin (Eds.), *Origins and development of schizophrenia* (pp. 5–11). Washington, DC: American Psychological Association.

Gould, R. A., & Clum, G. A. (1993). A meta-analysis of self-help treatment approaches. *Clinical Psychology Review, 13,* 169–186.

Grabe, H. J., Spitzer, C., Schwahn, C., Marcinek, A., Frahnow, A., et al. (2009). Serotonin transporter gene (SLC6A4) promoter polymorphisms and the susceptibility to Posttraumatic Stress Disorder in the general population. *American Journal of Psychiatry, 166,* 926–933.

Grabe, S., & Hyde, J. S. (2006). Ethnicity and body dissatisfaction among women in the United States: A meta-analysis. *Psychological Bulletin, 132,* 622–640.

Grady, D. (2006, October 24). Self-portraits chronicle a descent into Alzheimer's. *New York Times.* Retrieved February 21, 2007, from www.nytimes.com/2006/10/24/health/24alzh.html

Graff, G. (1989). A Starr is reborn. Retrieved July 16, 2002, from http://members.aol.com/applescruff33/ringoastarrisreborninterview.html

Graham, K. G. (1976, April). Interview with Little Edie. *Interview Magazine* In A. Mayles (Director/Producer) & D. Mayles (Director/Producer), *Grey Gardens* (disc 2).

Grant, B. F. (2000). Estimates of U.S. children exposed to alcohol abuse and dependence in the family. *American Journal of Public Health, 90,* 112–115.

Grant, B. F., Goldstein, R. B., Chou, S. P., Huang, B., Stinson, F. S., et al. (2008). Sociodemographic and psychopathologic predictors of first incidence of DSM-IV substance use, mood, and anxiety Disorders: Results from the Wave 2 National Epidemiologic Survey on Alcohol and Related Conditions. *Molecular Psychiatry, 13,* 1–16.

Grant, B. F., Hasin, D. S., Stinson, F. S., Dawson, D. A., Chou, S. P., et al. (2004). Prevalence, correlates, and disability of personality disorders in the United States: Results from the National Epidemiologic Survey on Alcohol and Related Conditions. *Journal of Clinical Psychiatry, 65,* 948–958.

Grant, B. F., Stinson, F. S., Dawson, D. A., Chou, S. P., Ruan, W. J., & Pickering, R. P. (2004). Co-occurrence of 12-month alcohol and drug use disorders and personality disorders in the United States: Results from the National Epidemiologic Survey on Alcohol and Related Conditions. *Archives of General Psychiatry, 61,* 361–368.

Grant, J. E., Menard, W., Pagano, M. E., Fay, C., & Phillips, K. A. (2005). Substance use disorders in individuals with body dysmorphic disorder. *Journal of Clinical Psychiatry, 66,* 309–316.

Grant, P. M., Huh, G. A., Perivoliotis, D., Stolar, N. M., & Beck, A. T. (2012). Randomized trial to evaluate the efficacy of cognitive therapy for low-functioning patients with schizophrenia. *Archives of General Psychiatry, 69,* 121–127.

Gratz, K. L., Rosenthal, M. Z., Tull, M. T., Lejuez, C. W., & Gunderson, J. G. (2006). An experimental investigation of emotion dysregulation in borderline personality disorder. *Journal of Abnormal Psychology, 115,* 850–855.

Gray, C. A. (1996) Social stories and comic strip conversations with students with Asperger syndrome and high functioning autism. In E. Schopler, G. B. Mesibov, & L. Kunce (Eds.), *Asperger syndrome and high functioning autism* (pp. 1–10). New York: Plenum.

Gray, J. A. (1987). Perspectives on anxiety and impulsiveness: A commentary. *Journal of Research in Personality, 21,* 493–509.

Gray, J. A. (1991). The neuropsychology of temperament. In J. Strelau & A. Angleitner (Eds.), *Explorations in temperament: International perspectives on theory and measurement* (pp. 105–128). New York: Plenum Press.

Graybar, S. R., & Boutilier, L. R. (2002). Nontraumatic pathways to borderline personality disorder. *Psychotherapy: Theory, Research, Practice, Training, 39,* 152–162.

Graziottin, A. (2007). Prevalence and evaluation of sexual health problems—HSDD in Europe. *Journal of Sexual Medicine, 4,* 211–219.

Green, A. R. (2004). MDMA: Fact and fallacy, and the need to increase knowledge in both the scientific and popular press. *Psychopharmacology, 173,* 231–233.

Green, J. G., McLaughlin, K. A., Berglund, P. A., Gruber, M. J., Sampson, N. A., et al. (2010). National Comorbidity Survey Replication I: Associations With First Onset of *DSM-IV* Disorders. *Arch Gen Psychiatry, 67,* 113–123.

Green, J. P., & Lynn, S. J. (1995). Hypnosis, dissociation, and simultaneous-task performance. *Journal of Personality and Social Psychology, 69,* 728–735.

Green, M. F. (2001). *Schizophrenia revealed: From neurons to social interactions.* New York: W. W. Norton.

Green, M. F. (2007). Cognition, drug treatment, and functional outcome in schizophrenia: A tale of two transitions. *American Journal of Psychiatry, 164,* 992–994.

Green, R. (1974). The behaviorally feminine male child: Pretranssexual? Pretransvestic? Prehomosexual? Preheterosexual? In R. C. Friedman, R. M. Richart, R. L. Vande Wiele, & L. O. Stern (Eds.), *Sex differences in behavior.* (pp. 33–52). Oxford, England: John Wiley & Sons.

Green, R. (1987). Gender identity in childhood and later sexual orientation: Follow-up of 78 males. In S. Chess & A. Thomas (Eds.), *Annual progress in child psychiatry and child development* (pp. 214–220). Philadelphia: Brunner/Mazel.

Green, R. (2000). Family cooccurrence of "gender dysphoria": Ten siblings or parent–child pairs. *Archives of Sexual Behavior, 29,* 499–507.

Greenberg, B. D., Altemus, M., & Murphy, D. L. (1997). The role of neurotransmitters and neurohormones in obsessive-compulsive disorder. *International Review of Psychiatry, 9,* 31–44.

Greenberg, B. D., Murphy, D. L., & Rasmussen, S. A. (2003) Neuroanatomically based approaches to obsessive-compulsive disorder. Neurosurgery and transcranial magnetic stimulation. *Psychiatric Clinics of North America, 23,* 671–686.

Greenberg, G. (2013). *Book of woe: The DSM and the unmasking of psychiatry.* New York: Blue Rider Press.

Greenberg, J. R., & Mitchell, S. A. (1983). *Object relations in psychoanalytic theory.* Cambridge, MA: Harvard University Press.

Greenberg, R. P. (2002). Reflections on the emperor's new drugs. *Prevention & Treatment, 5,* Article 27. Available on the World Wide Web: www.journals.apa. org/prevention/volume5/pre0050027c.html

Greenberg, R. P., & Fisher, S. (1989). Examining antidepressant effectiveness: Findings, ambiguities, and some vexing puzzles. In S. Fisher & R. P. Greenberg (Eds.), *The limits of biological treatments for psychological distress: Comparisons with psychotherapy and placebo* (pp. 1–37). Hillsdale, NJ: Lawrence Erlbaum.

Greene, E., Heilbrun, K., Fortune, W. H., & Nietzel, M. T. (2007). *Wrightsman's psychology and the legal system* (6th ed.). Belmont, CA: Thomson/Wadsworth.

Greene, R. L. (2000). *The MMPI-2: An interpretive manual* (2nd ed.). Needham Heights, MA: Allyn & Bacon.

Greenfield, S. F. (2002). Women and alcohol use disorders. *Harvard Review of Psychiatry, 10,* 76–85.

Greenhouse, L. (2006, February 22). Sect allowed to import its hallucinogenic tea. *New York Times.* Retrieved February 22, 2006, from www.nytimes.com/2006/02/22/politics/22scotus.html?_r=1&oref=slogin

Greenwood, T. A., & Kelsoe, J. R. (2003). Promoter and intronic variants affect the transcriptional regulation of the human dopamine transporter gene. *Genomics, 82,* 511–520.

Gregorian, R. S., Golden, K. A., Bahce, A., Goodman, C., Kwong, W. J., & Khan, Z. M. (2002). Antidepressant-induced sexual dysfunction. *The Annals of Pharmacotherapy, 36,* 1577–1589.

Gregory, R. J., & Remen, A. L. (2008). A manual-based psychodynamic therapy for treatment-resistant borderline personality disorder. *Psychotherapy: Theory, Research, Practice, Training, 45,* 15–27.

Greig, T. C., Bryson, G. J., & Bell, M. D. (2004). Theory of mind performance in schizophrenia: Diagnostic, symptom, and neuropsychological correlates. *Journal of Nervous and Mental Disorders, 192,* 12–18.

Grigorenko, E. L. (2001). Developmental dyslexia: An update on genes, brains, and environments. *Journal of Child Psychology and Psychiatry, 42,* 91–125.

Grilo, C. M., & McGlashan, T. H. (2005). Course and outcome of personality disorders. In Oldham, John M. (Ed.); Skodol, Andrew E. (Ed.); Bender, Donna S. (Ed.). *The American Psychiatric Publishing Textbook of Personality Disorders.* (pp. 103–115). Washington, DC, US: American Psychiatric Publishing, Inc.

Grilo, C. M., Pagano, M. E., Stout, R. L., Markowitz, J. C., Ansell, E. B., et al. (2012). Stressful life events predict eating disorder relapse following remission: Six-year prospective outcomes. *International Journal of Eating Disorders, 45*(2), 185–192.

Grilo, C. M., Sanislow, C. A., Gunderson, J. G., Pagano, M. E., Yen, S., et al. (2004). Two-year stability and change of schizotypal, borderline, avoidant, and obsessive-compulsive personality disorders. *Journal of Consulting and Clinical Psychology, 72,* 767–775.

Grimes, K., & Walker, E. F. (1994). Childhood emotional expressions, educational attainments, and age at onset of illness in schizophrenia. *Journal of Abnormal Psychology, 103,* 784–790.

Grisaru, N., Amir, M., Cohen, H., & Kaplan, Z. (1998). Effect of transcranial magnetic stimulation in posttraumatic stress disorder: A preliminary study. *Biological Psychiatry, 44,* 52–55.

Grisso, T., & Appelbaum, P. S. (1995). The MacArthur Treatment Competence Study: III. Abilities of patients to consent to psychiatric and medical treatment. *Law and Human Behavior, 19,* 149–174.

Grocholewski, A., Kliem, S., & Heinrichs, N. (2012). Selective attention to imagined facial ugliness is specific to body dysmorphic disorder. *Body Image, 9,* 261–269.

Gropalis, M., Bleichhardt, G., Hiller, W., & Witthöft, M. (2013). Specificity and modifiability of cognitive biases in hypochondriasis. *Journal of Consulting and Clinical Psychology, 81*(3), 558–565.

Grove, L. (2005, May 25). Tom to Brooke: Don't be a woman of substance. *New York Daily News.* Retrieved January 18, 2007, from www.nydailynews.com/news/gossip/story/312036p-266946c.html

Gruber, K. J., & Taylor, M. F. (2006). A family perspective for substance abuse: Implications from the literature. *Journal of Social Work Practice in the Addictions, 6,* 1–29.

Grucza, R. A., Przybeck, T. R., & Cloninger, C. R. (2007). Prevalence and correlates of binge eating disorder in a community sample. *Comprehensive Psychiatry, 48,* 124–131.

Guan, L., Wang, B., Chen, Y., Yang, L., Li, J., & Qian, Q. (2009). A high-density single-nucleotide polymorphism screen of 23 candidate genes in attention deficit hyperactivity disorder: Suggesting multiple susceptibility genes among Chinese Han population. *Molecular Psychiatry, 14,* 546–554.

Guarnaccia, P. J. (1997a). A cross-cultural perspective on anxiety disorders. In S. Friedman (Ed.), *Cultural issues in the treatment of anxiety* (pp. 3–20). New York: Guilford Press.

Guarnaccia, P. J. (1997b). Social stress and psychological distress among Latinos in the United States. In I. Al-Issa & M. Tousignant (Eds.), *Ethnicity, immigration, and psychopathology* (pp. 71–94). New York: Plenum Press.

Gude, T., Hoffart, A., Hedley, L., & Ro, O. (2004). The dimensionality of dependent personality disorder. *Journal of Personality Disorders, 18,* 604–610.

Gujar, S. K., Maheshwari, S., Bjorkman-Burtscher, I., & Sundgren, P. C. (2005). Magnetic resonance spectroscopy. *Journal of Neuroophthalmology, 25,* 217–226.

Guller, Y., Ferrarelli, F., Shackman, A. J., Sarasso, S., Peterson, M. J., et al. (2012). Probing thalamic integrity in schizophrenia using concurrent transcranial magnetic stimulation and functional magnetic resonance imaging. *Archives of General Psychiatry, 69,* 662–671.

Gunderson, J. G., Daversa, M. T., Grilo, C. M., McGlashan, T. H., Zanarini, M. C., et al. (2006). Predictors of 2-year outcome for patients with borderline personality disorder. *American Journal of Psychiatry, 163,* 822–826.

Gunderson, J. G., Morey, L. C., Stout, R. L., Skodol, A. E., Shea, M. T., et al. (2004). Major depressive disorder and borderline personality disorder revisited: Longitudinal interactions. *Journal of Clinical Psychiatry, 65,* 1049–1056.

Gunderson, J. G., Stout, R. L., McGlashan, T. H., Shea, M. T., Morey, L. C., et al. (2011). Ten-year course of borderline personality disorder: Psychopathology and function from the collaborative longitudinal personality disorders study. *Archives of General Psychiatry, 68,* 827–837.

Gunderson, J. G., Weinberg, I., Daversa, M. T., Kueppenbender, K. D., Zanarini, M. C., et al. (2006). Descriptive and longitudinal observations on the relationship of borderline personality disorder and bipolar disorder. *American Journal of Psychiatry, 163,* 1173–1178.

Gunewardene, A., Huon, G. F., & Zheng, R. (2001). Exposure to Westernization and dieting: A cross-cultural study. *International Journal of Eating Disorders, 29,* 289–293.

Gunnell, D., Saperia, J., & Ashby, D. (2005). Selective serotonin reuptake inhibitors (SSRIs) and suicide in adults: Meta-analysis of drug company data from placebo controlled, randomised controlled trials submitted to the MHRA's safety review. *British Medical Journal, 330,* 385–388.

Gur, R. C., Ragland, J. D., & Gur, R. E. (1997). Cognitive changes in schizophrenia—a critical look. *International Review of Psychiatry, 9,* 449–457.

Gur, R. E., Turetsky, B. I., Loughead, J., Snyder, W., Kohler, C., Elliott, M., et al. (2007). Visual attention circuitry in schizophrenia investigated with oddball event-related functional Magnetic Resonance Imaging. *American Journal of Psychiatry, 164,* 442–449.

Guralnik, O., Giesbrecht, T., Knutelska, M., Sirroff, B., & Simeon, D. (2007). Cognitive functioning in depersonalization disorder. *Journal of Nervous and Mental Disease, 195,* 983–988.

Guralnik, O., Schmeidler, J., & Simeon, D. (2000). Feeling unreal: Cognitive processes in depersonalization. *American Journal of Psychiatry, 157,* 103–109.

Gureje, O., Ustun, T. B., & Simon, G. E. (1997). The syndrome of hypochondriasis: A cross-national study in primary care. *Psychological Medicine, 27,* 1001–1010.

Gurman, A. S. (2000). Family therapy. In A. E. Kazdin (Ed.), *Encyclopedia of psychology* (Vol. 3, pp. 329–333). Washington, DC: American Psychological Association.

Gurvits, T. V., Shenton, M. E., Hokama, H., & Ohta, H. (1996). Magnetic resonance imaging study of hippocampal volume in chronic, combat-related posttraumatic stress disorder. *Biological Psychiatry, 40,* 1091–1099.

Guthrie, R. M., & Bryant, R. A. (2005). Auditory startle response in firefighters before and after trauma exposure. *American Journal of Psychiatry, 162,* 283–290.

Gutierrez, R., Atkinson, J. H., & Grant, I. (1994). "Mild neurocognitive disorder: Needed addition to the nosology of cognitive impairment (organic mental) disorders": Erratum. *The Journal of Neuropsychiatry and Clinical Neurosciences, 6*(1), 75–86.

Gyulai, L., Abass, A., Broich, K., & Reilley, J. (1997). I-123 lofetamine single-photon computer emission tomography in rapid cycling bipolar disorder: A clinical study. *Biological Psychiatry, 41,* 152–161.

Haber, J. (2000). Management of substance abuse and dependence problems in families. In M. A. Naegle & C. E. D'Avanzo (Eds.), *Addictions & substance abuse: Strategies for advanced practice nursing* (pp. 305–331). Englewood Cliffs, NJ: Prentice Hall.

Haber, J., Hamera, E., Hillyer, D., Limandri, B., Panel, S., et al. (2003). Advanced practice psychiatric nurses: 2003 legislative update. *Journal of the American Psychiatric Nurses Association, 9,* 205–216.

Haber, J. R., Jacob, T., & Heath, A. C. (2005). Paternal alcoholism and offspring conduct disorder: Evidence for the "common genes" hypothesis. *Twin Research and Human Genetics, 8,* 120–131.

Hackett, G. I. (2008). Erectile dysfunction predicts cardiovascular risk in men. *British Medical Journal, 337,* a2166.

Haeffel, G. J., & Hames, J. L. (in press). Cognitive vulnerability to depression can be contagious. *Clinical Pyschological Science, np.*

Hakko, H., Räsänen, P., & Tiihonen, J. (1998). Secular trends in the rates and seasonality of violent and nonviolent suicide occurrences in Finland during 1980–95. *Journal of Affective Disorders, 50,* 49–54.

Halbreich, U., & Kahn, L. (2001). Role of estrogen in the aetiology and treatment of mood disorders. *CNS Drugs, 15,* 797–817.

Hall, W. D., & Lynskey, M. (2005). Is cannabis a gateway drug? Testing hypotheses about the relationship between cannabis use and the use of other illicit drugs. *Drug and Alcohol Review, 24,* 39–48.

Halligan, P. W., Athwal, B. S., Oakley, D. A., & Frackowiak, R. S. J. (2000). The functional anatomy of a hypnotic paralysis: Implications for conversion hysteria. *Lancet, 355,* 986–987.

Halligan, P. W., Bass, C., & Wade, D. T. (2000). New approaches to conversion hysteria: Functional imaging may improve understanding and reduce morbidity. *British Medical Journal, 320,* 1488–1489.

Hallmayer, J. (2000). The epidemiology of the genetic liability for schizophrenia. *Australian & New Zealand Journal of Psychiatry, 34*(Suppl.), S47–S55.

Hallmayer, J., Cleveland, S., Torres, A., Phillips, J., Cohen, B., et al. (2011). Genetic Heritability and shared environmental factors among twin pairs with autism. *Archives of General Psychiatry, 68,* 1095–1102.

Hallowell, E. M., & Ratey, J. J. (1994). *Driven to distraction: Recognizing and coping with attention deficit disorder from childhood through adulthood.* New York: Touchstone.

Halmi, K. A. (1995). Current concepts and definitions. In G. I. Szmukler, C. Dare, & J. Treasure (Eds.), *Handbook of eating disorders: Theory, treatment and research* (pp. 29–42). Oxford, England: John Wiley & Sons.

Halmi, K. A., Agras, W. S., Mitchell, J., Wilson, G. T., Crow, S., et al. (2002). Relapse predictors of patients with bulimia nervosa who achieved abstinence through cognitive behavioral therapy. *Archives of General Psychiatry, 59,* 1105–1109.

Halmi, K. A., Sunday, S. R., Klump, K. L., Strober, M., Leckman, J. F., et al. (2003). Obsessions and compulsions in anorexia nervosa subtypes. *International Journal of Eating Disorders, 33,* 308–319.

Halmi, K. A., Sunday, S. R., Strober, M., Kaplan, A., Woodside, D. B., et al. (2000). Perfectionism in anorexia nervosa: Variation by clinical subtype, obsessionality, and pathological eating behavior. *American Journal of Psychiatry, 157,* 1799–1805.

Hamilton, M. E., Voris, J. C., Sebastian, P. S., Singha, A. K., Krejci, L. P., et al. (1998). Money as a tool to extinguish conditioned responses to cocaine in addicts. *Journal of Clinical Psychology, 54,* 211–218.

Hamilton, S. R. (2008). Schizophrenia candidate genes: Are we really coming up blank? *American Journal of Psychiatry, 165,* 420–423.

Hanewinkel, R., Sargent, J. D., Poelen, E. A. P., Scholte, R., Florek, E., et al. (2012). Alcohol consumption in movies and adolescent binge drinking in 6 European countries. *Pediatrics, 129,* 709–720.

Hankin, B. L., Abramson, L. Y., Miller, N., & Haeffel, G. J. (2004). Cognitive vulnerability-stress theories of depression: Examining affective specificity in the prediction of depression versus anxiety in three prospective studies. *Cognitive Therapy and Research, 28,* 309–345.

Hanna, G. L., Fischer, D. J., & Fluent, T. E. (2006). Separation anxiety disorder and school refusal in children and adolescents. *Pediatrics in Review, 27,* 56–63.

Hanrahan, F., Field, A. P., Jones, F. W., & Davey, G. C. L. (2013). A meta-analysis of cognitive therapy for worry in generalized anxiety disorder. *Clinical Psychology Review, 33*(1), 120–132.

Hansen, N. B., Lambert, M. J., & Forman, E. M. (2002). The psychotherapy dose–response effect and its implications for treatment delivery services. *Clinical Psychology: Science and Practice, 9,* 329–343.

Hansenne, M., Pitchot, W., Pinto, E., Reggers, J., Scantamburlo, G., et al. (2002). 5-HT1A dysfunction in borderline personality disorder. *Psychological Medicine, 32,* 935–941.

Hanson, R. K., Bloom, I., & Stephenson, M. (2004). Evaluating community sex offender treatment programs: A 12-year follow-up of 724 offenders. *Canadian Journal of Behavioural Science, 36,* 87–96.

Happé, F. G. E. (1994). An advanced test of theory of mind: Understanding of story characters' thoughts and feelings by able autistic, mentally handicapped, and normal children and adults. *Journal of Autism and Developmental Disorders, 24,* 129–154.

Hardan, A. Y., Muddasani, S., Vernulapalli, M., Keshavan, M. S., & Minshew, N. J. (2006). An MRI study of increased cortical thickness in autism. *American Journal of Psychiatry, 163,* 1290–1292.

Harden, B. L., & Lubetsky, M. (2005). Pharmacotherapy in autism and related disorders. *School Psychology Quarterly, 20,* 155–171.

Hare, R. D. (1993). *Without conscience: The disturbing world of the psychopaths among us.* New York, NY: Pocket Books.

Hare, R. D. (1997). Psychopathy: A clinical construct whose time has come. *Criminal Justice and Behavior, 23,* 25–54.

Hare, R. D. (2003). *Manual for the Hare Psychopathy Checklist* (2nd ed. rev.). Toronto, Canada: Multi-Health Systems.

Harford, T. C., Chen, C. M., Saha, T. D., Smith, S. M., Hasin, D. S., & Grant, B. F. (2013). An item response theory analysis of DSM-IV diagnostic criteria for personality disorders: Findings from the National Epidemiologic Survey on Alcohol and Related Conditions. *Personality Disorders: Theory, Research, and Treatment.*

Harrington, R., Fudge, H., Rutter, M., Pickles, A., & Hill, J. (1990). Adult outcomes of childhood and adolescent depression: I. Psychiatric status. *Archives of General Psychiatry, 47,* 465–473.

Harris, M. G., Henry, L. P., Harrigan, S. M., Purcell, R., Schwartz, O. S., Farrelly, S. E., et al. (2005). The relationship between duration of untreated psychosis and outcome: An eight-year prospective study. *Schizophrenia Research, 79,* 85–93.

Harrison, K., & Hefner, V. (2006). Media exposure, current and future body ideals, and disordered eating among preadolescent girls: A longitudinal panel study. *Journal of Youth and Adolescence, 35,* 153–163.

Hart, S. D. (1998). The role of psychopathy in assessing risk for violence: Conceptual and methodological issues. *Legal and Criminological Psychology, 3,* 121–137.

Hart, S. D., & Hare, R. D. (1989). Discriminant validity of the Psychopathy Checklist in a forensic psychiatric population. *Psychological Assessment, 1,* 211–218.

Hartley, H. (2006). The "pinking" of Viagra culture: Drug industry efforts to create and repackage sex drugs for women. *Sexualities, 9,* 363–378.

Hartmann, H. (1939). *Ego psychology and the problem of adaptation.* New York: International Universities Press.

Hartung, C. M., & Widiger, T. A. (1998). Gender differences in the diagnosis of mental disorders: Conclusions and controversies of the DSM-IV. *Psychological Bulletin, 123,* 260–278.

Harvey, A. G., & Bryant, R. A. (2002). Acute stress disorder: A synthesis and critique. *Psychological Bulletin, 128,* 886–902.

Harvey, P. D. (2005a). Aging in healthy individuals. In *Schizophrenia in late life: Aging effects on symptoms and course of illness* (pp. 17–34). Washington, DC: American Psychological Association.

Harvey, P. D. (2005b). Dementia and schizophrenia: Similarities and differences. In *Schizophrenia in late life: Aging effects on symptoms and course of illness* (pp. 101–116). Washington, DC: American Psychological Association.

Harvey, P. D. (2005c). Late-onset schizophrenia. In *Schizophrenia in late life: Aging effects on symptoms and course of illness* (pp. 89–99). Washington, DC: American Psychological Association.

Haskett, M. E., Nears, K., Ward, C. S., & McPherson, A. V. (2006). Diversity in adjustment of maltreated children: Factors associated with resilient functioning. *Clinical Psychology Review, 26,* 796–812.

Hasler, G., Drevets, W. C., Manji, H. K., & Charney, D. S. (2004). Discovering endophenotypes for major depression. *Neuropsychopharmacology, 29,* 1765–1781.

Havey, J. M., Olson, J. M., McCormick, C., & Cates, G. L. (2005). Teachers' perceptions of the incidence and management of attention-deficit hyperactivity disorder. *Applied Neuropsychology, 12,* 120–127.

Hawke, J. L., Wadsworth, S. J., & DeFries, J. C. (2006). Genetic influences on reading difficulties in boys and girls: The Colorado twin study. *Dyslexia: An International Journal of Research and Practice, 12,* 21–29.

Hawkins, J., Catalano, R., & Miller, J. (1992). Risk and protective factors for alcohol and other drug problems in adolescence and early adulthood: Implications for substance abuse prevention. *Psychological Bulletin, 112,* 64–105.

Hayden, D. (2003). *Pox: Genius, madness, and the mysteries of syphilis.* New York: Basic Books.

Heath, A. C., Madden, P. A. F., Bucholz, K. K., Nelson, E. C., Todorov, A., et al. (2003). Genetic and environmental risks of dependence on alcohol, tobacco, and other drugs. In R. Plomin, J. C. DeFries, I. W. Craig, & P. McGuffin (Eds.), *Behavioral genetics in the postgenomic era* (pp. 309–334). Washington, DC: American Psychological Association.

Heatherton, T. F., & Baumeister, R. F. (1991). Binge eating as escape from self-awareness. *Psychological Bulletin, 110,* 86–108.

Heaton, R. K., Grant, I., & Matthews, C. G. (1991). Comprehensive norms for an expanded Halstead-Reitan Battery: Demographic corrections, research findings, and clinical applications. Odessa, FL: Psychological Assessment Resources.

Heil, P., & Simons, D. (2008). Multiple paraphilias: Prevalence, etiology, assessment, and treatment. In D. R. Laws & W. T. O'Donohue (Eds.), *Sexual deviance: Theory, assessment, and treatment* (2nd ed., pp. 527–556). New York: Guilford Press.

Heilbrun, K., Nezu, C. M., Keeney, M., Chung, S., & Wasserman, A. L. (1998). Sexual offending: Linking assessment, intervention, and decision making. *Psychology, Public Policy, and Law, 4,* 138–174.

Heim, A., & Westen, D. (2005). Theories of personality and personality disorders. In J. M. Oldham, A. E. Skodol, & D. S. Bender (Eds.), *The American Psychiatric Publishing textbook of personality disorders* (pp. 17–33). Washington, DC: American Psychiatric Publishing.

Heiman, J. R. (2000). Orgasmic disorders in women. In S. R. Leiblum & R. C. Rosen (Eds.), *Principles and practice of sex therapy* (3rd ed., pp. 118–153). New York: Guilford Press.

Heiman, J. R. (2002a). Psychologic treatments for female sexual dysfunction: Are they effective and do we need them? *Archives of Sexual Behavior, 31,* 445–450.

Heiman, J. R. (2002b). Sexual dysfunction: Overview of prevalence, etiological factors, and treatments. *Journal of Sex Research, 39,* 73–78.

Heiman, J. R., & Meston, C. M. (1997). Evaluating sexual dysfunction in women. *Clinical Obstetrics and Gynecology, 40,* 616–629.

Heimberg, R. G., Dodge, C. S., Hope, D. A., Kennedy, C. R., Zollo, L. J., & Becker, R. E. (1990). Cognitive behavioral group treatment for social phobia: Comparison with a credible placebo control. *Cognitive Therapy and Research, 14,* 1–23.

Heimberg, R. G., Liebowitz, M. R., Hope, D. A., Schneier, F. R., Holt, C. S., et al. (1998). Cognitive behavioral group therapy vs phenelzine therapy for social phobia: 12-week outcome. *Archives of General Psychiatry, 55*, 1133–1141.

Heimberg, R. G., Stein, M. B., Hiripi, E., & Kessler, R. C. (2000). Trends in the prevalence of social phobia in the United States: A synthetic cohort analysis of changes over four decades. *European Psychiatry, 15*, 29–37.

Heinlen, K. T., Welfel, E. R., Richmond, E. N., & O'Donnell, M. S. (2003). The nature, scope, and ethics of psychologists' e-therapy Web sites: What consumers find when surfing the Web. *Psychotherapy: Theory, Research, Practice, Training, 40*, 112–124.

Heinrichs, M., Wagner, D., Schoch, W., Soravia, L. M., Hellhammer, D. H., & Ehlert, U. (2005). Predicting posttraumatic stress symptoms from pretraumatic risk factors: A 2-year prospective follow-up study in firefighters. *American Journal of Psychiatry, 162*, 2276–2286.

Heinssen, R. K., Perkins, D. O., Appelbaum, P. S., & Fenton, W. S. (2001). Informed consent in early psychosis research: NIMH workshop, November 15, 2000. *Schizophrenia Bulletin, 27*, 571–584.

Heinz, A. (2000). Dopaminhypothese der Schizophrenien: Neue Befunde fur eine alte Theorie. [The dopamine hypothesis of schizophrenia: New findings for an old theory]. *Nervenarzt, 71*, 54–57.

Hellström, K., & Öst, L. (1995). One-session therapist directed exposure vs two forms of manual directed self-exposure in the treatment of spider phobia. *Behaviour Research and Therapy, 33*, 959–965.

Hellstrom, W. J. G., Nehra, A., Shabsigh, R., & Sharlip, I. D. (2006). Premature ejaculation: The most common male sexual dysfunction. *Journal of Sexual Medicine, 3*, 1–3.

Helms, J. E., & Cook, D. A. (1999). *Using race and culture in counseling and psychotherapy: Theory and process.* Needham Heights, MA, US, Allyn & Bacon.

Helverskov, J. L., Clausen, L., Mors, O., Frydenberg, M., Thomsen, P. H., & Rokkedal, K. (2010). Trans-diagnostic outcome of eating disorders: A 30-month follow-up study of 629 patients. *European Eating Disorders Review, 18*, 453–463.

Henderson, C., Roux, A. V. D., Jacobs, D. R., Jr., Kiefe, C. I., West, D., & Williams, D. R. (2005). Neighbourhood characteristics, individual level socioeconomic factors, and depressive symptoms in young adults: The CARDIA study. *Journal of Epidemiology & Community Health, 59*, 322–328.

Hendin, H. (1995). Assisted suicide, euthanasia, and suicide prevention: The implications of the Dutch experience. *Suicide and Life-Threatening Behavior, 25*, 193–204.

Henggeler, S. W., Schoenwald, S. K., Borduin, C. M., Rowland, M. D., & Cunningham, P. B. (1998). *Multisystemic treatment of antisocial behavior in children and adolescents.* New York: Guilford Press.

Henneman, W. J. P., Sluimer, J. D., Barnes, J., van der Flier, W. M., Cluimer, I. C., et al. (2009). Hippocampal atrophy rates in Alzheimer's disease. *Neurology, 72*, 999–1007.

Henning, K. R., & Frueh, B. C. (1996). Cognitive-behavioral treatment of incarcerated offenders. *Criminal Justice and Behavior, 23*, 523–541.

Henquet, C., Krabbendam, L., Spauwen, J., Kaplan, C., Lieb, R., et al. (2005). Prospective cohort study of cannabis use, predisposition for psychosis, and psychotic symptoms in young people. *British Medical Journal, 330*, 11–16.

Hepp, U., Kraemer, B., Schnyder, U., Miller, N., & Delsignore, A. (2005). Psychiatric comorbidity in gender identity disorder. *Journal of Psychosomatic Research, 58*, 259–261.

Herba, C. M., Tremblay, R. E., Boivin, M., Liu, X., Mongeau, C., et al. (in press). Maternal depressive symptoms and children's emotional problems: Can early child care help children of depressed mothers? *JAMA Psychiatry.*

Herbert, M.R. (2005). Large brains in autism: The challenge of pervasive abnormality. *The Neuroscientist, 11*, 417–440.

Herek, G. M., & Garnets, L. D. (2007). Sexual orientation and mental health. *Annual Review of Clinical Psychology, 3*, 105–127.

Herholz, K. (1996). Neuroimaging in anorexia nervosa. *Psychiatry Research, 62*, 105–110.

Herman, J. (1992). *Trauma and recovery.* New York: Basic Books.

Hermelin, B. (2001). *Bright splinters of the mind: A personal story of research with autistic savants.* London: Jessica Kingsley.

Hershman, D. J., & Lieb, J. (1988). *The key to genius/manic-depression and the creative life.* New York: Prometheus.

Hershman, D. J., & Lieb, J. (1998). *Manic depression and creativity.* New York: Prometheus.

Hertz-Picciotto, I., & Delwiche, L. (2009). The rise in autism and the role of age at diagnosis. *Epidemiology, 20*, 84–90.

Heruti, R. J., Levy, A., Adunski, A., & Ohry, A. (2002). Conversion motor paralysis disorder: Overview and rehabilitation model. *Spinal Cord, 40*, 327–334.

Herzog, D. B., & Delinsky, S. S. (2001). Classification of eating disorders. In R. H. Striegel-Moore & L. Smolak (Eds.), *Eating disorders: Innovative directions in research and practice* (pp. 31–50). Washington, DC: American Psychological Association.

Herzog, D. B., Dorer, D. J., Keel, P. K., Selwyn, S. E., Ekeblad, E. R., et al. (1999). Recovery and relapse in anorexia and bulimia nervosa: A 7.5-year follow-up study. *Journal of the American Academy of Child & Adolescent Psychiatry, 38*, 829–837.

Hesselbrock, V. (1986). Family history of psychopathology in alcoholics: A review and issues. In R. Meyer (Ed.), *Psychopathology and Addictive Disorders* (pp. 41–56). New York: Guilford Press.

Hesslinger, B., Tebartz van Elst, L., Thiel, T., Haegele, K., Hennig, J., & Ebert, D. (2002) Frontoorbital volume reductions in adult patients with attention deficit hyperactivity disorder. *Neuroscience Letters, 328*, 319–321.

Hestad, K., Ellertsen, B., & Klove, H. (1998). Neuropsychological assessment in old age. In Nordhus, I. H. (Ed); VandenBos, G. R. (Ed); Berg, S. (Ed); Fromholt, P. (Ed), *Clinical Geropsychology.* (pp. 259–288). Washington, DC: American Psychological Association.

Hettema, J., Steele, J., & Miller, W. R. (2005). Motivational interviewing. *Annual Review of Clinical Psychology, 1*, 91–111.

Hettema, J. M., Neale, M. C., & Kendler, K. S. (2001). A review and meta-analysis of the genetic epidemiology of anxiety disorders. *American Journal of Psychiatry, 158*, 1568–1578.

Hettema, J. M., Prescott, C. A., & Kendler, K. S. (2001). A population-based twin study of generalized anxiety disorder in men and women. *Journal of Nervous & Mental Disease, 189*, 413–420.

Heyman, I., Mataiz-Cols, D., & Fineberg, N. A. (2006). Obsessive-compulsive disorder. *British Medical Journal, 333*, 424–429.

Hicks, K. M. (2005). The "new view" approach to women's sexual problems. Medscape. Retrieved September 28, 2007, from www.medscape.com/viewprogram/4705_pnt

Hidalgo, R. B., & Davidson, R. T. (2000). Selective serotonin reuptake inhibitors in post-traumatic stress disorder. *Journal of Psychopharmacology, 14*, 70–76.

Hiday, V. A. (2003). Outpatient commitment: The state of empirical research on its outcomes. *Psychology, Public Policy, and Law, 9*, 8–32.

Hiday, V. A., & Ray, B. (2010). Arrests two years after exiting a well-established mental health court. *Psychiatric Services, 61*(5), 463–468.

Hiday, V. A., & Wales, H. W. (2003). Civil commitment and arrests. *Current Opinion in Psychiatry, 16*, 575–580.

Higgenbotham, H. N., West, S., & Forsyth, D. (1988). *Psychotherapy and behavior change: Social, cultural and methodological perspectives.* New York: Pergamon.

Higgins, S. T., & Silverman, K. (1999). *Motivating behavior change among illicit-drug abusers: Research on contingency management interventions.* Washington, DC: American Psychological Association.

Higgins, S. T., Budney, A. J., Bickel, W. K., Hughes, J. R., Foerg, F., & Badger, G. (1993). Achieving cocaine abstinence with a behavioral approach. *American Journal of Psychiatry, 150*, 763–769.

Higgins, S. T., Heil, S. H., & Lussier, J. P. (2004). Clinical implications of reinforcement as a determinant of substance use disorders. *Annual Review of Psychology, 55*, 431–461.

Higuchi, S., Matsushita, S., Murayama, M., Takagi, S., & Hayashida, M. (1995). Alcohol and aldehyde dehydrogenase polymorphisms and the risk for alcoholism. *American Journal of Psychiatry, 152*, 1219–1221.

Hildebrand, M., & de Ruiter, C. (2004). PCL-R psychopathy and its relation to DSM-IV-TR Axis I and II disorders in a sample of male forensic psychiatric patients in the Netherlands. *International Journal of Law and Psychiatry, 27*, 233–248.

Hilgard, E. R. (1994). Neodissociation theory. In S. J. Lynn & J. W. Rhue (Eds.), *Dissociation: Clinical and theoretical perspectives* (pp. 32–51). New York, Guilford Press.

Hill, C. E., & Lambert, M. J. (2004). Methodological issues in studying psychotherapy processes and outcomes. In M. J. Lambert (Ed.) *Bergin and Garfield's Handbook of Psychotherpy and Behavior Change* (5th edition). (pp. 84–135). New York: Wiley and Sons.

Hill, D. B., Rozanski, C., Carfagnini, J., & Willoughby, B. (2005). Gender identity disorders in childhood and adolescence: A critical inquiry. *Journal of Psychology & Human Sexuality, 17*, 7–33.

Hill, J. (2003). Early identification of individuals at risk for antisocial personality disorder. *British Journal of Psychiatry, 182*, s11–s14.

Hiller, W., Rief, W., & Fichter, M. M. (2002). Dimensional and categorical approaches to hypochondriasis. *Psychological Medicine, 32*, 707–718.

Hilts, D., Gawryl, M., Koenig, G., Dgetluck, N., Loewen, G., et al. (2012). EVP-6124, a selective alpha-7 partial agonist, has positive effects on cognition and clinical function in mild to moderate Alzheimer's disease patients: Results of a six-month, double-blind, placebo controlled, dose ranging study. *Alzheimer's Association International Conference (AAIC)*. Abstract 04-12-04.

Hilty, D. M., Bourgeois, J. A., Chang, C. H., & Servis, M. E. (2001). Somatization disorder. *Current Treatment Options in Neurology, 3*, 305–320.

Himle, J. A., Baser, R. E., Taylor, R. J., Campbell, R. D, & Jackson, J. S. (2009). Anxiety disorders among African Americans, blacks of Caribbean descent, and non-Hispanic whites in the United States. *Journal of Anxiety Disorders, 23*, pp. 578–590.

Hinrichsen, H., Wright, F., Waller, G., & Meyer, C. (2003). Social anxiety and coping strategies in the eating disorders. *Eating Behaviors, 4*, 117–126.

Hinshaw, S. P., Erhardt, D., Murphy, D. A., Greenstein, J. J., & Pelham, W. E. (1993). Part 7: Attention-deficit hyperactivity disorder. In V. B. Van Hasselt & M. Hersen (Eds.), *Handbook of behavior therapy and pharmacotherapy for children: A comparative analysis* (pp. 233–271). Needham Heights, MA: Allyn & Bacon.

Hinton, D., Hinton, S., Pham, T., Chau, H., & Tran, M. (2003). 'Hit by the wind' and temperature-shift panic among Vietnamese refugees. *Transcultural Psychiatry, 40*, 342–376.

Hinton, D., Hinton, S., Um, K., Chea, A. S., & Sak, S. (2002). The Khmer "weak heart" syndrome: Fear of death from palpitations. *Transcultural Psychiatry, 39*, 323–344.

Hinton, D., Um, K., & Ba, P. (2001). A unique panic-disorder presentation among Khmer refugees: The sore-neck syndrome. *Culture, Medicine and Psychiatry, 25*, 297–316.

Hirai, M., & Clum, G. A. (2006). A meta-analytic study of self-help interventions for anxiety problems. *Behavior Therapy, 37*, 99–111.

Hirai, M., & Clum, G. A. (2008). Self-help therapies for anxiety disorders. In P. L. Watkins & G. A. Clum (Eds.), *Handbook of self-help therapies* (pp. 77–107). New York: Lawrence Erlbaum Associates.

Hirschfeld, R. M., Keller, M. B., Panico, S., Arons, B. S., Barlow, D., et al. (1997). The National Depressive and Manic-Depressive Association consensus statement on the undertreatment of depression. *JAMA: Journal of the American Medical Association, 277*, 333–340.

Hochhalter, A. K., Sweeney, W. A., Savage, L. M., Bakke, B. L., & Overmier, J. B. (2001). Using animal models to address the memory deficits of Wernicke-Korsakoff syndrome. In M. E. Carroll & J. B. Overmier (Eds.), *Animal research and human health: Advancing human welfare through behavioral science* (pp. 281–292). Washington, DC: American Psychological Association.

Hoechstetter, K., Meinck, H. M., Henningsen, P., Scherg, M., & Rupp, A. (2002). Psychogenic sensory loss: Magnetic source imaging reveals normal tactile evoked activity of the human primary and secondary somatosensory cortex. *Neuroscience Letters, 323*, 137–140.

Hoehn-Saric, R., Hazlett, R. L., & McLeod, D. R. (1993). Generalized anxiety disorder with early and late onset of anxiety symptoms. *Comprehensive Psychiatry, 34*, 291–298.

Hoek, H. W., & van Hoeken, D. (2003). Review of the prevalence and incidence of eating disorders. *International Journal of Eating Disorders, 34*, 383–396.

Hoff, A. L., & Kremen, W. S. (2003). Neuropsychology in schizophrenia: An update. *Current Opinion in Psychiatry, 16*, 149–155.

Hoff, A., Kremen, W. S., Wieneke, M. H., Lauriello, J., Blankfeld, H. M., et al. (2001). Association of estrogen levels with neuropsychological performance in women with schizophrenia. *American Journal of Psychiatry, 158*, 1134–1139.

Hoffman, L. W. (1991). The influence of the family environment on personality: Accounting for sibling differences. *Psychological Bulletin, 110*, 187–203.

Hoffman, R. E., Boutros, N. N., Hu, S., Berman, R. M., Krystal, J. H., & Charney, D. S. (2000). Transcranial magnetic stimulation and auditory hallucinations in schizophrenia. *Lancet, 355*, 1073–1075.

Hoffman, R. E., Gueorguieva, R., Hawkins, K. A., Varanko, M., Boutros, N. N., et al. (2005). Temporoparietal transcranial magnetic stimulation for auditory hallucinations: Safety, efficacy and moderators in a fifty patient sample. *Biological Psychiatry, 58*, 97–104.

Hofmann, S. G., Moscovitch, D. A., & Heinrichs, N. (2002). Evolutionary mechanisms of fear and anxiety. *Journal of Cognitive Psychotherapy, 16*, 317–330.

Hoge, S., Poythress, N., Bonnie, R., Monahan, J., Eisenberg, M., & Feucht-Haviar, T. (1997). *The MacArthur Adjudicative Competence Study*: Diagnosis, psychopathology, and adjudicative competence-related abilities. *Behavioral Sciences and the Law, 15*, 329–345.

Hoge, S. K., Bonnie, R. J., Poythress, N., & Monahan, J. (1992). Attorney-client decision-making in criminal cases: Client competence and participation as perceived by their attorneys. *Behavioral Sciences & the Law, 10*, 385–394.

Hogue, A., Dauber, S., Samuolis, J., & Liddle, H. A. (2006). Treatment techniques and outcomes in multidimensional family therapy for adolescent behavior problems. *Journal of Family Psychology, 20*, 535–543.

Holder-Perkins, V., & Wise, T. N. (2001). Somatization disorder. In K. A. Phillips (Ed.), *Somatoform and factitious disorders* (pp. 1–26). Washington, DC: American Psychiatric Association.

Hollander, E., & Rosen, J. (2000). Impulsivity. *Journal of Psychopharmacology, 14*, S39–S44.

Hollander, E., Liebowitz, M. R., & Rosen, W. G. (1991). Neuropsychiatric and neuropsychological studies in obsessive-compulsive disorder. In J. Zohar, T. Insel, & S. Rasmussen (Eds.), *The psychobiology of obsessive-compulsive disorder.* (pp. 126–145). New York: Springer.

Hollier, L. M., McIntire, D. D., & Leveno, K. J. (1999). Outcome of twin pregnancies according to intrapair birth weight differences. *Obstetrics & Gynecology, 94*, 1006–1010.

Hollifield, M., Paine, S., Tuttle, L., & Kellner, R. (1999). Hypochondriasis, somatization, and perceived health and utilization of health care services. *Psychosomatics: Journal of Consultation and Liaison Psychiatry, 40*, 380–386.

Hollon, S. D., & Beck, A. T. (1994). Cognitive and cognitive-behavioral therapies. In A. E. Bergin & S. L. Garfield (Eds.), *Handbook of psychotherapy and behavior change* (4th ed., pp. 428–466). New York: John Wiley & Sons.

Hollon, S. D., & Beck, A. T. (2004). Cognitive and cognitive behavior therapies. In M. J. Lambert (Ed.), *Bergin and Garfield's handbook of psychotherapy and behavior change* (5th ed., pp. 447–492). New York: John Wiley & Sons.

Hollon, S. D., DeRubeis, R. J., Shelton, R. C., & Weiss, B. (2002). The emperor's new drugs: Effect size and moderation effects. *Prevention & Treatment, 5*, Article 28. www.journals.apa.org/prevention/volume5/pre0050028c.html

Hollon, S. D., DeRubeis, R. J., Shelton, R. C., Amsterdam, J. D., Salomon, R. M., et al. (2005). Prevention of relapse following cognitive therapy vs medications in moderate to severe depression. *Archives of General Psychiatry, 62*, 417–422.

Holthausen, E. A., Wiersma, D., Sitskoorn, M. M., Dingemans, P. M., Schene, A. H., & van den Bosch, R. J. (2003). Long-term memory deficits in schizophrenia: primary or secondary dysfunction? *Neuropsychology, 17*, 539–547.

Holtzheimer, P. E., III, & Avery, D. H. (2005). Focal brain stimulation for treatment-resistant depression: Transcranial magnetic stimulation, vagus-nerve stimulation, and deep-brain stimulation. *Primary Psychiatry, 12,* 57–64.

Holzman, P. S., Kringlen, E., Matthysse, S., Flanagan, S. D., Lipton, R. B., et al. (1988). A single dominant gene can account for eye tracking dysfunctions and schizophrenia in offspring of discordant twins. *Archives of General Psychiatry, 45,* 641–647.

Holzman, P. S., Solomon, C. M., Levin, S., & Waternaux, C. S. (1984). Pursuit eye movement dysfunctions in schizophrenia: Family evidence for specificity. *Archives of General Psychiatry 41,* 136–139.

Homma, A., Imai, Y., Tago, H., Asada, T., Shigeta, M., et al. (2008). Donepezil treatment of patients with severe Alzheimer's disease in a Japanese population: Results from a 24-week, double-blind, placebo-controlled, randomized trial. *Dementia and Geriatric Cognitive Disorders, 25,* 399–407.

Hong, L. E., Tagamets, M., Avila, M., Wonodi, I., Holcomb, H., & Thaker, G. K. (2005). Specific motion processing pathway deficit during eye tracking in schizophrenia: A performance-matched functional magnetic resonance imaging study. *Biological Psychiatry, 57,* 726–732.

Honig, A., Hofman, A., Rozendaal, N., & Dingemans, P. (1997). Psycho-education in bipolar disorder: Effect on expressed emotion. *Psychiatry Research, 72,* 17–22.

Hopper, K., Harrison, G., Janca, A., & Sartorius, N. (2007). *Recovery from schizophrenia: An international perspective. A Report from the WHO Collaborative Project, The International Study of Schizophrenia.* New York: Oxford University Press.

Hopwood, C. J., Thomas, K. M., Markon, K. E., Wright, A. G. C., & Krueger, R. F. (2012). DSM-5 personality traits and DSM–IV personality disorders. *Journal of Abnormal Psychology, 121,* 424–432.

Horan, W. P., & Blanchard, J. J. (2003). Neurocognitive, social, and emotional dysfunction in deficit syndrome schizophrenia. *Schizophrenia Research, 65,* 125–137.

Horesh, N., Amir, M., Kedem, P., Goldberger, Y., & Kotler, M. (1997). Life events in childhood, adolescence and adulthood and the relationship to panic disorder. *Acta Psychiatrica Scandinavica, 96,* 373–378.

Hornbacher, M. (1998). *Wasted: A memoir of anorexia and bulimia.* New York: Harper Perennial.

Hornbacher, M. (2008). *Madness: A bipolar life.* New York: Houghton Mifflin.

Horney, K. (1937). *The neurotic personality of our times.* Oxford, England: Norton.

Horowitz, L. M. (2004). Diffuse identity and lack of long-term direction: The histrionic personality disorder and other related disorders. In L. M. Horowitz (Ed.), *Interpersonal foundations of psychopathology* (pp. 189–203). Washington, DC: American Psychological Association.

Horvath, A. O., & Symonds, B. D. (1991). Relation between working alliance and outcome in psychotherapy: A meta-analysis. *Journal of Counseling Psychology, 38,* 139–149.

Horwath, E., & Weissman, M. M. (2000). The epidemiology and cross-national presentation of obsessive-compulsive disorder. *Psychiatric Clinics of North America, 23,* 493–507.

Horwath, E., Lish, J. D., Johnson, J., Hornig, C. D., & Weissman, M. M. (1993). Agoraphobia without panic: Clinical reappraisal of an epidemiologic finding. *American Journal of Psychiatry, 150,* 1496–1501.

Hough, W. G., & O'Brien, K. P. (2005). The effect of community treatment orders on offending rates. *Psychiatry, Psychology and Law, 12,* 411–423.

Houts, A. C. (2002). Discovery, invention, and the expansion of the modern Diagnostic and Statistical Manual of Mental Disorders. In L. E. Beutler & M. L. Malik (Eds.), *Rethinking the DSM: A psychological perspective* (pp. 17–65). Washington, DC: American Psychological Association.

Hovey, J. D. (1998). Acculturative stress, depression, and suicidal ideation among Mexican-American adolescents: Implications for the development of suicide prevention programs in schools. *Psychological Reports, 83,* 249–250.

Hovey, J. D. (2000). Acculturative stress, depression, and suicidal ideation in Mexican immigrants. *Cultural Diversity & Ethnic Minority Psychology, 6,* 134–151.

Hovey, J. D., & King, C. A. (1996). Acculturative stress, depression, and suicidal ideation among immigrant and second-generation Latino adolescents. *Journal of the American Academy of Child and Adolescent Psychiatry, 35,* 1183–1192.

Howard, K. I., Lueger, R. J., Maling, M. S., & Martinovich, Z. (1993). A phase model of psychotherapy outcome: Causal mediation of change. *Journal of Consulting & Clinical Psychology, 61,* 678–685.

Howsepian, A. A. (2011). Mental illness and firearm violence. *JAMA, 306*(9), 930.

Hoy, H. (2007, July 25). Prison castrations raise concerns. *The Prague Post.* Retrieved April 17, 2013, from www.praguepost.com

Hrabosky, J. I., Cash, T. F., Veale, D., Neziroglu, F., Soll, E. A., et al. (2009). Multidimensional body image comparisons among patients with eating disorders, body dysmorphic disorder, and clinical controls: A multisite study. *Body Image, 6*(3), 155–163.

Hsee, C. K., Hatfield, E., Carlson, J. G., & Chemtob, C. (1990). The effect of power on susceptibility to emotional contagion. *Cognition & Emotion, 4,* 327–340. Retrieved April 3, 2007, from http://transcripts.cnn.com/TRANSCRIPTS/0205/21/lt.24.html

Huang, Y. Y., & Kandel, E. R. (2007). 5-Hydroxytryptamine induces a protein kinase A/mitogen-activated protein kinase-mediated and macromolecular synthesis-dependent late phase of long-term potentiation in the amygdala. *Journal of Neuroscience, 27,* 3111–3119.

Hubbard, R. L., Marsden, M. E., Rachal, J. V., Harwood, H. G., Cavanaugh, E. R., & Ginzburg, H. M. (1989). *Drug abuse treatment: A national study of effectiveness* (pp. 90–92). Chapel Hill: University of North Carolina Press, 1989.

Hudson, C. G. (2005). Socioeconomic status and mental illness: Tests of the social causation and selection hypotheses. *American Journal of Orthopsychiatry, 75,* 3–18.

Hudson, J., & Rapee, R. M. (2001). Parent–child interactions and anxiety disorders: An observational study. *Behaviour Research and Therapy, 39,* 1411–1427.

Hudson, J. I., Hiripi, E., Pope, H. G., Jr., & Kessler, R. C. (2007). The prevalence and correlates of eating disorders in the National Comorbidity Survey Replication. *Biological Psychiatry, 61,* 348–358.

Hudziak, J. J., Derks, E. M., Althoff, R. R., Copeland, W., & Boomsma, D. I. (2005). The genetic and environmental contributions to oppositional defiant behavior: A multi-informant twin study. *Journal of the American Academy of Child & Adolescent Psychiatry, 44,* 907–914.

Huether, G., Zhou, D., Schmidt, S., Wiltfang, J., & Eckart, R. (1997). Long-term food restriction down-regulates the density of serotonin transporters in the rat frontal cortex. *Biological Psychiatry, 41,* 1174–1180.

Hugdahl, K. (2001). *Psychophysiology: The mind-body perspective* (2nd ed.). Cambridge, MA: Harvard University Press.

Hughes, C., Kumari, V., Soni, W., Das, M., Binneman, B., et al. (2003). Longitudinal study of symptoms and cognitive function in chronic schizophrenia. *Schizophrenia Research, 59,* 137–146.

Hui, C. H., & Triandis, H. C. (1986). Individualism-collectivism: A study of cross-cultural researchers. *Journal of Cross-Cultural Psychology, 17,* 225–248.

Hui, L. K., Ng, R. M. K., Pau, L., & Yip, K. C. (2012). Relationship of cognitions and symptoms of agoraphobia in Hong Kong Chinese: A combined quantitative and qualitative study. *International Journal of Social Psychiatry, 58*(2), 153–165.

Humfleet, G. L., & Haas, A. L. (2004). Is marijuana use becoming a "gateway" to nicotine dependence? *Addiction, 99,* 5–6.

Hummingbird. (1999). First person account: Schizophrenia, substance abuse, and HIV. *Schizophrenia Bulletin, 25,* 863–866.

Humphreys, K., & Moos, R. H. (2007). Encouraging posttreatment self-help group involvement to reduce demand for continuing care services: Two-year clinical and utilization outcomes. *Alcoholism: Clinical and Experimental Research, 31,* 64–68.

Humphreys, K., Winzelberg, A., & Klaw, E. (2000). Psychologists' ethical responsibilities in Internet-based groups: Issues, strategies, and a call for dialogue. *Professional Psychology: Research and Practice, 31,* 493–496.

Hunt, I. M., Kapur, N., Windfuhr, K., Robinson, J., Bickley, H., et al. (National Confidential Inquiry into Suicide and Homicide by People with Mental Illness). (2006). Suicide in schizophrenia: Findings from a national clinical survey. *Journal of Psychiatric Practice, 12*, 139–147.

Hunter, E. C. M., Baker, D., Phillips, M. L., Sierra, M., & David, A. S. (2005). Cognitive-behaviour therapy for depersonalisation disorder: An open study. *Behaviour Research and Therapy, 43*, 1121–1130.

Hunter, E. C. M., Phillips, M. L., Chalder, T., Sierra, M., & David, A. S. (2003). Depersonalisation disorder: A cognitive-behavioural conceptualisation. *Behaviour Research and Therapy, 41*, 1451–1467.

Huntjens, R. J. C., Peters, M. L., Postma, A., Woertman, L., Effting, M., & van der Hart, O. (2005). Transfer of newly acquired stimulus valence between identities in dissociative identity disorder (DID). *Behaviour Research and Therapy, 43*, 243–255.

Huntjens, R. J. C., Peters, M. L., Woertman, L., Bovenschen, L. M., Martin, R. C., & Postma, A. (2006). Inter-identity amnesia in dissociative identity disorder: A simulated memory impairment? *Psychological Medicine, 36*, 857–863.

Huntjens, R.J.C., Peters, M., Woertman, L., van der Hart, O., & Postma, A. (2007). Memory transfer for trauma-related words between identities in dissociative identity disorder. *Behaviour Research and Therapy, 45*, 775–789.

Huntjens, R. J. C., Postma, A., Peters, M. L., Woertman, L., & van der Hart, O. (2003). Interidentity amnesia for neutral, episodic information in dissociative identity disorder. *Journal of Abnormal Psychology, 112*, 290–297.

Hurd, M. D., Martorell, P., Delavande, A., Mullen, K. J., &Langa, K. M. (2013). Monetary costs of dementia in the United States. *The New England Journal of Medicine, 368*, 1326–1334.

Hurt, R. D., Offord, K. P., Croghan, I. T., Gomez-Dahl, L., Kottke, T. E., et al. (1996). Mortality following inpatient addictions treatment: Role of tobacco use in a community-based cohort. *Journal of the American Medical Association, 275*, 1097–1103.

Husted, D. S., & Shapira, N. A. (2004). A review of the treatment for refractory obsessive-compulsive disorder: From medicine to deep brain stimulation. *CNS Spectrums, 9*, 833–847.

Huttenlocher, P. R. (2002). *Neural plasticity: The effects of environment on the development of the cerebral cortex.* Cambridge, MA: Harvard University Press.

Hybels, C. F., Blazer, D. G., Pieper, C. F., Burchett, B. M., Hays, J. C., et al. (2006). Sociodemographic characteristics of the neighborhood and depressive symptoms in older adults: Using multilevel modeling in geriatric psychiatry. *American Journal of Geriatric Psychiatry, 14*, 498–506.

Hyde, J. S., Mezulis, A. H., & Abramson, L. Y. (2008). The ABCs of depression: Integrating affective, biological, and cognitive models to explain the emergence of the gender difference in depression. *Psychological Review, 115*, 291–313.

Hyman, S. E. (2001). A 28-year-old man addicted to cocaine. *Journal of the American Medical Association, 286*, 2586–2594.

Hyman, S. E., (2005). Addiction: A disease of learning and memory. *American Journal of Pyschiatry, 162*, 1414–1422.

Hyman, S. E. (2011). Grouping diagnoses of mental disorders by their common risk factors. *The American Journal of Psychiatry, 168*(1), 1–3.

Hyman, S. E., & Nestler, E. J. (1993). *The molecular foundations of psychiatry.* Washington, DC: American Psychiatric Press.

Hyman, S. M., Gold, S. N., & Cott, M. A. (2003). Forms of social support that moderate PTSD in childhood sexual abuse survivors. *Journal of Family Violence, 18*, 295–300.

Iacono, W. G., Moreau, M., Beiser, M., Fleming, J. A. E., & Lin, T. (1992). Smooth-pursuit eye tracking in first-episode psychotic patients and their relatives. *Journal of Abnormal Psychology, 101*, 104–116.

Igartua, K. J., Gill, K., & Montoro, R. (2003). Internalized homophobia: A factor in depression, anxiety, and suicide in the gay and lesbian population. *Canadian Journal of Community Mental Health, 22*, 15–30.

Ikeuchi, T., Kaneko, H., Miyashita, A., Nozaki, H., Kasuga, K., et al. (2008). Mutational analysis in early-onset familial dementia in the Japanese population: The role of PSEN1 and MAPT R406W mutations. *Dementia and Geriatric Cognitive Disorders, 26*, 43–49.

Ikonomovic, M. D., Klunk, W. E., Abrahamson, E. E., Mathis, C. A., Price, J. C., et al. (2008). Post-mortem correlates of in vivo PiB-PET amyloid imaging in a typical case of Alzheimer's disease. *Brain: A Journal of Neurology, 131*, 1630–1645.

Ilgen, M. A., & Hutchison, K. E. (2005). A history of major depressive disorder and the response to stress. *Journal of Affective Disorders, 86*, 143–150.

Inaba, A., Thoits, P. A., Ueno, K., Gove, W. R., Evenson, R. J., & Sloan, M. (2005). Depression in the United States and Japan: Gender, marital status, and SES patterns. *Social Science & Medicine, 61*, 2280–2292.

Insel, T. (2013). *Transforming diagnosis. NIMH director's blog.* Retrieved May 21, 2013, from www.nimh.nih.gov/about/director/2013/transforming-diagnosis.shtml

Insel, T. R. (1992). Toward a neuroanatomy of obsessive-compulsive disorder. *Archives of General Psychiatry, 49*, 739–744.

Insel, T. R., & Winslow, J. T. (1990). Neurobiology of obsessive-compulsive disorder. In M. A. Jenike, L. Baer, & W. E. Minichiello (Eds.), *Obsessive-compulsive disorders: Theory and management.* (pp. 118–131). Chicago: Year Book Medical.

Intrator, J., Hare, R., Strizke, P., & Brichtswein, K. (1997). A brain imaging (single photon emission computerized tomography) study of semantic and affective processing in psychopaths. *Biological Psychiatry, 42*, 96–103.

Ireland, T., & Widom, C. S. (1994). Childhood victimization and risk for alcohol and drug arrests. *International Journal of the Addictions, 29*, 235–274.

Ironson, G. I., Freund, B., Strauss, J. L., & Williams, J. (2002). A comparison of two treatments for traumatic stress: A community based study of EMDR and prolonged exposure. *Journal of Clinical Psychology, 58*, 113–128.

Isometsä, E. T. (2000). Suicide. *Current Opinion in Psychiatry, 13*, 143–147.

Ito, K. L., & Maramba, G. G. (2002). Therapeutic beliefs of Asian American therapists: Views from an ethnic-specific clinic. *Transcultural Psychiatry, 39*, 33–73.

Ivarsson, T., Larsson, B., & Gillberg, C. (1998). A 2–4 year follow-up of depressive symptoms, suicidal ideation, and suicide attempts among adolescent psychiatric inpatients. *European Child and Adolescent Psychiatry, 7*, 96–104.

Ivry, R. B., Spencer, R. M., Zelaznik, H. N., & Diedrichsen, J. (2002). The cerebellum and event timing. In S. M. Highstein & W. T. Thach (Eds.). *The cerebellum: Recent developments in cerebellar research* (pp. 302–317). New York: New York Academy of Sciences.

Jackson v. Indiana, 406 U.S. 715 (1972).

Jackson, J., Fiddler, M., Kapur, N., Wells, A., Tomenson, B., & Creed, F. (2006). Number of bodily symptoms predicts outcome more accurately than health anxiety in patients attending neurology, cardiology, and gastroenterology clinics. *Journal of Psychosomatic Research, 60*, 357–363.

Jacobi, C., Hayward, C., de Zwaan, M., Kraemer, H. C., & Agras, W. S. (2004). Coming to terms with risk factors for eating disorders: Application of risk terminology and suggestions for a general taxonomy. *Psychological Bulletin, 130*, 19–65.

Jacobs, M. K., Christensen, A., Snibbe, J. R., Dolezal-Wood, S., Huber, A., & Polterok, A. (2001). A comparison of computer-based versus traditional individual psychotherapy. *Professional Psychology: Research & Practice, 32*, 92–96.

Jacobs, S.-E., Thomas, W., & Lang, S. (1997). *Two-spirit people: Native American gender identity, sexuality, and spirituality.* Champaign: University of Illinois Press.

Jacobsen, L. K., Southwick, S. M., & Kosten, T. R. (2001). Substance use disorders in patients with posttraumatic stress disorder: A review of the literature. *American Journal of Psychiatry, 158*, 1184–1190.

Jacobson, N. S., Martell, C. R., & Dimidjian, S. (2001). Behavioral activation treatment for depression: Returning to contextual roots. *Clinical Psychology: Science and Practice, 8*, 255–270.

Jacobson, S. W., Carr, L. G., Croxford, J., Sokol, R. J., Li, T.-K., & Jabobson, J. L. (2006). Protective effect of the alcohol dehydrogenase-ADH1B allele in children exposed to alcohol during pregnancy. *Journal of Pediatrics, 148*, 30–37.

Jaffee v. Redmond, 518 U.S. 1 (1996).

Jain, M., Palacio, L. G., Castellanos, F. X., Palacio, J. D., Pineda, D., et al. (2007). Attention-deficit/hyperactivity disorder and comorbid disruptive behavior disorders: Evidence of pleiotropy and new susceptibility loci. *Biological Psychiatry, 61,* 1329–1339.

Jakupcak, M., Osborne, T. L., Michael, S., Cook, J. W., & McFall, M. (2006). Implications of masculine gender role stress in male veterans with posttraumatic stress disorder. *Psychology of Men & Masculinity, 7,* 203–211.

Jamison, K. R. (1989). Mood disorders and patterns of creativity in British writers and artists. *Psychiatry, 52,* 125–134.

Jamison, K. R. (1993). *Touched with fire: Manic-depressive illness and the artistic temperament.* New York: Free Press.

Jamison, K. R. (1995). *An unquiet mind: A memoir of moods and madness.* New York: Vintage Books.

Jamison, K. R., Gerner, R. H., Hammen, C., & Padesky, C. (1980). Clouds and silver linings: Positive experiences associated with primary affective disorders. *American Journal of Psychiatry, 137,* 198–202.

Jamison, R. N., & Walker, L. S. (1992). Illness behavior in children of chronic pain patients. *International Journal of Psychiatry in Medicine, 22,* 329–342.

Janet, P. (1907). *The major symptoms of hysteria.* New York: Macmillan.

Jang, K. L., Paris, J., Zweig-Frank, H., & Livesley, W. J. (1998). Twin study of dissociative experience. *Journal of Nervous and Mental Disease, 186,* 345–351.

Jang, K. L., Vernon, P. A., & Livesley, W. J. (2001). Behavioural-genetic perspectives on personality function. *The Canadian Journal of Psychiatry, 46,* 234–244.

Janoff-Bulman, R. (1995). *Victims of violence.* In G. S. Everly, Jr., & J. M. Lating (Eds.), *Psychotraumatology: Key papers and core concepts in post-traumatic stress* (pp. 73–86). New York: Plenum Press.

Jansen, A., Nederkoorn, C., & Mulkens, S. (2005). Selective visual attention for ugly and beautiful body parts in eating disorders. *Behaviour Research and Therapy, 43,* 183–196.

Jansen, K. L., & Darracot-Cankovic, R. (2001). The nonmedical use of ketamine, part two: A review of problem use and dependence. *Journal of Psychoactive Drugs 33,* 151–158.

Jansiewicz, E. M., Goldberg, M. C., Newschaffer, C. J., Denckla, M. B., Landa, R., & Mostofsky, S. H. (2006). Motor signs distinguish children with high functioning autism and Asperger's syndrome from controls. *Journal of Autism and Developmental Disorders, 36,* 613–621.

Janssen, I., Krabbendam, L., Jolles, J., & van Os, J. (2003). Alterations in theory of mind in patients with schizophrenia and non-psychotic relatives. *Acta Psychiatrica Scandinavica, 108,* 110–117.

Janus, E. S. (2003). Treatment and the civil commitment of sex offenders. In B. J. Winick & J. Q. La Fond (Eds.), *Protecting society from sexually dangerous offenders: Law, justice, and therapy* (pp. 119–129). Washington, DC: American Psychological Association.

Jarret, R. B., Kraft, D., Doyle, J., Foster, B. M., Eaves, G. G., & Silver, P. C. (2001). Preventing recurrent depression using cognitive therapy with and without a continuation phase: A randomized clinical trial. *Archives of General Psychiatry, 58,* 381–388.

Jarvis, E. (1998). Schizophrenia in British immigrants: Recent findings, issues and implications. *Transcultural Psychiatry, 35,* 39–74.

Jasper, F. J. (2003). Working with dissociative fugue in a general psychotherapy practice: A cautionary tale. *American Journal of Clinical Hypnosis, 45,* 311–322.

Javeline, D. (1999). Response effects in polite cultures: A test of acquiescence in Kazakhstan. *Public Opinion Quarterly, 63,* 1–28.

Jefferys, D. E., & Castle, D. J. (2003). Body dysmorphic disorder—a fear of imagined ugliness. *Australian Family Physician, 32,* 722–755.

Jenike, M., Baer, L., & Minichiello, W. (Eds.) (1998). *Obsessive-compulsive disorders: Practical management.* St. Louis: Mosby.

Jenike, M. A. (1984). Obsessive-compulsive disorder: A question of a neurologic lesion. *Comprehensive Psychiatry, 25,* 298–304.

Jenkins-Hall, K., & Sacco, W. P. (1991). Effects of client race and depression on evaluations by white therapists. *Journal of Social Clinical Psychology, 10,* 322–333.

Jennings, J. M., Dagenbach, D., Engle, C. M., & Funke, L. J. (2007). Age-related changes and the attention network task: An examination of alerting, orienting, and executive function. *Aging, Neuropsychology, and Cognition, 14,* 353–369.

Jensen, P. S., Hinshaw, S. P., Kraemer, H. C., Lenora, N., Newcorn, J. H., et al. (2001). ADHD comorbidity findings from the MTA study: Comparing comorbid subgroups. *Journal of the American Academy of Child & Adolescent Psychiatry, 40,* 147–158.

Jerome, L. W., & Zaylor, C. (2000). Cyberspace: Creating a therapeutic environment for telehealth applications. *Professional Psychology: Research & Practice, 31,* 478–483.

Jessen, G., Steffensen, P., & Jensen, B. (1998). Seasons and meteorological factors in suicidal behaviour: Findings and methodological considerations from a Danish study. *Archives of Suicide Research, 4,* 263–280.

Ji, J., Kleinman, A., & Becker, A. E. (2001). Suicide in contemporary China: A review of China's distinctive suicide demographics in their sociocultural context. *Harvard Review of Psychiatry, 9,* 1–12.

Jianlin, J. (2000). Suicide rates and mental health services in modern China. *Crisis, 21,* 118–121.

Jimerson, D. C., Lesem, M. D., Kaye, W. H., & Brewerton, T. D. (1992). Low serotonin and dopamine metabolite concentrations in cerebrospinal fluid from bulimic patients with frequent binge episodes. *Archives of General Psychiatry, 49,* 132–138.

Joe, G. W., Simpson, D. D., & Broome, K. M. (1999). Retention and patient engagement models for different treatment modalities in DATOS. *Drug and Alcohol Dependence, 57,* 113–125.

Johanson, A., Risberg, J., Tucker, D. M., & Gustafson, L. (2006). Changes in frontal lobe activity with cognitive therapy for spider phobia. *Applied Neuropsychology, 13,* 34–41.

Johns, A. (2001). Psychiatric effects of cannabis. *British Journal of Psychiatry, 178,* 116–122.

Johns, L. C., Hemsley, D., & Kuipers, E. (2002). A comparison of auditory hallucinations in a psychiatric and non-psychiatric group. *British Journal of Clinical Psychology, 41,* 81–86.

Johnson, B. A., & Ait-Daoud, N. (2000). Neuropharmalogical treatments for alcoholism: Scientific basis and clinical findings. *Psychopharmacology, 149,* 327–344.

Johnson, C. L., Lund, B. C., & Yates, W. R. (2003). Recovery rates for anorexia nervosa. *American Journal of Psychiatry, 160,* 798.

Johnson, C. P., Myers, S. M., & The Council on Children with Disabilities. (2007). Identification and evaluation of children with autism spectrum disorders. *Pediatrics, 120,* 1183–1215.

Johnson, J. G., Bromley, E., & McGeoch, P. G. (2005). Role of childhood experiences in the development of maladaptive and adaptive personality traits. In J. M. Oldham, A. E. Skodol, & D. S. Bender, Donna S. (Eds.), *The American Psychiatric Publishing textbook of personality disorders* (pp. 209–221). Washington, DC: American Psychiatric Publishing.

Johnson, J. G., Cohen, P., Chen, H., Kasen, S., & Brook, J. S. (2006). Parenting behaviors associated with risk for offspring personality disorder during adulthood. *Archives of General Psychiatry, 63,* 579–587.

Johnson, J. G., Cohen, P., Dohrenwend, B. P., Link, B. G., & Brook, J. S. (1999). A longitudinal investigation of social causation and social selection processes involved in the association between socioeconomic status and psychiatric disorders. *Journal of Abnormal Psychology, 108,* 490–499.

Johnson, J. G., Cohen, P., Kasen, S., & Brook, J. S. (2002). Childhood adversities associated with risk for eating disorders or weight problems during adolescence or early adulthood. *American Journal of Psychiatry, 159,* 394–400.

Johnson, J. G., Cohen, P., Kasen, S., & Brook, J. S. (2006a). Dissociative disorders among adults in the community, impaired functioning, and axis I and II comorbidity. *Journal of Psychiatric Research, 40,* 131–140.

Johnson, J. G., Cohen, P., Kasen, S., & Brook, J. S. (2006b). Personality disorders evident by early adulthood and risk for anxiety disorders during middle adulthood. *Journal of Anxiety Disorders, 20,* 408–426.

Johnson, J. G., Cohen, P., Kasen, S., Skodol, A. E., Hamagami, F., & Brook, J. S. (2000). Age-related change in personality disorder trait levels between early adolescence and adulthood: A community-based longitudinal investigation. *Acta Psychiatrica Scandinavica, 102,* 265–275.

Johnson, J. G., Cohen, P., Kotler, L., Kasen, S., & Brook, J. S. (2002). Psychiatric disorders associated with risk for the development of eating disorders during adolescence and early adulthood. *Journal of Consulting and Clinical Psychology, 70*, 1119–1128.

Johnson, S. D. (2008). Substance use, post-traumatic stress disorder and violence. *Current Opinion in Psychiatry, 21*, 242–246.

Johnson, S. L., & Miller, I. (1997). Negative life events and time to recovery from episodes of bipolar disorder. *Journal of Abnormal Psychology, 106*, 449–457.

Johnson, S. L., & Roberts, J. E. (1995). Life events and bipolar disorder: Implications from biological theories. *Psychological Bulletin, 117*, 434–449.

Johnston, C., & Freeman, W. (1997). Attributions for child behavior in parents of children with behavior disorders and children with attention-deficit/hyperactivity disorder. *Journal of Consulting and Clinical Psychology, 65*, 636–645.

Joiner, T., Coyne, J. C., & Blalock, J. (1999). On the interpersonal nature of depression: Overview and synthesis. In T. Joiner & J. C. Coyne (Eds.), *The interactional nature of depression: Advances in interpersonal approaches* (pp. 3–19). Washington, DC: American Psychological Association.

Joiner, T. E. (1994). Contagious depression: Existence, specificity to depressed symptoms, and the role of reassurance seeking. *Journal of Personality & Social Psychology, 67*, 287–296.

Joiner, T. E., Jr. (1996). A confirmatory factor-analytic investigation of the tripartite model of depression and anxiety in college students. *Cognitive Therapy and Research, 20*, 521–539.

Jones H. E., Johnson, R. E., Bigelow, G. E., Silverman, K., Mudric, T., & Strain, E. C. (2004). Safety and efficacy of L-tryptophan and behavioral incentives for treatment of cocaine dependence: A randomized clinical. *American Journal on Addictions, 13*, 421–437.

Jones, M. K., & Menzies, R. G. (1995). The etiology of fear of spiders. *Anxiety, Stress & Coping: An International Journal, 8*, 227–234.

Jones, S. (2004). Psychotherapy of bipolar disorder: A review. *Journal of Affective Disorders, 80*, 101–114.

Joormann, J., & Gotlib, I. H. (2006). Is this happiness I see? Biases in the identification of emotional facial expressions in depression and social phobia. *Journal of Abnormal Psychology, 115*, 705–714.

Jope, R. S. (1999). Anti-bipolar therapy: Mechanism of action of lithium. *Molecular Psychiatry, 4*, 117–128.

Jose, P. E., & Brown, I. (2008). When does the gender difference in rumination begin? Gender and age differences in the use of rumination by adolescents. *Journal of Youth and Adolescence, 37*, 180–192.

Joseph, R. (1999). The neurology of traumatic "dissociative" amnesia: Commentary and literature review. *Child Abuse and Neglect, 23*, 715–727.

Joseph, S., Williams, R., & Yule, W. (1995). Psychosocial perspectives on post-traumatic stress. *Clinical Psychology Review, 15*, 515–544.

Joshi, K. G., Frierson, R. L., & Gunter, T. D. (2006). Shared psychotic disorder and criminal responsibility: A review and case report of folie à trois. *Journal of the American Academy of Psychiatry and the Law, 34*, 511–517.

Joyce, P. R., McKenzie, J. M., Luty, S. E., Mulder, R. T., Carter, J. D., et al. (2003). Temperament, childhood environment and psychopathology as risk factors for avoidant and borderline personality disorders. *Australian and New Zealand Journal of Psychiatry, 37*, 756–764.

Judd, L. L., Akiskal, H. S., Schettler, P. J., Coryell, W., Maser, J., Rice, J. A., et al. (2003). The comparative clinical phenotype and long term longitudinal episode course of bipolar I and II: A clinical spectrum or distinct disorders? *Journal of Affective Disorders, 73*, 19–32.

Judd, L. L., Kessler, R. C., Paulhus, M. P., Zeller, P. V., Wittchen, H. U., & Kinovac, J. L. (1998). Cormorbidity as a fundamental feature of generalized anxiety diorders: Results from the National Comorbidity Study (NCS). *Acta Psychiatrica Scandinavia, 393*(Suppl.), 6–11.

Judd, L. L., Schettler, P. J., Akiskal, H. S., Coryell, W., Leon, A. C., et al. (2008). Residual symptom recovery from major affective episodes in bipolar disorders and rapid episode relapse/recurrence. *Archives of General Psychiatry, 65*, 386–394.

Juengling, F. D., Schmahl, C., Hesslinger, B., Ebert, D., Bremner, J. D., et al. (2003). Positron emission tomography in female patients with borderline personality disorder. *Journal of Psychiatry Research, 37*, 109–115.

Jung, C. G. (1983). *The essential Jung* (A. Storr, Ed.). Princeton, NJ: Princeton University Press.

Just, N., & Alloy, L. B. (1997). The response styles theory of depression: Tests and an extension of the theory. *Journal of Abnormal Psychology, 106*, 221–229.

Kafka, M. P. (2000). The paraphilia-related disorders: Nonparaphilic hypersexuality and sexual compulsivity/addiction. In S. R. Leiblum & R. C. Rosen (Eds.), *Principles and practice of sex therapy* (3rd ed., pp. 471–503). New York: Guilford Press.

Kafka, M. P. (2003). The monoamine hypothesis for the pathophysiology of paraphilic disorders: An update. *Annals of the New York Academy of Science, 989*, 86–94.

Kafka, M. P., & Hennen, J. (2000). Psychostimulant augmentation during treatment with selective serotonin reuptake inhibitors in men with paraphilia-related disorders: A case series. *Journal of Clinical Psychiatry, 61*, 664–670.

Kagan, J. (1989). Temperamental contributions to social behavior. *American Psychologist, 44*, 668–674.

Kagan, R. M., & Reid, W. J. (1986). Critical factors in the adoption of emotionally disturbed youths. *Child Welfare Journal, 65*, 63–73.

Kahan, D., Polivy, J., & Herman, C. P. (2003). Conformity and dietary disinhibition: A test of the ego-strength model of self-regulation. *International Journal of Eating Disorders, 33*, 165–171.

Kahn, E. (1998). A critique of nondirectivity in the person-centered approach. *Journal of Humanistic Psychology, 39*, 94–110.

Kahn, R. S., Fleischhacker, W. W., Boter, H., Davidson, M., Vergouwe, Y., et al. (2008). Effectiveness of antipsychotic drugs in first-episode schizophrenia and schizophreniform disorder: An open randomised clinical trial. *Lancet, 371*, 1085–1097.

Kahn, R. S., Khoury, J., Nichols, W. C., & Lanphear, B. P. (2003). Role of dopamine transporter genotype and maternal prenatal smoking in childhood hyperactive-impulsive, inattentive, and oppositional behaviors. *Journal of Pediatrics, 143*, 104–110.

Kahn, R. S., Linszen, D. H., van Os, J., Wiersma, D., Bruhheman, R., et al. (2011). Evidence that familial liability for psychosis is expressed as differential sensitivity to cannabis: An analysis of patient–sibling and sibling–control pairs. *Archives of General Psychiatry, 68*, 138–147.

Kalaria, R. N., & Ballard, C. (1999). Overlap between pathology of Alzheimer disease and vascular dementia. *Alzheimer Disease & Associated Disorders, 13*, S115–S123.

Kales, H. C., Chen, P., Blow, F. C., Welsh, D. E., & Mellow, A. M. (2005). Rates of clinical depression diagnosis, functional impairment, and nursing home placement in coexisting dementia and depression. *American Journal of Geriatric Psychiatry, 13*, 441–449.

Kalisvaart, K. J., de Jonghe, J. F. M., Bogaards, M. J., Vreeswijk, R., Egberts, T. C. G., et al. (2005). Haloperidol prophylaxis for elderly hip-surgery patients at risk for delirium: A randomized placebo-controlled study. *Journal of the American Geriatrics Society, 53*, 1658–1666.

Kalivas, P. W., & Volkow, N. D. (2005). The neural basis of addiction: A pathology of motivation and choice. *American Journal of Psychiatry, 162*, 1403–1413.

Kaltiala-Heino, R., Kosunen, E., & Rimpela, M. (2003). Pubertal timing, sexual behaviour and self-reported depression in middle adolescence. *Journal of Adolescence, 26*, 531–545.

Kaltiala-Heino, R., Rimpelä, M., Rantanen, P., & Rimpelä, A. (2000). Bullying at school—an indicator of adolescents at risk for mental disorders. *Journal of Adolescence, 23*, 661–674.

Kameya, Y. (2001). How Japanese culture affects the sexual functions of normal females. *Journal of Sex & Marital Therapy, 27*, 151–152.

Kandel, D., & Logan, J. (1984). Patterns of drug use from adolescence to young adulthood: Periods of risk for initiation, continued use and discontinuation. *American Journal of Public Health, 74*, 660–666.

Kandel, D. B. (2002). *Stages and pathways of drug involvement: Examining the gateway hypothesis.* Cambridge, England: Cambridge University Press.

Kandel, D. B., & Yamaguchi, K. (1985). Developmental patterns of the use of legal, illegal and medically prescribed psychotropic drugs from adolescence to young adulthood. In C. L. Jones & R. Battjes (Eds.), *Etiology of drug abuse: Implications for prevention* (pp. 193–235). Washington DC: Superintendent of Documents, U.S. Government Printing Office. [NIDA Research Monograph 56, DHHS Pub. No. ADM 85–1335.]

Kandel, D. B., & Yamaguchi, K. (1999). Developmental stages of involvement in substance abuse. In P. J. Ott, R. E. Tarter, & R. T. Ammerman (Eds.), *Sourcebook on substance abuse: Etiology epidemiology, assessment and treatment* (pp. 50–74). New York: Allyn & Bacon.

Kandel, E. R., Schwartz, J. H., & Jessell, T. M. (Eds.). (2007). *Principles of neural science* (5th ed.). New York: Elsevier Science.

Kaniasty, K., & Norris, F. H. (1992). Social support and victims of crime: Matching event, support, and outcome. *American Journal of Community Psychology, 20*, 211–241.

Kaniasty, K. Z., Norris, F. H., & Murrell, S. A. (1990). Received and perceived social support following natural disaster. *Journal of Applied Social Psychology, 20*, 85–114.

Kansas v. Crane, 122 S. Ct. 867 (2002).

Kansas v. Hendricks, 521 U.S. 346 (1997).

Kaplan, A. (2007a). Hoarding: Studies characterize phenotype, demonstrate treatment. *Psychiatric Times, 24*(6). Retrieved February 25, 2009, from www.psychiatrictimes.com/showArticle.jhtml?articleId=199202770

Kaplan, A. (2007b). Mental illness in US Latinos addressed in survey, outreach efforts. *Psychiatric Times, 24*, n.p. Retrieved April 3, 2007, from www.psychiatrictimes.com/showArticle.jhtml;jsessionid=0V0Y2JR5R5C X0QSNDLPCKH0CJUNN2JVN?articleID=198001928&pgno=2

Kaplan, H. S. (1981). *The new sex therapy.* New York: Brunner/Mazel.

Kaplan, H. S. (1987). *Sexual aversion, sexual phobias, and panic disorder.* New York: Brunner/Mazel.

Kaplan, H. S. (1989). *How to overcome premature ejaculation.* New York: Brunner-Routledge.

Kaplan, H. S. (1995). Sexual aversion disorder: The case of the phobic virgin, or an abused child grows up. In R. C. Rosen & S. R. Leiblum (Eds.), *Case studies in sex therapy* (pp. 65–80). New York: Guilford Press.

Kaplan, L. J. (1991). *Female perversions.* Northvale, NJ: Jason Aronson.

Kapur, N., & Graham, K. S. (2002). Recovery of memory function in neurological disease. In A. D. Baddeley, M. D. Kopelman, & B. A. Wilson (Eds.), *Handbook of memory disorders* (2nd ed., pp. 233–248). Chichester, England: Wiley.

Kapur, N., Glisky, E. L., & Wilson, B. A. (2004). External memory aids and computers in memory rehabilitation. In A. D. Baddeley, M. D. Kopelman, & B. A. Wilson (Eds.), *Essential handbook of memory disorders for clinicians* (pp. 301–328). New York: Wiley.

Kapur, S. (2003). Psychosis as a state of aberrant salience: A framework linking biology, phenomenology, and pharmacology in schizophrenia. *American Journal of Psychiatry, 160*, 13–23.

Kapur, S. & Seeman, P. (2002) NMDA receptor antagonists ketamine and PCP have direct effectson the deopamine D(2) and serotonin 5-HT(2) receptors: Implications for models of schizophrenia. *Molecular Psychiatry, 7*, 837–844.

Kar, N. (2005). Chronic koro-like symptoms— two case reports. *BioMed Central Psychiatry, 5*, 34. Retrieved February 19, 2007, from www.pubmedcentral. nih.gov/articlerender. fcgi?artid=1266381

Karkowski, L. M., & Kendler, K. S. (1997). An examination of the genetic relationship between bipolar and unipolar illness in an epidemiological sample. *Psychiatric Genetics, 7*, 159–163.

Karlin, B. E., Duffy, M., & Gleaves, D. H. (2008).Patterns and predictors of mental health service use and mental illness among older and younger adults in the United States. *Psychological Services, 5*,275–294.

Karlsson, R. (2005). Ethnic matching between therapist and patient in psychotherapy: An overview of findings, together with methodological and conceptual issues. *Cultural Diversity and Ethnic Minority Psychology, 11*, 113–129.

Kasckow, J. W., Baker, D., & Geracioti, T. D., Jr. (2001). Corticotropin-releasing hormone in depression and post-traumatic stress disorder. *Peptides, 22*, 845–851.

Kasper, S., & Resinger, E. (2001). Panic disorder: The place of benzodiazepines and selective serotonin reuptake inhibitors. *European Neuropsychopharmacology, 11*, 307–321.

Katerndahl, D., Burge, S., & Kellogg, N. (2005). Predictors of development of adult psychopathology in female victims of childhood sexual abuse. *Journal of Nervous and Mental Disease, 193*, 258–264.

Katz, P. S. (2012). Antidepressants no easy fix in primary care. *ACP Internist*, January. Accessed on January 29, 2013 from http://www.acpinternist. org/archives/2012/01/antidepressants.htm

Kaufer, D. I. (2002). Pharmacologic therapy of dementia with Lewy bodies. *Journal of Geriatric Psychiatry and Neurology, 15*, 224–232.

Kaufman, A. S., Kaufman, J. C., & McLean, J. E. (1995). Factor structure of the Kaufman Adolescent and Adult Intelligence Test (KAIT) for Whites, African Americans, and Hispanics. *Educational and Psychological Measurement, 55*, 365–376.

Kavanagh, D. J. (1992). Recent developments in expressed emotion and schizophrenia. *British Journal of Psychiatry, 160*, 601–620.

Kavirajan, H. (2009). Memantine: A comprehensive review of safety and efficacy. *Expert Opinion in Drug Safety, 8*, 89–109.

Kaye, W. H., Bailer, U. F., Frank, G. K., Wagner, A., & Henry, S. E. (2005). Brain imaging of serotonin after recovery from anorexia and bulimia nervosa. *Physiology & Behavior, 86*, 15–17.

Kaye, W. H., Barbarich, N. C., Putnam, K., Gendall, K. A., Fernstrom, J., et al. (2003). Anxiolytic effects of acute tryptophan depletion in anorexia nervosa. *International Journal of Eating Disorders, 33*, 257–267.

Kaye, W. H., Bulik, C. M., Thornton, L., Barbarich, N., Masters, K., & Price Foundation Collaborative Group. (2004). Comorbidity of anxiety disorders with anorexia and bulimia nervosa. *American Journal of Psychiatry, 161*, 2215–2221.

Kaye, W. H., Frank, G. K., Bailer, U. F., & Henry, S. E. (2005). Neurobiology of anorexia nervosa: Clinical implications of alterations of the function of serotonin and other neuronal systems. *International Journal of Eating Disorders, 37*, S15–S19.

Kaye, W. H., Gendall, K. A., Fernstrom, M. H., Fernstrom, J. D., McConaha, C. W., & Weltzin, T. E. (2000). Effects of acute tryptophan depletion on mood in bulimia nervosa. *Biological Psychiatry, 47*, 151–157.

Kazdin, A. E. (1994). Methodology, design, and evaluation in psychotherapy research. In A. E. Bergin & S. L. Garfield (Eds.), *Handbook of psychotherapy and behavior change* (4th ed., pp. 19–71). Oxford, England: John Wiley & Sons.

Kazdin, A. E. (1995). *Conduct disorders in childhood and adolescence* (2nd ed.). Thousand Oaks, CA: Sage Publications.

Kazdin, A. E., & Weisz, J. R. (1998). Identifying and developing empirically supported child and adolescent treatments. *Journal of Consulting and Clinical Psychology, 66*, 19–36.

KCI. (2007, June–July). *KCI: The Anti-Meth Site.* Methamphetamine: Stories and letters of the hidden costs. Retrieved October 10, 2007, from www.kci.org/meth_info/letters/2007/June-July_2007.htm

Keane, T. M., & Barlow, D. H. (2002). Posttraumatic stress disorder. In D. H. Barlow (Ed.), *Anxiety and its disorders: The nature and treatment of anxiety and panic* (2nd ed., pp. 418–452). New York: Guilford Press.

Keane, T. M., Scott, W. O., Chavoya, G. A., Lamparski, D. M., & Fairbank, J. A. (1985). Social support in Vietnam veterans with posttraumatic stress disorder: A comparative analysis. *Journal of Consulting and Clinical Psychology, 53*, 95–102.

Keane, T. M., Zimering, R. T., & Caddell, J. M. (1985). A behavioral formulation of posttraumatic stress disorder in Vietnam veterans. *The Behavior Therapist, 8*, 9–12.

Keck, P. E., Jr., & McElroy, S. L. (2003). Redefining mood stabilization. *Journal of Affective Disorders, 73*, 163–169.

Keck, P. E., Orsulak, P. J., Cutler, A. J., Sanchez, R., Torbeyns, A., et al. (CN138–135 Study Group). (2009). Aripiprazole monotherapy in the treatment of acute bipolar I mania: A randomized, double-blind, placebo- and lithium-controlled study. *Journal of Affective Disorders, 112*, 36–49.

Keck, P. E., Pope, H. G., Hudson, J. I., McElroy, S. L., Yurgelun-Todd, D., & Hundert, E. M. (1990). A controlled study of phenomenology and family history in outpatients with bulimia nervosa. *Comprehensive Psychiatry, 31*, 275–283.

Keefe, R. S., Bilder, R. M., Davis, S. M., Harvey, P. D., Palmer, B. W., et al. (2007). Neurocognitive effects of antipsychotic medications in patients with chronic schizophrenia in the CATIE trial. *Archives of General Psychiatry, 64*, 633–647.

Keefe, R. S. E., Arnold, M. C., Bayen, U. J., & Harvey, P. D. (1999). Source monitoring deficits in patients with schizophrenia: A multinomial modelling analysis. *Psychological Medicine, 29*, 903–914.

Keefe, R. S. E., Bollini, A. M., & Silva, S. G. (1999). Do novel antipsychotics improve cognition? A report of a meta-analysis. *Psychiatric Annals, 29*, 623–629.

Keefe, R. S. E., Eesley, C. E., & Poe, M. P. (2005). Defining a cognitive function decrement in schizophrenia. *Biological Psychiatry, 57*, 688–691.

Keefe, R. S. E., Silva, S. G., Perkins, D. O., & Lieberman, J. A. (1999). The effects of atypical antipsychotic drugs on neurocognitive impairment in schizophrenia: A review and meta-analysis. *Schizophrenia Bulletin, 25*, 201–222.

Keefe, R. S. E., Sweeney, J. A., Gu, H., Hamer, R. M., Perkins, D. O., et al. (2007). Effects of olanzapine, quetiapine, and risperidone on neurocognitive function in early psychosis: A randomized, double-blind 52-week comparison. *American Journal of Psychiatry, 164*, 1061–1071.

Keefe, R. S. E., Young, C. A., Rock, S. L., Purdon, S. E., Gold, J. M., et alp. (2006). One-year double-blind study of the neurocognitive efficacy of olanzapine, risperidone, and haloperidol in schizophrenia. *Schizophrenia Research, 81*, 1–15.

Keel, P. K., Brown, T. A., Holm-Denoma, J., & Bodell, L. P. (2011). Comparison of DSM-IV versus proposed DSM-5 diagnostic criteria for eating disorders: Reduction of eating disorder not otherwise specified and validity. *International Journal of Eating Disorders, 44*(6), 553–560.

Keel, P. K., Dorer, D. J., Eddy, K. T., Franko, D., Charatan, D. L., & Herzog, D. B. (2003). Predictors of mortality in eating disorders. *Archives of General Psychiatry, 60*, 179–183.

Keel, P. K., Dorer, D. J., Franko, D. L., Jackson, S. C., & Herzog, D. B. (2005). Postremission predictors of relapse in women with eating disorders. *American Journal of Psychiatry, 162*, 2263–2268.

Keel, P. K., & Haedt, A. (2008). Evidence-based psychosocial treatments for eating problems and eating disorders. *Journal of Clinical Child and Adolescent Psychology, 37*, 39–61.

Keel, P. K., Heatherton, T. F., Dorer, D. J., Joiner, T. E., & Zalta, A. K. (2006). Point prevalence of bulimia nervosa in 1982, 1992, and 2002. *Psychological Medicine, 36*, 119–127.

Keel, P. K., & Klump, K. L. (2003). Are eating disorders culture-bound syndromes? Implications for conceptualizing their etiology. *Psychological Bulletin, 129*, 747–769.

Keel, P. K., & Mitchell, J. E. (1997). Outcome in bulimia nervosa. *American Journal of Psychiatry, 154*, 313–321.

Keel, P. K., Mitchell, J. E., Miller, K. B., Davis, T. L., & Crow, S. J. (1999). Long-term outcome of bulimia nervosa. *Archives of General Psychiatry, 56*, 63–69.

Keery, H., Boutelle, K., van den Berg, P., & Thompson, J. K. (2005). The impact of appearance-related teasing by family members. *Journal of Adolescent Health, 37*, 120–127.

Keith, J. A., & Midlarsky, E. (2004). Anorexia nervosa in postmenopausal women: Clinical and empirical perspectives. *Journal of Mental Health and Aging, 10*, 287–299.

Keith, S., Regier, D., & Rae, D. (1991). Schizophrenic disorderes. In L. N. Robins & D. S. Rae (Eds.), *Psychiatric disorders in America: The Epidemiological Catchment Area Study.* New York: Free Press.

Keller, M. B., & Hanks, D. L. (1994). The natural history and heterogeneity of depressive disorders: Implications for rational antidepressant therapy. *Journal of Clinical Psychiatry, 55*, 25–31.

Keller, W. R., Kum, L. M., Wehring, H. J., Koola, M. M., Buchanan, R. W., & Kelly, D. L. (2013). A review of anti-inflammatory agents for symptoms of schizophrenia. *Journal of Psychopharmacology, 27*(4), 337–342.

Kelley, M.L., & Fals-Stewart, W. (2002). Couple-versus individual-based therapy for alcohol and drug abuse: Effects on children's psychosocial functioning. *Journal of Consulting & Clinical Psychology, 70*, 417–427.

Kelsey, J. E., Newport, J., & Nemeroff, C. B. (2006). *Principles of psychopharmacology for mental health professionals.* Hoboken, NJ: John Wiley & Sons.

Keltikangas-Järvinen, L., Puttonen, S., Kivimäki, M., Rontu, R., & Lehtimäki, T. (2006). Cloninger's temperament dimensions and epidermal growth factor A61G polymorphism in Finnish adults. *Genes, Brain & Behavior, 5*, 11–18.

Kemp, S. (2000). Psychology: The Middle Ages. In A. E. Kazdin (Ed.), *Encyclopedia of psychology* (Vol. 6, pp. 382–385). Washington, DC: American Psychological Association.

Kenardy, J., & Taylor, C. B. (1999). Expected versus unexpected panic attacks: A naturalistic prospective study. *Journal of Anxiety Disorders, 13*, 435–445.

Kenardy, J., Fried, L., Kraemer, H. C., & Taylor, C. B. (1992). Psychological precursors of panic attacks. *British Journal of Psychiatry, 160*, 668–673.

Kendall, P. C., Holmbeck, G. N., & Verduin, T. (2004). Methodology, design, and evaluation in psychotherapy research. In M. J. Lambert (Ed.), *Bergin & Garfield's handbook of psychotherapy and behavior change* (5th ed., pp. 16–43). New York: John Wiley & Sons.

Kendell, R., & Jablensky, A. (2003). Distinguishing between the validity and utility of psychiatric diagnoses. *American Journal of Psychiatry, 160*, 4–12.

Kendler, K. S. (1983) Overview: A current perspective on twin studies of schizophrenia. *American Journal of Psychiatry 140*, 1413–1425.

Kendler, K. S. (2008). Explanatory models for psychiatric illness. *American Journal of Psychiatry, 165*, 695–702.

Kendler, K. S., Aggen, S. H., Knudsen, G. P., Røysamb, E., Neale, M. C., & Reichborn-Kjennerud, T. (2011). The structure of genetic and environmental risk factors for syndromal and subsyndromal common DSM-IV Axis I and all Axis II disorders. *The American Journal of Psychiatry, 168*(1), 29–39.

Kendler, K. S., & Diehl, S. R. (1993). The genetics of schizophrenia: A current genetic-epidemiologic perspective. *Schizophrenia Bulletin, 19*, 87–112.

Kendler, K. S., Bulik, C. M., Silberg, J., Hettema, J. M., Myers, J., & Prescott, C. A. (2000). Childhood sexual abuse and adult psychiatric and substance use disorders in women: An epidemiological and cotwin control analysis. *Archives of General Psychiatry, 57*, 953–959.

Kendler, K. S., Gardner, C. O., Gatz, M., & Pedersen, N. L. (2007). The sources of co-morbidity between major depression and generalized anxiety disorder in a Swedish national twin sample. *Psychological Medicine, 37*, 453–462.

Kendler, K. S., Jacobson, K. C., Myers, J., & Prescott, C. A. (2002). Sex differences in genetic and environmental risk factors for irrational fears and phobias. *Psychological Medicine, 32*, 209–217.

Kendler, K. S., Karkowski, L. M., & Prescott, C. A. (1999a). Causal relationship between stressful life events and the onset of major depression. *American Journal of Psychiatry, 156*, 837–848.

Kendler, K. S., Karkowski, L. M., & Prescott, C. A. (1999b). Fears and phobias: Reliability and heritability. *Psychological Medicine, 29*, 539–553.

Kendler, K. S., Kuhn, J. W., Vittum, J., Prescott, C. A., & Riley, B. (2005). The interaction of stressful life events and a serotonin transporter polymorphism in the prediction of episodes of major depression: A replication. *Archives of General Psychiatry, 62*, 529–535.

Kendler, K. S., MacLean, C., Neale, M., Kessler, R. C., Heath, A. C. & Eaves, L. (1991). The genetic epidemiology of bulimia nervosa. *American Journal of Psychiatry, 148*, 1627–1637.

Kendler, K. S., Myers, J., & Prescott, C. A. (2002). The etiology of phobias: An evaluation of the stress-diathesis model. *Archives of General Psychiatry, 59*, 242–248.

Kendler, K. S., Myers, J., Prescott, C. A., & Neale, M. C. (2001). The genetic epidemiology of irrational fears and phobias in men. *Archives of General Psychiatry, 58*, 257–265.

Kendler, K. S., Neale, M. C., Kessler, R. C., Heath, A. C., & Eaves, L. J. (1992). The genetic epidemiology of phobias in women: The interrelationship of agoraphobia, social phobia, situational phobia, and simple phobia. *Archives of General Psychiatry, 49*, 273–281.

Kendler, K. S., Neale, M. C., Kessler, R. C., Heath, A. C., & Eaves, L. J. (1993). Panic disorder in women: A population-based twin study. *Psychological Medicine, 23*, 397–406.

Kendler, K. S., Neale, M. C., & Walsh, D. (1995). Evaluating the spectrum concept of schizophrenia in the Roscommon Family Study. *American Journal of Psychiatry, 152*, 749–754.

Kendler, K. S., Ohlsson, H., Sundquist, K., & Sundquist, J. (2013). Within-family environmental transmission of drug abuse: A Swedish national study. *JAMA Psychiatry, 70*, 235–242.

Kendler, K. S., Prescott, C. A., Neale, M. C., & Pedersen, N. L. (1997). Temperance board registration for alcohol abuse in a national sample of Swedish male twins, born 1902–1949. *Archives of General Psychiatry, 54*, 178–184.

Kendler, K. S., Sundquist, K., Ohlsson, H., Palmér, K., Maes, H., et al. (2013). Genetic and familial environmental influences on the risk for drug abuse. *JAMA Psychiatry, 70*, 690–697.

Kendler, K. S., Walters, E. E., Truett, K. R., Heath, A. C., Neale, M. C., et al. (1995). A twin-family study of self-report symptoms of panic-phobia and somatization. *Behavior Genetics 25*, 499–515.

Kennedy, N., Boydell, J., Kalidindi, S., Fearon, P., Jones, P. B., et al. (2005). Gender differences in incidence and age at onset of mania and bipolar disorder over a 35-year period in Camberwell, England. *American Journal of Psychiatry, 162*, 257–262.

Kennedy, S. H., Javanmard, M., & Vaccarino, F. J. (1997). A review of functional neuroimaging in mood disorders: Positron emission tomography and depression. *The Canadian Journal of Psychiatry, 42*, 467–475.

Kenny, P. J., & Markou, A. (2004). The ups and downs of addiction: Role of metabotropic glutamate receptors. *Trends in Pharmacological Science, 25*, 265–272.

Kernberg, O. (1967). Borderline Personality Organization. *Journal of the American Psychoanalytic Association, 15*, 641–685.

Kernberg, O. F. (1986). *Severe personality disorders: Psychotherapeutic strategies.* New Haven, CT: Yale University Press.

Kerns, K. A., McInerney, R. J., & Wilde, N. J. (2001). Time reproduction, working memory, and behavioral inhibition in children with ADHD. *Child Neuropsychology, 7*, 21–31.

Keshavan, M. S., Anderson, S. A., & Pettegrew, J. W. (1994). Is schizophrenia due to excessive synaptic pruning in the prefrontal cortex? The Feinberg hypothesis revisited. *Journal of Psychiatric Research, 28*, 239–265.

Keski-Rahkonen, A., Hoek, H. W., Susser, E. S., Linna, M. S., Sihvola, E., et al. (2007). Epidemiology and course in anorexia nervosa in the community. *American Journal of Psychiatry, 164*, 1259–1265.

Kessels, R. P. C., & de Haan, E. H. F. (2003). Implicit learning in memory rehabilitation: A meta-analysis on errorless learning and vanishing cues methods. *Journal of Clinical and Experimental Neuropsychology, 25*, 805–814.

Kessing, L. V., Agerbo, E., & Mortensen, P. B. (2004). Major stressful life events and other risk factors for first admission with mania. *Bipolar Disorders, 6*, 122–129.

Kessler, H. R. (2006). The bedside neuropsychological examination. In P. J. Snyder, P. D. Nussbaum, & D. L. Robins (Eds.), *Clinical neuropsychology: A pocket handbook for assessment* (2nd ed., pp. 75–101). Washington, DC: American Psychological Association.

Kessler, R. C. (2003). Epidemiology of women and depression. *Journal of Affective Disorders, 74*, 5–13.

Kessler, R. C., Adler, L., Barkley, R., Biederman, J., Conners, C. K., et al. (2006). The prevalence and correlates of adult ADHD in the United States: Results from the National Comorbidity Survey replication. *American Journal of Psychiatry, 163*, 716–723.

Kessler, R. C., Akiskal, H. S., Ames, M., Birnbaum, H., Greenberg, P., et al. (2006). Prevalence and effects of mood disorders on work performance in a nationally representative sample of U.S. workers. *American Journal of Psychiatry, 163*, 1561–1568.

Kessler, R. C., Berglund, P., Demler, O., Jin, R., Koretz, D., et al. (2003). The epidemiology of major depressive disorder: Results from the National Comorbidity Survey Replication (NCS-R). *JAMA: Journal of the American Medical Association, 289*, 3095–3105.

Kessler, R. C., Berglund, P., Demler, O., Jin, R., & Walters, E. E. (2005). Lifetime prevalence and age-of-onset distributions of DSM-IV disorders in the National Comorbidity Survey Replication. *Archives of General Psychiatry, 62*, 593–602.

Kessler, R. C., Berglund, P. A., Chiu, W. T., Deitz, A. C., Hudson, J. I., et al. (2013). The prevalence and correlates of binge eating disorder in the world health organization world mental health surveys. *Biological Psychiatry, 73*, 904–914.

Kessler, R. C., Borges, G., & Walters, E. E. (1999). Prevalence of and risk factors for lifetime suicide attempts in the National Comorbidity Survey. *Archives of General Psychiatry, 56*, 617–626.

Kessler, R. C., Brandenburg, N., Lane, M., Roy-Byrne, P., Stang, P. D., et al. (2005). Rethinking the duration requirement for generalized anxiety disorder: Evidence from the National Comorbidity Survey Replication. *Psychological Medicine, 35*, 1073–1082.

Kessler, R. C., Chiu, W. T., Demler, O., & Walters, E. E. (2005). Prevalence, severity, and comorbidity of 12-Month DSM-IV disorders in the National Comorbidity Survey Replication. *Archives of General Psychiatry, 62*, 617–627.

Kessler, R. C., Foster, C. L., Saunders, W. B., & Stang, P. E. (1995). Social consequences of psychiatric disorders I: Educational attainment. *American Journal of Psychiatry, 152*, 1026–1032.

Kessler, R. C., & Frank, R. G. (1997). The impact of psychiatric disorders on work loss days. *Psychological Medicine, 27*, 861–873.

Kessler, R. C., McGonagle, K. A., Zhao, S., Nelson, C. B., Hughes, M., et al. (1994). Lifetime and 12-month prevalence of DSM-III-R psychiatric disorders in the United States. *Archives of General Psychiatry, 51*, 8–19.

Kessler, R. C., Mickelson, K. D., & Williams, D. R. (1999). The prevalence, distribution, and mental health correlates of perceived discrimination in the United States. *Journal of Health and Social Behavior, 40*, 208–230.

Kessler, R. C., Sonnega, A., Bromet, E., Hughes, M., & Nelson, C. B. (1995). Posttraumatic stress disorder in the National Comorbidity Survey. *Archives of General Psychiatry, 52*, 1048–1060.

Keuneman, R., Weerasundera, R., & Castle, D. (2002). The role of ECT in schizophrenia. *Australasian Psychiatry, 10*, 385–388.

Keyes, C. L. M. (2007). Promoting and protecting mental health as flourishing: A complementary strategy for improving national mental health. *American Psychologist, 62*, 95–108.

Keyes, K. M., Schulenberg, J. E., O'Malley, P. M., Johnston, L. D., Bachman, J. G., et al. (2012). Birth cohort effect on adolescent alcohol use: The influence of social norms from 1976 to 2007. *Archives of General Psychiatry, 69*, 1257–1266.

Keys, A., Brozek, J., Henschel, A., Mickelsen, O., & Taylor, H. L. (1950). *The biology of human starvation* (Vols. 1–2). Oxford, England: University of Minnesota Press.

Khalifa, N., & von Knorring, A. (2003). Prevalence of tic disorders and Tourette syndrome in a Swedish school population. *Developmental Medicine & Child Neurology, 45*, 315–319.

Khan A., Leventhal, R. M., Khan, S. R., & Brown, W. A. (2002). Severity of depression and response to antidepressants and placebo: An analysis of the Food and Drug Administration database. *Journal of Clinical Psychopharmacology, 22*, 40–45.

Khan, A., Warner, H. A., & Brown, W. A. (2000). Symptom reduction and suicide risk in patients treated with placebo in antidepressant clinical trials: An analysis of the Food and Drug Administration database. *Archives of General Psychiatry, 57*, 311–317.

Khashan, A. S., Abel, K. M., McNamee, R., Pedersen, M. G., Webb, R. T., et al. (2008). Higher risk of offspring schizophrenia following antenatal maternal exposure to severe adverse life events. *Archives of General Psychiatry, 65*, 146–152.

Kho, K. H., VanVreeswijk, M. F., & Murre, J. M. J. (2006). A retrospective controlled study into memory complaints reported by depressed patients after treatment with electroconvulsive therapy and pharmacotherapy or pharmacotherapy only. *Journal of ECT, 22*, 199–205.

Kiefer, F., Jahn, H., Tarnaske, T., Helwig, H., Briken, P., et al. (2003). Comparing and combining naltrexone and acamprosate in relapse prevention of alcoholism: A double-blind, placebo-controlled study. *Archives of General Psychiatry, 60*, 92–99.

Kiehl, K. A., Smith, A. M., Hare, R. D., Mendrek, A., Forster, B. B., et al. (2001). Limbic abnormalities in affective processing by criminal psychopaths as revealed by functional magnetic resonance imaging. *Biological Psychiatry, 50*, 677–684.

Kieseppä, T., Partonen, T., Haukka, J., Kaprio, J., & Lönnqvis, J. (2004). High concordance of bipolar I disorder in a nationwide sample of twins. *American Journal of Psychiatry, 161*, 1814–1821.

Kihlstrom, J. F. (2001). Dissociative disorders. In P. B. Sutker & H. E. Adams (Eds.), *Comprehensive handbook of psychopathology* (3rd ed., pp. 259–276). New York: Kluwer Academic/Plenum.

Kihlstrom, J. F. (2002a). Demand characteristics in the laboratory and the clinic: Conversations and collaborations with subjects and patients. *Prevention and Treatment, 5*, Article 36c.

Kihlstrom, J. F. (2002b). To honor Kraepelin: From symptoms to pathology in the diagnosis of mental illness. In L. E. Beutler & M. L. Malik (eds.), *Rethinking the DSM: A psychological perspective* (pp. 279–303). Washington, DC: American Psychological Association.

Kihlstrom, J. R. (2005). Dissociative disorders. *Annual Review of Clinical Psychology, 1*, 227–253.

Kiliç, B. G., Sener, S., Koçkar, A. I., & Karakas, S. (2007). Multicomponent attention deficits in attention deficit hyperactivity disorder. *Psychiatry and Clinical Neurosciences, 61*, 142–148.

Killaspy, H., Bebbington, P., Blizard, R., Johnson, S., Nolan, F., et al. (2006). The REACT study: Randomised evaluation of assertive community treatment in north London. *BMJ: British Medical Journal, 332*, 815–820.

Killen, J. D., Fortmann, S. P., Murphy Jr., G. M., Hayward, C., Arredondo, C., et al. (2006). Extended treatment with Bupropion SR for cigarette smoking cessation. *Journal of Consulting and Clinical Psychology, 74*, 286–294.

Kilpatrick, D. G., Acierno, R., Saunders, B., Resnick, H. S., Best, C. L., et al. (2000). Risk factors for adolescent substance abuse and dependence: Data from a national sample. *Journal of Consulting and Clinical Psychology, 68*, 19–30.

Kilpatrick, D. G., Koenen, K. C., Ruggiero, K. J., Acierno, R., Galea, S., et al. (2007). The serotonin transporter genotype and social support and moderation of posttraumatic stress disorder and depression in hurricane-exposed adults. *American Journal of Psychiatry, 164*, 1693–1699.

Kim, J.-H., & Lennon, S. J. (2007). Mass media and self-esteem, body image, and eating disorder tendencies. *Clothing and Textiles Research Journal, 25*, 3–23.

Kim, J-J., Lee, M. C., Kim, J., Kim, I. Y., Kim, S. I., et al. (2001). Grey matter abnormalities in obsessive-compulsive disorder: Statistical parametric mapping of segmented magnetic resonance images. *British Journal of Psychiatry, 179*, 330–334.

Kim, M., Kwon, J. S., Kang, S., Youn, T., & Kang, K. (2004). Impairment of recognition memory in schizophrenia: Event-related potential study using a continuous recognition task. *Psychiatry and Clinical Neurosciences, 58*, 465–472.

Kimball, M. M. (2000). From "Anna O." to Bertha Pappenheim: Transforming private pain into public action. *History of Psychology, 3*, 20–43.

Kimble, G. A. (1981). Biological and cognitive constraints of learning. In L. T. Benjamin, Jr. (Ed.), *The G. Stanley Hall lecture series* (Vol. 1). Washington, DC: American Psychological Association.

King, B. H. (1990). Hypothesis: Involvement of the serotonergic system in the clinical expression of monosymptomatic hypochondriasis. *Pharmacopsychiatry, 23*, 85–89.

King, L. A., King, D. W., Fairbank, J. A., Keane, T. M., & Adams, G. A. (1998). Resilience-recovery factors in post-traumatic stress disorder among female and male Vietnam veterans: Hardiness, postwar social support, and additional stressful life events. *Journal of Personality and Social Psychology, 74*, 420–434.

King, D. W., King, L. A., Foy, D. W., Keane, T. M., & Fairbank, J. A. (1999). Posttraumatic stress disorder in a national sample of female and male Vietnam veterans: Risk factors, war-zone stressors, and resilience-recovery variables. *Journal of Abnormal Psychology, 108*, 164–170.

King, S. A., Engi, S., & Poulos, S. T. (1998). Using the Internet to assist therapy. *British Journal of Guidance and Counselling, 26*, 43–52.

Kirk, J. M., Doty, P., & de Wit, H. (1998). Effects of expectancies on subjective responses to oral d-tetrahydrocannabinol. *Pharmacology, Biochemistry and Behavior, 59*, 287–293.

Kirk, S. A., & Hsieh, D. K. (2004). Diagnostic consistency in assessing conduct disorder: An experiment on the effect of social context. *American Journal of Orthopsychiatry, 74*, 43–55.

Kirkpatrick, B., Buchanan, R. W., McKenney, P. D., Alphs, L. D., & Carpenter, W. T., Jr. (1989). The Schedule for the Deficit Syndrome: An instrument for research in schizophrenia. *Psychiatry Research, 30*, 119–123.

Kirmayer, L. J., & Looper, K. J. (2006). Abnormal illness behaviour: Physiological, psychological and social dimensions of coping with distress. *Current Opinion in Psychiatry, 19*, 54–60.

Kirsch, I. (2010). *The emperor's new drugs: Exploding the antidepressant myth.* New York: 2010.

Kirsch, I., & Lynn, S. J. (1998). Dissociation theories of hypnosis. *Psychological Bulletin, 123*, 100–111.

Kirsch, I., & Lynn, S. J. (1999). Automaticity in clinical psychology. *American Psychologist, 54*, 504–515.

Kirsch, I., & Sapirstein, G. (1998). Listening to Prozac but hearing placebo: A meta-analysis of antidepressant medication. *Prevention & Treatment, 1*, Article 0002a.

Kirsch, I., & Sapirstein, G. (1999). Listening to Prozac but hearing placebo: A meta-analysis of antidepressant medications. In I. Kirsch (Ed.), *How expectancies shape experience* (pp. 303–320). Washington, DC: American Psychological Association.

Kirsch, I., Moore, T. J., Scoboria, A., & Nicholls, S. S. (2002). The emperor's new drugs: An analysis of antidepressant medication data submitted to the U.S. Food and Drug Administration. *Prevention & Treatment, 5*, Article 23. Available on the World Wide Web: www.journals.apa.org/prevention/volume5/pre0050023a.html

Kirsch, I., Scoboria, A., & Moore, T. J. (2002). Antidepressants and placebos: Secrets, revelations, and unanswered questions. *Prevention & Treatment, 5*, n.p.

Kirsch, L. G., & Becker, J. V. (2006). Sexual offending: Theory of problem, theory of change, and implications for treatment effectiveness. *Aggression and Violent Behavior, 11*, 208–224.

Kirschenbaum, H., & Jourdan, A. (2005). The current status of Carl Rogers and the person-centered approach. *Psychotherapy: Theory, Research, Practice, Training, 42*, 37–51.

Kitzmann, K. M. (2000). Effects of marital conflict on subsequent triadic family interactions and parenting. *Developmental Psychology, 36*, 3–13.

Kjernisted, K. D., Enns, M. W., & Lander, M. (2002). An open-label clinical trial of nefazodone in hypochondriasis. *Psychosomatics: Journal of Consultation and Liaison Psychiatry, 43*, 290–294.

Klassen, A. F., Miller, A., & Fine, S. (2006). Agreement between parent and child report of quality of life in children with attention-deficit/hyperactivity disorder. *Child: Care, Health and Development, 32*, 397–406.

Klein, C. A. (2011). Cloudy confidentiality: Clinical and legal implications of cloud computing in health care. *Journal of the American Academy of Psychiatry and the Law, 39*(4), 571–578.

Klein, D. A., & Walsh, B. T. (2005). Translational approafches to understanding anorexia nervosa. *International Journal of Eating Disorders, 37*, S10–S14.

Klein, D. F. (1993). False suffocation alarms, spontaneous panics, and related conditions: An integrative hypothesis. *Archives of General Psychiatry, 50*, 306–317.

Klein, D. N. (2008). Classification of depressive disorders in the DSM-V: Proposal for a two-dimension system. *Journal of Abnormal Psychology, 117*, 552–560.

Klein, D. N., Santiago, N. J., Vivian, D., Blalock, J. A., Kocsis, J. H., et al. (2004). Cognitive-behavioral analysis system of psychotherapy as a maintenance treatment for chronic depression. *Journal of Consulting & Clinical Psychology, 72*, 681–688.

Klein, D. N., Shankman, S. A., & Rose, S. (2006). Ten-year prospective follow-up study of the naturalistic course of dysthymic disorder and double depression. *American Journal of Psychiatry, 163*, 872–880.

Klein, E., Kreinin, I., Chistyakov, A., Koren, D., Mecz, L., et al. (1999). Therapeutic efficacy of right prefrontal slow repetitive transcranial magnetic stimulation in major depression: A double-blind controlled study. *Archives of General Psychiatry, 56,* 315–320.

Klein, M. (1932). *The Psycho-analysis of children.* London: Hogarth.

Kleinfield, N. R., & Roane, K. R. (1999, January 11). Subway killing casts light on suspect's mental torment. *The New York Times,* p. A1.

Kleinknecht, R. A. (2002). Comments on: Non-associative fear acquisition: A review of the evidence from retrospective and longitudinal research. *Behaviour Research and Therapy, 40,* 159–163.

Kleinman, A. (1988). *Rethinking psychiatry: From cultural category to personal experience.* New York: Free Press.

Kleinplatz, P. J. (2001). A critical evaluation of sex therapy: Room for improvement. In P. J. Kleinplatz (Ed.), *New directions in sex therapy: Innovations and alternatives* (pp. xi–xxxiii). Philadelphia: Taylor and Rutledge.

Klerman, G. L., & Weissman, M. M. (Eds.). (1993). *New applications of interpersonal psychotherapy.* Washington, DC: American Psychiatric Association.

Klerman, G. L., Weismann, M. M., Rounsaville, B. J., & Chevron, E. S. (1984). *Interpersonal psychotherapy for depression.* New York: Basic Books.

Klin, A., Pauls, D., Schultz, R., & Volkmar, F. (2005). Three diagnostic approaches to Asperger syndrome: Implications for research. *Journal of Autism and Developmental Disorders, 35,* 221–234.

Klinger, L. G., Dawson, G., & Renner, P. (2003). Autistic disorder. In E. J. Mash & R. A. Barkley (Eds.), *Child psychopathology* (2nd ed., pp. 409–454). New York: Guilford Press.

Klonsky, E. D. (2008). What is emptiness? Clarifying the 7th criterion for borderline personality disorder. *Journal of Personality Disorders, 22,* 418–426.

Klosko, J. S., Barlow, D. H., Tassinari, R., & Cerny, J. A. (1990). A comparison of alprazolam and behavior therapy in treatment of panic disorder. *Journal of Consulting and Clinical Psychology, 58,* 77–84.

Kluft, R. P. (1999). An overview of the psychotherapy of dissociative identity disorder. *American Journal of Psychotherapy, 53,* 289–319.

Klump, K. L., Wonderlich, S., Lehoux, P., Lilenfeld, L. R. R., & Bulik, C. M. (2002). Does environment matter? A review of nonshared environment and eating disorders. *International Journal of Eating Disorders, 31,* 118–135.

Knapp, C. (1997). *Drinking: A love story.* New York: Dial Press.

Knapp, C. (2003). *Appetites: Why women want.* New York: Counterpoint.

Knopman, D. S., Boeve, B. F., & Petersen, R. C. (2003). Essentials of the proper diagnoses of mild cognitive impairment, dementia, and major subtypes of dementia. *Mayo Clinic Proceedings, 78,* 1290–1308.

Knox, K. L., Litts, D. A., Talcott, G. W., Feig, J. C., & Caine, E. D. (2003). Risk of suicide and related adverse outcomes after exposure to a suicide prevention programme in the US Air Force: Cohort study. *British Medical Journal, 327,* 1376–1380.

Koenigsberg, H. W., Reynolds, D., Goodman, M., New, A. S., Mitropoulou, V., et al. (2003). Risperidone in the treatment of schizotypal personality disorder. *Journal of Clinical Psychiatry, 64,* 628–634.

Koenigsberg, H. W., Woo-Ming, A. M., & Siever, L. J. (2007). Psychopharmacological treatment of personality disorders. In P. E. Nathan & J. M. Gorman (Eds.), *A guide to treatments that work* (3rd ed., pp. 659–680). New York: Oxford University Press.

Kohen, R., Neumaier, J. F., Hamblin, M. W., & Edwards, E. (2003). Congenitally learned helpless rats show abnormalities in intracellular signaling. *Biological Psychiatry, 53,* 520–529.

Kohn, R. (2002). Belonging to two worlds: The experience of migration. Commentary. *South African Psychiatry Review, 5,* 6–8.

Kohut, H. (1971). *Analysis of the self: Systematic approach to treatment of narcissistic personality disorders.* New York: International Universities Press.

Kohut, H. (1977). *The restoration of the self.* New York: International Universities Press.

Kojima, S., Nagai, N., Nakabeppu, Y., Muranaga, T., Deguchi, D., et al. (2005). Comparison of regional cerebral blood flow in patients with anorexia nervosa before and after weight gain. *Psychiatry Research: Neuroimaging, 140,* 251–258.

Köksal, F., Domjan, M., Kurt, A., Sertel, Ö., Örüng, S., et al. (2004). An animal model of fetishism. *Behaviour Research and Therapy, 42,* 1421–1434.

Kolodny, R., Masters, W., & Johnson, V. (1979). *A textbook of sexual medicine.* Boston: Little Brown and Company.

Kolur, U. S., Reddy, Y. C. J., John, J. P., Kandavel, T., & Jain, S. (2006). Sustained attention and executive functions in euthymic young people with bipolar disorder. *British Journal of Psychiatry, 189,* 453–458.

Kong, L. L., Allen, J. J. B., & Glisky, E. L. (2008). Interidentity memory transfer in dissociative identity disorder. *Journal of Abnormal Psychology, 117,* 686–692.

Konick, L. C., & Friedman, L. (2001). Meta-analysis of thalamic size in schizophrenia. *Biological Psychiatry, 49,* 28–38.

Konigsberg, E., & Farmer, A. (2008, February 20). Father tells of slaying suspect's long ordeal. *The New York Times.* Retrieved July 21, 2008, from www.nytimes.com/2008/02/20/nyregion/20commit.html?8br

Konstantareas, M. M. (2006). Social skills training in high functioning autism and Asperger's disorder. *Hellenic Journal of Psychology, 3,* 39–56.

Koob, G. F., & Bloom, F. E. (1988). Cellular and molecular mechanisms of drug dependence. *Science, 242,* 715–723.

Koob, G. F., & Le Moal, M. (2008). Addiction and the brain antireward system. *Annual Review of Psychology, 59,* 29–53.

Koob, G. F., Sanna, P. P., & Bloom, F. E. (1998). Neuroscience of addiction. *Neuron, 21,* 467–476.

Kopelman, M. D. (1999). Clinical and neuropsychological studies of patients with amnesic disorders. In M. A. Ron & A. S. David (Eds.), *Disorders of mind and brain* (Vol. 1, pp. 147–176). Cambridge: Cambridge University Press.

Kopelman, M. D. (2002). Psychogenic fugue. In A. D. Baddeley, M. D. Kopelman, & B. A. Wilson (Eds.), *The handbook of memory disorders* (2nd ed., pp. 451–471). Chichester, England: Wiley.

Koplewicz, H. S., Shatkin, J. P., Kadison, R., Nielsen, J., Girard, K., & Sood, A. A. (2007). *College mental health.* Symposium 24 at the American Academy of Child & Adolescent Psychiatry 54th Annual Meeting, October 23–28, 2007.

Koponen, S., Taiminen, T., Portin, R., Himanen, L., Isoniemi, H., et al. (2002). Axis I and II psychiatric disorders after traumatic brain injury: A 30-year follow-up study. *American Journal of Psychiatry, 159,* 1315–1321.

Kosslyn, S. M., & Koenig, O. (1995). *Wet mind: The new cognitive neuroscience.* New York: Free Press.

Kosslyn, S. M., Thompson, W. L., & Ganis, G. (2006). *The case for mental imagery.* New York: Oxford University Press.

Kosslyn, S. M., Thompson, W. L., Costantini-Ferrando, M. F., Alpert, N. M., & Spiegel, D. (2000). Hypnotic visual illusion alters color processing in the brain. *American Journal of Psychiatry, 157,* 1279–1284.

Kouri, E. M., & Pope, H. G. (2000). Abstinence symptoms during withdrawal from chronic marijuana use. *Experimental & Clinical Psychopharmacology, 8,* 483–492.

Kovnick, J. A., Appelbaum, P. S., Hoge, S. K., & Leadbetter, R. A. (2003). Competence to consent to research among long-stay inpatients with chronic schizophrenia. *Psychiatric Services, 54,* 1247–1252.

Koyama, T., Tachimori, H., Osada, H., Takeda, T., & Kurita, H. (2007). Cognitive and symptom profiles in Asperger's syndrome and high-functioning autism. *Psychiatry and Clinical Neurosciences, 61,* 99–104.

Kozlowska, K. (2005). Healing the disembodied mind: Contemporary models of conversion disorder. *Harvard Review of Psychiatry, 13,* 1–13.

Kraaij, V., & Garnefski, N. (2002). Negative life events and depressive symptoms in late life: Buffering effects of parental and partner bonding? *Personal Relationships, 9,* 205–214.

Krabbendam, L., & Aleman, A. (2003). Cognitive rehabilitation in schizophrenia: A quantitative analysis of controlled studies. *Psychopharmacology, 169,* 376–382.

Kram, M. L., Kramer, G. L., Steciuk, M., Ronan, P. J., & Petty, F. (2000). Effects of learned helplessness on brain GABA receptors. *Neuroscience Research, 38,* 193–198.

Kransny, L., Williams, B. J., Provencal, S., & Ozonoff, S. (2003). Social skills interventions for the autism spectrum: Essential ingredients and a model curriculum. *Child and Adolescent Psychiatric Clinics of North America, 12,* 107–122.

Kratochvil, C. J., Greenhill, L. L., March, J. S., Burke, W. J., & Vaughan, B. S. (2004). Current opinion: The role of stimulants in the treatment of preschool children with attention-deficit hyperactivity disorder. *CNS Drugs, 18,* 957–966.

Kratochvil, C. J., Heiligenstein, J. H., Dittmann, R., Spencer, T. J., Biederman, J., et al. (2002). Atomoxetine and methylphenidate treatment in children with ADHD: A prospective, randomized, open-label trial. *Journal of the American Academy of Child & Adolescent Psychiatry, 41,* 776–784.

Kraus, G., & Reynolds, D. J. (2001). The "A-B-C's" of the Cluster B's: Identifying, understanding, and treating Cluster B personality disorders. *Clinical Psychology Review, 21,* 345–373.

Kravitz, H. M., Fawcett, J., McGuire, M., Kravitz, G. S., & Whitney, M. (1999). Treatment attrition among alcohol-dependent men: Is it related to novelty seeking personality traits? *Journal of Clinical Psychopharmacology, 19,* 51–56.

Kremen, W. S., Koenen, K. C., Boake, C., Purcell, S., Eisen, S. A., et al. (2007). Pretrauma cognitive ability and risk for posttraumatic stress disorder. *Archives of General Psychiatry, 64,* 361–368.

Krijn, M., Emmelkamp, P. M. G., Biemond, R., de Wilde de Ligny, C., Schuemie, M. J., & van der Mast, C. A. P. G. (2004). Treatment of acrophobia in virtual reality: The role of immersion and presence. *Behaviour Research and Therapy, 42,* 229–239.

Kring, A. M., & Neale, J. M. (1996). Do schizophrenic patients show a disjunctive relationship among expressive, experiential, and psychophysiological components of emotion? *Journal of Abnormal Psychology, 105,* 249–257.

Kringelbach, M. L., Araujo, I., & Rolls, E. T. (2001). Face expression as a reinforcer activates the orbitofrontal cortex in an emotion-related reversal task. *Neuroimage, 13*(6), S433.

Kroenke, K. (2003). Patients presenting with somatic complaints: Epidemiology, psychiatric co-morbidity and management. *International Journal of Methods in Psychiatric Research, 12,* 34–43.

Kruh, I. P., Frick, P. J., & Clements, C. B. (2005). Historical and personality correlates to the violence patterns of juveniles tried as adults. *Criminal Justice and Behavior, 32,* 69–96.

Kruijver, F. P., Zhou, J. N., Pool, C. W., Hofman, M. A., Gooren, L. J. G., & Swaab, D. F. (2000). Male-to-female transsexuals have female neuron numbers in a limbic nucleus. *Journal of Clinical Endocrinology and Metabolism, 85,* 2034–2041.

Kruijver, I. P. M., Kerkstra, A., Francke, A. L., Bensing, J. M., & van de Wiel, H. B. M. (2000). Evaluation of communication training programs in nursing care: A review of the literature. *Patient Education and Counseling, 39,* 129–145.

Krupinski, J., Tiller, J. W. G., Burrows, G. D., & Mackenzie, A. (1998). *Predicting suicide risk among young suicide attempters.* In R. J. Kosky, H. S. Eshkevari, R. D. Goldney, & R. Hassan (Eds.), *Suicide prevention: The global context* (pp. 93–97). New York: Plenum Press.

Krupnick, J. L., Sotsky, S. M., Simmens, S., Moyer, J., Elkin, I., et al. (1996). The role of the therapeutic alliance in psychotherapy and pharmacotherapy outcome: Findings in the National Institute of Mental Health Treatment of Depression Collaborative Research Program. *Journal of Consulting and Clinical Psychology, 64,* 532–539.

Krystal, J. H., Perry, E. B., Jr., Gueorguieva, R., Belger, A., Madonick, S. H., et al. (2005). Comparative and interactive human psychopharmacologic effects of ketamine and amphetamine: Implications for glutamatergic and dopaminergic model psychoses and cognitive function. *Archives of General Psychiatry, 62,* 985–995.

Ksir, C. (2000). Drugs. In A. E. Kazdin (Ed.), *Encyclopedia of psychology* (Vol. 3, pp. 98–101). Washington, DC: American Psychological Association.

Kuboki, T., Nomura, S., Ide, M., Suematsu, H., & Araki, S. (1996). Epidemiological data on anorexia nervosa in Japan. *Psychiatry Research, 62,* 11–16.

Kuhl, B. A., Kahn, I., Dudukovic, N. M., & Wagner, A. D. (2008). Overcoming suppression in order to remember: Contributions from anterior cingulated and ventrolateral prefrontal cortex. *Cognitive, Affective, & Behavioral Neuroscience, 8,* 211–221.

Kulhara, P., & Chakrabarti, S. (2001). Culture and schizophrenia and other psychotic disorders. *Psychiatric Clinics of North America, 24,* 449–464.

Kulkarni, J., de Castella, A., Fitzgerald, P. B., Gurvich, C. T., Bailey, M., et al. (2008). Estrogen in severe mental illness: A potential new treatment approach. *Archives of General Psychiatry, 65,* 955–960.

Kumari, V., & Postma, P. (2005). Nicotine use in schizophrenia: The self-medication hypotheses. *Neuroscience & Biobehavioral Reviews, 29,* 1021–1034.

Kumpulainen, K., Räsänen, E., Henttonen, I., Almqvist, F., Kresanov, K., et al. (1998). Bullying and psychiatric symptoms among elementary school-age children. *Child Abuse & Neglect, 22,* 705–717.

Kundert, D. K., & Trimarchi, C. L. (2006). Pervasive developmental disorders. In L. Phelps (Ed.), *Chronic health-related disorders in children: Collaborative medical and psychoeducational interventions* (pp. 213–235). Washington, DC: American Psychological Association.

Kunen, S., Niederhauser, R., Smith, P. O., Morris, J. A., & Marx, B. D. (2005). Race disparities in psychiatric rates in emergency departments. *Journal of Consulting & Clinical Psychology, 73,* 116–126.

Kunert, H. J., Druecke, H. W., Sass, H., & Herpertz, S. C. (2003). Frontal lobe dysfunctions in borderline personality disorder? Neuropsychological findings. *Journal of Personality Disorders, 17,* 497–509.

Kuntsche, E., Simons-Moroton, B., Fotiou, A., ter Bogt, T., & Kokkevi, A. (2009). Decrease in adolescent cannabis use from 2002 to 2006 and links to evenings out with friends in 31 European and North American Countries and Regions. *Archives of Pediatric Adolescent Medicine, 163,* 119–125.

Kupfer, D. J. (2012). Dr. Kupfer defends DSM-5. *Medscape,* June 1. Retrieved May 21, 2013, from www.medscape.com/viewarticle/764735

Kupfer, D. J., First, M. B., & Regier, D. A. (Eds.). (2002). *A research agenda for DSM-V.* Washington, DC: American Psychiatric Association.

Kurihara, T., Kato, M., Reverger, R., & Yagi, G. (2000). Outcome of schizophrenia in a non-industrialized society: Comparative study between Bali and Tokyo. *Acta Psychiatrica Scandinavica, 101,* 148–152.

Kurtz, M. M., & Mueser, K. T. (2008). A meta-analysis of controlled research on social skills training for schizophrenia. *Journal of Consulting and Clinical Psychology, 76,* 491–504.

Kurtz, M. M., Seltzer, J. C., Shagan, D. S., Thime, W. R., & Wexler, B. E. (2007). Computer-assisted cognitive remediation in schizophrenia: What is the active ingredient? *Schizophrenia Research, 89,* 251–260.

Kushner, M. G., Riggs, D. S., Foa, E. B., & Miller, S. (1992). Perceived controllability and the development of PTSD in crime victims. *Behaviour Research and Therapy, 31,* 105–110.

Kutchins, H., & Kirk, S. A. (1997). *Making us crazy: DSM: The psychiatric bible and the creation of mental disorders.* New York: Free Press.

La Rue, A., & Watson, J. (1998). Psychological assessment of older adults. *Professional Psychology: Research and Practice, 29,* 5–14.

Laakso, M., Vaurio, O., Koivisto, E., Savolainen, L., Eronen, M., & Aronen, H. J. (2001). Psychopathy and the posterior hippocampus. *Brain Behavior and Research, 118,* 187–193.

Labott, S. M., & Wallach, H. R. (2002). Malingering dissociative identity disorder: Objective and projective assessment. *Psychological Reports, 90,* 525–538.

Laffaye, C., McKellar, J. D., Ilgen, M. A., & Moos, R. H. (2008). Predictors of 4-year outcome of community residential treatment for patients with substance use disorders. *Addiction, 103,* 671–680.

Lagges, A. M., & Dunn, D. W. (2003). Depression in children and adolescents. *Neurologic Clinics, 21,* 953–960.

Lahey, B. B., Loeber, R., Burke, J. D., & Applegate, B. (2005). Predicting future antisocial personality disorder in males from a clinical assessment in childhood. *Journal of Consulting and Clinical Psychology, 73,* 389–399.

Lahey, B. B., McBurnett, K., & Loeber, R. (2000). Are attention-deficit/hyperactivity disorder and oppositional defiant disorder developmental precursors to conduct disorder? In A. J. Sameroff, M. Lewis, & S. M. Miller (Eds.), *Handbook of developmental psychopathology* (2nd ed., pp. 431–446). Dordrecht, Netherlands: Kluwer Academic.

Lahey, B. B., Pelham, W. E., Loney, J., Lee, S. S., & Willcutt, E. (2005). Instability of the DSM-IV subtypes of ADHD from preschool through elementary school. *Archives of General Psychiatry, 62,* 896–902.

Lahti, M., Pesonen, A.-K., Räikköönen, K., Heinonen, K., Wahlbeck, K., et al. (2012). Temporary separation from parents in early childhood and serious personality disorders in adult life. *Journal of Personality Disorders, 26*(5), 751–762.

Lake v. Cameron, 124 U.S. App. D. C. 264; 364 F.2d 657; 1966 U.S. App. LEXIS 6103 (1966).

Laks, J., & Engelhardt, E. (2008). Reports in pharmacological treatments in geriatric psychiatry: Is there anything new or just adding to old evidence? *Current Opinion in Psychiatry, 21,* 562–567.

Lam, A. G., & Sue, S. (2001). Client diversity. *Psychotherapy: Theory, Research, Practice, Training, 38,* 479–486.

Lam, D. H., Bright, J., Jones, S., Hayward, P., Schuck, N., Chisholm, D., & Sham, P. (2000). Cognitive therapy for bipolar illness—a pilot study of relapse prevention. *Cognitive Therapy and Research, 24,* 503–520.

Lam, K., Marra, C., & Salzinger, K. (2005). Social reinforcement of somatic versus psychological description of depressive events. *Behaviour, Research and Therapy,* 1203–1218.

Lam, R. W., Bartley, S., Yatham, L. N., Tam, E. M., & Zis, A. P. (1999). Clinical predictors of short-term outcome in electroconvulsive therapy. *The Canadian Journal of Psychiatry/La Revue canadienne de psychiatrie, 44,* 158–163.

Lamb, W. K., & Jones, E. E. (1998). *A meta-analysis of racial matching in psychotherapy.* Unpublished manuscript, University of California–Berkeley.

Lamb, K., Pies, R., & Zisook, S. (2010). The bereavement exclusion for the diagnosis of major depression: To be, or not to be. *Psychiatry, 7*(7), 19–25.

Lambert, K., & Kinsley, C. H. (2005). *Clinical neuroscience.* New York: Worth.

Lambert, M. J. (Ed.). (2004). *Bergin & Garfield's handbook of psychotherapy and behavior change* (5th ed.). New York: John Wiley & Sons.

Lambert, M. J., & Bergin, A. E. (1994). The effectiveness of psychotherapy. In A. E. Bergin & S. L. Garfield (Eds.), *Handbook of psychotherapy and behavior change* (4th ed., pp. 143–189). Oxford, England: John Wiley & Sons.

Lambert, M. J., & Ogles, B. M. (2004). The efficacy and effectiveness of psychotherapy. In M. J. Lambert (Ed.), *Bergin and Garfield's handbook of psychotherapy and behavior change* (5th ed., pp. 139–193). New York: John Wiley & Sons.

Lambert, M. J., Hansen, N. B., & Finch, A. E. (2001). Patient-focused research: Using patient outcome data to enhance treatment effects. *Journal of Consulting & Clinical Psychology, 69,* 159–172.

Lambrou, C., Veale, D., & Wilson, G. (2012). Appearance concerns comparisons among persons with body dysmorphic disorder and nonclinical controls with and without aesthetic training. *Body Image, 9,* 86–92.

Lampropoulos, G. K. (2001). Bridging technical eclecticism and theoretical integration: Assimilative integration. *Journal of Psychotherapy Integration, 11,* 5–19.

Lanctôt, K. L., Herrmann, N., Yau, K. K., Kahn, L. R., Liu, B. A., et al. (2003). Efficacy and safety of cholinesterase inhibitors in Alzheimer's disease: A meta-analysis. *Canadian Medical Association Journal, 169,* 557–564.

Landa, R. J., Holman, K. C., & Garrett-Mayer, E. (2007). Social and communication development in toddlers with early and later diagnosis of autism spectrum disorders. *Archives of General Psychiatry, 64,* 853–864.

Landen, M., Walinder, J., Hambert, G., & Lundstrom B. (1998). Factors predictive of regret in sex reassignment. *Acta Psychiatrica Scandinavica, 97,* 284–289.

Lane, S. D., Cherek, D. R., Pietras, C. J., & Steinberg, J. L. (2005). Performance of heavy marijuana-smoking adolescents on a laboratory measure of motivation. *Addictive Behaviors, 30,* 815–828.

Lang, P. J. (1995). The emotion probe: Studies of motivation and attention. *American Psychologist, 50,* 372–385.

Lang, R. A., Langevin, R., Checkley, K. L., & Pugh, G. (1987). Genital exhibitionism: Courtship disorder or narcissism? *Canadian Journal of Behavioural Science/Revue canadienne des sciences du comportement, 19,* 216–232.

Langa, K. M., Foster, N. L., & Larson, E. B. (2004). Mixed dementia: Emerging concepts and therapeutic implications. *JAMA: Journal of the American Medical Association, 292,* 2901–2908.

Langdon, R., & Coltheart, M. (2001). Visual perspective-taking and schizotypy: Evidence for a simulation-based account of mentalizing in normal adults. *Cognition, 82,* 1–26.

Lange, A., van de Ven, J.-P., Schrieken, B., & Emmelkamp, P. M. G. (2001). Interapy. Treatment of posttraumatic stress through the Internet: A controlled trial. *Journal of Behavior Therapy & Experimental Psychiatry, 32,* 73–90.

Langenbucher, J. W., Labouvie, E., Martin, C. S., Sanjuan, P. M., Bavly, L., et al. (2004). An application of item response theory analysis to alcohol, cannabis, and cocaine criteria in DSM-IV. *Journal of Abnormal Psychology, 113,* 72–80.

Langer, S. J., & Martin, J. I. (2004). How dresses can make you mentally ill: Examining gender identity disorder in children. *Child & Adolescent Social Work Journal, 21,* 5–23.

Langevin, R. (2006). Acceptance and completion of treatment among sex offenders. *International Journal of Offender Therapy and Comparative Criminology, 50,* 402–417.

Langevin, R., Paitich, D., Ramsay, G., Anderson, C., Kamrad, J., et al. (1979). Experimental studies of the etiology of genital exhibitionism. *Archives of Sexual Behavior, 8,* 307–331.

Langton, C. M., Barbaree, H. E., Harkins, L., & Peacock, E. J. (2006). Sex offenders' response to treatment and its association with recidivism as a function of psychopathy. *Sexual Abuse: Journal of Research and Treatment, 18,* 99–120.

Lanphear, B. P., Vorhees, C. V., & Bellinger, D. C. (2005) Protecting children from environmental toxins. Public Library of Science Medicine, e61. Retrieved January 17, 2007, from http://medicine.plosjournals.org/perlserv/?request=get-document&doi=10.1371%2Fjournal.pmed.0020061

Large, M., Sharma, S., Compton, M. T., Slade, T., & Nielssen, O. (2011). Cannabis use and earlier onset of psychosis: A systematic meta-analysis. *Archives of General Psychiatry, 68,* 555–561.

Larkin, J., Rice, C., & Russell, V. (1999). Sexual harassment, education and the prevention of disordered eating. In N. Piran, M. Levine, & C. Steiner-Adair (Eds.), *Preventing eating disorders: A handbook of intervention and special challenges* (pp. 194–207). Philadelphia: Brunner/Mazel.

Larson, C. L., Schaefer, H. S., Siegle, G. J., Jackson, C. A. B., Anderle, M. J., & Davidson, R. J. (2006). Fear is fast in phobic individuals: Amygdala activation in response to fear-relevant stimuli. *Biological Psychiatry, 60,* 410–417.

Larson, K., Russ, S. A., Kahn, R. S., & Halfon, N. (2011). Patterns of comorbidity, functioning, and service use for US children with ADHD, 2007. *Pediatrics, 127,* 462–470.

Laruelle, M., Abi-Dargham, A., Casanova, M. F., Toti, R., Weinberger, D. R., & Kleinman, J. E. (1993). Selective abnormalities of prefrontal serotonergic receptors in schizophrenia: A postmortem study. *Archives of General Psychiatry, 50,* 810–818.

Larzelere, R. E., & Kuhn, B. R. (2005). Comparing child outcomes of physical punishment and alternative disciplinary tactics: A meta-analysis. *Clinical Child and Family Psychology Review, 8,* 1–37.

LaSalle, V. H., Cromer, K. R., Nelson, K. N., Kazuba, D., Justement, L., & Murphy, D. L. (2004). Diagnostic interview assessed neuropsychiatric disorder comorbidity in 334 individuals with obsessive-compulsive disorder. *Depression and Anxiety, 19,* 163–173.

Lau, A., & Zane, N. (2000). Examining the effects of ethnic-specific services: An analysis of cost-utilization and treatment outcome for Asian American clients. *Journal of Community Psychology, 28,* 63–77.

Laucht, M., Skowronek, M. H., Becker, K., Schmidt, M. H., Esser, G., et al. (2007). Interacting effects of the dopamine transporter gene and psychosocial adversity on attention-deficit/hyperactivity disorder symptoms among year-olds from a high-risk community sample. *Archives of General Psychiatry, 64,* 585–590.

Laumann, E., Gagnon, J. H., Michael, R. T., & Michaels, S. (1994). *The social organization of sexuality: Sexual practices in the United States.* Chicago: University of Chicago Press.

Laumann, E. O., Paik, A., & Rosen, R. C. (1999). Sexual dysfunction in the United States: Prevalence and predictors. *Journal of the American Medical Association, 281,* 537–544.

Lauriello, J., & Bustillo, J. (2001). Medication treatments for schizophrenia: Translating research findings into better outcomes. *Journal of Psychiatric Practice, 7,* 260–265.

LaVeist, T. A., Nickerson, K. J., & Bowie, J. V. (2000). Attitudes about racism, medical mistrust and satisfaction with care among African American and White cardiac patients. *Medical Care Research and Review, 57,* 146–161.

Laws, D. R., & Marshall, W. L. (1991). Masturbatory reconditioning with sexual deviates: An evaluative review. *Advances in Behaviour Research & Therapy, 13,* 13–25.

Lawson, J., Baron-Cohen, S., & Wheelwright, S. (2004). Empathising and systemising in adults with and without Asperger syndrome. *Journal of Autism and Developmental Disorders, 34,* 301–310.

Lazev, A. B., Herzog, T. A., & Brandon, T. H. (1999). Classical conditioning of environmental cues to cigarette smoking. *Experimental and Clinical Psychopharmacology, 7,* 56–63.

Le Couteur, A., Bailey, A., Goode, S., Pickles, A., Robertson, S., et al. (1996). A broader phenotype of autism: The clinical spectrum in twins. *Journal of Child Psychology and Psychiatry, 37,* 785–801.

le Grange, D., & Eisler, I. (2009). Family interventions in adolescent anorexia nervosa. *Child and Adolescent Psychiatric Clinics of North America, 18,* 159–173.

Leavitt, F. (1997). False attribution of suggestibility to explain recovered memory of childhood sexual abuse following extended amnesia. *Child Abuse and Neglect, 21,* 265–272.

Leccese, A. P. (1991). *Drugs and society: Behavioral medicines and abusable drugs.* Englewood Cliffs, NJ: Prentice Hall.

Leckman, J. E., Denys, D., Simpson, H. B., Mataix-Cols, D., Hollander, E., et al. (2010). Obsessive-compulsive disorder: A review of the diagnostic criteria and possible subtype and dimensional specifiers for DSM-V. *Depression & Anxiety, 27,* 507–527.

Ledley, D. R., & Heimberg, R. G. (2006). Cognitive vulnerability to social anxiety. *Journal of Social & Clinical Psychology, 25,* 755–778.

LeDoux, J. E. (1996). *The emotional brain: The mysterious underpinnings of emotional life.* New York: Simon & Schuster.

LeDoux, J. E. (2000). Emotion circuits in the brain. *Annual Review of Neuroscience, 23,* 155–184.

Lee, A. M., & Lee, S. (1996). Disordered eating and its psychosocial correlates among Chinese adolescent females in Hong Kong. *International Journal of Eating Disorders, 20,* 177–183.

Lee, B. Y., & Newberg, A. B. (2005). Religion and health: A review and critical analysis. *Zygon, 40,* 443–468.

Lee, C., Gavriel, H., Drummond, P., Richards, J., & Greenwald, R. (2002). Treatment of post-traumatic stress disorder: A comparison of stress inoculation training with prolonged exposure and eye movement desensitization and reprocessing. *Journal of Clinical Psychology, 58,* 1071–1089.

Lee, D. O. (2004). Menstrually related self-injurious behavior in adolescents with autism. *Journal of the American Academy of Child & Adolescent Psychiatry, 43,* 1193.

Lee, P. W. H., Lieh Mak, F., Yu, K. K., & Spinks, J. A. (1991). Pattern of outcome in schizophrenia in Hong Kong. *Acta Psychiatrica Scandinavica. 84,* 346–352.

Lee, S. H., & Oh, D. S. (1999). Offensive type of social phobia: Cross-cultural perspectives. *International Medical Journal, 6,* 271–279.

Lee, S., Chiu, H. F., & Chen, C. (1989). Anorexia nervosa in Hong Kong: Why not more in Chinese? *British Journal of Psychiatry, 154,* 683–688.

Lee, S., Ho, T. P., & Hsu, L. K. (1993). Fat phobic and non-fat phobic anorexia nervosa: A comparative study of 70 Chinese patients in Hong Kong. *Psychological Medicine, 23,* 999–1017.

Lee, S., Hsu, L. G., & Wing, Y. K. (1992). Bulimia nervosa in Hong Kong Chinese patients. *British Journal of Psychiatry, 161,* 545–551.

Lee, S., & Lee, A. M. (2000). Disordered eating in three communities of China: A comparative study of female high school students in Hong Kong, Shenzhen, and rural Hunan. *International Journal of Eating Disorders, 27,* 317–327.

Lee, S., Ng, K. L. Kwok, K. P. S., & Tsang, A. (2009). Prevalence and correlates of social fears in Hong Kong. *Journal of Anxiety Disorders, 23,* 327–332.

Lee S. A. (1997). Chinese perspective of somatoform disorders. *Journal of Psychosomatic Research, 43,* 115–119.

Lee, Y. H. (2008). The diagnosis of borderline personality disorder in Asian cultures. *Dissertation Abstracts International B: Sciences and Engineering, 68*(12), 8402B.

Leenaars, A. A. (1988). Are women's suicides really different from men's? *Women & Health, 14,* 17–33.

Leenaars, A. A. (2003). Can a theory of suicide predict all "suicides" in the elderly? *Crisis: The Journal of Crisis Intervention and Suicide Prevention, 24,* 7–16.

Leentjens, A. F., & Diefenbacher, A. (2006). A survey of delirium guidelines in Europe. *Journal of Psychosomatic Research, 61,* 123–128.

Leentjens, A. F. G., & van der Mast, R. C. (2005). Delirium in elderly people: An update. *Current Opinion in Psychiatry, 18,* 325–330.

Leff, J., Berkowitz, R., Shavit, N., Strachan, A., Glass, I., & Vaughn, C. (1990). A trial of family therapy versus a relatives' group for schizophrenia. Two-year follow-up. *British Journal of Psychiatry, 157,* 571–577.

LeGris, J., & van Reekum, R. (2006). Neuropsychological correlates of borderline personality disorder and suicidal behavior. *Canadian Journal of Psychiatry, 51,* 131–142.

Lehman, A. F., Steinwachs, K. M., & Survey Co-Investigators of the PORT Project. (1998). Patterns of usual care for schizophrenia: Initial results from the Schizophrenia Patient Outcomes Research Team (PORT) Client Survey. *Schizophrenia Bulletin, 24,* 11–20.

Lehrer, P. M., & Woolfolk, R. L. (1994). Respiratory system involvement in Western relaxation and self-regulation. In B. H. Timmons & R. Ley (Eds.), *Behavioral and psychological approaches to breathing disorders* (pp. 191–203). New York: Plenum Press.

Leibenluft, E. (2008). Chronobiological evaluation of rapid-cycling bipolar disorder. NIMH Grant Number: 1Z01MH02614-07. Manuscript in preparation.

Leibenluft, E., Albert, P. S., Rosenthal, N. E., & Wehr, T. A. (1996). Relationship between sleep and mood in patients with rapid-cycling bipolar disorder. *Psychiatry Research, 63,* 161–168.

Leiblum, S. R., & Segraves, R. T. (2000). Sex therapy with aging adults. In S. R. Leiblum & R. C. Rosen (Eds), *Principles and practice of sex therapy* (3rd ed., pp. 423–448). New York: Guilford Press.

Leiblum, S. R., Pervin, L. A., & Campbell, E. H. (1989). The treatment of vaginismus: Success and failure. In S. R. Leiblum & R. C. Rosen (Eds.), *Principles and practice of sex therapy: Update for the 1990s* (2nd ed., pp. 113–138). New York: Guilford Press.

Leighton, A. H., & Hughes, C. C. (1955). Notes on Eskimos patterns of suicide. *Southwestern Journal of Anthropology, 11,* 327–338.

Leising, D., Sporberg, D., & Rehbein, D. (2006). Characteristic interpersonal behavior in dependent and avoidant personality disorder can be observed within very short interaction sequences. *Journal of Personality Disorders, 20,* 319–330.

Lelewer, N. (1994). *Something's not right: One family's struggle with learning disabilities.* Acton, MA: VanderWyk & Burnham.

Lemche, E., Surguladze, S. A., Giampietro, V. P., Anilkumar, A., Brammer, M. J., et al. (2007). Limbic and prefrontal responses to facial emotion expressions in depersonalization. *Neuroreport, 18,* 473–477.

Lenox, R. H., & Hahn, C. G. (2000). Overview of the mechanism of action of lithium in the brain: 50-year update. *Journal of Clinical Psychiatry, 61,* 5–15.

Lenze, E. J., Mulsant, B. H., Mohlman, J., Shear, M. K., Dew, M. A., et al. (2005). Generalized anxiety disorder in late life: Lifetime course and comorbidity with major depressive disorder. *American Journal of Geriatric Psychiatry, 13,* 77–80.

Lenzenweger, M. F. (1999). Stability and change in personality disorder features: The Longitudinal Study of Personality Disorders. *Archives of General Psychiatry, 56,* 1009–1015.

Lenzenweger, M. F. (2006). The longitudinal study of personality disorders: History, design considerations, and initial findings. *Journal of Personality Disorders, 20*, 645–670.

Lenzenweger, M. F., Johnson, M. D., & Willett, J. B. (2004). Individual growth curve analysis illuminates stability and change in personality disorder features: The longitudinal study of personality disorders. *Archives of General Psychiatry, 61*, 1015–1024.

Leone, P., Pocock, D., & Wise, R. A. (1991). Morphine-dopamine interaction: Ventral tegmental morphine increases nucleus accumbens dopamine release. *Pharmacology Biochemistry & Behavior, 39*, 469–472.

Letonoff, E. J., Williams, T. R., & Sidhu, K. S. (2002). Hysterical paralysis: A report of three cases and a review of the literature. *Spine, 27*, E441–E445.

Leuchter, A. F., Cook, I. A., Witte, E. A., Morgan, M., & Abrams, M. (2002). Change in brain function of depressed subjects during treatment with placebo. *American Journal of Psychiatry, 159*, 122–129.

Leung, K. S., & Cottler, L. B. (2008). Ecstasy and other club drugs: A review of recent epidemiologic studies. *Current Opinion in Psychiatry, 21*, 234–241.

Lev-Ran, S., Imtiaz, S., Rehm, J., & Le Foll, B. (2013). Exploring the association between lifetime prevalence of mental illness and transition from substance use to substance use disorders: Results from the National Epidemiologic Survey of Alcohol and Related Conditions (NESARC). *The American Journal on Addictions, 22,* 93–98.

Levenson, J. S. (2004). Sexual predator civil commitment: A comparison of selected and released offenders. *International Journal of Offender Therapy and Comparative Criminology, 48*, 638–648.

Levin, A. (2007). Multiple physical illnesses common in Iraq war veterans with PTSD. *Psychiatric News, 42*(2), 4.

Levin, R. J. (1994). Human male sexuality: Appetite and arousal, desire and drive. In C. R. Legg & D. A. Booth (Eds.), *Appetite: Neural and behavioural bases* (pp. 127–164). New York: Oxford University Press.

Levine, M. P., & Harrison, K. (2004). Media's role in the perpetuation and prevention of negative body image and disordered eating. In J. K. Thompson (Ed.), *Handbook of eating disorders and obesity* (pp. 695–717). Hoboken, NJ: John Wiley & Sons.

Levine, S. B. (1988). Intrapsychic and individual aspects of sexual desire. In S. R. Leiblum & R. C. Rosen (Eds.), *Sexual desire disorders* (pp. 21–44). New York: Guilford Press.

Levine, S. Z., Lurie, I., Kohn, R., & Levav, I. (2011). Trajectories of the course of schizophrenia: From progressive deterioration to amelioration over three decades. *Schizophrenia Research, 126*(1–3), 184–191.

Levitan, C., Ward, P. B., & Catts, S. V. (1999). Superior temporal gyral volumes and laterality correlates of auditory hallucinations in schizophrenia. *Biological Psychiatry, 46*, 955–962.

Levitt, E. E., Moser, C., & Jamison, K. V. (1994). The prevalence and some attributes of females in the sadomasochistic subculture: A second report. *Archives of Sexual Behavior, 23*, 465–473.

Levy, T. M., & Orlans, M. (1999). Kids who kill: Attachment disorder, antisocial personality and violence. *The Forensic Examiner, 8*, 19–24.

Levy, T. M., & Orlans, M. (2000). Attachment disorder as an antecedent to violence and antisocial patterns in children. In T. M. Levy (Ed.), *Handbook of attachment interventions* (pp. 1–26). San Diego, CA: Academic Press.

Lewinsohn, P. M. (1974). A behavioral approach to depression. In R. J. Friedman & M. M. Katz (Eds.), *The psychology of depression: Contemporary theory and research* (pp. 157–186). Washington, DC: Winston.

Lewinsohn, P. M., & Essau, C. A. (2002). Depression in adolescents. In I. H. Gotlib & C. L. Hammen (Eds.), *Handbook of depression.* (pp. 541–559). New York: Guilford Press.

Lewinsohn, P. M., Allen, N. B., Seeley, J. R., & Gotlib, I. H. (1999). First onset versus recurrence of depression: Differential processes of psychosocial risk. *Journal of Abnormal Psychology, 108*, 483–489.

Lewinsohn, P. M., Rohde, P., Klein, D. N., & Seeley, J. R. (1999). Natural course of adolescent major depressive disorder: I. Continuity into young adulthood. *Journal of the American Academy of Child & Adolescent Psychiatry, 38*, 56–63.

Lewinsohn, P. M., Rohde, P., Seeley, J. R., & Fischer, S. A. (1993). Age-cohort changes in the lifetime occurrence of depression and other mental disorders. *Journal of Abnormal Psychology, 102*, 110–120.

Lewis, D. A., & Moghaddam, B. (2006). Cognitive dysfunction in schizophrenia: Convergence of gamma-aminobutyric acid and glutamate alterations. *Archives of Neurology, 63*, 1372–1376.

Lewis, D. O., Yeager, C. A., Swica, Y., Pincus, J. H., & Lewis, M. (1997). Objective documentation of child abuse and dissociation in 12 murderers with dissociative identity disorder. *American Journal of Psychiatry, 154*, 1703–1710.

Lewis, P. A., & Critchley, H. D. (2003). Mood-dependent memory. *Trends in Cognitive Sciences, 7*, 431–433.

Lewontin, R. C. (1976). Race and intelligence. In N. J. Block & G. G. Dworkin (Eds.), *The IQ controversy* (pp. 78–92). New York: Pantheon Books.

Leyman, L., De Raedt, R., Schacht, R., & Koster, E. H. W. (2007). Attentional biases for angry faces in unipolar depression. *Psychological Medicine, 37*, 393–402.

Leyton, M., Okazawa, H., Diksic, M., Paris, J., Rosa, P., et al. (2001). Brain regional alpha-[C-11] methyl-(L)-tryptophan trapping in impulsive subjects with borderline personality disorder. *American Journal of Psychiatry, 158*, 775–782.

Li, D., Chokka, P., & Tibbo, P. (2001). Toward an integrative understanding of social phobia. *Journal of Psychiatry & Neuroscience, 26*, 190–202.

Li, D., Sham, P. C., Owen, M. J., & He, L. (2006). Meta-analysis shows significant association between dopamine system genes and attention deficit hyperactivity disorder (ADHD). *Human Molecular Genetics, 15*, 2276–2284.

Li, S-C., Lindenberger, U., & Sikström, S. (2001). Aging cognition: From neuro-modulation to representation. *Trends in Cognitive Sciences, 5*, 479–486.

Liberman, R. P., & Robertson, M. J. (2005). A pilot, controlled skills training study of schizotypal high school students. *Verhaltenstherapie, 15*, 176–180.

Lichtenstein, P., & Annas, P. (2000). Heritability and prevalence of specific fears and phobias in childhood. *Journal of Child Psychology & Psychiatry & Allied Disciplines, 41*, 927–937.

Liddle, P. F., Friston, K. J., Frith, C. D., Hirsch, S. R., Jones, T., & Frackowiak, R. S. (1992). Patterns of cerebral blood flow in schizophrenia. *British Journal of Psychiatry, 160*, 179–186.

Lieb, K., Zanarini, M. C., Schmahl, C., Linehan, M. M., & Bohus, M. (2004). Borderline personality disorder. *Lancet, 364*, 453–461.

Lieb, R., Becker, E., & Altamura, C. (2005). The epidemiology of generalized anxiety disorder in Europe. *European Neuropsychopharmacology, 15*, 445–452.

Lieber, C. S. (2003). Relationships between nutrition, alcohol use, and liver disease. *Alcohol Research & Health, 27*, 220–231.

Lieberman, J. A. (1999). Is schizophrenia a neurodegenerative disorder? A clinical and pathophysiological perspective. *Biological Psychiatry, 46*, 729–739.

Lierberman, J. A. (2011). Psychiatric diagnosis in the lab: How far off are we? *Psychiatric Times*, September 28. Retrieved November 15, 2011, from www.medscape.com/viewarticle/750288.

Lieberman, J. A., Stroup, T. S., McEvoy, J. P., Swartz, M. S., Rosenheck, R. A., et al. (for the Clinical Antipsychotic Trials of Intervention Effectiveness (CATIE) Investigators). (2005). Effectiveness of antipsychotic drugs in patients with chronic schizophrenia. *New England Journal of Medicine, 353*, 1209–1223.

Liebowitz, M. R. (1999). Update on the diagnosis and treatment of social anxiety disorder. *Journal of Clinical Psychiatry, 60*(Suppl. 18), 22–26.

Lilenfeld, L. R., & Kaye, W. H. (1998). Genetic studies of anorexia and bulimia nervosa. In H. Hoek, J. Treasure, & M. Katzman (Eds.), *Neurobiology in the treatment of eating disorders* (pp. 169–194). Chichester, England: John Wiley & Sons.

Lilienfeld, S. O., Wood, J. M., & Garb, H. N. (2000). The scientific status of projective techniques. *Psychological Science in the Public Interest, 1*, 27–66.

Lilienfeld, S. O., Kirsch, I., Sarbin, T. R., Lynn, S. J., Chaves, J. F., et al. (1999). Dissociative identity disorder and the sociocognitive model: Recalling the lessons of the past. *Psychological Bulletin, 125*, 507–523.

Lin, E. H. B., Katon, W. J., Simon, G. E., Von Korff, M., Bush, T. M., et al. (2000). Low-intensity treatment of depression in primary care: Is it problematic? *General Hospital Psychiatry, 22,* 78–83.

Lin, K. M., & Cheung, F. (1999). Mental health issues for Asian Americans. *Psychiatric Services 50,* 774–780.

Lin, K. M., Cheung, F., Smith, M., & Poland, R. E. (1997). The use of psychotropic medications in working with Asian patients. In E. Lee (Ed.), *Working with Asian Americans: A guide for clinicians* (pp. 388–399). New York: Guilford Press.

Lindblom, K. M., Linton, S. J., Fedeli, C., & Bryngelsson, I. (2006). Burnout in the working population: Relations to psychosocial work factors. *International Journal of Behavioral Medicine, 13,* 51–59.

Linde, K., Berner, M. M., & Kriston, L. (2008). St. John's wort for major depression. *Cochrane Database of Systematic Reviews,* Issue 4. Art. No.: CD000448.

Linde, K., Berner, M., Egger, M., & Mulrow, C. (2005). St John's wort for depression: Meta-analysis of randomised controlled trials. *British Journal of Psychiatry, 186,* 99–107.

Linde, P. (2002). *Of spirits and madness: An American psychiatrist in Africa.* New York: McGraw-Hill.

Linehan, M. M. (1981). A social-behavioral analysis of suicide and parasuicide: Implications for clinical assessment and treatment. In J. Clarkin & H. Glazer (Eds.), *Depression: Behavioral and directive intervention strategies* (pp. 229–294). New York: Garland Press.

Linehan, M. M. (1993). *Cognitive-behavioral treatment of borderline personality disorder.* New York: Guilford Press.

Linehan, M. M., & Heard, H. L. (1999). Borderline personality disorder: Costs, course, and treatment outcomes. In N. E. Miller & K. M. Magruder (Eds.), *Cost-effectiveness of psychotherapy: A guide for practitioners, researchers, and policymakers* (pp. 291–305). New York: Oxford University Press.

Linehan, M. M., & Kehrer, C. A. (1993). Borderline personality disorder. In D. H. Barlow (Ed.), *Clinical handbook of psychological disorders: A step-by-step treatment manual* (2nd ed., pp. 396–441). New York: Guilford Press.

Linehan, M. M., Comtois, K. A., Murray, A. M., Brown, M. Z., Gallop, R. J., et al. (2006). Two-year randomized controlled trial and follow-up of dialectical behavior therapy vs therapy by experts for suicidal behaviors and borderline personality disorder. *Archives of General Psychiatry, 63,* 757–766.

Linehan, M. M., Schmidt, H., III, Dimeff, L. A., Craft, J. C., Kanter, J., & Comtois, K. A. (1999). Dialectical behavior therapy for patients with borderline personality disorder and drug-dependence. *The American Journal on Addictions, 8,* 279–292.

Lingford-Hughes, A., & Nutt, D. (2000). Alcohol and drug abuse. *Current Opinion in Psychiatry, 13,* 291–298.

Lipsanen, T., Korkeila, J., Peltola, P., Järvinen, J., Langen, K., & Lauerma, H. (2004). Dissociative disorders among psychiatric patients: Comparison with a nonclinical sample. *European Psychiatry, 19,* 53–55.

Lipsitz, J. D., Barlow, D. H., Mannuzza, S., Hofmann, S. G., & Fyer, A. J. (2002). Clinical features of four DSM-IV-specific phobia subtypes. *Journal of Nervous and Mental Disease, 190,* 471–478.

Littell, J. H., & Girvin, H. (2002). Stages of change: A critique. *Behavior Modification, 26,* 223–273.

Litz, B. T., Engel, C. C., Bryant, R. A., & Papa, A. (2007). A randomized, controlled proof-of-concept trial of an Internet-based, therapist-assisted self-management treatment for posttraumatic stress disorder. *American Journal of Psychiatry, 164,* 1676–1683.

Livesley, W. J. (2001). Conceptual and taxonomic issues. In W. J. Livesley (Ed.), *Handbook of personality disorders: Theory, research, and treatment* (pp. 3–38). New York: Guilford Press.

Livesley, W. J. (2007). An integrated approach to the treatment of personality disorder. *Journal of Mental Health, 16,* 131–148.

Livesley, W. J., Jang, K. L., & Vernon, P. A. (1998). Phenotypic and genetic structure of traits delineating personality disorder. *Archives of General Psychiatry, 55,* 941–948.

Livingston, G., Johnston, K., Katona, C., Paton, J., & Lyketsos, C. G. (Old Age Task Force of the World Federation of Biological Psychiatry). (2005). Systematic review of psychological approaches to the management of neuropsychiatric symptoms of dementia. *American Journal of Psychiatry, 162,* 1996–2021.

Lock, J. (2004). Family approaches for anorexia nervosa and bulimia nervosa. In J. K. Thompson (Ed.), *Handbook of eating disorders and obesity* (pp. 218–231). Hoboken, NJ: John Wiley & Sons.

Lock, J., Le Grange, D., Agras, W. S., & Dare, C. (2001). Treatment manual for anorexia nervosa: A family-based approach. *Family Therapy, 29,* 190–191.

Locker, D., Thomson, W. M., & Poulton, R. (2001). Psychological disorder, conditioning experiences, and the onset of dental anxiety in early adulthood. *Journal of Dental Research, 80,* 1588–1592.

Loeber, R., & Farrington, D. P. (2000). Young children who commit crime: Epidemiology, developmental origins, risk factors, early interventions, and policy implications. *Development and Psychopathology, 12,* 737–762.

Loening-Baucke, V. (1996). Encopresis and soiling. *Pediatric Clinics of North America, 43,* 279–298.

Loewenstein, R. J. (1994). Diagnosis, epidemiology, clinical course, treatment, and cost effectiveness of treatment for dissociative disorders and MPD: Report submitted to the Clinton Administration Task Force on Health Care Financing Reform. *Dissociation: Progress in the Dissociative Disorders, 7,* 3–11.

Loney, B. R., Frick, P. J., Clements, C. B., Ellis, M. L., & Kerlin, K. (2003). Callous-unemotional traits, impulsivity, and emotional processing in adolescents with antisocial behavior problems. *Journal of Clinical Child and Adolescent Psychology, 32,* 66–80.

Loney, B. R., Frick, P. J., Ellis, M., & McCoy, M. G. (1998). Intelligence, callous-unemotional traits, and antisocial behavior. *Journal of Psychopathology and Behavioral Assessment, 20,* 231–247.

Loo, C. (2004). Transcranial magnetic stimulation: Promise for the future? *Australasian Psychiatry, 12,* 409–410.

Looper, K. J., & Kirmayer, L. J. (2002). Behavioral medicine approaches to somatoform disorders. *Journal of Consulting and Clinical Psychology, 70,* 810–827.

Lopez, S. R., Nelson, K. A., Polo, J. A., Jenkins, J., Karno, M., & Snyder, K. (1998, August). *Family warmth and the course of schizophrenia of Mexican Americans and Anglo Americans.* Paper presented at the International Congress of Applied Psychology, San Francisco.

LoPiccolo, J., & Friedman, J. M. (1988). Broad-spectrum treatment of low sexual desire: Integration of cognitive, behavioral, and systemic therapy. In S. R. Leiblum & R. C. Rosen (Eds.), *Sexual desire disorders* (pp. 107–144). New York: Guilford Press.

LoPiccolo, J., & Stock, W. E. (1986). Treatment of sexual dysfunction. *Journal of Consulting and Clinical Psychology, 54,* 158–167.

Lorenz, J., Kunze, K., & Bromm, B. (1998). Differentiation of conversive sensory loss and malingering by P300 in a modified oddball task. *Neuroreport, 9,* 187–191.

Lorge, E. (2008, January 31). Army responds to rising suicide rates. *Army Behavioral Health.* Retrieved December 2, 2008, from www.behavioralhealth.army.mil/news/20080131armyrespondstosuicide.html

Lorimer, P. A., Simpson, R. L., Myles, B. S., & Ganz, J. B. (2002). The use of social stories as a preventative behavioral intervention in a home setting with a child with autism. *Journal of Positive Behavior Interventions, 4,* 53–60.

Lougee, L., Perlmutter, S. J., Nicolson, R., Garvey, M. A., & Swedo, S. E. (2000). Psychiatric disorders in first-degree relatives of children with pediatric autoimmune neuropsychiatric disorders associated with streptococcal infections (PANDAS). *Journal of the American Academy of Child & Adolescent Psychiatry, 39,* 1120–1126.

Louis, M., & Kowalski, S. D. (2002). Use of aromatherapy with hospice patients to decrease pain, anxiety, and depression and to promote an increased sense of well-being. *American Journal of Hospice & Palliative Care, 19,* 381–386.

Lowe, M. R., Gleaves, D. H., DiSimone-Weiss, R. T., Furgueson, C., Gayda, C. A., et al. (1996). Restraint, dieting, and the continuum model of bulimia nervosa. *Journal of Abnormal Psychology, 105,* 508–517.

Luborsky, L., Barber, J., Siqueland, L., McLellan, A. T., & Woody, G. (1997). Establishing a therapeutic alliance with substance abusers. In L. S. Onken, J. D. Blaine, & J. J. Boren (Eds.), *Beyond the therapeutic alliance: Keeping the drug-dependent individual in treatment* (pp. 223–240). National Institute on Drug Abuse Research Monograph 165. NIH publication no. 97–4142. Washington: DC: U.S. Government Printing Office.

Luborsky, L., Diguer, L., Seligman, D. A., Rosenthal, R., Krause, E. D., et al. (1999). The researcher's own therapy allegiances: A "wild card" in comparisons of treatment efficacy. *Clinical Psychology: Science & Practice 6*, 95–106.

Luborsky, L., Rosenthal, R., Diguer, L., Andrusyna, T. P., Berman, J. S., et al. (2002). The dodo bird verdict is alive and well—mostly. *Clinical Psychology: Science and Practice, 9*, 2–12.

Luborsky, L., Singer, B., & Luborsky, L. (1975). Comparative studies of psychotherapies: Is it true that "everyone has won and all must have prizes"? *Archives of General Psychiatry, 32*, 995–1008.

Luby, J. L., Sullivan, J., Belden, A., Stalets, M., Blankenship, S., & Spitznagel, E. (2006). An observational analysis of behavior in depressed preschoolers: Further validation of early-onset depression. *Journal of the American Academy of Child & Adolescent Psychiatry, 45*, 203–212.

Lucka, I. (2006). Depressive disorders in patients suffering from anorexia nervosa. *Archives of Psychiatry and Psychotherapy, 8*, 55–61.

Luczak, S. E., Elvine-Kreis, B., Shea, S. H., Carr, L. G., & Wall, T. L. (2002). Genetic risk for alcoholism relates to level of response to alcohol in Asian-American men and women. *Journal of Studies on Alcohol, 63*, 74–82.

Luczak, S. E., Wall, T. L., Shea, S. H., Byun, S. M., & Carr, L. G. (2001). Binge drinking in Chinese, Korean, and White college students: Genetic and ethnic group differences. *Psychology of Addictive Behaviors, 15*, 306–309.

Ludman, E. J., Simon, G. E., Tutty, S., & Von Korff, M. (2007). A randomized trial of telephone psychotherapy and pharmacotherapy for depression: Continuation and durability of effects. *Journal of Consulting and Clinical Psychology, 75*, 257–266.

Lund, B. C., Hernandez, E. R., Yates, W. R., Mitchell, J. R., McKee, P. A., & Johnson, C. L. (2009). Rate of inpatient weight restoration predicts outcome in anorexia nervosa. *International Journal of Eating Disorders, 42*, 301–305.

Lundberg, P., Cantor-Graae, E., Kahima, M., & Östergren, P. (2007). Delusional ideation and manic symptoms in potential future emigrants in Uganda. *Psychological Medicine, 37*, 505–512.

Lundgren, J. D., Danoff-Burg, S., & Anderson, D. A. (2004). Cognitive-behavioral therapy for bulimia nervosa: An empirical analysis of clinical significance. *International Journal of Eating Disorders, 35*, 262–274.

Lundh, L., & Öst, L. (1996). Recognition bias for critical faces in social phobics. *Behaviour Research & Therapy, 34*, 787–794.

Lutz, W., Martinovich, Z., Howard, K. I., & Leon, S. C. (2002). Outcome management, expected treatment response, and severity-adjusted provider filing in outpatient psychotherapy. *Journal of Clinical Psychology, 58*, 1291–1304.

Lykken, D. T. (1995). *The antisocial personalities.* Mahwah, NJ: Erlbaum.

Lykouras, L. (1999). Pharmacotherapy of social phobia: A critical assessment. *Psychiatriki, 10*, 35–41.

Lyle, S., Grizzell, M., Willmott, S., Benbow, S., Clark, M., & Jolley, D. (2008). Treatment of a whole population sample of Alzheimer's disease with donepezil over a 4-year period: Lessons learned. *Dementia and Geriatric Cognitive Disorders, 25*, 226–231.

Lynch, D. J., McGrady, A., Nagel, R., & Zsembik, C. (1999). Somatization in family practice: Comparing 5 methods of classification. *Primary Care Companion to the Journal of Clinical Psychiatry, 1*, 85–89.

Lynch, W. C., Heil, D. P., Wagner, E., & Havens, M. D. (2008). Body dissatisfaction mediates the association between body mass index and risky weight control behaviors among White and Native American adolescent girls. *Appetite, 51*, 210–213.

Lynn, S. J., Lilienfeld, S. O., Merckelbach, H., Giesbrecht, T., & van der Kloet, D. (2012). Dissociation and dissociative disorders: Challenging conventional wisdom. *Current Directions in Psychological Science, 21*, 48–53.

Lynskey, M. T., Heath, A. C., Nelson, E. C., Bucholz, K. K., Madden, P. A. F., et al. (2002). Genetic and environmental contributions to cannabis dependence in a national young adult twin sample. *Psychological Medicine, 32*, 195–207.

Lyon, H. M., Startup, M., & Bentall, R. P. (1999). Social cognition and the manic defense: Attributions, selective attention, and self-schema in bipolar affective disorder. *Journal of Abnormal Psychology, 108*, 273–282.

Lyons, M. J., Eisen, S. A., Goldberg, J., True, W., Lin, N., et al. (1998). A registry-based twin study of depression in men. *Archives of General Psychiatry, 55*, 468–472.

Lyons, M. J., Goldberg, J., Eisen, S.A., True, W., Tsuang, M.T., et al. (1993) Do genes influence exposure to trauma? A twin study of combat. *American Journal of Medical Genetics, 48*, 22–27.

Lyons-Ruth, K., Holmes, B. M., Sasvari-Szekely, M., Ronai, Z., Nemoda, Z., & Pauls, D. (2007). Serotonin transporter polymorphism and borderline or antisocial traits among low-income young adults. *Psychiatric Genetics, 17*, 339–343.

Lyoo, I. K., Han, M. H., & Cho, D. Y. (1998). A brain MRI study in subjects with borderline personality disorder. *Journal of Affective Disorders, 50*, 235–243.

Maaranen, P., Tanskanen, A., Honkalampi, K., Haatainen, K., Hintikka, J., & Viinamäki, H. (2005). Factors associated with pathological dissociation in the general population. *Australian and New Zealand Journal of Psychiatry, 39*, 387–394.

MacArthur Research Network on Mental Health and the Law. (2001a). *The MacArthur Adjudicative Competence Study.* Retrieved January 21, 2006, from www.macarthur.virginia.edu/adjudicate.html

MacArthur Research Network on Mental Health and the Law. (2001b). *The MacArthur Coercion Study.* Retrieved October 27, 2006, from www.macarthur.virginia.edu/coercion.html

MacArthur Research Network on Mental Health and the Law. (2001c). *The MacArthur Violence Risk Assessment Study.* Retrieved January 24, 2006, from www. macarthur.virginia.edu/risk.html

Macaskill, N. D., & Macaskill, A. (1996). Rational-emotive therapy plus pharmacotherapy versus pharmacotherapy alone in the treatment of high cognitive dysfunction depression. *Cognitive Therapy & Research, 20*, 575–592.

MacCabe, J. H., Wicks, S., Löfving, S., David, A. S., Berndtsson, Å., et al. (2013). Decline in cognitive performance between ages 13 and 18 years and the risk for psychosis in adulthood. *JAMA Psychiatry, 70*, 361–270.

MacDonald, P. A., Antony, M. M., MacLeod, C. M., & Richter, M. M. (1997). Memory and confidence in memory judgments among individuals with obsessive compulsive disorder and nonclinical controls. *Behaviour Research and Therapy, 35*, 497–505.

Macedo, C. E., Martinez, R. C., Albrechet-Souza, L., Molina, V. A., & Brandao, M. L. (2007). 5-HT2- and D1-mechanisms of the basolateral nucleus of the amygdala enhance conditioned fear and impair unconditioned fear. *Behavioural Brain Research, 177*, 100–108.

MacKay, D. G., & Ahmetzanov, M. V. (2005). Emotion, memory, and attention in the taboo Stroop paradigm: An experimental analogue of flashbulb memories. *Psychological Science, 16*, 25–32.

MacKenzie, K. R. (2001). Group psychotherapy. In W. J. Livesley (Ed.), *Handbook of personality disorders: Theory, research, and treatment* (pp. 497–526). New York: Guilford Press.

Mackie, S., Shaw, P., Lenroot, R., Pierson, R., Greenstein, D. K., et al. (2007). Cerebellar development and clinical outcome in attention deficit hyperactivity disorder. *American Journal of Psychiatry, 164*, 647–655.

Macklin, M. L., Metzger, L. J., Litz, B. T., McNally, R. J., Lasko, N. B., et al. (1998). Lower precombat intelligence is a risk factor for posttraumatic stress disorder. *Journal of Consulting and Clinical Psychology, 66*, 323–326.

Maden, A., Scott, F., Burnett, R., Lewis, G. H., & Skapinakis, P. (2004). Offending in psychiatric patients after discharge from medium secure units: Prospective national cohort study. *BMJ: British Medical Journal, 328*, 1534.

Maes, H. H., Silberg, J. L., Neale, M. C., & Eaves, L. J. (2007). Genetic and cultural transmission of antisocial behavior: An extended twin parent model. *Twin Research and Human Genetics, 10*, 136–150.

Magarinos, M., Zafar, U., Nissenson, K., & Blanco, C. (2002). Epidemiology and treatment of hypochondriasis. *CNS Drugs, 16,* 9–22.

Magee, W. J., Eaton, W. W., Wittchen, H., McGonagle, K. A., & Kessler, R. C. (1996). Agoraphobia, simple phobia, and social phobia in the national comorbidity survey. *Archives of General Psychiatry, 53,* 159–168.

Maier, M. A., Bernier, A., Pekrun, R., Zimmermann, P., Strasser, K., & Grossmann, K. E. (2005). Attachment state of mind and perceptual processing of emotional stimuli. *Attachment & Human Development, 7,* 67–81.

Mailis-Gagnon, A., Giannoylis, I., Downar, J., Kwan, C. L., Mikulis, D. J., et al. (2003). Altered central somatosensory processing in chronic pain patients with "hysterical" anesthesia. *Neurology, 13,* 1501–1507.

Main, M., & Solomon, J. (1986). Discovery of an insecure-disorganized/disoriented attachment pattern. In T. B. Brazelton & M. W. Yogman (Eds.), *Affective development in infancy* (pp. 95–124). Westport, CT: Ablex.

Malan, D. H. (1976). *The frontier of brief psychotherapy: An example of the convergence of research and clinical practice.* New York: Plenum Medical.

Malatesta, V. J., & Adams, H. E. (2001). Sexual dysfunctions. In P. B. Sutker & H. E. Adams (Eds.), *Comprehensive handbook of psychopathology* (3rd ed., pp. 713–748). New York: Academic/Plenum.

Maldonado, J. R., & Spiegel, D. (2001). Conversion disorder. In K. A. Phillips (Ed.), *Somatoform and factitious disorders* (pp. 95–128). Washington, DC: American Psychiatric Association.

Malik, M. L., & Beutler, L. E. (2002). The emergence of dissatisfaction with the DSM. In L. E. Beutler & M. L. Malik (Eds.), *Rethinking the DSM: A psychological perspective* (pp. 3–15). Washington, DC: American Psychological Association.

Malik, S., & Velazquez, J. (2002, July/August). Cultural competence and the "New Americans." *Children's Voice.* Retrieved September 1, 2005, from www.cwla. org/articles/default.htm.

Malkoff-Schwartz, S., Frank, E., et al. (1998). Stressful life events and social rhythm disruption in the onset of manic depressive bipolar episodes: A preliminary investigation. *Archives of General Psychiatry, 55,* 702–707.

Mancebo, M. C., Eisen, J. L., Grant, J. E., & Rasmussen, S. A. (2005). Obsessive compulsive personality disorder and obsessive compulsive disorder: Clinical characteristics, diagnostic difficulties, and treatment. *Annals of Clinical Psychiatry, 17,* 197–204.

Manfro, G. G., Otto, M. W., McArdle, E. T., Worthington III, J. J., Rosenbaum, J. F., & Pollak, M. H. (1996). Relationship of antecedent stressful life events to childhood and family history of anxiety and the course of panic disorder. *Journal of Affective Disorders, 41,* 135–139.

Mannuzza, S., Klein, R. G., Abikoff, H., & Moulton, J. L., III. (2004). Significance of childhood conduct problems to later development of conduct disorder among children with ADHD: A prospective follow-up study. *Journal of Abnormal Child Psychology, 32,* 565–573.

Mantovani, A., Lisanby, S. H., Pieraccini, F., Ulivelli, M., Castrogiovanni, P., & Rossi, S. (2006). Repetitive transcranial magnetic stimulation (rTMS) in the treatment of obsessive-compulsive disorder (OCD) and Tourette's syndrome (TS). *International Journal of Neuropsychopharmacology, 9,* 95–100.

Maramba, G. G., & Hall, G. C. N. (2002). Meta-analyses of ethnic match as a predictor of dropout, utilization, and level of functioning. *Cultural Diversity and Ethnic Minority Psychology, 8,* 290–297.

Marano, H. E. (2003). Bedfellows: Insomnia and depression. *Psychology Today,* July/August, n.p. Retrieved May 4, 2007, from http://psychologytoday.com/articles/pto-20030715-000001.html

Marazziti, D., Dell'Osso, L., Presta, S., Pfanner, C., Rossi, A., Masala, U., et al. (1999). Platelet [3H]paroxetine binding in patients with OCD-related disorders. *Psychiatry Research, 89,* 223–228.

Marcus, S. M., Young, E. A., Kerber, K. B., Kornstein, S., Farabaugh, A. H., et al. (2005). Gender differences in depression: Findings from the STAR*D study. *Journal of Affective Disorders, 87,* 141–150.

Marder, S. R., Davis, J. M., & Chouinard, G. (1997). The effects of risperidone on the five dimensions of schizophrenia derived by factor analysis: Combined results of the North American trials. *Journal of Clinical Psychiatry, 58,* 538–546.

Marengo, J. T., Harrow, M., Lannin-Kettering, I. B., & Wilson, A. (1985). The assessment of bizarre-idiosyncratic thinking: A manual for scoring responses to verbal tests. In M. Harrow & D. Quinlan (Eds.), *Disordered thinking and schizophrenic psychopathology* (pp. 394–449). New York: Gardner Press.

Margraf, J., Ehlers, A., Roth, W. T., Clark, D. B, Sheikh, J., et al. (1991). How "blind" are double-blind studies? *Journal of Consulting and Clinical Psychology, 59,* 184–187.

Maric, N., Krabbendam, L., Vollebergh, W., de Graaf, R., & van Os, J. (2003). Sex differences in symptoms of psychosis in a non-selected, general population sample. *Schizophrenia Research, 63,* 89–95.

Marino, C., Citterio, A., Giorda, R., Facoetti, A., Menozzi, G., et al. (2007). Association of short-term memory with a variant within DYX1C1 in developmental dyslexia. *Genes, Brain & Behavior, 6,* 640–646.

Maris, R. W. (2002). Suicide. *The Lancet, 360,* 319–326.

Markowitsch, H. J. (1999). Functional neuroimaging correlates of functional amnesia. *Memory, 7,* 561–583.

Markowitsch, H. J., Fink, G. R., Thöne, A., Kessler, J., & Heiss, W.–D. (1997). A PET study of persistent psychogenic amnesia covering the whole life span. *Cognitive Neuropsychiatry, 22,* 135–158.

Markowitz, J. C. (2005). Interpersonal therapy. In J. M. Oldham, A. E. Skodol, & D. S. Bender (Eds.). *The American Psychiatric Publishing textbook of personality disorders* (pp. 321–334). Washington, DC: American Psychiatric Publishing.

Markowitz, J. C., Skodol, A. E., & Bleiberg, K. (2006). Interpersonal psychotherapy for borderline personality disorder: Possible mechanisms of change. *Journal of Clinical Psychology, 62,* 431–444.

Markowitz, J. C., Skodol, A. E., Petkova, E., Xie, H., Cheng, J., et al. (2005). Longitudinal comparison of depressive personality disorder and dysthymic disorder. *Comprehensive Psychiatry, 46,* 239–245.

Marks, I. M. (1969). *Fears and phobias.* New York: Academic Press.

Marks, I., Lovell, K., Noshirvani, H., Livanou, M., & Thrasher, S. (1998). Treatment of posttraumatic stress disorder by exposure and/or cognitive restructuring: A controlled study. *Archives of General Psychiatry, 55,* 317–325.

Marlatt, G. A., & Gordon, J. R. (Eds.). (1985). *Relapse prevention: Maintenance strategies in the treatment of addictive behaviors.* New York: Guilford Press.

Marques, L., Alegria, M., Becker, A., Chen, C., Fang, A., et al. (2011). Comparative prevalence, correlates of impairment, and service utilization for eating disorders across US ethnic groups: Implications for reducing ethnic disparities in health care access for eating disorders. *International Journal of Eating Disorders, 44,* 412–420.

Marsella, A., Friedman, M., & Spain, E. (1996). Ethnocultural aspects of posttraumatic stress disorder: An overview of issues and research directions. In A. Marsella, M. Friedman, E. Gerrity, & R. Scurfield (Eds.), *Ethnocultural aspects of posttraumatic stress disorder: Issues, research, and clinical applications* (pp. 105–130). Washington, DC: American Psychological Association.

Marshall, C. R., Harcourt-Brown, S., Ramus, F., & van der Lely, H. K. (2008). The link between prosody and language skills in children with specifi c language impairment (SLI) and/or dyslexia. *International Journal of Language Communication Disorders, 23,* 1–23.

Marshall, J. C., Halligan, P. W., Fink, G. R., Wade, D. T., & Frackowiak, R. S. (1997). The functional anatomy of a hysterical paralysis. *Cognition, 64,* B1–B8.

Marshall, M., Lewis, S., Lockwood, A., Drake, R., Jones, P., & Croudace, T. (2005). Association between duration of untreated psychosis and outcome in cohorts of first-episode patients. *Archives of General Psychiatry, 62,* 975–983.

Marshall, R. D., Schneier, F. R., Lin, S., Simpson, H. B., Vermes, D., & Leibowitz, M. (2000). Childhood trauma and dissociative symptoms in panic disorder. *American Journal of Psychiatry, 157,* 451–453.

Marshall, R. D., Spitzer, R., & Liebowitz, M. R. (1999). Review and critique of the new DSM-IV diagnosis of acute stress disorder. *American Journal of Psychiatry, 156,* 1677–1685.

Marshall, W. L. (1997). Pedophilia: Psychopathology and theory. In D. R. Laws, & W. T. O'Donohue (Eds.), *Sexual deviance: Theory, assessment, and treatment.* (pp. 152–174). New York: Guilford Press.

Marshall, W. L., O'sullivan, C., & Fernandez, Y. M. (1996). The enhancement of victim empathy among incarcerated child molesters. *Legal and Criminological Psychology, 1,* 95–102.

Marteinsdottir, I., Tillfors, M., Furmark, T., Anderberg, U. M., & Ekselius, L. (2003). Personality dimensions measured by the Temperament and Character Inventory (TCI) in subjects with social phobia. *Nordic Journal of Psychiatry, 57,* 29–35.

Marten, P. A., Brown, T. A., Barlow, D. H., Borkovec, T. D., Shear, M. K., & Lydiard, R. B. (1993). Evaluation of the ratings comprising the associated symptom criterion of DSM-III-R generalized anxiety disorder. *Journal of Nervous and Mental Disease, 181,* 676–682.

Martens, W. H. J. (2005). Multidimensional model of trauma and correlated antisocial personality disorder. *Journal of Loss & Trauma, 10,* 115–129.

Martin, D. (2002, January 25). Edith Bouvier Beale, 84, "Little Edie," Dies. *The New York Times,* p. A20.

Martin, D. J., Garske, J. P., & Davis, M. K. (2000). Relationship of alliance with outcome and other variables. *Journal of Consulting and Clinical Psychology, 68,* 438–450.

Martin, N. C., Levy, F., Pieka, J., & Hay, D. A. (2006). A genetic study of attention deficit hyperactivity disorder, conduct disorder, oppositional defiant disorder and reading disability: Aetiological overlaps and implications. *International Journal of Disability, Development and Education, 53,* 21–34.

Martin-Soelch, C. (2009). Is depression associated with dysfunction of the central reward system? Biochemical Society Transactions, 37(Pt 1), 313–317.

Martinez, C., Rietbrock, S., Wise, L., Ashby, D., Chick, J., et al. (2005). Antidepressant treatment and the risk of fatal and non-fatal self harm in first episode depression: nested case-control study. *British Medical Journal, 330,* 389–393.

Martínez-Arán, A., Vieta, E., Colom, F., Reinares, M., Benabarre, A., et al. (2000). Cognitive dysfunctions in bipolar disorder: Evidence of neuropsychological disturbances. *Psychotherapy & Psychosomatics, 69,* 2–18.

Martínez-Arán, A., Vieta, E., Colom, F., Torrent, C., Reinares, M., et al. (2005). Do cognitive complaints in euthymic bipolar patients reflect objective cognitive impairment? *Psychotherapy and Psychosomatics, 74,* 295–302.

Martorano, J. T. (1984). The psychological treatment of Anna O. In M. Rosenbaum & M. Muroff (Eds.), *Anna O.: Fourteen contemporary reinterpretations* (pp. 85–100). New York: Free Press.

Mascolo, M., Trent, S., Colwell, C., & Mehler, P. S. (2012). What the emergency department needs to know when caring for patients with eating disorders. *International Journal of Eating Disorders, 45,* 977–981.

Maslach, C. (2003). Job burnout: New directions in research and intervention. *Current Directions in Psychological Science, 12,* 189–192.

Maslow, A. H. (1968). *Toward a psychology of being* (2nd ed.). Oxford, England: D. Van Nostrand.

Masters, W. H., & Johnson, V. E. (1966). *Human sexual response.* Oxford, England: Little, Brown.

Masters, W. H., & Johnson, V. E. (1970). *Human sexual inadequacy.* New York: Bantam Books.

Mataix-Cols, D., do Rosario-Campos, M. C., & Leckman, J. F. (2005). A multidimensional model of obsessive-compulsive disorder. *American Journal of Psychiatry, 162,* 228–238.

Mather, C. (2005). Accusations of genital theft: A case from northern Ghana. *Culture, Medicine and Psychiatry, 29,* 33–52.

Mathew, S. J., Coplan, J. D., & Gorman, J. M. (2001). Neurobiological mechanisms of social anxiety disorder. *American Journal of Psychiatry, 158,* 1558–1567.

Mathews, A., Mogg, K., May, J., & Eysenck, M. (1989). Implicit and explicit memory bias in anxiety. *Journal of Abnormal Psychology, 98,* 236–240.

Mathews, M., Basily, B., & Mathews, M. (2006). Better outcomes for schizophrenia in non-Western countries. *Psychiatric Services, 57,* 143–144.

Matijevic, T., Knezevic, J., Slavica, M., & Pavelic, J. (2009). Rett syndrome: From the gene to the disease. *European Neurology, 61,* 3–10.

Matson, J. L., Minshawi, N. F., Gonzalez, M. L., & Mayville, S. B. (2006). Relationship of comorbid problem behaviors to social skills in persons with profound mental retardation. *Behavior Modification, 30,* 496–506.

Matsunaga, H., Maebayashi, K., Hayashida, K., Okino, K., Matsui, T., et al. (2007). Symptom structure in Japanese patients with obsessive-compulsive disorder. *American Journal of Psychiatry, 165,* 251–253.

Matt, G. E., Vazquez, C., & Campbell, W. K. (1992). Mood-congruent recall of affectively toned stimuli: A meta-analytic review. *Clinical Psychology Review, 12,* 227–255.

Maughan, B., & Rutter, M. (2001). Antisocial children grown up. In J. Hill & B. Maughan (Eds.), *Conduct disorders in childhood and adolescence* (pp. 507–552). New York: Cambridge University Press.

Maurer, K. (2001). Overview of the oestrogen protection hypothesis in schizophrenia 2001 [abstract S47]. *Archives of Women's Mental Health, 3(suppl 2),* 12.

Maurer, K., & Häfner, H. (1995). Methodological aspects of onset assessment in schizophrenia. *Schizophrenia Research, 15,* 265–276.

Mauro, T. (2007, January 4). Rehnquist FBI File sheds new light on drug dependence, confirmation battles. *Legal Times.* Retrieved August 1, 2007, from www.law.com/jsp/law/LawArticleFriendly.jsp?id=1167818524831

Mausner-Dorsch, H., & Eaton, W. W. (2000). Psychosocial work environment and depression: Epidemiologic assessment of the demand-control model. *American Journal of Public Health, 90,* 1765–1770.

Mayer, P., & Ziaian, T. (2002). Suicide, gender, and age variations in India: Are women in Indian society protected from suicide? *Crisis, 23,* 98–103.

Mayou, R., & Farmer, A. (2002). Functional somatic symptoms and syndromes. *British Medical Journal, 325,* 265–268.

Mayou, R., Kirmayer, L. J., Simon, G., Kroenke, K., & Sharpe, M. (2005). Somatoform disorders: Time for a new approach in DSM-V. *American Journal of Psychiatry, 162,* 847–855.

Mays, V. M., & Cochran, S. D. (2001). Mental health correlates of perceived discrimination among lesbian, gay, and bisexual adults in the United States. *American Journal of Public Health, 91,* 1869–1876.

Maysles, A. (Director). (2006). *The Beales of Grey Gardens.* Available from The Criterion Collection, New York, NY.

Maysles, D., & Maysles, A. (1976). *Grey Gardens* [Motion picture]. (Available from The Criterion Collection, Irvington, NY).

McAnulty, R. D., Adams, H. E., & Dillon, J. (2001). Sexual deviations: Paraphilias. In P. B. Sutker & H. E. Adams (Eds.), *Comprehensive handbook of psychopathology* (3rd ed., pp. 749–773). New York: Academic/Plenum.

McArthur, J. C., Haughey, N., Gartner, S., Conant, K., Pardo, C., et al. (2003). Human immunodeficiency virus-associated dementia: An evolving disease. *Journal of Neurovirology, 9,* 205–221.

McBride, W. J., Murphy, J. M., Lumeng, L., & Li, T.-K. (1990). Serotonin, dopamine and GABA involvement in alcohol drinking of selectively bred rats. *Alcohol, 7,* 199–205.

McCabe, M. P., & Ricciardelli, L. A. (2001a). Body image and body change techniques among young adolescent boys. *European Eating Disorders Review, 9,* 335–347.

McCabe, M. P., & Ricciardelli, L. A. (2001b). Parent, peer and media influences on body image and strategies to both increase and decrease body size among adolescent boys and girls. *Adolescence, 36,* 225–240.

McCabe, O. L. (2004). Crossing the quality chasm in behavioral health care: The role of evidence-based practice. *Professional Psychology: Research & Practice, 35,* 571–579.

McCandliss, B., Cohen, L., & Dehaene, S. (2003). The visual word form area: Expertise in reading in the fusiform gyrus. *Trends in Cognitive Sciences, 7,* 293–299.

McCook, A. (2002, October 8). More suicide deaths in high altitude U.S. states. *Reuters Health.* Retrieved November 4, 2002, from www.nlm.nih.gov/medlineplus/news/fullstory_9779.html

McDermott, E., & de Silva, P. (2005). Impaired neuronal glucose uptake in pathogenesis of schizophrenia—can GLUT 1 and GLUT 3 deficits explain imaging, post-mortem and pharmacological findings? *Medical Hypotheses, 65,* 1076–1081.

McDermott, S., Moran, R., Platt, T., Issac, T., Wood, H., & Dasari, S. (2005). Depression in adults with disabilities, in primary care. *Disability and Rehabilitation: An International, Multidisciplinary Journal, 27,* 117–123.

McElwain, J. & Paisner, D. (2008). *The game of my life.* New York: New American Library.

McElroy, S. L., Altshuler, L. L., Suppes, T., Keck, P. E., Jr., Frye, M. A., et al. (2001). Axis I psychiatric comorbidity and its relationship to historical illness variables in 288 patients with bipolar disorder. *American Journal of Psychiatry, 158,* 420–426.

McElroy, S. L., Casuto, L. S., Nelson, E. B., Lake, K. A., Soutullo, C. A., et al. (2000). Placebo-controlled trial of sertraline in the treatment of binge eating disorder. *American Journal of Psychiatry, 157,* 1004–1006.

McEvoy, J. P., Lieberman, J. A., Perkins, D. A., Hamer, R. M., Gu, H., et al. (2007). Efficacy and tolerability of olanzapine, quetiapine, and risperidone in the treatment of early psychosis: A randomized, double-blind 52-week comparison. *American Journal of Psychiatry, 164,* 1050–1060.

McEvoy, J. P., Lieberman, J. A., Stroup, T. S., Rosenheck, R., Swartz, M. S., et al. (for the CATIE Investigators). (2006). Effectiveness of clozapine versus olanzapine, quetiapine, and risperidone in patients with chronic schizophrenia who did not respond to prior atypical antipsychotic treatment. *American Journal of Psychiatry, 163,* 600–612.

McEvoy, M., Mahoney, A., Perini, S. J., & Kingsep, P. (in press). Changes in postevent processing and metacognitions during cognitive behavioral group therapy for social phobia. *Journal of Anxiety Disorders, np.*

McEwen, B. S. (2001). Commentary on PTSD discussion. *Hippocampus, 11,* 82–84.

McFarlane, A. C., Atchison, M., & Yehuda, R. (1997). The acute stress response following motor vehicle accidents and its relations to PTSD. *Annals of the New York Academy of Science, 821,* 437–441.

McFarlane, W. R., Cornblatt, B., & Carter, C. S. (2012). Early intervention in psychosis: Rationale, results and implications for treatment of adolescents at risk. *Adolescent Psychiatry, 2(2),* 125–139.

McGlashan, T. H., & Fenton, W. S. (1993). Subtype progression and pathophysiologic deterioration in early schizophrenia. *Schizophrenia Bulletin, 19,* 71–84.

McGlashan, T. H., & Hoffman, R. E. (2000). Schizophrenia as a disorder of developmentally reduced synaptic connectivity. *Archives of General Psychiatry, 57,* 637–648.

McGlashan, T. H., Grilo, C. M., Skodol, A. E., Gunderson, J. G., Shea, M. T., et al. (2000). The Collaborative Longitudinal Personality Disorders Study: Baseline Axis I/II and II/II diagnostic co-occurrence. *Acta Psychiatrica Scandinavica, 102,* 256–264.

McGoldrick, M., Giordano, J., & Pearce, J. K. (Eds.). (1996). *Ethnicity and family therapy* (2nd ed.). New York: Guilford Press.

McGorry, P. (2001). Early psychosis—Gender aspects of treatment. Presentation at 1st World Congress on Women's Mental Health, March 27–31, Berlin, Germany.

McGorry, P. D. (2010). Risk syndromes, clinical staging and DSM V: New diagnostic infrastructure for early intervention in psychiatry. *Schizophrenia Research, 120*(1–3), 49–53.

McGorry, P. D. (2012). Truth and reality in early intervention. *Australian and New Zealand Journal of Psychiatry, 46*(4), 313–316.

McGorry, P. D., & Edwards, J. (2002). Response to "The prevention of schizophrenia: What interventions are safe and effective?" *Schizophrenia Bulletin, 28,* 177–180.

McGorry, P. D., Yung, A. R., Phillips, L. J., Yuen, H. P., Francey, S., et al. (2002). Randomized controlled trial of interventions designed to reduce the risk of progression to first-episode psychosis in a clinical sample with subthreshold symptoms. *Archives of General Psychiatry, 59,* 921–928.

McGough, J. J., & Barkley, R. A. (2004). Diagnostic controversies in adult attention deficit hyperactivity disorder. *American Journal of Psychiatry, 161,* 1948–1956.

McGough, J. J., & McCracken, J. T. (2006). Adult attention deficit hyperactivity disorder: Moving beyond DSM-IV. *American Journal of Psychiatry, 163,* 1673–1675.

McGowin, D. (1993). *Living in the labyrinth: A personal journal through the maze of Alzheimer's.* New York: Delacorte Press.

McGrath, J. J. (2006). Variations in the incidence of schizophrenia: Data versus dogma. *Schizophrenia Bulletin, 32,* 195–197.

McGrath, P. J., Stewart, J. W., Quitkin, F. M., Chen, Y., Alpert, J. E., et al. (2006). Predictors of relapse in a prospective study of fluoxetine treatment of major depression. *American Journal of Psychiatry, 163,* 1542–1548.

McGue, M., & Iacono, W. G. (2005). The association of early adolescent problem behavior with adult psychopathology. *American Journal of Psychiatry, 162,* 1118–1124.

McGue, M., Pickens, R. W., & Svikis, D. S. (1992). Sex and age effects on the inheritance of alcohol problems: A twin study. *Journal of Abnormal Psychology, 101,* 3–17.

McGuffin, P., Katz, R., Aldrich, J., & Bebbington, P. (1988). The Camberwell Collaborative Depression Study. II. Investigation of family members. *British Journal of Psychiatry, 152,* 766–774.

McGuffin, P., Rijsdijk, F., Andrew, M., Sham, P., Katz, R., & Cardno, A. (2003). The heritability of bipolar affective disorder and the genetic relationship to unipolar depression. *Archives of General Psychiatry, 60,* 497–502.

McGurk, S. R., Twamley, E. W., Sitzer, D. I., McHugo, G. J., & Mueser, K. T. (2007). A meta-analysis of cognitive remediation in schizophrenia. *American Journal of Psychiatry, 164,* 1791–1802.

McHugh, P. (1993). Multiple personality disorder. *Harvard Medical School Mental Health Letter, 10,* 4–6.

McHugh, P. R., & Slavney, P. R. (2012). Mental illness—Comprehensive evaluation or checklist? *New England Journal of Medicine, 366,* 1853–1855.

McHugh, P. R., & Treisman, G. (2007). PTSD: A problematic diagnostic category. *Journal of Anxiety Disorders, 21,* 211–222.

McInerney, R. J., & Kerns, K. A. (2003). Time reproduction in children with ADHD: Motivation matters. *Child Neuropsychology, 9,* 91–108.

McIntosh, J. L. (2003). *U.S.A. suicide: Official final data 2001.* Retrieved January 19, 2004, from www.suicidology.org/associations/1045/files/2001datapg.pdf

McIntosh, V. V. W., Jordan, J., Carter, F. A., Luty, S. E., McKenzie, J. M., et al. (2005). Three psychotherapies for anorexia nervosa: A randomized, controlled trial. *American Journal of Psychiatry, 162,* 741–747.

McKay, D., & Neziroglu, F. (1996). Social skills training in a case of obsessive-compulsive disorder with schizotypal personality disorder. *Journal of Behavior Therapy and Experimental Psychiatry, 27,* 189–194.

McKendrick, K., Sullivan, C., Banks, S., & Sacks, S. (2007). Modified therapeutic community treatment for offenders with MICA disorders: Antisocial personality disorder and treatment outcomes. *Journal of Offender Rehabilitation, 44,* 133–159.

McKenna, K. (2004). *Talk to her: Interview.* Seattle, WA: Fantagraphics Books.

McKetin, R., Lubman, D. I., Baker, A. L., Dawe, S. & Ali, R. L. (2013). Dose-related psychotic symptoms in chronic methamphetamine users: Evidence from a prospective longitudinal study. *JAMA Psychiatry, 70,* 319–324.

McLeod, D. S., Koenen, K. C., Meyer, J. M., Lyons, M. J., Eisen, S., et al. (2001). Genetic and environmental influences on the relationship among combat exposure, posttraumatic stress disorder symptoms, and alcohol use. *Journal of Traumatic Stress, 14,* 259–275.

McMullin, R. E. (1986). *Handbook of cognitive therapy techniques.* New York: Norton.

McNally, R. J. (1994). *Panic disorder: A critical analysis.* New York: Guilford Press.

McNally, R. J. (2002). On nonassociative fear emergence. *Behaviour Research and Therapy, 40,* 169–172.

McNally, R. J. (2003) Progress and controversy in the study of posttraumatic stress disorder. *Annual Review of Psychology, 54,* 229–252.

McNally, R. J. (2007). Can we solve the mysteries of the National Vietnam Veterans Readjustment Study? *Journal of Anxiety Disorders, 21,* 192–200.

McNally, R. J., & Kohlbeck, P. A. (1993). Reality monitoring in obsessive-compulsive disorder. *Behaviour Research and Therapy, 31,* 249–253.

McNally, R. J., & Shin, L. M. (1995). Association of intelligence with severity of posttraumatic stress disorder symptoms in Vietnam combat veterans. *American Journal of Psychiatry, 152,* 936–938.

McNally, R. J., Lasko, N. B., Macklin, M. L., & Pitman, R. K. (1995). Autobiographical memory disturbance in combat-related posttraumatic stress disorder. *Behaviour Research and Therapy, 33,* 619–630.

McNamara, B., Ray, J. L., Arthurs, O. J., & Boniface S. (2001). Transcranial magnetic stimulation for depression and other psychiatric disorders. *Psychological Medicine, 31,* 1141–1146.

McNeil, T. F., Cantor-Graae, E., & Weinberger, D. R. (2000). Relationship of obstetric complications and differences in size of brain structures in monozygotic twin pairs discordant for schizophrenia. *American Journal of Psychiatry, 157,* 203–212.

McNiel, D. E., & Binder, R. L. (2007). Effectiveness of a mental health court in reducing criminal recidivism and violence. *American Journal of Psychiatry, 164,* 1395–1403.

McQuiston, J. T. (1995, February 17). Commuter killing trial goes to jury: Ferguson gives incoherent summation. *Houston Chronicle,* p. A2.

McRae, A. L., Budney, A. J., & Brady, K. T. (2003). Treatment of marijuana dependence: A review of the literature. *Journal of Substance Abuse Treatment, 24,* 369–376.

McSherry, B., & Keyzer, P. (Eds.). (2011). *International perspectives on forensic mental health. Dangerous people: Policy, prediction, and practice.* New York: Routledge/Taylor & Francis Group.

McWilliams, S., Hill, S., Mannion, N., Fetherston, A., Kinsella, A., & O'Callaghan, E. (2012). Schizophrenia: A five-year follow-up of patient outcome following psycho-education for caregivers. *European Psychiatry, 27*(1), 56–61.

Meana, J. J., Barturen, F., & Garcia-Sevilla, J. J. (1992). 1a-sub-2-adrenoceptors in the brain of suicide victims: Increased receptor density associated with major depression. *Biological Psychiatry, 31,* 471–490.

Meares, R., Mendelsohn, F. A., & Milgrom-Friedman, J. (1981). A sex difference in the seasonal variation of suicide rate: A single cycle for men, two cycles for women. *British Journal of Psychiatry, 138,* 321–325.

Medford, N., Brierley, B., Brammer, M., Bullmore, E. T., David, A. S., & Phillips, M. L. (2006). Emotional memory in depersonalization disorder: A functional MRI study. *Psychiatry Research, 148,* 93–102.

Mednick, S. A., Gabrielli, W. F., & Hutchings, B. (1984). Genetic influences in criminal convictions: Evidence from an adoption cohort. *Science, 224,* 891–894.

Mednick, S. A., Watson, J. B., Huttunen, M., Cannon, T. D., Katila, H., et al. (1998). A two-hit working model of the etiology of schizophrenia. In M. F. Lenzenweger & R. H. Dworkin (Eds.), *Origins and development of schizophrenia: Advances in experimental psychopathology* (pp. 27–66). Washington, DC: American Psychological Association.

Meehl, P. (1960). The cognitive activity of the clinician. *American Psychologist, 15,* 19–27.

Meehl, P. E. (1962). Schizotaxia, schizotypy, schizophrenia. *American Psychologist, 12,* 827–838.

Mehler, P. S. (2001). Diagnosis and care of patients with anorexia nervosa in primary care settings. *Annals of Internal Medicine, 134,* 1048–1059.

Mehler, P. S. (2003). Osteoporosis in anorexia nervosa: Prevention and treatment. *International Journal of Eating Disorders, 33,* 113–126.

Mehta, M. M., Moriarty, K. J., Proctor, D., Bird, M., & Darling, W. (2006). Alcohol misuse in older people: Heavy consumption and protean presentations. *Journal of Epidemiology & Community Health, 60,* 1048–1052.

Meier, M. H., Caspi, A., Ambler, A., Harrington, H., Houts, R., et al. (2012). Persistent cannabis users show neuropsychological decline from childhood to midlife. *PNAS Proceedings of the National Academy of Sciences of the United States of America, 109,* E2657–E2664.

Melartin, T. K., Rytsälä, H. J., Leskelä, U. S., Lestelä-Mielonen, P. S., Sokero, T. P., & Isometsä, E. T. (2004). Severity and comorbidity predict episode duration and recurrence of DSM-IV major depressive disorder. *Journal of Clinical Psychiatry, 65,* 810–819.

Melfi, C., Croghan, T., Hanna, M., & Robinson, R. (2000). Racial variation in antidepressant treatment in a Medicaid population. *Journal of Clinical Psychiatry, 61,* 16–21.

Melinder, M. R., & Barch, D. M. (2003). The influence of a working memory load manipulation on language production in schizophrenia. *Schizophrenia Bulletin, 29,* 473–485.

Mellon, M. W., & McGrath, M. L. (2000). Empirically supported treatments in pediatric psychology: Nocturnal enuresis. *Journal of Pediatric Psychology, 25,* 193–214.

Meloy, J. R. (1988). *The psychopathic mind: Origins, dynamics, and treatment.* Northvale, NJ: Aronson.

Mendez, M. F., & Cummings, J. L. (2004). Neuropsychiatric aspects of aphasia. In S. C. Yudofsky & R. E. Hales (Eds.), *Essentials of neuropsychiatry and clinical neurosciences* (pp. 189–200). Arlington, VA: American Psychiatric Publishing.

Mennin, D. S., Turk, C. L., Heimberg, R. G., & Carmin, C. (2004). Regulation of emotion in generalized anxiety disorder. In M. A. Reinecke & D. A. Clark (Eds.), *Cognitive therapy across the lifespan: Evidence and practice* (pp. 60–89). New York: Cambridge University Press.

Menzies, R. G., & Clarke, J. C. (1993a). The etiology of childhood water phobia. *Behaviour Research and Therapy, 31,* 499–501.

Menzies, R. G., & Clarke, J. C. (1993b). The etiology of fear of heights and its relationship to severity and individual response patterns. *Behaviour Research and Therapy, 31,* 355–365.

Menzies, R. G., & Clarke, J. C. (1995a). The etiology of phobias: A nonassociative account. *Clinical Psychology Review, 15,* 23–48.

Menzies, R. G., & Clarke, J. C. (1995b). The etiology of acrophobia and its relationship to severity and individual response patterns. *Behaviour Research and Therapy, 33,* 795–803.

Menzies, R. G., & Parker, L. (2001). The origins of height fear: An evaluation of neoconditioning explanations. *Behaviour Research and Therapy, 39,* 185–199.

Mercer, C. H., Fenton, K. A., Johnson, A. M., Wellings, K., Macdowall, W., et al. (2003). Sexual function problems and help seeking behaviour in Britain: National probability sample survey. *British Medical Journal, 327,* 426–427.

Merckelbach, H., Devilly, G. J., & Rassin, E. (2002). Alters in dissociative identity disorder: Metaphors or genuine entities? *Clinical Psychology Review, 22,* 481–497.

Merikangas, K. R., Akiskal, H. S., Angst, J., Greenberg, P. E., Hirschfeld, R. M. A., et al. (2007). Lifetime and 12-month prevalence of bipolar spectrum disorder in the National Comorbidity Survey Replication. *Archives of General Psychiatry, 64,* 543–552.

Merikangas, K. R., Jin, R., He, J. P., Kessler, R. C., Lee, S., et al. (2011). Prevalence and correlates of bipolar spectrum disorder in the world mental health survey initiative. *Archives of General Psychiatry, 68,* 241–251.

Merskey, H. (2004). Somatization, hysteria, or incompletely explained symptoms? *Canadian Journal of Psychiatry, 49,* 649–651.

Messer, S. B. (1992). A critical examination of belief structures in integrative and eclectic psychotherapy. In J. C. Norcross & M. R. Goldfried (Eds.), *Handbook of psychotherapy integration* (pp. 130–165). New York: Basic Books.

Messer, S. B. (2003). Introduction to the special issue on assimilative integration. *Journal of Psychotherapy Integration, 11,* 1–4.

Messer, S. B. (2004). Evidence-based practice: Beyond empirically supported treatments. *Professional Psychology: Research & Practice, 35,* 580–588.

Messer, S. B., & Wampold, B. E. (2002). Let's face facts: Common factors are more potent than specific therapy ingredients. *Clinical Psychology: Science and Practice, 9,* 21–25.

Messias, E., & Kirkpatrick, B. (2001). Summer birth and deficit schizophrenia in the Epidemiological Catchment Area study. *Journal of Nervous and Mental Disease, 189,* 608–612.

Meston, C. M., Hull, E., Levin, R. J., & Sipski, M. (2004). Disorders of orgasm in women. *Journal of Sexual Medicine, 1,* 66–68.

Metalsky, G. I., Joiner, T. E., Hardin, T. S., & Abramson, L. Y. (1993). Depressive reactions to failure in a naturalistic setting: A test of the hopelessness and self-esteem theories of depression. *Journal of Abnormal Psychology, 102,* 101–109.

Meuret, A. E., Rosenfield, D., Wilhelm, F. H., Zhou, E., Conrad, A., et al. (2011). Do unexpected panic attacks occur spontaneously? *Biological Psychiatry, 70,* 985–991.

Meyer, B. (2002). Personality and mood correlates of avoidant personality disorder. *Journal of Personality Disorders, 16,* 174–188.

Meyer, G. J. (2002a). Exploring possible ethnic differences and bias in the Rorschach Comprehensive System. *Journal of Personality Assessment, 78,* 104–129.

Meyer, G. J. (2002b). Implications of information-gathering methods for a refined taxonomy of psychopathology. In L. E. Beutler & M. L. Malik (Eds.), *Rethinking the DSM: A psychological perspective* (pp. 69–105). Washington, DC: American Psychological Association.

Meyer, G. J., & Archer, R. P. (2001). The hard science of Rorschach research: What do we know and where do we go? *Psychological Assessment, 13,* 486–502.

Meyer, J. A., Mundy, P. C., van Hecke, A. V., & Durocher, J. S. (2006). Social attribution processes and comorbid psychiatric symptoms in children with Asperger syndrome. *Autism, 10,* 383–402.

Meyer, R. G., & Weaver, C. M. (2006). *Law and mental health: A case-based approach.* New York: Guilford Press.

Meyer, U. (2013). Developmental neuroinflammation and schizophrenia. *Progress in Neuro-Psychopharmacology & Biological Psychiatry, 42,* 20–34.

Mezey, G. & Robbins, I. (2001). Usefulness and validity of post-traumatic stress disorder as a psychiatric category. *British Medical Journal, 323,* 561–563.

Mezulis, A. H., Abramson, L. Y., Hyde, J. S., & Hankin, B. L. (2004). Is there a universal positivity bias in attributions? A meta-analytic review of individual, developmental, and cultural differences in the self-serving attributional bias. *Psychological Bulletin, 130,* 711–747.

Micallef, J., & Blin, O. (2001). Neurobiology and clinical pharmacology of obsessive-compulsive disorder. *Clinical Neuropharmacology, 24,* 191–207.

Michael, N., Erfrth, A., Ohrmann, P., Gössling, M., Arold, V., et al. (2003). Acute mania is accompanied by elevated glutamate/glutamine levels within the left dorsolateral prefrontal cortex. *Psychopharmacology, 168,* 344–346.

Middleton, K. L., Willner, J., & Simmons, K. M. (2002). Natural disasters and post-traumatic stress disorder symptom complex: Evidence from the Oklahoma tornado outbreak. *International Journal of Stress Management, 9,* 229–236.

Midence, K., & Hargreaves, I. (1997). Psychosocial adjustment in male-to-female transsexuals: An overview of the research evidence. *Journal of Psychology: Interdisciplinary and Applied, 131,* 602–614.

Miethe, T. D., Lu, H., & Reese, E. (2000). Reintegrative shaming and recidivism risk in drug court: Explanations for some unexpected findings. *Crime and Delinquency, 46,* 522–541.

Mikkelsen, E. J. (2001). Enuresis and encopresis: Ten years of progress. *Journal of the American Academy of Child & Adolescent Psychiatry, 40,* 1146–1158.

Miklowitz, D. J. (2004). The role of family systems in severe and recurrent psychiatric disorders: A developmental psychopathology view. *Development and Psychopathology, 16,* 667–688.

Miklowitz, D. J. (2008). Adjunctive psychotherapy for bipolar disorders: State of the evidence. *American Journal of Psychiatry, 165,* 1408–1419.

Miklowitz, D. J., George, E. L., Richards, J. A., Simoneau, T. L., & Suddath, R. L. (2003). A randomized study of family-focused psychoeducation and pharmacotherapy in the outpatient management of bipolar disorder. *Archives of General Psychiatry, 60,* 904–912.

Miklowitz, D. J., Goldstein, M. J., Nuechterlein, K. H., Snyder, K. S., & Mintz, J. (1988). Family factors and the course of bipolar affective disorder. *Archives of General Psychiatry, 45,* 225–231.

Miklowitz, D. J., Otto, M. W., Frank, E., Reilly-Harrington, N. A., Kogan, J. N., et al. (2007). Intensive psychosocial intervention enhances functioning in patients with bipolar depression: Results from a 9-month randomized controlled trial. *American Journal of Psychiatry, 164,* 1340–1347.

Miklowitz, D. J., Simoneau, T. L., George, E. L., Richards, J. A., Kalbag, A., et al. (2000). Family-focused treatment of bipolar disorder: 1-year effects of a psychoeducational programme in conjunction with pharmacotherapy. *Biological Psychiatry 48,* 582–592.

Mikton, C., & Grounds, A. (2007). Cross-cultural clinical judgment bias in personality disorder diagnosis by forensic psychiatrists in the UK: A case-vignette study. *Journal of Personality Disorders, 21,* 400–417.

Mikulincer, M. (1994). *Human learned helplessness: A coping perspective.* New York: Plenum Press.

Milak, M. S., Parsey, R. V., Keilp, J., Oquendo, M. A., Malone, K. M., & Mann, J. J. (2005). Neuroanatomic correlates of psychopathologic components of major depressive disorder. *Archives of General Psychiatry, 62,* 397–408.

Milich, R. (1994). The response of children with ADHD to failure: If at first you don't succeed, do you try, try, again? *School Psychology Review, 23,* 11–18.

Miller, J. J., Fletcher, K., & Kabat-Zinn, J. (1995). Three-year follow-up and clinical implications of a mindfulness meditation-based stress reduction intervention in the treatment of anxiety disorders. *General Hospital Psychiatry, 17,* 192–200.

Miller, J. L., Schmidt, L. A., Vaillancourt, T., McDougall, P., & Laliberte, M. (2006). Neuroticism and introversion: A risky combination for disordered eating among a non-clinical sample of undergraduate women. *Eating Behaviors, 7,* 69–78.

Miller, M. (2002). Resilience elements in students with learning disabilities. *Journal of Clinical Psychology, 58,* 291–298.

Miller, R., & Mason, S. E. (2002). *Diagnosis: Schizophrenia.* New York: Columbia University Press.

Miller, W. R. (2001). Motivational enhancement therapy: Description of counseling approach. In J. J. Boren, L. S. Onken, & K. M. Carroll (Eds.), *Approaches to drug abuse counseling* (pp. 89–93). Bethesda, MD: National Institute on Drug Abuse. Available atwww.dualdiagnosis. org/library/nida_00-4151/8.html

Miller, W. R., & Rollnick, S. (1992). *Motivational interviewing* (2nd ed.). New York: Guilford Press.

Miller, W. R., & Seligman, M. E. (1973). Depression and the perception of reinforcement. *Journal of Abnormal Psychology, 82,* 62–73.

Miller, W. R., & Seligman, M. E. (1975). Depression and learned helplessness in man. *Journal of Abnormal Psychology, 84,* 228–238.

Millet, B., Leclaire, M., Bourdel, M. C., Loo, H., Tezcan, E., & Kuloglu, M. (2000). Comparison of sociodemographic, clinical and phenomenological characteristics of Turkish and French patients suffering from obsessive-compulsive disorder. *Canadian Journal of Psychiatry, 45,* 848.

Millon, T. (1981). *Disorders of personality, DSM-III: Axis II.* New York: Wiley.

Millon, T. (1998). DSM-IV narcissistic personality disorder: Historical reflections and future directions. In E. Ronningstam (Ed.), *Disorders of narcissism: Diagnostic, clinical, and empirical implications* (pp. 75–101). Washington, DC: American Psychiatric Press.

Millon, T., & Davis, R. D. (2000). *Personality disorders in modern life.* New York: Wiley.

Mills, T. C., Paul, J., Stall, R., Pollack, L., Canchola, J., et al. (2004). Distress and depression in men who have sex with men: The Urban Men's Health Study. *American Journal of Psychiatry, 161,* 278–285.

Milos, G., Kuenzli, C., Soelch, C. M., Schumacher, S., Moergeli, H., & Mueller-Pfeiffer, C. (2013). How much should I eat? Estimation of meal portions in anorexia nervosa. *Appetite, 63,* 42–47.

Milos, G., Spindler, A., Ruggiero, G., Klaghofer, R., & Schnyder, U. (2002). Comorbidity of obsessive-compulsive disorders and duration of eating disorders. *International Journal of Eating Disorders, 31,* 284–289.

Minde, K. (2003). Assessment and treatment of attachment disorders. *Current Opinion in Psychiatry, 16,* 377–381.

Mineka, S., Cook, M., & Miller, S. (1984). Fear conditioned with escapable and inescapable shock: Effects of a feedback stimulus. *Journal of Experimental Psychology: Animal Behavior Processes, 10,* 307–323.

Mineka, S., Watson, D., & Clark, L. A. (1998). Comorbidity of anxiety and unipolar mood disorders. *Annual Review of Psychology, 49,* 377–412.

Mineka, S., & Zinbarg, R. (1995). Conditioning and ethological models of social phobia. In R. G. Heimberg, M. R. Liebowitz, D. A. Hope, & F. R. Schneier (Eds.), *Social phobia: Diagnosis, assessment, and treatment* (pp. 134–162). New York: Guilford Press.

Miniño, A. M., Arias, E., Kochanek, K. D., Murphy, S. L., & Smith, B. L. (2002). Deaths: Final data for 2000. *National Vital Statistics Reports, 50*(15). Hyattsville, MD: National Center for Health Statistics.

Minshew, N. J., & Williams, D. L. (2007). The new neurobiology of autism: Cortex, connectivity, and neuronal organization. *Archives of Neurology, 64*, 945–950.

Mintz, A. R., Dobson, K. S., & Romney, D. M. (2003). Insight in schizophrenia: A meta-analysis. *Schizophrenia Research, 61*, 75–88.

Minuchin, S. (1974). *Families and family therapy.* Cambridge, MA: Harvard University Press.

Minuchin, S., Rosman, B. L., & Baker, L. (1978). *Psychosomatic families: Anorexia nervosa in context.* Oxford, England: Harvard University Press.

Miranda, J., Azocar, F., Organista, K. C., Dwyer, E., & Areane, P. (2003). Treatment of depression among impoverished primary care patients from ethnic minority groups. *Psychiatric Services, 54*, 219–225.

Miranda, J., Azocar, F., Organista, K., Dwyer, E., & Areane, P. (2000). Treatment of depression in disadvantaged medical patients. Presented at the tenth NIMH international conference on Mental Health Problems in the General Health Care Sector. Bethesda, Maryland.

Mirsky, A. F., & Quinn, O. W. (1988). The Genain quadruplets. *Schizophrenia Bulletin, 14*, 595–612.

Mirsky, A. F., Bieliauskas, L. A., French, L. M., Van Kammen, D. P., Joensson, E., & Sedvall, G. (2000). A 39-year followup on the Genain quadruplets. *Schizophrenia Bulletin, 26*, 699–708.

Mirsky, A., F., Quinn, O. W., DeLisi, L. E., Schwerdt, P., & Buchsbaum, M. S. (1987). The Genain quadruplets: A 25-year follow-up of four monozygous women discordant for the severity of schizophrenic illness. In N. E. Miller & G. D. Cohen (Eds.), *Schizophrenia and aging: Schizophrenia, paranoia, and schizophreniform disorders in later life* (pp. 83–94). New York: Guilford Press.

Misra, S., & Ganzini, L. (2004). Capacity to consent to research among patients with bipolar disorder. *Journal of Affective Disorders, 80*, 115–123.

Mitchell, A. J. (2007). Understanding medication discontinuation in depression. *Psychiatric Times, 24.* Retrieved October 20, 2008, from www.psychiatrictimes.com/display/article/10168/54731

Mitchell, J., O'Neil, J. P., Janabi, M., Marks, S. M., Jagust, W. J., & Fields, H. L. (2012). Alcohol consumption induces endogenous opioid release in the human orbitofrontal cortex and nucleus accumbens. *Science Translational Medicine, 4*, 116ra6.

Mitchell, J. E., Peterson, C. B., Myers, T., & Wonderlich, S. (2001). Combining pharmacotherapy and psychotherapy in the treatment of patients with eating disorders. *Psychiatric Clinics of North America, 24*, 315–323.

Mittal, V. A., Neumann, C., Saczawa, M., & Walker, E. F. (2008). Longitudinal progression of movement abnormalities in relation to psychotic symptoms in adolescents at high risk of schizophrenia. *Archives of General Psychiatry, 65*, 165–171.

Mittendorfer-Rutz, E., Rasmussen, F., & Wasserman, D. (2004). Restricted fetal growth and adverse maternal psychosocial and socioeconomic conditions as risk factors for suicidal behaviour of offspring: A cohort study. *Lancet, 364*, 1135–1140.

Mittleman, M. A., Lewis, R. A., Maclure, M., Sherwood, J. B., & Muller, J. E. (2001). Triggering myocardial infarction by marijuana. *Circulation, 103*, 2805–2809.

Miura, Y., Mizuno, M., Yamashita, C., Watanabe, K., Murakami, M., & Kashima, H. (2004). Expressed emotion and social functioning in chronic schizophrenia. *Comprehensive Psychiatry, 45*, 469–474.

Modell, J. G., Mountz, J. M., Curtis, G. C., & Greden, J. F. (1989). Neurophysiologic dysfunction in basal ganglia/limbic striatal and thalamocortical circuits as a pathogenetic mechanism of obsessive-compulsive disorder. *Journal of Neuropsychiatry & Clinical Neurosciences, 1*, 27–36.

Modell, S., Huber, J., Holsboer, F., & Lauer, C. J. (2003). The Munich Vulnerability Study on Affective Disorders: Risk factors for unipolarity versus bipolarity. *Journal of Affective Disorders, 74*, 173–184.

Moffitt, T. E. (2003). Life-course-persistent and adolescence-limited antisocial behavior: A 10-year research review and a research agenda. In B. B. Lahey, T. E. Moffitt, & A. Caspi (Eds.), *Causes of conduct disorder and juvenile delinquency* (pp. 49–75). New York: Guilford Press.

Moffitt, T. E., & Caspi, A. (2001). Childhood predictors differentiate life-course persistent and adolescence-limited antisocial pathways among males and females. *Development and Psychopathology, 13*, 355–375.

Moffitt, T. E., Caspi, A., Harrington, H., & Milne, B. J. (2002). Males on the life-course-persistent and adolescence-limited antisocial pathways: Follow-up at age 26 years. *Development and Psychopathology, 14*, 179–207.

Moffitt, T. E., Caspi, A., Harrington, H., Milne, B. J., Melchior, M., et al. (2007). Generalized anxiety disorder and depression: Childhood risk factors in a birth cohort followed to age 32. *Psychological Medicine, 37*, 441–452.

Mogg, K., & Bradley, B. P. (2005). Attentional bias in generalized anxiety disorder versus depressive disorder. *Cognitive Therapy and Research, 29*, 29–45.

Mogg, K., Bradley, B. P., & Williams, R. (1995). Attentional bias in anxiety and depression: The role of awareness. *British Journal of Clinical Psychology, 34*, 17–36.

Mogg, K., Millar, N., & Bradley, B. P. (2000). Biases in eye movements to threatening facial expressions in generalized anxiety disorder and depressive disorder. *Journal of Abnormal Psychology, 109*, 695–704.

Mohr, D. C., Hart, S. L., Julian, L., Catledge, C., Honos-Webb, L., et al. (2005). Telephone-administered psychotherapy for depression. *Archives of General Psychiatry, 62*, 1007–1014.

Molfese, D. L. (2000). Predicting dyslexia at 8 years of age using neonatal brain responses. *Brain and Language, 72*, 238–245.

Monahan, J., & Steadman, H. J. (Eds.). (1994). *Violence and mental disorder: Developments in risk assessment.* Chicago: Chicago: University of Chicago Press.

Monahan, J., Steadman, H., Silver, E., Appelbaum, P. S., Robbins, P. C., et al. (2001). *Rethinking risk assessment: The MacArthur study of mental disorder and violence.* New York: Oxford University Press.

Moncrieff, J. (2001). Are antidepressants overrated? A review of methodological problems in antidepressant trials. *Journal of Nervous and Mental Disease, 189*, 288–295.

Moncrieff, J. (2002). The antidepressant debate. *British Journal of Psychiatry, 180*, 193–194.

Moncrieff, J., & Kirsch, I. (2005). Efficacy of antidepressants in adults. *British Medical Journal, 331*, 155–157.

Moncrieff, J., Wessely, S., & Hardy, R. (2001). Antidepressants using active placebos. *Cochrane Database Systematic Review, 2*, CD003012.

Mond, J. M., Hay, P. J., Rodgers, B., & Owen, C. (2006). An update on the definition of "excessive exercise" in eating disorders research. *International Journal of Eating Disorders, 39*, 147–153.

Monk, C. S., Nelson, E. E., McClure, E. B., Mogg, K., Bradley, B. P., et al. (2006). Ventrolateral prefrontal cortex activation and attentional bias in response to angry faces in adolescents with generalized anxiety disorder. *American Journal of Psychiatry, 163*, 1091–1097.

Monroe, S. M., & Simons, A. D. (1991). Diathesis-stress theories in the context of life-stress research: Implications for the depressive disorders. *Psychological Bulletin, 110*, 406–425.

Monroe, S. M., Rohde, P., Seeley, J. R., & Lewinsohn, P. M. (1999). Life events and depression in adolescence: Relationship loss as a prospective risk factor for first onset of major depressive disorder. *Journal of Abnormal Psychology, 108*, 606–661.

Montano, C. B. (1994). Recognition and treatment of depression in a primary care setting. *Journal of Clinical Psychiatry, 55*(12, Suppl), 18–34.

Montgomery, S. A., Schatzberg, A. F., Guelfi, J. D., Kasper, S., Nemeroff, C., et al. (2001). Pharmacotherapy of depression and mixed states in bipolar disorder. *Journal of Affective Disorders, 59*(Suppl. 1), S39–S56.

Monti, P. M., Abrams, D. B., Kadden, R. M., & Cooney, N. L. (1989). *Treating alcohol dependence: A coping skills training guide in the treatment of alcoholism.* New York: Guilford Press.

Moore, C. (2006). *George & Sam: Two boys, One family, and autism.* New York: St. Martin's Press.

Moore, T. H. M., Zammit, S., Lingford-Hughest, A., Barnes, T. R. E., Jones, P. B., et al. (2007). Cannabis use and risk of psychotic or affective mental health outcomes: A systematic review. *Lancet, 370*, 319–328.

Moos, R., & Moos, B. (1986). *Family Environment Scale Manual* (2nd ed.). Palo Alto, CA: Consulting Psychologists Press.

Moos, R. H., & Moos, B. S. (2004). Long-term influence of duration and frequency of participation in Alcoholics Anonymous on individuals with alcohol use disorders. *Journal of Consulting and Clinical Psychology, 72*, 81–90.

Moos, R. H., & Timko, C. (2008). Outcome research on 12-step and other self-help programs. In M. Galanter & H. D. Kleber (Eds.), *The American Psychiatric Publishing textbook of substance abuse treatment* (4th ed., pp. 511–521). Arlington, VA: American Psychiatric Publishing.

Moradi, B., Dirks, D., & Matteson, A. V. (2005). Roles of sexual objectification experiences and internalization of standards of beauty in eating disorder symptomatology: A test and extension of objectification theory. *Journal of Counseling Psychology, 52*, 420–428.

Moran, P. (1999). The epidemiology of antisocial personality disorder. *Social Psychiatry and Psychiatric Epidemiology, 34*, 231–242.

Morey, L. C., Alexander, G. M., & Boggs, C. (2005). Gender. In J. M. Oldham, A. E. Skodol, & D. S. Bender (Eds.), *The American Psychiatric Publishing textbook of personality disorders* (pp. 541–559). Washington, DC: American Psychiatric Publishing.

Morey, L. C., Hopwood, C. J., Markowitz, J. C., Gunderson, J. G., Grilo, C. M., et al. (2012). Comparison of alternative models for personality disorders, II: 6-, 8- and 10-year follow-up. *Psychological Medicine, 42*(8), 1705–1713.

Morey, L. C., Warner, M. B., Shea, M. T., Gunderson, J. G., Sanislow, C. A., et al. (2003). The representation of four personality disorders by the schedule for nonadaptive and adaptive personality dimensional model of personality. *Psychological Assessment, 15*, 326–332.

Morey, R. A., Inan, S., Mitchell, T. V., Perkins, D. O., Lieberman, J. A., & Belger, A. (2005). Imaging frontostriatal function in ultra-high-risk, early, and chronic schizophrenia during executive processing. *Archives of General Psychiatry, 62*, 254–262.

Morgan, C. D., & Murray, H. A. (1935). A method for investigating fantasies: The Thematic Apperception Test. *Archives of Neurological Psychiatry, 34*, 289–306.

Morgan, J. F., & Crisp, A. H. (2000). Use of leukotomy for intractable anorexia nervosa: A long-term follow-up study. *International Journal of Eating Disorders, 27*, 249–258.

Moritz, S., & Woodward, T. S. (2006). The contribution of metamemory deficits to schizophrenia. *Journal of Abnormal Psychology, 115*, 15–25.

Morris, N. (1986). *Insanity defense* (National Institute of Justice Crime File Study Guide). Washington, DC: U.S. Department of Justice, National Institute of Justice/Criminal Justice Reference Service.

Mort, J. R., & Aparasu, R. R. (2002). Prescribing of psychotropics in the elderly: Why is it so often inappropriate? *CNS Drugs, 16*, 99–109.

Mörtberg, E., Karlsson, A., Fyring, C., & Sundin, Ö. (2006). Intensive cognitive-behavioral group treatment (CBGT) of social phobia: A randomized controlled study. *Journal of Anxiety Disorders, 20*, 646–660.

Mortensen, P. B., Pedersen, C. B., Westergaard, T., Wohlfahrt, J., Ewald, H., et al. (1999). Effects of family history and place and season of birth on the risk of schizophrenia. *New England Journal of Medicine, 340*, 603–608.

Moscicki, E. (2001). Epidemiology of suicide. In S. Goldsmith(Ed.), *Risk factors for suicide* (pp. 1–4). Washington, DC: National Academy Press.

Moscicki, E. K. (1995). Epidemiology of suicidal behavior. In M. M. Silverman & R. W. Maris (Eds.), *Suicide prevention: Toward the year 2000* (pp. 22–35). New York: Guilford Press.

Moscicki, E. K. (1997). Identification of suicide risk factors using epidemiologic studies. *Psychiatric Clinics of North America, 20*, 499–517.

Moser, C. (2001). Paraphilia: A critique of a confused concept. In P. J. Kleinplatz (Ed.), *New directions in sex therapy: Innovations and alternatives* (pp. 91–108). Philadelphia: Taylor and Rutledge.

Moser, C. (2009). When is an unusual sexual interest a mental disorder? *Archives of Sexual Behavior, 38*, 323–325.

Moser, C.,& Devereux, M. (2012). Sexual medicine, sex therapy, and sexual health care. In P. J. Kleinplatz (Ed.), *New Directions in Sex Therapy* (2nd ed., pp. 127–139). New York: Routledge.

Moser, C., & Kleinplatz, P. J. (2005). DSM-IV-TR and the paraphilias: An argument for removal. *Journal of Psychology & Human Sexuality, 17*, 91–109.

Mosher, P. W., & Swire, P. P. (2002). The ethical and legal implications of Jaffee v. Redmond and the HIPAA medical privacy rule for psychotherapy and general psychiatry. *Psychiatric Clinics of North America, 25*, 575–584.

Moussaoui, D., el Kadiri, M. Agoub, M., Tazi, I., & Kadri, N. (1999). Depression, suicidal ideation and schizophrenia. *Encephale, 25*, 9–11.

Mowrer, O. H. (1939). A stimulus–response analysis of anxiety and its role as a reinforcing agent. *Psychological Review, 46*, 553–565.

Mowrer, O. H. (1947). On the dual nature of learning: A re-interpretation of "conditioning" and "problem-solving." *Harvard Educational Review, 17*, 102–148.

Moyers, T. (2003). Motivational interviewing. In J. L. Sorensen, R. A. Rawson, J. Guydish, & J. E. Zweben (Eds.), *Drug abuse treatment through collaboration: Practice and research partnerships that work* (pp. 139–150). Washington, DC: American Psychological Association.

Moynihan, R. (2003). The making of a disease: Female sexual dysfunction. *British Medical Journal, 326*, 45–47.

Mrazek, P., & Haggerty, R. (1994). *Reducing risks for mental disorders: Frontiers for preventive intervention research*. Washington, DC: National Academy Press.

Mrug, S., Hoza, B., Gerdes, A. C., Hinshaw, S., Arnold, L. E., et al. (2009). Discriminating between children with ADHD and classmates using peer variables. *Journal of Attention Disorders, 12*, 372–380.

Mueser, K. T., Bond, G. R., Drake, R. E., & Resnick, S. G. (1998). Models of community care for severe mental illness: A review of research on case management. *Schizophrenia Bulletin, 24*, 37–74.

Mueser, K. T., Goodman, L. B., Trumbetta, S. L., Rosenberg, S. D., Osher, F. C., et al. (1998). Trauma and posttraumatic stress disorder in severe mental illness. *Journal of Consulting and Clinical Psychology, 66*, 493–499.

Muhle, R., Trentacoste, S. V., & Rapin, I. (2004). The genetics of autism. *Pediatrics, 113*, e472–e486.

Muir, S. L., Wertheim, E. H., & Paxton, S. J. (1999). Adolescent girls' first diets: Triggers and the role of multiple dimensions of self-concept. *Eating Disorders: The Journal of Treatment & Prevention, 7*, 259–227.

Mulas, F., Capilla, A., Fernández, S., Etchepareborda, M. C., Campo, P., et al. (2006). Shifting-related brain magnetic activity in attention-deficit/hyperactivity disorder. *Biological Psychiatry, 59*, 373–379.

Mulder, R. T., & Joyce, P. R. (1997). Temperament and the structure of personality disorder symptoms. *Psychological Medicine, 27*, 99–106.

Mulholland, A. M., & Mintz, L. B. (2001). Prevalence of eating disorders among African American women. *Journal of Counseling Psychology, 48*, 111–116.

Mullen, R. (2003). The problem of bizarre delusions. *Journal of Nervous and Mental Disease, 191*, 546–548.

Muller, J., & Roberts, J. E. (2005). Memory and attention in obsessive-compulsive disorder: A review. *Journal of Anxiety Disorders, 19*, 1–28.

Muller, N., & Schwarz, M. (2006). Schizophrenia as an inflammation-mediated dysbalance of glutamatergic neurotransmission. *Neurotox Research, 10*, 131–148.

Müller, T., Mannel, M., Murck, H., & Rahlfs, V. W. (2004). Treatment of somatoform disorders with St. John's wort: A randomized, double-blind and placebo-controlled trial. *Psychosomatic Medicine, 66*, 538–547.

Mulvany, F., O'Callaghan, E., Takei, N., Byrne, M., Fearon, P., & Larkin, C. (2001). Effect of social class at birth on risk and presentation of schizophrenia: Case-control study. *BMJ: British Medical Journal, 323*, 1398–1401.

Munafò, M. R., Clark, T. G., Roberts, K. H., & Johnstone, E. C. (2006). Neuroticism mediates the association of the serotonin transporter gene with lifetime major depression. *Neuropsychobiology, 53,* 1–8.

Mundo, E., Richter, M. A., Sam, F., Macciardi, F., & Kennedy, J. L. (2000). Is the 5-HT-sub(1Dβ) receptor gene implicated in the pathogenesis of obsessive-compulsive disorder? *American Journal of Psychiatry, 157,* 1160–1161.

Mundo, E., Walker, M., Tims, H., Macciardi, F., & Kennedy, J. L. (2000). Lack of linkage disequilibrium between serotonin transporter protein gene (SLC6A4) and bipolar disorder. *American Journal of Medical Genetics, 96,* 379–383.

Munroe, R. L., & Gauvain, M. (2001). Why the paraphilias? Domesticating strange sex. *Cross-Cultural Research: The Journal of Comparative Social Science, 35,* 44–64.

Murias, M. A., Webb, S. J., Merkle, K., Greenson, J., & Dawson, G. (2006, October 14). Spontaneous EEG coherence in adults with autism. Poster presented at *Neuroscience 2006* Georgia World Congress Center.

Murphy, L. J., & Mitchell, D. L. (1998). When writing helps to heal: E-mail as therapy. *British Journal of Guidance and Counseling, 26,* 21–32.

Murray, C. J. L., & Lopez, A. D. (Eds.). (1996). *The global burden of disease. A comprehensive assessment of mortality and disability from diseases, injuries, and risk factors in 1990 and projected to 2020.* Cambridge, MA: Harvard School of Public Health.

Murray, H. A. (1943). *Thematic Apperception Test manual.* Cambridge, MA: Harvard University Press.

Murray, L. A., Whitehouse, W. G., & Alloy, L. B. (1999). Mood congruence and depressive deficits in memory: A forced-recall analysis. *Memory, 7,* 175–196.

Myers, J. E. B. (1998). Legal issues in child abuse and neglect practice. Thousand Oaks, CA: Sage.

Myin-Germeys, I., Delespaul, P. A. E. G., & deVries, M. W. (2000). Schizophrenia patients are more emotionally active than is assumed based on their behavior. *Schizophrenia Bulletin, 26,* 847–853.

Nahas, Z., Kozel, F. A., Li, X., Anderson, B., & George, M. S. (2003). Left prefrontal transcranial magnetic stimulation (TMS) treatment of depression in bipolar affective disorder: A pilot study of acute safety and efficacy. *Bipolar Disorders, 5,* 40–47.

Nahas, Z., Kozel, F. A., Li, X., Anderson, B., George, M. S. (2003). Left prefrontal transcranial magnetic stimulation (TMS) treatment of depression in bipolar affective disorder: A pilot study of acute safety and efficacy. *Bipolar Disorders, 5,* 40–47.

Narrow, W. E., & Kuhl, E. A. (2011). Clinical significance and disorder thresholds in DSM-5: The role of disability and distress. In D. A. Regier, W. E. Narrow, E. A. Kuhl, & D. J. Kupfer (Eds.), *The Conceptual Evolution of DSM-5* (pp. 147–162). Arlington, VA: American Psychiatric Publishing.

Nathan, P. E., Skinstad, A. H., & Dolan, S. L. (2000). Clinical psychology II. Psychological treatments: Research and practice. In K. Pawlik & M.R. Rosenzweig (Eds.), *International handbook of psychology* (pp. 429–451). Thousand Oaks, CA: Sage Publications.

Nathan, P. E., Stuart, S. P., & Dolan, S. L. (2000). Research on psychotherapy efficacy and effectiveness: Between Scylla and Charybdis? *Psychological Bulletin, 126,* 964–981.

National Center for Health Statistics. (2008). *Diagnosed attention deficit hyperactivity disorder and learning disability: United States, 2004–2006.* DHHS Publication No. (PHS) 2008-1565, Series 10, No. 237. Retrieved February 15, 2009, from www.cdc.gov/nchs/data/series/sr_10/sr10_237.pdf

National Collaborating Centre for Mental Health. (2005) Post-Traumatic Stress Disorder. The Management of PTSD in Adults and Children in Primary and Secondary Care. *NICE Clinical Guidelines, 26.* Leicester, UK: Gaskell.

National Committee for Quality Assurance. (2007). *The state of health care quality 2007.* Washington, DC: Author.

National Depressive and Manic Depressive Association. (2002). *Suicide prevention.* Retrieved Month 01, 2003, from www.ndmda.org/suicide.html

National Institute on Aging. (2003). *Alzheimer's disease: Unraveling the mystery.* NIH Pub. No: 02-3782. Retrieved December 4, 2007, from www.nia.nih.gov/NR/rdonlyres/A294D332-71A2-4866-BDD7-A0DF216DAAA4/0/Alzheimers_Disease_Unraveling_the_Mystery.pdf

National Institute on Alcohol Abuse and Alcoholism, National Advisory Council. (2004). NIAAA Council approves definition of binge drinking. *NIAAA Newsletter, 3.* Retrieved February 22, 2006, from http://pubs.niaaa.nih.gov/publications/Newsletter/winter2004/Newsletter_Number3.htm#council

National Institute on Alcohol Abuse and Alcoholism. (2005). What is alcoholism? Retrieved December 12, 2005, from www.niaaa.nih.gov/FAQs/General-English/FAQ1.htm

National Institute on Alcohol Abuse and Alcoholism. (2012). FAQs for the General Public. Retrieved March 8, 2012, from www.niaaa.nih.gov/FAQs/General-English/Pages/default.aspx

National Institute on Drug Abuse. (1999). *Principles of drug addiction treatment: A research-based guide* [NIH Publication No. 00-4180]. Bethesda, MD: Author.

National Institute on Drug Abuse. (2000). *The brain: Understanding neurobiology through the study of addiction.* [NIH Publication No. 00-4871]. Bethesda, MD: Author.

National Institute on Drug Abuse. (2001). *NIDA research report series: Hallucinogens and dissociative drugs* [NIH Publication No. 01-4209]. Retrieved December 24, 2008, from www.drugabuse.gov/PDF/PODAT/PODAT.pdf

National Institute on Drug Abuse. (2003). *Drug use among racial/ethnic minorities* [NIH Publication No. 03-3888]. Bethesda, MD: Author.

National Institute on Drug Abuse. (2004). *NIDA research report series: Cocaine: Abuse and addiction* [NIH publication number 99-4342]. Bethesda, MD: Author.

National Institute on Drug Abuse. (2005a). *NIDA research report series: Heroin: Abuse and addiction* [NIH Publication No. 05-4165]. Bethesda, MD: Author.

National Institute on Drug Abuse. (2005b). *NIDA research report series: Marijuana abuse* [NIH publication number 05-3859]. Bethesda, MD: Author.

National Institute on Drug Abuse. (2005c). *NIDA research report series: Prescription drugs: Abuse and addiction* [NIH Publication No. 05-4881]. Bethesda, MD: Author.

National Institute on Drug Abuse. (2006a). NIDA InfoFacts: Costs to society. Retrieved March 12, 2009, from www.drugabuse.gov/Infofacts/costs.html

National Institute on Drug Abuse. (2006b). NIDA InfoFacts: Methylphenidate (Ritalin). Retrieved March 12, 2009, from www.drugabuse.gov/Infofacts/ADHD.html

National Institute on Drug Abuse. (2006c). NIDA research report series: Tobacco addiction [NIH Publication No. 06-4342]. Bethesda, MD: Author.

National Institute on Drug Abuse. (2007a). NIDA InfoFacts: Cigarettes and Other Tobacco Products. Retrieved March 12, 2009, from www.drugabuse.gov/Infofacts/tobacco.html

National Institute on Drug Abuse. (2007b). NIDA InfoFacts: Crack and cocaine. Retrieved March 12, 2009, from www.drugabuse.gov/Infofacts/cocaine.html

National Institute on Drug Abuse. (2007c). NIDA InfoFacts: Heroin. Retrieved March 12, 2009, from www.drugabuse.gov/Infofacts/heroin.html

National Institute on Drug Abuse. (2007d). NIDA InfoFacts: LSD. Retrieved March 12, 2009, from www.drugabuse.gov/pdf/infofacts/Hallucinogens08.pdf

National Institute on Drug Abuse. (2007e). NIDA InfoFacts: MDMA (Ecstasy). Retrieved March 12, 2009, from www.drugabuse.gov/Infofacts/ecstasy.html

National Institute on Drug Abuse. (2007f). NIDA InfoFacts: PCP (Phencyclidine). Retrieved March 12, 2009, from www.drugabuse.gov/Infofacts/hallucinogens.html

National Institute on Drug Abuse. (2007g). *The science of addiction: Drugs, brains, and behavior* [NIH Publication No. 07-5605]. Bethesda, MD: Author.

National Institute on Drug Abuse. (2008a). NIDA InfoFacts: Nationwide trends. Retrieved December 20, 2008, from www.drugabuse.gov/Infofacts/NationTrends08.pdf

National Institute on Drug Abuse. (2008b). NIDA InfoFacts: MDMA (Ecstasy). Retrieved December 20, 2008, from www.drugabuse.gov /PDF/Infofacts/MDMA08.pdf

National Institute on Drug Abuse. (2008c). NIDA InfoFacts: Methamphetamine. Retrieved December 20, 2008, from www.drugabuse.gov /Infofacts/methamphetamine.html

National Institute on Drug Abuse. (2008d). NIDA InfoFacts: Hallucinogens—LSD, peyote, psilocybin and PCP. Retrieved December 20, 2008, from www.drugabuse.gov/Infofacts /hallucinogens.html

National Institute on Drug Abuse. (2008e). InfoFacts: Prescription and over-the-counter medications. Retrieved December 23, 2008, from www.nida.nih.gov/PDF/Infofacts/PainMed08.pdf

National Institute on Drug Abuse. (2008f). NIDA InfoFacts: Treatment approaches for drug addiction. Retrieved December 24, 2008, from www.nida.nih.gov/PDF/InfoFacts/ Treatment08.pdf

National Institute on Drug Abuse. (2012). DrugFacts: Synthetic Cathinones ("Bath Salts"). Retrieved December 16, 2012, from www. drugabuse.gov/publications/drugfacts/synthetic- cathinones-bath-salts

Naughton, A. M., Maguire, S. A., Mann, M. K., Lumb, R. C., Tempest, V., et al. (in press). Emotional, behavioral and develpmenta features indicative of neglect or emotional abuse in preschool children. *JAMA Pediatrics.*

Nazareth, I., Boynton, P., & King, M. (2003). Problems with sexual function in people attending London general practitioners: Cross sectional study. *British Medical Journal, 327,* 423–426.

Neal-Barnett, A. M., & Smith Sr., J. (1997). African Americans. In S. Friedman (Ed.), *Cultural issues in the treatment of anxiety.* (pp. 154–174). New York: Guilford Press.

Neale, M. C., Walter, E. E., Eaves, L. J., Kessler, R. C., Heath, A. C., & Kendler, K. S. (1994). Genetics of blood-injury fears and phobias: A population-based twin study. *American Journal of Medical Genetics, 54,* 326–334.

Neale, T. (2008). ICAD: Biomarkers may help identify pre-clinical Alzheimer's. *Medscape.* Retrieved July 31, 2008, from www. medpagetoday.com/MeetingCoverage/ICAD/ tb/10323.

Nebelkopf, E., & Phillips, M. (2004). *Healing and mentat health for Native Americans: Speaking in red.* Walnut Creek, CA: Altamira Press.

Neighbors, H. W., Trierweiler, S. J., Ford, B. C., & Muroff, J. R. (2003). Racial differences in DSM-IV-TR diagnosis using a semi-structured instrument: The importance of clinical judgment in the diagnosis of African Americans. *Journal of Health & Social Behavior, 44,* 237–256.

Nelson, M. D., Saykin, A. J., Flashman, L. A., & Riordan, H. J. (1998). Hippocampal volume reduction in schizophrenia as assessed by magnetic resonance imaging: A meta-analytic study. *Archives of General Psychiatry, 55,* 433–440.

Nemeroff, C. (1998). The neurobiology of depression. *Scientific American, 278,* 28–35.

Nemeroff, C. B. (2008). Recent findings in the pathophysiology of depression. *Focus, 6,* 3–14.

Nemeroff, C. J., Stein, R. I., Diehl, N. S., & Smilack, K. M. (1994). From the Cleavers to the Clintons: Role choices and body orientation as reflected in magazine article content. *International Journal of Eating Disorders, 16,* 167–176.

Nestadt, G., Samuels, J., Riddle, M., Bienvenu, J., Liang, K-Y., et al. (2000). A family study of obsessive-compulsive disorder. *Archives of General Psychiatry, 57,* 358–363.

Nestler, E. J. (1997). Schizophrenia: An emerging pathophysiology. *Nature, 385,* 578–579.

Neuman, R. J., Lobos, E., Reich, W., Henderson, C. A., Sun, L. W., & Todd, R. D. (2007). Prenatal smoking exposure and dopaminergic genotypes interact to cause a severe ADHD subtype. *Biological Psychiatry, 61,* 1320–1328.

Neumann, C., & Walker, E. F. (1996). Childhood neuromotor soft signs, behavior problems, and adult psychopathology. In T. Ollendick & R. Prinz (Eds.), *Advances in clinical child psychology* (pp. 173–203). New York: Plenum Press.

Neumark-Sztainer, D., Wall, M., Larson, N., Eisenberg, M., & Loth, K. (2011). Dieting and disordered eating behaviors from adolescence to young adulthood: Findings from a 10-year longitudinal study. *Journal of the American Dietetic Association, 111,* 1004–1111.

Neumeister, A., Charney, D. S., & Drevets, W. C. (2005). Depression and the hippocampus. *American Journal of Psychiatry, 162,* 1057.

Neumeister, A., Wood, S., Bonne, O., Nugent, A. C., Luckenbaugh, D. A., et al. (2005). Reduced hippocampal volume in unmedicated, remitted patients with major depression versus control subjects. *Biological Psychiatry, 57,* 935–937.

New, A. S., Hazlett, E. A., Buchsbaum, M. S., Goodman, M., Koenigsberg, H. W., & Iskander, L. (2003). M-CPP PET and impulsive aggression in borderline personality disorder. *Biological Psychiatry, 53,* 104S.

New York Psychiatric Institute. (2006). Retrieved November 1, 2006, from http://nypisys. cpmc.columbia.edu/anxiety/PTSDCASE.HTM

Newman, C. F., Leahy, R. L., Beck, A. T., Reilly-Harrington, N. A., & Gyulai, L. (2002). *Bipolar disorder: A cognitive therapy approach.* Washington, DC: American Psychological Association.

Newman, M. G., Kenardy, J., Herman, S., & Taylor, C. B. (1997). Comparison of palmtop- computer-assisted brief cognitive-behavioral treatment to cognitive behavioral treatment for panic disorder. *Journal of Consulting and Clinical Psychology, 65,* 178–183.

Newton, T. F., Roache, J. D., De La Garza II, R., Fong, T., Wallace, C. L., et al. (2006). Bupropion reduces methamphetamine-induced subjective effects and cue-induced craving. *Neuropsychopharmacology, 31,* 1537–1544.

Nezu, C. M., Nezu, A. M., & Gill-Weiss, M. J. (1992). Psychopathology in persons with mental retardation: Clinical guidelines for assessment and treatment. Champaign, IL: Research Press.

Ng, C. H. (1997). The stigma of mental illness in Asian cultures. *Australian and New Zealand Journal of Psychiatry, 31,* 382–390.

Nguyen, H. H. (2006). Acculturation in the United States. In D. L. Sam & J. W. Berry (Eds.), *The Cambridge handbook of acculturation psychology* (pp. 311–330). New York: Cambridge University Press.

Nicdao, E. G., Hong, S., & Takeuchi, D. T. (2007). Prevalence and correlates of eating disorders among Asian Americans: Results from the National Latino and Asian American Study. *International Journal of Eating Disorders, 40,* S22–S26.

Nicholas, M., Obler, L., Albert, M., & Goodglass, H. (1985). Lexical retrieval in healthy aging. *Cortex, 21,* 595–606.

Nichols, M. (2000). Special populations. In S. R. Leiblum & R. C. Rosen (Eds.), *Principles and practice of sex therapy* (3rd ed., pp. 335–367). New York: Guilford Press.

Nickel, M. K., Muehlbacher, M., Nickel, C., Kettler, C., Gil, F. P., et al. (2006). Aripiprazole in the treatment of patients with borderline personality disorder: A double-blind, placebo- controlled study. *American Journal of Psychiatry, 163,* 833–838.

Nield, L. S., & Kamat, D. (2004). Enuresis: How to evaluate and treat. *Clinical Pediatrics, 43,* 409–415.

Nigg, J. T. (2006a). Temperament and developmental psychopathology. *Journal of Child Psychology and Psychiatry, 47,* 395–422.

Nigg, J. T. (2006b). *What causes ADHD? Toward a multi-path model for understanding what goes wrong and why.* New York: Guilford Press.

Nigg, J. T., & Goldsmith, H. H. (1994). Genetics of personality disorders: Perspectives from personality and psychopathology research. *Psychological Bulletin, 115,* 346–380.

Nigg, J. T., Hinshaw, S. P., & Huang- Pollock, C. (2006). Disorders of attention and impulse regulation. In D. Cicchetti & D. J. Cohen (Eds.), *Developmental psychopathology, Vol. 3: Risk, disorder, and adaptation* (2nd ed., pp. 358–403). Hoboken, NJ: John Wiley & Sons.

Nigg, J., Nikolas, M., Friderici, K., Park, L., & Zucker, R. A. (2007). Genotype and neuropsychological response inhibition as resilience promoters for attention-deficit/ hyperactivity disorder, oppositional defiant disorder, and conduct disorder under conditions of psychosocial adversity. *Development and Psychopathology, 19,* 767–786.

Nitschke, J. B., Dixon, G. E., Sarinopoulos, I., Short, S. J., Cohen, J. D., et al. (2006). Altering expectancy dampens neural response to aversive taste in primary taste cortex. *Nature Neuroscience, 9,* 435–442.

Nobre, P. J., & Pinto-Gouveia, J. (2006). Dysfunctional sexual beliefs as vulnerability factors for sexual dysfunction. *Journal of Sex Research, 43,* 68–75.

Nock, M. K., Borges, G., Bromet, E. J., Alonso, J., Angermeyer, M., et al. (2008). Cross-national prevalence and risk factors for suicidal ideation, plans and attempts. *British Journal of Psychiatry, 192,* 98–105.

Nock, M. K., Kazdin, A. E., Hiripi, E., & Kessler, R. C. (2006). Prevalence, subtypes, and correlates of DSM-IV conduct disorder in the National Comorbidity Survey replication. *Psychological Medicine, 36,* 699–710.

Nolan, S. A., & Mineka, S. (1997, November). Verbal, nonverbal, and genderrelated factors in the interpersonal consequences of depression and anxiety. Presented at the annual meeting of the Association for the Advancement of Behavior Therapy, Miami Beach, FL.

Nolen-Hoeksema, S. (1987). Sex differences in unipolar depression: Evidence and theory. *Psychological Bulletin, 101,* 259–282.

Nolen-Hoeksema, S. (2000). The role of rumination in depressive disorders and mixed anxiety/depressive symptoms. *Journal of Abnormal Psychology, 109,* 504–511.

Nolen-Hoeksema, S. (2001). Gender differences in depression. *Current Directions in Psychological Science, 10,* 173–176.

Nolen-Hoeksema, S., & Girgus, J. (1994). The emergence of gender differences in depression during adolescence. *Psychological Bulletin, 115,* 424–443.

Nolen-Hoeksema, S., & Morrow, J. (1991). A prospective study of depression and posttraumatic stress symptoms after a natural disaster: The 1989 Loma Prieta earthquake. *Journal of Personality and Social Psychology, 61,* 115–121.

Nolen-Hoeksema, S., & Morrow, J. (1993). Effects of rumination and distraction on naturally occurring depressed mood. *Cognition & Emotion, 7,* 561–570.

Nomura, M., Kusumi, I., Kaneko, M., Masui, T., Daiguji, M., et al. (2006). Involvement of a polymorphism in the 5-HT2A receptor gene in impulsive behavior. *Psychopharmacology, 187,* 30–35.

Norasakkunkit, V., Kitayama, S., & Uchida, Y. (2012). Social anxiety and holistic cognition: Self-focused social anxiety in the United States and other-focused social anxiety in Japan. *Journal of Cross-Cultural Psychology, 43,* 742–757.

Norberg, M. M., Krystal, J. H., & Tolin, D. F. (2008). A meta-analysis of D-cycloserine and the facilitation of fear extinction and exposure therapy. *Biological Psychiatry, 63,* 1118–1126.

Norcross, J. C., Hedges, M., & Castle, P. H. (2002). Psychologists conducting psychotherapy in 2001: A study of the Division 29 membership. *Psychotherapy: Theory, Research, Practice, Training, 39,* 97–102.

Norcross, J. C., Sayette, M. A., Mayne, T. J., Karg, R. S., & Turkson, M. A. (1998). Selecting a doctoral program in professional psychology: Some comparisons among PhD counseling, PhD clinical, and PsyD clinical psychology programs. *Professional Psychology: Research and Practice, 29,* 609–614.

Nordling, N., Sandnabba, N. K., & Santtila, P. (2000). The prevalence and effects of self-reported childhood sexual abuse among sadomasochistically oriented males and females. *Journal of Child Sexual Abuse, 9,* 53–63.

Norman, P. (1997). *Shout! The Beatles in their generation.* New York: Fireside.

Norman, R. M. G., Malla, A. K., McLean, T. S., McIntosh, E. M., Neufeld, R. W. J., et al. (2002). An evaluation of a stress management program for individuals with schizophrenia. *Schizophrenia Research, 58,* 293–303.

Norris, F. H., Murphy, A. D., Baker, C. K., Perilla, J. L., Rodriguez, F. G., & Rodriguez, J. D. J. G. (2003). Epidemiology of trauma and posttraumatic stress disorder in Mexico. *Journal of Abnormal Psychology, 112,* 646–656.

Norris, F. H., Perilla, J. L., & Murphy, A. D. (2001). Postdisaster stress in the United States and Mexico: A cross-cultural test of the multicriterion conceptual model of posttraumatic stress disorder. *Journal of Abnormal Psychology, 110,* 553–563.

Nowinski, J. (2003). Self-help groups. In J. L. Sorensen, R. A. Rawson, J. Guydish & J. E. Zweben (Eds.). *Drug abuse treatment through collaboration: Practice and research partnerships that work* (pp. 55–70). Washington, DC: American Psychological Association.

Noyes, R., Jr., Happel, R. L., & Yagla, S. J. (1999). Correlates of hypochondriasis in a nonclinical population. *Psychosomatics, 40,* 461–469.

Noyes, R., Jr., Holt, C. S., Happel, R. L., Kathol, R. G., & Yagla, S. J. (1997). A family study of hypochondriasis. *Journal of Nervous and Mental Disorders, 185,* 223–232.

Noyes, R., Jr., Stuart, S. P., & Watson, D. B. (2008). A reconceptualization of the somatoform disorders. *Psychosomatics: Journal of Consultation Liaison Psychiatry, 49,* 14–22.

Nuechterlein, K. H. (1991). Vigilance in schizophrenia and related disorders. In S. R. Steinhauer, J. H. Gruzelier, & J. Zubin (Eds.), *Neuropsychology, psychophysiology, and information processing* (pp. 397–433). New York: Elsevier Science.

Nurnberger, J. I. Jr., Wiegand, R., Bucholz, K., O'Connor, S., Meyer, E. T., et al. (2004). A family study of alcohol dependence: Coaggregation of multiple disorders in relatives of alcohol-dependent probands. *Archives of General Psychiatry, 61,* 1246–1256.

Nutt, D., & Lawson, C. (1992). Panic attacks: A neurochemical overview of models and mechanisms. *British Journal of Psychiatry, 160,* 165–178.

Nutt, D. J. (2001). Neurobiological mechanisms in generalized anxiety disorder. *Journal of Clinical Psychiatry, 62,* 22–27.

Nutt, D. J. (2008). Relationship of neurotransmitters to the symptoms of major depressive disorder. *Journal of Clinical Psychiatry, 69* (Suppl E1), 4–7.

Nuttbrock, L., Hwahng, S., Bockting, W., Rosenblum, A., Mason, H., et al. (2010). Psychiatric impact of gender-related abuse across the life course of male to female transgender persons. *Journal of Sex Research, 47,* 12–23.

Oakland, T., Mpofu, E., Glasgow, K., & Jumel, B. (2003). Diagnosis and administrative interventions for students with mental retardation in Australia, France, United States, and Zimbabwe 98 years after Binet's first intelligence test. *International Journal of Testing, 3,* 59–75.

Oakley, D. A. (1999). Hypnosis and conversion hysteria: A unifying model. *Cognitive Neuropsychiatry, 4,* 243–265.

O'Brien, C. P. (2005). Anticraving medications for relapse prevention: A possible new class of psychoactive medications. *American Journal of Psychiatry, 162,* 1423–1431.

O'Brien, C. P., Volkow, N., & Li, T. (2006). What's in a word? Addiction versus dependence in DSM-V. *American Journal of Psychiatry, 163,* 764–765.

O'Connor v. Donaldson, 422 U.S. 563 (1975).

O'Connor, M. G., & Lafleche, G. (2006). Amnesic syndromes. In P. J. Snyder, P. D. Nussbaum, & D. L. Robins (Eds.), *Clinical neuropsychology: A pocket handbook for assessment* (2nd ed., pp. 463–488). Washington, DC: American Psychological Association.

O'Connor, R. C., Sheehy, N. P., & O'Connor, D. B.. (1999). A thematic analysis of suicide notes. *Crisis: The Journal of Crisis Intervention and Suicide Prevention, 20,* 106–114.

Odgers, C. L., Caspi, A., Nagin, D., Piquero, A. R., Slutske, W. S., et al. (2008). Is it important to prevent early exposure to drugs and alcohol among teens? *Psychological Science, 19,* 1037–1044.

Ofovwe, C. E., Ofovwe, G. E., & Meyer, A. (2006). The prevalence of attention-deficit/hyperactivity disorder among school-aged children in Benin City, Nigeria. *Journal of Child and Adolescent Mental Health, 18,* 1–5.

Ogawa, K., Miya, M., Watarai, A., Nakazawa, K. M., Yuasa, S., & Utena, H. (1987). A long-term follow up study of schizophrenia in Japan—with special reference to the course of social adjustment. *British Journal of Psychiatry, 151,* 758–765.

Ogden, C. A., Rich, M. E., Schork, N. J., Paulus, M. P., Geyer, M. A., et al. (2004). Candidate genes, pathways and mechanisms for bipolar (manic-depressive) and related disorders: An expanded convergent functional genomics approach. *Molecular Psychiatry, 9,* 1007–1029.

Ogden, C. L., Fryar, C. D., Carroll, M. D., & Flegal, K. M. (2004, October 27). Mean Body Weight, Height, and Body Mass Index, United States 1960–2002. Advance Data from Vital and Health Statistics, 347, Table 10, p. 12. Retrieved May 27, 2009 from http://www.cdc.gov/nchs/data/ad/ad347.pdf

Ogloff, J. R., Wong, S., & Greenwood, A. (1990). Treating criminal psychopaths in a therapeutic community program. *Behavioral Sciences & the Law, 8,* 181–190.

Ogloff, J. R. P. (2006). Psychopathy/antisocial personality disorder conundrum. *Australian and New Zealand Journal of Psychiatry, 40,* 519–528.

Ogundipe, T., & Shankar, C. (2013). Too dangerous to be NGRI? *Journal of the American Academy of Psychiatry and the Law, 41*(1), 140–142.

Öhman, A. (1986). Face the beast and fear the face: Animal and social fears as prototypes for evolutionary analyses of emotion. *Psychophysiology, 23*, 123–145.

Öhman, A., Fredrikson, M., Hugdahl, K., & Rimmo, P.-A. (1976). The premise of equipotentiality in human classical conditioning: Conditioned electrodermal responses to potentially phobic stimuli. *Journal of Experimental Psychology: General, 105*, 313–337.

Okubo, Y., Suhara, T., Suzuki, K., Kobayashi, K., Inoue, O., Terasaki, O., et al. (1997). Decreased prefrontal dopamine D1 receptors in schizophrenia revealed by PET. *Nature, 385*, 578–579.

Olde Hartman, T. C., Borghuis, M. S., Lucassen, P. L. B. J., can de Laar, F. A., Speckens, A. E., & van Weel, C. (2009). Medically unexplained symptoms, somatization disorder, and hypochondriasis: Course and Progrnoisis. A systematic review. *Journal of Psychosomatic Research, 66*, 363–377.

Oldham, J. M. (2005). Personality disorders: Recent history and future directions. In J. M. Oldham, A. E. Skodol, & D. S. Bender (Eds.), *The American Psychiatric Publishing textbook of personality disorders* (pp. 3–16). Washington, DC: American Psychiatric Publishing.

Oldham, J. M., Skodol, A. E., Kellman, H. D., Hyler, S. E., Doidge, N., et al. (1995). Comorbidity of Axis I and Axis II disorders. *American Journal of Psychiatry, 152*, 571–578.

Olds, J., & Milner, P. (1954). Positive reinforcement produced by electrical stimulation of the septal area and other regions of rat brain. *Journal of Comparative and Physiological Psychology, 47*, 419–427.

Olesen, P. J., Westerberg, H., & Klingberg, T. (2003). Increased prefrontal and parietal activity after training of working memory. *Nature Neuroscience, 7*(1), 75–79.

Olino, T. M., Klein, D. N., Lewinsohn, P. M., Rohde, P., & Seeley, J. R. (2008). Longitudinal associations between depressive and anxiety disorders: A comparison of two trait models. *Psychological Medicine, 38*, 353–363.

Olivardia, R. (2007). Muscle dysmorphia: Characteristics, assessment, and treatment. In J. K. Thompson, J. Kevin, & G. Cafri (Eds.), *The muscular ideal: Psychological, social, and medical perspectives* (pp. 123–139). Washington, DC: American Psychological Association.

Olson, D. H., McCubbin, H. I., Barnes, H., Larsen, A., Muxen, M., & Wilson, M. (1985). *Family inventories.* St. Paul, MN: Family Social Science, University of Minnesota.

Olson, I. R., Page, K, Moore, K., Chatterjee, A., & Verfaellie, M. (2006). Working memory for conjunctions relies on the medial temporal lobe. *Journal of Neuroscience, 26*, 4596–4601.

Olson, R., Forsberg, H., Gayan, J., & DeFries, J. (1999). A behavioral-genetic analysis of reading disabilities and component processes. In R. Klein & P. McMullen (Eds.), *Converging methods for understanding reading and dyslexia* (pp. 133–153). Cambridge, MA: MIT Press.

Olver, M., & Wong, S. C. P. (2009). Therapeutic responses of psychopathic sexual offenders: Treatment attrition, therapeutic change, and long-term recidivism. *Journal of Consulting and Clinical Psychology, 77*, 328–336.

O'Malley, P. G., Jackson, J. L., Santoro, J., Tomkins, G., Balden, E., & Kroenke, K. (1999). Antidepressant therapy for unexplained symptoms and symptom syndromes. *Journal of Family Practice, 48*, 980–990.

O'Malley, P. M., Johnston, L. D., & Bachman, J. G. (1999). Epidemiology of substance abuse in adolescence. In P. J. Ott, R. E. Tarter, & R. T. Ammerman (Eds.), *Sourcebook on substance abuse: Etiology, epidemiology, assessment, and treatment* (pp. 14–31). Needham Heights, MA: Allyn & Bacon.

O'Malley, S. S., Jaffe, A. J., Chang, G., & Schottenfeld, R. S. (1992). Naltrexone and coping skills therapy for alcohol dependence: A controlled study. *Archives of General Psychiatry, 49*, 881–887.

O'Neill, M. L., Lidz, V., & Heilbrun, K. (2003). Adolescents with psychopathic characteristics in a substance abusing cohort: Treatment process and outcomes. *Law and Human Behavior, 27*, 299–313.

Oniszczenko, W., & Dragan, W. L. (2005). Association between dopamine D4 receptor exon III polymorphism and emotional reactivity as a temperamental trait. *Twin Research and Human Genetics, 8*, 633–637.

Oniszczenko, W., Zawadzki, B., Strelau, J., Riemann, R., Angleitner, A., & Spinath, F. M. (2003). Genetic and environmental determinants of temperament: A comparative study based on Polish and German samples. *European Journal of Personality, 17*, 207–220.

Oosterbaan, D. B., van Balkom, A. J., van Boeijen, C. A., de Meij, T. G., & van Dyck, R. (2001). An open study of paroxetine in hypochondriasis. *Progress in Neuro-Psychopharmacology & Biological Psychiatry, 25*, 1023–1033.

Open Minds. (1999). Over 72% of insured Americans are enrolled in MBHOs: Magellan Behavioral Health continues to dominate the market. *Open Minds: The Behavioral Health and Social Service Industry Analyst, 11*, 9.

Oquendo, M. A., Baca-García, E., Mann, J., & Giner, J. (2008). Issues for DSM-V: Suicidal behavior as a separate diagnosis on a separate axis. *American Journal of Psychiatry, 165*, 1383–1384.

Oquendo, M. A., Bongiovi-Garcia, N. E., Galfalvy, H., Goldberg, P. H., Grunebaum, M. F., et al. (2007). Sex differences in clinical predictors of suicidal acts after major depression: A prospective study. *American Journal of Psychiatry, 164*, 134–141.

Orr, S. P., & Pitman, R. K. (1993). Psychophysiologic assessment of attempts to simulate posttraumatic stress disorder. *Biological Psychiatry, 33*, 127–129.

Orr, S. P., Metzger, L. J., & Pitman, R. K. (2002). Psychophysiology of post-traumatic stress disorder. *Psychiatric Clinics of North America, 25*, 271–293.

Orr, S. P., Pitman, R. K., Lasko, N. B., & Herz, L. R. (1993). Psychophysiological assessment of posttraumatic stress disorder imagery in World War II and Korean combat veterans. *Journal of Abnormal Psychology, 102*, 152–159.

Osborne, C. & Wise, T. (2005). Paraphilias. In R. Balon & T. Segraves (Eds.), *Handbook of sexual dysfunction.* Boca Raton, FL: Taylor & Francis.

Osmond, M., Wilkie, M., & Moore, J. (2001). *Behind the smile: My journey out of postpartum depression.* New York: Warner.

Öst, L. (1992). Blood and injection phobia: Background and cognitive, physiological, and behavioral variables. *Journal of Abnormal Psychology, 101*, 68–74.

Öst, L., Brandberg, M., & Alm, T. (1997). One versus five sessions of exposure in the treatment of flying phobia. *Behaviour Research and Therapy, 35*, 987–996.

Öst, L. G., Ferebee, I., & Furmark, T. (1997). One-session group therapy of spider phobia: Direct versus indirect treatments. *Behaviour Research & Therapy, 35*, 721–732.

Öst, L., Fellenius, J., & Sterner, U. (1991). Applied tension, exposure in vivo, and tension-only in the treatment of blood phobia. *Behaviour Research and Therapy, 29*, 561–574.

Öst, L., Salkovskis, P. M., & Hellström, K. (1991). One-session therapist-directed exposure vs. self-exposure in the treatment of spider phobia. *Behavior Therapy, 22*, 407–422.

Öst, L., Svensson, L., Hellström, K., & Lindwall, R. (2001). One-session treatment of specific phobias in youths: A randomized clinical trial. *Journal of Consulting and Clinical Psychology, 69*, 814–824.

Osuch, E. A., Benson, B. E., Luckenbaugh, D. A., Garaci, D. A., Post, R. M., & McCann, U. (2008). Repetitive TMS combined with exposure therapy for PTSD: a preliminary study. *Journal of Anxiety Disorders, 23*, 54–59.

Ott, S. L., Roberts, S., Rock, D., Allen, J., & Erlenmeyer-Kimling, L. (2002). Positive and negative thought disorder and psychopathology in childhood among subjects with adulthood schizophrenia. *Schizophrenia Research, 58*, 231–239.

Otte, C., Kellner, M., Arlt, J., Jahn, H., Holsboer, F., & Wiedemann, K. (2002). Prolactin but not ACTH increases during sodium lactate-induced panic attacks. *Psychiatry Research, 109*, 201–205.

Otto, M. W. (2002). The dose and delivery of psychotherapy: A commentary on Hansen et al. *Clinical Psychology: Science and Practice, 9*, 348–349.

Otto, M. W., Pollack, M. H., Sachs, G. S., O'Neil, C. A., & Rosenbaum, J. (1992). Alcohol dependence in panic disorder patients. *Journal of Psychiatric Research, 26,* 29–38.

Otto, M. W., Wilhelm, S., Cohen, L. S., & Harlow, B. L. (2001). Prevalence of body dysmorphic disorder in a community sample of women. *American Journal of Psychiatry, 158,* 2061–2063.

Otto, R. K. (2000). Assessing and managing violence risk in outpatient settings. *Journal of Clinical Psychology, 56,* 1239–1262.

Ousley, L., Cordero, E. D., & White, S. (2008). Eating disorders and body image of undergraduate men. *Journal of American College Health, 56,* 617–621.

Overmier, J. B., & Seligman, M. E. (1967). Effects of inescapable shock upon subsequent escape and avoidance responding. *Journal of Comparative and Physiological Psychology, 63,* 28–33.

Owen, M. J., O'Donovan, M. C., Thapar, A., & Craddock, N. (2011). Neurodevelopmental hypothesis of schizophrenia. *British Journal of Psychiatry, 198,* 173–175.

Oxford, M., Cavell, T. A., & Hughes, J. N. (2003). Callous/unemotional traits moderate the relation between ineffective parenting and child externalizing problems: A partial replication and extension. *Journal of Clinical Child and Adolescent Psychology, 32,* 577–585.

Oxnam, R. B. (2005). *A fractured mind: My life with multiple personality disorder.* New York: Hyperion Books.

Ozcan, M. E., Shivakumar, G., & Suppes, T. (2006). Treating rapid cycling bipolar disorder with novel medications. *Current Psychiatry Reviews, 2,* 361–369.

Ozkan, M., & Altindag, A. (2005). Comorbid personality disorders in subjects with panic disorder: Do personality disorders increase clinical severity? *Comprehensive Psychiatry, 46,* 20–26.

Ozonoff, S., & Jensen, J. (1999). Specific executive function profiles in three neurodevelopmental disorders. *Journal of Autism and Developmental Disorders, 29,* 171–177.

Ozonoff, S., Macari, S., Young, G. S., Goldring, S., Thompson, M., & Rogers, S. J. (2008). Atypical object exploration at 12 months of age is associated with autism in a prospective sample. *Autism, 12,* 457–472.

Ozonoff, S., Rogers, S. J., & Hendren, R. L. (2003). *Autism spectrum disorders: A research review for practitioners.* Arlington, VA: American Psychiatric Publishing.

Packman, W. L., Marlitt, R. E., Bongar, B., & Pennuto, T. O. (2004). A comprehensive and concise assessment of suicide risk. *Behavioral Sciences & the Law, 22,* 667–680.

Packnett, E. R., Gubata, M. E., Cowan, D. N., & Niebuhr, D. W. (2012). Temporal trends in the epidemiology of disabilities related to posttraumatic stress disorder in the U.S. Army and Marine Corps from 2005–2010. *Journal of Traumatic Stress, 25,* 485–493.

Pagnin, D., de Queiroz, V., Pini, S., & Cassano, G. B. (2004). Efficacy of ECT in depression: A meta-analytic review. *Journal of ECT, 20,* 13–20.

Palazzoli, M. S. (1974). Self-starvation: From the intrapsychic to the transpersonal approach to anorexia nervosa. (A. Pomerans, Trans.). Oxford, England: Chaucer.

Palazzoli, M. S. (1988). The family of the anorexic patient: A model system. In M. S. Palazzoli & M. Selvini (Eds.), *The work of Mara Selvini Palazzoli* (A. Pomerans, Trans., pp. 183–197). Lanham, MD: Jason Aronson.

Pallanti, S., Hollander, E., & Goodman, W. K. (2004). A qualitative analysis of nonresponse: Management of treatment-refractory obsessive-compulsive disorder. *Journal of Clinical Psychiatry, 65,* 6–10.

Pallister, E., & Waller, G. (2008). Anxiety in the eating disorders: Understanding the overlap. *Clinical Psychology Review, 28,* 366–386.

Palmer, R. H., Button, T. M., Rhee, S. H., Corley, R. P., Young, S. E., et al. (2012). Genetic etiology of the common liability to drug dependence: Evidence of common and specific mechanisms for DSM-IV dependence symptoms. *Drug Alcohol Dependence, 123*(Suppl.), S24–S32.

Palmer, R. L. (2003). Concepts of eating disorders. In J. Treasure, U. Schmidt, & E. van Furth (Eds.), *Handbook of eating disorders* (pp. 1–10). Chichester, England: Wiley.

Palmer, R. L., Birchall, H., Damani, S., Gatward, N., McGrain, L., & Parker, L. (2003). A dialectical behavior therapy program for people with an eating disorder and borderline personality disorder—Description and outcome. *International Journal of Eating Disorders, 33,* 281–286.

Paniagua, F. A. (2001). *Diagnosis in a multicultural context.* Thousand Oaks, CA: Sage Publications.

Pancheri, P., Scapicchio, P., & Dell Chiaie, R. (2002). A double-blind, randomized parallel-group, efficacy and safety study of intramuscular S-adenosyl-L-methionine 1,4-butanedisulphonate (SAMe) versus imipramine in patients with major depressive disorder. *International Journal of Neuropsychopharmacology, 5,* 287–294.

Pantelis, C., Velakoulis, D., McGorry, P. D., Wood, S. J., Suckling, J., et al. (2003). Neuroanatomical abnormalities before and after onset of psychosis: A cross-sectional and longitudinal MRI comparison. *Lancet, 361,* 281–288.

Papadimitriou, G. N., Calabrese, J. R., Dikeos, D. G., & Christodoulou, G. N. (2005). Rapid cycling bipolar disorder: Biology and pathogenesis. *International Journal of Neuropsychopharmacology, 8,* 281–292.

Papapetropoulos, S., Gonzalez, J., Lieberman, A., Villar, J. M., & Mash, D. C. (2005). Dementia in Parkinson's disease: A post-mortem study in a population of brain donors. *International Journal of Geriatric Psychiatry, 20,* 418–422.

Papp, L. A., Klein, D. F., & Gorman, J. M. (1993). Carbon dioxide hypersensitivity, hyperventilation, and panic disorder. *American Journal of Psychiatry, 150,* 1149–1157.

Papp, L. A., Martinez, J. M., Klein, D. F., Coplan, J. D., Norman, R. G., et al. (1997). Respiratory psychophysiology of panic disorder: Three respiratory challenges in 98 subjects. *American Journal of Psychiatry, 154,* 1557–1565.

Paquette, V., Lévesque, J., Mensour, B., Leroux, J. M., Beaudoin, G., et al. (2003). "Change the mind and you change the brain": Effects of cognitive-behavioral therapy on the neural correlates of spider phobia. *Neuroimage, 18,* 401–409.

Parasuraman, R., Nestor, P. G., & Greenwood, P. (1989). Sustained-attention capacity in young and older adults. *Psychology and Aging, 4,* 339–345.

Pardini, D., Obradovic, J., & Loeber, R. (2006). Interpersonal callousness, hyperactivity/impulsivity, inattention, and conduct problems as precursors to delinquency persistence in boys: A comparison of three grade-based cohorts. *Journal of Clinical Child and Adolescent Psychology, 35,* 46–59.

Pardini, D. A. (2006). The callousness pathway to severe violent delinquency. *Aggressive Behavior, 32,* 590–598.

Pardini, D. A., Lochman, J. E., & Frick, P. J. (2003). Callous/unemotional traits and social-cognitive processes in adjudicated youths. *Journal of the American Academy of Child & Adolescent Psychiatry, 42,* 364–371.

Paris, J. (1993). The treatment of borderline personality disorder in light of the research on its long term outcome. *The Canadian Journal of Psychiatry, 38,* 28–34.

Paris, J. (1996). Cultural factors in the emergence of borderline pathology. *Psychiatry: Interpersonal and Biological Processes, 59,* 185–192.

Paris, J. (1999). Borderline personality disorder. In T. Millon, P. H. Blaney, & R. D. Davis (Eds), *Oxford textbook of psychopathology* (pp. 628–652). New York: Oxford University Press.

Paris, J. (2001). Psychosocial adversity. In W. J. Livesley (Ed.), *Handbook of personality disorders: Theory, research, and treatment* (pp. 231–241). New York: Guilford Press.

Paris, J. (2003). *Personality disorders over time: Precursors, course, and outcome.* Arlington, VA: American Psychiatric Publishing.

Paris, J. (2005). A current integrative perspective on personality disorders. In J. M. Oldham, A. E. Skodol, & D. S. Bender (Eds.), *The American Psychiatric Publishing textbook of personality disorders* (pp. 119–128). Washington, DC: American Psychiatric Publishing.

Paris, J. (2008). Clinical trials of treatment for personality disorders. *Psychiatric Clinics of North America, 31,* 517–526.

Paris, J., & Zweig-Frank, H. (2001). The 27-year follow-up of patients with borderline personality disorder. *Comprehensive Psychiatry, 42,* 482–487.

Parker, G., Gladstone, G., & Chee, K. T. (2001). Depression in the planet's largest ethnic group: The Chinese. *American Journal of Psychiatry, 158,* 857–864.

Parner, E. T., Schendel, D. E., & Thorsen, P. (2008). Autism prevalence trends over time in Denmark. *Archives of Pediatrics & Adolescent Medicine, 162,* 1150–1156.

Parpura, V., & Haydon, P. G. (2000). Physiological astrocytic calcium levels stimulate glutamate release to modulate adjacent neurons. *Proceedings of the National Academy of Sciences USA, 97,* 8629–8634.

Parrott, A. C. (2002). Recreational Ecstasy/MDMA, the serotonin syndrome, and serotonergic neurotoxicity. *Pharmacology, Biochemistry & Behavior, 71,* 837–844.

Parsons v. Alabama, 81 Ala. 577, So. 854 (1886).

Partin, J. C., Hamill, S. K., Fischel, J. E., & Partin, J. S. (1992). Painful defecation and fecal soiling in children. *Pediatrics, 89,* 1007–1009.

Partnership for a Drug-Free America. (2007). *Agony from Ecstasy.* Retrieved October 20, 2007, from www.drugfree.org/Portal/Stories/Agony

Patel, V., Abas, M., Broadhead, J., Todd, C., & Reeler, A. (2001). Depression in developing countries: Lessons from Zimbabwe. *British Medical Journal, 322,* 482–484.

Patkar, A. A., Pae, C., & Masand, P. S. (2006). Transdermal selegiline: The new generation of monoamine oxidase inhibitors. *CNS Spectrum, 11,* 363–375.

Pattij, T., & Vanderschuren, L. J. (2008). The neuropharmacology of impulsive behaviour. *Trends in Pharmacological Sciences, 29,* 192–199.

Pauli, P., Wiedemann, G., & Montoya, P. (1998). Covariation bias in flight phobics. *Journal of Anxiety Disorders, 12,* 555–565.

Pauls, D. L., Alsobrook, J. P., Goodman, W., Rasmussen, S., & Leckman, J. F. (1995). A family study of obsessive-compulsive disorder. *American Journal of Psychiatry, 152,* 76–84.

Pauls, D. L., Raymond, C. L., & Robertson, M. (1991). The genetics of obsessive-compulsive disorder: A review. In J. Zohar, T. Insel, & S. Rasmussen (Eds.), *The psychobiology of obsessive-compulsive disorder* (pp. 89–100). New York: Springer.

Pavlov, I. (1936). *Lectures on conditioned reflexes.* Oxford, England: Liveright.

Pavlov, I. P. (1927). *Conditioned reflexes: An investigation of the physiological activity of the cerebral cortex* (Trans. G.V. Anrep). London: Oxford University Press.

Paxton, S. J., Schutz, H. K., Wertheim, E. H., & Muir, S. L. (1999). Friendship clique and peer influences on body image concerns, dietary restraint, extreme weight-loss behaviors, and binge eating in adolescent girls. *Journal of Abnormal Psychology, 108,* 255–266.

Pelc, K., Kornreich, C., Foisy, M. L., & Dan, B. (2006). Recognition of emotional facial expressions in attention-deficit hyperactivity disorder. *Pediatric Neurology, 35,* 93–97.

Penadés, R., Catalán, R., Salamero, M., Boget, T., Puig, O., Guarch, J., & Gastó, C. (2006). Cognitive remediation therapy for outpatients with chronic schizophrenia: A controlled and randomized study. *Schizophrenia Research, 87,* 323–331.

Penders, T. M., Gestring, R. E., & Vilensky, D. A. (2012). Excited delirium following use of synthetic cathinones (bath salts). *General Hospital Psychiatry, 34,* 647–650.

Pengilly, J. W., & Dowd, E. T. (2000). *Hardiness and social support as moderator of stress in college students. Journal of Clinical Psychology, 56,* 813–820.

Penn, D. L., & Combs, D. (2000). Modification of affect perception deficits in schizophrenia. *Schizophrenia Research, 46,* 217–229.

Pennebaker, J. W. (1999). The effects of traumatic disclosure on physical and mental health: The values of writing and talking about upsetting events. *International Journal of Emergency Mental Health, 1,* 9–18.

Perälä, J., Suvisaari, J., Saarni, S. I., Kuoppasalmi, K., Isometsä, E., et al. (2007). Lifetime prevalence of psychotic and bipolar I disorders in a general population. *Archives of General Psychiatry, 64,* 19–28.

Perez, M., & Joiner, T. E., Jr. (2003). Body image dissatisfaction and disordered eating in black and white women. *International Journal of Eating Disorders, 33,* 342–350.

Perez, M., Voelz, Z. R., Pettit, J. W., & Joiner Jr., T. E. (2002). The role of acculturative stress and body dissatisfaction in predicting bulimic symptomatology across ethnic groups. *International Journal of Eating Disorders, 31,* 442–454.

Perilla, J. L., Norris, F. H., & Lavizzo, E. A. (2002). Ethnicity, culture, and disaster response: Identifying and explaining ethnic differences in PTSD six months after Hurricane Andrew. *Journal of Social & Clinical Psychology, 21,* 20–45.

Perkins, B. R., & Rouanzoin, C. C. (2002). A critical evaluation of current views regarding eye movement desensitization and reprocessing (EMDR): Clarifying points of confusion. *Journal of Clinical Psychology, 58*(1), 77–97.

Perkins, D. O. (1999). Adherence to antipsychotic medications. *Journal of Clinical Psychiatry, 60,* 25–30.

Perkins, H. W. (1997). College student misperceptions of alcohol and other drug use norms among peers. In *Designing alcohol and other drug prevention programs in higher education: Bringing theory into practice* (pp. 177–206). Newton, MA: Higher Education Center for Alcohol and Other Drug Abuse and Violence Prevention.

Perkonigg, A., Kessler, R. C., Storz, S., & Wittchen, H. U. (2000). Traumatic events and post-traumatic stress disorder in the community: Prevalence, risk factors and comorbidity. *Acta Psychiatrica Scandinavica, 101,* 46–59.

Perlick, D., & Silverstein, B. (1994). Faces of female discontent: Depression, disordered eating, and changing gender roles. In P. Fallon M. Katzman, & S. C. Wooley (Eds.), *Feminist perspectives on eating disorders* (pp. 77–93). New York: Guilford Press.

Perlin, M. L. (2000a). The competence to plead guilty and the competence to waive counsel. In M. L. Perlin (Ed.), *The hidden prejudice: Mental disability on trial* (pp. 205–221). Washington, DC: American Psychological Association.

Perlin, M. L. (2000b). The right to refuse treatment. In M. L. Perlin (ed.) *The Hidden Prejudice: Mental Disability on Trial.* (pp. 125–156). Washington, DC: American Psychological Association.

Perlin, M. L. (2000c). Involuntary civil commitment law. In M L. Perlin, (Ed.), *The Hidden Prejudice: Mental Disability on Trial.* (pp. 79–112). Washington, DC, US: American Psychological Association.

Perlin, M. L. (2003). Therapeutic jurisprudence and outpatient commitment law: Kendra's Law as case study. *Psychology, Public Policy, and Law, 9,* 183–208.

Perlis, M. L., Giles, D. E., Buysse, D. J., Tu, X., & Kupfer, D. J. (1997). Self-reported sleep disturbance as a prodromal symptom in recurrent depression. *Journal of Affective Disorders, 42,* 209–212.

Perlis, M. L., Smith, L. J., Lyness, J. M., Matteson, S. R., Pigeon, W. R., et al. (2006). Insomnia as a risk factor for onset of depression in the elderly. *Behavioral Sleep Medicine, 4,* 104–113.

Perlis, R. H., Ostacher, M. J., Patel, J. K., Marangell, L. B., Zhang, H., et al. (2006). Predictors of recurrence in bipolar disorder: Primary outcomes from the Systematic Treatment Enhancement Program for Bipolar Disorder (STEP-BD). *American Journal of Psychiatry, 163,* 217–224.

Perlstein, W. M., Carter, C. S., Noll, D. C., & Cohen, J. D. (2001). Relation of prefrontal cortex dysfunction to working memory and symptoms in schizophrenia. *American Journal of Psychiatry, 158,* 1105–1113.

Perroud, N., Nicastro, R., Jermann, F., & Huguelet, P. (2012). Mindfulness skills in borderline personality disorder patients during dialectical behavior therapy: Preliminary results. *International Journal of Psychiatry in Clinical Practice, 16,* 189–196.

Pescosolido, B. A., Monahan, J., Link, B. G., Stueve, A., & Kikuzawa, S. (1999). The public's view of the competence, dangerousness, and need for legal coercion of persons with mental health problems. *American Journal of Public Health, 89,* 1339–1345.

Peter, M., Schuurmans, H., Vingerhoets, A. J. J. M., Smeets, G., Verkoeijen, P., & Arntz, A. (2013). Borderline personality disorder and emotional intelligence. *Journal of Nervous and Mental Disease, 201*(2), 99–104.

Petersen, R. C., & O'Brien, J. (2006). Mild cognitive impairment should be considered for DSM-V. *Journal of Geriatric Psychiatry and Neurology, 19,* 147–154.

Peterson, C., & Seligman, M. E. (1984). Causal explanations as a risk factor for depression: Theory and evidence. *Psychological Review, 91,* 347–374.

Peterson, C. B., Crow, S. J., Swanson, S. A., Crosby, R. D., Wonderlich, S. A., et al. (2011). Examining the stability of DSM–IV and empirically derived eating disorder classification: Implications for DSM-5. *Journal of Consulting and Clinical Psychology, 79,* 777–783.

Peterson, T. J., Feldman, G., Harley, R., Fresco, D. M., Graves, L., et al. (2007). Extreme response style in recurrent and chronically depressed patients: Change with antidepressant administration and stability during continuation treatment. *Journal of Consulting and Clinical Psychology, 75*, 145–153.

Petkova, E., Quitkin, F. M., McGrath, P. J., Stewart, J. W., & Klein, D. F. (2000). A method to quantify rater bias in antidepressant trials. *Neuropsychopharmacology, 22*, 559–565.

Petry, N. M., Stinson, F. S., & Grant, B. F. (2005). Comorbidity of DSM-IV pathological gambling and other psychiatric disorders: Results from the National Epidemiologic Survey on Alcohol and Related Conditions. *Journal of Clinical Psychiatry, 66*, 564–574.

Petry, N. M., Weinstock, J., & Alessi, S. M. (2011). A randomized trial of contingency management delivered in the context of group counseling. *Journal of Consulting and Clinical Psychology, 79*(5), 686–696.

Petty, F., Kramer, G. L., & Wilson, L. (1992). Prevention of learned helplessness: In vivo correlation with cortical serotonin. *Pharmacology, Biochemistry and Behavior, 43*, 361–367.

Pfäfflin, F. (2010). The surgical castration of detained sex offenders amounts to degrading treatment. *Recht & Psychiatrie 28*, 2010, 179–182.

Pfammatter, M., Junghan, U. M., & Brenner, H. D. (2006). Efficacy of psychological therapy in schizophrenia: Conclusions from meta-analyses. *Schizophrenia Bulletin, 32*, S64–S80.

Pfennig, A., Frye, M. A., Köberle, U., & Bauer, M. (2004). The mood spectrum and hypothalamic-pituitary-thyroid axis. *Primary Psychiatry, 11*, 42–47.

Pflanz, S. (2008). *Talking paper on Air Force Suicide Prevention Program*. Retrieved December 2, 2008, from www.afspp.afms.mil/idc/groups/public/documents/afms/ctb_101896.pdf

Phan, K. L., Fitzgerald, D. A., Nathan, P. J., & Tancer, M. E. (2006). Association between amygdala hyperactivity to harsh faces and severity of social anxiety in generalized social phobia. *Biological Psychiatry, 59*, 424–429.

Phelps E. A., O'Connor, K. J., Cunningham, W. A., Funayama, E. S., Gatenby, J. C., et al. (2000). Performance on indirect measures of race evaluation predicts amygdala activation. *Journal of Cognitive Neuroscience, 12*, 729–738.

Phelps, L., Brown, R. T., & Power, T. J. (2002). Tics and Tourette's disorder. In L. Phelps, R. T. Brown, & T. J. Power (Eds.), *Pediatric psychopharmacology: Combining medical and psychosocial interventions* (pp. 203–229). Washington, DC: American Psychological Association.

Phillips, K. A. (2000). Body dysmorphic disorder: Diagnostic controversies and treatment challenges. *Bulletin of the Menninger Clinic, 64*, 18–35.

Phillips, K. A. (2001). Body dysmorphic disorder. In K. A. Phillips (Ed.), *Somatoform and factitious disorders* (pp. 67–94). Washington, DC: American Psychiatric Press.

Phillips, K. A., & Diaz, S. F. (1997). Gender differences in body dysmorphic disorder. *Journal of Nervous and Mental Disease, 185*, 570–577.

Phillips, K. A., & Hollander, E. (2008). Treating body dysmorphic disorder with medication: Evidence, misconceptions, and a suggested approach. *Body Image, 5*, 13–27.

Phillips, K. A., & Najjar, F. (2003). An open-label study of citalopram in body dysmorphic disorder. *Journal of Clinical Psychiatry, 64*, 715–720.

Phillips, K. A., Albertini, R. S., & Rasmussen S. A. (2002). A randomized placebo-controlled trial of fluoxetine in body dysmorphic disorder. *Archives of General Psychiatry, 59*, 381–388.

Phillips, K. A., Coles, M. E., Menard, W., Yen, S., Fay, C., & Weisberg, R. B. (2005). Suicidal ideation and suicide attempts in body dysmorphic disorder. *Journal of Clinical Psychiatry, 66*, 717–725.

Phillips, K. A., McElroy, S. L., Keck, P. E., Jr., Hudson, J. I., & Pope, H. G., Jr. (1994). A comparison of delusional and nondelusional body dysmorphic disorder in 100 cases. *Psychopharmacology Bulletin, 30*, 179–186.

Phillips, K. A., Menard, W., & Fay, C. (2006). Gender similarities and differences in 200 individuals with body dysmorphic disorder. *Comprehensive Psychiatry, 47*, 77–87.

Phillips, K. A., Menard, W., Fay, C., & Pagano, M. E. (2005). Psychosocial functioning and quality of life in body dysmorphic disorder. *Comprehensive Psychiatry, 46*, 254–260.

Phillips, K. A., Pagano, M. E., Menard, W., & Stout, R. L. (2006). A 12-month follow-up study of the course of body dysmorphic disorder. *American Journal of Psychiatry, 163*, 907–908.

Phillips, K. A., Pagano, M. E., Menard, W., Fay, C., & Stout, R. L. (2005). Predictors of remission from body dysmorphic disorder: A prospective study. *Journal of Nervous and Mental Disease, 193*, 564–567.

Phillips, K. A., Quinn, G., & Stout, R. L. (2008). Functional impairment in body dysmorphic disorder: A prospective, follow-up study. *Journal of Psychiatric Research, 42*, 701–707.

Phillips, M. (2001, September 22–26). *The participation of China to the WHO/SUPREMISS project*. Paper read at the XXIst Congress of the International Association for Suicide Prevention, Chennai, India.

Phillips, M. L., & Frank, E. (2006). Redefining bipolar disorder: Toward DSM-V. *American Journal of Psychiatry, 163*, 1135–1136.

Phillips, M. L., & Sierra, M. (2003). Depersonalization disorder: A functional neuroanatomical perspective. *Stress, 6*, 157–165.

Phillips, M. L., Medford, N., Senior, C., Bullmore, E. T., Suckling, J., et al. (2001). Depersonalization disorder: Thinking without feeling. *Psychiatry Research, 108*, 145–160.

Phillips, M. R., Li, X., & Zhang, Y. (2002). Suicide rates in China, 1995–99. *The Lancet, 359*, 835–840.

Phillips, M. R., West, C. L., Shen, Q., & Zheng, Y. (1998). Comparison of schizophrenic patients' families and normal families in China, using Chinese versions of FACES-II and the Family Environment Scales. *Family Process, 37*, 95–106.

Piasecki, M., Antonuccio, D. O., Steinagel, G., & Kohlenberg, B. S. (2002). Penetration of the blind in a controlled study of Paxil used to treat cocaine addiction. *Journal of Behavior Therapy and Experimental Psychiatry, 33*, 67–71.

Piasecki, M. P., Antonuccio, D. O., Steinagel, G. M., Kohlenberg, B. S., & Kapadar, K. (2002). Penetrating the blind in a study of an SSRI. *Journal of Behavior Therapy and Experimental Psychiatry, 33*, 67–71.

Picciotto, M. R. (1998). Common aspects of the action of nicotine and other drugs of abuse. *Drug and Alcohol Dependence, 51*, 165–172.

Pich, E. M., Pagliusi, S. R., Tessari, M., Talabot-Ayer, D., van Huijsduijnen, R. H., & Chiamulera, C. (1997). Common neural substrates for the addictive properties of nicotine and cocaine. *Science, 275*, 83–86.

Pies, R. W. (2013). Bereavement does not immunize against major depression. *Medscape.* Retrieved on January 29, 2013 from http://www.medscape.com/viewarticle/777960_print

Pigott, T. A. (1996). OCD: Where the serotonin selectivity story begins. *Journal of Clinical Psychiatry, 57*, 11–20.

Pigott, T. A. (1999). Gender differences in the epidemiology and treatment of anxiety disorders. *Journal of Clinical Psychiatry, 60* (Suppl. 18), 4–15.

Pigott, T, A., Myers, K. R., & Williams, D. A. (1996). Obsessive-compulsive disorder: A neuropsychiatric perspective. In R. M. Rapee (Ed.), *Current controversies in the anxiety disorders.* (pp. 13–160). New York: Guilford Press.

Pihl, R. O. (1999). Substance abuse: Etiological considerations. In T. Millon, P. H. Blaney, & R. D. Davis (Eds.), *Oxford textbook of psychopathology* (pp. 249–276). New York: Oxford University Press.

Pihl, R. O., & Peterson, J. B. (1995). Alcoholism: The role of different motivational systems. *Journal of Psychiatry & Neuroscience, 20*, 372–396.

Pike, K. M. (1998). Long-term course of anorexia nervosa: Response, relapse, remission, and recovery. *Clinical Psychology Review, 18*, 447–475.

Pike, K. M., Devlin, M. J., & Loeb, K. L. (2004). Cognitive-behavioral therapy in the treatment of anorexia nervosa, bulimia nervosa, and binge eating disorder. In J. K. Thompson (Ed.), *Handbook of eating disorders and obesity* (pp. 130–162). Hoboken, NJ: John Wiley & Sons.

Pike, K. M., & Walsh, T. (1996). Ethnicity and eating disorders: Implications for incidence and treatment. *Psychopharmacology Bulletin, 32*, 265–274.

Pike, K. M., Walsh, B. T., Vitousek, K., Wilson, G. T., & Bauer, J. (2003). Cognitive behavior therapy in the posthospitalization treatment of anorexia nervosa. *American Journal of Psychiatry, 160*, 2046–2049.

Pilkonis, P. A., & Krause, M. S. (1999). Summary: Paradigms for psychotherapy outcome research. *Journal of Clinical Psychology, 55*, 201–205.

Pilling, S., Bebbington, P., Kuipers, E., Garety, P., Geddes, J., Orbach, G., & Morgan, C. (2002). Psychological treatments in schizophrenia: I. Meta-analysis of family intervention and cognitive behaviour therapy. *Psychological Medicine, 32*, 763–782.

Pillmann, F., Haring, A., Balzuweit, S., & Marneros, A. (2002). A comparison of DSM-IV brief psychotic disorder with "positive" schizophrenia and healthy controls. *Comprehensive Psychiatry, 43*, 385–392.

Pilowsky, D. J., Wickramaratne, P., Nomura, Y., & Weissman, M. M. (2006). Family discord, parental depression, and psychopathology in offspring: 20-year follow-up. *Journal of the American Academy of Child & Adolescent Psychiatry, 45*, 452–460.

Pincus, A. L., & Wilson, K. R. (2001). Interpersonal variability in dependent personality. *Journal of Personality, 69*, 223–251.

Pine, D. S., Wasserman, G. A., Miller, L., Coplan, J. D., Bagiella, E., et al. (1998). Heart period variability and psychopathology in urban boys at risk for delinquency. *Psychophysiology, 35*, 521–529.

Pineda, D. A., Palacio, L. G., Puerta, I. C., Merchán, V., Arango, C. P., et al. (2007). Environmental influences that affect attention-deficit/hyperactivity disorder: Study of a genetic isolate. *European Child & Adolescent Psychiatry, 16*, 337–346.

Piñeros, M., Rosselli, D., & Calderon, C. (1998). An epidemic of collective conversion and dissociation disorder in an indigenous group of Colombia: Its relation to cultural change. *Social Science & Medicine, 46*, 1425–1428.

Pinkerman, J. E., Haynes, J. P., & Keiser, T. (1993). Characteristics of psychological practice in juvenile court clinics. *American Journal of Forensic Psychology, 11*, 3–12.

Piper, A., & Merskey, H. (2004a). The persistence of folly: A critical examination of dissociative identity disorder. Part I. The excesses of an improbable concept. *Canadian Journal of Psychiatry, 49*, 592–600.

Piper, A., & Merskey, H. (2004b). The persistence of folly: A critical examination of dissociative identity disorder. Part II. The defense and decline of multiple personality or dissociative identity disorder. *Canadian Journal of Psychiatry, 49*, 678–683.

Piper, W. E., & Joyce, A. S. (2001). Psychosocial treatment outcome. In W. J. Livesley (Ed.), *Handbook of personality disorders: Theory, research, and treatment* (pp. 323–343). New York: Guilford Press.

Piper, W. E., & Ogrodniczuk, J. S. (2005). Group treatment. In J. M. Oldham, A. E. Skodol, & D. S. Bender (Eds.), *The American Psychiatric Publishing textbook of personality disorders* (pp. 347–357). Washington, DC: American Psychiatric Publishing.

Piran, N., Jasper, K., & Pinhas, L. (2004). Feminist therapy and eating disorders. In J. K. Thompson (Ed.), *Handbook of eating disorders and obesity* (pp. 263–278). Hoboken, NJ: John Wiley & Sons.

Pissiota, A., Frans, O., Michelgård, A., Appel, L., Långström, B., et al. (2003). Amygdala and anterior cingulate cortex activation during affective startle modulation: a PET study of fear. *European Journal of Neuroscience, 18*, 1325–1331.

Pithers, W. D. (1990). Relapse prevention with sexual aggressors: A method for maintaining therapeutic gain and enhancing external supervision. In W. L. Marshall, D. R. Laws, & H. E. Barbaree (Eds.), *Handbook of sexual assault: Issues, theories, and treatment of the offender* (pp. 343–361). New York: Plenum Press.

Pitman, R. K., & Delahanty, D. L. (2005). Conceptually driven pharmacologic approaches to acute trauma. *CNS Spectrums, 10*, 99–106.

Pitman, R. K., Shin, L. M., & Rauch, S. L. (2001). Investigating the pathogenesis of posttraumatic stress disorder with neuroimaging. *Journal of Clinical Psychiatry, 62*, 47–54.

Pitschel-Walz, G., Leucht, S., Baeuml, J., Kissling, W., & Engel, R. R. (2001). The effect of family interventions on relapse and rehospitalization in schizophrenia—A meta-analysis. *Schizophrenia Bulletin, 27*, 73–92.

Pitts, F. M., & McClure, J. N. (1967). Lactate metabolism anxiety neurosis. *New England Journal of Medicine, 277*, 1329–1336.

Plassman, B. L., Langa, K. M., Fisher, G. G., Heeringa, S. G., Weir, D. R., et al. (2007). Prevalence of dementia in the United States: The Aging, Demographics, and Memory Study. *Neuroepidemiology, 29*, 125–132.

Plaze, M., Bartrés-Faz, D., Martinot, J., Januel, D., Bellivier, F., et al. (2006). Left superior temporal gyrus activation during sentence perception negatively correlates with auditory hallucination severity in schizophrenia patients. *Schizophrenia Research, 87*, 109–115.

Pliszka, S. R. (2007). Pharmacologic treatment of attention-deficit/hyperactivity disorder: Efficacy, safety and mechanisms of action. *Neuropsychology Review, 17*, 61–72.

Pliszka, S. R., Matthews, T. L., Braslow, K. J., & Watson, M. A. (2006). Comparative effects of methylphenidate and mixed salts amphetamine on height and weight in children with attention-deficit/hyperactivity disorder. *Journal of the American Academy of Child & Adolescent Psychiatry, 45*, 520–526.

Plomin, R., DeFries, J. C., Craig, I. W., & McGuffin, P. (Eds.). (2003). *Behavioral genetics in the postgenomic era.* Washington, DC: APA Books.

Plomin, R., DeFries, J. C., McClearn, G. E., & Rutter, M. (1997). *Behavioral genetics* (3rd ed.). New York: Freeman.

Plotsky, P. M., Thrivikraman, K. V., Nemeroff, C. B., Caldji, C., Sharma, S., & Meaney, M. J. (2005). Long-term consequences of neonatal rearing on central corticotropin-releasing factor systems in adult male rat offspring. *Neuropsychopharmacology. 30*, 2192–2204.

Pluess, M., Conrad, A., & Wilhelm, F. H. (2009). Muscle tension in generalized anxiety disorder: A critical review of the literature. *Journal of Anxiety Disorders, 23*, 1–11.

Poewe, W., Wolters, E., & Emre, M. (2006). Long-term benefits of rivastigmine in dementia associated with Parkinson's disease: An active treatment extension study. *Movement Disorders, 21*, 456–461.

Polanczyk, G., & Rohde, L. A. (2007). Epidemiology of attention-deficit/hyperactivity disorder across the lifespan. *Current Opinion in Psychiatry, 20*, 386–392.

Polanczyk, G., de Lima, M. S., Horta, B. L., Biederman, J., Rohde, L. A. (2007). The worldwide prevalence of ADHD: A systematic review and metaregression analysis. *American Journal of Psychiatry, 164*, 942–948.

Polivy, J. (1996). Psychological consequences of food restriction. *Journal of the American Dietetic Association, 96*, 589–592.

Polivy, J., & Herman, C. P. (1985). Dieting and binge eating: A causal analysis. *American Psychologist, 40*, 193–204.

Polivy, J., & Herman, C. P. (1993). Etiology of binge eating: Psychological mechanisms. In C. G. Fairburn, & G. T. Wilson (Eds.), *Binge eating: Nature, assessment, and treatment* (pp. 173–205). New York: Guilford Press.

Polivy, J., & Herman, C. P. (2002). Causes of eating disorders. *Annual Review of Psychology, 53*, 187–213.

Pollak, S. D., Cicchetti, D., Hornung, K., & Reed, A. (2000). Recognizing emotion in faces: Developmental effects of child abuse and neglect. *Developmental Psychology, 36*, 679–688.

Pollock, V. E., Briere, J., Schneider, L., Knop, J., Mednick, S. A., & Goodwin, D. W. (1990). Childhood antecedents of antisocial behavior: Parental alcoholism and physical abusiveness. *American Journal of Psychiatry, 147*, 1290–1293.

Pomeroy, C. (2004). Assessment of medical status and physical factors. In J. K. Thompson (Ed.), *Handbook of eating disorders and obesity* (pp. 81–111). Hoboken, NJ: John Wiley & Sons.

Poortinga, Y. H. (1995). Cultural bias in assessment: Historical and thematic issues. *European Journal of Psychological Assessment, 11*, 140–146.

Pope, H. G., Phillips, K. A., & Olivardia, R. (2000). *The Adonis complex: The secret crisis of male body obsession.* Sydney: Free Press.

Pope, H. G., & Yurgelin-Todd D. (1996). The residual cognitive effects of heavy marijuana use in college students. *JAMA: Journal of the American Medical Association, 275*, 521–527.

Pope, H. G., Gruber, A. J., Hudson, J. I., Huestis, M. A., & Yurgelun-Todd, D. (2001). Neuropsychological performance in long-term cannabis users. *Archives of General Psychiatry, 58*, 909–915.

Pope, H. G., Jr., Gruber, A. J., Choi, P., Olivardia, R., & Phillips, K. A. (1997). Muscle dysmorphia: An underrecognized form of body dysmorphic disorder. *Psychosomatics: Journal of Consultation and Liaison Psychiatry, 38*, 548–557.

Pope, H. G., Jr., Gruber, A. J., Mangweth, B., Bureau, B., deCol, C., et al. (2000). Body image perception among men in three countries. *American Journal of Psychiatry, 157,* 1297–1301.

Pope, H. G., Jr., Oliva, P. S., Hudson, J. I., Bodkin, J. A., & Gruber, A. J. (1999). Attitudes toward DSM-IV-TR dissociative disorders diagnoses among board-certified American psychiatrists. *American Journal of Psychiatry, 156,* 321–323.

Pope, H. G., Jr., Poliakoff, M. B., Parker, M. P., Boynes, M., & Hudson, J. I. (2007). Is dissociative amnesia a culture-bound syndrome? Findings from a survey of historical literature. *Psychological Medicine, 37,* 225–233.

Porter, R. (2002). *Madness: A brief history.* New York: Oxford University Press.

Porter, V. R., Buxton, W. G., Fairbanks, L. A., Strickland, T., O'Connor, S. M., et al. (2003). Frequency and characteristics of anxiety among patients with Alzheimer's disease and related dementias. *Journal of Neuropsychiatry & Clinical Neurosciences, 15,* 180–186.

Potter, G. G., & Steffens, D. C. (2007, November 1). Depression and cognitive impairment in older adults. *Psychiatric Times, 24.* Retrieved January 10, 2008, from www.psychiatrictimes.com/showArticle. jhtml;jsessionid=Z3DNXGDTE ZBJAQSNDLO SKH0CJUNN2JVN?articleId=202602111

Poulet, E., Brunelin, J., Bediou, B., Bation, R., Forgeard, L., et al. (2005). Slow transcranial magnetic stimulation can rapidly reduce resistant auditory hallucinations in schizophrenia. *Biological Psychiatry, 57,* 188–191.

Poulton, R., & Menzies, R. G. (2002). Non-associative fear acquisition: A review of the evidence from retrospective and longitudinal research. *Behaviour Research and Therapy, 40,* 127–149.

Poulton, R., Menzies, R. G., Craske, M. G., Langley, J. D., & Silva, P. A. (1999). Water trauma and swimming experiences up to age 9 and fear of water at age 18: A longitudinal study. *Behaviour Research and Therapy, 37,* 39–48.

Powell, R. A., & Gee, T. L. (1999). The effects of hypnosis on dissociative identity disorder: A reexamination of the evidence. *Canadian Journal of Psychiatry, 44,* 914–916.

Power, K. G., McGoldrick, T., Brown, K., Buchanan, R., Sharp, D., et al. (2002). A controlled comparison of eye movement desensitization and reprocessing versus exposure plus cognitive restructuring, versus waiting list in the treatment of posttraumatic stress disorder. *Journal of Clinical Psychology and Psychotherapy, 9,* 299–318.

Powers, M. B., & Emmelkamp, P. M. G. (2008). Virtual reality exposure therapy for anxiety disorders: A meta-analysis. *Journal of Anxiety Disorders, 22,* 561–569.

Powers, P. S., Santana, C. A., & Bannon, Y. S. (2002). Olanzapine in the treatment of anorexia nervosa: An open label trial. *International Journal of Eating Disorders, 32,* 146–154.

Pratt, B., & Woolfenden, S. (2002). Interventions for preventing eating disorders in children and adolescents. *Cochrane Database of Systematic Reviews (2):* CD002891.

Prazeres, A. M., Nascimento, A. L., & Fontenelle, L. F. (2013). Cognitive-behavioral therapy for body dysmorphic disorder: A review of its efficacy. *Neuropsychiatric Disease and Treatment, 9,* Article ID 307-316.

Pressman, L. J., Loo, S. K., Carpenter, E. M., Asarnow, J. R., Lynn, D., et al. (2006). Relationship of family environment and parental psychiatric diagnosis to impairment in ADHD. *Journal of the American Academy of Child & Adolescent Psychiatry, 45,* 346–354.

Preti, A. (2003). Unemployment and suicide. *Journal of Epidemiology & Community Health, 57,* 557–558.

Pretzer, J. L., & Beck, A. T. (2005). A cognitive theory of personality disorders. In M. F. Lenzenweger & J. F. Clarkin (Eds.), *Major theories of personality disorder* (2nd ed., pp. 43–113). New York: Guilford Press.

Price, B. H., Baral, I., Cosgrove, G. R., Rauch, S. L., Nierenberg, A. A., et al H. (2001). Improvement in severe self-mutilation following limbic leucotomy: A series of 5 consecutive cases. *Journal of Clinical Psychiatry, 62,* 925–932.

Price, D. D., Finniss, D. G., & Benedetti, F. (2008). A comprehensive review of the placebo effect: Recent advances and current thought. *Annual Review of Psychology, 59,* 565–590.

Price, R. W. (2003). Editorial comment: Diagnosis of focal brain lesions—old lessons retaught. *AIDS Reader, 13,* 553.

Prichard, Z. M., Jorm, A. F., Mackinnon, A., & Easteal, S. (2007). Association analysis of 15 polymorphisms within 10 candidate genes for antisocial behavioural traits. *Psychiatric Genetics, 17,* 299–303.

Pridmore, S., Chambers, A., & McArthur, M. (2005). Neuroimaging in psychopathy. *Australian and New Zealand Journal of Psychiatry, 39,* 856–865.

Prien, R. F. & Kocsis, J. H. (1995). Long-term treatment of mood disorders. In *Psychopharmacology: the Fourth Generation of Progress.* F. E. Bloom & D. J. Kupfer (Eds.), (pp. 1067–1079). New York: Raven Press.

Priest, D. (2008). Soldier suicides at record level. *Washington Post, 130*(422).

Prince, M., Bryce, R., Albanese, E., Wimo, A., Ribeiro, W., & Ferri, C. P. (2013). The global prevalence of dementia: A systematic review and metaanalysis. *Alzheimer's & Dementia, 9*(1), 63–75.

Prins, A., Kaloupek, D. G., & Keane, T. M. (1995). Psychophysiological evidence for autonomic arousal and startle in traumatized adult populations. In M. J. Friedman D. S. Charney, & A. Y. Deutch (Eds.), *Neurobiological and clinical consequences of stress: From normal adaptation to posttraumatic stress disorder* (pp. 291–314). Philadelphia: Lippincott Williams & Wilkins.

Prochaska, J. O., Norcross, J. C., & DiClemente, C. C. (2007). *Changing for good.* New York: Morrow.

Prochaska, J. O., Velicer, W. F., Rossi, J. S., Goldstein, M. G., Marcus, B. H., et al. (1994). Stages of change and decisional balance for 12 problem behaviors. *Health Psychology, 13,* 39–46.

Project MATCH Research Group. (1997). Matching alcoholism treatments to patient heterogeneity: Project MATCH posttreatment drinking outcomes. *Journal of Studies on Alcohol, 58,* 7–29.

Project MATCH Research Group. (1998). Matching alcoholism treatments to patient heterogeneity: Project MATCH three-year drinking outcomes. *Alcoholism: Clinical & Experimental Research, 22,* 1300–1311.

Project search. (2006). *The Advance* (APSE newsletter), *17.* Retrieved August 2, 2007, from www.apse.org/docs/falladvance2006.pdf

Propper, C., & Moore, G. A. (2006). The influence of parenting on infant emotionality: A multi-level psychobiological perspective. *Developmental Review, 26,* 427–460.

Pruett, M. K., Insabella, G. M., & Gustafson, K. (2005). The Collaborative Divorce Project: A court-based intervention for separating parents with young children. *Family Court Review, 43,* 38–51.

Przeworski, A., & Newman, M. G. (2004). Palmtop computer-assisted group therapy for social phobia. *Journal of Clinical Psychology, 60,* 179–188.

Puente, A. E. (2003). Neuropsychology: Introducing aging into the study of brain and behavior. In S. K. Whitbourne & J. C. Cavanaugh (Eds.), *Integrating aging topics into psychology: A practical guide for teaching* (pp. 29–42). Washington, DC: American Psychological Association.

Pull, C. B. (2005). Current status of virtual reality exposure therapy in anxiety disorders. *Current Opinion in Psychiatry, 18,* 7–14.

Putnam, F. W. (1989). Pierre Janet and modern views of dissociation. *Journal of Traumatic Stress, 2,* 413–429.

Putnam, F. W. (1995). Development of dissociative disorders. In: D. Cicchetti & D. J. Cohen (Eds.), *Developmental psychopathology* (Vol. 2, pp. 581–608). New York: Wiley.

Putnam, F. W., & Loewenstein, R. J. (1993). Treatment of multiple personality disorder: A survey of current practices. *American Journal of Psychiatry, 150,* 1048–1052.

Putnam, F. W., Helmers, K., Horowitz, L. A., & Trickett, P. K. (1995). Hypnotizability and dissociativity in sexually abused girls. *Child Abuse & Neglect, 19,* 645–655.

Pyszczynski, T., & Greenberg, J. (1987). Self-regulatory perseveration and the depressive self-focusing style: A self-awareness theory of reactive depression. *Psychological Bulletin, 102,* 1–17.

Qin, P., & Mortensen, P. B. (2001). Specific characteristics of *suicide* in China. *Acta Psychiatrica Scandinavica, 103,* 117–121.

Quattrocchi, M. R., & Schopp, R. F. (2005). *Tarasaurus rex:* A standard of care that could not adapt. *Psychology, Public Policy, and Law, 11,* 109–137.

Quinn, P. O. (2005). Treating adolescent girls and women with ADHD: Gender-specific issues. *Journal of Clinical Psychology, 61,* 579–587.

Quinta Gomes, A. L., & Nobre, P. (2012). Early maladaptive schemas and sexual dysfunction in men. *Archives of Sexual Behavior, 41*(1), 311–320.

Rabheru, K. (2001). The use of electroconvulsive therapy in special patient populations. *The Canadian Journal of Psychiatry/ La Revue canadienne de psychiatrie, 46,* 710–719.

Rabin, L. A., Wishart, H. A., Fields, R. B., & Saykin, A. J. (2006). The dementias. In P. J. Snyder, P. D. Nussbaum, & D. L. Robins (Eds.), *Clinical neuropsychology: A pocket handbook for assessment* (2nd ed., pp. 210–239). Washington, DC: American Psychological Association.

Rachman, S. (1997). A cognitive theory of obsessions. *Behaviour Research and Therapy, 35,* 793–802.

Radomsky, A. S., Rachman, S., & Hammond, D. (2001). Memory bias, confidence and responsibility in compulsive checking. *Behaviour Research and Therapy, 39,* 813–822.

Raimo, E. B., Roemer, R. A., Moster, M., & Shan, Y. (1999). Alcohol-induced depersonalization. *Biological Psychiatry, 45,* 1523–1526.

Raine, A. (2002). Biosocial studies of antisocial and violent behavior in children and adults: A review. *Journal of Abnormal Child Psychology, 30,* 311–326.

Raine, A. (2006). Schizotypal personality: Neurodevelopmental and psychosocial trajectories. *Annual Review of Clinical Psychology, 2,* 291–326.

Raine, A., Brennan, P., Mednick, B., & Mednick, S. A. (1996). High rates of violence, crime, academic problems, and behavioral problems in males with both early neuromotor deficits and unstable family environments. *Archives of General Psychiatry, 53,* 544–549.

Raine, A., Buchsbaum, M., & LaCasse, L. (1997). Brain abnormalities in murderers indicated by positron emission tomography. *Biological Psychiatry, 42,* 495–508.

Raine, A., Lencz, T., Bihrle, S., LaCasse, L, & Colletti, P. (2000). Reduced prefrontal gray matter volume and reduced autonomic activity in antisocial personality disorder. *Archives of General Psychiatry, 57,* 119–127.

Raine, A., Lencz, T., Taylor, K., Hellige, J. B., Bihrle, S., et al. (2003). Corpus callosum abnormalities in psychopathic antisocial individuals. *Archives of General Psychiatry, 60,* 1134–1142.

Raine, A., Meloy, J. R., Bihrle, S., Stoddard, J., LaCasse, L., & Buchsbaum, M. S. (1998). Reduced prefrontal and increased subcortical brain functioning assessed using positron emission tomography in predatory and affective murderers. *Behavioral Sciences & the Law, 16*(3), 319–332.

Rajkowska, G. (1997). Morphometric methods for studying the prefrontal cortex in suicide victims and psychiatric patients. *Annals of the New York Academy of Sciences, 836,* 253–268.

Rajska-Neumann, A., & Wieczorowska-Tobis, K. (2007). Polypharmacy and potential inappropriateness of pharmacological treatment among community-dwelling elderly patients. *Archives of Gerontology and Geriatrics, 44,* 303–309.

Rakoff, D. (2002, December 29). The lives they lived; The debutante's staying-in party. *The New York Times.*

Raleigh, M. J., McGuire, M. T., Brammer, G. L., & Yuwiler, A. (1984). Social and environmental influences on blood serotonin concentrations in monkeys. *Archives of General Psychiatry, 41,* 405–410.

Ramaekers, J. G., Kauert, G., van Ruitenbeek, P., Theunissen, E. L., Schneider, E., & Moeller, M. R. (2006). High-potency marijuana impairs executive function and inhibitory motor control. *Neuropsychopharmacology, 31,* 2296–2303.

Ramafedi, G. (1999). Suicide and sexual orientation: Nearing the end of a controversy? *Archives of General Psychiatry, 56,* 885–886.

Ramanathan, S., Balasubramanian, N., & Krishnadas, R. (2013). Macroeconomic environment during infancy as a possible risk factor for adolescent behavioral problems. *JAMA Psychiatry, 70*(2), 218–225.

Ramirez, M., III. (1999). *Multicultural psychotherapy: An approach to individual and cultural differences* (2nd ed.). Needham Heights, MA: Allyn & Bacon.

Ramírez-Esparza, N., Gosling, S. D., Benet-Martínez, V., Potter, J. P., & Pennebaker, J. W. (2006). Do bilinguals have two personalities? A special case of cultural frame switching. *Journal of Research in Personality, 40,* 99–120.

Ramus, F. Rosen, S., Dakin, S., Day, B., Castellote, J., et al. (2003). Theories of developmental dyslexia: Insights from a multiple case study of dyslexic adults. *Brain, 126,* 841–865.

Rand Corporation. (2001). Retrieved October 27, 2006, from www.rand.org/news/Press/ ca.mental.htmlRedlich, A. D., Steadman, H. J., Monahan, J., Petrila, J., & Griffin, P. A. (2005). The second generation of mental health courts. *Psychology, Public Policy, and Law, 11,* 527–538.

Rao, U., Dahl, R. E., Ryan, N. D., Birmaher, B., Williamson, D. E., Rao, R., & Kaufman, J. (2002). Heterogeneity in EEG sleep findings in adolescent depression: Unipolar versus bipolar clinical course. *Journal of Affective Disorders, 70,* 273–280.

Rao V., & Lyketsos, C. G. (1998). Delusions in Alzheimer's disease. *Journal of Neuropsychiatry & Clinical Neurosciences, 10,* 373–382.

Rapee, R. M., & Abbott, M. J. (2006). Mental representation of observable attributes in people with social phobia. *Journal of Behavior Therapy and Experimental Psychiatry, 37,* 113–126.

Rapee, R. M., & Heimberg, R. G. (1997). A cognitive-behavioral model of anxiety in social phobia. *Behaviour Research and Therapy, 35,* 741–756.

Raphael, F. J., & Lacey, J. H. (1992). Sociocultural aspects of eating disorders. *Annals of Medicine, 24,* 293–296.

Rapoport, J. L. (1991). Recent advances in obsessive-compulsive disorder. *Neuropsychopharmacology, 5,* 1–10.

Rapoport, J. L., Giedd, J. N., Blumenthal, J., Hamburger, S., Jeffries, N., et al. (1999). Progressive cortical change during adolescence in childhood-onset schizophrenia: A longitudinal magnetic resonance imaging study. *Archives of General Psychiatry, 56,* 649–654.

Rapoport, M. J., Mamdani, M., & Herrmann, N. (2006). Electroconvulsive therapy in older adults: 13-year trends. *The Canadian Journal of Psychiatry/La Revue canadienne de psychiatrie, 51,* 616–619.

Raskin, M., Talbott, J. A., & Meyerson, A. T. (1966). Diagnosis of conversion reactions: Predictive value of psychiatric criteria. *Journal of the American Medical Association, 197,* 530–534.

Rasmussen, H. B., Timm, S., Wang, A. G., Soeby, K., Lublin, H., et al. (2006). Association between the CCR5 32-bp deletion allele and late onset of schizophrenia. *American Journal of Psychiatry, 163,* 507–511.

Rasmussen, P. R. (2005). The avoidant prototype. In P. R. Rasmussen (Ed.), *Personality-guided cognitive-behavioral therapy* (pp. 191–213). Washington, DC: American Psychological Association.

Rauch, S. L., Dougherty, D. D., Cosgrove, G. R., Cassem, E. H., Alpert, N. M., et al. (2001). Cerebral metabolic correlates as potential predictors of response to anterior cingulotomy for obsessive compulsive disorder. *Biological Psychiatry, 50,* 659–667.

Rauch, S. L., Dougherty, D. D., Malone, D., Rezai, A., Friehs, G., et al. (2006). A functional neuroimaging investigation of deep brain stimulation in patients with obsessive-compulsive disorder. *Journal of Neurosurgery, 104,* 558–565.

Rauch, S. L., Jenike, M. A., Alpert, N. M., Baer, L., Breiter, H. C., et al. (1994). Regional cerebral blood flow measured during symptom provocation in obsessive-compulsive disorder using oxygen 15-labeled carbon dioxide and positron emission tomography. *Archives of General Psychiatry, 51,* 62–70.

Rauch, S. L., Savage, C. R., Alpert, N. M., Miguel, E. C., Baer, L., et al. (1995). A positron emission tomographic study of simple phobic symptom provocation. *Archives of General Psychiatry, 52,* 20–28.

Rauch, S. L., Savage, C. R., Brown, H. D., Curran, T., Alpert, N. M., et al. (1995). A PET investigation of implicit and explicit sequence learning. *Human Brain Mapping, 3,* 271–286.

Rauch, S. L., Shin, L. M., & Phelps, E. A. (2006). Neurocircuitry models of posttraumatic stress disorder and extinction: Human neuroimaging research—past, present, and future. *Biological Psychiatry, 60,* 376–382.

Rauch, S. L., van der Kolk, B. A., Fisler, R. E., & Alpert, N. M. (1996). A symptom provocation study of posttraumatic stress disorder using positron emission tomography and script-driven imagery. *Archives of General Psychiatry, 53,* 380–387.

Rauch, S. L., Whalen, P. J., Shin, L. M., McInerney, S. C., Macklin, M. L., et al. (2000). Exaggerated amygdala response to masked facial stimuli in posttraumatic stress disorder: A functional MRI study. *Biological Psychiatry, 47,* 769–776.

Raymond, N. C., Coleman, E., Ohlerking, F., Christenson, G. A., & Miner, M. (1999). Psychiatric comorbidity in pedophilic sex offenders. *American Journal of Psychiatry, 156,* 786–788.

Ready, D. J., Pollack, S., Rothbaum, B. O., & Alarcon, R. D. (2006). Virtual reality exposure for veterans with posttraumatic stress disorder. *Journal of Aggression, Maltreatment & Trauma, 12,* 199–220.

Rebec, G. V. (2000). Cocaine. In A. E. Kazdin (Ed.), *Encyclopedia of psychology* (Vol. 2, pp. 130–131). Washington, DC: American Psychological Association.

Rector, N. A., & Beck, A. T. (2002a). A clinical review of cognitive therapy for schizophrenia. *Current Psychiatry Report, 4,* 284–292.

Rector, N. A., & Beck, A. T. (2002b). Cognitive therapy for schizophrenia: From conceptualisation to intervention. *Canadian Journal of Psychiatry, 47,* 39–48.

Rector, N. A., Seeman, M. V., & Segal, Z. V. (2003). Cognitive therapy of schizophrenia: A preliminary randomized controlled trial. *Schizophrenia Research, 63,* 1–11.

Reger, G. M., & Gahm, G. A. (2008). Virtual reality exposure therapy for active duty soldiers. *Journal of Clinical Psychology, 64,* 940–946.

Regier, D. A., Farmer, M. E., Rae, D. S., Locke, B. Z., Keith, S. J., et al. (1990). Comorbidity of mental disorders with alcohol and other drug abuse: Results from the Epidemiologic Catchment Area (ECA) study. *Journal of the American Medical Association, 264,* 2511–2518.

Regier, D. A., Narrow, W. E., Rae, D. S., Manderscheid, R. W., Locke, B. Z., & Goodwin, F. K. (1993). The de facto US mental and addictive disorders service system: Epidemiologic Catchment Area prospective 1-year prevalence rates of disorders and services. *Archives of General Psychiatry, 50,* 85–94.

Rehm, L. P. (2002). How can we better disentangle placebo and drug effects? *Prevention & Treatment, 5,* Article 31. http://www.journals.apa.org/prevention/volume5/pre0050031c.html

Reich, J. (2000). The relationship of social phobia to avoidant personality disorder: A proposal to reclassify avoidant personality disorder based on clinical empirical findings. *European Psychiatry, 15,* 151–159.

Reichenberg, A., Gross, R., Weiser, M., Bresnahan, M., Silverman, J., et al. (2006). Advancing paternal age and autism. *Archives of General Psychiatry, 63,* 1026–1032.

Reichenberg, A., Rieckmann, N., & Harvey, P. D. (2005). Stability in schizophrenia symptoms over time: Findings from the Mount Sinai Pilgrim Psychiatric Center longitudinal study. *Journal of Abnormal Psychology, 114,* 363–372.

Reid, G., Aitken, C., Beyer, L., & Crofts, N. (2001). Ethnic communities' vulnerability to involvement with illicit drugs. *Drugs: Education, Prevention & Policy, 8,* 359–374.

Reifman, A., & Windle, M. (1995). Adolescent suicidal behaviors as a function of depression, hopelessness, alcohol use, and social support: A longitudinal investigation. *American Journal of Community Psychology, 23,* 329–354.

Reiland, R. (2004). *Get me out of here: My recovery from borderline personality pisorder.* Center City, MN: Hazeldon.

Reinberg, A. (2011). CDC: Half of Americans will suffer from mental health woes. *USA Today,* September 9, 2011. Retrieved November 15, 2011, from http://yourlife.usatoday.com/health/medical/mentalhealth/story/2011-09-05/CDC-Half-of-Americans-will-suffer-from-mental-health-woes/50250702/1

Reinders, A. A., Nijenhuis, E. R., Paans, A. M., Korf, J., Willemsen, A. T., & den Boer, J. A. (2003). One brain, two selves. *Neuroimage, 20,* 2119–2125.

Reiner, R. (2008). Integrating a portable biofeedback device into clinical practice for patients with anxiety disorders: Results of a pilot study. *Applied Psychophysiology and Biofeedback, 33,* 55–61.

Reisberg, B., Ferris, S. H., de Leon, M. J., & Crook, T. (1982). The Global Deterioration Scale for the assessment of primary degenerative dementia. *American Journal of Psychiatry, 139,* 1136–1139.

Reiss, S. (1991). Expectancy model of fear, anxiety, and panic. *Clinical Psychology Review, 11,* 141–153.

Reiss, S., & McNally, R. J. (1985). Expectancy model of fear. In S. Reiss and R. R. Bootzin (Eds.), *Theoretical issues in behavior therapy* (pp. 107–121). New York: Academic Press.

Reitan, R. M. (1958). Validity of the Trail Making Test as an indicator of organic brain damage. *Perceptual and Motor Skills, 8,* 271–276.

Reitan, R. M., & Davison, L. A. (1974). *Clinical neuropsychology: Current status and applications. The series in clinical psychology* (Vol. 2). Washington, DC: V. H. Winston.

Relkin, N., Bettger, L., Tsakanikas, D., & Ravdin, L. (2012). Three-year follow-up on the IVIG for Alzheimer's phase II study. *Alzheimer's Association International Conference.* Abstract P3-381. Presented July 17, 2012.

Remafedi, G. (1999). Sexual orientation and youth suicide. *JAMA: Journal of the American Medical Association, 282,* 1291–1292.

Rende, R., & Plomin, R. (1992). Diathesis–stress models of psychopathology: A quantitative genetic perspective. *Applied & Preventative Psychology, 1,* 177–182.

Renner, L. M., & Slack, K. S. (2006). Intimate partner violence and child maltreatment: Understanding intra- and intergenerational connections. *Child Abuse & Neglect, 30,* 599–617.

Rennie v. Klein, 462 F. Supp. 1131; 1978 U.S. Dist. LEXIS 14441 (1978).

Resnick, H. S., Kilpatrick, D. G., Dansky, B. S., Saunders, B. E., & Best, C. L. (1993). Prevalence of civilian trauma and posttraumatic stress disorder in a representative national sample of women. *Journal of Consulting and Clinical Psychology, 61,* 984–991.

Ressler, K. J., Rothbaum, B. O., Tannenbaum, L., Anderson, P., Graap, K., et al. (2004). Cognitive enhancers as adjuncts to psychotherapy: Use of D-cycloserine in phobic individuals to facilitate extinction of fear. *Archives of General Psychiatry, 61,* 1136–1144.

Rettew, D. C., & McKee, L. (2005). Temperament and its role in developmental psychopathology. *Harvard Review of Psychiatry, 13,* 14–27.

Rettew, D. C., Doyle, A. C., Kwan, M., Stanger, C., & Hudziak, J. J. (2006). Exploring the boundary between temperament and generalized anxiety disorder: A receiver operating characteristic analysis. *Journal of Anxiety Disorders, 20,* 931–945.

Reynolds, C. A., Raine, A., Mellingen, K., Venables, P. H., & Mednick, S. A. (2000.) Three-factor model of schizotypal personality: Invariance across culture, gender, religious affiliation, family adversity, and psychopathology. *Schizophrenia Bulletin, 26,* 603–618.

Reynolds, S., Stiles, W. B., Barkham, M., Shapiro, D. A., Hardy, G. E., & Rees, A. (1996). Acceleration of changes in session impact during contrasting time-limited psychotherapies. *Journal of Consulting and Clinical Psychology, 64,* 577–586.

Rhode, P., Lewinsohn, P. M., Klein, D. N., Seeley, J. R., & Gau, J. M. (2013). Key characteristics of major depressive disorder occurring in childhood, adolescence, emerging adulthood, and adulthood. *Clinical Psychological Science, 1,* 41–53.

Ricca, V., Mannucci, E., Mezzani, B., Di Bernardo, M., Zucchi, T., et al. (2001). Psychopathological and clinical features of outpatients with an eating disorder not otherwise specified. *Eating & Weight Disorders, 6,* 157–165.

Ricciardelli, L. A., & McCabe, M. P. (2001). Self-esteem and negative affect as moderators of sociocultural influences on body dissatisfaction strategies to decrease weight and strategies to increase muscle tone among adolescent boys and girls. *Sex Roles, 44,* 189–207.

Ricciardelli, L. A., McCabe, M. P., Lillis, J., & Thomas, K. (2006). A Longitudinal Investigation of the Development of Weight and Muscle Concerns Among Preadolescent Boys. *Journal of Youth and Adolescence, 35,* 177–187.

Riccio, C. A., Wolfe, M., Davis, B., Romine, C., George, C., & Lee, D. (2005). Attention-deficit hyperactivity disorder: Manifestation in adulthood. *Archives of Clinical Neuropsychology, 20,* 249–269.

Rice, F., Harold, G., & Thaper, A. (2002). The genetic aetiology of childhood depression: A review. *Journal of Child Psychology & Psychiatry, 43,* 65–79.

Rice, M. E., Harris, G., & Cormier, C. (1992). An evaluation of a maximum security therapeutic community for psychopaths and other mentally disordered offenders. *Law and Human Behavior; 16*, 399–412.

Rice, M. J., & Moller, M. D. (2006). Wellness outcomes of trauma psychoeducation. *Archives of Psychiatric Nursing, 20*, 94–102.

Richards, J. C., Edgar, L. V., & Gibbon, P. (1996). Cardiac acuity in panic disorder. *Cognitive Therapy and Research, 20*, 361–376.

Richards, R., Kinney, D. K., Lunde, I., Benet, M., & Merzel, A. P. C. (1988). Creativity in manic-depressives, cyclothymes, their normal relatives, and control subjects. *Journal of Abnormal Psychology 97*, 281–288.

Rieber, R. W. (1999). Hypnosis, false memory and multiple personality: A trinity of affinity. *History of Psychiatry, 10*, 3–11.

Rief, W., & Nanke, A. (1999). Somatization disorder from a cognitive-psychobiological perspective. *Current Opinion in Psychiatry, 12*, 733–738.

Rief, W., Heuser, J., Mayrhuber, E., Stelzer, I., Hiller, W., & Fichter, M. M. (1996). The classification of multiple somatoform symptoms. *Journal of Nervous and Mental Disease, 184*, 680–687. Rosenbloom, M., Sullivan, E.V., & Pfefferbaum, A. (2003). Using magnetic resonance imaging and diffusion tensor imaging to assess brain damage in alcoholics. *Alcohol Research & Health 27*, 146–152.

Ries, R. K., Galanter, M., & Tonigan, J. S. (2008). Twelve-step facilitation. In M. Galanter, & H. D. Kleber, (Eds.), *The American Psychiatric Publishing textbook of substance abuse treatment (4th ed.).* (pp. 373–386). Arlington, VA: American Psychiatric Publishing, Inc.

Rifkin, A., Ghisalbert, D., Dimatou, S., Jin, C., & Sethi, M. (1998). Dissociative identity disorder in psychiatric inpatients. *American Journal of Psychiatry, 155*, 844–845.

Rihmer, Z. (2007). Suicide risk in mood disorders. *Current Opinion in Psychiatry, 20*, 17–22.

Rihmer, Z., Rutz, W., Pihlgren, H., & Pestality, P. (1998). Decreasing tendency of seasonality in suicide may indicate lowering rate of depressive suicides in the population. *Psychiatry Research, 81*, 233–240.

Riley, E. A., Clemson, L., Sitharthan, G., & Diamond, M. (2013). Surviving a gender variant childhood: The views of transgender adults on the needs of gender variant children and their parents. *Journal of Sex and Marital Therapy, 39*, 241–263.

Riley, E. P., & McGee, C. L. (2005). Fetal alcohol spectrum disorders: An overview with emphasis on changes in brain and behavior. *Experimental Biology and Medicine, 230*, 357–365.

Ringman, J. M., & Cummings, J. L. (2006). Current and emerging pharmacological treatment options for dementia. *Behavioral Neurology, 17*, 5–16.

Rinne, T., de Kloet, E. R., Wouters, L., Goekoop, J. G., DeRijk, R. H., & van den Brink, W. (2002). Hyperresponsiveness of hypothalamic-pituitary adrenal axis to combined dexamethasone/corticotropin-releasing hormone challenge in female borderline personality disorder subjects with a history of sustained childhood abuse. *Biological Psychiatry, 52*, 1102–1112.

Riskind, J. H., & Alloy, L. B. (2006). Cognitive vulnerability to psychological disorders: Overview of theory, design, and methods. *Journal of Social & Clinical Psychology, 25*, 705–725.

Riskind, J. H., Moore, R., & Bowley, L. (1995). The looming of spiders: The fearful perceptual distortion of movement and menace. *Behavior Research and Therapy, 33*, 171–178.

Ritchie, C. W., Ames, D., Clayton, T., & Lai, R. (2004). Meta-analysis of randomized trials of the efficacy and safety of donepezil, galantamine, and rivastigmine for the treatment of Alzheimer disease. *American Journal of Geriatric Psychiatry, 12*, 358–369.

Ritchie, K., & Lovestone, S. (2002). The dementias. *Lancet, 360*, 1767–1769.

Ritterband, L. M., Gonder-Frederick, L. A., Cox, D. J., Clifton, A. D., West, R. W., & Borowitz, S. M. (2003). Internet interventions: In review, in use, and into the future. *Professional Psychology: Research & Practice, 34*, 527–534.

Rivas-Vazquez, R. A. (2001). Antidepressants as first-line agents in the current pharmacotherapy of anxiety disorders. *Professional Psychology: Research and Practice, 32*, 101–104.

Rivas-Vazquez, R. A., Rice, J., & Kalman, D. (2003). Pharmacotherapy of obesity and eating disorders. *Professional Psychology: Research & Practice, 34*, 562–566.

Robbins, T. W. (2000). Chemical neuromodulation of frontal-executive functions in humans and other animals. *Experimental Brain Research, 133*, 130–138.

Robbins, T. W., & Everitt, B. J. (1999a). Drug addiction: Bad habits add up. *Nature, 398*, 567–570.

Robbins, T. W., & Everitt, B. J. (1999b). Interaction of the dopaminergic system with mechanisms of associative learning and cognition: Implications for drug abuse. *Psychological Science, 10*, 199–202.

Roberson-Nay, R., Eaves, L. J., Hettema, J. M., Kendler, K. S., & Silberg, J. L. (2012). Childhood separation anxiety disorder and adult onset panic attacks share a common genetic diathesis. *Depression and Anxiety, 29*(4), 320–327.

Roberts, A. L., Rosario, M., Corliss, H. L., Koenen, K. C., & Austin, S. B. (2012). Childhood gender nonconformity: A risk indicator for childhood abuse and posttraumatic stress in youth. *Pediatrics, 129*, 410–417.

Robins, C. J., Ivanoff, A. M., & Linehan, M. M. (2001). Dialectical behavior therapy. In W. J. Livesley (Ed.), *Handbook of personality disorders: Theory, research, and treatment* (pp. 437–459). New York: Guilford Press.

Robins, L. N., & Regier, D. A. (1991). *Psychiatric disorders in America: The Epidemiological Catchment Area Study.* New York: Free Press.

Robinson, D., Woerner, M. G., Alvir, J. M., Bilder, R., Goldman, R., et al. (1999). Predictors of relapse following response from a first episode of schizophrenia or schizoaffective disorder. *Archives of General Psychiatry, 56*, 241–247.

Robinson, J., Sareen, J., Cox, B. J., & Bolton, J. M. (2011). Role of self-medication in the development of comorbid anxiety and substance use disorders. *Archives of General Psychiatry, 68*, 800–807.

Robinson, M. S., & Alloy, L. B. (2003). Negative cognitive styles and stress-reactive rumination interact to predict depression: A prospective study. *Cognitive Therapy and Research, 27*, 275–292.

Robinson, T., & Valcour, F. (1995). The use of depo-provera in the treatment of child molesters and sexually compulsive males. *Sexual Addiction & Compulsivity, 2*, 277–294.

Rodewald, F., Dell, P. F., Wilhelm-Gößling, C., & Gast, U. (2011). Are major dissociative disorders characterized by a qualitatively different kind of dissociation? *Journal of Trauma & Dissociation, 12*, 9–24.

Roelofs, K., Hooguin, K. A. L., Keijers, G. P. J., Näring, G. W. B., Moene, G. C., & Sandijck, P. (2002). Hypnotic susceptibility in patients With conversion disorder. *Journal of Abnormal Psychology, 111*, 390–395.

Roelofs, K., Spinhoven, P., Sandijck, P., Moene, F. C., & Hooguin, K. A. L. (2005). The impact of early trauma and recent life events on symptom severity in patients with conversion disorder. *Journal of Nervous and Mental Disease, 193*, 508–514.

Roelofs, K., van Galen, G. P., Keijsers, G. P., & Hooguin, C. A. (2002). Motor initiation and execution in patients with conversion paralysis. *Acta Psychologica, 110*, 21–34.

Roesler, A. & Witztum, E. (2000). Pharmacotherapy of paraphilias in the next millennium. *Behavioral Sciences & the Law, 18*, 43–56.

Rogan, R. G., & Hammer, M. R. (1998). An exploratory study of message affect behavior: A comparison between African Americans and Euro-Americans. *Journal of Language and Social Psychology, 17*, 449–464.

Rogers, C. R. (1942). *Counseling and psychotherapy: Newer concepts in practice.* Oxford, England: Houghton Mifflin.

Rogers, C. R. (1951). *Client-centered therapy: Its current practice, implications, and theory.* Boston: Houghton Mifflin.

Rogers, S. J. (1998). Neuropsychology of autism in young children and its implications for early intervention. *Mental Retardation and Developmental Disabilities Research Reviews, 4*, 104–112.

Rohde, D. (1999a, October 16). Jury hears a confession in killing. *The New York Times*, p. B2.

Rohde, D. (1999b, March 4). Man claims "ghost" drove him to push woman to her death. *The New York Times*, p. B2.

Rohde, D. (1999c, October 9). Witness tearfully describes fatal subway shoving. *The New York Times* p. B2,.

Rohde, D. (2000, February 23). For retrial, subway defendant goes off medication. *The New York Times*, p. B1.

Roisman, G. I., & Fraley, R. C. (2006). The limits of genetic influence: A behavior-genetic analysis of infant-caregiver relationship quality and temperament. *Child Development, 77*, 1656–1667.

Romach, M. K., & Sellers, E. M. (1991). Management of the alcohol withdrawal syndrome. *Annual Review of Medicine, 42*, 323–340.

Romero, M. P., & Wintemute, G. J. (2002). The epidemiology of firearm suicide in the United States. *Journal of Urban Health, 79*, 39–48.

Room, R., & Makela K. (2000). Typologies of the cultural position of drinking. *Journal of Studies on Alcohol, 61*, 475–483.

Rosa, A. R., Marco, M., Fachel, J. M. G., Kapczinski, F., Stein, A. T., & Barros, H. M. T. (2007). Correlation between drug treatment adherence and lithium treatment attitudes and knowledge by bipolar patients. *Progress in Neuro-Psychopharmacology & Biological Psychiatry, 31*, 217–224.

Rosa, M. A., Gattaz, W. F., Pascual-Leone, A., Fregni, F., Rosa, M. O., et al. (2006). Comparison of repetitive transcranial magnetic stimulation and electroconvulsive therapy in unipolar non-psychotic refractory depression: A randomized, single-blind study. *International Journal of Neuropsychopharmacology, 9*, 667–676.

Rosanoff, A. J. (1914). A study of brain atrophy in relation to insanity. *American Journal of Insanity, 71*, 101–132.

Rosario-Campos, M. C., Leckman, J. F., Mercadante, M. T., Shavitt, R. G., da Silva Prado, H., et al. (2001). Adults with early-onset obsessive-compulsive disorder. *American Journal of Psychiatry 158*, 1899–1903.

Roscoe, W. (1993). How to become a berdache: Toward a unified analysis of gender diversity. In G. Herdt (Ed.), *Third sex, third gender: Beyond sexual dimorphism in culture and history* (pp. 329–372). New York: Zone Books.

Rosen, G. D., Bai, J., Wang, Y., Fiondella, C. G., Threlkeld, S. W., et al. (2007). Disruption of neuronal migration by RNAi of Dyx1c1 results in neocortical and hippocampal malformations. *Cerebral Cortex, 17*, 2562–2572.

Rosen, J. B., & Donley, M. P. (2006). Animal studies of amygdala function in fear and uncertainty: Relevance to human research. *Biological Psychology, 73*, 49–60.

Rosen, R. C., & Beck, J. G. (1988). *Patterns of sexual arousal: Psychophysiological processes and clinical applications.* New York: Guilford Press.

Rosen, R. C., & Leiblum, S. R. (1989). Assessment and treatment of desire disorders. In S. R. Leiblum & R. C. Rosen (Eds.), *Principles and practice of sex therapy: Update for the 1990s* (2nd ed., pp. 19–47). New York: Guilford Press.

Rosen, R. C., & Leiblum, S. R. (Eds.). (1995). *Case studies in sex therapy.* New York: Guilford Press.

Rosen, R. C., Taylor, J. F., Leiblum, S. R., & Bachmann, G. A. (1993). Prevalence of sexual dysfunction in women: Results of a survey study of 329 women in an outpatient gynecological clinic. *Journal of Sex & Marital Therapy, 19*, 171–188.

Rosenbaum, B., Valbak, K., Harder, S., Knudsen, P., Koster, A., et al. (2005). The Danish National Schizophrenia Project: Prospective, comparative longitudinal treatment study of first-episode psychosis. *British Journal of Psychiatry, 186*, 394–399.

Rosenbaum, J. F., Arana, G. W., Hyman, S. E., Labbate, L. A., & Fava, M. (2005). *Handbook of psychiatric drug therapy* (5th ed.). New York: Lippincott, Williams, & Wilkins.

Rosenberg, H. (1993). Prediction of controlled drinking by alcoholics and problem drinkers. Psychological Bulletin, 113, 129–139.

Rosenberg, H. (2002). Controlled drinking. In: Hersen M., Sledge W.H. (Eds). *Encyclopedia of psychotherapy.* New York: Elsevier Science.

Rosenberg, H., & Melville, J. (2005). Controlled drinking and controlled drug use as outcome goals in British treatment services. *Addiction Research and Theory, 13*, 85–92.

Rosenberg, R. S. (2013a). DSM-5: A "living document" dead on arrival. *Psychology Today.* Retrieved May 21, 2013, from www.psychologytoday.com/blog/the-superheroes/201305/dsm-5-living-document-dead-arrival

Rosenberg, R. S. (2013b). Abnormal is the new normal. *Slate,* April 12. Retrieved May 21, 2013, from www.slate.com/articles/health_and_science/medical_examiner/2013/04/diagnostic_and_statistical_manual_fifth_edition_why_will_half_the_u_s_population.html

Rosenbloom, M., Sullivan, E. V., & Pfefferbaum, A. (2003). Using magnetic resonance imaging and diffusion tensor imaging to assess brain damage in alcoholics. *Alcohol Research & Health 27*, 146–152.

Rosenfarb, I. S., Bellack, A. S., & Aziz, N. (2006). Family interactions and the course of schizophrenia in African American and White patients. *Journal of Abnormal Psychology, 115*, 112–120.

Rosenthal, D. (Ed.). (1963). *The Genain quadruplets: A case study and theoretical analysis of heredity and environment in schizophrenia.* New York: Basic Books.

Rosenthal, R. (1991). *Meta-analytic procedures for social research.* Beverly Hills, CA: Sage Publications.

Rospenda, K. (2002). Workplace harassment, services utilization, and drinking outcomes. *Journal of Occupational Health Psychology, 7*, 141–155.

Ross, C. A., Miller, S. D., Bjornson, L., Reagor, P., Fraser, G. A., & Anderson, G. (1991). Abuse histories in 102 cases of multiple personality disorder. *The Canadian Journal of Psychiatry/La Revue canadienne de psychiatrie, 36*, 97–101.

Ross, L. K., Arnsberger, P., & Fox, P. J. (1998). The relationship between cognitive functioning and disease severity with depression in dementia of the Alzheimer's type. *Aging & Mental Health, 2*, 319–327.

Ross, L. T., & Hill, E. M. (2004). Comparing alcoholic and nonalcoholic parents on the family unpredictability scale. *Psychological Reports, 94*, 1385–1391.

Rossiter, E. M., & Agras, W. S. (1990). An empirical test of the DSM-III-R definition of binge. *International Journal of Eating Disorders, 9*, 513–518.

Roth, A., & Fonagy, P. (2005). *What works for whom: A critical review of psychotherapy research* (2nd ed.). New York,: Guilford Press.

Rothbaum, B. O., Anderson, P., Zimand, E., Hodges, L., Lang, D., & Wilson, J. (2006). Virtual reality exposure therapy and standard (in vivo) exposure therapy in the treatment of fear of flying. *Behavior Therapy, 37*, 80–90.

Rothbaum, B. O., Hodges, L., Anderson, P. L., Price, L., & Smith, S. (2002). Twelve-month follow-up of virtual reality and standard exposure therapies for the fear of flying. *Journal of Consulting & Clinical Psychology, 70*, 428–432.

Rothbaum, B. O., Hodges, L., Smith, S., Lee, J. H., & Price, L. (2001). A controlled study of virtual reality exposure therapy for the fear of flying. *Journal of Consulting & Clinical Psychology, 68*, 1020–1026.

Rothbaum, F., Weisz, J., Pott, M., Miyake, K., & Morelli, G. (2000). Attachment and culture: Security in the United States and Japan. *American Psychologist, 55*, 1093–1104.

Rothenberg, A. (2001). Bipolar illness, creativity, and treatment. *Psychiatric Quarterly, 72*, 131–147.

Rothman, A. J., Haddock, G., & Schwarz, N. (2001). "How many partners is too many?" Shaping perceptions of personal vulnerability. *Journal of Applied Social Psychology, 31*, 2195–2214.

Rothman, E. (1995, December 15). What's in a name? *Focus Online: News from Harvard Medical, Dental, and Public Health Schools.* Retrieved April 25, 2007, from http://focus. hms.harvard.edu/1995/Dec15_1995/On_ Becoming_A_Doctor.html

Rouillon, F. (1997). Epidemiology of panic disorder. *Human Psychopharmacology: Clinical and Experimental, 12*, S7–S12.

Rouse v. Cameron, 373 F.2d 451 (D. C. Cir. 1966); later proceeding, 387 F.2d 241 (1967).

Roy, A. (1980). Hysteria. *Journal of Psychosomatic Research, 24*, 53–56.

Rubia, K., Smith, A. B., Brammer, M. J., & Taylor, E. (2007). Temporal lobe dysfunction in medication-naïve boys with attention-deficit/hyperactivity disorder during attention allocation and its relation to response variability. *Biological Psychiatry, 62*, 999–1006.

Rubin, L., Fitts, M., & Becker, A. E. (2003) Whatever feels good in my soul: Body ethics and aesthetics among African American and Latina women. *Culture, Medicine, and Psychiatry, 27*, 49–75.

Rubinsztein, J. D., Michael, A., Paykel, E. S., & Sahakian, B. J. (2000). Cognitive impairment in remission of bipolar affective disorder. *Psychological Medicine, 30*, 1025–1036.

Ruffolo, J. S., Phillips, K. A., Menard, W., Fay, C., & Weisberg, R. B. (2006). Comorbidity of body dysmorphic disorder and eating disorders: Severity of psychopathology and body image disturbance. *International Journal of Eating Disorders, 39,* 11–19.

Ruiz-Sancho, A. M., Smith, G. W., & Gunderson, J. G. (2001). Psychoeduational approaches. In W. J. Livesley (Ed.), *Handbook of personality disorders: Theory, research, and treatment* (pp. 460–474). New York: Guilford Press.

Rund, B. R., Melle, I., Friis, S., Larsen, T. K., Midboe, L. J., Oet al. (2004). Neurocognitive dysfunction in first-episode psychosis: Correlates with symptoms, premorbid adjustment, and duration of untreated psychosis. *American Journal of Psychiatry, 161,* 466–472.

Ruscio, A. M., Seitchik, A. E., Gentes, E. L., Jones, J. D., & Hallion, L. S. (2011). Perseverative thought: A robust predictor of response to emotional challenge in generalized anxiety disorder and major depressive disorder. *Behaviour Research and Therapy, 49,* 867–874.

Rush, A. J., Zimmerman, M., Wisniewski, S. R., Fava, M., Hollon, S. D., et al. (2005). Comorbid psychiatric disorders in depressed outpatients: Demographic and clinical features. *Journal of Affective Disorders, 87,* 43–55.

Russell, C. J., & Keel, P. K. (2002). Homosexuality as a specific risk factor for eating disorders in men. *International Journal of Eating Disorders, 31,* 300–306.

Russell, M. (1990). Prevalence of alcoholism among children of alcoholics. In M. Windle, & J. S. Searles (Eds.), *Children of alcoholics: Critical perspectives* (pp. 9–38). New York: Guilford Press.

Russell, T. A., Reynaud, E., Herba, C., Morris, R., & Corcoran, R. (2006). Do you see what I see? Interpretations of intentional movement in schizophrenia. *Schizophrenia Research, 81,* 101–111.

Rutherford, M. D., Baron-Cohen, S., & Wheelwright, S. (2002). Reading the mind in the voice: A study with normal adults and adults with Asperger syndrome and high functioning autism. *Journal of Autism and Developmental Disorders, 32,* 189–194.

Rutter, M. (2003). Poverty and Child Mental Health: Natural experiments and social causation. *JAMA: Journal of the American Medical Association, 290,* 2063–2064.

Rutter, M. L. (1999). Psychosocial adversity and child psychopathology. *British Journal of Psychiatry, 174,* 480–493.

Rutter, M., & Maughan, B. (1997). Psychosocial adversities in childhood and adult psychopathology. *Journal of Personality Disorders, 11,* 4–18.

Rutter, M., & Quinton, D. (1984). Parental psychiatric disorder: Effects on children. *Psychological Medicine, 14,* 853–880.

Ruwaard, J., Lange, A., Bouwman, M., Broeksteeg, J., & Schrieken, B. (2007). E-mailed standardized cognitive behavioural treatment of work-related stress: A randomized controlled trial. *Cognitive Behaviour Therapy, 36,* 179–192.

Ryan, D., & Carr, A. (2001). A study of the differential effects of Tomm's questioning styles on therapeutic alliance. *Family Process, 40,* 67–77.

Rybakowski, F., Slopien, A., Dmitrzak-Weglarz, M., Czerski, P., Rajewski, A., & Hauser, J. (2006). The 5-HT2A -1438 A/G and 5-HTTLPR polymorphisms and personality dimensions in adolescent anorexia nervosa: Association study. *Neuropsychobiology, 53,* 33–39.

Saatcioglu, O., Erim, R., & Cakmak, D. (2006). Role of family in alcohol and substance abuse. *Psychiatry and Clinical Neurosciences, 60,* 125–132.

Saba, G., Verdon, C. M., Kalalou, K., Rocamora, J. F., Dumortier, G., et al. (2006). Transcranial magnetic stimulation in the treatment of schizophrenic symptoms: A double blind sham controlled study. *Journal of Psychiatric Research, 40,* 147–152.

Sabourin, M. E., Cutcomb, S. D., Crawford, H. J., & Pribram, K. (1990–1991). EEG correlates of hypnotic susceptibility and hypnotic trance: Spectral analysis and coherence. *International Journal of Psychophysiology, 10,* 125–142.

Sachdev, P. S. (1985). Koro epidemic in north-east India. *Australia New Zealand Journal of Psychiatry, 19,* 433–438.

Sachs, G. S. (2006). A review of agitation in mental illness: Burden of illness and underlying pathology. *Journal of Clinical Psychiatry, 67*(Suppl. 10), 5–12.

Sachs-Ericsson, N., Plant, E. A., & Blazer, D. G. (2005). Racial differences in the frequency of depressive symptoms among community dwelling elders: The role of socioeconomic factors. *Aging & Mental Health, 9,* 201–209.

Sackheim, H. A., Devanand, D. P., & Nobler, M. S. (1995). Electroconvulsive therapy. In F. E. Bloom & D. J. Kupfer (Eds.), *Psychopharmacology: The Fourth Generation of Progress.* New York: Raven Press. pp. 1123–1141.

Sackheim, H. A., Haskett, R. F., Mulsant, B. H., Thase, M. E., Mann, J. J., et al. (2001). Continuation pharmacotherapy in the prevention of relapse following electroconvulsive therapy: A randomized controlled trial. *Journal of the American Medical Association, 285,* 1299–1307.

Sacktor, N., Nakasujja, N., Skolasky, R., Robertson, K., Wong, M., et al. (2006). Antiretroviral therapy improves cognitive impairment in HIV+ individuals in sub-Saharan Africa. *Neurology, 67,* 311–314.

Sadeghi, M., & Fakhrai, A. (2000). Transsexualism in female monozygotic twins: A case report. *Australian and New Zealand Journal of Psychiatry, 34,* 862–864.

Sadock, B. J., & Sadock, V. A. (2007). *Kaplan and Sadock's synopsis of psychiatry: Behavioral sciences/clinical psychiatry* (10th ed.). Philadelphia: Lippincott, Williams, & Wilkins.

Sadock, V. (1995). Psychotropic drugs and sexual dysfunction. *Primary Psychiatry, 4,* 16–17.

Safer, D. L., Telch, C. F., & Agras, W. S. (2001). Dialectical behavior therapy for bulimia nervosa. *American Journal of Psychiatry, 158,* 632–634.

Safren, S. A., Sprich, S., Mimiaga, M. J., Surman, C., Knouse, L., et al. (2010). Cognitive behavioral therapy vs relaxation with educational support for medication-treated adults with ADHD and persistent symptoms. *JAMA, 304*(8):875–880.

Saha, S., Chant, D., Welham, J., & McGrath, J. (2005). A systematic review of the prevalence of schizophrenia. *PLoS Medicine, 2,* e141.

Saladin, M. E. & Santa Ana, E. J. (2004). Controlled drinking: More than just a controversy. *Current Opinion in Psychiatry, 17,* 175–187.

Salamone, J. D. (2002). Antidepressants and placebos: Conceptual problems and research strategies. *Prevention & Treatment, 5,* Article 24. www.journals.apa.org/prevention/volume5/pre0050024c.html

Salekin, R. (2002). Psychopathy and therapeutic pessimism: Clinical lore or clinical reality? *Clinical Psychology Review, 22,* 79–112.

Salekin, R., Worley, C., & Grimes, R. (2010). Treatment of psychopathy: A review and brief introduction to the mental model approach for psychopathy. *Behavioral Sciences and the Law, 28,* 235–266.

Salkovskis, P. M. (1985). Obsessional-compulsive problems: A cognitive-behavioural analysis. *Behaviour Research and Therapy, 23,* 571–583.

Salkovskis, P. M. (1988). Phenomenology, assessment, and the cognitive model of panic. In S. Rachman & J. D. Maser (Eds.), *Panic: Psychological perspectives* (pp. 111–136). Hillsdale, NJ: Lawrence Erlbaum.

Salkovskis, P. M. (1996). The cognitive approach to anxiety: Threat beliefs, safety-seeking behavior, and the special case of health anxiety and obsessions. In P. M. Salkovskis (Ed.), *Frontiers of cognitive therapy* (pp. 48–74). New York: Guilford Press.

Salkovskis, P. M., & Campbell, P. (1994). Thought suppression induces intrusion in naturally occurring negative intrusive thoughts. *Behaviour Research and Therapy, 32,* 1–8.

Salmán, E., Diamond, K., Jusino, C., Sánchez-LaCay, A., & Liebowitz, M. R. (1997). Hispanic Americans. In S. Friedman (Ed.), *Cultural issues in the treatment of anxiety* (pp. 59–80). New York: Guilford Press.

Salo, R., Buonocore, M. H., Leamon, M., Natsuaki, Y., Waters, K., et al. (2011). Extended findings of brain metabolite normalization in MA-dependent subjects across sustained abstinence: A proton MRS study. *Drug and Alcohol Dependence, 113,* 133–138.

Salthouse, T. A. (2001). General and specific age-related influences on neuropsychological variables. In F. Boiler & S. Cappa (Eds.), *Handbook of neuropsychology: Vol. 6. Aging and dementia.* (pp. 39–50) London: Elsevier.

Salthouse, T. A. (2005). Relations between cognitive abilities and measures of executive functioning. *Neuropsychology, 19,* 532–545.

Samuels, J., Eaton, W. W., Bienvenu, O. J., III, Brown, C., Costa, P. T., Jr., & Nestadt, G. (2002). Prevalence and correlates of personality disorders in a community sample. *British Journal of Psychiatry, 180,* 536–542.

Sánchez, H. G. (2001). Risk factor model for suicide assessment and intervention. *Professional Psychology: Research and Practice, 32*, 351–358.

Sandberg, S. (2002). *Hyperactivity and attention disorders of childhood.* New York: Cambridge University Press.

Sanders, A. R., Duan, J., Levinson, D. F., Shi, J., He, D., et al. (2008). No significant association of 14 candidate genes with schizophrenia in a large European ancestry sample: Implications for psychiatric genetics. *American Journal of Psychiatry, 165*, 497–506.

Sanderson, W. C., & Barlow, D. H. (1990). A description of patients diagnosed with DSM-III-R generalized anxiety disorder. *Journal of Nervous and Mental Disease, 178*, 588–591.

Sands, J. R., & Harrow, M. (1999). Depression during the longitudinal course of schizophrenia. *Schizophrenia Bulletin, 25*, 157–171.

Sanfilipo, M., Lafargue, T., Rusinek, H., Arena, L., Loneragan, C., et al. (2002). Cognitive performance in schizophrenia: Relationship to regional brain volumes and psychiatric symptoms. *Psychiatry Research: Neuroimaging, 116*, 1–23.

Sansone, R. A., & Sansone, L. A. (2011). Personality pathology and its influence on eating disorders. *Innovations in Clinical Neuroscience, 8*, 14–18.

Santangelo, S. L., & Tsatsanis, K. (2005). What is known about autism: Genes, brain, and behavior. *American Journal of Pharmacogenomics, 5*, 71–92.

Santhiveeran, J., & Grant, B. (2005). Use of communication tools and fee-setting in e-therapy: A Web site survey. *Social Work in Mental Health, 4*, 31–45.

Santisteban, D. A., Muir-Malcolm, J. A., Mitrani, V. B., & Szapocznik, J. (2002). Integrating the study of ethnic culture and family psychology intervention science. In H. A. Liddle, D. A. Santisteban, R. F. Levant, & J. H. Bray (Eds), *Family psychology: Science-based interventions* (pp. 331–351). Washington, DC: American Psychological Association.

Sapolsky, R. M. (1996). Why stress is bad for your brain. *Science, 273*, 749–750.

Sapolsky, R. M. (1997). *Why zebras don't get ulcers.* New York: Freeman.

Sar, V., Akyuz, G., & Dogan, O. (2007). Prevalence of dissociative disorders among women in the general population. *Psychiatry Research, 149*, 169–176.

Sarbin, T. R. (1995). On the belief that one body may be host to two or more personalities. *International Journal of Clinical and Experimental Hypnosis, 43*, 163–183.

Sareen, J., Campbell, D. W., Leslie, W. D., Malisza, K. L., Stein, M. B., et al. (2007). Striatal function in generalized social phobia: A functional magnetic resonance imaging study. *Biological Psychiatry, 61*, 396–404.

Sareen, J., Stein, M. B., Cox, B. J., & Hassard, S. T. (2004). Understanding comorbidity of anxiety disorders with antisocial behavior: Findings from two large community surveys. *Journal of Nervous and Mental Disease, 192*, 178–186.

Sarísoy, G., Böke, Ö., Arík, A. C., & Sahin, A. R. (2008). Panic disorder with nocturnal panic attacks: Symptoms and comorbidities. *European Psychiatry, 23*, 195–200.

Sarró, R. (1956). Spain as the cradle of psychiatry. In *Centennial papers: Saint Elizabeth's Hospital 1855–1955* (pp. 85–96). Washington, DC: Centennial Commission, Saint Elizabeth's Hospital.

Sartor, C. E., Grant, J. D., Lynskey, M. T., McCutcheon, V. V., Waldron, M., et al. (2012). Common heritable contributions to low-risk trauma, high-risk trauma, posttraumatic stress disorders, and major depression. *Archives of General Psychiatry, 69*, 293–299.

Satcher, D. (1999). *The Surgeon General's call to action to prevent suicide, 1999.* Washington, DC: U.S. Public Health Service.

Satterfield, J. H. (1987). Childhood diagnostic and neurophysiological predictors of teenage arrest rates: An 8-year prospective study. In S. A. Mednick, T. E. Moffit, & S. A. Stack (Eds.), *The causes of crime: New biological approaches* (pp. 146–167). Cambridge, England: Cambridge University Press.

Sattler, J. M. (1982). *Assessment of children's intelligence and special abilities* (2nd ed.). Boston: Allyn & Bacon.

Saudino, K. J. (2005). Special article: Behavioral genetics and child temperament. *Journal of Developmental & Behavioral Pediatrics, 26*, 214–223.

Saulsman, L. M., & Page, A. C. (2004). The five-factor model and personality disorder empirical literature: A meta-analytic review. *Clinical Psychology Review, 23*, 1055–1085.

Sava, F. A., Yates, B. T., Lupu, V., Szentagotai, A., & David, D. (2009). Cost-effectiveness and cost-utility of cognitive therapy, rational emotive behavioral therapy, and fluoxetine (Prozac) in treating clinical depression: A randomized clinical trial. *Journal of Clinical Psychology, 65*, 36–52.

Saxena, S., & Rauch, S. L. (2000). Functional neuroimaging and the neuroanatomy of obsessive-compulsive disorder. *Psychiatric Clinics of North America, 23*, 563–586.

Saxena, S., Brody, A. L., Schwartz, J. M., & Baxter, L. R. (1998). Neuroimaging and frontal-subcortical circuitry in obsessive-compulsive disorder. *British Journal of Psychiatry, 173*, 26–37.

Scahill, L., & Schwab-Stone, M. (2000). Epidemiology of ADHD in school-age children. *Child and Adolescent Psychiatric Clinics of North America, 9*, 541–555.

Scarmeas, N., Brandt, J., Blacker, D., Albert, A., Hadjigerogious, G., et al. (2007). Disruptive behavior as a predictor in Alzheimer's disease. *Archives of Neurology, 64*, 1755–1761.

Scarpa, A., Haden, S. C., & Hurley, J. (2006). Community violence victimization and symptoms of posttraumatic stress disorder: The moderating effects of coping and social support. *Journal of Interpersonal Violence, 21*, 446–469.

Scarr, S., & McCartney, K. (1983). How people make their own environments: A theory of genotype-environment effects. *Child Development, 54*, 424–435.

Schachter, S., & Latane, B. (1964). Crime, cognition, and the autonomic nervous system. *Nebraska Symposium on Motivation, 12*, 221–275.

Schacter, D. L., Kaszniak, A. K., Kihlstrom, J. F., & Valdiserri, M. (1991). The relation between source memory and aging. *Psychology and Aging, 6*, 559–568.

Schacter, D. L., Koutstaal, W., & Norman, K. A. (1997). False memories and aging. *Trends in Cognitive Sciences, 1*, 229–236.

Schaefer, K. (Interviewer). (2003, May 29). Ideastream Focus on Mental Health: Frese Family Album. [Radio broadcast]. Cleveland, OH: WPCN.

Schafe, G. E., & LeDoux, J. E. (2004). The neural basis of fear. In M. S. Gazzaniga (Ed.), *The cognitive neurosciences* (3rd ed.), (pp. 987–1003). Cambridge, MA: MIT Press.

Schatzberg, A. F. (2000). Clinical efficacy of reboxetine in major depression. *Journal of Clinical Psychiatry, 61*, 31–38.

Schechter, R., & Grether, J. K. (2008). Continuing increases in autism reported to California's developmental services system: Mercury in retrograde. *Archives of General Psychiatry, 65*, 19–24.

Schena, M., Shalon, D., Davis, R. W., & Brown, P. O. (1995). Quantitative monitoring of gene expression patterns with a complementary DNA microarray. *Science, 270*, 467–470.

Scherrer, J. F., True, W. R., Xian, H., Lyons, M. J., Eisen, S. A., et al. (2000). Evidence for genetic influences common and specific to symptoms of generalized anxiety and panic. *Journal of Affective Disorders, 57*, 25–35.

Schildkraut, J. J. (1965). The catecholamine hypothesis of affective disorders: A review of supporting evidence. *American Journal of Psychiatry, 122*, 509–522.

Schmahl, C. G., Elzinga, B. M., Vermetten, E., Sanislow, C., McGlashan, T. H., & Bremner, J. D. (2003). Neural correlates of memories of abandonment in women with and without borderline personality disorder. *Biological Psychiatry, 54*, 142–151.

Schmahl, C. G., Vermetten, E., Elzinga, B. M., & Bremner, J. D. (2004). A positron emission tomography study of memories of childhood abuse in borderline personality disorder. *Biological Psychiatry, 55*, 759–765.

Schmahl, C. G., Vermetten, E., Elzinga, B. M., & Douglas, B. J. (2003). Magnetic resonance imaging of hippocampal and amygdala volume in women with childhood abuse and borderline personality disorder. *Psychiatry Research, 122*, 193–198.

Schmaling, K. B., & Hernandez, D. V. (2005). Detection of depression among low-income Mexican Americans in primary care. *Journal of Health Care for the Poor and Underserved, 16*, 780–790.

Schmidt, N. B., Lerew, D. R., & Jackson, R. J. (1997). The role of anxiety sensitivity in the pathogenesis of panic: Prospective evaluation of spontaneous panic attacks during acute stress. *Journal of Abnormal Psychology, 106*, 355–364.

Schmitt, D. P., Alcalay, L., Allensworth, M., Allik, J., Ault, L., et al. (2004). Patterns and universals of adult romantic attachment across 62 regions: Are models of self and other pancultural constructs? *Journal of Cross-cultural Psychology, 35*(4), 367–402.

Schneck, C. D., Miklowitz, D. J., Miyahara, S., Araga, M., Wisniewski, S., et al. (2008). The prospective course of rapid-cycling bipolar disorder: Findings from the STEP-B. *American Journal of Psychiatry, 165*, 370–377.

Schneider, F., Gur, R. C., Koch, K., Backes, V., Amunts, K., et al. (2006). Impairment in the specificity of emotion processing in schizophrenia. *American Journal of Psychiatry, 163*, 442–447.

Schneider, F., Habel, U., Kessler, C., Posse, S., Grodd, W., & Muller-Gartner, H. (2000). Functional imaging of conditioned aversive emotional responses in antisocial personality disorder. *Neuropsychobiology, 42*, 192–201.

Schneider, F. R., Blanco, C., Antia, S. X., & Liebowitz, M. R. (2002). The social anxiety spectrum. *Psychiatric Clinics of North America, 25*, 757–774.

Schneider, L. S., Dagerman, K., & Insel, P. S. (2006a). Efficacy and adverse effects of atypical antipsychotics for dementia: Meta-analysis of randomized, placebo-controlled trials. *American Journal of Geriatric Psychiatry, 14*, 191–210.

Schneider, L. S., Dagerman, K. S., & Insel, P. (2006b). Risk of death with atypical antipsychotic drug treatment for dementia: Meta-analysis of randomized placebo-controlled trials: Reply. *JAMA: Journal of the American Medical Association, 295*, 496–497.

Schneider, M., Retz, W., Coogan, A., Thome, J., & Rösler, M. (2006). Anatomical and functional brain imaging in adult attention-deficit/hyperactivity disorder (ADHD)—a neurological view. *European Archives of Psychiatry and Clinical Neuroscience, 256*(Suppl. 1): I/32–I/41.

Schneider, S., Blatter-Meunier, J., Herren, C., Adornetto, C., In-Albon, T., & Lavallee, K. (2011). Disorder-specific cognitive-behavioral therapy for separation anxiety disorder in young children: A randomized waiting-list-controlled trial. *Psychotherapy and Psychosomatics, 80*(4), 206–215.

Schneider-Axmann, T., Kamer, T., Moroni, M., Maric, N., Tepest, R., et al. (2006). Relation between cerebrospinal fluid, gray matter and white matter changes in families with schizophrenia. *Journal of Psychiatric Research, 40*, 646–655.

Schnurr, P. P., Friedman, M. J., Engel, C. C., Foa, E. B., Shea, M. T., et al. (2007). Cognitive behavioral therapy for posttraumatic stress disorder in women: A randomized controlled trial. *JAMA: Journal of the American Medical Association, 297*, 820–830.

Schnurr, P. P., Friedman, M. J., Foy, D. W., Shea, M. T., Hsieh, F. Y., et al. (2003). Randomized trial of trauma-focused group therapy for posttraumatic stress disorder: Results from a Department of Veterans Affairs cooperative study. *Archives of General Psychiatry, 60*, 481–489.

Schoevers, R. A., Beekman, A. T. F., Deeg, D. J. H., Jonker, C., & van Tilburg, W. (2003). Comorbidity and risk-patterns of depression, generalised anxiety disorder and mixed anxiety-depression in later life: Results from the AMSTEL study. *International Journal of Geriatric Psychiatry, 18*, 994–1001.

Schoevers, R. A., van Tilburg, W., Beekman, A. T. F., & Deeg, D. J. H. (2005). Depression and generalized anxiety disorder: Co-occurrence and longitudinal patterns in elderly patients. *American Journal of Geriatric Psychiatry, 13*, 31–39.

Schonfeldt-Lecuona, C., Connemann, B. J., Spitzer, M., & Herwig, U. (2003). Transcranial magnetic stimulation in the reversal of motor conversion disorder. *Psychotherapy & Psychosomatics, 72*, 286–288.

Schopp, R. F. (1991). The psychotherapist's duty to protect the public: The appropriate standard and the foundation in legal theory and empirical premises. *Nebraska Law Review, 70*, 327–360.

Schopp, R. F., & Quattrocchi, M. R. (1984). Tarasoff, the doctrine of special relationships and the psychotherapist's duty to warn. *The Journal of Psychiatry and Law, 12*, 13–37.

Schore, A. N. (2003). *Affect dysregulation and disorders of the self.* New York: Norton.

Schrimsher, G. W., Billingsley, R. L., Jackson, E. F., & Moore, B. D., III. (2002). Caudate nucleus volume asymmetry predicts attention-deficit hyperactivity disorder (ADHD) symptomatology in children. *Journal of Child Neurolology, 17*, 877–884.

Schrof, J. M., & Schultz, S. (1999, March 8). Melancholy nation. *U.S. News and World Report*, pp. 56–63.

Schuckit, M. A. (1999). New findings on the genetics of alcoholism. *JAMA: Journal of the American Medical Association, 281*, 1875–1876.

Schulenberg, J., Wadsworth, K. N., O'Malley, P. M., Bachman, J. G., & Johnston, L. D. (1996). Adolescent risk factors for binge drinking during the transition to young adulthood: Variable- and pattern-centered approaches to change. *Developmental Psychology, 32*, 659–674.

Schulte-Körne, G. (2001). Genetics of reading and spelling disorder. *Journal of Child Psychology and Psychiatry, 42*, 985–997.

Schulte-Korne, G., & Remschmidt, H. (1996). Familial clustering of conversion disorder. *Nervenartz, 67*, 794–798.

Schultze-Lutter, F., Schimmelmann, B. G., Ruhrmann, S., & Michel, C. (2013). 'A rose is a rose is a rose', but at-risk criteria differ. *Psychopathology, 46*(2), 75–87.

Schwalberg, M. D., Barlow, D. H., Alger, S. A., & Howard, L. J. (1992). Comparison of bulimics, obese binge eaters, social phobics, and individuals with panic disorder on comorbidity across DSM-III-R anxiety disorders. *Journal of Abnormal Psychology, 101*, 675–681.

Schwartz, J. M., Stoessel, P. W., Baxter, L. R., Martin, K. M., & Phelps, M. E. (1996). Systematic changes in cerebral glucose metabolic rate after successful behavior modification treatment of obsessive-compulsive disorder. *Archives of General Psychiatry, 53*, 109–113.

Schwartz, R. C. (2001). Racial profiling in medical research. *New England Journal of Medicine, 344*, 1392–1393.

Schwarz, N. (1999). Self-reports: How the questions shape the answers. *American Psychologist, 54*, 93–105.

Schwarz, N., Knäuper, B., Hippler, H. J., Noelle-Neumann, E., & Clark, F. (1991). Rating scales: Numeric values may change the meaning of scale labels. *Public Opinion Quarterly, 55*, 570–582.

Schwitzer, G. (2012). Amyloid & Alzheimer's: The cause-and-effect question often missed. *Health News Watchdog Blog, August 15*. Retrieved August 15, 2012, from www.medpagetoday.com/GarySchwitzer/34202

Sclar, D. A., Robison, L. M., Skaer, T. L, & Galin, R. S. (1999). Ethnicity and the prescribing of antidepressant pharmacotherapy: 1992–1995. *Harvard Review of Psychiatry, 7*, 29–36.

Scogin, F., Bynum, J., Stephens, G., & Calhoon, S. (1990). Efficacy of self-administered treatment programs: Meta-analytic review. *Professional Psychology: Research and Practice, 21*, 42–47.

Scott, D. J., Stohler, C. S., Egnatu, C. M., Wang, H., Koeppe, R. A., & Zubieta, J. (2008). Placebo and nocebo effects are defined by opposite opioid and dopaminergic responses. *Archives of General Psychiatry, 65*, 220–231.

Scott, J., & Gutierrez, M. J. (2004). The current status of psychological treatments in bipolar disorders: A systematic review of relapse prevention. *Bipolar Disorders, 6*, 498–503.

Scott, J., Stanton, B., Garland, A., & Ferrier, I. N. (2000). Cognitive vulnerability in patients with bipolar disorder. *Psychological Medicine, 30*, 467–472.

Scott, W. D., Ingram, R. E., & Shadel, W. G. (2003). Hostile and sad moods in dysphoria: Evidence for cognitive specificity in attributions. *Journal of Social & Clinical Psychology, 22*, 233–252.

Seedat, S., Stein, M. B., & Forde, D. R. (2003). Prevalence of dissociative experiences in a community sample: Relationship to gender, ethnicity, and substance use. *Journal of Nervous and Mental Disease, 191*, 115–120.

Seeman, M. V. (2000). Women and psychosis. *Medscape Women's Health, 5*, n.p. Retrieved February 9, 2009, from www.medscape.com/viewarticle/408912

Seeman, M., & Lang, M. (1990) The role of estrogens in schizophrenia gender differences. *Schizophrenia Bulletin, 16*, 185–194.

Segal, D. L. (2003). Abnormal psychology. In S. K. Whitbourne & J. C. Cavanaugh (Eds.), *Integrating aging topics into psychology: A practical guide for teaching* (pp. 141–158). Washington, DC: American Psychological Association.

Segal, Z. V., Pearson, J. L., & Thase, M. E. (2003). Challenges in preventing relapse in major depression: Report of a National Institute of Mental Health Workshop on state of the science of relapse prevention in major depression. *Journal of Affective Disorders, 77,* 97–108.

Segrin, C., & Abramson, L. Y. (1994). Negative reactions to depressive behaviors: A communication theory analysis. *Journal of Abnormal Psychology, 103,* 655–668.

Segrin, C., & Dillard, J. P. (1992). The interactional theory of depression: A meta-analysis of the research literature. *Journal of Social & Clinical Psychology, 11,* 43–70.

Segui, J., Maruez, M., Garcia, L., Canet, J., Salvador-Carulla, L., & Ortiz, M. (2000). Depersonalization in panic disorder: A clinical study. *Comprehensive Psychiatry, 41,* 172–178.

Seidman, L. J., Faraone, S. V., Goldstein, J. M., Kremen, W. S., Horton, N. J., et al. (2002). Left hippocampal volume as a vulnerability indicator for schizophrenia: A magnetic resonance imaging morphometric study of nonpsychotic first-degree relatives. *Archives of General Psychiatry, 59,* 839–849.

Seil, D. (1996). Transsexuals: The boundaries of sexual identity and gender. In R. P. Cabaj & T. S. Stein (Eds.), *Textbook of Homosexuality and Mental Health.* (pp. 743–762). Washington, DC: American Psychiatric Press.

Seivewright, H., Tyrer, P., & Johnson, T. (2002). Change in personality status in neurotic disorders. *Lancet, 359,* 2253–2254.

Sell v. United States, 539 U.S. 166 (2003). (No. 02-5664).

Selten, J., Cantor-Graae, E., & Kahn, R. S. (2007). Migration and schizophrenia. *Current Opinion in Psychiatry, 20,* 111–115.

Semkovska, M., & McLoughlin, D. M. (2010). Objective cognitive performance associated with electroconvulsive therapy for depression: a systematic review and meta-analysis. *Biological Psychiatry, 68*(6), 568–577.

Sentell, J. W., Lacroix, M., Sentell, J. V., & Finstuen, K. (1997). Predictive patterns of suicidal behavior: The United States armed services versus the civilian population. *Military Medicine, 162,* 162–171.

Sereny, G., Sharma, V., Holt. J., & Gordis, E. (1986). Mandatory supervised Antabuse therapy in an outpatient alcoholism program: A pilot study. *Alcoholism, 10,* 290–292.

Sergi, M. J., Rassovsky, Y., Nuechterlein, K. H., & Green, M. F. (2006). Social perception as a mediator of the influence of early visual processing on functional status in schizophrenia. *American Journal of Psychiatry, 163,* 448–454.

Serin, R. C. (1991). Psychopathy and violence in criminals. *Journal of Interpersonal Violence, 6,* 423–431.

Serra, M., Althaus, M., de Sonneville, L. M. J., Stant, A. D., Jackson, A. E., & Minderaa, R. B. (2003). Face recognition in children with a pervasive developmental disorder not otherwise specified. *Journal of Autism and Developmental Disorders, 33,* 303–317.

Seto, M. C., & Barbaree, H. E. (1999). Psychopathy, treatment behavior, and sex offender recidivism. *Journal of Interpersonal Violence, 14,* 1235–1248.

Shabsigh, R., Seftel, A. D., Kloner, R. A., Rosen, R. C., & Montorsi, F. (2003). The emerging frontier for management of erectile sysfunction: Strategies for patient care on the horizon. Symposium held at the Hilton Chicago in Chicago on April 25, 2003.

Shadish, W. R., Cook, T. D., & Campbell, D. T. (2002). *Experimental and quasi-experimental designs for causal inference.* Boston: Houghton Mifflin.

Shadish, W. R., Navarro, A. M., Matt, G. E., & Phillips, G. (2000). The effects of psychological therapies under clinically representative conditions: A meta-analysis. *Psychological Bulletin, 126,* 512–529.

Shaffer, G. W., & Lazarus, R. S. (1952). Historical development. In G. W. Shaffer & R. S. Lazarus (Eds.), *Fundamental concepts in clinical psychology* (pp. 1–31). New York: McGraw-Hill.

Shafran, R., Thordarson, D. S., & Rachman, S. (1996). Thought-action fusion in obsessive compulsive disorder. *Journal of Anxiety Disorders, 10,* 379–391.

Shah, N., Passi, V., Bryson, S., & Agras, W. S. (2005). Patterns of eating and abstinence in women treated for bulimia nervosa. *International Journal of Eating Disorders, 38,* 330–334.

Shalev, A. Y., Ankri, Y., Israeli-Shalev, Y., Peleg, T., Adessky, R., & Freedman, S. (2012). Prevention of posttraumatic stress disorder: Results from the Jerusalem trauma outreach and prevention study. *Archives of General Psychiatry, 69,* 166–176.

Shalev, A. Y., Peri, T., Canetti, L., & Schreiber, S. (1996). Predictors of PTSD in injured trauma survivors: A prospective study. *American Journal of Psychiatry, 153,* 219–225.

Shalev, A. Y., Sahar, T., Freedman, S., Peri, T., Glick, N., et al. (1998). A prospective study of heart rate response following trauma and the subsequent development of posttraumatic stress disorder. *Archives of General Psychiatry, 55,* 553–559.

Shapira, B., Tubi, N., Drexler, H., Lidsky, D., Calev, A., & Lerer, B. (1998). Cost and benefit in the choice of ECT schedule: Twice versus three times weekly ECT. *British Journal of Psychiatry, 172,* 44–48.

Shapiro, A. K. (1964). Factors contributing to the placebo effect: Their significance for psychotherapy. *American Journal of Psychotherapy, 18,* 73–88.

Shapiro, A. K., & Morris, L. A. (1978). The placebo effect in medical and psychological therapies. In S. L. Garfield & A. E. Bergin (Eds.), *Handbook of psychotherapy and behavior change: An empirical analysis* (2nd ed.). New York: John Wiley & Sons.

Shapiro, F. (2001). *Eye movement desensitization and reprocessing: Basic principles, protocols and procedures* (2nd ed.). New York: Guilford Press.

Shapiro, F., & Maxfield, L. (2002). Eye movement desensitization and reprocessing (EMDR): Information processing in the treatment of trauma. *In Session: Psychotherapy in Practice, 58*(8), 933–946.

Shattuck, P. T., Seltzer, M. M., Greenberg, J. S., Orsmond, G. I., Bolt, D., et al. (2007). Change in autism symptoms and maladaptive behaviors in adolescents and adults with an autism spectrum disorder. *Journal of Autism and Developmental Disorders, 37,* 1735–1747.

Shavitt, R. G., Hounie, A. G., Campos, M. C. R., & Miguel, E. C. (2006). Tourette's syndrome. *Psychiatric Clinics of North America, 29,* 471–486.

Shaw, D. S., Winslow, E. B., Owens, E. B., & Hood, N. (1998). Young children's adjustment to chronic family adversity: A longitudinal study of low-income families. *Journal of the American Academy of Child & Adolescent Psychiatry, 37,* 545–553.

Shaw, H., Ramirez, L., Trost, A., Randall, P., & Stice, E. (2004). Body image and eating disturbances across ethnic groups: More similarities than differences. *Psychology of Addictive Behaviors, 18,* 12–18.

Shaw, H., Stice, E., & Becker, C. B. (2009). Preventing eating disorders. *Child and Adolescent Psychiatric Clinics of North America, 18,* 199–207.

Shaw-Zirt, B., Popali-Lehane, L., Chaplin, W., & Bergman, A. (2005). Adjustment, social skills, and self-esteem in college students with symptoms of ADHD. *Journal of Attention Disorders, 8,* 109–120.

Shaywitz, B. A., Lyon, G. R., & Shaywitz, S. E. (2006). The role of functional magnetic resonance imaging in understanding reading and dyslexia. *Developmental Neuropsychology, 30,* 613–632.

Shaywitz, B. A., Shaywitz, S. E., Blachman, B. A., Pugh, K. R., Fulbright, R. K., et al. (2004). Development of left occipitotemporal systems for skilled reading in children after a phonologically-based intervention. *Biological Psychiatry, 55,* 926–933.

Shaywitz, B. A., Shaywitz, S. E., Pugh, K. R., Mencl, W. E., Fulbright, R. K., et al. (2002). Disruption of posterior brain systems for reading in children with developmental dyslexia. *Biological Psychiatry, 52,* 101–110.

Shea, M. T., Elkin, I., Imber, S. D., Sotsky, S. M., Watkins, J. T., et al. (1992). Course of depressive symptoms over follow-up: Findings from the National Institute of Mental Health Treatment of Depression Collaborative Research Program. *Archives of General Psychiatry, 49,* 782–787.

Shea, M. T., Stout, R. L., Yen, S., Pagano, M. E., Skodol, A. E., et al. (2004). Associations in the course of personality disorders and Axis I disorders over time. *Journal of Abnormal Psychology, 113,* 499–508.

Shear, K., Jin, R., Ruscio, A. M., Walters, E. E., & Kessler, R. C. (2006). Prevalence and correlates of estimated DSM-IV child and adult separation anxiety disorder in the National Comorbidity Survey replication. *American Journal of Psychiatry, 163,* 1074–1083.

Shearin, E. N., & Linehan, M. M. (1994). Dialectical behavior therapy for borderline personality disorder: Theoretical and empirical foundations. *Acta Psychiatrica Scandinavica, 89,* 61–68.

Sheehy, G. (1972, January 10). The secret of Grey Gardens. *New York Magazine,* pp. 24–30.

Sheehy, G. (2006). A return to Grey Gardens. *New York Magazine,* November 6. Retrieved December 27, 2006, from www.nymag.com/arts/theater/features/23484/

Sheets, E., & Craighead, W. E. (2007). Toward an empirically based classification of personality pathology. *Clinical Psychology: Science and Practice, 14,* 77–93.

Shepherd, G. M. (1999). Information processing in dendrites. In M. J. Zigmond, F. E. Bloom, S. C. Landis, J. L. Roberts, & L. R. Squire (Eds.), *Fundamental neuroscience* (pp. 363–388). New York: Academic Press.

Shepherd, M. D., Schoenberg, M., Slavich, S., Wituk, S., Warren, M., & Meissen, G. (1999). Continuum of professional involvement in self-help groups. *Journal of Community Psychology, 27,* 39–53.

Sher, K. J., Grekin, E. R., & Williams, N. A. (2005). The development of alcohol use disorders. *Annual Review of Clinical Psychology, 1,* 493–523.

Sher, K. J., Trull, T. J., Bartholow, B. D., & Vieth, A. (1999). Personality & alcoholism: Issues, methods and etiological processes. In K. E. Leonard & H. T. Blane (Eds.), *Psychological theories of drinking and alcoholism.* (pp. 54–105). New York: Guilford Press.

Sherman, M. D., Zanotti, D. K., & Jones, D. E. (2005). Key elements in couples therapy with veterans with combat-related posttraumatic stress disorder. *Professional Psychology: Research and Practice, 36,* 626–633.

Shevlin, M., Dorahy, M. J., & Adamson, G. (2007). Trauma and psychosis: an analysis of the National Comorbidity Survey. *American Journal of Psychiatry, 164,* 166–169.

Shi, Z., Bureau, J.-F., Easterbrooks, M. A., Zhao, X., & Lyons-Ruth, K. (2012). Childhood maltreatment and prospectively observed quality of early care as predictors of antisocial personality disorder features. *Infant Mental Health Journal, 33,* 55–69.

Shiah, L., Chao, C., Mao, W., & Chuang, Y. (2006). Treatment of paraphilic sexual disorder: The use of topiramate in fetishism. *International Clinical Psychopharmacology, 21,* 241–243.

Shifren, J. L., Russo, P. A., Segreti, A., & Johannes, C. B. (2008). Sexual problems and distress in United States women: Prevalence and correlates. *Obstetrical Gynecology, 112,* 970–978.

Shin, L. M., Kosslyn, S. M., McNally, R. J., Alpert, N. M., Thompson, W. L., et al. (1997). Visual imagery and perception in posttraumatic stress disorder: A positron emission tomographic investigation. *Archives of General Psychiatry, 54,* 233–241.

Shin, L. M., McNally, R. J., Kosslyn, S. M., Thompson, W. L., Rauch, S. L., et al. (1999). Regional cerebral blood flow during script-driven imagery in childhood sexual abuse-related PTSD: A PET investigation. *American Journal of Psychiatry, 156,* 575–584.

Shin, L. M., Shin, P. S., Heckers, S., Krangel, T. S., Macklin, M. L., et al. (2004). Hippocampal function in posttraumatic stress disorder. *Hippocampus, 14,* 292–300.

Shin, L. M., Wright, C. I., Cannistraro, P. A., Wedig, M. M., McMullin, K., et al. (2005). A functional magnetic resonance imaging study of amygdala and medial prefrontal cortex responses to overtly presented fearful faces in posttraumatic stress disorder. *Archives of General Psychiatry, 62,* 273–281.

Shindel, A. W., & Moser, C. (2011). Why are the paraphilias mental disorders? *The Journal of Sexual Medicine, 8*(3), 927–929.

Shiraishi, H., Suzuki, A., Fukasawa, T., Aoshima, T., Ujiie, Y., et al. (2006). Monoamine oxidase A gene promoter polymorphism affects novelty seeking and reward dependence in healthy study participants. *Psychiatric Genetics, 16,* 55–58.

Shooka, A., Al-Haddad, M. K., & Raees, A. (1998). OCD in Bahrain: A phenomenological profile. *International Journal of Social Psychiatry, 44,* 147–154.

Shor-Posner, G., Lecusay, R., Miguez-Burbano, M. J., Quesada, J., Rodriguez, A., et al. (2000). Quality of life measures in the Miami HIV-1 infected drug abusers cohort: Relationship to gender and disease status. *Journal of Substance Abuse, 11,* 395–404.

Shrout, P. E., Canino, G. J., Bird, H. R., Rubio-Stipec, M., Bravo, M., & Burnam, M. A. (1992). Mental health status among Puerto Ricans, Mexican Americans, and non-Hispanic whites. *American Journal of Community Psychology, 20,* 729–752.

Siberski, J. (2013). Dementia and DSM-5: Changes, cost, and confusion. *Aging Well, 5,* 12.

Sibille, E., Arango, V., Galfalvy, H. C., Pavlidis, P., Erraji-Benchekroun, L., et al. (2004). Gene expression profiling of depression and suicide in human prefrontal cortex. *Neuropsychopharmacology, 29,* 351–361.

Siegel, S. (1988). State dependent learning and morphine tolerance. *Behavioral Neuroscience, 102,* 228–232.

Siegel, S., & Ramos, B. M. C. (2002). Applying laboratory research: Drug anticipation and the treatment of drug addiction. *Experimental and Clinical Psychopharmacology, 10,* 162–183.

Siegel, S., Baptista, M. A. S., Kim, J. A., McDonald, R. V., & Weise-Kelly, L. (2000). Pavlovian psychopharmacology: The associative basis of tolerance. *Experimental and Clinical Psychopharmacology, 8,* 276–293.

Sierra, M., & Berrios, G. E. (1998). Depersonalization: Neurobiological perspectives. *Biological Psychiatry, 44,* 898–908.

Sierra, M., Phillips, M. L., Ivin, G., Krystal, J., & David, A. S. (2003). A placebo-controlled, cross-over trial of lamotrigine in depersonalization disorder. *Journal of Psychopharmacology, 17,* 103–105.

Sierra, M., Senior, C., Dalton, J., McDonough, M., Bond, A., et al. (2002). Autonomic response in depersonalization disorder. *Archives of General Psychiatry, 59,* 833–838.

Siever, L. J., & Davis, K. L. (1991). A psychobiological perspective on the personality disorders. *American Journal of Psychiatry, 148,* 1647–1658.

Siever, L. J., & Davis, K. L. (2004). The pathophysiology of schizophrenia disorders: Perspectives from the spectrum. *American Journal of Psychiatry, 161,* 398–413.

Sifneos, P. E. (1992). *Short-term anxiety-provoking psychotherapy: A treatment manual.* New York: Basic Books.

Sigman, M., Spence, S. J., & Wang, A. T. (2006). Autism from developmental and neuropsychological perspectives. *Annual Review of Clinical Psychology, 2,* 327–355.

Sigmon, S. T., Pells, J. J., Boulard, N. E., Whitcomb-Smith, S., Edenfield, T. M., et al. (2005). Gender differences in self-reports of depression: The response bias hypothesis revisited. *Sex Roles, 53,* 401–411.

Sigvardsson, S., Bohman, M., & Cloninger, C. R. (1996). Replication of the Stockholm Adoption Study of alcoholism: Confirmatory cross-fostering analysis. *Archives of General Psychiatry, 53,* 681–687.

Silber, T. J. (2004). Ipecac abuse, morbidity and mortality: Is it time to repeal its over the counter status? paper presented at the conference on eating disorders, April 29–May 2, Orlando FL. [Abstract in the *International Journal of eating Disorders, 35,* 375.]

Silk, T. J., Rinehart, N., Bradshaw, J. L., Tonge, B., Egan, G., et al. (2006). Visuospatial processing and the function of prefrontal-parietal networks in autism spectrum disorders: A functional MRI study. *American Journal of Psychiatry, 163,* 1440–1443.

Silver, E., & Teasdale, B. (2005). Mental disorder and violence: An examination of stressful life events and impaired social support. *Social Problems, 52,* 62–78.

Silverman, K., Chutuape, M. A., Bigelow, G. E., & Stitzer, M. L. (1999). Voucher-based reinforcement of cocaine abstinence in treatment-resistant methadone patients: Effects of reinforcement magnitude. *Psychopharmacology, 146,* 128–138.

Silverman, K., Robles, E., Mudric, T., Bigelow, G. E., & Stitzer, M. L. (2004). A randomized trial of long-term reinforcement of cocaine abstinence in methadone-maintained patients who inject drugs. *Journal of Consulting Clinical Psychology, 72,* 839–854.

Silverman, K., Svikis, D., Robles, E., Stitzer, M. L., & Bigelow, G. E. (2001). A reinforcement-based therapeutic workplace for the treatment of drug abuse: Six-month abstinence outcomes. *Experimental & Clinical Psychopharmacology, 9,* 14–23.

Silverstein, J. L. (1989). Origins of psychogenic vaginismus. *Psychotherapy and Psychosomatics, 52,* 197–204.

Silverstein, M. L. (2007). Descriptive psychopathology and theoretical viewpoints: Dependent, histrionic, and antisocial personality disorders. In M. L. Silverstein, *Disorders of the self: A personality-guided approach* (pp. 145–170). Washington, DC: American Psychological Association.

Silverstein, S. M., Hatashita-Wong, M., Solak, B. A., Uhlhaas, P., Landa, Y., et al. (2005). Effectiveness of a two-phase cognitive rehabilitation intervention for severely impaired schizophrenia patients. *Psychological Medicine, 35,* 829–837.

Sim, L., & Zeman, J. (2005). Emotion regulation factors as mediators between body dissatisfaction and bulimic symptoms in early adolescent girls. *Journal of Early Adolescence, 25,* 478–496.

Simeon, D., Guralnik, O., Hazlett, E. A., Spiegel-Cohen, J., Hollander, E., & Buchsbaum M. S. (2000). Feeling unreal: A PET study of depersonalization disorder. *American Journal of Psychiatry, 157,* 1782–1788.

Simeon, D., Guralnik, O., Knutelska, M., Yehuda, R., & Schmeidler, J. (2003). Basal norepinephrine in depersonalization disorder. *Psychiatry Research, 121,* 93–97.

Simeon, D., Guralnik, O., Schmeidler, J., Sirof, B., & Knutelska, M. (2001). The role of childhood interpersonal trauma in depersonalization disorder. *American Journal of Psychiatry, 158,* 1027–1033.

Simeon, D., Knutelska, M., Nelson, D., & Guralnik, O. (2003). Feeling unreal: A depersonalization disorder update of 117 cases. *Journal of Clinical Psychiatry, 64,* 990–997.

Simeon, D., Stein, D. J., & Hollander E. (1998). Treatment of depersonalization disorder with clomipramine. *Biological Psychiatry, 15,* 302–303.

Simkins, S., Hawton, K., Yip, P. S. F., & Yam, C. H. K. (2003). Seasonality in suicide: A study of farming suicides in England and Wales. *Crisis: The Journal of Crisis Intervention and Suicide Prevention, 24,* 93–97.

Simon, G. E., & Gureje, O. (1999). Stability of somatization disorder and somatization symptoms among primary care patients. *Archives of General Psychiatry, 56,* 90–95.

Simoni-Wastila, L., Ritter, G., & Strickler, G. (2004). Gender and other factors associated with the nonmedical use of abusable prescription drugs. *Substance Use & Misuse, 39,* 1–23.

Simons, R. L., Murry, V., McLoyd, V., Lin, K., Cutrona, C., & Conger, R. D. (2002). Discrimination, crime, ethnic identity, and parenting as correlates of depressive symptoms among African American children: A multilevel analysis. *Development and Psychopathology, 14,* 371–393.

Simos, P. G., Fletcher, J. M., Sarkari, S., Billingsley, R. L., Denton, C., & Papanicolaou, A. C. (2007). Altering the brain circuits for reading through intervention: A magnetic source imaging study. *Neuropsychology, 21,* 485–496.

Simpson, D. D. (1984) National treatment system evaluation based on the drug abuse reporting program (DARP) follow-up research. *NIDA Research Monograph, 51,* 29–41.

Simpson, D. D., Joe, G. W., & Broome, K. M. (2002). A national 5-year follow-up of treatment outcomes for cocaine dependence. *Archives of General Psychiatry, 59,* 538–544.

Simpson, M. E., & Conklin, G. H. (1989). Socio-economic development, suicide and religion: A test of Durkheim's theory of religion and suicide *Social Forces, 67,* 945–964.

Siok, W. T., Perfetti, C. A., Jin, Z., & Tan, L. H. (2004). Biological abnormality of impaired reading is constrained by culture. *Nature, 431,* 71–76.

Siqueland, L., Rynn, M., & Diamond, G. S. (2005). Cognitive behavioral and attachment based family therapy for anxious adolescents: Phase I and II studies. *Journal of Anxiety Disorders, 19,* 361–381.

Siris, S. G. (2001). Suicide and schizophrenia. *Journal of Psychopharmacology, 15,* 127–135.

Skaer, T. L., Sclar, D. A., & Robison, L. M. (2008). Trend in anxiety disorders in the USA 1990–2003. *Primary Care & Community Psychiatry, 13,* 1–7.

Skeels, H., & Dye, H. (1939). A study of the effects of differential stimulation on mentally retarded children. *American Journal of Mental Deficiency, 44,* 114–136.

Skeem, J. L., & Mulvey, E. P. (2001). Psychopathy and community violence among civil psychiatric patients: Results from the MacArthur violence risk assessment study. *Journal of Consulting and Clinical Psychology, 69,* 358–374.

Skinner, B. F. (1965). *Science and human behavior.* New York: Free Press.

Skinner, B. F. (1986). What is wrong with daily life in the Western world? *American Psychologist, 41,* 568–574.

Skinner, B. F. (1987). Whatever happened to psychology as the science of behavior? *American Psychologist, 42,* 780–786.

Skinner, H. A. (1995). Critical issues in the diagnosis of substance use disorders. In J. D. Blaine, A. M. Horton, & L. H. Towle (Eds.), *Diagnosis and severity of drug abuse and dependence.* (NIH Publication No. 95–3884).

Skodol, A. E. (2005). Manifestations, clinical diagnosis, and comorbidity. In J. M. Oldham, A. E. Skodol, & D. S. Bender (Eds.), *The American Psychiatric Publishing textbook of personality disorders* (pp. 57–87). Washington, DC: American Psychiatric Publishing.

Skodol, A. E., Gunderson, J. G., McGlashan, T. H., Dyck, I. R., Stout, R. L., et al. (2002). Functional impairment in patients with schizotypal, borderline, avoidant, or obsessive-compulsive personality disorder. *American Journal of Psychiatry, 159,* 276–283.

Skodol, A. E., Gunderson, J. G., Shea, M. T., McGlashan, T. H., Morey, L. C., et al. (2005). The Collaborative Longitudinal Personality Disorders Study (CLPS): Overview and implications. *Journal of Personality Disorders, 19,* 487–504.

Skodol, A. E., Oldham, J. M., & Gallaher, P. E. (1999). Axis II comorbidity of substance use disorders among patients referred for treatment of personality disorders. *American Journal of Psychiatry, 156,* 733–738.

Skodol, A. E., Oldham, J. M., Hyler, S. E., Kellman, H. D., Doidge, N., & Davies, M. (1993). Comorbidity of DSM-III-R eating disorders and personality disorders. *International Journal of Eating Disorders, 14,* 403–416.

Skodol, A. E., Oldham, J. M., Hyler, S. E., Stein, D. J., Hollander, E., et al. (1995). Patterns of anxiety and personality disorder comorbidity. *Journal of Psychiatric Research, 29,* 361–374.

Skodol, A. E., Pagano, M. E., Bender, D. S., Shea, M. T., Gunderson, J. G., et al. (2005). Stability of functional impairment in patients with schizotypal, borderline, avoidant, or obsessive-compulsive personality disorder over two years. *Psychological Medicine, 35,* 443–451.

Skodol, A. E., Siever, L. J., Livesley, W. J., Gunderson, J. G., Pfohl, B., & Widiger, T. A. (2002). The borderline diagnosis II: Biology, genetics, and clinical course. *Biological Psychiatry, 51,* 951–963.

Slavich, G. M., & Cole, S. W. (2013). The emerging field of human social genomics. *Clinical Psychological Science, 1,* 331–348.

Slavich, G. M., Monroe, S. M., & Gotlib, I. H. (2011). Early parental loss and depression history: Associations with recent life stress in major depressive disorder. *Journal of Psychiatric Research, 45*(9), 1146–1152.

Sleek, S. (1997). Treating people who live life on the borderline. *APA Monitor, 7,* 20–22.

Sloan, D. M., Mizes, J. S., & Epstein, E. M. (2005). Empirical classification of eating disorders. *Eating Behaviors, 6,* 53–62.

Slomkowski, C., Klein, R. G., & Mannuzza, S. (1995). Is self-esteem an important outcome in hyperactive children? *Journal of Abnormal Child Psychology, 23,* 303–315.

Slomski, A. (2012). A trip on "bath salts" is cheaper than meth or cocaine but much more dangerous. *JAMA, 308,* 2445–2446.

Slotema, C. W., Blom, J. D., Hoek, H. W., & Sommer, I. E. C. (2010). Should we expand the toolbox of psychiatric treatment methods to include repetitive transcranial magnetic stimulation (rTMS)? *Journal of Clinical Psychiatry, 71,* 873–884.

Slutske, W. S., Heath, A. C., Dinwiddie, S. H., Madden, P. A. F., Bucholz, K. K., et al. (1997). Modeling genetic and environmental influences in the etiology of conduct disorder: A study of 2,682 adult twin pairs. *Journal of Abnormal Psychology, 106,* 266–279.

Small, G. W., Kepe, V., Ercoli, L. M., Siddarth, P., Bookheimer, S. Y., et al. (2006). PET of brain amyloid and tau in mild cognitive impairment. *New England Journal of Medicine, 355,* 2652–2653.

Smeets, G., de Jong, P. J., & Mayer, B. (2000). If you suffer from a headache, then you have a brain tumour: Domain-specific reasoning "bias" and hypochondriasis. *Behavioral Research and Therapy, 38,* 763–776.

Smith A. (2000). An fMRI investigation of frontal lobe functioning in psychopathy and schizophrenia during a go/no go task (Doctoral dissertation, The University of British Columbia, Canada). *Dissertation Abstracts International B, Physical Sciences and Engineering. 61* (01), 128.

Smith, D. C., Hall, J. A., Williams, J. K., An, H., & Gotman, N. (2006). Comparative efficacy of family and group treatment for adolescent substance abuse. *American Journal on Addictions, 15,* 131–136.

Smith, E. E., & Kosslyn, S. M. (2006). *Cognitive psychology: Mind and brain.* Upper Saddle River, NJ: Prentice Hall.

Smith G. R., Jr., Monson, R. A., & Ray, D. C. (1986). Patients with multiple unexplained symptoms: Their characteristics, functional health, and health care utilization. *Archives of Internal Medicine, 146,* 69–72.

Smith, K. A., Fairburn, C. G., & Cowen, P. J. (1999). Symptomatic relapse in bulimia nervosa following acute tryptophan depletion. *Archives of General Psychiatry, 56,* 171–176.

Smith, L. M., Chang, L., Yonekura, M. L., Gilbride, K., Kuo, J., et al. (2001). Brain proton magnetic resonance spectroscopy and imaging in children exposed to cocaine in utero. *Pediatrics, 107,* 227–231.

Smith, R. C., Gardiner, J. C., Lyles, J. S., Sirbu, C., Dwamena, F. C., et al. (2005). Exploration of DSM-IV-TR criteria in primary care patients with medically unexplained symptoms. *Psychosomatic Medicine, 67,* 123–129.

Smith, T. C., Ryan, M. A. K., Wingard, D. L., Slymen, D. J., Sallis, J. F., & Kritz-Silverstein, D. (2008). New onset and persistent symptoms of posttraumatic stress disorder self reported after deployment and combat exposures: Prospective population based US military cohort study. *British Medical Journal, 336,* 366–371.

Smith, Y. L. S., van Goozen, S. H. M., & Cohen-Kettenis, P. T. (2001). Adolescents with gender identity disorder who were accepted or rejected for sex reassignment surgery: A prospective follow-up study. *Journal of the American Academy of Child & Adolescent Psychiatry, 40,* 472–481.

Smith, Y. L. S., van Goozen, S. H. M., Kuiper, A. J., & Cohen-Kettenis, P. T. (2005). Sex reassignment: Outcomes and predictors of treatment for adolescent and adult transsexuals. *Psychological Medicine, 35,* 89–99.

Smolak, L., & Murnen, S. K. (2004). A feminist approach to eating disorders. In J. K. Thompson (Ed.), *Handbook of eating disorders and obesity* (pp. 590–605). Hoboken, NJ: John Wiley & Sons.

Smoller, J. W., Finn, C., & White, C. (2000). The genetics of anxiety disorders: An overview. *Psychiatric Annals, 30,* 745–753.

Snitz, B. E., Weissfeld, L. A., Lopez, O. L., Kuller, L. H., Saxton, J., M., et al. (2013). Cognitive trajectories associated with β-amyloid deposition in the oldest-old without dementia. *Neurology, 80,* 1378–1384.

Snow, A. L., Dani, R., Souchek, J., Sullivan, G., Ashton, C. M., & Kunik, M. E. (2005). Comorbid psychosocial symptoms and quality of life in patients with dementia. *American Journal of Geriatric Psychiatry, 13,* 393–401.

Snowden, L. R. (2007). Explaining mental health treatment disparities: Ethnic and cultural differences in family involvement. *Culture, Medicine and Psychiatry, 31,* 389–402.

Snowden, L. R., & Cheung, F. K. (1990). Use of inpatient mental health services by members of ethnic minority groups. *American Psychologist, 45,* 347–355.

Snowden, L. R., & Pingitore, D. (2002). Frequency and scope of mental health service delivery to African Americans in primary care. *Mental Health Services Research, 4,* 123–130.

Snyder, L. B., Milici, F. F., Slater, M., Sun, H., & Strizhakova, Y. (2006). Effects of alcohol advertising exposure on drinking among youth. *Archives of Pediatric Adolescent Medicine, 160,* 18–24.

Soares, J. C. (2000). Recent advances in the treatment of bipolar mania, depression, mixed states, and rapid cycling. *International Clinical Psychopharmacology, 15,* 183–196.

Sobell, M. B. & Sobell, L. C. (2006). Obstacles to the adoption of low risk drinking goals in the treatment of alcohol problems in the United States: A commentary. Addiction Research and Theory, 14, 19–24.

Söderlund, G., Sikström, S., & Smart, A. (2007). Listen to the noise: Noise is beneficial for cognitive performance in ADHD. *Journal of Child Psychology and Psychiatry, 48,* 840–847.

Solanto, M. V. (2002). Dopamine dysfunction in AD/HD: Integrating clinical and basic neuroscience research. *Behavioural Brain Research 130,* 65–71.

Soloff, P. H. (2000). Psychopharmacology of borderline personality disorder. *Psychiatric Clinics of North America, 23,* 169–192.

Soloff, P. H., Kelly, T. M., Strotmeyer, S. J., Malone, K. M., & Mann, J. J. (2003). Impulsivity, gender, and response to fenfluramine challenge in borderline personality disorder. *Psychiatry Research, 119,* 11–24.

Soloff, P. H., Meltzer, C. C., Becker, C., Greer, P. J., Kelly, T. M., & Constantine, D. (2003). Impulsivity and prefrontal hypometabolism in borderline personality disorder. *Psychiatry Research, 123,* 153–163.

Soloff, P. H., Meltzer, C. C., Greer, P. J., Constantine, D., & Kelly, T. M. (2000). A fenfluramine-activated FDG-PET study of borderline personality disorder. *Biological Psychiatry, 47,* 540–547.

Solomon, D. A., Keller, M. B., Leon, A. C., Mueller, T. I., Lavori, P. W., et al. (2000). Multiple recurrences of major depressive disorder. *American Journal of Psychiatry, 157,* 229–233.

Somers, J. M., Goldner, E. M., Waraich, P., & Hsu, L. (2006). Prevalence and incidence studies of anxiety disorders: A systematic review of the literature. *Canadian Journal of Psychiatry, 51,* 100–113.

Sonuga-Barke, E. J. S., Thompson, M., Abikoff, H., Klein, R., & Brotman, L. M. (2006). Nonpharmacological interventions for preschoolers with ADHD: The case for specialized parent training. *Infants & Young Children 19,* 142–153.

Soomro, G. M., Altman, D., Rajagopal, S., & Oakley-Browne, M. (2008). Selective serotonin re-uptake inhibitors (SSRIs) versus placebo for obsessive compulsive disorder (OCD). *Cochrane Database of Systematic Reviews, 2008, 1,* Article Number CD001765.

Sorkin, A., Weinshall, D., Modai, I., & Peled, A. (2006). Improving the accuracy of the diagnosis of schizophrenia by means of virtual reality. *American Journal of Psychiatry, 163,* 512–520.

Soto, O. R. (2003, November 8). Stalker of actress to be freed from jail. *San Diego Union-Tribune.* Retrieved September 25, 2008, from www.signonsandiego.com/news/metro/20031106-9999_2m6stalk.html

Sourander, A., Ronning, J., Brunstein-Klomek, A., Gyllenberg, D., Kumpulainen, K., et al. (2009). Childhood bullying behavior and later psychiatric hospital and psychopharmacologic treatment. *Archives of General Psychiatry, 66,* 1005–1012.

South, S. C., & DeYoung, N. J. (2013). Behavior genetics of personality disorders: Informing classification and conceptualization in DSM-5. *Personality Disorders: Theory, Research, and Treatment, 4,* 270–283.

South, S. C., & Krueger, R. F. (2011). Genetic and environmental influences on internalizing psychopathology vary as a function of economic status. *Psychological Medicine, 41,* 107–117.

Southard, E. E. (1910). A study of the dementia praecox group in the light of certain cases showing anomalies or scleroses in particular brain regions. *American Journal of Insanity, 67,* 119–176.

Southwick, S. M., Bremner, D., Krystal, J. H., & Charney, D. S. (1994). Psychobiologic research in post-traumatic stress disorder. *Psychiatric Clinics of North America, 17,* 251–264.

Southwick, S. M., Krystal, J. H., Morgan, C. A., Johnson, D., Nagy, L. M., et al. (1993). Abnormal noradrenergic function in posttraumatic stress disorder. *Archives of General Psychiatry, 50,* 266–274.

Sowell, E. R., Thompson, P. M., Welcome, S. E., Henkenius, A. L., Toga, A. W., & Peterson, B. S. (2003). Cortical abnormalities in children and adolescents with attention-deficit hyperactivity disorder. *Lancet, 362,* 1699–1707.

Spanos, N. P. (1994). Multiple identity enactments and multiple personality disorder: A sociocognitive perspective. *Psychological Bulletin, 116,* 143–165.

Sparén, P., Vågerö, D., Shestov, D. B., Plavinskaja, S., Parfenova, N., et al. (2004). Long term mortality after severe starvation during the siege of Leningrad: Prospective cohort study. *British Medical Journal, 328,* 11.

Spector, A., Davies, S., Woods, B., & Orrell, M. (2000). Reality orientation for dementia: A systematic review of the evidence of effectiveness from randomized controlled trials. *The Gerontologist, 40,* 206–212.

Spector, I. P., & Carey, M. P. (1990). Incidence and prevalence of the sexual dysfunctions: A critical review of the empirical literature. *Archives of Sexual Behavior, 19,* 389–408.

Spiegel, D., Bierre, P., & Rootenberg, J. (1989). Hypnotic alteration of somatosensory perception. *American Journal of Psychiatry, 146,* 749–754.

Spiegel, D., Cutcomb, S., Ren, C., & Pribram, K. (1985). Hypnotic hallucination alters evoked potentials. *Journal of Abnormal Psychology, 94,* 249–255.

Spiegel, D., Loewenstein, R. J., Lewis-Fernandez, R., Sar, V., Simeon, D., et al. (2011). Dissociative disorders in DSM-5. *Depression and Anxiety, 28,* 824–852.

Spiegel, H. (1974). The grade 5 syndrome: The highly hypnotizable person. *International Journal of Clinical and Experimental Hypnosis, 22,* 303–319.

Spielberger, C. D., & Rickman, R. L. (1990). Assessment of state and trait anxiety in cardiovascular disorders. In D. G. Byrne and R. H. Rosenman (Eds.), *Anxiety and the heart* (pp. 73–92). New York: Hemisphere Publishing.

Spielmans, G. I., Berman, M. I., & Usitalo, A. N. (2011). Psychotherapy versus second generation antidepressants in the treatment of depression: A meta-analysis. *Journal of Nervous and Mental Disease, 199*(3), 142–149.

Spira, A. P., & Edelstein, B. A. (2006). Behavioral interventions for agitation in older adults with dementia: An evaluative review. *International Psychogeriatrics, 18,* 195–225.

Spitz, B. (2005). *The Beatles: The biography.* New York: Little, Brown.

Spitzer, R. L., First, M. B., & Wakefield, J. C. (2007). Saving PTSD from itself in DSM-V. *Journal of Anxiety Disorders, 21,* 233–241.

Spitzer, R. L., First, M. B., Williams, J. B. W., & Gibbon, M. (2002). *DSM-IV-TR Casebook.* Washington, DC: American Psychiatric Publishers.

Spoor, S. T. P., Bekker, M. H. J., Van Strien, T., & van Heck, G. L. (2007). Relations between negative affect, coping, and emotional eating. *Appetite, 48,* 368–376.

Sporn, A., & Lisanby, S. H. (2006). Non-pharmacological treatment modalities in children and adolescents: A review of electro-convulsive therapy, transcranial magnetic stimulation, vagus nerve stimulation, magnetic seizure therapy, and deep brain stimulation. *Clinical Neuropsychiatry: Journal of Treatment Evaluation, 3,* 230–244.

Spreen, O., & Strauss, E. (1998). *A compendium of neuropsychological tests: Administration norms and commentary* (2nd ed.). New York: Oxford University Press.

Sprock, J., Rader, T. J., Kendall, J. P., & Yoder, C. Y. (2000). Neuropsychological functioning in patients with borderline personality disorder. *Journal of Clinical Psychology, 56,* 1587–1600.

Squire, L. R. (2004). Memory systems of the brain: A brief history and current perspective. *Neurobiology of Learning and Memory, 82,* 171–177.

Squire, L. R., & Kandel, E. (2000). *Memory: From mind to molecules.* New York: Scientific American Library.

Sramek, J. J., Frackiewicz, E. J., & Cutler, N. R. (1997). Efficacy and safety of two dosing regimens of buspirone in the treatment of outpatients with persistent anxiety. *Clinical Therapeutics, 19,* 498–506.

Staba, D. (2004). Hollywood kid Carrie Fisher and her best awful. *BP Magazine,* Fall. Retrieved December 24, 2011, from www.bphope.com/Item.aspx/280/hollywood-kid-carrie-fisher-and-her-best-awful

Stack, S. (1983). The effect of religious commitment of suicide: A cross-national analysis. *Journal of Health and Social Behavior, 24,* 362–274.

Stack, S., & Wasserman, I. (1992). The effect of religion on suicide ideology: An analysis of the networks perspective *Journal of Scientific Study of Religion, 31,* 457–466.

Stafford, J., & Lynn, S. J. (2002). Cultural scripts, memories of childhood abuse, and multiple identities: A study of role-played enactments. *International Journal of Clinical and Experimental Hypnosis, 50,* 67–85.

Stafford, M. R., Jackson, H., Mayo-Wilson, E., Morrison, A. P., & Kendall, T. (2013). Early interventions to prevent psychosis: Systematic review and meta-analysis. *BMJ: British Medical Journal, 346,* Article ID f185.

Staines, G. L., Magura, S., Foote, J., Deluca, A., & Kosanke, N. (2001). Polysubstance use among alcoholics. *Journal of Addictive Diseases, 20,* 53–69.

Stålenheim, E. G., & von Knorring, L. (1996). Psychopathy and Axis I and Axis II psychiatric disorders in a forensic psychiatric population in Sweden. *Acta Psychiatrica Scandinavica, 94,* 217–223.

Stanton, M. D. (1981). Strategic approaches to family therapy. In A. S. Gurman & D. P. Kniskern (Eds.), *Handbook of family therapy* (pp. 361–402). New York: Brunner/Mazel.

Stanton, M. D., & Shadish, W. R. (1997). Outcome, attrition, and family-couples treatment for drug abuse: A meta-analysis and review of the controlled, comparative studies. *Psychological Bulletin, 122,* 170–191.

Staples, J., Rellini, A. H., & Roberts, S. P. (2012). Avoiding experiences: Sexual dysfunction in women with a history of sexual abuse in childhood and adolescence. *Archives of Sexual Behavior, 41*(2), 341–350.

Starcevic, V., & Berle, D. (2013). Cyberchondria: Towards a better understanding of excessive health-related Internet use. *Expert Review of Neurotherapeutics, 13*(2), 205–213.

Starker, S. (1988). Psychologists and self-help books: Attitudes and prescriptive practices of clinicians. *American Journal of Psychotherapy, 42,* 448–455.

Stark-Wroblewski, K., Yanico, B. J., & Lupe, S. (2005). Acculturation, internalization of Western appearance norms, and eating pathology among Japanese and Chinese international student women. *Psychology of Women Quarterly, 29,* 38–46.

Statistics Canada. (2005). *Selected leading causes of death by sex, 1997.* Retrieved December 3, 2006, from www.statcan. ca/english/Pgdb/health36.htm

Steadman, H., Mulvey, E., Monahan, J., Robbins, P., Appelbaum, P., et al. (1998). Violence by people discharged from acute psychiatric inpatient facilities and by others in the same neighborhoods. *Archives of General Psychiatry, 55,* 393–401.

Steadman, H. J., McGreevy, M. A., Morrissey, J. P., Callahan, L. A., Robbins, P. C., & Cirincione, C. (1993). *Before and after Hinckley: Evaluating insanity defense reform.* New York: Guilford Press.

Stefansson, H., Rujescu, D., Cichon, S., Pietiläinen, O. P., Ingason, A., et al. (2008). Large recurrent microdeletions associated with schizophrenia. *Nature, 455,* 232–236.

Steffenburg, S., Gillberg, C., Hellgren, L., Andersson, L., Gillberg, I. C., et al. (1989). A twin study of autism in Denmark, Finland, Iceland, Norway and Sweden. *Journal of Child Psychology and Psychiatry, 30,* 405–416.

Stefulj, J., Büttner, A., Kubat, M., Zill, P., Balija, M., et al. (2004). 5HT-2C receptor polymorphism in suicide victims: Association studies in German and Slavic populations. *European Archives of Psychiatry & Clinical Neuroscience, 254,* 224–227.

Stein, A., Woolley, H., Cooper, S., Winterbottom, J., Fairburn, C. G., & Cortina-Borja, M. (2006). Eating habits and attitudes among 10-year-old children of mothers with eating disorders: Longitudinal study *British Journal of Psychiatry, 189,* 324–329.

Stein, A., Woolley, H., Senior, R., Hertzmann, L., Lovel, M., et al. (2006). Treating disturbances in the relationship between mothers with bulimic eating disorders and their infants: A randomized, controlled trial of video feedback. *American Journal of Psychiatry, 163,* 899–906.

Stein, D. J. (2008). Depression, anhedonia, and psychomotor symptoms: the role of dopaminergic neurocircuitry. *CNS Spectrums, 3,* 561–565.

Stein, D. J., Koenen, K. C., Friedman, M. J., Hill, E., McLaughlin, K. A., et al. (2013). Dissociation in posttraumatic stress disorder: Evidence from the World Mental Health Surveys. *Biological Psychiatry, 73*(4), 302–312.

Stein, D. J., & Matsunaga, H. (2006). Specific phobia: A disorder of fear conditioning and extinction. *CNS Spectrums, 11,* 248–251.

Stein, D. J., Seedat, S., van der Linden, G. J. H., & Zungu-Dirwayi, N. (2000). Selective serotonin reuptake inhibitors in the treatment of post-traumatic stress disorder: A meta-analysis of randomized controlled trials. *International Clinical Psychopharmacology, 15*(Suppl. 2), S31–S39.

Stein, D. J., Westenberg, H. G. M., & Liebowitz, M. R. (2002). Social anxiety disorder and generalized anxiety disorder: Serotonergic and dopaminergic neurocircuitry. *Journal of Clinical Psychiatry, 63*, 12–19.

Stein, D., Weizman, A., & Bloch, Y. (2006). Electroconvulsive therapy and Transcranial Magnetic Stimulation: Can they be considered valid modalities in the treatment of pediatric mood disorders? *Child and Adolescent Psychiatric Clinics of North America, 15*, 1035–1056.

Stein, L. I., & Test, M. A. (1980). Alternative to mental hospital treatment: I. Conceptual model, treatment program, and clinical evaluation. *Archives of General Psychiatry, 37*, 392–397.

Stein, M. B., & Gelernter, J. (2010). Genetic basis of social anxiety disorder. In S. G. Hofmann & P. M. DiBartolo (Eds.), *Social anxiety: Clinical, developmental, and social perspectives* (2nd ed.) (pp. 313–322). San Diego: CA: Elsevier Academic Press.

Stein, M. B., Jang, K. L., & Livesley, W. J. (2002). Heritability of social anxiety-related concerns and personality characteristics: A twin study. *Journal of Nervous and Mental Disease, 190*, 219–224.

Stein, M. B., Kerridge, C., Dimsdale, J. E., & Hoyt, D. B. (2007). Pharmacotherapy to prevent PTSD: Results from a randomized controlled proof-of-concept trial in physically injured patients. *Journal of Traumatic Stress, 20*, 923–932.

Stein, M. B., McQuaid, J. R., Pedrelli, P., Lenox, R., & McCahill, M. E. (2000). Posttraumatic stress disorder in the primary care medical setting. *General Hospital Psychiatry, 22*, 261–269.

Steinberg, M. (1994). *Handbook for the assessment of dissociation.* Washington, DC: American Psychiatric Publishers.

Steinberg, M. (2001). *The stranger in the mirror: Dissociation—The hidden epidemic.* Washington, DC: American Pyschiatric Publishing.

Steiner, B. W. (1985). *Gender dysphoria: Development, research, management.* New York: Plenum Press.

Steiner, M., Dunn, E., & Born, L. (2003). Hormones and mood: From menarche to menopause and beyond. *Journal of Affective Disorders, 74*, 67–83.

Steinfeld, B. I., & Keyes, J. A. (2011). Electronic medical records in a multidisciplinary health care setting: A clinical perspective. *Professional Psychology: Research and Practice, 42*(6), 426–432.

Steinhausen, H. (2002). The outcome of anorexia nervosa in the 20th century. *American Journal of Psychiatry, 159*, 1284–1293.

Steketee, G., & White, K. (1990). *When once is not enough.* Oakland, CA: New Harbinger Publications.

Stephens, J. H., Richard, P., & McHugh, P. R. (1999). Suicide in patients hospitalized for schizophrenia: 1913–1940. *Journal of Nervous and Mental Disease, 187*, 10–14.

Stermac, L. E., & Segal, Z. V. (1989). Adult sexual contact with children: An examination of cognitive factors. *Behavior Therapy, 20*, 573–584.

Stevens, J., Harman, J. S., & Kelleher, K. J. (2005). Race/ethnicity and insurance status as factors associated with ADHD treatment patterns. *Journal of Child and Adolescent Psychopharmacology, 15*, 88–96.

Stevens, M. C., Pearlson, G. D., & Kiehl, K. A. (2007). An fMRI auditory oddball study of combined-subtype attention deficit hyperactivity disorder. *American Journal of Psychiatry, 164*, 1737–1749.

Stevens, S., Gerlach, A. L., & Rist, F. (2008). Effects of alcohol on ratings of emotional facial expressions in social phobics. *Journal of Anxiety Disorders, 22*, 940–948.

Stevenson, J., Asherson, P., Hay, D., Levy, F., Swanson, J., et al. (2005). Characterizing the ADHD phenotype for genetic studies. *Developmental Science, 8*, 115–121.

Stewart, J., deWit, H., & Eikelbloom, R. (1984). Role of unconditioned and conditioned drug effects in the self-administration of opiates and stimulants. *Psychological Review, 91*, 251–268.

Stewart, S. (1996). Alcohol abuse in individuals exposed to trauma: A critical review. *Psychological Bulletin, 120*, 83–112.

Stewart, S., Zvolensky, M. J., & Eifert, G. H. (2001). Negative-reinforcement drinking motives mediate the relation between anxiety sensitivity and increased drinking behavior. *Personality & Individual Differences, 31*, 157–171.

Stewart, W. F., Ricci, J. A., Chee, E., Hahn, S. R., & Morganstein, D. (2003). Cost of lost productive work time among US workers with depression. *JAMA: Journal of the American Medical Association, 289*, 3135–3144.

Stice, E., & Hoffman, E. (2004). Eating disorder prevention programs. In J. K. Thompson (Ed.), *Handbook of eating disorders and obesity* (pp. 33–57). Hoboken, NJ: John Wiley & Sons.

Stice, E., Marti, C. N., & Rohde, P. (2013). Prevalence, incidence, impairment, and course of the proposed DSM-5 eating disorder diagnoses in an 8-year prospective community study of young women. *Journal of Abnormal Psychology, 122*(2), 445–457.

Stice, E., Maxfield, J., & Wells, T. (2003). Adverse effects of social pressure to be thin on young women: An experimental investigation of the effects of "fat talk." *International Journal of Eating Disorders, 34*, 108–117.

Stice, E., Schupak-Neuberg, E., Shaw, H. E., & Stein, R. I. (1994). Relation of media exposure to eating disorder symptomatology: An examination of mediating mechanisms. *Journal of Abnormal Psychology, 103*, 836–840.

Stice, E., & Shaw, H. (2004). Eating disorder prevention programs: A meta-analytic review. *Psychological Bulletin, 130*, 206–227.

Stice, E., Shaw, H., & Marti, C. N. (2006). A meta-analytic review of eating disorder prevention programs: Encouraging findings. *Annual Review of Clinical Psychology, 3*, 233–257.

Stinson, F. S., Dawson, D. A., Chou, S. P., Smith, S., Goldstein, R. B., et al. (2007). The epidmiology of DSM-IV specific phobia in the USA: Result from the National Epidemiologic Survey on Alcohol and Related Conditions. *Psychological Medicine, 37*, 1047–1059.

Stitzer, M., & Petry, N. (2006). Contingency management for treatment of substance abuse. *Annual Review of Clinical Psychology, 2*, 411–434.

Stock, W., & Moser, C. (2001). Feminist sex therapy in the age of Viagra. In P. J. Kleinplatz (Ed.), *New directions in sex therapy: Innovations and alternatives* (pp. 130–162) Philadelphia: Taylor and Rutledge.

Stone, A. B. (1993). Treatment of hypochondriasis with clomipramine. *Journal of Clinical Psychiatry, 54*, 200–201.

Stone, A. L., Storr, C. L., & Anthony, J. C. (2006). Evidence for a hallucinogen dependence syndrome developing soon after onset of hallucinogen use during adolescence. *International Journal of Methods in Psychiatric Research, 15*, 116–130.

Stone, J., Carson, A., Aditya, H., Prescott, R., Zaubi, M., et al. (2009). The role of physical injury in motor and sensory conversion symptoms: A systematic and narrative review. *Journal of Psychosomatic Research, 66*, 383–390.

Stone, J., LaFrance, W. C., Levenson, J. L., & Sharpe, M. (2010). Issues for DSM-5 conversion disorder. *American Journal of Psychiatry, 167*, 626–627.

Stone, J., Zeman, A., Simonotto, E., Meyer, M., Azuma, R., et al. (2007). fMRI in patients with motor conversion symptoms and controls with simulated weakness. *Psychosomatic Medicine, 69*, 961–969.

Strain, B. A. (2003). Influence of gender bias on the diagnosis of borderline personality disorder. *Dissertation Abstracts International B: Sciences and Engineering, 64* (6), 2941B.

Strain, E. C., Bigelow, G. E., Liebson, I. A., & Stitzer, M. L. (1999). Moderate- vs high-dose methadone in the treatment of opioid dependence: A randomized trial. *JAMA: Journal of the American Medical Association, 281*, 1000–1005.

Strakowski, S. M., Adler, C. M., & DelBello, M. P. (2002). Volumetric MRI studies of mood disorders: Do they distinguish unipolar and bipolar disorder? *Bipolar Disorders, 4*, 80–88.

Strakowski, S. M., & Frances, A. J. (2012). What's wrong with DSM-5? *Medscape,* June 1. Retrieved May 21, 2013, from www.medscape.com/viewarticle/763886

Strakowski, S. M., Shelton, R. C., & Kolbrener, M. L. (1993). The effects of race and comorbidity on clinical diagnosis in patients with psychosis. *Journal of Clinical Psychiatry, 54*, 96–102.

Straube, T., Mentzel, H., & Miltner, W. H. R. (2006). Neural mechanisms of automatic and direct processing of phobogenic stimuli in specific phobia. *Biological Psychiatry, 59,* 162–170.

Striegel-Moore, R. H. (1993). Etiology of binge eating: A developmental perspective. In C. G. Fairburn & G. T. Wilson (Eds.), *Binge eating: Nature, assessment, and treatment* (pp. 144–172). New York: Guilford Press.

Striegel-Moore, R. H., & Cachelin, F. M. (2001). Etiology of eating disorders in women. *Counseling Psychologist, 29,* 635–661.

Striegel-Moore, R. H., Dohm, F. A., Kraemer, H. C., Taylor, C. B., Daniels, S., et al. (2003). Eating disorders in White and Black women. *American Journal of Psychiatry, 160,* 1326–1331.

Striegel-Moore, R. H., Silberstein, L. R., & Rodin, J. (1986). Toward an understanding of risk factors for bulimia. *American Psychologist, 41,* 246–263.

Strober, M. (1995). Family-genetic influences on anorexia nervosa and bulimia nervosa. In K. D. Brownell & C. G. Fairburn (Eds.), *Eating disorders and obesity: A comprehensive handbook.* New York: Guilford Press.

Strober, M., Freeman, R., Lampert, C., Diamond, J., & Kaye, W. (2000). Controlled family study of anorexia nervosa and bulimia nervosa: Evidence of shared liability and transmission of partial syndromes. *American Journal of Psychiatry, 157,* 393–401.

Strupp, H., & Binder, J. (1984). *Psychotherapy in a new key: A guide to time-limited dynamic psychotherapy.* New York: Basic Books.

Stuart, G. L., Moore, T. M., Ramsey, S. E., & Kahler, C. W. (2003). Relationship aggression and substance use among women court-referred to domestic violence intervention programs. *Addictive Behaviors, 28,* 1603–1610.

Stuart, S., & Noyes, R., Jr. (2005). Treating hypochondriasis with interpersonal psychotherapy. *Journal of Contemporary Psychotherapy, 35,* 269–283.

Stuart, S., Noyes, R., Jr., Starcevic, V., & Barsky, A. (2008). Integrative approach to somatoform disorders combining interpersonal and cognitive-behavioral theory and techniques. *Journal of Contemporary Psychotherapy, 38,* 45–53.

Stunkard, A., Allison, K., & Lundgren, J. (2008). Issues for DSM-V: Night eating syndrome. *American Journal of Psychiatry, 165,* 424.

Stuss, D. T., Alexander, M. P., Palumbo, C. L., Buckle, L., Sayer, L., & Pogue, J. (1994). Organizational strategies with unilateral or bilateral frontal lobe injury in word learning tasks. *Neuropsychology, 8,* 355–373.

Styron, W. (1990). *Darkness visible: A memoir of madness.* New York: Random House.

Subramaniam, P., & Woods, B. (2012). The impact of individual reminiscence therapy for people with dementia: Systematic review. *Expert Review of Neurotherapeutics, 12*(5), 545–555.

Substance Abuse and Mental Health Services Administration. (2000). *National household survey on drug abuse main findings 1998: Office of applied studies.* Rockville, MD: National Clearinghouse for Alcohol and Drug Information.

Substance Abuse and Mental Health Services Administration. (2008). *Results from the 2007 national survey on drug use and health: National findings.* (Office of Applied Studies, NSDUH Series H-34, DHHS Publication No. SMA 08-4343). Rockville, MD: Department of Health and Human Services. Retrieved December 18, 2008, from http://oas.samhsa.gov/nsduh/2k7nsduh/2k7Results.pdf

Substance Abuse and Mental Health Services Administration. (2004). *Results from the 2003 national survey on drug use and health: National findings.* [NHSDA Series H-25. DHHS Pub. No. (SMA) 04-3964]. Rockville, MD: Department of Health and Human Services.

Substance Abuse and Mental Health Services Administration, Office of Applied Studies. (2008). *National survey on drug use and health, 2003 and 2004.* Retrieved October 20, 2008, from www.oas.samhsa.gov/NSDUH/2k4nsduh/2k4tabs/Sect6peTabs1to81.htm#tab6.59a

Substance Abuse and Mental Health Services Administration (SAMHSA). (2010). *Results from the 2009 National Survey on Drug Use and Health: Volume I. Summary of National Findings.* Retrieved March 8, 2012, from www.oas.samhsa.gov/NSDUH/2k9NSDUH/2k9Results.htm#7.1

Substancemisuse.net. (2007). Debbie's story. Retrieved August 2, 2007, from www.substancemisuse.net/problem-users/pustories/debbiesstory.htm

Sue, S., Fujino, D. C., Hu, L. T., Takeuchi, D. T., & Zane, N. W. S. (1991). Community mental health services for ethnic minority groups: A test of the cultural responsiveness hypothesis. *Journal of Consulting and Clinical Psychology, 59,* 533–540.

Sue, S., Kuraski, K. S., & Srinivasan, S. (1999). Ethnicity, gender, and cross-cultural issues in clinical research. In P. C. Kendall, J. N. Butcher, & G. N. Holmbeck (Eds.), *Handbook of research methods in clinical psychology* (2nd ed., pp. 54–71). Hoboken, NJ: John Wiley & Sons.

Sue, S., Zane, N., & Young, K. (1994). Research on psychotherapy with culturally diverse populations. In A. E. Bergin & S. L. Garfield (Eds.), *Handbook of psychotherapy and behavior change* (4th ed., pp. 783–817). Oxford, England: John Wiley & Sons.

Suh, J. J., Pettinati, H. M., Kampman, K. M., & O'Brien, C. P. (2006). The status of disulfiram: A half of a century later. *Journal of Clinical Psychopharmacology, 26,* 290–302.

Sullins, E. S. (1991). Emotional contagion revisited: Effects of social comparison and expressive style on mood convergence. *Personality and Social Psychology Bulletin, 17,* 166–174.

Sullivan, G. M., Mann, J. J., Oquendo, M. A., Lo, E. S., Cooper, T. B., & Gorman, J. M. (2006). Low cerebrospinal fluid transthyretin levels in depression: Correlations with suicidal ideation and low serotonin function. *Biological Psychiatry, 60,* 500–506.

Sullivan, H. S. (1953). *The interpersonal theory of psychiatry.* New York: W. W. Norton.

Sullivan, P. F., Bulik, C. M., & Kendler, K. S. (1998). The epidemiology and classification of bulimia nervosa. *Psychological Medicine, 28,* 599–610.

Sulpy, D., & Schweighardt, R. (1994). *Drugs, divorces, and a slipping image: The unauthorized story of the Beatles' "Get Back" sessions.* Princeton Junction, NJ: The 910.

Sultan, S., Andronikof, A., Réveillère, C., & Lemmel, G. (2006). A Rorschach stability study in a nonpatient adult sample. *Journal of Personality Assessment, 87,* 330–348.

Summerfield, D. (2001). The invention of post-traumatic stress disorder and the social usefulness of a psychiatric category. *British Medical Journal, 322,* 95–98.

Sundgot-Borgen, J. (1999). Eating disorders among male and female elite athletes. *British Journal of Sports Medicine, 33,* 434.

Sundquist, A. (1999). First person account: Family psychoeducation can change lives. *Schizophrenia Bulletin, 25,* 619–621.

Sung, M., Erkanli, A., Angold, A., & Costello, E. J. (2004). Effects of age at first substance use and psychiatric comorbidity on the development of substance use disorders. *Drug and Alcohol Dependence, 75,* 287–299.

Surguladze, S. A., Young, A. W., Senior, C., Brébion, G., Travis, M. J., & Phillips, M. L. (2004). Recognition accuracy and response bias to happy and sad facial expressions in patients with major depression. *Neuropsychology, 18,* 212–218.

Sutker, P. D., & Allain, A. N., Jr. (2001). Antisocial personality disorder. In H. E. Adams & P. B. Sutker (Eds.), *Comprehensive handbook of psychopathology* (3rd ed., pp. 445–490). New York: Kluwer Academic/Plenum.

Sutton, C. T., & Broken Nose, M. A. (1996). American Indian families: An overview. In M. McGoldrick, J. Giordano, & J. K. Pearce (Eds.), *Ethnicity and family therapy* (2nd ed., pp. 31–44). New York: Guilford Press.

Svartberg, M., & Stiles, T. C. (1991). Comparative effects of short-term psychodynamic psychotherapy: A meta-analysis. *Journal of Consulting & Clinical Psychology, 59,* 704–714.

Swaab, D. F. (2003). *The human hypothalamus: Basic and clinical aspects. Part 1: Nuclei of the human hypothalamus.* Amsterdam: Elsevier.

Swaggart, B., Gagnon, E., Bock, S. J., Earles, T. L., Quinn, C., & Myles, B. S. (1995). Using social stories to teach social and behavioral skills to children with autism. *Focus on Autistic Behavior, 10,* 1–16.

Swanson, J., Flodman, P., Kennedy, J., Spence, M. A., Moyzis, R., et al. (2000). Dopamine genes and ADHD. *Neuroscience and Biobehavioral Reviews, 24,* 21–25.

Swanson, J. M., & Volkow, N. D. (2002). Pharmacokinetic and pharmacodynamic properties of stimulants: Implications for the design of new treatments for ADHD. *Behavioural Brain Research, 130,* 73–78.

Swanson, J. M., Casey, B. J., Nigg, J., Castellanos, F. X., Volkow, N. D., & Taylor, E. (2004). Clinical and cognitive definitions of attention deficits in children with attention-deficit/hyperactivity disorder. In M. I. Posner (Ed.), *Cognitive neuroscience of attention* (pp. 430–445). New York: Guilford.

Swanson, J. M., Kinsbourne, M., Nigg, J., Lanphear, B., Stefanatos, G. A., et al. (2007). Etiologic subtypes of attention-deficit/hyperactivity disorder: Brain imaging, molecular genetic and environmental factors and the dopamine hypothesis. *Neuropsychology Review, 17,* 39–59.

Swanson, J. W. (1994). Mental disorder, substance abuse, and community violence: an epidemiological approach. In J. Monahan & H. J. Steadman (Eds.), *Violence and mental disorder: Developments in risk assessment* (pp. 101–136). Chicago: University of Chicago Press.

Swanson, J. W., Swartz, M. S., Van Dorn, R. A., Elbogen, E. B., Wagner, H. R., et al. (2006). A national study of violent behavior in persons with schizophrenia. *Archives of General Psychiatry, 63,* 490–499.

Swartz, H. A. (1999). Interpersonal psychotherapy. In M. Hersen, & A. S. Bellack (Eds.), *Handbook of comparative interventions for adult disorders* (2nd ed., pp. 139–155). Hoboken, NJ: John Wiley & Sons.

Swartz, M. S., Swanson, J. W., Hiday, V. A., Wagner, H. R., Burns, B. J., & Borum, R. (2001). A randomized controlled trial of out patient commitment in North Carolina. *Psychiatric Services, 52,* 325–329.

Swartz, M. S., Wagner, H. R., Swanson, J. W., Stroup, T. S., McEvoy, J. P., et al. (2006). Substance use in persons with schizophrenia: Baseline prevalence and correlates from the NIMH CATIE study. *Journal of Nervous and Mental Disease, 194,* 164–172.

Swedo, S. E., Leonard, H. L., Garvey, M., Mittleman, B., Allen, A. J., et al. (1998). Pediatric autoimmune neuropsychiatric disorders associated with streptococcal infections: Clinical description of the first 50 cases. *American Journal of Psychiatry, 155,* 264–271.

Sweeney, P. D., Anderson, K., & Bailey, S. (1986). Attributional style in depression: A meta-analytic review. *Journal of Personality and Social Psychology, 50,* 974–991.

Swendsen, J. D., Merikangas, K. R., Canino, G. J., Kessler, R. C., Rubio-Stipec, M., & Anglst, J. (1998). The comorbidity of alcoholism with anxiety and depressive disorders in four geographic communities. *Comprehensive Psychiatry, 39,* 176–184.

Swenne, I. (2000). Heart risk associated with weight loss in anorexia nervosa and eating disorders: Electrocardiographic changes during the early phase of refeeding. *Acta Paediatrica, 89,* 447–452.

Swica, Y., Lewis, D. O., & Lewis, M. (1996). Child abuse and dissociative identity disorder/multiple personality disorder: The documentation of childhood maltreatment and the corroboration of symptoms. *Child and Adolescent Psychiatric Clinics of North America, 5,* 431–447.

Swift, A., & Wright, M. O. (2000). Does social support buffer stress for college women: When and how? *Journal of College Student Psychotherapy, 14,* 23–42.

Sykes, R. (2006). Somatoform disorders in DSM-IV: Mental or physical disorders? *Journal of Psychosomatic Research, 60,* 341–344.

Syvalathi, E. K. G. (1994). Biological factors in schizophrenia: Structural and functional aspects. *British Journal of Psychiatry, 164*(Suppl. 23), 9–14.

Szapocznik, J., Hervis, O., & Schwartz, S. (2003). *Brief strategic family therapy for adolescent drug abuse.* (NIH Publication 03-4751). Bethesda, MD: National Institute on Drug Abuse.

Szasz, T. S. (1960). The myth of mental illness. *American Psychologist, 15,* 113–118.

TADS Team (2007). The Treatment for Adolescents with Depression Study (TADS): Long-term effectiveness and safety outcomes. *Archives of General Psychiatry, 64,* 1132–1144.

Tager-Flusberg, H. (1999). A psychological approach to understanding the social and language impairments in autism. *International Review of Psychiatry, 11,* 325–334.

Takano, A., Shiga, T., Kitagawa, N., Koyama, T., Katoh, C., et al. (2001). Abnormal neuronal network in anorexia nervosa studied with I-123-IMP SPECT. *Psychiatry Research, 107,* 45–50.

Takeshita, J. (1997). Psychosis. In W-S. Tseng & J. Streltzer (Eds.), Culture and psychopathology: A guide to clinician assessment (pp. 124–138). New York: Brunner/Mazel.

Tamminga, C. A. (2006). Practical treatment information for schizophrenia. *American Journal of Psychiatry, 163,* 563–565.

Tan, H. M., Tong, S. F., & Ho, C. C. K. (2012). Men's health: Sexual dysfunction, physical, and psychological health—Is there a link? *Journal of Sexual Medicine, 9*(3), 663–671.

Tanda, G., Pontieri, F., & Di Chiara, G. (1997). Cannabinoid and heroin activation of mesolimbic dopamine transmission by a common opioid receptor mechanism. *Science, 276,* 2048–2050.

Tandon, R., Keshavan, M. S., & Nasrallah, H. A. (2008). Schizophrenia, "just the facts": What we know in 2008. 2. Epidemiology and etiology. *Schizophrenia Research, 102,* 1–18.

Tang, T. Z., & DeRubeis, R. J. (1999). Sudden gains and critical sessions in cognitive-behavioral therapy for depression. *Journal of Consulting and Clinical Psychology, 67,* 894–904.

Tani, P., Lindberg, N., Appelberg, B., Wendt, T. N., Wendt, L. V., & Porkka-Heiskanen, T. (2006). Clinical neurological abnormalities in young adults with Asperger syndrome. *Psychiatry and Clinical Neurosciences, 60,* 253–255.

Tanielian, T., & Jaycox, L. H. (2008). *Invisible wounds of war: Psychological and cognitive injuries, their consequences, and services to assist recovery.* Rand Center for Military Health Policy Research. Retrieved September 4, 2008, from www.rand.org/pubs/monographs/2008/RAND_MG720.sum.pdf

Tanofsky-Kraff, M., & Wilfley, D. E. (2010). Interpersonal psychotherapy for the treatment of eating disorders. In W. S. Agras (Ed.), *Oxford library of psychology. The Oxford handbook of eating disorders* (pp. 348–372). New York: Oxford University Press.

Tantleff-Dunn, S., Gokee-LaRose, J., & Peterson, R. D. (2004). Interpersonal psychotherapy for the treatment of anorexia nervosa, bulimia nervosa, and binge eating disorder. In J. K. Thompson (Ed.), *Handbook of eating disorders and obesity* (pp. 163–185). Hoboken, NJ: John Wiley & Sons.

Tarasoff v. Regents of the University of California, 529 P.2d 553 (Cal. 1974).

Tarasoff v. Regents of the University of California, 551 P.2d 334 (Cal. 1976).

Tareen, A., Hodes, M., & Rangel, L. (2005). Non-fat-phobic anorexia nervosa in British South Asian adolescents. *International Journal of Eating Disorders, 37,* 161–165.

Tariot, P. N., Farlow, M. R., Grossberg, G. T., Graham, S. M., McDonald, S., & Gergel, I. (2004). Memantine treatment in patients with moderate to severe Alzheimer disease already receiving donepezil: A randomized controlled trial. *Journal of the American Medical Association, 291,* 317–324.

Tarrier, N., & Bobes, J. (2000). The importance of psychosocial interventions and patient involvement in the treatment of schizophrenia. *International Journal of Psychiatry in Clinical Practice, 4,* S35–S51.

Tarrier, N., Kinney, C., McCarthy, E., Wittkowski, A., Yusupoff, L., et al. (2001). Are some types of psychotic symptoms more responsive to cognitive-behavior therapy? *Behavioural & Cognitive Psychotherapy, 29,* 45–55.

Tarrier, N., Pilgrim, H., Sommerfield, C., Faragher, B., Reynolds, M., et al. (1999). A randomized trial of cognitive therapy and imaginal exposure in the treatment of chronic posttraumatic stress disorder. *Journal of Consulting & Clinical Psychology, 67,* 13–18.

Tarullo, A. R., & Gunnar, M. R. (2006). Child maltreatment and the developing HPA axis. *Hormones and Behavior, 50,* 632–639.

Task Force on Promotion and Dissemination of Psychological Procedures. (1995). Training in and dissemination of empirically-validated psychological treatments: Report and recommendations. *The Clinical Psychologist, 48,* 3–23.

Tate, D. F., & Zabinski, M. F. (2004). Computer and Internet applications for psychological treatment: Update for clinicians. *Journal of Clinical Psychology, 60,* 209–220.

Tauscher, J., Bagby, R. M., Javanmard, M., Christensen, B. K., Kasper, S., & Kapur, S. (2001). Inverse relationship between serotonin 5-HT(1A) receptor binding and anxiety: A [(11) C]WAY-100635 PET investigation in healthy volunteers. *American Journal of Psychiatry, 158,* 1326–1328.

Taylor, C. T., & Alden, L. E. (2006). Parental overprotection and interpersonal behavior in generalized social phobia. *Behavior Therapy, 37,* 14–24.

Taylor, C. T., Laposa, J. M., & Alden, L. E. (2004). Is avoidant personality disorder more than just social avoidance? *Journal of Personality Disorders, 18,* 571–594.

Taylor, J. Y., Caldwell, C. H., Baser, R. E., Faison, N., & Jackson, J. S. (2007). Prevalence of eating disorders among Blacks in the national survey of American life. *International Journal of Eating Disorders, 40,* S10–S14.

Taylor, S. (1996). Meta-analysis of cognitive-behavioral treatment for social phobia. *Journal of Behavior Therapy and Experimental Psychiatry, 27,* 1–9.

Taylor, S. (2000). *Understanding and treating panic disorder: Cognitive-behavioural approaches.* New York: Wiley.

Taylor, S., Asmundson, G. J. G., & Coons, M. J. (2005). Current directions in the treatment of hypochondriasis. *Journal of Cognitive Psychotherapy, 19,* 285–304.

Taylor, S., Fedoroff, I. C., Koch, W. J., Thordarson, D. S., Fecteau, G., & Nicki, R. M. (2001). Posttraumatic stress disorder arising after road traffic collisions: Patterns of response to cognitive-behavior therapy. *Journal of Consulting & Clinical Psychology, 69,* 541–551.

Taylor, S., & Rachman, S. J. (1994). Klein's suffocation theory of panic. *Archives of General Psychiatry, 51,* 505–506.

Taylor, S., Thordarson, D. S., Maxfield, L., Fedoroff, I. C., Lovell, K., & Ogrodniczuk, J. (2003). Comparative efficacy, speed, and adverse effects of three PTSD treatments: Exposure therapy, EMDR, and relaxation training. *Journal of Consulting and Clinical Psychology, 71,* 330–338.

Taylor, S., Woody, S., Koch, W. J., McLean, P. D., & Anderson, K. W. (1996). Suffocation false alarms and efficacy of cognitive behavioral therapy for panic disorder. *Behavior Therapy, 27,* 115–126.

Tcheremissine, O. V., Lane, S. D., Cherek, D. R., & Pietras, C. J. (2003). Impulsiveness and other personality dimensions in substance use disorders and conduct disorders. *Addictive Disorders & Their Treatment, 2,* 1–7.

Teasdale, J. D. (1983). Negative thinking in depression: Cause, effect, or reciprocal relationship. *Advances in Behaviour Research & Therapy, 5,* 3–25.

Teasdale, J. D., & Barnard, P. J. (1993). *Affect, cognition, and change: Re-modelling depressive thought.* Hillsdale, NJ: Lawrence Erlbaum.

Teasdale, J. D., Moore, R. G., Hayhurst, H., Pope, M., Williams, S., & Segal, Z. V. (2002). Metacognitive awareness and prevention of relapse in depression: empirical evidence. *Journal of Consulting and Clinical Psychology, 70,* 275–287.

Tebartz van Elst, L., Hesslinger, B., Thiel, T., Geiger, E., Haegele, K., et al. (2003). Frontolimbic brain abnormalities in patients with borderline personality disorder: A volumetric magnetic resonance imaging study. *Biological Psychiatry, 54,* 163–171.

Teicher, M. H., Andersen, S. L., Polcari, A., Anderson, C. M., & Navalta, C. P. (2002). Developmental neurobiology of childhood stress and trauma. *Psychiatric Clinics of North America, 25,* 397–426.

Teicher, M. H., Andersen, S. L., Polcari, A., Anderson, C. M., Navalta, C. P., & Kim, D. M. (2003). The neurobiological consequences of early stress and childhood maltreatment. *Neuroscience & Biobehavioral Reviews, 27,* 33–44.

Tek, C., Kirkpatrick, B., Kelly, C., & McCreadie, R. G. (2001). Summer birth and deficit schizophrenia in Nithsdale, Scotland. *Journal of Nervous and Mental Disease, 189,* 613–617.

Telch, C. F., Agras, W. S., & Linehan, M. M. (2001). Dialectical behavior therapy for binge eating disorder. *Journal of Consulting and Clinical Psychology, 69,* 1061–1065.

Temple, E., Deutsch, G. K., Poldrack, R. A., Miller, S. L., Tallal, P., et al. (2003). Neural deficits in children with dyslexia ameliorated by behavioral remediation: Evidence from functional MRI. *Proceedings of the National Academy of Sciences, USA, 100,* 2860–2865.

Tengström, A., Hodgins, S., & Kullgren, G. (2001). Men with schizophrenia who behave violently: The usefulness of an early- versus late-start offender typology. *Schizophrenia Bulletin, 27,* 205–218.

Tennant, C. (2002). Life events, stress and depression: A review of the findings. *Australian & New Zealand Journal of Psychiatry, 36,* 173–182.

Tennen, H., & Herzberger, S. (1987). Depression, self-esteem, and the absence of self-protective attributional biases. *Journal of Personality and Social Psychology, 52,* 72–80.

ter Kuile, M., van Lankveld, J. J. D. M., de Groot, E., Melles, R., Neffs, J., & Zandbergen, M. (2007). Cognitive-behavioral therapy for women with lifelong vaginismus: Process and prognostic factors. *Behaviour Research and Therapy, 45,* 359–373.

Teves, D., Videen, T. O., Cryer, P. E., & Powers, W. J. (2004) Activation of human medial prefrontal cortex during autonomic responses to hypoglycemia. *Proceedings of the National Academy of Sciences USA, 101,* 6217–6221.

Thase, M. E. (2002). Antidepressant effects: The suit may be small, but the fabric is real. *Prevention & Treatment, 5,* Article 32. www.journals.apa.org/prevention/volume5/pre0050032c.html

Thase, M. E., Greenhouse, J. B., Frank, E., Reynolds, C. F., III, Pilkonis, P. A., et al. (1997). Treatment of major depression with psychotherapy or psychotherapy–pharmacotherapy combinations. *Archives of General Psychiatry, 54,* 1009–1015.

The Hughes legacy: Scramble for the billions. (1976, April 19). *Time Magazine.* Retrieved June 28, 2007, from www.time.com/time/magazine/article/0,9171,914059,00.html

Thom, A., Sartory, G., & Joehren, P. (2000). Comparison between one-session psychological treatment and benzodiazepine in dental phobia. *Journal of Consulting & Clinical Psychology, 68,* 378–387.

Thomas, G. V. (1994). Mixed personality disorder with passive-aggressive and avoidant features. In P. T. Costa, Jr., & T. A. Widiger (Eds.), *Personality disorders and the five-factor model of personality* (pp. 211–215). Washington, DC: American Psychological Association.

Thompson v. County of Alameda, 614 P.2d 728 (Cal. 1980).

Thompson, J. K. (1990). *Body image disturbance: Assessment and treatment.* New York: Pergamon Press.

Thompson, J. K., & Smolak, L. (2001). *Body image, eating disorders, and obesity in youth: Assessment, prevention, and treatment.* Washington, DC: American Psychological Association.

Thompson, J. K., & Stice, E. (2001). Thin-ideal internalization: Mounting evidence for a new risk factor for body-image disturbance and eating pathology. *Current Directions in Psychological Science, 10,* 181–183.

Thompson, J. K., Heinberg, L. J., Altabe, M., & Tantleff-Dunn, S. (1999). *Exacting beauty: Theory, assessment, and treatment of body image disturbance.* Washington, DC: American Psychological Association.

Thompson, J. M., Gallagher, P., Hughes, J. H., Watson, S., Gray, J. M., et al. (2005). Neurocognitive impairment in euthymic patients with bipolar affective disorder. *British Journal of Psychiatry, 186,* 32–40.

Thompson, P. M., Hayashi, K. M., Simon, S. L., Geaga, J. A., Hong, M. S., et al. (2004). Structural abnormalities in the brains of human subjects who use methamphetamine. *Journal of Neuroscience, 24,* 6028–6036.

Thompson, R. F. (1993). *The brain, a neuroscience primer* (2nd ed.). New York: W. H. Freeman.

Thompson, S. B. N. (2003). General anaesthesia and cognitive functioning. *Chinese Journal of Clinical Psychology, 11,* 71–72.

Thompson, W. W., Price, C., Goodson, B., Shay, D. K., Benson, P., et al. (2007). Early thimerosal exposure and neuropsychological outcomes at 7 to 10 years. *New England Journal of Medicine, 357,* 1281–1292.

Thomsen, P. H., Ebbesen, C., & Persson, C. (2001). Long-term experience with citalopram in the treatment of adolescent OCD. *Journal of the American Academy of Child & Adolescent Psychiatry, 40,* 895–902.

Thorberg, F. A., & Lyvers, M. (2006). Negative Mood Regulation (NMR) expectancies, mood, and affect intensity among clients in substance disorder treatment facilities. *Addictive Behaviors, 31,* 811–820.

Thorn, B. L., & Gilbert, L. A. (1998). Antecedents of work and family role expectations of college men. *Journal of Family Psychology, 12,* 259–267.

Tidey, J. W., Rohsenow, D. J., Kaplan, G. B., & Swift, R. M. (2005). Cigarette smoking topography in smokers with schizophrenia and matched non-psychiatric controls. *Drug and Alcohol Dependence, 80,* 259–265.

Tiefer, L. (1987). Social constructionism and the study of human sexuality. In P. Shaver & C. Hendrick (Eds.), *Sex and gender* (pp. 70–94). Thousand Oaks, CA: Sage Publications.

Tiefer, L. (1991). Historical, scientific, clinical and feminist criticisms of "the human sexual response cycle" model. *Annual Review of Sex Research, 2,* 1–23.

Tiefer, L. (2001). Feminist critique of sex therapy: Foregrounding the politics of sex. In P. J. Kleinplatz (Ed.), *New directions in sex therapy: Innovations and alternatives.* Philadelphia: Taylor and Rutledge.

Tienari, P., Wahlberg, K., & Wynne, L. C. (2006). Finnish Adoption Study of Schizophrenia: Implications for family interventions. *Families, Systems, & Health, 24,* 442–451.

Tienari, P., Wynne, L. C., Läksy, K., Moring, J., Nieminen, P., et al. (2003). Genetic boundaries of the schizophrenia spectrum: Evidence from the Finnish adoptive family study of schizophrenia. *American Journal of Psychiatry, 160,* 1587–1594.

Tienari, P., Wynne, L. C., Moring, J., Lahti, I., Naarala, M., et al. (1994). The Finnish adoptive family study of schizophrenia. Implications for family research. *British Journal of Psychiatry, 164,* 20–26.

Tihonen, J., Lönnqvist, J. Wahlbeck, K., Klaukka, T., Tanskanen, A., & Kaukka, J. (2006). Antidepressants and the risk of suicide, attempted suicide, and overall mortality in a nationwide cohort. *Archives of General Psychiatry, 63,* 1358–1367.

Tillfors, M., Furmark, T., Ekselius, L., & Fredrikson, M. (2004). Social phobia and avoidant personality disorder: One spectrum disorder? *Nordic Journal of Psychiatry, 58,* 147–152.

Tillfors, M., Furmark, T., Marteinsdottir, I., Fischer, H., Pissiota, A., et al. (2001). Cerebral blood flow in subjects with social phobia during stressful speaking tasks: A PET study. *American Journal of Psychiatry, 158,* 1220–1226.

Timko, C., DeBenedetti, A., & Billow, R. (2006). Intensive referral to 12-step self-help groups and 6-month substance use disorder outcomes. *Addiction, 101,* 678–688.

Tisher, M., & Dean, S. (2000). Family therapy with the elderly. *Australian and New Zealand Journal of Family Therapy, 21,* 94–101.

Toft, T., Fink, P., Oernboel, E., Christensen, K., Frostholm, L., & Olesen, F. (2005). Mental disorders in primary care: Prevalence and co-morbidity among disorders. Results from the Functional Illness in Primary Care (FIP) study. *Psychological Medicine, 35,* 1175–1184.

Tolin, D. F., & Foa, E. B. (2006). Sex differences in trauma and posttraumatic stress disorder: A quantitative review of 25 years of research. *Psychological Bulletin, 132,* 959–992.

Tolin, D. F., Worhunsky, P., & Maltby, N. (2006). Are "obsessive" beliefs specific to OCD? A comparison across anxiety disorders. *Behaviour Research and Therapy, 44,* 469–480.

Tollison, C. D., & Adams, H. E. (1979). *Sexual disorders: Treatment, theory, and research.* New York: Gardner.

Tomarken, A. J., Mineka, S., & Cook, M. (1989). Fear-relevant selective associations and covariation bias. *Journal of Abnormal Psychology, 98,* 381–394.

Tomkins, D. M., & Sellers, E. M. (2001). Addiction and the brain: The role of neurotransmitters in the cause and treatment of drug dependence. *Canadian Medical Association Journal, 164,* 817–821.

Torgersen, S. (2005). Epidemiology. In J. M. Oldham, A. E. Skodol, & D. S. Bender (Eds.), *The American Psychiatric Publishing textbook of personality disorders* (pp. 129–141). Washington, DC: American Psychiatric Publishing.

Torgersen, S., Kringlen, E., & Cramer, V. (2001). The prevalence of personality disorders in a community sample. *Archives of General Psychiatry, 58,* 590–596.

Torgersen, S., Lygren, S., Oien, P. A., Skre, I., Onstad, S., et al. (2000). A twin study of personality disorders. *Comprehensive Psychiatry, 41,* 416–425.

Torgersen, S. G. (1983). Genetic factors in anxiety disorders. *Archives of General Psychiatry, 40,* 1085–1089.

Torrens, M., & Martín-Santos, R. (2000). Why do people abuse alcohol and drugs? *Current Opinion in Psychiatry, 13,* 285–289.

Torrens, M., Fonseca, F., Mateu, G., & Farré, M. (2005). Efficacy of antidepressants in substance use disorders with and without comorbid depression: A systematic review and meta-analysis. *Drug and Alcohol Dependence, 78,* 1–22.

Torrey, E. F. (2001). *Surviving schizophrenia: A manual for families, consumers, and providers* (4th ed.). New York: Quill.

Torrey, E. F. (2002). Studies of individuals with schizophrenia never treated with antipsychotic medications: A review. *Schizophrenia Research, 58,* 101–115.

Tost, H., Vollmert, C., Brassen, S., Schmitt, A., Dressing, H., & Braus, D. F. (2004). Pedophilia: Neuropsychological evidence encouraging a brain network perspective. *Medical Hypotheses, 63,* 528–531.

Towbin, K. E., Mauk, J. E., & Batshaw, M. L. (2002). Pervasive developmental disorders. In M. L. Batshaw (Ed.), *Children with disabilities* (5th ed., pp. 365–387). Baltimore: Brookes Publishing.

Tozzi, F., Thornton, L. M., Klump, K. L., Fichter, M. M., Halmi, K. A., et al. (2005). Symptom fluctuation in eating disorders: Correlates of diagnostic crossover. *American Journal of Psychiatry, 162,* 732–740.

Tractenberg, R. E., Weiner, M. F., Patterson, M. B., Teri, L., & Thal, L. J. (2003). Comorbidity of psychopathological domains in community-dwelling persons with Alzheimer's disease. *Journal of Geriatric Psychiatry and Neurology, 16,* 94–99.

Trestman, R. L., Keefe, R. S. E., Mitropoulou, V., Harvey, P. D., deVegvar, M. L., et al. (1995). Cognitive function and biological correlates of cognitive performance in schizotypal personality disorder. *Psychiatry Research, 59,* 127–136.

Trierweiler, S. J., Muroff, J. R., Jackson, J. S., Neighbors, H. W., & Munday, C. (2005). Clinician race, situational attributions, and diagnoses of mood versus schizophrenia disorders. *Cultural Diversity & Ethnic Minority Psychology, 11,* 351–364.

Trimble, J. E. (1994). Cultural variations in the use of alcohol and drugs. In W. J. Lonner & R. S. Malpass (Eds.), *Psychology and culture* (pp. 79–84). Boston: Allyn & Bacon.

True, W. R., Rice, J., Eisen, S. A., Heath, A. C., Goldberg, J., et al. (1993). A twin study of genetic and environmental contributions to liability for posttraumatic stress symptoms. *Archives of General Psychiatry, 50,* 257–264.

Trull, T. J., & Durrett, C. A. (2005). Categorical and dimensional models of personality disorder. *Annual Review of Clinical Psychology, 1,* 355–380.

Trull, T. J., Vergés, A., Wood, P. K., Jahng, S., & Sher, K. J. (2012). The structure of Diagnostic and Statistical Manual of Mental Disorders (4th edition, text revision) personality disorder symptoms in a large national sample. *Personality Disorders: Theory, Research, and Treatment, 3*(4), 355–369.

Tsai, S., Hong, C., Yu, Y. W.-Y., Chen, T., Wang, Y., & Lin, W. (2004). Association study of serotonin 1B receptor (A-161T) genetic polymorphism and suicidal behaviors and response to fluoxetine in major depressive disorder. *Neuropsychobiology, 50,* 235–238.

Tsoi, W. F., & Wong, K. E. (1991). A 15 year follow up study of Chinese schizophrenic patients. *Acta Psychiatrica Scandinavica. 84,* 217–220.

Tsuang, M. T., Bar, J. L., Harley, R. M., & Lyons, M. J. (2001). The Harvard Twin Study of Substance Abuse: What we have learned. *Harvard Review of Psychiatry, 9,* 267–279.

Tsuang, M. T., Stone, W. S., & Faraone, S. V. (2000). Toward reformulating the diagnosis of schizophrenia. *American Journal of Psychiatry, 157,* 1041–1050.

Tsuang, M. T., Van Os, J., Tandon, R., Barch, D. M., Bustillo, J., et al. (in press). Attenuated psychosis syndrome in dsm-5. *Schizophrenia Research.* Advanced online publication.

Tsuchiya, K. J., Agerbo, E., & Mortensen, P. B. (2005). Parental death and bipolar disorder: A robust association was found in early maternal suicide. *Journal of Affective Disorders, 86,* 151–159.

Tsuchiya, K. J., Takagai, S., Kawai, M., Matsumoto, H., Nakamura, K., et al. (2005). Advanced paternal age associated with an elevated risk for schizophrenia in offspring in a Japanese population. *Schizophrenia Research, 76,* 337–342.

Tucker, D., & Brakel, S. J. (2012). DSM-5 paraphilic diagnoses and SVP law. *Archives of Sexual Behavior, 41*(3), 533.

Turetsky, B. I., Moberg, P. J., Mozley, L. H., Moelter, S. T., Agrin, R. N., et al. (2002). Memory-delineated subtypes of schizophrenia: Relationship to clinical, neuroanatomical, and neurophysiological measures. *Neuropsychology, 16,* 481–490.

Turkington, D., Kingdon, D., & Weiden, P. J. (2006). Cognitive behavior therapy for schizophrenia. *American Journal of Psychiatry, 163,* 365–373.

Turnbull, J. D., Heaslip, S., & McLeod, H. A. (2000). Pre-school children's attitudes to fat and normal male and female stimulus figures. *International Journal of Obesity, 24,* 1705–1706.

Turner, H., & Bryant-Waugh, R. (2004). Eating disorder not otherwise specified (eating disorder NOS): Profiles of clients presenting at a community eating disorder service. *European Eating Disorders Review, 12,* 18–26.

Turner, R. M. (1994). Borderline, narcissistic, and histrionic personality disorders. In M. Hersen & R. T. Ammerman (Eds.), *Handbook of prescriptive treatments for adults* (pp. 393–420). New York: Plenum Press.

Turner, S. M., & Beidel, D. C. (1988). *Treating obsessive-compulsive disorder.* Elmsford, NY: Pergamon Press.

Turner, T. (1989). Rich and mad in Victorian England. *Psychological Medicine, 19,* 29–44.

Tuthill, R. W. (1996). Hair lead levels related to children's classroom attention-deficit behavior. *Archives of Environmental Health, 51,* 214–220.

Twenge, J. M. (2000). The age of anxiety? Birth cohort change in anxiety and neuroticism, 1952–1993. *Journal of Personality and Social Psychology, 79,* 1007–1021.

Tye, C., Mercure, E., Ashwood, K. L., Azadi, B., Asherson, P., et al. (2013). Neurophysiological responses to faces and gaze direction differentiate children with ASD, ADHD and ASD + ADHD. *Developmental Cognitive Neuroscience, 5,* 71–85.

Tyrer, P. (2002). Nidotherapy: A new approach to the treatment of personality disorder. *Acta Psychiatrica Scandinavica, 105,* 469–472.

Tyrer, P., & Johnson, T. (1996). Establishing the severity of personality disorder. *American Journal of Psychiatry, 153,* 1593–1597.

Tyrer, P., Gunderson, J., Lyons, M., & Tohen, M. (1997). Extent of comorbidity between mental state and personality disorders. *Journal of Personality Disorders, 11,* 242–259.

Tyson, A. S. (2008, September 5). Soldiers' suicide rate on pace to set record. *The Washington Post,* p. A02.

U.S. Census Bureau. (2000). *Changing shape of the nation's income distribution, 1947–1998.* Retrieved April 4, 2001, from http://www.census.gov/prod/2000pubs/p60-204.pdf

U.S. Census Bureau. (2001) *Census 2000 redistricting [Public Law 94–171] summary file.* Washington, DC: Author.

U.S. Department of Health and Human Services. (1999). *Mental health: A report of the Surgeon General.* Rockville: MD: Author. Retrieved January 15, 2007, from http://mentalhealth.samhsa.gov/cre/ch2.asp

U.S. Department of Health and Human Services. (2001). *Mental health: Culture, race, and ethnicity. A supplement to mental health: A report of the Surgeon General.* Rockville, MD: U.S. Department of Health and Human Services, Substance Abuse and Mental Health Services Administration, Center for Mental Health Services. Retrieved October 12, 2008, from www.surgeongeneral.gov/library/mentalhealth/cre/sma-01-3613.pdf

U.S. Department of Health and Human Services, Office of the Secretary. (2002). Standards for privacy of individually identifiable health information. *Federal Register, 67:* 53182–53273.

U.S. National Library of Medicine. (2005). The balance of passions. In *History of medicine and disease: Emotions and disease.* Retrieved February 19, 2007, from http://www.nlm.nih.gov/hmd/emotions/balance.html

United Nations International Drug Control Programme. (1997). *World drug report.* Oxford: Oxford University Press.

United States v. Comstock, No. 08-1224 (2010).

United States Public Health Service. (2001). *Mental health: Culture, race, and ethnicity. A supplement to mental health: A report of the Surgeon General.* Retrieved January 12, 2007, from www.surgeongeneral.gov/library/mentalhealth/cre/

Unwin, G. L., & Deb, S. (2011). Efficacy of atypical antipsychotic medication in the management of behaviour problems in children with intellectual disabilities and borderline intelligence: A systematic review. *Research in Developmental Disabilities, 32*(6), 2121–2133.

Urbszat, D., Herman, C. P., & Polivy, J. (2002). Eat, drink, and be merry, for tomorrow we diet: Effects of anticipated deprivation on food intake in restrained and unrestrained eaters. *Journal of Abnormal Psychology, 111,* 396–401.

Vaginismus.com. (2007). Burning and tightness from no apparent cause: Lynn. Retrieved October 1, 2007, from www.vaginismus.com/vaginismus-stories

Vaiva, G., Ducrocq, F., Jezequel, K., Averland, B., Lestavel, P., et al. (2003). Immediate treatment with propranolol decreases posttraumatic stress disorder two months after trauma. *Biological Psychiatry, 54,* 947–949.

Vajk, F. C., Craighead, W. E., Craighead, L. W., & Holley, C. (1997, November). Risk of major depression as a function of response styles to depressed mood. Poster presented at the annual meeting of the Association for the Advancement of Behavior Therapy, Miami Beach, FL.

Valera, E. M., Faraone, S. V., Murray, K. E., & Seidman, L. J. (2007). Meta-analysis of structural imaging findings in attention-deficit/hyperactivity disorder. *Biological Psychiatry, 61*(12), 1361–1369.

Van Allen, J., & Roberts, M. C. (2011). Critical incidents in the marriage of psychology and technology: A discussion of potential ethical issues in practice, education, and policy. *Professional Psychology: Research and Practice, 42*(6), 433–439.

van Balkom, A. J. L. M., Bakker, A., Spinhoven, P., Blaauw, B. M. J. W., et al. (1997). A meta-analysis of the treatment of panic disorder with or without agoraphobia: A comparison of psychopharmacological, cognitive-behavioral, and combination treatments. *Journal of Nervous and Mental Disease, 185,* 510–516.

van den Bosch, L. M. C., Koeter, M. W. J., Stijnen, T., Verheul, R., & van den Brink, W. (2005). Sustained efficacy of dialectical behaviour therapy for borderline personality disorder. *Behaviour Research and Therapy, 43,* 1231–1241.

van den Bosch, L. M. C., Koeter, M. W. J., Stijnen, T., Verheul, R., & van den Brink, W. (2005). Sustained efficacy of dialectical behaviour therapy for borderline personality disorder. *Behaviour Research and Therapy, 43,* 1231–1241.

van den Heuvel, O. A., van de Wetering, B. J., Veltman, D. J., & Pauls, D. L. (2000). Genetic studies of panic disorder: A review. *Journal of Clinical Psychiatry, 61,* 756–766.

van den Heuvel, O. A., Veltman, D. J., Groenewegen, H. J., Witter, M. P., Merkelbach, J., et al. (2005). Disorder-specific neuroanatomical correlates of attentional bias in obsessive-compulsive disorder, panic disorder, and hypochondriasis. *Archives of General Psychiatry, 62*, 922–933.

van der Kloet, D., Giesbrecht, T., Lynn, S. J., Merckelbach, H., & de Zutter, A. (2012). Sleep normalization and decrease in dissociative experiences: Evaluation in an inpatient sample. *Journal of Abnormal Psychology, 121*(1), 140–150.

van der Kloet, D., Merckelbach, H., Giesbrecht, T., & Lynn, S. J. (2012). Fragmented sleep, fragmented mind: The role of sleep in dissociative disorders. *Perspectives on Psychological Science, 7*, 159–175.

Van der Linden, G. J. H., Stein, D. J., & van Balkom, A. J. L. M. (2000). The efficacy of the selective serotonin reuptake inhibitors for social anxiety disorder (social phobia): A meta-analysis of randomized controlled trials. *International Clinical Psychopharmacology, 15*(Suppl. 2), S15–S23.

Van der Linden, G., Van Heerden, B., Warwick, J., Wessels, C., Van Kradenburg, J., et al. (2000). Functional brain imaging and pharmacotherapy in social phobia: Single photon emission computer tomography before and after treatment with the selective serotonin reuptake inhibitor citalopram. *Progress in Neuro-Psychopharmacology & Biological Psychiatry, 24*, 419–438.

van Duijl, M., Cardeña, E., & de Jong, J. (2005). The validity of DSM-IV-TR dissociative disorders categories in southwest Uganda. *Transcultural Psychiatry, 42*, 219–241.

van Elst, L. T., Valerius, G., Büchert, M., Thiel, T., Rüsch, N., et al. (2005). Increased prefrontal and hippocampal glutamate concentration in schizophrenia: Evidence from a magnetic resonance spectroscopy study. *Biological Psychiatry, 58*, 724–730.

van Erp, T. G. M., Saleh, P. A., Rosso, I. M., Huttunen, M., Lönnqvist, J., et al. (2002). Contributions of genetic risk and fetal hypoxia to hippocampal volume in patients with schizophrenia or schizoaffective disorder, their unaffected siblings, and healthy unrelated volunteers. *American Journal of Psychiatry, 159*, 1514–1520.

Van Gerwen, L. J., Spinhoven, P., & Van Dyck, R. (2006). Behavioral and cognitive group treatment for fear of flying: A randomized controlled trial. *Journal of Behavior Therapy and Experimental Psychiatry, 37*, 358–371.

van Heeringen, K. (2003). The neurobiology of suicide and suicidality. *Canadian Journal of Psychiatry, 48*, 292–300.

van Os, J., & Delespaul, P. (2003). Psychosis research at Maastricht University, The Netherlands. *British Journal of Psychiatry, 183*, 559–560.

Van Thiel, D. H., Tarter, R. E., Rosenblum, E., & Gavaler, J. S. (1988). Ethanol, its metabolism and gonadal effects: Does sex make a difference? *Advances in Alcohol and Substance Abuse 7*, 131–169.

Van Velzen, C. J. M., Emmelkamp, P. M. G., & Scholing, A. (1997). The impact of personality disorders on behavioral treatment outcome for social phobia. *Behaviour Research and Therapy, 35*, 889–900.

van Zuiden, M., Geuze, E., Willemen, H. L. D. M., Vermetten, E., Maas, M., et al. (2011). Pre-existing high glucocorticoid receptor number predicting development of posttraumatic stress symptoms after military deployment. *American Journal of Psychiatry, 168*, 89–96.

Vance, A., Silk, T. J., Casey, M., Rinehart, N. J., Bradshaw, J. L., et al. (2007). Right parietal dysfunction in children with attention deficit hyperactivity disorder, combined type: A functional MRI study. *Molecular Psychiatry, 12*, 826–832.

Vansteenwegen, D., Vervliet, B., Hermans, D., Thewissen, R., & Eelen, P. (2007). Verbal, behavioural and physiological assessment of the generalization of exposure-based fear reduction in a spider-anxious population. *Behaviour Research and Therapy, 45*, 291–300.

Vaughn, C., & Leff, J. (1976). Measurement of expressed emotion in the families of psychiatric patients. *British Journal of Social and Clinical Psychology, 15*, 1069–1177.

Vaughan, K., Armstrong, M.F., Gold, R., O'Connor, N., Jenneke, W., & Tarrier, N. (1994). A trial of eye movement desensitization compared to image habituation training and applied muscle relaxation in post-traumatic stress disorder. *Journal of Behavior Therapy & Experimental Psychiatry, 25*, 283–291.

Veale, D., De Haro, L., & Lambrou, C. (2003). Cosmetic rhinoplasty in body dysmorphic disorder. *British Journal of Plastic Surgery, 56*, 546–551.

Veale, D., Ennis, M., & Lambrou, C. (2002). Possible association of body dysmorphic disorder with an occupation or education in art and design. *American Journal of Psychiatry, 159*, 1788–90.

Vehmanen, L., Kaprio, J., & Loennqvist, J. (1995). Twin studies on concordance for bipolar disorder. *Psychiatria Fennica, 26*, 107–116.

Velakoulis, D., Pantelis, C., McGorry, P. D., Dudgeon, P., Brewer, W., et al. (1999). Hippocampal volume in first-episode psychoses and chronic schizophrenia: A high resolution magnetic resonance imaging study. *Archives of General Psychiatry, 56*, 133–141.

Veling, W., Susser, E, van Os, J., Machenbach, J. P., Selten, J.-P., & Hoek, H. W. (2012). Ethnic density of neighborhoods and incidence of psychotic disorders among immigrants. *American Journal of Psychiatry, 165*, 66–73.

Ventura, J., Nuechterlein, K. H., Lukoff, D., & Hardesty, J. P. (1989). A prospective study of stressful life events and schizophrenic relapse. *Journal of Abnormal Psychology, 98*, 407–411.

Verdoux, H., Sorbara, F., Gindre, C., Swendsen, J. D., & van Os, J. (2003). Cannabis use and dimensions of psychosis in a nonclinical population of female subjects. *Schizophrenia Research, 59*, 77–84.

Verduin, T. L., & Kendall, P. C. (2003). Differential occurrence of comorbidity within childhood anxiety disorders. *Journal of Clinical Child and Adolescent Psychology, 32*, 290–295.

Verheul, R., & Widiger, T. A. (2004). A meta-analysis of the prevalence and usage of the personality disorder not otherwise specified (PDNOS) diagnosis. *Journal of Personality Disorders, 18*, 309–319.

Verheul, R., Bartak, A., & Widiger, T. A. (2007). Prevalence and construct validity of personality disorder not otherwise specified (PDNOS). *Journal of Personality Disorders, 21*, 359–370.

Verheul, R., van den Brink, W., & Geerlings, P. (1999). A three-pathway psychobiological model of craving for alcohol. *Alcohol Alcoholism, 34*, 197–222.

Verkes, R. J., Gijsman, H. J., Pieters, M. S. M., Schoemaker, R. C., de Visser, S., et al. (2001). Cognitive performance and serotonergic function in users of Ecstasy. *Psychopharmacology, 153*, 196–202.

Victor, M., Adams, R. D., & Collins, G. H. (1989). *The Wernicke-Korsakoff syndrome and related neurological disorders due to alcoholism and malnutrition* (2nd ed.). Philadelphia: F. A. Davis.

Vidal, C. N., Rapoport, J. L., Hayashi, K. M., Geaga, J. A., Sui, Y., et al. (2006). Dynamically spreading frontal and cingulate deficits mapped in adolescents with schizophrenia. *Archives of General Psychiatry, 63*, 25–34.

Viding, E., Blair, R. J. R., Moffitt, T. E., & Plomin, R. (2005). Evidence for substantial genetic risk for psychopathy in 7-year-olds. *Journal of Child Psychology and Psychiatry, 46*, 592–597.

Vidyasagar, T. R. (2005). Attentional gating in primary visual cortex: A physiological basis for dyslexia. *Perception, 34*, 903–911.

Vieweg, R., & Shawcross, C. R. (1998). A trial to determine any difference between two and three times a week ECT in the rate of recovery from depression. *Journal of Mental Health (UK), 7*, 403–409.

Vijayakumar, L., John, S., Pirkis, J., & Whiteford, H. (2005). Suicide in developing countries. 2. Risk factors. *Crisis, 26*, 112–119.

Villaseñor, Y., & Waitzkin, H. (1999). Limitations of a structured psychiatric diagnostic instrument in assessing somatization among Latino patients in primary care. *Medical Care, 37*, 637–646.

Vinckenbosch, E., Robichon, F., & Eliez, S. (2005). Gray matter alteration in dyslexia: Converging evidence from volumetric and voxel-by-voxel MRI analyses. *Neuropsychologia, 43,* 324–331.

Viney, W. (2000). Dix, Dorothea Lynde. In A. E. Kazdin (Ed.), *Encyclopedia of psychology* (Vol. 3, pp. 65–66). Washington, DC: American Psychological Association.

Visser, S. N., Bitsko, R. H., Danielson, M. L., Perou, R., & Blumberg, S. J. (2010). Increasing Prevalence of parent-reported attention-deficit/hyperactivity disorder among children—United States, 2003 and 2007. *Morbidity and Mortality Weekly Report (MMWR), 59,* 1439–1443.

Vita, A., De Peri, L., Silenzi, C., & Dieci, M. (2006). Brain morphology in first-episode schizophrenia: A meta-analysis of quantitative magnetic resonance imaging studies. *Schizophrenia Research, 82,* 75–88.

Vogel, M., Busse, S., Freyberger, H. J., & Grabe, H. J. (2006). Dopamine D3 receptor and schizophrenia: A widened scope for the immune hypothesis. *Medical Hypotheses, 67,* 354–358.

Voglmaier, M. M., Seidman, L. J., Niznikiewicz, M. A., Dickey, C. C., Shenton, M. E., & McCarley, R. W. (2000). Verbal and nonverbal neuropsychological test performance in subjects with schizotypal personality disorder. *American Journal of Psychiatry, 157,* 787–793.

Vohs, K. D., & Heatherton, T. F. (2000). Self-regulatory failure: A resource-depletion approach. *Psychological Science, 11,* 249–254.

Voineskos, A. M., Foussias, G., Lerch, J., Felsky, D., Remington, G., et al. (2013). Neuroimaging evidence for the deficit subtype of schizophrenia. *JAMA Psychiatry, 70,* 472–480.

Volkow, N. D., Chang, L., Wang, G.-J., Fowler, J. S., Ding, Y.-S., et al. (2001). Low level of brain dopamine D2 receptors in methamphetamine abusers: Association with metabolism in the orbitofrontal cortex. *American Journal of Psychiatry, 158,* 2015–2021.

Volkow, N. D., Chang, L., Wang, G., Fowler, J. S., Franceschi, D., Sedler, M. J., et al. (2001a). Higher cortical and lower subcortical metabolism in detoxified methamphetamine abusers. *American Journal of Psychiatry, 158,* 383–389.

Volkow, N. D., Chang, L., Wang, G. J., Fowler, J. S., Franceschi, D., Sedler, M., et al. (2001b). Loss of dopamine transporters in methamphetamine abusers recovers with protracted abstinence. *Journal of Neuroscience, 21,* 9414–9418.

Volkow, N. D., Tancredi, L. R., Grant, C., & Gillespie, H. (1995). Brain glucose metabolism in violent psychiatric patients: A preliminary study. *Psychiatry Research: Neuroimaging, 61,* 243–253.

Volkow, N. D., Wang, G., Fowler, J. S., & Ding, Y. (2005). Imaging the effects of methylphenidate on brain dopamine: New model on its therapeutic actions for attention-deficit/hyperactivity disorder. *Biological Psychiatry, 57,* 1410–1415.

Volkow, N. D., Wang, G.-J., Fowler, J. S., Logan, J., Gatley, S. J., et al. (1999). Prediction of reinforcing responses to psychostimulants in humans by brain dopamine D2 receptor levels. *American Journal of Psychiatry, 156,* 1440–1443.

Volkow, N. D., Wang, G., Newcorn, J., Telang, F., Solanto, M. V., et al. (2007). Depressed dopamine activity in caudate and preliminary evidence of limbic involvement in adults with attention-deficit/hyperactivity disorder. *Archives of General Psychiatry, 64,* 932–940.

Völlum, B., Richardson, P., Stirling, J., Elliott, R., Dolan, M., et al. (2004). Neurobiological substrates of antisocial and borderline personality disorder: Preliminary results of a functional fMRI study. *Criminal Behaviour and Mental Health, 14,* 39–54.

Von Holle, A., Pinheiro, A. P., Thornton, L. M., Klump, K. L., Berrettini, W. H., et al. (2008). Temporal patterns of recovery across eating disorder subtypes. *Australian and New Zealand Journal of Psychiatry, 42,* 108–117.

von Zerssen, D., Leon, C. A., Moller, H., Wittchen, H., Pfister, H., & Sartorius, N. (1990). Care strategies for schizophrenic patients in a transcultural comparison. *Comprehensive Psychiatry, 31,* 398–408.

Voth, H. M., & Orth, M. H. (1973). *Psychotherapy and the role of the environment.* New York: Behavioral Press.

Vuchinich, R. E. & Tucker, J. A. (1996). Alcoholic relapse, life events, and behavioral theories of choice: A prospective analysis. *Experimental and Clinical Psychopharmacology, 4,* 19–28.

Vuilleumier, P., Chicherio, C., Assal, F., Schwartz, S., Slosman, D., & Landis, T. (2001). Functional neuroanatomical correlates of hysterical sensorimotor loss. *Brain, 124,* 1077–1090.

Waas, G. A., & Kleckler, D. M. (2000). Play therapy. In A. E. Kazdin (Ed.), *Encyclopedia of psychology* (Vol. 6, pp. 218–223). Washington, DC: American Psychological Association.

Waber, R. L., Shiv, B., Carmon, Z., & Ariely, D. (2008). Research letter: Commericial features of placebo and therapeutic efficacy. *Journal of the American Medical Association, 299*(9), 1016–1017.

Wada, T., Kawakatsu, S., Komatani, A., Okuyama, N., & Otani, K. (1999). Possible association between delusional disorder, somatic type and reduced regional cerebral blood flow. *Progress in Neuro-Psychopharmacology & Biological Psychiatry, 23,* 353–357.

Wade, D., Harrigan, S., Harris, M. G., Edwards, J., & McGorry, P. D. (2006). Treatment for the initial acute phase of first-episode psychosis in a real-world setting. *Psychiatric Bulletin, 30,* 127–131.

Wade, T. D. (2007). Epidemiology of eating disorders: Creating opportunities to move the current classification paradigm forward. *International Journal of Eating Disorders, 40,* S27–S30.

Wade, T. D., Bergin, J. L., Tiggemann, M., Bulik, C. M., & Fairburn, C. G. (2006). Prevalence and long-term course of lifetime eating disorders in an adult Australian twin cohort. *Australian and New Zealand Journal of Psychiatry, 40,* 121–128.

Wadsworth, S. J., Olson, R. K., Pennington, B. F., & DeFries, J. C. (2000). Differential genetic etiology of reading disability as a function of IQ. *Journal of Learning Disabilities, 33,* 192–199.

Wager, T. D., Rilling, J. K., Smith, E. E., Sokolik, A., Casey, K. L., et al. (2004). Placebo-induced changes in fMRI in the anticipation and experience of pain, *Science, 303,* 1162–1167.

Wagner, P. S. (1996). First person account: A voice from another closet. *Schizophrenia Bulletin, 22,* 399–401.

Wagner, P. S., & Spiro, C. S. (2005). *Divided minds: Twin sisters and their journey through schizophrenia.* New York: St. Martin's Press.

Wahl, O. F. (1999). Mental health consumers' experience of stigma. *Schizophrenia Bulletin, 25,* 467–478.

Wahlbeck, K., Forsén, T., Osmond, C., Barker, D. J. P., & Eriksson, J. G. (2001). Association of schizophrenia with low maternal body mass index, small size at birth and thinness during childhood. *Archives of General Psychiatry, 58,* 48–52.

Waismann, R., Fenwick, P. B., Wilson, G. D., Hewett, T. D., & Lumsden, J. (2003). EEG responses to visual erotic stimuli in men with normal and paraphilic interests. *Archives of Sexual Behavior, 32,* 135–144.

Wakefield, J. C. (2010). Misdiagnosing normality: Psychiatry's failure to address the problem of false positive diagnoses of mental disorder in a changing professional environment. *Journal of Mental Health, 19,* 337–351.

Wakefield, J. C., & First, M. B. (2012). Validity of the bereavement exclusion to major depression: Does the empirical evidence support the proposal to eliminate the exclusion of DSM-5? *World Psychiatry, 11,* 3–10.

Walach, H., & Maidhof, C. (1999). Is the placebo effect dependent on time? A meta-analysis. In I. Kirsch (Ed.), *How Expectancies Shape Experience* (pp. 321–332). Washington, DC: American Psychological Association.

Walcott, D. D., Pratt, H. D., & Patel, D. R. (2003). Adolescents and eating disorders: Gender, racial, ethnic, sociocultural and socioeconomic issues. *Journal of Adolescent Research, 18,* 223–243.

Waldeck, T. L., & Miller, L. S. (2000). Social skills deficits in schizotypal personality disorder. *Psychiatry Research, 93,* 237–246.

Waldman, I. D., & Gizer, I. R. (2006). The genetics of attention deficit hyperactivity disorder. *Clinical Psychology Review, 26,* 396–432.

Waldman, M., Nicholson, S., Adilov, N., & Williams, J. (2008). Autism prevalence and precipitation rates in California, Oregon, and Washington counties. *Archives of Pediatric Adolescent Medicine, 162,* 1026–1034.

Waldron, V. R., Lavitt, M., & Kelley, D. (2000). The nature and prevention of harm in technology-mediated self-help settings: Three exemplars. *Journal of Technology in Human Services, 17*, 267–293.

Walker, E. F., & Diforio, D. (1997). Schizophrenia: A neural diathesis-stress model. *Psychological Review, 104*, 667–685.

Walker, E. F., Grimes, K. E., Davis, D., & Smith, A. (1993). Childhood precursors of schizophrenia: Facial expressions of emotion. *American Journal of Psychiatry, 150*, 1654–1660.

Walker, E. F., Logan, C. B., & Walder, D. (1999). Indicators of neurdevelopmental abnormality in schizotypal personality disorder. *Psychiatric Annals, 29*, 132–136.

Walker, E. F., Savoie, T., & Davis, D. (1994). Neuromotor precursors of schizophrenia. *Schizophrenia Bulletin, 148*, 661–666.

Walker, E. F., Walder, D. J., & Reynolds, F. (2001). Developmental changes in cortisol secretion in normal and at-risk youth. *Development & Psychopathology, 13*, 721–732.

Walker, E., Kestler, L., Bollini, A., & Hochman, K. M. (2004). Schizophrenia: Etiology and course. *Annual Review of Psychology, 55*, 401–430.

Walker, Z., & Stevens, T. (2002). Dementia with Lewy bodies: Clinical characteristics and diagnostic criteria. *Journal of Geriatric Psychiatry and Neurology, 15*, 188–194.

Wallace, C., Mullen, P. E., & Burgess, P. (2004). Criminal offending in schizophrenia over a 25-year period marked by deinstitutionalization and increasing prevalence of comorbid substance use disorders. *American Journal of Psychiatry, 161*, 716–727.

Waller, N. G., & Shaver, P. R. (1994). The importance of nongenetic influences on romantic love styles: A twin-family study. *Psychological Science, 5*, 268–274.

Wallien, M. S. C., Zucker, K. J., Steensma, T. D., & Cohen-Kettenis, P. T. (2008). 2D:4D finger-length ratios in children and adults with gender identity order. *Hormones and Behavior, 54*, 450–454.

Walling, M.K., Reiter, R.C., O'Hara, M.W., Milburn, A.K., Lilly, G. & Vincent, S.D. (1994). Abuse history and chronic pain in women: I. Prevalences of sexual abuse and physical abuse. *Obstetrics and Gynecology, 84*, 193–199.

Walls, J. (2005). *The glass castle.* New York: Scribner's.

Walsh, A. E., Oldman, A. D., Franklin, M., Fairburn, C. G., & Cowen, P. J. (1995). Dieting decreases plasma tryptophan and increases the prolactin response to d-fenfluramine in women but not men. *Journal of Affective Disorders, 21*, 89–97.

Walsh, B. T. (1993). Binge eating in bulimia nervosa. In C. G. Fairburn & G. T. Wilson (Eds.), *Binge eating: Nature, assessment, and treatment* (pp. 37–49). New York: Guilford Press.

Walsh, B. T., & Kahn, C. B. (1997). Diagnostic criteria for eating disorders: Current concerns and future directions. *Psychopharmacology Bulletin, 33*, 369–372.

Walsh, B. T., Kaplan, A. S., Attia, E., Olmsted, M., Parides, M., et al. (2006). Fluoxetine after weight restoration in anorexia nervosa: A randomized controlled trial. *Journal of the American Medical Association, 295*, 2605–2612.

Walsh, B. T., Seidman, S. N., Sysko, R., & Gould, M. (2002). Placebo response in studies of major depression: Variable, substantial, and growing. *JAMA: Journal of the American Medical Association, 287*, 1840–1847.

Walsh, B. T., Wilson, G. T., Loeb, K. L., Devlin, M. J., Pike, K. M., et al. (1997). Medication and psychotherapy in the treatment of bulimia nervosa. *American Journal of Psychiatry, 154*, 523–531.

Walsh, E., Buchanan, A., & Fahy, T. (2002). Violence and schizophrenia: Examining the evidence. *British Journal of Psychiatry, 180*, 490–495.

Wampold, B. E. (2001a). *The Great Psychotherapy Debate: Models, Methods, and Findings.* Mahwah, NJ, US: Lawrence Erlbaum Associates, Publishers.

Wampold, B. E. (2001b). Practical interpretations of outcome research in psychotherapy through the examination of effect sizes. *Clinician's Research Digest, Supp. 24*, n.p.

Wampold, B. E. (2010). The research evidence for common factors models: A historically situated perspective. In B. L. Duncan, S. D. Miller, B. E. Wampold, & M. A. Hubble (Eds.), *The heart and soul of change: Delivering what works in therapy* (2nd ed., pp. 49–81). Washington D.C.: American Psychiatric Association.

Wampold, B. E., & Bhati, K. S. (2004). Attending to the omissions: A historical examination of evidence-based practice movements. *Professional Psychology: Research & Practice, 35*, 563–570.

Wang, G.-J., Volkow, N. D., Chang, L., Miller, E., Sedler, M., et al. (2004). Partial recovery of brain metabolism in methamphetamine abusers after protracted abstinence. *American Journal of Psychiatry, 161*, 242–248.

Wang, P. S., Lane, M., Olfson, M., Pincus, H. A., Wells, K. B., & Kessler, R. C. (2005). Twelve-month use of mental health services in the United States: Results from the National Comorbidity Survey Replication. *Archives of General Psychiatry, 62*, 629–640.

Wansink, B., & Ittersum, K. (2005). Shape of glass and amount of alcohol poured: Comparative study of effect of practice and concentration. *British Medical Journal, 331*, 1512–1514.

Ward, O. B. (1992). Fetal drug exposure and sexual differentiation of males. In A. A. Gerall, H. Moltz, & I. L. Ward (Eds.), *Sexual differentiation* (pp. 181–219). New York: Plenum Press.

Warner, R. (2002). Response to McGorry and Edwards. *Schizophrenia Bulletin, 28*, 181–185.

Waslick, B. D., Kandel, R., & Kakouros, A. (2002). Depression in children and adolescents: An overview. In D. Shaffer & B. Waslick (Eds.), *The many faces of depression in children and adolescents* (pp. 1–36). Arlington, VA: American Psychiatric Publishing.

Wasserman, D., & Varnick A. (1998). Reliability of statistics on violent death and suicide in the Former USSR, 1970–1990. *Acta Psychiatrica Scandinavica Supplement, 394*, 34–41.

Wassermann, E. M., Epstein, C. M., Ziemann, U., Walsh, V., Paus, T., & Lisanby, S. H. (2008). *Oxford handbook of transcranial stimulation.* New York, NY: Oxford University Press.

Watanabe, Y., Someya, T., & Nawa, H. (2010). Cytokine hypothesis of schizophrenia pathogenesis: Evidence from human studies and animal models. *Psychiatry and Clinical Neurosciences, 64*(3), 217–230.

Waters, M. (2000). Psychologists spotlight growing concern of higher suicide rates among adolescents. *Monitor on Psychology, 31*, n.p.

Watkins, P. C. (2002). Implicit memory bias in depression. *Cognition and Emotion, 16*, 381–402.

Watson, J. B. (1931). *Behaviorism* (2nd ed.). Oxford, England: Kegan Paul.

Watson, J. B., & Rayner, R. (1920). Conditioned emotional reactions. *Journal of Experimental Psychology, 3*, 1–14.

Watson, J. C., Goldman, R. N., & Greenberg, L. S. (2007). *Case studies in emotion-focused treatment of depression: A comparison of good and poor outcomes.* Washington, DC: American Psychological Association.

Wattar, U., Sorensen, P., Buemann, I., Birket-Smith, M., Salkovskis, P. M., et al. (2005). Outcome of cognitive-behavioural treatment for health anxiety (hypochondriasis) in a routine clinical setting. *Behavioural and Cognitive Psychotherapy, 33*, 165–175.

Watts-English, T., Fortson, B. L., Gibler, N., Hooper, S. R., & DeBellis, M. D. (2006). The psychobiology of maltreatment in childhood. *Journal of Social Issues, 62*, 717–736.

WCPN. (2006). A conversation with Fred Frese. Retrieved August 9, 2007, from http://www.wcpn.org/specials/mentalhealth/features/0529fred_frese.html

Webb, A., Lind, P. A., Kalmijn, J., Feller, H. S., Smith, T. L., et al. (2011). The investigation into CYP2E1 in relation to the level of response to alcohol through a combination of linkage and association analysis. *Alcoholism: Clinical & Experimental Research, 35*, 10–18.

Wechsler, H., & Kuo, M. (2003). Watering down the drinks: The moderating effect of college demographics on alcohol use of high-risk groups. *American Journal of Public Health, 93,* 1929–1933.

Wechsler, H., Dowdall, G. W., Maenner, G., Gledhill-Hoyt, J., & Lee, H. (1998). Changes in binge drinking and related problems among American college students between 1993 and 1997. *Journal of American College Health, 47,* 57–68.

Wechsler, H., Fulop, M., Padilla, A., Lee, H., & Patrick, K. (1997). Binge drinking among college students: A comparison of California with other states. *Journal of American College Health, 45,* 273–277.

Wechsler, H., Lee, J. E., Nelson, T. F., & Kuo, M. (2002). Underage college students' drinking behavior, access to alcohol, and the influence of deterrence policies. *Journal of American College Health, 50,* 223–236.

Wegner, D. M., Schneider, D. J., Carter, S. R., & White, T. L. (1987). Paradoxical effects of thought suppression. *Journal of Personality & Social Psychology, 53,* 5–13.

Weiden, P. J., & Zygmunt, A. (1997). Medication noncompliance in schizophrenia: Part I, assessment. *Journal of Practical Psychiatry and Behavioral Health, 3,* 106–112.

Weinberger, D. R., & Lipska, B. K. (1995). Cortical maldevelopment, antipsychotic drugs, and schizophrenia: A search for common ground. *Schizophrenia Research, 16,* 87–110.

Weinberger, J. (1995). Common factors aren't so common: The common factors dilemma. *Clinical Psychology: Science and Practice, 2,* 45–69.

Weinstein, N. (1993). Testing four competing theories of health-protective behavior. *Health Psychology, 12,* 324–333.

Weinstein, N. D. (1984). Why it won't happen to me: Perceptions of risk factors and illness susceptibility. *Health Psychology, 3,* 431–457.

Weintraub, E., & Robinson, C. (2000). A case of monosymptomatic hypochondriacal psychosis treated with olanzapine. *Annals of Clinical Psychiatry, 12,* 247–249.

Weiser, M., Reichenberg, A., Grotto, I., Yasvitzky, R., Rabinowitz, J., et al. (2004). Higher rates of cigarette smoking in male adolescents before the onset of schizophrenia: A historical-prospective cohort study. *American Journal of Psychiatry, 161,* 1219–1223.

Weisman, A. G. (1997). Understanding cross-cultural prognostic variability for schizophrenia. *Cultural Diversity and Mental Health, 3,* 23–35.

Weisman, A. G., Rosales, G., Kymalainen, J., & Armesto, J. (2005). Ethnicity, family cohesion, religiosity and general emotional distress in patients with schizophrenia and their relatives. *Journal of Nervous and Mental Disease, 193,* 359–368.

Weiss, L. A., Shen, Y., Korn, J. M., Arking, D. E., Miller, D. T., et al. (2008). Association between microdeletion and microduplication at 16p11.1 and autism. *New England Journal of Medicine, 358,* 667–675.

Weissman, M. M., Bland, R. C., Canino, G. J., Greenwald, S., Hwu, H. G., et al. (1994). The cross national epidemiology of obsessive compulsive disorder: The Cross National Collaborative Group. *Journal of Clinical Psychiatry, 55,* 5–10.

Weissman, M. M., Bland, R. C., Canino, G. J., Greenwald, S., Hwu, H. G., et al. (1999). Prevalence of suicide ideation and suicide attempts in nine countries. *Psychological Medicine, 29,* 9–17.

Weissman, M. M., Bruce, M. L., Leaf, P. J., Florio, L., & Holzer, C. (1991). Affective disorders. In L. N. Robins & D. A. Regier (Eds.), *Psychiatric disorders in America* (pp. 53–80). New York: Free Press.

Weissman, M. M., Markowitz, J. C., & Klerman, G. L. (2000). *Comprehensive guide to interpersonal therapy.* New York: Basic Books.

Weissman, M. M., Pilowsky, D. J., Wickramaratne, P. J., Talati, A., Wisniewski, S. R., et al. (2006). Remissions in maternal depression and child psychopathology: A STAR*D-child report. *JAMA: Journal of the American Medical Association, 295,* 1389–1398.

Weissman, M. M., Wickramaratne, P., Nomura, Y., Warner, V., Pilowsky, D., & Verdeli, H. (2006). Offspring of depressed parents: 20 years later. *American Journal of Psychiatry, 163,* 1001–1008.

Weissman, M. M., Wolk, S., Goldstein, R. B., Moreau, D., Adams, P., et al. (1999). Depressed adolescents grown up. *JAMA: Journal of the American Medical Association, 281,* 1707–1713.

Weissman, M. M., Wolk, S., Wickramaratne, P., Goldstein, R. B., Adams, P., et al. (1999). Children with prepubertal-onset major depressive disorder and anxiety grown up. *Archives of General Psychiatry, 56,* 794–801.

Weisz, J. R., Jensen-Doss, A., & Hawley, K. M. (2006). Evidence-based youth psychotherapies versus usual clinical care. *American Psychologist, 61,* 671–689.

Weisz, J. R., McCarty, C. A., Eastman, K. L., Chaiyasit, W., & Suwanlert, S. (1997). Developmental psychopathology and culture: Ten lessons from Thailand. In S. S. Luthar, J. A. Burack, D. Cicchetti, & J. R. Weisz (Eds.), *Developmental psychopathology: Perspectives on adjustment, risk, and disorder* (pp. 568–592). New York: Cambridge University Press.

Weisz, J. R., Suwanlert, S., Chaiyasit, W., & Walter, B. R. (1987). Over- and undercontrolled referral problems among children and adolescents from Thailand and the United States: The *wat* and *wai* of cultural differences. *Journal of Consulting and Clinical Psychology, 55,* 719–726.

Welkenhuysen-Gybels, J., Billiet, J., & Cambré, B. (2003). Adjustment for acquiescence in the assessment of the construct equivalence of Likert-type score items. *Journal of Cross-Cultural Psychology, 34,* 702–722.

Weltzin, T. E., Weisensel, N., Franczyk, D., Burnett, K., Klitz, C., & Bean, P. (2005). Eating disorders in men: Update. *Journal of Men's Health & Gender, 2,* 186–193.

Wender, P. H., Kety, S. S., Rosenthal, D., Schulsinger, F., Ortmann, J., & Luhde, I. (1986). Psychiatric disorders in the biological and adoptive families of adopted individuals with affective disorders. *Archives of General Psychiatry, 43,* 923–929.

Wender, P. H., Rosenthal, D., Kety, S. S., Schulsinger, F., & Weiner, J. (1973). Social class and psychopathology in adoptees: A natural experimental method for separating the role of genetic and experimental factors. *Archives of General Psychiatry, 28,* 318–325.

Wenner, J. S. (1971). John Lennon interview with *Rolling Stone* magazine. Retrieved March 12, 2009, from www.members.tripod.com/~taz4158/johnint.html

Wenzel, A., & Cochran, C. K. (2006). Autobiographical memories prompted by automatic thoughts in panic disorder and social phobia. *Cognitive Behaviour Therapy, 35,* 129–137.

Wenzel, A., Brown, G. K., & Beck, A. T. (2009). *Cognitive therapy for suicidal patients: Scientific and clinical applications.* (pp. 53–77). Washington, DC: American Psychological Association.

Wenzel, A., Chapman, J. E., Newman, C. F., Beck, A. T., & Brown, G. K. (2006). Hypothesized mechanisms of change in cognitive therapy for borderline personality disorder. *Journal of Clinical Psychology, 62,* 503–516.

Wenzlaff, R. M., & Beevers, C. G. (1998). Depression and interpersonal responses to others' moods: The solicitation of negative information about happy people. *Personality & Social Psychology Bulletin, 24,* 386–398.

Werch, C. E., & Anzalone, D. A. (1995). Stage theory and research on tobacco, alcohol, and other drug use. *Journal of Drug Education, 25,* 81–98.

Werneke, U., Horn, O., & Taylor, D. M. (2004). How effective is St. John's wort? The evidence revisited. *Journal of Clinical Psychiatry, 65,* 611–617.

Werner, S., Malaspina, D., & Rabinowitz, J. (2007). Socioeconomic status at birth is associated with risk of schizophrenia: Population-based multilevel study. *Schizophrenia Bulletin, 33,* 1373–1378.

Werstiuk, E. S., Coote, M., Griffith, L., Shannon, H., & Steiner, M. (1996). Effects of electroconvulsive therapy on peripheral adrenoceptors, plasma, noradrenaline, MHPG, and cortisol in depressed patients. *British Journal of Psychiatry, 169,* 758–765.

Werth, J. L., Jr., Welfel, E. R., & Benjamin, G. A. H. (Eds.). (2009). *The duty to protect: Ethical, legal, and professional considerations for mental health professionals.* Washington, DC: American Psychological Press.

Wertz, J. M., & Sayette, M. A. (2001). A review of the effects of perceived drug use opportunity on self-reported urge. *Experimental and Clinical Psychopharmacology, 1,* 3–13.

Wesner, R. B., & Noyes, R. (1991). Imipramine: An effective treatment for illness phobia. *Journal of Affective Disorders, 22,* 43–48.

West, S. G. (2009). Alternatives to random experiments. *Current Directions in Psychological Science, 18,* 299–304.

Westen, D., & Morrison, K. (2001). A multidimensional meta-analysis of treatments for depression, panic, and generalized anxiety disorder: An empirical examination of the status of empirically supported treatments. *Journal of Consulting and Clinical Psychology, 69,* 875–899.

Westen, D., & Shedler, J. (2000). A prototype matching approach to diagnosing personality disorders: Toward DSM-V. *Journal of Personality Disorders, 14,* 109–126.

Westen, D., & Weinberger, J. (2004). When clinical description becomes statistical prediction. *American Psychologist, 59,* 595–613.

Westen, D., Heim, A. K., Morrison, K., Patterson, M., & Campbell, L. (2002). Simplifying diagnosis using a prototype-matching approach: Implications for the next edition of the DSM. In L. E. Beutler & M. L. Malik (Eds.), *Rethinking the DSM: A psychological perspective* (pp. 221–250). Washington, DC: American Psychological Association.

Westen, D., Novotny, C. M., & Thompson-Brenner, H. (2004). The empirical status of empirically supported psychotherapies: Assumptions, findings, and reporting in controlled clinical trials. *Psychological Bulletin, 130,* 631–663.

Westen, D., Novotny, C. M., & Thompson-Brenner, H. (2005). EBP? EST: Reply to Crits-Christoph et al. (2005) and Weisz et al. (2005). *Psychological Bulletin, 131,* 427–433.

Westerlund, E. (1992). *Women's sexuality after childhood incest.* New York: W. W. Norton & Co.

Wexler, B. E., & Bell, M. D. (2005). Cognitive remediation and vocational rehabilitation for schizophrenia. Schizophrenia Bulletin, 31, 931–941.

Wexler, B. E., Gottschalk, C. H., Fulbright, R. K., Prohovnik, I., Lacadie, C. M., et al. (2001). Functional magnetic resonance imaging of cocaine craving. *American Journal of Psychiatry, 158,* 86–95.

Wexler, B. E., Hawkins, K. A., Rounsaville, B., Anderson, M., Sernyak, M. J., & Green, M. F. (1997). Normal neurocognitive performance after extended practice in patients with schizophrenia. Schizophrenia Research, 26, 173–180.

Weyerer, S., & Wiedenmann, A. (1995). Economic factors and the rate of suicide in Germany between 1881 to 1989. *Psychological Report, 76,* 1331–1341.

Whalen, C. K, Henker, B., Ishikawa, S. S., Jamner, L. D., Floro, J. N., et al. (2006). An electronic diary study of contextual triggers and ADHD: Get ready, get set, get mad. *Journal of the American Academy of Child Adolescent Psychiatry, 45,* 166–174.

Whitaker, R. (2002). *Mad in America: Bad science, bad medicine, and the enduring mistreatment of the mentally ill.* Cambridge, MA: Perseus.

White, H. R., Jarrett, N., Valencia, E. Y., Loeber, R., & Wei, E. (2007). Stages and sequences of initiation and regular substance use in a longitudinal cohort of black and white male adolescents. *Journal of Studies on Alcohol and Drugs, 68,* 173–181.

White, J. M., & Ryan, C. F. (1996). Pharmacological properties of ketamine. *Drug and Alcohol Review, 15,* 145–155.

White, K., Kando, J., Park, T., Waternaux, C., & Brown, W. A. (1992). Side effects and the "blindability" of clinical drug trials. *American Journal of Psychiatry, 149,* 1730–1731.

White, K. H., & Barlow, D. H. (2002). Panic disorder and agoraphobia. In D.H. Barlow (Ed.), *Clinical handbook of psychological disorders* (2nd ed., pp. 328–379). New York: Guilford Press.

White, M.A., Grilo, C. M., O'Malley, S. S., & Potenza, M. N. (2010). Clinical case discussion: Binge eating disorder, obesity, and tobacco smoking. *Journal of Addiction Medicine, 4,* 11–19. Retrieved June 11, 2013, from www.ncbi.nlm.nih.gov/pmc/articles/PMC2860740/

White, R. W. (1948). *The abnormal personality: A textbook.* New York: Ronald Press.

Whitehead, W. E. (2006). Hypnosis for irritable bowel syndrome: The empirical evidence of therapeutic effects. *International Journal of Clinical and Experimental Hypnosis, 54,* 7–20.

Whitlock, J. L., Powers, J. L., & Eckenrode, J. (2006). The virtual cutting edge: The Internet and adolescent self-injury. *Developmental Psychology, 42,* 407–417.

Whittinger, N. S., Langley, K., Fowler, T. A., Thomas, H. V., & Thapar, A. (2007). Clinical precursors of adolescent conduct disorder in children with attention-deficit/hyperactivity disorder. *Journal of the American Academy of Child & Adolescent Psychiatry, 46,* 179–187.

WHO World Mental Health Survey Consortium. (2004). Prevalence, severity, and unmet need for treatment of mental disorders in the World Health Organization World Mental Health Surveys. *JAMA: Journal of the American Medical Association, 291,* 2581–2590.

Wiborg, I. M., & Dahl, A. A. (1997). The recollection of parental rearing styles in patients with panic disorder. *Acta Psychiatrica Scandinavica, 96,* 58–63.

Wiborg, I. M., Falkum, E., Dahl, A. A., & Gullberg, C. (2005). Is harm avoidance an essential feature of patients with panic disorder? *Comprehensive Psychiatry, 46,* 311–314.

Wickramaratne, P., Gameroff, M. J., Pilowsky, D. J., Hughes, C. W., Garber, J., et al. (2011). Children of depressed mothers 1 year after remission of maternal depression: Findings From the STAR*D-Child Study. *American Journal of Psychiatry, 168,* 593–602.

Wicks, S., Hjern, A., & Dalman, C. (2010). Social risk or genetic liability for psychosis? A study of children born in Sweden and reared by adoptive parents. *The American Journal of Psychiatry, 167,* 1240–1246.

Widiger, T. A., & Corbitt, E. M. (1997). Comorbidity of antisocial personality disorder with other personality disorders. In D. M. Stoff, J. Breiling, &J. D. Maser (Eds.), *Handbook of antisocial behavior* (pp. 75–82). Hoboken: John Wiley.

Widiger, T. A., & Costa, P. T., Jr. (2002). Five-factor model personality disorder research. In P. T. Costa, Jr., & T. A. Widiger (Eds.), *Personality disorders and the five-factor model of personality* (2nd ed., pp. 59–87). Washington, DC: American Psychological Association.

Widiger, T. A., Costa, P. T., Jr., & McCrae, R. R. (2002). A proposal for Axis II: Diagnosing personality disorders using the five-factor model. In P. T. Costa, Jr., & T. A. Widiger (Eds.), *Personality disorders and the five-factor model of personality* (2nd ed., pp. 431–456). Washington, DC: American Psychological Association.

Widiger, T. A., & Frances, A. J. (1989). Epidemiology, diagnosis, and comorbidity of borderline personality disorder. In A. Tasman, R. E. Hales, & A. J. Frances (Eds.), *Review of psychiatry* (Vol. 8). Washington, DC: American Psychiatric Press.

Widiger, T. A., & Lowe, J. R. (2008). A dimensional model of personality disorder: Proposal for DSM-V. *Psychiatric Clinics of North America, 31,* 363–378.

Widiger, T. A., & Mullins-Sweatt, S. N. (2005). Categorical and dimensional models of personality disorders. In J. M. Oldham, A. E. Skodol, & D. S. Bender (Eds.), *The American Psychiatric Publishing textbook of personality disorders* (pp. 35–53). Washington, DC: American Psychiatric Publishing.

Widiger, T. A., & Trull, T. J. (1993). Borderline and narcissistic personality disorders. In P. B. Sutker & H. E. Adams (Eds.), *Comprehensive handbook of psychopathology* (2nd ed., pp. 371–394). New York: Plenum Press.

Widiger, T. A., & Trull, T. J. (2007). Plate tectonics in the classification of personality disorder: Shifting to a dimensional model. *American Psychologist, 62,* 71–83.

Widom, C. S., DuMont, K., & Czaja, S. J. (2007). A prospective investigation of major depressive disorder and comorbidity in abused and neglected children grown up. *Archives of General Psychiatry, 64,* 49–56.

Wiedemann, G., Pauli, P., Dengler, W., Lutzenberger, W., Birbaumer, N., & Buchkremer, G. (1999). Frontal brain asymmetry as a biological substrate of emotions in patients with panic disorders. *Archives of General Psychiatry, 56,* 78–84.

Wigal, T., Greenhill, L., Chuang, S., McGough, J., Vitiello, B., A., et al. (2006). Safety and tolerability of methylphenidate in preschool children with ADHD. *Journal of the American Academy of Child and Adolescent Psychiatry, 45,* 1294–1303.

Wilberg, T., Karterud, S., Pedersen, G., & Urnes, O. (2009). The impact of avoidant personality disorder on psychosocial functioning is substantial. *Nordic Journal of Psychiatry, 30,* 1–7.

Wilfley, D. E., Agras, W. S., Telch, C. F., Rossiter, E. M., Schneider, J. A., et al. (1993). Group cognitive-behavioral therapy and group interpersonal psychotherapy for the nonpurging bulimic individual: A controlled comparison. *Journal of Consulting and Clinical Psychology, 61,* 296–305.

Wilfley, D. E., Iacovino, J. M., & Van Buren, D. J. (2012). Interpersonal psychotherapy for eating disorders. In J. C. Markowitz & M. M. Weissman (Eds.), *Casebook of interpersonal psychotherapy* (pp. 125–148). New York: Oxford University Press.

Wilk, C. M., Gold, J. M., McMahon, R. P., Humber, K., Iannone, V. N., & Buchanan, R. W. (2005). No, it is not possible to be schizophrenic yet neuropsychologically normal. Neuropsychology, 19, 778–786.

Wilkinson, D. J. C., Thompson, J. M., Lambert, G. W., Jennings, G. L., Schwarz, R. G., et al. (1998). Sympathetic activity in patients with panic disorder at rest, under laboratory mental stress, and during panic attacks. *Archives of General Psychiatry, 55,* 511–520.

Williams, D. R., & Williams-Morris, R. (2000). Racism and mental health: The African American experience. *Ethnicity & Health, 5,* 243–268.

Williams, J., Hadjistavropoulos, T., & Sharpe, D. (2006). A meta-analysis of psychological and pharmacological treatments for body dysmorphic disorder. *Behaviour Research and Therapy, 44,* 99–111.

Williams, J. M. G., Watts, F. N., MacLeod, C. & Mathews, A. (1997). *Cognitive Psychology and Emotional Disorders* (2nd ed.). Chichester, England: Wiley.

Williams, R. J., & Chang, S. Y. (2000). A comprehensive and comparative review of adolescent substance abuse treatment outcome. *Clinical Psychology: Science & Practice, 7,* 138–166.

Williams, T. (2012). "Suicides Outpacing War Deaths for Troops." *New York Times,* June 9, p. A10. Retrieved May 30, 2013, from www.nytimes.com/2012/06/09/us/suicides-eclipse-war-deaths-for-us-troops.html?_r=0

Williamson, D. A., Womble, L. G., Smeets, M. A. M., Netemeyer, R. G., Thaw, J. M., et al. (2002). Latent structure of eating disorder symptoms: A factor analytic and taxometric investigation. *American Journal of Psychiatry, 159,* 412–418.

Williamson-Catania, J. (2007). Genetics of neurodegenerative disease: Alzheimer's diease, frontotemporal dementia. In K. L. Bell (Dir.), *Dementia: Update for the practitioner.* Columbia University College of Physicians and Surgeons, Continuing Medical Education. Retrieved December 20, 2007, from http://ci.columbia.edu/c1182/web/sect_8/c1182_s8_2.html

Wilson, B. A. (1999). *Case studies in neuropsychological rehabilitation.* New York: Oxford University Press.

Wilson, B. A. (2004). Management and remediation of memory probems in brain-injured adults. In A. D. Baddeley, M. D. Kopelman, & B. A. Wilson (eds.), *Essential handbook of memory disorders for clinicians* (pp. 199–226). New York: Wiley.

Wilson, G. T., & Fairburn, C. G. (2007). Treatments for eating disorders. In P. Nathan & J. M. Gorman (Eds.), *A guide to treatments that work* (3rd ed., pp. 579–609). New York: Oxford University Press.

Wilson, G. T., Fairburn, C., Agras, W. S., Walsh, B. T., & Kraemer, H. (2002). Cognitive-behavioral therapy for bulimia nervosa: Time course and mechanisms of change. *Journal of Consulting & Clinical Psychology, 70,* 267–274.

Wilson, G. T., Nathan, P. E., O'Leary, K. D., & Clark, L. A. (1996). *Abnormal psychology: Integrating perspectives.* Boston: Allyn & Bacon.

Wilson, G. T., & Sysko, R. (2009). Frequency of binge eating episodes in bulimia nervosa and binge eating disorder: Diagnostic considerations. *International Journal of Eating Disorders, 42,* 603–610.

Wilson, I., Duszynski, K., & Mant, A. (2003). A 5-year follow-up of general practice patients experiencing depression. *Family Practice, 20,* 685–689.

Wilson, J. K., & Rapee, R. M. (2006). Self-concept certainty in social phobia. *Behaviour Research and Therapy, 44,* 113–136.

Wilson, J. S., & Costanzo, P. R. (1996). A preliminary study of attachment, attention, and schizotypy in early adulthood. *Journal of Social & Clinical Psychology, 15,* 231–260.

Wilson, R. I., & Nicoll, R. A. (2001). Endogenous cannabinoids mediate retrograde signaling at hippocampal synapses. *Nature, 410,* 588–592.

Wilson, W., Mathew, R., Turkington, T., Hawk, T., Coleman, R. E., & Provenzale, J. (2000). Brain morphological changes and early marijuana use: a magnetic resonance and positron emission tomography study. *Journal of Addictive Diseases, 19,* 1–22.

Windle, M., & Windle, R. C. (2012). Early onset problem behaviors and alcohol, tobacco, and other substance use disorders in young adulthood. *Drug and Alcohol Dependence, 121*(1–2), 152–158.

Winerip, M. (1999a, May 23). Bedlam on the street. *The New York Times.*

Winerip, M. (1999b, October 18). Oddity and normality vie in subway killer's confession. *The New York Times,* p. B1.

Winfree, L. T., & Bernat, F. P. (1998). Social learning, self-control, and substance abuse by eighth grade students: A tale of two cities. *Journal of Drug Issues, 28,* 539–338.

Winick, B. J. (2003). A therapeutic jurisprudence assessment of sexually violent predator laws. In B. J. Winick & J. Q. La Fond (Eds.), *Protecting society from sexually dangerous offenders: Law, justice, and therapy* (pp. 317–331). Washington, DC: American Psychological Association.

Winnicott, D. W. (1958). *Through paediatrics to psycho-analysis: Collected papers.* New York: Basic Books, 1958.

Winzelberg, A., & Humphreys, K. (1999). Should patients' religiosity influence clinicians' referral to 12-step self-help groups? Evidence from a study of 3,018 male substance abuse patients. *Journal of Consulting and Clinical Psychology, 67,* 790–794.

Wirshing, D. A., Sergi, M. J., & Mintz, J. (2005). A videotape intervention to enhance the informed consent process for medical and psychiatric treatment research. *American Journal of Psychiatry, 162,* 186–188.

Wisco, B. E., & Nolen-Hoeksema, S. (2009). The interaction of mood and rumination in depression: Effects on mood maintenance and mood-congruent autobiographical memory. *Journal of Rational-Emotive & Cognitive-Behavior Therapy, 27*(3), 144–159.

Wise, T. N., & Birket-Smith, M. (2002). The somatoform disorders for DSM-V: The need for changes in process and content. *Psychosomatics: The Journal of Consultation and Liaison Psychiatry, 43,* 437–440.

Wiseman, C. V., Sunday, S. R., Klapper, F., Harris, W. A., & Halmi, K. A. (2001). Changing patterns of hospitalization in eating disorder patients. *International Journal of Eating Disorders, 30,* 69–74.

Wisner, K. L., Perel, J. M., Peindl, K. S., & Hanusa, B. H. (2004). Timing of depression recurrence in the first year after birth. *Journal of Affective Disorders, 78,* 249–252.

Wisner, K. L., Sit, D. K. Y., McShea, M. C., Rizzo, D. M., Zoretich, R. A., et al. (2013). Onset timing, thoughts of self-harm and diagnoses in postpartum women with screen-positive depression findings. *JAMA Psychiatry, 70,* 490–498.

Wittchen, H. U., & Hoyer, J. (2001). Generalized anxiety disorder: Nature and course. *Journal of Clinical Psychiatry, 62,* 15–19.

Wohl, M., & Gorwood, P. (2007). Paternal ages below or above 35 years old are associated with a different risk of schizophrenia in the offspring. *European Psychiatry, 22,* 22–26.

Wolchik, S. A., Sandler, I. N., Millsap, R. E., Plummer, B. A., Greene, S. M., et al. (2002). Six-year follow-up of preventive interventions for children of divorce: A randomized controlled trial. *JAMA: Journal of the American Medical Association, 288,* 1874–1881.

Wolpe, J. (1997). Thirty years of behavior therapy. *Behavior Therapy, 28,* 633–635.

Wonderlich, S., & Mitchell, J. E. (2001). The role of personality in the onset of eating disoders and treatment implications. *Psychiatric Clinics of North America, 24,* 249–258.

Wong, E. C., Kim, B. S. K., Zane, N. W. S., Kim, I. J., & Huang, J. S. (2003). Examining culturally based variables associated with ethnicity: Influences on credibility perceptions of empirically supported interventions. *Cultural Diversity & Ethnic Minority Psychology, 9,* 88–96.

Wong, J. L., Wetterneck, C., & Klein, A. (2000). Effects of depressed mood on verbal memory performance versus self-reports of cognitive difficulties. *International Journal of Rehabilitation & Health, 5,* 85–97.

Wong, S. C. P., Gordon, A., Gu, D., Lewis, K. & Olver, M. E. (2012). The Effectiveness of violence reduction treatment for psychopathic offenders: Empirical evidence and a treatment model. *International Journal of Forensic Mental Health, 11,* 336–349.

Wood, J. M., Lilienfeld, S. O., Nezworski, M. T., & Garb, H. N. (2001). Coming to grips with negative evidence for the comprehensive system for the Rorschach: A comment on Gacono, Loving, and Bodholdt; Ganellen; and Bornstein. *Journal of Personality Assessment, 77,* 48–70.

Wood, J. M., Nezworski, M. T., Garb, H. N., & Lilienfeld, S. O. (2001). Problems with the norms of the comprehensive system for the Rorschach: Methodological and conceptual considerations. *Clinical Psychology: Science & Practice, 8,* 397–402.

Woodall, W. G., Delaney, H. D., Kunitz, S. J., Westerberg, V. S., & Zhao, H. (2007). A randomized trial of a DWI intervention program for first offenders: Intervention outcomes and interactions with antisocial personality disorder among a primarily American-Indian sample. *Alcoholism: Clinical and Experimental Research, 31,* 974–987.

Woods, B. (2004). Reducing the impact of cognitive impairment in dementia. In A. D. Baddeley, M. D. Kopelman, & B. A. Wilson (Eds.), *Essential handbook of memory disorders for clinicians* (pp. 285–300) New York: Wiley.

Woods, B., Spector, A., Jones, C., Orrell, M., & Davies, S. (1998). Reminiscence therapy for dementia. *Cochrane Database of Systematic Reviews, 3:* CD001120. DOI: 10.1002/14651858. CD001120.pub2.

Woods, S. W., Morgenstern, H., Saksa, J. R., Walsh, B. C., Sullivan, M. C., et al. (2010). Incidence of tardivedyskinesia with atypical versus conventional antipsychotic medication: A prospective cohort study. *Journal of Clinical Psychiatry, 71,* 463–474.

Woody, E. Z., & Bowers, K. S. (1994). A frontal assault on dissociated control. In S. J. Lynn & J. W. Rhue (Eds.), *Dissociation: Clinical and theoretical perspectives* (pp. 52–79). New York: Guilford Press.

Wool, C. A., & Barsky, A. J. (1994). Do women somatize more than men? Gender differences in somatization. *Psychosomatics: Journal of Consultation and Liaison Psychiatry, 35,* 445–452.

Woollett, K., & Maguire, E. A. (2011). Acquiring "the knowledge" of London's layout drives structural brain changes. *Current biology, 21*(24), 2109-2114.

World Health Organization. (1948) *Constitution of the World Health Organization.* Retrieved January 26, 2009, from Jawww.searo. who.int/LinkFiles/About_ SEARO_const.pdf.

World Health Organization. (1999). *Figures and facts about suicide.* Technical Report. Geneva: Author.

World Health Organization. (2002a). *Distribution of suicides rates (per 100,000) by gender and age, 2000.* Retrieved February 22, 2009, from www.who.int/mental_health/prevention/suicide/ suicide_rates_chart/en/index.html

World Health Organization. (2002b). *World report on violence and health.* Retrieved October 20, 2008, from www.who.int/violence_injury_ prevention/violence/global_ campaign/en/ chap7.pdf

World Health Organization. (2008). *Depression.* Retrieved October 20, 2008, from www.who.int/mental_health/management/ depression/definition/en/

World Health Organization. (2009). *Definition of an older or elderly person.* Retrieved February 21, 2009, from www.who.int/healthinfo/survey/ ageingdefnolder/en/index.html

Wright, L. (2007). *My life at Grey Gardens: Thirteen months and beyond.* Lois Wright.

Wright, S., & Klee, H. (2001). Violent crime, aggression and amphetamine: What are the implications for drug treatment services? *Drugs: Education, Prevention & Policy, 8,* 73–90.

Wrightsman, L. S., & Fulero, S. M. (2005). *Forensic psychology* (2nd ed.). Belmont, CA: Wadsworth.

Wu, K. D., Clark, L. A., & Watson, D. (2006). Relations between obsessive-compulsive disorder and personality: Beyond Axis I-Axis II comorbidity. *Journal of Anxiety Disorders, 20,* 695–717.

Wuerker, A. K., Long, J. D., Haas, G. L., & Bellack, A. S. (2002). Interpersonal control, expressed emotion, and change in symptoms in families of persons with schizophrenia, Schizophrenia Research, 58, 281–292.

Wyatt v. Stickney, 334 F. Supp. 1341 (M. D. Ala. 1971).

Wykes, T., Reeder, C., Williams, C., Corner, J., Rice, C., & Everitt, B. (in press). Are the effects of cognitive remediation therapy (CRT) durable? Results from an exploratory trial in schizophrenia. *Schizophrenia Research, 61,* 163–174.

Wynne, L. C., Tienari, P., Nieminen, P., Sorri, A., Lahti, I., et al. (2006). I. Genotype-environment interaction in the schizophrenia spectrum: Genetic liability and global family ratings in the Finnish Adoption Study. *Family Process, 45,* 419–434.

Xiao, Z., Yan, H., Wang, Z., Zou, Z., Xu, Y., et al. (2006). Trauma and dissociation in China. *American Journal of Psychiatry, 163,* 1388–1391.

Xu, B., Roos, J. L., Levy, S., van Rensburg, E. J., Gogos, J. A., & Karalorgou, M. (2008). Strong association of de novo copy number mutations with sporadic schizophrenia. *Nature Genetics, 40,* 880–885.

Yang, L. H., Phillips, M. R., Licht, D. M., & Hooley, J. M. (2004). Causal attributions about schizophrenia in families in China: Expressed emotion and patient relapse. *Journal of Abnormal Psychology, 113,* 592–602.

Yang, Y., Glenn, A. L., & Raine, A. (2008). Brain abnormalities in antisocial individuals: Implications for the law. *Behavioral Sciences & the Law, 26*(1), 65–83.

Yates, P. M., Hucker, S. J., & Kingston, D. A. (2008). Sexual sadism: Psychopathy and theory. In D. R. Laws & W. T. O'Donohue (Eds.), *Sexual deviance: Theory, assessment, and treatment* (2nd ed., pp. 213–230). New York: Guilford Press.

Yehuda, R., Boisoneau, D., Lowy, M. T., & Giller, E. L. (1995). Dose-response changes in plasma cortisol and lymphocyte glucocorticoid receptors following dexamethasone administration in combat veterans with and without posttraumatic stress disorder. *Archives of General Psychiatry, 52,* 583–593.

Yehuda, R., Giller, E. L., Southwick, S. M., Lowy, M. T., & Mason, J. W. (1991). Hypothalamic-pituitary-adrenal dysfunction in posttraumatic stress disorder. *Biological Psychiatry, 30,* 1031–1048.

Yehuda, R., Kahana, B., Binder-Brynes, K., Southwick, S. M., Mason, J. W., & Giller, E. L. (1995). Low urinary cortisol excretion in Holocaust survivors with posttraumatic stress disorder. *American Journal of Psychiatry, 152,* 982–986.

Yehuda, R., Teicher, M. H., Trestman, R. L., Levengood, R. A., & Siever, L. J. (1996). Cortisol regulation in posttraumatic stress disorder and major depression: A chronobiological analysis. *Biological Psychiatry, 40,* 79–88.

Yen, S., Sr., Shea, M. T., Battle, C. L., Johnson, D. M., Zlotnick, C., et al. (2002). Traumatic exposure and posttraumatic stress disorder in borderline, schizotypal, avoidant and obsessive-compulsive personality disorders: Findings from the Collaborative Longitudinal Personality Disorders Study. *Journal of Nervous and Mental Disease, 190,* 510–518.

Yildiz, A., Vieta, E., Leucht, S., & Baldessarini, R. J. (2011). Efficacy of antimanic treatments: Meta-analysis of randomized, controlled trials. *Neuropsychopharmacology, 36,* 375–389.

Yip, P. S. F., Callanan, C., & Yuen, H. P. (2000). Urban/rural and gender differentials in suicide rates: East and west. *Journal of Affective Disorders, 57,* 99–106.

Yip, P. S. F., Chao, A., & Ho, T. P. (1998). A re-examination of seasonal variation in suicides in Australia and New Zealand. *Journal of Affective Disorders, 47,* 141–150.

Yip, P. S. F., Yang, K. C. T., & Qin, P. (2006). Seasonality of suicides with and without psychiatric illness in Denmark. *Journal of Affective Disorders, 96,* 117–121.

Yoo, H. J., Kim, M., Ha, J. H., Chung, A., Sim, M. E., et al. (2006). Biogenetic temperament and character and attention deficit hyperactivity disorder in Korean children. *Psychopathology, 39,* 25–31.

Yoon, T., Okada, J., Jung, M. W., & Kim, J. J. (2008). Prefrontal cortex and hippocampus subserve different components of working memory in rats. *Learning & Memory, 15,* 97–105.

Young, D. M. (2001). Depression. In W. S. Tseng & J. Streltzer (Eds.), *Culture and psychopathology: A guide to clinical assessment* (pp. 28–45). New York: Brunner/Mazel.

Young, J. E. (1990). *Cognitive therapy for personality disorders: A schema-focused approach.* Sarasota, FL: Professional Resource Exchange.

Young, K. S. (2005). An empirical examination of client attitudes towards online counseling. *CyberPsychology & Behavior, 8,* 172–177.

Yovel, I., & Mineka, S. (2005). Emotion-congruent attentional biases: The perspective of hierarchical models of emotional disorders. *Personality and Individual Differences, 38,* 785–795.

Yudofsky, S. C. (2005). *Fatal Flaws: Navigating Destructive Relationships With People with Disorders of Personality and Character.* Washington, DC, US: American Psychiatric Publishing, Inc.

Zabinski, M. F., Pung, M. A., Wilfley, D. E., Eppstein, D. L., Winzelberg, A. J., et al. (2001). Reducing risk factors for eating disorders: Targeting at-risk women with a computerized psychoeducational program. *International Journal of Eating Disorders, 29,* 401–408.

Zabinski, M. F., Wilfley, D. E., Calfas, K. J, Winzelberg, A. J., & Taylor, C. B. (2004). An interactive psychoeducational intervention for women at risk of developing an eating disorder. *Journal of Consulting and Clinical Psychology, 72,* 914–919.

Zadina, J. N., Corey, D. M., Casbergue, R. M., Lemen, L. C., Rouse, J. C., et al. (2006). Lobar asymmetries in subtypes of dyslexic and control subjects. *Journal of Child Neurology, 21,* 922–931.

Zalsman, G., Frisch, A., Apter, A., & Weizman, A. (2002). Genetics of suicidal behavior: Candidate association genetic approach. *Israel Journal of Psychiatry & Related Sciences, 39,* 252–261.

Zamboanga, B. L., Bean, J. L., Pietras, A. C., & Pabón, L. C. (2005). Subjective evaluations of alcohol expectancies and their relevance to drinking game involvement in female college students. *Journal of Adolescent Health, 37,* 77–80.

Zammit, S., Allebeck, P., Andreasson, S., Lundberg, I., & Lewis, G. (2002). Self reported cannabis use as a risk factor for schizophrenia in Swedish conscripts of 1969: Historical cohort study. *British Medical Journal, 325,* 1199–1212.

Zammit, S., Allebeck, P., Dalman, C., Lundberg, I., Hemmingson, T., et al. (2003). Paternal age and risk for schizophrenia. *British Journal of Psychiatry, 183,* 405–408.

Zanarini, M. C., & Gunderson, J. G. (1997). Differential diagnosis of antisocial and borderline personality disorders. In D. M. Stoff, J. Breiling, & J. D. Maser (Eds.), *Handbook of antisocial behavior* (pp. 83–91). Hoboken, NJ: John Wiley.

Zanarini, M. C., Frankenburg, F. R., DeLuca, C. J., Hennen, J., Khera, G. S., & Gunderson, J. G. (1998). The pain of being borderline: Dysphoric states specific to borderline personality disorder. *Harvard Review of Psychiatry, 6,* 201–207.

Zanarini, M. C., Frankenburg, F. R., Hennen, J., Reich, D. B., & Silk, K. R. (2004). Axis I comorbidity in patients with borderline personality disorder: 6-year follow-up and prediction of time to remission. *American Journal of Psychiatry, 161,* 2108–2114.

Zanarini, M. C., Frankenburg, F. R., Hennen, J., Reich, B., & Silk, K. R. (2005). The McLean Study of Adult Development (MSAD): Overview and implications of the first six years of prospective follow-up. *Journal of Personality Disorders, 19,* 505–523.

Zanarini, M. C., Frankenburg, F. R., Hennen, J., Reich, D. B., & Silk, K. R. (2006). Prediction of the 10-year course of borderline personality disorder. *American Journal of Psychiatry, 163,* 827–832.

Zanarini, M. C., Frankenburge, F. R., Reich, B, & Fitzmaurice, G. (2010). Time to attainment of recovery from borderline personality disorder and stability of recovery: A 10-year prospective follow-up study. *American Journal of Psychiatry, 167,* 663–667.

Zanarini, M. C., Frankenburg, F. R., Reich, D. B., Silk, K. R., Hudson, J. I., & McSweeney, L. B. (2006). The subsyndromal phenomenology of borderline personality disorder: A 10-year follow-up study. *American Journal of Psychiatry, 164,* 929–935.

Zanarini, M. C., Gunderson, J. G., & Frankenburg, F. R. (1989). Axis I phenomenology of borderline personality disorder. *Comprehensive Psychiatry, 30,* 149–156.

Zane, N., Hall, G. C. N., Sue, S., Young, K., & Nunez, J. (2004). Research on psychotherapy with culturally diverse populations. In M. J. Lambert (Ed.), *Bergin and Garfield's handbook of psychotherapy and behavior change* (5th ed., pp. 805–821). New York: John Wiley & Sons.

Zarrinpar, A., Deldin, P., and Kosslyn, S. M. (2006). Effects of depression on sensory/motor vs. central processing in visual mental imagery. *Cognition & Emotion, 20,* 737–758.

Zeeck, A., Weber, S., Sandholz, A., Joos, A., & Hartmann, A. (2011). Stability of long-term outcome in bulimia nervosa: A 3-year follow-up. *Journal of Clinical Psychology, 67,* 318–327.

Zhan, C., Sangl, J., Bierman, A., Miller, M., Friedman, B., et al. (2001). Potentially inappropriate medication use in the community-dwelling elderly: Findings from the 1996 medical expenditure panel survey. *Journal of the American Medical Association, 286,* 2823–2829.

Zhang, A., & Snowden, L. R. (1999). Ethnic characteristics of mental disorders in five U.S. communities. *Cultural Diversity and Ethnic Minority Psychology, 5,* 134–146.

Zhang, A. Y., Snowden, L. R., & Sue, S. (1998). Differences between Asian and White Americans' help seeking and utilization patterns in the Los Angeles area. *Journal of Community Psychology, 26,* 317–326.

Zhang, L., ChangR. C.-C., Chu, L.-W., &Mak, H. K.-F. (2012). Current neuroimaging techniques in Alzheimer's disease and applications in animal models. *American Journal of Nuclear Medicine and Molecular Imaging, 2,* 386–404.

Zhang, X. Y., Zhou, D. F., Cao, L. Y., Wu, G. Y., & Shen, Y. C. (2005). Cortisol and cytokines in chronic and treatment-resistant patients with schizophrenia: Association with psychopathology and response to antipsychotics. *Neuropsychopharmacology, 30,* 1532–1538.

Zhu, Y., Wang, K., Zhang, J., Long, Y., Su, L., & Zhou, M. (2003). A survey on tic disorder of children aged 6–15 years. *Chinese Mental Health Journal, 17,* 363–366.

Zhukov, D. A., & Vinogradova, E. P. (1998). Agonistic behavior during stress prevents the development of learned helplessness in rats. *Neuroscience and Behavioral Physiology, 28,* 206–210.

Ziatas, K., Durkin, K., & Pratt, C. (2003). Differences in assertive speech acts produced by children with autism, Asperger syndrome, specific language impairment, and normal development. *Development and Psychopathology, 15,* 73–94.

Ziegler, F. J., Imboden, J. B., & Meyer, E. (1960). Contemporary conversion reactions: A clinical study. *American Journal of Psychiatry, 116,* 901–910.

Zimmerman, M., & Chelminski, I. (2003). Generalized anxiety disorder in patients with major depression: Is DSM-IV's hierarchy correct? *American Journal of Psychiatry, 160,* 504–521.

Zipfel, S., Loewe, B., Reas, D. L., Deter, H.-C., & Herzog, W. (2000). Long-term prognosis in anorexia nervosa: Lessons from a 21-year follow-up study. *Lancet, 355,* 721–722.

Zisook, S., Shear, K., & Kendler, K. S. (2007). Validity of the bereavement exclusion criterion for the diagnosis of major depressive episode. *World Psychiatry, 6,* 102–107.

Zittel, C., & Westen, D. (1998). Conceptual issues and research findings on borderline personality disorder: What every clinician should know. *In Session, 4,* 5–20.

Zlotnick, C., Miller, I. W., Pearlstein, T., Howard, M., & Sweeney, P. (2006). A preventive intervention for pregnant women on public assistance at risk for postpartum depression. *American Journal of Psychiatry, 163,* 1443–1445.

Zornberg, G. L., Buka, S. L., & Tsuang, M. T. (2000). Hypoxic-ischemia-related fetal/neonatal complications and risk of schizophrenia and other nonaffective psychoses: A 19-year longitudinal study. *American Journal of Psychiatry 157,* 196–202.

Zorumski, C. F. (2005). Neurobiology, neurogenesis, and the pathology of psychopathology. In C. F. Zorumski & E. H. Rubin (Eds.), *Psychopathology in the genome and neuroscience era* (pp. 175–187). Washington, DC: American Psychiatric Publishing.

Zubieta, J.-K., Huguelet, P., O'Neil, R. L., & Giordani, B. J. (2001). Cognitive function in euthymic bipolar I disorder. *Psychiatry Research, 102,* 9–20.

Zucker, K. J. (2005). Gender identity disorder in children and adolescents. *Annual Review of Clinical Psychology, 1,* 467–492.

Zucker, K. J., & Bradley, S. J. (1995). *Gender identity disorder and psychosexual problems in children and adolescents.* New York: Guilford Press.

Zucker, K. J., Wild, J., Bradley, S. J., & Lowry, C. B. (1993). Physical attractiveness of boys with gender identity disorder. *Archives of Sexual Behavior, 22,* 23–36.

Zuckerman, M. (1991a). Biotypes for basic personality dimensions? "The Twilight Zone" between genotype and social phenotype. In J. Strelau & A. Angleitner (Eds.), *Explorations in temperament: International perspectives on theory and measurement* (pp. 129–146). New York: Plenum Press.

Zuckerman, M. (1991b). *Psychobiology of personality.* New York: Cambridge University Press.

Zuckerman, M. (1994). *Behavioural expressions and biosocial bases of sensation seeking.* New York: Cambridge University Press.

Zuckerman, M. (1999). Antisocial personality disorder. In M. Zuckerman, *Vulnerability to psychopathology: A biosocial model* (pp. 209–253). Washington, DC: American Psychological Association.

CHAPTER 1

Figure 1.3: The Diathesis-Stress Model. American Psychological Association. Copyright © 1991 American Psychological Association.

CHAPTER 2

Table 2.3: Cognitive Distortions, adapted from Feeling Good: The New Mood Therapy, by David Burns, 1980. Adaptation of Table 3-1: Definitions of Cognitive Distortions (abridged from ten to six) from *Feeling Good: The New Mood Therapy* by David D. Burns, M.D. Copyright © 1980 by David D. Burns, M.D. Reprinted by permission of HarperCollins Publishers.

CHAPTER 3

Table 3.1: The 22 Categories of Mental Disorders in DSM-5. From the Diagnostic and Statistical Manual of Mental Disorders.

Table 3.4: Table: MMPI-2 Scales. Sample of MMPI-2 Scales. Excerpted from the MMPI®-2 (Minnesota Multiphasic Personality Inventory®-2) Manual for Administration, Scoring, and Interpretation, Revised Edition. Copyright © 2001 by the Regents of the University of Minnesota. Items excerpted from the MMPI®-2 Booklet of Abbreviated Items. Copyright © 2005 by the Regents of the University of Minnesota. Used by permission of the University of Minnesota Press. All rights reserved. "MMPI" and "Minnesota Multiphasic Personality Inventory" are trademarks owned by the Regents of the University of Minnesota.

Figure 3.3: Figure: Rates of Serious Mental Illness Across Countries. From WHO World Mental Health Survey Consortium. Copyright © 2004 American Medical Association. All rights reserved.

CHAPTER 4

Table 4.2: Information Provided for Obtaining Informed Consent. Copyright © American Psychological Association.

Table 4.4: Ethical Guidelines for Research on Experimental Treatments. Copyright © American Psychological Association.

CHAPTER 5

Excerpts from *An Unquiet Mind* by Kay Redfield Jamison, Copyright © 1995 by Kay Redfield Jamison. Used by permission of Alfred A. Knopf, a division of Random House, Inc.

CHAPTER 6

Excerpt from *The Earl Campbell Story*, by Earl Campbell and John Ruane, published by ECW Press Ltd., 1999, 9781550223910. Reprinted by permission.

Figure 6.5: Heritablities of Specific Phobias, by K.S. Kendler, L.M. Karkowski, and C.A. Prescott, from "Fears and Phobias: Reliability and Heritability." *Psychological Medicine*, 29, 539–553, 1999. Copyright © 1999 Cambridge University Press. Reprinted with the permission of Cambridge University Press.

Table 6.8: Table: Interoceptive Exposure Exercises for Treatment of Panic Disorder, from CCC/Guilford Publications, Inc. Clinical Handbook of Psychological Disorders: A Step-by-step Treatment Manual by Barlow, David H. Reproduced with permission of GUILFORD PUBLICATIONS, INCORPORATED in the format Book via Copyright Clearance Center.

Table 6.3: DSM-5 Criteria for a Panic Attack. American Psychiatric Association. Reprinted with permission from The Diagnostic and Statistical Manual of Mental Disorders, Fifth Edition (Copyright 2013) American Psychiatric Association.

CHAPTER 9

Table 9.1: The Twelve Steps of Alcoholics Anonymous. The Twelve Steps are reprinted with permission of Alcoholics Anonymous World Services, Inc. ("AAWS") Permission to reprint the Twelve Steps does not mean that AAWS has reviewed or approved the contents of this publication, or that AAWS necessarily agrees with the views expressed herein. A.A. is a program of recovery from alcoholism only-use of the Twelve Steps in connection with programs and activities which are patterned after A.A., but which address other problems, or in any other non-A.A. context, does not imply otherwise.

Figure 9.6: Figure from BSCS. (2003). Understanding Alcohol: Investigations into Biology & Behavior. NIH publication No. 04-4991. Copyright © 2003 by BSCS. All rights reserved. Used with permission.

CHAPTER 10

Excerpts from pp. 6, 27, 40, 44, 102, 195-6, 284 (518 words) from WASTED: A MEMOIR OF ANOREXIA AND BULIMIA by MARYA HORNBACHER. Copyright © 1998 by Marya Hornbacher Beard. Reprinted by permission of HarperCollins Publishers.

CHAPTER 13

Excerpt from *Get Me Out of Here: My Recovery from Borderline Personality Disorder* by Reiland, Rachel. Reproduced with permission of Hazelden in the format republish in a book via Copyright Clearance Center.

CHAPTER 15

Excerpts from Excerpts from "Psychological Assessment of Older Adults" by Asenath La Rue and Jennifer Watson from Professional Psychology: Research and Practice, 29, 5-14, 1998. Copyright © 1998 by the American Psychological Association. Adapted with permission. The use of this information does not imply endorsement by the publisher.

CHAPTER 16

Excerpt from "Jury hears a confession in killing" by D. Rohde, *The New York Times*, October 16, 1999, © 1999. The New York Times. All rights reserved. Used by permission and protected by the Copyright Laws of the United States. The printing, copying, redistribution, or retransmission of the Material without express written permission is prohibited.

Excerpt from "Witness tearfully describes fatal subway shoving" by D. Rohde, The New York Times, October 9, 1999, © 1999. *The New York Times*. All rights reserved. Used by permission and protected by the Copyright Laws of the United States. The printing, copying, redistribution, or retransmission of the Material without express written permission is prohibited.

Tables of Diagnostic Criteria for Disorders throughout this book are reprinted with permission from the Diagnostic and Statistical Manual of Mental Disorders, Fifth Edition, (Copyright ©2013). American Psychiatric Association. All Rights Reserved.